D1205513

INTERACTIVE CASEBOOK SERIES℠

CRIMINAL PROCEDURE: INVESTIGATIVE

A Contemporary Approach

THIRD EDITION

―――――――――

Russell L. Weaver
PROFESSOR OF LAW & DISTINGUISHED UNIVERSITY SCHOLAR
UNIVERSITY OF LOUISVILLE
LOUIS D. BRANDEIS SCHOOL OF LAW

John M. Burkoff
PROFESSOR OF LAW EMERITUS
UNIVERSITY OF PITTSBURGH SCHOOL OF LAW

Catherine Hancock
GEOFFREY C. BIBLE & MURRAY H. BRING PROFESSOR OF CONSTITUTIONAL LAW
TULANE UNIVERSITY SCHOOL OF LAW

―――――――――

WEST
ACADEMIC
PUBLISHING

Interactive Casebook Series is a servicemark registered in the U.S. Patent and Trademark Office.

© 2015, 2018 LEG, Inc. d/b/a West Academic
© 2021 LEG, Inc. d/b/a West Academic
    444 Cedar Street, Suite 700
    St. Paul, MN 55101
    1-877-888-1330

West, West Academic Publishing, and West Academic are trademarks of West Publishing Corporation, used under license.

Printed in the United States of America

ISBN: 978-1-68467-882-2

To Laurence, Ben and Kate, with love

RLW

Dedicated with love to Nancy, Amy & Sean,
David & Emmy, Emma, Molly,
Hannah, and Cyrus

JMB

For Peter, Elizabeth, Caitlin & Alex, Margaret & Josh

CH

Preface

This third edition of our interactive criminal procedure casebook continues the tradition of our prior criminal procedure casebook (which went through five editions in a non-interactive format), but continues to a third edition in the interactive format.

As with the prior books, our primary goal was to create a "teacher's book"—a book that contains thought provoking problems (referred to as "hypos" in the Interactive Casebook Series) designed to stimulate thought and produce interesting classroom discussion. The hypos are woven throughout the chapters and are designed to help students learn doctrine, illuminate trends in the law, and ultimately produce better learning. A secondary goal was to include a focus on teaching "skills." Many of the hypos place students in practical situations that they are likely to encounter in practice, and therefore encourage students to think about how they might handle those situations in real-life.

However, the interactive format allows us to offer a number of other features, including live hyperlinks and the ability to access the material interactively. Students will also find a variety of boxes in the text of the principal cases, Some of these boxes involve "food for thought" questions that will help them to understand how to address the more complex questions that arise in the "points for discussion" material and in the hypotheticals. The boxes also provide information about topics such as the attorneys' strategies in the cases and links to online sources that illustrate various facets of the litigation. There are also "FYI," and "Take Note" boxes. Also included are multiple choice questions that allow students to test their understanding and comprehension of the issues presented.

As with any book, tradeoffs are necessary. In order to prevent the book from being unduly voluminous and unwieldy, we have chosen not to include encyclopedic notes and references like those found in other books. The inclusion of too many notes impedes learning. Moreover, in the criminal procedure area, students have numerous high-quality secondary sources available to them, and students can consult those sources for expanded scholarly discussions of the law. By limiting the scope of notes, we were able to include more hypotheticals and to provide greater opportunity for critical thinking.

We welcome input from faculty and students who use this book. You can contact us at the following e-mail addresses: Professor Russell Weaver (russ.weaver@louisville.edu); Professor John Burkoff (burkoff@pitt.edu); and Professor Catherine Hancock (chancock@law.tulane.edu).

We give thanks to the many people who assisted us in the creation and revision of this book, including our research assistants and secretaries. We are particularly grateful to students who helped us find and correct errors.

Finally, we are thankful to our spouses, significant others, and children who supported us through the various stages of this project.

RLW, JMB, CH

Acknowledgments

Excerpts from the following articles have been reprinted by permission:

James M. Anderson, Maya Buenaventura, & Paul Heaton, *The Effects of Holistic Defense on Criminal Justice Outcomes,* 132 Harv. L. Rev. 819, 821–24, 882–86 (2019).

Eric Fish, *Against Adversary Prosecution,* 103 Iowa L. Rev. 1419, 1420–23, 1424–26 (2018).

Monroe Freedman & Abbe Smith, *Misunderstanding Lawyer's Ethics (Book Review of Daniel Markovits, A Modern Legal Ethics: Adversary Ethics in a Democratic Age (2008)),* 108 Mich. L. Rev. 925, 925–26, 927, 929, 931–34, 935–36, 937–38 (2010).

Bruce Green & Ellen Yaroshefsky, *Prosecutorial Accountability 2.0,* 92 Notre Dame L. Rev. 51, 114–16 (2016). Vol. 92 NOTRE DAME LAW REVIEW, Page 51 (2016). Reprinted with permission. © Notre Dame Law Review, University of Notre Dame.

W. William Hodes, *Seeking the Truth Versus Telling the Truth at the Boundaries of the Law: Misdirection, Lying, and "Lying With an Explanation,"* 44 S. Tex. L. Rev. 53, 57–62 (2002).

Richard Klein, *The Role of Defense Counsel in Ensuring a Fair Justice System,* 36 The Champion 38, 38–39, 43–44 (June 2012).

Daniel Markovits, *Adversary Advocacy and the Authority of Adjudication,* 75 Fordham L. Rev. 1367, 1367–1369, 1370, 1391–1393, 1395 (2006).

Robert P. Mosteller, *Why Defense Attorneys Cannot, But Do, Care About Innocence,* 50 Santa Clara L. Rev. 1, 3–4, 40–41, 58–59, 60–62 (2010).

Deborah L. Rhode, *The Future of the Legal Profession: Institutionalizing Ethics,* 44 Case W. Res. L. Rev. 665, 667–73 (1994).

This article originally appeared as Daniel Richman, *Prosecutors and Their Agents, Agents and Their Prosecutors,* 103 COLUM. L. REV. 749, 756–763, 786–790 (2003). Reprinted by permission.

Abbe Smith, *Defending Those People*, 10 OHIO ST. J. CRIM. L. 277, 283–285, 287–288, 290–291, 298, 300, 301 (2012).

Features of This Casebook

Throughout the book you will find various text boxes on either side of the page. These boxes provide information that will help you to understand a case or cause you to think more deeply about an issue.

 For More Information These boxes point you to resources to consult for more information on a subject.

 What's That? These boxes explain the meaning of special legal terms that appear in the main text. Black's Law Dictionary definitions may be accessed by clicking on the hyperlinked term in the text.

 Take Note Here you will be prompted to take special notice of something that deserves further thought or attention.

 See It These boxes point you to visual information that is relevant to the material in the text.

 It's Latin to Me The law is fond of Latin terms and phrases; when you encounter these for the first time, this box will explain their meaning.

 Food for Thought These boxes pose questions that prompt you to think about issues raised by the material.

 Practice Pointer Here you will find advice relevant to legal practice typically inspired by the actions (or inactions) of legal counsel in the cases or simply prompted by an important issue being discussed.

 FYI A self-explanatory category that shares useful or simply interesting information relevant to material in the text.

 Hear It These boxes point you to an audio file that is relevant to the material in the text.

 Ethical Issue These boxes present relevant real-world situations that potentially cause ethical conflicts and pose questions relating to those situations.

Go Online If there are relevant online resources that are worth consulting in relation to any matter being discussed, these boxes will direct you to them.

 Test Your Knowledge These boxes contain hyperlinks to online assessment questions that will help you test your understanding of the material in each chapter.

 Global View These boxes offer comparative and international law perspectives.

 Who's That? These boxes provide biographical information about a person mentioned in the text.

 Major Themes A discussion of some of the deeper themes and issues pertaining to the topic covered in that chapter.

 Make the Connection When concepts or discussions that pertain to information covered in other law school courses appear in a case or elsewhere in this text, often you will find this text box to indicate the course in which you can study those topics. Here you may also be prompted to connect information in the current case to material that you have covered elsewhere in this course.

Table of Contents

Chapter 3   *The Right to Counsel*...39

Table of Cases

The principal cases are in **bold** type.
Cases cited or discussed in the text are in roman type.
References are to pages. Cases cited in principal cases
and within other quoted materials are not included.

Page numbers 859–1468, set out below,
are found in Weaver, Burkoff, and Hancock's
Criminal Procedure, A Contemporary Approach (3rd ed. 2021).

CRIMINAL PROCEDURE: INVESTIGATIVE

A Contemporary Approach

THIRD EDITION

CHAPTER 1

Introduction to the Criminal Justice Process

Lawyers who work in the criminal justice system rely on many sources of law, including the constitutional case law of the United States Supreme Court. These important federal precedents are part of the bedrock knowledge of defense counsel and prosecutors who practice in municipal, state and federal courts, and roughly a dozen precedential criminal procedure decisions are handed down by the Court every year. This case law is the primary source material in most criminal procedure casebooks, but the significance of the Court's rulings can be difficult to understand in context because of the narrow doctrinal focus exhibited in any

Go Online

You can see just what cases are going to be or have been argued at the Supreme Court's website. *See* http://www.supremecourt.gov/.

one individual decision. The Court's opinions rarely describe the procedures and lawyering activities that occurred *before* a case is briefed and argued in the rarified forum of the Court's chambers. Each opinion usually gives the reader only a tiny glimpse of the large backdrop of law, custom, and practice that surrounds each case. This Chapter provides a brief overview of that backdrop, which practicing lawyers take for granted as a frame of reference for understanding the Court's precedents.

A. Sources of Law That Create Legal Rights for Criminal Defendants & Regulate the Procedures of the Criminal Justice System

Certain federal constitutional rights are available to all defendants who are charged with crimes. These rights are established in particular provisions of the Bill of Rights, such as the Fourth, Fifth, Sixth, and Eighth Amendments, and by the Due Process and Equal Protection Clauses of the Fourteenth Amendment. A defendant in a federal prosecution is also entitled to rights that are provided by federal statutes, such as the federal Code of Criminal Procedure, 18 U.S.C. § 3001 *et seq.*

A defendant in a state prosecution is entitled to invoke not only federal constitutional rights, but also rights provided by state statutes or state codes of criminal procedure. More importantly, state defendants also have *state* constitutional rights that may provide greater protections than federal constitutional rights. Most state constitutions have provisions that are similar to the Bill of Rights, and each state's highest appellate court is the final authority on the meaning of these provisions. From a state court's point of view, federal Supreme Court interpretations of a particular right may provide a model for interpretation of the state constitutional version of that right. However, the federal approach is sometimes rejected by state courts whose state constitutions have been interpreted as providing greater protections for state court defendants. While many rulings by the United States Supreme Court are "borrowed" by state supreme courts as interpretations of parallel state constitutional provisions, some rulings are rejected by state courts that interpret their state provisions as intended to provide greater protections.

Make the Connection

This important point may be clearer to you when you read about particular federal constitutional rights later in this casebook. For example, in Chapter 4, you will discover that, under the Fourth Amendment, federal law enforcement officers need neither probable cause nor a warrant in order to use a canine sniff for drugs or explosives. However, some state supreme courts have interpreted their state constitutions as requiring either probable cause or reasonable suspicion before state law enforcement officers can use canines for this purpose.

In effect, the federal constitution creates a "floor" that establishes the minimum rights that must be recognized in *all* criminal prosecutions and criminal investigations, but the state courts are free to establish their own higher "floors" that establish greater protections and rights that will be enforced in state prosecutions. From a defense counsel's perspective, representation of a client in a particular state court requires a bedrock knowledge of that state's constitutional and statutory law, in order to raise all relevant state-law claims in tandem with arguments based on the federal constitution. State prosecutors also must possess the same bedrock knowledge in order to enable them to respond to all of these claims.

In addition to constitutional and statutory law, there are other sources of law that create rights for criminal defendants or regulate the criminal justice process in important ways. One case-law source is the body of judge-made rules that derive from a court's "supervisory" authority over the criminal court system and its evidentiary rules. One statutory source is the rules of court adopted by judges to govern procedure in particular courts. These sources exist in both federal and state jurisdictions. There are also "local" sources of law that create rights and regulate criminal procedure, such as city ordinances and municipal court rules.

Occasionally, it may be unclear whether a person is charged with a "crime," or only with a "civil" offense that does not entitle him or her to state and federal constitutional and statutory rights reserved for *criminal* defendants. When the Congress or a state legislature labels a sanction as criminal, courts recognize that this permits a defendant to invoke such rights. However, if the legislature labels a sanction as civil, this does not end the inquiry. The Supreme Court has ruled that it is theoretically possible for a defendant to persuade a court to treat a proceeding as criminal (sometimes "quasi-criminal") despite its legislative classification as civil. However, it is usually very difficult for defense counsel to win such an argument without strong evidence that the statutory scheme is punitive in purpose or effect.

While the Supreme Court's federal constitutional precedents have been likened to a "code" of criminal procedure, they are neither as systematic nor as comprehensive as a legislative code. Instead, they reveal the Court's historical preoccupation with particular issues that raise fundamental questions about fairness in the treatment of people who are investigated for and charged with crime, and about the needs of law enforcement officers and officials to investigate and prosecute crimes effectively. For example, the Prohibition era provided the setting for the Court's early development of Fourth Amendment law defining police powers to conduct searches and seizures, and the focus on the prosecution of drug crimes in recent decades has spurred the Court to establish many new Fourth Amendment precedents. Moreover, those precedents are concentrated in particular fields of criminal procedure, so that some fields are heavily influenced by them and other fields are not. Even in fields where many precedents exist, the Court's decisions often provide sketchy guidance for lower courts that must attempt to interpret and enforce these holdings. Thus, in most areas of criminal procedure, the Court's decisions provide only a starting point for analyzing some issues

When state legislatures and courts consider the need to define or interpret statutory codes governing criminal procedure, they are often influenced by the Federal Rules of Criminal Procedure and other federal statutes, and by the American Bar Association (ABA) Standards

Go Online

You can view the most recent federal statistics on criminal victimization rates of U.S. residents at http://www.bjs.gov/index.cfm?ty=pbse&sid=6. After declining 62% from 1994 to 2015, the number of violent-crime victims increased from 2015 to 2016, and again from 2016 to 2018. Among U.S. residents age 12 or older, the number of violent-crime victims rose from 2.7 million in 2015 to 3.3 million in 2018. This overall rise was driven by increases in the number of victims of rape or sexual assault, aggravated assault, and simple assault. From 2015 to 2018, the portion of U.S. residents age 12 or older who were victims of violent crime rose from 0.98% to 1.18% (up 20%). The total number of times people experienced violent crime rose from 5.0 million in 2015 to 6.4 million in 2018, while the rate of violent victimization rose from 18.6 to 23.2 victimizations per 1,000 persons age 12 or older. https://www.bjs.gov/content/pub/pdf/cv18_sum.pdf.

for Criminal Justice. They may also be influenced by the American Law Institute's Model Code of Pre-Arraignment Procedure. However, there is no real pressure for the "nationalization" of criminal procedure doctrine and practice, in part because of the long history of state and local autonomy and diversity in this field. In fact, the politicization of "law and order" issues in recent decades has created the opposite kind of pressure for constant local experimentation with criminal procedure rules. Public criticism of the weaknesses of the criminal justice system is a permanent feature of the modern legal landscape, and political calls for reform of the system have affected many aspects of criminal procedure, ranging from the election of state supreme court justices based on their doctrinal views to legislative attempts to repeal or restrict various criminal procedure rules that benefit defendants, such as the writ of *habeas corpus* and exclusionary rules of evidence.

B. Prosecution Systems

1. Multiple Jurisdictions, Major & Minor Crimes

When a person commits a criminal act, he or she may violate simultaneously the criminal law of multiple jurisdictions, such as federal and state laws, or state laws and municipal ordinances. According to the Court's Double Jeopardy doctrine, multiple prosecutions for the same act by different "sovereign" governments are not prohibited by the Constitution. *See, e.g., Gamble v. United States*, <u>139 S.Ct. 1960, 1964 (2019)</u>: "We have long held that a crime under one sovereign's laws is not 'the same offence' as a crime under the laws of another sovereign. Under this 'dual-sovereignty' doctrine, a State may prosecute a defendant under state law even if the Federal Government has prosecuted him for the same conduct under a federal statute. Or the reverse may happen."

It is possible, however, that a statute of limitations may bar prosecution in one jurisdiction, or that prosecution in one jurisdiction may be particularly advantageous because of the penalty, the procedural rules, or for some other reason. Or, some prosecutors may lack resources that other prosecutors possess, and this difference may influence the timing and outcome of decisions to prosecute in only one or both jurisdictions.

In federal and state jurisdictions, most prosecutions are for minor crimes. While the definition of a "minor" crime is not uniform among the states, in most states a misdemeanor cannot be punished for more than one year in prison. Fewer than one tenth of state prosecutions are for felonies. By contrast, about one third of federal prosecutions are for felonies. Not surprisingly states have established different procedures to deal with the millions of minor-crime prosecutions that occur every year.

For example, a defendant who is charged with a misdemeanor may not be entitled to a preliminary hearing, grand jury review, pretrial discovery, or a jury trial. Also, prosecutions for minor crimes may be tried in municipal court before a magistrate who may not be a lawyer.

2. The Gap Between Law & Practice

When lawyers practice criminal law, they often find that the criminal procedure rules "on the books" may not reflect reality, and that a defendant's rights may be rarely invoked or enforced. This may be the result of defense counsel's advice to waive these rights, as when a defendant pleads guilty and thereby waives the right to trial by jury and the privilege against self-incrimination, among others. Or defense counsel may lack the resources to pursue all potential legal arguments available to an indigent defendant, or counsel may act inadequately under ABA standards but still not be "ineffective" under federal constitutional standards. It may be that defense counsel lacks evidence that will persuade a judge or prosecutor to accept a defendant's claim, as when a judge credits a police officer's testimony concerning an event and rejects the defendant's testimony. Even when a defendant has a good claim, he or she may nonetheless have no right to the assistance of appointed counsel to pursue such a claim. According to Supreme Court precedents, the Sixth Amendment guarantees trial counsel for indigent defendants only when he or she will receive a jail or prison sentence. For appeals, the Fourteenth Amendment guarantees indigent defendants a right to counsel only for the first appeal. Defendants who seek to pursue claims in other circumstances have no federal constitutional right to counsel, although they may have such rights based on state constitutional or statutory law.

The gap between law and practice also is created by the decentralized nature of prosecution systems. The federal system is the most centralized institution, because police and prosecutors generally answer to a single prosecutorial authority, the Department of Justice (DOJ) (although some federal agencies also have their own prosecution units). The DOJ attempts to create some uniformity among its agents through the promulgation of policy positions to be followed by all United States Attorneys' Offices and, for example, all Drug Enforcement Administration officers. By contrast, in state prosecution systems, police and prosecutors often work for different authorities, so that police actions may not be authorized by prosecutors, but only by the police department. Typically, state prosecutors have "territorial" jurisdiction over a particular county (which often overlaps with the jurisdiction of certain local prosecutors or city attorneys), and a variety of police departments also have overlapping jurisdictions within the same territory. This collection of autonomous groups in the prosecution system makes it difficult for uniform policies or practices to be implemented without the cooperation of all of the agents in the system.

Finally, both police and prosecutors are vested with considerable discretion, which further widens the gap between law and practice. For example, the police have substantial discretion to ignore criminal acts, or to arrest one person for a certain crime but not another person who has committed exactly the same crime. Prosecutors have discretion in their charging decisions, and in plea bargaining. Some of the Supreme Court's remedies for constitutional violations by police and prosecutors are assumed to be necessary in order to create incentives for these law enforcement agents and officials to adhere to constitutional obligations. Yet even the existence of incentives cannot always insure the proper recognition and enforcement of constitutional rights on the streets, or for that matter, in court.

C. The Roles of Prosecutors & Defense Counsel in Various Stages of a Criminal Prosecution

1. The Pre-Arrest Investigation Stage

One goal of most pre-arrest investigations, whether conducted by police or by prosecutors working together with police, is to obtain evidence that will satisfy the "probable cause" standard required both for arrest and for judicial validation of any decision to charge a person with a crime. This standard does not require as much evidence as the "preponderance" (more likely than not) standard for proving liability in a typical civil case. But the probable cause standard requires more proof than the lower "reasonable suspicion" standard that allows police to stop, question, frisk, and briefly detain people during pre-arrest investigations. A second goal of most pre-arrest investigations is to obtain sufficient evidence to satisfy the "beyond a reasonable doubt" standard required ultimately for conviction at trial. If this kind of evidence cannot be obtained before an arrest is made, then police and prosecutors will attempt to obtain it by using a variety of investigatory techniques after the arrest.

A prosecutor's first contact with a case usually occurs after police have engaged in some investigative procedures following the report of a crime, i.e. it is reactive not proactive, or after police have arrested a person following a report and investigation. Police may not be able to make a crime-scene arrest, but they usually will interview the victim and any witnesses and collect evidence in order to preserve a record for later prosecution. Unlike the police activities portrayed in television dramas, investigations for most crimes do not go beyond these simple activities. When further investigation is required, prosecutors may be asked to participate in police efforts to obtain a warrant for searches and seizures of a person's home, or in interviews of witnesses or interrogations of a suspect who may not be in custody. Occasionally, prosecutors may participate in investigations of unreported crimes. They may help supervise "sting" operations, for example, or advise the police concerning the use of undercover police agents or informants, or surveillance techniques such as electronic monitoring. Prosecutors may also investigate crimes through the use of grand jury proceedings, and use subpoenas to compel witnesses to testify and provide evidence to grand juries.

Defense counsel usually will not play a role in pre-arrest investigative activities by prosecutors and police, unless called upon to do so by a client. For example, a person with retained counsel may ask for advice concerning

> **Food for Thought**
>
> Would our criminal justice system be fairer, do you think, if prosecutors were more involved in pre-arrest investigative activities?

the advisability of agreeing to a police interview, and may agree to the interview only in the presence of counsel. A witness who is required to appear before a grand jury may consult retained counsel during breaks in the proceedings. A person who believes he or she may be the "target" of a grand jury investigation may employ retained counsel to communicate with prosecutors in order to protect his or her interests, to gain immunity, or to attempt to influence the ultimate charging decision.

2. The Arrest Stage

There are two different kinds of arrests: a non-custodial "citation" arrest, and the "full-custody" arrest. Both require probable cause, but the citation arrest is typically used only for minor offenses such as traffic crimes. Most states and municipalities authorize police to issue an arrest citation for such crimes, in their discretion, and to release the arrested person after giving them the citation. The arrestee has the obligation to respond to the citation, either by pleading guilty and paying a fine, or by appearing in court to contest guilt. Even for minor offenses, however, police may retain the discretion to perform a full-custody arrest, and usually they will follow this practice when arresting a person for a serious crime. After forcibly detaining the arrestee, the police will take him or her to the police station for "booking," and then the arrestee will be jailed or possibly released to await the outcome of the prosecutor's review and decision to charge.

Most arrests are made without warrants, as authorized by the Supreme Court's precedents which establish a variety of exceptions to the Fourth Amendment's warrant requirement. Thus, police will seek an arrest warrant from a magistrate only when they are required to do so by law, or when there is some practical reason to do so. Prosecutors may work together with police in preparing the documents to present to a magistrate. The request for a warrant must be supported by sworn affidavits describing the investigation that led the police to believe there is probable cause that a crime has been committed by a particular person. The magistrate's hearing on the police request for an arrest warrant is *ex parte* and defense counsel usually have no role to play in this procedure.

The power to make a full-custody arrest carries with it other powers. It entitles police to perform a full search of the arrestee's person at the scene of arrest, and to search the passenger compartment of a car when arresting a driver. Once a person is in custody, even more intrusive body searches may be allowed for arrestees who are going to be jailed. Even though these searches may be made without probable cause, a warrantless arrest must be based upon probable cause that will be reviewed by a magistrate at a hearing after the arrest. The Supreme Court's precedents establish 48 hours as the maximum deadline for such a hearing, but most states have significantly shorter deadlines.

It's Latin to Me

Ex parte. On or from one party only, usually without notice to or argument from the adverse party.

3. The Booking & Jailing Stage

People who have been subjected to a full-custody arrest will also undergo the booking process, which usually occurs at the police station or jail. The purpose of booking is to allow the police to keep a record of arrests, and to obtain photographs and fingerprints of arrestees. There is no connection between booking and the formal "charging" process, which occurs later. During booking, the arrestee is asked to supply biographical information, such as name and address, but should not be asked questions about the crime. After booking, police may allow people who are arrested for minor crimes to post "bail" immediately, and to be released on their own recognizance, pending the outcome of later decisions whether or not to file formal charges against them. However, people who lack the money to post bail will be jailed, as will people who are charged with serious crimes. Someone who is jailed may be subjected to a thorough search of his or her person, and a complete inventory of the new arrestee's possessions may be performed. State or local law, or police custom or practice may allow an arrestee to telephone a lawyer or a friend at this stage, but an arrested person who is indigent may not have contact with appointed defense counsel until the arraignment stage.

In 2009, 62% of felony defendants in the 75 largest counties were released prior to case disposition. About 1 in 10 detained defendants (4% of defendants overall) was denied bail. Nearly half (45%) of murder defendants were denied bail, compared to 8% or less of defendants charged with other offenses. About half (49%) of all releases used private surety bonds, the most common method of pretrial release. About 2 in 5 pretrial releases did not require posting of any type of bond. Overall, detained defendants had a median bail amount of $25,000, compared to $6,000 for released defendants. Detained murder defendants had the highest median bail amount ($1,000,000), followed by detained rape defendants ($100,000). Among defendants who were released, about 3 in 10 (29%) committed some type of misconduct while released, and 17% missed a scheduled court appearance, resulting in a bench warrant being issued. Brian A. Reaves, U.S. Department of Justice, Office of Justice Programs, Bureau of Justice Statistics Special Report, "Felony Defendants in Large Urban Counties, 2009—Statistical Tables" (December 2013), https://www.bjs.gov/content/pub/pdf/fdluc09.pdf.

4. The Post-Arrest Investigation Stage

After an arrest, a prosecutor may participate in the same kinds of investigative activity that precedes an arrest, such as witness interviews or interrogations, and the procuring of search warrants. Additionally, a prosecutor may participate in activities that usually occur only after arrest, such as a "lineup," where police require the arrestee to stand with a group of people who roughly resemble him or her, and ask a witness to attempt to identify the person who committed the crime. An indigent arrestee has no *per se* right to have appointed counsel present during a lineup. Not until the initiation of formal "adversarial judicial proceedings" does such a right to counsel exist. Nor does the arrestee have a right to have appointed counsel present at a photographic "showup," where police show a witness an "array" of photographs which includes a picture of the defendant, and ask the witness to attempt to identify the guilty party. A prosecutor also may participate in the interrogation of an arrested person, who is now entitled to *Miranda* warnings due to the existence of "custodial" interrogation. An arrestee may invoke the right to counsel by asking for a lawyer during an interrogation, thereby precluding further interrogation until counsel is present.

5. The Decision to Bring a Formal Charge by Filing a Complaint

When a person is arrested, the police have, in a sense, "charged" that person with committing a crime, but that is not a formal charge that will serve as the basis of a prosecution. The prosecution does not actually begin until a "complaint" is filed, either by the prosecutor or by the police. Many arrests do not result in the filing of complaint. In some cases, a supervising police officer will decide that no charge should be pursued. In many jurisdictions, a prosecutor will make this decision, although it is possible that the decision to drop a case may not be made until after the defendant's "first appearance," or even later, after the filing of an information or issuance of an indictment. When a prosecutor decides to drop a charge, it is often due to insufficient admissible evidence, or because of the unavailability of witnesses whose testimony is believed to be necessary for conviction. In making charging decisions, a prosecutor also may decide to change the original charge, or to add additional charges. It is common for a prosecutor to review all felony arrests before deciding which charges to pursue by filing a complaint, and to allow police to file a complaint for most misdemeanor charges without a prosecutor's review.

When a complaint is filed either by a prosecutor or by a police officer, the arrestee is now a "defendant." The complaint usually sets forth a description of the crime and a citation to the criminal code offense being charged. Either the police or the victim will sign the complaint, and swear to the truth of its allegations. The act of filing the complaint is not necessarily accompanied by other immediate formal judicial proceedings. However, this filing sets other procedures in motion under state or local law, such as the requirement that a defendant must make a "first appearance" in court within a certain time period. If the defendant is not in jail, there may be a time lapse of several days before this hearing, but any defendant in jail must be brought "promptly" before a magistrate. Further, if a defendant is arrested without a warrant, the validity of probable cause for the arrest must also be determined promptly by a magistrate.

FYI

"Between 1990 and 2009, more than 3 in 5 felony defendants were charged with either a drug offense or property offense, and about 1 in 4 was charged with a violent offense. The percentage of defendants charged with a violent offense in 2009 (25%) approached that observed in 1990 (27%) after dropping to a low of 23% in 2004 and 2005. Drug defendants represented 33% of felony cases in both 1990 and 2009, but they accounted for 37% of cases between 1996 and 2006." Brian A. Reaves, "Felony Defendants in Large Urban Counties, 2009," (December 2013), https://www.bjs.gov/content/pub/pdf/fdluc09.pdf.

If the crime is a misdemeanor, the complaint will remain the "charging instrument" for the prosecutor, and the case usually will be tried in a lower-level court. However, if the crime is a felony, the complaint will be replaced with a different instrument after proceedings in the lower-level court are finished, and the case proceeds to the "court of original jurisdiction," where the trial will occur. In cases where the grand jury is involved, that charging document will be an "indictment," and in other cases, that document is called an "information." Defense counsel usually does not play a role at the charging stage, unless he or she has been retained by a client to communicate with the prosecutor and to attempt to negotiate the disposition of the charge.

6. The Defendant's First Appearance in Court

The defendant's first appearance in court occurs after the complaint is filed. This initial hearing—sometimes called the "presentment"—before the magistrate may occur as early as a few hours after arrest, or as late as several days after the arrest, depending on the defendant's custodial status and the nature of the arrest. Usually, the hearing has three purposes. First, the magistrate informs the defendant of the charges set forth in the complaint, and typically describes the defendant's various rights, such as the right to remain silent and the right to counsel. Second, the magistrate must determine whether the defendant is indigent, and ask an indigent defendant whether he or she wishes to be represented by appointed counsel. Most defendants are indigent. Most often, these defendants will be represented by attorneys employed by a state or local public defender agency. However, some jurisdictions continue to use a system of appointing attorneys from the private Bar. A few jurisdictions allow a private law firm or other group to contract for indigent representation.

Finally, the magistrate sets bail for the defendant at this hearing, assuming that this is necessary because the defendant is in custody. The magistrate may require the defendant to post cash or a bond that is obtained from a professional bonding agency. In the alternative, the magistrate may decide to release a defendant, but impose conditions on that release. Some states allow the magistrate to perform a fourth function at this hearing: to review the grounds for probable cause for a warrantless arrest. For misdemeanor cases triable in the magistrate's court, a fifth function of the first appearance is to ask for the defendant's plea on the record. It is possible for a misdemeanor defendant to plead guilty, assuming that any right to counsel and other rights are properly waived. The magistrate's acceptance of a guilty plea is regulated by standards set forth in constitutional precedents as well as statutory law. In felony cases, the

> **FYI**
>
> "Indigent defense involves the use of publicly financed counsel to represent criminal defendants who are unable to afford private counsel. At the end of their case approximately 66% of felony Federal defendants and 82% of felony defendants in large State courts were represented by public defenders or assigned counsel." Caroline Wolf Harlow, U.S. Department of Justice, Office of Justice Programs, Bureau of Justice Statistics Special Report, "Defense Counsel in Criminal Cases," (November 2000), http://www.bjs.gov/content/pub/pdf/dccc.pdf.

defendant's plea on the record will occur at the arraignment. While indigent defendants will not be represented by appointed counsel at the first appearance, retained defense counsel may participate in the hearing.

7. The Preliminary Hearing or Grand Jury Stage

The preliminary hearing (sometimes called a preliminary examination) usually will usually be the first stage where an indigent defendant will be represented by appointed counsel, and thus for most defendants, it will be the first -proceeding where the prosecutor and the defense counsel meet formally as adversaries. However, a preliminary hearing may not occur for a variety of reasons. A prosecutor may decide not to pursue the charge and file a *nolle prosequi* motion in order to have the complaint dismissed. Defense counsel may advise a client to plead guilty, and to waive the preliminary hearing in anticipation of the plea. Or, a prosecutor in some few jurisdictions may decide to avoid the disadvantages of a preliminary hearing by seeking an indictment from a grand jury.

It's Latin to Me

Nolle prosequi. A legal notice that a lawsuit or prosecution has been abandoned.

The primary disadvantage of a preliminary hearing, from a prosecutor's point of view, is that it provides advantages to defense counsel. Specifically, it allows defense counsel to cross-examine the "probable cause" witnesses who testify at the hearing, and thereby obtain a formal record that may be used for impeachment of these witnesses at trial. Defense counsel may also discover a prosecutor's evidence or strategy that would otherwise be difficult to learn about before trial. Typically, defense does not present evidence at a preliminary hearing, in order to avoid the very disadvantages that may provoke a prosecutor to avoid such a hearing. By taking the same witnesses to a secret grand jury proceeding where defense counsel is absent, the prosecutor, in jurisdictions permitting this avenue, may obtain a finding of probable cause while avoiding the need to have a magistrate to make this determination at a preliminary hearing.

See It

Do you want to view a preliminary hearing? Here's one you can watch involving a defendant accused of murdering his girlfriend and her unborn child. *See* https://www.youtube.com/watch?v=aJeomZoeSyE.

Even if the prosecutor does decide to go forward with a preliminary hearing, and to minimize the exposure of witnesses by presenting only a small amount of evidence, it is the rare case where a magistrate rejects a complaint for lack of probable cause. After all, another magistrate has previously concluded that probable cause existed for the arrest, and unless other evidence casts doubt upon that determination, the result of this second probable cause determination will be the same.

CHAPTER 1 *Introduction to the Criminal Justice Process*   13

Once this decision is made, there are two possible routes that the prosecution will take, depending on the requirements of state law. In a majority of states, the defendant will then be "bound over" to the trial court, where the prosecutor will file an "information" which supplants the complaint.

In a few states and in federal prosecutions, the defendant must be "bound over" to the grand jury, so that an indictment may issue from that body which supplants the complaint. In states where a prosecutor has the option of using the grand jury or filing an information, the latter procedure is typically used. If the grand jury option must be used, the grand jury is required to make an independent determination of probable cause, based on a prosecutor's presentation of evidence. Defense counsel do not have access to these secret proceedings. It is a rare case where a grand jury refuses to indict a defendant, whether or not the grand jury's proceeding was preceded by a preliminary hearing.

Once an indictment is issued or an information is filed, Supreme Court precedents impose certain limitations on a prosecutor's subsequent investigative activities. For example, if undercover police agents deliberately elicit incriminating statements from a defendant at this stage, such statements will not be admissible at trial on the charged offense. If a prosecutor wishes to conduct a lineup at this point, and does so in the absence of counsel, any identification obtained at the lineup will likewise be inadmissible.

8. The Arraignment Stage

The arraignment has two functions. At this hearing, the judge informs defendant of the felony charges in the indictment or information, and defendant is asked to enter a plea to the charges. Most defendants will enter a plea of not guilty, and the judge will then set the case for trial. An indigent defendant is entitled to representation by appointed counsel at arraignment. If counsel has not been appointed and defendant asks for counsel, this will bar further police interrogation about the charged crime until counsel is present, but will not necessarily cut off questioning about other crimes.

Once the arraignment occurs, plea negotiations may begin, although in some cases they may occur even earlier (or later). Defense counsel may advise a defendant to plead guilty because of the benefits offered by a prosecutor in

See It

Do you want to view an arraignment? Here's one you can watch involving a defendant charged with eight counts of attempted murder; five counts of terrorism, six counts of intimidation with a dangerous weapon; eight counts of assault on a peace officer with the intent to inflict serious injury; and eight counts of assault on a peace officer by use or display of a dangerous weapon. *See* https://www.youtube.com/watch?v=EKJLBNteq9U.

exchange for a plea, whether in the form of an agreement to reduce charges or to recommend a lower sentence. However, a prosecutor may decline to offer such benefits, especially for serious charges. Most cases are nonetheless resolved by guilty pleas, but the rate of pleas varies among jurisdictions and between crimes. If no guilty plea occurs, a prosecutor may either dismiss the charges or continue to investigate the case and prepare for trial. The prosecutor will seek discovery material from the defense as permitted by statutory law, such as a list of trial witnesses. In some jurisdictions, the defense must give the prosecution notice of the intent to raise certain defenses at trial, such as alibi or insanity. The prosecutor may also rely on expert witnesses to assist with forensic evidence, or with preparation for rebuttal of certain defenses.

Ideally, if defense counsel has the resources and time to investigate a case thoroughly, he or she may hire a private investigator to assist in interviewing witnesses and collecting evidence. Counsel will interview the defendant, examine the police report, and seek discovery of exculpatory material from the prosecutor, as well as other discovery material allowed by state or federal law, such as a list of trial witnesses. Counsel may seek to have an expert appointed for an indigent defendant to assist in trial preparation relating to crucial issues.

Defense counsel should attempt to follow the A.B.A. Criminal Justice Defense Function Standards concerning the proper representation of a criminal defendant. There are especially complex duties of preparation required by the A.B.A. Standards for capital cases. However, appointed defense counsel are sometimes burdened with large caseloads and have few or no resources for investigating a case thoroughly. In some jurisdictions, there are caps on the maximum fees that appointed counsel may receive, such as $1,000 for all the work involved in preparing and trying a capital case. In a few jurisdictions, these caps have been challenged on constitutional grounds, and legislative and judicial responses to these challenges have sometimes created resulted in increased resources available to defense counsel

FYI

The 4th edition of the A.B.A. Criminal Justice Defense Function Standards, adopted in 2015, can be found at https://www.americanbar.org/groups/criminal_justice/standards/DefenseFunctionFourthEdition/.

9. The Pre-Trial Motions Stage

As part of defense counsel's investigation of a case, certain pre-trial motions may be filed, such as a motion to compel disclosure of evidence, or for the appointment of expert witnesses to testify at trial concerning a defense like insanity. Other motions will be made in order to pursue a defendant's claims that the police or prosecutor violated the constitution or statutory law. These motions include a motion to exclude inadmissible evidence at trial, usually referred to as a "motion to suppress" evidence. Other standard motions include a motion to quash the indictment because of particular defects, a motion for reduction of bail, and a motion *in limine* to limit the prosecutor's examination of witnesses in some way.

It's Latin to Me

Motion in limine. A pretrial request that certain inadmissible evidence not be referred to or offered at trial.

Most motions to suppress are filed in order to exclude materials seized in unconstitutional searches, or incriminating statements by the defendants obtained in unconstitutional interrogations, or pre-trial identifications by witnesses obtained in an unconstitutional manner. In the small percentage of cases where a motion to suppress is granted, this ruling may result in a prosecutor's filing a *nolle prosequi* motion to dismiss, because the prosecutor now believes there is insufficient evidence of proof of guilt "beyond a reasonable doubt" to obtain a conviction at trial. However, the prosecutor may obtain additional evidence later and proceed with the same charge against the same defendant again, because the protection of the Double Jeopardy Clause does not attach until the jury is sworn at trial.

See It

Do you want to view a suppression hearing? Here's one you can watch involving a defendant charged with DUI (driving under the influence). *See* https://www.youtube.com/watch?v=NhmkC87Kzg4.

10. The Trial Stage

Defendants are guaranteed the right to a speedy trial, and some defendants will receive a trial within the time limits set by federal or state statutes, which often require that the trial occur within six months of the indictment. However, defense counsel may advise a defendant to waive the right to a speedy trial in order to have more time for pretrial preparation. Even where the right is not waived, a statutory exception to the required deadline may apply.

Defense counsel and a prosecutor will conduct *voir dire* of the jury in most states, although in some state courts and the federal courts, the judge

FYI

Of 100 defendants arraigned on serious felony charges in the 75 largest urban counties in the U.S., only 4 of them will actually go to trial. Sixty-five will plead guilty; 23 will have their cases dismissed; and 8 will be diverted or have some other outcome. Thomas H. Cohen and Tracey Kyckelhahn, U.S. Department of Justice, Office of Justice Programs, Bureau of Justice Statistics Bulletin, "Felony Defendants in Large Urban Counties, 2006," (May 2010), http://www.bjs.gov/content/pub/pdf/fdluc06.pdf.

conducts *voir dire*. Based on the information obtained from juror questionnaires and the answers obtained from jurors during *voir dire* questioning, the prosecutor and defense counsel will challenge jurors "for cause" and with "peremptory challenges." This process is regulated by Supreme Court precedents governing jury selection, as well as by statutory laws that define the grounds for challenges and limit each side to a certain number of peremptory challenges.

Most cases are tried to a jury, although defense counsel may advise the defendant to waive the right to a jury trial in some cases. Only a small percentage of trials end in a mistrial because the jury cannot agree on a verdict. Supreme Court precedents limit the right to jury trial to cases where the maximum sentence is more than six months in prison, but some states provide for this right in other cases. The jury verdict must be unanimous, although Supreme Court precedents prior to 2020 allowed for non-unanimous, state court criminal verdicts. Most states also require a jury of twelve for serious felonies and capital cases, and some states use six-person juries for misdemeanors or less serious felonies. The Court's precedents hold that a unanimous jury of six is the smallest size that can be used for a criminal trial. Most trials end in conviction, and the conviction rates vary significantly for different crimes.

11. The Sentencing Stage

In most states, a convicted defendant in a non-capital case will be sentenced by the trial judge, but in a few states, the jury will sentence the defendant. In a capital case, the jury has the responsibility of choosing between life and death. Some states have adopted complex sentencing guidelines for non-capital cases, modeled on the federal sentencing guidelines. These guidelines, or the existence of statutory "mandatory minimum" sentences, may influence or limit the discretion of a sentencing judge.

An indigent defendant is entitled to representation by appointed counsel at the sentencing hearing, which is usually held some weeks after the trial so that the probation department may prepare a presentence report for the judge. This report will

Food for Thought

Would our system be fairer if the newly-convicted defendant was typically sentenced by the same jury of peers that just found him or her guilty, rather than by the trial judge?

contain information about the defendant's history that the probation officer believes may be relevant to sentencing. At sentencing, defense counsel may try to challenge information in the report, and may produce new information for the judge's consideration. Usually, however, the role of a defense counsel and prosecutor is confined to argument concerning the appropriate exercise of judicial discretion, based on the facts in the presentence report. Defendants convicted of misdemeanors often receive a fine or community service, or both, instead of a jail sentence, but most defendants convicted of serious felonies receive a substantial prison sentence. Once a sentence is imposed, the state corrections system takes on the responsibility for administering it. The availability of parole and "good time" may mean that a defendant will not serve the same time as the sentence that is imposed by the judge.

12. The Appeal Stage

When a defendant appeals a conviction, Supreme Court precedents hold that this action does not implicate Double Jeopardy rights if the reversal is on a ground other than the sufficiency of the evidence. Accordingly, the defendant-appellant may usually be tried again if the conviction is reversed. The Court's precedents also hold that an indigent defendant is entitled to appointed counsel to pursue the first appeal "of right." While there is no federal constitutional right to such an appeal itself, all states have a long tradition of providing this right. For a state defendant, this appeal usually lies in an intermediate appellate court, or in the state supreme court of if there are no such intermediate courts in that state. For a federal defendant, the appeal lies in the federal Circuit Court of Appeals. In most states with intermediate appellate courts, once the defendant loses the first appeal of right, a further appeal to the state supreme court will be heard only if that court exercises its discretion and decides to hear the case. Supreme Court precedents do not establish a right to appointed counsel for indigent defendants for this second discretionary appeal, or for subsequent stages, such as the pursuit of a writ of certiorari to the Supreme Court. Only after the appeal process is exhausted will the conviction be termed "final." At that point, a convicted defendant may pursue the inaptly named "post-conviction remedies," available in state and federal courts.

13. The "Post-Conviction" Remedies Stage

Once a conviction is final, a state defendant usually must pursue his claims by filing a petition in the state trial court, seeking state "*habeas*" or "*coram nobis*" relief. A defendant may seek an evidentiary hearing on such claims, and some states provide that indigents have a right to appointed counsel at this stage. Even in states that do not provide counsel automatically at this stage, a trial court may decide to appoint counsel in a particular case in order to have the merits of the case briefed and argued, or in order to provide representation at the evidentiary hearing. Most requests for evidentiary hearings at this stage, however, are not granted. If a hearing is granted, it will be conducted as a civil proceeding. The losing party may appeal to the intermediate appellate court, and then to the state supreme court. At this point, a losing defendant usually will have "exhausted" his or her available post-conviction remedies in state court, and may file a petition for a writ of *habeas corpus* in federal district court, in order to pursue federal constitutional claims. A federal defendant begins the post-conviction process by filing that petition at the outset in federal district court. In non-capital cases, post-conviction relief is granted in a very small percentage of cases. In capital cases, however, there is a higher percentage of cases where relief is granted, especially in some federal circuits.

Executive Summary

Constitutional Criminal Procedure Rights. The Bill of Rights, especially the Fourth, Fifth, Sixth, and Eighth Amendments, through the Due Process and Equal Protection Clauses of the Fourteenth Amendment, is the source of most of the rights that individuals possess relating to law enforcement activity and in the criminal justice system.

State Constitutional Criminal Procedure Rights. State constitutions are often interpreted as providing greater individual rights in the criminal justice setting that Bill of Rights provisions as interpreted by the Supreme Court.

Dual Sovereignty. Multiple prosecutions for the same criminal act by the federal and state governments are not prohibited by the Constitution.

Prosecutors Are Generally Reactive Not Proactive. Most criminal activity comes to the attention of prosecutors after reports from law enforcement agents rather than resulting from a concerted investigative effort.

Charging Documents. An accused person may face charges filed in an "information" issued after a preliminary hearing or, in some states and in federal prosecutions, as a result of an "indictment" issued by a grand jury.

Discovery in Criminal Cases. The preliminary hearing is the principal means of discovery of the information possessed by the prosecution in criminal cases.

Most Defendants Do Not Actually Go to Trial. Most criminal defendants do not ultimately stand trial on the charges filed against them. Most defendants plead guilty instead, although many have the charges against them dismissed.

Finality of Convictions. A conviction is not "final" until the final appeal has concluded or the opportunity to appeal has lapsed. Even then, a convicted defendant may seek to initiate post-conviction proceedings, such as seeking a writ of *habeas corpus*.

Major Themes

a. Law and Practice Often Different—The rights a particular Bill of Rights provides and the rights individuals actually receive may not be—and often are not—the same thing.

b. Discretion Pervasive—Law enforcement officers and prosecutors have wide discretion in who and how they investigate suspected criminal activity and in what and when criminal charges are filed.

c. Indigents Disadvantaged—Criminal defendants who have sufficient means to retain their own counsel, post bail, and hire experts and investigators, have an advantage over indigent defendants who have a limited entitlement to such things.

d. Plea Bargaining Is the Name of the Game—Most criminal defendants facing serious charges end up pleading guilty to lesser charges as a result of their acceptance of a plea bargain.

For More Information

- William J. Brennan, Jr., *The Bill of Rights and the States: The Revival of State Constitutions As Guardians of Individual Rights*, 61 N.Y.U. L. Rev. 535 (1986).

- Russell L. Weaver, John M. Burkoff, Catherine Hancock & Steven I. Friedland, Principles of Criminal Procedure Ch. 1 (7th ed. 2021).

- Catherine M. Grosso & Barbara O'Brien, *Grounding Criminal Procedure*, 20 J. Gender Race & Just. 53 (2017).

- Wayne LaFave, Jerold Israel, Nancy King & Orin Kerr, Criminal Procedure 6th ed. (West Academic Publishing 2016).

- Anna Lvovsky, *The Judicial Presumption of Police Expertise*, 130 Harv. L. Rev. 1995 (2017).

- Alexandra Natapoff, *Misdemeanors*, 85 S. Cal. L. Rev. 1313 (2012).

- Robert E. Scott & William J. Stuntz, *Plea Bargaining As Contract*, 101 Yale L.J. 1909 (1992).

- William J. Stuntz, *The Pathological Politics of Criminal Law*, 100 Mich. L. Rev. 505 (2001).

- William J. Stuntz, *The Uneasy Relationship Between Criminal Procedure and Criminal Justice*, 107 Yale L.J. 1 (1997).

Test Your Knowledge

To assess your understanding of the material in this chapter, <u>click here</u> to take a quiz.

CHAPTER 2

Fourteenth Amendment Due Process

A. Incorporation of the Bill of Rights

Federal criminal procedure, like other exercises in national governance, are subject to the United States Constitution. Notwithstanding the Bill of Rights' comprehensive and uncontroverted pertinence to federal investigative, prosecutorial and adjudicative processes, its applicability to the states is a more recent and debated phenomenon.[1]

Adoption of the Fourteenth Amendment represented a fundamental redistribution of power from the state to the national government. Although that Amendment heightened the federal interest in and responsibility over civil rights, debate has persisted over whether the amendment enhanced the significance of the Bill of Rights and made it applicable to the states. U.S. Supreme Court opinions have advanced several analytical methods for determining whether the Bill of Rights applies to the states.

In the first half of the twentieth century, the leading method for determining how and whether the Bill of Rights was applicable to the states through the Fourteenth Amendment was the "fundamental rights" approach. The Bill of Rights is regarded as protecting rights that are fundamental, and provides a reference point for measuring which state practices are so shocking to the conscience that they are inconsistent with the concept of "ordered liberty." *Palko v. Connecticut*, 302 U.S. 319 (1937). The court evaluated each case under a totality of circumstances approach. For example, long before the Court held in *Gideon v. Wainwright* that the Sixth Amendment required the appointment of counsel for state felony defendants, it had held that the Sixth Amendment right to counsel was not a "fundamental right" which the states had to follow. In other words, it did not "shock the conscience" for a state to refuse appointment of counsel for indigent defendants accused of felonies. *Betts v. Brady*, 316 U.S. 455 (1942). Decisions like *Betts* produced criticism that the rights of a state defendant were substantially limited in comparison with a federal defendant.

The second method used to evaluate the applicability of the Bill of Rights to the states through the Fourteenth Amendment is the "total incorporation" approach

---

[1]   U.S. Const., Amend. XIX. The history of Reconstruction is discussed comprehensively in Charles Fairman, VII History of the Supreme Court of the United States, Reconstruction and Reunion (1987).

under which all the protections of the Bill of Rights apply to the states. Critics of this approach relied on the lack of legislative history of the Bill of Rights to support any legislative intent that all protections should be applied to the states. Although Justice Hugo Black was unable to convince a majority of his colleagues that the total incorporation approach was the proper course, his advocacy nevertheless influenced the "selective incorporation" approach used by the current Court.

In *Duncan v. Louisiana*, <u>391 U.S. 145 (1968)</u>, Justice White described the difference between the approaches:

FYI

Selective incorporation represents a hybrid or compromise between the earlier analytical methods. Its advocates believe that Fourteenth Amendment Due Process includes rights which are essential to "ordered liberty," and that the protections in the Bill of Rights are the only fundamental protections. They also find that the fundamental rights approach is too subjective and unstructured.

In one sense recent cases applying provisions of the first eight Amendments to the States represent a new approach to the "incorporation" debate. Earlier the Court can be seen as having asked, when inquiring into whether some particular procedural safeguard was required of a State, if a civilized system could be imagined that would not accord the particular protection. For example, *Palko v. State of Connecticut* stated: "The right to trial by jury and the immunity from prosecution except as the result of an indictment may have value and importance. Even so, they are not of the very essence of a scheme of ordered liberty. Few would be so narrow or provincial as to maintain that a fair and enlightened system of justice would be impossible without them." Recent cases, on the other hand, have proceeded upon the valid assumption that state criminal processes are not imaginary and theoretical schemes but actual systems bearing virtually every characteristic of the common-law system that has been developing contemporaneously in England and in this country. The question thus is whether given this kind of system a particular procedure is fundamental—whether, that is, a procedure is necessary to an Anglo-American regime of ordered liberty. It is this sort of inquiry that can justify the conclusions that state courts must exclude evidence seized in violation of the Fourth Amendment, *Mapp v. State of Ohio*; and that state prosecutors may not comment on a defendant's failure to testify, *Griffin v. State of California*.

Of each of these determinations that a constitutional provision originally written to bind the Federal Government should bind the States as well it might be said that the limitation in question is not necessarily fundamental

to fairness in every criminal system that might be imagined but is fundamental in the context of the criminal processes maintained by the American
States. When the inquiry is approached in this way the question whether
the States can impose criminal punishment without granting a jury trial
appears quite different from the way it appeared in the older cases opining that States might abolish jury trial. A criminal process which was fair
and equitable but used no juries is easy to imagine. It would make use
of alternative guarantees and protections which would serve the purposes
that the jury serves in the English and American systems. Yet no American
State has undertaken to construct such a system. Instead, every American
State, including Louisiana, uses the jury extensively, and imposes very serious punishments only after a trial at which the defendant has a right to a
jury's verdict. In every State, including Louisiana, the structure and style of
the criminal process—the supporting framework and the subsidiary procedures—are of the sort that naturally complement jury trial, and have developed in connection with and in reliance upon jury trial.

To determine whether a particular Bill of Rights protection applies to the states
under the selective incorporation approach, it is necessary to look at 1) the entirety
of the right, not just as it applies to a particular set of facts (as with the fundamental
rights approach), and 2) whether the provision is fundamental to Anglo-American
jurisprudence. In *Malloy v. Hogan*, 378 U.S. 1 (1964), Justice Brennan observed that
if the right applies to the states, all aspects of the right will apply to every state case as
it applies to every federal case:

> The Fourteenth Amendment guaranteed the petitioner the protection of
> the Fifth Amendment's privilege against self-incrimination, and under the
> applicable federal standard, the state court erred in holding that the privi-
> lege was not properly invoked. The state urges that the availability of the
> federal privilege to a witness in a state inquiry is to be determined according
> to a less stringent safeguard than is applicable in a federal proceeding. We
> disagree. The guarantees aspects of the Bill of Rights are all to be enforced
> against the States under the Fourteenth Amendment according to the same
> standards that protect those personal rights against federal encroachment.
> The Court thus has rejected the notion that the Fourteenth Amendment
> applies to the States only a "watered-down, subjective version of the indi-
> vidual guarantees of the Bill of Rights."

Despite criticism that the selective incorporation approach is arbitrary and prevents local experimentation, it was the basis for applying most of the Bill of Rights
protections to the states in the second half of the twentieth century. Of the Bill of
Rights provisions related to criminal procedure, the Court has refused to find that
only two portions are expressly applicable to the states through the Fourteenth

Amendment. The Eighth Amendment prohibition on excessive bail, although it may be regarded by the Court as fundamental, is not applicable to the states. As recently as the 1990s, the Court has held that the Fifth Amendment requirement for a grand jury indictment in felony cases is inapplicable to the states. *Albright v. Oliver*, 510 U.S. 266 (1994).

McDonald v. City of Chicago, Illinois

561 U.S. 742 (2010).

JUSTICE ALITO announced the judgment of the Court.

In *District of Columbia v. Heller*, 554 U.S. 570 (2008), we held that the Second Amendment protects the right to keep and bear arms for the purpose of self-defense, and we struck down a District of Columbia law that banned the possession of handguns in the home. The city of Chicago and the village of Oak Park, a Chicago suburb, have laws that are similar to the District of Columbia's, but Chicago and Oak Park argue that their laws are constitutional because the Second Amendment has no application to the States. We have previously held that most of the provisions of the Bill of Rights apply with full force to both the Federal Government and the States. Applying the standard that is well established in our case law, we hold that the Second Amendment right is fully applicable to the States.

The Bill of Rights, including the Second Amendment, originally applied only to the Federal Government. In *Barron ex rel. Tiernan v. Mayor of Baltimore*, 7 Pet. 243, 8 L.Ed. 672 (1833), the Court, in an opinion by Chief Justice Marshall, explained that this question was "of great importance" but "not of much difficulty." In less than four pages, the Court firmly rejected the proposition that the first eight Amendments operate as limitations on the States, holding that they apply only to the Federal Government. The constitutional Amendments adopted in the aftermath of the Civil War fundamentally altered our country's federal system. The provision at issue in this case, § 1 of the Fourteenth Amendment, provides, among other things, that a State may not abridge "the privileges or immunities of citizens of the United States" or deprive "any person of life, liberty, or property, without due process of law." The Court eventually initiated what has been called a process of "selective incorporation," i.e., the Court began to hold that the Due Process Clause fully incorporates particular rights contained in the first eight Amendments. The Court inquired whether a particular Bill of Rights guarantee is fundamental to our scheme of ordered liberty and system of justice.

The Court also shed any reluctance to hold that rights guaranteed by the Bill of Rights met the requirements for protection under the Due Process Clause. The

Court eventually incorporated almost all of the provisions of the Bill of Rights. Only a handful of the Bill of Rights protections remain unincorporated. Finally, the Court abandoned the notion that the Fourteenth Amendment applies to the States only a watered-down, subjective version of the individual guarantees of the Bill of Rights," stating that it would be "incongruous" to apply different standards "depending on whether the claim was asserted in a state or federal court." Instead, the Court decisively held that incorporated Bill of Rights protections "are all to be enforced against the States under the Fourteenth Amendment according to the same standards that protect those personal rights against federal encroachment."

With this framework in mind, we now turn to whether the Second Amendment right to keep and bear arms is incorporated in the concept of due process. In answering that question, we must decide whether the right to keep and bear arms is fundamental to our scheme of ordered liberty, or whether this right is "deeply rooted in this Nation's history and tradition." Our decision in *Heller* points unmistakably to the answer. In *Heller*, we held that the Second Amendment protects the right to possess a handgun in the home for the purpose of self-defense. Unless considerations of *stare decisis* counsel otherwise, a provision of the Bill of Rights that protects a right that is fundamental from an American perspective applies equally to the Federal Government and the States. We therefore hold that the Due Process Clause of the Fourteenth Amendment incorporates the Second Amendment right recognized in *Heller*.

Points for Discussion

a. Incorporated Rights

These decisions are cited by the *McDonald* Court as those in which the Court "eventually incorporated almost all of the provisions of the Bill of Rights": "With respect to the First Amendment, *see Everson v. Board of Ed. of Ewing*, 330 U.S. 1 (1947) (Establishment Clause); *Cantwell v. Connecticut*, 310 U.S. 296 (1940) (Free Exercise Clause); *De Jonge v. Oregon*, 299 U.S. 353 (1937) (freedom of assembly); *Gitlow v. New York*, 268 U.S. 652 (1925) (free speech); *Near v. Minnesota ex rel. Olson*, 283 U.S. 697 (1931) (freedom of the press). With respect to the Fourth Amendment, *see Aguilar v. Texas*, 378 U.S. 108 (1964) (warrant requirement); *Mapp v. Ohio*, 367 U.S. 643 (1961) (exclusionary rule); *Wolf v. Colorado*, 338 U.S. 25 (1949) (freedom from unreasonable searches and seizures). With respect to the Fifth Amendment, *see Benton v. Maryland*, 395 U.S. 784 (1969) (Double Jeopardy Clause); *Malloy v. Hogan*, 378 U.S. 1 (1964) (privilege against self-incrimination); *Chicago, B. & Q.R. Co. v. Chicago*, 166 U.S. 226 (1897) (Just Compensation Clause). With respect to the Sixth Amendment, *see Duncan v. Louisiana*, 391 U.S. 145 (1968) (trial by jury in criminal cases); *Washington v. Texas*, 388 U.S. 14 (1967) (compulsory process); *Klopfer v. North Carolina*, 386 U.S. 213 (1967) (speedy trial); *Pointer v. Texas*, 380 U.S. 400 (1965) (right to confront adverse witness); *Gideon v. Wainwright*, 372 U.S. 335 (1963) (assistance of counsel); *In re Oliver*, 333 U.S. 257 (1948) (right to a public trial). With respect to the Eighth Amendment, *see Robinson v. California*, 370 U.S. 660 (1962) (cruel and unusual punishment); *Schilb v. Kuebel*, 404 U.S. 357 (1971) (prohibition against excessive bail)."

b. Rights Not Fully Incorporated

The *McDonald* Court cited these decisions to illustrate the "handful of the Bill of Rights protections that remain unincorporated": "In addition to the right to keep and bear arms (and the Sixth Amendment right to a unanimous jury verdict), the only rights not fully incorporated are 1) the Third Amendment's protection against quartering of soldiers; 2) the Fifth Amendment's grand jury indictment requirement; 3) the Seventh Amendment right to a jury trial in civil cases; and 4) the Eighth Amendment's prohibition on excessive fines." The Sixth Amendment right to a unanimous jury has now been incorporated.

B. Retroactivity

Constitutional interpretation that generates a new rule of law presents an issue with respect to scope of application. Traditionally, the Court has allowed a prevailing litigant to be the beneficiary of a new rule. Initial determinations that illegally seized evidence must be excluded from trial, *Mapp v. Ohio*, 367 U.S. 643 (1961), or that persons in custodial interrogation must be informed of certain rights they possess, *Miranda v. Arizona*, 384 U.S. 436 (1966). thus redounded to the benefit of the individuals who first prevailed. Application at least to the prevailing litigant is justified for purposes of satisfying the case or controversy requirement and providing inducement for challenges that may improve the law.

Beyond a party whose case engendered a constitutional rule change, the scope of a new principle's operation has been widely debated especially in recent decades. During the 1960s, as federal case law became increasingly protective of defendant's rights, the Court asserted that the benefit of a new rule would not extend to persons whose convictions became final prior to its adoption. In *Linkletter v. Walker*, 381 U.S. 618, 637 (1965), the Court thus applied the exclusionary rule in a forward-looking fashion except to the extent the litigant and persons had not played out the full string of appeals. Reluctance to allow greater retroactivity reflected the sense that such a distribution of benefits would subvert the interest of finality, generate numerous retrials and undermine good-faith reliance by police and courts on the existing state of constitutional law.

Pursuant to the *Linkletter* doctrine, the benefits of a new rule did not extend to *habeas corpus* petitioners but could be claimed by persons whose cases still were on direct review. Further tightening of retroactivity principles occurred thereafter. Non-retroactivity (except for the litigant) reflected the work of a Court that, in expanding the ambit of defendants' rights, locked onto prospectivity as a device for minimizing disruption of and costs to the criminal justice system. *See, e.g., Jenkins v. Delaware*, <u>395 U.S. 213 (1969)</u>. Whatever virtues the Court attached to such a premise, however, were not consensually acknowledged. In *Desist v. United States*, Justice Harlan argued that prospectivity was a handmaiden of arbitrariness and judicial overreaching. Responding to a majority decision refus-

FYI

In *Stovall v. Denno*, the Court determined that a newly imposed requirement of counsel at lineups governed only police activity that post-dated the new rule. *Stovall v. Denno*, <u>388 U.S. 293, 299–301 (1967)</u>. Like claims would not be heard, therefore, even if asserted in cases for which a final judgment had not been rendered.

ing to apply retroactively a rule requiring counsel at certain line-ups, Harlan concluded that he could no longer "accept the rule first announced two years ago in *Stovall v. Denno*, and reaffirmed today, which permits this Court to apply a 'new' constitutional rule entirely prospectively, while making an exception only for the particular litigant whose case was chosen as the vehicle for establishing that rule. Indeed, I have concluded that *Linkletter* was right in insisting that all 'new' rules of constitutional law must, at a minimum, be applied to all those cases which are still subject to direct review by this Court at the time the 'new' decision is handed down. He went on to argue that:

> Matters of basic principle are at stake. In the classical view of constitutional adjudication, criminal defendants cannot come before this Court simply to request largesse. This Court is entitled to decide constitutional issues only when the facts of a particular case require their resolution for a just adjudication on the merits. We do not release a criminal from jail because we like to do so, or because we think it wise to do so, but because the government has offended constitutional principle in the conduct of his case. When another similarly situated defendant comes before us, we must grant the same relief or give a principled reason for acting differently. We depart from this basic judicial tradition when we simply pick and choose from among similarly situated defendants those who alone will receive the benefit of a "new" rule of constitutional law.

The unsound character of the rule reaffirmed today is perhaps best exposed by considering the following hypothetical. Imagine that the Second Circuit in the present case had anticipated the line of reasoning this Court subsequently pursued in *Katz v. United States*, concluding—as this Court there did—that "the underpinnings of *Olmstead* and *Goldman* have been so eroded by our subsequent decisions that the 'trespass' doctrine there enunciated can no longer be regarded as controlling." Would we have reversed the case on the ground that the principles the Second Circuit had announced—though identical with those in *Katz*—should not control because *Katz* is not retroactive? To the contrary, I venture to say that we would have taken satisfaction that the lower court had reached the same conclusion we subsequently did in *Katz*. If a "new" constitutional doctrine is truly right, we should not reverse lower courts which have accepted it; nor should we affirm those which have rejected the very arguments we have embraced. Anything else would belie the truism that it is the task of this Court, like that of any other, to do justice to each litigant on the merits of his own case. It is only if our decisions can be justified in terms of this fundamental premise that they may properly be considered the legitimate products of a court of law, rather than the commands of a super-legislature. Re-examination of prior developments in the field of retroactivity leads me irresistibly to the conclusion that the only solid disposition of this case lies in vacating the judgment of the Court of Appeals and in remanding this case to that court for further consideration in light of *Katz*. *Desist v. United States*, 394 U.S. 244 (1969).

Harlan's reasoning had long-term significance. In *Griffith v. Kentucky*, the Court determined that a new rule should be applied to all cases pending on direct review. It observed that:

> In Justice Harlan's view, and now in ours, failure to apply a newly declared constitutional rule to criminal cases pending on direct review violates basic norms of constitutional adjudication. First, it is a settled principle that this Court adjudicates only "cases" and "controversies." Unlike a legislature, we do not promulgate new rules of constitutional criminal procedure on a broad basis. Rather, the nature of judicial review requires that we adjudicate specific cases, and each case usually becomes the vehicle for announcement of a new rule. But after we have decided a new rule in the case selected, the integrity of judicial review requires that we apply that rule to all similar cases pending on direct review. Justice Harlan observed:

> > "If we do not resolve all cases before us on direct review in light of our best understanding of governing constitutional principles, it is difficult to see why we should so adjudicate any case at all. In truth, the Court's assertion of power to disregard current law in adjudicating cases before us that have not already run the full course of appellate review, is quite simply an assertion that our constitutional function is not one of adjudication but in effect of legislation."

> As a practical matter, we cannot hear each case pending on direct review and apply the new rule. But we fulfill our judicial responsibility by in-

structing the lower courts to apply the new rule retroactively to cases not yet final. Thus, it is the nature of judicial review that precludes us from "simply fishing one case from the stream of appellate review, using it as a vehicle for pronouncing new constitutional standards, and then permitting a stream of similar cases subsequently to flow by unaffected by that new rule."

Second, selective application of new rules violates the principle of treating similarly situated defendants the same. As we pointed out in *United States v. Johnson*, the problem with not applying new rules to cases pending on direct review is "the actual inequity that results when the Court chooses which of many similarly situated defendants should be the chance beneficiary" of a new rule. Although the Court had tolerated this inequity for a time by not applying new rules retroactively to cases on direct review, we noted: "The time for toleration has come to an end." *Griffith v. Kentucky*, 479 U.S. 314, 322 (1987).

Although arguing for retroactivity in cases in which convictions had not been finalized, Justice Harlan also distinguished collateral review from direct review. Given the unique purpose of the writ of *habeas corpus*, to ensure that states comply with federal principles at the time they were in force, he identified no logic for retroactivity in collateral proceedings except when punished conduct was beyond a state's law-making power or so fundamental as to be an implication of "ordered liberty." In *Teague v. Lane*, 489 U.S. 288 (1989), a plurality subscribed to Harlan's argument that retroactivity generally should not extend to *habeas* actions. This determination was notable not only for its investment in Harlan's thesis but for further narrowing the possibility of retroactivity in *habeas* proceedings.

The Court noted two limited exceptions suggested by Justice Harlan to the general prohibition on announcing or applying new rules in collateral proceedings. First, a new rule should be applied retroactively if it places "certain kinds of primary, private individual conduct beyond the power of the criminal law-making authority to proscribe." The second exception was that a new rule should be applied retroactively if it requires the observance of "watershed rules of criminal procedure." Although *Teague* did not generate a majority opinion, the reasoning of the O'Connor plurality was adopted soon thereafter in *Penry v. Lynaugh*, 492 U.S. 302, 314 (1989).

A critical determinant of retroactivity is whether a principle is driven by precedent or establishes a new rule. The *Linkletter* doctrine reflected Blackstonian theory that regarded new rulings as a discovery of the law as it actually existed. The *Teague* decision and its progeny rejected the notion that the law is decoded, and instead accepted the prior legal condition as a reality. In *Yates v. Aiken*, 484 U.S. 211, 216 (1988), the Court distinguished between a result generated by a rule that breaks new ground and an outcome that is dictated by precedent. It referenced Harlan's understanding "that most collateral attacks on final judgments should be resolved by reference to the state of the law at the time of the petitioner's conviction, and his sense that many 'new' holdings are merely applications of principles that were well settled at the time of conviction."

Justice Harlan in *Desist* distinguished between rules that were genuinely new and holdings that applied established principles to different factual settings. In *Teague*, the plurality stressed that a new rule is announced "if the result was not *dictated* by precedent existing at the time the defendant's conviction became final." 489 U.S. at 301. Whatever room the *Teague* and *Penry* decisions left for results ordained by existing precedent, was compressed further in *Butler v. McKellar*, 494 U.S. 407 (1990). The *McKellar* Court determined that a rule was new "if the outcome was susceptible to debate among reasonable minds." The depiction of a new rule elicited criticism by dissenting justices and commentators to the effect that the majority had gutted the writ of *habeas corpus* and thus "infringed upon legislative prerogatives." 494 U.S. at 432 (Brennan, J., dissenting). Supporting that perspective is the fact that the Court typically does not grant review unless reasonable minds differ over the applicability of existing law.

Butler v. McKellar

494 U.S. 407 (1990).

CHIEF JUSTICE REHNQUIST delivered the opinion of the Court.

Petitioner Horace Butler was convicted and sentenced to death for the murder of Pamela Lane. After his conviction became final on direct appeal, Butler collaterally attacked his conviction by way of a petition for federal *habeas corpus*. Butler relied on our decision in *Arizona v. Roberson*, decided after his conviction became final. We have held that a new decision generally is not applicable in cases on collateral review unless the decision was dictated by precedent existing at the time the petitioner's conviction became final. We hold that our ruling in *Roberson* was not so dictated and that Butler's claim is not within either of two narrow exceptions to the general rule.

We held in *Roberson* that the Fifth Amendment bars police-initiated interrogation following a suspect's request for counsel in the context of a separate investigation. On Butler's motion for reconsideration, the original Fourth Circuit panel considered Butler's new contention that *Roberson* requires suppression of his statements taken in the separate investigation of Lane's murder. Although the panel conceded that the substance of its prior conclusion "was cast into immediate and serious doubt" by our subsequent decision in *Roberson*, it nevertheless determined that Butler was not entitled to the retroactive benefit of *Roberson*. According to the panel, the *Edwards-*

Roberson limitations on police interrogation are only tangentially related to the truth-finding function. They are viewed most accurately as part of the prophylactic protection of the Fifth Amendment right to counsel created to be "guidelines" for the law enforcement profession. The interrogation of Butler, while unquestionably contrary to present "guidelines," was conducted in strict accordance with established law at the time. The panel, therefore, denied Butler's petition for rehearing. A majority of the Circuit Judges denied, over a dissent, Butler's petition for a rehearing en banc. We granted certiorari, and now affirm.

The "new rule" principle validates reasonable, good-faith interpretations of existing precedents made by state courts even though they are shown to be contrary to later decisions. Butler contends that *Roberson* did not establish a new rule and is, therefore, available to support his *habeas* petition. Butler argues that *Roberson* was merely an application of *Edwards* to a slightly different set of facts. In support of his position, Butler points out that the majority had said that *Roberson's* case was directly controlled by *Edwards*. But the fact that a court says that its decision is within the "logical compass" of an earlier decision, or indeed that it is "controlled" by a prior decision, is not conclusive for purposes of deciding whether the current decision is a "new rule." Courts frequently view their decisions as being "controlled" or "governed" by prior opinions even when aware of reasonable contrary conclusions reached by other courts. In *Roberson*, for instance, the Court found *Edwards* controlling but acknowledged a significant difference of opinion on the part of several lower courts that had considered the question previously. That the outcome in *Roberson* was susceptible to debate among reasonable minds is evidenced further by the differing positions taken by the judges of the Courts of Appeals for the Fourth and Seventh Circuits noted previously. It would not have been an illogical or even a grudging application of *Edwards* to decide that it did not extend to the facts of *Roberson*. We hold, therefore, that *Roberson* announced a "new rule."

The question remains whether the new rule in *Roberson* nevertheless comes within one of the two recognized exceptions under which a new rule is available on collateral review. Under the first exception, "a new rule should be applied retroactively if it places 'certain kinds of primary, private individual conduct beyond the power of the criminal law-making authority to proscribe.'" This exception is clearly inapplicable. The proscribed conduct in the instant case is capital murder, the prosecution of which is, to put it mildly, not prohibited by the rule in *Roberson*. Nor did *Roberson* address any "categorical guarantees accorded by the Constitution" such as a prohibition on the imposition of a particular punishment on a certain class of offenders. Under the second exception, a new rule may be applied on collateral review "if it requires the observance of those procedures that are 'implicit in the concept of ordered liberty.'" *Teague*, however, discerned a latent danger in relying solely on this famous language from *Palko*: "Were we to employ the *Palko* test without more, we would be doing little more than importing into a very different context the terms of the debate over incorporation. Reviving the *Palko* test now, in this area of law, would be unnecessarily anachronistic." We believe that Justice Harlan's concerns about the difficulty in identifying both the existence and the value of accuracy-enhancing procedural rules can be addressed by limiting the scope of the second exception to those new procedures without which the likelihood of an accurate conviction is seriously diminished. "Because we operate from the premise that such procedures would be so central to an accurate determination of innocence or guilt, we believe it unlikely that many such components of basic due process have yet to emerge."

Because a violation of *Roberson*'s added restrictions on police investigatory procedures would not seriously diminish the likelihood of obtaining an accurate determination—indeed, it may increase that likelihood—we conclude that *Roberson* did not establish any principle that would come within the second exception.

The judgment of the Court of Appeals is therefore *Affirmed.*

[JUSTICE BRENNAN dissented, joined by JUSTICES MARSHALL, BLACKMUN and STEVENS. He argued that the Court had narrowed the window for identifying a new rule in *habeas* proceedings. *Roberson* was not a "new rule," dictated by prior precedent, and therefore, should be retroactively applicable to cases on collateral review.]

Whorton v. Bockting

549 U.S. 406 (2007).

JUSTICE ALITO delivered the opinion of the Court.

This case presents the question whether, under the rules set out in *Teague v. Lane*, 489 U.S. 288 (1989), our decision in *Crawford v. Washington*, 541 U.S. 36 (2004), is retroactive to cases already final on direct review. We hold that it is not.

Respondent Marvin Bockting lived in Las Vegas, Nevada, with his wife, Laura Bockting, their 3-year-old daughter Honesty, and Laura's 6-year-old daughter from a previous relationship, Autumn. One night, while respondent was at work, Autumn awoke from a dream crying, but she refused to tell her mother what was wrong, explaining: "Daddy said you would make him leave and that he would beat my butt if I told you." After her mother reassured her, Autumn said that respondent had frequently forced her to engage in numerous and varied sexual acts with him. The next day, Laura Bockting confronted respondent and asked him to leave the house. He did so but denied any wrongdoing. Two days later, Laura called a rape crisis hotline and brought Autumn to the hospital for an examination. At the hospital, Detective Charles Zinovitch from the Las Vegas Metropolitan Police Department Sexual Assault Unit attempted to interview Autumn but found her too distressed to discuss the assaults. Detective Zinovitch then ordered a rape examination, which revealed strong physical evidence of sexual assaults. Two days later, Detective Zinovitch interviewed Autumn in the presence of her mother, and at that time, Autumn provided a detailed description of acts of sexual assault carried out by respondent; Autumn also demonstrated those acts using anatomically correct dolls. Respondent was then arrested, and a state grand jury indicted him on four counts of sexual assault on a minor under 14 years of age.

At respondent's preliminary hearing, Autumn testified that she understood the difference between a truth and a lie, but she became upset when asked about the assaults. Although she initially agreed that respondent had touched her in a way that "she didn't think he was supposed to touch her," she later stated that she could not remember how respondent had touched her or what she had told her mother or the detective. The trial court, found the testimony of Laura Bockting and Detective Zinovitch to be sufficient to hold respondent for trial. At trial, the court held a hearing outside the presence of the jury to determine whether Autumn could testify. After it became apparent that Autumn was too distressed to be sworn in, the State moved under Nev.Rev.Stat. § 51.385 (2003) to allow Laura Bockting and Detective Zinovitch to recount Autumn's statements regarding the sexual assaults. Under the Nevada statute, out-of-court statements made by a child under 10 years of age describing acts of sexual assault or physical abuse of the child may be admitted if the court finds that the child is unavailable or unable to testify and that "the time, content and circumstances of the statement provide sufficient circumstantial guarantees of trustworthiness." Over defense counsel's objection that admission of this testimony would violate the Confrontation Clause, the trial court found sufficient evidence of reliability to satisfy § 51.385. As a result of this ruling, Laura Bockting and Detective Zinovitch were permitted at trial to recount Autumn's out-of-court statements about the assaults. Laura Bockting also testified that respondent was the only male who had had the opportunity to assault Autumn. In addition, the prosecution introduced evidence regarding Autumn's medical exam. Respondent testified in his own defense and denied the assaults, and the defense brought out the fact that Autumn, unlike many children her age, had acquired some knowledge about sexual acts, since she had seen respondent and her mother engaging in sexual intercourse and had become familiar with sexual terms. The jury found respondent guilty of three counts of sexual assault on a minor under the age of 14, and the trial court imposed two consecutive life sentences and another concurrent life sentence.

Respondent took an appeal to the Nevada Supreme Court, which handed down its final decision more than a decade before *Crawford*. In analyzing respondent's contention that the admission of Autumn's out-of-court statements violated his Confrontation Clause rights, the Nevada Supreme Court looked to *Ohio v. Roberts*, 448 U.S. 56 (1980), which was then the governing precedent of this Court. *Roberts* held that the Confrontation Clause permitted the admission of a hearsay statement made by a declarant who was unavailable to testify if the statement bore sufficient indicia of reliability, either because the statement fell within a firmly rooted hearsay exception or because there were "particularized guarantees of trustworthiness" relating to the statement in question. Applying *Roberts*, the Nevada Supreme Court held that the admission of Autumn's statements was constitutional because the circumstances surrounding the making of the statements provided particularized guarantees of trustworthiness. The Court cited the "natural spontaneity" of Autumn's initial statements to her mother, her reiteration of the same account to Detective Zinovitch several days later, her use of anatomically correct dolls to demonstrate the assaults, and her detailed descriptions of sexual acts with which a 6-year-old would generally not be familiar.

Respondent then filed a petition for a writ of *habeas corpus* with the United States District Court for the District of Nevada. While this appeal was pending, we issued our opinion in *Crawford*, in which we overruled *Roberts* and held that "testimonial statements of witnesses absent from trial" are admissible "only where the declarant is unavailable, and only where the defendant has had a prior opportunity to cross-examine the witness." We noted that the outcome in *Roberts*—as well as the outcome in all similar cases decided by this Court—was consistent with the rule announced in *Crawford*, but we concluded that the interpretation of the Confrontation Clause set out in *Roberts* was unsound in several respects. First, we observed that *Roberts* potentially excluded too much testimony because it imposed Confrontation Clause restrictions on nontestimonial hearsay not governed by that Clause. At the same time, we noted, the *Roberts* test was too "malleable" in permitting the admission of *ex parte* testimonial statements.

On appeal from the denial of his petition for writ of *habeas corpus*, respondent contended that if the rule in *Crawford* had been applied to his case, Autumn's out-of-court statements could not have been admitted into evidence and the jury would not have convicted him. Respondent further argued that *Crawford* should have been applied to his case because the rule was either (1) an old rule in existence at the time of his conviction or (2) a "watershed" rule that implicated "the fundamental fairness and accuracy of the criminal proceeding." *Saffle v. Parks*, 494 U.S. 484, 495 (1990). A divided panel of the Ninth Circuit reversed the District Court, holding that *Crawford* applies retroactively to cases on collateral review. The panel's decision conflicts with the decision of every other Court of Appeals and State Supreme Court that has addressed this issue. We granted certiorari to resolve this conflict.

In *Teague* and subsequent cases, we laid out the framework to be used in determining whether a rule announced in one of our opinions should be applied retroactively to judgments in criminal cases that are already final on direct review. Under the *Teague* framework, an old rule applies both on direct and collateral review, but a new rule is generally applicable only to cases that are still on direct review. A new rule applies retroactively in a collateral proceeding only if (1) the rule is substantive or

(2) the rule is a " 'watershed rule of criminal procedure' implicating the fundamental fairness and accuracy of the criminal proceeding." *Saffle, supra,* at 495 (quoting *Teague, supra,* at 311 (plurality opinion)).

In this case, it is undisputed that respondent's conviction became final on direct appeal well before *Crawford* was decided. We therefore turn to the question whether *Crawford* applied an old rule or announced a new one. A new rule is defined as "a rule that was not '*dictated* by precedent existing at the time the defendant's conviction became final.'" *Saffle, supra,* at 488 (quoting *Teague, supra,* at 301 (plurality opinion)). Applying this definition, it is clear that *Crawford* announced a new rule. The *Crawford* rule was not "dictated" by prior precedent. Quite the opposite is true. The *Crawford* rule is flatly inconsistent with the prior governing precedent, *Roberts,* which *Crawford* overruled. "The explicit overruling of an earlier holding no doubt creates a new rule." *Saffle, supra,* at 488. *Crawford* was quick to note that "the rationales" of our prior decisions had been inconsistent with the *Crawford* rule. "The 'new rule' principle validates reasonable, good-faith interpretations of existing precedents made by state courts even though they are shown to be contrary to later decisions." *Lockhart v. Fretwell,* 506 U.S. 364 (1993). Prior to *Crawford,* "reasonable jurists" could have reached the conclusion that the *Roberts* rule was the rule that governed the admission of hearsay statements made by an unavailable declarant.

Because *Crawford* announced a "new rule" and because it is clear and undisputed that the rule is procedural and not substantive, that rule cannot be applied in this collateral attack on respondent's conviction unless it is a " 'watershed rule of criminal procedure' implicating the fundamental fairness and accuracy of the criminal proceeding." *Saffle,* 494 U.S., at 495 (quoting *Teague,* 489 U.S., at 311 (plurality opinion)). This exception is "extremely narrow." We have observed that it is "unlikely" that any such rules "have yet to emerge," *ibid.* In the years since *Teague,* we have rejected every claim that a new rule satisfied the requirements for watershed status. *See, e.g., Summerlin, supra* (rejecting retroactivity for *Ring v. Arizona,* 536 U.S. 584 (2002)); *Beard v. Banks,* 542 U.S. 406 (2004) (rejecting retroactivity for *Mills v. Maryland,* 486 U.S. 367 (1988)); *O'Dell, supra* (rejecting retroactivity for *Simmons v. South Carolina,* 512 U.S. 154 (1994)); *Gilmore v. Taylor,* 508 U.S. 333 (1993) (rejecting retroactivity for a new rule relating to jury instructions on homicide); *Sawyer v. Smith,* 497 U.S. 227 (1990) (rejecting retroactivity for *Caldwell v. Mississippi,* 472 U.S. 320 (1985)).

In order to qualify as watershed, a new rule must meet two requirements. First, the rule must be necessary to prevent "an impermissibly large risk" of an inaccurate conviction. *Summerlin, supra,* at 356. Second, the rule must "alter our understanding of the bedrock procedural elements essential to the fairness of a proceeding." *Ibid.* We consider each of these requirements in turn.

The *Crawford* rule does not satisfy the first requirement relating to an impermissibly large risk of an inaccurate conviction. To be sure, the *Crawford* rule reflects the Framers' preferred mechanism (cross-examination) for ensuring that inaccurate out-of-court testimonial statements are not used to convict an accused. But in order for a new rule to meet the accuracy requirement, "it is not enough to say that the rule is aimed at improving the accuracy of trial," *Sawyer*, 497 U.S., at 242 or that the rule "is directed toward the enhancement of reliability and accuracy in some sense." Instead, the question is whether the new rule remedied "an 'impermissibly large risk' " of an inaccurate conviction.

Guidance in answering this question is provided by *Gideon v. Wainwright*, 372 U.S. 335 (1963), to which we have repeatedly referred in discussing the meaning of the *Teague* exception. In *Gideon*, the only case that we have identified as qualifying under this exception, the Court held that counsel must be appointed for any indigent defendant charged with a felony. When a defendant who wishes to be represented by counsel is denied representation, *Gideon* held, the risk of an unreliable verdict is intolerably high. *See Mickens v. Taylor*, 535 U.S. 162 (2002). The new rule announced in *Gideon* eliminated this risk. The *Crawford* rule is in no way comparable to the *Gideon* rule. The *Crawford* rule is much more limited in scope, and the relationship of that rule to the accuracy of the fact-finding process is far less direct and profound. *Crawford* overruled *Roberts* because *Roberts* was inconsistent with the original understanding of the meaning of the Confrontation Clause, not because the Court reached the conclusion that the overall effect of the *Crawford* rule would be to improve the accuracy of fact finding in criminal trials. Indeed, in *Crawford* we recognized that even under the *Roberts* rule, this Court had never specifically approved the introduction of testimonial hearsay statements. Accordingly, it is not surprising that the overall effect of *Crawford* with regard to the accuracy of fact-finding in criminal cases is not easy to assess.

With respect to *testimonial* out-of-court statements, *Crawford* is more restrictive than was *Roberts*, and this may improve the accuracy of fact-finding in some criminal cases. Specifically, under *Roberts*, there may have been cases in which courts erroneously determined that testimonial statements were reliable. But whatever improvement in reliability *Crawford* produced in this respect must be considered together with *Crawford*'s elimination of Confrontation Clause protection against the admission of unreliable out-of-court non-testimonial statements. Under *Roberts*, an out-of-court non-testimonial statement not subject to prior cross-examination could not be admitted without a judicial determination regarding reliability. Under *Crawford*, on the other hand, the Confrontation Clause has no application to such statements and therefore permits their admission even if they lack indicia of reliability.

It is thus unclear whether *Crawford*, on the whole, decreased or increased the number of unreliable out-of-court statements that may be admitted in criminal trials. But the question is not whether *Crawford* resulted in some net improvement in the accuracy of fact-finding in criminal cases. Rather, "the question is whether testimony admissible under *Roberts* is so much more unreliable than that admissible under *Crawford* that the *Crawford* rule is one without which the likelihood of an accurate conviction is *seriously* diminished." *Crawford* did not effect a change of this magnitude.

The *Crawford* rule also did not "alter our understanding of the *bedrock procedural elements* essential to the fairness of a proceeding." This requirement cannot be met simply by showing that a new procedural rule is *based on* a "bedrock" right. We have frequently held that the *Teague* bar to retroactivity applies to new rules that are based on "bedrock" constitutional rights. Similarly, "that a new procedural rule is 'fundamental' in some abstract sense is not enough." *Summerlin*, 542 U.S., at 352. Instead, in order to meet this requirement, a new rule must itself constitute a previously unrecognized bedrock procedural element that is essential to the fairness of a proceeding. In this case, it is apparent that the rule announced in *Crawford*, while certainly important, is not in the same category with *Gideon*. *Gideon* effected a profound and "sweeping" change. The *Crawford* rule simply lacks the "primacy" and "centrality" of the *Gideon* rule, and does not qualify as a rule that "altered our understanding of the bedrock procedural elements essential to the fairness of a proceeding," *Sawyer*, 497 U.S., at 242.

In sum, we hold that *Crawford* announced a "new rule" of criminal procedure and that this rule does not fall within the *Teague* exception for watershed rules. We therefore reverse the judgment of the Court of Appeals and remand the case for further proceedings consistent with this opinion.

It is so ordered.

Executive Summary

Application of the Bill of Rights to the States. Although the provisions of the Bill of rights were originally conceived as limitations on the power, many of these rights were held applicable against the states during the twentieth century.

Decisions Regarding Incorporation & Applicability. To determine whether a Bill of Rights protection applies to the states under the selective incorporation approach, it is necessary to look at 1) the entirety of the right, not just as it applies to a particular set of facts (as with the fundamental rights approach), and 2) whether the provision is fundamental to Anglo-American jurisprudence.

Incorporation of Criminal Rights. A number of criminal process provisions have been applied to the states, including the Fourth Amendment's prohibition against unreasonable searches and seizures, the Fifth Amendment's prohibitions against double jeopardy, compelled self-incrimination, and the Sixth Amendment's right to trial by jury, to compulsory process, to a speedy and public trial, the assistance of counsel, and to prohibitions against excessive bail and cruel and unusual punishment.

Retroactivity of New Constitutional Rules. When the courts announce a new constitutional rule, questions arise regarding whether the new rule should be retroactively applied. In general, the courts have been reluctant to extend the benefits of a new rule to someone whose conviction was final prior to announcement of the new rule. However, the benefits of a new rule were sometimes applied to those whose convictions were on direct review at the time the rule is announced.

Major Themes

a.   **Incorporation of Rights**—Many provisions of the Bill of Rights have been incorporated into the Fourteenth Amendment, and are therefore applicable to the states.

b.   **Retroactivity**—Whenever the courts announce a new constitutional rule, questions can arise regarding whether the rule should be applied retroactively to convictions that are already final. As a general rule, new rules are not applied retroactively except to cases that are still pending at the time that the new rule is announced.

For More Information

- WAYNE R. LAFAVE, JEROLD H. ISRAEL, NANCY J. KING & ORIN S. KERR, CRIMINAL PROCEDURE (6th ed. 2017).

- RUSSELL L. WEAVER, JOHN M. BURKOFF, CATHERINE HANCOCK & STEVEN I. FRIEDLAND, PRINCIPLES OF CRIMINAL PROCEDURE Ch. 2 (7th ed. 2021).

Test Your Knowledge

To access your understanding of the material in this chapter, <u>click here</u> to take a quiz.

CHAPTER 3

The Right to Counsel

A. Generally

In 1938, the United States Supreme Court held that federal defendants who could not afford an attorney had a constitutional right to appointed counsel under the Sixth Amendment. *Johnson v. Zerbst*, 304 U.S. 458 (1938). Justice Black, writing for the majority, emphasized that "the Sixth Amendment stands as a constant admonition that if the constitutional safeguards it provides be lost, justice will not 'still be done.' It embodies a realistic recognition of the obvious truth that the average defendant does not have the professional legal skills to protect himself when brought before a tribunal with power to take his life or liberty, wherein the prosecution is presented by experienced and learned counsel. The Sixth Amendment withholds from federal courts, in all criminal proceedings, the power and authority to deprive an accused of his life or liberty unless he has or waives the assistance of counsel."

Betts v. Brady

316 U.S. 455 (1942).

MR. JUSTICE ROBERTS delivered the opinion of the Court.

Smith Betts was indicted for robbery in the Circuit Court of Carroll County, Maryland. Due to lack of funds he was unable to employ counsel, and so informed the judge at his arraignment. He requested that counsel be appointed for him. The judge advised him that this could not be done as it was not the practice in Carroll County to appoint counsel for indigent defendants save in prosecutions for murder and rape.

Without waiving his asserted right to counsel the petitioner pleaded not guilty and elected to be tried without a jury. At his request witnesses were summoned in his behalf. He cross-examined the State's witnesses and examined his own. The latter gave testimony tending to establish an alibi. Although afforded the opportunity, he did not take the witness stand. The judge found him guilty and imposed a sentence of eight years.

Was the petitioner's conviction and sentence a deprivation of his liberty without due process of law, in violation of the Fourteenth Amendment, because of the court's refusal to appoint counsel at his request?

The Sixth Amendment of the national Constitution applies only to trials in federal courts. The due process clause of the Fourteenth Amendment does not incorporate, as such, the specific guarantees found in the Sixth Amendment although a denial by a State of rights or privileges specifically embodied in that and others of the first eight amendments may, in certain circumstances, or in connection with other elements, operate, in a given case, to deprive a litigant of due process of law in violation of the Fourteenth. The phrase due process of law formulates a concept less rigid and more fluid than those envisaged in other specific and particular provisions of the Bill of Rights. Its application is less a matter of rule. Asserted denial is to be tested by an appraisal of the totality of facts in a given case. That which may, in one setting, constitute a denial of fundamental fairness, shocking to the universal sense of justice, may, in other circumstances, and in the light of other considerations, fall short of such denial. In the application of such a concept there is always the danger of falling into the habit of formulating the guarantee into a set of hard and fast rules the application of which in a given case may be to ignore the qualifying factors therein disclosed.

The question we are now to decide is whether due process of law demands that in every criminal case, whatever the circumstances, a State must furnish counsel to an indigent defendant. Is the furnishing of counsel in all cases whatever dictated by natural, inherent, and fundamental principles of fairness? The answer to the question may be found in the common understanding of those who have lived under the Anglo-American system of law. By the Sixth Amendment the people ordained that, in all criminal prosecutions, the accused should "enjoy the right to have the Assistance of Counsel for his defense." We have construed the provision to require appointment of counsel in all cases where a defendant is unable to procure the services of an attorney, and where the right has not been intentionally and competently waived. Though, as we have noted, the Amendment lays down no rule for the conduct of the States, the question recurs whether the constraint laid by the Amendment upon the national courts expresses a rule so fundamental and essential to a fair trial, and so, to due process of law, that it is made obligatory upon the states by the Fourteenth Amendment. Relevant data on the subject are afforded by constitutional and statutory provisions subsisting in the colonies and the states prior to the inclusion of the Bill of Rights in the national Constitution, and in the constitutional, legislative, and judicial history of the States to the present date.

The Constitutions of the thirteen original States, as they were at the time of federal union, exhibit great diversity in respect of the right to have counsel in criminal cases. It is evident that the constitutional provisions to the effect that a defendant should be "allowed" counsel or should have a right "to be heard by himself and his counsel," or that he might be heard by "either or both," at his election, were intended to do away with the rules which denied representation, in whole or in part, by counsel in criminal prosecutions, but were not aimed to compel the State to provide counsel for a defendant.

The constitutions of all the States, presently in force, save that of Virginia, contain provisions with respect to the assistance of counsel in criminal trials. Those of nine States may be said to embody a guarantee textually the same as that of the Sixth Amendment, or of like import. In the fundamental law of most States, however, the language used indicates only that a defendant is not to be denied the privilege of representation by counsel of his choice.

This demonstrates that, in the great majority of the States, it has been the considered judgment of the people, their representatives and their courts that appointment of counsel is not a fundamental right, essential to a fair trial.

On the contrary, the matter has generally been deemed one of legislative policy. In the light of this evidence, we are unable to say that the concept of due process incorporated in the Fourteenth Amendment obligates the States, whatever may be their own views, to furnish counsel in every such case. Every court has power, if it deems proper, to appoint counsel where that course seems to be required in the interest of fairness.

In this case there was no question of the commission of a robbery. The State's case consisted of evidence identifying the petitioner as the perpetrator. The defense was an alibi. Petitioner called and examined witnesses to prove that he was at another place at the time of the commission of the offense. The simple issue was the veracity of the testimony for the State and that for the defendant. As Judge Bond says, the accused was not helpless, but was a man forty-three years old, of ordinary intelligence, and ability to take care of his own interests on the trial of that narrow issue. He had once before been in a criminal court, pleaded guilty to larceny and served a sentence and was not wholly unfamiliar with criminal procedure.

Make the Connection

Recall the discussion in Chapter 2(A) of the pre-incorporation "fundamental rights" approach to determining individual rights in the states. This is a perfect example. The Court here won't require states to respect Bill of Rights provisions unless they are "fundamental and necessary" to due process or "shocking to the universal sense of justice." What does this actually mean in this setting? What significance do you think we should give today to the fact that, when the Constitution was adopted, indigent defendants did not have the right to counsel?

It is quite clear that in Maryland, if the situation had been otherwise and it had appeared that the petitioner was, for any reason, at a serious disadvantage by reason of the lack of counsel, a refusal to appoint would have resulted in the reversal of a judgment of conviction.

Food for Thought

Is this accurate? Do you believe that a person who previously pleaded guilty in a criminal matter would now be somewhat familiar with criminal procedure? Really?

To deduce from the due process clause a rule binding upon the states in this matter would be to impose upon them a requirement without distinction between criminal charges of different magnitude or in respect of courts of varying jurisdiction. "Presumably it would be argued that trials in the Traffic Court would require it." And indeed it was said by petitioner's counsel both below and in this court, that as the Fourteenth Amendment extends the protection of due process to property as well as to life and liberty, if we hold with the petitioner, logic would require the furnishing of counsel in civil cases involving property.

As we have said, the Fourteenth Amendment prohibits the conviction and incarceration of one whose trial is offensive to the common and fundamental ideas of fairness and right, and while want of counsel in a particular case may result in a conviction lacking in such fundamental fairness, we cannot say that the Amendment embodies an inexorable command that no trial for any offense, or in any court, can be fairly conducted and justice accorded a defendant who is not represented by counsel.

The judgment is *Affirmed.*

MR. JUSTICE BLACK, dissenting, with whom MR. JUSTICE DOUGLAS and MR. JUSTICE MURPHY concur.

The petitioner, a farm hand, out of a job and on relief, was indicted in a Maryland state court on a charge of robbery. He was too poor to hire a lawyer. He so informed the court and requested that counsel be appointed to defend him. His request was denied. Put to trial without a lawyer, he conducted his own defense, was found guilty, and was sentenced to eight years' imprisonment. The court below found that the petitioner had "at least an ordinary amount of intelligence." It is clear from his examination of witnesses that he was a man of little education.

If this case had come to us from a federal court, it is clear we should have to reverse it, because the Sixth Amendment makes the right to counsel in criminal cases inviolable by the Federal Government. I believe that the Fourteenth Amendment made the Sixth applicable to the states. But this view, although often urged in dissents, has never been accepted by a majority of this Court and is not accepted today.

This Court has declared that due process of law is denied if a trial is conducted in such manner that it is "shocking to the universal sense of justice" or "offensive to the common and fundamental ideas of fairness and right." On another occasion, this Court has recognized that whatever is "implicit in the concept of ordered liberty" and "essential to the substance of a hearing" is within the procedural protection afforded by the constitutional guaranty of due process. The right to counsel in a criminal proceeding is "fundamental."

An historical evaluation of the right to a full hearing in criminal cases, and the dangers of denying it, were set out in the *Powell v. Alabama*, 287 U.S. 45 (1932), case, where this Court said: "What does a hearing include? Historically and in practice, in our own country at least, it has always included the right to the aid of counsel when desired and provided by the party asserting the right. Even the intelligent and educated layman lacks both the skill and knowledge adequately to prepare his defense, even though he have a perfect one. He requires the guiding hand of counsel in every step in the proceedings against him. Without it, though he be not guilty, he faces the danger of conviction because he does not know how to establish his innocence."

A practice cannot be reconciled with "common and fundamental ideas of fairness and right," which subjects innocent men to increased dangers of conviction merely because of their poverty. Whether a man is innocent cannot be determined from a trial in which, as here, denial of counsel has made it impossible to conclude, with any satisfactory degree of certainty, that the defendant's case was adequately presented.

Gideon v. Wainwright

372 U.S. 335 (1963).

MR. JUSTICE BLACK delivered the opinion of the Court.

Petitioner was charged in a Florida state court with having broken and entered a poolroom with intent to commit a misdemeanor. This offense is a felony under Florida law. Appearing in court without funds and without a lawyer, petitioner asked the court to appoint counsel for him, whereupon the following colloquy took place:

"The COURT: Mr. Gideon, I am sorry, but I cannot appoint Counsel to represent you in this case. Under the laws of the State of Florida, the only time the Court can appoint Counsel to represent a Defendant is when that person is charged with a capital offense. I am sorry, but I will have to deny your request to appoint Counsel to defend you in this case.

"The DEFENDANT: The United States Supreme Court says I am entitled to be represented by Counsel."

Put to trial before a jury, Gideon conducted his defense about as well as could be expected from a layman. He made an opening statement to the jury, cross-examined the State's witnesses, presented witnesses in his own defense, declined to testify himself, and made a short argument "emphasizing his innocence to the charge contained in the Information filed in this case." The jury returned a verdict of guilty, and petitioner was sentenced to serve five years in the state prison. Gideon subsequently filed a *habeas corpus* petition attacking his conviction on the ground that the trial court's refusal to appoint counsel for him was unconstitutional. The Florida Supreme Court denied him any relief without opinion. Since 1942, when *Betts v. Brady* was decided by a divided Court, the problem of a defendant's federal constitutional right to counsel in a state court has been a continuing source of controversy and litigation in both state and federal courts.

The Sixth Amendment provides: "In all criminal prosecutions, the accused shall enjoy the right to have the Assistance of Counsel for his defense." We have construed this to mean that in federal courts counsel must be provided for defendants unable to employ counsel unless the right is competently and intelligently waived. *Betts* argued that this right is extended to indigent defendants in state courts by the Fourteenth Amendment. In response the Court stated that, while the Sixth Amendment laid down "no rule for the conduct of the States, the question recurs whether the constraint laid by the Amendment upon the national courts expresses a rule so fundamental and essential to a fair trial, and so, to due process of law, that it is made obligatory upon the States by the Fourteenth Amendment." In order to decide whether the Sixth Amendment's guarantee of counsel is of this fundamental nature, the Court in *Betts* set out and considered "relevant data on the subject afforded by constitutional and statutory provisions subsisting in the colonies and the states prior to the inclusion of the Bill of Rights in the national Constitution, and in the constitutional, legislative, and judicial history of the States to the present date." On the basis of this historical data the Court concluded that "appointment of counsel is not a fundamental right, essential to a fair trial." It was for this reason the *Betts* Court refused to accept the contention that the Sixth Amendment's guarantee of counsel for indigent federal defendants was extended to or, in the words of that Court, "made obligatory upon the states by the Fourteenth Amendment." Plainly, had the Court concluded that appointment of counsel for an indigent criminal defendant was "a fundamental right, essential to a fair trial," it would have held that the Fourteenth Amendment requires appointment of counsel in a state court, just as the Sixth Amendment requires in a federal court.

See It

You can watch the legendary actor, Henry Fonda, do a terrific job of playing the role of Clarence Gideon in the 1980 made-for-TV film, *Gideon's Trumpet*, based on the book by Anthony Lewis. *See* http://www.imdb.com/title/tt0080789/.

We accept *Betts v. Brady*'s assumption, based as it was on our prior cases, that a provision of the Bill of Rights which is "fundamental and essential to a fair trial" is made obligatory upon the States by the Fourteenth Amendment. We think the Court in *Betts* was wrong, however, in concluding that the Sixth Amendment's guarantee of counsel is not one of these fundamental rights.

The fact is that in deciding as it did—that "appointment of counsel is not a fundamental right, essential to a fair trial"—the Court in *Betts v. Brady* made an abrupt break with its own well-considered precedents. In returning to these old precedents, sounder we believe than the new, we but restore constitutional principles established to achieve a fair system of justice. Not only these precedents but also reason and reflection require us to recognize that in our adversary system of criminal justice, any person haled into court, who is too poor to hire a lawyer, cannot be assured a fair trial unless counsel is provided for him. This seems to us to be an obvious truth. Governments, both state and federal, quite properly spend vast sums of money to establish machinery to try defendants accused of crime. Lawyers to prosecute are everywhere deemed essential to protect the public's interest in an orderly society. Similarly, there are few defendants charged with crime, few indeed, who fail to hire the best lawyers they can get to prepare and present their defenses. That government hires lawyers to prosecute and defendants who have the money hire lawyers to defend are the strongest indications of the wide-spread belief that lawyers in criminal courts are necessities, not luxuries. The right of one charged with crime to counsel may not be deemed fundamental and essential to fair trials in some countries, but it is in ours. From the very beginning, our state and national constitutions and laws have laid great emphasis on procedural and substantive safeguards designed to assure fair trials before impartial tribunals in which every defendant stands equal before the law. This noble ideal cannot be realized if the poor man charged with crime has to face his accusers without a lawyer to assist him. A defendant's need for a lawyer is nowhere better stated than in the moving words of Mr. Justice Sutherland in *Powell v. Alabama*, 287 U.S. 45 (1932):

> "The right to be heard would be, in many cases, of little avail if it did not comprehend the right to be heard by counsel. Even the intelligent and educated layman has small and sometimes no skill in the science of law. If charged with crime, he is incapable, generally, of determining for himself whether the indictment is good or bad. He is unfamiliar with the rules of evidence. Left without the aid of counsel he may be put on trial without a proper charge, and convicted upon incompetent evidence, or evidence irrelevant to the issue or otherwise inadmissible. He lacks both the skill and knowledge adequately to prepare his defense, even though he have a perfect one. He requires the guiding hand of counsel at every step in the proceedings against him. Without it, though he be not guilty, he faces the danger of conviction because he does not know how to establish his innocence."

The Court in *Betts v. Brady* departed from the sound wisdom upon which the Court's holding in *Powell v. Alabama* rested. Florida, supported by two other States, has asked that *Betts v. Brady* be left intact. Twenty-two States, as friends of the Court, argue that *Betts* was "an anachronism when handed down" and that it should now be overruled.

We agree. *Reversed.*

MR. JUSTICE HARLAN, concurring.

Food for Thought

Why do you think that the Attorneys General from twenty-two states filed an *Amicus* Brief *in Gideon's behalf* rather than supporting the state of Florida? Do you think they were simply convinced at this point in time that *Betts* was wrongly decided? Or could they have had some tactical motivation for taking this position?

When we hold a right or immunity to be "implicit in the concept of ordered liberty" and thus valid against the States, we do not automatically carry over an entire body of federal law and apply it in full sweep to the States. Any such concept would disregard the frequently wide disparity between the legitimate interests of the States and of the Federal Government, the divergent problems that they face, and the significantly different consequences of their actions.

Points for Discussion

a. Providing Indigent Services

Representation for the literally millions of indigent criminal defendants charged in state and federal court each year is provided through a public-defender or contract-attorney system, or simply by an appropriate judge or judicial officer assigning the indigent's defense to a private attorney by order of appointment. In 2007, 964 public defender offices across the nation received nearly 6 million indigent defense cases. Misdemeanor cases accounted for about 40% of all cases received by state-based public defender offices and about 50% of the cases received by county-based offices. Donald J. Farole, Jr. & Lynn Langton, Public Defender Offices, 2007—Statistical Tables (Revised) (U.S. Dept. Of Justice, Bur. Of Justice Statistics, Nov. 2009), https://www.bjs.gov/index.cfm?ty=pbdetail&iid=1758.

County-based public defender offices received more than 4 million cases in 2007. About three-quarters (73%) of county-based public defender offices exceeded the maximum recommended limit of cases received per attorney in 2007. County-based offices employed a median of 7 litigating public defenders. Donald J. Farole, Jr. & Lynn Langton, County-based and Local Public Defender Offices, 2007 (U.S. Dept.

Of Justice, Bur. Of Justice Statistics, Sept. 2010), https://www.bjs.gov/content/pub/pdf/clpdo07.pdf. State governments spent $2.3 billion on indigent defense in 2012. Erinn Herberman and Tracey Kyckelhahn, State Government Indigent Defense Expenditures, FY 2008–2012—Updated (U.S. Dept. Of Justice, Bur. Of Justice Statistics, October 24, 2014), http://www.bjs.gov/content/pub/pdf/sgide0812.pdf.

Court-appointed counsel represented 66% of federal felony defendants in 1998. U.S. Dept. of Justice, Bur. of Justice Statistics, Defense Counsel in Criminal Cases (November 2000). However,

federal appellate and district judges express high regard for public defenders but low regard for court-appointed counsel and retained counsel. Retained counsel represent 25% and court-appointed counsel 33% of federal criminal defendants. If the quality of legal representation matters to criminal case outcomes, as recent studies suggest, a majority of indigent federal criminal defendants may be serving longer sentences by virtue of not having been represented by a federal public defender. The Constitution has been interpreted to place a floor under the quality of assistance of counsel tolerated in criminal cases, but one federal district judge described the work of defense attorneys other than public defenders as "exceedingly poor."

Richard A. Posner & Albert H. Yoon, *What Judges Think of the Quality of Legal Representation*, 63 STANFORD LAW REVIEW 317, 341–42 (2011).

> **FYI**
>
> "Of the 28 states and the District of Columbia that had state-administered indigent defense systems in 2013: Twenty-seven states and the District of Columbia had either governmental or nongovernmental public defenders providing representation for indigent clients; Eight states and the District of Columbia required indigent clients to pay both an application fee to receive representation and recoupment for legal services provided; In nine states the governor appointed the chief executives of the indigent defense delivery system; Six states reported fewer than 10 full-time equivalent investigators on staff for public defender offices. Between 2007 and 2013, 16 of the 22 states with state administered public defender offices increased the number of full-time equivalent litigating attorneys. In 2013, state-administered systems closed an estimated 2,696,950 criminal, appellate, civil, and juvenile cases." Suzanne M. Strong, State-Administered Indigent Defense Systems, 2013 (U.S. Dept. of Justice, Bur. Of Justice Statistics (November 16, 2016), https://www.bjs.gov/index.cfm?ty=pbdetail&iid=5826.

Unfortunately, skyrocketing caseloads and inadequate funding for such programs has led to what some commentators deem "a crisis of extraordinary proportions in many states throughout the country." Richard Klein & Robert Spangenberg, *The Indigent Defense Crisis* 25 (ABA Section of Criminal Justice 1993). *See also id.* ("Justice often does not reach impoverished urban centers or poor rural counties where limited funding for indigent defense cannot provide effective representation to those accused of crime."); Stephen B. Bright, *Turning Celebrated Principles Into Reality*, CHAMPION 6 (January/February 2003):

> No constitutional right is celebrated so much in the abstract and observed so little in reality as the right to counsel. While leaders of the judiciary, legal profession and government give speeches every Law Day about the essential role of lawyers in protecting the individual rights of people accused of crimes, many states have yet to create and fund adequately independent programs for providing legal representation. As a result, some people—even people accused of felonies—enter guilty pleas and are sentenced to imprisonment without any representation. Others languish in jail for weeks or months—often for longer than any sentence they would receive—before being assigned a lawyer. Many receive only perfunctory representation—sometimes nothing more than hurried conversations with a court-appointed lawyer outside the courtroom or even in open court—before entering a guilty plea or going to trial. The poor person who is wrongfully convicted may face years in prison, or even execution, without any legal assistance to pursue avenues of post-conviction review.

See also Ethan Bronner, *Right to Lawyer Can Be Empty Promise for Poor*, New York Times p. A1 (March 16, 2013) ("The Legal Services Corporation says there are more than 60 million Americans—35 percent more than in 2005—who qualify for its services. But it calculates that 80 percent of the legal needs of the poor go unmet."); Attorney General Eric Holder, Jr., *Defendants' legal rights undermined by budget cuts*, Washington Post (August 22, 2013) ("Despite the promise of the court's ruling in *Gideon*, the U.S. indigent defense systems—which provide representation to those who cannot afford it—are in financial crisis, plagued by crushing caseloads and insufficient resources.").

Food for Thought

Do these comments and statistics make you wonder whether the *Gideon* decision has actually worked to accomplish what the Court thought or hoped that it would accomplish? Should more public monies be spent on indigent defense services? Is this realistic as a political matter?

See further Matt Apuzzo, *Holder Backs Suit in New York Faulting Legal Service for Poor*, New York Times p. A1 (Sept. 25, 2014):

> Attorney General Eric H. Holder Jr., who last year declared a crisis in America's legal-defense system for the poor, is supporting a class-action lawsuit that accuses Gov. Andrew M. Cuomo and the State of New York of perpetuating a system that violates the rights of people who cannot afford to hire lawyers. The lawsuit claims that public defenders in New York are so

overworked and overmatched that poor people essentially receive no legal defense at all. It describes a system in which indigent defendants navigate courts nearly alone, relying on spotty advice from lawyers who do not have the time or money to investigate their cases or advise them properly. Because of substandard legal aid, children are taken from their parents, defendants in minor cases are jailed for long periods and people are imprisoned for crimes for which they might have been acquitted, the civil rights lawyers who filed the suit said.

Although the United States is not a party to the case, Mr. Holder is using the same core legal arguments as the plaintiffs and the weight of the federal government to resolve what he sees as deep-seated unfairness in local criminal courts. His views will bring national attention to a case that has mainly been of interest in New York. After Mr. Holder weighed in last year in a similar case in Washington State, the judge strongly rebuked the public-defense systems in two cities there and ordered improvements.

If the New York lawsuit succeeds, the state could be forced to take over the public-defense system, which is now run by county governments. Such an outcome would also quite likely encourage similar lawsuits, and, in turn, additional intervention by the Justice Department.

Mr. Holder has made the right to legal representation part of a broad effort to address inequities in the criminal justice system. He has pushed to reduce harsh sentences that were adopted during the country's crack epidemic, for example, and to eliminate mandatory-minimum sentences for nonviolent drug crimes.

"To truly guarantee adequate representation for low-income de-

FYI

Difficulties in providing indigent services does not necessarily equate with lesser quality services. *See, e.g.,* Brian J. Ostrom & Jordan Bowman, "Examining the Effectiveness of Indigent Defense Team Services: A Multisite Evaluation of Holistic Defense in Practice, Project Summary," p. 49, U.S. Dept. of Justice, Office of Justice Programs (February 2020), https://www.ncjrs.gov/pdffiles1/nij/grants/254549.pdf: "The enhanced efficiency gained by holistic and traditional public defenders in Minnesota does not come at the expense of their clients. Public defenders, both holistic and traditional, are as successful as privately retained attorneys in achieving favorable outcomes for their clients. The conviction rates, dismissal rates, acquittal rates at trial, charge reduction rates, incarceration rates, and length of prison sentences for their clients are similar to the outcomes associated with privately retained counsel, with few substantive differences."

fendants, we must ensure that public defenders' caseloads allow them to do an effective job," Mr. Holder said in a statement. "The Department of Justice is committed to addressing the inequalities that unfold every day in

America's courtrooms."

And, finally, see Sara Mayeux, "Our Rickety Public Defense System Has Finally Collapsed. Here's How to Fix It," The Nation (May 9, 2016), https://www.thenation.com/article/archive/our-rickety-public-defense-system-has-finally-collapsed-heres-how-to-fix-it/:

> The persistence of crisis conditions in indigent defense suggests that the causes are deeply entrenched, and not a temporary reflection of shifting political views or economic vicissitudes. One long-term historical factor helping to explain America's weak commitment to indigent defense is the legal profession's own prestige hierarchy, which has long valorized advising corporations more than helping ordinary people. A second factor undermining indigent defense is simply the structure of American federalism. The New Orleans judge who recently ordered the release of defendants awaiting counsel wrote, by way of explanation, that "constitutional rights are not contingent on budget demands." But in practice, constitutional rights are often hamstrung by state-level budgets.

b. Excessive Caseloads & Appointments

In *State ex rel. Missouri Public Defender Com'n v. Waters*, 370 S.W.3d 592 (Mo. 2012), the Missouri Supreme Court ruled that a trial court exceeded its lawful authority by appointing the state public defender's office to represent a defendant in contravention of an administrative rule permitting a district defender office to decline additional appointments when it has been certified as being on limited availability after exceeding its caseload capacity for at least three consecutive calendar months. The court reasoned that overburdened defense counsel is ineffective counsel and

> simply put, a judge may not appoint counsel when the judge is aware that, for whatever reason, counsel is unable to provide effective representation to a defendant. Effective, not just pro forma, representation is required by the Missouri and federal constitutions.

Does this make sense to you? Should (can?) courts force state or local governments to spend more on indigent defense, essentially making a "political" choice as between public spending priorities?

c. Who Is an "Indigent"?

The Supreme Court has never defined "indigency" for purposes of an indigent criminal defendant's right to the appointment of counsel. States use varying formulae and income levels to define indigency for these purposes. The American Bar Association, in ABA Standards for Criminal Justice, Providing Defense Services Standard

5–7.1 (3d ed. 1992), has recommended the following standard be applied: "Counsel should be provided to persons who are financially unable to obtain adequate representation without substantial hardship. Counsel should not be denied because of a person's ability to pay part of the cost of representation, because friends or relatives have resources to obtain counsel, or because bond has been or can be posted."

d. Making the Indigent's Family Pay

The Massachusetts Supreme Judicial Court has held that rules of court requiring the income of an otherwise indigent's defendant's girlfriend and mother to be attributed to him did not violate his right to counsel, and that it was not unconstitutional to place the burden of proving indigency on the defendant himself. *Com. v. Fico*, 462 Mass. 737, 971 N.E.2d 275 (2012). *See also Com. v. Porter*, 462 Mass. 724, 971 N.E.2d 291 (2012) (rule allowing defendant's spouse's income to be attributed to him for purposes of determining indigency held constitutional); *Com. v. Mortimer*, 462 Mass. 749, 971 N.E.2d 283 (2012) (rule allowing defendant's spouse's income to be attributed to him for purposes of determining indigency held constitutional). Is this fair? What do you think?

Food for Thought

Can public defenders refuse to take additional cases until they are "caught up" with existing cases, and simply ask judges to appoint private attorneys at state expense? What else can they do? Should they (can they) sue the state (their employers) for relief? *See, e.g.,* Dave Collins, *Public defenders feel squeeze: Conn. cuts create caseload worries*, BOSTON GLOBE (July 21, 2011), ("The public defenders' office cut all 30 of its per diem independent contractor positions last week, including 16 lawyers, and laid off 12 temporary employees, including seven lawyers. All 42 of those workers helped keep caseload levels down, but needed to be cut regardless of any union savings deal. To meet the savings mandated by the Legislature, the public defenders' office is proposing laying off 24 full-time employees and eliminating another nine jobs through attrition or retirements. The agency has not decided yet how many of those positions will be lawyers or when the job cuts will be made."); Deborah Yetter, *State's Public Defender Can't Refuse Cases, Court Rules*, LOUISVILLE COURIER-JOURNAL, A-1, c. 1–6 (Sept. 20, 2008).

Argersinger v. Hamlin

407 U.S. 25 (1972).

MR. JUSTICE DOUGLAS delivered the opinion of the Court.

Petitioner, an indigent, was charged in Florida with carrying a concealed weapon, an offense punishable by imprisonment up to six months, a $1,000 fine, or both. The Florida Supreme Court followed the line we marked out in *Duncan v. Louisiana*, 391

U.S. 145, 159, as respects the right to trial by jury and held that the right to court-appointed counsel extends only to trials "for non-petty offenses punishable by more than six months imprisonment." We reverse.

The right to trial by jury, also guaranteed by the Sixth Amendment by reason of the Fourteenth, was limited by Duncan to trials where the potential punishment was imprisonment for six months or more. But the right to trial by jury has a different genealogy and is brigaded with a system of trial to a judge alone. While there is historical support for limiting the "deep commitment" to trial by jury to "serious criminal cases," there is no such support for a similar limitation on the right to assistance of counsel.

The Sixth Amendment extended the right to counsel beyond its common-law dimensions. But there is nothing in the language of the Amendment, its history, or in the decisions of this Court, to indicate that it was intended to embody a retraction of the right in petty offenses wherein the common law previously did require that counsel be provided.

The assistance of counsel is often a requisite to the very existence of a fair trial. The requirement of counsel may well be necessary for a fair trial even in a petty-offense prosecution. We are by no means convinced that legal and constitutional questions involved in a case that actually leads to imprisonment even for a brief period are any less complex than when a person can be sent off for six months or more.

Beyond the problem of trials and appeals is that of the guilty plea, a problem which looms large in misdemeanor as well as in felony cases. Counsel is needed so that the accused may know precisely what he is doing, so that he is fully aware of the prospect of going to jail or prison, and so that he is treated fairly by the prosecution.

In addition, the volume of misdemeanor cases, far greater in number than felony prosecutions, may create an obsession for speedy dispositions, regardless of the fairness of the result. We must conclude, therefore, that the problems associated with misdemeanor and petty offenses often require the presence of counsel to insure the accused a fair trial. Mr. Justice Powell suggests that these problems are raised even in situations where there is no prospect of imprisonment. We need not consider the requirements of the Sixth Amendment as regards the right to counsel where loss of liberty is not involved, however, for here petitioner was in fact sentenced to jail. And, as we said in *Baldwin*, "the prospect of imprisonment for however short a time will seldom be viewed by the accused as a trivial or 'petty' matter and may well result in quite serious repercussions affecting his career and his reputation."

We hold, therefore, that absent a knowing and intelligent waiver, no person may be imprisoned for any offense, whether classified as petty, misdemeanor, or felony, unless he was represented by counsel at his trial.

We do not sit as an ombudsman to direct state courts how to manage their affairs but only to make clear the federal constitutional requirement. How crimes should be classified is largely a state matter. The fact that traffic charges technically fall within the category of "criminal prosecutions" does not necessarily mean that many of them will be brought into the class where imprisonment actually occurs.

Food for Thought

Does this holding make sense? How can a judge sensibly and fairly make the decision whether or not he or she is going to sentence the defendant (if convicted) to at least a day in jail *in advance of hearing the facts*?

Under the rule we announce today, every judge will know when the trial of a misdemeanor starts that no imprisonment may be imposed, even though local law permits it, unless the accused is represented by counsel. He will have a measure of the seriousness and gravity of the offense and therefore know when to name a lawyer to represent the accused before the trial starts.

The run of misdemeanors will not be affected by today's ruling. But in those that end up in the actual deprivation of a person's liberty, the accused will receive the benefit of "the guiding hand of counsel" so necessary when one's liberty is in jeopardy.

Food for Thought

Is representation by a law student in criminal proceedings sufficient to meet the Sixth Amendment guarantee of the right to counsel? Would you want to have your spleen removed by a medical student? Is there a difference? What do you think? When he was alive, should we have arranged for a medical student to perform an endoscopy on Chief Justice Burger and *then* ask him if he thought this was adequate medical care? Too late now.

Reversed.

MR. CHIEF JUSTICE BURGER, concurred in the result. MR. JUSTICE BRENNAN, with whom MR. JUSTICE DOUGLAS and MR. JUSTICE STEWART joined, concurred, adding:

Law students may provide an important source of legal representation for the indigent. More than 125 of the country's 147 accredited law schools have established clinical programs in which faculty supervised students aid clients in a variety of civil and criminal matters. These programs supplement practice rules enacted in 38 States authorizing students to practice law under prescribed conditions.

Most of these regulations permit students to make supervised court appearances as defense counsel in criminal cases.

Given the huge increase in law school enrollments over the past few years, law students can be expected to make a significant contribution, quantitatively and qualitatively, to the representation of the poor in many areas.

MR. JUSTICE POWELL, with whom MR. JUSTICE REHNQUIST joins, concurring in the result.

Food for Thought

Do you agree with Justice Powell? Was a "bright-line rule" really necessary here? Bright line rules are often appealing because they are seemingly easy to apply. However, sometimes these rules create anomalous results. It's hard to create a "one size fits all rule" and have it make sense in every situation. Case-by-case approaches, on the other hand, can produce unpredictable results and can be hard to apply. Which is better in this specific situation?

The flat six-month rule of the Florida court and the equally inflexible rule of the majority opinion apply to all cases within their defined areas regardless of circumstances. It is precisely because of this mechanistic application that I find these alternatives unsatisfactory. Due process embodies principles of fairness rather than immutable line drawing as to every aspect of a criminal trial.

While counsel is often essential to a fair trial, this is by no means a universal fact. Some petty offense cases are complex; others are exceedingly simple. Where the possibility of a jail sentence is remote and the probable fine seems small, or where the evidence of guilt is overwhelming, the costs of assistance of counsel may exceed the benefits. It is anomalous that the Court's opinion today will extend the right of appointed counsel to indigent defendants in cases where the right to counsel would rarely be exercised by nonindigent defendants. I would hold that the right to counsel in petty-offense cases is not absolute but is one to be determined by the trial courts exercising a judicial discretion on a case-by-case basis.

Points for Discussion

a. Right to Counsel for Fines?

In *Scott v. Illinois*, 440 U.S. 367 (1979), Scott was convicted of theft and fined $50 after a bench trial in which he was unrepresented. The Illinois statute set the maximum penalty for theft at a $500 fine and/or one year in jail. Scott challenged his conviction on the basis that *Argersinger* required the state to provide counsel whenever imprisonment was an *authorized* penalty. The Court rejected this challenge: "The central premise of *Argersinger*—that actual imprisonment is a penalty different in kind from fines or the mere threat of imprisonment—is eminently sound and warrants adoption of actual imprisonment as the line defining the constitutional right to appointment of counsel." Justice Brennan dissented: "The offense of 'theft' is certainly not a 'petty' one. It is punishable by a sentence of up to one year in jail. It carries the moral stigma associated with common-law crimes traditionally recognized as indicative of moral depravity. Scott's right to the assistance of appointed counsel is thus plainly mandated by the logic of the Court's prior cases, including Argersinger itself."

b. Suspended Sentences

In *Alabama v. Shelton*, 535 U.S. 654 (2002), the Supreme Court ruled 5-to-4 that the *Argersinger* and *Scott* day-in-jail rule applies to defendants who receive suspended sentences rather than actual incarceration. Shelton was convicted of assault and sentenced to 30 days in jail, but the trial court immediately suspended the sentence, placing him on probation for two years. The majority held that "the Sixth Amendment right to appointed counsel, as delineated in *Argersinger* and *Scott*, applies to a defendant in Shelton's situation. We hold that a suspended sentence that may 'end up in the actual deprivation of a person's liberty' may not be imposed unless the defendant was accorded 'the guiding hand of counsel' in the prosecution for the crime charged." The Court added that "a suspended sentence is a prison term imposed for the offense of conviction. Once the prison term is triggered, the defendant is incarcerated not for the probation violation, but for the underlying offense. The uncounseled conviction at that point 'results in imprisonment'; it 'ends up in the actual deprivation of a person's liberty.' This is precisely what the Sixth Amendment, as interpreted in *Argersinger* and *Scott*, does not allow."

c. Sentence Enhancement with Uncounseled Conviction

In *Baldasar v. Illinois*, 446 U.S. 222 (1980), the Supreme Court held that an uncounseled misdemeanor conviction, although lawful under *Scott*, could not be used to enhance a defendant's sentence for a subsequent misdemeanor conviction into a felony conviction under a sentencing enhancement statute. Subsequently, however, the Court reversed itself, overruling *Baldasar* and holding that "an uncounseled misdemeanor conviction, valid under *Scott* because no prison term was imposed, is also valid when used to enhance punishment at a subsequent conviction." *Nichols v. United States*, 511 U.S. 738, 749 (1994).

d. When Right to Counsel Attaches

Gideon and *Scott* focus upon the right to counsel at trial. The text of the Sixth Amendment embraces, however, "all criminal prosecutions," not just criminal trials. The Supreme Court has ruled, accordingly, that the right to counsel attaches prior to trial at any "critical stage of the criminal prosecution" after the "initiation of adversary judicial criminal proceedings—whether by way of formal charge, preliminary hearing, indictment, information, or arraignment." *Kirby v. Illinois*, <u>406 U.S. 682, 683, 689 (1972)</u>. A proceeding is a critical stage of the prosecution when "potential substantial prejudice to the defendant's rights inheres in the particular confrontation," and "the ability of counsel can help avoid that prejudice." *United States v. Wade*, <u>388 U.S. 218, 227 (1967)</u>. The right to counsel applies, for example, when a defendant appears at a sentencing proceeding, *Mempa v. Rhay*, <u>389 U.S. 128 (1967)</u>, when a defendant appears at a preliminary hearing, *Coleman v. Alabama*, <u>399 U.S. 1 (1970)</u>, and when a defendant first appears before a judge to be "told of the formal accusation against him and restrictions are imposed on his liberty," *Rothgery v. Gillespie County, Texas*, <u>554 U.S. 191, 194 (2008)</u>.

>
> **FYI**
>
> Based on California's Constitution, California's Supreme Court has decided indigent defendants are entitled to counsel during provisional appeals of in even minor criminal cases. *See Gardner v. Superior Court*, <u>6 Cal.5th 998, 245 Cal. Rptr.3d 58, 436 P.3d 946 (Cal. 2019)</u>.

e. Choosing Retained Defense Counsel

A criminal defendant with adequate resources has the right to retain counsel of his or her choice. *United States v., Gonzalez-Lopez*, <u>548 U.S. 140 (2006)</u>; *Chandler v. Fretag*, <u>348 U.S. 3 (1954)</u>. However, such retained counsel must be admitted to practice in the jurisdiction in which the trial is being held, unless the trial court exercises its discretion to grant counsel special admission to the Bar for purposes of that trial only ("*pro hac vice* admission"). *Leis v. Flynt*, <u>439 U.S. 438 (1979)</u>.

>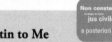
> **It's Latin to Me**
>
> *Pro hac vice.* A lawyer who has not been admitted to practice in a particular jurisdiction but who is admitted there temporarily for the purpose of conducting a particular case.

> **FYI**
>
> A trial court's order denying defendant the use of his retained counsel because counsel could not be available for three hours as he was attending a disciplinary proceeding was held to be a Sixth Amendment violation, and grounds for reversal of defendant's convictions and death sentence, entitling him to a new trial. *See Randolph v. Wetzel*, <u>2020 WL 2745722 (M.D. Pa. 2020)</u> ("The Sixth Amendment to the United States Constitution protects a criminal defendant's right to counsel of choice. Although this right is not absolute, it is not to be lightly abrogated. In the instant case, the trial court's "unreasoning and arbitrary insistence upon expeditiousness in the face of a justifiable request for delay" violated Randolph's constitutional right to counsel of choice.").

f.   Indigents Have No Right to Choose Counsel

Unlike criminal defendants who have adequate resources to employ their own counsel, indigent defendants do not have a right to "choose" their counsel. As the Court explained in *Wheat v. United States*, 486 U.S. 153, 159 (1988), "the essential aim of the Sixth Amendment is to guarantee an effective advocate for each criminal defendant rather than to insure that a defendant will inexorably be represented by the lawyer whom he prefers. A defendant may not insist on representation by an attorney he cannot afford or who for other reasons declines to represent the defendant." A judge may, however, as a discretionary matter, appoint an attorney that an indigent defendant desires, assuming that such attorney is available and agrees to accept the (typically minimal) compensation that is provided for such appointed services.

Moreover, 18 U.S.C. § 3599 entitles indigent federal criminal defendants to the appointment of counsel in capital cases, including *habeas corpus* proceedings. In *Christeson v. Roper*, 574 U.S. 373 (2015), a majority of the Supreme Court held that a federal district court abused its discretion in denying a *habeas* petitioner's request for substitution of his federally-appointed counsel due to counsel's conflict of interest. Such motions for appointment of new counsel should be evaluated in the "interests of justice," the majority ruled, and substitution of counsel was necessary under that standard in *Christeson* where appointed counsel labored under what the Court deemed an "obvious conflict of interest."

Hypo 1: *License Revocation*

Does a respondent in a driver's license revocation proceeding have a right to appointed counsel? Would your answer be any different if the judge made it clear in advance that no jail time would be imposed?

Hypo 2: *Post-Verdict Motions*

After the criminal trial has concluded and the defendant has been convicted, does the defendant have a continuing right to be represented by appointed counsel for purposes of filing post-trial motions, like a motion for new trial, for example? What if the defendant represented himself at trial, waiving his right to appointed trial counsel? In that case, should his waiver mean that he has also lost the right to have counsel appointed to make post-trial motions for him? *See State v. Pitts*, 131 Hawai'i 537, 319 P.3d 456 (2014).

Hypo 3: *Special Relationship with Counsel*

Defendants Emily and William Harris, members of the "Symbionese Liberation Army," were charged with kidnaping, robbery, assault with a deadly weapon and false imprisonment. Defendants asked the trial judge to appoint attorneys Susan Johnson and Leonard Weinberg to represent them. Both attorneys were willing to undertake the representation, had represented defendants in a prior related proceeding, and purported to have a special relationship with defendants. Many of the witnesses in the prior proceeding were likely to be witnesses in this proceeding. The defendants also asserted that these attorneys shared their political and social beliefs so that there was a sense of mutual trust and confidence between them. In their view, to appoint "strangers" in whom they had no such confidence and trust would be to deprive them of a true representation of their interests. Should the judge grant defendants' motion to appoint these attorneys? How would you argue this case for the State? How might defendants respond? How would you rule? Suppose that the judge felt that it would be better to appoint other attorneys based on their reputation among the local bench and bar, their experience in the trial of capital cases, and the fact that the other attorneys were certified as criminal law specialists by the State Bar? *See Harris v. Superior Court*, 19 Cal.3d 786, 140 Cal. Rptr. 318, 567 P.2d 750 (In Banc, 1977).

Hypo 4: *Physical Assault on Counsel*

When should a trial judge deny an indigent defendant the right to counsel and force him or her to proceed pro se? Suppose that a defendant told his appointed counsel "I know how to get rid of you," and later physically assaulted him. If you were the judge, how should you proceed? If counsel wants to withdraw, should you release him, and, if so, are you obligated to appoint alternate counsel for the defendant, or can you force him to proceed *pro se*? *See State v. Holmes*, 302 S.W.3d 831 (Tenn. 2010).

B. Waiver of the Right to Counsel

Faretta v. California

422 U.S. 806 (1975).

MR. JUSTICE STEWART delivered the opinion of the Court.

The Sixth and Fourteenth Amendments of our Constitution guarantee that a person brought to trial in any state or federal court must be afforded the right to the assistance of counsel before he can be validly convicted and punished by imprisonment. This clear constitutional rule has emerged from a series of cases decided here over the last 50 years. The question before us now is whether a defendant in a state criminal trial has a constitutional right to proceed *without* counsel when he voluntarily and intelligently elects to do so. Stated another way, the question is whether a State may constitutionally hale a person into its criminal courts and there force a lawyer upon him, even when he insists that he wants to conduct his own defense. It is not an easy question, but we have concluded that a State may not constitutionally do so.

Anthony Faretta was charged with grand theft in an information filed in the Superior Court of Los Angeles County, Cal. At the arraignment, the Superior Court Judge assigned to preside at the trial appointed the public defender to represent Faretta. Well before the date of trial, however, Faretta requested that he be permitted to represent himself. Questioning by the judge revealed that Faretta had once represented himself in a criminal prosecution, that he had a high school education, and that he did not want to be represented by the public defender because he believed that office was "very loaded down with a heavy case load." The judge responded that he believed Faretta was "making a mistake" and emphasized that in further proceedings Faretta would receive no special favors. Nevertheless, after establishing that Faretta wanted to represent himself and did not want a lawyer, the judge, in a "preliminary ruling," accepted Faretta's waiver of the assistance of counsel. The judge indicated, however, that he might reverse this ruling if it later appeared that Faretta was unable adequately to represent himself.

Several weeks thereafter, but still prior to trial, the judge *sua sponte* held a hearing to inquire into Faretta's ability to conduct his own defense, and questioned him specifically about both the hearsay rule and the state law governing the challenge of potential jurors. After

> **It's Latin to Me**
>
> *Sua sponte.* Without prompting or suggestion; on its own motion.

consideration of Faretta's answers, and observation of his demeanor, the judge ruled that Faretta had not made an intelligent and knowing waiver of his right to the assistance of counsel, and also ruled that Faretta had no constitutional right to conduct his own defense. The judge, accordingly, reversed his earlier ruling permitting self-representation and again appointed the public defender to represent Faretta. Faretta's subsequent request for leave to act as co-counsel was rejected, as were his efforts to make certain motions on his own behalf. Throughout the subsequent trial, the judge required that Faretta's defense be conducted only through the appointed lawyer from the public defender's office. At the conclusion of the trial, the jury found Faretta guilty as charged, and the judge sentenced him to prison. The California Court of Appeal affirmed the trial judge's ruling that Faretta had no federal or state constitutional right to represent himself.

In the federal courts, the right of self-representation has been protected by statute since the beginnings of our Nation. In *Adams v. U. S. ex rel. McCann*, 317 U.S. 269, 279 (1942), the Court recognized that the Sixth Amendment right to the assistance of counsel implicitly embodies a "correlative right to dispense with a lawyer's help." The defendant in that case, indicted for federal mail fraud violations, insisted on conducting his own defense without benefit of counsel. He also requested a bench trial and signed a waiver of his right to trial by jury. The prosecution consented to the waiver of a jury, and the waiver was accepted by the court. The defendant was convicted, but the Court of Appeals reversed the conviction on the ground that a person accused of a felony could not competently waive his right to trial by jury except upon the advice of a lawyer. This Court reversed and reinstated the conviction, holding that "an accused, in the exercise of a free and intelligent choice, and with the considered approval of the court, may waive trial by jury, and so likewise may he competently and intelligently waive his Constitutional right to assistance of counsel."

Food for Thought

Why would a defendant want to proceed *pro se*? How can such a decision make sense? After all, few defendants are well versed in the criminal law, the rules of evidence, or in criminal procedure. So, how can they effectively represent themselves (or think that they can)?

The *Adams* case does not, of course, necessarily resolve the issue before us. It held only that "the Constitution does not force a lawyer upon a defendant." Whether the Constitution forbids a State from forcing a lawyer upon a defendant is a different question. But the Court in *Adams* did recognize, albeit in dictum, an affirmative right of self-representation:

> "The right to assistance of counsel and the correlative right to dispense with a lawyer's help are not legal formalisms. They rest on considerations that go to the substance of an accused's position before the law.

"What were contrived as protections for the accused should not be turned into fetters. To deny an accused a choice of procedure in circumstances in which he, though a layman, is as capable as any lawyer of making an intelligent choice, is to impair the worth of great Constitutional safeguards by treating them as empty verbalisms.

"When the administration of the criminal law is hedged about as it is by the Constitutional safeguards for the protection of an accused, to deny him in the exercise of his free choice the right to dispense with some of these safeguards is to imprison a man in his privileges and call it the Constitution."

This Court's past recognition of the right of self-representation, the federal-court authority holding the right to be of constitutional dimension, and the state constitutions pointing to the right's fundamental nature form a consensus not easily ignored. We confront here a nearly universal conviction, on the part of our people as well as our courts, that forcing a lawyer upon an unwilling defendant is contrary to his basic right to defend himself if he truly wants to do so. This consensus is soundly premised. The right of self-representation finds support in the structure of the Sixth Amendment, as well as in the English and colonial jurisprudence from which the Amendment emerged. Because Sixth Amendment rights are basic to our adversary system of criminal justice, they are part of the "due process of law" that is guaranteed by the Fourteenth Amendment to defendants in the criminal courts of the States. The Sixth Amendment does not provide merely that a defense shall be made for the accused; it grants to the accused personally the right to make his defense. It is the accused, not counsel, who must be "informed of the nature and cause of the accusation," who must be "confronted with the witnesses against him," and who must be accorded "compulsory process for obtaining witnesses in his favor." Although not stated in the Amendment in so many words, the right to self-representation—to make one's own defense personally—is thus necessarily implied by the structure of the Amendment. The right to defend is given directly to the accused; for it is he who suffers the consequences if the defense fails.

The counsel provision supplements this design. It speaks of the "assistance" of counsel, and an assistant, however expert, is still an assistant. The language and spirit of the Sixth Amendment contemplate that counsel, like the other defense tools guaranteed by the Amendment, shall be an aid to a willing defendant—not an organ of the State interposed between an unwilling defendant and his right to defend himself personally. To thrust counsel upon the accused, against his considered wish, thus violates the logic of the Amendment. In such a case, counsel is not an assistant, but a master; and the right to make a defense is stripped of the personal character upon which the Amendment insists. It is true that when a defendant chooses to have a lawyer manage and present his case, law and tradition may allocate to the counsel the power to make binding decisions of trial strategy in many areas. This allocation can only be justified, however, by the defendant's consent, at the outset, to accept counsel as his representative. An unwanted counsel "represents" the defendant only through a tenuous and unacceptable legal fiction. Unless the accused has acquiesced in such representation, the defense presented is not the defense guaranteed him by the Constitution, for, in a very real sense, it is not *his* defense.

There can be no blinking the fact that the right of an accused to conduct his own defense seems to cut against the grain of this Court's decisions holding that the Constitution requires that no accused can be convicted and imprisoned unless he has been accorded the right to the assistance of counsel. For it is surely true that the basic thesis of those decisions is that the help of a lawyer is essential to assure the defendant a fair trial. And a strong argument can surely be made that the whole thrust of those decisions most inevitably lead to the conclusion that a State may constitutionally impose a lawyer upon even an unwilling defendant.

But it is one thing to hold that every defendant, rich or poor, has the right to the assistance of counsel, and quite another to say that a State may compel a defendant to accept a lawyer he does not want. The value of state-appointed counsel was not unappreciated by the Founders, yet the notion of compulsory counsel was utterly foreign to them. And whatever else may be said of those who wrote the Bill of Rights, surely there can be no doubt that they understood the inestimable worth of free choice.

It is undeniable that in most criminal prosecutions defendants could better defend with counsel's guidance than by their own unskilled efforts. But where the defendant will not voluntarily accept representation by counsel, the potential advantage of a lawyer's training and experience can be realized, if at all, only imperfectly. To force a lawyer on a defendant can only lead him to believe that the law contrives against him. Moreover, it is not inconceivable that in some rare instances, the defendant might in fact present his case more effectively by conducting his own defense. Personal liberties are not rooted in the law of averages. The right to defend is personal. The defendant, and not his lawyer or the State, will bear the personal consequences of a conviction. It is the defendant, therefore, who must be free personally to decide whether in his particular case counsel is to his advantage. And although he may conduct his own defense ultimately to his own detriment,

Take Note

This is an important footnote. After the Court legitimized the concept of "standby counsel" here, the use of this technique became commonplace where defendants decided to "go *pro se*" in serious cases.

his choice must be honored out of "that respect for the individual which is the life-blood of the law."[46]

Is it *really* so foolish to want to represent oneself? *See, e.g.,* Erica J. Hashimoto, *Defending the Right to Self Representation: An Empirical Look at the* Pro Se *Felony Defendant*, 85 N.C. L. Rev. 423, 423–24 (2007):

> The data undermine both the assumption that most felony pro se defendants are ill-served by the decision to self-represent and the theory that most pro se defendants suffer from mental illness. Somewhat surprisingly, the data indicate that pro se felony defendants in state courts are convicted at rates equivalent to or lower than the conviction rates of represented felony defendants, and the vast majority of pro se felony defendants—nearly 80%—did not display outward signs of mental illness.

> The data also suggest an alternative explanation for the pro se phenomenon. The small, self-selected group of felony defendants who choose to represent themselves may make that choice because of legitimate concerns about court-appointed counsel. Without the right to represent themselves, those defendants would be in the untenable position of being represented by inadequate counsel with no alternative.When an accused manages his own defense, he relinquishes, as a purely factual matter, many of the traditional benefits associated with the right to counsel. For this reason, in order to represent himself, the accused must "knowingly and intelligently" forgo those relinquished benefits. Although a defendant need not himself have the skill and experience of a lawyer in order competently and intelligently to choose self-representation, he should be made aware of the dangers and disadvantages of self-representation, so that the record will establish that "he knows what he is doing and his choice is made with eyes open."

Here, weeks before trial, Faretta clearly and unequivocally declared to the trial judge that he wanted to represent himself and did not want counsel. The record affirmatively shows that Faretta was literate, competent, and understanding, and that he was voluntarily exercising his informed free will. The trial judge had warned Faretta that he thought it was a mistake not to accept the assistance of counsel, and that Faretta would be required to follow all the "ground rules" of trial procedure. We need make no assessment of how well or poorly Faretta had mastered the intricacies of the

---

[46] We are told that many criminal defendants representing themselves may use the courtroom for deliberate disruption of their trials. But the right of self-representation has been recognized from our beginnings by federal law and by most of the States, and no such result has thereby occurred. Moreover, the trial judge may terminate self-representation by a defendant who deliberately engages in serious and obstructionist misconduct. Of course, a State may—even over objection by the accused—appoint a 'standby counsel' to aid the accused if and when the accused requests help, and to be available to represent the accused in the event that termination of the defendant's self-representation is necessary.

The right of self-representation is not a license to abuse the dignity of the courtroom. Neither is it a license not to comply with relevant rules of procedural and substantive law. Thus, whatever else may or may not be open to him on appeal, a defendant who elects to represent himself cannot thereafter complain that the quality of his own defense amounted to a denial of "effective assistance of counsel."

hearsay rule and the California code provisions that govern challenges of potential jurors on *voir dire*. For his technical legal knowledge, as such, was not relevant to an assessment of his knowing exercise of the right to defend himself.

In forcing Faretta, under these circumstances, to accept against his will a state-appointed public defender, the California courts deprived him of his constitutional right to conduct his own defense. Accordingly, the judgment before us is vacated.

MR. CHIEF JUSTICE BURGER, with whom MR. JUSTICE BLACKMUN and MR. JUSTICE REHNQUIST join, dissenting.

This case is another example of the judicial tendency to constitutionalize what is thought "good." That effort fails on its own terms here, because there is nothing desirable or useful in permitting every accused person, even the most uneducated and inexperienced, to insist upon conducting his own defense to criminal charges. If we were to assume that there will be widespread exercise of the newly discovered constitutional right to self-representation, it would almost certainly follow that there will be added congestion in the courts and that the quality of justice will suffer.

MR. JUSTICE BLACKMUN, with whom THE CHIEF JUSTICE and MR. JUSTICE REHNQUIST join, dissenting.

I fear that the right to self-representation constitutionalized today frequently will cause procedural confusion without advancing any significant strategic interest of the defendant. I therefore dissent. Although the Court indicates that a pro se defendant necessarily waives any claim he might otherwise make of ineffective assistance of counsel, the opinion leaves open a host of other procedural questions. Must every defendant be advised of his right to proceed *pro se*? If so, when must that notice be given? If a defendant has elected to exercise his right to proceed *pro se*, does he still have a constitutional right to assistance of standby counsel? How soon must a defendant decide between proceeding by counsel or *pro se*? Must he be allowed to switch in midtrial? If there is any truth to the old proverb that "one who is his own lawyer has a fool for a client," the Court by its opinion today now bestows a *constitutional* right on one to make a fool of himself.

Point for Discussion

On Appeal

In *State v. Rafey*, <u>167 Wash.2d 644, 652, 222 P.3d 86, 89 (2009)</u>, the Washington Supreme Court recognized a convicted defendant's right to proceed *pro se* under the State of Washington's Constitution: "In both trial and appellate proceedings, courts must carefully balance the dissonant rights to counsel and to self-representation when a defendant seeks to proceed *pro se*." However, the court also warned that the right must be asserted in a timely manner. Are appellate proceedings so different from trial court proceedings that courts should *not* recognize a right to *pro se* representation in that setting? What do you think?

Hypo 1: *The Unabomber Case*

You are the federal judge assigned to hear the "Unabomber case." The defendant, Theodore Kaczynski, is the individual who was charged with having murdered a number of people with mail bombs. Defendant wants to conduct his own defense, but his own attorneys question his competency. The reality is that Kaczynski is very bright, but his sanity is questionable (to put it mildly). How do you decide whether Kaczynski is competent to represent himself? How much weight should you give to the fact that Kaczynski may not be insane, but is, any event, clearly not in sound mental health?

See It

Here's how the FBI described this case: "How do you catch a twisted genius who aspires to be the perfect, anonymous killer—who builds untraceable bombs and delivers them to random targets, who leaves false clues to throw off authorities, who lives like a recluse in the mountains of Montana and tells no one of his secret crimes? That was the challenge facing the FBI and its investigative partners, who spent nearly two decades hunting down this ultimate lone wolf bomber." *See* https://www.fbi.gov/history/famous-cases/unabomber.

Hypo 2: *Non-Investigating Great Advocate*

Defendant was represented at trial by a public defender. On several occasions during the trial, defendant expressed dissatisfaction with counsel's performance. Prior to jury selection, defendant filed a motion to dismiss his attorney. He claimed that his attorney was not investigating the case adequately. Defense counsel acknowledged the existence of some problems in investigating matters related to the case, but the judge nonetheless denied defendant's motion, noting that the defendant's attorney had been a "great advocate" for his client. Did the judge act properly? *State v. Flanagan*, 293 Conn. 406, 978 A.2d 64 (2009).

Iowa v. Tovar

541 U.S. 77 (2004).

JUSTICE GINSBURG delivered the opinion of the Court.

The Sixth Amendment safeguards to an accused who faces incarceration the right to counsel at all critical stages of the criminal process. The entry of a guilty plea, whether to a misdemeanor or a felony charge, ranks as a "critical stage" at which the right to counsel adheres. Waiver of the right to counsel, as of constitutional rights in the criminal process generally, must be a "knowing, intelligent act done with sufficient awareness of the relevant circumstances." This case concerns the extent to which a trial judge, before accepting a guilty plea from an uncounseled defendant, must elaborate on the right to representation.

Hear It

You can hear the oral argument in *Tovar* at http://www.oyez.org/cases/2000-2009/2003/2003_02_1541.

Beyond affording the defendant the opportunity to consult with counsel prior to entry of a plea and to be assisted by counsel at the plea hearing, must the court, specifically: (1) advise the defendant that "waiving the assistance of counsel in deciding whether to plead guilty entails the risk that a viable defense will be overlooked"; and (2) "admonish" the defendant "that by waiving his right to an attorney he will lose the opportunity to obtain an independent opinion on whether, under the facts and applicable law, it is wise to plead guilty"? The Iowa Supreme Court held both warnings essential to the "knowing and intelligent" waiver of the Sixth Amendment right to the assistance of counsel.

We hold that neither warning is mandated by the Sixth Amendment. The constitutional requirement is satisfied when the trial court informs the accused of the nature of the charges against him, of his right to be counseled regarding his plea, and of the range of allowable punishments attendant upon the entry of a guilty plea.

On November 2, 1996, respondent Felipe Edgardo Tovar, then a 21-year-old college student, was arrested in Ames, Iowa, for operating a motor vehicle while under the influence of alcohol (OWI). At arraignment, the court's inquiries of Tovar began: "Mr. Tovar appears without counsel and I see, Mr. Tovar, that you waived application for a court appointed attorney. Did you want to represent yourself at today's hearing?" Tovar replied: "Yes, sir." The court soon after asked: "How did you wish to plead?" Tovar answered: "Guilty." Tovar affirmed that he had not been promised anything or threatened in any way to induce him to plead guilty.

Conducting the guilty plea colloquy required by the Iowa Rules of Criminal Procedure, the court explained that, if Tovar pleaded not guilty, he would be entitled to a speedy and public trial by jury, and would have the right to be represented at that trial by an attorney, who "could help Tovar select a jury, question and cross-examine the State's witnesses, present evidence, if any, in his behalf, and make arguments to the judge and jury on his behalf." By pleading guilty, the court cautioned, "not only would Tovar give up his right to a trial of any kind on the charge against him, he would give up his right to be represented by an attorney at that trial." The court further advised Tovar that, if he entered a guilty plea, he would relinquish the right to remain silent at trial, the right to the presumption of innocence, and the right to subpoena witnesses and compel their testimony.

Turning to the particular offense with which Tovar had been charged, the court informed him that an OWI conviction carried a maximum penalty of a year in jail and a $1,000 fine, and a minimum penalty of two days in jail and a $500 fine. Tovar affirmed that he understood his exposure to those penalties. The court next explained that, before accepting a guilty plea, the court had to assure itself that Tovar was in fact guilty of the charged offense. To that end, the court informed Tovar that the OWI charge had only two elements: first, on the date in question, Tovar was operating a motor vehicle in the State of Iowa; second, when he did so, he was intoxicated. Tovar confirmed that he had been driving on the night he was apprehended and that he did not dispute the results of the intoxilyzer test administered by the police that night, which showed that his blood alcohol level exceeded the legal limit nearly twice over.

After the plea colloquy, the court asked Tovar if he still wished to plead guilty, and Tovar affirmed that he did. The court then accepted Tovar's plea, observing that there was "a factual basis" for it, and that Tovar had made the plea "voluntarily, with a full understanding of his rights, and of the consequences of pleading guilty."

On December 30, 1996, Tovar appeared for sentencing on the OWI charge. Noting that Tovar was again in attendance without counsel, the court inquired: "Mr. Tovar, did you want to represent yourself at today's hearing or did you want to take some time to hire an attorney to represent you?" Tovar replied that he would represent himself. The court then engaged in essentially the same plea colloquy on the suspension charge as it had on the OWI charge the previous month. After accepting Tovar's guilty plea, the court imposed the minimum sentence of two days in jail and a $500 fine, plus a surcharge and costs.

On March 16, 1998, Tovar was convicted of OWI for a second time. He was represented by counsel in that proceeding, in which he pleaded guilty. On December 14, 2000, Tovar was again charged with OWI, this time as a third offense. Represented by an attorney, Tovar pleaded not guilty.

In March 2001, through counsel, Tovar filed a motion arguing that Tovar's first OWI conviction, in 1996, could not be used to enhance the December 2000 OWI charge from a second-offense aggravated misdemeanor to a third-offense felony. Tovar did not allege that he was unaware at the November 1996 arraignment of his right to counsel prior to pleading guilty and at the plea hearing. Instead, he maintained that his 1996 waiver of counsel was invalid—not "full knowing, intelligent, and voluntary"—because he "was never made aware by the court of the dangers and disadvantages of self-representation."

The court denied Tovar's motion. Tovar then waived his right to a jury trial and was found guilty. On the OWI third-offense charge, he received a 180-day jail term, with all but 30 days suspended, three years of probation, and a $2,500 fine plus surcharges and costs. The Iowa Court of Appeals affirmed, but the Supreme Court of Iowa reversed, holding that the colloquy preceding acceptance of Tovar's 1996 guilty plea had been constitutionally inadequate. We granted certiorari and we now reverse.

The Sixth Amendment secures to a defendant who faces incarceration the right to counsel at all "critical stages" of the criminal process. A plea hearing qualifies as a "critical stage."

Because Tovar received a two-day prison term for his 1996 OWI conviction, he had a right to counsel both at the plea stage and at trial had he elected to contest the charge.

A person accused of crime, however, may choose to forgo representation. While the Constitution does not force a lawyer upon a defendant, it does require that any waiver of the right to counsel be knowing, voluntary, and intelligent. Tovar contends that his waiver of counsel at his first OWI plea hearing, was insufficiently informed, and therefore constitutionally invalid. In particular, he asserts that the trial judge did not elaborate on the value, at that stage of the case, of an attorney's advice and the dangers of self-representation in entering a plea.

Take Note

Note that, without much fanfare, the Court confirmed here that indigents have the right to counsel at guilty plea hearings.

We have described a waiver of counsel as intelligent when the defendant "knows what he is doing and his choice is made with eyes open." We have not, however, prescribed any formula or script to be read to a defendant who states that he elects to proceed without counsel. The information a defendant must possess in order to make an intelligent election will depend on a range of case-specific factors, including the defendant's education or sophistication, the complex or easily grasped nature of the charge, and the stage of the proceeding.

In Tovar's case, he first indicated that he waived counsel at his Initial Appearance, affirmed that he wanted to represent himself at the plea hearing, and declined the court's offer of "time to hire an attorney" at sentencing, when it was still open to him to request withdrawal of his plea. Does the Sixth Amendment require a court to give a rigid and detailed admonishment to a *pro se* defendant pleading guilty of the usefulness of an attorney, that an attorney may provide an independent opinion whether it is wise to plead guilty and that without an attorney the defendant risks overlooking a defense? This Court recently explained, in reversing a lower court determination that a guilty plea was not voluntary: "The law ordinarily considers a waiver knowing, intelligent, and sufficiently aware if the defendant fully understands the nature of the right and how it would likely apply in general in the circumstances—even though the defendant may not know the specific detailed consequences of invoking it." We have similarly observed: "If the defendant lacked a full and complete appreciation of all of the consequences flowing from his waiver, it does not defeat the State's showing that the information it provided to him satisfied the constitutional minimum."

In a collateral attack on an uncounseled conviction, it is the defendant's burden to prove that he did not competently and intelligently waive his right to the assistance of counsel. Tovar has never claimed that he did not fully understand the charge or the range of punishment for the crime prior to pleading guilty. Further, he has never "articulated with precision" the additional information counsel could have provided, given the simplicity of the charge. Nor does he assert that he was unaware of his right to be counseled prior to and at his arraignment. He suggests only that he "may have been under the mistaken belief that he had a right to counsel at trial, but not if he was merely going to plead guilty."

Food for Thought

As extensive as waiver-of-the-right-to-counsel colloquies may appear in theory, the reality is that many trial judges "fly through" them, and many other judges openly encourage such waivers. What effect to you think that the *Tovar* decision will have on that practical reality?

We note, finally, that States are free to adopt by statute, rule, or decision any guides to the acceptance of an uncounseled plea they deem useful. We hold only that the two admonitions the Iowa Supreme Court ordered are not required by the Federal Constitution.

For the reasons stated, the judgment of the Supreme Court of Iowa is reversed.

Indiana v. Edwards

554 U.S. 164 (2008).

JUSTICE BREYER delivered the opinion of the Court.

This case focuses upon a criminal defendant whom a state court found mentally

Hear It

You can hear the oral argument in *Edwards* at http://www.oyez.org/cases/2000-2009/2007/2007_07_208.

competent to stand trial if represented by counsel but not mentally competent to conduct that trial himself. We must decide whether in these circumstances the Constitution forbids a State from insisting that the defendant proceed to trial with counsel, the State thereby denying the defendant the right to represent himself. We conclude that the Constitution does not forbid a State so to insist.

In July 1999 Ahmad Edwards tried to steal a pair of shoes from an Indiana department store. After he was discovered, he drew a gun, fired at a store security officer, and wounded a bystander. He was caught and then charged with attempted murder, battery with a deadly weapon, criminal recklessness, and theft. His mental condition subsequently became the subject of three competency proceedings and two self-representation requests, mostly before the same trial judge:

1. First Competency Hearing: August 2000. Five months after Edwards' arrest, his court-appointed counsel asked for a psychiatric evaluation. After hearing psychiatrist and neuropsychologist witnesses (in February 2000 and again in August 2000), the court found Edwards incompetent to stand trial and committed him to Logansport State Hospital for evaluation and treatment.

2. Second Competency Hearing: March 2002. Seven months after his commitment, doctors found that Edwards' condition had improved to the point where he could stand trial. Several months later, however, but still before trial, Edwards' counsel asked for another psychiatric evaluation. In March 2002, the judge held a competency hearing, considered additional psychiatric evidence, and (in April) found that Edwards, while "suffering from mental illness," was "competent to assist his attorneys in his defense and stand trial for the charged crimes."

3. Third Competency Hearing: April 2003. Seven months later but still before trial, Edwards' counsel sought yet another psychiatric evaluation of his client. And, in April 2003, the court held yet another competency hear-

ing. Edwards' counsel presented further psychiatric and neuropsychological evidence showing that Edwards was suffering from serious thinking difficulties and delusions. A testifying psychiatrist reported that Edwards could understand the charges against him, but he was "unable to cooperate with his attorney in his defense because of his schizophrenic illness"; "his delusions and his marked difficulties in thinking make it impossible for him to cooperate with his attorney." In November 2003, the court concluded that Edwards was not then competent to stand trial and ordered his recommitment to the state hospital.

4.   First Self-Representation Request and First Trial: June 2005. About eight months after his commitment, the hospital reported that Edwards' condition had again improved to the point that he had again become competent to stand trial. And almost one year after that Edwards' trial began. Just before trial, Edwards asked to represent himself. He also asked for a continuance, which, he said, he needed in order to proceed pro se. The court refused the continuance. Edwards then proceeded to trial represented by counsel. The jury convicted him of criminal recklessness and theft but failed to reach a verdict on the charges of attempted murder and battery.

5.   Second Self-Representation Request and Second Trial: December 2005. The State decided to retry Edwards on the attempted murder and battery charges. Just before the retrial, Edwards again asked the court to permit him to represent himself. Referring to the lengthy record of psychiatric reports, the trial court noted that Edwards still suffered from schizophrenia and concluded that "with these findings, he's competent to stand trial but I'm not going to find he's competent to defend himself." The court denied Edwards' self-representation request. Edwards was represented by appointed counsel at his retrial. The jury convicted Edwards on both of the remaining counts.

Subsequently, the Indiana Supreme Court concluded that this Court's precedents, namely, *Faretta,* and *Godinez v. Moran,* 509 U.S. 389 (1993), required the State to allow *Edwards* to represent himself. Our examination of this Court's precedents convinces us that those precedents frame the question presented, but they do not answer it. The two cases that set forth the Constitution's "mental competence" standard, *Dusky v. United States,* 362 U.S. 402 (1960), and *Drope v. Missouri,* 420 U.S. 162 (1975), specify that the Constitution does not permit trial of an individual who lacks "mental competency." *Dusky* defines the competency standard as including both (1) "whether" the defendant has "a rational as well as factual understanding of the proceedings against him" and (2) whether the defendant "has sufficient present ability to consult with his lawyer with a reasonable degree of rational understanding." *Drope* repeats that standard, stating that it "has long been accepted that a person whose mental condition is such that he lacks the capacity to understand the nature and object of the proceedings against him, to consult with counsel, and to assist in preparing his defense may not be subjected to a trial." Neither case considered the mental competency issue presented here, namely, the relation of the mental competence standard to the right of self-representation.

The Court's foundational "self-representation" case, *Faretta*, held that the Sixth and Fourteenth Amendments include a "constitutional right to proceed without counsel when" a criminal defendant "voluntarily and intelligently elects to do so." The sole case in which this Court considered mental competence and self-representation together is *Godinez*. That case focused upon a borderline-competent criminal defendant who had asked a state trial court to permit him to represent himself and to change his pleas from not guilty to guilty. The state trial court had found that the defendant met *Dusky's* mental competence standard, that he "knowingly and intelligently" waived his right to assistance of counsel, and that he "freely and voluntarily" chose to plead guilty. And the state trial court had consequently granted the defendant's self-representation and change-of-plea requests. This Court "rejected the notion that competence to plead guilty or to waive the right to counsel must be measured by a standard that is higher than (or even different from) the *Dusky* standard." The decision to plead guilty, we said, "is no more complicated than the sum total of decisions that a represented defendant may be called upon to make during the course of a trial." Hence "there is no reason to believe that the decision to waive counsel requires an appreciably higher level of mental functioning than the decision to waive other constitutional rights." And even assuming that self-representation might pose special trial-related difficulties, "the competence that is required of a defendant seeking to waive his right to counsel is the competence to waive the right, not the competence to represent himself."

Godinez does not answer the question before us now. In *Godinez*, the higher standard sought to measure the defendant's ability to proceed on his own to enter a guilty plea; here the higher standard seeks to measure the defendant's ability to conduct trial proceedings. To put the matter more specifically, the *Godinez* defendant sought only to change his pleas to guilty, he did not seek to conduct trial proceedings, and his ability to conduct a defense at trial was expressly not at issue.

We assume that a criminal defendant has sufficient mental competence to stand trial (i.e., the defendant meets *Dusky's* standard) and that the defendant insists on representing himself during that trial. We ask whether the Constitution permits a State to limit that defendant's self-representation right by insisting upon representation by counsel at trial on the ground that the defendant lacks the mental capacity to conduct his trial defense unless represented.

Several considerations taken together lead us to conclude that the answer to this question is yes. First, the Court's precedent points slightly in the direction of our affirmative answer. The Court's "mental competency" cases set forth a standard that focuses directly upon a defendant's "present ability to consult with his lawyer," a "capacity to consult with counsel," and an ability "to assist counsel in preparing his defense." These standards assume representation by counsel and emphasize the importance of counsel. They thus suggest (though do not hold) that an instance in which a defendant who would choose to forgo counsel at trial presents a very different set of circumstances, which in our view, calls for a different standard.

Second, the nature of the problem before us cautions against the use of a single mental competency standard for deciding both (1) whether a defendant who is represented by counsel can proceed to trial and (2) whether a defendant who goes to trial must be permitted to represent himself. Mental illness itself is not a unitary concept. It varies in degree. It can vary over time. It interferes with an individual's functioning at different times in different ways. The history of this case illustrates the complexity of the problem. In certain instances an individual may well be able to satisfy *Dusky*'s mental competence standard, for he will be able to work with counsel at trial, yet at the same time he may be unable to carry out the basic tasks needed to present his own defense without the help of counsel.

Third, in our view, a right of self-representation at trial will not "affirm the dignity" of a defendant who lacks the mental capacity to conduct his defense without the assistance of counsel. To the contrary, given that defendant's uncertain mental state, the spectacle that could well result from his self-representation at trial is at least as likely to prove humiliating as ennobling. Moreover, insofar as a defendant's lack of capacity threatens an improper conviction or sentence, self-representation in that exceptional context undercuts the most basic of the Constitution's criminal law objectives, providing a fair trial.

Further, proceedings must not only be fair, they must appear fair to all who observe them. An amicus brief reports one psychiatrist's reaction to having observed a patient (a patient who had satisfied *Dusky*) try to conduct his own defense: "How in the world can our legal system allow an insane man to defend himself?" The application of *Dusky*'s basic mental competence standard can

FYI

Only a *minority* of states have followed Indiana's lead and determined that the competency standard to be met in order for a defendant to proceed *pro se* should be set higher than the competency standard to be met for merely standing trial represented by counsel.

help in part to avoid this result. But given the different capacities needed to proceed to trial without counsel, there is little reason to believe that *Dusky* alone is sufficient. At the same time, the trial judge, particularly one such as the trial judge in this case, who presided over one of *Edwards'* competency hearings and his two trials, will often prove best able to make more fine-tuned mental capacity decisions, tailored to the individualized circumstances of a particular defendant.

We consequently conclude that the Constitution permits judges to take realistic account of the particular defendant's mental capacities by asking whether a defendant who seeks to conduct his own defense at trial is mentally competent to do so. That is to say, the Constitution permits States to insist upon representation by counsel for those competent enough to stand trial under Dusky but who still suffer from severe mental illness to the point where they are not competent to conduct trial proceedings by themselves.

Indiana has also asked us to adopt, as a measure of a defendant's ability to conduct a trial, a more specific standard that would "deny a criminal defendant the right to represent himself at trial where the defendant cannot communicate coherently with the court or a jury." We are sufficiently uncertain, however, as to how that particular standard would work in practice to refrain from endorsing it as a federal constitutional standard here. We need not now, and we do not, adopt it.

Indiana has also asked us to overrule *Faretta*. We decline to do so. We recognize that judges have sometimes expressed concern that *Faretta*, contrary to its intent, has led to trials that are unfair. But recent empirical research suggests that such instances are not common. *See, e.g.,* Hashimoto, Defending the Right of Self-Representation: An Empirical Look at the *Pro Se* Felony Defendant, 85 N.C.L.Rev. 423, 427, 428 (2007) (noting that of the small number of defendants who chose to proceed pro se, roughly 0.3% to 0.5%" of the total, state felony defendants in particular "appear to have achieved higher felony acquittal rates than their represented counterparts in that they were less likely to have been convicted of felonies"). At the same time, instances in which the trial's fairness is in doubt may well be concentrated in the 20 percent or so of self-representation cases where the mental competence of the defendant is also at issue. If so, today's opinion, assuring trial judges the authority to deal appropriately with cases in the latter category, may well alleviate those fair trial concerns.

Food for Thought

Is it *fair* to convict a *pro se* defendant of a crime when any reasonable person could see that he or she did not have the slightest idea what he or she was doing? What do you think?

For these reasons, the judgment of the Supreme Court of Indiana is vacated, and JUSTICE SCALIA, with whom JUSTICE THOMAS joins, dissenting.

The Constitution guarantees a defendant who knowingly and voluntarily waives the right to counsel the right to proceed pro se at his trial. A mentally ill defendant who knowingly and voluntarily elects to proceed pro se instead of through counsel receives a fair trial that comports with the Fourteenth Amendment. The Court today concludes that a State may nonetheless strip a mentally ill defendant of the right to represent himself when that would be fairer. In my view the Constitution does not permit a State to substitute its own perception of fairness for the defendant's right to make his own case before the jury—a specific right long understood as essential to a fair trial.

Because I think a defendant who is competent to stand trial, and who is capable of knowing and voluntary waiver of assistance of counsel, has a constitutional right to conduct his own defense, I respectfully dissent.

Points for Discussion

a. *Pro Se* Defendants, Mental Illness, & the Challenge for Trial Judges

Pro se defendants with mental problems are a real challenge for trial judges. Not only might such defendants do crazy and/or disruptive things in court, but the judge may have a reasonable fear that their lack of legal skills might lead to an unfair result. It is not surprising then to find trial judges, after *Edwards*, turning down an increasing number of putative *pro se* defendants' requests to represent themselves on competency grounds. Not only because it's "easier" on the judge, but also because of the judge's (perfectly legitimate) fears and doubts about the fairness of the proceedings. That said, as the *Edwards* Court made clear, *Faretta* is still good law. Criminal defendants do still have a constitutional right to represent themselves.

> **FYI**
>
> In *United States v. Balsiger*, 910 F.3d 942 (7th Cir. 2018), after defendant's lawyer died, he insisted on hiring a lawyer who would not be available for 18 months. Even though the trial judge made it clear that he would not delay the trial for 18 months, defendant repeatedly refused to choose another attorney. The judge did indicate that, if defendant chose another attorney, he would grant a continuance for a reasonable period of time so that counsel could prepare for trial. Finally, when defendant continued to fail to choose an alternate attorney, the judge concluded that he had waived his right to counsel and forced him to proceed *pro se*. The Seventh Circuit found that this was not a violation of his Sixth Amendment right to counsel: "The district court's decision to deny the continuance was neither unreasonable nor arbitrary."

b. Waiver by Silence

What constitutes a good waiver? Suppose that the defendant fails to assert the right to counsel, and proceeds to represent himself or herself at trial. Has there been a waiver by virtue of the mere failure to make such an assertion? No. The Court has made it clear that such a waiver will not be presumed from mere silence. Trial judges, accordingly, need to take pains to make sure that waivers are clear on the record.

c. Good Waivers

The *Faretta* Court talked about a "knowing and intelligent" waiver of counsel and the *Tovar* Court similarly spoke of a waiver made by a defendant who "knows what he is doing." But *Tovar* and *Faretta* don't *really* require that a defendant make an "intelligent" choice in the dictionary meaning of that word. As Justice Blackmun pointed out in his dissent in *Faretta*, few decisions to waive counsel can be regarded as truly intelligent in that sense. In most instances, criminal defendants do not know the rules of evidence, and have studied neither criminal law nor criminal procedure. Under these circumstances, can even a fully competent defendant make a truly "knowing" and "intelligent" waiver of the right to counsel? In any event, the Supreme Court requires only that the defendant be competent to make the waiver, and that he or she has been given sufficient information on which to base the waiver decision.

FYI

In *United States v. Watts*, 896 F.3d 1245 (11th Cir. 2018), defendant elected to proceed *pro se*, and decided that he would not testify in his own defense. Defendant changed his mind after both sides had rested in terms of their production of evidence. After the court refused to reopen the case so that he could testify, defendant objected that the trial judge did not adequately explain his right to testify. The 11th Circuit disagreed, noting that defendant was able to consult with his former attorney (who remained present in an advisory role) before deciding not to testify.

Hypo 1: *Judge's Dilemma*

Assuming that defendants are entitled to make a less than (truly) intelligent choice, how should they do so? A robbery defendant has stated that he is aware of his right to counsel, but that he prefers to proceed *pro se*. In light of *Faretta*'s requirement that a waiver be "knowing and intelligent," how should the trial judge proceed? Should the judge accept his request at face value? Should the judge interrogate him about his knowledge of the rules of evidence and the criminal law? Should it matter that the accused did not know, or was not able to recall, most (or any) of the exceptions to the hearsay rule? For that matter, can you recall them?

Hypo 2: *Judge's Dilemma #2*

If a *pro se* defendant has a valid objection to inadmissible evidence introduced by the prosecutor but fails to make the objection (because he or she doesn't know the applicable law), should the trial judge act *sua sponte* to keep the evidence out? Should the judge inform the *pro se* defendant of the law? Or should the judge say nothing and simply permit the prosecution to introduce otherwise inadmissible evidence

Hypo 3: *Defendant Changes His Mind*

Where an indigent defendant has waived his right to counsel multiple times, but then changes his mind after trial, and decides that he does want counsel after all for purposes of filing a motion for new trial, should the trial judge have the discretion to deny that request? Or must the trial judge grant that request automatically? What do you think is the appropriate rule given the existing precedent? *See Marshall v. Rodgers,* 569 U.S. 58 (2013).

Exercise: *Pro Se Request*

You are the law clerk to a trial judge. Defendant Jane Jones has been charged with arson in your court and has demanded to proceed *pro se* at trial. She was examined by a clinical psychologist one year ago who found that Jones suffered from "an active psychotic disorder of a paranoid type" and has "auditory hallucinations, delusions of a bizarre and persecutory nature, and is intent on using the legal process as a vehicle for acting out many of her paranoid psychotic preoccupations." After interrogating Jones at length, your judge has told you that she believes that Jones understands the seriousness of the charge filed against her and comprehends the disadvantages of proceeding *pro se,* and that Jones told her that although she heard voices in the past, she no longer does. The file also discloses that Jones has extensive familiarity with the courts in that she has previously filed seventeen motions in state court, eleven in federal court, and has instituted two Court of Claims actions, one for damages for false arrest and the other for an assault allegedly committed on her at a state mental institution. Your judge has asked you to provide her with a bench memo (of no longer than 5 double-spaced pages) that summarizes the applicable federal law on this subject and recommends to her whether or not she should permit Jones to proceed *pro se.*

* * *

The *Faretta* Court indicated in a footnote that trial judges could appoint "standby counsel" to assist *pro se* defendants in presenting their cases, or simply to be available when and if the *pro se* defendant decides that he or she would rather be represented by counsel. As the following decision illustrates, however, standby counsel's appropriate role remains controversial.

McKaskle v. Wiggins

465 U.S. 168 (1984).

JUSTICE O'CONNOR delivered the opinion of the Court.

In *Faretta v. California*, this Court recognized a defendant's Sixth Amendment right to conduct his own defense. The Court also held that a trial court may appoint

Hear It

You can hear the oral argument in *McKaskle* at http://www.oyez.org/cases/1980-1989/1983/1983_82_1135.

"standby counsel" to assist the *pro se* defendant in his defense. Today we must decide what role standby counsel who is present at trial over the defendant's objection may play consistent with the protection of the defendant's *Faretta* rights.

Carl Edwin Wiggins was convicted of robbery and sentenced to life imprisonment as a recidivist. In his petition for federal *habeas corpus* relief, Wiggins argued that standby counsel's conduct deprived him of his right to present his own defense, as guaranteed by *Faretta*. The Court of Appeals held that Wiggins' Sixth Amendment right of self-representation was violated by the unsolicited participation of overzealous standby counsel: "The rule that we establish today is that court-appointed standby counsel is 'to be seen, but not heard.' By this we mean that he is not to compete with the defendant or supersede his defense. Rather, his presence is there for advisory purposes only, to be used or not used as the defendant sees fit." We do not accept the Court of Appeals' rule, and reverse its judgment.

A defendant's right to self-representation plainly encompasses certain specific rights to have his voice heard. The *pro se* defendant must be allowed to control the organization and content of his own defense, to make motions, to argue points of law, to participate in *voir dire*, to question witnesses, and to address the court and the jury at appropriate points in the trial. The record reveals that Wiggins was in fact accorded all of these rights.

Before trial Wiggins moved the trial court to order preparation of a transcript of the first trial. He, not standby counsel, then waived receipt of the transcript and announced ready for trial. He filed and argued at least 12 *pro se* motions in pretrial proceedings. Wiggins alone conducted the defense's *voir dire* of prospective jurors and made the opening statement for the defense to the jury.

Wiggins filed numerous *pro se* motions in the course of the trial. He cross-examined the prosecution's witnesses freely, and registered his own objections. Throughout the trial Wiggins selected the witnesses for the defense, examined them, decided that certain questions would not be asked by the defense, and decided which witnesses would not be called. Against counsel's advice, Wiggins announced that the defense rested. Wiggins filed his own requested charges to the jury, and made his own objections to the court's suggested charge. He obtained the removal of one of the court's proposed charges over counsel's express objection, approved the verdict form supplied to the jury, and gave a closing argument to the and he argued his case to the jury at that stage as well.

Wiggins' complaint is directed not at limits placed on *his* participation in the trial, for there clearly were none. Wiggins contends that his right to present his defense *pro se* was impaired by the distracting, intrusive, and unsolicited participation of counsel throughout the trial.

Faretta's logic indicates that no absolute bar on standby counsel's unsolicited participation is appropriate or was intended. The right to appear *pro se* exists to affirm the dignity and autonomy of the accused and to allow the presentation of what may, at least occasionally, be the accused's best possible defense. Both of these objectives can be achieved without categorically silencing standby counsel.

In determining whether a defendant's *Faretta* rights have been respected, the primary focus must be on whether the defendant had a fair chance to present his case in his own way. *Faretta* itself dealt with the defendant's affirmative right to participate, not with the limits on standby counsel's additional involvement. The specific rights to make his voice heard that Wiggins was plainly accorded form the core of a defendant's right of self-representation.

We recognize, nonetheless, that the right to speak for oneself entails more than the opportunity to add one's voice to a cacophony of others. As Wiggins contends, the objectives underlying the right to proceed *pro se* may be undermined by unsolicited and excessively intrusive participation by standby counsel. In proceedings before a jury the defendant may legitimately be concerned that multiple voices "for the defense" will confuse the message the defendant wishes to convey, thus defeating *Faretta*'s objectives. Accordingly, the *Faretta* right must impose some limits on the extent of standby counsel's unsolicited participation.

First, the *pro se* defendant is entitled to preserve actual control over the case he chooses to present to the jury. This is the core of the *Faretta* right. If standby counsel's participation over the defendant's objection effectively allows counsel to make or substantially interfere with any significant tactical decisions, or to control the questioning of witnesses, or to speak instead of the defendant on any matter of importance, the *Faretta* right is eroded.

Take Note

The ABA in its Criminal Justice Standards, The Defense Function, Standard 4-5.3(b) (4th ed. 2015), has recommended that "defense counsel whose duty is to assist a *pro se* accused only when the accused requests assistance may bring to the attention of the accused steps that could be potentially beneficial or dangerous to the accused, but should not actively participate in the conduct of the defense unless requested by the accused or as directed to do so by the court."

Second, participation by standby counsel without the defendant's consent should not be allowed to destroy the jury's perception that the defendant is representing himself. The defendant's appearance in the status of one conducting his own defense is important in a criminal trial, since the right to appear *pro se* exists to affirm the accused's individual dignity and autonomy. In related contexts the courts have recognized that a defendant has a right to be present at all important stages of trial, that he may not normally be forced to appear in court in shackles or prison garb, and that he has a right to present testimony in his own behalf. Appearing before the jury in the status of one who is defending himself may be equally important to the *pro se* defendant. From the jury's perspective, the message conveyed by the defense may depend as much on the messenger as on the message itself. From the defendant's own point of view, the right to appear *pro se* can lose much of its importance if only the lawyers in the courtroom know that the right is being exercised.

Participation by standby counsel outside the presence of the jury engages only the first of these two limitations. A trial judge, who in any event receives a defendant's original *Faretta* request and supervises the protection of the right throughout the trial, must be considered capable of differentiating the claims presented by a *pro se* defendant from those presented by standby counsel. Accordingly, the appearance of a *pro se* defendant's self-representation will not be unacceptably undermined by counsel's participation outside the presence of the jury.

Thus, *Faretta* rights are adequately vindicated in proceedings outside the presence of the jury if the *pro se* defendant is allowed to address the court freely on his own behalf and if disagreements between counsel and the *pro se* defendant are resolved in the defendant's favor whenever the matter is one that would normally be left to the discretion of counsel.

Most of the incidents of which Wiggins complains occurred when the jury was not in the courtroom. In the jury's absence Wiggins' two standby counsel frequently explained to the trial judge their views and points of disagreement with Wiggins. Counsel made motions, dictated proposed strategies into the record, registered objections to the prosecution's testimony, urged the summoning of additional witnesses, and suggested questions that the defendant should have asked of witnesses. On several occasions Wiggins expressly adopted standby counsel's initiatives.

On several other occasions Wiggins strongly opposed the initiatives of counsel. He resisted counsel's suggestion that the trial be postponed so that the transcript of his prior trial could be prepared, and he waived counsel's right to a 10-day preparation period, which counsel wished to invoke. In the course of a pretrial discussion concerning a discovery request Wiggins indignantly demanded that counsel not participate further without invitation. Later, Wiggins successfully opposed the inclusion in the jury instructions of a charge that counsel felt should be included.

The most acrimonious exchange between standby counsel Graham and Wiggins occurred in the course of questioning a witness on *voir dire*. Wiggins suggests this exchange was typical of counsel's overbearing conduct, but he fails to place the incident in context. Wiggins had expressly agreed to have Graham conduct the *voir dire*, but Wiggins attempted to take over the questioning in midstream. Plainly exasperated, Graham used profanity and curtly directed Wiggins to "sit down."

Though several of these incidents are regrettable, we are satisfied that counsel's participation outside the presence of the jury fully satisfied the first standard we have outlined. Wiggins was given ample opportunity to present his own position to the court on every matter discussed. He was given time to think matters over, to explain his problems and concerns informally, and to speak to the judge off the record. Standby counsel participated actively, but for the most part in an orderly manner. Equally important, all conflicts between Wiggins and counsel were resolved in Wiggins' favor. The trial judge repeatedly explained to all concerned that Wiggins' strategic choices, not counsel's, would prevail. Not every motion made by Wiggins was granted, but in no instance was counsel's position adopted over Wiggins' on a matter that would normally be left to the defense's discretion.

Participation by standby counsel in the presence of the jury is more problematic. It is here that the defendant may legitimately claim that excessive involvement by counsel will destroy the appearance that the defendant is acting *pro se*. This, in turn, may erode the dignitary values that the right to self-representation is intended to promote and may undercut the defendant's presentation to the jury of his own most effective defense. Nonetheless, we believe that a categorical bar on participation by standby counsel in the presence of the jury is unnecessary.

In measuring standby counsel's involvement against the standards we have described, it is important not to lose sight of the defendant's own conduct. A defendant can waive his *Faretta* rights. Participation by counsel with a *pro se* defendant's express approval is, of course, constitutionally unobjectionable. A defendant's invitation to counsel to participate in the trial obliterates any claim that the participation in question deprived the defendant of control over his own defense. Such participation also diminishes any general claim that counsel unreasonably interfered with the defendant's right to appear in the status of one defending himself.

Although this is self-evident, it is also easily overlooked. A defendant like Wiggins, who vehemently objects at the beginning of trial to standby counsel's very presence in the courtroom, may express quite different views as the trial progresses. Even when he insists that he is not waiving his *Faretta* rights, a *pro se* defendant's solicitation of or acquiescence in certain types of participation by counsel substantially undermines later protestations that counsel interfered unacceptably.

The record in this case reveals that Wiggins' *pro se* efforts were undermined primarily by his own, frequent changes of mind regarding counsel's role. *Faretta* does not require a trial judge to permit "hybrid" representation of the type Wiggins was actually allowed. But if a defendant is given the opportunity and elects to have counsel appear before the court or jury, his complaints concerning counsel's subsequent unsolicited participation lose much of their force. A defendant does not have a constitutional right to choreograph special appearances by counsel. Once a *pro se* defendant invites or agrees to any substantial participation by counsel, subsequent appearances by counsel must be presumed to be with the defendant's acquiescence, at least until the defendant expressly and unambiguously renews his request that standby counsel be silenced.

Faretta rights are also not infringed when standby counsel assists the *pro se* defendant in overcoming routine procedural or evidentiary obstacles to the completion of some specific task, such as introducing evidence or objecting to testimony, that the defendant has clearly shown he wishes to complete. Nor are they infringed when counsel merely helps to ensure the defendant's compliance with basic rules of courtroom protocol and procedure. In neither case is there any significant interference with the defendant's actual control over the presentation of his defense. The likelihood that the defendant's appearance in the status of one defending himself will be eroded is also slight, and in any event it is tolerable. A defendant does not have a constitutional right to receive personal instruction from the trial judge on courtroom procedure. Nor does the Constitution require judges to take over chores for a *pro se* defendant that would normally be attended to by trained counsel as a matter of course.

Accordingly, we make explicit today what is already implicit in *Faretta*: A defendant's Sixth Amendment rights are not violated when a trial judge appoints standby counsel—even over the defendant's objection—to relieve the judge of the need to explain and enforce basic rules of courtroom protocol or to assist the defendant in overcoming routine obstacles that stand in the way of the defendant's achievement of his own clearly indicated goals. Participation by counsel to steer a defendant through the basic procedures of trial is permissible even in the unlikely event that it somewhat undermines the *pro se* defendant's appearance of control over his own defense.

At Wiggins' trial a significant part of standby counsel's participation both in and out of the jury's presence involved basic mechanics of the type we have described—informing the court of the whereabouts of witnesses, supplying Wiggins with a form needed to elect to go to the jury at the punishment phase of trial, explaining to Wiggins that he should not argue his case while questioning a witness, and so on. When Wiggins attempted to introduce a document into evidence, but failed to mark it for identification or to lay a predicate for its introduction, counsel, at the trial court's suggestion, questioned the witness to lay an appropriate predicate, and Wiggins then resumed his examination. Similarly, the trial judge repeatedly instructed Wiggins to consult with counsel, not with the court, regarding the appropriate procedure for summoning witnesses.

Notwithstanding Wiggins' several general objections to the presence and participation of counsel, we find these aspects of counsel's involvement irreproachable. None interfered with Wiggins' actual control over his defense; none can reasonably be thought to have undermined Wiggins' appearance before the jury in the status of a *pro se* defendant.

Putting aside participation that was either approved by Wiggins or attendant to routine clerical or procedural matters, counsel's unsolicited comments in front of the jury were infrequent and for the most part innocuous. On two occasions Graham interrupted a witness' answer to a question put by Wiggins. The first interruption was trivial. When the second was made the jury was briefly excused and subsequently given a cautionary instruction as requested by Graham. Wiggins made no objection. Standby counsel also moved for a mistrial three times in the presence of the jury. Each motion was in response to allegedly prejudicial questions or comments by the prosecutor. Wiggins did not comment on the first motion, but he opposed the following two. All three motions were immediately denied by the trial court. Regrettably, counsel used profanity to express his exasperation on the second occasion. Finally, counsel played an active role at the punishment phase of the trial. The record supplies no explanation for the sudden change in this regard. Wiggins made no objection to counsel's participation in this phase of the trial. We can only surmise that by then Wiggins had concluded that appearing *pro se* was not in his best interests.

The statements made by counsel during the guilt phase of the trial, in the presence of the jury and without Wiggins' express consent, occupy only a small portion of the transcript. Most were of an unobjectionable, mechanical sort. While standby counsel's participation at Wiggins' trial should not serve as a model for future trials, we believe that counsel's involvement fell short of infringing on Wiggins' *Faretta* rights. Wiggins unquestionably maintained actual control over the presentation of his own defense at all times.

We are also persuaded that Wiggins was allowed to appear before the jury in the status of one defending himself. At the outset the trial judge carefully explained to the jury that Wiggins would be appearing *pro se*. Wiggins, not counsel, examined prospective jurors on *voir dire*, cross-examined the prosecution's witnesses, examined his own witnesses, and made an opening statement for the defense. Wiggins objected to the prosecutor's case at least as often as did counsel. If Wiggins closing statement to the jury had to compete with one made by counsel, it was only because Wiggins agreed in advance to that arrangement.

By contrast, counsel's interruptions of Wiggins or witnesses being questioned by Wiggins in the presence of the jury were few and perfunctory. Most of counsel's uninvited comments were directed at the prosecutor. Such interruptions present little threat to a defendant's *Faretta* rights, at least when the defendant's view regarding those objections has not been clearly articulated. On the rare occasions that disagreements between counsel and Wiggins were aired in the presence of the jury the trial judge consistently ruled in Wiggins' favor. This was a pattern more likely to reinforce than to detract from the appearance that Wiggins was controlling his own defense. The intrusions by counsel at Wiggins' trial were simply not substantial or frequent enough to have seriously undermined Wiggins' appearance before the jury in the status of one representing himself.

Faretta affirmed the defendant's constitutional right to appear on stage at his trial. We recognize that a *pro se* defendant may wish to dance a solo, not a *pas de deux*. Standby counsel must generally respect that preference. But counsel need not be excluded altogether, especially when the participation is outside the presence of the jury or is with the defendant's express or tacit consent. The defendant in this case was allowed to make his own appearances as he saw fit. In our judgment counsel's unsolicited involvement was held within reasonable limits.

Food for Thought

The majority concludes that its new test for the limits on standby counsel's participation was not violated in this case. Do you think this conclusion was correct, i.e. even if the test is just fine, was it really satisfied on these facts?

The judgment of the Court of Appeals is therefore *Reversed*.

JUSTICE WHITE, with whom JUSTICE BRENNAN and JUSTICE MARSHALL join, dissenting.

The continuous and substantial intervention of standby counsel, despite Wiggins' repeated demands that he play a passive role, could not have had "anything but a negative impact on the jury. It also destroyed Wiggins' own perception that he was conducting *his* defense."

Under the Court's new test, it is necessary to determine whether the *pro se* defendant retained "actual control over the case he chose to present to the jury," and whether standby counsel's participation "destroyed the jury's perception that the defendant was representing himself." Although this test purports to protect all of the values underlying our holding in *Faretta*, it is unclear whether it can achieve this result.

As long as the *pro se* defendant is allowed his say, the first prong of the Court's test accords standby counsel at a bench trial or any proceeding outside the presence of a jury virtually untrammeled discretion to present any factual or legal argument to which the defendant does not object.

Although the Court is more solicitous of a *pro se* defendant's interests when standby counsel intervenes before a jury, the test's second prong suffers from similar shortcomings. To the extent that trial and appellate courts can discern the point at which counsel's unsolicited participation substantially undermines a *pro se* defendant's appearance before the jury, a matter about which I harbor substantial doubts, their decisions will, to a certain extent, "affirm the accused's individual dignity and autonomy." But they will do so incompletely, for in focusing on how the jury views the defendant, the majority opinion ignores *Faretta*'s emphasis on the defendant's own perception of the criminal justice system, and implies that the Court actually adheres to the result-oriented harmless error standard it purports to reject.

As a guide for standby counsel and lower courts, moreover, the Court's two-part test is clearly deficient. Instead of encouraging counsel to accept a limited role, the Court plainly invites them to participate despite their clients' contrary instructions until the clients renew their objections and trial courts draw the line. Trial courts required to rule on *pro se* defendants' objections to counsel's intervention also are left at sea. They clearly must prevent standby counsel from

> **Food for Thought**
>
> What more could the trial court have done in this case to protect Wiggin's pro se rights? One thing it could have done was to order standby counsel to remain silent, at least in front of the jury, unless spoken to or requested to speak by the defendant. Obviously, the majority was unwilling to impose that requirement. Would that have been a better result?

overtly muzzling their pro se clients and resolve certain conflicts in defendants' favor. But the Court's opinion places few, if any, other clear limits on counsel's uninvited participation; instead it requires trial courts to make numerous subjective judgments concerning the effect of counsel's actions on defendants' *Faretta* rights.

In short, I believe that the Court's test is unworkable and insufficiently protective of the fundamental interests we recognized in *Faretta*.

Hypo 1: *Meddling Law Professor*

Suppose that you graduated from law school, passed the bar (*congratulations*!), and were appointed to represent an indigent defendant in a criminal case. Your criminal procedure professor, interested to see how much you learned in law school, comes to observe. Unhappy with your performance, the professor offers interjections and suggestions while you are trying the case. Is a court likely to tolerate the professor's conduct? If not, should the court be any more willing to tolerate such conduct when a *pro se* defendant is involved as counsel? Is there a dispositive difference in these two situations?

Hypo 2: *Judicial Instructions*

Suppose that you are the judge in a criminal case involving a *pro se* defendant and standby counsel. Prior to trial, would you give standby counsel any special instructions regarding his or her role? What instructions? Suppose that counsel subsequently intrudes in the case inappropriately. How should you (still the trial judge) respond?

Hypo 3: *Standby Counsel's Role in Penalty Phase*

Defendant, who proceeded *pro se* at trial, was convicted of murder and faced the possibility of a death sentence. During the penalty phase of the proceeding, he elected not to present any evidence and instead relied in mitigation on the fact that he had confessed to some unsolved crimes and took responsibility for the murder for which he had been convicted. Standby counsel conducted his own mitigation investigation, and introduced mitigation evidence over defendant's objections, *inter alia*, establishing that defendant "was under the emotional or mental disturbance of cocaine dependency, and an antisocial personality disorder." Defendant was sentenced to death. Were the actions of standby counsel in presenting mitigation evidence over defendant's objections justified? Or did they unduly infringe upon defendant's Sixth Amendment right to proceed *pro se*? *Barnes v. State*, 29 So.3d 1010 (Fla. 2010).

Hypo 4: *Pro Se Defendant at Sidebar?*

Attorneys often "approach the Bench" and have conversations with the trial judge about various issues. This is called meeting "at sidebar." If a *pro se* defendant has standby counsel, should that *pro se* defendant have a right to participate in these sidebar conferences discussing legal issues instead of or in addition to standby counsel? Would it or should it make any difference if the defendant had previously been disruptive in court? *See Allen v. Com.*, 410 S.W.3d 125 (Ky. 2013).

C. Ineffective Assistance of Counsel

In *Powell v. Alabama*, 287 U.S. 45 (1932), the United States Supreme Court made it clear that a criminal defendant's constitutional right to counsel includes the right to the "effective" assistance of counsel.

However, the Court did not establish a test to determine when defense counsel violates the Sixth Amendment due to ineffective assistance of counsel until 1984.

Powell v. Alabama was the Supreme Court's decision in the widely-publicized "Scottsboro Boys" case, in which nine African-American teenagers were prosecuted for the rape of two white women. The trial court purported to appoint "all the members of the bar" to represent the defendants. But, despite the theoretical abundance of defense counsel, the reality was that no local lawyer would represent them. As a result, they were unrepresented at arraignment, and they were still unrepresented as late as the morning of trial. At that point, the judge hastily forced two lawyers to serve as counsel, but neither attorney was given time to prepare for trial, which began immediately. Unsurprisingly, the Scottsboro Boys were quickly convicted in a one-day trial and some were sentenced to death, and others received life sentences. But, in what can be seen as one of the earliest civil-rights decisions in this country, the Supreme Court reversed, holding that not only did the defendants have the right to counsel, but they were also entitled to the *effective* assistance of counsel, a right which they clearly had not received. (*Postscript:* Justice was only temporary. The defendants were re-convicted on remand, even though, in hindsight, the charges against them were clearly ludicrous and fabricated.)

See It

Watch and listen to Emory's Charles Howard Candler Professor and Chair of African American Studies, Carol Anderson, movingly discuss the extraordinary circumstances of this case. *See* https://www.youtube.com/watch?v=TmsYL-mqx3wg.

Strickland v. Washington

466 U.S. 668 (1984).

JUSTICE O'CONNOR delivered the opinion of the Court.

This case requires us to consider the proper standards for judging a criminal defendant's contention that the Constitution requires a conviction or death sentence to be set aside because counsel's assistance at the trial or sentencing was ineffective.

During a 10-day period in September 1976, respondent planned and committed three groups of crimes, which included three brutal stabbing murders, torture, kidnaping, severe assaults, attempted murders, attempted extortion, and theft. After his two accomplices were arrested, respondent surrendered to police and voluntarily gave a lengthy statement confessing to the third of the criminal episodes. The State of Florida indicted respondent for kidnaping and murder and appointed an experienced criminal lawyer to represent him.

Hear It

You can hear the oral argument in *Strickland* at http://www.oyez.org/cases/1980-1989/1983/1983_82_1554.

Counsel actively pursued pretrial motions and discovery. He cut his efforts short, however, and he experienced a sense of hopelessness about the case, when he learned that, against his specific advice, respondent had also confessed to the first two murders. By the date set for trial, respondent was subject to indictment for three counts of first-degree murder and multiple counts of robbery, kidnaping for ransom, breaking and entering and assault, attempted murder, and conspiracy to commit robbery. Respondent waived his right to a jury trial, again acting against counsel's advice, and pleaded guilty to all charges, including the three capital murder charges.

In the plea colloquy, respondent told the trial judge that, although he had committed a string of burglaries, he had no significant prior criminal record and that at the time of his criminal spree he was under extreme stress caused by his inability to support his family. He also stated, however, that he accepted responsibility for the crimes. The trial judge told respondent that he had "a great deal of respect for people who are willing to step forward and admit their responsibility" but that he was making no statement at all about his likely sentencing decision.

Counsel advised respondent to invoke his right under Florida law to an advisory jury at his capital sentencing hearing. Respondent rejected the advice and waived the right. He chose instead to be sentenced by the trial judge without a jury recommendation.

In preparing for the sentencing hearing, counsel spoke with respondent about his background. He also spoke on the telephone with respondent's wife and mother, though he did not follow up on the one unsuccessful effort to meet with them. He did not otherwise seek out character witnesses for respondent. Nor did he request a psychiatric examination, since his conversations with his client gave no indication that respondent had psychological problems.

Counsel decided not to present and hence not to look further for evidence concerning respondent's character and emotional state. That decision reflected trial counsel's sense of hopelessness about overcoming the evidentiary effect of respondent's confessions to the gruesome crimes. It also reflected the judgment that it was advisable to rely on the plea colloquy for evidence about respondent's background and about his claim of emotional stress: the plea colloquy communicated sufficient information about these subjects, and by forgoing the opportunity to present new evidence on these subjects, counsel prevented the State from cross-examining respondent on his claim and from putting on psychiatric evidence of its own.

Counsel also excluded from the sentencing hearing other evidence he thought was potentially damaging. He successfully moved to exclude respondent's "rap sheet." Because he judged that a presentence report might prove more detrimental than helpful, as it would have included respondent's criminal history and thereby would have undermined the claim of no significant history of criminal activity, he did not request that one be prepared.

At the sentencing hearing, counsel's strategy was based primarily on the trial judge's remarks at the plea colloquy as well as on his reputation as a sentencing judge who thought it important for a convicted defendant to own up to his crime. Counsel argued that respondent's remorse and acceptance of responsibility justified sparing him from the death penalty. Counsel also argued that respondent had no history of criminal activity and that respondent committed the crimes under extreme mental or emotional disturbance, thus coming within the statutory list of mitigating circumstances. He further argued that respondent should be spared death because he had surrendered, confessed, and offered to testify against a codefendant and because respondent was fundamentally a good person who had briefly gone badly wrong in extremely stressful circumstances. The State put on evidence and witnesses largely for the purpose of describing the details of the crimes. Counsel did not cross-examine the medical experts who testified about the manner of death of respondent's victims.

The trial judge found several aggravating circumstances with respect to each of the three murders. He found that all three murders were especially heinous, atrocious, and cruel, all involving repeated stabbings. All three murders were committed in the course of at least one other dangerous and violent felony, and since all involved robbery, the murders were for pecuniary gain. All three murders were committed to avoid arrest for the accompanying crimes and to hinder law enforcement. In the course of one of the murders, respondent knowingly subjected numerous persons to a grave risk of death by deliberately stabbing and shooting the murder victim's sisters-in-law, who sustained severe—in one case, ultimately fatal—injuries.

With respect to mitigating circumstances, the trial judge made the same findings for all three capital murders. First, although there was no admitted evidence of prior convictions, respondent had stated that he had engaged in a course of stealing. In any case, even if respondent had no significant history of criminal activity, the aggravating circumstances "would still clearly far outweigh" that mitigating factor. Second, the judge found that, during all three crimes, respondent was not suffering from extreme mental or emotional disturbance and could appreciate the criminality of his acts. Third, none of the victims was a participant in, or consented to, respondent's conduct. Fourth, respondent's participation in the crimes was neither minor nor the result of duress or domination by an accomplice. Finally, respondent's age (26) could not be considered a factor in mitigation, especially when viewed in light of respondent's planning of the crimes and disposition of the proceeds of the various accompanying thefts.

In short, the trial judge found numerous aggravating circumstances and no (or a single comparatively insignificant) mitigating circumstance. He therefore sentenced respondent to death on each of the three counts of murder and to prison terms for the other crimes. The Florida Supreme Court upheld the convictions and sentences. In subsequent postconviction proceedings, a federal district court denied Strickland's petition for *habeas corpus*, but the court of appeals reversed.

In a long line of cases that includes *Powell v. Alabama*, 287 U.S. 45 (1932), *Johnson v. Zerbst*, 304 U.S. 458 (1938), and *Gideon v. Wainwright*, 372 U.S. 335 (1963), this Court has recognized that the Sixth Amendment right to counsel exists, and is needed, in order to protect the fundamental right to a fair trial. A fair trial is one in which evidence subject to adversarial testing is presented to an impartial tribunal for resolution of issues defined in advance of the proceeding. The right to counsel plays a crucial role in the adversarial system embodied in the Sixth Amendment, since access to counsel's skill and knowledge is necessary to accord defendants the ample opportunity to meet the case of the prosecution to which they are entitled.

The Court has recognized that "the right to counsel is the right to the effective assistance of counsel." Government violates the right to effective assistance when it interferes in certain ways with the ability of counsel to make independent decisions about how to conduct the defense. Counsel, however, can also deprive a defendant of the right to effective assistance, simply by failing to render "adequate legal assistance."

The Court has not elaborated on the meaning of the constitutional requirement of effective assistance in cases presenting claims of "actual ineffectiveness." In giving meaning to the requirement, however, we must take its purpose—to ensure a fair trial—as the guide. The benchmark for judging any claim of ineffectiveness must be whether counsel's conduct so undermined the proper functioning of the adversarial process that the trial cannot be relied on as having produced a just result.

The same principle applies to a capital sentencing proceeding such as that provided by Florida law. A capital sentencing proceeding like the one involved in this case is sufficiently like a trial in its adversarial format and in the existence of standards for decision, that counsel's role in the proceeding is comparable to counsel's role at trial—to ensure that the adversarial testing process works to produce a just result under the standards governing decision. For purposes of describing counsel's duties, therefore, Florida's capital sentencing proceeding need not be distinguished from an ordinary trial.

> **Food for Thought**
>
> Given the potential consequences of a capital sentencing hearing—*a sentence of death*—wouldn't it have been reasonable to have required defense counsel to do more than to provide merely *adequate* representation?

A convicted defendant's claim that counsel's assistance was so defective as to require reversal of a conviction or death sentence has two components. First, the defendant must show that counsel's performance was deficient. This requires showing that counsel made errors so serious that counsel was not functioning as the "counsel" guaranteed the defendant by the Sixth Amendment. Second, the defendant must show that the deficient performance prejudiced the defense. This requires showing that counsel's errors were so serious as to deprive the defendant of a fair trial, a trial whose result is reliable. Unless a defendant makes both showings, it cannot be said that the conviction or death sentence resulted from a breakdown in the adversary process that renders the result unreliable.

The proper standard for attorney performance is that of reasonably effective assistance. When a convicted defendant complains of the ineffectiveness of counsel's assistance, the defendant must show that counsel's representation fell below an objective standard of reasonableness. More specific guidelines are not appropriate. The Sixth Amendment refers simply to "counsel," not specifying particular requirements of effective assistance. It relies instead on the legal profession's maintenance of standards sufficient to justify the law's presumption that counsel will fulfill the role in the adversary process that the Amendment envisions. The proper measure of attorney performance remains simply reasonableness under prevailing professional norms.

Representation of a criminal defendant entails certain basic duties. Counsel's function is to assist the defendant, and hence counsel owes the client a duty of loyalty, a duty to avoid conflicts of interest. From counsel's function as assistant to the defendant derive the overarching duty to advocate the defendant's cause and the more particular duties to consult with the defendant on important decisions and to keep the defendant informed of important developments in the course of the prosecution. Counsel also has a duty to bring to bear such skill and knowledge as will render the trial a reliable adversarial testing process.

These basic duties neither exhaustively define the obligations of counsel nor form a checklist for judicial evaluation of attorney performance. In any case presenting an ineffectiveness claim, the performance inquiry must be whether counsel's assistance was reasonable considering all the circumstances. Prevailing norms of practice as reflected in American Bar Association standards and the like, *e.g.*, ABA Standards for Criminal Justice 4–1.1 to 4–8.6 (2d ed. 1980) ("The Defense Function"), are guides to determining what is reasonable, but they are only guides. No particular set of detailed rules for counsel's conduct can satisfactorily take account of the variety of circumstances faced by defense counsel or the range of legitimate decisions regarding how best to represent a criminal defendant. Moreover, the purpose of the effective assistance guarantee of the Sixth Amendment is not to improve the quality of legal representation, although that is a goal of considerable importance to the legal system. The purpose is simply to ensure that criminal defendants receive a fair trial.

Judicial scrutiny of counsel's performance must be highly deferential. It is all too tempting for a defendant to second-guess counsel's assistance after conviction or adverse sentence, and it is all too easy for a court, examining counsel's defense after it has proved unsuccessful, to conclude that a particular act or omission of counsel was unreasonable. A fair assessment of attorney performance requires that every effort be made to eliminate the distorting effects of hindsight, to reconstruct the circumstances of counsel's challenged conduct, and to evaluate the conduct from counsel's perspective at the time. Because of the difficulties inherent in making the evaluation, a court must indulge a strong presumption that counsel's conduct falls within the wide range of reasonable professional assistance; that is, the defendant must overcome the presumption that, under the circumstances, the challenged action "might be considered sound trial strategy." There are countless ways to provide effective assistance in any given case. Even the best criminal defense attorneys would not defend a particular client in the same way.

The availability of intrusive post-trial inquiry into attorney performance or of detailed guidelines for its evaluation would encourage the proliferation of ineffectiveness challenges. Criminal trials resolved unfavorably to the defendant would increasingly come to be followed by a second trial, this one of counsel's unsuccessful defense. Counsel's performance and even willingness to serve could be adversely affected. Intensive scrutiny of counsel and rigid requirements for acceptable assistance could dampen the ardor and impair the independence of defense counsel, discourage the acceptance of assigned cases, and undermine the trust between attorney and client.

Thus, a court deciding an actual ineffectiveness claim must judge the reasonableness of counsel's challenged conduct on the facts of the particular case, viewed as of the time of counsel's conduct. A convicted defendant making a claim of ineffective assistance must identify the acts or omissions of counsel that are alleged not to have been the result of reasonable professional judgment. The court must then determine whether, in light of all the circumstances, the identified acts or omissions were outside the wide range of professionally competent assistance. In making that determination, the court should keep in mind that counsel's function, as elaborated in prevailing professional norms, is to make the adversarial testing process work in the particular case. At the same time, the court should recognize that counsel is strongly presumed to have rendered adequate assistance and made all significant decisions in the exercise of reasonable professional judgment.

These standards require no special amplification in order to define counsel's duty to investigate, the duty at issue in this case. As the Court of Appeals concluded, strategic choices made after thorough investigation of law and facts relevant to plausible options are virtually unchallengeable; and strategic choices made after less than complete investigation are reasonable precisely to the extent that reasonable professional judgments support the limitations on investigation. In other words, counsel has a duty to make reasonable investigations or to make a reasonable decision that makes particular investigations unnecessary. In any ineffectiveness case, a particular decision not to investigate must be directly assessed for reasonableness in all the circumstances, applying a heavy measure of deference to counsel's judgments.

The reasonableness of counsel's actions may be determined or substantially influenced by the defendant's own statements or actions. Counsel's actions are usually based, quite properly, on informed strategic choices made by the defendant and on information supplied by the defendant. In particular, what investigation decisions are reasonable depends critically on such information. For example, when the facts that support a certain potential line of defense are generally known to counsel because of what the defendant has said, the need for further investigation may be considerably diminished or eliminated altogether. And when a defendant has given counsel reason to believe that pursuing certain investigations would be fruitless or even harmful, counsel's failure to pursue those investigations may not later be challenged as unreasonable. In short, inquiry into counsel's conversations with the defendant may be critical to a proper assessment of counsel's investigation decisions, just as it may be critical to a proper assessment of counsel's other litigation decisions.

An error by counsel, even if professionally unreasonable, does not warrant setting aside the judgment of a criminal proceeding if the error had no effect on the judgment. The purpose of the Sixth Amendment guarantee of counsel is to ensure that a defendant has the assistance necessary to justify reliance on the outcome of the proceeding. Accordingly, any deficiencies in counsel's performance must be prejudicial to the defense in order to constitute ineffective assistance under the Constitution.

Conflict of interest claims aside, actual ineffectiveness claims alleging a deficiency in attorney performance are subject to a general requirement that the defendant affirmatively prove prejudice. The government is not responsible for, and hence not able to prevent, attorney errors that will result in reversal of a conviction or sentence. Attorney errors come in an infinite variety and are as likely to be utterly harmless in a particular case as they are to be prejudicial. They cannot be classified according to likelihood of causing prejudice. Nor can they be defined with sufficient precision to inform defense attorneys correctly just what conduct to avoid. Representation is an art, and an act or omission that is unprofessional in one case may be sound or even brilliant in another. Even if a defendant shows that particular errors of counsel were unreasonable, therefore, the defendant must show that they actually had an adverse effect on the defense.

It is not enough for the defendant to show that the errors had some conceivable effect on the outcome of the proceeding. Virtually every act or omission of counsel would meet that test, and not every error that conceivably could have influenced the outcome undermines the reliability of the result of the proceeding.

The appropriate test for prejudice finds its roots in the test for materiality of exculpatory information not disclosed to the defense by the prosecution, and in the test for materiality of testimony made unavailable to the defense by Government deportation of a witness. The defendant must show that there is a reasonable probability that, but for counsel's unprofessional errors, the result of the proceeding would have been different. A reasonable probability is a probability sufficient to undermine confidence in the outcome.

In making the determination whether the specified errors resulted in the required prejudice, a court should presume, absent challenge to the judgment on grounds of evidentiary insufficiency, that the judge or jury acted according to law. An assessment of the likelihood of a result more favorable to the defendant must exclude the possibility of arbitrariness, whimsy, caprice, "nullification," and the like. A defendant has no entitlement to the luck of a lawless decisionmaker, even if a lawless decision cannot be reviewed. The assessment of prejudice should proceed on the assumption that the decisionmaker is reasonably, conscientiously, and impartially applying the standards that govern the decision. It should not depend on the idiosyncracies of the particular decisionmaker, such as unusual propensities toward harshness or leniency. Although these factors may actually have entered into counsel's selection of strategies and, to that limited extent, may thus affect the performance inquiry, they are irrelevant to the prejudice inquiry. Thus, evidence about the actual process of decision, if not part of the record of the proceeding under review, and evidence about, for example, a particular judge's sentencing practices, should not be considered in the prejudice determination.

The governing legal standard plays a critical role in defining the question to be asked in assessing the prejudice from counsel's errors. When a defendant challenges a conviction, the question is whether there is a reasonable probability that, absent the errors, the fact-finder would have had a reasonable doubt respecting guilt. When a defendant challenges a death sentence such as the one at issue in this case, the question is whether there is a reasonable probability that, absent the errors, the sentencer—including an appellate court, to the extent it independently reweighs the evidence—would have concluded that the balance of aggravating and mitigating circumstances did not warrant death.

In making this determination, a court hearing an ineffectiveness claim must consider the totality of the evidence before the judge or jury. A verdict or conclusion only weakly supported by the record is more likely to have been affected by errors than one with overwhelming record support. Taking the unaffected findings as a given, and taking due account of the effect of the errors on the remaining findings, a court making the prejudice inquiry must ask if the defendant has met the burden of showing that the decision reached would reasonably likely have been different absent the errors.

A number of practical considerations are important for the application of the standards we have outlined. Most important, in adjudicating a claim of actual ineffectiveness of counsel, a court should keep in mind that the principles we have stated do not establish mechanical rules. Although those principles should guide the process of decision, the ultimate focus of inquiry must be on the fundamental fairness of the proceeding whose result is being challenged. In every case the court should be concerned with whether, despite the strong presumption of reliability, the result of the particular proceeding is unreliable because of a breakdown in the adversarial process that our system counts on to produce just results.

Take Note

Note that to defeat a claim of ineffectiveness, all the government must do is to establish that the defendant has failed to satisfy *either* one of these tests, not both.

To the extent that this has already been the guiding inquiry in the lower courts, the standards articulated today do not require reconsideration of ineffectiveness claims rejected under different standards. With regard to the prejudice inquiry, only the strict outcome-determinative test, among the standards articulated in the lower courts, imposes a heavier burden on defendants than the tests laid down today. The difference, however, should alter the merit of an ineffectiveness claim only in the rarest case.

Although we have discussed the performance component of an ineffectiveness claim prior to the prejudice component, there is no reason for a court deciding an ineffective assistance claim to approach the inquiry in the same order or even to address both components of the inquiry if the defendant makes an insufficient showing on one. If it is easier to dispose of an ineffectiveness claim on the ground of lack of sufficient prejudice, which we expect will often be so, that course should be followed. Courts should strive to ensure that ineffectiveness claims not become so burdensome to defense counsel that the entire criminal justice system suffers as a result.

Application of the governing principles is not difficult in this case. The facts as described above make clear that the conduct of respondent's counsel at and before respondent's sentencing proceeding cannot be found unreasonable. They also make clear that, even assuming the challenged conduct of counsel was unreasonable, respondent suffered insufficient prejudice to warrant setting aside his death sentence.

With respect to the performance component, the record shows that respondent's counsel made a strategic choice to argue for the extreme emotional distress mitigating circumstance and to rely as fully as possible on respondent's acceptance of responsibility for his crimes. Although counsel understandably felt hopeless about respondent's prospects, nothing in the record indicates that counsel's sense of hopelessness distorted his professional judgment. Counsel's strategy choice was well within the range of professionally reasonable judgments, and the decision not to seek more character or psychological evidence than was already in hand was likewise reasonable.

The trial judge's views on the importance of owning up to one's crimes were well known to counsel. The aggravating circumstances were utterly overwhelming. Trial counsel could reasonably surmise from his conversations with respondent that character and psychological evidence would be of little help. Respondent had already been able to mention at the plea colloquy the substance of what there was to know about his financial and emotional troubles. Restricting testimony on respondent's character to what had come in at the plea colloquy ensured that contrary character and psychological evidence and respondent's criminal history, which counsel had successfully moved to exclude, would not come in. On these facts, there can be little question, even without application of the presumption of adequate performance, that trial counsel's defense, though unsuccessful, was the result of reasonable professional judgment.

With respect to the prejudice component, the lack of merit of respondent's claim is even more stark. The evidence that respondent says his trial counsel should have offered at the sentencing hearing would barely have altered the sentencing profile presented to the sentencing judge. At most this evidence shows that numerous people who knew respondent thought he was generally a good person and that a psychiatrist and a psychologist believed he was under considerable emotional stress that did not rise to the level of extreme disturbance. Given the overwhelming aggravating factors, there is no reasonable probability that the omitted evidence would have changed the conclusion that the aggravating circumstances outweighed the mitigating circumstances and, hence, the sentence imposed. Indeed, admission of the evidence respondent now offers might even have been harmful to his case: his "rap sheet" would probably have been admitted into evidence, and the psychological reports would have directly contradicted respondent's claim that the mitigating circumstance of extreme emotional disturbance applied to his case.

Failure to make the required showing of either deficient performance or sufficient prejudice defeats the ineffectiveness claim. Here there is a double failure. More generally, respondent has made no showing that the justice of his sentence was rendered unreliable by a breakdown in the adversary process caused by deficiencies in counsel's assistance. Respondent's sentencing proceeding was not fundamentally unfair.

We conclude, therefore, that the District Court properly declined to issue a writ of *habeas corpus*. The judgment of the Court of Appeals is accordingly *Reversed*.

JUSTICE MARSHALL, dissenting.

My objection to the performance standard adopted by the Court is that it is so malleable that, in practice, it will either have no grip at all or will yield excessive variation in the manner in which the Sixth Amendment is interpreted and applied by different courts.

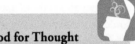

Food for Thought

Is the *Strickland* ineffectiveness test a sensible and fair one? Is it unreasonably difficult for a defendant to satisfy? Does or should the Sixth Amendment right to counsel require *more* from a defense representative?

I object to the prejudice standard adopted by the Court for two independent reasons. First, it is often very difficult to tell whether a defendant convicted after a trial in which he was ineffectively represented would have fared better if his lawyer had been competent. Seemingly impregnable cases can sometimes be dismantled by good defense counsel. On the basis of a cold record, it may be impossible for a reviewing court confidently to ascertain how the government's evidence and arguments would have stood up against rebuttal and cross-examination by a shrewd, well-prepared lawyer. The difficulties of estimating prejudice after the fact are exacerbated by the possibility that evidence of injury to the defendant may be missing from the record precisely because of the incompetence of defense counsel. In view of all these impediments to a fair evaluation of the probability that the outcome of a trial was affected by ineffectiveness of counsel, it seems to me senseless to impose on a defendant whose lawyer has been shown to have been incompetent the burden of demonstrating prejudice.

Second and more fundamentally, the assumption on which the Court's holding rests is that the only purpose of the constitutional guarantee of effective assistance of counsel is to reduce the chance that innocent persons will be convicted. In my view, the guarantee also functions to ensure that convictions are obtained only through fundamentally fair procedures. The majority contends that the Sixth Amendment is not violated when a manifestly guilty defendant is convicted after a trial in which he was represented by a manifestly ineffective attorney. I cannot agree. Every defendant is entitled to a trial in which his interests are vigorously and conscientiously advocated by an able lawyer.

Points for Discussion

a.　Extrinsic Ineffectiveness

In a companion case to *Strickland, United States v. Cronic*, 466 U.S. 648 (1984), the Supreme Court rejected defendant's "extrinsic" claims of defense counsel's ineffectiveness in all but the rarest of cases. "Extrinsic" claims are those that focus upon alleged general problems with counsel or the case (e.g. counsel was too young and/or inexperienced, the case was too complex for this attorney and/or there was too little time to prepare) without accompanying claims of "actual" incidents of ineffectiveness. Cronic was indicted on mail fraud charges involving the transfer of over $9,400,000 in checks between banks in Florida and Oklahoma during a 4-month period. Shortly before the scheduled trial date, retained counsel withdrew. The court then appointed a young lawyer with a real estate practice to represent Cronic, but allowed counsel only 25 days for pretrial preparation even though it had taken the Government over four and one-half years to investigate the case and it had reviewed thousands of documents during that time. Cronic was subsequently convicted on 11 of the 13 counts in the indictment and received a 25-year sentence. The court of appeals overturned Cronic's conviction based on five extrinsic factors: "(1) The time afforded for investigation and preparation; (2) the experience of counsel; (3) the gravity of the charge; (4) the complexity of possible defenses; and (5) the accessibility of witnesses to counsel." The Supreme Court reversed, however, holding that a criminal defendant can "make out a claim of ineffective assistance only by pointing to specific errors made by trial counsel."

b.　Ineffectiveness Claims in *Habeas Corpus* Proceedings

In *Kimmelman v. Morrison*, 477 U.S. 365 (1986), the Court refused to extend *Stone v. Powell*, 428 U.S. 465 (1976) to Sixth Amendment claims of ineffectiveness. In *Stone*, the Court held that exclusionary rule arguments relating to Fourth Amendment violations could not be asserted on collateral review in federal *habeas corpus* proceedings if the defendant had a full and fair opportunity to raise the issues in state court. In *Kimmelman*, the Court held that this rule did not apply to claims of ineffective assistance where the principal allegation and manifestation of inadequate representation was counsel's failure to file a timely motion to suppress evidence allegedly obtained in violation of the Fourth Amendment.

c. Ethics & Ineffectiveness

In *Nix v. Whiteside*, <u>475 U.S. 157 (1986)</u>, Whiteside was convicted of second degree murder. At trial, Whiteside claimed self-defense and wanted to testify that he had seen something metallic (presumably a gun) in the victim's hand. However, Whiteside's attorney concluded that the testimony would be perjury and "advised him that if he did do that it would be my duty to advise the Court of what he was doing and that I felt he was committing perjury." Counsel also stated that he would attempt to withdraw from representing Whiteside if he insisted on committing perjury. Following his conviction, Whiteside sought a writ of *habeas corpus*, claiming that the attorney's conduct deprived him of effective assistance of counsel. The Court rejected this argument:

> An attorney's ethical duty to advance the interests of his client is limited by an equally solemn duty to comply with the law and standards of professional conduct; it specifically ensures that the client may not use false evidence. Whether counsel's conduct is seen as a successful attempt to dissuade his client from committing the crime of perjury, or whether seen as a 'threat' to withdraw from representation and disclose the illegal scheme, his representation of Whiteside falls well within accepted standards of professional conduct and the range of reasonable professional conduct acceptable under *Strickland*.

Hypo 1: Cronic *Problems*

Does the *Cronic* presumption of effective assistance in the absence of a showing of actual, prejudicial errors make sense? When defense counsel is inexperienced and is given insufficient time and resources to prepare his case, is it really fair to simply presume that counsel functioned effectively? Shouldn't ineffective assistance be presumed sometimes? What if defendant's counsel showed up for trial drunk and occasionally went to sleep during the trial. In such a situation, should defendant really have to show that counsel committed specific errors in order to gain reversal?

Hypo 2: *Defense Counsel Ten Minutes Late*

Defendant Donald was charged, *inter alia*, with felony murder. At trial, his defense counsel returned late from a break in the proceedings, totally missing ten minutes of the trial. Donald was convicted and subsequently sentenced to life imprisonment. Do you think that defense counsel's absence during ten minutes of the trial was (or should be deemed to be) ineffective assistance under *Cronic*, entitling Donald to a new trial? *See Woods v. Donald*, 575 U.S. 312 (2015).

Hypo 3: *Missing Counsel*

Suppose that a defendant's attorney recommends that he talk to the police to explain his alibi to robbery/murder charges. However, counsel mistakenly believes that he cannot remain in the room during the questioning and therefore leaves. Notwithstanding counsel's absence, defendant explains his alibi and it leads the police to two witnesses who testify against him. Defendant is convicted. Should his conviction be reversed for ineffective assistance of counsel? *See People v. Frazier*, 2008 WL 782593 (Mich. Ct. App. 2008).

Hypo 4: *Failure to Object to Leg Restraints*

Was defense counsel ineffective under *Cronic* for failing to object to the fact that defendant was standing trial for first-degree murder while being forced by the sheriff to wear a leg restraint under his pants leg which prevented him from fully straightening his leg? Does it—should it—matter that the shackle was not visible to the jury? *See Zink v. State*, 278 S.W.3d 170 (Mo. 2009).

> ### Hypo 5: *Limiting Communication with a Client*
>
> Suppose that a criminal defendant is "physically intimidating" and "verbally abusive" towards his court-appointed attorney. May the lawyer place limitations on the client's ability to communicate with the lawyer, including only scheduled appointments and written communications. In imposing such limitations, can the lawyer meet his obligation to have "meaningful communication with the client?" *See* N.Y. State Bar Ass'n Commission on Professional Ethics, Op. 1144 (Jan. 29, 2018).

Missouri v. Frye

566 U.S. 134 (2012).

JUSTICE KENNEDY delivered the opinion of the Court.

The Sixth Amendment, applicable to the States by the terms of the Fourteenth Amendment, provides that the accused shall have the assistance of counsel in all criminal prosecutions. The right to counsel is the right to effective assistance of counsel. This case arises in the context of claimed ineffective assistance that led to the lapse of a prosecution offer of a plea bargain, a proposal that offered terms more lenient than the terms of the guilty plea entered later. The initial question is whether the constitutional right to counsel extends to the negotiation and consideration of

Hear It

You can hear the oral argument in *Frye* at http://www.oyez.org/cases/2010-2019/ 2011/2011_10_444.

plea offers that lapse or are rejected. If there is a right to effective assistance with respect to those offers, a further question is what a defendant must demonstrate in order to show that prejudice resulted from counsel's deficient performance.

In August 2007, respondent Galin Frye was charged with driving with a revoked license. Frye had been convicted for that offense on three other occasions, so the State of Missouri charged him with a class D felony, which carries a maximum term of imprisonment of four years. On November 15, the prosecutor sent a letter to Frye's counsel offering a choice of two plea bargains. The prosecutor first offered to recommend a 3-year sentence if there was a guilty plea to the felony charge, without a recommendation regarding probation but with a recommendation that Frye serve 10 days in jail as so-called "shock" time. The second offer was to reduce the charge to a misdemeanor and, if Frye pleaded guilty to it, to recommend a 90-day sentence.

The misdemeanor charge of driving with a revoked license carries a maximum term of imprisonment of one year. The letter stated both offers would expire on December 28. Frye's attorney did not advise Frye that the offers had been made. The offers expired.

Frye's preliminary hearing was scheduled for January 4, 2008. On December 30, 2007, less than a week before the hearing, Frye was again arrested for driving with a revoked license. At the January 4 hearing, Frye waived his right to a preliminary hearing on the charge arising from the August 2007 arrest. He pleaded not guilty at a subsequent arraignment but then changed his plea to guilty. There was no underlying plea agreement. The state trial court accepted Frye's guilty plea. The prosecutor recommended a 3-year sentence, made no recommendation regarding probation, and requested 10 days shock time in jail. The trial judge sentenced Frye to three years in prison.

Frye filed for postconviction relief in state court. He alleged his counsel's failure to inform him of the prosecution's plea offer denied him the effective assistance of counsel. At an evidentiary hearing, Frye testified he would have entered a guilty plea to the misdemeanor had he known about the offer. A state court denied the postconviction motion, but the Missouri Court of Appeals reversed.

It is well settled that the right to the effective assistance of counsel applies to certain steps before trial. The "Sixth Amendment guarantees a defendant the right to have counsel present at all 'critical' stages of the criminal proceedings." Critical stages include arraignments, postindictment interrogations, postindictment lineups, and the entry of a guilty plea. With respect to the right to effective counsel in plea negotiations, a proper beginning point is to discuss two cases from this Court considering the role of counsel in advising a client about a plea offer and an ensuing guilty plea: *Hill v. Lockhart*, 474 U.S. 52 (1985); and *Padilla v. Kentucky*, 559 U.S. 356 (2010).

Hill established that claims of ineffective assistance of counsel in the plea bargain context are governed by the two-part test set forth in *Strickland*. In *Hill*, the decision turned on the second part of the *Strickland* test. There, a defendant who had entered a guilty plea claimed his counsel had misinformed him of the amount of time he would have to serve before he became eligible for parole. But the defendant had not alleged that, even if adequate advice and assistance had been given, he would have elected to plead not guilty and proceed to trial. Thus, the Court found that no prejudice from the inadequate advice had been shown or alleged.

In *Padilla*, the Court again discussed the duties of counsel in advising a client with respect to a plea offer that leads to a guilty plea. *Padilla* held that a guilty plea, based on a plea offer, should be set aside because counsel misinformed the defendant of the immigration consequences of the conviction. The Court made clear that "the negotiation of a plea bargain is a critical phase of litigation for purposes of the Sixth

Amendment right to effective assistance of counsel." It also rejected the argument made by petitioner in this case that a knowing and voluntary plea supersedes errors by defense counsel.

When a plea offer has lapsed or been rejected, no formal court proceedings are involved. This underscores that the plea-bargaining process is often in flux, with no clear standards or time lines and with no judicial supervision of the discussions between prosecution and defense. Indeed, discussions between client and defense counsel are privileged. So the prosecution has little or no notice if something may be amiss and perhaps no capacity to intervene in any event. And, as noted, the State insists there is no right to receive a plea offer. For all these reasons, the State contends, it is unfair to subject it to the consequences of defense counsel's inadequacies, especially when the opportunities for a full and fair trial, or, as here, for a later guilty plea albeit on less favorable terms, are preserved.

The State's contentions are neither illogical nor without some persuasive force, yet they do not suffice to overcome a simple reality. Ninety-seven percent of federal convictions and ninety-four percent of state convictions are the result of guilty pleas. The reality is that plea bargains have become so central to the administration of the criminal justice system that defense counsel have responsibilities in the plea bargain process, responsibilities that must be met to render the adequate assistance of counsel that the Sixth Amendment requires in the criminal process at critical stages. Because ours is for the most part a system of pleas, not a system of trials, it is insufficient simply to point to the guarantee of a fair trial as a backstop that inoculates any errors in the pretrial process. "To a large extent, horse trading between prosecutor and defense counsel determines who goes to jail and for how long. That is what plea bargaining is. It is not some adjunct to the criminal justice system; it is the criminal justice system." Scott & Stuntz, Plea Bargaining as Contract, 101 Yale L. J. 1909, 1912 (1992). In today's criminal justice system, therefore, the negotiation of a plea bargain, rather than the unfolding of a trial, is almost always the critical point for a defendant.

Take Note

Don't miss this important point. The five-justice majority in Frye recognized explicitly that plea bargaining—not an actual criminal trial—is "the name of the game" in U.S. criminal justice. That is how most criminal prosecutions are resolved, namely through pleas not in trials. Once the majority reached this conclusion, the holding that ineffective-assistance-of-counsel rules apply was ineluctable.

To note the prevalence of plea bargaining is not to criticize it. The potential to conserve valuable prosecutorial resources and for defendants to admit their crimes and receive more favorable terms at sentencing means that a plea agreement can benefit both parties. In order that these benefits can be realized, however, criminal defendants require effective counsel during plea negotiations. Anything less might deny a defendant effective representation by counsel at the only stage when legal aid and advice would help him.

The inquiry then becomes how to define the duty and responsibilities of defense counsel in the plea bargain process. This is a difficult question. Bargaining is, by its nature, defined to a substantial degree by personal style. The alternative courses and tactics in negotiation are so individual that it may be neither prudent nor practicable to try to elaborate or define detailed standards for the proper discharge of defense counsel's participation in the process. This case presents neither the necessity nor the occasion to define the duties of defense counsel in those respects, however. Here the question is whether defense counsel has the duty to communicate the terms of a formal offer to accept a plea on terms and conditions that may result in a lesser sentence, a conviction on lesser charges, or both.

This Court now holds that, as a general rule, defense counsel has the duty to communicate formal offers from the prosecution to accept a plea on terms and conditions that may be favorable to the accused. Any exceptions to that rule need not be explored here, for the offer was a formal one with a fixed expiration date. When defense counsel allowed the offer to expire without advising the defendant or allowing him to consider it, defense counsel did not render the effective assistance the Constitution requires. Under *Strickland*, the question then becomes what, if any, prejudice resulted from the breach of duty.

To show prejudice from ineffective assistance of counsel where a plea offer has lapsed or been rejected because of counsel's deficient performance, defendants must demonstrate a reasonable probability they would have accepted the earlier plea offer had they been afforded effective assistance of counsel. Defendants must also demonstrate a reasonable probability the plea would have been entered without the prosecution canceling it or the trial court refusing to accept it, if they had the authority to exercise that discretion under state law. To establish prejudice in this instance, it is necessary to show a reasonable probability that the end result of the criminal process would have been more favorable by reason of a plea to a lesser charge or a sentence of less prison time. In a case, such as this, where a defendant pleads guilty to less favorable terms and claims that ineffective assistance of counsel caused him to miss out on a more favorable earlier plea offer, *Strickland*'s inquiry into whether "the result of the proceeding would have been different," requires looking not at whether the defendant would have proceeded to trial absent ineffective assistance but whether he would have accepted the offer to plead pursuant to the terms earlier proposed.

In order to complete a showing of *Strickland* prejudice, defendants who have shown a reasonable probability they would have accepted the earlier plea offer must also show that, if the prosecution had the discretion to cancel it or if the trial court had the discretion to refuse to accept it, there is a reasonable probability neither the prosecution nor the trial court would have prevented the offer from being accepted or implemented. This further showing is of particular importance because a defendant has no right to be offered a plea, nor a federal right that the judge accept it. It can be assumed that in most jurisdictions prosecutors and judges are familiar with the boundaries of acceptable plea bargains and sentences. So in most instances it should not be difficult to make an objective assessment as to whether or not a particular fact or intervening circumstance would suffice, in the normal course, to cause prosecutorial withdrawal or judicial nonapproval of a plea bargain. The determination that there is or is not a reasonable probability that the outcome of the proceeding would have been different absent counsel's errors can be conducted within that framework.

These standards must be applied to the instant case. As regards the deficient performance prong of *Strickland*, the Court of Appeals found the "record is void of any evidence of any effort by trial counsel to communicate the formal Offer to Frye during the Offer window, let alone any evidence that Frye's conduct interfered with trial counsel's ability to do so." On this record, it is evident that Frye's attorney did not make a meaningful attempt to inform the defendant of a written plea offer before the offer expired. The Missouri Court of Appeals was correct that "counsel's representation fell below an objective standard of reasonableness." The Court of Appeals erred, however, in articulating the precise standard for prejudice in this context. As noted, a defendant in Frye's position must show not only a reasonable probability that he would have accepted the lapsed plea but also a reasonable probability that the prosecution would have adhered to the agreement and that it would have been accepted by the trial court. Frye can show he would have accepted the offer, but there is strong reason to doubt the prosecution and the trial court would have permitted the plea bargain to become final.

There appears to be a reasonable probability Frye would have accepted the prosecutor's original offer of a plea bargain if the offer had been communicated to him, because he pleaded guilty to a more serious charge, with no promise of a sentencing recommendation from the prosecutor.

The Court of Appeals failed, however, to require Frye to show that the first plea offer, if accepted by Frye, would have been adhered to by the prosecution and accepted by the trial court. Whether the prosecution and trial court are required to do so is a matter of state law, and it is not the place of this Court to settle those matters. The Court has established the minimum requirements of the Sixth Amendment as interpreted in *Strickland*, and States have the discretion to add procedural protections under state law if they choose. A State may choose to preclude the prosecution from withdrawing a plea offer once it has been accepted or perhaps to preclude a trial court from rejecting a plea bargain. In Missouri, it appears a plea offer once accepted by the defendant can be withdrawn without recourse by the prosecution. The extent of the trial court's discretion in Missouri to reject a plea agreement appears to be in some doubt.

Food for Thought

How in the world can the defendant prove whether the prosecution would have honored its bargain? Or whether the Court would accept it? Are proofs like this too high a burden for a defendant who has not been advised of a favorable plea bargain to meet?

We remand for the Missouri Court of Appeals to consider these state-law questions, because they bear on the federal question of *Strickland* prejudice. If, as the Missouri court stated here, the prosecutor could have canceled the plea agreement, and if Frye fails to show a reasonable probability the prosecutor would have adhered to the agreement, there is no *Strickland* prejudice. Like-

wise, if the trial court could have refused to accept the plea agreement, and if Frye fails to show a reasonable probability the trial court would have accepted the plea, there is no *Strickland* prejudice. In this case, given Frye's new offense for driving without a license on December 30, 2007, there is reason to doubt that the prosecution would have adhered to the agreement or that the trial court would have accepted it at the January 4, 2008, hearing, unless they were required by state law to do so.

The judgment of the Missouri Court of Appeals is vacated, and the case is remanded for further proceedings not inconsistent with this opinion.

JUSTICE SCALIA, with whom THE CHIEF JUSTICE, JUSTICE THOMAS, and JUSTICE ALITO join, dissenting.

The Court acknowledges that Frye's conviction was untainted by attorney error. Given the ultimate focus of our ineffective-assistance cases on the fundamental fairness of the proceeding whose result is being challenged, that should be the end of the matter.

The plea-bargaining process is a subject worthy of regulation, since it is the means by which most criminal convictions are obtained. It happens not to be, however, a subject covered by the Sixth Amendment, which is concerned not with the fairness of bargaining but with the fairness of conviction. The Constitution is not an all-purpose tool for judicial construction of a perfect world; and when we ignore its text in order to make it that, we often find ourselves swinging a

Food for Thought

Was Justice Scalia correct? Is "fairness" the "ultimate focus" of the Court's ineffective assistance cases?

sledge where a tack hammer is needed. In this case, the Court's sledge may require the reversal of perfectly valid, eminently just, convictions. I respectfully dissent.

Point for Discussion

Poor Advice

In the companion case of *Lafler v. Cooper*, <u>566 U.S. 156 (2012)</u>, the same 5-to-4 majority of the Supreme Court, applied *Strickland* to a situation where a favorable plea offer was reported to the client (unlike Frye), but, on poor advice of counsel, was rejected. "In these circumstances," the majority ruled, "a defendant must show that but for the ineffective advice of counsel there is a reasonable probability that the plea offer would have been presented to the court (i.e., that the defendant would have accepted the plea and the prosecution would not have withdrawn it in light of intervening circumstances), that the court would have accepted its terms, and that the conviction or sentence, or both, under the offer's terms would have been less severe than under the judgment and sentence that in fact were imposed." Deficient performance was conceded, and the Court found prejudice because "respondent received a minimum sentence 3½ times greater than he would have received under the plea." That said, the majority added:

> Even if a defendant shows ineffective assistance of counsel has caused the rejection of a plea leading to a trial and a more severe sentence, there is the question of what constitutes an appropriate remedy.

> The specific injury suffered by defendants who decline a plea offer as a result of ineffective assistance of counsel and then receive a greater sentence as a result of trial can come in at least one of two forms. In some cases, the sole advantage a defendant would have received under the plea is a lesser sentence. This is typically the case when the charges that would have been admitted as part of the plea bargain are the same as the charges the defendant was convicted of after trial. In this situation the court may conduct an evidentiary hearing to determine whether the defendant has shown a reasonable probability that but for counsel's errors he would have accepted the plea. If the showing is made, the court may exercise discretion in determining whether the defendant should receive the term of imprisonment the government offered in the plea, the sentence he received at trial, or something in between.

> In some situations it may be that resentencing alone will not be full redress for the constitutional injury. If, for example, an offer was for a guilty plea to a count or counts less serious than the ones for which a defendant was convicted after trial, or if a mandatory sentence confines a judge's sen-

tencing discretion after trial, a resentencing based on the conviction at trial may not suffice. In these circumstances, the proper exercise of discretion to remedy the constitutional injury may be to require the prosecution to reoffer the plea proposal. Once this has occurred, the judge can then exercise discretion in deciding whether to vacate the conviction from trial and accept the plea or leave the conviction undisturbed.

* * *

Since the reasonableness of defense counsel's conduct is a very fact-specific inquiry under *Strickland*, sometimes it may be perfectly reasonable for counsel to engage in counter-intuitive conduct for good reasons, e.g. actually conceding the defendant's guilt or abandoning an insanity defense. Then again, defense counsel's strategic decisions are not entirely immune from second guessing. In this regard, consider the following Supreme Court decisions:

Florida v. Nixon

543 U.S. 175 (2004).

JUSTICE GINSBURG delivered the opinion of the Court.

This capital case concerns defense counsel's strategic decision to concede, at the guilt phase of the trial, the defendant's commission of murder, and to concentrate the defense on establishing, at the penalty phase, cause for sparing the defendant's life. Any concession of that order, the Florida Supreme Court held, made without the defendant's express consent—however gruesome the crime and despite the strength of the evidence of guilt—automatically ranks as prejudicial ineffective assistance of counsel necessitating a new trial. We reverse the Florida Supreme Court's judgment.

Defense counsel undoubtedly has a duty to discuss potential strategies with the defendant. *See Strickland v. Washington*, 466 U.S. 668 (1984). But when a defendant, informed by counsel, neither consents nor objects to the course counsel describes as the most promising means to avert a sentence of death, counsel is not automatically barred from pursuing that course. The reasonableness of counsel's performance, after consultation with the defendant yields no response, must be judged in accord with the inquiry generally applicable to ineffective-assistance-of-counsel claims: Did counsel's representation "fall below an objective standard of reasonableness"? The Florida Supreme Court erred in applying, instead, a presumption of deficient performance, as well as a presumption of prejudice; that latter presumption, we have instructed, is reserved for cases in which counsel fails meaningfully to oppose the prosecution's case. A presumption of prejudice is not in order based solely on a defendant's failure to provide express consent to a tenable strategy counsel has adequately disclosed to and discussed with the defendant.

On Monday, August 13, 1984, near a dirt road in the environs of Tallahassee, Florida, a passing motorist discovered Jeanne Bickner's charred body. Bickner had been tied to a tree and set on fire while still alive. Her left leg and arm, and most of her hair and skin, had been burned away. The next day, police found Bickner's car, abandoned on a Tallahassee street corner, on fire. Police arrested 23-year-old Joe Elton Nixon later that morning, after Nixon's brother informed the sheriff's office that Nixon had confessed to the murder.

Questioned by the police, Nixon described in graphic detail how he had kidnaped Bickner, then killed her. He recounted that he had approached Bickner, a stranger, in a mall, and asked her to help him jumpstart his car. Bickner offered Nixon a ride home in her 1973 MG sports car. Once on the road, Nixon directed Bickner to drive to a remote place; en route, he overpowered her and stopped the car. Nixon next put Bickner in the MG's trunk, drove into a wooded area, removed Bickner from the car, and tied her to a tree with jumper cables. Bickner pleaded with Nixon to release her, offering him money in exchange. Concerned that Bickner might identify him, Nixon decided to kill her. He set fire to Bickner's personal belongings and ignited her with burning objects. Nixon drove away in the MG, and later told his brother and girlfriend what he had done. He burned the MG on Tuesday, August 14, after reading in the newspaper that Bickner's body had been discovered.

The State gathered overwhelming evidence establishing that Nixon had committed the murder in the manner he described. In late August 1984, Nixon was indicted in Leon County, Florida, for first-degree murder, kidnaping, robbery, and arson. Assistant public defender Michael Corin, assigned to represent Nixon, filed a plea of not guilty and deposed all of the State's potential witnesses. Corin concluded, given the strength of the evidence, that Nixon's guilt was not "subject to any reasonable dispute." Corin thereupon commenced plea negotiations, hoping to persuade the prosecution to drop the death penalty in exchange for Nixon's guilty pleas to all charges. Negotiations broke down when the prosecutors indicated their unwillingness to recommend a sentence other than death.

Faced with the inevitability of going to trial on a capital charge, Corin turned his attention to the penalty phase, believing that the only way to save Nixon's life would be to present extensive mitigation evidence centering on Nixon's mental instability. Experienced in capital defense, Corin feared that denying Nixon's commission of the kidnaping and murder during the guilt phase would compromise Corin's ability to persuade the jury, during the penalty phase, that Nixon's conduct was the product of his mental illness. Corin concluded that the best strategy would be to concede guilt, thereby preserving his credibility in urging leniency during the penalty phase.

Corin attempted to explain this strategy to Nixon at least three times. Although Corin had represented Nixon previously on unrelated charges and the two had a good relationship in Corin's estimation, Nixon was generally unresponsive during their discussions. He never verbally approved or protested Corin's proposed strategy. Corin eventually exercised his professional judgment to pursue the concession strategy. As he explained: "There are many times lawyers make decisions because they have to make them because the client does nothing."

When Nixon's trial began on July 15, 1985, his unresponsiveness deepened into disruptive and violent behavior. On the second day of jury selection, Nixon pulled off his clothing, demanded a black judge and lawyer, refused to be escorted into the courtroom, and threatened to force the guards to shoot him. An extended on-the-record colloquy followed Nixon's bizarre behavior, during which Corin urged the trial judge to explain Nixon's rights to him and ascertain whether Nixon understood the significance of absenting himself from the trial. Corin also argued that restraining Nixon and compelling him to be present would prejudice him in the eyes of the jury. When the judge examined Nixon on the record in a holding cell, Nixon stated he had no interest in the trial and threatened to misbehave if forced to attend. The judge ruled that Nixon had intelligently and voluntarily waived his right to be present at trial.

The guilt phase of the trial thus began in Nixon's absence. In his opening statement, Corin acknowledged Nixon's guilt and urged the jury to focus on the penalty phase:

> "In this case, there won't be any question, none whatsoever, that my client, Joe Elton Nixon, caused Jeannie Bickner's death. That fact will be proved to your satisfaction beyond any doubt.

> "This case is about the death of Joe Elton Nixon and whether it should occur within the next few years by electrocution or maybe its natural expiration after a lifetime of confinement.

> "Now, in arriving at your verdict, in your penalty recommendation, for we will get that far, you are going to learn many facts about Joe Elton Nixon. Some of those facts are going to be good. That may not seem clear to you at this time. But, and sadly, most of the things you learn of Joe Elton Nixon are not going to be good. But, I'm suggesting to you that when you have seen all the testimony, heard all the testimony and the evidence that has been shown, there are going to be reasons why you should recommend that his life be spared."

During its case in chief, the State introduced the tape of Nixon's confession, expert testimony on the manner in which Bickner died, and witness testimony regarding Nixon's confessions to his relatives and his possession of Bickner's car and personal effects. Corin cross-examined these witnesses only when he felt their statements needed clarification and he did not present a defense case. Corin did object to the introduction of crime scene photographs as unduly prejudicial and actively contested several aspects of the jury instructions during the charge conference. In his closing argument, Corin again conceded Nixon's guilt and reminded the jury of the importance of the penalty phase: "I will hope to argue to you and give you reasons not that Mr. Nixon's life be spared one final and terminal confinement forever, but that he not be sentenced to die." The jury found Nixon guilty on all counts.

At the start of the penalty phase, Corin argued to the jury that "Joe Elton Nixon is not normal organically, intellectually, emotionally or educationally or in any other way." Corin presented the testimony of eight witnesses. Relatives and friends described Nixon's childhood emotional troubles and his erratic behavior in the days preceding the murder. A psychiatrist and a psychologist addressed Nixon's antisocial personality, his history of emotional instability and psychiatric care, his low IQ, and the possibility that at some point he suffered brain damage. The State presented little evidence during the penalty phase, simply incorporating its guilt-phase evidence by reference, and introducing testimony, over Corin's objection, that Nixon had removed Bickner's underwear in order to terrorize her.

In his closing argument, Corin emphasized Nixon's youth, the psychiatric evidence, and the jury's discretion to consider any mitigating circumstances; Corin urged that, if not sentenced to death, "Joe Elton Nixon would never be released from confinement." The death penalty, Corin maintained, was appropriate only for "intact human beings," and "Joe Elton Nixon is not one of those. He's never been one of those. He never will be one of those." Corin concluded: "You know, we're not around here all that long. And it's rare when we have the opportunity to give or take life. And you have that opportunity to give life. And I'm going to ask you to do that. Thank you." After deliberating for approximately three hours, the jury recommended that Nixon be sentenced to death.

In accord with the jury's recommendation, the trial court imposed the death penalty. Notably, at the close of the penalty phase, the court commended Corin's performance during the trial, stating that "the tactic employed by trial counsel was an excellent analysis of the reality of his case." The evidence of guilt "would have persuaded any jury beyond all doubt," and "for trial counsel to have inferred that Mr. Nixon was not guilty would have deprived counsel of any credibility during the penalty phase." The Florida Supreme Court subsequently reversed, finding ineffective assistance of counsel.

We granted certiorari to resolve an important question of constitutional law, i.e., whether counsel's failure to obtain the defendant's express consent to a strategy of conceding guilt in a capital trial automatically renders counsel's performance deficient, and whether counsel's effectiveness should be evaluated under *Cronic* or *Strickland*. We now reverse the judgment of the Florida Supreme Court.

An attorney undoubtedly has a duty to consult with the client regarding important decisions, including questions of overarching defense strategy. That obligation, however, does not require counsel to obtain the defendant's consent to every tactical decision. But certain decisions regarding the exercise or waiver of basic trial rights are of such moment that they cannot be made for the defendant by a surrogate. A defendant, this Court affirmed, has "the ultimate authority" to determine "whether to plead guilty, waive a jury, testify in his or her own behalf, or take an appeal." Concerning those decisions, an attorney must both consult with the defendant and obtain consent to the recommended course of action.

FYI

The Florida Supreme Court's decision in *Nixon* led to calls for the impeachment of three of the justices who decided that case. Given the outcome of the Supreme Court's unanimous ruling in *Nixon*, reversing the Florida Supreme Court, do you think that those calls were justified?

Corin was obliged to, and in fact several times did, explain his proposed trial strategy to Nixon. Given Nixon's constant resistance to answering inquiries put to him by counsel and court, Corin was not additionally required to gain express consent before conceding Nixon's guilt. The two evidentiary hearings conducted by the Florida trial court demonstrate beyond doubt that Corin fulfilled his duty of consultation by informing Nixon of counsel's proposed strategy and its potential benefits. Nixon's characteristic silence each time information was conveyed to him, in sum, did not suffice to render unreasonable Corin's decision to concede guilt and to home in, instead, on the life or death penalty issue.

Food for Thought

Suppose that, instead of remaining unresponsive, Nixon insisted that he was actually innocent (in the face of the same, overwhelming contrary evidence)? Would or should defense counsel in that instance have gone "all out" to try (futilely) to establish his innocence, thus creating a much higher risk of a death sentence?

Corin's concession of Nixon's guilt does not rank as a failure to function in any meaningful sense as the Government's adversary. Although such a concession in a run-of-the-mine trial might present a closer question, the gravity of the potential sentence in a capital trial and the proceeding's two-phase structure vitally affect counsel's strategic calculus. Attorneys representing capital defendants face daunting challenges in developing trial strategies, not least because the defendant's guilt is often clear. Prosecutors are more likely to seek the death penalty, and to refuse to accept a plea to a life sentence, when the evidence is overwhelming and the crime heinous. In such cases, "avoiding execution may be the best and only realistic result possible."

Counsel therefore may reasonably decide to focus on the trial's penalty phase, at which time counsel's mission is to persuade the trier that his client's life should be spared. Unable to negotiate a guilty plea in exchange for a life sentence, defense counsel must strive at the guilt phase to avoid a counterproductive course. In this light, counsel cannot be deemed ineffective for attempting to impress the jury with his candor and his unwillingness to engage in a useless charade.

> **Food for Thought**
>
> What if this had not been a capital case. Should the Court's ultimate holding have been the same? If Nixon had faced a potential sentence of 5 to 10 years in jail, for example, would defense counsel have been justified in sacrificing any chance at an acquittal, however remote, for a chance at arguing for a reduced sentence subsequently? What do you think?

To summarize, in a capital case, counsel must consider in conjunction both the guilt and penalty phases in determining how best to proceed. When counsel informs the defendant of the strategy counsel believes to be in the defendant's best interest and the defendant is unresponsive, counsel's strategic choice is not impeded by any blanket rule demanding the defendant's explicit consent. Instead, if counsel's strategy, given the evidence bearing on the defendant's guilt, satisfies the *Strickland* standard, that is the end of the matter; no tenable claim of ineffective assistance would remain.

Reversed.

Points for Discussion

a. Concession of Guilt over Defendant's Objections

In a more recent decision where "in contrast to *Nixon*, the defendant vociferously insisted that he did not engage in the charged acts and adamantly objected to any admission of guilt," the Supreme Court reached a different conclusion:

> We hold that a defendant has the right to insist that counsel refrain from admitting guilt, even when counsel's experienced-based view is that confessing guilt offers the defendant the best chance to avoid the death penalty. Guaranteeing a defendant the right "to have the Assistance of Counsel for his defence," the Sixth Amendment so demands. With individual liberty—and, in capital cases, life—at stake, it is the defendant's prerogative, not counsel's, to decide on the objective of his defense: to admit guilt in the

hope of gaining mercy at the sentencing stage, or to maintain his innocence, leaving it to the State to prove his guilt beyond a reasonable doubt.

McCoy v. Louisiana, 138 S.Ct. 1500 (U.S. 2018).

The Court in *McCoy* explained its reasoning for this different result than in *Nixon* as follows:

> Just as a defendant may steadfastly refuse to plead guilty in the face of overwhelming evidence against her, or reject the assistance of legal counsel despite the defendant's own inexperience and lack of professional qualifications, so may she insist on maintaining her innocence at the guilt phase of a capital trial. These are not strategic choices about how best to achieve a client's objectives; they are choices about what the client's objectives in fact are.

> In contrast, "Nixon's attorney did not negate Nixon's autonomy by overriding Nixon's desired defense objective, for Nixon never asserted any such objective. Nixon 'was generally unresponsive' during discussions of trial strategy, and 'never verbally approved or protested' counsel's proposed approach. Nixon complained about the admission of his guilt only after trial. McCoy, in contrast, opposed [his defense counsel's] assertion of his guilt at every opportunity, before and during trial, both in conference with his lawyer and in open court."

Does this distinction make sense to you? Recall that Nixon never actually agreed to his counsel's concession of his guilt. Does or should that make a difference?

b.   Advice About Defense

In *Knowles v. Mirzayance,* 556 U.S. 111 (2009), the Supreme Court concluded that defense counsel's advice to his client that he withdraw his insanity defense because it was "doomed to fail"—advice that was accepted by his client—was also not ineffective assistance of counsel. As the Court made clear, "we are aware of no 'prevailing professional norms' that prevent counsel from recommending that a plea be withdrawn when it is almost certain to lose. The law does not require counsel to raise every available nonfrivolous defense. Counsel also is not required to have a tactical reason—above and beyond a reasonable appraisal of a claim's dismal prospects for success—for recommending that a weak claim be dropped altogether." What do you think? Was this really the *effective* assistance of counsel?

Rompilla v. Beard

545 U.S. 374 (2005).

JUSTICE SOUTER delivered the opinion of the Court.

This case calls for specific application of the standard of reasonable competence required on the part of defense counsel by the Sixth Amendment. We hold that even when a capital defendant's family members and the defendant himself have suggested that no mitigating evidence is available, his lawyer is bound to make reasonable efforts to obtain and review material that counsel knows the prosecution will probably rely on as evidence of aggravation at the sentencing phase of trial.

On the morning of January 14, 1988, James Scanlon was discovered dead in a bar he ran in Allentown, Pennsylvania, his body having been stabbed repeatedly and set on fire. Rompilla was indicted for the murder and related offenses, and the Commonwealth gave notice of intent to ask for the death penalty. Two public defenders were assigned to the case.

The jury at the guilt phase of trial found Rompilla guilty on all counts, and during the ensuing penalty phase, the prosecutor sought to prove three aggravating factors to justify a death sentence: that the murder was committed in the course of another felony; that the murder was committed by torture; and that Rompilla had a significant history of felony convictions indicating the use or threat of violence. The Commonwealth presented evidence on all three aggravators, and the jury found all proven. Rompilla's evidence in mitigation consisted of relatively brief testimony: five of his family members argued in effect for residual doubt, and beseeched the jury for mercy, saying that they believed Rompilla was innocent and a good man. Rompilla's 14-year-old son testified that he loved his father and would visit him in prison. The jury acknowledged this evidence to the point of finding, as two factors in mitigation, that Rompilla's son had testified on his behalf and that rehabilitation was possible. But the jurors assigned the greater weight to the aggravating factors, and sentenced Rompilla to death. The Supreme Court of Pennsylvania affirmed both conviction and sentence. Subsequently, a District Court granted Rompilla's *habeas corpus* petition on ineffectiveness grounds, and the Third Circuit Court of Appeals reversed. We granted certiorari, and now reverse.

Ineffective assistance under *Strickland* is deficient performance by counsel resulting in prejudice, with performance being measured against an "objective standard of reasonableness," "under prevailing professional norms." This case, like some others recently, looks to norms of adequate investigation in preparing for the sentencing phase of a capital trial, when defense counsel's job is to counter the State's evidence of aggravated culpability with evidence in mitigation. In judging the defense's investigation, as in applying *Strickland* generally, hindsight is discounted by pegging adequacy to counsel's perspective at the time investigative decisions are made, and by giving a heavy measure of deference to counsel's judgments.

A standard of reasonableness applied as if one stood in counsel's shoes spawns few hard-edged rules, and the merits of a number of counsel's choices in this case are subject to fair debate. This is not a case in which defense counsel simply ignored their obligation to find mitigating evidence, and their workload as busy public defenders did not keep them from making a number of efforts, including interviews with Rompilla and some members of his family, and examinations of reports by three mental health experts who gave opinions at the guilt phase. None of the sources proved particularly helpful.

Rompilla's own contributions to any mitigation case were minimal. Counsel found him uninterested in helping, as on their visit to his prison to go over a proposed mitigation strategy, when Rompilla told them he was "bored being here listening" and returned to his cell. To questions about childhood and schooling, his answers indicated they had been normal, save for quitting school in the ninth grade. There were times when Rompilla was even actively obstructive by sending counsel off on false leads.

The lawyers also spoke with five members of Rompilla's family (his former wife, two brothers, a sister-in-law, and his son), and counsel testified that they developed a good relationship with the family in the course of their representation. The third and final source tapped for mitigating material was the cadre of three mental health witnesses who were asked to look into Rompilla's mental state as of the time of the offense and his competency to stand trial, but their reports revealed "nothing useful" to Rompilla's case, and the lawyers consequently did not go to any other historical source that might have cast light on Rompilla's mental condition.

When new counsel entered the case to raise Rompilla's postconviction claims, however, they identified a number of likely avenues the trial lawyers could fruitfully have followed in building a mitigation case. School records are one example, which trial counsel never examined in spite of the professed unfamiliarity of the several family members with Rompilla's childhood, and despite counsel's knowledge that Rompilla left school after the ninth grade. Others examples are records of Rompilla's juvenile and adult incarcerations, which counsel did not consult, although they were aware of their client's criminal record. And while counsel knew from police reports provided in pretrial discovery that Rompilla had been drinking heavily at the time of his offense, and although one of the mental health experts reported that Rompilla's troubles with alcohol merited further investigation, counsel did not look for evidence of a history of dependence on alcohol that might have extenuating significance.

Before us, trial counsel and the Commonwealth respond to these unexplored possibilities by emphasizing this Court's recognition that the duty to investigate does not force defense lawyers to scour the globe on the off-chance something will turn up; reasonably diligent counsel may draw a line when they have good reason to think further investigation would be a waste. The Commonwealth argues that the information trial counsel gathered from Rompilla and the other sources gave them sound reason to think it would have been pointless to spend time and money on the additional investigation espoused by postconviction counsel, and we can say that there is room for debate about trial counsel's obligation to follow at least some of those potential lines of enquiry. There is no need to say more, however, for a further point is clear and dispositive: the lawyers were deficient in failing to examine the court file on Rompilla's prior conviction.

There is an obvious reason that the failure to examine Rompilla's prior conviction file fell below the level of reasonable performance. Counsel knew that the Commonwealth intended to seek the death penalty by proving Rompilla had a significant history of felony convictions indicating the use or threat of violence, an aggravator under state law. Counsel further knew that the Commonwealth would attempt to establish this history by proving Rompilla's prior conviction for rape and assault, and would emphasize his violent character by introducing a transcript of the rape victim's testimony given in that earlier trial. There is no question that defense counsel were on notice, since they acknowledge that a "plea letter," written by one of them four days prior to trial, mentioned the prosecutor's plans. It is also undisputed that the prior conviction file was a public document, readily available for the asking at the very courthouse where Rompilla was to be tried.

It is clear, however, that defense counsel did not look at any part of that file, including the transcript, until warned by the prosecution a second time. In a colloquy the day before the evidentiary sentencing phase began, the prosecutor again said he would present the transcript of the victim's testimony to establish the prior conviction.

With every effort to view the facts as a defense lawyer would have done at the time, it is difficult to see how counsel could have failed to realize that without examining the readily available file they were seriously compromising their opportunity to respond to a case for aggravation. The prosecution was going to use the dramatic facts of a similar prior offense, and Rompilla's counsel had a duty to make all reasonable efforts to learn what they could about the offense. Reasonable efforts certainly included obtaining the Commonwealth's own readily available file on the prior conviction to learn what the Commonwealth knew about the crime, to discover any mitigating evidence the Commonwealth would downplay and to anticipate the details of the aggravating evidence the Commonwealth would emphasize. Without making reasonable efforts to review the file, defense counsel could have had no hope of knowing whether the prosecution was quoting selectively from the transcript, or whether there were circumstances extenuating the behavior described by the victim. The obligation to get the file was particularly pressing here owing to the similarity of the violent prior offense to the crime charged and Rompilla's sentencing strategy stressing residual doubt. Without making efforts to learn the details and rebut the relevance of the earlier crime, a convincing argument for residual doubt was certainly beyond any hope.

At argument the most that Pennsylvania (and the United States as amicus) could say was that defense counsel's efforts to find mitigating evidence by other means excused them from looking at the prior conviction file. And that, of course, is the position taken by the state postconviction courts. Without specifically discussing the prior case file, they too found that defense counsel's efforts were enough to free them from any obligation to enquire further.

We think this conclusion of the state court fails to answer the considerations we have set out, to the point of being an objectively unreasonable conclusion. It flouts prudence to deny that a defense lawyer should try to look at a file he knows the prosecution will cull for aggravating evidence, let alone when the file is sitting in the trial courthouse, open for the asking. No reasonable lawyer would forgo examination of the file thinking he could do as well by asking the defendant or family relations whether they recalled anything helpful or damaging in the prior victim's testimony. Nor would a reasonable lawyer compare possible searches for school reports, juvenile records, and evidence of drinking habits to the opportunity to take a look at a file disclosing what the prosecutor knows and even plans to read from in his case. Questioning a few more family members and searching for old records can promise less than looking for a needle in a haystack, when a lawyer truly has reason to doubt there is any needle there. But looking at a file the prosecution says it will use is a sure bet: whatever may be in that file is going to tell defense counsel something about what the prosecution can produce.

The dissent thinks this analysis creates a "rigid, per se" rule that requires defense counsel to do a complete review of the file on any prior conviction introduced, but that is a mistake. Counsel fell short here because they failed to make reasonable efforts to review the prior conviction file, despite knowing that the prosecution intended to introduce Rompilla's prior conviction not merely by entering a notice of conviction into evidence but by quoting damaging testimony of the rape victim in that case. The unreasonableness of attempting no more than they did was heightened by the easy availability of the file at the trial courthouse, and the great risk that testimony about a similar violent crime would hamstring counsel's chosen defense of residual doubt.

Since counsel's failure to look at the file fell below the line of reasonable practice, there is a further question about prejudice, that is, whether "there is a reasonable probability that, but for counsel's unprofessional errors, the result of the proceeding would have been different." We think Rompilla has shown beyond any doubt that counsel's lapse was prejudicial; Pennsylvania, indeed, does not even contest the claim of prejudice.

If the defense lawyers had looked in the file on Rompilla's prior conviction, it is uncontested they would have found a range of mitigation leads that no other source had opened up. In the same file with the transcript of the prior trial were the records of Rompilla's imprisonment on the earlier conviction, which defense counsel testified she had never seen. The prison files pictured Rompilla's childhood and mental health very differently from anything defense counsel had seen or heard. An evaluation by a corrections counselor states that Rompilla was "reared in the slum environment of Allentown, Pa. vicinity. He early came to the attention of juvenile authorities, quit school at 16, and started a series of incarcerations in and out Penna. often of assaultive nature and commonly related to over-indulgence in alcoholic beverages." The same file discloses test results that the defense's mental health experts would have viewed as pointing to schizophrenia and other disorders, and test scores showing a third grade level of cognition after nine years of schooling.

The accumulated entries would have destroyed the benign conception of Rompilla's upbringing and mental capacity defense counsel had formed from talking with Rompilla himself and some of his family members, and from the reports of the mental health experts. With this information, counsel would have become skeptical of the impression given by the five family members and would unquestionably have gone further to build a mitigation case. Further effort would presumably have unearthed much of the material postconviction counsel found, including testimony from several members of Rompilla's family, whom trial counsel did not interview. Judge Sloviter dissenting in the Third Circuit, summarized this evidence:

> "Rompilla's parents were both severe alcoholics who drank constantly. His mother drank during her pregnancy with Rompilla, and he and his brothers eventually developed serious drinking problems. His father, who had a vicious temper, frequently beat Rompilla's mother, leaving her bruised and black-eyed, and bragged about his cheating on her. His parents fought violently, and on at least one occasion his mother stabbed his father. He was abused by his father who beat him when he was young with his hands, fists, leather straps, belts and sticks. All of the children lived in terror. There were no expressions of parental love, affection or approval. Instead, he was subjected to yelling and verbal abuse. His father locked Rompilla and his brother Richard in a small wire mesh dog pen that was filthy and excrement filled. He had an isolated background, and was not allowed to visit other children or to speak to anyone on the phone. They had no indoor plumbing in the house, he slept in the attic with no heat, and the children were not given clothes and attended school in rags."

The jury never heard any of this and neither did the mental health experts who examined Rompilla before trial. While they found "nothing helpful to Rompilla's case," their postconviction counterparts, alerted by information from school, medical, and prison records that trial counsel never saw, found plenty of " 'red flags' " pointing up a need to test further. When they tested, they found that Rompilla "suffers from organic brain damage, an extreme mental disturbance significantly impairing several of his cognitive functions." They also said that "Rompilla's problems relate back to his childhood, and were likely caused by fetal alcohol syndrome and that Rompilla's capacity to appreciate the criminality of his conduct or to conform his conduct to the law was substantially impaired at the time of the offense."

These findings in turn would probably have prompted a look at school and juvenile records, all of them easy to get, showing, for example, that when Rompilla was 16 his mother "was missing from home frequently for a period of one or several weeks at a time." The same report noted that his mother "has been reported . . . frequently under the influence of alcoholic beverages, with the result that the children have always been poorly kept and on the filthy side which was also the condition of the home at all times." School records showed Rompilla's IQ was in the mentally retarded range.

Food for Thought

It may well be the case that the key fact to know in this case, like *Nixon*, is that this is a capital case. Is it possible that the Court is *sub silentio* requiring more of counsel in such cases than in non-capital cases given the gravity and finality of the potential penalty? If that is indeed the case, do you think that is an inappropriate approach? And if that is what a majority of the Court is really doing, should it just say so directly?

This evidence adds up to a mitigation case that bears no relation to the few naked pleas for mercy actually put before the jury, and although we suppose it is possible that a jury could have heard it all and still have decided on the death penalty, that is not the test. It goes without saying that the undiscovered mitigating evidence, taken as a whole, might well have influenced the jury's appraisal of Rompilla's culpability, and the likelihood of a different result if the evidence had gone in is sufficient to undermine confidence in the outcome actually reached at sentencing, *Strickland*.

The judgment of the Third Circuit is reversed, and Pennsylvania must either retry the case on penalty or stipulate to a life sentence.

JUSTICE O'CONNOR, concurring.

I write separately to put to rest one concern. The dissent worries that the Court's opinion "imposes on defense counsel a rigid requirement to review all documents in what it calls the 'case file' of any prior conviction that the prosecution might rely on at trial." But the Court's opinion imposes no such rule. Rather, today's decision simply applies our longstanding case-by-case approach to determining whether an attorney's performance was unconstitutionally deficient under *Strickland*. Trial counsel's performance in Rompilla's case falls short under that standard, because the attorneys' behavior was not "reasonable considering all the circumstances." In particular, there were three circumstances which made the attorneys' failure to examine Rompilla's prior conviction file unreasonable.

First, Rompilla's attorneys knew that their client's prior conviction would be at the very heart of the prosecution's case. The prior conviction went not to a collateral matter, but rather to one of the aggravating circumstances making Rompilla eligible for the death penalty. Second, the prosecutor's planned use of the prior conviction threatened to eviscerate one of the defense's primary mitigation arguments. Rompilla was convicted on the basis of strong circumstantial evidence. His lawyers structured the entire mitigation argument around the hope of convincing the jury that residual doubt about Rompilla's guilt made it inappropriate to impose the death penalty. In announcing an intention to introduce testimony about Rompilla's similar prior offense, the prosecutor put Rompilla's attorneys on notice that the prospective defense on mitigation likely would be ineffective and counterproductive. Third, the attorneys' decision not to obtain Rompilla's prior conviction file was not the result of an informed tactical decision about how the lawyers' time would best be spent. Their failure to obtain the crucial file was the result of inattention, not reasoned strategic judgment. As a result, their conduct fell below constitutionally required standards.

JUSTICE KENNEDY, with whom THE CHIEF JUSTICE, JUSTICE SCALIA, and JUSTICE THOMAS join, dissenting.

Today the Court brands two committed criminal defense attorneys as ineffective—"outside the wide range of professionally competent counsel"—because they did not look in an old case file and stumble upon something they had not set out to find. To reach this result, the majority imposes on defense counsel a rigid requirement to review all documents in what it calls the "case file" of any prior conviction that the prosecution might rely on at trial.

The majority's analysis contains barely a mention of *Strickland* and makes little effort to square today's holding with our traditional reluctance to impose rigid requirements on defense counsel. While the Court disclaims any intention to create a bright-line rule, this affords little comfort. The Court's opinion makes clear it has imposed on counsel a broad obligation to review prior conviction case files where those priors are used in aggravation—and to review every document in those files if not every single page of every document, regardless of the prosecution's proposed use for the prior conviction.

One of the primary reasons this Court has rejected a checklist approach to effective assistance of counsel is that each new requirement risks distracting attorneys from the real objective of providing vigorous advocacy as dictated by the facts and circumstances in the particular case. The Court's rigid requirement that counsel always review the case files of convictions the prosecution seeks to use at trial will be just such a distraction.

Food for Thought

The dissenters say this case creates a "rigid requirement." The majority say it does not. Which side is correct? Isn't it true after decision in *Rompilla* that defense counsel in a capital case must always look at the file documents relating to a prior offense if the prosecution indicates that it intends to rely on that conviction for purposes of sentence enhancement? If it is true, is that an inappropriate result?

Points for Discussion

a.   AEDPA

A 5-to-4 majority of the Supreme Court ruled in *Williams v. Taylor*, <u>529 U.S. 362, 412 (2000)</u>, that the Antiterrorism & Effective Death Penalty Act of 1996 ("AEDPA"), <u>28 U.S.C. § 2254</u>, "places a new constraint on the power of a federal *habeas* court to grant a state prisoner's application for a writ of *habeas corpus* with respect to claims adjudicated on the merits in state court." More particularly, the Court held, under this new provision,

> the writ may issue only if one of the following two conditions is satisfied— the state-court adjudication resulted in a decision that (1) "was contrary to clearly established Federal law, as determined by the Supreme Court of the United States," or (2) "involved an unreasonable application of clearly established Federal law, as determined by the Supreme Court of the United States." Under the "contrary to" clause, a federal *habeas* court may grant the writ if the state court arrives at a conclusion opposite to that reached by this Court on a question of law or if the state court decides a case differently than this Court has on a set of materially indistinguishable facts. Under the "unreasonable application" clause, a federal *habeas* court may grant the writ if the state court identifies the correct governing legal principle from this Court's decisions but unreasonably applies that principle to the facts of the prisoner's case.

Subsequently, the Supreme Court added that " 'clearly established Federal law' for purposes of the AEDPA includes only the holdings, as opposed to the *dicta*, of this Court's decisions." *See White v. Woodall*, <u>572 U.S. 415, 419 (2014)</u>. And the Supreme

Court has also advised that the AEDPA also "prohibits the federal courts of appeals from relying on their own precedent to conclude that a particular constitutional principle is 'clearly established.'" *See Lopez v. Smith*, 574 U.S. 1, 2 (2014). More recently, the Supreme Court has opined that where a state court decision being reviewed in *habeas* proceedings includes little or no reasoning, "the federal court should 'look through' the unexplained decision to the last related state-court decision that does provide a relevant rationale. It should then presume that the unexplained decision adopted the same reasoning. But the State may rebut the presumption by showing that the unexplained affirmance relied or most likely did rely on different grounds than the lower state court's decision, such as alternative grounds for affirmance that were briefed or argued to the state supreme court or obvious in the record it reviewed." *Wilson v. Sellers*, 138 S. Ct. 1188, 1192 (2018).

Most significantly, the fact that a state court may have made an *incorrect* constitutional ruling on an ineffectiveness inquiry no longer suffices—under this AEDPA provision—to entitle a defendant to *habeas corpus* relief. *See, e.g. Woodford v. Visciotti*, 537 U.S. 19 (2002) ("Under the 'unreasonable application' clause, a federal *habeas* court may not issue the writ simply because that court concludes in its independent judgment that the state-court decision applied *Strickland* incorrectly. Rather, it is the *habeas* applicant's burden to show that the state court applied *Strickland* to the facts of his case in an objectively unreasonable manner.").

> **FYI**
>
> The Seventh Circuit has held that the Wisconsin Court of Appeals' conclusion that defense counsel's failure to produce for trial an individual who defendant claimed was the perpetrator of the home invasion and robbery for which he was convicted did not constitute deficient performance was an unreasonable application of clearly established federal law since there would have been strong corroboration of some "damning evidence" supporting this allegation had that individual testified. *Cook v. Foster*, 948 F.3d 896 (7th Cir. 2020).

In *Rompilla*, the dissenters argued that "the Pennsylvania Supreme Court gave careful consideration to Rompilla's Sixth Amendment claim and concluded that 'counsel reasonably relied upon their discussions with Rompilla and upon their experts to determine the records needed to evaluate his mental health and other potential mitigating circumstances.' This decision was far from unreasonable under the AEDPA." The majority concluded, however, not only that defense counsel were ineffective, but that the state court decision finding them *not* to have been ineffective "was contrary to, or involved an unreasonable application of, clearly established Federal law, as determined by the Supreme Court of the United States," pursuant to the AEDPA. What do you think? Do you agree?

See also Sexton v. Beaudreaux, 138 S. Ct. 2555, 2558 (2018), quoting *Harrington v. Richter*, 562 U.S. 86, 102 (2011) ("When, as here, there is no reasoned state-court decision on the merits, the federal court 'must determine what arguments or theories . . . could have supported the state court's decision; and then it must ask whether it is possible fairminded jurists could disagree that those arguments or theories are inconsistent with the holding in a prior decision of this Court.' ").

b. Decisional Consistency

Why was defense counsels' decision to focus on mitigation in the penalty phase of a capital case held in *Nixon* to be reasonable and the same decision held to be unreasonable in *Rompilla*? Does this difference in result make sense to you?

c. Limited Records for Review

In *Cullen v. Pinholster*, 563 U.S. 170 (2011), the Supreme Court ruled that an ineffectiveness inquiry in a federal *habeas corpus* proceeding under the AEDPA (*see* Point a, above) is limited to the record that was before the state court that adjudicated the claim on the merits; evidence that was presented only to the federal *habeas* court may not be considered. The *Cullen* majority conceded that "this test is 'difficult to meet,' and it is a 'highly deferential standard for evaluating state-court rulings, which demands that state-court decisions be given the benefit of the doubt.' "

The Supreme Court has also made clear that "whether a state court's decision resulted from an unreasonable legal or factual conclusion under the AEDPA does not require that there be an opinion from the state court explaining the state court's reasoning. Where a state court's decision is unaccompanied by an explanation, the *habeas* petitioner's burden still must be met by showing there was no reasonable basis for the state court to deny relief." *Harrington v. Richter*, 562 U.S. 86 (2011).

d. Mentally Ill Clients

In its 2007 decision in *Schriro v. Landrigan*, 550 U.S. 465 (2007), a 5-to-4 majority of the Supreme Court held that a federal district court did not abuse its discretion in declining to order a *habeas corpus* evidentiary hearing in a case where counsel failed to present significant mitigating evidence at a capital sentencing hearing where that failure was due to defendant's express request. As the majority pointed out, "it was not objectively unreasonable for the district court to conclude that a defendant who refused to allow the presentation of any mitigating evidence could not establish *Strickland* prejudice based on his counsel's failure to investigate further possible mitigating evidence." In dissent, Justice Stevens argued, however, that

> significant mitigating evidence—evidence that may well have explained respondent's criminal conduct and unruly behavior at his capital sentencing hearing—was unknown at the time of sentencing. Only years later did respondent learn that he suffers from a serious psychological condition that

sheds important light on his earlier actions. The reason why this and other mitigating evidence was unavailable is that respondent's counsel failed to conduct a constitutionally adequate investigation.

What do you think? Should a mentally ill defendant's decisions against interest divest him of any opportunity to establish ineffective assistance after the fact?

e.   Adequate Investigations

In *Bobby v. Van Hook*, 558 U.S. 4 (2009), the Supreme Court found that counsel was *not* ineffective for failing to adequately investigate and to present additional mitigating evidence at a capital sentencing hearing when defense counsel did present a great deal of evidence, but there could have been more:

> "Despite all the mitigating evidence the defense did present, Van Hook and the Court of Appeals fault his counsel for failing to find more. What his counsel did discover, the argument goes, gave them 'reason to suspect that much worse details existed,' and that suspicion should have prompted them to interview other family members-his stepsister, two uncles, and two aunts-as well as a psychiatrist who once treated his mother, all of whom 'could have helped his counsel narrate the true story of Van Hook's childhood experiences.' But there comes a point at which evidence from more distant relatives can reasonably be expected to be only cumulative, and the search for it distractive from more important duties. Given all the evidence they unearthed from those closest to Van Hook's upbringing and the experts who reviewed his history, it was not unreasonable for his counsel not to identify and interview every other living family member or every therapist who once treated his parents. This is not a case in which the defendant's attorneys failed to act while potentially powerful mitigating evidence stared them in the face or would have been apparent from documents any reasonable attorney would have obtained. It is instead a case, like *Strickland* itself, in which defense counsel's 'decision not to seek more' mitigating evidence from the defendant's background 'than was already in hand' fell 'well within the range of professionally reasonable judgments.' "

Do you think this decision is consistent with the decision in *Rompilla*?

f.   Advice on Deportation Risk

In *Padilla v. Kentucky*, 559 U.S. 356 (2010), the Supreme Court ruled that in order to satisfy the performance prong of *Strickland*, "counsel must inform her client whether his guilty plea carries a risk of deportation." Padilla claimed that his counsel not only failed to advise him about the deportation consequences of his guilty plea to charged marijuana offenses, but told him that he did not have to worry about immigration status since he had been in the country so long. This advice was incorrect and, after his conviction, Padilla did indeed face deportation.

The Court held that "advice regarding deportation is not categorically removed from the ambit of the Sixth Amendment right to counsel. *Strickland* applies to Padilla's claim." That does not mean, the Court added, that criminal defense counsel must become experts on immigration law. Rather, "a criminal defense attorney need do no more than advise a noncitizen client that pending criminal charges may carry a risk of adverse immigration consequences."

The Supreme Court subsequently ruled that *Padilla* does not apply retroactively. *Chaidez v. United States*, 568 U.S. 342 (2013). Hence, a person whose conviction became final before *Padilla* was decided could not benefit from that decision.

g. Don't Skimp on Experts

In *Hinton v. Alabama*, 571 U.S. 263 (2014), the Supreme Court unanimously found the conduct of defense counsel deficient where he failed to request additional funds to replace an inadequate "firearms and toolmark" expert. In *Hinton*, forensic comparisons of bullets recovered from the homicide defendant's revolver was critical evidence tying him to the crime scene. Operating under the mistaken belief that he could pay no more than $1,000, counsel went looking for a well-regarded expert, but found only one person who was willing to take the case for that amount of money. Counsel hired that expert even though he did not have the expertise he thought he needed, concluding that—for that amount of money—he was "stuck" with him. As expected, the expert's testimony was weak and largely discredited, defendant was convicted, and subsequently sentenced to death.

The Court concluded that defense counsel "knew that he needed more funding to present an effective defense, yet he failed to make even the cursory investigation of the state statute providing for defense funding for indigent defendants that would have revealed to him that he could receive reimbursement not just for $1,000 but for 'any expenses reasonably incurred.' An attorney's ignorance of a point of law that is fundamental to his case combined with his failure to perform basic research on that point is a quintessential example of unreasonable performance under *Strickland*."

That finding of inadequate performance did not, in and of itself, establish ineffective assistance. The case was remanded for a determination whether this deficient performance actually prejudiced the defendant. What would the defendant have to prove on remand to show that this deficient performance prejudiced him?

* * *

What exactly constitutes "prejudice" under *Strickland*? Consider the following decisions:

Glover v. United States

531 U.S. 198 (2001).

JUSTICE KENNEDY delivered the opinion of the Court.

Petitioner, Paul Glover, contends that the trial court erred in a Sentencing Guidelines determination. The legal error, petitioner alleges, increased his prison sentence by at least 6 months and perhaps by 21 months. We must decide whether this would be "prejudice" under *Strickland v. Washington*, 466 U.S. 668 (1984). We reverse and remand for further proceedings.

Glover was the Vice President and General Counsel of the Chicago Truck Drivers, Helpers, and Warehouse Workers Union (Independent). Glover used his control over the union's investments to enrich himself and his co-conspirators through kickbacks. The presentence investigation report recommended that the convictions for labor racketeering, money laundering, and tax evasion be grouped together under United States Sentencing Commission, Guidelines Manual § 3D1.2 (Nov.1994), which allows the grouping of "counts involving substantially the same harm." The District Court ruled that the money laundering counts should not be grouped with Glover's other offenses. Glover's attorneys did not submit papers or offer extensive oral arguments contesting the no-grouping argument and, accordingly, Glover's offense level was increased by two levels, yielding a concomitant increase in the sentencing range. Glover was sentenced to 84 months in prison, which was in the middle of the Guidelines range of 78 to 97 months. On appeal, Glover's counsel (the same attorneys who represented him in District Court) did not raise the grouping issue. A short time after argument on Glover's appeal, a different panel of the Seventh Circuit held that, under some circumstances, grouping of money laundering offenses with other counts was proper under § 3D1.2. *United States v. Wilson*, 98 F.3d 281 (1996). A month later, the Seventh Circuit affirmed his conviction and sentence.

Glover filed a *pro se* motion to correct his sentence. The failure of his counsel to press the grouping issue, he argued, was ineffective assistance. The performance of counsel, he contended, fell below a reasonable standard both at sentencing, when his attorneys did not with any clarity or force contest the Government's argument, and on appeal, when they did not present the issue in their briefs or call the *Wilson* decision to the panel's attention following the oral argument. He further argued that absent the ineffective assistance, his offense level would have been two levels lower, yielding a Guidelines sentencing range of 63 to 78 months. Under this theory, the 84-month sentence he received was an unlawful increase of anywhere between 6 and 21 months.

The District Court denied Glover's motion and the Court of Appeals affirmed. It appears the Seventh Circuit relied on *Lockhart v. Fretwell*, 506 U.S. 364 (1993). *Lockhart* holds that in some circumstances a mere difference in outcome will not suffice to establish prejudice. But this Court explained last Term that our holding in Lockhart does not supplant the *Strickland* analysis. Our jurisprudence suggests that any amount of actual jail time has Sixth Amendment significance. *Argersinger v. Hamlin*, 407 U.S. 25 (1972).

Take Note

As difficult as it may sometimes be to establish the prejudice prong of the *Strickland* test, it is not impossible as the decision in *Glover* illustrates.

The Seventh Circuit's rule is not well considered in any event, because there is no obvious dividing line by which to measure how much longer a sentence must be for the increase to constitute substantial prejudice. Although the amount by which a defendant's sentence is increased by a particular decision may be a factor to consider in determining whether counsel's performance in failing to argue the point constitutes ineffective assistance, under a determinate system of constrained discretion such as the Sentencing Guidelines it cannot serve as a bar to a showing of prejudice. We hold that the Seventh Circuit erred in engrafting this additional requirement onto the prejudice branch of the *Strickland* test. This is not a case where trial strategies, in retrospect, might be criticized for leading to a harsher sentence. Here we consider the sentencing calculation itself, a calculation resulting from a ruling which, if it had been error, would have been correctable on appeal. We express no opinion on the ultimate merits of Glover's claim because the question of deficient performance is not before us, but it is clear that prejudice flowed from the asserted error in sentencing.

The judgment of the Seventh Circuit is reversed.

Buck v. Davis

137 S.Ct. 759 (2017).

CHIEF JUSTICE ROBERTS delivered the opinion of the Court.

A Texas jury convicted petitioner Duane Buck of capital murder. Under state law, the jury could impose a death sentence only if it found that Buck was likely to commit acts of violence in the future. Buck's attorney called a psychologist to offer his opinion on that issue. The psychologist testified that Buck probably would not engage in violent conduct. But he also stated that one of the factors pertinent in assessing a person's propensity for violence was his race, and that Buck was statistically more likely to act violently because he is black. The jury sentenced Buck to death.

Buck contends that his attorney's introduction of this evidence violated his Sixth Amendment right to the effective assistance of counsel. The Sixth Amendment right to counsel is the right to the effective assistance of counsel. A defendant who claims to have been denied effective assistance must show both that counsel performed deficiently and that counsel's deficient performance caused him prejudice.

Strickland's first prong sets a high bar. A defense lawyer navigating a criminal proceeding faces any number of choices about how best to make a client's case. The lawyer has discharged his constitutional responsibility so long as his decisions fall within the "wide range of professionally competent assistance." It is only when the lawyer's errors were "so serious that counsel was not functioning as the 'counsel' guaranteed by the Sixth Amendment" that *Strickland*'s first prong is satisfied.

The District Court determined that, in this case, counsel's performance fell outside the bounds of competent representation. We agree. Counsel knew that Dr. Quijano's report reflected the view that Buck's race disproportionately predisposed him to violent conduct; he also knew that the principal point of dispute during the trial's penalty phase was whether Buck was likely to act violently in the future. Counsel nevertheless (1) called Dr. Quijano to the stand; (2) specifically elicited testimony about the connection between Buck's race and the likelihood of future violence; and (3) put into evidence Dr. Quijano's expert report that stated, in reference to factors bearing on future dangerousness, "Race. Black: Increased probability."

Given that the jury had to make a finding of future dangerousness before it could impose a death sentence, Dr. Quijano's report said, in effect, that the color of Buck's skin made him more deserving of execution. It would be patently unconstitutional for a state to argue that a defendant is liable to be a future danger because of his race. No competent defense attorney would introduce such evidence about his own client.

To satisfy *Strickland*, a litigant must also demonstrate prejudice—"a reasonable probability that, but for counsel's unprofessional errors, the result of the proceeding would have been different." Accordingly, the question before the District Court was whether Buck had demonstrated a reasonable probability that, without Dr. Quijano's testimony on race, at least one juror would have harbored a reasonable doubt about whether Buck was likely to be violent in the future. The District Court concluded that Buck had not made such a showing. We disagree.

In arguing that the jury would have imposed a death sentence even if Dr. Quijano had not offered race-based testimony, the State primarily emphasizes the brutality of

Buck's crime and his lack of remorse. A jury may conclude that a crime's vicious nature calls for a sentence of death. In this case, however, several considerations convince us that it is reasonably probable—notwithstanding the nature of Buck's crime and his behavior in its aftermath—that the proceeding would have ended differently had counsel rendered competent representation.

Dr. Quijano testified on the key point at issue in Buck's sentencing. True, the jury was asked to decide two issues—whether Buck was likely to be a future danger, and, if so, whether mitigating circumstances nevertheless justified a sentence of life imprisonment. But the focus of the proceeding was on the first question. Much of the penalty phase testimony was directed to future dangerousness, as were the summations for both sides. The jury, consistent with the focus of the parties, asked during deliberations to see the expert reports on dangerousness.

Deciding the key issue of Buck's dangerousness involved an unusual inquiry. The jurors were not asked to determine a historical fact concerning Buck's conduct, but to render a predictive judgment inevitably entailing a degree of speculation. Buck, all agreed, had committed acts of terrible violence. Would he do so again?

Buck's prior violent acts had occurred outside of prison, and within the context of romantic relationships with women. If the jury did not impose a death sentence, Buck would be sentenced to life in prison, and no such romantic relationship would be likely to arise. A jury could conclude that those changes would minimize the prospect of future dangerousness.

But one thing would never change: the color of Buck's skin. Buck would always be black. And according to Dr. Quijano, that immutable characteristic carried with it an "increased probability" of future violence. Here was hard statistical evidence—from an expert—to guide an otherwise speculative inquiry.

And it was potent evidence. Dr. Quijano's testimony appealed to a powerful racial stereotype—that of black men as "violence prone." In combination with the substance of the jury's inquiry, this created something of a perfect storm. Dr. Quijano's opinion coincided precisely with a particularly noxious strain of racial prejudice, which itself coincided precisely with the central question at sentencing. The effect of this unusual confluence of factors was to provide support for making a decision on life or death on the basis of race.

This effect was heightened due to the source of the testimony. Dr. Quijano took the stand as a medical expert bearing the court's imprimatur. The jury learned at the outset of his testimony that he held a doctorate in clinical psychology, had conducted evaluations in some 70 capital murder cases, and had been appointed by the trial judge (at public expense) to evaluate Reasonable jurors might well have valued his opinion concerning the central question before them.

For these reasons, we cannot accept the District Court's conclusion that the introduction of any mention of race during the penalty phase was "de minimis." There were only two references to race in Dr. Quijano's testimony—one during direct examination, the other on cross. But when a jury hears expert testimony that expressly makes a defendant's race directly pertinent on the question of life or death, the impact of that evidence cannot be measured simply by how much air time it received at trial or how many pages it occupies in the record. Some toxins can be deadly in small doses.

The effect of Dr. Quijano's testimony on Buck's sentencing cannot be dismissed as "de minimis." Buck has demonstrated prejudice.

The judgment of the United States Court of Appeals for the Fifth Circuit is reversed, and the case is remanded for further proceedings consistent with this opinion.

> **FYI**
>
> *Consider* Lisa M. Saccomano, *Defining the Proper Role of "Offender Characteristics" in Sentencing Decisions: A Critical Race Theory Perspective*, 56 AM. CRIM. L. REV. 1693 (2019) ("I argue that white cultural values are deeply embedded in the practice of weighing offender characteristic factors at sentencing, such that judges often cite the incidents of privilege in mitigation, e.g., educational attainment and employment status. Similarly, judges often cite the incidents of disadvantage in aggravation.").

Points for Discussion

a. Quick Plea Advice Not Ineffective

In *Premo v. Moore*, 562 U.S. 115 (2011), the Supreme Court concluded that a state postconviction court's conclusion that defense counsel did not perform deficiently in advising his client, Moore, to enter a quick no-contest plea to felony murder, without having brought a motion to suppress one of his confessions, was neither an unreasonable application of clearly established federal law, nor was the conclusion that he was not prejudiced unreasonable:

> The state court here reasonably could have determined that Moore would have accepted the plea agreement even if his confession had been ruled inadmissible. By the time the plea agreement cut short investigation of Moore's crimes, the State's case was already formidable and included two witnesses to an admissible confession. Had the prosecution continued to investigate, its case might well have become stronger. At the same time, Moore faced grave punishments. His decision to plead no contest allowed him to avoid a possible sentence of life without parole or death. The bargain counsel struck was thus a favorable one—the statutory minimum for the

charged offense—and the decision to forgo a challenge to the confession may have been essential to securing that agreement.

b.   Insufficient Investigation Not Necessarily Prejudicial

In *Wong v. Belmontes*, 558 U.S. 15 (2009), the Court held that Belmontes was not prejudiced by the fact that defense counsel may have been ineffective for failing to investigate and present sufficient mitigating evidence during the penalty phase of his capital trial:

> It is hard to imagine expert testimony and additional facts about Belmontes' difficult childhood outweighing the facts of the victim's murder. It becomes even harder to envision such a result when the evidence that Belmontes had committed another murder—'the most powerful imaginable aggravating evidence,' is added to the mix. The notion that the result could have been different if only counsel had put on more than the nine witnesses he did, or called expert witnesses to bolster his case, is fanciful.

However, the Supreme Court subsequently emphasized that "we have never limited the prejudice inquiry under *Strickland* to penalty phase cases in which there was only 'little or no mitigation evidence' presented." *Sears v. Upton*, 561 U.S. 945 (2010). As the *Sears* Court explained:

> To assess the probability of a different outcome under *Strickland*, we consider the totality of the available mitigation evidence—both that adduced at trial, and the evidence adduced in the *habeas* proceeding—and reweigh it against the evidence in aggravation. That standard will necessarily require a court to "speculate" as to the effect of the new evidence—regardless of how much or how little mitigation evidence was presented during the initial penalty phase. This is the proper prejudice standard for evaluating a claim of ineffective representation in the context of a penalty phase mitigation investigation.

Why do you think that so many Supreme Court ineffective-assistance-of-counsel decisions arise out of capital sentencing hearings? Is it because counsel in that setting is often so bad or because judges are less concerned about achieving finality in those cases? Or is neither of those reasons persuasive?

c.   Changing Technology & Ineffectiveness

In *Wright v. Van Patten*, 552 U.S. 120 (2008), the Supreme Court concluded that defense counsel's participation in a plea hearing (no contest) by speaker phone—rather than in person—was not presumptively prejudicial to his client: "Our precedents do not clearly hold that counsel's participation by speaker phone should be treated as a complete denial of counsel, on par with total absence. Even if we agree with Van Patten that a lawyer physically present will tend to perform better than one on the phone, it does not necessarily follow that mere telephone contact amounted to total absence or prevented counsel from assisting the accused, so as to entail application of *Cronic*. The question is not whether counsel in those circumstances will perform less well than he otherwise would, but whether the circumstances are likely to result in such poor performance that an inquiry into its effects would not be worth the time." Do you agree? Should the same result apply when defense counsel appears at trial by way of video conferencing? Or, sometime in the (distant?) future, defense counsel "appears" virtually, but not corporally?

d.   Convicting the Innocent

A 2014 study estimates that if all death-sentenced defendants remained under sentence of death indefinitely, at least 4.1% of them would ultimately be exonerated. *See* Samuel R. Gross, Barbara O'Brien, Chen Huc, and Edward H. Kennedy, Proceedings of the National Academy of Science of the United States of America, *Rate of false conviction of criminal defendants who are sentenced to death*, http://www.pnas.org/content/111/20/7230.full (2014). As of June 1, 2020, 2,622 individuals have been found to have been wrongly convicted of a crime since 1989, and later cleared of all the charges against them based on new evidence of innocence. *See* National Registry of Exonerations, https://www.law.umich.edu/special/exoneration/Pages/about.aspx. *See also, e.g.*, Illinois abolishes death penalty; cites wrongful convictions, The Washington Times (March 9, 2011) ("Illinois abolished the death penalty Wednesday, more than a decade after the state imposed a moratorium on executions out of concern that innocent people could be put to death by a justice system that had wrongly condemned 13 men."). Does this suggest that the Court's approach to ineffective assistance is too strict, too difficult to establish? But, on the other hand, aren't *some* erroneous convictions inevitable? Or not?

e.   Structural Error & Ineffectiveness

Some trial errors are known as "structural errors," errors that cannot be deemed to be harmless. The purpose of the structural error doctrine is to ensure that certain basic, constitutional guarantees define the framework of any criminal trial. One such basic constitutional guarantee is the right to a public trial.

In *Weaver v. Massachusetts*, 137 S.Ct. 1899 (2017), the issue arose of the relationship between this kind of structural error and an ineffectiveness claim. During Weaver's trial on state criminal charges, the courtroom was completely occupied by potential jurors and closed to the public for two days of the jury selection process. Defense counsel neither objected to the closure at trial nor raised the issue on direct review. As a result, the Court was faced with "the question whether invalidation of the conviction is required, or if the prejudice inquiry is altered when the structural error is raised in the context of an ineffective-assistance-of-counsel claim."

The Court reasoned that

> although the public-trial right is structural, it is subject to exceptions. Though these cases should be rare, a judge may deprive a defendant of his right to an open courtroom by making proper factual findings in support of the decision to do so. The fact that the public-trial right is subject to these exceptions suggests that not every public-trial violation results in fundamental unfairness. Thus, when a defendant raises a public-trial violation via an ineffective-assistance-of-counsel claim, *Strickland* prejudice is not shown automatically. Instead, the burden is on the defendant to show either a reasonable probability of a different outcome in his or her case or to show that the particular public-trial violation was so serious as to render his or her trial fundamentally unfair.

Hence, the Supreme Court ruled, "in the context of a public-trial violation during jury selection, where the error is neither preserved nor raised on direct review but is raised later via an ineffective-assistance-of-counsel claim, the defendant must demonstrate prejudice to secure a new trial." In *Weaver*, the Court held that Weaver failed to do this, i.e. he did not establish a reasonable probability that the jury would not have convicted him if his attorney had objected to the closure of the courtroom.

Do you think this is a sensible test? Why should a defendant whose trial was subject to a structural error, the failure to receive a basic constitutional guarantee, have to prove that he or she was prejudiced thereby? More importantly, just how would a defendant go about proving such prejudice? As Justice Breyer, joined by Justice Kagan, argued in dissent:

> In my view, we should not require defendants to take on a task that is normally impossible to perform. Nor would I give lower courts the unenviably complex job of deciphering which structural errors really undermine fundamental fairness and which do not—that game is not worth the candle. I would simply say that just as structural errors are categorically insusceptible to harmless-error analysis on direct review, so too are they categorically insusceptible to actual-prejudice analysis in Strickland claims. A showing that an attorney's constitutionally deficient performance produced a structural error should consequently be enough to entitle a defendant to relief.

What do you think?

f. Failure to File Appeal

In *Garza v. Idaho*, <u>139 S.Ct. 738 (2019)</u>, the Supreme Court held that "prejudice is presumed when counsel's constitutionally deficient performance deprives a defendant of an appeal that he otherwise would have taken." Indeed, the *Garza* Court found ineffective assistance to have existed in the absence of a prejudice inquiry simply because "Garza's attorney rendered deficient performance by not filing the notice of appeal in light of Garza's clear requests." Or as the Court restated the underlying point, "the rule is the one compelled by our precedent: When counsel's deficient performance forfeits an appeal that a defendant otherwise would have taken, the defendant gets a new opportunity to appeal." The *Garza* Court added, "we hold today that this presumption applies even when the defendant has signed an appeal waiver."

Hypo 1: *Failure to Challenge Government's Use of Flawed Scientific Evidence*

Defense counsel failed to challenge the government's use of Comparative Bullet Lead Analysis (CBLA) at defendant's first-degree murder trial in 1995. Although no longer generally accepted after 2003, CBLA evidence was commonly used at that time. Was defense counsel ineffective for failing to challenge the prosecution's use of that questionable evidence? Does it make sense to judge the reasonableness of defense counsel's conduct many years later, in hindsight? *See Maryland v. Kulbicki*, <u>136 S.Ct. 2 (2015)</u>.

Hypo 2: *Failure to Suppress*

Defendant is on trial for possession of narcotics. The prosecution has overwhelming evidence of guilt in the form of cocaine found in defendant's home. However, the evidence was obtained as a result of an illegal search. As in *Premo*, set out above, defense counsel fails to file a suppression motion and defendant is convicted. Was counsel ineffective under either *Strickland* or *Cronic*? *See, e.g., State v. Silvers*, <u>587 N.W.2d 325 (Neb. 1998)</u>.

Hypo 3: *Demeaning Client*

Should ineffectiveness be presumed where counsel referred to his client with a racist epithet and told him that he "hoped he gets life?" Counsel also stated that, if defendant "insists on going to trial," he would be "very ineffective." *See Frazer v. United States,* 18 F.3d 778 (9th Cir.1994).

Hypo 4: *Failure to Reveal Plea Offer*

The prosecution offered defendant's counsel a ten year plea deal on charges of felony murder, robbery and conspiracy. However, counsel failed to convey the offer to defendant in a timely manner. After defendant took the stand and testified in her own behalf, the prosecutor withdrew the offer. Was counsel ineffective for failing to convey the plea offer in a timely manner? *See Helmedach v. Commissioner,* 329 Conn. 726, 189 A.3d 1173 (2018).

Hypo 5: *Failure to Appear*

Do you think that criminal defense counsel should be deemed to be automatically ineffective when he failed to show up for most of the direct and cross-examination of an important prosecution witness—a victim—without any excuse for his absence? What if counsel failed to show up for any of the cross-examination? Would it make any difference in your analysis if counsel was prepared to finish the cross-examination, but asked for a recess to review what he had missed before proceeding? *See McKnight v. State,* 320 S.C. 356, 465 S.E.2d 352 (1995).

Hypo 6: *Prior Convictions*

Defendant is convicted of armed robbery. He had been convicted of this crime twice before. During *voir dire,* defense counsel asked the members of the venire whether they could judge defendant fairly and with an open mind if they learned he had been convicted of armed robbery twice previously. At no other point in the trial was the subject of defendant's prior convictions mentioned. Was counsel ineffective because he mentioned them during *voir dire*?

Hypo 7: *Failure to Advise*

Defense counsel failed to inform his client, who was considering pleading guilty to a drug offense, that the client's prior conviction for a narcotics paraphernalia offence would qualify as a sentencing enhancement mandating imprisonment for not less than five years. On advice of counsel, defendant pled guilty to manufacturing methamphetamine, second offense, and was sentenced to seven years' imprisonment. After *Padilla*, discussed above, was this ineffective assistance of counsel? *See Berry v. State*, 381 S.C. 630, 675 S.E.2d 425 (2009).

Hypo 8: *Failure to Call Eyewitness*

Do you think that trial counsel was ineffective where he failed to call an eyewitness to the shooting at issue even though he knew that her statements would contradict the eyewitness upon whom the prosecution's entire case relied, he knew that she had not identified the defendant on the night of the shooting, and he also knew that the witness had not identified the defendant later when she examined a photo array? Can you think of any tactical reason at all why counsel might have failed to put a witness like this on the stand? *See State v. Jenkins*, 355 Wis.2d 180, 848 N.W.2d 786 (2014).

Hypo 9: *You Get What You Pay for*

Massachusetts suffered from a shortage of lawyers willing to accept indigent appointments. The trial court concluded that the unavailability of lawyers was directly related to inadequate levels of compensation. Suppose that you are a trial court judge and you have a number of indigent defendants who are entitled to counsel but who remain unrepresented. What remedies are available to you? Should you: 1) order attorneys to accept indigent cases at prevailing compensation rates; 2) order the state to pay attorneys more for indigent representation; or 3) order that defendants be released and their cases be dismissed without prejudice? *See Lavallee v. Justices in the Hampden Superior Court*, 442 Mass. 228, 812 N.E.2d 895 (2004).

Hypo 10: *Investigating Ineffective Assistance*

You were recently admitted to the Bar of your state and are engaged in an active criminal law practice. As *pro bono* work, you take an occasional "innocence case," one in which you have serious doubts about whether someone was fairly convicted of a crime. One day, J.T. Booker comes to see you about his brother, John, who is on death row having been convicted of a brutal rape and murder. J.T. tells you that John could not have committed the rape or the murder because he was in another city at the time of the crime. J.T. is so sincere, and so convinced of his brother's innocence, that you decide to take the case. Suppose that you may want to pursue an ineffective assistance of claim with respect to trial counsel's performance. What steps would you take in order to decide whether ineffective assistance actually existed, and whether you should assert this claim? What types of evidence would be useful to you? How would you go about obtaining such evidence? How would you begin?

Hypo 11: *Failure to Advise Defendant to Be Contrite*

Defendant pled guilty to Assault Second Degree and Endangering the Welfare of a Child. Counsel, who met with his client only briefly and for the very first time on the day of sentencing, had not discussed with him the desirability of his expressing his contrition for the crimes he committed. The sentencing judge sentenced defendant to 18 years in prison, emphasizing as a basis for the heavy sentence defendant's lack of contrition in his allocution. Was defense counsel ineffective for not advising his client to express his contrition or, if he wasn't actually contrite, not to engage in allocution? *See Harden v. State*, 180 A.3d 1037 (Del. 2018).

Exercise: *IAC Claim*

Defendant Larry Hall was convicted at trial along with a codefendant, G., of the rape and murder of a young woman. The crime was one of a series of similar, seemingly-random abductions, rapes, and grisly murders of young women which took place during 1981 and 1982. Hall's defense at trial—which was apparently not credited by the jury—was strictly one of factual innocence. Hall was sentenced to death. His conviction and death sentence were affirmed on direct appeal.

Hall has now sought postconviction relief in state court, arguing that he is entitled to a new trial because of the ineffective assistance of his trial counsel, Kyle LaBomba (which he did not raise in his direct appeal since LaBomba was also his appellate counsel and failed to question his own ineffectiveness). The postconviction court denied Hall the opportunity for an evidentiary hearing on his claim of LaBomba's ineffectiveness, concluding that he did not make a sufficient showing of arguable ineffectiveness to justify such a hearing. Hall has appealed this decision to a state appellate court, arguing that he is entitled to a hearing. Attached to his appeal papers are affidavits from a number of psychiatrists which claim that he was psychotic and "psychologically adrift" at the time of the rape and murder for which he was sentenced to death and, further, that he was under the influence of the co-defendant, Linda Sanders, who initiated all of the crimes and "possessed a Charles Manson-like persona, subjugating Hall to her will."

Hall argues that LaBomba was ineffective in that he failed to raise any psychiatric defenses at trial. More important, Hall argues in his appeal papers that LaBomba failed even to obtain any psychiatric evaluation of Hall to assess whether or not such a defense might be tenable. It is Hall's argument that he is at least entitled to an evidentiary hearing at which he should be given an opportunity to show that LaBomba was constitutionally ineffective in failing to investigate and raise psychiatric defenses to these charges.

Half of you will be assigned to the defense, half to the prosecution. Prepare a brief (1 to 2 pages) outline of the arguments which support your side of the issue on appeal whether Hall should be entitled to such an evidentiary hearing on LaBomba's ineffectiveness.

D. Conflicts of Interest

In *Strickland*, the Court stated that when an attorney represents clients with conflicting interests, a limited presumption of incompetence can arise. *Cuyler* squarely presents that issue.

Cuyler v. Sullivan

446 U.S. 335 (1980).

MR. JUSTICE POWELL delivered the opinion of the Court.

The question presented is whether a state prisoner may obtain a federal writ of *habeas corpus* by showing that his retained defense counsel represented potentially conflicting interests.

Hear It

You can hear the oral argument in *Cuyler* at http://www.oyez.org/cases/1970-1979/1979/1979_78_1832.

Respondent John Sullivan was indicted with Gregory Carchidi and Anthony DiPasquale for the first-degree murders of John Gorey and Rita Janda. The victims, a labor official and his companion, were shot to death in Gorey's second-story office at the Philadelphia headquarters of Teamsters' Local 107. Francis McGrath, a janitor, saw the three defendants in the building just before the shooting. They appeared to be awaiting someone, and they encouraged McGrath to do his work on another day. McGrath ignored their suggestions. Shortly afterward, Gorey arrived and went to his office. McGrath then heard what sounded like firecrackers exploding in rapid succession. Carchidi, who was in the room where McGrath was working, abruptly directed McGrath to leave the building and to say nothing. McGrath hastily complied. When he returned to the building about 15 minutes later, the defendants were gone. The victims' bodies were discovered the next morning.

Two privately retained lawyers, G. Fred DiBona and A. Charles Peruto, represented all three defendants throughout the state proceedings that followed the indictment. Sullivan accepted representation from the two lawyers retained by his codefendants because he could not afford to pay his own lawyer. At no time did Sullivan or his lawyers object to the multiple representation. Sullivan was the first defendant to come to trial. The evidence against him was entirely circumstantial, consisting primarily of McGrath's testimony. At the close of the Commonwealth's case, the defense rested without presenting any evidence. The jury found Sullivan guilty and fixed his penalty at life imprisonment. The Pennsylvania Supreme Court affirmed his conviction by an equally divided vote. Sullivan's codefendants, Carchidi and DiPasquale, were acquitted at separate trials. In subsequent postconviction proceedings, a federal district court denied Sullivan's request for *habeas corpus* relief, but the Third Circuit Court of Appeals reversed, finding a conflict of interest sufficient to raise Sixth Amendment concerns.

We come to Sullivan's claim that he was denied the effective assistance of counsel guaranteed by the Sixth Amendment because his lawyers had a conflict of interest. In

Holloway v. Arkansas, 435 U.S. 475 (1978), a single public defender represented three defendants at the same trial. The trial court refused to consider the appointment of separate counsel despite the defense lawyer's timely and repeated assertions that the interests of his clients conflicted. This Court recognized that a lawyer forced to represent codefendants whose interests conflict cannot provide the adequate legal assistance required by the Sixth Amendment. Given the trial court's failure to respond to timely objections, however, the Court did not consider whether the alleged conflict actually existed. It simply held that the trial court's error unconstitutionally endangered the right to counsel.

Holloway requires state trial courts to investigate timely objections to multiple representation. But nothing in our precedents suggests that the Sixth Amendment requires state courts themselves to initiate inquiries into the propriety of multiple representation in every case. Defense counsel have an ethical obligation to avoid conflicting representations and to advise the court promptly when a conflict of interest arises during the course of trial. Absent special circumstances, therefore, trial courts may assume either that multiple representation entails no conflict or that the lawyer and his clients knowingly accept such risk of conflict as may exist. Unless the trial court knows or reasonably should know that a particular conflict exists, the court need not initiate an inquiry.

> **FYI**
>
> The *Holloway* Court established that where counsel has brought the issue of potential conflict to a trial court's attention and the trial court failed properly to respond to the motion, e.g. by failing to either grant it or to ascertain the potentiality of a conflict at an appropriate hearing, in contrast to ordinary ineffectiveness inquiries, reversal of a defendant's conviction is "automatic," even in the absence of a demonstration of prejudice. As the Supreme Court subsequently reiterated this rule: "*Holloway* creates an automatic reversal rule where defense counsel is forced to represent codefendants over his timely objection, unless the trial court has determined that there is no conflict." *Mickens v. Taylor*, 535 U.S. 162, 168 (2002).

Holloway reaffirmed that multiple representation does not violate the Sixth Amendment unless it gives rise to a conflict of interest. Since a possible conflict inheres in almost every instance of multiple representation, a defendant who objects to multiple representation must have the opportunity to show that potential conflicts impermissibly imperil his right to a fair trial. But unless the trial court fails to afford such an opportunity, a reviewing court cannot presume that the possibility for conflict has resulted in ineffective assistance of counsel. Such a presumption would preclude multiple representation even in cases where "a common defense gives strength against a common attack."

In order to establish a violation of the Sixth Amendment, a defendant who raised no objection at trial must demonstrate that an actual conflict of interest adversely affected his lawyer's performance. In *Glasser v. United States*, 315 U.S. 60 (1942), for example, the record showed that defense counsel failed to cross-examine a prosecution witness whose testimony linked Glasser with the crime and failed to resist the presentation of arguably inadmissible evidence. The Court found that both omissions resulted from counsel's desire to diminish the jury's perception of a codefendant's guilt. Indeed, the evidence of counsel's "struggle to serve two masters could not seriously be doubted." Since this actual conflict of interest impaired Glasser's defense, the Court reversed his conviction.

> **FYI**
>
> American Bar Association Standards for Criminal Justice Defense Function Standard 4–1.7(d) (4th ed. 2015) provides as follows:
>
> Except where necessary to secure counsel for preliminary matters such as initial hearings or applications for bail, a defense counsel (or multiple counsel associated in practice) should not undertake to represent more than one client in the same criminal case. When there is not yet a criminal case, such multiple representation should be engaged in only when, after careful investigation and consideration, it is clear either that no conflict is likely to develop at any stage of the matter, or that multiple representation will be advantageous to each of the clients represented and that foreseeable conflicts can be waived.

Glasser established that unconstitutional multiple representation is never harmless error. Once the Court concluded that Glasser's lawyer had an actual conflict of interest, it refused "to indulge in nice calculations as to the amount of prejudice" attributable to the conflict. The conflict itself demonstrated a denial of the right to have the effective assistance of counsel. Thus, a defendant who shows that a conflict of interest actually affected the adequacy of his representation need not demonstrate prejudice in order to obtain relief. But until a defendant shows that his counsel actively represented conflicting interests, he has not established the constitutional predicate for his claim of ineffective assistance.

The Court of Appeals granted Sullivan relief because he had shown that the multiple representation in this case involved a possible conflict of interest. We hold that the possibility of conflict is insufficient to impugn a criminal conviction. In order to demonstrate a violation of his Sixth Amendment rights, a defendant must establish that an actual conflict of interest adversely affected his lawyer's performance. Sullivan believes he should prevail even under this standard. He emphasizes Peruto's admission that the decision to rest Sullivan's defense reflected a reluctance to expose witnesses who later might have testified for the other defendants. The petitioner, on the other hand, points to DiBona's contrary testimony and to evidence that Sullivan himself wished to avoid taking the stand. Since the Court of Appeals did not weigh these conflicting contentions under the proper legal standard, its judgment is vacated and the case is remanded for further proceedings consistent with this opinion.

MR. JUSTICE BRENNAN, concurring in the result.

Upon discovery of joint representation, the duty of the trial court is to ensure that the defendants have not unwittingly given up their constitutional right to effective counsel. This is necessary since it is usually the case that defendants will not know what their rights are or how to raise them. Had the trial record in the present case shown that respondent made a knowing and intelligent choice of joint representation, I could accept the Court's standard for a postconviction determination as to whether respondent in fact was denied effective assistance. Here, however, where there is no evidence that the court advised respondent about the potential for conflict or that respondent made a knowing and intelligent choice to forgo his right to separate counsel, I believe that respondent, who has shown a significant possibility of conflict, is entitled to a presumption that his representation in fact suffered.

MR. JUSTICE MARSHALL, concurring in part and dissenting in part.

If the possibility of the inconsistent interests of the clients was brought home to the court by means of an objection at trial, the court may not require joint representation. But if no objection was made at trial, the appropriate inquiry is whether a conflict actually existed during the course of the representation. Because it is the simultaneous representation of conflicting interests against which the Sixth Amendment protects a defendant, he need go no further than to show the existence of an actual conflict. An actual conflict of interests negates the unimpaired loyalty a defendant is constitutionally entitled to expect and receive from his attorney. In the present case Peruto's testimony, if credited by the court, would be sufficient to make out a case of ineffective assistance by reason of a conflict of interests under even a restrictive reading of the Court's standard.

Points for Discussion

a. Disqualification Motions

It has become increasingly common for prosecutors to file pretrial motions to disqualify defense counsel. Such motions may be aimed at preventing counsel from engaging in the simultaneous representation of all or any one or more of multiple codefendants. Trial courts hearing such motions have the inherent judicial authority to oversee the conduct of the Bar, including the power to grant or deny such motions to disqualify. Typically, trial courts considering such motions in criminal cases look for guidance both to Sixth Amendment law and to applicable lawyer ethics code provisions relating to impermissible conflicts of interests.

b. Representation by Law Firm Partners

In *Burger v. Kemp*, 483 U.S. 776 (1987), petitioner was convicted of capital murder and sentenced to death. Petitioner claimed that his lawyer had a conflict of interest because his law partner represented petitioner's coindictee. Although the Supreme Court assumed that "two law partners are considered as one attorney," the Court refused to presume ineffective assistance. "We presume prejudice only if the defendant demonstrates that counsel 'actively represented conflicting interests' and that 'an actual conflict of interest adversely affected his lawyer's performance.' " The Court found that petitioner was unable to satisfy this standard:

> Petitioner argues that the joint representation adversely affected the quality of the counsel he received in two ways: Leaphart did not negotiate a plea agreement resulting in a life sentence, and he failed to take advantage of petitioner's lesser culpability when compared with his coindictee Stevens. We find that neither argument provides a basis for relief.

> The notion that the prosecutor would have been receptive to a plea bargain is completely unsupported in the record. The evidence of both defendants' guilt, including their confessions, and eyewitness and tangible evidence, was overwhelming and uncontradicted; the prosecutor had no need for petitioner's eyewitness testimony to persuade the jury to convict Stevens and to sentence him to death. Mr. Burger tried to negotiate a plea with the district attorney for a life sentence. He flatly refused to even discuss it in any terms.

> The argument that his partner's representation of Stevens inhibited Leaphart from arguing petitioner's lesser culpability because such reliance would be prejudicial to Stevens is also unsupported. Because the trials were separate, Leaphart would have had no particular reason for concern about the possible impact of the tactics in petitioner's trial on the outcome of Stevens' trial.

c. *Mickens v. Taylor*

In *Mickens v. Taylor*, <u>535 U.S. 162 (2002)</u>, involving defense counsel who had been representing his client's victim at the time of the victim's death, Justice Scalia ruled for the 5-to-4 majority that reversal need not be automatic every time a trial court fails to inquire into a potential conflict:

> The rule applied when the trial judge is not aware of the conflict (and thus not obligated to inquire) is that prejudice will be presumed only if the conflict has significantly affected counsel's performance—thereby rendering the verdict unreliable, even though *Strickland* prejudice cannot be shown. The trial court's awareness of a potential conflict neither renders it more likely that counsel's performance was significantly affected nor in any other way renders the verdict unreliable. Since this was not a case in which (as in *Holloway*) counsel protested his inability simultaneously to represent

multiple defendants; and since the trial court's failure to make the *Sullivan*-mandated inquiry does not reduce the petitioner's burden of proof; it was at least necessary, to void the conviction, for petitioner to establish that the conflict of interest adversely affected his counsel's performance.

Suppose that, in *Mickens*, the attorney had informed the trial judge of his prior representation of Hall, stated that he was conflicted, asked to be replaced, and the trial judge dismissed the request without further inquiry. Would automatic reversal be required in that case?

d. Waiver of Conflicts

In *Wheat v. United States*, 486 U.S. 153 (1988), defendant Wheat was charged with participating in a drug distribution conspiracy. Also charged were Gomez-Barajas and Bravo, who were represented by attorney Iredale. Gomez-Barajas was tried and acquitted on drug charges overlapping with those against Wheat. To avoid a trial on other charges, Gomez-Barajas offered to plead guilty to tax evasion and illegal importation of merchandise. At the commencement of Wheat's trial, the plea had not been accepted and could have been withdrawn. Bravo decided to plead guilty to one count of transporting marijuana. After the plea was accepted, Iredale notified the court that he had been asked to defend Wheat. When the Government objected because of a possible conflict of interest, the trial court refused to allow the representation. Wheat's conviction was upheld on appeal:

> A defendant may not insist on retaining an attorney who has a previous or ongoing relationship with an opposing party, even when the opposing party is the Government. Where a court justifiably finds an actual conflict of interest, it may decline a proffer of waiver, and insist that defendants be separately represented. The court must be allowed substantial latitude in refusing waivers of conflicts of interest not only in those rare cases where an actual conflict may be demonstrated before trial, but in the more common cases where a potential for conflict exists which may or may not burgeon into an actual conflict as the trial progresses.

e. Sex with Clients

In *Commonwealth v. Stote*, 456 Mass. 213, 922 N.E.2d 768 (2010), the Supreme Judicial Court of Massachusetts concluded that no unconstitutional conflict of interest existed where defense counsel at trial was discovered to have had an intimate relationship with an assistant district attorney (ADA) in the appellate division of the prosecutor's office, and a previous intimate relationship with the actual trial prosecutor. The court found that no *actual* conflict of interest existed with respect to the ongoing relationship as both defense counsel and the ADA swore that no confidential information about defendant was disclosed, and there was nothing in the record to suggest otherwise. The ADA added, moreover, that she had no involvement in the Commonwealth's appeal and knew nothing about the case, and this averment was corroborated by the trial prosecutor. Moreover, the court found that no conflict of interest existed with respect to defense counsel's prior relationship, which had ended seventeen years before trial, noting that "the trial judge pointed out that defense counsel 'had no hesitation whatsoever in lambasting the trial prosecutor for her alleged transgressions at trial' and concluded that 'he vigorously represented the defendant both at trial and on appeal.' "

Do these conclusions make sense to you? Does the fact that defense counsel "lambasted" the prosecutor at trial, for example, really indicate the absence of a conflict? What if defense counsel and the trial prosecutor were married or simply living together? Would that or should that make a difference? Should the defendant at least have been informed of that fact? What do you think?

Hypo 1: *Counsel Facing Disciplinary Complaints*

Defendants filed state bar disciplinary complaints against their respective defense counsel the week before trial. They claimed that their counsel had refused their requests to file motions to dismiss based upon speedy trial objections. Counsel moved to withdraw the day before trial based upon the conflict presented by the disciplinary complaints, but the trial court denied their requests finding no merit to their speedy trial claims. Defendants were convicted of mail fraud, conspiracy to commit mail fraud, aggravated identity theft, conspiracy to commit identity theft, and illegal monetary transactions. They now claim they were denied the effective assistance of counsel based on the conflict of interest posed by the pending disciplinary complaints against their lawyers. Were they? *United States v. Gandy*, 926 F.3d 248 (6th Cir. 2019).

Hypo 2: *Retained Counsel & Ineffectiveness*

Should a non-indigent defendant be able to complain that his or her retained counsel was "ineffective?" As a general rule, non-indigent defendants have the right to choose the counsel they prefer (subject, of course, to their ability to pay the attorney's fees and the attorney's willingness to take the case). If the non-indigent chooses poorly and counsel commits prejudicial error, should that conviction be reversed for ineffectiveness?

Hypo 3: *Lump Sum Fees & Conflicts*

Has defense counsel rendered ineffective assistance of counsel as a result of a conflict of interest when he was paid a lump sum amount for his representation of a client rather than on an hourly basis? Defendant argued that this compensation agreement created an inherent and irreconcilable conflict of interest because both counsel's compensation and the costs for investigative and expert services were covered by a lump sum fee. Defendant asserted that this circumstance created a financial disincentive for counsel to adequately investigate and prepare his case. What do you think? *See People v. Doolin*, 45 Cal.4th 390, 87 Cal. Rptr.3d 209, 198 P.3d 11 (2009).

E. The *Griffin-Douglas* Doctrine

In *Griffin v. Illinois*, 351 U.S. 12 (1956), the Supreme Court concluded that an indigent prisoner appealing from conviction in state court had a Fourteenth Amendment right (under both the due process and equal protection clauses) to a free transcript of the trial proceedings where such transcripts were often a practical necessity for securing an appeal. In a plurality opinion, writing for four justices, Justice Black concluded that "there can be no equal justice where the kind of trial a man [*sic*] gets depends on the amount of money he has. Destitute defendants must be afforded as adequate appellate review as defendants who have money enough to buy transcripts."

Thereafter, the Court held in *Douglas v. California*, 372 U.S. 353 (1963), a companion case to *Gideon*, that indigent convicted defendants have a Fourteenth Amendment right (under both the due process and equal protection clauses) to the assistance of counsel on a first appeal where the state has granted them the right to appeal (as opposed to those instances where entitlement to appeal is only discretionary). Justice Douglas opined that "where the merits of the one and only appeal an indigent has as of right are decided without benefit of counsel, we think an unconstitutional line has been drawn between rich and poor."

> **Food for Thought**
>
> As then-Justice Rehnquist acknowledged in *Ross v. Moffitt*, indigent defendants are "somewhat handicapped' as compared to more affluent defendants by that decision, requiring only an "adequate"—but not an *equal*—opportunity to present one's claims. Does the Constitution require that the government address and relieve such handicaps?

Subsequently, the Court declined to extend this so-called "*Griffin-Douglas* Doctrine" so as to require a Fourteenth Amendment entitlement to counsel by indigents in discretionary state appeals and applications for review to the Supreme Court, holding that "the duty of the State under our cases is not to duplicate the legal arsenal that may be privately retained by a criminal defendant in a continuing effort to reverse his conviction, but only to assure the indigent defendant an adequate opportunity to present his claims fairly in the context of the State's appellate process." *Ross v. Moffitt*, 417 U.S. 600, 616 (1974).

The Supreme Court's 2005 decision in *Halbert v. Michigan* made it clear, however, that *Ross* did not supplant the Court's *Griffin-Douglas* commitment to equal justice for rich and poor:

Halbert v. Michigan

545 U.S. 605 (2005).

JUSTICE GINSBURG delivered the opinion of the Court.

In 1994, Michigan voters approved a proposal amending the State Constitution to provide that "an appeal by an accused who pleads guilty or nolo contendere shall be by leave of the court." Thereafter, several Michigan state judges began to deny appointed appellate counsel to indigents convicted by plea. Rejecting challenges based on the Equal Protection and Due Process Clauses of the Fourteenth Amendment to the Federal Constitution, the Michigan Supreme Court upheld this practice.

Hear It

You can hear the oral argument in *Halbert* at http://www.oyez.org/cases/2000-2009/2004/2004_03_10198.

Petitioner Antonio Dwayne Halbert, convicted on his plea of nolo contendere, sought the appointment of counsel to assist him in applying for leave to appeal to the Michigan Court of Appeals. The state trial court and the Court of Appeals denied Halbert's requests for appointed counsel, and the Michigan Supreme Court declined review.

Michigan Court of Appeals review of an application for leave to appeal, Halbert contends, ranks as a first-tier appellate proceeding requiring appointment of counsel under *Douglas v. California*, 372 U.S. 353 (1963). Michigan urges that appeal to the State Court of Appeals is discretionary and, for an appeal of that order, *Ross v. Moffitt*, 417 U.S. 600 (1974), holds counsel need not be appointed. Today, we conclude that Halbert's case is properly ranked with *Douglas* rather than *Ross*. Accordingly, we hold that the Due Process and Equal Protection Clauses require the appointment of counsel for defendants, convicted on their pleas, who seek access to first-tier review in the Michigan Court of Appeals.

The Federal Constitution imposes on the States no obligation to provide appellate review of criminal convictions. Having provided such an avenue, however, a State may not "bolt the door to equal justice" to indigent defendants. *Griffin* held that, when a State conditions an appeal from a conviction on the provision of a trial transcript, the State must furnish free transcripts to indigent defendants who seek to appeal. *Douglas* relied on *Griffin*'s reasoning to hold that, in first appeals as of right, States must appoint counsel to represent indigent defendants. *Ross* held, however, that a State need not appoint counsel to aid a poor person in discretionary appeals to the State's highest court, or in petitioning for review in this Court.

Cases on appeal barriers encountered by persons unable to pay their own way, we have observed, "cannot be resolved by resort to easy slogans or pigeonhole analysis." Our decisions in point reflect both equal protection and due process concerns. The equal protection concern relates to the legitimacy of fencing out would-be appellants based solely on their inability to pay core costs, while the due process concern homes in on the essential fairness of the state-ordered proceedings.

Two considerations were key to our decision in *Douglas* that a State is required to appoint counsel for an indigent defendant's first-tier appeal as of right. First, such an appeal entails an adjudication on the "merits." Second, first-tier review differs from subsequent appellate stages at which the claims have once been presented by appellate counsel and passed upon by an appellate court.

In *Ross*, we explained why the rationale of *Douglas* did not extend to the appointment of counsel for an indigent seeking to pursue a second-tier discretionary appeal to the North Carolina Supreme Court or, thereafter, certiorari review in this Court. The North Carolina Supreme Court, in common with this Court we perceived, does not sit as an error-correction instance. Principal criteria for state high court review, we noted, included "whether the subject matter of the appeal has significant public interest, whether the cause involves legal principles of major significance to the jurisprudence of the State, and whether the decision below is in probable conflict" with the court's precedent. Further, we pointed out, a defendant who had already benefitted from counsel's aid in a first-tier appeal as of right would have, "at the very least, a transcript or other record of trial proceedings, a brief on his behalf in the Court of Appeals setting forth his claims of error, and in many cases an opinion by the Court of Appeals disposing of his case."

Halbert's case is framed by these two prior decisions of this Court concerning state-funded appellate counsel, *Douglas* and *Ross*. The question before us is essentially one of classification: With which of those decisions should the instant case be aligned? We hold that *Douglas* provides the controlling instruction. Two aspects of the Michigan Court of Appeals' process following plea-based convictions lead us to that conclusion. First, in determining how to dispose of an application for leave to appeal, Michigan's intermediate appellate court looks to the merits of the claims made in the application. Second, indigent defendants pursuing first-tier review in the Court of Appeals are generally ill equipped to represent themselves.

A defendant who pleads guilty or nolo contendere in a Michigan court does not thereby forfeit all opportunity for appellate review. Although he relinquishes access to an appeal as of right, he is entitled to apply for leave to appeal, and that entitlement is officially conveyed to him. Of critical importance, the tribunal to which he addresses his application, the Michigan Court of Appeals, unlike the Michigan Supreme Court, sits as an error-correction instance.

Whether formally categorized as the decision of an appeal or the disposal of a leave application, the Court of Appeals' ruling on a plea-convicted defendant's claims provides the first, and likely the only, direct review the defendant's conviction and sentence will receive. Parties like Halbert, however, are disarmed in their endeavor to gain first-tier review. As the Court in *Ross* emphasized, a defendant seeking State Supreme Court review following a first-tier appeal as of right earlier had the assistance of appellate counsel. The attorney appointed to serve at the intermediate appellate court level will have reviewed the trial court record, researched the legal issues, and prepared a brief reflecting that review and research. The defendant seeking second-tier review may also be armed with an opinion of the intermediate appellate court addressing the issues counsel raised. A first-tier review applicant, forced to act *pro se*, will face a record unreviewed by appellate counsel, and will be equipped with no attorney's brief prepared for, or reasoned opinion by, a court of review.

Persons in Halbert's situation are particularly handicapped as self-representatives. Approximately 70% of indigent defendants represented by appointed counsel plead guilty, and 70% of those convicted are incarcerated. Sixty-eight percent of the state prison population did not complete high school, and many lack the most basic literacy skills. Seven out of ten inmates fall in the lowest two out of five levels of literacy— marked by an inability to do such basic tasks as write a brief letter to explain an error on a credit card bill, use a bus schedule, or state in writing an argument made in a lengthy newspaper article. Many, Halbert among them, have learning disabilities and mental impairments.

Navigating the appellate process without a lawyer's assistance is a perilous endeavor for a layperson, and well beyond the competence of individuals, like Halbert, who have little education, learning disabilities, and mental impairments. Appeals by defendants convicted on their pleas may involve myriad and often complicated substantive issues, and may be no less complex than other appeals. One who pleads guilty or nolo contendere may still raise on appeal constitutional defects that are irrelevant to his factual guilt, double jeopardy claims requiring no further factual record, jurisdictional defects, challenges to the sufficiency of the evidence at the preliminary examination, preserved entrapment claims, mental competency claims, factual basis claims, claims that the state had no right to proceed in the first place, including claims that a defendant was charged under an inapplicable statute, and claims of ineffective assistance of counsel.

While the State has a legitimate interest in reducing the workload of its judiciary, providing indigents with appellate counsel will yield applications easier to comprehend. Michigan's Court of Appeals would still have recourse to summary denials of leave applications in cases not warranting further review. And when a defendant's case presents no genuinely arguable issue, appointed counsel may so inform the court.

For the reasons stated, we vacate the judgment of the Michigan Court of Appeals and remand the case for further proceedings not inconsistent with this opinion.

JUSTICE THOMAS, with whom JUSTICE SCALIA joins, and with whom the CHIEF JUSTICE joins in part, dissenting.

The majority holds that Michigan's system is constitutionally inadequate. It finds that all plea-convicted indigent defendants have the right to appellate counsel when seeking leave to appeal. *Douglas*, however, does not support extending the right to counsel to any form of discretionary review, as *Ross v. Moffitt*, and later cases make clear. Moreover, Michigan has not engaged in the sort of invidious discrimination against indigent defendants that *Douglas* condemns. Michigan has done no more than recognize the undeniable difference between defendants who plead guilty and those who maintain their innocence, in an attempt to divert resources from largely frivolous appeals to more meritorious ones. The majority substitutes its own policy preference for that of Michigan voters, and it does so based on an untenable reading of *Douglas*.

Today the Court confers on defendants convicted by plea a right nowhere to be found in the Constitution or this Court's cases. It does so at the expense of defendants whose claims are, on average, likely more meritorious. I respectfully dissent.

* * *

One of the most significant applications of the *Griffin-Douglas* Doctrine in the criminal justice system involves the question of what assistance—other than defense counsel—the government must provide to indigent defendants.

Ake v. Oklahoma

470 U.S. 68 (1985).

JUSTICE MARSHALL delivered the opinion of the Court.

The issue in this case is whether the Constitution requires that an indigent defendant have access to the psychiatric examination and assistance necessary to prepare an effective defense based on his mental condition, when his sanity at the time of the offense is seriously in question.

Late in 1979, Glen Burton Ake was arrested and charged with murdering a couple and wounding their two children. His behavior at arraignment, and in other prearraignment incidents at the jail, was so bizarre that the trial judge, *sua sponte*, ordered him to be examined by a psychiatrist "for the purpose of advising with the Court as to his impressions of whether the Defendant may need an extended period of mental observation." The examining psychiatrist reported: "At times Ake appears to be frankly delusional. He claims to be the 'sword of vengeance' of the Lord and that he will sit at the left hand of God in heaven." He diagnosed Ake as a probable paranoid schizophrenic and recommended a prolonged psychiatric evaluation to determine whether Ake was competent to stand trial.

In March, Ake was committed to a state hospital to be examined with respect to his "present sanity," i.e., his competency to stand trial. On April 10, less than six months after the incidents for which Ake was indicted, the chief forensic psychiatrist at the state hospital informed the court that Ake was not competent to stand trial. The court then held a competency hearing, at which a psychiatrist testified:

> "Ake is a psychotic. His psychiatric diagnosis was that of paranoid schizophrenia—chronic, with exacerbation, that is with current upset, and that in addition he is dangerous. Because of the severity of his mental illness and because of the intensities of his rage, his poor control, his delusions, he requires a maximum security facility within—I believe—the State Psychiatric Hospital system."

The court found Ake to be a "mentally ill person in need of care and treatment" and incompetent to stand trial, and ordered him committed to the state mental hospital.

Six weeks later, the chief forensic psychiatrist informed the court that Ake had become competent to stand trial. At the time, Ake was receiving 200 milligrams of Thorazine, an antipsychotic drug, three times daily, and the psychiatrist indicated that, if Ake continued to receive that dosage, his condition would remain stable. The State then resumed proceedings against Ake.

At a pretrial conference in June, Ake's attorney informed the court that his client would raise an insanity defense. To enable him to prepare and present such a defense adequately, the attorney stated, a psychiatrist would have to examine Ake with respect to his mental condition at the time of the offense. During Ake's 3-month stay at the state hospital, no inquiry had been made into his sanity at the time of the offense, and, as an indigent, Ake could not afford to pay for a psychiatrist. Counsel asked the court either to arrange to have a psychiatrist perform the examination, or to provide funds to allow the defense to arrange one. The trial judge rejected counsel's argument that the Federal Constitution requires that an indigent defendant receive the assistance of a psychiatrist when that assistance is necessary to the defense, and he denied the motion for a psychiatric evaluation at state expense.

Ake was tried for two counts of murder in the first degree, a crime punishable by death in Oklahoma, and for two counts of shooting with intent to kill. At the guilt phase of trial, his sole defense was insanity. Although defense counsel called to the stand and questioned each of the psychiatrists who had examined Ake at the state hospital, none testified about his mental state at the time of the offense because none had examined him on that point. The prosecution, in turn, asked each of these psychiatrists whether he had performed or seen the results of any examination diagnosing Ake's mental state at the time of the offense, and each doctor replied that he had not. As a result, there was no expert testimony for either side on Ake's sanity at the time of the offense. The jurors were then instructed that Ake could be found not guilty by reason of insanity if he did not have the ability to distinguish right from wrong at the time of the alleged offense. They were further told that Ake was to be presumed sane at the time of the crime unless he presented evidence sufficient to raise a reasonable doubt about his sanity at that time. If he raised such a doubt in their minds, the jurors were informed, the burden of proof shifted to the State to prove sanity beyond a reasonable doubt. The jury rejected Ake's insanity defense and returned a verdict of guilty on all counts.

At the sentencing proceeding, the State asked for the death penalty. No new evidence was presented. The prosecutor relied significantly on the testimony of the state psychiatrists who had examined Ake, and who had testified at the guilt phase that Ake was dangerous to society, to establish the likelihood of his future dangerous behavior. Ake had no expert witness to rebut this testimony or to introduce on his behalf evidence in mitigation of his punishment. The jury sentenced Ake to death on each of the two murder counts, and to 500 years' imprisonment on each of the two counts of shooting with intent to kill.

The Oklahoma Court of Criminal Appeals upheld Ake's conviction on appeal. We hold that when a defendant has made a preliminary showing that his sanity at the time of the offense is likely to be a significant factor at trial, the Constitution requires that a State provide access to a psychiatrist's assistance on this issue if the defendant cannot otherwise afford one.

This Court has long recognized that when a State brings its judicial power to bear on an indigent defendant in a criminal proceeding, it must take steps to assure that the defendant has a fair opportunity to present his defense. This elementary principle, grounded in significant part on the Fourteenth Amendment's due process guarantee of fundamental fairness, derives from the belief that justice cannot be equal where, simply as a result of his poverty, a defendant is denied the opportunity to participate meaningfully in a judicial proceeding in which his liberty is at stake. In recognition of this right, this Court held almost 30 years ago that once a State offers to criminal defendants the opportunity to appeal their cases, it must provide a trial transcript to an indigent defendant if the transcript is necessary to a decision on the merits of the appeal. *Griffin v. Illinois*, 351 U.S. 12 (1956). Since then, this Court has held that an indigent defendant may not be required to pay a fee before filing a notice of appeal of his conviction, that an indigent defendant is entitled to the assistance of counsel at trial, and on his first direct appeal as of right, and that such assistance must be effective.

Meaningful access to justice has been the consistent theme of these cases. We recognized long ago that mere access to the courthouse doors does not by itself assure a proper functioning of the adversary process, and that a criminal trial is fundamentally unfair if the State proceeds against an indigent defendant without making certain that he has access to the raw materials integral to the building of an effective defense. Thus, while the Court has not held that a State must purchase for the indigent defendant all the assistance that his wealthier counterpart might buy, it has often reaffirmed that fundamental fairness entitles indigent defendants to "an adequate opportunity to present their claims fairly within the adversary system." To implement this principle, we have focused on identifying the basic tools of an adequate defense or appeal, and we have required that such tools be provided to those defendants who cannot afford to pay for them.

To say that these basic tools must be provided is, of course, merely to begin our inquiry. In this case we must decide whether, and under what conditions, the participation of a psychiatrist is important enough to preparation of a defense to require the State to provide an indigent defendant with access to competent psychiatric assistance in preparing the defense. Three factors are relevant to this determination. The first is the private interest that will be affected by the action of the State. The second is the governmental interest that will be affected if the safeguard is to be provided. The third is the probable value of the additional or substitute procedural safeguards that are sought, and the risk of an erroneous deprivation of the affected interest if those safeguards are not provided.

The private interest in the accuracy of a criminal proceeding that places an individual's life or liberty at risk is almost uniquely compelling. Indeed, the host of safeguards fashioned by this Court over the years to diminish the risk of erroneous conviction stands as a testament to that concern. The interest of the individual in the outcome of the State's effort to overcome the presumption of innocence is obvious and weighs heavily in our analysis.

We consider, next, the interest of the State. Oklahoma asserts that to provide Ake with psychiatric assistance on the record before us would result in a staggering burden to the State. We are unpersuaded by this assertion. Many States, as well as the Federal Government, currently make psychiatric assistance available to indigent defendants, and they have not found the financial burden so great as to preclude this assistance. This is especially so when the obligation of the State is limited to provision of one competent psychiatrist, as it is in many States, and as we limit the right we recognize today. At the same time, it is difficult to identify any interest of the State, other than that in its economy, that weighs against recognition of this right. The State's interest in prevailing at trial—unlike that of a private litigant—is necessarily tempered by its interest in the fair and accurate adjudication of criminal cases. Thus, also unlike a private litigant, a State may not legitimately assert an interest in maintenance of a strategic advantage over the defense, if the result of that advantage is to cast a pall on the accuracy of the verdict obtained. We therefore conclude that the governmental interest in denying Ake the assistance of a psychiatrist is not substantial, in light of the compelling interest of both the State and the individual in accurate dispositions.

Last, we inquire into the probable value of the psychiatric assistance sought, and the risk of error in the proceeding if such assistance is not offered. We begin by considering the pivotal role that psychiatry has come to play in criminal proceedings. More than 40 States, as well as the Federal Government, have decided either through legislation or judicial decision that indigent defendants are entitled, under certain circumstances, to the assistance of a psychiatrist's expertise. These statutes and court decisions reflect a reality that we recognize today, namely, that when the State has made the defendant's mental condition relevant to his criminal culpability and to the punishment he might suffer, the assistance of a psychiatrist may well be crucial to the defendant's ability to marshal his defense. In this role, psychiatrists gather facts, through professional examination, interviews, and elsewhere, that they will share with the judge or jury; they analyze the information gathered and from it draw plausible conclusions about the defendant's mental condition, and about the effects of any disorder on behavior; and they offer opinions about how the defendant's mental condition might have affected his behavior at the time in question.

Psychiatry is not an exact science, and psychiatrists disagree widely and frequently on what constitutes mental illness, on the appropriate diagnosis to be attached to given behavior and symptoms, on cure and treatment, and on likelihood of future dangerousness. Perhaps because there often is no single, accurate psychiatric conclusion on legal insanity in a given case, juries remain the primary fact-finders on this issue, and they must resolve differences in opinion within the psychiatric profession on the basis of the evidence offered by each party. When jurors make this determination about issues that inevitably are complex and foreign, the testimony of psychiatrists can be crucial and a virtual necessity if an insanity plea is to have any chance of success. In so saying, we neither approve nor disapprove the widespread reliance on psychiatrists but instead recognize the unfairness of a contrary holding in light of the evolving practice.

Food for Thought

In this day and age when it may appear that no two psychological experts ever hold the same viewpoint, what accounts for the lower courts' reluctance to provide such services? The obvious answer is the slippery slope. If you provide a psychiatrist, then won't you need to provide investigators, and medical examiners, and accident reconstruction professionals, and ballistics experts, and DNA specialists, and jury consultants, etc., etc. When have you left the realm of "basic tools' and simply provided a "defense consultant" (as Justice Rehnquist worries in his omitted dissent). At a time when it stretches governmental units' budgets simply to provide indigents with appointed counsel, where would the money come from for such "extravagances"?

The foregoing leads inexorably to the conclusion that, without the assistance of a psychiatrist to conduct a professional examination on issues relevant to the defense, to help determine whether the insanity defense is viable, to present testimony, and to assist in preparing the cross-examination of a State's psychiatric witnesses, the risk of an inaccurate resolution of sanity issues is extremely high. With such assistance, the defendant is fairly able to present at least enough information to the jury, in a meaningful manner, as to permit it to make a sensible determination.

We therefore hold that when a defendant demonstrates to the trial judge that his sanity at the time of the offense is to be a significant factor at trial, the State must, at a minimum, assure the defendant access to a competent psychiatrist who will conduct an appropriate examination and assist in evaluation, preparation, and presentation of the defense. This is not to say, of course, that the indigent defendant has a constitutional right to choose a psychiatrist of his personal liking or to receive funds to hire his own. Our concern is that the indigent defendant have access to a competent psychiatrist for the purpose we have discussed, and as in the case of the provision of counsel we leave to the States the decision on how to implement this right.

Ake also was denied the means of presenting evidence to rebut the State's evidence of his future dangerousness. The foregoing discussion compels a similar conclusion in the context of a capital sentencing proceeding, when the State presents psychiatric evidence of the defendant's future dangerousness. We have repeatedly recognized the defendant's compelling interest in fair adjudication at the sentencing phase of a capital case. The State, too, has a profound interest in assuring that its ultimate sanction is not erroneously imposed, and we do not see why monetary considerations should be more persuasive in this context than at trial.

We turn now to apply these standards to the facts of this case. On the record before us, it is clear that Ake's mental state at the time of the offense was a substantial factor in his defense, and that the trial court was on notice of that fact when the request for a court-appointed psychiatrist was made. In addition, Ake's future dangerousness was a significant factor at the sentencing phase. The state psychiatrist who treated Ake at the state mental hospital testified at the guilt phase that, because of his mental illness, Ake posed a threat of continuing criminal violence. This testimony raised the issue of Ake's future dangerousness, which is an aggravating factor under Oklahoma's capital sentencing scheme, and on which the prosecutor relied at sentencing. We therefore conclude that Ake also was entitled to the assistance of a psychiatrist on this issue and that the denial of that assistance deprived him of due process.

Accordingly, we reverse and remand for a new trial.

Point for Discussion

Volunteer Psychologist Insufficient

In *McWilliams v. Dunn*, 137 S.Ct. 1790 (2017), a 5-to-4 majority of the Supreme Court held that Alabama failed to meet its obligations under *Ake v. Oklahoma* to provide a capital murder defendant, McWilliams, with access to a mental health expert to assist in the evaluation, preparation, and presentation of his defense at sentencing. Alabama argued that the State was exempted from its obligations under *Ake* because McWilliams already had the assistance of a psychologist from the University of Alabama who had volunteered to help defense counsel "in her spare time." Justice Breyer ruled for the majority that "even if the episodic assistance of an outside volunteer could relieve the State of its constitutional duty to ensure an indigent defendant access to meaningful expert assistance, no lower court has held or suggested that that psychologist was available to help, or might have helped, McWilliams at the judicial sentencing proceeding, the proceeding here at issue. Alabama does not refer to any specific record facts that indicate that she was available to the defense at this time."

"No one denies that the conditions that trigger application of *Ake* are present," the majority added, as "McWilliams is and was an 'indigent defendant,' his 'mental condition' was 'relevant to the punishment he might suffer,' and that 'mental condition,' i.e., his 'sanity at the time of the offense,' was 'seriously in question.'" Consequently, the Constitution, as interpreted in *Ake*, required the State to provide

McWilliams with "access to a competent psychiatrist who will conduct an appropriate examination and assist in evaluation, preparation, and presentation of the defense."

Hypo 1: *Additional Assistance*

Defendant James Kelly was convicted of the robbery, rape and murder of a college student who was working as a pizza delivery person and who had delivered a pizza to Kelly's girlfriend's apartment. He was sentenced to death. On appeal, Kelly contended that the trial judge erred by denying his pretrial request for provision of a private investigator and other experts. The trial judge had concluded that *Ake* does not give a defendant a constitutional right to any expert other than a psychiatrist. Kelly argued that, although he had consensual sex with the victim, he did not kill her, and that a private investigator would have enabled him to find key (unnamed) witnesses who would have helped to confirm his story. Moreover, he argued that he should have been provided with: 1) a forensic expert to assess the truthfulness of the prosecution's forensic experts (who "matched" his DNA with DNA found in the victim's vagina and on the victim's underwear and jeans); and 2) a medical expert to "go over" the medical examiner's report. Do you think that the trial court's ruling was correct? *See Rogers v. Oklahoma*, 890 P.2d 959 (Okla. Cr. App. 1995).

Hypo 2: *Transcript of Co-Defendant's Trial*

Should a defendant have the right under the *Griffin-Douglas* Doctrine to be provided with a free copy of his *co-defendant's* trial transcript when the two of them have had separate trials but the facts all arose out of the same incident? *See State v. Scott*, 131 Hawai'i 333, 319 P.3d 252 (2013).

Executive Summary

Right to Counsel. People have a right to the assistance of counsel for their defense at all critical stages of the proceedings when they are charged with a criminal offense, and if they are indigent and cannot afford counsel, one will be appointed for them.

Indigent Appointments. Indigent criminal defendants are only entitled to appointment of counsel when they will receive a punishment of at least one day in jail, whether or not that sentence is suspended.

Waiver of Right to Counsel. A waiver of the right to counsel must be knowing and intelligent.

Right to Proceed *Pro Se*. Competent criminal defendants have the right to waive the assistance of counsel and to represent themselves at trial (deemed "proceeding *pro se*").

Standby Counsel. Standby counsel may be appointed to assist a *pro se* criminal defendant in his or her defense, but counsel must endeavor to preserve the *pro se* defendant's actual control over the case, and is not allowed to destroy the jury's perception that the defendant is representing himself or herself.

Ineffective Assistance of Counsel. To obtain a reversal of a conviction on grounds of ineffective assistance under the seminal *Strickland* decision, a convicted defendant must show *both* that defense counsel's performance was deficient in that it fell below an objective standard of reasonableness *and* that counsel's deficient performance was prejudicial in that there was a reasonable probability that, absent counsel's errors, the fact-finder would have had a reasonable doubt respecting his or her guilt.

Conflicts of Interest. In order to establish ineffectiveness based upon defense counsel's conflict of interest, a defendant who raised no objection at trial must demonstrate that an actual conflict of interest adversely affected his or her lawyer's performance.

Other Assistance Beyond Counsel. An indigent criminal defendant has a right under the Fourteenth Amendment to assistance other than representation by a lawyer when that assistance constitutes a basic tool of an adequate defense or appeal, such as access to a psychological expert where defendant's sanity will be a significant issue at trial.

Major Themes

a. Indigent Representation Unequal—Although indigent criminal defendants are entitled to appointed counsel, they do not have the right to counsel of their choice, nor representation at every point in the proceedings, nor the full array of resources available to someone who can afford to retain his or her own attorney.

b. Ineffectiveness Difficult to Establish—Although criminal defendants are entitled to receive the effective assistance of counsel, ineffectiveness under the *Strickland* two-part test is extremely difficult to establish, and very few convictions are reversed on this basis.

For More Information

- AMERICAN BAR ASSOCIATION, *GIDEON'S* BROKEN PROMISE: AMERICA'S CONTINUING QUEST FOR EQUAL JUSTICE (2004).

- MARY SUE BACKUS & PAUL MARCUS, THE RIGHT TO COUNSEL IN CRIMINAL CASES: A NATIONAL CRISIS (2006).

- JOHN M. BURKOFF & NANCY M. BURKOFF, INEFFECTIVE ASSISTANCE OF COUNSEL (Thomson Reuters/West, annual editions).

- DAVID COLE, NO EQUAL JUSTICE (1999).

- David Harris, *The Constitution and Truth Seeking: A New Theory on Expert Services for Indigent Defendants,* 83 J. CRIM. L. & C. 469 (1992).

- Bruce R. Jacob, *Memories of and Reflections About Gideon v. Wainwright,* 33 STETSON L. REV. 181 (2003).

- Janet Moore, *The Antidemocratic Sixth Amendment,* 91 WASH. L. REV. 1705 (2016).

- Shaun Ossei-Owusu, *The Sixth Amendment Facade: The Racial Evolution of the Right to Counsel,* 167 U. PA. L. REV. 1161 (2019).

- Anne Bowen Poulin, *The Role of Standby Counsel in Criminal Cases: In the Twilight Zone of the Criminal Justice System,* 75 N.Y.U. L. REV. 676 (2000).

- John Rappaport, *The Structural Function of the Sixth Amendment Right to Counsel of Choice,* 2016 SUP. CT. REV. 117 (2016).

- Abbe Smith, *The Difference in Criminal Defense and the Difference It Makes,* 11 WASH.U. J.L.& POL'Y 83 (2003).

- Ken Strutin, *From Poverty to Personhood:* Gideon *Unchained,* 45 MITCHELL HAMLINE L. REV. 266 (2019).

- JAMES TOMKOVICZ, THE RIGHT TO THE ASSISTANCE OF COUNSEL (Greenwood Press 2002).

- RUSSELL L. WEAVER, JOHN M. BURKOFF, CATHERINE HANCOCK & STEVEN I. FRIEDLAND, PRINCIPLES OF CRIMINAL PROCEDURE Ch. 3 (7th ed. 2021).

Test Your Knowledge

To assess your understanding of the material in this chapter, click here to take a quiz.

CHAPTER 4

Arrest, Search & Seizure

A. Search Warrants

1. The Warrant Preference

The Supreme Court has instructed law enforcement officers and lower courts that it has a strong "preference" that warrants should be used even where a warrantless search would otherwise be constitutional. As the Court explained in a key 1984 decision:

> Because a search warrant provides the detached scrutiny of a neutral magistrate, which is a more reliable safeguard against improper searches than the hurried judgment of a law enforcement officer engaged in the often competitive enterprise of ferreting out crime, we have expressed a strong preference for warrants and declared that in a doubtful or marginal case a search under a warrant may be sustainable where one without it may fail.

United States v. Leon, <u>468 U.S. 897, 913–14 (1984)</u>, quoting *United States v. Chadwick*, <u>433 U.S. 1, 9 (1977)</u> (*Chadwick* quoting *Johnson v. United States*, <u>333 U.S. 10, 14 (1948)</u>), and *United States v. Ventresca*, <u>380 U.S. 102, 106 (1965)</u>.

> **Food for Thought**
>
> It is easy enough to point out that we want neutral magistrates—not the officers themselves—to make the probable cause determination necessary prior to a search or seizure. But why do you think that is the case? Don't we trust police officers? Should we?

2. The Warrant Requirement

The Supreme Court has also long established that a warrant "requirement" is—at least as a matter of theory—one of the first principles of its Fourth Amendment jurisprudence. As the Court explained in *Thompson v. Louisiana,* <u>469 U.S. 17, 19–20 (1984)</u>, *quoting Katz v. United States*, <u>389 U.S. 347, 357 (1967)</u>:

In a long line of cases, this Court has stressed that searches conducted outside the judicial process, without prior approval by judge or magistrate, are per se unreasonable under the Fourth Amendment-subject only to a few specifically established and well delineated exceptions. In all cases outside the exceptions to the warrant requirement the Fourth Amendment requires the interposition of a neutral and detached magistrate between the police and the "persons, houses, papers and effects" of the citizen.

Practice Pointer

Despite the fact that the warrant requirement is and remains such a firm theoretical fixture of Fourth Amendment law, the truth of the matter is that, in actual practice, the number of searches justified under one of the "few specifically established and well delineated exceptions" to the warrant requirement far outnumber the number of searches actually undertaken with a warrant. In short, while only a relatively few exceptions to the warrant requirement exist, most searches fall within these exceptional categories. As a result, a more useful and practical way to view this rule of law is to use the following rule of practice, even if it puts the cart before the horse: if a search is not justified by one of the warrant requirement "exceptions," then a search warrant must be obtained.

Why are warrants required? The Court answered this question in *Skinner v. Railway Labor Executives' Ass'n,* <u>489 U.S. 602, 621–22 (1989)</u> as follows:

An essential purpose of a warrant requirement is to protect privacy interests by assuring citizens subject to a search or seizure that such intrusions are not the random or arbitrary acts of government agents. A warrant assures the citizen that the intrusion is authorized by law, and that it is narrowly limited in its objectives and scope. A warrant also provides the detached and neutral scrutiny of a neutral magistrate, and thus ensures an objective determination whether an intrusion is justified in any given case.

3. Obtaining Warrants

In most jurisdictions, any law enforcement or prosecuting officer is authorized to apply for a search warrant simply by taking an application for a search warrant to a magistrate authorized by law to issue warrants. Typically, the application must include an attachment of one or more written affidavits. In such affidavits, the affiant must have sworn under oath to facts sufficient to establish

See It

What does a search warrant look like? Take a look at a blank federal search warrant. *See* <u>http://www.uscourts.gov/ sites/default/files/ao093.pdf</u>. What does a search warrant application look like? Take a look at a blank federal search warrant application. *See* <u>http://www. uscourts.gov/forms/law-enforcement-grand-jury-and-prosecution-forms/ application-search-warrant</u>.

probable cause to believe both that the items to be listed for seizure in the warrant are in fact evidence of specified criminal activity, and that these items are presently located at the premises for which the search warrant is being sought.

In addition, under F.R.Cr.P. 41(d)(3), "a magistrate judge may issue a warrant based on information communicated by telephone or other reliable electronic means." Many states have similar court rule provisions.

Exercise: *Preparing Affidavit*

You are an FBI Special Agent working in New York City. You have recently been contacted by e-mail by a confidential informant (CI), who has not revealed his or her identity to you, but who sent you information by e-mail six months ago identifying by name and address a person the CI said was selling sexually explicit images of children over the internet. (This is a federal crime. *See* FYI at right.). A subsequent investigation of that individual by your office revealed that he was indeed engaged in such criminal activity and criminal charges have been filed against him. In the message you have just received, the CI has stated as follows:

> I've got another scoop for you guys. In the past week, I've downloaded 67 GIF image files from a guy calling himself Nick9795 who is operating on USOL, the "United States OnLine" computer service. I paid Nick9795 $19.95 twice to gain access to these files. All of the pictures were of young children (boys and girls) engaged in gross sex acts with grown women. I hacked around in the USOL files and I think that Nick9795 is a guy named Gary Durham who lives in Oswego. GO GET HIM!!!

18 U.S.C. § 2252(A) provides, inter alia, that "any person who—(1) knowingly transports or ships using any means or facility of interstate or foreign commerce or in or affecting interstate or foreign commerce by any means including by computer or mails, any visual depiction, if—
(A) the producing of such visual depiction involves the use of a minor engaging in sexually explicit conduct; and (b) such visual depiction is of such conduct; (2) knowingly receives, or distributes, any visual depiction using any means or facility of interstate or foreign commerce or that has been mailed, or has been shipped or transported in or affecting interstate or foreign commerce or through the mails, contain any visual depiction that has been mailed, or has been shipped or transported using any means or facility of interstate or foreign commerce or in or affecting interstate or foreign commerce, or which was produced using materials which have been mailed or so shipped or transported, by any means including by computer, if—(i) the producing of such visual depiction involves the use of a minor engaging in sexually explicit conduct; and (ii) such visual depiction is of such conduct; Shall be punished as provided in subsection (b) of this section."

You have located four people named Gary Durham who live in Oswego, New York, and have placed a "dialed number recorder" (DNR) (a device which records outgoing phone numbers) on each of their home telephone lines. The DNR on one of the phone lines, a line belonging to Gary Durham of 234 Ash Street in Oswego, indicates numerous phone calls have been placed in the last three months to telephone numbers associated with USOL dial-in services. Accordingly, you have decided to obtain a search warrant to search 234 Ash Street for child pornography.

Go Online

For information about the FBI's Violent Crimes Against Children/Online Predators Program, *see* https://www.fbi.gov/investigate/violent-crime/cac.

You have tried to find out both the identity of "Nick 9795" and the frequency of his or her usage of USOL services. However, you have contacted USOL and they have refused to give you that information, citing customer privacy concerns. You have decided, accordingly, that you need to obtain a search warrant to search USOL's files in order to seize the file of "Nick9795."

Your class will be divided in half. The first group should prepare an affidavit based on the information set forth above to attempt to support the issuance of a search warrant for the Gary Durham residence in Oswego.

The second group should prepare an affidavit based on the information set forth above which will support the issuance of a search warrant for the "Nick9795" file at the offices of USOL.

(If, in preparing your affidavit, you decide that you do not possess sufficient information to support the issuance of a search warrant, you should include all the relevant information that you do possess in your affidavit, but add a separate page at the end of this assignment discussing what additional investigative techniques you would use in order to turn up additional information which would be sufficient to support the issuance of such a search warrant.)

4. Challenging Warrants

After a search has been made pursuant to a warrant, defense counsel can subsequently challenge the lawfulness of the search based upon the insufficiency of the supporting affidavit in two different ways. First, defense counsel can argue that the supporting affidavit *on its face* did not establish sufficient probable cause to support issuance of the warrant (and, hence, that the evidence seized pursuant to execution of the warrant must be suppressed as the fruits of an unconstitutional search). Second, defense counsel can try to challenge the accuracy or veracity of the statements in the affidavit which on their face establish probable cause. However, as the following Supreme Court decision makes clear, it is very difficult for counsel to win such a challenge, to "*go behind*" the warrant.

Franks v. Delaware

438 U.S. 154 (1978).

MR. JUSTICE BLACKMUN delivered the opinion of the Court.

This case presents an important and longstanding issue of Fourth Amendment law. Does a defendant in a criminal proceeding ever have the right, under the Fourth and Fourteenth Amendments, subsequent to the ex parte issuance of a search warrant, to challenge the truthfulness of factual statements made in an affidavit supporting the warrant?

In the present case the Supreme Court of Delaware held, as a matter of first impression for it, that a defendant under no circumstances may so challenge the veracity of a sworn statement used by police to procure a search warrant. We reverse, and we hold that, where the defendant makes a substantial prelimi-nary showing that a false statement knowingly and intentionally, or with reckless disregard for the truth, was included by the affiant in the warrant affidavit, and if the allegedly false state-ment is necessary to the finding of prob-able cause, the Fourth Amendment requires that a hearing be held at the

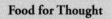

Food for Thought

Why do you think that the Delaware Supreme Court ruled below that a de-fendant could *never* "go behind" a search warrant affidavit? *Never!* Doesn't such a ruling mean that a search warrant could be issued based entirely upon lies and/ or conjecture? How do the majority and dissenting Justices deal with this issue?

defendant's request. In the event that at that hearing the allegation of perjury or reckless disregard is established by the defendant by a preponderance of the evidence, and, with the affidavit's false material set to one side, the affidavit's remaining content is insufficient to establish probable cause, the search warrant must be voided and the fruits of the search excluded to the same extent as if probable cause was lacking on the face of the affidavit.

Whether the Fourth and Fourteenth Amendments, and the derivative exclusion-ary rule ever mandate that a defendant be permitted to attack the veracity of a warrant affidavit after the warrant has been issued and executed, is a question that encounters conflicting values. The bulwark of Fourth Amendment protection, of course, is the Warrant Clause, requiring that, absent certain exceptions, police obtain a warrant from a neutral and disinterested magistrate before embarking upon a search. In deciding today that, in certain circumstances, a challenge to a warrant's veracity must be permitted, we derive our ground from language of the Warrant Clause itself, which surely takes the affiant's good faith as its premise: "No Warrants shall issue, but upon probable cause, supported by Oath or affirmation." Judge Frankel, in United States v. Halsey, 257 F. Supp. 1002, 1005 (S.D.N.Y. 1966), aff'd, Docket No. 31369 (CA2, June 12, 1967), put the matter simply: "When the Fourth Amendment demands a factual showing sufficient to comprise 'probable cause,' the obvious assumption is that there will be a *truthful* showing." This does not mean "truthful" in the sense that every fact recited in the warrant affidavit is necessarily correct, for probable cause may be founded upon hearsay and upon information received from informants, as well as upon information within the affiant's own knowledge that sometimes must be garnered hastily. But surely it is to be "truthful" in the sense that the information put forth is believed or appropriately accepted by the affiant as true. Because it is the magistrate who must determine independently whether there is probable cause, it would be an unthinkable imposition upon his authority if a warrant affidavit, revealed after the fact to contain a deliberately or recklessly false statement, were to stand beyond impeachment.

In saying this, however, one must give cognizance to competing values that lead us to impose limitations. They perhaps can be best addressed by noting the arguments of respondent and others against allowing veracity challenges. First, respondent argues that the exclusionary rule is not a personal constitutional right, but only a judicially created remedy extended where its benefit as a deterrent promises to outweigh the societal cost of its use; that the Court has declined to apply the exclusionary rule when illegally seized evidence is used to impeach the credibility of a defendant's testimony, is used in a grand jury proceeding, or is used in a civil trial; and that the Court similarly has restricted application of the Fourth Amendment exclusionary rule in federal *habeas corpus* review of a state conviction. Respondent argues that applying the exclusionary rule to another situation-the deterrence of deliberate or reckless untruthfulness in a warrant affidavit-is not justified for many of the same reasons that led to the above restrictions; interfering with a criminal conviction in order to deter official misconduct is a burden too great to impose on society.

Second, respondent argues that a citizen's privacy interests are adequately protected by a requirement that applicants for a warrant submit a sworn affidavit and by the magistrate's independent determination of sufficiency based on the face of the affidavit.

Third, it is argued that the magistrate already is equipped to conduct a fairly vigorous inquiry into the accuracy of the factual affidavit supporting a warrant application. He may question the affiant, or summon other persons to give testimony at the warrant proceeding. The incremental gain from a post-search adversary proceeding, it is said, would not be great.

Fourth, it is argued that it would unwisely diminish the solemnity and moment of the magistrate's proceeding to make his inquiry into probable cause reviewable in regard to veracity. The less final, and less deference paid to, the magistrate's determination of veracity, the less initiative will he use in that task.

Fifth, it is argued that permitting a post-search evidentiary hearing on issues of veracity would confuse the pressing issue of guilt or innocence with the collateral question as to whether there had been official misconduct in the drafting of the affidavit.

Sixth and finally, it is argued that a post-search veracity challenge is inappropriate because the accuracy of an affidavit in large part is beyond the control of the affiant. An affidavit may properly be based on hearsay, on fleeting observations, and on tips received from unnamed informants whose identity often will be properly protected from revelation under McCray v. Illinois, 386 U.S. 300 (1967).

None of these considerations is trivial. Indeed, because of them, the rule announced today has a limited scope, both in regard to when exclusion of the seized evidence is mandated, and when a hearing on allegations of misstatements must be accorded. But neither do the considerations cited by respondent and others have a fully controlling weight; we conclude that they are insufficient to justify an absolute ban on post-search impeachment of veracity. On this side of the balance, also, there are pressing considerations:

First, a flat ban on impeachment of veracity could denude the probable-cause requirement of all real meaning. The requirement that a warrant not issue "but upon probable cause, supported by Oath or affirmation," would be reduced to a nullity if a police officer was able to use deliberately falsified allegations to demonstrate probable cause, and, having misled the magistrate, then was able to remain confident that the ploy was worthwhile.

Second, the hearing before the magistrate not always will suffice to discourage lawless or reckless misconduct. The pre-search proceeding is necessarily ex parte, since the subject of the search cannot be tipped off to the application for a warrant lest he destroy or remove evidence. The usual reliance of our legal system on adversary proceedings itself should be an indication that an ex parte inquiry is likely to be less vigorous.

Third, the alternative sanctions of a perjury prosecution, administrative discipline, contempt, or a civil suit are not likely to fill the gap.

Fourth, allowing an evidentiary hearing, after a suitable preliminary proffer of material falsity, would not diminish the importance and solemnity of the warrant-issuing process. Our reluctance today to extend the rule of exclusion beyond instances of deliberate misstatements, and those of reckless disregard, leaves a broad field where the magistrate is the sole protection of a citizen's Fourth Amendment rights, namely, in instances where police have been merely negligent in checking or recording the facts relevant to a probable-cause determination.

Fifth, the claim that a post-search hearing will confuse the issue of the defendant's guilt with the issue of the State's possible misbehavior is footless. The hearing will not be in the presence of the jury. An issue extraneous to guilt already is examined in any probable-cause determination or review of probable cause.

Sixth and finally, as to the argument that the exclusionary rule should not be extended to a "new" area, we cannot regard any such extension really to be at issue here. Despite the deep skepticism of Members of this Court as to the wisdom of extending the exclusionary rule to collateral areas, such as civil or grand jury proceedings, the Court has not questioned, in the absence of a more efficacious sanction, the continued application of the rule to suppress evidence from the State's case where a Fourth Amendment violation has been substantial and deliberate. We see no principled basis for distinguishing between the question of the sufficiency of an affidavit, which also is subject to a post-search reexamination, and the question of its integrity.

Food for Thought

Does the result of this balancing-of-interests analysis make sense to you? Would you have reached a different conclusion? Why?

In sum, and to repeat with some embellishment what we stated at the beginning of this opinion: There is, of course, a presumption of validity with respect to the affidavit supporting the search warrant. To mandate an evidentiary hearing, the challenger's attack must be more than conclusory and must be supported by more than a mere desire to cross-examine. There must be allegations of deliberate falsehood or of reckless disregard for the truth, and those allegations must be accompanied by an offer of proof. They should point out specifically the portion of the warrant affidavit that is claimed to be false; and they should be accompanied by a statement of supporting reasons. Allegations of negligence or innocent mistake are insufficient. The deliberate falsity or reckless disregard whose impeachment is permitted today is only that of the affiant, not of any nongovernmental informant. Finally, if these requirements are met, and if, when material that is the subject of the alleged falsity or reckless disregard is set to one side, there remains sufficient content in the warrant affidavit to support a finding of probable cause, no hearing is required. On the other hand, if the remaining content is insufficient, the defendant is entitled, under the Fourth and Fourteenth Amendments, to his hearing. Whether he will prevail at that hearing is, of course, another issue.

Because of Delaware's absolute rule, its courts did not have occasion to consider the proffer put forward by petitioner Franks. The judgment of the Supreme Court of Delaware is reversed.

MR. JUSTICE REHNQUIST, with whom THE CHIEF JUSTICE joins, dissenting.

If the function of the warrant requirement is to obtain the determination of a neutral magistrate as to whether sufficient grounds have been urged to support the issuance of a warrant, that function is fulfilled at the time the magistrate concludes that the requirement has been met. Like any other determination of a magistrate, of a court, or of countless other fact-finding tribunals, the decision may be incorrect as a matter of law. Even if correct, some inaccurate or falsified information may have gone into the making of the determination. But unless we are to exalt as the *ne plus ultra* of our system of criminal justice the absolute correctness of every factual determination made along the tortuous route from the filing of the complaint or the issuance of an indictment to the final determination that a judgment of conviction was properly obtained, we shall lose perspective as to the purposes of the system as well as of the warrant requirement of the Fourth and Fourteenth Amendments.

> **Take Note**
>
> Don't miss the point made by the majority that even if an affidavit averment is shown to have been a deliberate, out-and-out lie on the part of the affiant, the warrant is still not necessarily defective. If a sufficient offer of proof is made by the defendant that the affidavit in question contains deliberately or recklessly-made misstatements or fails to include such omissions, the subsequent procedure is that the court holding a *Franks* hearing must consider the affidavit, redacted to strike the appropriate material and to add the appropriate omitted material, and consider whether or not the affidavit—as so redacted—establishes sufficient probable cause to search the specified premises for the specified objects of the search. If it does, then despite whatever lies that may have been included, the search warrant is still good and the exclusionary rule inapplicable. If probable cause does not exist in the affidavit as redacted, the warrant is defective and the exclusionary rule applies to all evidence derived from its execution.

> **Food for Thought**
>
> Do you agree with then-Justice Rehnquist? Isn't there some virtue in finality, even if the issuing magistrate got it wrong only because he or she was misled?

Point for Discussion

Omission of Information

The *Franks* test for determining when defense counsel may successfully "go behind" statements in a warrant affidavit also applies to an affiant's reckless or intentional *omission* of material information from an affidavit. If the affiant knows-and intentionally or recklessly withholds-information from an affidavit which would have cast doubt upon the existence of probable cause had it been considered by the issuing magistrate, the search warrant is defective and the fruits of its execution may be suppressed.

Hypo 1: *Omitted Information About Search Target's Incarceration*

A drive-by shooting occurred in Santa Maria, California. Shots were fired from a vehicle into an occupied home, striking and injuring a young boy. Informants told the police that the occupants were formerly associated with the Tangas gang and that the shooting was a reaction to their disassociation from the gang. Police officers obtained a list of names of alleged Tangas members believed to be closely associated with the suspected shooters. Based on this and other information, an officer obtained a "multiple location gang association warrant," authorizing a search of seven individuals' homes based upon the belief that these individuals might be harboring weapons or evidence related to the shooting. The warrant affidavit failed to disclose, however, that Javier Bravo, Jr., one of the seven individuals, was at that time and for over six months, incarcerated in the California prison system and therefore not only was he not present in the Bravo home when the warrant was executed, but he could not have been involved in the shooting or the storage of weapons used in it. Assuming that evidence of criminal activity was seized in the execution of that warrant and criminal charges brought against one of the occupants of the Bravo home, could that occupant suppress the evidence based upon the omission of this information relating to Bravo's incarceration from the warrant application? Does it matter that the officer who prepared the affidavit did not know that Bravo was in custody? Should it matter? *See Bravo v. City of Santa Maria*, 665 F.3d 1076 (9th Cir. 2011).

Hypo 2: *Powder Not Crack Cocaine*

Eugenio Negron sold crack cocaine to an undercover police officer. After he was arrested, Negron agreed to cooperate with the police and told them that he had recently bought fifty grams of "drugs" from a person he knew only as "Fat Back," who resided at 50 Putnam Circle. Based on this information, officers obtained a warrant to search that address and discovered 17.4 kilograms of *powder* cocaine. Fat Back (who turned out to be Jimmy Rosario) was arrested and now seeks to suppress the seized cocaine, arguing that the affidavit used to obtain the search warrant was inaccurate as the affiant averred that Negron had bought 50 grams of "crack cocaine" from Rosario, when Negron later testified that he bought 50 grams of powder cocaine from him. The officer who prepared the affidavit conceded that he had simply assumed that the purchase was of crack cocaine because Negron had been arrested carrying crack cocaine. Is this misstatement sufficient to support suppression of the cocaine seized under *Franks*? See *United States v. Rosario*, 810 F. Supp.2d 375 (D. Mass. 2011).

Exercise: *Motion to Suppress Based on Bad Affidavit*

Take home and review one of the affidavits prepared previously in the earlier Chapter 4 Exercise. You are now defense counsel representing Durham after the search pursuant to a search warrant based upon this affidavit has taken place (and has produced evidence that the U.S. Attorney's Office seeks to use against Durham in a federal criminal prosecution). Assuming that the warrant issued based solely upon this affidavit (and ignoring any standing issues that might be present), prepare a Brief in Support of Defendant Durham's Motion to Suppress (of no more than 5 pages in length) contending that the affidavit was either insufficient to support the warrant on its face and/or that it was recklessly or intentionally misleading within the meaning of *Franks*.

5. The Particularity Requirement

The Fourth Amendment expressly requires that "no Warrants shall issue, but upon probable cause, and particularly describing the place to be searched, and the persons or things to be seized." The Supreme Court has made clear that "the uniformly applied rule is that a search conducted pursuant to a warrant that fails to conform to the particularity requirement of the Fourth Amendment is unconstitutional." *Massachusetts v. Sheppard*, 468 U.S. 981, 988 n. 5 (1984).

To answer the question just *how* particular a description of the place to be searched must be to satisfy the particularity requirement, the Supreme Court has adopted the following test: "It is enough if the description is such that the officer with a search warrant can with reasonable effort ascertain and identify the place intended." *Steele v. U.S. No. 1*, 267 U.S. 498, 503 (1925). As to the things to be seized, the Supreme Court has stated that if the language in a search warrant description is so imprecise as to have an "indiscriminate sweep," the search warrant is, accordingly, "constitutionally intolerable." *Stanford v. Texas*, 379 U.S. 476, 486 (1965).

United States v. Grubbs

547 U.S. 90 (2006).

JUSTICE SCALIA delivered the opinion of the Court.

Federal law enforcement officers obtained a search warrant for respondent's house on the basis of an affidavit explaining that the warrant would be executed only after a controlled delivery of contraband to that location. We address two challenges to the constitutionality of this anticipatory warrant.

Respondent Jeffrey Grubbs purchased a videotape containing child pornography from a Web site operated by an undercover postal inspector. Officers from the Postal Inspection Service arranged a controlled delivery of a package containing the videotape to Grubbs' residence. A postal inspector submitted a search warrant application to a Magistrate Judge for the Eastern District of California, accompanied by an affidavit describing the proposed operation in detail. The affidavit stated:

Hear It

You can hear the oral argument in *Grubbs* at http://www.oyez.org/cases/2000-2009/2005/2005_04_1414.

"Execution of this search warrant will not occur unless and until the parcel has been received by a person(s) and has been physically taken into the residence. At that time, and not before, this search warrant will be executed by me and other United States Postal inspectors, with appropriate assistance from other law enforcement officers in accordance with this warrant's command."

In addition to describing this triggering condition, the affidavit referred to two attachments, which described Grubbs' residence and the items officers would seize. These attachments, but not the body of the affidavit, were incorporated into the requested warrant. The affidavit concluded: "Based upon the foregoing facts, I respectfully submit there exists probable cause to believe that the items set forth in Attachment B to this affidavit and the search warrant, will be found at Grubbs' residence, which residence is further described at Attachment A."

The Magistrate Judge issued the warrant as requested. Two days later, an undercover postal inspector delivered the package. Grubbs' wife signed for it and took the unopened package inside. The inspectors detained Grubbs as he left his home a few minutes later, then entered the house and commenced the search. Roughly 30 minutes into the search, Grubbs was provided with a copy of the warrant, which included both attachments but not the supporting affidavit that explained when the warrant would be executed. Grubbs consented to interrogation by the postal inspectors and admitted ordering the videotape. He was placed under arrest, and various items were seized, including the videotape. After moving unsuccessfully to suppress evidence seized during the search of his residence, Grubbs pleaded guilty to one count of receiving a visual depiction of a minor engaged in sexually explicit conduct, but reserved his right to appeal the denial of his motion to suppress. The Court of Appeals for the Ninth Circuit reversed.

An anticipatory warrant is a warrant based upon an affidavit showing probable cause that at some future time (but not presently) certain evidence of crime will be located at a specified place. Most anticipatory warrants subject their execution to some condition precedent other than the mere passage of time-a so-called "triggering condition." The affidavit at issue here, for instance, explained that "execution of the search warrant will not occur unless and until the parcel containing child pornography has been received by a person(s) and has been physically taken into the residence." If the government were to execute an anticipatory warrant before the triggering condition occurred, there would be no reason to believe the item described in the warrant could be found at the searched location; by definition, the triggering condition which establishes probable cause has not yet been satisfied when the warrant is issued. Grubbs argues that for this reason anticipatory warrants contravene the Fourth Amendment's provision that "no Warrants shall issue, but upon probable cause."

We reject this view, as has every Court of Appeals to confront the issue. Probable cause exists when there is a fair probability that contraband or evidence of a crime will be found in a particular

Take Note

Despite the prior unanimity in Courts of Appeals decisions on this point, *Grubbs* is notable because it is the *first* Supreme Court decision to expressly hold anticipatory warrants to be constitutional in the appropriate circumstances.

place. Because the probable-cause requirement looks to whether evidence will be found when the search is conducted, all warrants are, in a sense, "anticipatory." In the typical case where the police seek permission to search a house for an item they believe is already located there, the magistrate's determination that there is probable cause for the search amounts to a prediction that the item will still be there when the warrant is executed.

Anticipatory warrants are, therefore, no different in principle from ordinary warrants. They require the magistrate to determine (1) that it is now probable that (2) contraband, evidence of a crime, or a fugitive will be on the described premises (3) when the warrant is executed. It should be noted, however, that where the anticipatory warrant places a condition (other than the mere passage of time) upon its execution, the first of these determinations goes not merely to what will probably be found if the condition is met. (If that were the extent of the probability determination, an anticipatory warrant could be issued for every house in the country, authorizing search and seizure if contraband should be delivered-though for any single location there is no likelihood that contraband will be delivered.) Rather, the probability determination for a conditioned anticipatory warrant looks also to the likelihood that the condition will occur, and thus that a proper object of seizure will be on the described premises. In other words, for a conditioned anticipatory warrant to comply with the Fourth Amendment's requirement of probable cause, two prerequisites of probability must be satisfied. It must be true not only that if the triggering condition occurs there is a fair probability that contraband or evidence of a crime will be found in a particular place, but also that there is probable cause to believe the triggering condition will occur. The supporting affidavit must provide the magistrate with sufficient information to evaluate both aspects of the probable-cause determination.

In this case, the occurrence of the triggering condition—successful delivery of the videotape to Grubbs' residence—would plainly establish probable cause for the search. In addition, the affidavit established probable cause to believe the triggering condition would be satisfied. Although it is possible that Grubbs could have refused delivery of the videotape he had ordered, that was unlikely. The Magistrate therefore had a substantial basis for concluding that probable cause existed.

Take Note

Note the risk that exists when law enforcement officers obtain an anticipatory warrant, i.e. that the triggering condition upon which the warrant is based must *actually* occur; if it doesn't, the warrant is defective and unconstitutional.

The Ninth Circuit invalidated the anticipatory search warrant at issue here because the warrant failed to specify the triggering condition. The Fourth Amendment's particularity requirement, it held, "applies with full force to the conditions precedent to an anticipatory search warrant."

The Fourth Amendment, however, does not set forth some general "particularity requirement." It specifies only two matters that must be "particularly described" in the warrant: "the place to be searched" and "the persons or things to be seized." We have previously rejected efforts to expand the scope of this provision to embrace unenumerated matters.

Because the Fourth Amendment does not require that the triggering condition for an anticipatory search warrant be set forth in the warrant itself, the Court of Appeals erred in invalidating the warrant at issue here. The judgment of the Court of Appeals is reversed, and the case is remanded for further proceedings consistent with this opinion.

JUSTICE ALITO took no part in the consideration or decision of this case. JUSTICE SOUTER, with whom JUSTICE STEVENS and JUSTICE GINSBURG join, concurring in part and concurring in the judgment.

Practice Pointer

Even though the *Grubbs* decision holds that the Fourth Amendment does not require that the triggering condition in an anticipatory warrant be particularized in the warrant itself (as opposed to the affidavit, where it needs to be included in order to establish prospective probable cause), it nonetheless *should* be included as a matter of good practice. That's the dissenters' real concern, namely that an anticipatory warrant that doesn't particularize the triggering condition will end up being executed by officers who don't realize that there is such a condition and they might execute the warrant before the condition takes place, thus rendering the warrant defective.

The Court notes that a warrant's failure to specify the place to be searched and the objects sought violates an express textual requirement of the Fourth Amendment, whereas the text says nothing about a condition placed by the issuing magistrate on the authorization to search (here, delivery of the package of contraband). That textual difference is, however, no authority for neglecting to specify the point or contingency intended by the magistrate to trigger authorization, and the government should beware of banking on the terms of a warrant without such specification. The notation of a starting date was an established feature even of the objectionable 18th-century writs of assistance.

FYI

Contrary to the holding in *Grubbs*, Iowa's Supreme Court, applying its own state constitution, rejected the idea that search warrants could be based upon "future events." However, when federal officials conducted a valid search under *Grubbs*, based on an anticipatory warrant, the court held that the fruits of that search were admissible in a state court proceeding. *State v. Ramirez*, 895 N.W.2d 884 (Iowa 2017).

An issuing magistrate's failure to mention that condition can lead to several untoward consequences with constitutional significance. To begin with, a warrant that fails to tell the truth about what a magistrate authorized cannot inform the police officer's responsibility to respect the limits of authorization, a failing assuming real significance when the warrant is not executed by the official who applied for it and happens to know the unstated condition. The peril is that if an officer simply takes such a warrant on its face and makes the ostensibly authorized search before the unstated condition has been met, the search will be held unreasonable.

Hypo 1: *Wrong Resident*

An anticipatory search warrant was issued to search William Perkins' residence after a package DEA officers believed contained methamphetamine (due to a dog sniff) was delivered by an undercover agent. When the package was actually delivered to his home, however, Perkins was not there and it was accepted instead by his fiancée. Nonetheless, the officers immediately executed the warrant after she accepted the package, and they seized the methamphetamine that was inside the package and charged Perkins with its possession. Was this warrant lawfully executed since Perkins did not accept the package himself? Should the officers have waited for Perkins to come home? *See United States v. Perkins*, 887 F.3d 272 (6th Cir. 2018).

Hypo 2: *Cell Phone Search*

Based on a finding of probable cause, a judge issues a warrant to search a cell phone for evidence of defendant's drug dealing or his firing of a weapon. Must the warrant specify particular parts of the phone that may be searched, or may the warrant simply authorize the police to search the phone? What do you think? *See United States v. Bishop*, 910 F.3d 335 (7th Cir. 2018), *cert. denied*, 139 S.Ct. 1590 (2019).

Hypo 3: *Particularity & John Doe's DNA*

Following a serious sex crime (forcible rape), although police did not know the name of the perpetrator of the crime, they were able to isolate and identify his DNA from sperm found on the victim. Shortly before the statute of limitations expired, although the police were still unable to identify the perpetrator, they applied for a "John Doe" arrest warrant based on the perpetrator's DNA profile. Shortly thereafter, a police lab technician was able to match John Doe's DNA to that of a man found in a police database. The particularity requirement applies in the same fashion to arrest as to search warrants. Was it satisfied here, by a John Doe warrant that identified a suspect not by name, but only by his DNA profile? *See People v. Robinson,* 47 Cal.4th 1104, 104 Cal.Rptr.3d 727, 224 P.3d 55 (2010).

Hypo 4: *Seizing Safes*

Pursuant to a warrant authorizing them to search for stolen and forged checks, the police searched defendant's home. During the search, they found two locked safes capable of holding checks. Police seized the safes and transported them to the police station. When they were opened, they were found to contain methamphetamine. Defendant filed a motion to suppress on the basis that the safes were not particularly described in the search warrant and, hence, they could not be seized in order to be searched back at the police station. Is this a good argument? What if the safes had been unlocked or open when the police officers searched the home? Could they have been searched at that time? *See State v. Powell,* 306 S.W.3d 761 (Tex. Crim. App. 2010).

If executing officers mistakenly search the wrong search premises, i.e. a place not particularly described in the search warrant, that does not necessarily mean that the search is unconstitutional (or that the fruits of the search must be suppressed).

Maryland v. Garrison

480 U.S. 79 (1987).

Justice Stevens delivered the opinion of the Court.

Baltimore police officers obtained and executed a warrant to search the person of Lawrence McWebb and "the premises known as 2036 Park Avenue third floor apartment." When the police applied for the warrant and when they conducted the search pursuant to the warrant, they reasonably believed that there was only one apartment on the premises described in the warrant. In fact, the third floor was divided into two apartments, one occupied by McWebb and one by respondent Garrison. Before the officers executing the warrant became aware that they were in a separate apartment occupied by respondent, they had discovered the contraband that provided the basis for respondent's conviction for violating Maryland's Controlled Substances Act. The question presented is whether the seizure of that contraband was prohibited by the Fourth Amendment.

There is no question that the warrant was valid and was supported by probable cause. The trial court found, and the two appellate courts did not dispute, that after making a reasonable investigation, including a verification of information obtained from a reliable informant, an exterior examination of the three-story building at 2036 Park Avenue, and an inquiry of the utility company, the officer who obtained the warrant reasonably concluded that there was only one apartment on the third floor and that it was occupied by McWebb. Only after respondent's apartment had been entered and heroin, cash, and drug paraphernalia had been found did any of the officers realize that the third floor contained two apartments. As soon as they became aware of that fact, the search was discontinued. All of the officers reasonably believed that they were searching McWebb's apartment. No further search of respondent's apartment was made.

The manifest purpose of the particularity requirement was to prevent general searches. By limiting the authorization to search to the specific areas and things for which there is probable cause to search, the requirement ensures that the search will be carefully tailored to its justifications, and will not take on the character of the wide-ranging exploratory searches the Framers intended to prohibit. Thus, the scope of a lawful search is defined by the object of the search and the places in which there is probable cause to believe that it may be found. Just as probable cause to believe that a stolen lawnmower may be found in a garage will not support a warrant to search an upstairs bedroom, probable cause to believe that undocumented aliens are being transported in a van will not justify a warrantless search of a suitcase.

In this case there is no claim that the "persons or things to be seized" were inadequately described or that there was no probable cause to believe that those things might be found in "the place to be searched" as it was described in the warrant. With the benefit of hindsight, however, we now know that the description of that place was broader than appropriate because it was based on the mistaken belief that there was only one apartment on the third floor of the building at 2036 Park Avenue. The question is whether that factual mistake invalidated a warrant that undoubtedly would have been valid if it had reflected a completely accurate understanding of the building's floor plan.

Food for Thought

The police did not have probable cause to search Garrison's apartment. Was it really appropriate to interpret the Particularity Clause in such a way that its constitutional privacy protections are no longer present just because a police officer has made a mistake? What do you think?

Plainly, if the officers had known, or even if they should have known, that there were two separate dwelling units on the third floor of 2036 Park Avenue, they would have been obligated to exclude respondent's apartment from the scope of the requested warrant. But we must judge the constitutionality of their conduct in light of the information available to them at the time they acted. Those items of evidence that emerge after the warrant is issued have no bearing on whether or not a warrant was validly issued. Just as the discovery of contraband cannot validate a warrant invalid when issued, so is it equally clear that the discovery of facts demonstrating that a valid warrant was unnecessarily broad does not retroactively invalidate the warrant. The validity of the warrant must be assessed on the basis of the information that the officers disclosed, or had a duty to discover and to disclose, to the issuing Magistrate. On the basis of that information, we agree with the conclusion of all three Maryland courts that the warrant, insofar as it authorized a search that turned out to be ambiguous in scope, was valid when it issued.

The question whether the execution of the warrant violated respondent's constitutional right to be secure in his home is somewhat less clear. If the officers had known, or should have known, that the third floor contained two apartments before they entered the living quarters on the third floor, and thus had been aware of the error in the warrant, they would have been obligated to limit their search to McWebb's apartment. Moreover, as the officers recognized, they were required to discontinue the search of respondent's apartment as soon as they discovered that there were two separate units on the third floor and therefore were put on notice of the risk that they might be in a unit erroneously included within the terms of the warrant. The officers' conduct and the limits of the search were based on the information available as the search proceeded. While the purposes justifying a police search strictly limit the permissible extent of the search, the Court has also recognized the need to allow some latitude for honest mistakes that are made by officers in the dangerous and difficult process of making arrests and executing search warrants. The objective facts available to the officers at the time suggested no distinction between McWebb's apartment and the third-floor premises.

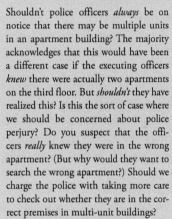

Food for Thought

Shouldn't police officers *always* be on notice that there may be multiple units in an apartment building? The majority acknowledges that this would have been a different case if the executing officers *knew* there were actually two apartments on the third floor. But *shouldn't* they have realized this? Is this the sort of case where we should be concerned about police perjury? Do you suspect that the officers *really* knew they were in the wrong apartment? (But why would they want to search the wrong apartment?) Should we charge the police with taking more care to check out whether they are in the correct premises in multi-unit buildings?

For that reason, the officers properly responded to the command contained in a valid warrant even if the warrant is interpreted as authorizing a search limited to McWebb's apartment rather than the entire third floor. Prior to the officers' discovery of the factual mistake, they perceived McWebb's apartment and the third-floor premises as one and the same; therefore their execution of the warrant reasonably included the entire third floor.[13]

The judgment of the Court of Appeals is reversed.

JUSTICE BLACKMUN, with whom JUSTICE BRENNAN and JUSTICE MARSHALL join, dissenting.

Even if one accepts the majority's view that there is no Fourth Amendment violation where the officers' mistake is reasonable, it is questionable whether that standard was met in this case. The place at issue here is a small multiple-occupancy building. Such forms of habitation are now common in this country, particularly in neighborhoods with changing populations and of declining affluence. Accordingly, any analysis of the "reasonableness" of the officers' behavior here must be done with this context in mind. In the Court's view, the "objective facts" did not put the officers on notice that they were dealing with two separate apartments on the third floor until the moment, considerably into the search after they had rummaged through a dresser and a closet in respondent's apartment and had discovered evidence incriminating him, when they realized their "mistake." The Court appears to base its conclusion that the officers' error here was reasonable on the fact that neither McWebb nor respondent ever told the officers during the search that they lived in separate apartments.

In my view, however, the "objective facts" should have made the officers aware that there were two different apartments on the third floor well before they discovered the incriminating evidence in respondent's apartment. Before McWebb happened to drive up while the search party was preparing to execute the warrant, one of the officers, Detective Shea, somewhat disguised as a construction worker, was already on the porch of the row house and was seeking to gain access to the locked first-floor door that permitted entrance into the building. From this vantage point he had time to observe the seven mailboxes and bells; indeed, he rang all seven bells, apparently in an effort to summon some resident to open the front door to the search party. A reasonable officer in Detective Shea's position, already aware that this was a multi-unit building and now armed with further knowledge of the number of units in the structure, would have conducted at that time more investigation to specify the exact location of McWebb's apartment before proceeding further. For example, he might have questioned another resident of the building.

A reasonable officer would have realized the mistake in the warrant during the moments following the officers' entrance to the third floor. In the open doorway to

---

[13]   We expressly distinguish the facts of this case from a situation in which the police know there are two apartments on a certain floor of a building, and have probable cause to believe that drugs are being sold out of that floor, but do not know in which of the two apartments the illegal transactions are taking place. A search pursuant to a warrant authorizing a search of the entire floor under those circumstances would present quite different issues from the ones before us in this case.

his apartment, they encountered respondent, clad in pajamas and wearing a half-body cast as a result of a recent spinal operation. It appears that respondent, together with McWebb and the passenger from McWebb's car, were shepherded into McWebb's apartment across the vestibule from his own. Once again, the officers were curiously silent. The informant had not led the officers to believe that anyone other than McWebb lived in the third-floor apartment; the search party had McWebb, the person targeted by the search warrant, in custody when it gained access to the vestibule; yet when they met respondent on the third floor, they simply asked him who he was but never where he lived. Had they done so, it is likely that they would have discovered the mistake in the warrant before they began their search.

Finally and most importantly, even if the officers had learned nothing from respondent, they should have realized the error in the warrant from their initial security sweep. Once on the third floor, the officers first fanned out through the rooms to conduct a preliminary check for other occupants who might pose a danger to them. As the map of the third floor demonstrates, the two apartments were almost a mirror image of each other-each had a bathroom, a kitchen, a living room, and a bedroom. Given the somewhat symmetrical layout of the apartments, it is difficult to imagine that, in the initial security sweep, a reasonable officer would not have discerned that two apartments were on the third floor, realized his mistake, and then confined the ensuing search to McWebb's residence.

Points for Discussion

a. Particularity & Affidavits

When faced with a challenge at a suppression hearing to the particularity of the description contained in a search warrant, courts generally look both to the actual descriptive language in the warrant itself and to the description contained in any accompanying affidavits, if such affidavits are physically attached to the warrant (and thus available to the executing officers for their consultation) and incorporated by suitable words of reference. Where there has been no such incorporation by reference, however, a warrant that does not otherwise satisfy the particularity requirement is unconstitutional. *See Groh v. Ramirez,* 540 U.S. 551 (2004).

b. Errors in Description

An error in the description of the place to be searched or the things to be seized in a search warrant does not render the warrant defective provided that other descriptive information in the warrant establishes with reasonable certainty the place to be searched or the things to be seized. *See, e.g., United States v. Brobst,* 558 F.3d 982, 992 (9th Cir. 2009) ("31 Driftwood Lane, Woods Bay, Montana" instead of "32877 Driftwood Lane, Bigfork, Montana" error OK where both the mailbox and the sign on the tree in front of the searched residence bore the search target's name); *United States v. Hang Le-Thy Tran,* 433 F.3d 472, 479–81 (6th Cir. 2006) ("937 28th Street S.W." instead of "931 28th Street S.W." error OK where executing officers knew correct address and mistake was typographic error); *State v. Grant,* 52 So.3d 149, 151–54 (La. Ct. App. 5 Cir. 2010) (434 Ocean Ave. instead of 474 Ocean Ave. and description of premises to be searched as a wooden structure with a tan door instead of stucco concrete structure with a white door errors held OK where "there was no reasonable probability that the wrong residence would be searched"); *State v. Stelly,* 304 Neb. 33, 932 N.W.2d 857, 868–69 (2019) (incorrect description of mobile phone as "ZTE" cell phone instead of "LG" cell phone held OK where latter was clearly the one lying near dead body); *People v. DeWitt,* 107 A.D.3d 1452, 1452–53, 967 N.Y.S.2d 547 (2013) (error in listing particularly-described vehicle under the heading "Persons" instead of "Vehicles" held OK).

c. Badly-Described Items & Properly-Described Items

Where an item to be seized has not been particularly described, a search warrant which has otherwise been lawfully obtained and executed remains constitutional with respect to any remaining items to be seized that have been properly described in the warrant. *See, e.g., State v. Tucker,* 133 N.H. 204, 575 A.2d 810, 813–15 (1990) (Opinion of former Justice Souter before he was appointed to the Supreme Court) ("it is not apparent why the public interest in prosecuting crime should be taxed by suppressing any evidence beyond that obtained under the ostensible authority of the warrant's unduly general element"). In addition, those items not "particularly described" may be seizable under the plain view doctrine.

d. Overbreadth in Description

The Supreme Court has upheld the seizure of a sawed off shotgun pursuant to a warrant description of "all firearms," even though the executing officers knew that the shooting under investigation was committed with a different "black sawed off shotgun with a pistol grip." As the Court reasoned, "even if the scope of the warrant were overbroad in authorizing a search for all guns when there was information only about a specific one, that specific one was a sawed-off shotgun with a pistol grip, owned by a known gang member, who had just fired the weapon five times in public in an attempt to murder another person. Under these circumstances-set forth in the warrant-it would not have been unreasonable for an officer to conclude that there was a 'fair probability' that the sawed-off shotgun was not the only firearm Bowen owned. And it certainly would have been reasonable for an officer to assume that Bowen's sawed-off shotgun was illegal. Evidence of one crime is not always evidence of several, but given Bowen's possession of one illegal gun, his gang membership, his willingness to use the gun to kill someone, and his concern about the police, a reasonable officer could conclude that there would be additional illegal guns among others that Bowen owned." *Messerschmidt v. Millender,* 565 U.S. 535, 548–49 (2012).

Hypo 1: *Searches of Multi-Unit Buildings*

Law enforcement officers had probable cause to believe that defendant Will Nelson Clark was dealing drugs from inside a multi-unit building at 1015 Fairfield Avenue and also from the front porch of that building. Accordingly, they obtained a search warrant to search the entire premises of that building, including "any and all persons present at this location during execution of said search warrant, all rooms, contents of those rooms, including any computers and hard drives of same, hallways, stairways, storage areas, basement, attic areas, closets, any and all locked and secured areas, locked safes or containers and porches to said address." In one of the downstairs apartments belonging to defendant Clark, executing officers seized a quantity of drugs, which subsequently tested as cocaine base, approximately $1703 in cash, and various items of drug paraphernalia. Was this a valid search? *See United States v. Clark,* 638 F.3d 89 (2d Cir. 2011). *See also State v. Rodrigues,* 145 Hawai'i 487, 454 P.3d 428, 435–38 (2019) ("Because the search warrant in this case failed to satisfy the particularity requirement of article I, section 7 of the Hawai'i Constitution, it was invalid. A search warrant for a multiple-occupancy building will be held invalid if it fails to describe the particular subunit to be searched.").

Hypo 2: *Search for "Ladies' Costume Jewelry"*

A search warrant authorized executing officers to seize, *inter alia,* "lady's [sic] costume jewelry" from Jose Garcia-Perlera's apartment. The police possessed probable cause to believe that Garcia-Perlera had broken into and ransacked a victim's home, stealing money, a laptop computer, and multiple items of costume jewelry. Was this warrant description sufficiently particular to justify the seizure of jewelry in the apartment, even non-costume jewelry? What do you think? *See Garcia-Perlera v. State,* 197 Md.App. 534, 14 A.3d 1164 (2011).

Hypo 3: *Search for "Stolen Items"*

A confidential informant who had provided reliable information in the past told police officers that he had seen "stolen items" at the residence of Sedric Sutton. The officers obtained a search warrant to search Sutton's home and found narcotics, $4,995 in cash, a handgun, and two digital scales. Sutton seeks to suppress these items, arguing that the search warrant was lacking in particularity. What result? Does it matter to this result that the executing officers did not find any "stolen items?" *See Sutton v. State*, 238 So.3d 1150 (Miss. 2018).

Hypo 4: *Searches of Computers*

Based on probable cause to believe that Payton was selling narcotics, a warrant was issued for the search of his home. The warrant particularly described "sales ledgers showing narcotics transactions such as pay/owe sheets," as well as "financial records of the person(s) in control of the residence or premises, bank accounts, loan applications, and income and expense records," but it did not explicitly authorize the search of computers. During the search, the police found no evidence relating to narcotics, but they did find a computer that was on with the screen saver activated. An officer moved the mouse and observed what he believed to be child pornography. The police then seized the computer on the grounds that they had the right to check it for records relating to drug transactions, and that they found the child pornography in "plain view" when they did. Payton claimed that, without specific authorization, the police had no right to examine his computer. Is he right? Did the search warrant authorize the officers to look at information on Payton's computer? Would it have made a difference if the officers had specified in their search warrant application that the records they were seeking might be in hard copy or electronic form? *See United States v. Payton*, 573 F.3d 859 (9th Cir. 2009).

Go Online

In the last couple of decades, searches and seizures of computers have posed a number of extremely complicated legal questions for courts and prosecutors and defense attorneys, as well. The law continues to develop on this subject, probably no faster than computer technology itself continues to develop. You might be interested in taking a look at the Justice Department's snapshot view of the developing law in this area. *See* Computer Crime and Intellectual Property Section, Criminal Division, U.S. Dept. of Justice, "Searching and Seizing Computers and Obtaining Electronic Evidence in Criminal Investigations" (Office of Legal Education, Executive Office for United States Attorneys 2009), http://www.justice.gov/criminal/cybercrime/docs/ssmanual2009.pdf. *See also* Office of the Attorney General, Memorandum: "Intake and Charging Policy for Computer Crime Matters" (September 11, 2014), https://www.justice.gov/criminal-ccips/file/904941/download; Office of Legal Education, Executive Office for United States Attorneys, "Prosecuting Computer Crimes," https://www.justice.gov/sites/default/files/criminal-ccips/legacy/2015/01/14/ccmanual.pdf.

Hypo 5: *Warrants to Hack Computers*

The Government applied for a search warrant targeting a computer allegedly used to violate federal bank fraud, identity theft, and computer security laws. Unknown persons were alleged to have committed these crimes using a particular email account via an unknown computer at an unknown location. The search was to be accomplished by contacting the Target Computer via a counterfeit email address, and then surreptitiously installing software designed not only to extract certain stored electronic records but also to generate user photographs and location information over a 30-day period. In other words, the Government sought a warrant "to hack" a computer suspected of criminal use. Does this application for a warrant raise particularity issues? Should this warrant application be granted? If a warrant application was denied on this basis, how else could the Government ever find this computer? *See In re Warrant to Search a Target Computer at Premises Unknown*, 958 F. Supp.2d 753 (S.D. Tex. 2013).

Hypo 6: *Searches of Data Files on Phones*

Law enforcement officers obtained a search warrant to search for "any or all files" on defendant's cell phone that constituted the offense of public indecency. Do you think that this description of the items to be seized was sufficiently particular to withstand constitutional scrutiny? Would there or should there be any data files that could not or should not be searched using this description? What do you think? *See United States v. Winn*, 79 F. Supp.3d 904 (S.D. Il. 2015).

Hypo 7: *Searches of Photographic Files on Phones*

Law enforcement officers obtained a search warrant to search defendant's iPhone for evidence of communications that would link him and another suspect to a shooting that occurred in the Hyde Park section of Boston. During the course of that search, the Government searched not only his contact lists and text messages, but also his photograph files. Defense counsel argues that photographs found in that search that linked defendant to the shooting had to be suppressed because there was no probable cause to search the iPhone's photograph files. Was defense counsel correct? If not, is there any limit to the data which the Government could lawfully search on that phone? Should there be? *See Com. v. Dorelas,* 473 Mass. 496, 43 N.E.3d 306, 313–314 (2016).

Hypo 8: *Forcing Manufacturers to Enable Government to Search Phones*

Assuming that Government agents have probable cause to suspect that data relevant to the commission of a crime is contained in data stored in a "locked" smartphone, should the Government have the right to force the phones' manufacturer to "unlock" that phone and "let them in?" Does it or should it matter that the Government has obtained a search warrant for the phone? *See, e.g., In re Apple, Inc.,* 149 F.Supp.3d 341 (E.D.N.Y. 2016). Does it or should it make a difference that the Government may be able to unlock that phone without the manufacturer's assistance, *e.g.* by employing a "hacker?" *See, e.g.,* Katie Benner & Eric Lichtblau, "U.S. Says It Has Unlocked iPhone Without Apple," New York Times p. A1 (March 28, 2016). *See also* Sara Morrison, "Why Attorney General Bill Barr is mad at Apple: The FBI didn't need Apple's help to crack a suspected terrorist's iPhone, but it's demanding it anyway," VOX (May 18, 2020), https://www.vox.com/recode/2020/5/18/21262731/fbi-apple-unlock-iphone-encryption-bill-barr-alshamrani.

Hypo 9: *Particularity & Roving Wiretaps*

Federal and New Jersey law each contain a "roving wiretap" provision that allows law enforcement officers, under certain circumstances, to intercept communications on newly-discovered telephone facilities used by a wiretap target, without first returning to the judge who issued the wiretap warrant. A criminal defendant challenged this roving wiretap provision, claiming that because it does not require law enforcement to identify a telephone facility with particularity and get court approval in advance, it violates both the Fourth Amendment and New Jersey constitutional law. Does it? What do you think? If a search target moved from one house to another, should a search warrant for the target in the first, particularized house, automatically move to the next house, without having to go back to the issuing judge for approval? *See State v. Feliciano,* 224 N.J. 351, 132 A.3d 1245 (2016).

6. Warrant Execution

Wilson v. Arkansas

514 U.S. 927 (1995).

JUSTICE THOMAS delivered the opinion of the Court.

At the time of the framing, the common law of search and seizure recognized a law enforcement officer's authority to break open the doors of a dwelling, but generally indicated that he first ought to announce his presence and authority. In this case, we hold that this common-law "knock and announce" principle forms a part of the reasonableness inquiry under the Fourth Amendment.

Hear It

You can hear the oral argument in *Wilson* at http://www.oyez.org/cases/1990-1999/1994/1994_94_5707.

During November and December 1992, petitioner Sharlene Wilson made a series of narcotics sales to an informant acting at the direction of the Arkansas State Police. In late November, the informant purchased marijuana and methamphetamine at the home that petitioner shared with Bryson Jacobs. On December 30, the informant telephoned petitioner at her home and arranged to meet her at a local store to buy some marijuana. According to testimony presented below, petitioner produced a semiautomatic pistol at this meeting and waved it in the informant's face, threatening to kill her if she turned out to be working for the police. Petitioner then sold the informant a bag of marijuana.

The next day, police officers applied for and obtained warrants to search petitioner's home and to arrest both petitioner and Jacobs. Affidavits filed in support of the warrants set forth the details of the narcotics transactions and stated that Jacobs had previously been convicted of arson and firebombing. The search was conducted later that afternoon. Police officers found the main door to petitioner's home open. While opening an unlocked screen door and entering the residence, they identified themselves as police officers and stated that they had a warrant. Once inside the home, the officers seized marijuana, methamphetamine, valium, narcotics paraphernalia, a gun, and ammunition. They also found petitioner in the bathroom, flushing marijuana down the toilet. Petitioner and Jacobs were arrested and charged with delivery of marijuana, delivery of methamphetamine, possession of drug paraphernalia, and possession of marijuana.

Before trial, petitioner filed a motion to suppress the evidence seized during the search. Petitioner asserted that the search was invalid on various grounds, including that the officers had failed to "knock and announce" before entering her home. The trial court summarily denied the suppression motion. After a jury trial, petitioner was convicted of all charges and sentenced to 32 years in prison. The Arkansas Supreme Court affirmed, finding "no authority for petitioner's theory that the knock and announce principle is required by the Fourth Amendment." We granted certiorari to resolve the conflict among the lower courts as to whether the common-law knock-and-announce principle forms a part of the Fourth Amendment reasonableness inquiry. We hold that it does, and accordingly reverse and remand.

The Fourth Amendment to the Constitution protects "the right of the people to be secure in their persons, houses, papers, and effects, against unreasonable searches and seizures." In evaluating the scope of this right, we have looked to the traditional protections against unreasonable searches and seizures afforded by the common law at the time of the framing. An examination of the common law of search and seizure leaves no doubt that the reasonableness of a search of a dwelling may depend in part on whether law enforcement officers announced their presence and authority prior to entering.

Although the common law generally protected a man's house as "his castle of defense and asylum," common-law courts long have held that "when the King is party, the sheriff (if the doors be not open) may break the party's house, either to arrest him, or to do other execution of the King's process, if otherwise he cannot enter." To this rule, however, common-law courts appended an important qualification:

> "But before he breaks it, he ought to signify the cause of his coming, and to make request to open doors, for the law without a default in the owner abhors the destruction or breaking of any house (which is for the habitation and safety of man) by which great damage and inconvenience might ensue to the party, when no default is in him; for perhaps he did not know of the process, of which, if he had notice, it is to be presumed that he would obey it."

Several prominent founding-era commentators agreed on this basic principle. According to Sir Matthew Hale, the "constant practice" at common law was that "the officer may break open the door, if he be sure the offender is there, if after acquainting them of the business, and demanding the prisoner, he refuses to open the door." William Hawkins propounded a similar principle: "the law doth never allow" an officer to break open the door of a dwelling "but in cases of necessity," that is, unless he "first signify to those in the house the cause of his coming, and request them to give him admittance." Sir William Blackstone stated simply that the sheriff may "justify breaking open doors, if the possession be not quietly delivered."

The common-law knock-and-announce principle was woven quickly into the fabric of early American law. Most of the States that ratified the Fourth Amendment had enacted constitutional provisions or statutes generally incorporating English common law, and a few States had enacted statutes specifically embracing the common-law view that the breaking of the door of a dwelling was permitted once admittance was refused.

Our own cases have acknowledged that the common law principle of announcement is "embedded in Anglo-American law," but we have never squarely held that this principle is an element of the reasonableness inquiry under the Fourth Amendment. We now so hold. Given the longstanding common-law endorsement of the practice of announcement, we have little doubt that the Framers of the Fourth Amendment thought that the method of an officer's entry into a dwelling was among the factors to be considered in assessing the reasonableness of a search or seizure.

This is not to say, of course, that every entry must be preceded by an announcement. The Fourth Amendment's flexible requirement of reasonableness should not be read to mandate a rigid rule of announcement that ignores countervailing law enforcement interests. As even petitioner concedes, the common-law principle of announcement was never stated as an inflexible rule requiring announcement under all circumstances.

Take Note

Aside from the common law history recounted by Justice Thomas, it is useful to understand just why entries without the sort of notice required by the knock and announce doctrine are problematic as a matter of common sense in addition to common law. As the Wisconsin Supreme Court made the point, "the knock and announce rule has three primary justifications. First, it serves to protect the safety of police officers and others by warning the occupants of the officers' entrance. Second, it protects the occupants' limited privacy interests when the police already have a warrant. Third, it helps prevent the physical destruction of property." *State v. Stevens*, 511 N.W.2d 591, 594 (Wis. 1994), *cert. denied*, 515 U.S. 1102 (1995).

Because the common-law rule was justified in part by the belief that announcement generally would avoid "the destruction or breaking of any house by which great damage and inconvenience might ensue," courts acknowledged that the presumption in favor of announcement would yield under circumstances presenting a threat of physical violence. And courts have indicated that unannounced entry may be justified where police officers have reason to believe that evidence would likely be destroyed if advance notice were given.

We need not attempt a comprehensive catalog of the relevant countervailing factors here. For now, we leave to the lower courts the task of determining the circumstances under which an unannounced entry is reasonable under the Fourth Amendment. We simply hold that although a search or seizure of a dwelling might be constitutionally defective if police officers enter without prior announcement, law enforcement interests may also establish the reasonableness of an unannounced entry.

Respondent contends that the judgment below should be affirmed because the unannounced entry in this case was justified for two reasons. First, respondent argues that police officers reasonably believed that a prior announcement would have placed them in peril, given their knowledge that petitioner had threatened a government informant with a semiautomatic weapon and that Mr. Jacobs had previously been convicted of arson and firebombing. Second, respondent suggests that prior announcement would have produced an unreasonable risk that petitioner would destroy easily disposable narcotics evidence.

Take Note

It is important to recognize that the knock and announce doctrine consists of *three* separate and independent elements: a) announcement of the presence of the police (their "identity"); b) announcement of the police purpose (*e.g.,* "We've got a warrant to search your apartment!"); and c) delay prior to entry sufficient to permit the occupants to open the door. Failure by an executing officer to comply sufficiently with *any one* of these three requirements renders the warrant execution defective.

These considerations may well provide the necessary justification for the unannounced entry in this case. Because the Arkansas Supreme Court did not address their sufficiency, however, we remand to allow the state courts to make any necessary findings of fact and to make the determination of reasonableness in the first instance. The judgment of the Arkansas Supreme Court is reversed.

Points for Discussion

a. No Federal Exclusionary Remedy

As discussed in more detail in Chapter 8, the federal exclusionary rule does not apply in these situations. In *Hudson v. Michigan,* 547 U.S. 586 (2006), police waited only three to five seconds after knocking on a suspect's door before entering to execute a search warrant. Although the Court held that the police violated the "knock and announce" requirement, a majority of the Court also held that the evidence should not be excluded because the federal exclusionary rule does not apply to knock and announce violations.

b. State Exclusionary Rules

Some states, however, continue to apply an exclusionary rule in cases involving knock and announce violations pursuant to their own state constitutions. *See, e.g., State v. Rodriguez,* 399 N.J.Super. 192, 203, 943 A.2d 901, 908 (App. Div. 2008) ("Although conclusive as to the application of the Fourth Amendment, even if by the barest of margins, Hudson by no means governs the application of our state constitution to a knock and announce violation."); *State v. Jean-Paul,* 2013-NMCA-032, 295 P.3d 1072, 1076–77 (N.M. Ct. App. 2013) ("the remedy for any violation of Article II, Section 10's knock-and-announce requirement continues to be suppression of the evidence"); *State v. Majors,* 318 S.W.3d 850, 858–59 (Tenn. 2010) ("except in certain exigent circumstances, failure to comply with the rule in Tennessee is grounds for excluding any evidence seized under the search warrant.").

c. How Loud Is Loud Enough?

The announcement of identity and purpose need not be shouted, but it must be loud enough to be reasonably audible by the occupants of the search premises. *Compare United States v. Spriggs,* 996 F.2d 320, 322–23 (D.C. Cir.), *cert. denied,* 510 U.S. 938 (1993) (announcement held appropriate where it was "'slightly above a normal tone of voice'—and thus apparently sufficient to alert the residents of the apartment") *with People v. Ortiz,* 569 N.W.2d 653, 658–59 (Mich. Ct. App. 1997) (announcement held constitutionally deficient where "five persons within earshot and in varying positions could not hear' it; 'the notice given by the police was not reasonably calculated to provide notice to the occupants under the circumstances and was therefore inadequate").

Richards v. Wisconsin

520 U.S. 385 (1997).

JUSTICE STEVENS delivered the opinion of the Court.

In *Wilson v. Arkansas*, we held that the Fourth Amendment incorporates the common law requirement that police officers entering a dwelling must knock on the door and announce their identity and purpose before attempting forcible entry. At the same time, we recognized that the "flexible requirement of reasonableness should not be read to mandate a rigid rule of announcement that ignores countervailing law enforcement interests" and left "to the lower courts the task of determining the circumstances under which an unannounced entry is reasonable under the Fourth Amendment."

Hear It

You can hear the oral argument in *Richards* at http://www.oyez.org/cases/1990-1999/1996/1996_96_5955.

In this case, the Wisconsin Supreme Court concluded that police officers are never required to knock and announce their presence when executing a search warrant in a felony drug investigation. We disagree with the court's conclusion that the Fourth Amendment permits a blanket exception to the knock-and-announce requirement for this entire category of criminal activity.

On December 31, 1991, police officers in Madison, Wisconsin obtained a warrant to search Steiney Richards' hotel room for drugs and related paraphernalia. The search warrant was the culmination of an investigation that had uncovered substantial evidence that Richards was one of several individuals dealing drugs out of hotel rooms in Madison. The police requested a warrant that would have given advance authorization for a "no-knock" entry into the hotel room, but the magistrate explicitly deleted those portions of the warrant.

The officers arrived at the hotel room at 3:40 a.m. Officer Pharo, dressed as a maintenance man, led the team. With him were several plainclothes officers and at least one man in uniform. Officer Pharo knocked on Richards' door and, responding to the query from inside the room, stated that he was a maintenance man. With the chain still on the door, Richards cracked it open. Although there is some dispute as to what occurred next, Richards acknowledges that when he opened the door he saw the man in uniform standing behind Officer Pharo. He quickly slammed the door closed and, after waiting two or three seconds, the officers began kicking and ramming the door to gain entry to the locked room. At trial, the officers testified that they identified themselves as police while they were kicking the door in. When they finally did break into the room, the officers caught Richards trying to escape through the window. They also found cash and cocaine hidden in plastic bags above the bathroom ceiling tiles.

Richards sought to have the evidence from his hotel room suppressed on the ground that the officers had failed to knock and announce their presence prior to forcing entry into the room. The trial court denied the motion. The Wisconsin Supreme Court affirmed, concluding that exigent circumstances justifying a no-knock entry are always present in felony drug cases.

We recognized in *Wilson* that the knock-and-announce requirement could give way "under circumstances presenting a threat of physical violence," or "where police officers have reason to believe that evidence would likely be destroyed if advance notice were given." It is indisputable that felony drug investigations may frequently involve both of these circumstances. The question we must resolve is whether this fact justifies dispensing with case-by-case evaluation of the manner in which a search was executed.

The Wisconsin court explained its blanket exception as necessitated by the special circumstances of today's drug culture, and the State asserted at oral argument that the blanket exception was reasonable in "felony drug cases because of the convergence in a violent and dangerous form of commerce of weapons and the destruction of drugs." But creating exceptions to the knock-and-announce rule based on the "culture" surrounding a general category of criminal behavior presents at least two serious concerns.

First, the exception contains considerable overgeneralization. For example, while drug investigation frequently does pose special risks to officer safety and the preservation of evidence, not every drug investigation will pose these risks to a substantial degree.

A second difficulty with permitting a criminal-category exception to the knock-and-announce requirement is that the reasons for creating an exception in one category can, relatively easily, be applied to others. Armed bank robbers, for example, are, by definition, likely to have weapons, and the fruits of their crime may be destroyed without too much difficulty. If a per se exception were allowed for each category of criminal investigation that included a considerable-albeit hypothetical-risk of danger to officers or destruction of evidence, the knock-and-announce element of the Fourth Amendment's reasonableness requirement would be meaningless.

Thus, the fact that felony drug investigations may frequently present circumstances warranting a no-knock entry cannot remove from the neutral scrutiny of a reviewing court the reasonableness of the police decision not to knock and announce in a particular case. Instead, in each case, it is the duty of a court confronted with the question to determine whether the facts and circumstances of the particular entry justified dispensing with the knock-and-announce requirement.

In order to justify a "no-knock" entry, the police must have a reasonable suspicion that knocking and announcing their presence, under the particular circumstances, would be dangerous or futile, or that it would inhibit the effective investigation of the crime by, for example, allowing the destruction of evidence. This standard—as opposed to a probable cause requirement—strikes the appropriate balance between the legitimate law enforcement concerns at issue in the execution of search warrants and the individual privacy interests affected by no-knock entries. This showing is not high, but the police should be required to make it whenever the reasonableness of a no-knock entry is challenged.

Take Note

The *Richards* decision is important because it makes it clear that exigency-based exceptions (involving danger or destruction of evidence) to the knock-and-announce doctrine are not "automatic" (so called *per se* or "blanket" exceptions), i.e. exigency must be established individually in each particular case. But *Richards* is also important because it establishes the actual standard to be met by executing officers before exigency is recognized as an exception, namely a "*reasonable suspicion*" standard. Is this standard too low?

Although we reject the Wisconsin court's blanket exception to the knock-and-announce requirement, we conclude that the officers' no-knock entry into Richards' hotel room did not violate the Fourth Amendment. The circumstances in this case show that the officers had a reasonable suspicion that Richards might destroy evidence if given further opportunity to do so.

The judge who heard testimony at Richards' suppression hearing concluded that it was reasonable for the officers executing the warrant to believe that Richards knew, after opening the door to his hotel room the first time, that the men seeking entry to his room were the police. Once the officers reasonably believed that Richards knew who they were, the court concluded, it was reasonable for them to force entry immediately given the disposable nature of the drugs.

In arguing that the officers' entry was unreasonable, Richards places great emphasis on the fact that the magistrate who signed the search warrant for his hotel room deleted the portions of the proposed warrant that would have given the officers permission to execute a no-knock entry. But this fact does not alter the reasonableness of the officers' decision, which must be evaluated as of the time they entered the hotel room. At the time the officers obtained the warrant, they did not have evidence sufficient, in the judgment of the magistrate, to justify a no-knock warrant. Of course, the magistrate could not have anticipated in every particular the circumstances that would confront the officers when they arrived at Richards' hotel room.[4] These actual circumstances—petitioner's apparent recognition of the officers combined with the easily disposable nature of the drugs—justified the officers' ultimate decision to enter without first announcing their presence and authority.

Accordingly, although we reject the blanket exception to the knock-and-announce requirement for felony drug investigations, the judgment of the Wisconsin Supreme Court is affirmed.

> **Hear It**
>
> You can listen to the oral argument before the Supreme Court in the *Bailey* case at http://www.oyez.org/cases/2010-2019/2012/2012_11_770.

Point for Discussion

Futile Gestures

Note that the *Richards* decision includes a reference not only to danger and evidentiary destruction exceptions to the knock and announce requirement, but also refers to situations where announcing (and/or delaying) would be "futile." Although not cited expressly by the Court, there are a number of lower court decisions which hold that the knock and announce doctrine is excused where the giving of notice would be a "futile (or useless) gesture." *See, e.g., United States v. Metz*, 608 F.2d 147 (5th Cir. 1979), *cert. denied*, 449 U.S. 821 (1980) (failure to knock and announce held reasonable where one occupant was in police custody and yelled to other occupants inside that the police were standing outside); *United States v. Carter*, 792 Fed. Appx. 366, 369 (6th Cir. 2019), *cert. denied*, 2020 WL 1906601 (2020) ("Knock-and-announce rule applies only when officers enter by force; here, they were invited in."); *People v. Uhler*, 256 Cal. Rptr. 336 (Cal. Ct. App. 1989) (failure to delay after knock and announce held reasonable where occupants saw the executing officer through the screen door); *State v. Kelley*, 265 Neb. 563, 658 N.W.2d 279, 285–90 (2003) ("the deputies could reasonably infer that it would have been futile to knock and announce their identity and purpose for a substantial period of time given that Kelley's wife looked out the window and proceeded away from the directly adjacent door rather than responding to the deputies' knocking"). Indeed, the *Richards* case itself is, in application, at least in part, a "futile gesture" case as Richards had already seen a uniformed police officer in the hallway and slammed the door shut for that reason. (It is also an exigency-based, evidentiary-destruction exception case.)

---

[3] A number of States give magistrate judges the authority to issue "no-knock" warrants if the officers demonstrate ahead of time a reasonable suspicion that entry without prior announcement will be appropriate in a particular context. The practice of allowing magistrates to issue no-knock warrants seems entirely reasonable when sufficient cause to do so can be demonstrated ahead of time. But, as the facts of this case demonstrate, a magistrate's decision not to authorize a no-knock entry should not be interpreted to remove the officers' authority to exercise independent judgment concerning the wisdom of a no-knock entry at the time the warrant is being executed.

Hypo 1: *Entry After Anonymous Tip*

Police officers received an anonymous uncorroborated tip that a house contained a methamphetamine lab and firearms. Based on that tip, they obtained a warrant to search the house. Must the police knock and announce themselves before entering the residence? *See Doran v. Eckold,* 409 F.3d 958 (8th Cir.2005).

Hypo 2: *Entry After Surveillance Evidence*

Would your answer to Hypo 1 be affected by the fact that, before conducting the search, the police staked out the house and obtained additional evidence suggesting:

A) A certainty that a methamphetamine lab existed on the premises?

B) A certainty that firearms were present on the premises?

C) The presence of individuals with criminal records evidencing their prior commission of violent felonies?

Hypo 3: *What Was Being Flushed?*

Law enforcement officers executing a search warrant for narcotics broke down the door and entered forcibly after no one answered their announcement. As the officers entered, they heard a toilet running. They found 500 grams of crack cocaine in the residence, including some in the toilet. Do you think that the sound of a toilet flushing always justifies a forcible entry, i.e. that an occupant might be trying to destroy evidence? Does it matter that the officers did not actually hear the toilet running until after they entered? *See United States v. Williams,* 79 F. Supp.3d 888 (S.D. Ill. 2015).

Points for Discussion

a. Detention During Execution of Warrant

In *Ybarra v. Illinois,* 444 U.S. 85 (1979), the Supreme Court struck down an Illinois statute that authorized law enforcement officers to detain and search any person found on premises being searched pursuant to a search warrant. "The narrow scope of the *Terry* exception does not permit a frisk for weapons on less than reasonable belief or suspicion directed at the person to be frisked, even though that person happens to be on premises where an authorized narcotics search is taking place."

Nevertheless, in *Michigan v. Summers,* 452 U.S. 692 (1981), the Court upheld police detention of the occupant of a house while a search warrant for the house was being executed. The Court held that the "limited intrusion on the personal security" of the person detained was justified "by such substantial law enforcement interests" that the seizure could be made on articulable suspicion not amounting to probable cause.

In *Muehler v. Mena,* 544 U.S. 93 (2005), the Court ruled that—in the proper circumstances—an individual detained while a search warrant is being executed may be held for a period of 2 to 3 hours, and also may be handcuffed during that period. As Chief Justice Rehnquist explained for a majority of the Court:

> This was no ordinary search. The governmental interests in not only detaining, but using handcuffs, are at their maximum when, as here, a warrant authorizes a search for weapons and a wanted gang member resides on the premises. In such inherently dangerous situations, the use of handcuffs minimizes the risk of harm to both officers and occupants. Though this safety risk inherent in executing a search warrant for weapons was sufficient to justify the use of handcuffs, the need to detain multiple occupants made the use of handcuffs all the more reasonable.

Subsequently, in *Los Angeles County, California v. Rettele,* 550 U.S. 609 (2007), the Court upheld as reasonable the detention of two occupants of a house being searched (mistakenly as the police officers were in the wrong house) pursuant to search warrant. These occupants, a man and a woman, Rettele and Sadler, had been sleeping naked when the officers burst in. They were then made to stand naked at gunpoint for a few minutes with their hands up before being allowed to dress. The Court ruled as follows:

> In executing a search warrant officers may take reasonable action to secure the premises and to ensure their own safety and the efficacy of the search. The test of reasonableness under the Fourth Amendment is an objective one. Unreasonable actions include the use of excessive force or restraints that cause unnecessary pain or are imposed for a prolonged and unnecessary period of time.

> The orders by the police to the occupants, in the context of this lawful search, were permissible, and perhaps necessary, to protect the safety of the deputies. Blankets and bedding can conceal a weapon, and one of the

suspects was known to own a firearm, factors which underscore this point. The Constitution does not require an officer to ignore the possibility that an armed suspect may sleep with a weapon within reach.

The deputies needed a moment to secure the room and ensure that other persons were not close by or did not present a danger. Deputies were not required to turn their backs to allow Rettele and Sadler to retrieve clothing or to cover themselves with the sheets. This is not to say, of course, that the deputies were free to force Retelle and Sadler to remain motionless and standing for any longer than necessary. But there is no accusation that the detention here was prolonged. The deputies left the home less than 15 minutes after arriving.

The Fourth Amendment allows warrants to issue on probable cause, a standard well short of absolute certainly. Valid warrants will issue to search the innocent, and people like Rettele and Sadler unfortunately bear the cost. Officers executing search warrants on occasion enter a house when residents are engaged in private activity; and the resulting frustration, embarrassment, and humiliation may be real, as was true here. When officers execute a valid warrant and act in a reasonable manner to protect themselves from harm, however, the Fourth Amendment is not violated.

b.   Proximity of Detention to Search Premises

In *Bailey v. United States*, 568 U.S. 186 (2013), the Supreme Court ruled that "detentions incident to the execution of a search warrant are reasonable under the Fourth Amendment because the limited intrusion on personal liberty is outweighed by the special law enforcement interests at stake." But, the Court added, "once an individual has left the immediate vicinity of a premises to be searched, however, detentions must be justified by some other rationale." The *Bailey* Court ruled unconstitutional the stop of vehicle and a search of its occupants who had been seen five minutes earlier, exiting an apartment which was about to be searched. The stop took place about a mile away from the apartment. The Court found this sort of detention more intrusive than a detention at the scene of the search:

> Where officers arrest an individual away from his home, there is an additional level of intrusiveness. A public detention, even if merely incident to a search, will resemble a full-fledged arrest. As demonstrated here, detention beyond the immediate vicinity can involve an initial detention away from the scene and a second detention at the residence. In between, the individual will suffer the additional indignity of a compelled transfer back to the premises, giving all the appearances of an arrest. The detention here was more intrusive than a usual detention at the search scene. Bailey's car was

stopped; he was ordered to step out and was detained in full public view; he was handcuffed, transported in a marked patrol car, and detained further outside the apartment. These facts illustrate that detention away from a premises where police are already present often will be more intrusive than detentions at the scene.

Hence, the types of detentions held reasonable in *Summers* must be limited to the "immediate vicinity" of the search, which the search in *Bailey* was not:

> Limiting the rule in *Summers* to the area in which an occupant poses a real threat to the safe and efficient execution of a search warrant ensures that the scope of the detention incident to a search is confined to its underlying justification. Once an occupant is beyond the immediate vicinity of the premises to be searched, the search-related law enforcement interests are diminished and the intrusiveness of the detention is more severe.

> Here, petitioner was detained at a point beyond any reasonable understanding of the immediate vicinity of the premises in question; and so this case presents neither the necessity nor the occasion to further define the meaning of immediate vicinity. In closer cases courts can consider a number of factors to determine whether an occupant was detained within the immediate vicinity of the premises to be searched, including the lawful limits of the premises, whether the occupant was within the line of sight of his dwelling, the ease of reentry from the occupant's location, and other relevant factors.

Hypo: *Stop of Car away from Search Premises So as Not to Alert Occupants*

Local police officers obtained a search warrant to search an apartment at 117 Selman for narcotics. Before announcing and entering, they surveilled the location from a distance for a few minutes, and, while there, observed Daryl Nelson, who they knew lived in that apartment, arrive and a few minutes later, depart in a car. The officers quickly contacted nearby DEA agents who stopped Nelson's vehicle about one mile away from his apartment. One of the executing officers testified he wanted the vehicle stop made far enough away from the residence so that no other possible target would be alerted to the police presence and impending search. After the stop, Nelson eventually consented to a search of the car, and a bag of marijuana was found. Was the search warrant for narcotics in Nelson's apartment a sufficient basis for stopping him in his car one mile away? Can the bag of marijuana found in the car be suppressed? *State v. Nelson*, 215 So.3d 389 (La. Ct. App. 2 Cir. 2017).

c. Time Limits for Execution

A search warrant must be executed within the time period prescribed by the issuing magistrate, not to exceed the period established for execution of a search warrant in the applicable jurisdiction. This time limit, established by statute or court rule, is most commonly 10 days, although states have set limits as various as 2 to 60 days. *See, e.g.,* Fed. R. Crim. P. 41(e)(2)(A)(i) (federal time period not to exceed 14 days.)

d. Nighttime Execution

Most jurisdictions require law enforcement officers applying for a search warrant to be executed during the nighttime to make a special showing of necessity to search at that time. *See, e.g.,* Fed. R. Crim. P. 41(e)(2)(A)(ii) ("The warrant must command the officer to execute the warrant during the daytime, unless the judge for good cause expressly authorizes execution at another time."). In about half of these jurisdictions, however, law enforcement failures to follow nighttime search requirements have been held not to constitute error of a constitutional dimension. Although three justices of the Supreme Court held in 1974 that this requirement is a federal constitutional requirement, *Gooding v. United States,* 416 U.S. 430 (1974), this proposition has never been accepted by a majority of the Court.

Global View

The Brazilian Constitution of 1988, tit. II, chapt. I, art. 5 (XI), provides that homes may not be entered except by court order "during the day except in the event of 'flagrante delicto' or disaster, or to give help." Would this sort of provision be preferable to the U.S. Constitution's silence on this subject?

Hypo: *Nighttime Searches for Narcotics*

Police officers received numerous anonymous tips on a narcotics tip line that Todd Zeller, living at 114 24th Street South in Fargo, North Dakota, was selling methamphetamine from his home. They sent an undercover agent to the area and he made a "controlled buy" of meth from Zeller in the vicinity of that residence. The police then obtained a search warrant to search 114 24th Street South authorizing a nighttime search, and the warrant was executed at 4:00 am. Nighttime searches in North Dakota are only permitted when police demonstrate "reasonable cause" to search at night. The detective seeking the warrant included a special request for nighttime service authorization "to allow officers the ability to get closer to the residence before being detected under the cover of darkness." The affidavit also stated, "entry of law enforcement in this manner will be safer to those inside as well as the law enforcement officers executing the search warrant." Was this nighttime search justified? *See State v. Zeller*, 845 N.W.2d 6 (N.D. 2014).

United States v. Banks

540 U.S. 31 (2003).

JUSTICE SOUTER delivered the opinion of the Court.

Hear It

You can hear the oral argument in *Banks* at http://www.oyez.org/cases/2000-2009/2003/2003_02_473.

Officers executing a warrant to search for cocaine in respondent Banks's apartment knocked and announced their authority. The question is whether their 15-to-20-second wait before a forcible entry satisfied the Fourth Amendment. We hold that it did.

With information that Banks was selling cocaine at home, North Las Vegas Police Department officers and Federal Bureau of Investigation agents got a warrant to search his two-bedroom apartment. As soon as they arrived there, about 2 o'clock on a Wednesday afternoon, officers posted in front called out "police search warrant" and rapped hard enough on the door to be heard by officers at the back door. There was no indication whether anyone was home, and after waiting for 15 to 20 seconds with no answer, the officers broke open the front door with a battering ram. Banks was in the shower and testified that he heard nothing until the crash of the door, which brought him out dripping to confront the police. The search produced weapons, crack cocaine, and other evidence of drug dealing.

In response to drug and firearms charges, Banks moved to suppress evidence, arguing that the officers executing the search warrant waited an unreasonably short time before forcing entry, and so violated the Fourth Amendment. The District Court denied the motion, and Banks pleaded guilty, reserving his right to challenge the search on appeal. The Ninth Circuit Court of Appeals reversed in a 2-to-1 panel opinion.

We granted certiorari to consider how to go about applying the standard of reasonableness to the length of time police with a warrant must wait before entering without permission after knocking and announcing their intent in a felony case. We now reverse.

There has never been a dispute that these officers were obliged to knock and announce their intentions when executing the search warrant, an obligation they concededly honored. The Fourth Amendment says nothing specific about formalities in exercising a warrant's authorization, speaking to the manner of searching as well as to the legitimacy of searching at all simply in terms of the right to be "secure against unreasonable searches and seizures." Although the notion of reasonable execution must therefore be fleshed out, we have done that case by case, largely avoiding categories and protocols for searches. Instead, we have treated reasonableness as a function of the facts of cases so various that no template is likely to produce sounder results than examining the totality of circumstances in a given case; it is too hard to invent categories without giving short shrift to details that turn out to be important in a given instance, and without inflating marginal ones. We have, however, pointed out factual considerations of unusual, albeit not dispositive, significance.

Since most people keep their doors locked, entering without knocking will normally do some damage, a circumstance too common to require a heightened justification when a reasonable suspicion of exigency already justifies an unwarned entry. We have accordingly held that police in exigent circumstances may damage premises so far as necessary for a no-knock entrance without demonstrating the suspected risk in any more detail than the law demands for an unannounced intrusion simply by lifting the latch. Either way, it is enough that the officers had a reasonable suspicion of exigent circumstances.

This case turns on the significance of exigency revealed by circumstances known to the officers. Here the Government claims that a risk of losing evidence arose shortly after knocking and announcing. Although the police concededly arrived at Banks's door without reasonable suspicion of facts justifying a no-knock entry, they argue that announcing their presence started the clock running toward the moment of apprehension that Banks would flush away the easily disposable cocaine, prompted by knowing the police would soon be coming in.

Banks does not, of course, deny that exigency may develop in the period beginning when officers with a warrant knock to be admitted, and the issue comes down to whether it was reasonable to suspect imminent loss of evidence after the 15 to 20 seconds the officers waited prior to forcing their way. Though we agree with the dissenting opinion below that this call is a close one, we think that after 15 or 20 seconds without a response, police could fairly suspect that cocaine would be gone if they were reticent any longer. Courts of Appeals have, indeed, routinely held similar wait times to be reasonable in drug cases with similar facts including easily disposable evidence (and some courts have found even shorter ones to be reasonable enough).

A look at Banks's counterarguments shows why these courts reached sensible results, for each of his reasons for saying that 15 to 20 seconds was too brief rests on a mistake about the relevant enquiry: the fact that he was actually in the shower and did not hear the officers is not to the point, and the same is true of the claim that it might have taken him longer than 20 seconds if he had heard the knock and headed straight for the door. As for the shower, it is enough to say that the facts known to the police are what count in judging reasonable waiting time, and there is no indication that the police knew that Banks was in the shower and thus unaware of an impending search that he would otherwise have tried to frustrate.

And the argument that 15 to 20 seconds was too short for Banks to have come to the door ignores the very risk that justified prompt entry. True, if the officers were to justify their timing here by claiming that Banks's failure to admit them fairly suggested a refusal to let them in, Banks could at least argue that no such suspicion can arise until an occupant has had time to get to the door, a time that will vary with the size of the establishment, perhaps five seconds to open a motel room door, or several minutes to move through a townhouse. In this case, however, the police claim exigent need to enter, and the crucial fact in examining their actions is not time to reach the door but the particular exigency claimed. On the record here, what matters is the opportunity to get rid of cocaine, which a prudent dealer will keep near a commode or kitchen sink. The significant circumstances include the arrival of the police during the day, when anyone inside would probably have been up and around, and the sufficiency of 15 to 20 seconds for getting to the bathroom or the kitchen to start flushing cocaine down the drain. That is, when circumstances are exigent because a pusher may be near the point of putting his drugs beyond reach, it is imminent disposal, not travel time to the entrance, that governs when the police may reasonably enter; since the bathroom and kitchen are usually in the interior of a dwelling, not the front hall, there is no reason generally to peg the travel time to the location of the door, and no reliable basis for giving the proprietor of a mansion a longer wait than the resident of a bungalow, or an apartment like Banks's. And 15 to 20 seconds does not seem an unrealistic guess about the time someone would need to get in a position to rid his quarters of cocaine.

Once the exigency had matured, of course, the officers were not bound to learn anything more or wait any longer before going in, even though their entry entailed some harm to the building. The exigent need of law enforcement trumps a resident's interest in avoiding all property damage. One point in making an officer knock and announce, then, is to give a person inside the chance to save his door. That is why, in the case with no reason to suspect an immediate risk of frustration or futility in waiting at all, the reasonable wait time may well be longer when police make a forced entry, since they ought to be more certain the occupant has had time to answer the door. It is hard to be more definite than that. Suffice it to say that the need to damage property in the course of getting in is a good reason to require more patience than it would be reasonable to expect if the door were open. Police seeking a stolen piano may be able to spend more time to make sure they really need the battering ram.

The judgment of the Court of Appeals is reversed.

Food for Thought

How often do you think that police officers actually execute search warrants to look for stolen pianos, or anything else so large that it cannot be destroyed or hidden relatively quickly?

After the *Banks* decision, do you think that executing officers will *ever* really be required to delay more than 15 seconds? Can you answer your door in 15 seconds even when you're in the shower when they knock, and still hold on to your towel?

Go Online

But *see, e.g.,* "From antifreeze to a baby grand piano, police bust stolen merchandise ring," CTV News Toronto, June 27, 2014, http://toronto.ctvnews.ca/from-antifreeze-to-a-baby-grand-piano-police-bust-stolen-merchandise-ring-1.1889829. Do you suppose that searches for grand pianos happen more commonly in Canada?

Points for Discussion

a. Statutory vs. Constitutional Knock-and-Announce Requirements

Some states, like Florida, for example, have enacted knock-and-announce rules by statute rather than through judicial decision based upon the federal or state constitutions. In states like Florida, what then is the effect of the *Hudson* decision holding that the federal exclusionary rule does not apply, i.e. does it supplant the exclusionary rule that applies pursuant to a violation of the state knock-and-announce statute? *See State v. Cable,* 51 So.3d 434 (Fla. 2010).

b. When Is Destructive Behavior by Executing Officers Excessive?

In *United States v. Ramirez,* 523 U.S. 65, 71 (1998), the Supreme Court held that "excessive or unnecessary destruction of property in the course of a search may violate the Fourth Amendment, even though the entry itself is lawful and the fruits of the search are not subject to suppression." *See also, e.g., Ginter v. Stallcup,* 869 F.2d 384, 389 (8th Cir.1989) (there is a "Fourth Amendment right to be free from an unnecessarily destructive search and seizure. Thus, any destruction caused by law enforcement officers in the execution of a search or an arrest warrant must be necessary to effectively execute that warrant."); *Gurski v. New Jersey State Police Dept.,* 242 N.J.Super. 148, 576 A.2d 292, 299 (1990) ("No police officer in the course of executing a warrant can or should, without justification or sufficient reason, destroy private property, take or use any personal property of another without permission, or use abusive language."). But *see also, e.g., Parker v. Fantasia,* 425 F.Supp.3d 171, 190 (S.D.N.Y. 2019) ("Although Plaintiff submitted photographs of alleged damage with his Proposed Amended Complaint, those photographs, which are blurry and difficult to see, appear to depict nothing more than general disarray, and thus doom this claim.").

c. **Excessive Force in Making Seizures**

In *County of Los Angeles v. Mendez,* 137 S.Ct. 1539 (2017), a unanimous Supreme Court ruled that the operative question in excessive force cases is

> whether the totality of the circumstances justifies a particular sort of search or seizure. The reasonableness of the use of force is evaluated under an "objective" inquiry that pays careful attention to the facts and circumstances of each particular case. And the "reasonableness" of a particular use of force must be judged from the perspective of a reasonable officer on the scene, rather than with the 20/20 vision of hindsight. That inquiry is dispositive: When an officer carries out a seizure that is reasonable, taking into account all relevant circumstances, there is no valid excessive force claim.

The *Mendez* Court affirmed a lower court determination that deputies executing a search warrant did not act with excessive force when, after making a warrantless entry into a shack located behind the premises, they shot two individuals when one of them picked up what turned out to be a BB gun. The Court also reversed the Ninth Circuit Court of Appeals' holding that the officers were nonetheless liable for damages because the officers intentionally or recklessly "provoked" the violent confrontation. As the Court reasoned,

> the basic problem with the provocation rule is that it fails to stop there. Instead, the rule provides a novel and unsupported path to liability in cases in which the use of force was reasonable. Specifically, it instructs courts to look back in time to see if there was a different Fourth Amendment violation that is somehow tied to the eventual use of force. That distinct violation, rather than the forceful seizure itself, may then serve as the foundation of the plaintiff's excessive force claim.

> This approach mistakenly conflates distinct Fourth Amendment claims. Contrary to this approach, the objective reasonableness analysis must be conducted separately for each search or seizure that is alleged to be unconstitutional. An excessive force claim is a claim that a law enforcement officer carried out an unreasonable seizure through a use of force that was not justified under the relevant circumstances. It is not a claim that an officer used reasonable force after committing a distinct Fourth Amendment violation such as an unreasonable entry.

> By conflating excessive force claims with other Fourth Amendment claims, the provocation rule permits excessive force claims that cannot succeed on their own terms. That is precisely how the rule operated in this case. The District Court found (and the Ninth Circuit did not dispute) that the use of force by the deputies was reasonable. However, respondents were still

able to recover damages because the deputies committed a separate constitutional violation (the warrantless entry into the shack) that in some sense
set the table for the use of force. That is wrong.

d.   When Can Executing Officers Kill Animals Living on the Search Premises?

The Ninth Circuit Court of Appeals has held that the intentional killing of three
dogs, two of them "guard dogs" on search premises, one of them a Rottweiler, during
the execution of a search warrants on a Hells Angels clubhouse and residences was not
justified under the Fourth Amendment:

> Reasonableness is the touchstone of any seizure under the Fourth
> Amendment. Thus, to comply with the Fourth Amendment, the seizure-
> in this case, shooting and death-of the dogs must have been reasonable
> under the circumstances. We look to the totality of the circumstances to
> determine whether the destruction of property was reasonably necessary
> to effectuate the performance of the law enforcement officer's duties. To
> determine whether the shooting of the dogs was reasonable, we balance the
> nature and quality of the intrusion on the individual's Fourth Amendment
> interests against the countervailing governmental interests at stake.

> Here, the intrusion was severe. We have recognized that dogs are more
> than just a personal effect. The emotional attachment to a family's dog is
> not comparable to a possessory interest in furniture. The seizures were un-
> reasonable, in violation of the Fourth Amendment. Most important, both
> entry teams had a week to plan the execution of the entry. Despite advance
> knowledge of the presence of two guard dogs, the full extent of the plan to
> protect the entry team from the dogs was to either "isolate" or shoot the
> dogs. The officers had no specific plan for isolating the dogs.

> The contention that shooting the dogs was necessary to preserve stealth
> is unpersuasive. It was the officers' own method of entry that compromised
> their ability to effectuate a quiet entry. All of the above considerations sup-
> port the conclusion that the officers violated the plaintiffs' Fourth Amend-
> ment rights by unnecessarily shooting the dogs.

San Jose Chapter of Hells Angels Motorcycle Club v. City of San Jose, 402 F.3d
962 (9th Cir. 2005), *cert. denied,* 546 U.S. 1061 (2005).

Do you think that the Ninth Circuit was correct? Did these dogs pose a danger
to the executing officers and/or to the successful completion of the search that justified the officers' actions? This case was a civil rights action brought against the city

of San Jose for damages occasioned by the shooting of the dogs and other property damage that occurred during the raids. San Jose ultimately settled the case by paying $990,000, $530,000 of which was payment of the plaintiffs' attorneys' fees. *See also, e.g., Bullman v. City of Detroit, Michigan,* <u>787</u> Fed. Appx. 290, 299 (6th Cir. 2019) ("Shooting a dog is reasonable when, 'given all of the circumstances and viewed from the perspective of a reasonable officer at the scene, the [dogs] posed imminent threats to the officers.' ")

e. Scope of Search

The scope of a search undertaken pursuant to a warrant is strictly limited by the nature of the items sought in the warrant. *See, e.g., United States v. Jones,* <u>952 F.3d</u> <u>153 (4th Cir. 2020)</u> (warrant for marijuana justified search of safe in closet; "We hold that the magistrate, presented with evidence that Jones was illegally possessing and smoking marijuana in his house, had a substantial basis for concluding that probable cause existed to search the entire house for evidence of marijuana possession, even if the source of the smoke was a smoldering marijuana cigarette found in the kitchen trash can.")

FYI

Some executing officers have executed no-knock warrants while using so-called "flash-bang" devices (also called "stun grenades"). These devices produce an intense flash of light and a loud noise to briefly distract the occupants of search premises. The flash momentarily activates photoreceptor cells in peoples' eyes, making vision difficult for a few seconds. The blast also causes a temporary loss of hearing and balance. Most courts find the use of such flash-bang devices unreasonable where the executing officers neither possess a no-knock warrant nor face unexpected dangers upon entry.

See It

What does execution of a search warrant with a flash-bang device actually look and sound like? *See for yourself* at <u>https://www.</u> <u>youtube.com/watch?v=s4VJaNVHa88</u>.

Hypo 1: *Flash-Bang Device in Driveway*

Defendant Rockford argued that an entry into his and his parents' home to execute a search warrant was unconstitutional due to the executing officers' use of a flash-bang device outside in the driveway just prior to their knock, announce, delay, and entry by use of a battering ram. Defendant's mother, who was inside the home, testified that she mistook the sound of the flash-bang device for a problem with her furnace, that she did not hear knocking on the door before hearing the sound of the battering ram and seeing officers in her home, and that she was "scared to death" to encounter a police officer pointing a gun at her. Is this a violation of the knock-and announce doctrine? Does it matter, do you think, that the police may have made so much noise that no occupant could ever have heard their knock and announcement? *State v. Rockford*, 213 N.J. 424, 64 A.3d 514 (2013).

Hypo 2: *When Must a Search End?*

Police officers were lawfully inside defendant's home which he shared with his mother when they saw what they thought were three long guns near a staircase. Knowing that defendant's mother was a convicted felon and, thus, prohibited from possessing firearms, they obtained a warrant to search the home for prohibited weapons. Early in their search, the executing officers learned that the guns near the staircase were in fact "BB" guns. Nonetheless the officers continued the search and ultimately discovered cocaine. Can the cocaine be suppressed? Was it discovered during the lawful execution of a search warrant? What do you think? *State v. Schulz*, 164 N.H. 217, 55 A.3d 933 (2012).

B. Protected Fourth Amendment Interests

The Fourth Amendment protects people only against governmental "searches" and "seizures." For more than a century after the Fourth Amendment was adopted, there was little doubt regarding the meaning of the term "search." Those who suffered through the colonial period, and those who formulated and ratified the Fourth Amendment, were well aware of the British practices that led the new Americans to demand constitutional protections for security against "unreasonable searches and seizures." Colonial officials had conducted actual physical searches of "persons, houses, papers, and effects," and those physical searches were what the new Americans feared.

As a result, the Court's definition of the term "search" was consistent with these early understandings through the early twentieth century, and the Court's focus was on whether the government's action constituted a physical "trespass" into a "constitutionally protected area."

By the early twentieth century, however, this historical definition of the term search was becoming problematic. As new communications and electronic surveillance technologies were developed, the government was able to intrude into private areas without committing a physical trespass and without making any physical entry whatsoever into homes or offices. For example, in *Olmstead v. United States,* 277 U.S. 438 (1928), a closely divided Court held that governmental wiretapping of phones did not constitute a trespassory "search." The use of wiretaps to seize phone conversations did not constitute a "search" within the meaning of the Fourth Amendment because the police did not enter Olmstead's home, but rather listened in on public lines outside of Olmstead's house. The *Olmstead* dissenters disagreed, suggesting that new and developing technologies would require the Court to expand its definition of the term "search" beyond the material world of trespass. Otherwise, Fourth Amendment protections might lose their meaning and effectiveness. A dissenting Justice Brandeis argued that private telephone communications deserve no less Fourth Amendment protection than sealed letters, given the Framers' commitment to protect "Americans in their beliefs, their thoughts, their emotions, and their sensations." In his view, the Fourth Amendment guarantees the people "the right to be let alone," and therefore "every unjustifiable intrusion upon privacy, whatever the means employed," constitutes a violation of the Fourth Amendment.

For many years after *Olmstead* was decided, the Court continued to link privacy interests to trespassory intrusions. In *Goldman v. United States,* 316 U.S. 129 (1942), the Court held that no trespass was committed when agents placed a "detectaphone" device against a wall to amplify the sound waves coming from an adjoining office, and therefore there was no Fourth Amendment search. Justice Murphy's dissent criticized the failure of the trespass theory to cope with advancing surveillance technology: "Science has brought forth far more effective devices for the invasion of a person's privacy than the direct and obvious methods of oppression which were detested by our forebears and which inspired the Fourth Amendment. Whether the search of private quarters is accomplished by placing on the outer walls of the sanctum a detectaphone that transmits to the outside listener the intimate details of a private conversation, or by new methods of photography that penetrate walls or overcome distances, the privacy of the citizen is equally invaded by agents of the Government and intimate personal matters are laid bare to view." In *Silverman v. United States,* 365 U.S. 505 (1961), the Court found a Fourth Amendment violation, but only because governmental agents committed a trespass by inserting a "spike mike" a few inches into the common wall of a house in order to listen to conversations. Justice Douglas's concurrence emphasized that this technical trespass was not a principled basis for justifying Fourth Amendment protection of conversations in *Silverman* while denying it in *Goldman* and *Olmstead*.

1. Development of the Reasonable Expectation of Privacy Test

The Court began to alter its definition of the term "search" in the following case.

Katz v. United States

389 U.S. 347 (1967).

Mr. Justice Stewart delivered the opinion of the Court.

[Katz was convicted of transmitting wagering information by telephone. He made calls from telephone booths near his apartment. FBI agents placed a listening and recording device on top of and between the booths. From these devices, the agents obtained six recordings of about three minutes each, which were introduced at trial. The lower court assumed that the recordings did not violate the Fourth Amendment because "there was no physical entrance into the area occupied by" Katz.]

Katz has strenuously argued that the booth was a "constitutionally protected area." The Government has maintained with equal vigor that it was not. But this effort to decide whether or not a given "area," viewed in the abstract, is "constitutionally protected" deflects attention from the problem presented by this case. For the Fourth Amendment protects people, not places. What a person knowingly exposes to the public, even in his own home or office, is not a subject of Fourth Amendment protection. *See Lewis v. United States*, 385 U.S. 206 (1966). But what he seeks to preserve as private, even in an area accessible to the public, may be constitutionally protected.

The Government stresses that the telephone booth from which Katz made his calls was constructed partly of glass, so that he was as visible after he entered it as he would have been if he had remained outside. But what he sought to exclude when he entered the booth was not the intruding eye—it was the uninvited ear. He did not shed his right to do so simply because he made his calls from a place where he might be seen. No less than an individual in a business office, in a friend's apartment, or in a taxicab, a person in a telephone booth may rely upon the protection of the Fourth Amendment. One who occupies it, shuts the door

Food for Thought

How could the Court respond to the argument that Katz knowingly exposed his conversation to anyone working for the telephone company who could have listened to his call?

behind him, and pays the toll that permits him to place a call is surely entitled to assume that the words he utters into the mouthpiece will not be broadcast to the world. To read the Constitution more narrowly is to ignore the vital role that the public telephone has come to play in private communication.

The Government contends, however, that the activities of its agents in this case should not be tested by Fourth Amendment requirements, for the surveillance technique they employed involved no physical penetration of the telephone booth from which the petitioner placed his calls. It is true that the absence of such penetration was at one time thought to foreclose further Fourth Amendment inquiry, for that Amendment was thought to limit only searches and seizures of tangible property. But although a closely divided Court supposed in *Olmstead v. United States*, 277 U.S. 438 (1928), that surveillance without any trespass and without the seizure of any material object fell outside the ambit of the Constitution, we have since departed from the narrow view on which that decision rested. Indeed, we have expressly held that the Fourth Amendment governs not only the seizure of tangible items, but extends as well to the recording of oral statements overheard without any "technical trespass." *Silverman v. United States*, 365 U.S. 505, 511 (1961). Once it is recognized that the Fourth Amendment protects people—and not simply "areas"—against unreasonable searches and seizures it becomes clear that the reach of that Amendment cannot turn upon the presence or absence of a physical intrusion into any given enclosure.

We conclude that the underpinnings of *Olmstead* and *Goldman* have been so eroded by our subsequent decisions that the "trespass" doctrine can no longer be regarded as controlling. The Government's activities in electronically listening to and recording Katz's words violated the privacy upon which he justifiably relied while using the telephone booth and thus constituted a "search and seizure" within the meaning of the Fourth Amendment. The fact that the electronic device did not penetrate the wall of the booth can have no constitutional significance.

The question remaining is whether the search and seizure in this case complied with constitutional standards. It is clear that this surveillance was so narrowly circumscribed that a duly authorized magistrate could constitutionally have authorized, with appropriate safeguards, the very limited search and seizure that the Government assert took place. The Government urges that because its agents did no more here than they might properly have done with

Practice Pointer

In *Katz*, defense counsel initially argued that the Fourth Amendment provided absolute protection for conversations, echoing Justice Brandeis' *Olmstead* dissent. But at oral argument, defense counsel argued instead that the warrant procedure was both feasible and required for the lawful electronic surveillance of Katz's speech in the phone booth.

prior judicial sanction, we should validate their conduct. That we cannot do. The inescapable fact is that in this case, restraint was imposed by the agents themselves, not by a judicial officer. They were not required, before commencing their search, to present their estimate of probable cause for detached scrutiny by a neutral magistrate. They were not compelled, during the conduct of the search itself, to observe precise limits established in advance by a specific court order.

The Government urges the creation of a new exception. It argues that surveillance of a telephone booth should be exempted from the usual requirement of advance authorization by a magistrate upon a showing of probable cause. We cannot agree. Omission of such authorization "bypasses the safeguards provided by an objective predetermination of probable cause. And bypassing a neutral predetermination of the scope of a search leaves individuals secure from Fourth Amendment violations 'only in the discretion of the police.'" *Beck v. Ohio*, 379 U.S. 89, 96 (1964). These considerations do not vanish when the search in question is transferred from the setting of a home, an office, or a hotel room to that of a telephone booth. Wherever a man may be, he is entitled to know that he will remain free from unreasonable searches and seizures. The government agents here ignored a procedure that we hold to be a constitutional precondition of the kind of electronic surveillance involved in this case. Because the surveillance failed to meet that condition, and because it led to the petitioner's conviction, the judgment must be reversed. *It is so ordered.*

MR. JUSTICE HARLAN, concurring.

"The Fourth Amendment protects people, not places." The question, however, is what protection it affords to those people. Generally the answer to that question requires reference to a "place." My understanding is that there is a twofold requirement, first that a person have exhibited an actual (subjective) expectation of privacy and, second, that the expectation be one that society is prepared to recognize as "reasonable." Thus a man's home is, for most purposes, a place where he expects privacy, but objects, activities, or statements that he exposes to the "plain view" of outsiders are not "protected" because no intention to keep them to himself has been exhibited. On the other hand, conversations in the open would not be protected against being overheard, for the expectation of privacy under the circumstances would be unreasonable. "One who occupies (a telephone booth,) shuts the door behind him, and pays the toll that permits him to place a call is surely entitled to assume" that his con-

FYI

After *Olmstead*, Congress enacted a federal anti-wiretapping statute, which the Court interpreted in *Nardone v. United States*, 302 U.S. 379 (1937) as prohibiting the testimony of federal agents about illegally wiretapped conversations. But violations of federal and state wiretapping laws were widespread in later years. Following *Katz*, Congress enacted Title III of the Omnibus Crime Control and Safe Streets Act of 1968 to define the procedures for obtaining a wiretapping warrant, relying on the requirements for such warrants described in *Katz* and *Berger v. New York*, 388 U.S. 41 (1967).

versation is not being intercepted. The point is not that the booth is "accessible to the public" at other times, but that it is a temporarily private place whose momentary occupants' expectations of freedom from intrusion are recognized as reasonable.

Points for Discussion

a. Defining the Reasonable Expectation of Privacy (REOP) Test

The Court subsequently approved Justice Harlan's formula—requiring a subjective manifestation of an expectation of privacy that is objectively reasonable—as the expression of *Katz*'s holding.

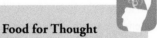

Food for Thought

An overnight guest has a REOP in a dwelling. But only people with a "property or possessory interest" in a car may challenge a police search of the car. These people include the owner or driver but not a mere passenger. Are these rulings consistent with *Katz*?

b. REOP & the Trespass Test

Although most post-*Katz* decisions focused on the "reasonable expectation of privacy" (REOP) test, the Court has emphasized that the *Katz* test "*added to*" rather than "*substituted for*" the physical trespass test. "For most of our history the Fourth Amendment was understood to embody a concern for government trespass upon the areas ("persons, houses, papers, and effects") it enumerates. *Katz* did not repudiate that understanding" or "erode the principle 'that when the Government does engage in physical intrusion of a constitutionally protected area in order to obtain information, that information may constitute a violation of the Fourth Amendment.'" *United States v. Jones*, 565 U.S. 400, 405 (2012). Thus, except for *Olmstead* and *Goldman*, pre-*Katz* precedents defining "constitutionally protected areas" remained good law after *Katz*. Indeed, *Katz* alluded to such precedents when noting the Fourth Amendment protection for people occupying a business office, a friend's apartment, a taxi cab, a home, or a hotel room. *See Lanza v. New York*, 370 U.S. 139, 143 (1962).

c. Privacy in the Home

The Court's precedents repeatedly endorse the principle that, "At the very core" of the Fourth Amendment "stands the right of a man to retreat into his own home and there be free from unreasonable governmental intrusion." *Silverman v. United States*, 365 U.S. 505, 515 (1961). In the post-*Katz* era, the Fourth Amendment's protection of the home from trespassory intrusions was extended to include intangible intrusions to obtain "information from the interior of the home" that "could not otherwise [be] obtained without physical intrusion into a constitutionally protected area." *Kyllo v. United States*, 533 U.S. 27, 34 (2001). The Court also recognized that "a person can have a legally sufficient interest in a place other than his own home" and that the "arcane distinctions" of property and tort law (between "guests, licensees, invitees and the like") do not control. *Rakas v. Illinois*, 439 U.S. 128, 142 (1978). In *Minnesota v. Olson*, 495 U.S. 91, 98 (1990), the Court held that overnight guests in a home have a REOP, reasoning that this rule "merely recognizes the everyday expectations of privacy that we all share," and validates "a longstanding social custom that serves functions recognized as valuable by society." The shelter and security of the host's home make it "a temporarily private place" for the guest as a "momentary occupant" whose expectations of freedom from intrusion are recognized as reasonable." But those who are merely "present with the consent of the householder" may not claim Fourth Amendment protection, such as visitors to a home who have no previous relationship with the homeowner and no purpose for their brief visit other than an illegal business transaction. *See Minnesota v. Carter*, 525 U.S. 83, 90 (1998). Does *Olson's* reasoning apply to a long-term acquaintance, who has visited a home numerous times as a social guest without staying overnight? If a tenant has not paid rent for several months but is still living in an apartment, when does she lose her REOP in that home?

d. Curtilage

In the Court's post-*Katz* precedents, the Court recognized that the land immediately surrounding and associated with a dwelling or protected structure constituted "curtilage" and therefore was protected under the Fourth Amendment. Curtilage was viewed as "part of the home itself for Fourth Amendment purposes," given its association with "intimate activity" and "the privacies of life," and therefore an expectation of privacy in curtilage could be deemed reasonable. Later in *United States v. Dunn*, 480 U.S. 294 (1987), the Court recognized that four factors typically provide the basis for lower courts to resolve curtilage questions: "[1] the proximity of the area claimed to be curtilage to the home; [2] whether the area is included within an enclosure surrounding the home; [3] the nature of the uses to which the area is put; and [4] the steps taken by the resident to protect the area from observation by people passing by."

Pre-*Katz* cases suggested that customs and social norms might allow a homeowner to confer an invitation or "implied license" on members of the public to make limited entry upon the curtilage of his or her dwelling. In *Florida v. Jardines*, 569 U.S. 1 (2013), the Court held that this implied license "typically permits a visitor to approach the home by the front path, knock promptly, wait briefly to be received, and then (absent invitation to linger longer) leave." Similarly, "a police officer not armed with a warrant may approach a home and knock, precisely because that is 'no more than any private citizen might do.'" *See Kentucky v. King*, 563 U.S. 452 (2011). Given earlier precedents recognizing curtilage as a "constitutionally protected area," however, *Jardines* emphasized that the Fourth Amendment prohibits physical intrusions upon the curtilage "to engage in conduct not explicitly or implicitly permitted by the homeowner." Therefore, the Court held that police officers violated that prohibition when they brought a trained drug-sniffing dog to the defendant's front porch "in the hopes of discovering incriminating evidence." The Court found it unnecessary to decide whether this police conduct violated the defendant's REOP in his curtilage and home. Instead, the Court relied on "the Fourth Amendment's property-rights baseline" in determining that "the background social norms that invite a visitor to the front door do not invite [any visitor] there to conduct a search." Since "the officers learned what they learned only by physically intruding on Jardines' property to gather evidence," this fact was "enough to establish that a search occurred" and that a warrant was required. Later in *Carrol v. Carman*, 574 U.S. 13 (2014), the Court recognized that lower courts have taken different approaches to deciding whether the police may approach other entrances to a home for a "knock and talk" (without a forensic narcotics dog).

e.   Undercover Agents & Informants

Katz cited *Lewis v. United States*, <u>385 U.S. 206 (1966)</u>, a case in which "a person knowingly exposed information to the public in his own home or office." *Lewis* held that defendant had no privacy interest in incriminating conversations with an undercover police officer, whom he had invited into his home to buy drugs. This invitation "converted" the home into a "commercial center to which outsiders are invited for purposes of unlawful business," and the agent did not "see, hear, or take anything in the home that was not intended by the defendant." Similarly, in *Hoffa v. United States*, <u>385 U.S. 293 (1966)</u>, a plurality held that defendant had no privacy interest in incriminating conversations he made in his hotel suite to an informant. Any expectation of Fourth Amendment protection from either type of monitoring was unreasonable when those conversations were "directed to" the informant or "knowingly carried on in his presence." The plurality declined to protect the "misplaced confidence" of the *Lewis* and *Hoffa* defendants that their associates "would not reveal their wrongdoing" by talking to government agents.

The Court affirmed the validity of both rulings in *United States v. White*, <u>401 U.S. 745 (1971)</u>. The informant in *White* wore a wire with a radio transmitter that allowed agents to both monitor and record his conversations with defendant in defendant's home and at other locations. The Court reasoned that this type of electronic surveillance was no different from the unwired surveillance in *Lewis* and *Hoffa*, and that an expectation of privacy from electronic surveillance would be unreasonable because anyone "contemplating illegal activities must realize and risk that his companions may be reporting to the police." Justice Harlan, joined by four justices, dissented and reasoned as follows:

> The impact of the practice of third-party bugging, must, I think, undermine that confidence and sense of security in dealing with one another that is characteristic of individual relationships between citizens in a free

society. It goes beyond the impact on privacy occasioned by the ordinary type of "informer" investigation upheld in *Lewis* and *Hoffa*. The argument of the plurality, that it is irrelevant whether secrets are revealed by the mere tattletale or the transistor, ignores the differences occasioned by third-party monitoring and recording which insures full and accurate disclosure of all that is said, free of the possibility of error and oversight that inheres in human reporting. The interest the plurality fails to protect is the expectation of the ordinary citizen, who has never engaged in illegal conduct in his life, that he may carry on his private discourse freely, openly, and spontaneously without measuring his every word against the connotations it might carry when instantaneously heard by others unknown to him and unfamiliar with his situation or analyzed in a cold, formal record played days, months, or years after the conversation. Interposition of a warrant requirement is designed not to shield "wrongdoers," but to secure a measure of privacy and a sense of personal security throughout our society.

f.   Private Search Doctrine

Katz referred approvingly to *Ex parte Jackson,* 96 U.S. 727 (1877), which held that letters and packages in the mail are protected by a REOP. In post-*Katz* cases, however, the Court recognized the "private search" doctrine which applies to situations in which a private actor opens an incriminating package and then turns it over to a government agent. In that situation, no REOP violation occurs unless the agent's subsequent intrusion is more extensive than that of the private actor. *See Walter v. United States,* 447 U.S. 649 (1980) (violation of REOP when private actor held film up to the light and agent later viewed the film on a projector); *United States v. Jacobsen,* 466 U.S. 109 (1984) (no violation of REOP when agent imitated the search of a FedEx employee who found white powder inside a package even though the agent also performed field test to determine that the powder was cocaine). The private search doctrine has been applied by lower courts to searches of computers, so that no warrant is required for an agent who stays within the scope of a prior actor's search.

Hypo 1: *Backpacks & Safety Deposit Boxes*

Although a safety deposit box is one of the most secure and private ways to protect property against the police or others, few individuals keep all of their valuables in safety deposit boxes. Suppose that a law student brings her backpack to class. If the backpack remains zipped, does she have a REOP in the contents of the backpack? If so, does the REOP continue to exist when the student leaves the classroom for five minutes? Would it matter whether the backpack is unzipped?

Hypo 2: *House Party*

Assume that Larry is a law student who decides to hold a party for all the students in his law school class, including their spouses or partners, and his friends. A total of 200 people actually attend the party. During the course of the evening, there is a constant flow of people in and out of Larry's home. Assume that Larry leaves marijuana cigarettes on the coffee table in his living room for the enjoyment of his guests, and that marijuana is an illegal drug. Does Larry have a REOP regarding the marijuana cigarettes on his coffee table?

Hypo 3: *Government Manipulation or Erosion of Privacy Expectations*

In *Smith v. Maryland*, 442 U.S. 735, 740 n.5 (1979), the Court observed that "if the Government were suddenly to announce on nationwide television that all homes henceforth would be subject to warrantless entry, individuals might not in fact entertain any actual expectation of privacy regarding their homes, papers and effects. But where an individual's subjective expectations have been 'conditioned' by influences alien to well-recognized Fourth Amendment freedoms, those subjective expectations obviously could play no meaningful role in ascertaining what the scope of Fourth Amendment protection was." However, even in the absence of such obvious government manipulation of privacy expectations of the citizenry, some forms of privacy erosion may lessen the collective social expectations of privacy in ways that would be accepted by the Court. If the government announces that it will place aural monitoring devices on public property outside each home and monitor all conversations in every house 24 hours a day, what reasoning could the Court use to find that this surveillance would violate reasonable expectations of privacy? *See* Anthony G. Amsterdam, *Perspectives on the Fourth Amendment*, 58 MINN. L. REV. 349 (1974). What less intrusive type of aural monitoring might be accepted by the Court as not violating a protected privacy interest?

2. Struggling to Define the REOP Test

When *Katz* was decided, one might have assumed that the decision signaled the Court's willingness to deal with the problem of advancing surveillance technology, especially given the potential breadth of the REOP test, and the Court's declaration that, "wherever a man may be, he is entitled to know that he will remain free from unreasonable searches and seizures." Indeed, in *Katz* itself, the REOP test allowed Katz to claim Fourth Amendment protections even though he would have received no protection under the trespass test. Paradoxically, in most of its subsequent decisions, the Court repeatedly has chosen to construe the REOP test narrowly.

a. Open Fields

In *Oliver v. United States,* 466 U.S. 170 (1984), the Court affirmed pre-*Katz* precedents that distinguished between protected curtilage and the unprotected land that lies beyond the curtilage, known as the "open fields." *See Hester v. United States,* 265 U.S. 57 (1924). *Oliver* held that a trespassory intrusion into a secluded area beyond the curtilege, which area was surrounded by a fence and "no trespassing" signs, did not constitute a search under the REOP test. Although couched in *Katz*'s language of "societal expectations," *Oliver*'s reasoning treated the REOP concept as affording only the same limited protection for "curtilage" land that was conferred by pre-*Katz* trespass theory and embedded in the English common law:

> In assessing the degree to which a search infringes upon individual privacy, the Court has given weight to such factors as the intention of the Framers of the Fourth Amendment, the uses to which the individual has put a location, and our societal understanding that certain areas deserve the most scrupulous protection from government invasion. The Amendment reflects the recognition of the Framers that certain enclaves should be free from arbitrary government interference. For example, the Court since the enactment of the Fourth Amendment has stressed "the overriding respect for the sanctity of the home that has been embedded in our traditions since the origins of the Republic." In contrast, open fields do not provide the setting for those intimate activities that the Amendment is intended to shelter from government interference or surveillance. There is no societal interest in protecting the privacy of those activities, such as the cultivation of crops, that occur in open fields. Moreover, as a practical matter these lands usually are accessible to the public and the police in ways that a home, an office, or commercial structure would not be. It is not generally true that fences or "No Trespassing" signs effectively bar the public from viewing open fields in rural areas. For these reasons, the asserted expectation of privacy in open fields is not an expectation "that society recognizes as reasonable."

Hypo: *Cluttered Yard*

Officer May observes Zeb's home from the sidewalk, notices that no defined pathway leads to the front door, and that the front yard is filled with obstructions, including stacked wood, a rusting truck, a wheelbarrow, garden tools, and bags of soil. Trees with thick foliage made it impossible to see into the house from the sidewalk. She decides to enter the front yard. After scrambling around obstructions, she reaches a small clear area in the back yard, where she peers into the nearest window, and notices marijuana plants inside the house. Does her conduct violate Zeb's REOP? Assume instead that Officer May sees that there is a clear pathway to Zeb's front door and that a driveway leads from the street to a carport in the back yard. So she walks down the driveway to the carport, peers into a different window, and then notices the marijuana plants inside the house. Does the analysis of the curtilage issue change? *See Commonwealth v. Dixon*, 482 S.E.3d 386 (Ky. 2015); *United States v. Alexander*, 888 F.3d 628 (2d Cir. 2018).

b. Third Party Doctrine

Post-*Katz* decisions raised the question of whether an individual can hold a REOP in information that he "voluntarily conveys" to a third party. The following case addresses that issue.

Smith v. Maryland

442 U.S. 735 (1979).

MR. JUSTICE BLACKMUN delivered the opinion of the Court.

[The police suspected Smith of robbing someone who afterwards received threatening and obscene phone calls. Smith fit the victim's description of the robber and his car was seen at the crime scene and noticed repeatedly in the victim's neighborhood. So the police asked the telephone company to install

See It

See http://s3-media2.fl.yelpcdn.com/bphoto/5Tyw352fdlXJt1aqUUTYQw/l.jpg for a photo of a pen register device.

a pen register to record the local telephone numbers dialed from Smith's landline in his home, as the company did not keep records for local calls. That same day, the pen register recorded one call made from Smith's landline to the victim, and the police obtained a search warrant and discovered evidence at his home. Smith argued that installation of the pen register constituted a "search" under *Katz*.]

Smith cannot claim that his "property" was invaded or that police intruded into a "constitutionally protected area." His claim is that, notwithstanding the absence of a trespass, the State infringed [his "legitimate expectation of privacy." Yet a pen register differs significantly from the listening device in *Katz*, for pen registers do not acquire the *contents* of communications. Given a pen register's limited capabilities, Smith's argument rests upon a claim that he had a "legitimate expectation of privacy" regarding the numbers he dialed on his phone. We doubt that people in general entertain any actual expectation of privacy in the numbers they dial. All telephone users realize that they must "convey" phone numbers to the telephone company, and that the phone company has the facilities for recording this information.

This Court consistently has held that a person has no legitimate expectation of privacy in information he voluntarily turns over to third parties. In *United States v. Miller*, 425 U.S. 435, 442 (1976), for example, the Court held that a bank depositor has no "legitimate 'expectation of privacy'" in financial information "voluntarily conveyed to banks and exposed to their employees in the ordinary course of business." Because the depositor assumed the risk of disclosure, the Court held that it would be unreasonable for him to expect his financial records to remain private. When he used his phone, Smith voluntarily conveyed numerical information to the telephone company and "exposed" that information to its equipment in the ordinary course of business. In so doing, Smith assumed the risk that the company would reveal to police the numbers he dialed.

The installation of the pen register, consequently, was not a "search," and no warrant was required. The judgment of the Maryland Court of Appeals is affirmed. *It is so ordered.*

Justice Stewart, with whom Justice Brennan joins, dissenting.

The information captured by such surveillance emanated from private conduct within a person's home or office—locations that without question are entitled to constitutional protection. Further, that information is an integral part of the telephonic communication that under *Katz* is entitled to constitutional protection, whether or not it is captured by a trespass into such an area. The numbers dialed from a private telephone are not without "content." I doubt there are any who would be happy to have broadcast to the world a list of the local or long distance numbers they have called. It easily could reveal the identities of the persons and places called, and thus reveal the most intimate details of a person's life.

Justice Marshall, with whom Justice Brennan joins, dissenting.

Privacy is not a discrete commodity, possessed absolutely or not at all. Those who disclose certain facts to a bank or phone company for a limited business purpose need not assume that this information will be released to other persons for other purposes.

The Court determines that individuals who convey information to third parties have "assumed the risk" of disclosure to the government. This analysis is misconceived. Implicit in the concept of assumption of risk is some notion of choice. Here, unless a person is prepared to forgo use of what for many has become a personal or professional necessity, he cannot help but accept the risk of surveillance. More fundamentally, to make risk analysis dispositive in assessing the reasonableness of privacy expectations would allow the government to define the scope of Fourth Amendment protection. Whether privacy expectations are legitimate within the meaning of *Katz* depends not on the risks an individual can be presumed to accept when imparting information to third parties, but on the risks he should be forced to assume in a free and open society. The prospect of unregulated government monitoring will undoubtedly prove disturbing even to those with nothing illicit to hide, and I am unwilling to insulate use of pen registers from independent judicial review.

Point for Discussion

Precedent for *Smith*'s Third Party Doctrine

In *Miller v. United States*, 425 U.S. 435 (1976), the Court tied the concepts of voluntary conveyance and knowing exposure to the declaration in *Katz* that, "What a person knowingly exposes to the public, even in his own home or office, is not a subject of Fourth Amendment protection." The federal agents in *Miller* obtained copies of the defendant's checks and bank records by means of subpoenas to banks where he had accounts. In rejecting the defendant's REOP argument, the *Miller* Court emphasized one rationale that went unmentioned in *Smith*, which was that the lack of REOP in bank records "was assumed by Congress" when enacting the Bank Secrecy Act of 1970 that required the banks to maintain the records. A similar rationale appeared in *Couch v. United States*, 409 U.S. 322, 335 (1973), to justify rejection of defendant's proposal that an "accountant-client" privilege should be recognized to support her REOP in documents held by her accountant on her behalf. The Court opined that "there can be little expectation of privacy where records are handed to an accountant, knowing that mandatory disclosure of much of the information therein is required in an income tax return."

c. **Beepers & GPS Devices**

United States v. Knotts

460 U.S. 276 (1983).

JUSTICE REHNQUIST delivered the opinion of the Court.

[Police officers suspected that Knotts' co-defendant Petschen might lead them to the site of a drug lab. So the officers arranged for a radio transmitter to be inserted in a five-gallon drum of chloroform that Petschen bought. The officers followed Petschens' car but could not maintain continual visual surveillance, and were forced to rely on the signals of the tracking beeper in the drum. The police did not use the beeper after determining it was in the general area of a secluded cabin owned and occupied by Knotts. The officers obtained a search warrant and found a drug lab inside the cabin. The five-gallon drum was outside the cabin. Knotts argued that the use of the tracking beeper in lieu of visual surveillance violated his reasonable expectation of privacy.]

A person traveling in an automobile on public thoroughfares has no reasonable expectation of privacy in his movements from one place to another. When Petschen traveled over the public streets he voluntarily conveyed to anyone who wanted to look the fact that he was traveling over particular roads in a particular direction, the fact of whatever stops he made, and the fact of his final destination when he exited from public roads onto private property.

As the owner of the cabin and surrounding premises to which Petschen drove, Knotts undoubtedly had the traditional expectation of privacy within a dwelling place insofar as the cabin was concerned. But no such expectation of privacy extended to the visual observation of the automobile arriving on his premises after leaving a public highway, nor to movements of objects such as the drum of chloroform outside the cabin in the "open fields."

Visual surveillance from public places along the car's route or adjoining Knotts' premises would have sufficed to reveal all of these facts to the police. The fact that the officers relied not only on visual surveillance but also on the use of the beeper does not alter the situation. Nothing in the Fourth Amendment prohibited the police from augmenting their sensory faculties with such enhancement as science and technology afforded them.

In *Smith v. Maryland*, 442 U.S. 735, 745 (1979), we said: "Smith voluntarily conveyed numerical information to the telephone company and 'exposed' that information to its equipment. In so doing, Smith assumed the risk that the company would reveal to police the numbers he dialed." Knotts does not actually quarrel with this analysis, though he expresses the generalized view that the result of the holding sought by the Government would be that "twenty-four hour surveillance of any citizen of this country will be possible, without judicial knowledge or supervision." If such dragnet type law enforcement practices as Knotts envisions should eventually occur, there will be time enough then to determine whether different constitutional principles may be applicable.

Nothing indicates that the beeper signal was received or relied upon after it had ended its automotive journey at rest on Knotts' land. There is no indication that the beeper was used to reveal information as to the movement of the drum within the cabin, or in any way that would not have been visible to the naked eye from outside the cabin.

There was neither a "search" nor a "seizure" within the contemplation of the Fourth Amendment. The judgment of the Court of Appeals is therefore *Reversed*.

Points for Discussion

a. Tracking Objects into Dwellings

In *United States v. Karo*, 468 U.S. 705 (1984), the Court held that the use of a tracking beeper violated a homeowner's reasonable expectation of privacy because police continued to monitor the location of the beeper until after it was taken inside a dwelling. This monitoring enabled them to determine whether the bottle (containing the beeper) remained in the dwelling. The Court reasoned that a search occurs when the Government "surreptitiously employs an electronic device to obtain information that it could not have obtained by observation from outside the curtilage of the house. The beeper tells the agent that a particular article is actually located at a particular time in the private residence and is in the possession of the person or persons whose residence is being watched." Thus, the beeper reveals "a critical fact about the interior of the premises" that the Government "could not have obtained without a warrant." By contrast, the beeper in *Knotts* "told the authorities nothing about the interior of Knotts' cabin." The information obtained in *Knotts* was "voluntarily conveyed to anyone who wanted to look," whereas in *Karo*, "the monitoring indicated that the beeper was inside the house, a fact that could not have been visually verified."

b. Revival of the Trespass Doctrine

In *United States v. Jones*, 565 U.S. 400 (2012), the police attached a GPS tracking device to the undercarriage of defendant's car. Instead of deciding the case under the REOP test, the Court surprised observers by producing a narrow holding that relied on the trespass test, and by invalidating both the warrantless attachment of the device and its use to monitor the movements of the defendant's car on public streets. The Court reasoned as follows:

> The Government contends that *Katz* shows that no search occurred here, since Jones had no "reasonable expectation of privacy" in the area of the Jeep accessed by Government agents (its underbody) and in the locations of the Jeep on the public roads, which were visible to all. But Jones's Fourth Amendment rights do not rise or fall with the *Katz* formulation. For most of our history the Fourth Amendment was understood to embody a particular concern for government trespass upon the areas ("persons, houses, papers, and effects") it enumerates. *Katz* did not repudiate that understanding [or] erode the principle "that, when the Government does engage in physical intrusion of a constitutionally protected area in order to obtain information, that intrusion may constitute a violation of the Fourth Amendment." *United States v. Knotts,* 460 U.S. 276, 286 (1983) (Brennan, J., concurring). What we apply is an 18th-century guarantee against unreasonable searches, which we believe must provide *at a minimum* the degree of protection it afforded when it was adopted. We do not make trespass the exclusive test. Situations involving merely the transmission of electronic signals without trespass would *remain* subject to *Katz* analysis.

d. Low-Flying Aircraft

California v. Ciraolo

476 U.S. 207 (1986).

CHIEF JUSTICE BURGER delivered the opinion of the Court.

[Police officers received an anonymous tip that marijuana was growing in Ciraolo's garden, but they could not see the yard's interior from the sidewalk because a ten-foot fence enclosed the yard. Therefore, they used an airplane to fly in navigable airspace at 1,000 feet over Ciraolo's house and backyard. This aerial view allowed them to see marijuana plants in the garden and they obtained a search warrant based on that information. Ciraolo argued that the aerial surveillance violated his REOP but his suppression motion was denied. The state appellate court reversed his conviction, finding that the flyover was not a routine patrol but involved a direct intrusion into the sanctity of the home.]

The State argues that Ciraolo has "knowingly exposed" his backyard to aerial observation, because all that was seen was visible to the naked eye from any aircraft flying overhead. The State analogizes its mode of observation to a knothole or opening in a fence; if there is an opening, the police may look. Ciraolo contends he has done all that can reasonably be expected to tell the world he wishes to maintain the privacy of his garden within the curtilage without covering his yard. Such covering, he argues, would defeat its purpose as an outside living area; he asserts he has not "knowingly" exposed himself to aerial views.

That the area is within the curtilage does not itself bar all police observation. The Fourth Amendment protection of the home has never been extended to require law enforcement officers to shield their eyes when passing by a home on public thoroughfares. Nor does the mere fact that an individual has taken measures to restrict some views of his activities preclude an officer's observations from a public vantage point where he has a right to be and which renders the activities clearly visible. *E.g. United States v. Knotts*, 460 U.S. 276 (1983). "What a person knowingly exposes to the public, even in his own home or office, is not a subject of Fourth Amendment protection." *Katz v. United States*, 389 U.S. 347, 351 (1967). Any member of the public flying in this airspace who glanced down could have seen everything that these officers observed. Ciraolo's expectation that his garden was protected from such observation is unreasonable and is not an expectation that society is prepared to honor. The Fourth Amendment simply does not require the police traveling in the public airways at this altitude to obtain a warrant in order to observe what is visible to the naked eye. *Reversed.*

JUSTICE POWELL, with whom JUSTICE BRENNAN, JUSTICE MARSHALL, and JUSTICE BLACKMUN join, dissenting.

The home is a place in which a subjective expectation of privacy virtually always will be legitimate. *United States v. Karo*, 468 U.S 705, 713–715 (1984). "At the very core of the Fourth Amendment stands the right of a person to retreat into his own home and there be free from unreasonable governmental intrusion." *Silverman v. United States*, 365 U.S. 505, 511 (1961). The Court finds support for its conclusion in *United States v. Knotts*, 460 U.S. 276 (1983), but its reasoning is flawed. First, the actual risk to privacy from commercial or pleasure aircraft is virtually nonexistent, as travelers normally obtain at most a fleeting, anonymous, and nondiscriminating glimpse of the landscape and buildings over which they pass. The risk that a passenger on a plane might observe private activities, and might connect those activities with particular people, is simply too trivial to protect against. People do not "knowingly expose" their residential yards "to the public" merely by failing to build barriers that prevent aerial surveillance. The activities under surveillance in *Knotts* took place on public streets, not in private homes. The activity in this case, by contrast, took place within the private area immediately adjacent to a home. Here, police conducted an overflight at low altitude solely for the purpose of discovering evidence of crime within a private enclave into which they were constitutionally forbidden to intrude at ground level without a warrant. We have consistently afforded heightened protection to a person's right to be left alone in the privacy of his house. The Court fails to enforce that right or to give any weight to the longstanding presumption that warrantless intrusions into the home are unreasonable. I dissent.

Point for Discussion

Limits on Flyovers

In a companion case, *Dow Chemical Co. v. United States,* 476 U.S. 227 (1986), government agents took photographs of the "business curtilage" of a chemical plant during a flyover at 1200 feet. The Court rejected defendant's REOP claim, reasoning that the camera was a "conventional, albeit precise, commercial camera commonly used in mapmaking." It was not "some unique sensory device that, for example, could penetrate the walls of buildings and record conversations in Dow's plants, offices or laboratories." The Government conceded, and the Court agreed, that "surveillance of private property by using highly sophisticated surveillance equipment not generally available to the public, such as satellite technology, might be constitutionally proscribed absent a warrant." Second, the Court observed that the photographs were "not so revealing of intimate details as to raise constitutional concerns." A plurality of the Court extended *Ciraolo's* reasoning in *Florida v. Riley,* 488 U.S. 445 (1989), in which an officer used a helicopter flyover at 400 feet to look down through the holes in the roof of a greenhouse in the defendant's curtilage. This naked-eye observation of the marijuana plants did not violate the defendant's REOP because "any member of the public could legally have been flying over Riley's property in a helicopter at the altitude of 400 feet and could have observed Riley's greenhouse." The Court noted that helicopters are not bound by the limits of navigable airspace imposed on airplanes, and there was no "intimation" either that the helicopter interfered with use of the curtilage or that "intimate details" were observed.

Food for Thought

The FAA's current rules require commercial drones to fly below 400 feet during the daytime within the operator's line of sight. Not long from now, there may be tens of thousands of drones in the air. What influence will this development have on the judicial resolution of the question whether to recognize a REOP from surveillance by police drones? Drone-related legislation has been enacted in more than 30 states and many statutes create prohibitions that apply to the use of surveillance drones by law enforcement entities. One typical exception is the scenario in which a warrant for using a drone is obtained based on probable cause. What other exceptions would be likely to be endorsed in these statutes? Or allowed based on a lack of REOP?

e. Garbage Collection

California v. Greenwood

<u>486 U.S. 35 (1988).</u>

JUSTICE WHITE delivered the opinion of the Court.

The issue is whether the Fourth Amendment prohibits the warrantless search and seizure of garbage left for collection outside the curtilage of a home. We conclude that it does not.

[When a police officer received a tip indicating that Greenwood might be engaged in narcotics trafficking at his house, she obtained the cooperation of the trash collector, who agreed to pick up the plastic garbage bags left on the curb in front of Greenwood's house, and then turn them over to the officer. When she searched through the trash, she found items related to narcotics use. This information was used to obtain a search warrant for Greenwood's house. When the warrant was executed, drugs were seized and Greenwood and others were arrested. The next month, the officer obtained access to the garbage bags again using the same method. A second search warrant was obtained based on the evidence of narcotics use in the second set of garbage bags. The second search of Greenwood's house led to another seizure of drugs and the second arrest of Greenwood and others.]

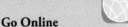

Go Online

The garbage search presented the Court with another technique that coincided with the development of other surveillance strategies during the era of the "war on drugs." For a chronology of the history of the "war on drugs" in the United States, assembled by the PBS Frontline program, *see* <u>http://www.pbs.org/wgbh/pages/frontline/shows/drugs/cron/</u>.

The warrantless search and seizure of the garbage bags left at the curb outside the Greenwood house would violate the Fourth Amendment only if the respondents manifested a subjective expectation of privacy in their garbage that society accepts as objectively reasonable. Respondents assert that they had, and exhibited, an expectation of privacy with respect to the trash that was searched by the police: The trash, which was placed on the street for collection at a fixed time, was contained in opaque plastic bags, which the garbage collector was expected to pick up, mingle with the trash of others, and deposit at the garbage dump. The trash was only temporarily on the street, and there was little likelihood that it would be inspected by anyone.

Here, respondents exposed their garbage to the public sufficiently to defeat their claim to Fourth Amendment protection. Plastic garbage bags left on or at the side of a public street are readily accessible to animals, children, scavengers, snoops, and other members of the public. Moreover, defendants placed their refuse at the curb for the express purpose of conveying it to a third party, the trash collector, who might himself have sorted through defendants' trash or permitted others, such as the police, to do so. Having deposited their garbage "in an area particularly suited for public inspection and, in a manner of speaking, public consumption, for the express purpose of having strangers take it," defendants could have had no reasonable expectation of privacy in the inculpatory items that they discarded.

Furthermore, the police cannot reasonably be expected to avert their eyes from evidence of criminal activity that could have been observed by any member of the public. We held in *Smith v. Maryland*, 442 U.S. 735 (1979), that an individual has no legitimate expectation of privacy in the numbers dialed on his telephone because he voluntarily conveys those numbers to the telephone company [and] "a person has no legitimate expectation of privacy in information he voluntarily turns over to third parties."

JUSTICE BRENNAN, with whom JUSTICE MARSHALL joins, dissenting:

A trash bag is "a common repository for one's personal effects" and is "inevitably associated with the expectation of privacy." A single bag of trash testifies eloquently to the eating, reading, and recreational habits of the person who produced it. A search of trash, like a search of the bedroom, can relate intimate details about sexual practices, health, and personal hygiene. Like rifling through desk drawers or intercepting phone calls, rummaging through trash can divulge the target's financial and professional status, political affiliations and inclinations, private thoughts, personal relationships, and romantic interests. It cannot be doubted that a sealed trash bag harbors telling evidence of the "intimate activity associated with the 'sanctity of a man's home and the privacies of life,'" which the Fourth Amendment is designed to protect. The mere *possibility* that unwelcome meddlers might open and rummage through the containers does not negate the expectation of privacy in their contents any more than the possibility of a burglary negates an expectation of privacy in the home; or the possibility of a private intrusion negates an expectation of privacy in an unopened package; or the possibility that an operator will listen in on a telephone conversation negates an expectation of privacy in the words spoken on the telephone. Nor is it dispositive that "defendants placed their refuse at the curb for the express purpose of conveying it to a third party, who might himself have sorted through the trash or permitted others, such as the police, to do so." Even the voluntary relinquishment of possession or control over an effect does not necessarily amount to a relinquishment of a privacy expectation in it. Were it otherwise, a letter or package would lose all Fourth Amendment protection when placed in a mailbox or other depository with the "express purpose" of entrusting it to the postal officer or a private carrier. Yet, it has been clear for at least 110 years that the possibility of such an intrusion does not justify a warrantless search by police in the first instance. *See Ex Parte Jackson*, 96 U.S. 727 (1878).

Point for Discussion

Luggage Surveillance

In *Bond v. United States,* 529 U.S. 334 (2000), the government invoked both *Smith* rationales in an attempt to defeat a bus passenger's claim that the surveillance technique of "luggage squeezes" violated a reasonable expectation of privacy. In *Bond,* a border patrol agent implemented this search method by walking down the aisle of a bus and squeezing each piece of soft luggage stored in the luggage bins above the passenger seats. Inside the defendant's canvas bag, the agent felt a "brick-like" object, and a search of the bag revealed a "brick" of methamphetamine wrapped in duct tape. The *Bond* Court concluded that the tactile intrusion of the "luggage squeeze" and the visual intrusion of flyover surveillance were not analogous: "Physically invasive inspection is simply more intrusive than purely visual inspection. When a bus passenger places a bag in an overhead bin, he expects that other passengers or bus employees may move it for one reason or another. Thus, a bus passenger clearly expects that his bag may be handled. He does not expect that other passengers or bus employees will, as a matter of course, feel the bag in an exploratory manner. But this is exactly what the agent did here. We therefore hold that the agent's physical manipulation of petitioner's bag violated the Fourth Amendment." The *Bond* dissenters would have relied on *Smith*'s rationales—conveyance to a third party and knowing exposure—to reject the *Bond* defendant's asserted expectation of privacy. What policy reasons may explain the *Bond* Court's refusal to extend these rationales to permit warrantless luggage squeezes?

f.   Canine Sniffs

Can the police use drug sniffing dogs to ferret out crime? Consider the following case.

United States v. Place

462 U.S. 696 (1983).

JUSTICE O'CONNOR delivered the opinion of the Court.

DEA agents, suspicious of Place's behavior, seized his luggage and subjected it to a canine sniff. In deciding whether the seizure was permissible, the Court was called on to decide whether the sniff constituted a search within the meaning of the Fourth Amendment.

The Fourth Amendment "protects people from unreasonable government intrusions into their legitimate expectations of privacy." A person possesses a privacy interest in the contents of personal luggage that is protected by the Fourth Amendment. A "canine sniff" by a well-trained narcotics detection dog, however, does not require opening the luggage. It does not expose noncontraband items that otherwise would remain hidden from public view, as does, for example, an officer's rummaging through the contents of the luggage. Thus, the manner in which information is obtained through this investigative technique is much less intrusive than a typical search. Moreover, the sniff discloses only the presence or absence of narcotics, a contraband item. Thus, despite the fact that the sniff tells the authorities something about the contents of the luggage, the information obtained is limited. This limited disclosure also ensures that the owner of the property is not subjected to the embarrassment and inconvenience entailed in less discriminate and more intrusive investigative methods. In these respects, the canine sniff is *sui generis*. We are aware of no other investigative procedure that is so limited both in the manner in which the information is obtained and in the content of the information revealed by the procedure. Therefore, we conclude that the particular course of investigation that the agents intended to pursue here—exposure of respondent's luggage, which was located in a public place, to a trained canine—did not constitute a "search" within the meaning of the Fourth Amendment.

Point for Discussion

Canine Sniffs During Traffic Stops

The Court observed in *Indianapolis v. Edmond,* 531 U.S. 32 (2000), that "the fact that officers walk a narcotics-detection dog around the exterior" of a car "does not establish a 'search.'" In *Illinois v. Caballes,* 543 U.S. 405 (2005), the Court held that "conducting a dog sniff of a car's exterior would not change the character of a traffic stop that is lawful at its inception and otherwise executed in a reasonable manner." The Court rejected defendant's argument that error rates "call into question the premise that drug-detection dogs will alert only to contraband." The *Caballes* dissenters disagreed, emphasizing that empirical evidence demonstrates "that the dog that alerts hundreds of times will be wrong dozens of times." They called for reconsideration of *Place* and urged that canine sniffs should be treated as "searches" when used during car stops for traffic crimes. In *Rodriguez v. United States,* 575 U.S. 348 (2015), the Court followed up on dicta in *Caballes* noting that a traffic stop would become unlawful if the dog sniff prolonged its duration beyond "the time reasonable required" to issue a ticket. The officer's stop in *Rodriguez* was held to be unlawful for that reason.

3. Evolving Constitutional Standards

As the foregoing cases suggest, most post-*Katz* decisions before 2001 concluded that the defendant did not possess a REOP, and therefore that there had been no invasion of the defendant's Fourth Amendment rights. The Court finally began to recognize that a new approach to the meaning of the Fourth Amendment was needed because new types of surveillance technology were emerging, including surveillance methods made possible by the internet. The Court's pre-internet interpretations of *Katz* had not been crafted with an awareness of the novel threats to privacy posed by these surveillance techniques. The following cases reveal how the Court attempted to develop new principles designed to come to grips with the new constitutional challenges created by evolving technologies in the post-internet era.

> ### Food for Thought
>
> Is the Court's focus on REOP and trespass misplaced? The text of the Fourth Amendment does not simply protect our right to be free from unreasonable searches and seizures, but rather our right to be secure against such intrusions. At the time of the founding, "secure" was defined as "protected from danger," or alternatively "free from fear." Imagine that a police officer tells you that your house will be raided for no reason whatsoever within the next five minutes. Is your Fourth Amendment right "to be secure" against an unreasonable search violated? If so, when? At the moment the officer notifies you that the search will occur? Or only once the search occurs? What if the search never occurs? *See* Luke M. Milligan, *The Forgotten Right to Be Secure*, 65 HASTINGS L.J. 713 (2014) (analyzing the original public meaning of the right "to be secure").

Kyllo v. United States

533 U.S. 27 (2001).

JUSTICE SCALIA delivered the opinion of the Court.

[An agent at the Department of Interior suspected that Kyllo was growing marijuana plants inside his home using high-intensity lamps. So agents used an Agema Thermovision 210 thermal imager to scan the home in order to detect and measure the heat that was emitted as infrared radiation. This device operated like a video camera showing heat images in shades of black, gray, and white. When the agents performed the scan at night from across the street, the garage roof and one side wall appeared to be relatively hot compared to the rest of the home, and substantially warmer than the other homes in the triplex. Based on information from the scan and other evidence, the agents obtained a search warrant and discovered more than 100 marijuana plants inside the home. The lower courts rejected Kyllo's claim that the warrantless use of the thermal imager to scan his home violated his reasonable expectation of privacy.]

Hear It

Listen to the oral argument before the Supreme Court in the *Kyllo* case at http://www.oyez.org/cases/2000-2009/2000/2000_99_8508.

This case presents the question whether the use of a thermal-imaging device aimed at a private home from a public street to detect relative amounts of heat within the home constitutes a "search" within the meaning of the Fourth Amendment. "At the very core" of the Fourth Amendment "stands the right of a man to retreat into his own home and there be free from unreasonable governmental intrusion." *Silverman v. United States*, 365 U.S. 505 (1961). With few exceptions, the question whether a warrantless search of a home is reasonable and hence constitutional must be answered no.

The permissibility of ordinary visual surveillance of a home used to be clear because, well into the twentieth century, our Fourth Amendment jurisprudence was tied to common-law trespass. We have since decoupled violation of a person's Fourth Amendment rights from trespassory violation of his property, but the lawfulness of warrantless visual surveillance of a home has still been preserved. We have previously reserved judgment as to how much technological enhancement of ordinary perception from such a vantage point, if any, is too much. The question we confront today is what limits there are upon this power of technology to shrink the realm of guaranteed privacy.

The *Katz* test—whether the individual has an expectation of privacy that society is prepared to recognize as reasonable—often has been criticized as circular, and hence subjective and unpredictable. But in the case of the search of the interior of homes, there is a ready criterion, with roots deep in the common law, of the minimal expectation of privacy that *exists*, and that is acknowledged to be *reasonable*. To withdraw protection of this minimum expectation would be to permit police technology to erode the privacy guaranteed by the Fourth Amendment. We think that obtaining by sense-enhancing technology any information regarding the interior of the home that could not otherwise have been obtained without physical "intrusion into a constitutionally protected area," *Silverman*, 365 U.S. at 512, constitutes a search—at least where (as here) the technology in question is not in general public use. This assures preservation of that degree of privacy against government that existed when the Fourth Amendment was adopted. On the basis of this criterion, the information obtained by the thermal imager in this case was the product of a search.

Take Note

The *Kyllo* opinion cited three examples of sophisticated technologies mentioned on the website of the National Law Enforcement and Corrections Technology Center. Included are a "Radar-Based Through-the-Wall Surveillance System," "Handheld Ultrasound Through the Wall Surveillance," and a "Radar Flashlight" to permit the detection of individuals "through interior building walls." For current projects, *see* https://justnet.org/About_NLECTC.html.

The Government maintains that thermal imaging must be upheld because it detected "only heat radiating from the external surface of the house." But just as a thermal imager captures only heat emanating from a house, so also a powerful directional microphone picks up only sound emanating from a house—and a satellite capable of scanning from many miles away would pick up only visible light emanating from a house. We rejected such a mechanical interpretation of the Fourth Amendment in *Katz*, where the eavesdropping device picked up only sound waves that reached the exterior of the phone booth. Reversing that approach would leave the homeowner at the mercy of advancing technology—including imaging technology that could discern all human activity in the home. While the technology used in the present case was relatively crude, the rule we adopt must take account of more sophisticated systems that are already in use or in development.

The Government also contends that the thermal imaging was constitutional because it did not "detect private activities occurring in private areas." The Fourth Amendment's protection of the home has never been tied to measurement of the quality or quantity of information obtained. There is no exception to the warrant requirement for the officer who barely cracks open the front door and sees nothing but the nonintimate rug on the vestibule floor. In the home, *all* details are intimate details, because the entire area is held safe from prying government eyes. Limiting the prohibition of thermal imaging to "intimate details" would not only be wrong in principle; it would be impractical in application. To begin with, there is no necessary connection between the sophistication of the surveillance equipment and the "intimacy" of the details that it observes. It might disclose, for example, at what hour each night the lady of the house takes her daily sauna and bath—a detail that many would consider "intimate"; and a much more sophisticated system might detect nothing more intimate than the fact that someone left a closet light on. We would have to develop a jurisprudence specifying which home activities are "intimate" and which are not. No police officer would be able to know *in advance* whether his through-the-wall surveillance picks up "intimate" details—and thus would be unable to know in advance whether it is constitutional.

Take Note

Justice Scalia's opinion noted that it is irrelevant whether neighbors or passersby may be able to detect heat emanating from a home, because "[t]he fact that equivalent information could sometimes be obtained by other means does not make lawful the use of means that violate the Fourth Amendment." Moreover, at the time of the heat scan by the agents, "no outside observer could have discerned the relative heat of Kyllo's home without thermal imaging" because it was nighttime.

The Fourth Amendment draws "a firm line at the entrance to the house." *Payton v. New York*, 445 U.S. 573, 590 (1980). That line must be not only firm but also bright—which requires clear specification of those methods of surveillance that require a warrant. We must take the long view, from the original meaning of the Fourth Amendment forward. Where, as here, the Government uses a device that is not in general public use, to explore details of the home that would previously have been unknowable without physical intrusion, the surveillance is a "search" and is presumptively unreasonable without a warrant.

The judgment of the Court of Appeals is reversed; the case is remanded for further proceedings consistent with this opinion. *It is so ordered.*

JUSTICE STEVENS, with whom THE CHIEF JUSTICE, JUSTICE O'CONNOR, and JUSTICE KENNEDY join, dissenting.

This case involves nothing more than off-the-wall surveillance by law enforcement officers to gather information exposed to the general public from the outside of a home. The ordinary use of the senses might enable a neighbor or passerby to notice the heat emanating from a building. Additionally, any member of the public might notice that one part of a house is warmer than another part or a nearby building if, for example, rainwater evaporates or snow melts at different rates across its surfaces. The notion that heat emissions from the outside of a dwelling are a private matter implicating the protections of the Fourth Amendment is not only unprecedented but also quite difficult to take seriously. Heat waves, like aromas that are generated in a kitchen, or in a laboratory or opium den, enter the public domain if and when they leave a building. A subjective expectation that they would remain private is not only implausible but also surely not "one that society is prepared to recognize as reasonable."

Just as "the police cannot reasonably be expected to avert their eyes from evidence of criminal activity that could have been observed by any member of the public," *Greenwood v. California*, 486 U.S. 35, 41 (1988), so too public officials should not have to avert their senses or their equipment from detecting emissions in the public domain such as excessive heat, traces of smoke, suspicious odors, odorless gases, airborne particulates, or radioactive emissions, any of which could identify hazards to the community. The countervailing privacy interest is at best trivial. Homes generally are insulated to keep heat in, rather than to prevent the detection of heat going out, and it does not seem that society will suffer from a rule requiring the rare homeowner who both intends to engage in uncommon activities that produce extraordinary amounts of heat, and wishes to conceal that production from outsiders, to make sure that the surrounding area is well insulated.

The Court has unfortunately failed to heed the counsel of judicial restraint and has endeavored to craft an all-encompassing rule for the future. It would be far wiser to give legislatures an unimpeded opportunity to grapple with these emerging issues rather than to shackle them with prematurely devised constitutional restraints. I respectfully dissent.

Hypo 1: *Sense-Enhancing Devices*

Assume that a police officer stands on a sidewalk, points a "powerful directional microphone" at a front window of a house, and eavesdrops on conversations in the living room. The government argues that the homeowner's REOP does not protect him against this surveillance because the microphone can be purchased for $100 at any retail store that sells electronics, and therefore, the device is in "general public use." How should the Court rule? As an alternate scenario, assume that the FBI obtains the assistance of an internet service provider in remotely activating a microphone and transmitter on the homeowner's cell phone, which is on a table in the living room. Then FBI agents use this microphone to eavesdrop on the conversations of people in the living room. What result under *Kyllo*?

Hypo 2: *Garage Door Opener & Key*

The police legally seize a garage door opener and keys as part of an arrest. Since the arrest is for a drug offense, and the police believe that the arrestee is dealing in drugs, they want to find out where he lives. They go to a condominium (the address on his driver's license), use the door opener on the garage door in the parking area, and insert the keys in the front door of the condominium. Both the opener and the key work. Have the police violated the arrestee's REOP? Would your answer be different if the arrestee lived in a single family home and the officers again try to garage door opener and the key? *See United States v. Correa*, 908 F.3d 208 (7th Cir. 2018).

* * *

In *Chimel v. California*, <u>395 U.S. 752 (1969)</u>, the Court held that the "search incident to arrest doctrine" allows police to make a warrantless search of an arrestee's person, as well as the area within their reach, for evidence or a weapon at the time of their arrest. In *United States v. Robinson*, <u>414 U.S. 218 (1973)</u>, the Court held that an officer could search a cigarette package in an arrestee's pocket after a custodial arrest for a traffic crime, even though no evidence (and arguably no weapon) could have been found in the package. In the following opinion, the Court examined whether cell phones should be treated differently than other containers like the cigarette package in *Robinson*.

Riley v. California

573 U.S. 373 (2014).

CHIEF JUSTICE ROBERTS delivered the opinion of the Court.

These cases raise a common question: whether the police may, without a warrant, search digital information on a cell phone seized from an individual who has been arrested. [After Riley was arrested, a police officer seized his cell phone and examined its contents as a search incident to arrest. The examination linked Riley to the Bloods gang and evidence linking him to gang violence. In a separate case, the police arrested Brima Wurie's cell phone, from which they obtained information about his residence, and ultimately searched the house, finding drugs.]

Cell phones are now such a pervasive and insistent part of daily life that the proverbial visitor from Mars might conclude they were an important feature of human anatomy. A smart phone of the sort taken from Riley was unheard of ten years ago; a significant majority of American adults now own such phones. Even less sophisticated phones like Wurie's have been around for less than 15 years. Both phones are based on technology nearly inconceivable just a few decades ago, when *United States v. Robinson*, 414 U.S. 218 (1973), was decided. *Robinson* regarded any privacy interests retained by an individual after arrest as significantly diminished by the fact of the arrest itself. Cell phones, however, place vast quantities of personal information literally in the hands of individuals.

Not every search "is acceptable solely because a person is in custody." *Maryland v. King*, 133 S. Ct. 1958, 1979 (2013). To the contrary, when "privacy-related concerns are weighty enough" a "search may require a warrant, notwithstanding the diminished expectations of privacy of the arrestee."

The United States asserts that a search of all data stored on a cell phone is "materially indistinguishable" from searches of physical items. Modern cell phones, as a category, implicate privacy concerns far beyond those implicated by the search of a cigarette pack, a wallet, or a purse. A conclusion that inspecting the contents of an arrestee's pockets works no substantial additional intrusion on privacy beyond the arrest itself may make sense as applied to physical items, but cell phones differ in both a quantitative and a qualitative sense from other objects that might be kept on an arrestee's person. Many of these devices are minicomputers that also happen to have the capacity to be used as a telephone. They could just as easily be called cameras, video players, rolodexes, calendars, tape recorders, libraries, diaries, albums, televisions, maps, or newspapers. One of the most notable distinguishing features of modern cell phones is their immense storage capacity. Before cell phones, a search of a person was limited by physical realities and tended to constitute only a narrow intrusion on privacy. Most people cannot lug around every piece of mail they have received for the past several months, every picture they have taken, or every book or article they have read—nor would they have any reason to attempt to do so. And if they did, they would have to drag behind them a trunk.

But the possible intrusion on privacy is not physically limited in the same way when it comes to cell phones. The current top-selling smart phone has a standard capacity of 16 gigabytes (and is available with up to 64 gigabytes). Sixteen gigabytes translates to millions of pages of text, thousands of pictures, or hundreds of videos. Cell phones couple that capacity with the ability to store many different types of information: Even the most basic phones that sell for less than $20 might hold photographs, picture messages, text messages, Internet browsing history, a calendar, a thousand-entry phone book, and so on. We expect that the gulf between physical practicability and digital capacity will only continue to widen in the future.

The storage capacity of cell phones has several interrelated consequences for privacy. First, a cell phone collects in one place many distinct types of information—an address, a note, a prescription, a bank statement, a video—that reveal much more in combination than any isolated record. Second, a cell phone's capacity allows even just one type of information to convey far more than previously possible. The sum of an individual's private life can be reconstructed through a thousand photographs labeled with dates, locations, and descriptions; the same cannot be said of a photograph or two of loved ones tucked into a wallet. Third, the data on a phone can date back to the purchase of the phone, or even earlier. A person might carry in his pocket a slip of paper reminding him to call Mr. Jones; he would not carry a record of all his communications with Mr. Jones for the past several months, as would routinely be kept on a phone.

Finally, there is an element of pervasiveness that characterizes cell phones but not physical records. Prior to the digital age, people did not typically carry a cache of sensitive personal information with them as they went about their day. Now the person who is not carrying a cell phone, with all that it contains, is the exception. Nearly three-quarters of smart phone users report being within five feet of their phones most of the time, with 12% admitting that they even use their phones in the shower. A decade ago police officers searching an arrestee might have occasionally stumbled across a highly personal item such as a diary. But those discoveries were likely to be few and far between. Today, by contrast, many of the more than 90% of American adults who own a cell phone keep on their person a digital record of nearly every aspect of their lives—from the mundane to the intimate. Allowing the police to scrutinize such records on a routine basis is quite different from allowing them to search a personal item or two in the occasional case.

Although the data stored on a cell phone is distinguished from physical records by quantity alone, certain types of data are also qualitatively different. An Internet search and browsing history can be found on an Internet-enabled phone and could reveal an individual's private interests or concerns—perhaps a search for certain symptoms of disease, coupled with frequent visits to WebMD. Data on a cell phone can also reveal where a person has been. Historic location information is a standard feature on many smart phones and can reconstruct someone's specific movements down to the minute, not only around town but also within a particular building.

Mobile application software on a cell phone, or "apps," offer a range of tools for managing detailed information about all aspects of a person's life. There are apps for Democratic Party news and Republican Party news; apps for alcohol, drug, and gambling addictions; apps for sharing prayer requests; apps for tracking pregnancy symptoms; apps for planning your budget; apps for every conceivable hobby or pastime; apps for improving your romantic life. There are popular apps for buying or selling just about anything, and the records of such transactions may be accessible on the phone indefinitely. There are over a million apps available in each of the two major app stores; the phrase "there's an app for that" is now part of the popular lexicon. The average smart phone user has installed 33 apps, which together can form a revealing montage of the user's life.

In 1926, Learned Hand observed that it is "a totally different thing to search a man's pockets and use against him what they contain, from ransacking his house for everything which may incriminate him." *United States v. Kirschenblatt*, 16 F. 2d 202, 203 (CA2). If his pockets contain a cell phone, that is no longer true. A cell phone search would typically expose to the government far *more* than the most exhaustive search of a house: A phone not only contains in digital form many sensitive records previously found in the home; it also contains a broad array of private information never found in a home in any form—unless the phone is.

To further complicate the scope of the privacy interests at stake, the data a user views on many modern cell phones may not in fact be stored on the device itself. Treating a cell phone as a container whose contents may be searched incident to an arrest is a bit strained as an initial matter. But the analogy crumbles entirely when a cell phone is used to access data located elsewhere, at the tap of a screen. That is what cell phones, with increasing frequency, are designed to do by taking advantage of "cloud computing." Cloud computing is the capacity of Internet-connected devices to display data stored on remote servers rather than on the device itself. Cell phone users often may not know whether particular information is stored on the device or in the cloud, and it generally makes little difference. Moreover, the same type of data may be stored locally on the device for one user and in the cloud for another.

California suggested that officers could search cell phone data if they could have obtained the same information from a pre-digital counterpart. But the fact that a search in the pre-digital era could have turned up a photograph or two in a wallet does not justify a search of thousands of photos in a digital gallery. The fact that someone could have tucked a paper bank statement in a pocket does not justify a search of every bank statement from the last five years. Such an analogue test would allow law enforcement to search a range of items contained on a phone, even though people would be unlikely to carry such a variety of information in physical form. In Riley's case, it is implausible that he would have strolled around with video tapes, photo albums, and an address book all crammed into his pockets. But because each of those items has a pre-digital analogue, police would be able to search a phone for all of those items—a significant diminution of privacy. In addition, an analogue test would launch courts on a difficult line-drawing expedition to determine which digital files are comparable to physical records. Is an e-mail equivalent to a letter? Is a voicemail equivalent to a phone message slip? It is not clear how officers could make these kinds of decisions before conducting a search, or how courts would apply the proposed rule after the fact.

We cannot deny that our decision will have an impact on the ability of law enforcement to combat crime. Cell phones have become important tools in facilitating coordination and communication among members of criminal enterprises, and can provide valuable incriminating information about dangerous criminals. Privacy comes at a cost. Our holding is not that the information on a cell phone is immune from search; it is instead that a warrant is generally required before such a search, even when a cell phone is seized incident to arrest. The warrant requirement is "an important working part of our machinery of government," not merely "an inconvenience to be somehow 'weighed' against the claims of police efficiency." *Coolidge v. New Hampshire*, 403 U. S. 443, 481 (1971). Recent technological advances similar to those discussed here have made the process of obtaining a warrant itself more efficient. *See McNeely*, 133 S. Ct. at 1561 (Roberts, C. J., concurring and dissenting) ("police officers can e-mail warrant requests to judges' iPads and judges have signed such warrants and e-mailed back in less than 15 minutes").Our cases have recognized that the Fourth Amendment was the founding generation's response to the reviled "general warrants" and "writs of assistance" of the colonial era, which allowed British officers to rummage through homes in an unrestrained search for evidence of criminal activity. Opposition to such searches was in fact one of the driving forces behind the Revolution itself. 10 Works of John Adams 247–248 (C. Adams ed. 1856). Modern cellphones are not just another technological convenience. With all they contain and all they may reveal, they hold for many Americans "the privacies of life." The fact that technology now allows an individual to carry such information in his hand does not make the information any less worthy of the protection for which the Founders fought. Our answer to the question of what police must do before searching a cell phone seized incident to an arrest is accordingly simple—get a warrant.

Food for Thought

Assume that police officers come upon a car that crashed into a lamppost late at night. The car is not occupied and the officers find a mobile phone in plain view on the front seat. When they open the car door and seize the phone, can they search the call log? Is this type of search and seizure different from the situation in *Riley? See United States v. Crumble,* 878 F.3d 656 (8th Cir. 2018). Alternatively, suppose that a fleeing suspect discards his cell phone. Does he retain a REOP in a discarded cell phone? *See United States v. Guerrero-Torres,* 762 Fed. Appx. 873 (11th Cir. 2019).

Point for Discussion

Protection for Electronic Communications

In 2014, the Missouri state constitution was amended by referendum to add "electronic communications and data" to the textual reference to protection for "persons, houses, papers, and effects." In 2015, California enacted the Electronic Communications Privacy Act which requires a warrant for "all digital content, location information, metadata, and access to devices like cell phones." Between 2017 to 2019, Maine, Nevada, and Minnesota enacted privacy legislation to regulate ISPs by prohibiting various kinds of disclosures of subscriber information without consent. *See generally* National Conference of State Legislatures (NCSL), *State Laws Related to Internet Privacy,* https://www.ncsl.org/research/telecommunications-and-information-technology/state-laws-related-to-internet-privacy.aspx#Consumer.

Hypo 1: *Seizing the Cell Phone*

Police were summoned to defendant's trailer after a woman was heard yelling "Stop!" At the trailer, they find defendant as well as an underdressed 16-year-old girl. In the course of an ensuring conversation, the girl admits that defendant's cell phone contains nude pictures of her as well as a video of her having sex with defendant. The police immediately seize the phone but do not search it until they obtain a warrant. Was the seizure permissible? *See United States v. Babcock,* 924 F.3d 1180 (11th Cir. 2019).

> ## Hypo 2: *Are Text Messages Different?*
>
> Suspecting that someone is involved in criminal activity, police investigators subpoena his internet service provider to compel the production of his cell phone text messages. Does *Smith v. Maryland* suggest that the suspect has no REOP in his text messages, because they were sent through a third party, and therefore, no Fourth Amendment violation occurs when police subpoena and read the messages? Can it be argued that the warrantless seizure of text messages is fundamentally different from the seizure of the dialed telephone numbers that are recorded by a pen register? Can text messages be analogized to ordinary mail sent through the post office, which is protected by *Katz*, so that the sender can assume that the messages will be read only by the recipient and not the carrier? *See Love v. State*, 543 S.W.3d 835 (Tex. Ct. Crim. App. 2016).

Carpenter v. United States

138 S.Ct. 2206 (2018).

CHIEF JUSTICE ROBERTS delivered the opinion of the Court.

In 2011, police arrested four men suspected of robbing Radio Shack and T-Mobile stores in Detroit. One of the men confessed that the group had robbed nine different stores in Michigan and Ohio. The suspect identified 15 accomplices and gave the FBI some of their cell phone numbers; the FBI reviewed his call records to identify additional numbers that he had called around the time of the robberies. Based on that information, the prosecutors applied for court orders under the Stored Communications Act to obtain cell phone records for petitioner Carpenter and others. That statute permits the Government to compel the disclosure of telecommunications records when it "offers specific and articulable facts showing that there are reasonable grounds to believe" that the records sought "are relevant and material to an ongoing criminal investigation." Federal Magistrates issued two orders directing Carpenter's wireless carriers—MetroPCS and Sprint—to disclose "cell/site sector information for Carpenter's telephone at call origination and at call termination for incoming and outgoing calls" during the four-month period when the string of robberies occurred. The first order sought 152 days of cell-site records from MetroPCS, which produced records spanning 127 days. The second order requested seven days of CSLI from Sprint, which produced two days of records covering the period when Carpenter's phone was in Ohio. The Government obtained 12,898 location points cataloging Carpenter's movements. Carpenter was charged with robbery and carrying a firearm during a federal crime of violence. Carpenter moved to suppress the cell-site data. The

District Court denied the motion. Carpenter was convicted. The Court of Appeals for the Sixth Circuit affirmed. We granted certiorari.

Although no single rubric definitively resolves which expectations of privacy are entitled to protection, the analysis is informed by historical understandings "of what was deemed an unreasonable search and seizure when [the Fourth Amendment] was adopted." *Carroll v. United States,* 267 U.S. 132, 149 (1925). On this score, our cases have recognized some basic guideposts. First, that the Amendment seeks to secure "the privacies of life" against "arbitrary power." *Boyd v. United States,* 116 U.S. 616, 630 (1886). Second, and relatedly, that a central aim of the Framers was "to place obstacles in the way of a too permeating police surveillance." *United States v. Di Re,* 332 U.S. 581, 595 (1948).

[This] case involves the Government's acquisition of wireless carrier cell-site records revealing the location of Carpenter's cell phone when it made or received calls. This sort of digital data—personal location information maintained by a third party—does not fit neatly under existing precedents. In *United States v. Knotts,* 460 U.S. 276 (1983), we [held that] the Government's use of a "beeper" to aid in tracking a vehicle did not constitute a search because "a person traveling in an automobile on public thoroughfares has no reasonable expectation of privacy in his movements." The movements of the vehicle and its destination had been "voluntarily conveyed to anyone who wanted to look." The Court emphasized that the "limited use which the government made of the signals from this particular beeper" during a discrete "automotive journey." Three decades later, in *United States v. Jones,* 565 U.S. 400 (2012), FBI agents installed a GPS tracking device on Jones's vehicle and monitored the vehicle's movements for 28 days. The Court decided the case based on the Government's physical trespass of the vehicle. Five Justices agreed that privacy concerns would be raised by "surreptitiously activating a stolen vehicle detection system" in Jones's car to track Jones or conducting GPS tracking of his cell phone. Since GPS monitoring of a vehicle tracks "every movement," "longer term GPS monitoring impinges on expectations of privacy"—regardless whether those movements were disclosed to the public at large.

The Court has drawn a line between what a person keeps to himself and what he shares with others. "A person has no legitimate expectation of privacy in information he voluntarily turns over to third parties." *Smith v. Maryland,* 442 U.S. 735, 743 (1979). That remains true "even if the information is revealed on the assumption that it will be used only for a limited purpose." *United States v. Miller,* 425 U.S. 435, 443 (1976). As a result, the Government is typically free to obtain such information from the recipient without triggering Fourth Amendment protections. This third-party doctrine largely traces its roots to *Miller.* Miller could "assert neither ownership nor possession" of the documents; they were "business records of the banks." The checks were "not confidential communications but negotiable instruments to be used in commercial transactions," and the bank statements contained information "exposed to bank employees in the ordinary course of business." Miller had "taken the risk, in revealing his affairs to another, that the information would be conveyed by that person to the Government." *Smith* applied the same principles in the context of information conveyed to a telephone company. The Court "doubted that people in general entertain any actual expectation of privacy in the numbers they dial." Telephone subscribers know that the numbers are used by the telephone company "for a variety of legitimate business purposes," including routing calls. Such an expectation "is not one that society is prepared to recognize as reasonable." *Smith* "voluntarily conveyed" the dialed numbers to the phone company by "exposing that information to its equipment in the ordinary course of business" and defendant "assumed the risk" that the company's records "would be divulged to police."

Much like GPS tracking of a vehicle, cell phone location information is detailed, encyclopedic, and effortlessly compiled. The fact that the individual continuously reveals his location to his wireless carrier implicates the third-party principle of *Smith* and *Miller*. But while the third-party doctrine applies to telephone numbers and bank records, it is not clear whether its logic extends to the qualitatively different category of cell-site records. When *Smith* was decided, few could have imagined a society in which a phone goes wherever its owner goes, conveying to the wireless carrier not just dialed digits, but a detailed and comprehensive record of the person's movements. We decline to extend *Smith* and *Miller* to cover these novel circumstances. Given the unique nature of cell phone location records, the fact that the information is held by a third party does not by itself overcome the user's claim to Fourth Amendment protection. An individual maintains a legitimate expectation of privacy in the record of his physical movements as captured through CSLI. The location information obtained from Carpenter's wireless carriers was the product of a search.

"What one seeks to preserve as private, even in an area accessible to the public, may be constitutionally protected." *Katz v. United States*, 389 U.S. 347, 351 (1967). Individuals have a reasonable expectation of privacy in the whole of their physical movements. Prior to the digital age, law enforcement might have pursued a suspect for a brief stretch, but doing so "for any extended period of time was difficult and costly and rarely undertaken." *Jones*, 565 U.S. at 429 (opinion of Alito, J.). For that reason, "society's expectation has been that law enforcement agents and others would not—and indeed could not—secretly monitor and catalogue every movement of an individual's car for a very long period." *Id.* at 430. Allowing government access to cell-site records contravenes that expectation. Although such records are generated for commercial purposes, that distinction does not negate Carpenter's anticipation of privacy in his physical location. Mapping a cell phone's location over the course of 127 days provides an all-encompassing record of the holder's whereabouts. The time-stamped data provides an intimate window into a person's life, revealing not only his particular movements, but through them his "familial, political, professional, religious, and sexual associations." These location records "hold the 'privacies of life.'" *Riley v. California*, 573 U.S. 373, 392 (2014). With the click of a button, Government can access each carrier's deep repository of historical location information at practically no expense. Historical cell-site records present even greater privacy concerns than GPS monitoring. Unlike the bugged container in *Knotts* or the car in *Jones*, a cell phone—almost a "feature of human anatomy," tracks nearly exactly the movements of its owner. While individuals regularly leave their vehicles, they carry cell phones beyond public thoroughfares and into private residences, doctor's offices, political headquarters, and other potentially revealing locales. When the Government tracks the location of a cell phone it achieves near perfect surveillance, as if it had attached an ankle monitor to the phone's user. In the past, attempts to reconstruct a person's movements were limited by a dearth of records and the frailties of recollection. With CSLI (cell site location information), the Government can travel back in time to retrace a person's whereabouts, subject only to the retention polices of the wireless carriers, which currently maintain records for up to five years. Because location information is continually logged for the 400 million devices in the United States—not just those belonging to persons who might come under investigation—this newfound tracking capacity runs against everyone. Police need not know in advance whether they want to follow a particular individual. The suspect has effectively been tailed every moment of every day for five years. Only the few without cell phones escape this tireless and absolute surveillance.

The accuracy of CSLI is rapidly approaching GPS-level precision. As the number of cell sites has proliferated, the geographic area covered by each cell sector has shrunk, particularly in urban areas. With new technology measuring the time and angle of signals hitting their towers, wireless carriers have the capability to pinpoint a phone's location within 50 meters. Accordingly, when the Government accessed CSLI from the wireless carriers, it invaded Carpenter's reasonable expectation of privacy in his physical movements.

The Government's [contends] that the third-party doctrine governs this case. In its view, cell-site records are "business records" created and maintained by the wireless carriers. The Government recognizes that this case features new technology, but asserts that the legal question turns on a garden-variety request for information from a third-party witness. The Government's position fails to contend with the seismic shifts in digital technology that made possible the tracking of not only Carpenter's location but also everyone else's, not for a short period but for years. Sprint and its competitors are not your typical witnesses. Unlike the nosy neighbor, they are ever alert, and their memory is nearly infallible. There is a world of difference between the limited types of personal information addressed in *Smith* and *Miller* and the exhaustive chronicle of location information casually collected by wireless carriers today. The Government thus is not asking for a straightforward application of the third-party doctrine, but instead a significant extension of it to a distinct category of information.

The third-party doctrine stems from the notion that an individual has a reduced expectation of privacy in information knowingly shared with another. But "diminished privacy interests does not mean that the Fourth Amendment falls out of the picture entirely." *Riley v. California*, 573 U.S. at 403. *Smith* and *Miller* did not rely solely on the act of sharing. They considered "the nature of the documents sought" to determine whether "there is a legitimate 'expectation of privacy' concerning their contents." *Smith* pointed out the limited capabilities of a pen register [which reveals] little in the way of "identifying information." *Miller* noted that checks were "not confidential communications but negotiable instruments used in commercial transactions." The Government fails to appreciate that there are no comparable limitations on CSLI. In *Knotts*, the Court relied on *Smith* to hold that an individual has no reasonable expectation of privacy in public movements that he "voluntarily conveyed to anyone who wanted to look." But five Justices agreed that longer term GPS monitoring of a vehicle traveling on public streets constitutes a search. This case is about a detailed chronicle of a person's physical presence compiled every day, every moment, over several years. Such a chronicle implicates privacy concerns beyond those considered in *Smith* and *Miller*. Neither does the second rationale underlying the third-party doctrine—voluntary exposure—hold up. Cell phones and the services they provide are "such a pervasive and insistent part of daily life" that carrying one is indispensable to participation in modern society. A cell phone logs a cell-site record without any affirmative act on the part of the user beyond powering up. Virtually any activity on the phone generates CSLI, including incoming calls, texts, or e-mails and countless other data connections that a phone automatically makes when checking for news, weather, or social media updates. Apart from disconnecting the phone, there is no way to avoid leaving a trail of location data. In no meaningful sense does the user voluntarily "assume the risk" of turning over a comprehensive dossier of his physical movements. We decline to extend *Smith* and *Miller* to the collection of CSLI. The fact that the Government obtained the information from a third party does not overcome Carpenter's claim to Fourth Amendment protection. The Government's acquisition of cell-site records was a search within the meaning of the Fourth Amendment.

We do not express a view on real-time CSLI or "tower dumps" (a download of information on all the devices that connected to a particular cell site during a particular interval). We do not disturb the application of *Smith* and *Miller* or call into question conventional surveillance techniques and tools, such as security cameras. Nor do we address other business records that might incidentally reveal location information. Further, our opinion does not consider other collection techniques involving foreign affairs or national security.

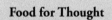

Food for Thought

Following *Riley* and *Carpenter*, what remains of the Third Party Doctrine? In what contexts will that doctrine apply?

Having found that the acquisition of Carpenter's CSLI was a search, the Government must generally obtain a warrant supported by probable cause before acquiring such records. Although the "ultimate measure of the constitutionality of a governmental search is 'reasonableness,' " warrantless searches are typically unreasonable where "a search is undertaken by law enforcement officials to discover evidence of criminal wrongdoing." *Vernonia School Dist. 47J v. Acton*, 515 U.S. 646, 652 (1995). "In the absence of a warrant, a search is reasonable only if it falls within a specific exception to the warrant requirement." *Riley*, 573 U.S. at 382. The Government acquired the cell-site records pursuant to a court order issued under the Stored Communications Act, which required the Government to show "reasonable grounds" for believing that the records were "relevant and material to an ongoing investigation." That showing falls short of the probable cause required for a warrant. The Court usually requires "some quantum of individualized suspicion" before a search or seizure may take place. Consequently, an order under Section 2703(d) of the Act is not a permissible mechanism for accessing historical cell-site records. Before compelling a wireless carrier to turn over a subscriber's CSLI, the Government's obligation is a familiar one—get a warrant.

Food for Thought

In an effort to catch criminals, a city decides to deploy police drones throughout the city. 24 hours a day, seven days a week, the city has hundreds of drones flying over the city. The drones only observe what is going on in public, and do not peer into houses or other private spaces. Under *Carpenter*, does the city's use of the drones constitute a search within the meaning of the Fourth Amendment?

Justice Alito contends that the warrant requirement simply does not apply when the Government acquires records using compulsory process. Given [the] lesser intrusion on personal privacy, the compulsory production of records is not held to the same probable cause standard. This Court's precedents set forth a categorical rule—separate and distinct from the third-party doctrine—subjecting subpoenas to lenient scrutiny without regard to the suspect's expectation of privacy in the records. But this Court has never held that the Government may subpoena third parties for records in which the suspect has a reasonable expectation of privacy. CSLI is an entirely different species of business record—something that implicates basic Fourth Amendment concerns about arbitrary government power much more directly than corporate tax or payroll ledgers. When confronting new digital technology, this Court has been careful not to uncritically extend existing precedents.

If the choice to proceed by subpoena provided a categorical limitation on Fourth Amendment protection, no type of record would ever be protected by the warrant requirement. Private letters, digital contents of a cell phone—any personal information reduced to document form, may be collected by subpoena for no reason other than "official curiosity." Justice Kennedy [leaves] open the question whether the warrant requirement applies "when the Government obtains the modern-day equivalents of an individual's own 'papers' or 'effects,' even when those papers or effects are held by a third party." That would be a sensible exception, because it would prevent the subpoena doctrine from overcoming any reasonable expectation of privacy. If the third-party doctrine does not apply to the "modern-day equivalents of an individual's own 'papers' or 'effects,' " then the implication is that the documents should receive full Fourth Amendment protection. We think that such protection should extend to a detailed log of a person's movements over several years. This is not to say that all orders compelling the production of documents will require a showing of probable cause. The Government will be able to use subpoenas to acquire records in the overwhelming majority of investigations. We hold only that a warrant is required in the rare case where the suspect has a legitimate privacy interest in records held by a third party.

Case-specific exceptions may support a warrantless search of an individual's cell-site records under certain circumstances. One well-recognized exception applies when "the exigencies of the situation make the needs of law enforcement so compelling that a warrantless search is objectively reasonable under the Fourth Amendment.' " *Kentucky v. King*, 563 U.S. 452, 460 (2011). Such exigencies include the need to pursue a fleeing suspect, protect individuals who are threatened with imminent harm, or prevent the imminent destruction of evidence. If law enforcement is confronted with an urgent situation, such fact-specific threats will likely justify the warrantless collection of CSLI. Lower courts have approved warrantless searches related to bomb threats, active shootings, and child abductions. While police must get a warrant when collecting CSLI to assist in the mine-run criminal investigation, the rule does not limit their ability to respond to an ongoing emergency.

As Justice Brandeis explained in his famous dissent, the Court is obligated—as "subtler and more far-reaching means of invading privacy have become available to the Government"—to ensure that the "progress of science" does not erode Fourth Amendment protections. *Olmstead v. United States*, 277 U.S. 438, 473 (1928). Here the progress of science has afforded law enforcement a powerful new tool to carry out its important responsibilities. At the same time, this tool risks Government encroachment of the sort the Framers, "after consulting the lessons of history," drafted the Fourth Amendment to prevent. *Di Re*, 332 U.S. at 595. We decline to grant the

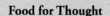

Food for Thought

Defendant was involved in a fatal car crash that the police believe that he caused. The police believe that data from the airbag control module (ACM) will provide useful information related to the accident such as the car's speed, brake status and throttle position. As a result, the police seize the ACM information without a warrant. Does the driver have a REOP in the data contained on the ACM? Must the police obtain a warrant in order to access that information? *See Mobley v. State*, 346 Ga. App. 641, 816 S.E.2d 769 (Ga. 2019).

state unrestricted access to a wireless carrier's database of physical location information. In light of the deeply revealing nature of CSLI, its depth, breadth, and comprehensive reach, and the inescapable and automatic nature of its collection, the fact that such information is gathered by a third party does not make it any less deserving of Fourth Amendment protection. The Government's acquisition of the cell-site records here was a search under that Amendment.

The judgment of the Court of Appeals is reversed, and the case is remanded for further proceedings consistent with this opinion.

It is so ordered.

JUSTICE KENNEDY, with whom JUSTICE THOMAS and JUSTICE ALITO join, dissenting.

The Court has twice held that individuals have no Fourth Amendment interests in business records which are possessed, owned, and controlled by a third party. So when the Government uses a subpoena to obtain bank records, telephone records, and credit card statements from the businesses that create and keep these records, the Government does not engage in a search of the business's customers within the meaning of the Fourth Amendment. Cell-site records are no different. Customers do not own, possess, control, or use the records, and for that reason have no reasonable expectation that they cannot be disclosed pursuant to lawful compulsory process.

The Court unhinges Fourth Amendment doctrine from the property-based concepts that have long grounded the analytic framework that pertains in these cases. In doing so it draws an unprincipled and unworkable line between cell-site records and financial and telephonic records. The Government can acquire a record of every credit card purchase and phone call a person makes over months or years without upsetting a legitimate expectation of privacy. But the Government crosses a constitutional line when it obtains a court's approval to issue a subpoena for more than six days of cell-site records in order to determine whether a person was within several hundred city blocks of a crime scene. That distinction is illogical. There is no basis for concluding that the Government interfered with information that the cell phone customer should have thought the law would deem owned or controlled by him. Cell-site records reveal the general location of the cell phone user. The information is imprecise because an individual cell-site covers a large geographic area. Major cell phone service providers keep cell-site records for long periods of time. Providers aggregate the records and sell them to third parties along with other information gleaned from cell phone usage. The market for cell phone data is in the billions of dollars.

The customary beginning point in any Fourth Amendment search case is whether the Government's actions constitute a "search" of defendant's person, house, papers, or effects, within the meaning of the constitution. The question is whether that search was reasonable. *Miller* and *Smith* hold that individuals lack any protected Fourth

Amendment interests in records possessed, owned, and controlled by a third party. As a matter of settled expectations, individuals have greater expectations of privacy in things and places that belong to them. Defendants could expect that third-party businesses could use the records the companies collected, stored, and classified as their own for any number of business and commercial purposes. The businesses were not bailees or custodians of the records. While a warrant allows the Government to enter and seize and make the examination itself, a subpoena simply requires the person to whom it is directed to make the disclosure. A subpoena provides the recipient the "opportunity to present objections" before complying, which further mitigates the intrusion. For those reasons a subpoena complies with the Fourth Amendment's reasonableness requirement so long as it is "sufficiently limited in scope, relevant in purpose, and specific in directive so that compliance will not be unreasonably burdensome." *Donovan v. Lone Steer, Inc.,* 464 U.S. 408, 415 (1984). Persons with no meaningful interests in the records sought by a subpoena have no rights to object to the records' disclosure—much less to assert that the Government must obtain a warrant. State and federal law enforcement subpoena credit card statements to develop probable cause to prosecute crimes ranging from drug trafficking and distribution to healthcare fraud to tax evasion. Subpoenas also may be used to obtain vehicle registration records, hotel records, employment records, and records of utility usage. Subpoenas also are used for investigatory purposes by state and federal grand juries, state and federal administrative agencies, and state and federal legislative bodies. Cell-site records are created, kept, classified, owned, and controlled by cell phone service providers, which aggregate and sell this information to third parties. Carpenter can "assert neither ownership nor possession" of the records and has no control over them.

Carpenter argues that he has Fourth Amendment interests in cell-site records because they are in essence his personal papers by operation of 47 U.S.C. § 222. That statute imposes restrictions on how providers may use "customer proprietary network information"—a term that encompasses cell-site records. The statute prohibits providers from disclosing personally identifiable cell-site records to private third parties. And it allows customers to request cell-site records from the provider. Carpenter's argument is unpersuasive for § 222 does not grant cell phone customers any meaningful interest in cell-site records. Nor does the statute provide customers any practical control over the records. Customers do not create the records; they have no say in whether or for how long the records are stored; and they cannot require the records to be modified or destroyed. In every legal and practical sense the "network information" regulated by § 222 is "proprietary" to the providers. Carpenter also may not claim a reasonable expectation of privacy. The cell phone service provider could use the information it collected, stored, and classified as its own for a variety of business and commercial purposes. This case does not involve property or a bailment. *Knotts* suggested that "different constitutional principles may be applicable" to "dragnet-type law enforcement practices." But the Court was referring to "twenty-four hour surveillance of any citizen without judicial knowledge or supervision." Cases like this one, where the

Government uses court-approved compulsory process to obtain records owned and controlled by a third party, are governed by *Miller* and *Smith*.

The Court errs when it concludes that cell-site records implicate greater privacy interests—and thus deserve greater—than financial records and telephone records. A person's movements are not particularly private as the Court recognized in *Knotts*. Today expectations of privacy in one's location are even less reasonable. Millions of Americans choose to share their location on a daily basis, whether by using a variety of location-based services on their phones, or by sharing their location with friends and the public at large via social media. And cell-site records disclose a person's location only in a general area. The records here revealed Carpenter's location within an area covering between a dozen and several hundred city blocks. By contrast, financial records and telephone records reveal what persons purchase and to whom they talk might disclose how much money they make; the political and religious organizations to which they donate; whether they have visited a psychiatrist, plastic surgeon, abortion clinic, or AIDS treatment center; whether they go to gay bars or straight ones; and who are their closest friends and family members. The troves of intimate information the Government can obtain using financial records and telephone records dwarfs what can be gathered from cell-site records. And the decision whether to transact with banks and credit card companies is no more or less voluntary than the decision whether to use a cell phone. "It is impossible to participate in the economic life of contemporary society without a bank account." But this Court has held that individuals do not have a reasonable expectation of privacy in financial records.

Cell phones make crimes easier to coordinate and conceal, while also providing the Government with new investigative tools that may have the potential to upset traditional privacy expectations. It is wise to defer to legislative judgments like the one embodied in § 2703(d) of the Stored Communications Act. Congress weighed the privacy interests at stake and imposed a judicial check to prevent executive overreach. The Court should be wary of upsetting that legislative balance and erecting constitutional barriers that foreclose further legislative instructions. The Court's holding that the Government must get a warrant to obtain more than six days of cell-site records limits the effectiveness of an important investigative tool for solving serious crimes. The long-term nature of many serious crimes, including serial crimes and terrorism offenses, necessitate the use of significantly more than six days of cell-site records.

The Court's holding is premised on cell-site records being a "distinct category of information" from other business records. But the Court does not explain what makes something distinct [and] the majority gives courts and law enforcement officers no indication how to determine whether any particular category of information falls on the financial-records side or the cell-site-records side of its newly conceived constitutional line. The Court's multifactor analysis—considering intimacy, comprehensiveness, expense, retrospectivity, and voluntariness—puts the law on a new and unstable foundation. Even if a distinct category of information is deemed to be more like cell-site records, courts and law enforcement officers will have to guess how much information can be requested before a warrant is required. By invalidating the Government's use of court-approved compulsory process, the Court calls into question the subpoena practices of federal and state grand juries, legislatures, and other investigative bodies.

JUSTICE THOMAS, dissenting.

By obtaining the cell-site records of MetroPCS and Sprint, the Government did not search Carpenter's property. He did not create the records, does not maintain them, cannot control them, and cannot destroy them. The records belong to MetroPCS and Sprint.

Katz has no basis in the text or history of the Fourth Amendment [and] it invites courts to make judgments about policy, not law. At the founding, "search" did not mean a violation of someone's reasonable expectation of privacy. Its ordinary meaning was "to look over or through for the purpose of finding something; to explore; to examine by inspection; as, to search the house for a book." *Kyllo v. United States*, 533 U.S. 27, 32 (2001). The word "privacy" does not appear in the Fourth Amendment (or anywhere in the Constitution). Instead, the Fourth Amendment references "the right of the people to be secure." It then limits it to "persons" and "houses, papers, and effects." By connecting the right to be secure to these four objects, "the text of the Fourth Amendment reflects its close connection to property." *Jones, supra*, at 405. The concept of security in property recognized by Locke and the English legal tradition appeared throughout the materials that inspired the Fourth Amendment. Adams [argued] that "property must be secured, or liberty cannot exist." *Discourse on Davila*, in 6 The Works of John Adams 280 C. Adams ed. 1851). Of course, the founding generation understood that, by securing their property, the Fourth Amendment would protect their privacy as well. But the Fourth Amendment does not justify *Katz*'s elevation of privacy as the *sine qua non* of the Amendment. As *Katz* recognized, the Fourth Amendment "cannot be translated into a general constitutional 'right to privacy,' " as its protections "often have nothing to do with privacy." The organizing constitutional idea of the founding era was property. In shifting the focus of the Fourth Amendment, *Katz* reads the words "persons, houses, papers, and effects" out of the text. The Founders decided to protect people from unreasonable searches and seizures of four specific things—persons, houses, papers, and effects. They identified those categories as "the objects of privacy protection to which the Constitution would extend, leaving further expansion to the people through their representatives in the legislature." *Minnesota v. Carter*, 525 U.S. 83, 97 (1998) (Scalia, J., concurring). Until today, our precedents have not acknowledged that individuals can claim a reasonable expectation of privacy in someone else's business records. The records are the business records of Sprint and MetroPCS. If someone stole these records, Carpenter does not argue that he could recover in a traditional tort action.

The common law required warrants for some types of searches and seizures, but not for many others. A subpoena for third-party documents was not a "search," and the common law did not limit the government's authority to subpoena third parties. The Founders would be confused by this Court's transformation of their common-law protection of property into a "warrant requirement" and a vague inquiry into "reasonable expectations of privacy." *Katz* has proved unworkable. *Katz* turns on society's current views about the reasonableness of various expectations of privacy. But the whole point of *Katz* was to "discredit" the relationship between the Fourth Amendment and property law, and this Court has repeatedly downplayed the importance of property law under *Katz*. Today, the Court makes no mention of property except to reject its relevance. As for "understandings that are recognized or permitted in society," our precedents do not explain who is included in "society," how we know what they "recognize or permit," and how much of society must agree before something constitutes an "understanding." Here, society might prefer a balanced regime that prohibits the Government from obtaining cell-site location information unless it can persuade a neutral magistrate that the information bears on an ongoing criminal investigation. That is precisely the regime Congress created. The Court invalidates this regime—the one that society actually created [through] "its elected representatives in Congress." Because *Katz* is a failed experiment, this Court is duty bound to reconsider it.

JUSTICE ALITO, with whom JUSTICE THOMAS joins, dissenting.

The Court ignores the distinction between an actual search and an order requiring a party to look through its own records and produce specified documents. The former, which intrudes on personal privacy more deeply, requires probable cause; the latter does not. Treating an order to produce like an actual search violates both the original understanding of the Fourth Amendment and more than a century of precedent. The Court [also] allows a defendant to object to the search of a third party's property. This is revolutionary. The Fourth Amendment protects "the right of the people to be secure in their persons, houses, papers, and effects", not the persons, houses, papers, and effects of others.

Compulsory process was familiar to the founding generation because it reflected "the ancient proposition" that "the public has a right to every man's evidence." *United States v. Nixon*, 418 U.S. 683, 709 (1974). By its terms, the Fourth Amendment does not apply to the compulsory production of documents, a practice that involves neither a physical intrusion into private space nor a taking of property by the state. "The Fourth Amendment was the founding generation's response to the reviled 'general warrants' and 'writs of assistance' of the colonial era, which allowed British officers to rummage through homes in an unrestrained search for evidence of criminal activity." *Riley v. California*, 573 U.S. 373, 403 (2014). A subpoena *duces tecum* permits a subpoenaed individual to conduct the search for the relevant documents himself, without law enforcement officers entering his home or rooting through his papers and effects. A showing of probable cause was not necessary so long as "the investigation is authorized by Congress, is for a purpose Congress can order, and the documents sought are relevant to the inquiry." Here the Government received the cell-site records pursuant to a court order. No search or seizure of Carpenter or his property occurred. The reason that we have never seen such a case is because—until today—defendants categorically had no "reasonable expectation of privacy" and no property interest in records belonging to third parties. Holding that subpoenas must meet the same standard as conventional searches will seriously damage their utility. Grand juries will be unable to demonstrate "the probable cause required for a warrant." If they are required to do so, many investigations will sputter and a host of criminals will be able to evade law enforcement's reach.

The Fourth Amendment guarantees "the right of the people to be secure in their persons, houses, papers, and effects." *Rakas v. Illinois*, 439 U.S. 128, 140 (1978). This Court has long insisted that [Fourth Amendment rights]y "may not be asserted vicariously," *id.* at 133. In this case, Carpenter has no meaningful control over the cell-site records, which are created, maintained, altered, used, and eventually destroyed by his cell service providers. Carpenter points to a provision of the Telecommunications Act that requires a provider to disclose cell-site records when a customer so requests. But a disclosure requirement is hardly sufficient to give someone an ownership interest in the documents. Nor does the Telecommunications Act give Carpenter a property right in the cell-site records simply because they are subject to confidentiality restrictions. Carpenter lacks any meaningful property-based connection to the cell-site records owned by his provider. Carpenter may not use the Fourth Amendment to exclude them. By holding otherwise, the Court allows Carpenter to object to the "search" of a third party's property.

All of this is unnecessary. In the Stored Communications Act, Congress restricts the misuse of cell-site records by cell service providers. The Act also restricts access by law enforcement. It permits law enforcement officers to acquire cell-site records only if they meet a heightened standard and obtain a court order. If the American people think that the Act is inadequate, they can turn to their elected representatives. Some of the greatest threats to individual privacy come from powerful private companies that collect and sometimes misuse vast quantities of data about the lives of ordinary Americans. If today's decision encourages the public to think that this Court can protect them from this looming threat to their privacy, the decision will mislead as well as disrupt.

JUSTICE GORSUCH, dissenting.

Once you disclose information to third parties, you forfeit any reasonable expectation of privacy you might have had. Why is someone's location when using a phone more sensitive than who he was talking to or what financial transactions he engaged in? Can the government demand a copy of your e-mails from Google or Microsoft without implicating your Fourth Amendment rights? Can it secure your DNA from 23andMe without a warrant or probable cause? *Smith* and *Miller* say yes. Countless scholars have concluded that the "third-party doctrine is horribly wrong."

[If *Katz's*] "reasonable expectation of privacy" test is supposed to be empirical, it's unclear why judges rather than legislators should conduct it. Legislators are responsive to their constituents and have institutional resources designed to help them discern and enact majoritarian preferences. Politically insulated judges are hardly the representative group you'd expect (or want) to be making empirical judgments for hundreds of millions of people. *Katz* has yielded an often unpredictable—and sometimes unbelievable—jurisprudence. *Smith* and *Miller* are two examples. The Court declines to say whether there is any sufficiently limited period of time "for which the Government may obtain an individual's historical location information free from Fourth Amendment scrutiny." But it tells us that access to seven days' worth of information does trigger Fourth Amendment scrutiny—even though here the carrier "produced only two days of records." Why seven days instead of three or one? The Court can't say whether the Fourth Amendment is triggered when the government collects "real-time CSLI or 'tower dumps' (a download of information on all the devices connected to a particular cell site during a particular interval)." But what distinguishes historical data from real-time data, or seven days of a single person's data from a download of everyone's data over some indefinite period of time? Why isn't a tower dump "too permeating police surveillance" and a dangerous tool of "arbitrary" authority? The Court tells us its decision does not "call into question conventional surveillance techniques and tools, such as security cameras." That raises questions about what techniques qualify as "conventional" and why those techniques would be okay if they lead to "permeating police surveillance" or "arbitrary police power."

Under [a] traditional approach, Fourth Amendment protections for your papers and effects do not automatically disappear just because you share them with third parties. Entrusting your stuff to others is a bailment. A bailee who uses the item in a different way than he's supposed to, or against the bailor's instructions, is liable for conversion. This approach is quite different from *Smith* and *Miller's* approach to reasonable expectations of privacy; whereas those cases extinguish Fourth Amendment interests once records are given to a third party, property law may preserve them. In *Ex parte Jackson*, 96 U.S. 727 (1878), this Court held that sealed letters placed in the mail are "as fully guarded from examination and inspection, except as to their form and weight, as if they were retained by the parties forwarding them." It did not matter that letters were bailed to a third party. The sender enjoyed the same Fourth Amendment protection as "when papers are subjected to search in one's own household." Just because you entrust your data—your modern-day papers and effects—to a third party may not mean you lose any Fourth Amendment interest in its contents. Few doubt that e-mail should be treated like the traditional mail it has supplanted.

I doubt that complete ownership or exclusive control of property is a necessary condition to assertion of a Fourth Amendment right. "People call a house 'their' home when legal title is in the bank, when they rent it, and even when they occupy it rent free." *Carter*, 525 U.S. at 95 (Scalia, J., concurring). That is why tenants and family members—though they have no legal title—have standing to complain about searches of the houses in which they live. Just because you have to entrust a third party with your data doesn't mean you should lose all Fourth Amendment protections. Use of technology is functionally compelled by the demands of modern life, and the fact that we store data with third parties may amount to a sort of involuntary bailment. If state legislators or courts say that a digital record has the attributes that normally make something property, that may supply a sounder basis for judicial decisionmaking than judicial guesswork about societal expectations. While positive law may help establish a person's Fourth Amendment interest there may be some circumstances where positive law cannot be used to defeat it. *Ex parte Jackson* said that "no law of Congress" could authorize letter carriers "to invade the secrecy of letters." 96 U.S. at 733. The post office couldn't impose a regulation dictating that those mailing letters surrender all legal interests in them once they're deposited in a mailbox. Nor does this mean protecting only the specific rights known at the founding; it means protecting their modern analogues too. I do not agree with the decision to keep *Smith* and *Miller* on life support.

Hypo 1: *Stingray Devices*

Federal and state law enforcement officials are now using a device known as a "stingray" or "IMSI catcher," which can imitate a cell phone tower and thereby interact with all nearby cell phones. Using radio waves, the stingray downloads the identifying data (IMSI or ESN) from all of the connected cell phones without going through the service provider. The stingray device can pinpoint the house in which a cell phone is located, even when no one is using the phone to make a call or obtain access to the internet. When stingray surveillance occurs, service to the connected cell phone is disrupted and it cannot be used. In order to obtain a stingray device from the manufacturer, a police department must sign a non-disclosure agreement, which is why the prevalence of stingray use remained secret until media revelations in 2014. Does the use of a stingray device constitute a "search" of the cell phones that are forced to connect to it? Does it matter whether the cell phone is in public or in a private home? If so, should the warrant requirement apply to stingray usage? How should a court respond if a prosecutor or police officer refuses to disclose evidence of stingray use, either to defense counsel or to the court, during court proceedings? *See United States v. Lambis*, 197 F. Supp. 3d 606 (S.D.N.Y. 2016); *United States v. Patrick*, 842 F.3d 540 (7th Cir. 2016).

Hypo 2: *Other Electronic Data*

After *Carpenter*, suppose that the police stop accessing historical cell site data. Can they "ping" a suspect's cell phone in order to ascertain his location, or does that constitute a "search" within the meaning of the Fourth Amendment? *See Commonwealth v. Almonor*, 482 Mass. 35, 120 N.E.3d 1183 (Mass. 2019). Likewise, is it a search when the police access email addresses, names, or internet protocol addresses from an ISP? *See United States v. Tolbert*, 326 F. Supp. 3d 1211 (D.N.M. 2018). What if they access and view publicly available peer-to-peer network (designed to allow the sharing of files between users of the network) files that contain child pornography? *See People v. Worrell*, 170 A.D.3d 1048, 96 N.Y.S.2d 269 (N.Y. App. 2019); *United States v. Norris*, 938 F.3d 1114 (9th Cir. 2019); *United States v. Hoeffener*, 950 F.3d 1037 (8th Cir. 2020).

Hypo 3: *Nationwide Camera Systems*

In 2002, the British government installed approximately 4.2 million cameras in public places to watch and monitor the populace in public places. This system allowed the government to monitor each person in London with 300 cameras each day. Following the London subway bombings in July 2005, the police made arrests based on information provided by the camera system. Cities such as Baltimore, Chicago, and New Orleans have received federal grants to install surveillance cameras. Assume that the U.S. decides to install a similar camera system, and a citizen's group sues claiming a loss of privacy in public spaces. After *Carpenter*, does the use of such a camera system violates the citizenry's reasonable expectation of privacy?

Hypo 4: *Facial Recognition*

Would it also be permissible for the police to combine the cameras with facial recognition technology? That technology involves a massive data base with the names and pictures of millions of people. As a result, the police can take the pictures with surveillance cameras, insert those pictures into facial recognition systems, and identity individuals that they observe in public. Under *Knotts*, are the police free to use these facial recognition technologies consistently with the Fourth Amendment?

Hypo 5: *Remotely Accessing Computers*

Using modern technology, the police have the ability to remotely access computers. Thus, an FBI agent in Washington, D.C., has the capacity to remotely access an individual's home computer in Kansas City, Missouri. The FBI has increasingly used such remote access techniques, and did so in connection with a "darknet" site called Playpen. The techniques allow the FBI to remotely install software on computers which sends their IP addresses back to the FBI. Does the use of remote techniques constitute a "search" within the meaning of the Fourth Amendment? What should be required for the use of such remote techniques?

Hypo 6: *License Plate Tracking*

The DEA has accumulated a database based on information received from "license plate reader" cameras located on major highways, including cameras operated by state and local law enforcement. The data provides information about the location and movement of vehicles in real time, and has resulted in the storage of hundreds of millions of records that can be accessed by police nationwide for their investigations. Initially, the DEA program focused on camera data from highways in states along the U.S. border, but the program was expanded to other states, and the DEA does not disclose the locations of the highway cameras used to collect the data. Although the data in the original program was preserved in the DEA database for two years, the data is saved now for only three months. Previously unknown details about the program were revealed in records obtained by the ACLU by means of a Freedom of Information Act request and shared with the media. Does this data gathering violate the REOP of motorists regarding their movements? If so, what kind of judicial supervision of the program should be required under the Fourth Amendment?

> ## Hypo 7: *NSA Surveillance*
>
> In the wake of Edward Snowden's revelations in 2013, two suits were filed challenging the constitutionality of the NSA's bulk telephony metadata surveillance program through which the government obtained the records of millions of domestic subscribers from internet service providers. The user data did not include the content of calls, but did include the phone numbers of callers and recipients, location data, and the time and duration of calls. Neither suit led to the finding that the NSA's program violated the Fourth Amendment. Other suits have challenged the NSA's PRISM program, which allows the government to investigate non-U.S. persons outside the country by obtaining from internet service providers (ISPs) the target's telephone and internet data, including emails, videos, voice chat, photos, and social networking data. Lower courts have upheld the "reasonableness" of the PRISM program based on the compelling interest in national security. Does the program involve a search under either the trespass test or the REOP test?

C. Probable Cause

Probable cause is an integral part of the Fourth Amendment's prohibition against unreasonable searches and seizures: "no Warrants shall issue, but upon probable cause, supported by Oath or affirmation." When the police obtain a warrant, the warrant must be based on probable cause. In addition, some exceptions to the warrant requirement also require probable cause (i.e., the automobile exception). *United States v. Leon*, 468 U.S. 897 (1984). What must be "probable?" When the police want to conduct a search, probable cause requires proof of two things: that the fruits, instrumentalities or evidence of crime exist, and that they can be found at the place to be searched. When the police want to arrest, probable cause requires proof that a crime was committed and that the person to be arrested committed it.

Applied literally, "probable cause" requires that something be "more probable than not." However, the courts have not applied the probable cause requirement literally. In *Draper v. United States,* 358 U.S. 307 (1959), the Court defined probable cause in the following way: "In dealing with probable cause, as the very name implies, we deal with probabilities. These are not technical; they are the factual and practical considerations of everyday life on which reasonable and prudent men, not legal technicians, act." Probable cause exists where "the facts and circumstances within the arresting officers' knowledge and of which they had reasonably trustworthy information are sufficient in themselves to warrant a man of reasonable caution in the belief that 'an offense has been or is being committed.'" *Carroll v. United States*, 267 U.S. 132 (1925).

Carroll v. United States

267 U.S. 132 (1925).

MR. CHIEF JUSTICE TAFT, delivered the opinion of the Court.

Section 25, title 2, of the National Prohibition Act, passed to enforce the Eighteenth Amendment, makes it unlawful to have or possess any liquor intended for use in violating the act.

Grand Rapids is about 152 miles from Detroit. Detroit and its neighborhood along the Detroit river, which is the international boundary, is one of the most active centers for introducing illegally into this country spirituous liquors for distribution into the interior. Prohibition agents were engaged in a regular patrol along the highways from Detroit to Grand Rapids to stop and seize liquor carried in automobiles. They knew or had convincing evidence to believe that the Carroll boys, as they called them, were "bootleggers" in Grand Rapids; i.e., that they were engaged in plying the unlawful trade of selling liquor in that city. [In September, 1921, undercover federal agents agreed to buy three cases of illegal whisky from the Carrolls who stated that they had to go to the east end of Grand Rapids to get the liquor and that they would be back in half an hour. The Carrolls left in an Oldsmobile roadster, but never returned.] The officers soon after [observed the Carrolls] going from Grand Rapids to Detroit, and attempted to follow them to see where they went, but they escaped observation. Two months later the officers suddenly met the same men on their way westward presumably from Detroit. They were in the same automobile they had been in the night when they tried to furnish whisky to the officers. They were coming from the direction of the great source of supply for their stock to Grand Rapids, where they plied their trade. The officers, when they saw the defendants, believed that they were carrying liquor, we can have no doubt, and we think it is equally clear that they had reasonable cause for thinking so. Emphasis is put on the statement by one of the officers that they were not looking for defendants at the particular time when they appeared. As soon as they appeared, the officers were entitled to use their reasoning faculties upon all the facts of which they had previous knowledge in respect to the defendants.

In light of this record, it is clear the officers here had justification for the search and seizure. The facts and circumstances within their knowledge and of which they had reasonably trustworthy information were sufficient in themselves to warrant a man of reasonable caution in the belief that intoxicating liquor was being transported in the automobile which they stopped and searched.

The judgment is affirmed.

The separate opinion of MR. JUSTICE MCREYNOLDS.

While quietly driving an ordinary automobile along a much frequented public road, plaintiffs in error were arrested by federal officers without a warrant and upon mere suspicion. The facts known by the officers were wholly insufficient to create a reasonable belief that they were transporting liquor contrary to law. The negotiation concerning three cases of whisky on September 29th was the only circumstance which could have subjected plaintiffs in error to any reasonable suspicion. No whisky was delivered, and it is not certain that they ever intended to deliver any. The arrest came 2 ½ months after the negotiation. Every act in the meantime is consistent with complete innocence. Has it come about that merely because a man once agreed to deliver whisky, but did not, he may be arrested whenever he ventures to drive an automobile on the road to Detroit!

Points for Discussion

a. Probable Cause for Possession

In *Maryland v. Pringle*, 540 U.S. 366 (2003), a police officer stopped a vehicle for speeding and noticed cocaine between the back seat and the arm rest. When all three passengers denied ownership, the officer arrested all three. The Court held that the officer had probable cause to arrest all of them despite their denials. Later, after being given a *Miranda* warning, Pringle admitted that the cocaine belonged to him and that he planned to sell it. Following his conviction, Pringle appealed, claiming that the admission was the illegal fruit of an unlawful arrest. The Court held that the officer had probable cause to arrest all three passengers: "We think it an entirely reasonable inference from these facts that any or all three of the occupants had knowledge of, and exercised dominion and control over, the cocaine. Thus a reasonable officer could conclude that there was probable cause to believe Pringle committed the crime of possession of cocaine, either solely or jointly."

b. Probable Cause & Trespassing Partiers

In *District of Columbia v. Wesby*, 138 S.Ct. 577 (2018), early one morning, police responded to a report regarding a raucous, late-night party at what should have been an unoccupied house, and ultimately arrested the people that they found in the house. The Court held that the police had probable cause to arrest the individuals for unlawful entry: "The officers found a group of people in a house that the neighbors had identified as vacant, that appeared to be vacant, and that the partygoers were treating as vacant. The group scattered, and some hid, at the sight of law enforcement. Their explanations for being at the house were full of holes. The source of their claimed invitation admitted that she had no right to be in the house, and the owner confirmed that fact. Even assuming the officers lacked actual probable cause to arrest the partygoers, the officers are entitled to qualified immunity because they 'reasonably but mistakenly concluded that probable cause was present.' "

Hypo 1: *Applying the Probable Cause Requirement*

Suppose that there is a street in your city where a large number of drug transactions occur. A significant percentage (in excess of 50%) of people on that street are either drug pushers or drug users who are purchasing drugs. Given these facts, do the police have "probable cause" to believe that everyone they find on the street is in possession of drugs? Would the police have probable cause to arrest those that they find suspiciously "hanging-out" on a street corner? What about a little old lady walking down the street pulling a shopping cart? If the police do not have probable cause as to everyone, how does the character of the street affect the probable cause determination in an individual case?

Hypo 2: *Refusing Consent*

Suppose that a police officer validly stops a motorist for a traffic violation (a burnt out taillight). After issuing the motorist a citation, the officer asks the motorist for permission to search the motorist's trunk, but the motorist refuses. The officer, who honestly believes that any law-abiding citizen would graciously consent to a search request, believes that the motorist has "something to hide. Otherwise, he would have given consent." Does the motorist's refusal give the officer probable cause to believe that the car contains contraband?

Hypo 3: *Retracting Consent*

Defendant is stopped for speeding. After checking defendant's driver's license and registration, the officer requests permission to search the car. The officer does so based on a "hunch" because he smelled a deodorizing agent which might indicate the presence of narcotics. When defendant opens the trunk, the officer sees a "heavily taped" cardboard box. When the officer presses on the box, defendant puts a briefcase on top of the box, closes the trunk, and states that the search is over. Based upon the circumstances, the officer thinks that he has probable cause to believe that defendant is in possession of narcotics. Does he? *See State v. Zelinske*, 108 N.M. 784, 779 P.2d 97 (App. 1989).

Hypo 4: *The "Pot Odor"*

When a police officer validly stops an automobile, he smells a marijuana scent emanating from the vehicle. Does the officer have probable cause to arrest the driver? *See State v. Grande*, 164 Wash.2d 135, 187 P.3d 248 (2008). Would it matter whether the state has a medical marijuana statute that allows individuals to possess marijuana for therapeutic medical reasons? *See State v. Senna*, 79 A.3d 45 (Vt. 2013).

Hypo 5: *Probable Cause?*

At midnight, an officer stops Digiovanni's car on an interstate highway because he is traveling too close to the car in front. In the ensuring stop, the driver produces a rental contract and a Massachusetts driver's license. Relying on his experience, the officer believes that the driver is involved in drug trafficking. In reaching that conclusion, he relies on several factors: two shirts hanging in the rear passenger compartment, a hygiene bag on the back seat, and the fact that the car interior is clean. The officer believes that non-drug traffickers on vacation would pack the shirts in a clothing bag, and he views the cleanness of the car as suspicious because "it is indicative of nonstop driving," and he regards the rental contract as indicative of drug trafficking activity because the car was rented in Fort Lauderdale Airport the previous day and was to be dropped off at Logan Airport in Boston, at a cost of $438. The officer views this rental as "implausible." Does the officer possess probable cause to believe that the driver is in possession of illegal drugs? *See United States v. Digiovanni*, 650 F.3d 498 (4th Cir. 2011).

Hypo 6: *More on Probable Cause?*

In the prior problem, assume that the driver is ordered to exit the car, and the officer asks questions concerning his travel plans. The driver states that he is traveling from Florida, where he spent the weekend with family, to Boston (where he lives), with a stop at his sister's residence in New York to pick up "some paintings and whatnot." The officer then asks the driver if he has any luggage in the car and if everything in the car belongs to him. The driver responds in the affirmative and says "oh boy" as he tosses his cigarette over the guardrail. The officer finds this remark "extremely suspicious," and asks the driver what is the matter, to which he replies, "it's just so hot." The officer then asks the driver if there is any marijuana in the car. The driver replies, "no sir. I never smoked marijuana in my life. It puts me to sleep." The officer asks the driver if there is any cocaine, heroin or methamphetamine in the car. The officer follows up with, "are you sure?" to which the driver replies, "I'm positive." Does the officer have probable cause to search the vehicle? How does the driver's nonsensical response (that he had "never" smoked marijuana because it puts him to sleep) enter into the analysis? *See United States v. Digiovanni*, 650 F.3d 498 (4th Cir. 2011).

Hypo 7: *Public Telephones & Drug Transactions*

A police detective knows that drug transactions are often arranged using public telephones, and that a particular public phone is frequently used for this purpose. One night, he sees a car parked near the phone, and also sees a man exit the car, make a short phone call, and then drive off. The officer follows the car which parks by the side of the road a short distance away. Another car pulls up nearby, a man leaves the other car and enters the first car, the two drive around the block, and the man returns to his vehicle. Although the officer does not witness an exchange of drugs or money during these events, he believes (based on his experience) that a drug transaction has taken place. Does the officer have probable cause to stop and search either or both vehicles? *See Commonwealth v. Levy*, 76 Mass. App. Ct. 617, 924 N.E.2d 771 (2010).

Hypo 8: *Computers Images of Child Pornography*

An officer finds McArthur masturbating in a public place, and arrests him for public indecency. In inventorying the contents of McArthur's wallet at the police station, the officer finds child pornography. Based on the photograph, and McArthur's public conduct, the police apply for a warrant to search his home. Is there probable cause to believe that McArthur has child pornography in his home? *See United States v. McArthur*, 573 F.3d 608 (8th Cir. 2009); *State v. Byrne*, 972 A.2d 633 (R.I. 2009). Would your view be different if McArthur had previously been convicted of committing two sex offenses (one involving sodomy on a minor), and he has been designated a sex offender?

Hypo 9: *Code Words*

Police, who suspect that Faagai runs a methamphetamine operation, obtain a warrant to intercept his phone calls. They hear a man (Penitani) ask another man (Mitchell) whether Faagai is "trustworthy." Afterwards, the police apprehend a woman with meth supplied by one of Penitani's agents, and intercept a text message from Penitani to Faagai stating, "Man thanks to this broad I lost ten large. Man sorry taking long with da tools bro." An officer testified that he believed that Penitani was stating that he had lost $10,000, and that "tools" referred to methamphetamine. The next day, FBI agents intercept a text message from Faagai to Penitani in which he states that he is going to Costco "to buy food for his house" and that if Penitani "gotta buy food for Penitani's house," they should meet at Costco. An FBI agent testified that he believed that Faagai was using "food" as a code word for "money," and that they agreed to meeting at 7-11 to obtain "tools." When the police arrive, the meeting is over and Faagai is leaving. Do the police have probable cause to search Faagai's car? *See United States v. Faagai* (9th Cir. 2017).

Spinelli v. United States

393 U.S. 410 (1969).

MR. JUSTICE HARLAN delivered the opinion of the Court.

William Spinelli was convicted of traveling to St. Louis, Missouri, from a nearby Illinois suburb with the intention of conducting gambling activities proscribed by Missouri law. Believing it desirable that the principles of *Aguilar v. Texas*, 378 U.S. 108 (1964), should be further explicated, we granted certiorari.

In *Aguilar*, a search warrant issued upon an affidavit of police officers who swore only that they had "received reliable information from a credible person and do believe" that narcotics were being illegally stored on the described premises. Recognizing that the constitutional requirement of probable cause can be satisfied by hearsay information, this Court held the affidavit inadequate for two reasons. First, the application failed to set forth any of the "underlying circumstances" necessary to enable the magistrate independently to judge the validity of the informant's conclusion that the narcotics were where he said they were. Second, the affiant-officers did not attempt to support their claim that their informant was "credible" or his information "reliable." The Government is, however, quite right in saying that the FBI affidavit in the present case is more ample than that in *Aguilar*. Not only does it contain a report from an anonymous informant, but it also contains a report of an independent FBI investigation which is said to corroborate the informant's tip. We are then, required to delineate the manner in which *Aguilar's* two-pronged test should be applied in these circumstances. The affidavit contained the following allegations:

1. The FBI kept track of Spinelli's movements on five days during the month of August 1965. On four of these occasions, Spinelli was seen crossing one of two bridges leading from Illinois into St. Louis, Missouri, between 11 a.m. and 12:15 p.m. On four of the five days, Spinelli was also seen parking his car in a lot used by residents of an apartment house at 1108 Indian Circle Drive in St. Louis, between 3:30 p.m. and 4:45 p.m.[6] On one day, Spinelli was followed further and seen to enter a particular apartment in the building.

2. An FBI check with the telephone company revealed that this apartment contained two telephones listed under the name of Grace P. Hagen, and carrying the numbers WYdown 4–0029 and WYdown 4–0136.

3. The application stated that "William Spinelli is known to this affiant and to federal law enforcement agents and local law enforcement agents as a bookmaker, an associate of bookmakers, a gambler, and an associate of gamblers."

4. Finally it was stated that the FBI "has been informed by a confidential reliable informant that William Spinelli is operating a handbook and accepting wagers and disseminating wagering information by means of the telephones which have been assigned the numbers WYdown 4–0029 and WYdown 4–0136."

Detailing the informant's tip has a fundamental place in this warrant application. Without it, probable cause could not be established. The first two items reflect only innocent-seeming activity and data. Spinelli's travels to and from the apartment building and his entry into a particular apartment on one occasion could hardly be taken as bespeaking gambling activity; and there is surely nothing unusual about an apartment containing two separate telephones. Many a householder indulges himself in this petty luxury. Finally, the allegation that Spinelli was "known" to the affiant and to other federal and local law enforcement officers as a gambler and an associate of gamblers is but a bald and unilluminating assertion of suspicion that is entitled to no weight in appraising the magistrate's decision.

So much indeed the Government does not deny. Rather, the Government claims that the informant's tip gives a suspicious color to the FBI's reports detailing Spinelli's innocent-seeming conduct and that, conversely, the FBI's surveillance corroborates the informant's tip, thereby entitling it to more weight. It is true, of course, that the

---

[6] No report was made as to Spinelli's movements during the period between his arrival in St. Louis at noon and his arrival at the parking lot in the late afternoon. Evidence indicated that Spinelli frequented the offices of his stockbroker during this period.

magistrate is obligated to render a judgment based upon a common-sense reading of the entire affidavit. We believe, however, that the "totality of circumstances" approach taken by the Court of Appeals paints with too broad a brush. Where, as here, the informer's tip is a necessary element in a finding of probable cause, its proper weight must be determined by a more precise analysis.

The informer's report must first be measured against *Aguilar*'s standards so that its probative value can be assessed. If the tip is found inadequate under *Aguilar*, the other allegations which corroborate the information contained in the hearsay report should then be considered. At this stage, however, the standards enunciated in *Aguilar* must inform the magistrate's decision. He must ask: Can it fairly be said that the tip, even when certain parts of it have been corroborated by independent sources, is as trust-worthy as a tip which would pass *Aguilar*'s tests without independent corroboration? *Aguilar* establishes that probable cause must be determined by a "neutral and detached magistrate," and not by "the officer engaged in the often competitive enterprise of ferreting out crime." A magistrate cannot properly discharge his constitutional duty if he relies on an informer's tip which—even when partially corroborated—is not as reliable as one which passes *Aguilar*'s requirements when standing alone.

Applying these principles, we first consider the weight to be given the informer's tip when it is considered apart from the rest of the affidavit. It is clear that a Commissioner could not credit it without abdicating his constitutional function. Though the affiant swore that his confidant was "reliable," he offered the magistrate no reason in support of this conclusion. Perhaps even more important is the fact that *Aguilar*'s other test has not been satisfied. The tip does not contain a sufficient statement of the underlying circumstances from which the informer concluded that Spinelli was running a bookmaking operation. We are not told how the FBI's source received his information—it is not alleged that the informant personally observed Spinelli at work or that he had ever placed a bet with him. Moreover, if the informant came by the information indirectly, he did not explain why his sources were reliable. In the absence of a statement detailing the manner in which the information was gathered, it is especially important that the tip describe the accused's criminal activity in sufficient detail that the magistrate may know that he is relying on something more substantial than a casual rumor circulating in the underworld or an accusation based merely on an individual's general reputation.

The detail provided by the informant in *Draper v. United States*, 358 U.S. 307 (1959), provides a suitable benchmark. While Hereford, the Government's informer in that case did not state the way in which he had obtained his information, he reported that Draper had gone to Chicago the day before by train and that he would return to Denver by train with three ounces of heroin on one of two specified mornings. Moreover, Hereford went on to describe, with minute particularity, the clothes that Draper would be wearing upon his arrival at the Denver station. A magistrate, when confronted with such detail, could reasonably infer that the informant had gained his information in a reliable way.[7] Such an inference cannot be made in the present case. Here, the only facts supplied were that Spinelli was using two specified telephones and that these phones were being used in gambling operations. This meager report could easily have been obtained from an offhand remark heard at a neighborhood bar.

Nor do we believe that the doubts *Aguilar* raises as to the report's reliability are adequately resolved by a consideration of the allegations detailing the FBI's independent investigative efforts. At most, these allegations indicated that Spinelli could have used the telephones specified by the informant for some purpose. This cannot by itself be said to support both the inference that the informer was generally trustworthy and that he had made his charge against Spinelli on the basis of information obtained in a reliable way. *Draper* provides a relevant comparison. Independent police work in that case corroborated more than one small detail that had been provided by the informant. The police, on meeting the inbound Denver train on the second morning specified by informer Hereford, saw a man whose dress corresponded precisely to Hereford's detailed description. It was then apparent that the informant had not been fabricating his report out of whole cloth; since the report was of the sort which in common experience may be recognized as having been obtained in a reliable way, it was perfectly clear that probable cause had been established.

We conclude that the informant's tip—even when corroborated to the extent indicated—was not sufficient to provide the basis for a finding of probable cause. This is not to say that the tip was so insubstantial that it could not properly have counted in the magistrate's determination. Rather, it needed some further support. When we look to the other parts of the application, however, we find nothing alleged which would permit the suspicions engendered by the informant's report to ripen into a judgment that a crime was probably being committed.

The judgment of the Court of Appeals is *reversed*.

Mr. Justice White, concurring.

The informant claimed the business involved gambling. Since his specific information about Spinelli using two phones with particular numbers had been verified, did not his allegation about gambling thereby become sufficiently more believable if the *Draper* principle is given any scope at all? I would think so, particularly since information from the informant which was verified was not neutral, irrelevant information but was material to proving the gambling allegation: two phones with different numbers in an apartment used away from home indicates a business use in an operation, like bookmaking, where multiple phones are needed. The *Draper* approach

---

[5]   While *Draper* involved the question whether the police had probable cause for an arrest without a warrant, the analysis required for this question is basically similar to that demanded when a magistrate considers whether a search warrant should issue.

would reasonably justify the issuance of a warrant in this case, particularly since the police had some awareness of Spinelli's past activities. The majority, while seemingly embracing *Draper*, confines that case to its own facts. I join the opinion of the Court and the judgment of reversal.

MR. JUSTICE BLACK, dissenting.

The affidavit given the magistrate was more than ample to show probable cause of the petitioner's guilt. The affidavit meticulously set out facts sufficient to show the following:

1. The petitioner had been shown going to and coming from a room in an apartment which contained two telephones listed under the name of another person. Nothing indicates that the apartment was of that large and luxurious type which could only be occupied by a person to whom it would be a "petty luxury" to have two separate telephones, with different numbers, both listed under the name of a person who did not live there.

2. The petitioner's car had been observed parked in the apartment's parking lot. This fact was highly relevant in showing that the petitioner was extremely interested in some enterprise which was located in the apartment.

3. The FBI had been informed by a reliable informant that the petitioner was accepting wagering information by telephones—the particular telephones located in the apartment the defendant had been repeatedly visiting. Unless the Court, going beyond the requirements of the Fourth Amendment, wishes to require magistrates to hold trials before issuing warrants, it is not necessary to have the affiant explain "the underlying circumstances from which the informer concluded that Spinelli was running a bookmaking operation."

4. The petitioner was known by federal and local law enforcement agents as a bookmaker and an associate of gamblers. Although the statement is hearsay that might not be admissible in a regular trial, everyone knows, unless he shuts his eyes to the realities of life, that this is a relevant fact which, together with other circumstances, might indicate a factual probability that gambling is taking place.

Food for Thought

The *Spinelli* decision discusses the decision in *Draper v. United States*. Is it clear to you why probable cause existed in *Draper*, but not in *Spinelli*? What additional facts would have been needed to establish probable cause in *Spinelli* under the *Draper* precedent?

The foregoing facts should be enough to constitute probable cause for anyone who does not believe that the only way to obtain a search warrant is to prove beyond a reasonable doubt that a defendant is guilty. Even *Aguilar* cannot support the contrary result.

Mr. Justice Fortas, dissenting.

A policeman's affidavit should not be judged as an entry in an essay contest. A policeman's affidavit is entitled to common-sense evaluation. The judgment of the Court of Appeals for the Eighth Circuit should be affirmed.

Make the Connection

Although *Spinelli* made clear that the police can use hearsay testimony in a probable cause hearing, the Court limited on the use of such testimony by imposing the *Aguilar-Spinelli* test. Ordinarily, when the police seek a warrant, they do so based on the testimony or affidavits of police officers. However, informants are an integral part of the investigative process, and are often relied on by police in their affidavits and testimony. The difficulty is that the testimony of informants is often "hearsay" (hearsay being defined as an out-of-court statement offered to prove the truth of the matter asserted in the statement). In criminal and civil trials, the use of hearsay is usually prohibited except when the statement fits into one of the many exceptions to the hearsay rule. By contrast, hearsay is usually admissible in a probable cause hearing. In *Draper v. United States*, 358 U.S. 307 (1959), the Court rejected petitioner's contention that "because hearsay is not legally competent evidence in a criminal trial, it could not legally have been considered, but should have been put out of mind" in deciding whether probable cause existed to arrest petitioner. The Court justified its holding by stating that there "is a large difference between the two things to be proved, guilt and probable cause, as well as between the tribunals which determine them, and therefore a like difference in the quanta and modes of proof required to establish them."

Hypo 1: *Corroboration of an Informer's Tip*

A veteran informer warns police that a suspect is going to make a cocaine delivery using a particular route. The tip provides the race and age of the suspect, as well as his name, and information regarding the suspect's vehicle, license plate number, the time of day and route that the suspect will take (going from Vermont to Pennsylvania). A police officer stakes out the route. When the officer observes a car and driver matching the description, he follows it. Under the *Aguilar-Spinelli* standards, does the officer have probable cause to stop and search the vehicle? *See State v. Robinson*, 185 Vt. 232, 969 A.2d 127 (2009).

Hypo 2: *The Repairman's Phone Call*

A landlord calls a repairman to fix a problem at a rental home. The repairman observes marijuana and other suspicious items in the house, lying in plain view, and calls the police. Based on the repairman's phone call, do the police have probable cause to obtain a warrant under the *Aguilar-Spinelli* standards Would it matter whether the repairman has previously given a tip? *See State v. Eisfeldt*, 163 Wash.2d 628, 185 P.3d 580 (2008).

Hypo 3: *The Eyewitness Report*

A woman is sweeping the front porch of her home when she sees a man walk onto a neighbor's porch and peer in the front door. The man then stops at another house and disappears. The woman later sees the man standing at a nearby bus stop where he has taken off his shirt and is using it to cover a television set. He is pacing nervously and is trying to hitchhike while waiting for the bus to arrive. The woman calls the police, tells them about the man's activities and location, and reports her suspicions of burglary. Officer Freeman, a twenty-year veteran, arrives five minutes later. He asks the man for identification which he cannot produce. When the officer asks about the television set, the man states that he bought the television set from someone in the neighborhood for $100. A "pat down" search for weapons reveals that the man (who is wearing only an undershirt) has brown wool gloves in his back pocket. The man is then arrested and searched. Did the officer have probable cause to arrest the man? Would it matter that, after the arrest, the owners of a house one block south of the woman's house report that their house has been burglarized and that a television set (the one found in the man's possession) has been stolen? *See People v. Quintero*, 657 P.2d 948 (Colo., En Banc, 1973).

Illinois v. Gates

462 U.S. 213 (1983).

JUSTICE REHNQUIST delivered the opinion of the Court.

Bloomingdale, Ill, is a suburb of Chicago located in DuPage County. On May 3, 1978, the Bloomingdale Police Department received by mail an anonymous handwritten letter which read as follows:

"This letter is to inform you that you have a couple in your town who make their living on selling drugs. They are Sue and Lance Gates, they live on Greenway, off Bloomingdale Rd. in the condominiums. Most of their buys are done in Florida. Sue his wife drives their car to Florida, where she leaves it to be loaded with drugs, then Lance flies down and drives it back. Sue flies back after she drops the car off in Florida. May 3 she is driving down there again and Lance will be flying down in a few days to drive it back. At the time Lance drives the car back he has the trunk loaded with over $100,000.00 in drugs. Presently they have over $100,000.00 worth of drugs in their basement. They brag about the fact they never have to work, and make their entire living on pushers. I guarantee if you watch them carefully you will make a big catch. They are friends with some big drugs dealers, who visit their house often.

Lance & Susan Gates
Greenway in Condominiums"

The letter was referred by the Chief of Police to Detective Mader, who decided to pursue the tip. Mader learned, from the Illinois Secretary of State, that an Illinois driver's license had been issued to one Lance Gates, residing at a stated address in Bloomingdale. He contacted a confidential informant, whose examination of certain financial records revealed a more recent address for the Gates, and he also learned from a police officer assigned to O'Hare Airport that "L. Gates" had made a reservation on Eastern Airlines flight 245 to West Palm Beach, Fla., scheduled to depart from Chicago on May 5 at 4:15 p.m.

Mader then made arrangements with an agent of the Drug Enforcement Administration for surveillance of the May 5 flight. The agent later reported to Mader that Gates had boarded the flight, and that federal agents in Florida had observed him arrive in West Palm Beach and take a taxi to the nearby Holiday Inn. They also reported that Gates went to a room registered to one Susan Gates and that, at 7:00 a.m. the next morning, Gates and an unidentified woman left the motel in a Mercury bearing Illinois license plates and drove northbound on an interstate frequently used by travelers to the Chicago area. In addition, the DEA agent informed Mader that the license plate number on the Mercury registered to a Hornet station wagon owned by Gates. The agent also advised Mader that the driving time between West Palm Beach and Bloomingdale was approximately 22 to 24 hours.

Mader signed an affidavit setting forth the foregoing facts, and submitted it to a judge of DuPage County, together with a copy of the anonymous letter. The judge thereupon issued a search warrant for the Gates' residence and their automobile. The judge, in deciding to issue the warrant, could have determined that the *modus operandi* of the Gates had been substantially corroborated. As the anonymous letter predicted, Lance Gates had flown from Chicago to West Palm Beach late in the afternoon of

May 5th, had checked into a hotel room registered in the name of his wife, and, at 7:00 a.m. the following morning, had headed north, accompanied by an unidentified woman, out of West Palm Beach on an interstate highway used by travelers from South Florida to Chicago in an automobile bearing a license plate issued to him.

At 5:15 a.m. on May 7th, only 36 hours after he had flown out of Chicago, Lance Gates, and his wife, returned to their home in Bloomingdale, driving the car in which they had left West Palm Beach some 22 hours earlier. The Bloomingdale police were awaiting them, searched the trunk of the Mercury, and uncovered approximately 350 pounds of marijuana. A search of the Gates' home revealed marijuana, weapons, and other contraband. The Illinois Circuit Court ordered suppression of all these items, on the ground that the affidavit failed to support the necessary determination of probable cause to believe that the Gates' automobile and home contained the contraband in question. The Illinois Appellate Court and the Supreme Court of Illinois affirmed.

The Illinois Supreme Court concluded—and we agree—that, standing alone, the anonymous letter would not provide the basis for a magistrate's determination that there was probable cause to believe contraband would be found in the Gates' car and home. The letter provides virtually nothing from which one might conclude that its author is either honest or his information reliable; likewise, the letter gives absolutely no indication of the basis for the writer's predictions regarding the Gates' criminal activities. Something more was required before a magistrate could conclude that there was probable cause to believe that contraband would be found in the Gates' home and car.

The Illinois Supreme Court also properly recognized that Detective Mader's affidavit might supplement the anonymous letter with information sufficient to permit a determination of probable cause. In holding that the affidavit did not contain sufficient additional information to sustain a determination of probable cause, the Illinois court applied a "two-pronged test," derived from our decision in *Spinelli v. United States*. The court understood *Spinelli* as requiring that the anonymous letter satisfy each of two independent requirements before it could be relied on. The letter, as supplemented by Mader's affidavit, first had to adequately reveal the "basis of knowledge" of the letter writer—the particular means by which he came by the information given in his report. Second, it had to provide facts sufficiently establishing either the "veracity" of the affiant's informant, or, alternatively, the "reliability" of the informant's report in this particular case.

The Illinois court, alluding to an elaborate set of legal rules that have developed among various lower courts to enforce the "two-pronged test,"[8] found that the test had not been satisfied. First, the "veracity" prong was not satisfied because, "there was simply no basis for concluding that the anonymous person who wrote the letter to the Bloomingdale Police Department was credible." The court indicated that corroboration by police of details contained in the letter might never satisfy the "veracity" prong, and in any event, could not do so if only "innocent" details are corroborated. In addition, the letter gave no indication of the basis of its writer's knowledge of the Gates' activities. The court understood *Spinelli* as permitting the detail contained in a tip to be used to infer that the informant had a reliable basis for his statements, but it thought that the anonymous letter failed to provide sufficient detail to permit such an inference. Thus, it concluded that no showing of probable cause had been made.

We agree that an informant's "veracity," "reliability" and "basis of knowledge" are all highly relevant in determining the value of his report. We do not agree, however, that these elements should be understood as entirely separate and independent requirements to be rigidly exacted in every case. Rather they should be understood simply as closely intertwined issues that may usefully illuminate the commonsense, practical question whether there is "probable cause" to believe that contraband or evidence is located in a particular place.

This totality of the circumstances approach is far more consistent with our prior treatment of probable cause than is any rigid demand that specific "tests" be satisfied by every informant's tip. Perhaps the central teaching of our decisions bearing on the probable cause standard is that it is a "practical, nontechnical conception." *Brinegar v. United States*, 338 U.S. 160, 176 (1949). These are not technical; they are the factual and practical considerations of everyday life on which reasonable and prudent men, not legal technicians, act." Our observation in *United States v. Cortez*, 449 U.S. 411, 418 621 (1981), regarding "particularized suspicion," is also applicable to the probable cause standard:

> The process does not deal with hard certainties, but with probabilities. Long before the law of probabilities was articulated as such, practical people formulated certain common-sense conclusions about human behavior; jurors as fact finders are permitted to do the same—and so are law enforcement officers. Finally, the evidence thus collected must be seen and weighed not

---

[8] The "veracity" prong of the *Spinelli* test has two "spurs"—the informant's "credibility" and the "reliability" of his information. Both the "basis of knowledge" prong and the "veracity" prong are treated as entirely separate requirements, which must be independently satisfied in every case in order to sustain a determination of probable cause. Some ancillary doctrines are relied on to satisfy certain of the foregoing requirements. For example, the "self-verifying detail" of a tip may satisfy the "basis of knowledge" requirement, although not the "credibility" spur of the "veracity" prong. Conversely, corroboration would seem not capable of supporting the "basis of knowledge" prong, but only the "veracity" prong.

in terms of library analysis by scholars, but as understood by those versed in the field of law enforcement.

As these comments illustrate, probable cause is a fluid concept—turning on the assessment of probabilities in particular factual contexts—not readily, or even usefully, reduced to a neat set of legal rules. Informants' tips doubtless come in many shapes and sizes from many different types of persons. As we said in *Adams v. Williams*, 407 U.S. 143, 147 (1972), "Informants' tips, like all other clues and evidence coming to a policeman on the scene may vary greatly in their value and reliability." Rigid legal rules are ill-suited to an area of such diversity. "One simple rule will not cover every situation."

Moreover, the "two-pronged test" directs analysis into two largely independent channels—the informant's "veracity" or "reliability" and his "basis of knowledge." There are persuasive arguments against according these two elements such independent status. They are better understood as relevant considerations in the totality of circumstances analysis that traditionally has guided probable cause determinations: a deficiency in one may be compensated for, in determining the overall reliability of a tip, by a strong showing as to the other, or by some other indicia of reliability.

If, for example, a particular informant is known for the unusual reliability of his predictions of certain types of criminal activities in a locality, his failure, in a particular case, to thoroughly set forth the basis of his knowledge surely should not serve as an absolute bar to a finding of probable cause based on his tip. Likewise, if an unquestionably honest citizen comes forward with a report of criminal activity—which if fabricated would subject him to criminal liability—we have found rigorous scrutiny of the basis of his knowledge unnecessary. Conversely, even if we entertain some doubt as to an informant's motives, his explicit and detailed description of alleged wrongdoing, along with a statement that the event was observed first-hand, entitles his tip to greater weight than might otherwise be the case. Unlike a totality of circumstances analysis, which permits a balanced assessment of the relative weights of all the various indicia of reliability (and unreliability) attending an informant's tip, the "two-pronged test" has encouraged an excessively technical dissection of informants' tips, with undue attention being focused on isolated issues that cannot sensibly be divorced from the other facts presented to the magistrate.

Finely-tuned standards such as proof beyond a reasonable doubt or by a preponderance of the evidence, useful in formal trials, have no place in the magistrate's decision. While an effort to fix some general, numerically precise degree of certainty corresponding to "probable cause" may not be helpful, it is clear that "only the probability, and not a prima facie showing, of criminal activity is the standard of probable cause."

We also have recognized that affidavits "are normally drafted by nonlawyers in the midst and haste of a criminal investigation. Technical requirements of elaborate specificity once exacted under common law pleading have no proper place in this area." Likewise, search and arrest warrants long have been issued by persons who are neither lawyers nor judges, and who certainly do not remain abreast of each judicial refinement of the nature of "probable cause." The rigorous inquiry into the *Spinelli* prongs and the complex superstructure of evidentiary and analytical rules that some have seen implicit in our *Spinelli* decision, cannot be reconciled with the fact that many warrants are—quite properly—issued on the basis of nontechnical, common-sense judgments of laymen applying a standard less demanding than those used in more formal legal proceedings. Given the informal, often hurried context in which it must be applied, the "built-in subtleties" of the "two-pronged test" are particularly unlikely to assist magistrates in determining probable cause.

After-the-fact scrutiny by courts of the sufficiency of an affidavit should not take the form of *de novo* review. A magistrate's "determination of probable cause should be paid great deference by reviewing courts." "A grudging or negative attitude by reviewing courts toward warrants," is inconsistent with the Fourth Amendment's strong preference for searches conducted pursuant to a warrant, "courts should not invalidate warrants by interpreting affidavits in a hyper technical, rather than a commonsense, manner."

If the affidavits submitted by police officers are subjected to the type of scrutiny some courts have deemed appropriate, police might well resort to warrantless searches, with the hope of relying on consent or some other exception to the warrant clause that might develop at the time of the search. In addition, the possession of a warrant by officers conducting an arrest or search greatly reduces the perception of unlawful or intrusive police conduct, by assuring "the individual whose property is searched or seized of the lawful authority of the executing officer, his need to search, and the limits of his power to search." Reflecting this preference for the warrant process, the traditional standard for review of an issuing magistrate's probable cause determination has been that so long as the magistrate had a "substantial basis for concluding" that a search would uncover evidence of wrongdoing, the Fourth Amendment requires no more. We think reaffirmation of this standard better serves the purpose of encouraging recourse to the warrant procedure and is more consistent with our traditional deference to the probable cause determinations of magistrates than is the "two-pronged test."

Finally, the direction taken by decisions following *Spinelli* poorly serves "the most basic function of any government": "to provide for the security of the individual and of his property." The strictures that inevitably accompany the "two-pronged test" cannot avoid seriously impeding the task of law enforcement. If that test must be rigorously applied in every case, anonymous tips seldom would be of greatly diminished value in police work. Ordinary citizens, like ordinary witnesses, generally do not provide extensive recitations of the basis of their everyday observations. Likewise, the veracity of persons supplying anonymous tips is by hypothesis unknown, and unknowable. As a result, anonymous tips seldom could survive a rigorous application of either of the *Spinelli* prongs. Yet, such tips, particularly when supplemented by independent police investigation, frequently contribute to the solution of otherwise "perfect crimes." While a conscientious assessment of the basis for crediting such tips is required by the Fourth Amendment, a standard that leaves virtually no place for anonymous citizen informants is not.

For these reasons, we conclude that it is wiser to abandon the "two-pronged test" established by our decisions in *Aguilar* and *Spinelli*. In its place we reaffirm the totality of the circumstances analysis that traditionally has informed probable cause determinations. The task of the issuing magistrate is simply to make a practical, common-sense decision whether, given all the circumstances set forth in the affidavit before him, including the "veracity" and "basis of knowledge" of persons supplying hearsay information, there is a fair probability that contraband or evidence of a crime will be found in a particular place. And the duty of a reviewing court is simply to ensure that the magistrate had a "substantial basis for concluding" that probable cause existed. We are convinced that this flexible, easily applied standard will better achieve the accommodation of public and private interests that the Fourth Amendment requires than does the approach that has developed from *Aguilar* and *Spinelli*.

Our earlier cases illustrate the limits beyond which a magistrate may not venture in issuing a warrant. A sworn statement of an affiant that "he has cause to suspect and does believe that" liquor illegally brought into the United States is located on certain premises will not do. *Nathanson v. United States*, 290 U.S. 41 (1933). The affidavit must provide the magistrate with a substantial basis for determining the existence of probable cause, and the wholly conclusory statement at issue in *Nathanson* failed to meet this requirement. An officer's statement that "affiants have received reliable information from a credible person and believe" that heroin is stored in a home, is likewise inadequate. *Aguilar v. Texas*, 378 U.S. 108 (1964). As in *Nathanson*, this is a mere conclusory statement that gives the magistrate virtually no basis at all for making a judgment regarding probable cause. Sufficient information must be presented to the magistrate to allow that official to determine probable cause; his action cannot be a mere ratification of the bare conclusions of others. In order to ensure that such an abdication of the magistrate's duty does not occur, courts must continue to conscientiously review the sufficiency of affidavits on which warrants are issued. But when we move beyond the "bare bones" affidavits present in cases such as *Nathanson* and *Aguilar*, this area simply does not lend itself to a prescribed set of rules, like that which had developed from *Spinelli*. Instead, the flexible, common-sense standard articulated in prior precedent better serves the purposes of the Fourth Amendment's probable cause requirement. Nothing in our opinion in any way lessens the authority of the magistrate to draw such reasonable inferences as he will from the material supplied to him by applicants for a warrant; indeed, he is freer than under the regime of *Aguilar* and *Spinelli* to draw such inferences, or to refuse to draw them if he is so minded.

Justice Brennan's criticism seems to be that magistrates should be restricted in their authority to make probable cause determinations by the standards laid down in *Aguilar* and *Spinelli*, and that such findings "should not be authorized unless there is some assurance that the information on which they are based has been obtained in a reliable way by an honest or credible person." However, under our opinion magistrates remain perfectly free to exact such assurances as they deem necessary, as well as those required by this opinion, in making probable cause determinations. Justice Brennan would apparently prefer that magistrates be restricted in their findings of probable cause by the development of an elaborate body of case law dealing with the *Spinelli* test. That such a labyrinthine body of judicial refinement bears any relationship to familiar definitions of probable cause is hard to imagine. Probable cause deals "with probabilities. These are not technical; they are the factual and practical considerations of everyday life on which reasonable and prudent men, not legal technicians, act."

Justice Brennan's dissent suggests that "words such as 'practical,' 'nontechnical,' and 'common sense,' are but code words for an overly-permissive attitude towards police practices in derogation of the rights secured by the Fourth Amendment." "Fidelity" to the commands of the Constitution suggests balanced judgment rather than exhortation. The highest "fidelity" is achieved neither by the judge who instinctively goes furthest in upholding even the most bizarre claim of individual constitutional rights, any more than it is achieved by a judge who instinctively goes furthest in accepting the most restrictive claims of governmental authorities. The task of this Court, as of other courts, is to "hold the balance true," and we think we have done that in this case.

Our decisions applying the totality of circumstances analysis outlined above have consistently recognized the value of corroboration of details of an informant's tip by independent police work. In *Jones v. United States, supra*, 362 U.S., at 269 we held that an affidavit relying on hearsay "is not to be deemed insufficient on that score, so long as a substantial basis for crediting the hearsay is presented." We went on to say that even in making a warrantless arrest an officer "may rely upon information received through an informant, rather than upon his direct observations, so long as the informant's statement is reasonably corroborated by other matters within the officer's knowledge." Likewise, we recognized the probative value of corroborative efforts of police officials in *Aguilar*—the source of the "two-pronged test"—by observing that if the police had made some effort to corroborate the informant's report at issue, "an entirely different case" would have been presented.

Our decision in *Draper v. United States*, 358 U.S. 307 (1959), however, is the classic case on the value of corroborative efforts of police officials. The showing of probable cause in the present case was fully as compelling as that in *Draper*. Even standing alone, the facts obtained through the independent investigation of Mader and the DEA at least suggested that the Gates were involved in drug trafficking. In addition to being a popular vacation site, Florida is well-known as a source of narcotics and other illegal drugs. Lance Gates' flight to Palm Beach, his brief, overnight stay in a motel, and apparent immediate return north to Chicago in the family car, conveniently awaiting him in West Palm Beach, is as suggestive of a pre-arranged drug run, as it is of an ordinary vacation trip.

In addition, the magistrate could rely on the anonymous letter, which had been corroborated in major part by Mader's efforts—just as had occurred in *Draper*. The Illinois court reasoned that *Draper* involved an informant who had given reliable information on previous occasions, while the honesty and reliability of the anonymous informant in this case were unknown to the Bloomingdale police. While this distinction might be an apt one at the time the police department received the anonymous letter, it became far less significant after Mader's independent investigative work occurred. The corroboration of the letter's predictions that the Gates' car would be in Florida, that Lance Gates would fly to Florida in the next day or so, and that he would drive the car north toward Bloomingdale all indicated, albeit not with certainty, that the informant's other assertions also were true. "Because an informant is right about some things, he is more probably right about other facts"—including the claim regarding the Gates' illegal activity. This may well not be the type of "reliability" or "veracity" necessary to satisfy some views of the "veracity prong" of *Spinelli*, but we think it suffices for the practical, common-sense judgment called for in making a probable cause determination. It is enough, for purposes of assessing probable cause, that "corroboration through other sources of information reduced the chances of a reckless or prevaricating tale," thus providing "a substantial basis for crediting the hearsay."

Finally, the anonymous letter contained a range of details relating not just to easily obtained facts and conditions existing at the time of the tip, but to future actions of third parties ordinarily not easily predicted. The letter writer's accurate information as to the travel plans of each of the Gates was of a character likely obtained only from the Gates themselves, or from someone familiar with their not entirely ordinary travel plans. If the informant had access to accurate information of this type a magistrate could properly conclude that it was not unlikely that he also had access to reliable information of the Gates' alleged illegal activities.[9] Of course, the Gates' travel plans might have been learned from a talkative neighbor or travel agent; under the "two-pronged test" developed from *Spinelli*, the character of the details in the anonymous letter might well not permit a sufficiently clear inference regarding the letter writer's "basis of knowledge." But probable cause does not demand the certainty we associate with formal trials. It is enough that there was a fair probability that the writer of the anonymous letter had obtained his entire story either from the Gates or someone they trusted. And corroboration of major portions of the letter's predictions provides just this probability. It is apparent, therefore, that the judge issuing the warrant had a "substantial basis for concluding" that probable cause to search the Gates' home and car existed. The judgment of the Supreme Court of Illinois therefore must be

Reversed.

JUSTICE WHITE, concurring in the judgment. I agree that the warrant should be upheld, but under the *Aguilar-Spinelli* framework. The Gates' activity was quite suspicious. Lance Gates' flight to Palm Beach, an area known to be a source of narcotics, the brief overnight stay in a motel, and apparent immediate return North, suggest a pattern that trained law-enforcement officers have recognized as indicative of illicit drug-dealing activity. Even had the corroboration related only to completely innocuous activities, this would not preclude the issuance of a valid warrant. The critical issue is not whether the activities observed by the police are innocent or suspicious. The proper focus should be on whether the actions of the suspects, whatever their nature, give rise to an inference that the informant is credible and that he obtained his information in a reliable manner. In *Draper*, the fact that the informer was able to predict, two days in advance, the exact clothing Draper would be wearing dispelled the possibility that his tip was just based on rumor or "an off-hand remark heard at a neighborhood bar." Probably Draper had planned in advance to wear these specific clothes so that an accomplice could identify him. A clear inference could therefore be drawn that the informant was either involved in the criminal scheme himself or that he otherwise had access to reliable, inside information.

As in *Draper*, the police investigation in the present case satisfactorily demonstrated that the informant's tip was as trustworthy as one that would alone satisfy the *Aguilar* tests. The tip predicted that Sue Gates would drive to Florida, that Lance Gates would fly there a few days after May 3, and that Lance would then drive the car

---

[9]   The dissent seizes on one inaccuracy in the anonymous informant's letter—its statement that Sue Gates would fly from Florida to Illinois, when in fact she drove—and argues that the probative value of the entire tip was undermined by this allegedly "material mistake." The dissent apparently adopts the rather implausible notion that persons dealing in drugs always stay at home, apparently out of fear that to leave might risk intrusion by criminals. The magistrate's determination that there might be drugs or evidence of criminal activity in the Gates' home was well-supported by the less speculative theory that if the informant could predict with considerable accuracy the somewhat unusual travel plans of the Gates, he probably also had a reliable basis for his statements that the Gates' kept a large quantity of drugs in their home and frequently were visited by other drug traffickers there.

back. After the police corroborated these facts, the magistrate could reasonably have inferred, as he apparently did, that the informant, who had specific knowledge of these unusual travel plans, did not make up his story and that he obtained his information in a reliable way.

It is not at all necessary to overrule *Aguilar-Spinelli* in order to reverse the judgment below. I am reluctant to approve any standard that does not expressly require, as a prerequisite to issuance of a warrant, some showing of facts from which an inference may be drawn that the informant is credible and that his information was obtained in a reliable way. The Court is correctly concerned with the fact that some lower courts have been applying *Aguilar-Spinelli* in an unduly rigid manner. I believe that with clarification of the rule of corroborating information, the lower courts are able to properly interpret *Aguilar-Spinelli* and avoid such unduly-rigid applications. It may prove to be the case that the only profitable instruction we can provide to magistrates is to rely on common sense. But the question whether a particular anonymous tip provides the basis for issuance of a warrant will often be a difficult one, and I would at least attempt to provide more precise guidance by clarifying *Aguilar-Spinelli* and the relationship of those cases with *Draper* before totally abdicating our responsibility in this area.

Justice Brennan, with whom Justice Marshall joins, dissenting.

Although I believe that the warrant is invalid even under the newly announced "totality of the circumstances" test, I write separately to dissent from the Court's unjustified and ill-advised rejection of the two-prong test for evaluating the validity of a warrant based on hearsay announced in *Aguilar* and refined in *Spinelli*.

In recognition of the judiciary's role as the only effective guardian of Fourth Amendment rights, this Court has developed a set of coherent rules governing a magistrate's consideration of a warrant application and the showings that are necessary to support a finding of probable cause. A neutral and detached magistrate, and not the police, should determine whether there is probable cause to support the issuance of a warrant. In order to emphasize the magistrate's role as an independent arbiter of probable cause and to insure that searches or seizures are not effected on less than probable cause, the Court has insisted that police officers provide magistrates with the underlying facts and circumstances that support the officers' conclusions.

The use of hearsay to support the issuance of a warrant presents special problems because informants, unlike police officers, are not regarded as presumptively reliable or honest. Moreover, the basis for an informant's conclusions is not always clear from an affidavit that merely reports those conclusions. If the conclusory allegations of a police officer are insufficient to support a finding of probable cause, surely the conclusory allegations of an informant should a fortiori be insufficient.

Properly understood, *Spinelli* stands for the proposition that corroboration of certain details in a tip may be sufficient to satisfy the veracity, but not the basis of knowledge, prong of *Aguilar*. *Spinelli* also suggests that in some limited circumstances considerable detail in an informant's tip may be adequate to satisfy the basis of knowledge prong of *Aguilar*. The rules drawn from the cases advance an important underlying substantive value: Findings of probable cause, and attendant intrusions, should not be authorized unless there is some assurance that the information on which they are based has been obtained in a reliable way by an honest or credible person. As applied to police officers, the rules focus on the way in which the information was acquired. As applied to informants, the rules focus both on the honesty or credibility of the informant and on the reliability of the way in which the information was acquired. An evaluation of affidavits based on hearsay involves a more difficult inquiry. This suggests a need to structure the inquiry in an effort to insure greater accuracy. The standards announced in *Aguilar*, as refined by *Spinelli*, fulfill that need. The standards inform the police of what information they have to provide and magistrates of what information they should demand. The standards also inform magistrates of the subsidiary findings they must make in order to arrive at an ultimate finding of probable cause. *Spinelli* directs the magistrate's attention to the possibility that the presence of self-verifying detail might satisfy *Aguilar*'s basis of knowledge prong and that corroboration of the details of a tip might satisfy *Aguilar*'s veracity prong. *Aguilar* and *Spinelli* assure the magistrate's role as an independent arbiter of probable cause, insure greater accuracy in probable cause determinations, and advance the substantive value identified above.

Both *Aguilar* and *Spinelli* dealt with tips from informants known at least to the police. And surely there is even more reason to subject anonymous informants' tips to the tests established by *Aguilar* and *Spinelli*. By definition nothing is known about an anonymous informant's identity, honesty, or reliability. Nor is there any basis for assuming that the information provided by an anonymous informant has been obtained in a reliable way. If we are unwilling to accept conclusory allegations from the police, who are presumptively reliable, or from informants who are known, at least to the police, there cannot possibly be any rational basis for accepting conclusory allegations from anonymous informants.

Police corroboration of the details of the tip might establish the reliability of the informant under *Aguilar*'s veracity prong, as refined in *Spinelli*, and the details in the tip might be sufficient to qualify under the "self-verifying detail" test established by *Spinelli* as a means of satisfying *Aguilar*'s basis of knowledge prong. The *Aguilar* and *Spinelli* tests must be applied to anonymous informants' tips, however, if we are to continue to insure that findings of probable cause, and attendant intrusions, are based on information provided by an honest or credible person who has acquired the information in a reliable way.

In light of the important purposes served by *Aguilar* and *Spinelli*, I would not reject the standards they establish. If anything, I simply would make more clear that *Spinelli*, properly understood, does not depart in any fundamental way from the test established by *Aguilar*. One can concede that probable cause is a "practical, nontechnical" concept without betraying the values that *Aguilar* and *Spinelli* reflect. *Aguilar* and *Spinelli* require the police to provide magistrates with certain crucial information. They also provide structure for magistrates' probable cause inquiries. Once a magistrate has determined that he has information before him that he can reasonably say has been obtained in a reliable way by a credible person, he has ample room to use his common sense and to apply a practical, nontechnical conception of probable cause.

The Court insists that the *Aguilar-Spinelli* standards are inconsistent with the fact that non-lawyers frequently serve as magistrates. To the contrary, the standards help to structure probable cause inquiries and, properly interpreted, may actually help a non-lawyer magistrate in making a probable cause determination. Of particular concern to all Americans must be that the Court gives virtually no consideration to the value of insuring that findings of probable cause are based on information that a magistrate can reasonably say has been obtained in a reliable way by an honest or credible person. Words such as "practical," "nontechnical," and "commonsense" are but code words for an overly permissive attitude towards police practices in derogation of the rights secured by the Fourth Amendment. Everyone shares the Court's concern over the horrors of drug trafficking, but under our Constitution only measures consistent with the Fourth Amendment may be employed by government to cure this evil.

By replacing *Aguilar* and *Spinelli* with a test that provides no assurance that magistrates, rather than the police, or informants, will make determinations of probable cause; imposes no structure on magistrates' probable cause inquiries; and invites the possibility that intrusions may be justified on less than reliable information from an honest or credible person, today's decision threatens to "obliterate one of the most fundamental distinctions between our form of government, where officers are under the law, and the police-state where they are the law."

JUSTICE STEVENS, with whom JUSTICE BRENNAN joins, dissenting.

The fact that Lance and Sue Gates made a 22-hour nonstop drive from West Palm Beach, Florida, to Bloomingdale, Illinois, only a few hours after Lance had flown to Florida provided persuasive evidence that they were engaged in illicit activity. That fact, however, was not known to the magistrate when he issued the warrant to search their home. What the magistrate did know at that time was that the anonymous informant had not been completely accurate in his or her predictions. The informant had indicated that "Sue drives their car to Florida *where she leaves it to be loaded up with drugs. Sue flies back after she drops the car off in Florida.*" Yet Detective Mader's affidavit reported that she "left the West Palm Beach area driving the Mercury northbound." The discrepancy between the informant's predictions and the facts known to Detective Mader is significant for three reasons. First, it cast doubt on the informant's hypothesis that the Gates already had "over $100,000 worth of drugs in their basement." The informant had predicted an itinerary that always kept one spouse in Bloomingdale, suggesting that the Gates did not want to leave their home unguarded because something valuable was hidden within. That inference obviously could not be drawn when it was known that the pair was actually together over a thousand miles from home. Second, the discrepancy made the Gates' conduct seem substantially less unusual than the informant had predicted it would be. It would have been odd if, as predicted, Sue had driven down to Florida on Wednesday, left the car, and flown right back to Illinois. But the mere facts that Sue was in West Palm Beach with the car,[10] that she was joined by her husband at the Holiday Inn on Friday,[11] and that the couple drove north together the next morning[12] are neither unusual nor probative of criminal activity. Third, the fact that the anonymous letter contained a material mistake undermines the reasonableness of relying on it as a basis for making a forcible entry into a private home.

Of course, the activities in this case did not stop when the magistrate issued the warrant. The Gates drove all night to Bloomingdale, the officers searched the car and found 400 pounds of marijuana, and then they searched the house. However, none of these subsequent events may be considered in evaluating the warrant, and the search of the house was legal only if the warrant was valid. I cannot accept the Court's casual conclusion that, before the Gates arrived in Bloomingdale, there was probable cause to justify a valid entry and search of a private home. No one knows who the informant in this case was, or what motivated him or her to write the note. Given that the note's predictions were faulty in one significant respect, and were corroborated by nothing except ordinary innocent activity, I must surmise that the Court's evaluation of the warrant's validity has been colored by subsequent events.

---

[10] The anonymous note suggested that she was going down on Wednesday, but for all the officers knew she had been in Florida for a month.

[11] Lance does not appear to have behaved suspiciously in flying down to Florida. He made a reservation in his own name and gave an accurate home phone number to the airlines. And Detective Mader's affidavit does not report that he did any of the other things drug couriers are notorious for doing, such as paying for the ticket in cash, dressing casually, looking pale and nervous, improperly filling out baggage tags, carrying American Tourister luggage, not carrying any luggage, or changing airlines en route.

[12] Detective Mader's affidavit hinted darkly that the couple had set out upon "that interstate highway commonly used by travelers to the Chicago area." But the same highway is also commonly used by travelers to Disney World, Sea World, and Ringling Brothers and Barnum and Bailey Circus World. It is also the road to Cocoa Beach, Cape Canaveral, and Washington, D.C. I would venture that each year dozens of perfectly innocent people fly to Florida, meet a waiting spouse, and drive off together in the family car.

Points for Discussion

a. Analyzing *Gates*

Does *Gates* abandon the *Aguilar-Spinelli* two-part test? What does the Court suggest in *Gates*? In thinking about this issue, consider *Massachusetts v. Upton*, 466 U.S. 727 (1984), decided the following year. That case also involved an anonymous tip, but the Massachusetts Supreme Judicial Court narrowly construed *Gates* and reversed Upton's conviction. The U.S. Supreme Court summarized the Massachusetts court's decision as follows: "The Massachusetts court apparently viewed *Gates* as merely adding a new wrinkle to the *Aguilar-Spinelli* two-pronged test: where an informant's veracity and/or basis of knowledge are not sufficiently clear, substantial corroboration of the tip may save an otherwise invalid warrant." The U.S. Supreme Court reversed: "In *Gates*, we did not merely refine or qualify the 'two-pronged test.' We rejected it as hyper technical and divorced from 'the factual and practical considerations of everyday life on which reasonable and prudent men, not legal technicians, act.' " "We conclude that it is wiser to abandon the 'two-pronged test' established by our decisions in *Aguilar* and *Spinelli*. In its place we reaffirm the totality-of-the-circumstances analysis that traditionally has informed probable-cause determinations."

b. Informer's Privilege

In *McCray v. Illinois*, 386 U.S. 300 (1967), petitioner was arrested for possession of narcotics and moved to suppress the evidence. Since the arrest was based on an informant's tip, petitioner sought to learn the informant's identity. The trial court denied the motion for disclosure, and the Court upheld the denial: "The informer is a vital part of society's defensive arsenal. We have repeatedly made clear that federal officers need not disclose an informer's identity in applying for an arrest or search warrant."

In *Roviaro v. United States*, 353 U.S. 53 (1957), defendant was convicted under the Narcotic Drugs Import and Export Act after the government refused to reveal the identity of an informant. Although the Court suggested that the decision to disclose should be made on a case-by-case basis, it held that the informant's identity should have been revealed in that case:

> The scope of the privilege is limited by its underlying purpose. Thus, where the disclosure of the contents of a communication will not tend to reveal the identity of an informer, the contents are not privileged. Likewise, once the identity of the informer has been disclosed to those who would have cause to resent the communication, the privilege is no longer applicable. A further limitation on the applicability of the privilege arises from the fundamental requirements of fairness. Where the disclosure of an informer's identity, or of the contents of his communication, is relevant and helpful to

the defense of an accused, or is essential to a fair determination of a cause, the privilege must give way. In these situations the trial court may require disclosure and, if the Government withholds the information, dismiss the action.

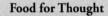

Food for Thought

In *Draper,* the Court emphasized that the informers' tip included great detail, and the police officer confirmed that detail. In *Gates,* there was also considerable detail in the tip, but were the police able to confirm the validity of the tip? Were there respects in which the tip was inaccurate? Should the inaccuracies be regarded as significant?

The problem is one that calls for balancing the public interest in protecting the flow of information against the individual's right to prepare his defense. Whether a proper balance renders nondisclosure erroneous must depend on the particular circumstances of each case, taking into consideration the crime charged, the possible defenses, the possible significance of the informer's testimony, and other relevant factors. The circumstances demonstrate that John Doe's possible testimony was highly relevant and might have been helpful to the defense. So far as petitioner knew, he and John Doe were

Food for Thought

Even if the Court could conclude that the Gates went to West Palm Beach to purchase more illegal drugs, was there probable cause to search their home? After all, the tip could be construed as suggesting that they always left someone at home to guard it. If, on this occasion, both flew to Florida and drove back, does that suggest that they might be out of drugs at home?

alone and unobserved during the crucial occurrence for which he was indicted. Unless petitioner waived his constitutional right not to take the stand in his own defense, John Doe was his one material witness. His testimony might have disclosed an entrapment. He might have thrown doubt upon petitioner's identity or on the identity of the package. He was the only witness who might have testified to petitioner's possible lack of knowledge of the contents of the package that he "transported" from the tree to John Doe's car. The desirability of calling John Doe as a witness, or at least interviewing him in preparation for trial, was a matter for the accused rather than the Government to decide. Finally, the Government's use against petitioner of his conversation with John Doe while riding in Doe's car particularly emphasizes the unfairness of the nondisclosure in this case. The only person, other than petitioner himself, who could controvert, explain or amplify Bryson's report of this important conversation was John Doe. Contradiction or amplification might have borne upon petitioner's knowledge of the contents of the package or might have tended to show an entrapment.

c.   **Drug Detection Dogs & Probable Cause**

In *Florida v. Harris*, 568 U.S. 237 (2013), the Court held that an "alert" by a drug-detection dog during a traffic stop provides probable cause to search a vehicle. In that case, a canine alerted at the driver's side door handle (suggesting that he smelled drugs there). In the ensuring search, the officer did not find any of the drugs that the dog was trained to detect (methamphetamine, marijuana, cocaine, heroin, and ecstasy), but did find 200 pseudoephedrine pills, 8,000 matches, a bottle of hydrochloric acid, two containers of antifreeze, and a coffee filter full of iodine crystals—all ingredients used in making methamphetamine. The officer then gave the driver a *Miranda* warning and he admitted to cooking meth at his home. The officer then arrested the driver for possession of pseudoephedrine for use in making meth. After the driver was released, the officer stopped him again, and the dog again alerted to the same door handle. This time, the officer discovered nothing of interest. At his trial, defendant moved to suppress evidence obtained from the first stop on the basis on the basis that the dog alert was unreliable because the dog had allegedly made two false positives on defendant's truck, and therefore did not provide the officer with probable cause to search the truck. The Court disagreed, noting that a dog's reliability should not be determined based on the dog's performance in actual traffic stops which can be deceiving because, if the dog failed to alert when drugs were present, nobody would know that drugs had been present. Conversely, if the dog alerted to vehicles in which the officer found no narcotics, "the dog may not have made a mistake at all. The dog may have detected substances that were too well hidden or present in quantities too small for the officer to locate. Or the dog may have smelled the residual odor of drugs previously in the vehicle or on the driver's person. Field data thus may markedly overstate a dog's real false positives." As a result, the Court held that a dog's reliability must be determined based on his performance in training exercises: "If a bona fide organization has certified a dog after testing his reliability in a controlled setting, a court can presume (subject to any conflicting evidence) that the dog's alert provides probable cause to search. The same is true, even in the absence of formal certification, if the dog has recently and successfully completed a training program that evaluated his proficiency in locating drugs." Given this particular dog's performance in training, the Court concluded that probable cause existed when the officer searched defendant's car. Two years earlier, the dog had successfully completed a 120-hour program in narcotics detection, and separately obtained a certification from an independent company. The Sheriff's Office required continuing training for the dog and his handler, and both satisfactorily completed another 40-hour training program one year earlier. Also, the handler worked with the dog four hours per week on exercises designed to keep his skills sharp. Throughout, the dog always performed at the highest level.

Hypo 1: *More on* Gates

In analyzing the *Gates* facts, the Court emphasized that the Gates left Palm Beach heading North on a highway that leads to Chicago, and that they drove all night. Was it appropriate for the Court to consider the fact that they drove all night since that fact could not have been known at the time that the warrant was issued? Although the Court could consider the fact that the Gates were headed North, how many options does one have from Palm Beach? Is it possible to go very far East, or very far South or West? Moreover, might the Gates have flown to West Palm Beach and driven to a nearby beach resort to the North? The highway did lead North, and therefore could take one to Chicago, but could the road also take one to many other places in Florida?

Food for Thought

In light of the *Gates* holding, would *Spinelli* be decided the same way today? In other words, applying the *Gates* "totality of the circumstances" test, rather than the two-pronged *Aguilar-Spinelli* test, would the Court be inclined to find that probable cause existed on the *Spinelli* facts?

Hypo 2: *Establishing Probable Cause*

A police detective, an eleven-year veteran with training and experience in narcotics investigations, learns from a confidential informant that there is "a dark skinned Hispanic male who is selling heroin" in varying amounts and prices in the city. The informant states that the heroin dealer walks with a pronounced limp, and that he can be reached at either of two telephone numbers. He also states that, if someone calls the dealer to purchase drugs, he will ask "how much" and then provide a location where he will meet a purchaser to exchange money for heroin. The dealer will arrive at the location either in a white Toyota sedan or in a "sharp looking" green Audi sedan with tinted windows and after-market wheels. When asked where the dealer keeps the drugs, the informant is unsure. If you are asked to advise the detective about how to proceed with the investigation, what would you advise? *See Commonwealth v. Escalera*, 462 Mass. 636, 970 N.E.2d 319 (2012).

Hypo 3: *The Tip*

The police receive an anonymous phone "tip" which states that a house is rented to Gary Moore; that Keith Umfleet has drugs stored in the refrigerator at the house; that Moore and Umfleet are eating a meal and afterwards plan to travel to Illinois to dispose of the drugs; that the parties own a red Volkswagen which they might drive to Illinois; that there is an incinerator located in the back of the apartment. After receiving the call, a police officer verifies that the house is rented and lived-in by Moore; that a red Volkswagen is parked outside; that there is an incinerator in the back of the apartment. The officer knows that Umfleet has a reputation as a previously arrested drug trafficker. Following the verification, the police stake out the house. While they do not see either Moore or Umfleet, they do see David Hill, a known drug user, walk "in and about the house." The officers also see an orange car pull into the parking lot, begin to look for a parking place, but drive off "in a very big hurry" when the driver spots the police. Do the police have "probable cause" to believe that the occupants of the apartment were in possession of drugs? *See State v. Wiley*, 522 S.W.2d 281 (Mo., En Banc, 1975).

Hypo 4: *Child Abuse Informant*

An anonymous tipster calls a child abuse hotline. She identifies Kendra D'Andrea and Willie Jordan as partners, provides D'Andrea's residential address, and identifies Jordan's employer by name. She informs the hotline that she received a message on her mobile phone containing photographs of D'Andrea and Jordan performing sexual acts on D'Andrea's eight-year-old daughter with her genitalia exposed. Based solely on the tip, do the police have probable cause to obtain a search warrant to search the residence? If not, what steps should they take to establish probable cause? *See United States v. D'Andrea*, 648 F.3d 1 (1st Cir. 2011).

Hypo 5: *The Suspected Cocaine Seller*

A police officer receives a tip about a black male named "Greg" who sells cocaine. The tip states that the seller drives a gold colored Mercedes to deliver the narcotics, and that he sells drugs only in the evening. The informant supplies the officer with Greg's cellular and home phone numbers, and the location where a narcotics sale will be made. The officer investigates the phone numbers and learns Greg's birthdate and driver's license number, and that a man named "Gregory Wallace" lives at the location associated with the phone numbers. Based on the tip and the investigation, do the police have probable cause to search the house? Would you reach a different conclusion if the police saw the informant enter the house to buy drugs, exit the house, and then they see Greg exit the house walking towards the informant with what appears to be drugs? *See Commonwealth v. Wallace*, 42 A.3d 1040 (Pa. 2012).

Hypo 6: *More on Suspected Cocaine Sellers*

Suppose that police receive an anonymous tip suggesting that a man by the name of Steve Clark, a white male, approximately 6' to 6'2" in height and weighing approximately 170–195 lbs., packages and distributes cocaine from 4242 Salmon Street in Philadelphia, and makes deliveries of cocaine in a white Pontiac Grand Am with a black roof, Pennsylvania license number FRG-5450. If the police go to that address, confirm that someone named "Steve Clark" lives there, find a Pontiac which matches that description bearing the stated license plate number, and see a man matching Steve's description leave the house, do they have probable cause to obtain a warrant to search the house? Do they need additional evidence? If so, what do they need? *See Commonwealth v. Clark*, 28 A.3d 1284 (Pa. 2011).

Hypo 7: *The Stash House*

Police receive an anonymous tip regarding a "narcotics stash house" and have the house under surveillance when they see an unidentified male arrive and enter the house. A few minutes later, the man leaves the house with a large white box that he places inside his truck. Police follow the truck which pulls over to the curb at a nearby street. The driver exits with the white box, walks over to a white GMC Envoy, and hands the box to a second unknown male (Cervantes). Cervantes drives his GMC Envoy to a nearby liquor store where he makes a purchase and drives away. Does the officer have probable cause to stop and search Cervantes's vehicle? *See United States v. Cervantes*, 678 F.3d 798 (9th Cir. 2012).

> ### Hypo 8: *The Tip*
>
> After the police arrest a high-ranking member of the West Hell Gang for possession of narcotics, he tells an officer that he knows where they can find some illegal guns. The gang is known for violence and is alleged to have been involved in the commission of several homicides and other shootings. The informant, who has recently been released on parole, believes and hopes that, by providing the information, the police will "go easier" on him. He then gives the police a precise address, tells them that the guns can be found in an abandoned car under the front seat. This particular informant has never provided the police with information in the past. Does the tip, offered under such circumstances, provide the police with probable cause to believe that illegal guns can be found in the vehicle? *See Harris v. O'Hare*, 770 F.3d 224 (2d Cir. 2014).

D. Warrantless Searches & Seizures

Despite the judicial preference for a warrant, the courts have established numerous exceptions to the warrant requirement. But the courts distinguish between arrests and searches. Even though warrantless arrests are generally permissible, warrantless searches are disfavored and regarded as "*per se* unreasonable subject only to a few specifically established and well-delineated exceptions." *Katz v. United States*, 389 U.S. 347, 357 (1967). In this section, we examine the exceptions and their underlying justifications.

1. Plain View Exception

The "plain view" exception is an often-used exception to the warrant requirement. When the police are conducting a lawful search, and are in a place where they have the right to be, they can view items that they find in plain view, and may also have the right to seize them. However, there have been debates regarding the scope of this exception.

Horton v. California

496 U.S. 128 (1990).

JUSTICE STEVENS delivered the opinion of the Court.

Pursuant to a warrant, an experienced police officer (Sergeant LaRault) searched Petitioner's home for the proceeds of a robbery. The officer did not find the stolen property. He did discover weapons in plain view and seized them. Specifically, he seized an Uzi machine gun, a .38-caliber revolver, two stun guns, a handcuff key, a San Jose Coin Club advertising brochure (the victim was the Treasurer of the Club), and a few items of clothing identified by the victim. LaRault testified that while he was searching for the stolen rings, he also was interested in finding other evidence connecting petitioner to the robbery. Thus, the seized evidence was not discovered "inadvertently."

The "plain-view" doctrine is an exception to the general rule that warrantless searches are presumptively unreasonable, but this characterization overlooks the important difference between searches and seizures. If an article is in plain view, neither its observation nor its seizure would involve any invasion of privacy. A seizure of the article, however, would obviously invade the owner's possessory interest. If "plain view" justifies an exception from an otherwise applicable warrant requirement, therefore, it must be an exception that is addressed to the concerns that are implicated by seizures rather than by searches.

In *Coolidge v. New Hampshire*, 403 U. S. 443, 481 (1971, Justice Stewart described two limitations on the plain view doctrine that he found implicit in its rationale: First, "plain view *alone* is never enough to justify the warrantless seizure of evidence," and second, "the discovery of evidence in plain view must be inadvertent." Justice Stewart's analysis of the "plain-view" doctrine did not command a majority, and a plurality of the Court has since made clear that the discussion is "not a binding precedent."

An essential predicate to any valid warrantless seizure of incriminating evidence is that the officer did not violate the Fourth Amendment in arriving at the place from which the evidence could be plainly viewed. There are two additional conditions that must be satisfied to justify the warrantless seizure. First, not only must the item be in plain view; its incriminating character must also be "immediately apparent." Second, not only must the officer be lawfully located in a place from which the object can be plainly seen, but he or she must also have a lawful right of access to the object itself.

Justice Stewart concluded that the inadvertence requirement was necessary to avoid a violation of the express constitutional requirement that a valid warrant must particularly describe the things to be seized. He explained: "The requirement of a warrant to seize imposes no inconvenience whatever, or at least none which is constitutionally cognizable in a legal system that regards warrantless searches as '*per se* unreasonable' in the absence of 'exigent circumstances.' If the initial intrusion is bottomed upon a warrant that fails to mention a particular object, though the police know its location and intend to seize it, then there is a violation of the express constitutional requirement of "Warrants particularly describing the things to be seized."

We find two flaws in this reasoning. First, evenhanded law enforcement is best achieved by the application of objective standards of conduct, rather than standards that depend upon the subjective state of mind of the officer. The fact that an officer is interested in an item of evidence and fully expects to find it in the course of a search should not invalidate its seizure if the search is confined in area and duration by the terms of a warrant or a valid exception to the warrant requirement. If the officer has knowledge approaching certainty that the item will be found, we see no reason why he or she would deliberately omit a particular description of the item to be seized from the application for a search warrant. Specification of the additional item could only permit the officer to expand the scope of the search. On the other hand, if he or she has a valid warrant to search for one item and merely a suspicion concerning the second, whether or not it amounts to probable cause, we fail to see why that suspicion should immunize the second item from seizure if it is found during a lawful search for the first.

Second, the suggestion that the inadvertence requirement is necessary to prevent the police from conducting general searches, or from converting specific warrants into general warrants, is not persuasive because that interest is already served by the requirements that no warrant issue unless it "particularly describes the place to be searched and the persons or things to be seized," and that a warrantless search be circumscribed by the exigencies which justify its initiation. Scrupulous adherence to these requirements serves the interests in limiting the area and duration of the search that the inadvertence requirement inadequately protects. Once those commands have been satisfied and the officer has a lawful right of access, however, no additional Fourth Amendment interest is furthered by requiring that the discovery of evidence be inadvertent. If the scope of the search exceeds that permitted by the terms of a validly issued warrant or the character of the relevant exception from the warrant requirement, the subsequent seizure is unconstitutional without more.

In this case, the scope of the search was not enlarged in the slightest by the omission of any reference to the weapons in the warrant. Indeed, if the three rings and other items named in the warrant had been found at the outset—or if petitioner had them in his possession and had responded to the warrant by producing them immediately—no search for weapons could have taken place.

The seizure of an object in plain view does not involve an intrusion on privacy. If the interest in privacy has been invaded, the violation must have occurred before the object came into plain view and there is no need for an inadvertence limitation on seizures to condemn it. The prohibition against general searches and general warrants serves primarily as a protection against unjustified intrusions on privacy. But reliance on privacy concerns that support that prohibition is misplaced when the inquiry concerns the scope of an exception that merely authorizes an officer with a lawful right of access to an item to seize it without a warrant.

In this case the items seized from petitioner's home were discovered during a lawful search authorized by a valid warrant. When they were discovered, it was immediately apparent to the officer that they constituted incriminating evidence. He had probable cause, not only to obtain a warrant to search for the stolen property, but also to believe that the weapons and handguns had been used in the crime he was investigating. The search was authorized by the warrant; the seizure was authorized by the "plain-view" doctrine. The judgment is affirmed.

It is so ordered.

JUSTICE BRENNAN, with whom JUSTICE MARSHALL joins, dissenting.

The inadvertent discovery requirement is essential if we are to take seriously the Fourth Amendment's protection of possessory interests as well as privacy interests. If an officer enters a house pursuant to a warrant to search for evidence of one crime when he is really interested only in seizing evidence relating to another crime, for which he does not have a warrant, his search is "pretextual" and the fruits of that search should be suppressed. Similarly, an officer might use an exception to the generally applicable warrant requirement, such as "hot pursuit," as a pretext to enter a home to seize items he knows he will find in plain view. Such conduct would be a deliberate attempt to circumvent the constitutional requirement of a warrant "particularly describing the place to be searched, and the persons or things to be seized," and cannot be condoned.

Points for Discussion

a. Immediately Apparent Requirement

In order for the plain view exception to apply, the criminal nature of the thing observed must be "immediately apparent." In *Minnesota v. Dickerson*, 508 U.S. 366 (1993), police officers stopped Dickerson and forced him to submit to a frisk. The frisk revealed no weapons, but the officer found a small lump in respondent's nylon jacket. The officer examined the lump with his fingers. By sliding the lump, the officer determined that it was crack cocaine in cellophane. The officer then reached into respondent's pocket and retrieved a small plastic bag containing one fifth of one gram of crack cocaine. Respondent was arrested and charged with possession of a controlled substance. The Court held that the seizure was invalid: "If a police officer lawfully pats down a suspect's outer clothing and feels an object whose contour or mass makes its identity immediately apparent, there has been no invasion of the suspect's privacy beyond that already authorized by the officer's search for weapons; if the object is contraband, its warrantless seizure would be justified by the same practical considerations that inhere in the plain-view context. Here, the officer determined that the lump was contraband only after 'squeezing, sliding and otherwise manipulating the contents of the defendant's pocket'—a pocket which the officer already knew contained no weapon. The officer's exploration of respondent's pocket after having concluded that it contained no weapon was unrelated to 'the sole justification of the search under *Terry*: the protection of the police officer and others nearby.' "

FYI

The plain view exception is frequently applied in situations like the one involved in Horton: a police officer has lawfully entered a house, finds evidence in plain view, and uses the exception to justify the seizure of the evidence. Illustrative is the holding in *Washington v. Chrisman*, 455 U.S. 1 (1982), in which a university police officer arrested a student for carrying a half-gallon bottle of gin on campus (state law prohibited the possession of alcoholic beverages by individuals under 21). After the student was handcuffed, the officer asked the student for identification which the student was unable to produce. The student then asked for permission to return to his dormitory room to retrieve his identification, and the officer accompanied the student to the room. At the room, the officer observed what appeared to be a pipe and marijuana seeds in plain view and seized them. The seizure was upheld.

b. Narcotics Balloon

In *Texas v. Brown*, 460 U.S. 730 (1983), Brown was stopped at a driver's license checkpoint, and was found holding an opaque, green party balloon which was knotted about one half inch from the tip. When Brown opened the glove compartment, the officer noticed that the compartment contained several small plastic vials, quantities of loose white powder, and an open bag of party balloons. The officer reached into the car and picked up the green balloon which seemed to contain a powdery substance within the tied-off portion of the balloon. Subsequent analysis revealed that the balloon contained heroin. The Court concluded that the heroin was "immediately apparent": "Officer Maples possessed probable cause to believe that the balloon in Brown's hand contained an illicit substance. Maples was aware, both from his participation in previous narcotics arrests and from discussions with

Food for Thought

Rambo Royster is walking down a public street smoking a marijuana joint. A police officer sees Royster and the joint. Does the plain view doctrine come into play in a situation like this? If so, how?

other officers, that balloons tied in the manner of the one possessed by Brown were frequently used to carry narcotics. This testimony was corroborated by a police department chemist who noted that it was "common" for balloons to be used in packaging narcotics. In addition, Maples was able to observe the contents of the glove compartment of Brown's car, which further suggested that Brown was engaged in activities that might involve possession of illicit substances. The fact that Maples could not see through the opaque fabric of the balloon is all but irrelevant: the distinctive character of the balloon itself spoke volumes as to its contents—particularly to the trained eye of the officer." Justice Stevens concurred: "The balloon could be one of those rare single-purpose containers which 'by their very nature cannot support any reasonable expectation of privacy because their contents can be inferred from their outward appearance.' "

Take Note

If an officer needs to move an object to determine whether it is "incriminating," the plain view doctrine does not apply. In *Arizona v. Hicks*, 480 U.S. 321 (1987), a bullet was fired into the floor of respondent's apartment, striking and injuring a man in the apartment below. When police officers entered respondent's apartment to search for the shooter, for other victims, and for weapons, one of the officers noticed expensive stereo components which seemed out of place in the squalid apartment. Suspecting that they were stolen, the officer moved some of the components so that he could read and record their serial numbers. The serial numbers allowed him to determine that the turntable had been stolen in an armed robbery. The Court concluded that the "moving" of the stereo equipment to view the serial numbers could not be justified under the plain view exception: "Inspecting those parts of the turntable that came into view during the search would not have constituted an independent search, because it would have produced no additional invasion of respondent's privacy interest. But taking action, which exposed to view concealed portions of the apartment or its contents, did produce a new invasion of respondent's privacy unjustified by the exigent circumstance that validated the entry. A search is a search, even if it happens to disclose nothing but the bottom of a turntable. 'The "plain view" doctrine may not be used to extend a general exploratory search from one object to another until something incriminating at last emerges.' " Justice Powell dissented: "The majority's distinction between 'looking' at a suspicious object in plain view and 'moving' it even a few inches trivializes the Fourth Amendment." Justice O'Connor also dissented: "If police officers have a reasonable, articulable suspicion that an object they come across during the course of a lawful search is evidence of crime, they may make a cursory examination of the object to verify their suspicion. The additional intrusion caused by an inspection of an item in plain view for its serial number is minuscule."

Hypo 1: *Marijuana on the Window Sill*

A police officer is walking down a public sidewalk when he observes three marijuana plants growing on the window sill inside a townhouse. Does the plain view exception apply? May the officer use the plain view doctrine to enter the house and seize the plants? If not, how does the exception apply?

Hypo 2: *"Plain Smell" Doctrine?*

Is there a "plain smell" doctrine analogous to the "plain view" doctrine? Suppose that a police officer stops a car that is traveling at excessive speed. When the occupant of the car rolls down the window, the officer smells marijuana smoke emanating from the window. Would the "plain smell" doctrine justify a search of the car? Might the officer be able to justify the search on other grounds?

Hypo 3: *Computers & Plain View*

The police have reason to believe that defendant is a child pornographer, and obtain a warrant to search his home for books and magazines containing child pornography. On entering defendant's house, the police find a computer that is linked to the internet. Because many pornographers now use the internet to obtain pictures of children, the police seize the computer on the theory that it reflects "evidence" of child pornography found in "plain view." Is the seizure valid? After the seizure, can the police enter the hard drive of the computer and search for evidence of child pornography?

Hypo 4: *More on Computers & Plain View*

In the prior problem, suppose that the police have probable cause to believe that defendant is using his computer to find and download child pornography, and particularly describe the computer as an item to be seized under the warrant. Following the seizure, as the police are going through defendant's computer files, they find a file titled "Bookmaking." Can the police search the "bookmaking" file on the assumption that it was found in "plain view" during the computer search, and is plainly evident of illegality? Does it matter whether the police are generally searching through the entire computer, or only examining files with titles suggesting that they might contain child pornography? *See United States v. Galpin*, 720 F.3d 436 (2d Cir. 2013).

Hypo 5: *Plain View During a "Knock and Talk"*

Suppose that the police believe that Fisher is operating a meth lab in his home. Lacking probable cause to obtain a warrant, the officers go to the house to conduct a "knock and talk" during which they knock on Fisher's door, talk to him, and see if he will consent to a search. During the "knock and talk," the officer (who is standing at Fisher's front door) happens to see meth-related items (e.g., pseudoephedrine) lying just inside the door on the coffee table. Does the "plain view" doctrine apply to the items? Does the officer have the right to enter the house and seize the items without a warrant? *See McClish v. Nugent*, 483 F.3d 1231 (11th Cir. 2007); *State v. Fisher*, 283 Kan. 272, 154 P.3d 455 (2007).

Hypo 6: *Plain View & the Dog Killing*

The police receive a frantic call from a woman, claiming that her neighbor is shooting at her dog. When the police arrive, defendant admits that he killed a dog, but claims that it was one of his own dogs, and that the police will "never find it." From the sidewalk, the police can see that a patch of ground on defendant's property, near his residence (20 feet away), has been dug up, and they also see a dog collar lying on top of the dirt. Can the dog bones lying beneath the fresh dirt be regarded as being in plain view? *See State v. Goulet*, 21 A.3d 302 (R.I. 2011).

Hypo 7: *More on Plain View*

The police, who are called to a residence that has been burglarized, notice that a window has been broken, presumably to effect entry. The owner asks the officers to do a sweep of the house in order to ensure that no intruder remains on the premises. The police take a dog with them. The dog "alerts" to a door, suggesting that there is a human behind the door. When the police open the door, they do not find a human. However, the dog sticks his nose into a plastic bag revealing to the officers the existence of marijuana. Can the officers seize the evidence under the plain view doctrine? Should the dog's actions be regarded as equivalent to the officer's decision to move the turntable (in order to ascertain serial numbers) in *Hicks*? Or should the dog's instinctive reactions be regarded as different for Fourth Amendment purposes? *See State v. Miller*, 367 N.C. 702, 766 S.E.2d 289 (2014).

Hypo 8: *The Credit Cards*

Suppose that the police arrest a man for smoking marijuana in his car. With probable cause to believe that there is marijuana in the vehicle, the police search the vehicle, including a leather bag that they find in the back seat. Although they do not find marijuana in the bag, they do find 15 credit cards. Given the large number of credit cards, can the police seize the cards on the basis that they constitute contraband in "plain view?" Does it matter what name is on the cards, and whether they correspond to the arrestee's name? Can the police examine the name on the cards to see if there is congruency? *See United States v. Saulsberry*, 878 F.3d 946 (10th Cir. 2017).

2. Search Incident to Legal Arrest

The search incident to legal arrest exception is one of the oldest and most well-established exceptions to the warrant requirement. It provides that, when the police make a legal arrest, they have the right to make a search incident to that arrest. Until 1976, there was uncertainty about the requirements for an arrest. Could an arrest be based solely on probable cause? Or, as under the search prong of the Fourth Amendment, is a warrant required?

Take Note

An arrest is the most serious form of seizure, and it occurs when the police take a suspect into custody in order to bring charges.

United States v. Watson

423 U.S. 411 (1976).

MR. JUSTICE WHITE delivered the opinion of the Court.

Based on information received from an informant, a federal postal inspector had reason to believe that Watson was in possession of credit cards stolen from the U.S. mail. The informant arranged to meet Watson in a restaurant. On the informant's signal (which indicated that Watson was in possession of the cards), federal inspectors closed in and arrested Watson for possession of stolen mail. After the arrest, Watson consented to a search of his car which revealed two more stolen credit cards. The court of appeals held that Watson's arrest was unconstitutional because the inspector acted without a warrant and granted Watson's motion to suppress the credit cards.

Under the Fourth Amendment, the people are to be "secure in their persons, houses, papers, and effects, against unreasonable searches and seizures, and no Warrants shall issue, but upon probable cause." The statute under which Watson was arrested represents a judgment by Congress that it is not unreasonable under the Fourth Amendment for postal inspectors to arrest without a warrant provided they have probable cause to do so. This was not an isolated or quixotic judgment of the legislative branch. Other federal law enforcement officers have been expressly authorized by statute for many years to make felony arrests on probable cause but without a warrant. This is true of United States marshals, and of agents of the Federal Bureau of Investigation, the Drug Enforcement Administration, the Secret Service, and the Customs Service.

There is nothing in the Court's prior cases indicating that under the Fourth Amendment a warrant is required to make a valid arrest for a felony. Indeed, the relevant decisions are uniformly to the contrary. "A police officer may arrest without warrant one believed by the officer upon reasonable cause to have been guilty of a felony." *Carroll v. United States*, 267 U.S. 132, 156 (1925). Cases construing the Fourth Amendment thus reflect the ancient common-law rule that a peace officer was permitted to arrest without a warrant for a misdemeanor or felony committed in his presence as well as for a felony not committed in his presence if there was reasonable ground for making the arrest. 10 HALSBURY'S LAWS OF ENGLAND 344–345 (3d ed. 1955). This has also been the prevailing rule under state constitutions and statutes.

Because the common-law rule authorizing arrests without a warrant generally prevailed in the States, it is important to note that in 1792 Congress invested United States marshals and their deputies with "the same powers in executing the laws of the United States, as sheriffs and their deputies in the several states have by law, in executing the laws of their respective states." The Second Congress thus saw no inconsistency between the Fourth Amendment and legislation giving United States marshals the same power as local peace officers to arrest for a felony without a warrant. This provision equating the power of federal marshals with those of local sheriffs was several times re-enacted and is today § 570 of Title 28 of the United States Code.

The balance struck by the common law in generally authorizing felony arrests on probable cause, but without a warrant, has survived substantially intact. It appears in almost all of the States in the form of express statutory authorization. The American Law Institute's model arrest statute authorizes an officer to take a person into custody if the officer has reasonable cause to believe that the person to be arrested has committed a felony, or has committed a misdemeanor or petty misdemeanor in his presence. The commentary to this section said: "The Code thus adopts the traditional and almost universal standard for arrest without a warrant."

This is the rule Congress has long directed its principal law enforcement officers to follow. Congress has plainly decided against conditioning warrantless arrest power on proof of exigent circumstances. Law enforcement officers may find it wise to seek arrest warrants where practicable to do so, and their judgments about probable cause may be more readily accepted where backed by a warrant issued by a magistrate. But we decline to transform this judicial preference into a constitutional rule when the judgment of the Nation and Congress has for so long been to authorize warrantless public arrests on probable cause rather than to encumber criminal prosecutions with endless litigation with respect to the existence of exigent circumstances, whether it was practicable to get a warrant, whether the suspect was about to flee, and the like.

Watson's arrest did not violate the Fourth Amendment, and the Court of Appeals erred in holding to the contrary.

MR. JUSTICE POWELL, concurring.

The historical momentum for acceptance of warrantless arrests, already strong at the adoption of the Fourth Amendment, has gained strength during the ensuing two centuries. Both the judiciary and the legislative bodies of this Nation repeatedly have placed their imprimaturs upon the practice and law enforcement agencies have developed their investigative and arrest procedures upon an assumption that warrantless arrests were valid so long as based upon probable cause. A constitutional rule permitting felony arrests only with a warrant or in exigent circumstances could severely hamper effective law enforcement. Good police practice often requires postponing an arrest, even after probable cause has been established, in order to place the suspect under surveillance or otherwise develop further evidence necessary to prove guilt to a jury. Additional investigative work could imperil the entire prosecution. Should the officers fail to obtain a warrant initially, and later be required by unforeseen circumstances to arrest immediately with no chance to procure a last-minute warrant, they would risk a court decision that the subsequent exigency did not excuse their failure to get a warrant in the interim since they first developed probable cause. If the officers attempted to meet such a contingency by procuring a warrant as soon as they had probable cause and then merely held it during their subsequent investigation, they would risk a court decision that the warrant had grown stale by the time it was used. Law enforcement personnel caught in this squeeze could ensure validity of their arrests only by obtaining a warrant and arresting as soon as probable cause existed, thereby foreclosing the possibility of gathering vital additional evidence from the suspect's continued actions.

MR. JUSTICE MARSHALL, with whom MR. JUSTICE BRENNAN joins, dissenting.

The Court relies on the English common-law rule of arrest and the many state and federal statutes following it. The substance of the ancient common-law rule provides no support for the far-reaching modern rule that the Court fashions on its model. A felony at common law and a felony today bear only slight resemblance. At common law, "No crime was considered a felony which did not occasion a total forfeiture of the offender's lands or goods or both." Today, "Any offense punishable by death or imprisonment for a term exceeding one year is a felony." 18 U.S.C. § 1. Only the most serious crimes were felonies at common law, and many crimes now classified as felonies under federal or state law were treated as misdemeanors. To make an arrest for any of these crimes at common law, the police officer was required to obtain a warrant, unless the crime was committed in his presence. Since many of these same crimes are commonly classified as felonies today, a warrant is no longer needed to make such arrests. The balance struck by the common law decreed that only in the most serious of cases could the warrant be dispensed with. This balance is not recognized when the common-law rule is unthinkingly transposed to our present classifications of criminal offenses.

A warrant is required in search situations not because of some high regard for property, but because of our regard for the individual, and his interest in his possessions and person. There can be no less invasion of privacy when the individual himself, rather than his property, is searched and seized. An unjustified arrest that forces the individual temporarily to forfeit his right to control his person and movements and interrupts the course of his daily business may be more intrusive than an unjustified search. "Being arrested and held by the police, even if for a few hours, is for most persons, awesome and frightening." ALI, Model Code of Pre-arraignment Procedure, Commentary 290–291 (1975). A warrant requirement for arrests would, of course, minimize the possibility that such an intrusion would occur on less than probable cause. For this reason, a warrant is required for searches. Surely there is no reason to place greater trust in the partisan assessment of a police officer that there is probable cause for an arrest than in his determination that probable cause exists for a search.

The concern that the warrant requirement would unduly burden law enforcement interests are wholly illusory. "It is the standard practice of the Federal Bureau of Investigation to obtain a warrant before making an arrest." The Government's assertion that a warrant requirement would impose an intolerable burden stems from the specious supposition that procurement of an arrest warrant would be necessary as soon as probable cause ripens. There is no requirement that a search warrant be obtained the moment police have probable cause to search. Police would not have to cut their investigation short the moment they obtain probable cause to arrest, nor would undercover agents be forced suddenly to terminate their work and forfeit their covers. Moreover, if in the course of the continued police investigation exigent circumstances develop that demand an immediate arrest, the arrest may be made without fear of unconstitutionality, so long as the exigency was unanticipated and not used to avoid the arrest warrant requirement. I respectfully dissent.

More than two decades after *Watson*, the Court addressed the legality of warrantless misdemeanor arrests in *Atwater v. City of Lago Vista*, 532 U.S. 318 (2001). Atwater was subjected to a full custodial arrest for a seatbelt violation punishable only by a fine. In upholding the arrest, the Court noted that early English statutes allowed the police to make warrantless misdemeanor arrests "for all sorts of relatively minor offenses unaccompanied by violence." Similar statutes existed in the District of Columbia and all 50 states, and the Court concluded that "the fact that many of the original States with such constitutional limitations continued to grant their own peace officers broad warrantless misdemeanor arrest authority undermines Atwater's contention that the founding generation meant to bar federal law enforcement officers from exercising the same authority." The Court found that there had been "two centuries of uninterrupted (and largely unchallenged) state and federal practice permitting warrantless arrests for misdemeanors not amounting to or involving breach of the peace." Justice O'Connor dissented, noting that "justifying a full arrest by the same quantum of evidence that justifies a traffic stop defies any sense of proportionality and is in serious tension with the Fourth Amendment's proscription of unreasonable seizures." She noted that a "custodial arrest exacts an obvious toll on an individual's liberty and privacy, even when the period of custody is relatively brief." In her view, "the penalty that may attach to any particular offense seems to provide the clearest and most consistent indication of the State's interest in arresting individuals suspected of committing that offense." Since the state imposed only a fine for driving without a seatbelt, "the State's interest in taking a person suspected of committing that offense into custody is surely limited, at best."

Points for Discussion

a. The Impact of State Law

In *Virginia v. Moore*, 553 U.S. 164 (2008), the Court rejected the idea that a police officer violates the Fourth Amendment by making an arrest based on probable cause but prohibited by state law (state law precluded a custodial arrest for driving on a suspended license unless the driver refuses to desist or the officer reasonably believes that the driver is likely to disregard a summons, or is likely to harm himself or others). In *Moore*, when the police conducted a search incident to arrest, they turned up cocaine. The Court noted that there was nothing to indicate that the Fourth Amendment "was intended to incorporate subsequently enacted statutes": "When an officer has probable cause to believe a person committed even a minor crime in his presence, the balancing of private and public interests is not in doubt. The arrest is constitutionally reasonable. The Fourth Amendment's meaning did not change with local law enforcement practices-even practices set by rule and state restrictions do not alter the Fourth Amendment's protections."

Take Note

What if a traffic arrest is used as a pretext for a car search? In *Arkansas v. Sullivan*, 532 U.S. 769 (2001), an officer stopped Sullivan for speeding as well as for having an improperly tinted windshield. After reviewing Sullivan's license, the officer realized that he was aware of "intelligence on Sullivan regarding narcotics." While Sullivan was trying unsuccessfully to locate his registration and insurance papers, the officer noticed a rusted roofing hatchet on the car's floorboard. The officer then arrested Sullivan for speeding, driving without registration and insurance documentation, carrying a weapon (the hatchet), and improper window tinting. The officer then searched the car and found a substance that appeared to be methamphetamine as well as drug paraphernalia. Sullivan was charged with various state-law drug offenses, unlawful possession of a weapon, and speeding, and moved to suppress the evidence on the basis that his arrest was merely a "pretext and sham to search" him. The Court rejected the challenge, noting that "subjective intentions play no role in ordinary, probable-cause Fourth Amendment analysis."

---

b. Arrests at Private Residences

In *Payton v. New York*, 445 U.S. 573 (1980), the Court struck down a New York law which authorized police officers to enter private residences without warrants, by force if necessary, to make routine felony arrests: "The Fourth Amendment has drawn a firm line at the entrance to the house. Absent exigent circumstances, that threshold may not reasonably be crossed without a warrant. An arrest warrant requirement may afford less protection than a search warrant requirement, but it will suffice to interpose the magistrate's determination of probable cause between the zealous officer and the citizen. If there is sufficient evidence of a citizen's participation in a felony to persuade a judicial officer that his arrest is justified, it is constitutionally reasonable to require him to open his doors to the officers of the law. An arrest warrant founded on probable cause implicitly carries with it the limited authority to enter a dwelling in which the suspect lives when there is reason to believe the suspect is within." Mr. Justice White dissented: "Warrantless arrest entries were firmly accepted at common law."

In *Steagald v. United States*, 451 U.S. 204 (1981), the Court held that a law enforcement officer may not search for the subject of an arrest warrant in the home of a third party without first obtaining a search warrant. *See also Minnesota v. Olson*, 495 U.S. 91 (1990).

In *Tennessee v. Garner*, 471 U.S. 1 (1985), the Court held that the Constitution prohibits the use of deadly force to make an arrest in most instances: "The use of deadly force is a self-defeating way of apprehending a suspect and so setting the criminal justice mechanism in motion. While the meaningful threat of deadly force might be thought to lead to the arrest of more live suspects by discouraging escape attempts, the presently available evidence does not support this thesis." The Court did hold that deadly force is permissible when the suspect "poses a threat of serious physical harm either to the officer or to others." In *Garner*, the suspect's youth, slightness, and lack of a weapon suggested that he did not pose a threat of physical danger to himself or others. As a result, the use of deadly force was deemed inappropriate. Justice O'Connor dissented: "The public interest in the use of deadly force as a last resort to apprehend a fleeing burglary suspect relates primarily to the serious nature of the crime. Household burglaries not only represent the illegal entry into a person's home, but also 'pose real risk of serious harm to others.' If apprehension is not immediate, it is likely that the suspect will not be caught." In *Scott v. Harris*, 550 U.S. 372 (2007), the Court held that a police officer could attempt to stop a fleeing motorist (who refused to yield to pursuing police) by ramming the motorist's car from behind even though the ramming ultimately rendered the motorist a paraplegic. The Court rejected the notion that the officer had used deadly force in contravention of *Garner*.

c. Stated Basis for Arrest

In *Devenpeck v. Alford*, 543 U.S. 146 (2004), a police officer possessed probable cause to believe that defendant had been impersonating a police officer. However, when the officer realized that defendant was recording their conversation, the officer decided to arrest defendant for violating the Washington Privacy Act, Wash. Rev.Code § 9.73.030 (1994). When the charges were dismissed, defendant filed suit under 42 U.S.C. § 1983, and also filed a state cause of action for unlawful arrest and imprisonment. The Court refused to accept the proposition that the probable cause inquiry is confined to the facts actually invoked at the time of arrest, but must be supported by known facts "closely related" to the offense that the officer invoked. The Court emphasized that the officer had probable cause to arrest defendant for impersonating a police officer, and chose not to charge for that offense solely because of a departmental policy against "stacking" charges. "We have consistently rejected a conception of the Fourth Amendment that would produce such haphazard results." "Subjective intent of the arresting officer, *however* it is determined (and of course subjective intent is *always* determined by objective means), is simply no basis for invalidating an arrest. Those are lawfully arrested whom the facts known to the arresting officers give probable cause to arrest."

In *Ashcroft v. al-Kidd,* 563 U.S. 731 (2011), plaintiff claimed that Attorney General Ashcroft had misused a material-witness warrant. Under federal law, a judge may order the arrest of a person whose testimony is regarded as "material in a criminal proceeding if it is shown that it may become impracticable to secure the presence of the person by subpoena." 18 U.S.C. § 3144. Abdullah al-Kidd (who was detained for 16 days and was under supervised revised relief for 14 months) sued, complaining that then-Attorney General John Ashcroft authorized federal officials to detain individuals with suspected ties to terrorist organizations. He contended that federal officials did not intend to call most of these individuals as witnesses, but instead detained them for having suspected terrorist ties because he lacked sufficient evidence to actually charge them with crimes. The Court held that "Fourth Amendment reasonableness 'is predominantly an objective inquiry,' and that the question is whether 'the circumstances, viewed objectively, justify the challenged action.' " If so, the governmental actor's subject intent is irrelevant. Since al-Kidd conceded that individualized suspicion supported the issuance of the material-witness arrest warrant, and did not assert that his arrest would have been unconstitutional absent the alleged pretextual use of the warrant, the Court found no Fourth Amendment violation, and concluded that there was no need to address the question of whether Ashcroft was entitled to qualified immunity. In *Alicea v. Thomas,* 815 F.3d 283 (7th Cir. 2016), the court held that the police acted unreasonably in ordering a dog to attack a burglary suspect.

Hypo 1: *"Knock and Talk" Arrest Under Payton*

Under *Payton*, *supra*, a police officer cannot arrest an individual at a private residence without a warrant. However, in *United States v. Santana*, 427 U.S. 38 (1976), the Court held that a suspect who was outside her home, and therefore knowingly exposed herself to "public view," and then retreated into the house, could be arrested without a warrant. Suppose that the police decide to conduct a "knock and talk" at Jane's house. While the police have probable cause to believe that Jane is a drug dealer, they do not have a warrant for her arrest and do not have a warrant to search the house. In response to the police knock, Jane opens the door and steps out onto the porch. Has Jane knowingly exposed herself to public view so that she can be arrested without a warrant? What if the police ask her to step outside and she does? *See McClish v. Nugent*, 483 F.3d 1231 (11th Cir. 2007).

Hypo 2: *Tasers & Unreasonable Force*

An 11-year-old girl, J.N., had been driving an ATV through the streets with another young passenger. J.N. had run several stop signs and was otherwise driving dangerously. When a police officer spotted J.N., he used his overhead lights and a siren to signal her to stop. J.N. responded by trying to escape on the ATV, and later abandoned the ATV to flee on foot. The officer chased J.N. on foot and finally caught up with her. According to J.N., she was never aggressive or threatening towards the officer, and she had already stopped attempting to flee, when she was tased. According to the officer, she was still trying to resist arrest. All agree that the officer used his taser multiple times against J.N. Given the circumstances, did the officer use excessive force against J.N.? *See Russell v. Virg-In*, 258 P.3d 795 (Alaska 2011).

* * *

Once a legal arrest occurs, the police are allowed to make a search incident to arrest. While the right to search is clear enough, the scope of the search can be open to debate. *Chimel v. California*, discussed in the following case, defined the conditions for, and parameters of, that search.

Riley v. California

573 U.S. 373 (2014).

CHIEF JUSTICE ROBERTS delivered the opinion of the Court.

[In separate incidents, David Riley and Brima Wurie were arrested. Both were carrying cell phones at the time and the arresting officers sought to search those phones incident to arrest. The search of Riley's phone turned up references to "CK," which stood for "Crips Killers," a slang term for the Bloods gang and eventually (through videos and other information contained on the phone) connected him to various crimes committed earlier. Wurie's phone was used to determine his home address, spark a further investigation, and led to a search of his home. Both Riley and Wurie challenged the police use of that evidence.]

The cases before us concern the reasonableness of a warrantless search incident to a lawful arrest. In 1914, this Court first acknowledged in dictum "the right on the part of the Government, always recognized under English and American law, to search the person of the accused when legally arrested to discover and seize the fruits or evidences of crime." *Weeks v. United States*, 232 U. S. 383, 392. Since that time, it has been well accepted that such a search constitutes an exception to the warrant requirement. The label "exception" is something of a misnomer as warrantless searches incident to arrest occur with far greater frequency than searches conducted pursuant to a warrant.

Although the existence of the exception for such searches has been recognized for a century, its scope has been debated for nearly as long. *See Arizona v. Gant*, 556 U. S. 332, 350 (2009). That debate has focused on the extent to which officers may search property found on or near the arrestee. Three related precedents set forth the rules governing such searches. The first, *Chimel v. California*, 395 U. S. 752 (1969), laid the groundwork for most of the existing search incident to arrest doctrine. Police officers in that case arrested Chimel inside his home and proceeded to search his entire three-bedroom house, including the attic and garage, in rooms and the contents of drawers. The Court crafted the following rule for assessing the reasonableness of a search incident to arrest: "When an arrest is made, it is reasonable for the arresting officer to search the person arrested in order to remove any weapons that the latter might seek to use in order to resist arrest or effect his escape. Otherwise, the officer's safety might well be endangered, and the arrest itself frustrated. In addition, it is entirely reasonable for the arresting officer to search for and seize any evidence on the arrestee's person in order to prevent its concealment or destruction. There is ample justification, therefore, for a search of the arrestee's person and the area 'within his immediate control'—construing that phrase to mean the area from within which he might gain possession of a weapon or destructible evidence." The extensive warrantless search of Chimel's home did not fit within this exception, because it was not needed to protect officer safety or to preserve evidence.

Four years later, in *United States v. Robinson*, 414 U. S. 218 (1973), the Court applied *Chimel* in the context of a search of the arrestee's person. A police officer had arrested Robinson for driving with a revoked license. The officer conducted a patdown search and felt an object that he could not identify in Robinson's coat pocket. He removed the object, which turned out to be a crumpled cigarette package, and opened it. Inside were 14 capsules of heroin. This Court held that "the authority to search the person incident to a lawful custodial arrest, while based upon the need to disarm and to discover evidence, does not depend on what a court may later decide was the probability in a particular arrest situation that weapons or evidence would in fact be found upon the person of the suspect." A "custodial arrest of a suspect based on probable cause is a reasonable intrusion under the Fourth Amendment; that intrusion being lawful, a search incident to the arrest requires no additional justification." Thus the search of Robinson was reasonable even though there was no concern about the loss of evidence, and the arresting officer had no specific concern that Robinson might be armed. "Having in the course of a lawful search come upon the crumpled package of cigarettes, the officer was entitled to inspect it." The search incident to arrest trilogy concludes with *Gant*, which analyzed searches of an arrestee's vehicle. *Gant* concluded that *Chimel* could authorize police to search a vehicle "only when the arrestee is unsecured and within reaching distance of the passenger compartment at the time of the search." *Gant* added, however, an independent exception for a warrantless search of a vehicle's passenger compartment "when it is 'reasonable to believe evidence relevant to the crime of arrest might be found in the vehicle.' "

These cases require us to decide how the search incident to arrest doctrine applies to modern cell phones. While *Robinson*'s categorical rule strikes the appropriate balance in the context of physical objects, neither of its rationales has much force with respect to digital content on cell phones. The two risks identified in *Chimel*—harm to officers and destruction of evidence—are present in all custodial arrests. There are no comparable risks when the search is of digital data. *Robinson* regarded any privacy interests retained by an individual after arrest as significantly diminished by the fact of the arrest itself. Cell phones, however, place vast quantities of personal information literally in the hands of individuals. A search of the information on a cell phone bears little resemblance to the type of brief physical search considered in *Robinson*. We therefore decline to extend *Robinson* to searches of data on cell phones, and hold that officers must generally secure a warrant before conducting such a search.

Digital data stored on a cell phone cannot be used as a weapon to harm an arresting officer or to effectuate the arrestee's escape. Law enforcement officers remain free to examine the physical aspects of a phone to ensure that it will not be used as a weapon—say, to determine whether there is a razor blade hidden between the phone and its case. Once an officer has secured a phone and eliminated any potential physical threats, data on the phone can endanger no one. Perhaps the same might have been said of the cigarette pack seized from Robinson's pocket. The officer in *Robinson* testified that he could not identify the objects in the cigarette pack but knew they were not cigarettes. Given that, a further search was a reasonable protective measure. No such unknowns exist with respect to digital data. The officers who searched Wurie's cell phone "knew exactly what they would find therein: data. They also knew that the data could not harm them."

The United States and California suggest that a search of cell phone data might help ensure officer safety in more indirect ways, for example by alerting officers that confederates of the arrestee are headed to the scene. There is undoubtedly a strong government interest in warning officers about such possibilities, but neither offers evidence to suggest that their concerns are based on actual experience. The proposed consideration would also represent a broadening of *Chimel*'s concern that an *arrestee himself* might grab a weapon and use it against an officer "to resist arrest or effect his escape." Any such threats from outside the arrest scene do not "lurk in all custodial arrests." *Chadwick*, 433 U. S., at 14–15. Accordingly, the interest in protecting officer safety does not justify dispensing with the warrant requirement across the board. To the extent dangers to arresting officers may be implicated in a particular case, they are better addressed through consideration of case-specific exceptions to the warrant requirement, such as the one for exigent circumstances. *See, e.g., Warden, Md. Penitentiary v. Hayden*, 387 U. S. 294 (1967)

Both Riley and Wurie concede that officers could have seized and secured their cell phones to prevent destruction of evidence while seeking a warrant. *See Illinois v.*

McArthur, 531 U. S. 326 (2001). Once law enforcement officers have secured a cell phone, there is no longer any risk that the arrestee will be able to delete incriminating data from the phone. Information on a cell phone may be vulnerable to two types of evidence destruction unique to digital data—remote wiping and data encryption. Remote wiping occurs when a phone, connected to a wireless network, receives a signal that erases stored data. This can happen when a third party sends a remote signal or when a phone is preprogrammed to delete data upon entering or leaving certain geographic areas (so-called "geofencing"). Encryption is a security feature that some modern cell phones use in addition to password protection. When such phones lock, data becomes protected by sophisticated encryption that renders a phone all but "unbreakable" unless police know the password. These broader concerns about the loss of evidence are distinct from *Chimel*'s focus on a defendant who responds to arrest by trying to conceal or destroy evidence within his reach. With respect to remote wiping, the Government's primary concern turns on the actions of third parties who are not present at the scene of arrest. Data encryption is even further afield. There, the Government focuses on the ordinary operation of a phone's security features, apart from *any* active attempt by a defendant or his associates to conceal or destroy evidence upon arrest. We have been given little reason to believe that either problem is prevalent. The briefing reveals only anecdotal examples of remote wiping triggered by an arrest. Similarly, the opportunities for officers to search a password-protected phone before data becomes encrypted are quite limited. Law enforcement officers are very unlikely to come upon such a phone in an unlocked state because most phones lock at the touch of a button or, as a default, after some very short period of inactivity.

In situations in which an arrest might trigger a remote-wipe attempt or an officer discovers an unlocked phone, the need to effect the arrest, secure the scene, and tend to other pressing matters means that law enforcement officers may well not be able to turn their attention to a cell phone right away. Cell phone data would be vulnerable to remote wiping from the time an individual anticipates arrest to the time any eventual search of the phone is completed, which might be at the station house hours later. Likewise, an officer who seizes a phone in an unlocked state might not be able to begin his search in the short time remaining before the phone locks and data becomes encrypted. Law enforcement is not without specific means to address the threat. Remote wiping can be prevented by disconnecting a phone from the network. Law enforcement officers can turn the phone off or remove its battery. If they are concerned about encryption or other potential problems, they can leave a phone powered on and place it in an enclosure that isolates the phone from radio waves. Such devices are commonly called "Faraday bags." They are essentially sandwich bags made of aluminum foil: cheap, lightweight, and easy to use. They may not be a complete answer to the problem, but they provide a reasonable response. In fact, a number of law enforcement agencies around the country already encourage the use of Faraday bags.

To the extent that law enforcement still has specific concerns about the potential loss of evidence in a particular case, there remain more targeted ways to address those concerns. If "the police are truly confronted with a 'now or never' situation,"—for example, circumstances suggesting that a defendant's phone will be the target of an imminent remote-wipe attempt—they may be able to rely on exigent circumstances to search the phone immediately. *Missouri v. McNeely*, 133 S. Ct. 1552(2013). If officers happen to seize a phone in an unlocked state, they may be able to disable a phone's automatic-lock feature in order to prevent the phone from locking and encrypting data. Such a preventive measure could be analyzed under *McArthur*, 531 U. S. 326, which approved officers' reasonable steps to secure a scene to preserve evidence while they awaited a warrant. Not every search "is acceptable solely because a person is in custody." *Maryland v. King*, 133 S. Ct. 1958, 1979 (2013).

The United States asserts that a search of data stored on a cell phone is "materially indistinguishable" from searches of physical items. Modern cell phones, as a category, implicate privacy concerns far beyond those implicated by the search of a cigarette pack, a wallet, or a purse. A conclusion that inspecting the contents of an arrestee's pockets works no substantial additional intrusion on privacy beyond the arrest itself may make sense as applied to physical items, but cell phones differ in both a quantitative and a qualitative sense from other objects that might be kept on an arrestee's person. The term "cell phone" is itself misleading; many of these devices are in fact minicomputers that also have the capacity to be used as a telephone. They could just as easily be called cameras, video players, rolodexes, calendars, tape recorders, libraries, diaries, albums, televisions, maps, or newspapers. One of the most notable distinguishing features of modern cell phones is their immense storage capacity. Before cell phones, a search of a person was limited by physical realities and tended as a general matter to constitute only a narrow intrusion on privacy. Most people cannot lug around every piece of mail they have received for the past several months, every picture they have taken, or every book or article they have read—nor would they have any reason to attempt to do so. If they did, they would have to drag behind them a trunk rather than a container the size of the cigarette package in *Robinson*. But the possible intrusion on privacy is not physically limited in the same way when it comes to cell phones. The current top-selling smart phone has a standard capacity of 16 gigabytes (and is available with up to 64 gigabytes). Sixteen gigabytes translates to millions of pages of text, thousands of pictures, or hundreds of videos. Cell phones couple that capacity with the ability to store many different types of information: Even the most basic phones that sell for less than $20 might hold photographs, picture messages, text messages, Internet browsing history, a calendar, a thousand-entry phone book, and so on. The gulf between physical practicability and digital capacity will only continue to widen in the future.

The storage capacity of cell phones has several interrelated consequences for privacy. First, a cell phone collects in one place many distinct types of information—an address, a note, a prescription, a bank statement, a video—that reveal much more in combination than any isolated record. Second, a cell phone's capacity allows even just one type of information to convey far more than previously possible. The sum of an individual's private life can be reconstructed through a thousand photographs labeled with dates, locations, and descriptions; the same cannot be said of a photograph or two of loved ones tucked into a wallet. Third, the data on a phone can date back to the purchase of the phone, or even earlier. A person might carry in his pocket a slip of paper reminding him to call Mr. Jones; he would not carry a record of all his communications with Mr. Jones for the past several months, as would routinely be kept on a phone.

Finally, there is an element of pervasiveness that characterizes cell phones but not physical records. Prior to the digital age, people did not typically carry a cache of sensitive personal information with them as they went about their day. Now it is the person who is not carrying a cell phone who is the exception. Nearly three-quarters of smart phone users report being within five feet of their phones most of the time, with 12% admitting that they even use their phones in the shower. A decade ago police officers searching an arrestee might have occasionally stumbled across a highly personal item such as a diary. Today, many of the more than 90% of American adults who own a cell phone keep on their person a digital record of nearly every aspect of their lives—from the mundane to the intimate. Allowing the police to scrutinize such records on a routine basis is quite different from allowing them to search a personal item or two in the occasional case.

The data stored on a cell phone is also qualitatively different. An Internet search and browsing history, for example, can be found on an Internet-enabled phone and could reveal an individual's private interests or concerns—perhaps a search for certain symptoms of disease, coupled with frequent visits to WebMD. Data on a cell phone can also reveal where a person has been. Historic location information is a standard feature on many smart phones and can reconstruct someone's specific movements down to the minute, not only around town but also within a particular building. *See United States v. Jones*, 132 S. Ct. 945 (2012) (Sotomayor, J., concurring).

Mobile application software on a cell phone, or "apps," offer a range of tools for managing detailed information about all aspects of a person's life. There are apps for Democratic Party news and Republican Party news; apps for alcohol, drug, and gambling addictions; apps for sharing prayer requests; apps for tracking pregnancy symptoms; apps for planning your budget; apps for every conceivable hobby or pastime; apps for improving your romantic life. There are popular apps for buying or selling just about anything, and the records of such transactions may be accessible on the phone indefinitely. There are over a million apps available in each of the two major app stores; the phrase "there's an app for that" is now part of the popular lexicon. The average smart phone user has installed 33 apps, which together can form a revealing montage of the user's life.

In 1926, Learned Hand observed that it is "a totally different thing to search a man's pockets and use against him what they contain, from ransacking his house for everything which may incriminate him." *United States v. Kirschenblatt*, 16 F. 2d 202, 203 (CA2). If his pockets contain a cell phone, that is no longer true. A cell phone search would typically expose to the government far *more* than the most exhaustive search of a house: A phone not only contains in digital form many sensitive records previously found in the home; it also contains a broad array of private information never found in a home in any form—unless the phone is.

To further complicate the scope of the privacy interests at stake, the data a user views on many modern cell phones may not in fact be stored on the device itself. Treating a cell phone as a container whose contents may be searched incident to an arrest is a bit strained. But the analogy crumbles when a cell phone is used to access data located elsewhere, at the tap of a screen. That is what cell phones, with increasing frequency, are designed to do by taking advantage of "cloud computing." Cloud computing is the capacity of Internet-connected devices to display data stored on remote servers rather than on the device itself. Cell phone users often may not know whether particular information is stored on the device or in the cloud, and it generally makes little difference. Moreover, the same type of data may be stored on the device for one user and in the cloud for another. The United States concedes that the search incident to arrest exception may not be stretched to cover a search of files accessed remotely—a search of files stored in the cloud. Such a search would be like finding a key in a suspect's pocket and arguing that it allowed law enforcement to unlock and search a house. Officers searching a phone's data would not typically know whether the information they are viewing was stored locally at the time of the arrest or has been pulled from the cloud. The Government suggests that officers could disconnect a phone from the network before searching the device. Alternatively, the Government proposes that law enforcement agencies "develop protocols to address" concerns raised by cloud computing. Probably a good idea, but the Founders did not fight a revolution to gain the right to government agency protocols. The possibility that a search might extend well beyond papers and effects in the physical proximity of an arrestee is yet another reason that the privacy interests here dwarf those in *Robinson*.

The United States and California offer various fallback options for permitting warrantless cell phone searches under certain circumstances. The United States proposes that the *Gant* standard be imported from the vehicle context, allowing a warrantless search of an arrestee's cell phone whenever it is reasonable to believe that the phone contains evidence of the crime of arrest. But *Gant* relied on "circumstances unique to the vehicle context" to endorse a search solely for the purpose of gathering evidence. Justice Scalia's *Thornton* opinion, on which *Gant* was based, explained that those unique circumstances are "a reduced expectation of privacy" and "heightened law enforcement needs" when it comes to motor vehicles. For reasons that we have explained, cell phone searches bear neither of those characteristics. A *Gant* standard would prove no practical limit when it comes to cell phone searches. In the vehicle context, *Gant* generally protects against searches for evidence of past crimes. In the cell phone context, it is reasonable to expect that incriminating information will be found on a phone regardless of when the crime occurred. Similarly, in the vehicle context *Gant* restricts broad searches resulting from minor crimes such as traffic violations. That would not necessarily be true for cell phones. It would be a particularly inexperienced or unimaginative law enforcement officer who could not come up with several reasons to suppose evidence of just about any crime could be found on a cell phone. Even an individual pulled over for something as basic as speeding might well have locational data dispositive of guilt on his phone. An individual pulled over for reckless driving might have evidence on the phone that shows whether he was texting while driving. The sources of potential pertinent information are virtually unlimited, so applying the *Gant* standard to cell phones would in effect give "police officers unbridled discretion to rummage at will among a person's private effects."

The United States also proposes a rule that would restrict the scope of a cell phone search to those areas of the phone where an officer reasonably believes that information relevant to the crime, the arrestee's identity, or officer safety will be discovered. This approach would again impose few meaningful constraints. The proposed categories would sweep in a great deal of information, and officers would not always be able to discern in advance what information would be found where.

We also reject the suggestion that officers should always be able to search a phone's call log. The Government relies on *Smith v. Maryland*, 442 U. S. 735 (1979), which held that no warrant was required to use a pen register at telephone company premises to identify numbers dialed by a particular caller. That case, however, concluded that the use of a pen register was not a "search" under the Fourth Amendment. There is no dispute here that the officers engaged in a search of Wurie's cell phone. Moreover, call logs typically contain more than just phone numbers; they include any identifying information that an individual might add, such as the label "my house" in Wurie's case.

California suggested that officers could search cell phone data if they could have obtained the same information from a pre-digital counterpart. But the fact that a search in the pre-digital era could have turned up a photograph or two in a wallet does not justify a search of thousands of photos in a digital gallery. The fact that someone could have tucked a paper bank statement in a pocket does not justify a search of every bank statement from the last five years. Such an analogue test would allow law enforcement to search a range of items contained on a phone, even though people would be unlikely to carry such a variety of information in physical form. In Riley's case, it is implausible that he would have strolled around with video tapes, photo albums, and an address book all crammed into his pockets. But because each of those items has a pre-digital analogue, police would be able to search a phone for all of those items—a significant diminution of privacy. In addition, an analogue test would launch courts on a difficult line-drawing expedition to determine which digital files are comparable to physical records. Is an e-mail equivalent to a letter? Is a voicemail equivalent to a phone message slip? It is not clear how officers could make these kinds of decisions before conducting a search, or how courts would apply the proposed rule after the fact.

We cannot deny that our decision will have an impact on the ability of law enforcement to combat crime. Cell phones have become important tools in facilitating coordination and communication among members of criminal enterprises, and can provide valuable incriminating information about dangerous criminals. Privacy comes at a cost. Our holding is not that the information on a cell phone is immune from search; it is that a warrant is generally required before such a search, even when a cell phone is seized incident to arrest. Our cases have recognized that the warrant requirement is "an important working part of our machinery of government," not merely "an inconvenience to be somehow 'weighed' against the claims of police efficiency." *Coolidge v. New Hampshire*, 403 U. S. 443, 481 (1971). Recent technological advances similar to those discussed here have, in addition, made the process of obtaining a warrant itself more efficient. *See McNeely*, 133 S. Ct. at 1561 (Roberts, C. J., concurring and dissenting) ("police officers can e-mail warrant requests to judges' iPads and judges have signed such warrants and e-mailed them back to officers in less than 15 minutes").

Even though the search incident to arrest exception does not apply to cell phones, other case-specific exceptions may still justify a warrantless search of a particular phone. "One well-recognized exception applies when " 'the exigencies of the situation' make the needs of law enforcement so compelling that a warrantless search is objectively reasonable under the Fourth Amendment." *Kentucky v. King*, 5131 S. Ct. at 1856. Such exigencies could include the need to prevent the imminent destruction of evidence in individual cases, to pursue a fleeing suspect, and to assist persons who are seriously injured or are threatened with imminent injury. In light of the exigent circumstances exception, there is no reason to believe that law enforcement officers will not be able to address some of the more extreme hypotheticals that have been suggested: a suspect texting an accomplice who, it is feared, is preparing to detonate a bomb, or a child abductor who may have information about the child's location on his cell phone. Such fact-specific threats may justify a warrantless search of cell phone data. The exigent circumstances exception requires a court to examine whether an emergency justified a warrantless search in each particular case.

Our cases have recognized that the Fourth Amendment was the founding generation's response to the reviled "general warrants" and "writs of assistance" of the colonial era, which allowed British officers to rummage through homes in an unrestrained search for evidence of criminal activity. Opposition to such searches was in fact one of the driving forces behind the Revolution itself. 10 Works of John Adams 247–248 (C. Adams ed. 1856). Modern cellphones are not just another technological convenience. With all they contain and all they may reveal, they hold for many Americans "the privacies of life." The fact that technology now allows an individual to carry such information in his hand does not make the information any less worthy of the protection for which the Founders fought. Our answer to the question of what police must do before searching a cell phone seized incident to an arrest is accordingly simple—get a warrant.

We reverse the judgment of the California Court of Appeal in No. 13–132 and remand the case for further proceedings not inconsistent with this opinion. We affirm the judgment of the First Circuit in No. 13–212.

It is so ordered.

JUSTICE ALITO, concurring in part and concurring in the judgment.

We should not mechanically apply the rule used in the predigital era to the search of a cell phone. Many cell phones now in use are capable of storing and accessing a quantity of information, some highly personal, that no person would ever have had on his person in hard-copy form. This calls for a new balancing of law enforcement and privacy interests. While the Court's approach leads to anomalies, I do not see a workable alternative. Law enforcement officers need clear rules regarding searches incident to arrest, and it would take many cases and many years for the courts to develop more nuanced rules. During that time, the nature of the electronic devices that ordinary Americans carry on their persons would continue to change.

I would reconsider the question presented here if either Congress or state legislatures, after assessing the legitimate needs of law enforcement and the privacy interests of cell phone owners, enact legislation that draws reasonable distinctions based on categories of information or perhaps other variables. Many forms of modern technology are making it easier and easier for both government and private entities to amass a wealth of information about the lives of ordinary Americans, and any ordinary Americans are choosing to make public much information that was seldom revealed to outsiders just a few decades ago. It would be unfortunate if privacy protection in the 21st century were left primarily to the federal courts using the blunt instrument of the Fourth Amendment. Legislatures, elected by the people, are in a better position than we are to assess and respond to the changes that have already occurred and those that almost certainly will take place in the future.

Points for Discussion

a. Search Incident to Arrest & Automobiles

For many years, there was uncertainty regarding how the search incident to legal arrest exception applied to someone who was arrested while traveling in an automobile. In *New York v. Belton*, 453 U. S. 454 (1981), the Court held that the arresting officer could search both the arrestee and the passenger compartment of the car, as well as any containers (e.g., purse or backpack) that the officer discovered in the passenger compartment during the search. To some extent, the *Belton* rule was nonsensical. At the time of the search in *Belton*, the suspect had been handcuffed and placed in the back seat of a patrol car. Moreover, because he was arrested for a traffic offense, there was no reason to believe that the vehicle contained evidence related to the offense. So, there was no possibility that the arrestee would be able to destroy evidence in the vehicle, or obtain a weapon that he could use to effectuate escape. In *Arizona v. Gant*, 556 U.S. 332 (2009), the Court overruled *Belton*, holding that the arresting officer can search the arrestee, but cannot search the vehicle unless it is "reasonable to believe evidence relevant to the crime of arrest might be found in the vehicle" or the arrestee is within reaching distance of the passenger compartment at the time of the search.

b. Civil Writs of Attachment

In *United States v. Phillips*, 834 F.3d 1176 (11th Cir. 2016), the court held that a search incident to legal arrest could be conducted in connection with the service of a civil writ of attachment.

Food for Thought

In some instances, the police might arrest one person who is traveling in a car, but not everyone. As a result, following the arrest, some of the former occupants of the car will re-enter it. Should the officers have the right to search the vehicle in order to make sure that it does not contain a weapon that the other occupants will be able to access? On what basis?

Hypo 1: Riley *& Digital Cameras*

Does *Riley's* analysis extend to the contents of digital cameras, or can they be searched without a warrant incident to an arrest? Do digital cameras store as much information as smart phones? Are they connected to the internet? But is the information stored on a smart phone potentially as sensitive as information stored on a smart phone? *See Commonwealth v. Mauricio*, 477 Mass. 588, 80 N.E.3d 318 (Mass. 2017).

Food for Thought

Suppose that a man believes that he is communicating with a young girl through Snapchat. In fact, he is communicating with an undercover police agent. The man agrees to meet the "girl" at a mall to help her buy underwear. When the man arrives, he is arrested. As part of a search incident to arrest, the police seize the man's cell phone. In order to make sure that the man is the person with whom he has been communicating, the agent sends a Snapchat message to the man's phone. The phone immediately lights up with a notification that the message has arrived. The agent can see the identification without entering the phone. Has the agent violated the man's Fourth Amendment rights by observing the notification? *See United States v. Brixen,* 908 F.3d 276 (7th Cir. 2018).

Hypo 2: *The Contemporaneousness Requirement*

Four police officers enter a hotel room (legally) to arrest a suspect. After the police handcuff her, and move her to the hallway outside the room, two officers re-enter the room and search it. The search extends to the dresser drawers and the suspect's purse (which was lying on the bed). In a drawer and in the purse, the police find contraband. Suppose that you represent the suspect, how can you argue that this search does not fit within the scope of the search incident to arrest exception? How might the state respond to these arguments? How would you expect the court to rule? *See State v. Gorup,* 279 Neb. 841, 782 N.W.2d 16 (2010); *People v. Perry,* 47 Ill.2d 402, 266 N.E.2d 330 (1971).

Hypo 3: *Probable Cause to Search the Vehicle*

Taylor's automobile rear-ends an SUV occupied by three U.S. marshals. One marshal alights and asks Taylor for his insurance information. The card that he produces has expired. While they are talking, Taylor suddenly indicates that he has to use the bathroom and urinates on a nearby tree. Based on this behavior, as well as the smell of alcohol on Taylor's breath and his unusual swaying back and forth, the deputy suspects that Taylor has been drinking. One of the other marshals calls the police who arrive shortly thereafter. After speaking with Taylor, the police conclude that Taylor is intoxicated based on his slurred speech, his swaying from side to side, the odor of alcohol coming from his person, the way he fumbles with his wallet while searching for his driver's license, and his statement that he consumed two beers about two hours earlier. The officer administers standard field sobriety tests which appellee fails. The police arrest Taylor for driving under the influence, place him in handcuffs, and put him in a patrol car for transport. Following the arrest, the officer searches the passenger compartment of Taylor's truck, looking for a current insurance card and evidence of alcohol consumption. Was the search valid? *See United States v. Taylor,* 49 A.3d 818, 821 (D.C.2012).

Hypo 4: *More on Probable Cause*

A police officer is searching for a man named in a warrant when he happens on another man who is acting in a "curious" way and appears to have something in his hand that he is manipulating. When the man spots the officer, he turns and begin to walk away carrying what appears to be a hamburger wrapper. The officer stops the man and runs a warrant check on him. The check reveals an outstanding warrant for the man and the officer tells him that he is under arrest. When the man drops the hamburger wrapper, and begins grinding it with his foot, the officer notices a baggie with what appear to be illegal pills. Does the officer have probable cause to search the man's truck (located nearby)? *See People v. Crum,* 312 P.3d 186 (Colo. 2013).

3. Booking Searches

After "booking" a suspect, the police usually conduct a "detention search" or "booking search" before placing him in the jail population. These "booking searches" were upheld in *Illinois v. Lafayette,* 462 U.S. 640 (1983), in which respondent was arrested for disturbing the peace after fighting with a theater manager. The search occurred in the booking room where the police found ten amphetamine pills inside a cigarette case. The Court concluded that it "is entirely proper for the police to remove and list or inventory property found on the person or in the possession of an arrested person who is to be jailed. A range of governmental interests support an inventory process. It is not unheard of for persons employed in police activities to steal property taken from arrested persons; similarly, arrested persons have been known to make false claims regarding what was taken from their possession at the stationhouse. A standardized procedure for making a list or inventory as soon as reasonable after reaching the stationhouse not only deters false claims but also inhibits theft or careless handling of articles taken from the arrested person. Arrested persons have also been known to injure themselves—or others—with belts, knives, drugs or other items on their person while being detained. Dangerous instrumentalities—such as razor blades, bombs, or weapons—can be concealed in innocent-looking articles taken from the arrestee's possession. Examining all the items removed from the arrestee's person or possession and listing or inventorying them is an entirely reasonable administrative procedure. It is immaterial whether the police actually fear any particular package or container; the need to protect against such risks arises independent of a particular officer's subjective concerns. Finally, inspection of an arrestee's personal property may assist the police in ascertaining or verifying his identity. In short, every consideration of orderly police administration benefiting both police and the public points toward the appropriateness of the examination of respondent's shoulder bag prior to his incarceration." In *United States v. Edwards*, 415 U.S. 800 (1974), the Court upheld a booking search that took place nearly ten hours after a defendant's arrest: "searches and seizures that could be made on the spot at the time of arrest may legally be conducted later when the accused arrives at the place of detention."

Florence v. Board of Chosen Freeholders of the County of Burlington

566 U.S. 318 (2012).

JUSTICE KENNEDY delivered the opinion of the Court, except as to Part IV.[2]

Correctional officials have a legitimate interest, indeed a responsibility, to ensure that jails are not made less secure by reason of what new detainees may carry in on their bodies. Facility personnel, other inmates, and the new detainee himself or herself may be in danger if these threats are introduced into the jail population. The term "jail" is used here in a broad sense to include prisons and other detention facilities. The specific measures being challenged involve whether every detainee admitted to the general population may be required to undergo a close visual inspection while undressed. In addressing this constitutional claim courts must defer to the judgment of correctional officials unless the record contains substantial evidence showing their policies are an unnecessary or un-justified response to problems of jail security. That showing has not been made in this case.

I

Seven years before, petitioner Albert Florence was arrested after fleeing from police officers in New Jersey. He was charged with obstruction of justice and use of a deadly weapon. Petitioner entered a plea of guilty to two lesser offenses and was sentenced to pay a fine in monthly installments. After he fell behind on his payments and failed to appear at an enforcement hearing, a bench warrant was issued for his arrest. He paid the outstanding balance less than a week later; but, for some unexplained reason, the warrant remained in a statewide computer database. Two years later, in New Jersey, petitioner and his wife were stopped in their automobile by a state trooper. Based on the outstanding warrant, the officer arrested petitioner and took him to the

---

[2]   Justice Thomas joins all but Part IV of the opinion.

Burlington County Detention Center. He was held for six days and then transferred to the Essex County Correctional Facility. Burlington County jail procedures required every arrestee to shower with a delousing agent. Officers would check arrestees for scars, marks, gang tattoos, and contraband as they disrobed. Petitioner claims he was also instructed to open his mouth, lift his tongue, hold out his arms, turn around, and lift his genitals. Petitioner shared a cell with at least one other person and interacted with other inmates following his admission to the jail.

The Essex County Correctional Facility is the largest county jail in New Jersey. It admits more than 25,000 inmates each year and houses about 1,000 gang members. All arriving detainees passed through a metal detector and waited in a group holding cell for a more thorough search. When they left the cell, they were instructed to remove their clothing while an officer looked for body markings, wounds, and contraband. Without touching the detainees, an officer looked at their ears, nose, mouth, hair, scalp, fingers, hands, arms, armpits, and other body openings. This policy applied regardless of the circumstances of the arrest, the suspected offense, or the detainee's behavior, demeanor, or criminal history. Petitioner alleges he was required to lift his genitals, turn around, and cough in a squatting position. After a mandatory shower, during which his clothes were inspected, petitioner was admitted to the facility. He was released the next day, when the charges against him were dismissed.

Petitioner sued the governmental entities, one of the wardens, and certain other defendants. The District Court concluded that any policy of "strip searching" nonindictable offenders without reasonable suspicion violated the Fourth Amendment. The United States Court of Appeals for the Third Circuit reversed. This Court granted certiorari.

The term "strip search" is imprecise. It may refer simply to the instruction to remove clothing while an officer observes from a distance; it may mean a visual inspection from a closer, more uncomfortable distance; it may include directing detainees to shake their heads or to run their hands through their hair to dislodge what might be hidden there; or it may involve instructions to raise arms, to display foot insteps, to expose the back of the ears, to move or spread the buttocks or genital areas, or to cough in a squatting position. There are no allegations that the detainees here were touched in any way as part of the searches.

II

The difficulties of operating a detention center must not be underestimated by the courts. *Turner v. Safley*, 482 U. S. 78 (1987). Jails (excluding prison facilities) admit more than 13 million inmates a year. The largest facilities process hundreds of people every day; smaller jails may be crowded on weekend nights, after a large police operation, or because of detainees arriving from other jurisdictions. Maintaining safety and order at these institutions requires the expertise of correctional officials, who must have substantial discretion to devise reasonable solutions to the problems they face. The Court has confirmed the importance of deference to correctional officials and explained that a regulation impinging on an inmate's constitutional rights must be upheld "if it is reasonably related to legitimate penological interests." *Turner, supra*, at 89. *Bell v. Wolfish*, 441 U. S. 520 (1979) addressed a rule requiring pretrial detainees in any correctional facility run by the Federal Bureau of Prisons "to expose their body cavities for visual inspection as a part of a strip search conducted after every contact visit with a person from outside the institution." Inmates at the federal Metropolitan Correctional Center in New York City argued there was no security justification for these searches. Officers searched guests before they entered the visiting room, and the inmates were under constant surveillance during the visit. There had been but one instance in which an inmate attempted to sneak contraband back into the facility. The Court nonetheless upheld the search policy. It deferred to the judgment of correctional officials that the inspections served not only to discover but also to deter the smuggling of weapons, drugs, and other prohibited items inside. The Court explained that there is no mechanical way to determine whether intrusions on an inmate's privacy are reasonable. The need for a particular search must be balanced against the resulting invasion of personal rights. Policies designed to keep contraband out of jails and prisons have been upheld in cases decided since *Bell*. In *Block v. Rutherford*, 468 U. S. 576 (1984), for example, the Court concluded that the Los Angeles County Jail could ban all contact visits because of the threat they posed.

There were "many justifications" for imposing a general ban rather than trying to carve out exceptions for certain detainees. It would be "difficult if not impossible" to identify "inmates who have propensities for violence, escape, or drug smuggling." This is made "even more difficult by the brevity of detention and the constantly changing nature of the inmate population." Deterring the possession of contraband depends in part on the ability to conduct searches without predictable exceptions. Inmates would adapt to any pattern or loopholes they discovered in the search protocol and then undermine the security of the institution. These cases establish that correctional officials must be permitted to devise reasonable search policies to detect and deter the possession of contraband in their facilities. *See Bell*, 441 U. S., at 546. The task of determining whether a policy is reasonably related to legitimate security interests is "peculiarly within the province and professional expertise of corrections officials." *Id.*, at 548. "In the absence of substantial evidence to indicate that the officials have exaggerated their response to these considerations courts should ordinarily defer to their expert judgment in such matters." *Block, supra*, at 584–585.

In many jails, officials seek to improve security by requiring some kind of strip search of everyone who is to be detained. These procedures have been used in different places throughout the country. Persons arrested for minor offenses may be among the detainees processed at these facilities. *Atwater v. Lago Vista*, 532 U. S. 318 (2001).

III

The question is whether undoubted security imperatives involved in jail supervision override the assertion that some detainees must be exempt from the more invasive search procedures at issue absent reasonable suspicion of a concealed weapon or other contraband. Deference must be given to the officials in charge of the jail unless there is "substantial evidence" demonstrating their response to the situation is exaggerated. Petitioner has not met this standard, and the record provides full justifications for the procedures used.

Correctional officials have a significant interest in conducting a thorough search as a standard part of the intake process. The admission of inmates creates numerous risks for facility staff, for the existing detainee population, and for a new detainee himself or herself. The danger of introducing lice or contagious infections, for example, is well documented. Persons just arrested may have wounds or other injuries requiring immediate medical attention. It may be difficult to identify and treat these problems until detainees remove their clothes for a visual inspection. Jails and prisons also face grave threats posed by the increasing number of gang members who go through the intake process. The groups recruit new members by force, engage in assaults against staff, and give other inmates a reason to arm themselves. Fights among feuding gangs can be deadly, and the officers who must maintain order are put in harm's way. These considerations provide a reasonable basis to justify a visual inspection for tattoos and other signs of gang affiliation. The identification and isolation of gang members before they are admitted protects everyone in the facility.

Detecting contraband concealed by new detainees, furthermore, is a most serious responsibility. Weapons, drugs, and alcohol all disrupt the safe operation of a jail. Correctional officers have had to confront arrestees concealing knives, scissors, razor blades, glass shards, and other prohibited items on their person, including in their body cavities. They have also found crack, heroin, and marijuana. The use of drugs can embolden inmates in aggression toward officers or each other; and trade in these substances can lead to violent confrontations.

There are many other kinds of contraband. The textbook definition of the term covers any unauthorized item. Everyday items can undermine security if introduced into a detention facility: "Lighters and matches are fire and arson risks or potential weapons. Cell phones are used to orchestrate violence and criminality both within and without jailhouse walls. Pills and medications enhance suicide risks. Chewing gum can block locking devices; hairpins can open handcuffs; wigs can conceal drugs and weapons." New Jersey Wardens Brief 8–9. Something as simple as a pen can pose a significant danger. Inmates commit more than 10,000 assaults on correctional staff every year and many more among themselves.

Contraband creates additional problems because scarce items, including currency, have value in a jail's culture and underground economy. Correctional officials inform us "the competition for such goods begets violence, extortion, and disorder." Gangs exacerbate the problem. They "orchestrate thefts, commit assaults, and approach inmates in packs to take the contraband from the weak." This puts the entire facility, including detainees being held for a brief term for a minor offense, at risk. Gangs coerce inmates who have access to the outside world, such as people serving their time on the weekends, to sneak things into the jail. These inmates, who might be thought to pose the least risk, have been caught smuggling prohibited items into jail. Concealing contraband often takes little time and effort. It might be done as an officer approaches a suspect's car or during a brief commotion in a group holding cell. Something small might be tucked or taped under an armpit, behind an ear, between the buttocks, in the instep of a foot, or inside the mouth or some other body cavity.

It is not surprising that correctional officials have sought to perform thorough searches at intake. Jails are often crowded, unsanitary, and dangerous places. There is a substantial interest in preventing any new inmate, either of his own will or as a result of coercion, from putting all who live or work at these institutions at even greater risk when he is admitted to the general population. Petitioner maintains there is little benefit to conducting these more invasive steps on a new detainee who has not been arrested for a serious crime or for any offense involving a weapon or drugs. In his view these detainees should be exempt from this process unless they give officers a particular reason to suspect them of hiding contraband. This standard would be unworkable. The seriousness of an offense is a poor predictor of who has contraband and it would be difficult in practice to determine whether individual detainees fall within the proposed exemption. People detained for minor offenses can turn out to be the most devious and dangerous criminals. Hours after the Oklahoma City bombing, Timothy McVeigh was stopped by a state trooper who noticed he was driving without a license plate. Police stopped serial killer Joel Rifkin for the same reason. One of the terrorists involved in the September 11 attacks was stopped and ticketed for speeding just two days before hijacking Flight 93. Reasonable correctional officials could conclude these uncertainties mean they must conduct the same thorough search of everyone who will be admitted to their facilities. Experience shows that people arrested for minor offenses have tried to smuggle prohibited items into jail, sometimes by using their rectal cavities or genitals for the concealment. They may have some of the same incentives as a serious criminal to hide contraband. A detainee might risk carrying cash, cigarettes, or a penknife to survive in jail. Others may make a quick decision to hide unlawful substances to avoid getting in more trouble at the time of their arrest. Officers at [one facility] discovered that a man arrested for driving under the influence had "2 dime bags of weed, 1 pack of rolling papers, 20 matches, and 5 sleeping pills" taped under his scrotum. A person booked on a misdemeanor charge of disorderly conduct managed to hide a lighter, tobacco, tattoo needles, and other prohibited items in his rectal cavity. Officials have discovered contraband hidden in body cavities of people arrested for trespassing, public nuisance, and shoplifting. There have been similar incidents at jails throughout the country.

Even if people arrested for a minor offense do not themselves wish to introduce contraband into a jail, they may be coerced into doing so by others. This could happen any time detainees are held in the same area, including in a van on the way to the station or in the holding cell of the jail. If a person arrested and detained for unpaid traffic citations is not subject to the same search as others, this will be known to other detainees with jail experience. A hardened criminal or gang member can, in just a few minutes, approach the person and coerce him into hiding the fruits of a crime, a weapon, or some other contraband. Exempting people arrested for minor offenses from a standard search protocol thus may put them at greater risk and result in more contraband being brought into the detention facility. This is a substantial reason not to mandate the exception petitioner seeks as a matter of constitutional law.

It also may be difficult to classify inmates by their current and prior offenses before the intake search. Jails can be even more dangerous than prisons because officials know so little about the people they admit at the outset. An arrestee may be carrying a false ID or lie about his identity. The officers who conduct an initial search often do not have access to criminal history records. And those records can be inaccurate or incomplete. Petitioner's rap sheet is an example. It did not reflect his previous arrest for possession of a deadly weapon. In the absence of reliable information it would be illogical to require officers to assume [that] arrestees do not pose a risk of smuggling something into the facility. The laborious administration of prisons would become less effective, and likely less fair and evenhanded, were the practical problems inevitable from the rules suggested by petitioner to be imposed as a constitutional mandate. Even if they had accurate information about a detainee's current and prior arrests, officers, under petitioner's proposed regime, would encounter serious implementation difficulties. They would be required, in a few minutes, to determine whether any of the underlying offenses were serious enough to authorize the more invasive search protocol. Other possible classifications based on characteristics of individual detainees also might prove to be unworkable or even give rise to charges of discriminatory application. Most officers would not be well equipped to make any of these legal determinations during the pressures of the intake process. To avoid liability, officers might be inclined not to conduct a thorough search in any close case, thus creating unnecessary risk for the entire jail population. Officers who interact with those suspected of violating the law have an "essential interest in readily administrable rules." The restrictions suggested by petitioner would limit the intrusion on the privacy of some detainees but at the risk of increased danger to everyone in the facility, including the less serious offenders themselves.

IV

This case does not require the Court to rule on the types of searches that would be reasonable in instances where a detainee will be held without assignment to the general jail population and without substantial contact with other detainees. The accommodations provided in these situations may diminish the need to conduct some aspects of the searches at issue. Petitioner's *amici* raise concerns about instances of officers engaging in intentional humiliation and other abusive practices. There also may be legitimate concerns about the invasiveness of searches that involve the touching of detainees. These issues are not implicated on the facts of this case.

V

The search procedures at the Burlington County Detention Center and the Essex County Correctional Facility struck a reasonable balance between inmate privacy and the needs of the institutions. The Fourth and Fourteenth Amendments do not require adoption of the framework of rules petitioner proposes. The judgment of the Court of Appeals for the Third Circuit is affirmed.

It is so ordered.

JUSTICE ALITO, concurring.

Most of those arrested for minor offenses are not dangerous, and most are released from custody prior to or at the time of their initial appearance. In some cases, the charges are dropped or arrestees are released either on their own recognizance or on minimal bail. Few are sentenced to incarceration. For these persons, admission to the general jail population, with the concomitant humiliation of a strip search, may not be reasonable, particularly if an alternative procedure is feasible. For example, the Federal Bureau of Prisons (BOP) segregates temporary detainees who are minor offenders from the general population.[1] The Court does not address whether it is always reasonable, without regard to the offense or the reason for detention, to strip search an arrestee before the arrestee's detention has been reviewed by a judicial officer.

JUSTICE BREYER, with whom JUSTICE GINSBURG, JUSTICE SOTOMAYOR, and JUSTICE KAGAN join, dissenting.

This case is limited to strip searches of arrestees entering a jail's general population, and involve close observation of the private areas of a person's body and for that reason constitute a far more serious invasion of that person's privacy. A search of an

---

[1]   According to BOP policy, prison and jail officials cannot subject persons arrested for misdemeanor or civil contempt offenses to visual body-cavity searches without their consent or without reasonable suspicion that they are concealing contraband. Those who are not searched must be housed separately from inmates in the general population.

individual arrested for a minor offense that does not involve drugs or violence—say a traffic offense, a regulatory offense, an essentially civil matter, or any other such misdemeanor—is an "unreasonable search" forbidden by the Fourth Amendment, unless prison authorities have reasonable suspicion to believe that the individual possesses drugs or other contraband.

Those confined in prison retain basic constitutional rights. In *Bell v. Wolfish*, the Court said:"The test of reasonableness under the Fourth Amendment is not capable of precise definition or mechanical application. In each case it requires a balancing of the need for the particular search against the invasion of personal rights that the search entails. Courts must consider the scope of the particular intrusion, the manner in which it is conducted, the justification for initiating it, and the place in which it is conducted." A strip search that involves a stranger peering without consent at a naked individual, and in particular at the most private portions of that person's body, is a serious invasion of privacy. Even when carried out in a respectful manner, and even absent any physical touching, such searches are inherently harmful, humiliating, and degrading. The harm to privacy interests would seem particularly acute where the person searched may have no expectation of being subject to such a search, say, because she had simply received a traffic ticket for failing to buckle a seatbelt, because he had not previously paid a civil fine, or because she had been arrested for a minor trespass.

Food for Thought

Suppose that a jail routinely strip searches all incoming prisoners. Ordinarily, each prisoner is strip searched individually. However, when there were a lot of incoming prisoners, the jail strip searches prisoners in groups of five. Is it permissible for the jail to do group strip searches? *See Sumpter v. Wayne*, 868 F.3d 473 (6th Cir. 2017).

I recognize: that managing a jail or prison is an "inordinately difficult undertaking," that prison regulations that interfere with important constitutional interests are generally valid as long as they are "reasonably related to legitimate penological interests," that finding injuries and preventing the spread of disease, minimizing the threat of gang violence, and detecting contraband are "legitimate penological interests," and that we normally defer to the expertise of jail and prison administrators in such matters. Nonetheless, the invasion of interests, must be "reasonably related" to the justifying "penological interest" and the need

Food for Thought

Suppose that you are the legal adviser to your city which does not routinely strip search everyone who is incarcerated in the city jail. Following the decision in *Florence*, city officials are debating whether they *should* routinely strip search all who are incarcerated, and have asked you for advice. How would you advise them? Are there less intrusive alternatives that would be preferable?

must not be "exaggerated." I have found no convincing reason indicating that, in the absence of reasonable suspicion, involuntary strip searches of those arrested for minor offenses are necessary to further the penal interests mentioned. There are strong reasons to believe they are not justified. The lack of justification for such a strip search is less obvious but no less real in respect to the detection of contraband. Neither the majority's opinion nor the briefs set forth any example of an instance in which contraband was smuggled into the general jail population during intake that could not have been discovered if the jail was employing a reasonable suspicion standard. It remains open whether it would be reasonable to admit an arrestee for a minor offense to the general jail population, and to subject her to the "humiliation of a strip search," prior to any review by a judicial officer.

Hypo 1: *Booking Searches & Non-Incarceration*

Suppose that a truck driver is stopped because his truck emits excess smoke. In checking the driver's license, a trooper learns that there are two warrants for the driver's arrest (one for failure to appear on a misdemeanor charge and the other for failure to pay a $25 fine for possession of marijuana). The trooper arrests the driver and takes him to the city jail. Jail procedures require complete processing of all arrestees, including a property inventory, whether or not the arrestee is able to post bail when the arrestee arrives at jail. The driver argues that any evidence found during the booking search should be excluded since the driver planned to immediately post bail. Does the state have a valid response to these arguments? *See Zehrung v. State*, 569 P.2d 189 (Alaska 1977).

Food for Thought

Everett Hoffman is arrested. At the station, the police want to search his backpack. Hoffman objects claiming that the police can serve their interest in "preservation of the defendant's property and protection of police from claims of lost or stolen property" by sealing the backpack in a plastic bag or box and placing it in a secure locker. Do the police have to accept Hoffman's suggestion or should they be allowed to search the backpack? What arguments can be made on Hoffman's behalf? How might the police respond?

Maryland v. King

569 U.S. 435 (2013).

Justice Kennedy delivered the opinion of the Court.

In 2003 a man concealing his face and armed with a gun broke into a woman's home in Maryland. He raped her. The police were unable to identify or apprehend the assailant, but they did obtain a sample of the perpetrator's DNA. In 2009 Alonzo King was arrested in Maryland, and charged with assault for menacing a group of people with a shotgun. As part of a routine booking procedure for serious offenses, his DNA sample was taken by applying a cotton swab or filter paper—known as a buccal swab—to the inside of his cheeks. The DNA was found to match the DNA taken from the rape victim. King was tried and convicted for the rape. The Court of Appeals of Maryland ruled that the DNA taken when King was booked for the 2009 charge was an unlawful seizure and set the rape conviction aside. This Court granted certiorari.

DNA technology is one of the most significant scientific advancements. Law enforcement, the defense bar, and the courts have acknowledged DNA testing's 'unparalleled ability both to exonerate the wrongly convicted and to identify the guilty. The current standard for forensic DNA testing relies on an analysis of the chromosomes located within the nucleus of all human cells. 'DNA material is composed of 'coding' and 'noncoding' regions. The coding regions are known as *genes* and contain the information necessary for a cell to make proteins. Non-protein-coding regions are not related directly to making proteins, and have been referred to as 'junk' DNA.' The adjective 'junk' may mislead for this is the DNA region used with near certainty to identify a person. The term indicates that this particular noncoding region, while useful and even dispositive for purposes like identity, does not show more far-reaching and complex characteristics like genetic traits. Many of the patterns found in DNA are shared among all people, so forensic analysis focuses on 'repeated DNA sequences scattered throughout the human genome,' known as 'short tandem repeats' (STRs). The alternative possibilities for the size and frequency of these STRs at any given point along a strand of DNA are known as 'alleles,' and multiple alleles are analyzed in order to ensure that a DNA profile matches only one individual. STR analysis makes it 'possible to determine whether a biological tissue matches a suspect with near certainty.' *Osborne, supra,* at 62.

The Act authorizes Maryland law enforcement authorities to collect DNA samples from 'an individual who is charged with a crime of violence or an attempt to commit a crime of violence; or burglary or an attempt to commit burglary.' Md. Pub. Saf. Code Ann. § 2–504(a)(3)(I) (Lexis 2011). Maryland law defines a crime of violence to include murder, rape, first-degree assault, kidnaping, arson, sexual assault, and a variety of other serious crimes. A DNA sample may not be processed or placed in a database before the individual is arraigned (unless the individual consents). A judicial officer ensures that there is probable cause to detain the arrestee on a qualifying serious offense. If 'all qualifying criminal charges are determined to be unsupported by probable cause the DNA sample shall be immediately destroyed.' DNA samples are also destroyed if 'a criminal action begun against the individual does not result in a conviction,' 'the conviction is finally reversed or vacated and no new trial is permitted,' or 'the individual is granted an unconditional pardon.' The Act also limits the information added to a DNA database and how it may be used. Specifically, no purpose other than identification is permissible: 'A person may not willfully test a DNA sample for information that does not relate to the identification of individuals as specified in this subtitle.' Tests for familial matches are also prohibited. The officers involved in taking and analyzing respondent's DNA sample complied with the Act.

Authorized by Congress and supervised by the Federal Bureau of Investigation, the Combined DNA Index System (CODIS) connects DNA laboratories at the local, state, and national level. Since its authorization in 1994, the CODIS system has grown to include all 50 States and a number of federal agencies. CODIS collects DNA profiles provided by local laboratories taken from arrestees, convicted offenders, and forensic evidence found at crime scenes. To participate in CODIS, a local laboratory must sign a memorandum of understanding agreeing to adhere to quality standards and submit to audits to evaluate compliance with the federal standards for scientifically rigorous DNA testing. One of the most significant aspects of CODIS is the standardization of the points of comparison in DNA analysis. The CODIS database is based on 13 loci at which the STR alleles are noted and compared. These loci make possible extreme accuracy in matching individual samples, with a 'random match probability of approximately 1 in 100 trillion (assuming unrelated individuals).' The CODIS loci are from the non-protein coding junk regions of DNA, and 'are not known to have any association with a genetic disease or any other genetic predisposition. Thus, the information in the database is only useful for human identity testing.' STR information is recorded only as a 'string of numbers'; and the DNA identification is accompanied only by information denoting the laboratory and the analyst responsible for the submission. In short, CODIS sets uniform national standards for DNA matching and then facilitates connections between local law enforcement agencies who can share more specific information about matched STR profiles.

All 50 States require the collection of DNA from felony convicts, and respondent does not dispute the validity of that practice. Twenty-eight States and the Federal Government have adopted laws authorizing the collection of DNA from some or all arrestees. Although those statutes vary in their particulars, their similarity means that this case implicates more than the specific Maryland law.

The framework for deciding the issue is well established. Using a buccal swab on the inner tissues of a person's cheek in order to obtain DNA samples is a search. A buccal swab is a far more gentle process than a venipuncture to draw blood. It involves but a light touch on the inside of the cheek; and although it can be deemed a search within the body of the arrestee, it requires no 'surgical intrusions beneath the skin.'

The ultimate measure of the constitutionality of a governmental search is 'reasonableness.'' *Vernonia School Dist. 47J v. Acton*, 515 U. S. 646, 652 (1995). In giving content to the inquiry whether an intrusion is reasonable, the Court has preferred 'some quantum of individualized suspicion as a prerequisite to a constitutional search or seizure. But the Fourth Amendment imposes no irreducible requirement of such suspicion.' *United States v. Martinez-Fuerte*, 428 U. S. 543, 560 (1976). In some circumstances, such as 'when faced with special law enforcement needs, diminished expectations of privacy, minimal intrusions, or the like, the Court has found that certain general, or individual, circumstances may render a warrantless search or seizure reasonable.' *Illinois v. McArthur*, 531 U. S. 326, 330 (2001). Those circumstances diminish the need for a warrant.

The Maryland DNA Collection Act provides that all arrestees charged with serious crimes must furnish the sample on a buccal swab. The arrestee is already in valid police custody for a serious offense supported by probable cause. The DNA collection is not subject to the judgment of officers whose perspective might be 'colored by their primary involvement in 'the often competitive enterprise of ferreting out crime.'' *Terry, supra*, at 12 (quoting *Johnson v. United States*, 333 U. S. 10, 14 (1948)). 'Both the circumstances justifying toxicological testing and the permissible limits of such intrusions are defined narrowly and specifically in the regulations that authorize them. In light of the standardized nature of the tests and the minimal discretion vested in those charged with administering the program, there are virtually no facts for a neutral magistrate to evaluate.' *Skinner, supra*, at 622. Here, the search falls within the category of cases this Court has analyzed by reference to the proposition that the 'touchstone of the Fourth Amendment is reasonableness, not individualized suspicion.' *Samson, supra*, at 855, n. 4.

Urgent government interests are not a license for indiscriminate police behavior. To say that no warrant is required is merely to acknowledge that 'rather than employing a *per se* rule of unreasonableness, we balance the privacy-related and law enforcement-related concerns to determine if the intrusion was reasonable.' *McArthur, supra*, at 331. This application of 'traditional standards of reasonableness' requires a court to weigh 'the promotion of legitimate governmental interests' against 'the degree to which the search intrudes upon an individual's privacy.' *Wyoming v. Houghton*, 526 U. S. 295, 300 (1999).

The legitimate government interest served by the Maryland DNA Collection Act is one that is well established: the need for law enforcement officers in a safe and accurate way to process and identify the persons and possessions they must take into custody. 'Probable cause provides legal justification for arresting a person suspected of crime, and for a brief period of detention to take the administrative steps incident to arrest.' *Gerstein v. Pugh*, 420 U. S. 103, 113 (1975). Also uncontested is the 'right of the Government to search the person of the accused when legally arrested.' *Weeks v. United States*, 232 U. S. 383, 392 (1914). The 'routine administrative procedures at a police station house incident to booking and jailing the suspect' derive from different origins and have different constitutional justifications than the search of a place. The interests are further different when an individual is formally processed into police custody. Then 'the law is in the act of subjecting the body of the accused to its physical dominion.' *People v. Chiagles*, 142 N. E. 583, 584 (1923) (Cardozo, J.). When probable cause exists to remove an individual from the normal channels of society and hold him in legal custody, DNA identification plays a critical role in serving those interests.

First, 'in every criminal case, it is known and must be known who has been arrested and who is being tried.' *Hiibel v. Sixth Judicial Dist. Court of Nev., Humboldt Cty.*, 542 U. S. 177, 191 (2004). 'A perpetrator will take unusual steps to conceal not only his conduct, but also his identity. Disguises used while committing a crime may be supplemented or replaced by changed names, and even changed physical features.' *Jones v. Murray*, 962 F. 2d 302, 307 (CA4 1992). An 'arrestee may be carrying a false ID or lie about his identity,' and 'criminal history records can be inaccurate or incomplete.' *Florence v. Board of Chosen Freeholders of County of Burlington*, 132 S. Ct. 1510, 1521 (2012). A suspect's criminal history is a critical part of his identity. It is a common occurrence that 'people detained for minor offenses turn out to be the most devious and dangerous criminals. Police already use routine and accepted means as varied as comparing the suspect's booking photograph to sketch artists' depictions of persons of interest, showing his mugshot to potential witnesses, and of course making a computerized comparison of the arrestee's fingerprints against electronic databases of known criminals and unsolved crimes. The only difference between DNA analysis and the accepted use of fingerprint databases is the unparalleled accuracy DNA provides. DNA collected from arrestees is an irrefutable identification of the person from whom it was taken. In this respect the use of DNA is no different than matching an arrestee's face to a wanted poster of a previously unidentified suspect; or matching tattoos to known gang symbols to reveal a criminal affiliation; or matching the arrestee's fingerprints to those recovered from a crime scene.

Second, law enforcement officers bear a responsibility for ensuring that the custody of an arrestee does not create inordinate 'risks for facility staff, for the existing detainee population, and for a new detainee.' *Florence, supra*, at 1518. 'Knowledge of identity may inform an officer that a suspect is wanted for another offense, or has a record of violence or mental disorder. On the other hand, knowing identity may help clear a suspect and allow the police to concentrate their efforts elsewhere.

Third, 'the Government has a substantial interest in ensuring that persons accused of crimes are available for trials.' *Bell v. Wolfish*, 441 U. S. 520, 534 (1979). A person who is arrested for one offense but knows that he has yet to answer for some past crime may be more inclined to flee the instant charges. A defendant who had committed a prior sexual assault might be inclined to flee on a burglary charge, knowing that a DNA sample would be taken from him after his conviction on the burglary charge that would tie him to the more serious charge of rape. A detainee who absconds from custody presents a risk to law enforcement officers, other detainees, victims of previous crimes, witnesses, and society at large.

Fourth, an arrestee's past conduct is essential to an assessment of the danger he poses to the public, and this will inform a court's determination whether the individual should be released on bail. Knowing that the defendant is wanted for a previous violent crime based on DNA identification is especially probative of the court's consideration of 'the danger of the defendant to the alleged victim, another person, or the community.' Even when release is permitted, the background identity of the suspect is necessary for determining what conditions must be met before release is allowed. The facts of this case are illustrative. When the DNA report linked him to the prior rape, it would be relevant to the conditions of his release. Even if an arrestee is released on bail, development of DNA identification revealing the defendant's unknown violent past can and should lead to the revocation of his conditional release.

Finally, in the interests of justice, the identification of an arrestee as the perpetrator of some heinous crime may have the salutary effect of freeing a person wrongfully imprisoned for the same offense. 'Prompt DNA testing would speed up apprehension of criminals before they commit additional crimes, and prevent the grotesque detention of innocent people.' J. Dwyer, P. Neufeld, & B. Scheck, Actual Innocence 245 (2000).

The Court has recognized that the 'governmental interests underlying a station-house search of the arrestee's person and possessions may in some circumstances be even greater than those supporting a search immediately following arrest.' *Lafayette*, 462 U. S., at 645. Thus, the Court has been reluctant to circumscribe the authority of the police to conduct reasonable booking searches. DNA identification represents an important advance in the techniques used by law enforcement to serve legitimate police concerns. Law enforcement agencies routinely have used scientific advancements in their standard procedures for the identification of arrestees. 'Police had been using photography to capture the faces of criminals almost since its invention.' S. Cole, Suspect Identities 20 (2001). Perhaps the most direct historical analogue to the DNA technology used to identify respondent is fingerprinting. DNA identification is an advanced technique superior to fingerprinting in many ways. A suspect who has changed his facial features to evade photographic identification or even one who has undertaken the more arduous task of altering his fingerprints cannot escape the revealing power of his DNA. Respondent's primary objection is that DNA identification is not as fast as fingerprinting. Prior to 1999, the processing of fingerprint submissions was largely a manual, labor-intensive process, taking weeks or months to process a single submission.' The question of how long it takes to process identifying information obtained from a valid search goes only to the efficacy of the search for its purpose of prompt identification, not the constitutionality of the search. Even so, the delay in processing DNA from arrestees is being reduced by rapid technical advances. Actual release of a serious offender as a routine matter takes weeks or months in any event.

Courts have confirmed that the Fourth Amendment allows police to take certain routine 'administrative steps incident to arrest—i.e., booking, photographing, and fingerprinting.' *McLaughlin,* 500 U. S., at 58. DNA identification of arrestees is 'no more than an extension of methods of identification long used in dealing with persons under arrest.' *Kelly*, 55 F. 2d, at 69. In the balance of reasonableness required by the Fourth Amendment, the Court must give great weight both to the significant government interest at stake in the identification of arrestees and to the unmatched potential of DNA identification to serve that interest.

The intrusion of a cheek swab to obtain a DNA sample is a minimal one. A significant government interest does not alone suffice to justify a search. The government interest must outweigh the degree to which the search invades an individual's legitimate expectations of privacy. The expectations of privacy of an individual taken into police custody 'necessarily are of a diminished scope.' *Bell*, 441 U. S., at 557. 'Both the person and the property in his immediate possession may be searched at the station house.' *United States v. Edwards*, 415 U. S. 800, 803 (1974). A search of the detainee's person when he is booked into custody may 'involve a relatively extensive exploration.' *Robinson*, 414 U. S., at 227. This is not to suggest that any search is acceptable solely because a person is in custody. Some searches, such as invasive surgery, or a search of the arrestee's home, involve either greater intrusions or higher expectations of privacy than are present in this case. A buccal swab involves an even more brief and still minimal intrusion. A gentle rub along the inside of the cheek does not break the skin, and it 'involves virtually no risk, trauma, or pain.' Nothing suggests that a buccal swab poses any physical danger whatsoever. A swab of this nature does not increase the indignity already attendant to normal incidents of arrest.

The processing of respondent's DNA sample's 13 CODIS loci did not intrude on respondent's privacy in a way that would make his DNA identification unconstitutional. The CODIS loci come from noncoding parts of the DNA that do not reveal the genetic traits of the arrestee. Even if non-coding alleles could provide some information, law enforcement officers analyze DNA for the sole purpose of generating a unique identifying number against which future samples may be matched. If future police analyze samples to determine, for instance, an arrestee's predisposition for a particular disease or other hereditary factors not relevant to identity, that case would present additional privacy concerns not present here. The Act provides statutory protections that guard against further invasion of privacy. The Act requires that 'only DNA records that directly relate to the identification of individuals shall be collected and stored.' The Court need not speculate about the risks posed 'by a system that did not contain comparable security provisions.' DNA identification of arrestees is a reasonable search that can be considered part of a routine booking procedure. The judgment of the Court of Appeals of Maryland is reversed.

It is so ordered.

JUSTICE SCALIA, with whom JUSTICE GINSBURG, JUSTICE SOTOMAYOR, and JUSTICE KAGAN join, dissenting.

While we have permitted searches without individualized suspicion, 'in none of these cases did we indicate approval of a search whose primary purpose was to detect evidence of ordinary criminal wrongdoing.' *Indianapolis v. Edmond*, 531 U. S. 32, 38 (2000). The Court elaborates at length the ways that the search here served the special purpose of 'identifying' King. If the purpose of this Act is to assess 'whether King should be released on bail,' why would it *possibly* forbid the DNA testing process to *begin* until King was arraigned? This search had nothing to do with establishing King's identity. King's DNA sample was not received by the Maryland State Police's Forensic Sciences Division until two weeks after his arrest. It sat in that office two months after it was received, and nearly three since King's arrest. The data from the tests were not available for several more weeks when the test results were entered into Maryland's DNA database, *together with information identifying the person from whom the sample was taken.* Meanwhile, bail had been set, King had engaged in discovery, and he had requested a speedy trial. It was not until four months after King's arrest that the for-warded sample transmitted (*without* identifying information) from the Maryland DNA database to the Federal Bureau of Investigation's national database was matched with a sample taken from the scene of an unrelated crime years earlier. King could not have been *identified* by this match. The FBI's DNA database consists of two distinct collections. The one to which King's DNA was submitted consists of DNA samples taken from known convicts or arrestees. The other collection consists of samples taken from crime scenes; the 'Unsolved Crimes Collection.' The Convict and Arrestee Collection contains only the DNA profile itself, the name of the agency that submitted it, the laboratory personnel who analyzed it, and an identification number for the specimen.

Food for Thought

Justice Scalia's dissent suggests the fear that states will expand their DNA testing to cover even minor offenses. Recall, when we studied arrest principles, we saw that individuals could be subjected to custodial arrest for relatively minor offenses (*e.g.*, failure to wear seat belts). Would the Maryland law be constitutional if it applied to *all* arrestees?

If one wanted to identify someone in custody using his DNA, the logical thing to do would be to compare that DNA against the Convict and Arrestee Collection. But that is not what was done. And that is because this search had nothing to do with identification.

The Maryland Act has a section helpfully entitled 'Purpose of collecting and testing DNA samples.' That provision lists five purposes for which DNA samples may be tested. The Court's imagined purpose is not among them. Instead, the law provides that DNA samples are collected and tested, as a matter of Maryland law, 'as part of an official investigation into a crime.' The attorney general of Maryland remarked that he 'looked forward to the opportunity to defend this important crime-fighting tool,' and praised the DNA database for helping to 'bring to justice violent perpetrators.'

Today's judgment will have the beneficial effect of solving more crimes; so would the taking of DNA samples from anyone who flies on an airplane. I doubt that the proud men who wrote the charter of our liberties would have been so eager to open their mouths for royal inspection.

Hypo 1: *Other Possible DNA Collections*

What if states decided to collect and store information related to all arrestees genetic traits and medical tendencies. Would the *King* decision allow the states to use DNA for these purposes? Are there justifications for doing so?

Hypo 2: *More on DNA Testing of Arrestees*

In *King*, the Maryland statute provided for DNA testing only after a judicial officer has made a probable cause determination and the arrestee has been charged with a crime. Would a DNA testing law be constitutional if it provided for DNA testing as soon as "immediately practicable" after a suspect is arrested? In other words, it required testing before a judicial officer determined that the state had probable cause to arrest the suspect? Does *King* suggest that the state has a valid interest in ascertaining the identity of those who have been arrested for a crime, but not yet charged? *See People v. Buza,* 180 Cal. Rptr. 3d 753 (Cal. App. 2014).

4. Automobile Exception

The automobile exception is one of the oldest exceptions to the warrant requirement. It provides that, when the police have probable cause to believe that an automobile contains the fruits, instrumentalities or evidence of crime, they may search the vehicle without a warrant.

California v. Carney

471 U.S. 386 (1985).

CHIEF JUSTICE BURGER delivered the opinion of the Court.

Drug Enforcement Agency Agent Robert Williams watched respondent, Charles Carney, approach a youth in downtown San Diego. The youth accompanied Carney to a Dodge Mini Motor Home parked in a nearby lot. Carney and the youth closed the window shades in the motor home. Agent Williams had previously received uncorroborated information that the same motor home was used by another person who was exchanging marihuana for sex. Williams, with assistance from other agents, kept the motor home under surveillance for the one and one-quarter hours that Carney and the youth remained inside. When the youth left the motor home, the agents stopped him. The youth told [them] that he had received marijuana in return for allowing Carney sexual contacts. At the agents' request, the youth returned to the motor home and knocked on its door; Carney stepped out. The agents identified themselves. Without a warrant or consent, one agent entered the motor home and observed marihuana, plastic bags, and a scale of the kind used in weighing drugs on a table. Agent Williams took Carney into custody and took possession of the motor home. A subsequent search of the motor home at the police station revealed additional marihuana in the cupboards and refrigerator. Respondent was convicted of possession of marihuana for sale. The California Supreme Court reversed. We granted certiorari. We reverse.

There are exceptions to the general rule that a warrant must be secured before a search is undertaken; one is the so-called "automobile exception." This exception was first set forth by the Court 60 years ago in *Carroll v. United States*, 267 U.S. 132 (1925). There, the Court recognized that the privacy interests in an automobile are constitutionally protected; however, it held that the ready mobility of the automobile justifies a lesser degree of protection of those interests. Our later cases have made clear that ready mobility is not the only basis for the exception. "Besides the element of mobility, less rigorous warrant requirements govern because the expectation of privacy with respect to one's automobile is significantly less than that relating to one's home or office."

Even in cases where an automobile was not immediately mobile, the lesser expectation of privacy resulting from its use as a readily mobile vehicle justified application of the vehicular exception. In some cases, the configuration of the vehicle contributed to the lower expectations of privacy; for example, we held in *Cardwell v. Lewis,* 417 U.S., at 590, that, because the passenger compartment of a standard automobile is relatively open to plain view, there are lesser expectations of privacy. But even when enclosed "repository" areas have been involved, we have concluded that the lesser expectations of privacy warrant application of the exception. We have applied the exception in the context of a locked car trunk, a sealed package in a car trunk, a closed compartment under the dashboard, the interior of a vehicle's upholstery, or sealed packages inside a covered pickup truck.

These reduced expectations of privacy derive not from the fact that the area to be searched is in plain view, but from the pervasive regulation of vehicles capable of traveling on the public highways. As we explained in *South Dakota v. Opperman,* 428 U.S. 364 (1976), an inventory search case: "Automobiles, unlike homes, are subjected to pervasive and continuing governmental regulation and controls, including periodic inspection and licensing requirements. As an everyday occurrence, police stop and examine vehicles when license plates or inspection stickers have expired, or if other violations, such as exhaust fumes or excessive noise, are noted, or if headlights or other safety equipment are not in proper working order."

The public is fully aware that it is accorded less privacy in its automobiles because of this compelling governmental need for regulation. In short, the pervasive schemes of regulation, which necessarily lead to reduced expectations of privacy, and the exigencies attendant to ready mobility justify searches without prior recourse to the authority of a magistrate so long as the overriding standard of probable cause is met.

When a vehicle is being used on the highways, or if it is readily capable of such use and is found stationary in a place not regularly used for residential purposes—temporary or otherwise—the two justifications for the vehicle exception come into play. First, the vehicle is obviously readily mobile by the turn of an ignition key, if not actually moving. Second, there is a reduced expectation of privacy stemming from its use as a licensed motor vehicle subject to a range of police regulation inapplicable to a fixed dwelling. At least in these circumstances, the overriding societal interests in effective law enforcement justify an immediate search before the vehicle and its occupants become unavailable. While it is true that respondent's vehicle possessed some, if not many of the attributes of a home, it is equally clear that the vehicle falls clearly within the scope of the exception. Respondent's motor home was readily mobile. Absent the prompt search and seizure, it could readily have been moved beyond the reach of the police. Furthermore, the vehicle was licensed to "operate on public streets; was serviced in public places; and was subject to extensive regulation and inspection." *Rakas v. Illinois,* 439 U.S. 128, 154 (1978) (Powell, J., concurring). And the vehicle was so situated that an objective observer would conclude that it was being used not as a residence, but as a vehicle.

Respondent urges us to distinguish his vehicle from other vehicles because it was capable of functioning as a home. In our mobile society, many vehicles used for transportation are being used not only for transportation but for shelter, *i.e.*, as a "home" or "residence." To distinguish between respondent's motor home and an ordinary sedan for purposes of the vehicle exception would require that we apply the exception depending upon the size of the vehicle and the quality of its appointments. Moreover, to fail to apply the exception to vehicles such as a motor home ignores the fact that a motor home lends itself easily to use as an instrument of illicit drug traffic and other illegal activity. In *United States v. Ross*, 456 U.S., at 822, we declined to distinguish between "worthy" and "unworthy" containers, noting that "the central purpose of the Fourth Amendment forecloses such a distinction." We decline today to distinguish between "worthy" and "unworthy" vehicles which are either on the public roads and highways, or situated such that it is reasonable to conclude that the vehicle is not being used as a residence.

Our application of the vehicle exception has never turned on the other uses to which a vehicle might be put. The exception has historically turned on the ready mobility of the vehicle, and on the presence of the vehicle in a setting that objectively indicates that the vehicle is being used for transportation.[17] These two requirements for application of the exception ensure that law enforcement officials are not unnecessarily hamstrung in their efforts to detect and prosecute criminal activity, and that the legitimate privacy interests of the public are protected. Applying the vehicle exception in these circumstances allows the essential purposes served by the exception to be fulfilled, while assuring that the exception will acknowledge legitimate privacy interests. This search was not unreasonable; it was plainly one that the magistrate could authorize if presented with these facts. The DEA agents had fresh, direct, uncontradicted evidence

Take Note

No exigent circumstances are needed for police to rely on the "automobile exception," only probable cause. In *Maryland v. Dyson*, 527 U.S. 465 (1999), the police had probable cause to believe that a vehicle contained illegal drugs, and they searched it without a warrant even though there was time to obtain one. The Maryland Court of Special Appeals invalidated the search on the basis that there were no exigent circumstances justifying the warrantless search. The U.S. Supreme Court reversed, noting that automobiles should be treated differently than homes, and that only probable cause is required to invoke the automobile exception.

---

[17]   We need not pass on the application of the vehicle exception to a motor home that is situated in a way or place that indicates that it is being used as a residence. Among the factors that might be relevant in determining whether a warrant would be required in such a circumstance is its location, whether the vehicle is readily mobile or elevated on blocks, whether the vehicle is licensed, whether it is connected to utilities, and whether it has convenient access to a public road.

that the respondent was distributing a controlled substance from the vehicle, apart from evidence of other possible offenses. The agents thus had abundant probable cause to enter and search the vehicle for evidence of a crime notwithstanding its possible use as a dwelling place.

The judgment of the California Supreme Court is *reversed.*

JUSTICE STEVENS, with whom JUSTICE BRENNAN and JUSTICE MARSHALL join, dissenting.

It is hardly unrealistic to expect experienced law enforcement officers to obtain a search warrant when one can easily be secured. Inherent mobility is not a sufficient justification for fashioning an exception to the warrant requirement, especially in the face of heightened expectations of privacy in the location searched. Motor homes, by their common use and construction, afford their owners a substantial and legitimate expectation of privacy when they dwell within. When a motor home is parked in a location removed from the public highway, society is prepared to recognize that the expectations of privacy within it are not unlike the expectations one has in a fixed dwelling. Such places may only be searched with a warrant based upon probable cause. Warrantless searches of motor homes are only reasonable when the motor home is traveling on the public streets or highways, or when exigent circumstances otherwise require an immediate search without the expenditure of time necessary to obtain a warrant. In this case, the motor home was parked in an off-street lot only a few blocks from the courthouse in downtown San Diego where dozens of magistrates were available to entertain a warrant application.[18]   The officers plainly had probable cause to arrest the respondent and search the motor home, and it is inexplicable why they eschewed the safe harbor of a warrant. The motor home in this case was designed to accommodate a breadth of ordinary everyday living. The State contends that officers in the field will have an impossible task determining whether or not other vehicles contain mobile living quarters. Surely the exteriors of these vehicles contain clues about their different functions which could alert officers in the field to the necessity of a warrant. A motor home is the functional equivalent of a hotel room, a vacation and retirement home, or a hunting and fishing cabin. The highest and most legitimate expectations of privacy associated with these temporary abodes should command the respect of this Court. A warrantless search of living quarters in a motor home is "presumptively unreasonable absent exigent circumstances."

---

[18]   In addition, a telephonic warrant was only 20 cents and the nearest phone booth away.

Points for Discussion

a. Curtilage & the Automobile Exception

In *Collins v. Virginia*, 138 S.Ct. 1663 (2018), the Court applied the automobile exception in the context of curtilage. A police officer saw a man on an orange and black motorcycle with an extended frame commit a traffic infraction, but the driver eluded the officer. A few weeks later, a second officer saw an orange and black motorcycle speeding, but the driver got away from him, too. The officers later learned that the motorcycle likely was stolen and in the possession of Collins. On Collins' Face-book profile, the police found pictures of an orange and black motorcycle parked at the top of a driveway. An officer tracked down the address, drove there, and observed (from the street) a motorcycle with an extended frame covered with a white tarp, parked at the same angle and in the same location on the driveway as in the Facebook photograph. Without a warrant, the officer walked onto the residential property to the top of the driveway where the motorcycle was parked, and pulled off the tarp, revealing a motorcycle that looked like the one from the speeding incident. He then ran a search of the license plate and vehicle identification numbers, which confirmed that the motorcycle was stolen. The officer then took a photograph, put the tarp back on, and left the property. Collins was later indicted by a grand jury for receiving stolen property. The Court held that the automobile exception did not apply:

Food for Thought

The Oregon Supreme Court has construed the Oregon Constitution as precluding use of the "automobile exception" to authorize a warrantless search of a defendant's vehicle when the vehicle is parked, immobile, and unoccupied at the time that the police encounter it in connection with a crime. The court held that the "constitution requires a warrant so that a disinterested branch of government—the judicial branch—and not the branch that conducts the search—the executive branch—makes the decision as to whether there is probable cause to search." The court went on to note that a neutral magistrate's evaluation of probable cause continued to be a desired goal, and the court did not anticipate that the police would rely on the automobile exception when advances in technology permitted quick and efficient electronic issuance of warrants. Is the Oregon approach preferable to the *Dyson* court's per se rule? *See State v. Kurokawa-Lasciak*, 351 Or. 179, 263 P.3d 336 (2011).

"The protection afforded curtilage is essentially a protection of families and personal privacy in an area intimately linked to the home, both physically and psychologically, where privacy expectations are most heightened." *California v. Ciraolo*, 476 U. S. 207, 212 (1986). Just like the front porch, side garden, or area "outside the front window," *Jardines*, 569 U. S., at 6, the driveway enclosure where Officer Rhodes searched the motorcycle constitutes "an area adjacent to the home and 'to which the activity of home life extends,'" and so is properly considered curtilage, *id.*, at 7 (quoting *Oliver*, 466 U. S., at 182). In physically intruding on the curtilage of Collins' home to search the motorcycle, Officer Rhodes not only invaded Collins' Fourth Amendment interest in the item searched, *i.e.,* the motorcycle, but also invaded Collins' Fourth Amendment interest in the curtilage of his home. To allow an officer to rely on the automobile exception to gain entry into a house or its curtilage for the purpose of conducting a vehicle search would unmoor the exception from its justifications, render hollow the core Fourth Amendment protection the Constitution extends to the house and its curtilage, and transform what was meant to be an exception into a tool with far broader application. So long as it is curtilage, a parking patio or carport into which an officer can see from the street is no less entitled to protection from trespass and a warrantless search than a fully enclosed garage. Virginia's proposed bright-line rule would grant constitutional rights to those persons with the financial means to afford residences with garages in which to store their vehicles but deprive those persons without such resources of any individualized consideration as to whether the areas in which they store their vehicles qualify as curtilage.

Justice Alito, dissenting argued that the "The Fourth Amendment prohibits 'unreasonable' searches" and what "the police did in this case was entirely reasonable. The motorcycle, when parked in the driveway, was just as mobile as it would have been had it been parked at the curb."

b. Delayed Automobile Searches

If the search of an automobile is delayed, the police may have time to obtain a warrant and arguably should be required to do so. However, in *Chambers v. Maroney,* 399 U.S. 42 (1970), the Court upheld a delayed search. Petitioner was riding in an automobile at the time of his arrest, but the vehicle was searched later at the police station rather than at the scene. The Court held that: "For constitutional purposes, we see no difference between seizing and holding a car before presenting the probable cause issue to a magistrate and carrying out an immediate search without a warrant. Given probable cause to search, either course is reasonable under the Fourth Amendment. The station wagon could have been searched on the spot when it was stopped since there was probable cause to search and it was a fleeting target for a search. The probable-cause factor still obtained at the station house and so did the mobility of the car. There is little to choose in terms of practical consequences between an immediate search without a warrant and the car's immobilization until a warrant is obtained."

In *United States v. Johns*, 469 U.S. 478 (1985), the police stopped and searched a vehicle based on probable cause. The police removed packages from the vehicle, and searched the packages several days later. The Court upheld the search: "We do not think that delay in the execution of the warrantless search is necessarily unreasonable. We do not suggest that police officers may indefinitely retain possession of a vehicle and its contents before they complete a vehicle search. Respondents have not even alleged, much less proved, that the delay in the search of packages adversely affected legitimate interests protected by the Fourth Amendment." Justice Brennan dissented: "A warrantless search occurring three days after seizure of a package found in an automobile violates the Fourth Amendment. There is simply no justification for departing from the Fourth Amendment warrant requirement under the circumstances of this case; no exigency precluded reasonable efforts to obtain a warrant prior to the search of the packages in the warehouse."

Food for Thought

In *Coolidge v. New Hampshire*, 403 U.S. 443 (1971), petitioner was arrested for murder at his home. His car, which was sitting on the front driveway, was impounded and towed to the police station. The car was searched two days later, as well as a year later. Evidence obtained from the search was admitted at petitioner's trial. In a plurality opinion, the Court held that the trial court erred in admitting the evidence: "The police had known for some time of the probable role of the Pontiac car in the crime. Coolidge was aware that he was a suspect, but he had been extremely cooperative throughout the investigation, and there was no indication that he meant to flee. He had ample opportunity to destroy any evidence he thought incriminating. There is no suggestion that, on the night in question, the car was being used for any illegal purpose, and it was regularly parked in the driveway of his house. The opportunity for search was thus hardly "fleeting." The objects that the police are assumed to have had probable cause to search for in the car were neither stolen nor contraband nor dangerous. The word "automobile" is not a talisman in whose presence the Fourth Amendment fades away and disappears. In short, by no possible stretch of the legal imagination can this be made into a case where "it is not practicable to secure a warrant," and the "automobile exception," despite its label, is simply irrelevant." Is the *Coolidge* reasoning still good law?

Hypo 1: *The Staged Accident*

The police have probable cause to make a warrantless search of an automobile for illegal drugs. However, because the owner is part of a drug ring, the police are reluctant to make a forcible search for fear of tipping off other members of the ring. Instead, the police stage a phony automobile accident (that causes minor damage, using an undercover police officer who appears to be drunk, and who is purportedly "arrested" at the scene of the accident). The real suspects are told to leave the keys in the vehicle and sit in the back of a police cruiser. After the suspects are seated, a "thief" (really a police operative) steals the vehicle. The police then search the vehicle and return it to the suspects. Did the police act permissibly? *See United States v. Alverez-Tejeda*, 491 F.3d 1013 (9th Cir. 2007).

Hypo 2: *The Drug Investigation*

Possessing probable cause to believe that defendant is a drug pusher, police obtain a warrant to search his house. As the police arrive at the house, the suspected pusher arrives in his car. In addition to searching the house (which did not reveal evidence of illegal drug activity), the police wish to search the vehicle. Based on the fact that the police had probable cause to believe that defendant was a drug pusher, and that he had drugs in his house (a belief that turned out to be inaccurate), did they have probable cause to believe that he had illegal drugs in his car? Would your analysis be different if, during the search of the house, the suspect's girlfriend informed police that defendant deals drugs out of his car? *See Commonwealth v. Fernandez*, 458 Mass. 137, 934 N.E.2d 810 (2010).

Hypo 3: *The Detached Camper*

A police officer, who observes "suspicious" behavior from a detached camper, comes closer in order to see what is happening. As she does, she smells a strong odor of marijuana, leading the officer to believe that she has probable cause to believe that marijuana can be found in the vehicle. However, the camper is not hooked up to a vehicle, is hooked up to an electrical outlet, and has its "stabilizing legs" extended and firmly in place. Can the officer search the camper without a warrant under the automobile exception? In other words, does that exception apply to a detached camper under these circumstances? *See State v. Otto*, 840 N.W.2d 589 (N.D. 2013).

California v. Acevedo

500 U.S. 565 (1991).

JUSTICE BLACKMUN delivered the opinion of the Court.

Officer Coleman of the Santa Ana, Cal., Police Department received a telephone call from a federal drug enforcement agent in Hawaii. The agent informed Coleman that he had seized a package containing marijuana which was to have been delivered to the Federal Express Office in Santa Ana and was addressed to J.R. Daza at 805 West Stevens Avenue in that city. The agent arranged to send the package to Coleman instead. Coleman was to take the package to the Federal Express office and arrest the person who arrived to claim it. Coleman received the package, verified its contents, and took it to the Senior Operations Manager at the Federal Express office. At about 10:30 a.m. a man, who identified himself as Jamie Daza, arrived to claim the package. He accepted it and drove to his apartment on West Stevens. He carried the package into the apartment. At 11:45 a.m., officers observed Daza leave the apartment and drop the box and paper that had contained the marijuana into a trash bin. Coleman at that point left the scene to get a search warrant. About 12:05 p.m., the officers saw Richard St. George leave the apartment carrying a blue knapsack which appeared to be half full. The officers stopped him as he was driving off, searched the knapsack, and found 1 ½ pounds of marijuana. At 12:30 p.m., respondent Charles Steven Acevedo arrived. He entered Daza's apartment, stayed for about 10 minutes, and reappeared carrying a brown paper bag that looked full. The officers noticed that the bag was the size of one of the wrapped marijuana packages sent from Hawaii. Acevedo walked to a silver Honda in the parking lot, placed the bag in the trunk of the car and started to drive away. Fearing the loss of evidence, officers in a marked police car stopped him. They opened the trunk and the bag, and found marijuana.

Respondent was charged with possession of marijuana for sale. When his motion to suppress was denied, he pleaded guilty but appealed the denial of his suppression motion. The California Court of Appeal's concluded that the marijuana should have been suppressed. We granted certiorari to reexamine the law applicable to a closed container in an automobile, a subject that has troubled courts and law enforcement officers since it was first considered in *United States v. Chadwick*, 433 U.S. 1 (1977).

In *United States v. Ross*, 456 U.S. 798 (1982), we held that a warrantless search of an automobile could include a search of a container or package found inside the car when such a search was supported by probable cause. The warrantless search of Ross' car occurred after an informant told the police that he had seen Ross complete a drug transaction using drugs stored in the trunk of his car. The police stopped the car, searched it, and discovered in the trunk a brown paper bag containing drugs. We decided that the search of Ross' car was not unreasonable under the Fourth Amendment: "The scope of a warrantless search based on probable cause is no narrower—and no broader—than the scope of a search authorized by a warrant supported by probable cause." Thus, "if probable cause justifies the search of a lawfully stopped vehicle, it justifies the search of every part of the vehicle and its contents that may conceal the object of the search." In *Ross*, we clarified the scope of the *Carroll* doctrine as properly including a "probing search" of compartments and containers within the automobile so long as the search is supported by probable cause.

Ross distinguished the *Carroll* doctrine from the separate rule that governed the search of closed containers. The Court had announced this separate rule, unique to luggage and other closed packages, bags, and containers, in *United States v. Chadwick*, 433 U.S. 1 (1977). In *Chadwick*, federal narcotics agents had probable cause to believe that a 200-pound double-locked footlocker contained marijuana. The agents tracked the locker as the defendants removed it from a train and carried it through the station to a waiting car. As soon as defendants lifted the locker into the trunk of the car, the agents arrested them, seized the locker, and searched it. In this Court, the United States did not contend that the locker's brief contact with the automobile's trunk sufficed to make the *Carroll* doctrine applicable. Rather, the United States urged that the search of movable luggage could be considered analogous to the search of an automobile. The Court rejected this argument because, it reasoned, a person expects more privacy in his luggage and personal effects than he does in his automobile. Moreover, it concluded that as "may often not be the case when automobiles are seized," secure storage facilities are usually available when the police seize luggage. In *Arkansas v. Sanders*, 442 U.S. 753 (1979), the Court extended *Chadwick*'s rule to apply to a suitcase actually being transported in the trunk of a car. In *Sanders*, the police had probable cause to believe a suitcase contained marijuana. They watched as defendant placed the suitcase in the trunk of a taxi and was driven away. The police pursued the taxi for several blocks, stopped it, found the suitcase in the trunk, and searched it. *Sanders* stressed the heightened privacy expectation in personal luggage and concluded that the presence of luggage in an automobile did not diminish the owner's expectation of privacy in his personal items.

In *Ross,* the Court endeavored to distinguish *Carroll*, which governed the *Ross* automobile search, and *Chadwick*, which governed the *Sanders* automobile search. It held that the *Carroll* doctrine covered searches of automobiles when the police had probable cause to search an entire vehicle, but that the *Chadwick* doctrine governed searches of luggage when the officers had probable cause to search only a container within the vehicle. Thus, in a *Ross* situation, the police could conduct a reasonable search under the Fourth Amendment without obtaining a warrant, whereas in a *Sanders* situation, the police had to obtain a warrant before they searched. *Ross* held that closed containers encountered by the police during a warrantless search of a car pursuant to the automobile exception could also be searched. Thus, *Ross* took the critical step of saying that closed containers in cars could be searched without a warrant because of their presence within the automobile. Despite the protection that *Sanders* purported to extend to closed containers, the privacy interest in those closed containers yielded to the broad scope of an automobile search.

The facts in this case closely resemble the facts in *Ross*. In *Ross*, the police had probable cause to believe that drugs were stored in the trunk of a particular car. Here, the police had probable cause to believe that respondent was carrying marijuana in a bag in his car's trunk. Furthermore, in *Ross*, as here, the drugs in the trunk were contained in a brown paper bag. *Ross* rejected *Chadwick*'s distinction between containers and cars. It concluded that the expectation of privacy in one's vehicle is equal to one's expectation of privacy in the container, and noted that "the privacy interests in a car's trunk or glove compartment may be no less than those in a movable container." It also recognized that it was arguable that the same exigent circumstances that permit a warrantless search of an automobile would justify the warrantless search of a movable container. In deference to the rule of *Chadwick* and *Sanders*, however, the Court put that question to one side.

We see no principled distinction in terms of either the privacy expectation or the exigent circumstances between the paper bag found by the police in *Ross* and the paper bag found by the police here. Furthermore, by attempting to distinguish between a container for which the police are specifically searching and a container which they come across in a car, we have provided only minimal protection for privacy and have impeded effective law enforcement. The line between probable cause to search a vehicle and probable cause to search a package in that vehicle is not always clear, and separate rules that govern the two objects to be searched may enable the police to broaden their power to make warrantless searches and disserve privacy interests. If the police know that they may open a bag only if they are actually searching the entire car, they may search more extensively than they otherwise would in order to establish the general probable cause required by *Ross*.

To the extent that the *Chadwick-Sanders* rule protects privacy, its protection is minimal. Law enforcement officers may seize a container and hold it until they obtain a search warrant. "Since the police, by hypothesis, have probable cause to seize the property, we can assume that a warrant will be routinely forthcoming in the overwhelming majority of cases.".

Finally, the search of a paper bag intrudes far less on individual privacy than does the incursion sanctioned long ago in *Carroll*. In that case, prohibition agents slashed the upholstery of the automobile. This Court nonetheless found their search to be reasonable under the Fourth Amendment. If destroying the interior of an automobile is not unreasonable, we cannot conclude that looking inside a closed container is. In light of the minimal protection to privacy afforded by the *Chadwick-Sanders* rule, and our serious doubt whether that rule substantially serves privacy interests, we now hold that the Fourth Amendment does not compel separate treatment for an automobile search that extends only to a container within the vehicle.

The *Chadwick-Sanders* rule not only has failed to protect privacy but also has confused courts and police officers and impeded effective law enforcement. The discrepancy between the two rules has led to confusion for law enforcement officers. For example, when an officer, who has developed probable cause to believe that a vehicle contains drugs, begins to search the vehicle and immediately discovers a closed container, which rule applies? Defendant will argue that the fact that the officer first chose to search the container indicates that his probable cause extended only to the container and that *Chadwick* and *Sanders* therefore require a warrant. On the other hand, the fact that the officer first chose to search in the most obvious location should not restrict the propriety of the search. The *Chadwick* rule, as applied in *Sanders*, has devolved into an anomaly such that the more likely the police are to discover drugs in a container, the less authority they have to search it. We have noted the virtue of providing " 'clear and unequivocal' guidelines to the law enforcement profession." The *Chadwick-Sanders* rule is the antithesis of a " 'clear and unequivocal' guideline."

The *Chadwick* dissenters predicted that the container rule would have "the perverse result of allowing fortuitous circumstances to control the outcome" of various searches. The rule was so confusing that within two years after *Chadwick*, this Court found it necessary to expound on the meaning of that decision and explain its application to luggage in general. It is better to adopt one clear-cut rule to govern automobile searches and eliminate the warrant requirement for closed containers set forth in *Sanders*. The interpretation of the *Carroll* doctrine set forth in *Ross* now applies to all searches of containers found in an automobile. In other words, the police may search without a warrant if their search is supported by probable cause.

Our holding today neither extends the *Carroll* doctrine nor broadens the scope of the permissible automobile search. It remains a "cardinal principle that 'searches conducted outside the judicial process, without prior approval by judge or magistrate, are *per se* unreasonable under the Fourth Amendment—subject only to a few specifically established and well-delineated exceptions.' " We held in *Ross*: "The exception recognized in *Carroll* is unquestionably one that is 'specifically established and well delineated.' "

We therefore interpret *Carroll* as providing one rule to govern all automobile searches. The police may search an automobile and the containers within it where they have probable cause to believe contraband or evidence is contained.

JUSTICE STEVENS, with whom JUSTICE MARSHALL joins, dissenting.

In *Chadwick*, we held that the privacy interest in luggage is "substantially greater than in an automobile." Indeed, luggage is specifically intended to safeguard the privacy of personal effects, unlike an automobile, "whose primary function is transportation." We then held that the mobility of luggage did not justify creating an additional exception to the Warrant Clause. Unlike an automobile, luggage can easily be seized and detained pending judicial approval of a search. Once the police have luggage "under their exclusive control, there is not the slightest danger that the luggage or its contents could be removed before a valid search warrant could be obtained. It is unreasonable to undertake the additional and greater intrusion of a search without a warrant".

To the extent there was any "anomaly" in our prior jurisprudence, the Court has "cured" it at the expense of creating a more serious paradox. Surely it is anomalous to prohibit a search of a briefcase while the owner is carrying it exposed on a public street yet to permit a search once the owner has placed the briefcase in the locked trunk of his car. One's privacy interest in one's luggage can certainly not be diminished by one's removing it from a public thoroughfare and placing it—out of sight—in a privately owned vehicle. Nor is the danger that evidence will escape increased if the luggage is in a car rather than on the street. In either location, if the police have probable cause, they are authorized to seize the luggage and to detain it until they obtain judicial approval for a search. Even if the warrant requirement does inconvenience the police to some extent, that fact does not distinguish this constitutional requirement from any other procedural protection secured by the Bill of Rights. It is merely a part of the price that our society must pay in order to preserve its freedom.

Hypo 1: *Scope of the Automobile Exception*

Does the automobile exception authorize a broad search? Does the answer to this question depend on the circumstances? Assume that the police have probable cause to believe that a suspect is carrying drugs: a) in his glove compartment; b) in the trunk of his car; c) in the left front wheel well; d) in the engine compartment; e) somewhere in the vehicle. Where may the police search in each of these situations?

Food for Thought

Suppose that the police have probable cause to believe that a woman in this criminal procedure class is carrying heroin in her purse. Absent exigent circumstances, may the police make a warrantless search of the purse when the woman is outside her vehicle? Does the situation change when she enters the vehicle with the purse?

Hypo 2: *The Marijuana Odor*

Just before midnight, Trooper Larsen notices that a vehicle driven by Tibbles has a defective taillight. When he approaches the car, he detects a strong marijuana odor. Although Tibbles produces a valid driver's license, he cannot find his vehicle registration. The trooper then informs Tibbles that he can smell marijuana and Tibbles replies that he does not have any in his possession. The trooper than asks Tibbles to step out of the car and searches him. The trooper does not find either marijuana or drug paraphernalia. Does the officer have probable cause to search the vehicle? *See State v. Tibbles*, 169 Wash.2d 364, 236 P.3d 885 (En Banc 2010).

5. Inventory Exception

The Court has also created an "inventory" exception to the warrant requirement. Inventory searches commonly occurs when the police impound a vehicle. The following case is illustrative.

Colorado v. Bertine

479 U.S. 367 (1987).

CHIEF JUSTICE REHNQUIST delivered the opinion of the Court.

A police officer in Boulder, Colorado, arrested respondent Steven Bertine for driving while under the influence of alcohol. After Bertine was taken into custody and before the arrival of a tow truck to take Bertine's van to an impoundment lot,[1] a backup officer inventoried the contents of the van. The officer opened a closed backpack in which he found controlled substances, cocaine paraphernalia, and a large amount of cash. Bertine was subsequently charged with driving while under the influence of alcohol, unlawful possession of cocaine with intent to dispense, sell, and distribute, and unlawful possession of methaqualone. We are asked to decide whether the Fourth Amendment prohibits the State from proving these charges with the evidence discovered during the inventory of Bertine's van. We hold that it does not.

The backup officer inventoried the van in accordance with local police procedures, which require a detailed inspection and inventory of impounded vehicles. He found the backpack directly behind the frontseat of the van. Inside the pack, the officer observed a nylon bag containing metal canisters. Opening the canisters, the officer discovered that they contained cocaine, methaqualone tablets, cocaine paraphernalia, and $700 in cash. In an outside zippered pouch of the backpack, he also found $210 in cash in a sealed envelope. After completing the inventory of the van, the officer had the van towed to an impound lot and brought the backpack, money, and contraband to the police station.

The Supreme Court of Colorado affirmed a lower court ruling granting Bertine's motion to suppress. The Colorado Supreme Court recognized that in *South Dakota v. Opperman*, 428 U.S. 364 (1976), we held inventory searches of automobiles to be consistent with the Fourth Amendment, and in *Illinois v. Lafayette*, 462 U.S. 640 (1983), we had held that the inventory search of personal effects of an arrestee at a police station was also permissible under that Amendment. The Supreme Court of Colorado felt, that our decisions holding searches of closed trunks and suitcases to

---

[1] Section 7–7–2(a)(4) of the Boulder Revised Code authorizes police officers to impound vehicles when drivers are taken into custody.

violate the Fourth Amendment, meant that *Opperman* and *Lafayette* did not govern this case. We granted certiorari.

Inventory searches are now a well-defined exception to the warrant requirement of the Fourth Amendment. An inventory search may be "reasonable" under the Fourth Amendment even though it is not conducted pursuant to a warrant based upon probable cause. In *Opperman*, this Court assessed the reasonableness of an inventory search of the glove compartment in an abandoned automobile impounded by the police. We found that inventory procedures serve to protect an owner's property while it is in the custody of the police, to insure against claims of lost, stolen, or vandalized property, and to guard the police from danger. In light of these strong governmental interests and the diminished expectation of privacy in an automobile, we upheld the search. Our cases accord deference to police caretaking procedures designed to secure and protect vehicles and their contents within police custody.

In the present case, as in *Opperman* and *Lafayette*, there was no showing that the police, who were following standardized procedures, acted in bad faith or for the sole purpose of investigation. In addition, the governmental interests justifying the inventory searches in *Opperman* and *Lafayette* are nearly the same as those which obtain here. In each case, the police were potentially responsible for the property taken into their custody. By securing the property, the police protected the property from unauthorized interference. Knowledge of the precise nature of the property helped guard against claims of theft, vandalism, or negligence. Such knowledge also helped to avert any danger to police or others that may have been posed by the property.

The Supreme Court of Colorado opined that *Lafayette* was not controlling because there was no danger of introducing contraband or weapons into a jail facility. *Lafayette*, however, did not suggest that the station-house setting of the inventory search was critical to our holding. Both in the present case and in *Lafayette*, the common governmental interests described above were served by the inventory searches.

The Supreme Court of Colorado also expressed the view that the search in this case was unreasonable because Bertine's van was towed to a secure, lighted facility and because Bertine himself could have been offered the opportunity to make other arrangements for the safekeeping of his property. But the security of the storage facility does not completely eliminate the need for inventorying; the police may still wish to protect themselves or the owners of the lot against false claims of theft or dangerous instrumentalities. While giving Bertine an opportunity to make alternative arrangements would undoubtedly have been possible, reasonable police regulations relating to inventory procedures administered in good faith satisfy the Fourth Amendment, even though courts might as a matter of hindsight be able to devise equally reasonable rules requiring a different procedure.[6]

The Supreme Court of Colorado thought it necessary to require that police, before inventorying a container, weigh the strength of the individual's privacy interest in the container against the possibility that the container might serve as a repository for dangerous or valuable items. We think that such a requirement is contrary to our decisions: "When a legitimate search is under way, and when its purpose and its limits have been precisely defined, nice distinctions between closets, drawers, and containers, in the case of a home, or between glove compartments, upholstered seats, trunks, and wrapped packages, in the case of a vehicle, must give way to the interest in the prompt and efficient completion of the task at hand." *United States v. Ross*, 456 U.S., at 821. We reaffirm these principles here: "a single familiar standard is essential to guide police officers who have only limited time and expertise to reflect on and balance the social and individual interests involved in the specific circumstances they confront." *Lafayette, supra*, 462 U.S., at 648.

Bertine argues that the inventory search of his van was unconstitutional because departmental regulations gave the police officers discretion to choose between impounding his van and parking and locking it in a public parking place. Nothing in *Opperman* or *Lafayette* prohibits the exercise of police discretion so long as that discretion is exercised according to standard criteria and on the basis of something other than suspicion of evidence of criminal activity. Here, the discretion afforded the Boulder police was exercised in light of standardized criteria, related to the feasibility and appropriateness of parking and locking a vehicle rather than impounding it.[7] There was no showing that the police chose to impound Bertine's van in order to investigate suspected criminal activity.

While both *Opperman* and *Lafayette* are distinguishable from the present case, we think that the principles enunciated in those cases govern the present one. The judgment of the Supreme Court of Colorado is therefore

Reversed.

JUSTICE BLACKMUN, with whom JUSTICE POWELL and JUSTICE O'CONNOR join, concurring.

---

[6]   The trial court found that the Police Department's procedures mandated the opening of closed containers and the listing of their contents. Our decisions have always adhered to the requirement that inventories be conducted according to standardized criteria.

[7]   Boulder Police Department procedures establish several conditions that must be met before an officer may pursue the park-and-lock alternative. For example, police may not park and lock the vehicle where there is reasonable risk of damage or vandalism to the vehicle or where the approval of the arrestee cannot be obtained. Not only do such conditions circumscribe the discretion of individual officers, but they also protect the vehicle and its contents and minimize claims of property loss.

Absence of discretion ensures that inventory searches will not be used as a purposeful and general means of discovering evidence of crime. It is permissible for police officers to open closed containers in an inventory search only if they are following standard police procedures that mandate the opening of such containers in every impounded vehicle. The Police Department's standard procedures did mandate the opening of closed containers and the listing of their contents.

JUSTICE MARSHALL, with whom JUSTICE BRENNAN joins, dissenting.

No standardized criteria limit a Boulder police officer's discretion. According to a departmental directive, after placing a driver under arrest, an officer has three options for disposing of the vehicle. First, he can allow a third party to take custody. Second, the officer or the driver (depending on the nature of the arrest) may take the car to the nearest public parking facility, lock it, and take the keys. Finally, the officer can do what was done in this case: impound the vehicle, and search and inventory its contents, including closed containers.

Under the first option, the police have no occasion to search the automobile. Under the "park and lock" option, "closed containers that give no indication of containing either valuables or a weapon may not be opened and the contents searched (*i.e.*, inventoried)." Only if the police choose the third option are they entitled to search closed containers in the vehicle. Where the vehicle is not itself evidence of a crime, as in this case, the police apparently have totally unbridled discretion as to which procedure to use. Consistent with this conclusion, Officer Reichenbach testified that such decisions were left to the discretion of the officer on the scene.

Once a Boulder police officer has made this initial discretionary decision to impound a vehicle, he is given little guidance as to which areas to search and what sort of items to inventory. The arresting officer testified as to what items would be inventoried: "That would I think be very individualistic as far as what an officer may or may not go into." These so-called procedures left the breadth of the "inventory" to the whim of the individual officer.

Inventory searches are not subject to the warrant requirement because they are conducted by the government as part of a "community caretaking" function, "totally divorced from the detection, investigation, or acquisition of evidence relating to the violation of a criminal statute." *Cady v. Dombrowski*, 413 U.S., at 441. Standardized procedures are necessary to ensure that this narrow exception is not improperly used to justify, after the fact, a warrantless investigative foray. Accordingly, to invalidate a search that is conducted without established procedures, it is not necessary to establish that the police actually acted in bad faith, or that the inventory was in fact a "pretext." Boulder's discretionary scheme is unreasonable because of the " 'grave danger' of abuse of discretion."

The Court greatly overstates the justifications for the inventory exception to the Fourth Amendment. *Opperman* relied on three governmental interests to justify the inventory search of an unlocked glove compartment in an automobile. The majority finds that "nearly the same" interests obtain in this case. The use of secure impoundment facilities effectively eliminates this concern.[6] As to false claims, "inventories are not a completely effective means of discouraging false claims, since there remains the possibility of accompanying such claims with an assertion that an item was stolen prior to the inventory or was intentionally omitted from the police records." Officer Reichenbach's inventory in this case would not have protected the police against claims lodged by respondent, false or otherwise. Indeed, the trial court's characterization of the inventory as "slip-shod" is the height of understatement. The third interest—protecting the police from potential danger—failed to receive the endorsement of a majority of the Court in *Opperman*. There is nothing in the nature of the offense for which respondent was arrested that suggests he was likely to be carrying weapons, explosives, or other dangerous items. Moreover, opening closed containers to inventory the contents can only increase the risk. "No sane individual inspects for booby-traps by simply opening the container." Thus, only the government's interest in protecting the owner's property actually justifies an inventory search of an impounded vehicle. I fail to see how preservation can even be asserted as a justification for the search in this case. The owner was "present to make other arrangements for the safekeeping of his belongings," yet the police made no attempt to ascertain whether in fact he wanted them to "safeguard" his property. Since respondent was charged with a traffic offense, he was unlikely to remain in custody for more than a few hours. He might well have been willing to leave his valuables unattended in the locked van for such a short period of time.

The Court completely ignores respondent's expectation of privacy in his backpack. Whatever his expectation of privacy in his automobile generally, our prior decisions clearly establish that he retained a reasonable expectation of privacy in the backpack and its contents. Indeed, the Boulder police officer who conducted the inventory acknowledged that backpacks commonly serve as repositories for personal effects. Thus, even if the governmental interests in this case were the same as those in *Opperman*, they would nonetheless be outweighed by respondent's comparatively greater expectation of privacy in his luggage.

---

[6] Respondent's vehicle was taken to a lighted, private storage lot with a locked 6-foot fence. The lot was patrolled by private security officers and police, and nothing had ever been stolen from a vehicle in the lot.

Point for Discussion

Departmental Policies

In *Florida v. Wells*, 495 U.S. 1 (1990), Wells was arrested for driving under the influence and his car was impounded. An inventory search at the impoundment facility revealed two marijuana cigarettes. It also turned up a locked suitcase which was found to contain a considerable quantity of marijuana. The record contained no evidence of any Highway Patrol policy on the opening of closed containers during inventory searches. The Court upheld the Florida Supreme Court's decision to exclude the evidence: "An inventory search must not be a ruse for a general rummaging in order to discover incriminating evidence. There is no reason to insist that inventory searches be conducted in a totally mechanical 'all or nothing' fashion. A police officer may be allowed latitude to determine whether a particular container should or should not be opened in light of the nature of the search and characteristics of the container itself. While policies of opening all containers or of opening no containers are unquestionably permissible, it would be equally permissible to allow the opening of closed containers whose contents officers are unable to ascertain from examining the containers' exteriors. The Florida Highway Patrol had no policy whatever with respect to the opening of closed containers encountered during an inventory search. Absent such a policy, the instant search was not sufficiently regulated to satisfy the Fourth Amendment."

Take Note

In order for an inventory search to be legal, the vehicle must have been legally impounded. Rules vary regarding the circumstances under which an impoundment is permitted. In *Cardwell v. Commonwealth*, 639 S.W.2d 549 (Ky.App.1982), defendant burglarized a home and stole guns and knives. Fleeing the scene, defendant was involved in an automobile accident and taken to a hospital. Although defendant told the police that his father would retrieve the car, the officer towed the vehicle since it protruded onto the road and constituted a hazard. Because the trunk's lock was broken, the officer searched the trunk to remove valuables and found two shotguns and a rifle marked with the name of the burglary victim. The officer then went to the victim's house where he found evidence of a break-in. When the officer returned to the car, he found one of the burglary victim's knives. Cardwell was arrested at the hospital where he later confessed to the crimes. The Court concluded that the impoundment was proper: "The vehicle was a safety hazard and had to be removed from the scene as soon as possible because of its damaged condition, its close proximity to the roadway, and its location on a curve with short visibility. These circumstances cause other motorists to be distracted, to look and gawk out of concerns for rendering aid or curiosity. It impedes traffic flow and constitutes a hazard upon the highway. The arrangement whereby his father would come from Louisville would create several hours delay while the vehicle was abandoned and exposed to the public on the roadway. The officer acted properly by ordering the impoundment and removal by a local wrecker. With the vehicle impounded and in a position to be removed from the scene, the trooper innocently discovered the fruits of the appellant's crimes. Finding the trunk lid loose, without a lock, the trooper did what we would expect a peace officer to do under like circumstances: to protect property as well as citizens. Keep in mind, appellant was not present. He was on his way to the hospital by ambulance." In *Florida v. White*, 526 U.S. 559 (1999), the police had probable cause to believe that a vehicle contained contraband. They seized the vehicle and subjected it to an inventory search. The Court held that the police do not need a warrant to seize an automobile from a public place when they have probable cause to believe that it contains forfeitable contraband.

Food for Thought

At 3:00 a.m., a police officer spots a heavily loaded car in a residential area. May the police officer pull the motorist over and inventory the contents of the car? Why? Why not?

Hypo 1: *Proof Requirements*

Do the police need either probable cause or reasonable suspicion in order to conduct an inventory search?

Food for Thought

Some state supreme courts have sometimes restricted the availability of inventory searches under their state constitutions. *Wagner v. Commonwealth*, 581 S.W.2d 352 (Ky. 1979). Shortly after the rape, the police apprehended Wagner and allowed him to lock and secure his car. However, when the victim pointed to her scarves and a spot of blood on the seat which she said was her blood. the police took Wagner to police headquarters for questioning and impounded his car. After Wagner was formally arrested, the police conducted an "inventory" search of his car "looking for evidence." The Kentucky Supreme Court invalidated the impoundment and the inventory search:

> "A vehicle may be impounded without a warrant in only four situations: 1) The owner or permissive user consents to the impoundment; 2)The vehicle, if not removed, constitutes a danger to other persons or property or the public safety[23] and the owner or permissive user cannot reasonably arrange for alternate means of removal; 3) The police have probable cause to believe both that the vehicle constitutes an instrumentality or fruit of a crime and that absent immediate impoundment the vehicle will be removed by a third party; or 4) The police have probable cause to believe that the vehicle contains evidence of a crime and that absent immediate impoundment the evidence will be lost or destroyed. So long as the only potential danger that might ensue from non-impoundment is danger to the safety of the vehicle and its contents no public interest exists to justify

---

[23]   An illegally parked vehicle would constitute a danger to public safety under this exception to the warrant requirement and could be impounded.

impoundment of the vehicle without the consent of its owner or permissive user. The driver, even though in police custody, is competent to decide whether to park the vehicle in a "bad" neighborhood and risk damage through vandalism or allow the police to take custody. Only when the vehicle if not removed poses a danger to other persons, property or the public safety does there exist a public interest to justify impoundment if the owner or permissive user is unable to reasonably arrange for a third party to provide for the vehicle's removal. Mere legal custody of an automobile by law enforcement officials does not automatically create a right to rummage about its interior. A routine police inventory of the contents of an impounded vehicle constitutes a substantial invasion of the zone of privacy of its owner or permissive user. It is an invasion additional to the intrusion upon his privacy interests occasioned by the impoundment itself. Such an inventory is impermissible unless the owner or permissive user consents or substantial necessities grounded upon public safety justify the search. If a vehicle is legally impounded and its owner or permissive user is present or otherwise known at the time the vehicle is seized no such need is ordinarily manifest. If the owner or permissive user does not consent to the routine inventory he will assume the risk that items obtained in the vehicle will be lost or stolen. The police merely lock up the vehicle and leave it in place until the owner or permissive user makes suitable arrangements for its removal. Concomitant with this right to prevent a routine inventory is the owner's or permissive user's right to have a representative present during any inventory that is authorized and his right to limit the inventory to only specific portions of the vehicle. If the police have probable cause, they can prevent the removal of the vehicle until a reasonable time has elapsed in which a warrant can be secured. Because the vehicle is in police custody there is no danger that any evidence it contains will be lost or stolen and hence no necessity to depart from the warrant requirement. If a warrant cannot be obtained no inventory can be undertaken unless the owner or permissive user consents. In this case the owner-driver of the seized vehicle was at police headquarters at the time of impoundment. Because neither a search warrant nor his consent was obtained prior rummaging through the interior of the car constituted an illegal search even though the car had been lawfully impounded. The evidence will be suppressed."

Wagner was overruled in *Cobb v. Commonwealth*, 509 S.W.3d 705 (Ky. 2017) (Kentucky law is no more expansive than federal law) In *Commonwealth v. Lagenella*, 83 A.3d 94 (Pa. 2013), the Pennsylvania Supreme Court interpreted Pennsylvania law as providing that a car that has been left legally parked following an arrest may not be impounded and inventoried when it does not present a danger to efficient or safe traffic flow or otherwise endanger the public. Are these state court approaches preferable?

Hypo 2: *The Permissibility of Impoundment*

Defendant is stopped for "reckless" driving after police officers observe him speeding and weaving in and out of traffic. Defendant pulls into a legal parking spot. A police officer decides to arrest him. May the police tow defendant's car to a police impoundment lot and conduct an inventory search? Should it matter whether the city or the police department have a policy on whether, and when, vehicles should be impounded and towed to impoundment lots? *See Baxter v. State*, 238 P.3d 934 (Okla. Crim. App. 2010).

Hypo 3: *Departmental Policies*

Ford was arrested and jailed for driving on a suspended driver's license. Since Ford's vehicle was obstructing traffic, the police officer called a tow truck to remove it. In conformity with departmental "policy," the officer conducted an inventory search of the vehicle before releasing it to the tow truck driver. The search yielded a sawed-off shotgun with a barrel length of 9 ½ inches and an overall length of 17 ½ inches. Subsequent investigation revealed that the weapon was not registered, and Ford was charged with violating the National Firearms Act. Ford challenges the inventory search on the basis that it was "a guise to justify a criminal investigatory search." Ford points to the fact that the department has no written policies regarding inventory searches, but rather only "customary" policies. Must a departmental policy be in writing to satisfy *Bertine*? On behalf of Ford, how can you argue that the policy must be in writing? How might the state respond? *See United States v. Ford*, 986 F.2d 57 (4th Cir.1993); *Clark v. Commonwealth*, 868 S.W.2d 101 (Ky.App.1993).

Hypo 4: *More on Impoundment*

A drug store is robbed of money and restricted drugs. The next morning, two police officers see an automobile make a quick turn at an intersection and proceed in the opposite direction. The officers follow the car which speeds up and disappears. Shortly thereafter the officers see Helm walking and stop him. After learning Helm's name, the officers ask him about the location of the car that he was driving. Helm replies, "What car?" After the police run a computer check and learn that there is an outstanding warrant for Helm's arrest, they arrest him and take him to jail where a search reveals a car key. Afterwards, the officers return to the area and find a 1978 silver Monte Carlo with a warm motor less than a block from the place of arrest. The key operates the ignition. Clothing and paraphernalia are observed lying in the back seat. The officers tow the vehicle for "safekeeping" based on police policy, as well as because it was in a high crime area. The officers search the trunk, which does not have a lock, and find a paper bag containing money and bottles of restricted drugs from the recently robbed drug store. Was the vehicle properly impounded? *See Helm v. Commonwealth*, 813 S.W.2d 816 (1991).

> ## Hypo 5: *Inventorying the Locked Bag*
>
> A police officer finds Vanya trespassing on school property and arrests him. As part of his standard procedure, the officer frisks the boy before placing him in the cruiser. During the frisk, the officer uncovers a 4 inch by 5 inch hard item, with a 90 degree angle, in the small of the boy's back. The boy reacts hostilely when the officer touches it. The object turns out to be a locked bag. The officer eventually opens the bag and finds money and marijuana. The police department's inventory policy provides, "Any container or article found on an arrestee's person or carried by him shall be opened and its contents inventoried." The juvenile argues that the policy is impermissibly vague because it "is silent with respect to locked containers versus closed containers." Was it permissible for the police to open the locked container? Does it matter whether they found a key to the bag, or whether they were forced to damage the bag in order to open it? *See Commonwealth v. Vanya V.*, 75 Mass. App. Ct. 370, 914 N.E.2d 339 (2009).

6. Consent

The consent exception is not really an "exception" to the warrant requirement. Any constitutional right can be waived, and citizens can waive their Fourth Amendment right to be free from governmental searches and seizures. Courts have struggled to determine what constitutes "consent."

Schneckloth v. Bustamonte

412 U.S. 218 (1973).

MR. JUSTICE STEWART delivered the opinion of the Court.

While on routine patrol at approximately 2:40 in the morning, Police Officer James Rand stopped an automobile when he observed that one headlight and its license plate light were burned out. Six men were in the vehicle. Joe Alcala and respondent, Robert Bustamonte, were in the front seat with Joe Gonzales, the driver. Three older men were seated in the rear. When Gonzales could not produce a driver's license, Rand asked if any of the other five had identification. Only Alcala produced a license, and he explained that the car was his brother's. After the six occupants had stepped out of the car at the officer's request and after two additional policemen arrived, Officer Rand asked Alcala if he could search the car. Alcala replied, "Sure, go ahead." Prior to the search no one was threatened with arrest and, according to Officer Rand's uncontradicted testimony, it "was all very congenial at this time." Gonzales testified that Alcala actually helped in the search of the car, by opening the trunk and glove compartment. In Gonzales' words: "The officer asked Joe (Alcala), 'Does the trunk open?' And Joe said, 'Yes.' He went to the car and got the keys and opened up the trunk." Wadded under the left rear seat, the police officers found three checks that had been stolen from a car wash. The trial judge denied the motion to suppress, and the checks were admitted at Bustamonte's trial. He was convicted.

A search authorized by consent is wholly valid but the State has the burden of proving that the consent was, in fact, freely and voluntarily given. *Bumper v. North Carolina*, 391 U.S. 543, 548. The precise question is what must the prosecution prove to demonstrate that a consent was "voluntarily" given. The most extensive exposition of the meaning of "voluntariness" has been developed in those cases in which the Court has had to determine the "voluntariness" of a defendant's confession for purposes of the Fourteenth Amendment. The significant fact about [those] decisions is that none turned on the presence or absence of a single controlling criterion; each reflected a careful scrutiny of the surrounding circumstances. In none of them did the Court rule that the Due Process Clause required the prosecution to prove as part of its initial burden that the defendant knew he had a right to refuse to answer the questions. While the state of the accused's mind, and the failure of the police to advise the accused of his rights, were certainly factors to be evaluated in assessing the "voluntariness" of an accused's responses, they were not in and of themselves determinative.

The question whether a consent to a search was in fact "voluntary" or was the product of duress or coercion, express or implied, is a question of fact to be determined from the totality of the circumstances. While knowledge of the right to refuse consent is one factor to be taken into account, the government need not establish such knowledge as the *sine qua non* of an effective consent. As with police questioning, two competing concerns must be accommodated in determining the meaning of a "voluntary" consent—the legitimate need for such searches and the equally important requirement of assuring the absence of coercion.

In situations where the police have some evidence of illicit activity, but lack probable cause to arrest or search, a search authorized by a valid consent may be the only means of obtaining important and reliable evidence. In the present case, while the police had reason to stop the car for traffic violations, the State does not contend that there was probable cause to search the vehicle or that the search was incident to a valid arrest of any of the occupants. Yet, the search yielded tangible evidence that served as a basis for a prosecution, and provided some assurance that others, wholly innocent of the crime, were not mistakenly brought to trial. In those cases where there is probable cause to arrest or search, but where the police lack a warrant, a consent search may still be valuable. If the search is conducted and proves fruitless, that in itself may convince the police that an arrest with its possible stigma and embarrassment is unnecessary, or that a far more extensive search pursuant to a warrant is not justified.

In short, a search pursuant to consent may result in considerably less inconvenience for the subject of the search, and, properly conducted, is a constitutionally permissible and wholly legitimate aspect of effective police activity.

But the Fourth and Fourteenth Amendments require that a consent not be coerced, by explicit or implicit means, by implied threat or covert force. No matter how subtly the coercion was applied, the resulting "consent" would be no more than a pretext for the unjustified police intrusion against which the Fourth Amendment is directed. The problem of reconciling the recognized legitimacy of consent searches with the requirement that they be free from any aspect of official coercion cannot be resolved by any infallible touchstone. To approve such searches without the most careful scrutiny would sanction the possibility of official coercion; to place artificial restrictions upon such searches would jeopardize their basic validity. Just as with confessions, the requirement of a "voluntary" consent reflects a fair accommodation of the constitutional requirements involved. In examining all the surrounding circumstances to determine if in fact the consent to search was coerced, account must be taken of subtly coercive police questions, as well as the possibly vulnerable subjective state of the person who consents. Those searches that are the product of police coercion can thus be filtered out without undermining the continuing validity of consent searches. In sum, there is no reason for us to depart in the area of consent searches, from the traditional definition of "voluntariness."

The approach of the Court of Appeals, that the State must affirmatively prove that the subject of the search knew that he had a right to refuse consent, would, in practice, create serious doubt whether consent searches could be conducted. There might be rare cases where it could be proved that a person in fact affirmatively knew of his right to refuse—such as where he announced to the police that if he didn't sign the consent form, "you police are going to get a search warrant;" or a case where by prior experience and training a person had clearly and convincingly demonstrated such knowledge. More commonly where there was no evidence of any coercion, explicit or implicit, the prosecution would be unable to demonstrate that the subject of the search in fact had known of his right to refuse consent. The very object of the inquiry—the nature of a person's subjective understanding—underlines the difficulty of the prosecution's burden. Any defendant who was the subject of a search authorized solely by his consent could effectively frustrate the introduction into evidence of the fruits of that search by simply failing to testify that he in fact knew he could refuse to consent. The near impossibility of meeting this prosecutorial burden suggests why this Court has never accepted any such litmus-paper test of voluntariness.

One alternative that would go far toward proving that the subject of a search did know he had a right to refuse consent would be to advise him of that right before eliciting his consent. That suggestion has been almost universally repudiated by both federal and state courts. It would be thoroughly impractical to impose on the normal consent search the detailed requirements of an effective warning. Consent searches are part of the standard investigatory techniques of law enforcement agencies. They normally occur on the highway, or in a person's home or office, and under informal and unstructured conditions. The circumstances that prompt the initial request to search may develop quickly or be a logical extension of investigative police questioning. The police may seek to investigate further suspicious circumstances or to follow up leads developed in questioning persons at the scene of a crime. These situations are a far cry from the structured atmosphere of a trial where, assisted by counsel, a defendant is informed of his trial rights. While surely a closer question, these situations are still immeasurably, far removed from "custodial interrogation" where, in *Miranda v. Arizona*, we found that the Constitution required certain now familiar warnings as a prerequisite to police interrogation. Consequently, we cannot accept the position that proof of knowledge of the right to refuse consent is a necessary prerequisite to demonstrating a "voluntary" consent. Rather it is only by analyzing all the circumstances of an individual consent that it can be ascertained whether in fact it was voluntary or coerced. It is this careful sifting of the unique facts and circumstances of each case that is evidenced in our prior decisions involving consent searches.

It is argued that to establish a "waiver" the State must demonstrate "an intentional relinquishment or abandonment of a known right or privilege." Our cases do not reflect an uncritical demand for a knowing and intelligent waiver in every situation where a person has failed to invoke a constitutional protection. Almost without exception, the requirement of a knowing and intelligent waiver has been applied only to those rights which the Constitution guarantees to a criminal defendant in order to preserve a fair trial. Hence, the standard of a knowing and intelligent waiver has most often been applied to test the validity of a waiver of counsel, either at trial, or upon a guilty plea. The Court has also applied the criteria to assess the effectiveness of a waiver of other trial rights such as the right to confrontation, to a jury trial, and to a speedy trial, and the right to be free from twice being placed in jeopardy. Guilty pleas have been carefully scrutinized to determine whether the accused knew and understood all the rights to which he would be entitled at trial, and that he had intentionally chosen to forgo them. The Court has evaluated the knowing and intelligent nature of the waiver of trial rights in trial-type situations, such as the waiver of the privilege against compulsory self-incrimination before an administrative agency or a congressional committee, or the waiver of counsel in a juvenile proceeding. The guarantees afforded a criminal defendant at trial also protect him at certain stages before the actual trial, and any alleged waiver must meet the strict standard of an intentional relinquishment of a "known" right. But the "trial" guarantees that have been applied to the "pretrial" stage of the criminal process are similarly designed to protect the fairness of the trial itself.

There is a vast difference between those rights that protect a fair criminal trial and the rights guaranteed under the Fourth Amendment. Nothing, either in the purposes behind requiring a "knowing" and "intelligent" waiver of trial rights, or in the practical application of such a requirement suggests that it ought to be extended to the constitutional guarantee against unreasonable searches and seizures. A strict standard of waiver has been applied to those rights guaranteed to a criminal defendant to insure that he will be accorded the greatest possible opportunity to utilize every facet of the constitutional model of a fair criminal trial. Any trial conducted in derogation of that model leaves open the possibility that the trial reached an unfair result precisely because all the protections specified in the Constitution were not provided. A prime example is the right to counsel. Without that right, a wholly innocent accused faces the real and substantial danger that simply because of his lack of legal expertise he may be convicted. The Constitution requires that every effort be made to see to it that a defendant in a criminal case has not unknowingly relinquished the basic protections that the Framers thought indispensable to a fair trial. The protections of the Fourth Amendment are of a wholly different order, and have nothing whatever to do with promoting the fair ascertainment of truth at a criminal trial. Rather, as Mr. Justice Frankfurter put it in *Wolf v. Colorado*, 338 U.S. 25, 27, the Fourth Amendment protects the "security of one's privacy against arbitrary intrusion by the police." Nor can it be said that a search, as opposed to an eventual trial, is somehow "unfair" if a person consents to a search. While the Fourth and Fourteenth Amendments limit the circumstances under which the police can conduct a search, there is nothing constitutionally suspect in a person's voluntarily allowing a search. The actual conduct of the search may be precisely the same as if the police had obtained a warrant. Unlike those constitutional guarantees that protect a defendant at trial, it cannot be said every reasonable presumption ought to be indulged against voluntary relinquishment. The community has a real interest in encouraging consent, for the resulting search may yield necessary evidence for the solution and prosecution of crime, evidence that may insure that a wholly innocent person is not wrongly charged with a criminal offense.

It would be next to impossible to apply to a consent search the standard of "an intentional relinquishment or abandonment of a known right or privilege." There must be examination into the knowing and understanding nature of the waiver, an examination that was designed for a trial judge in the structured atmosphere of a courtroom. It would be unrealistic to expect that in the informal, unstructured context of a consent search, a policeman, upon pain of tainting the evidence, could make the detailed type of examination demanded. If a diluted form of "waiver" were found acceptable, that would itself be ample recognition of the fact that there is no universal standard that must be applied in every situation where a person forgoes a constitutional right.[11] In short, there is nothing in the purposes or application of the waiver requirements of *Johnson v. Zerbst* that justifies, much less compels, the easy equation of a knowing waiver with a consent search. To make such an equation is to generalize from the broad rhetoric of some of our decisions, and to ignore the substance of the differing constitutional guarantees.

Much of what has already been said disposes of the argument that *Miranda* requires the conclusion that knowledge of a right to refuse is an indispensable element of a valid consent. In *Miranda* the Court found that the techniques of police questioning and the nature of custodial surroundings produce an inherently coercive situation. The Court concluded that "unless adequate protective devices are employed to dispel the compulsion inherent in custodial surroundings, no statement obtained from the defendant can truly be the product of his free choice." At another point the Court noted that "without proper safeguards the process of in-custody interrogation of persons suspected or accused of crime contains inherently compelling pressures which work to undermine the individual's will to resist and to compel him to speak where he would not otherwise do so freely."

In this case, there is no evidence of any inherently coercive tactics—either from the nature of the police questioning or the environment in which it took place. Indeed, since consent searches will normally occur on a person's own familiar territory, the specter of incommunicado police interrogation in some remote station house is simply inapposite. There is no reason to believe, under

Take Note

In *Florida v. Jimeno*, 500 U.S. 248 (1991), believing that respondent was carrying narcotics, a police officer asked for permission to search his car. Respondent consented, stating that he had nothing to hide. The officer found a folded brown paper bag containing a kilogram of cocaine on the floorboard. While the trial court held that the consent did not extend to the paper bag, the Court reversed: "Respondent granted Officer Trujillo permission to search his car, and did not place any explicit limitation on the scope of the search. It was objectively reasonable for the police to conclude that the general consent to search included consent to search containers within that car which might bear drugs including the paper bag lying on the car's floor." Justice Marshall dissented: "An individual has a heightened expectation of privacy in the contents of a closed container. It follows that an individual's consent to a search of the interior of his car cannot necessarily be understood as extending to containers in the car."

---

[11] Even a limited view of the demands of "an intentional relinquishment or abandonment of a known right or privilege" standard would inevitably lead to a requirement of detailed warnings before any consent search—a requirement all but universally rejected. As the Court stated in *Miranda* with respect to the privilege against compulsory self-incrimination: "We will not pause to inquire in individual cases whether the defendant was aware of his rights without a warning being given. Assessments of the knowledge the defendant possessed, based on information as to his age, education, intelligence, or prior contact with authorities, can never be more than speculation; a warning is a clear-cut fact." *Miranda v. Arizona,* 384 U.S., at 468.

circumstances such as are present here, that the response to a policeman's question is presumptively coerced; and there is, therefore, no reason to reject the traditional test for determining the voluntariness of a person's response. *Miranda*, of course, did not reach investigative questioning of a person not in custody, which is most directly analogous to the situation of a consent search, and it assuredly did not indicate that such questioning ought to be deemed inherently coercive.

It is also argued that the failure to require the Government to establish knowledge as a prerequisite to a valid consent, will relegate the Fourth Amendment to the special province of "the sophisticated versus the knowledgeable and the privileged." We cannot agree. The traditional definition of voluntariness has always taken into account evidence of minimal schooling, low intelligence, and the lack of any effective warnings to a person of his rights; and the voluntariness of any statement taken under those conditions has been carefully scrutinized to determine whether it was in fact voluntarily given.

We hold only that when the subject of a search is not in custody and the State attempts to justify a search on the basis of his consent, the Fourth and Fourteenth Amendments require that it demonstrate that the consent was in fact voluntarily given, and not the result of duress or coercion, express or implied. Voluntariness is a question of fact to be determined from all the circumstances, and while the subject's knowledge of a right to refuse is a factor to be taken into account, the prosecution is not required to demonstrate such knowledge as a prerequisite to establishing a voluntary consent.

The judgment must be *reversed.*

MR. JUSTICE BRENNAN, dissenting.

It wholly escapes me how our citizens can meaningfully be said to have waived something as precious as a constitutional guarantee without ever being aware of its existence. The Court's conclusion is supported neither by "linguistics," nor by "epistemology," nor by "common sense."

MR. JUSTICE MARSHALL, dissenting.

This Court has always scrutinized with great care claims that a person has foregone the opportunity to assert constitutional rights. Consent searches are permitted, not because such an exception to the requirements of probable cause and warrant is essential to proper law enforcement, but because we permit our citizens to choose whether or not they wish to exercise their constitutional rights. Our prior decisions simply do not support the view that a meaningful choice has been made solely because no coercion was brought to bear on the subject. I am at a loss to understand why consent "cannot be taken literally to mean a 'knowing' choice." I have difficulty comprehending how a decision made without knowledge of available alternatives can be treated as a choice at all.

If consent to search means that a person has chosen to forgo his right to exclude the police from the place they seek to search, it follows that his consent cannot be considered a meaningful choice unless he knew that he could in fact exclude the police. I can think of no other situation in which we would say that a person agreed to some course of action if he did not know that there was some other course he might have pursued. I would therefore hold that the prosecution may not rely on a purported consent to search if the subject of the search did not know that he could refuse to give consent.

Must the Government show that the subject knew of his rights, or must the subject show that he lacked such knowledge? Any fair allocation of the burden would require that it be placed on the prosecution. If the burden is placed on the defendant, all the subject can do is to testify that he did not know of his rights. I doubt that many trial judges will find for the defendant on the basis of that testimony. Precisely because the evidence is very hard to come by, courts have traditionally been reluctant to require a party to prove negatives such as the lack of knowledge. There are several ways by which the subject's knowledge of his rights may be shown. The subject may affirmatively demonstrate such knowledge by his responses at the time the search took place. Where the person giving consent is someone other than the defendant, the prosecution may require him to testify under oath. Denials of knowledge may be disproved by establishing that the subject had, in the recent past, demonstrated his knowledge of his rights, for example, by refusing entry when it was requested by the police. The prior experience or training of the subject might in some cases support an inference that he knew of his right to exclude the police.

The burden on the prosecutor would disappear, of course, if the police, at the time they requested consent to search, also told the subject that he had a right to refuse consent and that his decision to refuse would be respected. The Court contends that if an officer paused to inform the subject of his rights, the informality of the exchange would be destroyed. I doubt that a simple statement by an officer of an individual's right to refuse consent would do much except to alert the subject to a fact that he surely is entitled to know. For many years the agents of the Federal Bureau of Investigation have routinely informed subjects of their right to refuse when they request consent to search. Nothing disastrous would happen if the police, before requesting consent, informed the subject that he had a right to refuse consent and that his refusal would be respected. When the Court speaks of practicality, it really is talking of is the continued ability of the police to capitalize on the ignorance of citizens so as to accomplish by subterfuge what they could not achieve by relying only on the knowing relinquishment of constitutional rights.

"Under many circumstances a reasonable person might read an officer's 'May I' as the courteous expression of a demand backed by force of law." Consent is ordinarily given as acquiescence in an implicit claim of authority to search. Permitting searches in such circumstances, without any assurance that the subject knew that, by his consent, he was relinquishing his constitutional rights, is something that I cannot believe is sanctioned by the Constitution.

Point for Discussion

Duty to Advise

In *Ohio v. Robinette*, 519 U.S. 33 (1996), Robinette was lawfully stopped for speeding on an interstate highway and given a verbal warning. The officer asked Robinette whether he was carrying contraband. When Robinette answered in the negative, the officer asked for and obtained permission to search Robinette's car. The search revealed a small amount of marijuana and a contraband pill. The Court held that the officer was not required to tell Robinette that he was "free to go" before asking for consent to search the vehicle: "The Fourth Amendment test for a valid consent to search is that the consent be voluntary, and 'voluntariness is a question of fact to be determined from all the circumstances.' " Justice Stevens dissented: "When the officer had completed his task of either arresting or reprimanding the driver of the speeding car, his continued detention of that person constituted an illegal seizure. Because Robinette's consent to the search was the product of an unlawful detention, 'the consent was tainted by the illegality and was ineffective to justify the search.' " In Stevens' view, had the officer told Robinette that he was "free to go", this warning would have terminated the seizure and rendered the consent valid.

Food for Thought

In *State v. Johnson*, 68 N.J. 349, 346 A.2d 66 (1975), the New Jersey Supreme Court rejected *Schneckloth*'s holding in interpreting the New Jersey Constitution. The New Jersey Constitution's language tracks that of the Fourth Amendment, but the court construed it differently: "Many persons, perhaps most, would view the request of a police officer to make a search as having the force of law. Unless it is shown that the person knew that he had the right to refuse to accede to such a request, his assenting to the search is not meaningful. One cannot be held to have waived a right if he was unaware of its existence. However, in a non-custodial situation, such as here, the police would not necessarily be required to advise the person of his right to refuse to consent to the search." Does the New Jersey Supreme Court's holding in *Johnson* represent a preferable interpretation to the United States Supreme Court's holding in *Schneckloth*? *See also State v. Carty*, 170 N.J. 632, 790 A.2d 903 (2002), in which the New Jersey Supreme Court held that the police must have a "reasonable suspicion of criminal activity" before seeking a motorist's consent to search, and must also specifically inform the motorist of his right to refuse the consent. Is such a rule desirable? Should the police be required to have a "reasonable suspicion of criminal activity," or for that matter "probable cause," before requesting consent to search? In *State*

v. *Budd*, 185 Wash.2d 566, 374 P.3d 137 (En banc, 2016), the Washington Supreme Court held that, when police execute a "knock and talk" at a suspect's house, and request permission to search the house, they are required to advise the suspect of his/her right to refuse consent.

Hypo 1: *What Constitutes Consent?*

A narcotics detective receives a tip from a known narcotics user that unknown persons are smoking opium in the Europe Hotel. At the hotel, the detective smells a strong opium odor coming from Room #1. The officer knocks on the door and a voice inside asks who is there. "Lieutenant Belland" is the reply. There is a slight delay, some "shuffling or noise" in the room and then defendant opens the door. The officer says, "I want to talk to you." She then "steps back acquiescently and admits" him. The officer then says, "I want to talk to you about the opium smell in this room." She denies that there is such a smell. Then he says, "I want you to consider yourself under arrest because we are going to search the room." The search turns up opium and a smoking apparatus, the latter being warm from recent use. Did defendant "consent" to the officers entry and search? Based on *Schneckloth*, how might defendant argue that she did not consent? How might the prosecution respond? *See Johnson v. United States*, 333 U.S. 10 (1948).

Hypo 2: *Police Misrepresentations & Consent*

Petitioner lived with his grandmother, a 66-year-old widowed black woman, in a house located in a rural area at the end of an isolated road. Four white law enforcement officers go to the house and find the grandmother there with young children. One of the officers says "I have a warrant to search your house." The grandmother responds, "Go ahead," and opens the door. In the kitchen, the officers find a rifle that is later used as evidence against petitioner. Did the grandmother consent? Should it matter that the officers did not have a warrant? Would it matter whether the police had probable cause to obtain a warrant? Should it matter how the grandmother responded? Suppose that she had stated: a) "You don't need a warrant. I'd be happy to let you search"; b) "Well, if you have a warrant, I guess I'll have to let you search"; c) "I have no objection to you searching my house. You can look in any room or drawer in my house that you desire." In which of these situations does a valid consent exist? *See Bumper v. State of North Carolina*, 391 U.S. 543 (1968).

Food for Thought

Police discover "a little weed" on Pitts. At the time, Pitts is under arrest outside of his sister's house where he lives. Following the arrest, the police ask the sister for permission to search the house, explaining that she has the right to refuse consent. However, they also tell her that they will seek a warrant if she refuses to give consent, and will leave an officer to secure the house while the warrant is obtained. The sister, fearful that her son will return home and see the police, consents to the search. Was the consent coerced? *See State v. Pitts*, 978 A.2d 14, 2009 Vt. 51.

Hypo 3: *The Nature of the Misrepresentation*

Suppose that an undercover narcotics agent, after misrepresenting himself as a drug purchaser, is invited into John Preston's home to make a purchase. After the deal is consummated, the agent arrests Preston. At Preston's trial, the prosecution seeks to admit the purchase. Preston moves to suppress claiming that, because he did not realize that the agent was with law enforcement, his consent was not valid. Should the motion be granted? *See Lewis v. United States*, 385 U.S. 206 (1966).

Hypo 4: *More on the Nature of the Misrepresentation*

A detective receives a tip that defendant purchased child pornography over the internet. The detective speaks to defendant's credit card company and is informed that there is a disputed charge on defendant's account, that the account was closed, and that a new card was issued. The detective obtains defendant's new credit card number and computer screen name, and goes to defendant's residence under the guise of interviewing him about "possible fraudulent charges on his credit card." Defendant provides his credit card number to the detective who sees that it matches the one used to subscribe to a kiddie porn web site. The detective then asks defendant for permission to search his computer in regard to the fraudulent credit card charges. Defendant consents, and the detective inserts a forensic preview program into the computer and begins searching for kiddie porn rather than for fraudulent credit card charges. Was the consent to search valid when defendant was misled regarding the purpose of the search? *See People v. Prinzing*, 233 Ill.2d 587, 335 Ill.Dec. 643, 907 N.E.2d 87 (Ill. 2009).

Hypo 5: *The Scope of Consent*

Police stops defendant's vehicle for "excessively tinted" windows. When the officer notices fresh undercoating on the car, he asks for and obtains permission to search. When the officer pulls up some non-factory carpeting on the floor, and notices a small hole in the floorboard, the officer takes a crowbar and pries open the gas tank where he finds cocaine. Did defendant's consent justify the officer's use of the crowbar? Does it matter that the car was returned to defendant in a "materially different" condition that affected its "structural integrity?" Was the officer required to obtain additional permission before using the crowbar? *See People v. Gomez*, 5 N.Y.3d 416, 805 N.Y.S.2d 24, 838 N.E.2d 1271 (2005).

Food for Thought

Police stop a suspect because he is playing music too loudly. Aware that the suspect had previously been charged with narcotics offenses, the officer asked for permission to search the vehicle. The suspect consented. After the police searched the passenger compartment, but did not find anything incriminating, they decide to search under the hood of the car, and in particular to remove the air filter. Inside the filter, they find two guns. Did the suspect's permission to search the vehicle extend to the inside of the air filter? Does it matter that the suspect was present, but did not object when the police searched under the hood? *See Commonwealth v. Ortiz*, 478 Mass. 820, 90 N.E.3d 735 (Mass. 2018).

Hypo 6: *More on the Scope of Consent*

Suppose that a police officer stops a car for speeding. The officer asks for and obtains permission to search the vehicle. During the search, the officer finds a gift-wrapped box in the trunk. Is the officer required to obtain additional consent before opening the box? *See State v. Howell*, 284 Neb. 559, 822 N.W.2d 391 (2012). Likewise, suppose that the police are investigating the disappearance of a man's live-in girlfriend, and ask her boyfriend for permission to enter and "look around" their house. In the house, they find the keys to the girlfriend's car. Does the consent to "look around" include the right to open the car trunk (where the girlfriend's dead body was found)? *See State v. Bruce*, 412 S.C. 504, 772 S.E.2d 753 (S.C. 2015).

Hypo 7: *"Knock and Talk" Consent*

An informant tells police that Lucas (a 25-year-old college graduate) is growing marijuana in his home. Two plain clothes detectives visit Lucas to conduct a "knock and talk." When Lucas opens the door, they identify themselves as detectives, and Lucas invites them into the house where they smell burnt marijuana. One detective tells Lucas that he has heard there is marijuana in the house and that he will only write a citation if Lucas possesses drug paraphernalia or no more than a small amount of marijuana for personal use. The other detective notices a marijuana pipe on a shelf in plain view and asks if Lucas has any similar items. Lucas produces a box containing rolling papers, marijuana pipes, and marijuana residue, but denies that he has other drug-related items. The tone of this exchange is conversational, the detectives do not threaten arrest, and the detectives do not draw their weapons. After more police arrive, one detective asks Lucas to sign a consent form to allow a search of his house. The detective explains that probable cause exists to obtain a search warrant based on the marijuana pipe that was found in plain view, the marijuana aroma, the drug paraphernalia, and the information provided by the informant. When Lucas does not sign the form, the detectives conduct a protective sweep to secure the house in anticipation of obtaining a search warrant. At that point, Lucas says, "What do I have to sign?" The detective verbally reviews the consent form, informs Lucas of his right to refuse permission, and orally advises Lucas of his right to stop the search at any time. Lucas signs the consent form. The form provides that the detectives may search his residence for illegal controlled substances, drug paraphernalia, and "other material or records pertaining to narcotics." Was the consent valid? *See United States v. Lucas*, 640 F.3d 168 (6th Cir. 2011). Suppose that, during the search, the detectives find marijuana plants, each separately potted and named. The detectives then notice a laptop computer in the living room of the house. Near the laptop, a detective observes a handwritten marijuana plant "grow chart" with a numbered list of the named marijuana plants found in the bedroom closet, as well as height measurements, pot sizes, and notes. The chart is accompanied by a "to-do" list. Based on his training and experience, the detective knows that marijuana growers commonly keep similar data and digital photographs on computers and upload the information to the internet. The detective asks Lucas whether the computer is password-protected, and Lucas responds that it is not. When the detective accesses the laptop, he finds images of child pornography. Did Lucas' consent extend to the laptop? *See United States v. Lucas*, 640 F.3d 168 (6th Cir. 2011).

Hypo 8: *Collecting DNA*

Defendant is a suspect in a series of residential burglaries from which genetic material has been collected. When defendant is stopped for a traffic violation, his eyes are bloodshot and watery. Defendant performs sobriety tests and consents to a PAS breath test that requires him to place his mouth over the plastic tip of a PAS device and blow into it. Defendant is let go after passing all tests, but instead of discarding the mouthpiece of the PAS device, the police preserve it for DNA testing. The DNA links defendant to two burglaries. Was defendant's consent valid? *See People v. Thomas*, 200 Cal.App.4th 338, 132 Cal. Rptr.3d 714 (2011).

Hypo 9: *The Limits of Consent*

A suspect agrees to submit a DNA sample to police in order to exculpate himself as a suspect in a case. However, the police compare the suspect's DNA, not only against the DNA in the case for which he is a suspect, but against all of the DNA in a police data base. This comparison reveals that the suspect is guilty of another crime. When the police obtained a consensual sample of DNA from defendant, was it permissible for them to enter the DNA into the data base? *See Varriale v. State*, 119 A.3d 824 (Md. 2015), *cert. denied, Varriale v. Maryland*, 136 S.Ct. 898 (2016).

Hypo 10: *The Burglar's Consent*

A burglar breaks into a home. While the burglar is in the house, the police knock at the door. The burglar, being rather bold, opens the door. The police, assuming that the burglar is the owner of the house (or, otherwise, he wouldn't have opened the door), tell the burglar that they would like to search the house and ask for permission to do so. The burglar responds that he doesn't object to the search, but that he is just leaving for an urgent appointment. The burglar (whom the police still assume is the owner of the house) agrees to the search provided that two conditions are met: the burglar is free to leave for his appointment, and the police agree to lock up the house as they leave. If the police search the home and find illegal narcotics, can the evidence be admitted against the owner? On behalf of the owner, what arguments might you make? How might the state respond to those arguments? Does the following decision affect your analysis?

Illinois v. Rodriguez

497 U.S. 177 (1990).

JUSTICE SCALIA delivered the opinion of the Court.

Police were summoned to the residence of Dorothy Jackson in Chicago. They were met by Ms. Jackson's daughter, Gail Fischer, who showed signs of a severe beating. She told officers that she had been assaulted by respondent Edward Rodriguez earlier that day in an apartment on South California. Fischer stated that Rodriguez was asleep in the apartment, and she consented to travel there to unlock the door so that the officers could enter and arrest him. Fischer several times referred to the apartment as "our" apartment, and said that she had clothes and furniture there. It is unclear whether she indicated that she currently lived at the apartment, or only that she used to live there. Police officers drove to the apartment accompanied by Fischer. They did not obtain an arrest warrant for Rodriguez, nor did they seek a search warrant. Fischer unlocked the door with her key and gave the officers permission to enter. They moved through the door into the living room, where they observed in plain view drug paraphernalia and containers filled with white powder that they believed (correctly) to be cocaine. They proceeded to the bedroom, where they found Rodriguez asleep and discovered additional containers of white powder in two open attache cases. The officers arrested Rodriguez and seized the drugs and related paraphernalia. Rodriguez was charged with possession of a controlled substance with intent to deliver. The trial court's decision to grant Rodriguez's motion to suppress was affirmed on appeal.

The Fourth Amendment generally prohibits the warrantless entry of a person's home, whether to make an arrest or to search for specific objects. The prohibition does not apply, however, to situations in which voluntary consent has been obtained, either from the individual whose property is searched, or from a third party who possesses common authority over the premises. As we stated in *United States v. Matlock*, 415 U.S. 164 (1974), "common authority" rests "on mutual use of the property by persons generally having joint access or control for most purposes" The burden of establishing that common authority rests upon the State. That burden was not sustained. Although Fischer, with her two small children, had lived with Rodriguez, she had moved out almost a month before the search, and had gone to live with her mother. She took her and her children's clothing with her, though leaving behind some furniture and household effects. After July 1 she sometimes spent the night at Rodriguez's apartment, but never invited her friends there, and never went there herself when he was not home. Her name was not on the lease nor did she contribute to the rent. She had a key to the apartment, which she had taken without Rodriguez's knowledge (though she testified that Rodriguez had given her the key). On these facts the State has not established that Fischer had "joint access or control for most purposes."

Respondent asserts that permitting a reasonable belief of common authority to validate an entry would cause a defendant's Fourth Amendment rights to be "vicariously waived." We disagree. What Rodriguez is assured by the Fourth Amendment is not that no government search of his house will occur unless he consents; but that no such search will occur that is "unreasonable." There are various elements that can make a search of a person's house "reasonable"—one of which is the consent of the person or his cotenant. The essence of respondent's argument is that we should impose upon this element a requirement that we have not imposed upon other elements that regularly compel government officers to exercise judgment regarding the facts: namely, the requirement that their judgment be not only responsible but correct.

The fundamental objective that alone validates all unconsented government searches is the seizure of persons who have committed or are about to commit crimes, or of evidence related to crimes. But "reasonableness," with respect to this necessary element, does not demand that the government be factually correct in its assessment that that is what a search will produce. Warrants need only be supported by "probable cause," which demands no more than a proper "assessment of probabilities in particular factual contexts." *Illinois v. Gates*, 462 U.S. 213, 232 (1983). If a magistrate, based upon seemingly reliable but factually inaccurate information, issues a warrant for the search of a house in which the sought-after felon is not present, has never been present, and was never likely to have been present, the owner of that house suffers one of the inconveniences we all expose ourselves to as the cost of living in a safe society; he does not suffer a violation of the Fourth Amendment.

Another element often required in order to render an unconsented search "reasonable" is that the officer be authorized by a valid warrant. We have not held that "reasonableness" precludes error with respect to those factual judgments that law enforcement officials are expected to make. For example, in *Maryland v. Garrison*, we held the search unquestionably was objectively understandable and reasonable. The objective facts available to the officers at the time suggested no distinction between the suspect's apartment and the third-floor premises.

In order to satisfy the "reasonableness" requirement of the Fourth Amendment, what is generally demanded of the many factual determinations that must regularly be made by agents of the government—whether the magistrate issuing a warrant, the police officer executing a warrant, or the police officer conducting a search or seizure under one of the exceptions to the warrant requirement—is not that they always be correct, but that they be reasonable. As we put it in *Brinegar v. United States*, 338 U.S. 160, 176 (1949): "Because many situations which confront officers in the course of executing their duties are more or less ambiguous, room must be allowed for some mistakes on their part. But the mistakes must be those of reasonable men, acting on facts leading sensibly to their conclusions of probability."

We see no reason to depart from this general rule with respect to the authority to consent to a search. Whether the basis for such authority exists is the sort of recurring factual question to which law enforcement officials must be expected to apply their judgment; and all the Fourth Amendment requires is that they answer it reasonably. The Constitution is no more violated when officers enter without a warrant because they reasonably (though erroneously) believe that the person who has consented to their entry is a resident of the premises, than it is violated when they enter without a warrant because they reasonably (though erroneously) believe they are in pursuit of a violent felon who is about to escape.

What we hold today does not suggest that law enforcement officers may always accept a person's invitation to enter premises. Even when the invitation is accompanied by an explicit assertion that the person lives there, the surrounding circumstances could conceivably be such that a reasonable person would doubt its truth and not act upon it without further inquiry. As with other factual determinations bearing upon search and seizure, determination of consent to enter must "be judged against an objective standard: would the facts available to the officer at the moment 'warrant a man of reasonable caution in the belief' " that the consenting party had authority over the premises? If not, then warrantless entry without further inquiry is unlawful unless authority actually exists. But if so, the search is valid.

The Appellate Court found it unnecessary to determine whether the officers reasonably believed that Fischer had the authority to consent. We remand for consideration of that question.

So ordered.

JUSTICE MARSHALL, with whom JUSTICE BRENNAN and JUSTICE STEVENS join, dissenting.

A departure from the warrant requirement is not justified simply because an officer reasonably believes a third party has consented to a search of the defendant's home. Third-party consent searches are not based on an exigency and serve no compelling social goal. Police officers, when faced with the choice of relying on consent by a third party or securing a warrant, should secure a warrant and must therefore accept the risk of error should they instead choose to rely on consent. Third-party consent limits a person's ability to challenge the reasonableness of the search only because that person voluntarily has relinquished some of his expectation of privacy by sharing access or

Food for Thought

In light of the holding in *Rodriguez*, reconsider Hypo 10, *supra*, before *Rodriguez*, entitled "The Burglar's Consent."

control over his property with another person. A search conducted pursuant to an officer's reasonable but mistaken belief that a third party had authority to consent is thus on an entirely different constitutional footing from one based on the consent of a third party who in fact has such authority. Even if the officers reasonably believed that Fischer had authority to consent, she did not, and Rodriguez's expectation of privacy was therefore undiminished. Rodriguez accordingly can challenge the warrantless intrusion into his home as a violation of the Fourth Amendment.

Hypo 1: *The Sister's Consent*

School officials discover that a laptop computer is missing. Since the computer is equipped with tracking software, the police are able to trace the computer to a particular address. Officers go to that address, a house, and enter the vestibule without ringing the doorbell or announcing their presence, and knock on an inner door separating the vestibule from the rest of the home. A woman (the suspect's sister) welcomes the officers saying "Thank God you're all here." When asked whether the suspect is at home, she answers affirmatively, explaining that her brother has been "acting up" and cursing at her mother, and that she "was going to call the police anyway." The sister directs the officers upstairs, to a bedroom where they encounter a young man with a laptop. When asked whether it is his laptop, the young man answers that it is not. At this point, the suspect enters the room and says, "That's my laptop." The suspect moves to suppress the laptop at his trial, arguing that the initial police entry was invalid, and that the sister's consent did not extend to entry into his bedroom. Should the evidence be suppressed? *See In re Leroy,* 944 N.E.2d 1123 (2011).

Hypo 2: *Supervisors & Employees*

May a supervisor consent to a search of an employee's desk? Appellee was arrested for petty larceny. The police suspected that he stashed some of the loot in his office. With the consent of appellee's supervisor, the police search the desk (which was used only by defendant). The police find the loot in the drawer. Is a supervisor entitled to consent to the search of an employee's desk under these circumstances? What arguments might be made on behalf of appellee? How might the government respond? *See United States v. Blok,* 188 F.2d 1019 (D.C.Cir.1951).

Hypo 3: *More on Supervisors & Employees*

At the U.S. Mint in D.C., there was a loud noise that sounded like an explosion. An investigation reveals that a firecracker or other explosive had gone off. In an effort to find other fireworks possessed by Mint employees, the Captain of the security guard decides to search all employee lockers. In Donato's locker, he finds a bag of quarters. Donato is charged with embezzlement. Did the security guard, acting on behalf of Donato's employer, need Donato's consent to search the locker? Would it matter whether Mint regulations expressly state that "No mint lockers in mint institutions shall be considered to be private lockers," that all employee lockers are subject to inspection and will be regularly inspected by Mint security guards for sanitation purposes, and that Mint security guards have a master key that opens all employee lockers? *See United States v. Donato*, 269 F.Supp. 921 (E.D.Pa. 1967); *see also United States v. Oliver*, 630 F.3d 397 (5th Cir. 2011); *United States v. Purcell*, 526 F.3d 953 (6th Cir. 2008).

Hypo 4: *The Scope of Third Party Consent*

Stabile lived with Debbie Deetz, who believed that she was married to him (she was not), in a house secured by a mortgage in the name of Stabile's brother. Stabile defaulted on the loans and tried to mask his default by passing counterfeit checks. When police officers sought to question Stabile, he was not at home. Deetz invited the agents into the house. The officers asked Deetz for consent to search the house, provided her with a consent form, and informed her that she could refuse. Deetz reviewed the form for thirty minutes and signed so that she could find out about Stabile's finances. The agents then searched the house led by Deetz who provided the agents with documents and showed the agents several computers. Next to one computer, the agents found check stock, check writing software, photocopies of checks, copies of previously-passed fraudulent checks, two printers, and checks with an alias. The agents disconnected the hard drives. When one officer had difficulty removing a hard drive, Deetz provided the officer with a screwdriver from Stabile's toolbox. The officers left with six hard drives. Stabile claims that Deetz did not have authority to consent to a seizure of the computer. Is Stabile correct? Is the search invalid? *See United States v. Stabile*, 633 F.3d 219 (3d Cir. 2011).

Hypo 5: *Third Party Consent—Take Three*

Police, responding to a 911 call, find Hernandez' girlfriend (Elizabeth Romero), bruised, beaten, and visibly shaken. She tells police that Hernandez beat her and held her against her will until she escaped. She claims that she has been living with Hernandez for two weeks, that her personal belongings are in his apartment, that Hernandez has "lots of guns," and has stated that he "is not going to jail." When Hernandez appears, and spies the officers, he quickly walks into the corridor that leads to his apartment. When the police call Hernandez's cell phone, he denies that he is in his apartment and responds "with foul language." Believing that Hernandez is in his apartment, the deputies cordon off the area, but do not seek a warrant. At that point, Romero gives the police consent to enter the apartment to search for Hernandez. Romero states that there is one locked room in the apartment that she is not permitted to enter. The police find that the door to that room is locked. As part of a "protective sweep," an officer forces the locked door open. Did the officers act properly in entering the apartment and forcing the door? *See Hernandez v. State*, 98 So.3d 702 (Fl. App. 2012).

Hypo 6: *The Juvenile Center Director*

A juvenile is living at a transitional family center with his mother. When the director spots him with a gun, the director notifies the police and gives consent for the police to search his room. The director has a master key that opens every door in the shelter, and staff members have a master key that opens every room. Members of the staff have the right to enter any room "for professional business purposes (maintenance, room inspections, etc.)," but only with the knowledge of the director. If a "business professional," such as a repair person or exterminator, requires entry to a resident's room, he or she must be escorted by a staff member, with the director's approval. Shelter staff may conduct "room checks" at any time without warning to monitor compliance with the shelter's "Good Housekeeping Standard" and other rules and regulations, including those affecting health and safety. The manual has a "zero tolerance policy in regards to violent acts committed by residents" and provides that "any resident in possession of a weapon will be terminated immediately." The shelter "reserves the right to contact the Police should the situation warrant," but the manual does not state that the shelter director or a staff member may consent to a police search of a resident's room. Before entering the room, the police speak with the director and review the manual. Their entry is proceeded by the director who announces that she is conducting a room search. The search turns up the gun. The juvenile moves to suppress on the theory that the director lacked authority to consent to the search. Should the gun be suppressed? *See Commonwealth v. Porter*, 456 Mass. 254, 923 N.E.2d 36 (2010).

Georgia v. Randolph

547 U.S. 103 (2006).

JUSTICE SOUTER delivered the opinion of the Court.

The Fourth Amendment recognizes a valid warrantless entry and search of premises when police obtain the voluntary consent of an occupant who shares, or is reasonably believed to share, authority over the area in common with a co-occupant who later objects to the use of evidence so obtained. *Illinois v. Rodriguez*, 497 U.S. 177 (1990); *United States v. Matlock*, 415 U.S. 164 (1974). The question here is whether such an evidentiary seizure is lawful with the permission of one occupant when the other, who later seeks to suppress the evidence, is present at the scene and expressly refuses to consent.

Respondent Scott Randolph and his wife, Janet, separated in May 2001, when she left the marital residence in Georgia, and went to stay with her parents, taking their son and some belongings. In July, she returned to the house with the child, though the record does not reveal whether her object was reconciliation or retrieval of remaining possessions. On July 6, she complained to the police that after a domestic dispute her husband took their son away, and when officers reached the house she told them that her husband was a cocaine user whose habit had caused financial troubles. After the police arrived, Scott Randolph returned and explained that he had removed the child to a neighbor's house out of concern that his wife might take the boy out of the country again; he denied cocaine use, and countered that it was in fact his wife who abused drugs and alcohol. Sergeant Murray went with Janet Randolph to reclaim the child, and when they returned she not only renewed her complaints about her husband's drug use, but also volunteered that there were "items of drug evidence" in the house. Sergeant Murray asked Scott Randolph for permission to search the house, which he unequivocally refused. The sergeant turned to Janet Randolph for consent to search, which she readily gave. She led the officer upstairs to a bedroom that she identified as Scott's, where the sergeant noticed a drinking straw with a powdery residue he suspected was cocaine. He then [obtained] an evidence bag from his car and [called] the district attorney's office, who instructed him to stop the search and apply for a warrant. When Murray returned to the house, Janet Randolph withdrew her consent. The police took the straw to the police station, along with the Randolphs. After getting a search warrant, they returned to the house and seized further evidence of drug use, on the basis of which Scott Randolph was indicted for possession of cocaine. He moved to suppress the evidence, as products of a warrantless search. The trial court denied the motion. The Court of Appeals of Georgia reversed, and was sustained by the State Supreme Court. We granted certiorari and affirm.

To the Fourth Amendment rule ordinarily prohibiting the warrantless entry of a person's house as unreasonable *per se*, one "jealously and carefully drawn" exception recognizes the validity of searches with the voluntary consent of an individual possessing authority. None of our co-occupant consent-to-search cases has presented the further fact of a second occupant physically present and refusing permission to search, and later moving to suppress evidence so obtained.[2] The significance of such a refusal turns on the underpinnings of the co-occupant consent rule, as recognized since *Matlock*. The defendant in that case was arrested in the yard of a house where he lived with a Mrs. Graff and several of her relatives, and was detained in a squad car parked nearby. When the police went to the door, Mrs. Graff admitted them and consented to a search of the house. We said that "the consent of one who possesses common authority over premises or effects is valid as against the absent, nonconsenting person with whom that authority is shared." Consistent with our prior understanding that Fourth Amendment rights are not limited by the law of property, we explained that the third party's "common authority" is not synonymous with a technical property interest: "The authority which justified the third-party consent does not rest upon the law of property, with its attendant historical and legal refinement, but rests rather on mutual use of the property by persons generally having joint access or control for most purposes, so that it is reasonable to recognize that any of the co-inhabitants has the right to permit the inspection in his own right and that the others have assumed the risk that one of their number might permit the common area to be searched."

The constant element in assessing Fourth Amendment reasonableness in the consent cases is the great significance given to widely shared social expectations, which are naturally influenced by the law of property, but not controlled by its rules. *Matlock* not only holds that a solitary co-inhabitant may sometimes consent to a search of shared premises, but stands for the proposition that the reasonableness of such a search is in significant part a function of commonly held understandings about the authority that co-inhabitants may exercise in ways that affect each other's interests.

When someone comes to the door of a domestic dwelling with a baby at her hip, as Mrs. Graff did, she shows that she belongs there, and that fact standing alone is enough to tell a law enforcement officer or any other visitor that if she occupies the place along with others, she probably lives there subject to the assumption ten-

---

[2] Mindful of the multiplicity of living arrangements, we do not mean to suggest that the rule to be applied to them is varied.

ants usually make about their common authority when they share quarters. They understand that any one of them may admit visitors, with the consequence that a guest obnoxious to one may nevertheless be admitted in his absence by another. As *Matlock* put it, shared tenancy is understood to include an "assumption of risk," on which police officers are entitled to rely, and although some group living together might make an exceptional arrangement that no one could admit a guest without the agreement of all, the chance of such an eccentric scheme is too remote to expect visitors to investigate a particular household's rules before accepting an invitation to come in. So, *Matlock* relied on what was usual and placed no burden on the police to eliminate the possibility of atypical arrangements, in the absence of reason to doubt that the regular scheme was in place.

It is easy to imagine different facts on which, if known, no common authority could sensibly be suspected. A landlord or a hotel manager calls up no customary understanding of authority to admit guests without the consent of the current occupant. *See Chapman v. United States, supra* (landlord); *Stoner v. California*, 376 U.S. 483 (1964) (hotel manager). A tenant in the ordinary course does not take rented premises subject to any formal or informal agreement that the landlord may let visitors into the dwelling, and a hotel guest customarily has no reason to expect the manager to allow anyone but his own employees into his room. In these circumstances, neither state-law property rights, nor common contractual arrangements, nor any other source points to a common understanding of authority to admit third parties generally without the consent of a person occupying the premises. When it comes to searching through bureau drawers, there will be instances in which even a person clearly belonging on premises as an occupant may lack any perceived authority to consent; "a child of eight might well be considered to have the power to consent to the police crossing the threshold into that part of the house where any caller, such as a pollster or salesman, might well be admitted," 4 LaFave 8.4(c), at 207 (4th ed. 2004), but no one would reasonably expect such a child to be in a position to authorize anyone to rummage through his parents' bedroom.

A caller standing at the door of shared premises would have no confidence that one occupant's invitation was a sufficiently good reason to enter when a fellow tenant stood there saying, "stay out." Without some very good reason, no sensible person would go inside under those conditions. Fear for the safety of the occupant issuing the invitation, or of someone else inside, would be thought to justify entry, but the justification then would be the personal risk, the threats to life or limb, not the disputed invitation. The visitor's reticence would show not timidity but a realization that when people living together disagree over the use of their common quarters, a resolution must come through voluntary accommodation, not by appeals to authority. Unless the people living together fall within some recognized hierarchy, like a household of parent and child or barracks housing military personnel of different grades, there is no societal understanding of superior and inferior, a fact reflected in a standard formulation of domestic property law, that "each cotenant has the right to use and enjoy the entire property as if he or she were the sole owner, limited only by the same right in the other cotenants." 7 R. POWELL, POWELL ON REAL PROPERTY 50.031, p. 50–14 (M. Wolf gen. ed. 2005). The law does not ask who has the better side of the conflict; it simply provides a right to any co-tenant, even the most unreasonable, to obtain a decree partitioning the property (when the relationship is one of co-ownership) and terminating the relationship. In sum, there is no common understanding that one co-tenant generally has a right or authority to prevail over the express wishes of another, whether the issue is the color of the curtains or invitations to outsiders.

Since the co-tenant wishing to open the door to a third party has no recognized authority in law or social practice to prevail over a present and objecting co-tenant, his disputed invitation, without more, gives a police officer no better claim to reasonableness in entering than the officer would have in the absence of any consent at all. We have, after all, lived our whole national history with an understanding of "the ancient adage that a man's home is his castle to the point that the poorest man may in his cottage bid defiance to all the forces of the Crown," *Miller v. United States*, 357 U.S. 301 (1958). Disputed permission is thus no match for this central value of the Fourth Amendment. We recognize the consenting tenant's interest as a citizen in bringing criminal activity to light. And we understand a co-tenant's legitimate self-interest in siding with the police to deflect suspicion raised by sharing quarters with a criminal. But society can have the benefit of these interests without relying on a theory of consent that ignores an inhabitant's refusal to allow a warrantless search. The co-tenant acting on his own initiative may deliver evidence to the police, and can tell the police what he knows, for use before a magistrate in getting a warrant.[6] The reliance on a co-tenant's information instead of disputed consent accords with the law's general partiality toward "police action taken under a warrant as against searches and seizures without one," *United States v. Lefkowitz*, 285 U.S. 452 (1932).

No question has been raised about the authority of the police to enter a dwelling to protect a resident from domestic violence; so long as they have good reason to believe such a threat exists. (And since the police would then be lawfully in the premises, there is no question that they could seize any evidence in plain view or take further action supported by any consequent probable cause) The undoubted right of the police to enter in order to protect a victim has nothing to do with the question in this case, whether a search with the consent of one co-tenant is good against another, standing at the door and expressly refusing consent.[7] None of the cases cited by the

---

[6] The exchange of information like this in front of the objecting inhabitant may [create] an exigency that justifies immediate action on the police's part; if the objecting tenant cannot be incapacitated from destroying easily disposable evidence during the time required to get a warrant, a perceived need to act on the spot to preserve evidence may justify entry and search under the exigent circumstances exception.

[7] We understand the possibility that a battered individual will be afraid to express fear candidly, but this does not seem to be a reason to think such a person would invite the police into the dwelling to search for evidence against another.

dissent support its improbable view that recognizing limits on merely evidentiary searches would compromise the capacity to protect a fearful occupant. We therefore hold that a warrantless search of a shared dwelling for evidence over the express refusal of consent by a physically present resident cannot be justified as reasonable as to him on the basis of consent given to the police by another resident.

To ask whether the consenting tenant has the right to admit the police when a physically present fellow tenant objects is not to question whether some property right may be divested by the mere objection of another. It is, rather, whether customary social understanding accords the consenting tenant authority powerful enough to prevail over the co-tenant's objection. If a potential defendant with self-interest in objecting is in fact at the door and objects, the co-tenant's permission does not suffice for a reasonable search, whereas the potential objector, nearby but not invited to take part in the threshold colloquy, loses out. There is practical value in the simple clarity of complementary rules, one recognizing the co-tenant's permission when there is no fellow occupant on hand, the other according dispositive weight to the fellow occupant's contrary indication when he expresses it. It would needlessly limit the capacity of the police to respond if we were to hold that reasonableness required the police to take affirmative steps to find a potentially objecting co-tenant before acting on the permission they had already received. Every co-tenant consent case would turn into a test about the adequacy of the police's efforts to consult with a potential objector.

This case invites a straightforward application of the rule that a physically present inhabitant's express refusal of consent to a police search is dispositive as to him, regardless of the consent of a fellow occupant. The State does not argue that she gave any indication to the police of a need for protection inside the house that might have justified entry into the portion of the premises where the police found the powdery straw. Nor does the State claim that the entry and search should be upheld under the rubric of exigent circumstances.

The judgment of the Supreme Court of Georgia is therefore affirmed.

It is so ordered.

JUSTICE STEVENS, concurring.

When the Fourth Amendment was adopted, given the then-prevailing dramatic differences between the property rights of the husband and the far lesser rights of the wife, only the consent of the husband would matter. Assuming that both spouses are competent, neither one is a master possessing the power to override the other's constitutional right to deny entry to their castle.

JUSTICE BREYER, concurring.

The "totality of the circumstances" do not justify abandoning the Fourth Amendment's traditional hostility to police entry into a home without a warrant. If a possible abuse victim invites a responding officer to enter a home or consents to the officer's entry request, that invitation (or consent) could reflect the victim's fear about being left alone with an abuser. In that context, an invitation (or consent) would provide a special reason for immediate, rather than later, police entry. Today's decision will not adversely affect ordinary law enforcement practices.

CHIEF JUSTICE ROBERTS, with whom JUSTICE SCALIA joins, dissenting.

The rule the majority fashions provides protection on a random and happenstance basis, protecting, for example, a co-occupant who happens to be at the front door when the other occupant consents to a search, but not one napping or watching television in the next room. The correct approach recognizes that the Fourth Amendment protects privacy. If an individual shares information, papers, or places with another, he assumes the risk that the other person will in turn share access to that information or those papers or places with the government. Co-occupants have "assumed the risk that one of their number might permit a common area to be searched." *United States v. Matlock*, 415 U.S. 164 (1974). Just as Mrs. Randolph could walk upstairs, come down, and turn her husband's cocaine straw over to the police, she can consent to police entry and search of what is, after all, her home, too.

The majority assumes that an invited social guest who arrives at the door of a shared residence, and is greeted by a disagreeable co-occupant shouting "stay out," would simply go away. A relative or good friend of one of two feuding roommates might well enter the apartment over the objection of the other roommate. A guest who came to celebrate an occupant's birthday, or one who had traveled some distance for a particular reason, might not readily turn away simply because of a roommate's objection. The nature of the place itself is also pertinent: Invitees may react one way if the feuding roommates share one room, differently if there are common areas from which the objecting roommate could readily be expected to absent himself. The possible scenarios are limitless, and slight variations in the fact pattern yield vastly different expectations about whether the invitee might be expected to enter or to go away. Such shifting expectations are not a promising foundation on which to ground a constitutional rule.

The normal Fourth Amendment rule is that items discovered in plain view are admissible if the officers were legitimately on the premises; if the entry and search were reasonable "as to" Mrs. Randolph, based on her consent, it is not clear why the cocaine straw should not be admissible "as to" Mr. Randolph, as discovered in plain view during a legitimate search.

The question presented often arises when innocent cotenants seek to disassociate or protect themselves from ongoing criminal activity. There will be many cases in which a consenting co-occupant's wish to have the police enter is overridden by an objection from another present co-occupant. What does the majority imagine will happen when the consenting co-occupant is concerned about the other's criminal activity, once the door clicks shut? The objecting co-occupant may pause briefly to decide whether to destroy any evidence of wrongdoing or to inflict retribution on the consenting co-occupant first, but there can be little doubt that he will attend to both in short order. The majority's rule forbids police from entering to assist with a domestic dispute if the abuser whose behavior prompted the request for police assistance objects. It is far from clear that an exception for emergency entries suffices to protect the safety of occupants in domestic disputes. I respectfully dissent.

JUSTICE SCALIA, dissenting.

The issue is what to do when there is a *conflict* between two equals. It does not follow that the spouse who *refuses* consent should be the winner of the contest. Given the usual patterns of domestic violence, how often can police be expected to encounter the situation in which a man urges them to enter the home while a woman simultaneously demands that they stay out? The most common practical effect of today's decision is to give men the power to stop women from allowing police into their homes.

JUSTICE THOMAS, dissenting.

When a citizen leads police officers into a home shared with her spouse to show them evidence relevant to their investigation no Fourth Amendment search has occurred.

a. Removed Co-Occupant

Randolph was qualified by the holding in *Fernandez v. California*, 571 U.S. 292 (2014), which was similar to *Randolph* in that a co-occupant objected to allowing the police to search a house. However, after the objecting co-occupant was arrested and removed from the apartment house, the remaining occupant gave the police permission to enter and search. The removed co-occupant sought to suppress the results of the search. The court upheld the search:

> "This brings us to petitioner's argument that his objection, made at the threshold of the premises that the police wanted to search, remained effective until he changed his mind and withdrew his objection. This argument cannot be squared with the "widely shared social expectations" or "customary social usage" upon which *Randolph* was based. When the objecting occupant is standing at the threshold saying "stay out," a friend or visitor

invited to enter by another occupant can expect at best an uncomfortable scene and at worst violence if he or she tries to brush past the objector. But when the objector is not on the scene (and especially when it is known that the objector will not return during the course of the visit), the friend or visitor is much more likely to accept the invitation to enter.

Petitioner argues that an objection, once made, should last until it is withdrawn by the objector, but such a rule would be unreasonable. Suppose that a husband and wife owned a house as joint tenants and that the husband, after objecting to a search of the house, was convicted and sentenced to a 15-year prison term. Under petitioner's proposed rule, the wife would be unable to consent to a search of the house 10 years after the date on which her husband objected. We refuse to stretch *Randolph* to such strange lengths. Nor are we persuaded to hold that an objection lasts for a "reasonable" time. What interval of time would be reasonable in this context? A week? A month? A year? Ten years? Petitioner's rule would require the police and ultimately the courts to determine whether, after the passage of time, an objector still had "common authority" over the premises, and this would often be a tricky question. Suppose that an incarcerated objector and a consenting co-occupant were joint tenants on a lease. If the objector, after incarceration, stopped paying rent, would he still have "common authority," and would his objection retain its force? Would it be enough that his name remained on the lease? Would the result be different if the objecting and consenting lessees had an oral month-to-month tenancy? Another problem concerns the procedure needed to register a continuing objection. Would it be necessary for an occupant to object while police officers are at the door? Could a person like Randolph, suspecting that his estranged wife might invite the police to view his drug stash and paraphernalia, register an objection in advance? Could this be done by posting a sign in front of the house? Could a standing objection be registered by serving notice on the chief of police? Finally, there is the question of the particular law enforcement officers who would be bound by an objection. Would this include just the officers who were present when the objection was made? Would it also apply to other officers working on the same investigation? Would it extend to officers who were unaware of the objection? How about officers assigned to different but arguably related cases? Would it be limited by law enforcement agency?

Food for Thought

How does the Court's decision apply to a defendant who happens to be asleep when his wife agrees to allow the police to enter their residence, but who wakes up and immediately objects to the search. May the police continue with the search, or must they discontinue their efforts? How would you advise the police to act?

Justice Ginsburg, joined by two other justices, dissented.

In this case, the police could readily have obtained a warrant to search the shared residence. I would honor the Fourth Amendment's warrant requirement and hold that Fernandez' objection to the search did not become null upon his arrest and removal from the scene."

Hypo 1: *The Co-Occupant in the Patrol Car*

Defendant is arrested, handcuffed, and placed in the back of a patrol car. Suppose that the police ask defendant's wife for permission to search the house and she consents. Defendant, who is within earshot and realizes what is going on, yells out an objection. May the police enter? *See United States v. Henderson*, 536 F.3d 776 (7th Cir. 2008).

Food for Thought

Defendant, who was present when the police ask for permission to search her house for evidence of a meth lab, objects loudly. However, the husband pleads with the police to enter anyway because he fears that the meth chemicals are dangerous to his house, to him, and to their kids. May the police enter the house anyway? *See, e.g., United States v. Hendrix*, 595 F.2d 883 (D.C.Cir.1979).

Food for Thought

How would *Randolph* apply to a situation in which the police ask for permission to search an automobile, but one of the spouses objects while the other consents? Suppose that the driver consents while the passenger objects? Does the driver's consent carry more weight? Or, under *Randolph*, does the objection of one spouse preclude the authority to enter?

Hypo 2: *The Guest's Consent*

Believing that criminals are using a house to traffic narcotics, the police ask Chambers (who does not own the house, but is staying there with the permission of the owner) for permission to search the house for evidence of money laundering and drug trafficking. If Chambers consents, is the search valid if it reveals cocaine in the living room? What if the police find a boarded-up attic entryway, and Chambers consents to using a sledgehammer to dislodge the boards? In the attic, the police find nearly $1,000,000 in cash, more drugs, and ledgers. If you represent the owner of the house, how would you argue that the search is invalid? How might the state respond? *See United States v. Arreguin*, 735 F.3d 1168 (9th Cir. 2013); *United States v. Ibarra*, 948 F.2d 903 (5th Cir.1991).

Hypo 3: *The Grandmother's Consent*

In *Bumpers, supra,* the police searched a grandmother's home looking for a rifle allegedly used by her grandson in committing a rape. Can the grandmother consent to a search of her grandson's bedroom? Does it matter whether the grandson is present and objecting? *See United States v. Peyton*, 745 F.3d 546 (D.C. Cir. 2014).

Food for Thought

When a police officer makes a valid stop of an automobile, he obtains consent from the driver to search the vehicle. During the search, the officer comes upon a briefcase. A passenger in the vehicle asserts ownership of the briefcase, and asks the officer "Got a warrant for that?" Assume that the driver validly consented to the search of the vehicle, does the passenger's question constitute a revocation of consent regarding the briefcase, or was the meaning of the question ambiguous? Faced with the question, is the officer required to clarify whether the passenger is challenging the consent to search? *See State v. Wantland*, 2014 WI 58, 848 N.W.2d 810 (2014).

Hypo 4: *The Executive's Computer*

The police have reason to believe that a corporate executive is accessing child pornography from his office computer. The computer is owned by the company, but is protected by an individual password. However, the company's IT department has administrative access to all computers, monitors employee internet activity, and makes employees aware of the monitoring. Under such circumstances, does the CFO have authority to consent to a search of the executive's computer? *See United States v. Ziegler*, 474 F.3d 1184 (9th Cir. 2007).

Hypo 5: *Possession of Keys*

Defendant is arrested at a casino. While he is being taken away, he gives the keys to his vehicle to his girlfriend, and tells her: "lock it up and just wait for me." Despite the fact that the girlfriend possesses the keys to the vehicle, she is not listed on the rental agreement and is not insured. After repeated requests from the police, she consents to a search of the vehicle. Did she have the authority to consent? *See State v. Kurokawa-Lasciak*, 249 Or.App. 435, 278 P.3d 38 (2012).

Hypo 6: *The Overdue Rental Car*

Suppose that a man, who is driving a rental car, objects to a search of the vehicle. However, the rental car is overdue and the company has a right to repossess it. May the rental car company consent to a search of the car despite the driver's objections? *See United States v. Lumpkins*, 687 F.3d 1011 (8th Cir. 2012).

7. Administrative Inspections

A number of agencies regularly inspect buildings and worksites. Health inspectors enter restaurants to determine whether food preparation and service areas are clean, as well as to see whether food is being kept under healthy conditions. OSHA inspectors examine construction and factory sites to make sure that workers are employed in safe and healthy conditions. In some instances, administrative officials even seek to enter people's homes or yards (*e.g.*, child welfare officials enter a house looking for abused or neglected children).

FYI

Although the Fourth Amendment prohibits unreasonable searches and seizures, and therefore seems to provide homeowners and businessmen with some protection against administrative prying, until the 1960s there was doubt about whether the Fourth Amendment applied to administrative inspections. The Fourth Amendment clearly applies when the police search homes or businesses for evidence of criminal activity. However, prior to the following decision, many believed that administrative inspections were fundamentally different than police searches, and were not therefore subject to Fourth Amendment requirements.

Camara v. Municipal Court

387 U.S. 523 (1967).

MR. JUSTICE WHITE delivered the opinion of the Court.

Appellant Camara leased a ground floor apartment. City inspectors sought to inspect the apartment under § 503 of a San Francisco ordinance which authorized them to enter buildings "to perform any duty imposed upon them by the Municipal Code." When Camara refused to allow the inspectors to enter his apartment without a warrant, he was charged with violating § 507 of the ordinance which made it illegal to refuse to permit a lawful inspection.

The Fourth Amendment was designed to safeguard the privacy and security of individuals against arbitrary invasions by governmental officials. Except in certain carefully defined classes of cases, a search of private property without proper consent is "unreasonable" unless it has been authorized by a valid search warrant.

In *Frank v. State of Maryland*, 359 U.S. 360 (1959), this Court upheld the conviction of one who refused to permit a warrantless inspection of private premises for the purposes of locating and abating a suspected public nuisance. To the *Frank* majority, municipal fire, health, and housing inspection programs "touch at most upon the periphery of the important interests safeguarded by the Fourteenth Amendment's protection against official intrusion," because the inspections are merely to determine whether physical conditions exist which do not comply with minimum standards prescribed in local regulatory ordinances. Since the inspector does not ask that the property owner open his doors to a search for "evidence of criminal action" which may be used to secure the owner's criminal conviction, historic interests of "self-protection" jointly protected by the Fourth and Fifth Amendments are said not to be involved, but only the less intense "right to be secure from intrusion into personal privacy."

A routine inspection of the physical condition of private property is a less hostile intrusion than the typical policeman's search for the fruits and instrumentalities of crime. But we cannot agree that the Fourth Amendment interests at stake in these inspection cases are merely "peripheral." It is surely anomalous to say that the individual and his private property are fully protected by the Fourth Amendment only when the individual is suspected of criminal behavior. Even the most law-abiding citizen has a very tangible interest in limiting the circumstances under which the sanctity of his home may be broken by official authority, for the possibility of criminal entry under the guise of official sanction is a serious threat to personal and family security. And even accepting *Frank's* rather remarkable premise, inspections of the kind we are here considering do in fact jeopardize "self-protection" interests of the property owner. Like most regulatory laws, fire, health, and housing codes are enforced by criminal processes. In some cities, discovery of a violation by the inspector leads to a criminal complaint. Even in cities where discovery of a violation produces only an administrative compliance order, refusal to comply is a criminal offense, and the fact of compliance is verified by a second inspection, again without a warrant. Finally, refusal to permit an inspection is itself a crime, punishable by fine or even by jail sentence.

Appellee asserts that the warrant process could not function effectively in this field. The decision to inspect an entire municipal area is based upon legislative or administrative assessment of broad factors such as the area's age and condition. Unless the magistrate is to review such policy matters, he must issue a "rubber stamp" warrant which provides no protection at all to the property owner. These arguments unduly discount the purposes behind the warrant machinery contemplated by the Fourth Amendment. When the inspector demands entry, the occupant has no way of knowing whether enforcement of the municipal code involved requires inspection of his premises, no way of knowing the lawful limits of the inspector's power to search, and no way of knowing whether the inspector himself is acting under proper authorization. These are questions which may be reviewed by a neutral magistrate without any reassessment of the basic agency decision to canvass an area. Yet, only by refusing entry and risking a criminal conviction can the occupant challenge the inspector's decision to search. And even if the occupant possesses sufficient fortitude to take this risk, he may never learn any more about the reason for the inspection than that the law generally allows housing inspectors to gain entry. The practical effect of this system is to leave the occupant subject to the discretion of the official in the field. This is the discretion to invade private property which we have consistently circumscribed by a requirement that a disinterested party warrant the need to search.

The final justification suggested for warrantless administrative searches is that the health and safety of entire urban populations is dependent upon enforcement of minimum fire, housing, and sanitation standards, and that the only effective means of enforcing such codes is by routine systematized inspection of all physical structures. But the question is not whether these inspections may be made without a warrant. In assessing whether the public interest demands creation of a general exception to the Fourth Amendment's warrant requirement, the question is not whether the public interest justifies the type of search in question, but whether the authority to search should be evidenced by a warrant, which in turn depends in part upon whether the burden of obtaining a warrant is likely to frustrate the governmental purpose behind the search. It has nowhere been urged that fire, health, and housing code inspection programs could not achieve their goals within the confines of a reasonable search warrant requirement.

We hold that administrative searches of the kind at issue here are significant intrusions upon the interests protected by the Fourth Amendment, that such searches when authorized and conducted without a warrant procedure lack the traditional safeguards which the Fourth Amendment guarantees to the individual, and that the reasons put forth in *Frank* and other cases for upholding these warrantless searches are insufficient to justify so substantial a weakening of the Fourth Amendment's protections. Because of the nature of the municipal programs under consideration, these conclusions must be the beginning, not the end, of our inquiry.

In cases in which the Fourth Amendment requires that a warrant to search be obtained, "probable cause" is the standard by which a particular decision to search is tested against the constitutional mandate of reasonableness. To apply this standard, it is obviously necessary to focus upon the governmental interest which allegedly justifies official intrusion upon the constitutionally protected interests of the private citizen. In a criminal investigation, the police may undertake to recover specific stolen or contraband goods. But that public interest would hardly justify a sweeping search of an entire city in the hope that these goods might be found. A search for goods, even with a warrant, is "reasonable" only when there is "probable cause" to believe that they will be uncovered in a particular dwelling.

The inspection programs at issue are aimed at securing city-wide compliance with minimum physical standards for private property. The primary governmental interest at stake is to prevent even the unintentional development of conditions which are hazardous to public health and safety. Because fires and epidemics may ravage large urban areas, because unsightly conditions adversely affect the economic values of neighboring structures, numerous courts have upheld the police power of municipalities to impose and enforce such minimum standards even upon existing structures. In determining whether a particular inspection is reasonable—and thus in determining whether there is probable cause to issue a warrant for that inspection—the need for the inspection must be weighed in terms of these reasonable goals of code enforcement.

There is unanimous agreement among those most familiar with this field that the only effective way to seek universal compliance with the minimum standards required by municipal codes is through routine periodic inspections of all structures. It is here that the probable cause debate is focused, for the agency's decision to conduct an area inspection is unavoidably based on its appraisal of conditions in the area as a whole, not on its knowledge of conditions in each particular building. Appellee contends that, if the probable cause standard is adopted, the area inspection will be eliminated as a means of seeking compliance with code standards and the reasonable goals of code enforcement will be dealt a crushing blow.

There can be no ready test for determining reasonableness other than by balancing the need to search against the invasion which the search entails. A number of persuasive factors combine to support the reasonableness of area code-enforcement inspections. First, such programs have a long history of judicial and public acceptance. Second, the public interest demands that all dangerous conditions be prevented or abated, yet it is doubtful that any other canvassing technique would achieve acceptable results. Many such conditions—faulty wiring—are not observable from outside the building and indeed may not be apparent to the inexpert occupant himself. Finally, because the inspections are neither personal in nature nor aimed at the discovery of evidence of crime, they involve a relatively limited invasion of the urban citizen's privacy.

"Probable cause" to issue a warrant to inspect must exist if reasonable legislative or administrative standards for conducting an area inspection are satisfied with respect to a particular dwelling. Such standards, which will vary with the municipal program being enforced, may be based upon the passage of time, the nature of the building (*e.g.*, a multifamily apartment house), or the condition of the entire area, but they will not necessarily depend upon specific knowledge of the condition of the particular dwelling. It has been suggested that so to vary the probable cause test from the standard applied in criminal cases would be to authorize a "synthetic search warrant" and thereby to lessen the overall protections of the Fourth Amendment. We do not agree. The warrant procedure is designed to guarantee that a decision to search private property is justified by a reasonable governmental interest. But reasonableness is still the ultimate standard. If a valid public interest justifies the intrusion contemplated, then there is probable cause to issue a suitably restricted search warrant. Such an approach neither endangers time-honored doctrines applicable to criminal investigations nor makes a nullity of the probable cause requirement in this area. It merely gives full recognition to the competing public and private interests here at stake and, in so doing, best fulfills the historic purpose behind the constitutional right to be free from unreasonable government invasions of privacy.

Since our holding emphasizes the controlling standard of reasonableness, nothing we say is intended to foreclose prompt inspections, even without a warrant, that the law has traditionally upheld in emergency situations. *See North American Cold Storage Co. v. City of Chicago*, 211 U.S. 306 (seizure of unwholesome food); *Jacobson v. Commonwealth of Massachusetts*, 197 U.S. 11 (compulsory smallpox vaccination); *Compagnie Francaise de Navigation a Vapeur v. Louisiana State Board of Health*, 186 U.S. 380 (health quarantine); *Kroplin v. Truax*, 119 Ohio St. 610, 165 N.E. 498 (summary destruction of tubercular cattle). On the other hand, in the case of most routine area inspections, there is no compelling urgency to inspect at a particular time or on a particular day. Moreover, most citizens allow inspections of their property without a warrant. Thus, as a practical matter and in light of the Fourth Amendment's requirement that a warrant specify the property to be searched, it seems likely that warrants should normally be sought only after entry is refused unless there has been a citizen complaint or there is other satisfactory reason for securing immediate entry. Similarly, the requirement of a warrant procedure does not suggest any change in what seems to be the prevailing local policy, in most situations, of authorizing entry, but not entry by force, to inspect.

In this case, appellant has been charged with a crime for his refusal to permit housing inspectors to enter his leasehold without a warrant. There was no emergency demanding immediate access; in fact, the inspectors made three trips to the building in an attempt to obtain appellant's consent to search. Yet no warrant was obtained and thus appellant was unable to verify either the need for or the appropriate limits of the inspection. We therefore conclude that appellant had a constitutional right to insist that the inspectors obtain a warrant to search and that appellant may not constitutionally be convicted for refusing to consent to the inspection.

Judgment vacated and case remanded.

Hypo 1: *Applying* Camara

Although *Camara* involved a person's home, its holding extends to government inspections of businesses. Suppose that you are an attorney for the Occupational Safety & Health Administration (OSHA). You just received a call from Ms. Grace Harlow, a workplace inspector, assigned to the inspection of poultry factories. Tomorrow morning, Ms. Harlow plans to visit the Ajax Poultry Co. She wants to know whether she needs to obtain a warrant before going to the factory, or whether she can just show up. How would you advise Ms. Harlow? Does *Camara* force an inspector to begin every day at a judge's office seeking a warrant authorizing the search of a business or home?

Hypo 2: *The Factory Owner's Response*

Now, assume that you represent Ajax. You receive a call from Ajax's President Herb Deets indicating that a Ms. Harlow, an OSHA inspector, just "showed up" at Ajax's factory—unannounced and without a warrant. Mr. Deets wants to know whether he should allow the inspector to enter without a warrant. Mr. Deets feels that his plant is in compliance with OSHA regulations, but OSHA regulations are so strict that an overzealous inspector can always find a violation. Would it be advisable to give, or to refuse, consent? Advise Mr. Deets.

Hypo 3: *The Elevator Inspector & the Cocaine*

Suppose that an elevator inspector enters an office building to inspect an elevator. While there, he happens to notice crack cocaine lying in plain view. You are the lawyer for the agency for which the inspector works, and he calls you for advice. May the inspector seize the cocaine? Can he make arrests? How should he proceed?

City of Los Angeles v. Patel

576 U.S. 409 (2015).

JUSTICE SOTOMAYOR delivered the opinion of the Court.

Los Angeles Municipal Code (LAMC) § 41.49 requires hotel operators to record information about their guests, including: the guest's name and address; the number of people in each guest's party; the make, model, and license plate number of any guest's vehicle parked on hotel property; the guest's date and time of arrival and scheduled departure date; the room number assigned to the guest; the rate charged and amount collected for the room; and the method of payment. Guests without reservations, those who pay for their rooms with cash, and any guests who rent a room for less than 12 hours must present photographic identification at the time of check-in, and hotel operators are required to record the number and expiration date of that document. For those guests who check in using an electronic kiosk, the hotel's records must also contain the guest's credit card information. This information can be maintained in either electronic or paper form, but it must be "kept on the hotel premises in the guest reception or guest check-in area or in an office adjacent" thereto for a period of 90 days. Section 41.49(3)(a) states that hotel guest records "shall be made available to any officer of the Los Angeles Police Department for inspection," provided that "whenever possible, the inspection shall be conducted at a time and in a manner that minimizes any interference with the operation of the business." A hotel operator's failure to make his or her guest records available for police inspection is a misdemeanor punishable by up to six months in jail and a $1,000 fine. Respondents, a group of motel operators along with a lodging association, sued the city of Los Angeles challenging the constitutionality of § 41.49(3)(a). They sought declaratory and injunctive relief. The District Court entered judgment in favor of the City. A divided panel of the Ninth Circuit affirmed. On rehearing en banc, the Court of Appeals reversed. We granted certiorari and now affirm.

§ 41.49(3)(a) is facially unconstitutional because it fails to provide hotel operators with an opportunity for precompliance review. The Court has repeatedly held that "searches conducted outside the judicial process, without prior approval by a judge or a magistrate are *per se* unreasonable subject only to a few specifically established and well-delineated exceptions." *Arizona v. Gant*, 556 U.S. 332, 338 (2009). This rule "applies to commercial premises as well as to homes." *Marshall v. Barlow's, Inc.*, 436 U.S. 307, 312 (1978). Search regimes where no warrant is ever required may be reasonable where "special needs make the warrant and probable-cause requirement impracticable," and where the "primary purpose" of the searches is "distinguishable from the general interest in crime control," *Indianapolis v. Edmond*, 531 U.S. 32, 44 (2000). We assume that the searches authorized by § 41.49 serve a "special need" other than conducting criminal investigations: They ensure compliance with the recordkeeping requirement, which in turn deters criminals from operating on the hotels' premises. The Court has referred to this kind of search as an "administrative search." *Camara v. Municipal Court of City and County of San Francisco*, 387 U.S. 523, 534 (1967).

Absent consent, exigent circumstances, or the like, in order for an administrative search to be constitutional, the subject of the search must be afforded an opportunity to obtain precompliance review before a neutral decisionmaker. While the Court has never attempted to prescribe the exact form precompliance review must take, the City does not argue that § 41.49(3)(a) affords hotel operators any opportunity whatsoever. Section 41.49(3)(a) is, therefore, facially invalid. A hotel owner who refuses to give an officer access to his or her registry can be arrested on the spot. The Court has held that business owners cannot reasonably be put to this kind of choice. *Camara*, 387 U.S., at 533. Absent an opportunity for precompliance review, the ordinance creates an intolerable risk that searches authorized will exceed statutory limits, or be used as a pretext to harass hotel operators and their guests. Even if a hotel has been searched 10 times a day, every day, for three months, without any violation being found, the operator can only refuse to comply with an officer's demand to turn over the registry at his or her own peril.

We hold only that a hotel owner must be afforded an *opportunity* to have a neutral decisionmaker review an officer's demand to search the registry before he or she faces penalties for failing to comply. Actual review need only occur in those rare instances where a hotel operator objects to turning over the registry. This opportunity can be provided without imposing onerous burdens on those charged with an administrative scheme's enforcement. The searches authorized by § 41.49(3)(a) would be constitutional if they were performed pursuant to an administrative subpoena. These subpoenas, which are typically a simple form, can be issued by the individual seeking the record—here, officers in the field—without probable cause that a regulation is being infringed. Issuing a subpoena will usually be the full extent of an officer's burden because "the great majority of businessmen can be expected in normal course to consent to inspection without warrant." *Barlow's, Inc.*, 436 U.S., at 316.

In instances where a subpoenaed hotel operator believes that an attempted search is motivated by illicit purposes, respondents suggest it would be sufficient if he or she could move to quash the subpoena before any search takes place. A neutral decision-maker, including an administrative law judge, would then review the subpoenaed party's objections before deciding whether the subpoena is enforceable. Given the limited grounds on which a motion to quash can be granted, such challenges will likely be rare. In the even rarer event that an officer reasonably suspects that a hotel operator may tamper with the registry while the motion to quash is pending, he or she can guard the registry until the required hearing can occur, which ought not take long. *Illinois v. McArthur*, 531 U.S. 326 (2001). A 2002 report by the Department of Justice "identified approximately 335 existing administrative subpoena authorities held by various federal executive branch entities." In most contexts, business owners can be afforded at least an opportunity to contest an administrative search's propriety without unduly compromising the government's ability to achieve its regulatory aims. Of course administrative subpoenas are only one way in which an opportunity for precompliance review can be made available. But whatever the precise form, the availability of precompliance review alters the dynamic between the officer and the hotel to be searched, and reduces the risk that officers will use these administrative searches as a pretext to harass business owners.

Respondents have not challenged those parts of § 41.49 that require hotel operators to maintain guest registries containing certain information. Even absent legislative action to create a procedure along the lines discussed above, police will not be prevented from obtaining access to these documents. Hotel operators remain free to consent to searches of their registries and police can compel them to turn them over if they have a proper administrative warrant—including one that was issued *ex parte*—or if some other exception to the warrant requirement applies, including exigent circumstances.

The City contends that hotels are "closely regulated," and that the ordinance is facially valid under the more relaxed standard that applies to searches of this category of businesses. Over the past 45 years, the Court has identified only four industries that "have such a history of government oversight that no reasonable expectation of privacy could exist for a proprietor over the stock of such an enterprise," *See Barlow's, Inc.*, 436 U.S., at 313. Unlike liquor sales, *Colonnade*

FYI

In *New York v. Burger*, 482 U.S. 691, the Court took the extraordinary step of upholding warrantless searches of automobile junkyards by the police. The Court viewed the junkyards as constituting "closely regulated businesses," and upheld the searches even though they were being conducted by the police.

Catering Corp. v. United States, 397 U.S. 72 (1970), firearms dealing, *United States v. Biswell*, 406 U.S. 311, 311–312 (1972), mining, *Donovan v. Dewey*, 452 U.S. 594 (1981), or running an automobile junkyard, *New York v. Burger*, 482 U.S. 691 (1987), nothing inherent in the operation of hotels poses a clear and significant risk to the public welfare. *See, e.g., id., at 709* ("Automobile junkyards and vehicle dismantlers provide the major market for stolen vehicles and vehicle parts"); *Dewey*, 452 U.S., at 602 (describing the mining industry as "among the most hazardous in the country"). "The clear import of our cases is that the closely regulated industry is the exception." *Barlow's, Inc.*, 436 U.S., at 313. To classify hotels as pervasively regulated would permit what has always been a narrow exception to swallow the rule. The City refrains from arguing that § 41.49 itself renders hotels closely regulated. Nor do any of the other regulations—regulations requiring hotels to maintain a license, collect taxes, conspicuously post their rates, and meet certain sanitary standards—establish a comprehensive scheme of regulation that distinguishes hotels from numerous other businesses. All businesses in Los Angeles need a license to operate. While some regulations apply to a smaller set of businesses, these can hardly be said to have created a "comprehensive" scheme that puts hotel owners on notice that their "property will be subject to periodic inspections undertaken for specific purposes." *Burger*, 482 U.S., at 705, n. 16. Instead, they are more akin to the widely applicable minimum wage and maximum hour rules that the Court rejected as a basis for deeming "the entirety of American interstate commerce" to be closely regulated in *Barlow's, Inc*. If such general regulations were sufficient to invoke the closely regulated industry exception, it would be hard to imagine a type of business that would not qualify.

Petitioner attempts to recast this hodgepodge of regulations as a comprehensive scheme by referring to a "centuries-old tradition" of warrantless searches of hotels. Laws obligating inns to provide suitable lodging to all paying guests are not the same as laws subjecting inns to warrantless searches. Petitioner asserts that "for a long time, hotel owners left their registers open to widespread inspection." Setting aside that modern hotel registries contain sensitive information, such as driver's licenses and credit card numbers for which there is no historic analog, the fact that some hotels chose to make registries accessible to the public has little bearing on whether government authorities could have viewed these documents on demand without a hotel's consent. Even if hotels are pervasively regulated, § 41.49 would need to satisfy three additional criteria to be reasonable under the Fourth Amendment: (1) "There must be a 'substantial' government interest that informs the regulatory scheme pursuant to which the inspection is made"; (2) "the warrantless inspections must be 'necessary' to further the regulatory scheme"; and (3) "the statute's inspection program, in terms of the certainty and regularity of its application, must provide a constitutionally adequate substitute for a warrant." *Burger*, 482 U.S., at 702. Petitioner's interest in ensuring that hotels maintain accurate and complete registries might fulfill the first of these requirements, but § 41.49 fails the second and third prongs. The City claims that affording hotel operators any opportunity for precompliance review would fatally undermine the scheme's efficacy by giving operators a chance to falsify their records. This argument could be made regarding any recordkeeping requirement. Nothing precludes an officer from conducting a surprise inspection by obtaining an *ex parte* warrant or, where an officer reasonably suspects the registry would be altered, from guarding the registry pending a hearing on a motion to quash. *See Barlow's, Inc.,* 436 U.S., at 319–20. There is no basis to believe that resort to such measures will be needed to conduct spot checks in the vast majority of [hotels]. Section 41.49 is constitutionally deficient under the "certainty and regularity" prong of the closely regulated industries test because it fails sufficiently to constrain police officers' discretion as to which hotels to search and under what circumstances. While the Court has upheld inspection schemes of closely regulated industries that called for searches at least four times a year, or on a "regular basis," § 41.49 imposes no comparable standard. For the foregoing reasons, we agree that § 41.49(3)(a) is facially invalid insofar as it fails to provide any opportunity for precompliance review before a hotel must give its guest registry to the police for inspection. Accordingly, the judgment of the Ninth Circuit is affirmed.

It is so ordered.

JUSTICE SCALIA, with whom THE CHIEF JUSTICE and JUSTICE THOMAS join, dissenting.

In determining whether a business is closely regulated, this Court has looked to factors including the duration of the regulatory tradition, *Colonnade Catering Corp. v. United States,* 397 U.S. 72 (1970), *Donovan v. Dewey,* 452 U.S. 594 (1981); the comprehensiveness of the regulatory regime, and the imposition of similar regulations by other jurisdictions. These factors shed light on the expectation of privacy the owner of a business may reasonably have, which in turn affects the reasonableness of a warrantless search. Governments have long subjected motels to unique public duties, and have established inspection regimes to ensure compliance. "Innkeepers are bound to take, not merely ordinary care, but uncommon care, of the goods, money, and baggage of their guests," as travelers "are obliged to rely almost implicitly on the good faith of inn holders, who might have frequent opportunities of associating with ruffians and pilferers." At the time of the founding, searches—indeed, warrantless searches—of inns and similar places of public accommodation were commonplace. The regulatory tradition governing motels is not only longstanding, but comprehensive. Los Angeles imposes an occupancy tax upon transients who stay in motels, and makes the motel owner responsible for collecting it. It authorizes city officials "to enter a motel during business hours" in order to "inspect and examine" to determine whether these tax provisions have been complied with. It requires all motels to obtain a "Transient Occupancy Registration Certificate," which must be displayed on the premises. State law requires motels to "post in a conspicuous place a statement of rate or range of rates by the day for lodging," and forbids any charges in excess of those posted rates. Hotels must change bed linens between guests, and they must offer guests the option not to have towels and linens laundered daily. "Multiuse drinking utensils" may be placed in guest rooms only if they are "thoroughly washed and sanitized after each use" and "placed in protective bags." State authorities, like their municipal counterparts, "may at reasonable times enter and inspect any hotels, motels, or other public places" to ensure compliance. The regulatory regime is thus substantially *more* comprehensive than the regulations governing junkyards in *Burger*, where licensing, inventory-recording, and permit-posting requirements were found sufficient to qualify the industry as closely regulated. This evidence is surely enough to establish that "when a motel operator chooses to engage in this pervasively regulated business he does so with the knowledge that his business records will be subject to effective inspection." *United States v. Biswell*, 406 U.S. 311, 316 (1972).

Since we first concluded in *Colonnade Catering* that warrantless searches of closely regulated businesses are reasonable, we have only identified *one* industry as *not* closely regulated. Lower courts, have identified many more businesses as closely regulated: pharmacies, massage parlors, commercial-fishing operations, day-care facilities, nursing homes, jewelers, barbershops, and even rabbit dealers. Like automobile junkyards and catering companies that serve alcohol, many of these businesses are far from "intrinsically dangerous." The reason closely regulated industries may be searched without a warrant has nothing to do with the risk of harm they pose; rather, it has to do with the expectations of those who enter such a line of work. The City's ordinance easily satisfies the remaining *Burger* requirements: It furthers a substantial governmental interest, it is necessary to achieving that interest, and it provides an adequate substitute for a search warrant.

The private pain and public costs imposed by drug dealing, prostitution, and human trafficking are beyond contention, and motels provide an obvious haven for those who trade in human misery. Although law enforcement can enter a motel room without a warrant when exigent circumstances exist, the reason criminals use motel rooms is that they offer privacy and secrecy. The recordkeeping requirement operates by *deterring* crime. Criminals, who depend on the anonymity that motels offer, will balk when confronted with a motel's demand that they produce identification. And a motel's evasion of the recordkeeping requirement fosters crime. The warrantless inspection requirement provides a necessary incentive for motels to maintain their registers thoroughly and accurately: They never know when law enforcement might drop by to inspect. Motel operators who conspire with drug dealers and procurers may demand precompliance judicial review simply to buy time for making fraudulent entries in their guest registers.

The Court suggests that police could obtain an administrative subpoena to search a guest register and, if a motel moves to quash, the police could "guard the registry pending a hearing" on the motion. This proposal protects motels from government inspection of their registers by authorizing government agents to seize the registers or to upset guests by a prolonged police presence at the motel. The Court notes that police can obtain an *ex parte* warrant before conducting a register inspection. Presumably such warrants could issue without probable cause of wrongdoing by a particular motel. Even so, under this regime police would have to obtain an *ex parte* warrant before *every* inspection because law enforcement would have no way of knowing ahead of time which motels would refuse consent to a search upon request; and if they wait to obtain a warrant until consent is refused, motels will have the opportunity to falsify their guest registers while the police jump through the procedural hoops required to obtain a warrant. The costs of this always-get-a-warrant "alternative" would be prohibitive for a police force in one of America's largest cities, juggling numerous law-enforcement priorities, and confronting more than 2,000 motels within its jurisdiction. The fact that obtaining a warrant might be costly will not by itself render a warrantless search reasonable under the Fourth Amendment; but it can render a warrantless search *necessary* in the context of an administrative-search regime governing closely regulated businesses. The administrative search need only be reasonable.

Finally, the City's ordinance provides an adequate substitute for a warrant. Warrants "advise the owner of the scope and objects of the search, beyond which limits the inspector is not expected to proceed." *Barlow's*, 436 U.S., at 323. Ultimately, they protect against "devolving almost unbridled discretion upon executive and administrative officers, particularly those in the field, as to when to search and whom to search." *Ibid*. Nothing in the ordinance authorizes law enforcement to enter a nonpublic part

> **FYI**
>
> Even though *Camara* loosened the probable cause requirements for administrative searches, illegal inspections do occur. Sometimes, an agency obtains a warrant but the warrant was invalidly issued. In other cases, as in *Barlow*, the agency searches without a warrant when one is required. Or, as sometimes happens, the police conduct an illegal search and give the results to administrative officials.

of the motel. Compare this to the statute upheld in *Colonnade Catering*, which provided that "the Secretary or his delegate may enter, in the daytime, any building or place where any articles or objects subject to tax are made, produced, or kept, so far as it may be necessary for the purpose of examining said articles or objects." The Los Angeles ordinance—which limits warrantless police searches to the pages of a guest register in a public part of a motel—circumscribes police discretion in much more exacting terms than the laws we approved in our earlier cases. The Court claims that Los Angeles's ordinance does not adequately limit the *frequency* of searches. But the warrantless police searches of a business "10 times a day, every day, for three months" that the Court envisions under Los Angeles's regime are entirely consistent with the regimes in *Dewey* and *Burger*.

Point for Discussion

Trucker Checkpoints

In *United States v. Parker*, 583 F.3d 1049 (8th Cir. 2009), the court held that interstate trucking is a closely regulated industry so that state officials can stop truckers at checkpoints and make random inquiries regarding compliance with state truck regulation laws. In *Parker*, a police officer made a random check of a truck that was pulling a trailer containing three vehicles: a 2001 Ford Excursion, a 1995 Nissan Quest, and a 2000 Chevrolet Silverado. The check was a "Level 1 inspection" under the North American Standard Inspection Program (NASIP) that involved a check of the driver's logbook, bills of lading, insurance, and license. During the stop,

In *Marshall v. Barlow's Inc.*, 436 U.S. 307 (1978), the Court held that the Occupational Safety & Health Act, which authorized health and safety inspections of workplaces, did not authorize warrantless searches. The Court noted that virtually every business is subject to OSHA, and therefore an OSHA exception would eviscerate the Fourth Amendment warrant requirement. The Court also concluded that there was less need and justification for warrantless inspections.

the officer determined that the driver did not have a commercial license, and that his logbook was not up-to-date, and ordered defendant not to proceed for the next 10 hours. Although the officer did not require defendant to remain with the truck, he did remain and ultimately consented to a search of vehicles that he was transporting (which contained contraband drugs).

Food for Thought

Suppose that a state wants to ensure that adult film producers do not engage in child pornography. In an effort to implement that goal, the state enacts a law permitting warrantless searches of all film producers, and also requiring them to keep records regarding the ages of all actors. Given that films involve free speech, can film production be regarded as a closely regulated business? Is the state law valid? *See Free Speech Coalition, Inc. v. Attorney General*, 825 F.3d 149 (3d Cir. 2016).

Hypo 1: *Pawnbrokers & Special Metals*

Should a pawn broker that buys precious metals be treated as a "highly regulated" business? Suppose that the Ohio Precious Metals Dealers Act provides that all pawnbrokers must keep detailed records regarding all precious metals that they purchase, make the records available to the police on a daily basis, and give police the right to view the objects purchased as well as information regarding the sellers. The law was passed in an effort to help the police track down stolen property. Is the law valid? Suppose that the law requires pawnbrokers to give the police access, not only to their precious metals and precious metal records, but to their entire business? Would such a law be permissible under the Fourth Amendment? *See Liberty Coins, LLC v. Goodman*, 880 F.3d 274 (6th Cir. 2018).

Hypo 2: *McCown Iron*

OSHA officials have a long and complicated history with McCown Iron Works, an iron foundry in Idaho. When OSHA attempted to inspect McCown, John McCown, CEO and principal owner, refused to permit inspectors to enter. Later that year, in response to an employee complaint, OHSA made an unannounced visit to the foundry with a warrant. McCown refused entry and was held in contempt of court. The next year, when OSHA sent letters of inquiry to McCown, after receiving complaints from other employees, John McCown responded with a letter which stated that: "You have wasted my time and taxpayer money without improving safety. This is the problem with OSHA. It makes you look like fools and wastes everyone's time and money. Why don't you try to help employers by providing information about unsafe products and processes rather than acting like the Gestapo with secret informants and star courts." Despite the letters of inquiry, OSHA did not attempt to inspect McCown Iron. OSHA then sought a warrant to inspect McCown Iron's foundry. In its application, OSHA states that McCown was selected pursuant to its General Schedule System (GSS) which outlines OSHA's search policies and assigns each industry a nationwide Standard Industrial Classification (SIC) Code. OSHA also complies lists which show each industry employer with a lost work day injury rate (LWDI) at or above the national LWDI rate for their industries. From this list, inspection sites are selected randomly for each high rate industry. Based on the GSS, SIC and LWDI, a federal court issued a warrant. Suppose that you represent McCown Iron which is seeking advice. McCown would like to resist the subpoena. May it do so? On what grounds? Will McCown Iron suffer any special risks if it refuses to admit OSHA inspectors?

8. Stop & Frisk

Although the "stop and frisk" exception is one of the more recent exceptions to the warrant requirement, it has reshaped Fourth Amendment law in important respects.

Terry v. State of Ohio

392 U.S. 1 (1968).

MR. CHIEF JUSTICE WARREN delivered the opinion of the Court.

Petitioner Terry was convicted of carrying a concealed weapon and sentenced to one to three years in the penitentiary. Following denial of a motion to suppress, the prosecution introduced in evidence two revolvers and a number of bullets seized from Terry and a codefendant by Cleveland Police Detective Martin McFadden. At the hearing on the motion to suppress this evidence, Officer McFadden testified that while he was patrolling in plain clothes in downtown Cleveland at approximately 2:30 in the afternoon, his attention was attracted by two men, Chilton and Terry, standing on the corner of Huron Road and Euclid Avenue. He had never seen the two men before, and he was unable to say precisely what first drew his eye to them. However, he testified that he had been a policeman for 39 years and a detective for 35 and that he had been assigned to patrol this vicinity of downtown Cleveland for shoplifters and pickpockets for 30 years. He explained that he had developed routine habits of observation over the years and that he would "stand and watch people or walk and watch people at many intervals of the day." "Now, in this case when I looked over they didn't look right to me at the time." His interest aroused, Officer McFadden took up a post of observation in the entrance to a store 300 to 400 feet away from the two men. He saw one of the men leave the other and walk southwest on Huron Road, past some stores. The man paused for a moment and looked in a store window, then walked on a short distance, turned around and walked back to the corner, pausing to look in the same store window. He rejoined his companion at the corner, and the two conferred briefly. Then the second man went through the same series of motions, strolling down Huron Road, looking in the same window, walking on a short distance, turning back, peering in the store window again, and returning to confer with the first man. The two men repeated this ritual alternately between five and six times apiece, roughly a dozen trips. At one point, while the two were standing together, a third man approached them and engaged them briefly in conversation. This man then left the two others and walked west. Chilton and Terry resumed their measured pacing, peering and conferring. After 10 to 12 minutes, the two men walked off together, heading west, following the path taken earlier by the third man.

By this time Officer McFadden had become thoroughly suspicious. After observing their elaborately casual and oft-repeated reconnaissance of the store window, he suspected the two men of "casing a job, a stick-up," and he considered it his duty as a police officer to investigate further. He feared "they may have a gun." Officer McFadden followed Chilton and Terry and saw them stop in front of Zucker's store to talk to the same man who had conferred with them earlier. Deciding that the situation was ripe for direct action, Officer McFadden approached the three men, identified himself as a police officer and asked for their names. He was not acquainted with any of the three men, and he had received no information concerning them from any other source. When the men "mumbled something" in response to his inquiries, Officer McFadden grabbed petitioner Terry, spun him around so that they were facing the other two, with Terry between McFadden and the others, and patted down the outside of his clothing. In the left breast pocket of Terry's overcoat Officer McFadden felt a pistol. He reached inside, but was unable to remove the gun. At this point, keeping Terry between himself and the others, the officer ordered all three men to enter Zucker's store. As they went in, he removed Terry's overcoat completely, removed a .38-caliber revolver from the pocket and ordered all three men to face the wall with their hands raised. Officer McFadden proceeded to pat down the outer clothing of Chilton and the third man, Katz. He discovered another revolver in the outer pocket of Chilton's overcoat, but no weapons on Katz. The officer testified that he only patted the men down to see whether they had weapons, and that he did not put his hands beneath the outer garments of either Terry or Chilton until he felt their guns. He never placed his hands beneath Katz' outer garments. Officer McFadden seized Chilton's gun, asked the proprietor of the store to call a police wagon, and took all three men to the station, where Chilton and Terry were formally charged with carrying concealed weapons. We granted certiorari to determine whether the admission of the revolvers in evidence violated petitioner's rights under the Fourth Amendment, made applicable to the States by the Fourteenth.

Petitioner was entitled to the protection of the Fourth Amendment as he walked down the street in Cleveland. The question is whether in all the circumstances of this on-the-street encounter, his right to personal security was violated by an unreasonable search and seizure. This question thrusts to the fore difficult and troublesome issues regarding a sensitive area of police activity. It is frequently argued that in dealing with the rapidly unfolding and often dangerous situations on city streets the police are in need of an escalating set of flexible responses, graduated in relation to the amount of information they possess. For this purpose it is urged that distinctions should be made between a "stop" and an "arrest" (or a "seizure" of a person), and between a "frisk" and a "search." Thus, it is argued, the police should be allowed to "stop" a person and detain him briefly for questioning upon suspicion that he may be connected with criminal activity. Upon suspicion that the person may be armed, the police should have the power to "frisk" him for weapons. If the "stop" and the "frisk" give rise to probable cause to believe that the suspect has committed a crime, then the police should be empowered to make a formal "arrest," and a full incident "search" of the person. This scheme is justified in part upon the notion that a "stop" and a "frisk" amount to a mere "minor inconvenience and petty indignity," which can properly be imposed upon the citizen in the interest of effective law enforcement on the basis of a police officer's suspicion.

The argument is made that the authority of the police must be strictly circumscribed by the law of arrest and search as it has developed to date in the traditional jurisprudence of the Fourth Amendment. It is contended with some force that there is not—and cannot be—a variety of police activity which does not depend solely upon the voluntary cooperation of the citizen and yet which stops short of an arrest based upon probable cause to make such an arrest. The heart of the Fourth Amendment, the argument runs, is a severe requirement of specific justification for any intrusion upon protected personal security, coupled with a highly developed system of judicial controls to enforce upon the agents of the State the commands of the Constitution. We approach the issues in this case mindful of the limitations of the judicial function in controlling the myriad daily situations in which policemen and citizens confront each other on the street.

We turn our attention to the narrow question posed by the facts: whether it is always unreasonable for a policeman to seize a person and subject him to a limited search for weapons unless there is probable cause for an arrest. Our first task is to establish at what point in this encounter the Fourth Amendment becomes relevant. We must decide whether and when Officer McFadden "seized" Terry and whether and when he conducted a "search." It is quite plain that the Fourth Amendment governs "seizures" of the person which do not eventuate in a trip to the station house and prosecution for crime—"arrests" in traditional terminology. Whenever a police officer accosts an individual and restrains his freedom to walk away, he has "seized" that person. And it is nothing less than sheer torture of the English language to suggest that a careful exploration of the outer surfaces of a person's clothing all over his or her body in an attempt to find weapons is not a "search." Moreover, it is simply fantastic to urge that such a procedure performed in public by a policeman while the citizen stands helpless, perhaps facing a wall with his hands raised, is a "petty indignity." It is a serious intrusion upon the sanctity of the person, which may inflict great indignity and arouse strong resentment, and it is not to be undertaken lightly.

The danger in between a "stop" and an "arrest," or "seizure" of the person, and between a "frisk" and a "search" is twofold. It seeks to isolate from constitutional scrutiny the initial stages of the contact between the policeman and the citizen. By suggesting a rigid all-or-nothing model of justification and regulation under the Amendment, it obscures the utility of limitations upon the scope, as well as the initiation, of police action as a means of constitutional regulation. This Court has held past that a search which is reasonable at its inception may violate the Fourth Amendment by virtue of its intolerable intensity and scope. The scope of the search must be "strictly tied to and justified by" the circumstances which rendered its initiation permissible. The distinctions of classical "stop-and-frisk" theory thus serve to divert attention from the central inquiry under the Fourth Amendment—the reasonableness in all the circumstances of the particular governmental invasion of a citizen's personal security. "Search" and "seizure" are not talismans. We therefore reject the notions that the Fourth Amendment does not come into play at all as a limitation upon police conduct if the officers stop short of something called a "technical arrest" or a "full-blown search."

In this case there can be no question that Officer McFadden "seized" petitioner and subjected him to a "search" when he took hold of him and patted down the outer surfaces of his clothing. We must decide whether at that point it was reasonable for Officer McFadden to have interfered with petitioner's personal security as he did. In determining whether the seizure and search were "unreasonable" our inquiry is a dual one—whether the officer's action was justified at its inception, and whether it was reasonably related in scope to the circumstances which justified the interference in the first place.

We do not retreat from our holdings that the police must, whenever practicable, obtain advance judicial approval of searches and seizures through the warrant procedure, or that in most instances failure to comply with the warrant requirement can only be excused by exigent circumstances. But we deal here with an entire rubric of police conduct—necessarily swift action predicated upon the on-the-spot observations of the officer on the beat—which historically has not been, and as a practical matter could not be, subjected to the warrant procedure. Instead, the conduct involved in this case must be tested by the Fourth Amendment's general proscription against unreasonable searches and seizures.

Nonetheless, the notions which underlie both the warrant procedure and the requirement of probable cause remain fully relevant in this context. In order to assess the reasonableness of Officer McFadden's conduct as a general proposition, it is necessary "first to focus upon the governmental interest which allegedly justifies official intrusion upon the constitutionally protected interests of the private citizen," for there is "no ready test for determining reasonableness other than by balancing the need to search (or seize) against the invasion which the search (or seizure) entails." *Camara v. Municipal Court*, 387 U.S. 523, 534–535 (1967). In justifying the particular intrusion the police officer must be able to point to specific and articulable facts which, taken together with rational inferences from those facts, reasonably warrant that intrusion. The scheme of the Fourth Amendment becomes meaningful only when it is assured that at some point the conduct of those charged with enforcing the laws can be subjected to the more detached, neutral scrutiny of a judge who must evaluate the reasonableness of a particular search or seizure in light of the particular circumstances. In making that assessment it is imperative that the facts be judged against an objective standard: would the facts available to the officer at the moment of the seizure or the search "warrant a man of reasonable caution in the belief" that the action taken was appropriate? Anything less would invite intrusions upon constitutionally guaranteed rights based on nothing more substantial than inarticulate hunches, a result this Court has consistently refused to sanction. Simple "good faith on the part of the arresting officer is not enough. If subjective good faith alone were the test, the protections of the Fourth Amendment would evaporate, and the people would be 'secure in their persons, houses, papers and effects,' only in the discretion of the police."

Applying these principles, we consider the nature and extent of the governmental interests involved. One general interest is that of effective crime prevention and detection; it is this interest which underlies the recognition that a police officer may in appropriate circumstances and in an appropriate manner approach a person for purposes of investigating possibly criminal behavior even though there is no probable cause to make an arrest. It was this legitimate investigative function Officer McFadden was discharging when he decided to approach petitioner and his companions after he had observed Terry, Chilton, and Katz go through a series of acts, each of them perhaps innocent in itself, but which taken together warranted further investigation. There is nothing unusual in two men standing together on a street corner, perhaps waiting for someone. Nor is there anything suspicious about people in such circumstances strolling up and down the street, singly or in pairs. Store windows are made to be looked in. But the story is quite different where, as here, two men hover about a street corner for an extended period of time, at the end of which it becomes apparent that they are not waiting for anyone or anything; where these men pace alternately along an identical route, pausing to stare in the same store window roughly 24 times; where each completion of this route is followed immediately by a conference between the two men; where they are joined in one of these conferences by a third man who leaves swiftly; and where the two men follow the third and rejoin him a couple of blocks away. It would have been poor police work for an officer of 30 years' experience in the detection of thievery from stores in this same neighborhood to have failed to investigate this behavior further.

The crux of this case is not the propriety of Officer McFadden's taking steps to investigate petitioner's suspicious behavior, but whether there was justification for McFadden's invasion of Terry's personal security by searching him for weapons in the course of that investigation. We are concerned with more than the governmental interest in investigating crime; there is the more immediate interest of the police officer in taking steps to assure himself that the person with whom he is dealing is not armed with a weapon that could unexpectedly and fatally be used against him. Certainly it would be unreasonable to require that police officers take unnecessary risks in the performance of their duties. American criminals have a long tradition of armed violence, and every year in this country many law enforcement officers are killed in the line of duty, and thousands more are wounded. Virtually all of these deaths and a substantial portion of the injuries are inflicted with guns and knives.

We cannot blind ourselves to the need for law enforcement officers to protect themselves and other prospective victims of violence in situations where they may lack probable cause for an arrest. When an officer is justified in believing that the individual whose suspicious behavior he is investigating at close range is armed and presently dangerous to the officer or to others, it would be clearly unreasonable to deny the officer the power to take necessary measures to determine whether the person is in fact carrying a weapon and to neutralize the threat of physical harm.

We must still consider the nature and quality of the intrusion on individual rights which must be accepted if police officers are to be conceded the right to search for weapons in situations where probable cause to arrest for crime is lacking. Even a limited search of the outer clothing for weapons constitutes a severe, though brief, intrusion upon cherished personal security, and it must surely be an annoying, frightening, and perhaps humiliating experience. Petitioner contends that such an intrusion is permissible only incident to a lawful arrest, either for a crime involving the possession of weapons or for a crime the commission of which led the officer to investigate in the first place. However, this argument must be closely examined. Petitioner does not argue that a police officer should refrain from making any investigation of suspicious circumstances until such time as he has probable cause to make an arrest; nor does he deny that police officers in properly discharging their investigative function may find themselves confronting persons who might well be armed and dangerous. Moreover, he does not say that an officer is always unjustified in searching a suspect to discover weapons. Rather, he says it is unreasonable for the policeman to take that step until such time as the situation evolves to a point where there is probable cause to make an arrest. When that point has been reached, petitioner would concede the officer's right to conduct a search of the suspect for weapons, fruits or instrumentalities of the crime, or "mere" evidence, incident to the arrest.

There are two weaknesses in this line of reasoning. First, it fails to take account of traditional limitations upon the scope of searches, and thus recognizes no distinction in purpose, character, and extent between a search incident to an arrest and a limited search for weapons. The former, although justified in part by the acknowledged necessity to protect the arresting officer from assault with a concealed weapon, is also justified on other grounds, and can therefore involve a relatively extensive exploration of the person. A search for weapons in the absence of probable cause to arrest must, like any other search, be strictly circumscribed by the exigencies which justify its initiation. Thus it must be limited to that which is necessary for the discovery of weapons which might be used to harm the officer or others nearby, and may realistically be characterized as something less than a "full" search, even though it remains a serious intrusion. A second, and related, objection is that it assumes that the law of arrest has already worked out the balance between the particular interests involved here—the neutralization of danger to the policeman in the investigative circumstance and the sanctity of the individual. This is not so. An arrest is the initial stage of a criminal prosecution. It is intended to vindicate society's interest in having its laws obeyed, and it is inevitably accompanied by future interference with the individual's freedom of movement, whether or not trial or conviction ultimately follows. The protective search for weapons, on the other hand, constitutes a brief, though far from inconsiderable, intrusion upon the sanctity of the person. It does not follow that because an officer may lawfully arrest a person only when he is apprised of facts sufficient to warrant a belief that the person has committed or is committing a crime, the officer is equally unjustified, absent that kind of evidence, in making any intrusions short of an arrest. Moreover, a perfectly reasonable apprehension of danger may arise long before the officer is possessed of adequate information to justify taking a person into custody for the purpose of prosecuting him for a crime.

Our evaluation of the proper balance that has to be struck in this type of case leads us to conclude that there must be a narrowly drawn authority to permit a reasonable search for weapons for the protection of the police officer, where he has reason to believe that he is dealing with an armed and dangerous individual, regardless of whether he has probable cause to arrest the individual for a crime. The officer need not be absolutely certain that the individual is armed; the issue is whether a reasonably prudent man in the circumstances would be warranted in the belief that his safety or that of others was in danger. And in determining whether the officer acted reasonably in such circumstances, due weight must be given, not to his inchoate and unparticularized suspicion or "hunch," but to the specific reasonable inferences which he is entitled to draw from the facts in light of his experience.

We must now examine the conduct of Officer McFadden to determine whether his search and seizure of petitioner were reasonable, both at their inception and as conducted. He had observed Terry, together with Chilton and another man, acting in a manner he took to be preface to a "stick-up." On the facts and circumstances, a reasonably prudent man would have been warranted in believing petitioner was armed and thus presented a threat to the officer's safety while he was investigating his suspicious behavior. The actions of Terry and Chilton were consistent with McFadden's hypothesis that these men were contemplating a daylight robbery—which would be likely to involve the use of weapons—and nothing in their conduct from the time he first noticed them until the time he confronted them and identified himself as a police officer gave him sufficient reason to negate that hypothesis. Although the trio had departed the original scene, there was nothing to indicate abandonment of an intent to commit a robbery. Thus, when Officer McFadden approached the three men he had observed enough to make it quite reasonable to fear that they were armed; and nothing in their response to his hailing them, identifying himself as a police officer, and asking their names served to dispel that reasonable belief. We cannot say his decision at that point to seize Terry and pat his clothing for weapons was the product of a volatile or inventive imagination, or was undertaken simply as an act of harassment; the record evidences the tempered act of a policeman who in the course of an investigation had to make a quick decision as to how to protect himself and others from possible danger, and took limited steps to do so.

The manner in which the seizure and search were conducted is as vital a part of the inquiry as whether they were warranted at all. We need not develop at length the limitations which the Fourth Amendment places upon a protective seizure and search for weapons. These limitations will have to be developed in the concrete factual circumstances of individual cases. Suffice it to note that such a search, unlike a search without a warrant incident to a lawful arrest, is not justified by any need to prevent the disappearance or destruction of evidence of crime. The sole justification of the search is the protection of the police officer and others nearby, and it must therefore be confined in scope to an intrusion reasonably designed to discover guns, knives, clubs, or other hidden instruments for the assault of the police officer. The scope of the search in this case presents no serious problem in light of these standards. Officer McFadden patted down the outer clothing of petitioner and his two companions. He did not place his hands in their pockets or under the outer surface of their garments until he had felt weapons, and then he merely reached for and removed the guns. He never did invade Katz' person beyond the outer surfaces of his clothes, since he discovered nothing in his patdown which might have been a weapon. Officer McFadden confined his search strictly to what was minimally necessary to learn whether the men were armed and to disarm them once he discovered the weapons. He did not conduct a general exploratory search for whatever evidence of criminal activity he might find.

We conclude that the revolver seized from Terry was properly admitted in evidence against him. At the time he seized petitioner and searched him for weapons, Officer McFadden had reasonable grounds to believe that petitioner was armed and dangerous, and it was necessary for the protection of himself and others to take swift measures to discover the true facts and neutralize the threat of harm if it materialized. The policeman carefully restricted his search to what was appropriate to the discovery of the particular items which he sought. Each case of this sort will have to be decided on its own facts. We merely hold that where a police officer observes unusual conduct which leads him reasonably to conclude in light of his experience that criminal activity may be afoot and that the persons with whom he is dealing may be armed and presently dangerous, where in the course of investigating this behavior he identifies himself as a policeman and makes reasonable inquiries, and where nothing in the initial stages of the encounter serves to dispel his reasonable fear for his own or others' safety, he is entitled for the protection of himself and others in the area to conduct a carefully limited search of the outer clothing of such persons in an attempt to discover weapons which might be used to assault him. Such a search is a reasonable search under the Fourth Amendment, and any weapons seized may properly be introduced in evidence against the person from whom they were taken.

Affirmed.

MR. JUSTICE HARLAN, concurring.

A limited frisk incident to a lawful stop must often be rapid and routine. There is no reason why an officer, rightfully but forcibly confronting a person suspected of a serious crime, should have to ask one question and take the risk that the answer might be a bullet.

MR. JUSTICE DOUGLAS, dissenting.

The infringement on personal liberty of any "seizure" of a person can only be "reasonable" under the Fourth Amendment if we require the police to possess "probable cause" before they seize him. Only that line draws a meaningful distinction between an officer's mere inkling and the presence of facts within the officer's personal knowledge which would convince a reasonable man that the person seized has committed, is committing, or is about to commit a particular crime. To give the police greater power than a magistrate is to take a long step down the totalitarian path. Perhaps such a step is desirable to cope with modern forms of lawlessness. But if it is taken, it should be the deliberate choice of the people through a constitutional amendment.

Food for Thought

In *Florida v. J.L.*, 529 U.S. 266 (2000), the police received an anonymous tip that a young black male wearing a plaid shirt at a bus stop was carrying a gun. At the stop, the police find three young black males, including one who is wearing a plaid shirt. Except for the tip, the officers have no reason to believe that any of the males is engaged in illegal conduct. The officers immediately frisk the man in the plaid shirt, finds a gun in his pocket, and charges him with carrying a concealed firearm. The Court invalidated the search: "All the police had to go on in this case was the bare report of an unknown, unaccountable informant who neither explained how he knew about the gun nor supplied any basis for believing he had inside information about J.L. An accurate description of a subject's readily observable location and appearance will help the police correctly identify the person whom the tipster means to accuse. Such a tip, however, does not show that the tipster has knowledge of concealed criminal activity. Reasonable suspicion here requires that a tip be reliable in its assertion of illegality, not just in its tendency to identify a determinate person." The Court also rejected the state's contention that *Terry* should encompass a "firearms exception" permitting police to stop and frisk individuals for firearms. In light of the decisions that you have read, would *J.L.* be decided the same way today?

Points for Discussion

a. The "Bulge"

In *Pennsylvania v. Mimms*, 434 U.S. 106 (1966), the police stopped a vehicle because its license plate was expired. The officer approached the vehicle, asked the driver to step out, and also asked for the driver's license and registration. When the man exited the vehicle, the officer observed a "bulge" under the man's sports jacket, and decided to frisk him. In *Mimms*, the Court upheld the frisk. Even though the suspect was not acting suspiciously, the "bulge permitted the officer to conclude that Mimms was

Food for Thought

Would *Michigan v. Long* (referred to in the immediately preceding FYI box) justify the police in conducting a frisk when the police did not find a weapon (or have reason to believe that the driver had one), but the driver appeared to be nervous, was uncooperative, and verbally belligerent? *See Frazier v. Commonwealth*, 406 S.W.3d 448 (Ky. 2013). Would a frisk be allowed if the officer, during the course of a lawful stop, observes bullets in the car's ashtray? *See State v. Santos,* 64 A.3d 314 (R.I. 2013).

armed and thus posed a serious and present danger to the safety of the officer. In these circumstances, any man of 'reasonable caution' would likely have conducted the 'pat down.'"

b. The Recovering Drug Addict

In *Sibron v. New York*, 392 U.S. 40 (1968), a police officer continuously observed Sibron from 4:00 p.m. until midnight, observing him in conversation with known drug addicts. The officer could not overhear these conversations, and did not see anything pass between Sibron and the addicts. Late evening, Sibron enters a restaurant and begins eating with several known addicts. At that point, the officer approaches Sibron and states "You know what I am after." Sibron mumbles something and thrusts his hand into his pocket. The officer immediately reaches into the same pocket and finds several envelopes containing heroin. The Court rejected the idea that "persons who talk to narcotics addicts are engaged in the criminal traffic in narcotics" and found that the officer did not fear that Sibron was going for a weapon when he stuck his hand in his pocket. Justice Black dissented: "When Sibron, who had been approaching and talking to addicts for eight hours, reached his hand quickly to his left coat pocket, he might well be reaching for a gun. A policeman under such circumstances has to act in a split second; delay may mean death for him."

c. The Seated Suspect

In *Adams v. Williams*, 407 U.S. 143 (1972), a police officer, working in a high crime area, received a tip that an individual seated in a nearby car was carrying narcotics and had a gun in his waistband. The officer approached the vehicle, tapped on the window, and asked the driver to open his door. When the driver rolled down his window instead, the officer reached into the vehicle and retrieved a fully loaded revolver from the suspect's waistband. The Court upheld the decision to reach into the vehicle: "Under these circumstances the policeman's action in reaching to the spot where the gun was thought to be hidden constituted a limited intrusion designed to insure his safety, and we conclude that it was reasonable. The loaded gun was therefore admissible at Williams' trial." Justice Marshall dissented, arguing that there was insufficient basis for a frisk.

Food for Thought

Was it really necessary for the Court to create the stop and frisk exception? Did Officer McFadden have probable cause to arrest Terry and his cohorts? Did he have probable cause to search them? Even if McFadden possessed probable cause to search, based on what you have studied thus far, could he have searched Terry without a warrant? Should Officer McFadden have been forced to wait until Terry and his cohorts "made their move?"

d. Frisking Passengers

In *Arizona v. Johnson*, 555 U.S. 323 (2009), police were on patrol one evening in a neighborhood associated with the Crips gang. When an officer stopped and approached a vehicle, she noticed that one of the passengers was wearing a blue bandana associated with the Crips gang and had a scanner. She regarded the scanner as suspicious because few people carry scanners unless they are engaged in criminal activity or are trying to avoid the police. The passenger provided his name and volunteered that he lived in a nearby city associated with the Crips gang, as well as the fact that he had served time in prison for burglary. The Court held that, when an officer validly stops a vehicle, and develops reason to believe that a passenger is armed and dangerous, then the officer may pat down the passenger. The Court found sufficient basis for the pat down in the *Johnson* case.

e. The N.Y.P.D. Decree

In 2013, a federal judge concluded that the N.Y.P.D.'s stop and frisk policy disproportionately targeted blacks and Hispanics, and ordered the N.Y.P.D. to order additional training, and develop a "remedial process." *See Floyd v. City of New York*, 959 F. Supp.2d 540 (S.D.N.Y. 2013). The decree seemed to be inconsistent with U.S. Supreme Court precedent. *See Rizzo v. Goode*, 423 U.S. 362 (1976). The court of appeals eventually overturned the decree and ordered the judge removed from the case. *See Ligon v. City of New York*, 736 F.3d 231 (2d Cir. 2013). However, the City voluntarily agreed to limit the practice.

Hypo 1: *NRA Affiliations*

A police officer stops a pickup truck for speeding on a public highway and notices a "National Rifle Association" sticker on the back window. Even though the officer does not otherwise have a basis for concluding that the driver is "armed" and "dangerous," can the officer conduct a stop and frisk on the basis of the sticker? *See Estep v. Dallas County,* 310 F.3d 353 (5th Cir. 2002). In that same vein, suppose that a University of Louisville nursing student blogs about the importance of the right to bear arms, but does not advocate for violent or illegal conduct. When nursing school officials decide to dismiss the woman for blog comments that they regard as racist (the dismissal was later overturned by the courts), they want to subject her to a frisk before bringing her into the nursing school office. Based on the blog, and the woman's stated positions regarding the right to bear arms, can school officials assume that the woman is "armed and dangerous" and subject her to a weapons frisk?

Hypo 2: *Guns & Drug Deals*

The police have probable cause to believe that the driver of a vehicle has engaged in a drug deal. Do they have cause to frisk any passenger they find riding in the vehicle? *See State v. Lemert*, 843 N.W.2d 227 (Minn. 2014). What if the driver is wanted for commission of a violent crime (pistol whipping) and is a suspect in a shooting? If a solo officer attempts to arrest the driver, who is accompanied by three others, may he frisk all three of them? *See United States v. Howard*, 729 F.3d 665 (7th Cir. 2013).

Hypo 3: *The Fleeing Suspect*

While police officers are patrolling in a heavy narcotics trafficking area, defendant flees when he sees them. The officers chase defendant, catch him, and subject him to a pat-down search for weapons. During the frisk, an officer squeezes the bag defendant is carrying and feels a heavy, hard object similar to the shape of a gun. The officer then opens the bag and discovers a .38-caliber handgun with five live rounds of ammunition. Did the officer act properly? *See Illinois v. Wardlow*, 528 U.S. 119 (2000); *see also Mackey v. State*, 124 So.3d 176 (Fl. 2013).

Hypo 4: *Retaliation Killings & Frisks*

Boston police are patrolling city streets in an area plagued by gunfire in recent weeks. The night before, an individual was shot, and two individuals were killed in a nearby neighborhood. When the police see two unfamiliar men standing on a street corner, they approach them. When the men see the police, they begin to walk away. The officers follow the individuals and ask for their names, where they live, and what they are doing. One of the men states that he came to the area to visit a store on a particular street (no such store exists), and admits that he lives in the nearby area where the murders occurred the night before. Do the officers have sufficient cause to stop and frisk the suspects? *See Commonwealth v. Narcisse*, 73 Mass. App. Ct. 406, 898 N.E.2d 507 (2008).

Hypo 5: *The "One Plus" Rule*

Two police officers are patrolling in a high crime area one evening when they see a vehicle pull up to a gas station pump. When the driver does not leave the car, pump gas, or go into the convenience store, the officers regard the behavior as "unusual" and indicative of a drug transaction. When the vehicle leaves, the officers follow. The driver stops, exits, and walks over to a group of men who are talking and laughing. The officers recognize one of the men from prior drug arrests, but are unaware of whether he was convicted. The officers decide to approach the men, and they see that one of the men is openly wearing a gun in a holster (legal under state law). Based on their training, the officers believe that where there is one gun, there usually is another (the "one plus" rule). Do the officers have sufficient cause to stop and frisk the men? *See United States v. Black*, 707 F.3d 531 (4th Cir. 2013).

Hypo 6: *A Permissible Stop & Frisk?*

Plum, a 13-year police veteran is on routine patrol when he receives a police dispatch stating that an anonymous caller has reported a man with a handgun on a nearby street corner known for gang violence. The caller describes the individual as a tall, thin, dark-skinned male wearing a black jacket and a black and red cap. Plum arrives quickly, and sees three men standing on the corner. One of them is wearing a red jacket and a black and red cap. Except for the color of the jacket, the man matches the physical description relayed by the dispatcher. The man's jacket is open. Plum recognizes the man from prior narcotics investigations, and recalls that he has arrested the man on drug charges. Although Plum has not known the man to carry weapons, he knows that it is common for guns to be carried in connection with narcotics offenses. Plum is also aware that the man lives in the area and is associated with a group involved with handguns and shootings. On seeing Plum, all three men begin to walk away. The suspect seems quite nervous and moves his hand towards his waistband. Based on both the man's conduct, and the fact that he partially matches the anonymous caller's description of a man with a gun, Plum believes that the man might have a weapon concealed in his waistband. Plum directs the man to place his hands against a chain-link fence. Plum then lifts the man's tee-shirt and observes the top of a plastic bag (protruding above the waistband). Plum removes the bag and finds crack cocaine. Did Plum have adequate cause to conduct a stop and frisk? Was the scope of the frisk permissible? *See State v. Privott*, 203 N.J. 16, 999 A.2d 415 (2010).

Hypo 7: *The Gunfight & the Bullet-Riddled Car*

There is a gunfight in which a man is killed. A day later, police pull over a vehicle for an improper turn and demand identification. The officers know that Nolan (the passenger) is associated with a local gang. On approaching the driver's door, the arresting officer notices bullet holes in the car. After running data checks on the driver and the passenger, the officer notices that the homicide unit has put out a "locate" for Nolan. A "locate" means that an officer wishes to speak with the individual, but it does not give the officers authority to arrest the individual. At that point, the officer asks Nolan to get out of his car and stand near the back fender. Nolan goes past that area and sits on the curb. Nolan moves "very quickly" and grabs his waistband which is falling down, and the officer notices that there is something heavy in his pants. When asked if he has any weapons or other dangerous objects on his person, Nolan does not respond. Does the officer have sufficient cause to frisk Nolan? *See State v. Nolan*, 283 Neb. 50, 807 N.W.2d 520 (2012).

Hypo 8: *The Scope of a Stop & Frisk*

Suppose that a police officer has a valid basis for conducting a stop and frisk. During the course of the frisk, the officer feels a "hard object" in the suspect's left pants pocket. The suspect immediately tries to pull away when the officer touches it. The officer is uncertain what the object may be. May the officer remove the hard object from the suspect's pocket? *See United States v. Richardson*, 657 F.3d 521 (7th Cir. 2011); *see also United States v. I.E.V.*, 705 F.3d 430 (9th Cir. 2012).

Hypo 9: *Pretextual Stops*

When the driver of a late model convertible sees the police, he abruptly turns away and slides down, causing the police to become "suspicious" that the car is "a stolen vehicle." As the police follow, and run a registration check, the driver "reaches way down, as if to obtain an object or place an object under the right front seat." The movement causes the car to abruptly swerve across the center line, and the officers decide to conduct a traffic stop. The police admit that they did not stop the driver for a traffic offense, but rather because they were suspicious that the vehicle might be stolen and that the driver might have a weapon. As the officers approach the car, the driver "gets low in the seat" with his right arm positioned "low in his lap." At that point, the police order the driver to place his hands where they can see them and pull him from the car. The officers then frisk the driver and find an object in defendant's right jacket pocket which "felt like the butt of a small automatic." An officer then reaches into the pocket and finds only a "considerable sum of money folded in half," and a "plastic Baggi with a white powdery substance." Defendant is then placed under arrest for possession of a controlled substance. Did the police act properly? *See State v. Cotterman*, 544 S.W.2d 322 (Mo.App. 1976).

Hypo 10: *More Possible Stop & Frisk Scenarios*

A police officer, responding to a report of a domestic dispute, sees a man walking on the street near the site of the reported dispute. The officer does not know the man, and has no reason (other than the man's proximity to the dispute) to believe that he was involved in the dispute. The officer shines a spotlight on the man, exits his car, and tells the man to "stop." The man states that he is going to his cousin's house, and continues walking. Since the man is "fumbling in his pockets," the officer fears that he has a gun, pulls his own, and twice orders the man to remove his hands from his pockets. When the man keeps on walking, the officer sprays him in the face with pepper spray. Under *Terry*, did the officer act appropriately in attempting to stop the man and in using the pepper spray to accomplish the stop? *See State v. Garcia*, 147 N.M. 134, 217 P.3d 1032 (2009). Likewise, suppose that police receive a report that a young man is carrying a gun near the YWCA. The report does not indicate that the man is threatening or harassing anyone, or otherwise causing trouble. Besides, it is legal to possess a gun in that jurisdiction. The police respond and find someone matching the description of the man in the report. Do the police have grounds to conduct a stop and frisk? Suppose that, as the police approach the man, he turns and runs away. Do the police now have sufficient cause to subject the man to a stop and frisk? *See United States v. Brown*, 925 F.3d 1150 (9th Cir. 2019).

Safford Unified School District #1 v. Redding

<u>557 U.S. 364 (2009)</u>.

JUSTICE SOUTER delivered the opinion of the Court.

Savana Redding's mother filed suit against Safford Unified School District #1, and various school officials, for conducting a strip search in violation of Savana's Fourth Amendment rights. Petitioners moved for summary judgment, raising a defense of qualified immunity that [was] granted. The Ninth Circuit held that the strip search was unjustified under the Fourth Amendment test for searches of children by school officials set out in *New Jersey v. T. L. O.*, 469 U. S. 325 (1985). We granted certiorari, and now affirm in part, reverse in part, and remand.

The Fourth Amendment "right of the people to be secure in their persons against unreasonable searches and seizures" generally requires a law enforcement officer to have probable cause for conducting a search. In *T. L. O.*, we recognized that the school setting "requires some modification of the level of suspicion of illicit activity needed to justify a search," and held that for searches by school officials "a careful balancing of governmental and private interests suggests that the public interest is best served by a Fourth Amendment standard of reasonableness that stops short of probable cause." We have thus applied a standard of reasonable suspicion to determine the legality of a school administrators search of a student, and have held that a school search "will be permissible in its scope when the measures adopted are reasonably related to the objectives of the search and not excessively intrusive in light of the age and sex of the student and the nature of the infraction."

A number of cases on probable cause have an implicit bearing on the reliable knowledge element of reasonable suspicion, as we have attempted to flesh out the knowledge component by looking to the degree to which known facts imply prohibited conduct, the specificity of the information received, and the reliability of its source. At the end of the day, these factors cannot rigidly control, *Illinois v. Gates*, 462 U. S. 213 (1983), and the standards are "fluid concepts that take their substantive content from the particular contexts" in which they are being assessed. *Ornelas v. United States*, 517 U. S. 690, 696 (1996). Perhaps the best that can be said about the required knowledge component of probable cause for a law enforcement officer's evidence search is that it raise a "fair probability," *Gates*, 462 U. S., at 238, or a "substantial chance," of discovering evidence of criminal activity. The lesser standard for school searches could as readily be described as a moderate chance of finding evidence of wrongdoing.

In this case, the school's policies strictly prohibit the nonmedical use, possession, or sale of any drug on school grounds, including "any prescription or over-the-counter drug, except those for which permission to use in school has been granted pursuant to

Board policy."[3]   A week before Savana was searched, another student, Jordan Romero told the principal and Assistant Principal Wilson that "certain students were bringing drugs and weapons on campus," and that he had been sick after taking some pills that "he got from a classmate." On October 8, the same boy handed Wilson a white pill that he said Marissa Glines had given him. He told Wilson that students were planning to take the pills at lunch. Wilson learned from Peggy Schwallier, the school nurse, that the pill was Ibuprofen 400 mg, available only by prescription. Wilson then called Marissa out of class. Outside the classroom, Marissa's teacher handed Wilson the day planner, found within Marissa's reach, containing various contraband items. Wilson escorted Marissa back to his office. In the presence of Helen Romero, Wilson requested Marissa to turn out her pockets and open her wallet. Marissa produced a blue pill, several white ones, and a razor blade. Wilson asked where the blue pill came from, and Marissa answered, "I guess it slipped in when she gave me the IBU 400s." When Wilson asked whom she meant, Marissa replied, "Savana Redding." Wilson then enquired about the day planner and its contents; Marissa denied knowing anything about them. Wilson did not ask Marissa any follow-up questions to determine whether there was any likelihood that Savana presently had pills: neither asking when Marissa received the pills from Savana nor where Savana might be hiding them. Schwallier did not immediately recognize the blue pill, but information provided through a poison control hotline indicated that the pill was a 200-mg dose of an anti-inflammatory drug, generically called naproxen, available over the counter. Marissa was then subjected to a search of her bra and underpants by Romero and Schwallier, as Savana was later on. The search revealed no additional pills.

It was at this juncture that Wilson called Savana into his office and showed her the day planner. Their conversation established that Savana and Marissa were on friendly terms: while she denied knowledge of the contraband, Savana admitted that the day planner was hers and that she had lent it to Marissa. Wilson had other reports of their friendship from staff members, who had identified Savana and Marissa as part of an unusually rowdy group at the school's opening dance in August, during which alcohol and cigarettes were found in the girl's bathroom. Wilson had reason to connect the girls with this contraband, for Wilson knew that Jordan Romero had told the principal that before the dance, he had been at a party at Savana's house where alcohol was served. Marissa's statement that the pills came from Savana was thus sufficiently plausible to warrant suspicion that Savana was involved in pill distribution.

---

[3]   The Court said in *New Jersey v. T. L.O.,* 469 U. S. 325 (1985), that standards of conduct for schools are for school administrators to determine without second-guessing by courts lacking the experience to appreciate what may be needed. There is no need to explain the imperative of keeping drugs out of schools, or to explain the reasons for the school's rule banning all drugs, no matter how benign, without advance permission. Teachers are not pharmacologists trained to identify pills and powders, and an effective drug ban has to be enforceable fast. The plenary ban makes sense, and there is no basis to claim that the search was unreasonable owing to some defect or shortcoming of the rule it was aimed at enforcing.

This suspicion was enough to justify a search of Savana's backpack and outer clothing.[4]   If a student is reasonably suspected of giving out contraband pills, she is reasonably suspected of carrying them on her person and in the carryall. The look into Savana's bag, in her presence and in the relative privacy of Wilson's office, was not excessively intrusive, any more than Romero's subsequent search of her outer clothing.

A strip search followed. Romero and Schwallier directed Savana to remove her clothes down to her underwear, and then "pull out" her bra and the elastic band on her underpants. Although Romero and Schwallier stated that they did not see anything when Savana followed their instructions, we would not define strip search and its Fourth Amendment consequences in a way that would guarantee litigation about who was looking and how much was seen. The very fact of Savana's pulling her underwear away from her body in the presence of the two officials who were able to see her necessarily exposed her breasts and pelvic area to some degree, and both subjective and reasonable societal expectations of personal privacy support the treatment of such a search as categorically distinct, requiring distinct elements of justification on the part of school authorities for going beyond a search of outer clothing and belongings.

Savana's subjective expectation of privacy against such a search is inherent in her account of it as embarrassing, frightening, and humiliating. The reasonableness of her expectation is indicated by the consistent experiences of other young people similarly searched, whose adolescent vulnerability intensifies the patent intrusiveness of the exposure. The common reaction of these adolescents simply registers the obviously different meaning of a search exposing the body from the experience of nakedness or near undress in other school circumstances. Changing for gym is getting ready for play; exposing for a search is responding to an accusation reserved for suspected wrongdoers and fairly understood as so degrading that a number of communities have decided that strip searches in schools are never reasonable and have banned them no matter what the facts may be.

The indignity of the search does not, of course, outlaw it, but it does implicate the rule of reasonableness as stated in *T. L. O.*, that "the search as actually conducted be reasonably related in scope to the circumstances which justified the interference in the first place." The scope will be permissible when it is "not excessively intrusive in light of the age and sex of the student and the nature of the infraction." Here, the content of the suspicion failed to match the degree of intrusion. Wilson knew beforehand that the pills were prescription-strength ibuprofen and over-the-counter naproxen, common pain relievers equivalent to two Advil, or one Aleve. He must have been aware of the nature and limited threat of the specific drugs he was searching for, and while just about anything can be taken in quantities that will do real harm,

---

4   There is no question here that justification for the school officials' search was required in accordance with the *T.L.O.* standard of reasonable suspicion, for it is common ground that Savana had a reasonable expectation of privacy covering the personal things she chose to carry in her backpack, and that Wilson's decision to look through it was a "search" within the meaning of the Fourth Amendment.

Wilson had no reason to suspect that large amounts of the drugs were being passed around, or that individual students were receiving great numbers of pills.

Nor could Wilson have suspected that Savana was hiding common painkillers in her underwear. Petitioners suggest that "students hide contraband in or under their clothing," and cite a smattering of cases of students with contraband in their underwear. But a reasonable search that extensive calls for suspicion that it will pay off. But nondangerous school contraband does not raise the specter of stashes in intimate places, and there is no evidence of any general practice among Safford Middle School students of hiding that sort of thing in underwear; neither Jordan nor Marissa suggested to Wilson that Savana was doing that, and the preceding search of Marissa that Wilson ordered yielded nothing. Wilson never even determined when Marissa had received the pills from Savana; if it had been a few days before, that would weigh heavily against any reasonable conclusion that Savana presently had the pills on her person, much less in her underwear. In sum, what was missing from the suspected facts that pointed to Savana was any indication of danger to the students from the power of the drugs or their quantity, and any reason to suppose that Savana was carrying pills in her underwear. We think that the combination of these deficiencies was fatal to finding the search reasonable.

In so holding, we mean to cast no ill reflection on the assistant principal, for the record raises no doubt that his motive throughout was to eliminate drugs from his school and protect students from what Jordan Romero had gone through. Parents are known to overreact to protect their children from danger, and a school official with responsibility for safety may tend to do the same. The difference is that the Fourth Amendment places limits on the official, even with the high degree of deference that courts must pay to the educators professional judgment. We do mean, though, to make it clear that the *T. L. O.* concern to limit a school search to reasonable scope requires the support of reasonable suspicion of danger or of resort to underwear for hiding evidence of wrongdoing before a search can reasonably make the quantum leap from outer clothes and backpacks to exposure of intimate parts. The meaning of such a search, and the degradation its subject may reasonably feel, place a search that intrusive in a category of its own demanding its own specific suspicions.

A school official searching a student is "entitled to qualified immunity where clearly established law does not show that the search violated the Fourth Amendment." *Pearson v. Callahan*, 555 U. S. 223 (2009). To be established clearly, there is no need that "the very action in question have previously been held unlawful." *Wilson v. Layne*, 526 U. S. 603, 615 (1999). Even as to action less than an outrage, "officials can still be on notice that their conduct violates established law in novel factual circumstances." *Hope v. Pelzer*, 536 U. S. 730, 741 (2002). *T. L. O.* directed school officials to limit the intrusiveness of a search, "in light of the age and sex of the student and the nature of the infraction," and the intrusiveness of the strip search here cannot be seen as justifiably related to the circumstances. The strip search of Savana Redding was unreasonable and a violation of the Fourth Amendment, but petitioners are nevertheless protected from liability through qualified immunity. Our conclusions do not resolve the question of the liability of Safford Unified School District #1. The judgment of the Ninth Circuit is therefore affirmed in part and reversed in part, and this case is remanded for consideration of the *Monell* claim.

It is so ordered.

JUSTICE STEVENS, with whom JUSTICE GINSBURG joins, concurring in part and dissenting in part.

This is a case in which clearly established law meets clearly outrageous conduct. "It does not require a constitutional scholar to conclude that a nude search of a 13-year-old child is an invasion of constitutional rights of some magnitude."

JUSTICE GINSBURG, concurring in part and dissenting in part.

Assistant Principal Wilson's subjection of 13-year-old Savana Redding to a humiliating strip down search violated the Fourth Amendment.

JUSTICE THOMAS, concurring in the judgment in part and dissenting in part.

The search of Savana Redding did not violate the Fourth Amendment.

Take Note

In *New Jersey v. T.L.O.*, 469 U.S. 325 (1985), a teacher found two girls smoking in a lavatory. Both girls were taken to the Principal's office where they met with the Assistant Vice Principal, Mr. Choplick. When T.L.O. denied that she had been smoking, Choplick demanded to see her purse where he found cigarettes, rolling papers, marijuana and a substantial number of one-dollar bills. Afterwards, T.L.O. confessed to selling marijuana. Based on the confession and the evidence found during the search, delinquency charges were brought against T.L.O. The Court upheld the search, holding that the Fourth Amendment applies to searches by public school officials, but finding that such officials have greater latitude: "Against the child's interest in privacy must be set the substantial interest of teachers and administrators in maintaining discipline in the classroom and on school grounds. The school setting requires some easing of the restrictions to which searches by public authorities are ordinarily subject. The warrant requirement, would unduly interfere with the maintenance of the swift and informal disciplinary procedures needed in the schools. The legality of a search of a student should depend simply on the reasonableness, under all the circumstances, of the search. Determining the reasonableness of any search involves a twofold inquiry: first, one must consider whether the action was justified at its inception," and whether the search as actually conducted 'was reasonably related in scope to the circumstances which justified the interference in the first place.' Under ordinary circumstances, a search of a student by a teacher or other school official will be 'justified at its inception' when there are reasonable grounds for suspecting that the search will turn up evidence that the student has violated or is violating either the law or the rules of the school. Such a search will be permissible in its scope when the measures adopted are reasonably related to the objectives of the search and not excessively intrusive in light of the age and sex of the student and the nature of the infraction."

Food for Thought

In *Redding*, the school official suspected Savana of carrying prescription strength ibuprofen. Suppose that the school official had suspected Savana of carrying heroin or cocaine. Would that change in facts alter the analysis regarding the propriety of a strip search?

Hypo 1: *A Search for Weapons*

Would the search have been justified if the school official had suspected Savana of carrying detonator caps for explosives? Or are there less intrusive methods for searching for such weapons?

Hypo 2: *Canine Sniffs at Public Schools*

After determining that there is a "serious drug problem" with 80–200 incidents per year, a school district adopts a policy authorizing the police to enter the school to conduct random canine sniffs of student backpacks and lockers for evidence of contraband drugs. In adopting the policy, the district intended to "balance each student's right to privacy" with "the need to maintain an appropriate learning environment" while protecting "the safety and health of the district's faculty, staff and students." The policy states that "once a drug sniff is complete, the dog handler and dog will leave the area." A student's possessions will only be searched if a drug dog has twice alerted to them. Is the search justifiable under *Safford*? See *Burlison v. Springfield Public Schools*, 708 F.3d 1034 (8th Cir. 2013).

Hypo 3: *Searching the Student's Truck*

After discovering that a student left school without permission to go to his truck, which was parked on a residential street outside school grounds, the principal summoned the student to the office and searched him for drugs. Although the student claimed that he had gone to the truck simply to retrieve his wallet, the principal suspected that he might have retrieved drugs. However, no drugs were found. Based on the available evidence, did the principal have adequate grounds to search the truck even though it was not located on school property? *See J.P. v. Millard Public Schools,* 285 Neb. 890, 830 N.W.2d 453 (Neb. 2013).

Hypo 4: *Checking the Cell Phone*

During his freshman year in high school, G.C. began to have disciplinary problems, including drug use, anger and depression. Later, he was warned for excessive tardiness, disciplined for fighting in the boy's locker room, was caught with tobacco products at school, and confessed to being suicidal. A treatment counselor was very concerned and suggested that G.C. be committed to an institution. When G.C. violated the school's cell-phone policy by texting in class, a teacher confiscated the phone, and the principal read four text messages on the phone. The principal stated that he was worried because G.C. had engaged in angry outbursts. Was the phone search justifiable? *See G.C. v. Owensboro Public Schools,* 711 F.3d 623 (6th Cir. 2013).

* * *

In addition to authorizing a "frisk," *Terry* also authorizes the police to make an "investigative stop" which is a form of seizure. The Fourth Amendment prohibits not only unreasonable searches, but also unreasonable "seizures." The Court has recognized many different types of seizures ranging from an investigatory stop to an arrest. These seizures are subject to differing constitutional requirements.

FYI

Most seizures are investigative in nature and can be relatively brief. Roadside stops usually fit this description. However, the police also "seize" individuals for fingerprinting, lineups or interrogation purposes. What constitutes a seizure? When are such seizures valid? Consider the following cases.

United States v. Mendenhall

446 U.S. 544 (1980).

MR. JUSTICE STEWART announced the judgment of the Court and delivered an opinion, in which MR. JUSTICE REHNQUIST joined.

Respondent arrived at the Detroit Metropolitan Airport on a commercial airline flight from Los Angeles early in the morning. As she disembarked from the plane, she was observed by two agents of the DEA, who were at the airport for the purpose of detecting unlawful traffic in narcotics. After observing respondent's conduct, which appeared to the agents to be characteristic of persons unlawfully carrying narcotics, the agents approached her as she was walking through the concourse, identified themselves as federal agents, and asked to see her identification and airline ticket. Respondent produced her driver's license, which was in the name of Sylvia Mendenhall, and, in answer to a question, stated that she resided at the address appearing on the license. The airline ticket was in the name of "Annette Ford." When asked why the ticket bore a name different from her own, respondent stated that she "just felt like using that name." In response to a further question, respondent indicated that she had been in California only two days. Agent Anderson then identified himself as a federal narcotics agent and respondent "became quite shaken, extremely nervous. She had a hard time speaking." After returning the airline ticket and driver's license to her, Agent Anderson asked respondent if she would accompany him to the airport DEA office for further questions. She did so, although the record does not indicate a verbal response to the request. The office, which was located up one flight of stairs about 50 feet from where the respondent had first been approached, consisted of a reception area adjoined by three other rooms. At the office the agent asked respondent if she would allow a search of her person and handbag and told her that she had the right to decline the search if she desired. She responded: "Go ahead." She then handed Agent Anderson her purse, which contained a receipt for an airline ticket that had been issued to "F. Bush" three days earlier for a flight from Pittsburgh through Chicago to Los Angeles. The agent asked whether this was the ticket that she had used for her flight to California, and respondent stated that it was.

A female police officer then arrived to search respondent's person. She asked the agents if respondent had consented to be searched. The agents said that she had, and respondent followed the policewoman into a private room. There the policewoman asked respondent if she consented to the search, and respondent replied that she did. The policewoman explained that the search would require that respondent remove her clothing. Respondent stated that she had a plane to catch and was assured by the policewoman that if she were carrying no narcotics, there would be no problem. Respondent then began to disrobe without further comment. As respondent removed her clothing, she took from her undergarments two small packages, one of which appeared to contain heroin, and handed both to the policewoman. The agents then arrested respondent for possessing heroin. At her trial, respondent moved to suppress the heroin. The motion was denied.

The Government concedes that its agents had neither a warrant nor probable cause to believe that respondent was carrying narcotics when the agents conducted a search of respondent's person. It is the Government's position that the search was conducted pursuant to respondent's consent, and thus was excepted from the requirements of both a warrant and probable cause.

The Fourth Amendment's requirement that searches and seizures be founded upon an objective justification, governs all seizures of the person, "including seizures that involve only a brief detention short of traditional arrest." Accordingly, if respondent was "seized" when the DEA agents approached her on the concourse and asked questions of her, the agents' conduct in doing so was constitutional only if they reasonably suspected respondent of wrongdoing. But "not all personal intercourse between policemen and citizens involves 'seizures' of persons. Only when the officer, by means of physical force or show of authority, has in some way restrained the liberty of a citizen may we conclude that a 'seizure' has occurred." A person is "seized" only when, by means of physical force or a show of authority, his freedom of movement is restrained. Only when such restraint is imposed is there any foundation whatever for invoking constitutional safeguards. The purpose of the Fourth Amendment is not to eliminate all contact between the police and the citizenry, but "to prevent arbitrary and oppressive interference by enforcement officials with the privacy and personal security of individuals." As long as the person to whom questions are put remains free to disregard the questions and walk away, there has been no intrusion upon that person's liberty or privacy as would under the Constitution require some particularized and objective justification. Characterizing every street encounter between a citizen and the police as a "seizure," while not enhancing any interest secured by the Fourth Amendment, would impose wholly unrealistic restrictions upon a wide variety of legitimate law enforcement practices. The Court has acknowledged the need for police questioning as a tool in the effective enforcement of the criminal laws. "Without such investigation, those who were innocent might be falsely accused, those who were guilty might wholly escape prosecution, and many crimes would go unsolved. In short, the security of all would be diminished." *Schneckloth v. Bustamonte*, 412 U.S., at 225.

We conclude that a person has been "seized" within the meaning of the Fourth Amendment only if, in view of all of the circumstances surrounding the incident, a reasonable person would have believed that he was not free to leave.[8] Examples of circumstances that might indicate a seizure, even where the person did not attempt to leave, would be the threatening presence of several officers, the display of a weapon by an officer, some physical touching of the person of the citizen, or the use of language

---

[8]   The subjective intention of the DEA agent to detain respondent, had she attempted to leave, is irrelevant except insofar as that may have been conveyed to the respondent.

or tone of voice indicating that compliance with the officer's request might be compelled. In the absence of some such evidence, otherwise inoffensive contact between a member of the public and the police cannot, as a matter of law, amount to a seizure of that person.

On the facts of this case, no "seizure" occurred. The events took place in the public concourse. The agents wore no uniforms and displayed no weapons. They did not summon respondent to their presence, but instead approached her and identified themselves as federal agents. They requested, but did not demand to see respondent's identification and ticket. Such conduct without more, did not amount to an intrusion upon any constitutionally protected interest. Respondent was not seized simply by reason of the fact that the agents approached her, asked her if she would show them her ticket and identification, and posed to her a few questions. Nor was it enough that the person asking the questions was a law enforcement official. In short, nothing suggests that respondent had any objective reason to believe that she was not free to end the conversation in the concourse and proceed on her way, and for that reason we conclude that the agents' initial approach to her was not a seizure.

Food for Thought

Do you agree with the holding in *Mendenhall?* Would an ordinary person (one not schooled in criminal procedure), who is approached by the police in an airport, believe that she is "free to leave?" Could she respond to a police request by saying "Sorry, I'd love to chat with you, but I need to get a cup of coffee and don't really have time to chat. Perhaps next time." Or would the ordinary person more likely believe that she was required to submit to police questioning?

Our conclusion that no seizure occurred is not affected by the fact that respondent was not expressly told by the agents that she was free to decline to cooperate with their inquiry, for the voluntariness of her responses does not depend upon her having been so informed. We also reject the argument that the only inference to be drawn from the fact that respondent acted in a manner so contrary to her self-interest is that she was compelled to answer the agents' questions. It may happen that a person makes statements to law enforcement officials that he later regrets, but the issue in such cases is not whether the statement was self-protective, but rather whether it was made voluntarily.

Although we have concluded that the initial encounter between the DEA agents and respondent on the concourse at the Detroit Airport did not constitute an unlawful seizure, it is still arguable that respondent's Fourth Amendment protections were violated when she went from the concourse to the DEA office. Such a violation might in turn infect the subsequent search of the respondent's person. Whether respondent's consent to accompany the agents was in fact voluntary or was the product of duress or coercion, express or implied, is to be determined by the totality of all the circumstances, and is a matter which the Government has the burden of proving. The Government's evidence showed that respondent was not told that she had to go to the office, but was simply asked if she would accompany the officers. There were neither threats nor any show of force. Respondent had been questioned only briefly, and her ticket and identification were returned to her before she was asked to accompany the officers.

It is argued that the incident would reasonably have appeared coercive to respondent, who was 22 years old and had not graduated from high school. It is additionally suggested that respondent, a female and a Negro, may have felt unusually threatened by the officers, who were white males. While these factors were not irrelevant, neither were they decisive, and the totality of the evidence in this case was plainly adequate to support the finding that respondent voluntarily consented to accompany the officers to the DEA office.

Because the search of respondent's person was not preceded by an impermissible seizure of her person, it cannot be contended that her apparent consent to the search was infected by an unlawful detention. There remains to be considered whether respondent's consent to the search was for any other reason invalid. The District Court found that the "consent was freely and voluntarily given." There was more than enough evidence to sustain that view. First, respondent, who was 22 years old and had an 11th-grade education, was plainly capable of a knowing consent. Second, it is especially significant that respondent was twice expressly told that she was free to decline to consent to the search, and only thereafter explicitly consented. Although the Constitution does not require "proof of knowledge of a right to refuse as the *sine qua non* of an effective consent to a search," such knowledge was highly relevant to the determination that there had been consent. Perhaps more important, the fact that the officers themselves informed respondent that she was free to withhold her consent substantially lessened the probability that their conduct could reasonably have appeared to her to be coercive. Respondent has argued that she did in fact resist the search, relying principally on the testimony that when she was told that the search would require the removal of her clothing, she stated to the female police officer that "she had a plane to catch." But the trial court was entitled to view the statement as simply an expression of concern that the search be conducted quickly. Respondent had twice unequivocally indicated her consent to the search, and when assured by the police officer that there would be no problem if nothing were turned up by the search, she began to undress without further comment.

Respondent also argued that because she was within the DEA office when she consented to the search, her consent may have resulted from the inherently coercive nature of those surroundings. But there is no evidence that she was in any way coerced. In response to the argument that the respondent would not voluntarily have consented to a search that was likely to disclose the narcotics that she carried, the question is not whether the respondent acted in her ultimate self-interest, but whether she acted voluntarily.[9]

We conclude that the District Court's determination that respondent consented to the search of her person "freely and voluntarily" was sustained by the evidence.

It is so ordered.

MR. JUSTICE WHITE, with whom MR. JUSTICE BRENNAN, MR. JUSTICE MARSHALL, and MR. JUSTICE STEVENS join, dissenting.

Mendenhall undoubtedly was "seized" within the meaning of the Fourth Amendment when the agents escorted her from the public area of the terminal to the DEA office for questioning and a strip-search of her person. Although Mendenhall was not told that she was under arrest, she in fact was not free to refuse to go to the DEA office and was not told that she was. Once inside the office, Ms. Mendenhall would not have been permitted to leave without submitting to a strip-search. The Court's conclusion that the "totality of evidence was plainly adequate" to support a finding of consent can only be based on the notion that consent can be assumed from the absence of proof that a suspect resisted police authority. This is a notion that we have squarely rejected. The Government cannot rely solely on acquiescence to the officers' wishes to establish the requisite consent. Because Ms. Mendenhall was being illegally detained at the time of the search of her person, her suppression motion should have been granted in the absence of evidence to dissipate the taint.

Points for Discussion

a.   Seizures & Passengers

In *Brendlin v. California*, 551 U.S. 249 (2007), the Court held that when a police officer makes a traffic stop, the passenger of the vehicle (as well as the driver) is seized within the meaning of the Fourth Amendment. As a result, the passenger may challenge the constitutionality of the stop: "An officer who orders a car to pull over acts with an implicit claim of right based on fault of some sort, and a sensible person would not expect a police officer to allow people to come and go freely from the physical focal point of an investigation. If the likely wrongdoing is not the driving, the passenger will reasonably feel subject to suspicion owing to close association; but even when the wrongdoing is only bad driving, the passenger will expect to be subject to some scrutiny, and his attempt to leave the scene would be likely to prompt an objection from the officer that no passenger would feel free to leave. It is also reasonable for

---

[9]   Respondent may have thought she was acting in her self-interest by voluntarily cooperating with the officers in the hope of receiving more lenient treatment.

passengers to expect that a police officer at the scene of a crime, arrest, or investigation will not let people move around in ways that could jeopardize his safety."

> ### Take Note
>
> Following the decision in *Mendenhall*, the Court decided *Florida v. Royer*, 460 U.S. 491 (1983). *Royer* was factually similar to *Mendenhall* in that he was singled out because he fit a so-called "drug courier profile." He had purchased a one-way plane ticket to N.Y.C. and checked his bags with an identification tag using a name that was different than his own. Two agents approached Royer, asked to speak to him, and also asked for his plane ticket and driver's license. The ticket bore the name "Holt." Royer then became nervous and the detectives informed Royer that he was under suspicion for transporting narcotics. Without returning Royer's license or ticket, the detectives asked him to accompany them to the DEA office located in the airport. Royer did not respond, but followed them. The detectives also had his luggage removed from the plane and brought to the room. When asked to consent to a search of his luggage, Royer produced a key and opened it. The search produced illegal drugs. The Court held that Royer, unlike Mendenhall, had been "seized" within the meaning of the Fourth Amendment, because the police retained his identification and plane ticket and removed his luggage from the airplane. The Court noted that "statements given during a period of illegal detention are inadmissible even though voluntarily given if they are the product of the illegal detention and not the result of an independent act of free will: "Because Royer was being illegally detained when he consented to the search of his luggage, the consent was tainted by the illegality and was ineffective to justify the search."

b. Bus Sweeps

In *Florida v. Bostick*, 501 U.S. 429 (1991), two police officers, with badges, insignia and holstered pistols, boarded a bus from Miami to Atlanta during a stop in Fort Lauderdale. Without any articulable suspicion, the officers picked out defendant passenger and asked to inspect his ticket and identification. The ticket matched the defendant's identification and both were immediately returned to him. The officers then explained their presence as narcotics agents, and requested consent to search his luggage. The police specifically advised defendant that he had the right to refuse consent, and they did not threaten him. The Court concluded that defendant had not been "seized" within the meaning of the Fourth Amendment, and that his consent was therefore valid: "When police attempt to question a person who is walking down the street or through an airport lobby, it makes sense to inquire whether a reasonable person would feel free to continue walking. But when the person is seated on a bus and has no desire to leave, the degree to which a reasonable person would feel that he or she could leave is not an accurate measure of the coercive effect of the encounter." Justice Marshall dissented: "Officers who conduct suspicionless, dragnet-style sweeps put passengers to the choice of cooperating or of exiting their buses and possibly being stranded in unfamiliar locations. It is exactly because this 'choice' is no 'choice' at all that police engage this technique. The police may confront passengers without suspicion so long as they take simple steps, like advising the passengers confronted of their right to decline to be questioned, to dispel the aura of coercion and intimidation that pervades such encounters."

c. Factory Sweeps

In *Immigration and Naturalization Service v. Delgado*, 466 U.S. 210 (1984), under a warrant based on probable cause, the INS surveyed the work force at a plant looking for illegal aliens. Some agents positioned themselves near the buildings' exits while other agents dispersed throughout the factory to question employees at their work stations. The agents displayed badges, carried walkie-talkies, and carried holstered weapons. The agents approached employees, identified themselves, and asked one to three questions relating to citizenship. If an employee gave a credible reply that he was a U.S. citizen, the questioning ended, and the agent moved on to the next employee. If the employee gave an unsatisfactory response or admitted that he was an alien, the employee was asked to produce his immigration papers. During the survey, employees continued with their work and were free to walk about the factory. The Court rejected the employees' claim that they had been "seized": "When people are at work their freedom to move about has been meaningfully restricted, not by the actions of law enforcement officials, but by the workers' voluntary obligations to their employers. There is nothing to indicate that the stationing of agents near the factory doors showed the INS's intent to prevent people from leaving. The obvious purpose of the agents' presence at the factory doors was to insure that all persons in the factories were questioned. If mere questioning does not constitute a seizure when it occurs inside the factory, it is no more a seizure when it occurs at the exits. Respondents argue that the manner in which the surveys were conducted and the attendant disruption created a psychological environment which made them reasonably afraid they were not free to leave. It was obvious from the beginning that INS agents were only questioning people. Persons who simply went about their business in the workplace were not detained in any way. While persons who attempted to flee or evade the agents may eventually have been detained for questioning, respondents did not do so and were not in fact detained. The manner in which respondents were questioned, given its obvious purpose, could hardly result in a reasonable fear that respondents were not free to continue working or to move about the factory. The encounters with the INS agents were classic consensual encounters rather than Fourth Amendment seizures." Justice Brennan concurred in part and dissented in part: "It is fantastic to conclude that a reasonable person could ignore all that was occurring throughout the factory and,

Food for Thought

Given that Mendenhall must have known that she was carrying drugs in her clothes, how do you explain her decision to submit to a strip search? Was she acting voluntarily, or out of public spirit? Or did she not realize that she had the right to refuse?

when the INS agents reached him, have the temerity to believe that he was at liberty to refuse to answer their questions and walk away. Respondents' testimony paints a frightening picture of people subjected to wholesale interrogation under conditions designed not to respect personal security and privacy, but rather to elicit prompt answers from completely intimidated workers. These tactics amounted to seizures of respondents under the Fourth Amendment."

Hypo 1: *Applying the* Mendenhall *Test*

On your way home from this class, a police cruiser follows you for three blocks when the officer turns on his lights and siren. Believing that the officer wants you to stop, you pull off the road. The officer pulls over behind you and approaches your car. Under *Mendenhall*, have you been seized?

Hypo 2: *More on Applying the* Mendenhall *Test*

A robbery occurs at the campus book store. Shortly afterwards, the police search the campus for the robbers as well as for evidence. About this time, you are walking across campus on your way to this class. A police officer approaches you and says: "A robbery has just occurred at the campus book store, I'm looking for witnesses, and would like to ask you a few questions." Have you been "seized" within the meaning of the Fourth Amendment? Would you conclude that you have been "seized" if the officer regarded you as a possible suspect rather than as a witness? Is the officer's subjective intent relevant? What arguments can you make in support of the position that you have been "seized"?

Hypo 3: *The Border Patrol Encounter*

At night, border patrol agents stop two cars in the northbound lane of a highway that runs perpendicular to the Mexican border. As part of the stop, the officers turn on their emergency lights, and leave them flashing throughout the stop. One of the agents is carrying a flashlight which he shines at a passing vehicle. The officer, who is quite tall (6'9"), does not motion for the car to stop, but notices what appear to be individuals hiding on the floorboard of the vehicle. The driver of the passing vehicle decides to stop about 15' beyond the officer, and is apprehended for smuggling illegal aliens. When the officer shined his flashlight at the passing vehicle, was there a "stop" or "seizure" within the meaning of the Fourth Amendment? *See United States v. Al Nasser*, 555 F.3d 722 (9th Cir. 2009).

Food for Thought

Of course, the *Mendenhall* Court concluded that she was not "seized" within the meaning of the Fourth Amendment when the DEA agents approached her in the airport concourse. If there had been a seizure, the Court suggested that the initial seizure could have been justified based on a "reasonable suspicion" that Mendenhall was involved in criminal activity. Did the DEA agents have a reasonable suspicion regarding Mendenhall? What factors might have led the agents to believe that she was involved in criminal activity?

Hypo 4: *When Does a Seizure End?*

Two police officers see two adults sitting near a tree. The officers consider their presence "unusual" because the park is usually frequented only by children and the elderly at that time of day. Suppose that the police approach the man and the woman, demand identification to check their identities against a police data base, and determine that there is a restraining order that prevents the man from coming within 100 feet of the woman. The police arrest the man, return the woman's identification, and begin the process of taking the man into custody. During the following minutes there is casual conversation between the police officers and the woman regarding the restraining order (the woman states that she is trying to reconcile with the man). At some point, the officer asks the woman whether she would mind if he searches her purse. The woman permits the search which reveals crystal meth. For purposes of determining whether the woman voluntarily consented to a search of her purse, was the woman seized when the officer initially approached her and asked to see her identification? Did the seizure terminate when the officer returned the identification? *See State v. Ashbaugh*, 349 Or. 297, 244 P.3d 360 (2010).

California v. Hodari D.

499 U.S. 621 (1991).

JUSTICE SCALIA delivered the opinion of the Court.

Late one evening, Officers Brian McColgin and Jerry Pertoso were on patrol in a high-crime area of Oakland, California. They were in street clothes but wearing jackets with "Police" embossed on both front and back. As they rounded a corner, they saw four or five youths huddled around a small car parked at the curb. When the youths saw the officers' car approaching they apparently panicked, and took flight. Respondent, Hodari D., and one companion ran west through an alley; the others fled south. The red car headed south at a high rate of speed. The officers were suspicious and gave chase. McColgin remained in the car and continued south on 63rd Avenue; Pertoso left the car, ran north along 63rd, then west on Foothill Boulevard, and turned south on 62nd Avenue. Hodari, meanwhile, emerged from the alley onto 62nd and ran north. Looking behind as he ran, he did not turn and see Pertoso until the officer was almost upon him, whereupon he tossed away what appeared to be a small rock. A moment later, Pertoso tackled Hodari, handcuffed him, and radioed for assistance. Hodari was found to be carrying $130 in cash and a pager; and the rock he had discarded was found to be crack cocaine. In the juvenile proceeding brought against him, Hodari moved to suppress the evidence relating to the cocaine. The court denied the motion.

The only issue is whether, at the time he dropped the drugs, Hodari had been "seized" within the meaning of the Fourth Amendment. If so, respondent argues, the drugs were the fruit of that seizure and the evidence concerning them was properly excluded. If not, the drugs were abandoned by Hodari and lawfully recovered by the police, and the evidence should have been admitted.

The Fourth Amendment's protection against "unreasonable seizures" includes seizure of the person. From the time of the founding to the present, the word "seizure" has meant a "taking possession." For most purposes at common law, the word connoted not merely grasping, or applying physical force to, the animate or inanimate object in question, but actually bringing it within physical control. A ship still fleeing, even though under attack, would not be considered to have been seized as a war prize. To constitute an arrest, however—the quintessential "seizure of the person" under our Fourth Amendment jurisprudence—the mere grasping or application of physical force with lawful authority, whether or not it succeeded in subduing the arrestee, was sufficient. As one commentator has described it: "There can be constructive detention, which will constitute an arrest, although the party is never actually brought within the physical control of the party making an arrest. This is accomplished by merely touching, however slightly, the body of the accused, by the party making the arrest and for that purpose, although he does not succeed in stopping or holding him even for an instant; as where the bailiff had tried to arrest one who fought him off by a fork, the court said, 'If the bailiff had touched him, that had been an arrest' " A. CORNELIUS, SEARCH AND SEIZURE 163 (2d ed. 1930).

To say that an arrest is effected by the slightest application of physical force, despite the arrestee's escape, is not to say that for Fourth Amendment purposes there is a continuing arrest during the period of fugitivity. If Pertoso had laid his hands upon Hodari to arrest him, but Hodari had broken away and had then cast away the cocaine, it would hardly be realistic to say that that disclosure had been made during the course of an arrest. The present case is even further removed. It does not involve the application of any physical force; Hodari was untouched by Officer Pertoso at the time he discarded the cocaine. His defense relies upon the proposition that a seizure occurs "when the officer, by means of physical force or show of authority, has in some way restrained the liberty of a citizen." Hodari contends that Pertoso's pursuit qualified as a "show of authority" calling upon Hodari to halt. The question is whether, with respect to a show of authority as with respect to application of physical force, a seizure occurs even though the subject does not yield. We hold that it does not.

The language of the Fourth Amendment cannot sustain respondent's contention. The word "seizure" readily bears the meaning of a laying on of hands or application of physical force to restrain movement, even when it is ultimately unsuccessful. It does not remotely apply to the prospect of a policeman yelling "Stop, in the name of the law!" at a fleeing form that continues to flee. That is no seizure. Nor can the result respondent wishes to achieve be produced—indirectly by suggesting that Pertoso's uncomplied—with show of authority was a common-law arrest, and then appealing to the principle that all common-law arrests are seizures. An arrest requires either physical force or, where that is absent, submission to the assertion of authority. "Mere words will not constitute an arrest, while, on the other hand, no actual, physical touching is essential. The apparent inconsistency in the two parts of this statement is explained by the fact that an assertion of authority and purpose to arrest followed by submission of the arrestee constitutes an arrest. There can be no arrest without either touching or submission." Perkins, *The Law of Arrest*, 25 IOWA L.REV. 201, 206 (1940).

We do not think it desirable, even as a policy matter, to stretch the Fourth Amendment beyond its words and beyond the meaning of arrest. Street pursuits always place the public at some risk, and compliance with police orders to stop should be encouraged. Only a few of those orders will be without adequate basis, and since the addressee has no ready means of identifying the deficient ones it almost invariably is the responsible course to comply. Unlawful orders will not be deterred, by sanctioning through the exclusionary rule those of them that are not obeyed. Since policemen do not command "Stop!" expecting to be ignored, or give chase hoping to be outrun, it fully suffices to apply the deterrent to their genuine, successful seizures.

United States v. Mendenhall, 446 U.S. 544 (1980) says that a person has been seized "only if," not that he has been seized "whenever"; it states a necessary, but not a sufficient, condition for seizure—or, more precisely, for seizure effected through a "show of authority." *Mendenhall* establishes that the test for existence of a "show of authority" is an objective one: not whether the citizen perceived that he was being ordered to restrict his movement, but whether the officer's words and actions would have conveyed that to a reasonable person. Assuming that Pertoso's pursuit in the present case constituted a "show of authority" enjoining Hodari to halt, since Hodari did not comply with that injunction he was not seized until he was tackled. The cocaine abandoned while he was running was not the fruit of a seizure, and his motion to exclude it was properly denied. We reverse and remand for further proceedings not inconsistent with this opinion.

It is so ordered.

JUSTICE STEVENS, with whom JUSTICE MARSHALL joins, dissenting.

The officer's show of force—taking the form of a head-on chase—adequately conveyed the message that respondent was not free to leave. Here, respondent attempted to end "the conversation" before it began and soon found himself literally "not free to leave" when confronted by an officer running toward him head-on who eventually tackled him. There was an interval of time between the moment that respondent saw the officer fast approaching and the moment when he was tackled, and thus brought under the control of the officer. The same issue would arise if the show of force took the form of a command to "freeze," a warning shot, or the sound of sirens accompanied by a patrol car's flashing lights. In these situations, there may be a significant time interval between the initiation of the officer's show of force and the complete submission by the citizen. The Court concludes that the timing of the seizure is governed by the citizen's reaction, rather than by the officer's conduct. One consequence is that the point at which the interaction between citizen and police officer becomes a seizure occurs, not when a reasonable citizen believes he or she is no longer free to go, but, rather, only after the officer exercises control over the citizen. Interests in effective law enforcement and in personal liberty would be better served by adhering to a standard that "allows the police to determine in advance whether the conduct contemplated will implicate the Fourth Amendment." The constitutionality of a police officer's show of force should be measured by the conditions that exist at the time of the officer's action. The character of the citizen's response should not govern the constitutionality of the officer's conduct. In the present case, if Officer Pertoso had succeeded in tackling respondent before he dropped the rock of cocaine, the rock unquestionably would have been excluded as the fruit of the officer's unlawful seizure. Under the Court's analysis, the exclusionary rule has no application because an attempt to make an unconstitutional seizure is beyond the coverage of the Fourth Amendment, no matter how outrageous or unreasonable the officer's conduct may be.

Points for Discussion

a.   The Fleeing Motorist

A similar decision was rendered in *Hester v. United States*, 265 U.S. 57 (1924). During Prohibition, federal agents saw a moonshiner hand a customer a quart of whiskey. The agents tried to arrest both the moonshiner and the customer, but both fled. During the chase, both the moonshiner and the customer dropped various items of contraband. The police recovered the items and used them to convict the moonshiner of concealing alcohol in violation of federal law. The Court concluded that the items were properly admitted in evidence: "the defendant's own acts disclosed the contraband and there was no seizure in the sense of the law when the officers examined the contents of each after they had been abandoned."

b.   The Police Cruiser

In *Michigan v. Chesternut*, 486 U.S. 567 (1988), police officers were engaged in routine patrol in a marked police cruiser. When respondent saw the patrol car nearing the corner where he stood, he turned and began to run. The cruiser followed respondent "to see where he was going." The cruiser quickly caught up with respondent, drove alongside him for a short distance, and saw him discard a number of packets.

Food for Thought

Suppose that the officer shot Hodari to prevent his escape. Hodari was seriously wounded, unable to run away, and immediately fell to the ground. Before the officer could get to Hodari, he discarded a chunk of rock cocaine. The officer retrieved the cocaine and then subdued Hodari. At what point was Hodari seized? Was the cocaine obtained as a result of the seizure or afterwards? *See Tennessee v. Garner*, 471 U.S. 1 (1985).

The officers retrieved the packets, found that they contained pills which appeared to be codeine, and arrested respondent for possession of narcotics. During an ensuing search, the police discovered another packet of pills, a packet containing heroin, and a hypodermic needle. The Court upheld respondent's conviction for possession of illegal narcotics: "Respondent was not seized before he discarded the packets containing the controlled substance. The police conduct would not have communicated to the reasonable person an attempt to capture or otherwise intrude upon respondent's freedom of movement. The record does not reflect that the police activated a siren or flashers; or that they commanded respondent to halt, or displayed any weapons; or that they operated the car in an aggressive manner to block respondent's course or otherwise control the direction or speed of his movement. While the very presence of a police car driving parallel to a running pedestrian could be somewhat intimidating, this kind of police presence does not, standing alone, constitute a seizure. The police therefore were not required to have "a particularized and objective basis for suspecting respondent of criminal activity," in order to pursue him."

Hypo 1: *More on Fleeing Motorists*

Johnson stole an automobile and eluded police by traveling at high speeds. During this time, Johnson was followed by police cars with flashing lights. The chase ended when Johnson slammed into a police roadblock killing himself. The roadblock consisted of tractor-trailers placed across both lanes of a two-lane highway. The roadblock was "concealed" by the fact that it was around a bend in the road and was unilluminated. In addition, a police car, with its headlights on, had been placed between Johnson's oncoming vehicle and the truck, so that Johnson was "blinded." Johnson's heirs sued, claiming that the police had effected an unreasonable seizure in violation of the Fourth Amendment. In light of the holdings in *Mendenhall* and *Hodari D*, do you agree that Johnson was seized? If so, when did the seizure occur? What arguments might you make on behalf of Johnson's estate? How might the State respond? How should the Court rule? *See Brower v. County of Inyo*, 489 U.S. 593 (1989).

Hypo 2: *The Man & the Jacket*

Just after midnight, two police officers on routine patrol in a "high crime area" pull their marked vehicle alongside three young men who are walking. One officer explains to the men that they are "not in trouble," but that he would like to "talk to them" about some recent robberies. The officers then ask the men if they would agree to a pat-down for weapons. Two of the men reply that they have no objection, and one officer frisked them. The third man (Henson) also consented to a pat-down and placed his hands on the hood of the police car. However, before the officer could begin the frisk, the man started walking away. The officer then "grabbed the man's jacket," but the man "was able to wiggle out of it." The officer chased the man for about twenty yards until the man slipped and fell on the snow and the officer caught up with him. After a brief struggle, the officer placed the man in handcuffs. When was the man seized for purposes of the Fourth Amendment? *See Henson v. United States*, 55 A.3d 859 (D.C. Ct. App. 2012).

Hypo 3: *The Searchlight & the Pedestrian*

A police officer is patrolling in a high-crime area when he sees an individual standing next to a parked car. The officer shines his spotlight on the individual, exits his car walking briskly, and asks whether the suspect is on probation or parole. The individual does not resist or attempt to run away. Was the suspect "seized" when the officer exited the vehicle? *See People v. Garry*, 156 Cal.App.4th 1100, 67 Cal.Rptr.3d 849 (2007).

Food for Thought

Suppose that there is a history of racial tension in a particular city, and that tensions have been heightened by recent police shootings of African-American motorists. Around midnight, two white police officers approach an African-American man who is seated in his lawfully parked car in an effort to "find out what he is doing." Under the circumstances, has the man been seized? To what extent is the racial identity of the man, or the racial identity of the police officers, or the racial tensions, relevant to your answer? *See United States v. Washington*, 490 F.3d 765 (9th Cir. 2007).

Hypo 4: *The Smell of "Fresh Marijuana"*

After an anonymous tip that a woman and a man are smoking marijuana outside an apartment building, police officers proceeded to the location and found a properly parked vehicle with the windows down containing two people (a man and a woman) smoking cigarettes. The officers asked the passengers to exit the vehicle. One officer spoke to the man, and could detect the smell of marijuana. When the police called in a drug sniffing dog, the man admitted to possessing marijuana and showed the police where it could be found. Was the man "seized" within the meaning of the Fourth Amendment? If so, when did the seizure begin? *See State v. Joyce*, 159 N.H. 440, 986 A.2d 642 (2009).

* * *

Mendenhall makes clear that the police (or DEA agents or other governmental officials) can make an investigative stop when they have a reasonable suspicion that a suspect is involved in criminal activity. However, an investigative stop is a much more limited intrusion on individual privacy than a custodial arrest. In *Florida v. Royer*, 460 U.S. 491 (1983), a case that was factually similar (although distinguishable) from

Mendenhall, the Court noted that an "investigative detention must be temporary and last no longer than is necessary to effectuate the purpose of the stop," and should involve "the least intrusive means reasonably available to verify or dispel the officer's suspicion in a short period of time." The *Royer* Court held that the agents were free to stop Royer because they had reason to believe that he was carrying illegal drugs. However, because the officers removed Royer to the DEA office, and removed his luggage from the plane, the Court concluded that the "detention to which he was subjected was a more serious intrusion on his personal liberty than is allowable on mere suspicion of criminal activity."

Points for Discussion

a. Defining Reasonable Suspicion

In *Fields v. Swenson*, 459 F.2d 1064 (8th Cir.1972), late at night, two officers observed a station wagon at rest in an unlighted section of a parking lot near a hardware store. All nearby business establishments were closed. One of the officers was familiar with the area and had never seen the car before, but he recognized the license number as belonging to David Montgomery who he knew as a suspect in some burglaries. At 11:40 p.m., the officers see three persons approach the car "carrying something." One enters the car's back seat while the other two walk away. When the car is driven away, the police follow for several blocks and see the occupant of the rear seat take off a red jacket. When the officers stop the car, they observe a lady's handbag containing tools (hammers and other large tools) on the floor. The occu-

Take Note

In *United States v. Sokolow*, 490 U.S. 1 (1989), the Court held that "reasonable suspicion" involves "something more than an 'inchoate' and unparticularized suspicion or 'hunch,' " but "considerably less than proof of wrongdoing by a preponderance of the evidence." "Probable cause means 'a fair probability that contraband or evidence of a crime will be found,' and the level of suspicion required for a *Terry* stop is obviously less demanding than that for probable cause." In *United States v. Cortez*, 449 U.S. 411 (1981), the Court held that "reasonable suspicion" should be determined using a "totality of the circumstances" standard: "Based upon that whole picture the detaining officers must have a particularized and objective basis for suspecting the particular person stopped of criminal activity."

pants of the car are then placed under arrest for "investigation of burglary and larceny" and possession of burglary tools. The Court concluded that the police had a sufficient basis for an investigative stop.

b. 911 Calls & Reasonable Suspicion

In *Navarette v. California*, 572 U.S. 393 (2014), after a 911 caller reported that a vehicle had run her off the road, a police officer located the reported vehicle and executed a traffic stop. The Court held that the 911 call provided the officer with sufficient cause for the stop even though the tip was made anonymously, and there was no information regarding the informant's veracity or basis of knowledge. The Court found the tip "sufficiently reliable" for several reasons: "the caller claimed eyewitness knowledge of the alleged dangerous driving," adding "significant support" to "the tip's reliability," she reported "the incident soon after she was run off the road" (the Court regarded a "contemporaneous report" as "especially reliable"), and the caller used the 911 emergency system which permits the police to identify and trace callers, thereby providing "safeguards against making false reports with immunity."

FYI

In *Alabama v. White,* 496 U.S. 325 (1990), the Court held that police could rely on an anonymous tip in developing "reasonable suspicion." "Reasonable suspicion, like probable cause, is dependent upon both the content of information possessed by police and its degree of reliability." In considering the totality of the circumstances, "if a tip has a relatively low degree of reliability, more information will be required to establish the requisite quantum of suspicion than would be required if the tip were more reliable."

Therefore, the Court concluded that the tip provided the basis for concluding that the driver of the stopped vehicle was driving drunk or had been involved in "an isolated episode of past recklessness." Although the erratic driving might have been explainable as caused by an unruly child in the vehicle, the Court emphasized that reasonable suspicion "need not rule out the possibility of innocent conduct." Justice Scalia dissented, claiming that the Court's new rule suggests that "anonymous claims of a single instance of possibly careless or reckless driving, called in to 911, will support a traffic stop." He argued that the stop was not justified because the police knew nothing about the tipster, the conduct they observed was innocent, and the fact that the call was made to 911 was insufficient to assure reliability.

c. Drug Courier Profiles

In recent years, narcotics agents have increasingly relied on so-called "drug courier profiles" to establish the basis for an investigative stop. In *Mendenhall,* for example, detectives claimed that a profile focused their attention on Mendenhall:

> The agent testified that respondent's behavior fit the so-called "drug courier profile"—an informally compiled abstract of characteristics thought typical of persons carrying illicit drugs. The agents thought it relevant that (1) respondent was arriving on a flight from Los Angeles, a city believed by the agents to be the place of origin for much of the heroin brought to Detroit; (2) respondent was the last person to leave the plane, "appeared to be very nervous," and "completely scanned the whole area where the agents were standing"; (3) after leaving the plane respondent proceeded past the

baggage area without claiming any luggage; and (4) respondent changed airlines for her flight out of Detroit.

Mendenhall engaged in behavior that the agents believed was designed to evade detection. She deplaned only after all other passengers had left the aircraft. Agent Anderson testified that drug couriers often disembark last in order to have a clear view of the terminal so that they more easily can detect government agents. Once inside the terminal, respondent scanned the entire gate area and walked "very, very slowly" toward the baggage area. When she arrived there, she claimed no baggage. Instead, she asked a skycap for directions to the Eastern Airlines ticket counter located in a different terminal. Although she carried an American Airlines ticket for a flight from Detroit to Pittsburgh, she asked for an Eastern Airlines ticket. An airline employee gave her an Eastern Airlines boarding pass. Agent Anderson testified that drug couriers frequently travel without baggage and change flights en route to avoid surveillance. On the basis of these observations, the agents stopped and questioned respondent.

In *United States v. Sokolow*, 490 U.S. 1 (1989), the Court upheld the use of so-called "drug courier profiles": "A court sitting to determine the existence of reasonable suspicion must require the agent to articulate the factors leading to that conclusion, but the fact that these factors may be set forth in a 'profile' does not somehow detract from their evidentiary significance as seen by a trained agent."

d. Mistakes & Reasonable Suspicion

In *Heien v. North Carolina*, 574 U.S. 54 (2014), a police officer stopped a vehicle because of a faulty brake light, and checked the driver's license and registration. While undertaking these tasks, the officer became suspicious because the driver was acting nervously. The officer asked for and obtained consent to search the vehicle and found cocaine during the ensuing search. Heien, who was charged with attempted trafficking in cocaine, moved to suppress the cocaine on the basis that it did not violate state law to drive with only one working brake light. Therefore, so Heien argued, the stop was "objectively unreasonable," violated the Fourth Amendment, and the cocaine should have been suppressed. The Court disagreed. While the Court recognized that a traffic stop requires a "reasonable suspicion"—that is, "a particularized and objective basis for suspecting the particular person stopped" of breaking the law—the Court held that the "ultimate touchstone of the Fourth Amendment is reasonableness." The Court noted that "reasonable men make mistakes of law, and such mistakes are compatible with the concept of reasonable suspicion. Officers in the field must make factual assessments on the fly, and so deserve a margin of error. The Fourth Amendment tolerates only *reasonable* mistakes, and those mistakes—whether of fact or of law—must be *objectively* reasonable. Although the North Carolina statute at issue refers to '*a* stop lamp,' suggesting the need for only a single working brake light, it also provides that 'the stop lamp may be incorporated into a unit with one or more *other* rear lamps.' Another subsection of the same provision requires that vehicles 'have all originally equipped rear lamps or the equivalent in good working order,' arguably indicating that if a vehicle has multiple 'stop lamps,' all must be functional." The Court noted that there had been confusion in state court decisions construing the statute. Justice Sotomayor dissented, arguing that there "is nothing requiring us to hold that a reasonable mistake of law can justify a seizure under the Fourth Amendment, and quite a bit suggesting just the opposite."

e. Pretextual Stops

In *Whren v. United States*, 517 U.S. 806 (1996), two undercover police officers were patrolling in a "high drug area" when they saw respondent driving in an unusual manner and stopped him. Although respondent conceded that the officers had probable cause to stop him for traffic violations, he argued that it was a pretextual stop designed to search for drugs. The Court upheld the stop: "Prior cases foreclose any argument that the constitutional reasonableness of traffic stops depends on the actual motivations of the individual officers involved. The Constitution prohibits selective enforcement based on considerations such as race. But the constitutional basis for objecting to intentionally discriminatory application of laws is the Equal Protection Clause. Subjective intentions play no role in ordinary, probable-cause Fourth Amendment analysis."

Take Note

In *Muehler v. Mena*, 544 U.S. 93 (2005), during execution of a search warrant, the police handcuffed and detained an occupant of a house which they believed was occupied by a criminal gang. During the search, an officer asked the detainee about her immigration status, and the Court decided that this question did not constitute a separate seizure requiring reasonable suspicion, because "mere police questioning does not constitute a seizure." Instead, the Court emphasized that the duration of the questioning, not the content of the questioning, would be relevant in determining whether the detention was lawful. *Compare United States v. Stewart*, 473 F.3d 1265 (10th Cir. 2007) *with United States v. Mendez*, 467 F.3d 1162 (9th Cir. 2006).

f. Duration of Stop

In *United States v. Sharpe*, 470 U.S. 675 (1985), the Court rejected a court of appeals decision holding that investigative stops could not last longer than twenty minutes, noting that there is: "no rigid time limitation on *Terry* stops. While it is clear that 'the brevity of the invasion of the individual's Fourth Amendment interests is an important factor in determining whether the seizure is so minimally intrusive as to be justifiable on reasonable suspicion,' we need to consider the law enforcement purposes to be served by the stop as well as the time reasonably needed to effectuate those purposes." The Court went on: "In assessing whether a detention is too long to be justified as an investigative stop, it is appropriate to examine whether the police diligently pursued a means of investigation that was likely to confirm or dispel their suspicions quickly, during which time it was necessary to detain the defendant. A court making this assessment should consider whether the police are acting in a swiftly developing situation, and not indulge in unrealistic second-guessing. The question is not simply whether some other alternative was available, but whether the police acted unreasonably in failing to recognize or to pursue it."

g. Custodial Questioning

In *Dunaway v. New York*, 442 U.S. 200 (1979), the police viewed Dunaway as the prime suspect in a murder case, and decided to "pick him up" and "bring him in" for questioning. Dunaway was not told that he was under arrest, but the police stated that he would have been physically restrained had he attempted to leave. The Court held that probable cause was required: "The detention of petitioner was in important respects indistinguishable from a traditional arrest Any 'exception' that could cover a seizure as intrusive as that in this case would threaten to swallow the general rule that Fourth Amendment seizures are 'reasonable' only if based on probable cause."

h. Fingerprinting

In *Davis v. Mississippi*, 394 U.S. 721 (1969), Davis was convicted of rape and sentenced to life imprisonment based on fingerprints taken after a forced trip to the police station. The Court held that probable cause was required. Mr. Justice Stewart dissented: "Like the color of a man's eyes, his height, or his very physiognomy, the tips of his fingers are an inherent and unchanging characteristic of the man. We do not deal here with a confession wrongfully obtained or with property wrongfully seized. We deal, instead, with 'evidence' that can be identically reproduced and lawfully used at any subsequent trial." In *Hayes v. Florida*, 470 U.S. 811 (1985), in dicta, the Court suggested that a brief field detention for fingerprinting might be justified based only on a reasonable suspicion: "If there are articulable facts supporting a reasonable suspicion that a person has committed a criminal offense, that person may be stopped in order to identify him, to question him briefly, or to detain him briefly while attempting to obtain additional information."

Food for Thought

Consider the drug courier profile (referred to above) that DEA agents used to identify Mendenhall as a drug courier. Do you agree that Mendenhall's conduct was "suspicious?" In thinking about that issue, consider Justice White's dissent:

> No aspects of Ms. Mendenhall's conduct, either alone or in combination, were sufficient to provide reasonable suspicion that she was engaged in criminal activity. The fact that Ms. Mendenhall was the last person to alight from a flight originating in Los Angeles was plainly insufficient to provide a basis for stopping her. Nor was the fact that her flight originated from a "major source city," for the mere proximity of a person to areas with a high incidence of drug activity or to persons known to be drug addicts, does not provide the necessary reasonable suspicion for an investigatory stop. The DEA agents' observations that Ms. Mendenhall claimed no luggage and changed airlines were also insufficient to provide reasonable suspicion. Unlike Terry, where "nothing in the suspects' conduct from the time the officer first noticed them until the time he confronted them and identified himself as a police officer gave him sufficient reason to negate his hypothesis" of criminal behavior. Ms. Mendenhall's subsequent conduct negated any reasonable inference that she was traveling a long distance without luggage or changing her ticket to a different airline to avoid detection. Agent Anderson testified that he heard the ticket agent tell Ms. Mendenhall that her ticket to Pittsburgh already was in order and that all she needed was a boarding pass for the flight. Thus it should have been plain to an experienced observer that Ms. Mendenhall's failure to claim luggage was attributable to the fact that she was already ticketed through to Pittsburgh on a different airline. Because Agent Anderson's suspicion that Ms. Mendenhall was transporting narcotics could be based only on "his inchoate and unparticularized suspicion or 'hunch,' " rather than "specific reasonable inferences which he is entitled to draw from the facts in light of his experience," he was not justified in "seizing" Ms. Mendenhall.

Food for Thought

Is there a "reasonable suspicion of criminal activity" when a suspect 1) pays $2,100 for two airplane tickets from a roll of $20 bills; 2) travels under a name that does not match the name under which his telephone number is listed; 3) his original destination is Miami, a source city for illicit drugs; 4) he stayed in Miami for only 48 hours, even though a round-trip flight from Honolulu to Miami takes 20 hours; 5) he appeared nervous during his trip; and 6) he checked no luggage? *See United States v. Sokolow*, 490 U.S. 1 (1989).

Hypo 1: *Automobile Profiles?*

Suppose that the police create a "drug courier" profile for suspects that transport drugs between Miami and New York City or Boston by automobile. The profile focuses on cars coming from a "source city" (Miami) using a major "drug highway" (I-95). Because so many drivers on this highway tend to exceed the speed limit, and because drug couriers are anxious about being stopped, the profile suggests that drug couriers travel at or below the speed limit. Do the police have a "reasonable suspicion" that anyone meeting this profile is a "drug courier?"

Food for Thought

After *Mendenhall* and *Royer*, do narcotics agents have clear guidance about how they may act in airport situations? Suppose that the officers had approached Royer in the airport, and sought to ask him some questions, but Royer had refused to answer them, stating that he wants to get a cup of coffee and doesn't have time to talk to them and get the coffee. In light of the holding in *Royer*, what may the officers do next?

Hypo 2: *More on Defining Reasonable Suspicion*

Recall the *Digiovanni* problem in which a police officer stopped a car for following another car too closely. Even if the facts in that case did not provide the officer with probable cause to arrest Digiovanni, do they provide the police with a "reasonable suspicion" to believe that Digiovanni is in possession of illegal drugs? Recall that an officer saw two shirts hanging in the rear passenger compartment, a hygiene bag on the back seat, noticed that the interior of the car was clean, and the car was a rental. The officer viewed these facts as suggestive of drug trafficking activity. The rental contract indicated that the car was rented at Fort Lauderdale Airport the previous day and was to be dropped off at Logan International Airport in Boston, at a cost of $438. Does the officer have "reasonable suspicion" to continue the detention? If so, what is the officer allowed to do? *See United States v. Digiovanni*, 650 F.3d 498 (4th Cir. 2011). Does it matter that the officer asked Digiovanni if he had any luggage in the car and if everything in the car belonged to him, and Digiovanni responded in the affirmative. Then Digiovanni said, "Oh boy," as he tossed the cigarette he was smoking over the guardrail. The officer testified that he found this remark "extremely suspicious." The officer then asked Digiovanni what was the matter, to which

Digiovanni replied, "It's just so hot."Then the officer explained to Digiovanni that "people smuggle drugs and guns up and down I-95," and asked Digiovanni if there was any marijuana, cocaine or heroin in the car, and Digiovanni replied, "No sir. I never smoked marijuana in my life. It puts me to sleep." When the officer followed up with, "Are you sure?," Digiovanni replied, "I'm positive." Under these circumstances, does the officer possess a reasonable suspicion that Digiovanni is involved in drug trafficking? If so, what is the officer allowed to do next? How does Digiovanni's nonsensical response (that he had "never" smoked marijuana because it puts him to sleep) enter into the analysis? *See United States v. Digiovanni*, 650 F.3d 498 (4th Cir. 2011).

Hypo 3: *The Suspicious Rental Car*

A police officer, traveling on a highway, observes a driver unsafely pass another car. The officer stops the driver who appears to be "extremely nervous" and who does not maintain eye contact. The officer checks the driver's license and registration, as well as the rental car agreement. In talking to the driver, the officer learns that the car was rented in Las Vegas, Nevada (hundreds of miles away from the site of the stop in Kansas, and generally regarded by police as a "source city" for illegal drugs) the day before, that the driver is traveling to Indianapolis (hundreds of miles further) because he has to be at work the following day, and that the driver plans to return the car to Las Vegas two days later. The officer believes that these travel plans are "bizarre." By this time, the officer has written a citation for the traffic violation. Does the officer have a reasonable suspicion that the driver is involved in drug activity? If so, what may the officer do in order to verify (or dispel) his suspicions? *See United States v. White*, 584 F.3d 935 (10th Cir. 2009). If the officer has a drug sniffing dog with him, may he subject the vehicle and driver to a drug sniff? If the officer does not happen to have a drug sniffing dog with him, can he order the driver to follow him to the state highway patrol office about 9 miles away where a dog can conduct the sniff? While the officer could have waited for the dog to be brought to the scene, he believes that the sniff would occur much more quickly if it were conducted at the office, and orders the driver to follow him. Did he act properly?

Hypo 4: *Length of Stop*

Suppose that a police officer validly stops a suspect for a traffic violation. May the police officer extend the stop long enough to run a background check on the suspect to make sure who she is dealing with and to check for outstanding warrants? *See People v. Harris*, 886 N.E.2d 947 (2008). After the officer confirms the validity of the suspect's driver's license and the absence of outstanding warrants, the officer is writing a citation when another officer arrives and informs the first officer that the suspect is believed to be involved in drug activity. The first officer immediately stops writing the ticket, and goes to the suspect's car to question him about illegal drugs. After a brief conversation, the suspect consents to a search of the vehicle which turns up illegal narcotics and illegal firearms. Did the officer act permissibly in prolonging the search to ask about drugs and request consent to search? Did the officer have a "reasonable suspicion" on which to base the inquiry? *See United States v. Garner*, 961 F.3d 264 (2020); *United States v. Turvin*, 517 F.3d 1097 (9th Cir. 2008); *State v. Louthan*, 744 N.W.2d 454 (2008).

Hypo 5: *More on the Length of the Stop*

A police officer stopped Reyes for speeding and she stated that she was going to pick up her kids to drive them to school. The officer viewed that statement as odd because there were no passengers. The officer collected Reyes's license and registration and asked Reyes to join him in the patrol car. She initially refused. She eventually decided to comply, but carefully locked her vehicle (which the officer thought was unusual). As they talked, she stated that she started her trip in a city that was approximately three hours away, and that she was going to a city that was about 15 miles ahead. Finding it odd that Reyes would drive 3 ¼ hours to take kids to school, Reyes stated that the kids were not her own. Does the officer have sufficient cause to call in a canine unit? Suppose that the canine arrives before the officer finishes questioning Reyes? What if she is delayed 10 minutes? *See United States v. Reyes*, 960 F.3d 697 (5th Cir. 2020).

Hypo 6: *The Scope of the Stop*

One evening, an officer notices a van with illegal window tinting and executes a traffic stop. After the van stops, the officer notices that there is a "lot of shaking," so he immediately walks to the driver's side door. The officer find a male driver (Jackson), and he assumes that the man has switched seats because the female had been in the driver's seat. The officer states that, in his experience, such switching involves an attempt to hide or retrieve weapons. The driver admits that he switched places with the woman. When the officer asks the driver whether he has any weapons on him, the driver replies "no," and the officer finds no weapons in the ensuing patdown. However, the officer notices that the driver is nervous and that his heart is beating fast. The officer then handcuffs the female passenger while he places the driver in the back seat of his patrol car. The driver is told that he is not under arrest. The officer then searches the front passenger compartment of the van for weapons and finds whiskey under the van's rear floorboard, and a small hatchet beside the driver's seat. The officer also removes the cover of the horn on the steering wheel after noticing that it looks out of position. There, he discovers Ziploc bags containing a rock-like substance that turns out to be cocaine. Did the officer act properly in stopping the vehicle, frisking the occupants, and in searching the vehicle? *See Jackson v. United States*, 56 A.3d 1206 (D.C. App. 2012).

Hypo 7: *Drug Couriers?*

A police officer, assigned to a drug interdiction team, notices a green SUV on an interstate highway. Based on his experience, the officer suspects that the SUV is a rental vehicle because it is new, clean, has no window tinting, and no dealer insignia. The officer paces the vehicle and concludes that it is traveling 75 mph in a 70 mph zone. The officer also observes a white van traveling approximately four car lengths in front of the SUV at the same speed, and he suspects, based on the same indicators, that it is a rental vehicle as well. Both vehicles display Texas license plates, a "source state" for narcotics entering the state. In the officer's experience, a tandem driving formation of rental vehicles suggests a possible narcotics transporting arrangement. The officer travels beside the van and observes that the rear seats are folded down and that the driver appears to be nervous. Does the officer have sufficient justification to initiate a traffic stop of both vehicles? *See United States v. Allen*, 705 F.3d 367 (8th Cir. 2013).

Hypo 8: *More on Evaluating "Reasonable Suspicion"*

A police officer is on routine evening patrol in a "high-drug" and "high-crime area," where "multiple shootings" and "countless drug arrests" have taken place, when he notices two men standing next to a dumpster at a convenience store where "no trespassing signs" have been posted. As he approaches the store, the officer notices two men standing next to a pair of garbage dumpsters "toward the back" of the convenience store's side parking lot. The place where the men are standing is "not close" to the convenience store's front entrance. The men do not have shopping bags or any other items suggestive of recent purchases from the store. When the men see the officer, they "almost immediately" begin to walk away at a "fast pace," trying to "get away from the area." Although their path takes them past the convenience store's entrance, neither man attempts to enter the store. Suspecting that the men have been trespassing, the officer exits his vehicle and tells them that they are not free to go. Did the officer have a "reasonable suspicion" that the men were involved in criminal activity? *See United States v. Bumpers*, 705 F.3d 168 (4th Cir. 2013).

Hypo 9: *The Gun Shells*

A police officer responds to an unverified 911 call from a children's clothing store. The officer knows that there is drug activity in the surrounding area and that there have been several burglaries in this particular mall. When he arrives, a security guard tells the officer that a man has attempted to steal some clothing, and identifies a male who is walking quickly away from the store. There are six to eight people in the direction the guard points, but Griffin is the only one who fit the guard's description of "the black man in the green jacket and jeans." The officer follows the man who continuously looks over his shoulder and walk away briskly. The officer tells the man to stop. When the man disobeys and continues to walk away, the officer grabs the man's wrists, and states that he is investigating a petty theft. Even though the man denies stealing anything, the officer frisks the man in order to ensure his own safety. During the frisk, the officer feels what he "believes to be" batteries in the man's pocket. The officer does not reach into the pocket, but does find "it odd that someone is carrying batteries," he asks the man, "Hey, what's in your pocket? Why do you have batteries?" Griffin responded that the items are shotgun shells. The officer then asks the man if he has ever been to prison, and the man answers "yes." When the officer states that it is illegal for felons to possess weapons or ammunition, the man flees. Did the police officer act properly in asking the man the additional questions, or did he unduly prolong the seizure? *See United States v. Griffin*, 696 F.3d 1354 (11th Cir. 2012).

United States v. Place

462 U.S. 696 (1983).

Justice O'Connor delivered the opinion of the Court.

Respondent Place's behavior aroused the suspicions of law enforcement officers as he waited in line at the Miami International Airport to purchase a ticket to New York's LaGuardia Airport. As Place proceeded to the gate for his flight, agents approached him and requested his airline ticket and some identification. Place complied and consented to a search of the two suitcases he had checked. Because his flight was about to depart, however, the agents decided not to search the luggage. Prompted by Place's parting remark that he had recognized that they were police, the agents inspected the address tags on the checked luggage and noted discrepancies in the street addresses. Further investigation revealed that neither address existed and that the telephone number Place had given the airline belonged to a third address on the same street. On the basis of their encounter with Place and this information, the agents called Drug Enforcement Administration (DEA) authorities in New York to relay their information. Two DEA agents waited for Place at the arrival gate at LaGuardia Airport in New York. There again, his behavior aroused the suspicion of the agents. After he claimed his two bags and called a limousine, the agents decided to approach him. They identified themselves as federal narcotics agents, to which Place responded that he knew they were "cops" and had spotted them as soon as he had deplaned. One of the agents informed Place that, based on their own observations and information obtained from the Miami authorities, they believed that he might be carrying narcotics. The agents requested and received identification from Place—a New Jersey driver's license, on which the agents later ran a computer check that disclosed no offenses, and his airline ticket receipt. When Place refused to consent to a search of his luggage, one of the agents told him that they were going to take the luggage to a federal judge to try to obtain a search warrant and that Place was free to accompany them. Place declined, but obtained from one of the agents telephone numbers at which the agents could be reached. The agents then took the bags to Kennedy Airport, where they subjected the bags to a "sniff test" by a trained narcotics detection dog. The dog reacted positively to the smaller of the two bags but ambiguously to the larger bag. Approximately 90 minutes had elapsed since the seizure of respondent's luggage. Because it was late on a Friday afternoon, the agents retained the luggage until Monday morning, when they secured a search warrant from a magistrate for the smaller bag. Upon opening that bag, the agents discovered 1,125 grams of cocaine. Place was indicted for possession of cocaine with intent to distribute. The District Court denied Place's motion to suppress, but the court of appeals reversed.

The Court has viewed a seizure of personal property as *per se* unreasonable within the meaning of the Fourth Amendment unless it is accomplished pursuant to a judicial warrant issued upon probable cause and particularly describing the items to be seized. Where law enforcement authorities have probable cause to believe that a container holds contraband or evidence of a crime, but have not secured a warrant, the Court has interpreted the Amendment to permit seizure of the property, pending issuance of a warrant to examine its contents, if the exigencies of the circumstances demand it or some other recognized exception to the warrant requirement is present. For example, "objects such as weapons or contraband found in a public place may be seized by the police without a warrant," because, under these circumstances, the risk of the item's disappearance or use for its intended purpose before a warrant may be obtained outweighs the interest in possession.

The Government asks us to recognize the reasonableness under the Fourth Amendment of warrantless seizures of personal luggage from the custody of the owner on the basis of less than probable cause, for the purpose of pursuing a limited course of investigation, short of opening the luggage, that would quickly confirm or dispel the authorities' suspicion. Specifically, we are asked to apply the principles of *Terry* to permit seizures on the basis of reasonable, articulable suspicion, premised on objective facts, that the luggage contains contraband or evidence of a crime. In our view, such application is appropriate.

Where the authorities possess specific and articulable facts warranting a reasonable belief that a traveler's luggage contains narcotics, the governmental interest in seizing the luggage briefly to pursue further investigation is substantial. "The public has a compelling interest in detecting those who would traffic in deadly drugs for personal profit." In *Terry*, we described the governmental interests supporting the initial seizure of the person as "effective crime prevention and detection; it is this interest which underlies the recognition that a police officer may in appropriate circumstances and in an appropriate manner approach a person for purposes of investigating possibly criminal behavior even though there is no probable cause to make an arrest." Similarly, in *Michigan v. Summers* we identified three law enforcement interests that justified limited detention of the occupants of the premises during execution of a valid search warrant: "preventing flight in the event that incriminating evidence is found," "minimizing the risk of harm" both to the officers and the occupants, and "orderly completion of the search." The test is whether those interests are sufficiently "substantial," not whether they are independent of the interest in investigating crimes effectively and apprehending suspects. The context of a particular law enforcement practice may affect the determination whether a brief intrusion on Fourth Amendment interests on less than probable cause is essential to effective criminal investigation. Because of the inherently transient nature of drug courier activity at airports, allowing police to make brief investigative stops of persons at airports on reasonable suspicion of drug-trafficking substantially enhances the likelihood that police will be able to prevent the flow of narcotics into distribution channels.

Against this strong governmental interest, we must weigh the nature and extent of the intrusion upon the individual's Fourth Amendment rights when the police briefly detain luggage for limited investigative purposes. The intrusion on possessory interests occasioned by a seizure of one's personal effects can vary both in its nature and extent. The seizure may be made after the owner has relinquished control of the property to a third party or, as here, from the immediate custody and control of the owner. Moreover, the police may confine their investigation to an on-the-spot inquiry—for example, immediate exposure of the luggage to a trained narcotics detection dog—or transport the property to another location. Given the fact that seizures of property can vary in intrusiveness, some brief detentions of personal effects may be so minimally intrusive of Fourth Amendment interests that strong countervailing governmental interests will justify a seizure based only on specific articulable facts that the property contains contraband or evidence of a crime.

We conclude that when an officer's observations lead him reasonably to believe that a traveler is carrying luggage that contains narcotics, the principles of *Terry* and its progeny would permit the officer to detain the luggage briefly to investigate the circumstances that aroused his suspicion, provided that the investigative detention is properly limited in scope. The purpose for which respondent's luggage was seized was to arrange its exposure to a narcotics detection dog. If this investigative procedure is itself a search requiring probable cause, the seizure of respondent's luggage for the purpose of subjecting it to the sniff test—no matter how brief—could not be justified on less than probable cause. A "canine sniff" by a well-trained narcotics detection dog, however, does not require opening the luggage. It does not expose noncontraband items that otherwise would remain hidden from public view, as does, for example, an officer's rummaging through the contents of the luggage. Thus, the manner in which information is obtained through this investigative technique is much less intrusive than a typical search. Moreover, the sniff discloses only the presence or absence of narcotics, a contraband item. Despite the fact that the sniff tells the authorities something about the contents of the luggage, the information obtained is limited. This limited disclosure also ensures that the owner of the property is not subjected to the embarrassment and inconvenience entailed in less discriminate and more intrusive investigative methods. We conclude that the particular course of investigation that the agents intended to pursue here—exposure of respondent's luggage, which was located in a public place, to a trained canine—did not constitute a "search" within the meaning of the Fourth Amendment.

There is no doubt that the agents made a "seizure" of Place's luggage for purposes of the Fourth Amendment when, following his refusal to consent to a search, the agent told Place that he was going to take the luggage to a federal judge to secure issuance of a warrant. The premise of the Government's argument is that seizures of property are generally less intrusive than seizures of the person. While true in some circumstances, the precise type of detention we confront here is seizure of personal luggage from the immediate possession of the suspect for the purpose of arranging exposure to a narcotics detection dog. In the case of detention of luggage within the traveler's immediate possession, the police conduct intrudes on both the suspect's possessory interest in his luggage as well as his liberty interest in proceeding with his itinerary. The person whose luggage is detained is technically still free to continue his travels or carry out other personal activities pending release of the luggage. Moreover, he is not subjected to the coercive atmosphere of a custodial confinement or to the public indignity of being personally detained. Nevertheless, such a seizure can effectively restrain the person since he is subjected to the possible disruption of his travel plans in order to remain with his luggage or to arrange for its return. Therefore, when the police seize luggage from the suspect's custody, we think the limitations applicable to investigative detentions of the person should define the permissible scope of an investigative detention of the person's luggage on less than probable cause. Under this standard, it is clear that the police conduct here exceeded the permissible limits of a *Terry*-type investigative stop.

The length of the detention of Place's luggage precludes a conclusion that the seizure was reasonable in the absence of probable cause. The brevity of the invasion of the individual's Fourth Amendment interests is an important factor in determining whether the seizure is so minimally intrusive as to be justifiable on reasonable suspicion. Moreover, in assessing the effect of the length of the detention, we take into account whether the police diligently pursue their investigation. Here the New York agents knew the time of Place's scheduled arrival at LaGuardia, had ample time to arrange for their additional investigation, and thereby could have minimized the intrusion on respondent's Fourth Amendment interests. Although we decline to adopt any outside time limitation for a permissible *Terry* stop,[11] we have never approved a seizure of the person for the prolonged 90-minute period involved here and cannot do so on the facts presented by this case.

Although the 90-minute detention of respondent's luggage is sufficient to render the seizure unreasonable, the violation was exacerbated by the failure of the agents to accurately inform respondent of the place to which they were transporting his luggage, of the length of time he might be dispossessed, and of what arrangements would be made for return of the luggage if the investigation dispelled the suspicion. The detention of respondent's luggage went beyond the narrow authority possessed by

---

[28]   Cf. ALI, Model Code of Pre-Arraignment Procedure § 110.2(1) (1975)(recommending a maximum of 20 minutes for a *Terry* stop).

police to detain briefly luggage reasonably suspected to contain narcotics. Under the circumstances of this case, the seizure of respondent's luggage was unreasonable under the Fourth Amendment. Consequently, the evidence obtained from the subsequent search of his luggage was inadmissible, and Place's conviction must be reversed.

JUSTICE BRENNAN, with whom JUSTICE MARSHALL joins, concurring in the result.

The use of a balancing test in this case is inappropriate. First, the intrusion is no longer the "narrow" one contemplated by the *Terry* line of cases. In addition, the intrusion involves not only the seizure of a person, but also the seizure of property. The Court today has employed a balancing test 'to swallow the general rule that seizures of property are "reasonable" only if based on probable cause.' " Justice Blackmun's concern over "an emerging tendency on the part of the Court to convert the *Terry* decision into a general statement that the Fourth Amendment requires only that any seizure be reasonable," is certainly justified.

Point for Discussion

Seizing Mail

In *United States v. Van Leeuwen*, 397 U.S. 249 (1970), respondent mailed two 12-pound packages at a post office in the State of Washington, near the Canadian border, declaring that the packages contained coins addressed to post office boxes in California and Tennessee. Each package was sent airmail registered and insured for $10,000, so that they were not subject to discretionary inspection. When the postal clerk told the police that he was suspicious of the packages, an officer noticed that the return address was a vacant housing area and that the license plates of respondent's car were from British Columbia. Further investigation revealed that the California address was under investigation for trafficking in illegal coins. The Tennessee address was being investigated for the same crime. A customs official in Seattle thereupon obtained a search warrant, and the packages were opened and inspected. Respondent was subsequently tried for illegally importing gold coins. The Court upheld the seizure: "No interest protected by the Fourth Amendment was invaded by forwarding the packages the following day rather than the day when they were deposited. The significant Fourth Amendment interest was in the privacy of this first-class mail; and that privacy was not disturbed or invaded until the approval of the magistrate was obtained. Given the nature of the mailings, their suspicious character, the fact that there were two packages going to separate destinations, the

Food for Thought

In *Place*, suppose that you had been asked to advise the police about how to handle the investigation. What would you have advised them to do differently?

unavoidable delay in contacting the more distant of the two destinations, the distance between Mt. Vernon and Seattle—a 29-hour delay between the mailings and the service of the warrant cannot be said to be 'unreasonable' within the meaning of the Fourth Amendment."

Rodriguez v. United States

575 U.S. 348 (2015).

JUSTICE GINSBURG delivered the opinion of the Court.

Just after midnight, police officer Morgan Struble observed a Mercury Mountaineer veer slowly onto the shoulder of Nebraska State Highway 275 for seconds and then jerk back onto the road. Nebraska law prohibits driving on highway shoulders, and on that basis, Struble pulled the Mountaineer over. Struble is a K-9 officer and his dog Floyd was in his patrol car. Two men were in the Mountaineer: the driver, Denny Rodriguez, and a front-seat passenger, Scott Pollman. Struble approached the Mountaineer on the passenger's side. After Rodriguez identified himself, Struble asked him why he had driven onto the shoulder. Rodriguez replied that he had swerved to avoid a pothole. Struble then gathered Rodriguez's license, registration, and proof of insurance. Rodriguez decided to wait in his own vehicle. After running a records check on Rodriguez, Struble asked Pollman for his driver's license and began to question him about where the two men were coming from and where they were going. Pollman replied that they had traveled to Omaha, Nebraska, to look at a Ford Mustang that was for sale and that they were returning to Norfolk, Nebraska. Struble returned again to his patrol car, where he completed a records check on Pollman, and called for a second officer. Struble then began writing a warning ticket for Rodriguez for driving on the shoulder of the road. Struble returned to Rodriguez's vehicle a third time to issue the written warning. By 12:27 or 12:28 a.m., Struble had finished explaining the warning to Rodriguez, and had given back to Rodriguez and Pollman the documents obtained from them. Although justification for the traffic stop was "out of the way," Struble asked for permission to walk his dog around Rodriguez's vehicle. Rodriguez said no. Struble then instructed Rodriguez to turn off the ignition, exit the vehicle, and stand in front of the patrol car to wait for the second officer. Rodriguez complied. At 12:33 a.m., a deputy sheriff arrived. Struble retrieved his dog and led him twice around the Mountaineer. The dog alerted to the presence of drugs halfway through Struble's second pass. All told, seven or eight minutes had elapsed from the time Struble issued the written warning until the dog indicated the presence of drugs. A search of the vehicle revealed a large bag of methamphetamine.

Rodriguez was indicted on one count of possession with intent to distribute 50 grams or more of methamphetamine. He moved to suppress the evidence seized. The District Court denied Rodriguez's motion to suppress. The Eighth Circuit affirmed.

We granted certiorari to resolve whether police routinely may extend an otherwise-completed traffic stop, absent reasonable suspicion, in order to conduct a dog sniff.

A seizure for a traffic violation justifies a police investigation of that violation. "A relatively brief encounter," a routine traffic stop is "more analogous to a so-called '*Terry* stop' than to a formal arrest." *Knowles v. Iowa*, 525 U.S. 113, 117 (1998). Like a *Terry* stop, the tolerable duration of police inquiries in the traffic-stop context is determined by the seizure's "mission"—to address the traffic violation that warranted the stop, and attend to related safety concerns. *See also United States v. Sharpe*, 470 U.S. 675 (1985); *Florida v. Royer*, 460 U.S. 491 (1983) (plurality opinion). Because addressing the infraction is the purpose of the stop, it may "last no longer than is necessary to effectuate that purpose." Authority for the seizure thus ends when tasks tied to the traffic infraction are—or reasonably should have been—completed. *See Sharpe*, 470 U.S., at 686.

Our decisions in *Caballes* and *Johnson* heed these constraints. In *Illinois v. Caballes*, 543 U.S. 405 (2005), we concluded that the Fourth Amendment tolerated certain unrelated investigations that did not lengthen the roadside detention. *Johnson*, 555 U.S., at 327–328 (questioning); *Caballes*, 543 U.S., at 406 (dog sniff). In *Caballes*, however, we cautioned that a traffic stop "can become unlawful if it is prolonged beyond the time reasonably required to complete the mission" of issuing a warning ticket. We repeated that admonition in *Johnson:* The seizure remains lawful only "so long as unrelated inquiries do not measurably extend the duration of the stop." An officer, in other words, may conduct certain unrelated checks during an otherwise lawful traffic stop. But he may not do so in a way that prolongs the stop, absent the reasonable suspicion ordinarily demanded to justify detaining an individual. Beyond determining whether to issue a traffic ticket, an officer's mission includes "ordinary inquiries incident to the traffic stop." *Caballes*, 543 U.S., at 408. Typically such inquiries involve checking the driver's license, determining whether there are outstanding warrants against the driver, and inspecting the automobile's registration and proof of insurance. These checks serve the same objective as enforcement of the traffic code: ensuring that vehicles on the road are operated safely and responsibly. *See Prouse*, 440 U.S., at 658–659.

A dog sniff, by contrast, is a measure aimed at "detecting evidence of ordinary criminal wrongdoing." *Indianapolis v. Edmond*, 531 U.S. 32, 40–41 (2000). The Government acknowledged that a dog sniff, unlike the routine measures just mentioned, is not an ordinary incident of a traffic stop. Lacking the same close connection to roadway safety as the ordinary inquiries, a dog sniff is not fairly characterized as part of the officer's traffic mission. In *Mimms,* we reasoned that the government's "legitimate and weighty" interest in officer safety outweighs the "*de minimis*" additional intrusion of requiring a driver, already lawfully stopped, to exit the vehicle. The Eighth Circuit believed that the imposition here could be offset by the Government's "strong interest in interdicting the flow of illegal drugs along the nation's highways."

Unlike a general interest in criminal enforcement, the government's safety interest stems from the mission of the stop itself. Traffic stops are "especially fraught with danger to police officers," *Johnson,* 555 U.S., at 330, so an officer may need to take certain negligibly burdensome precautions in order to complete his mission safely. On-scene investigation into other crimes, however, detours from that mission. So too do safety precautions taken in order to facilitate such detours. Even assuming that the imposition here was no more intrusive than the exit order in *Mimms,* the dog sniff could not be justified on the same basis. Highway and officer safety are interests different in kind from the Government's endeavor to detect crime in general or drug trafficking in particular.

The Government argues that an officer may "incrementally" prolong a stop to conduct a dog sniff so long as the officer is reasonably diligent in pursuing the traffic-related purpose of the stop, and the overall duration of the stop remains reasonable in relation to the duration of other traffic stops involving similar circumstances. The reasonableness of a seizure, however, depends on what the police in fact do. If an officer can complete traffic-based inquiries expeditiously, then that is the amount of "time reasonably required to complete the stop's mission." *Caballes,* 543 U.S., at 407. As we said in *Caballes,* a traffic stop "prolonged beyond" that point is "unlawful." The critical question is not whether the dog sniff occurs before or after the officer issues a ticket, but whether conducting the sniff "prolongs"—*i.e.,* adds time to—"the stop."

The Magistrate Judge found that detention for the dog sniff in this case was not independently supported by individualized suspicion, and the District Court adopted the Magistrate Judge's findings. The question whether reasonable suspicion of criminal activity justified detaining Rodriguez beyond completion of the traffic infraction investigation, therefore, remains open for Eighth Circuit consideration on remand.

For the reasons stated, the judgment of the United States Court of Appeals for the Eighth Circuit is vacated, and the case is remanded for further proceedings consistent with this opinion.

It is so ordered.

JUSTICE THOMAS, with whom JUSTICE ALITO joins, and with whom JUSTICE KENNEDY joins as to all but Part III, dissenting.

Because the stop was reasonably executed, no Fourth Amendment violation occurred.

I

Approximately 29 minutes passed from the time Officer Struble stopped Rodriguez until his narcotics-detection dog alerted to the presence of drugs. That amount of time is hardly out of the ordinary for a traffic stop by a single officer of a vehicle containing multiple occupants even when no dog sniff is involved. During that time, Officer Struble conducted the ordinary activities of a traffic stop—he approached the vehicle, questioned Rodriguez about the observed violation, asked Pollman about their travel plans, ran serial warrant checks on Rodriguez and Pollman, and issued a written warning to Rodriguez. The fact that Officer Struble waited until after he gave Rodriguez the warning to conduct the dog sniff does not alter this analysis. Because "the use of a well-trained narcotics-detection dog generally does not implicate legitimate privacy interests," "conducting a dog sniff would not change the character of a traffic stop that is lawful at its inception and otherwise executed in a reasonable manner."

II

Caballes expressly anticipated that a traffic stop could be *reasonably* prolonged for officers to engage in a dog sniff. No Fourth Amendment violation had occurred in *Caballes,* where the "duration of the stop was entirely justified by the traffic offense and the ordinary inquiries incident to such a stop," but suggested a different result might attend a case "involving a dog sniff that occurred during an *unreasonably* prolonged traffic stop." The dividing line was whether the overall duration of the stop exceeded "the time reasonably required to complete the mission," not whether the duration of the stop "in fact" exceeded the time necessary to complete the traffic-related inquiries.

The majority's approach draws an artificial line between dog sniffs and other common police practices. Warrant checks are a constitutionally permissible part of a traffic stop, and the majority finds no fault in these measures. Yet its reasoning suggests the opposite. Such warrant checks look more like they are directed to "detecting evidence of ordinary criminal wrongdoing" than to "ensuring that vehicles on the road are operated safely and responsibly." Perhaps the existence of an outstanding warrant might make a driver less likely to operate his vehicle safely and responsibly on the road, but the same could be said about a driver in possession of contraband. A driver confronted by the police in either case might try to flee or become violent toward the officer. The majority suggests that a warrant check is an ordinary inquiry incident to a traffic stop because it can be used "to determine whether the apparent traffic violator is wanted for one or more previous traffic offenses." But such checks are a "manifestation of the 'war on drugs' motivation so often underlying routine traffic stops," and thus are very much like the dog sniff. The majority's reasoning appears to allow officers to engage in *some* questioning aimed at detecting evidence of ordinary criminal wrongdoing. But it is hard to see how such inquiries fall within the "seizure's 'mission' of addressing the traffic violation that warranted the stop," or "attending to related safety concerns." Its reasoning appears to come down to the principle that dogs are different.

A traffic stop based on reasonable suspicion, like all *Terry* stops, must be "justified at its inception" and "reasonably related in scope to the circumstances which justified the interference in the first place." *Hiibel,* 542 U.S., at 185. It also "cannot continue for an excessive period of time or resemble a traditional arrest." *Id.,* at 185–186. By contrast, a stop based on probable cause affords an officer considerably more leeway. In such seizures, an officer may engage in a warrantless arrest of the driver, a warrantless search incident to arrest of the driver, and a warrantless search incident to arrest of the vehicle if it is reasonable to believe evidence relevant to the crime of arrest might be found there. The *only* case involving a traffic stop based on probable cause that the majority cites is *Caballes.* But *Caballes* made clear that, in the context of a traffic stop supported by probable cause, "a dog sniff would not change the character of a traffic stop that is lawful at its inception and otherwise executed in a reasonable manner." Had Officer Struble arrested, handcuffed, and taken Rodriguez to the police station for his traffic violation, he would have complied with the Fourth Amendment. But because he made Rodriguez wait for seven or eight extra minutes until a dog arrived, he evidently committed a constitutional violation. Such a view of the Fourth Amendment makes little sense.

III

The Fourth Amendment permits an officer to conduct an investigative traffic stop when that officer has "a particularized and objective basis for suspecting the particular person stopped of criminal activity." Officer Struble testified that he first became suspicious that Rodriguez was engaged in criminal activity for a number of reasons. When he approached the vehicle, he smelled an "overwhelming odor of air freshener coming from the vehicle," which is, in his experience, "a common attempt to conceal an odor that people don't want to be smelled by the police." He observed that Rodriguez's passenger, Scott Pollman, appeared nervous. Pollman pulled his hat down low, puffed nervously on a cigarette, and refused to make eye contact with him. The officer thought he was "more nervous than your typical passenger" who "doesn't have anything to worry about because they didn't commit a traffic violation." Officer Struble's interactions with the vehicle's occupants only increased his suspicions. When he asked Rodriguez why he had driven onto the shoulder, Rodriguez claimed that he swerved to avoid a pothole. But that story could not be squared with Officer Struble's observation of the vehicle slowly driving off the road before being jerked back onto it. When Officer Struble asked Pollman where they were coming from and where they were going, Pollman told him they were traveling from Omaha, Nebraska, back to Norfolk, Nebraska, after looking at a vehicle they were considering purchasing. Pollman told the officer that he had neither seen pictures of the vehicle nor confirmed title before the trip. As Officer Struble explained, it "seemed suspicious" to him "to drive approximately two hours late at night to see a vehicle sight unseen to possibly buy it," and to go from Norfolk to Omaha to look at it because "usually people leave Omaha to go get vehicles, not the other way around" due to higher Omaha taxes. These facts, taken together, easily meet our standard for reasonable suspicion. Acts that, by themselves, might be innocent can, when taken together, give rise to reasonable suspicion. Officer Struble possessed probable cause to stop Rodriguez for driving on the shoulder, and he executed the subsequent stop in a reasonable manner.

JUSTICE ALITO, dissenting.

Officer Struble could have conducted the dog sniff while one of the tasks that the Court regards as properly part of the traffic stop was still in progress, but that sequence would have entailed unnecessary risk. When occupants of a vehicle who know that their vehicle contains a large amount of illegal drugs see that a drug-sniffing dog has alerted for the presence of drugs, they will almost certainly realize that the police will then proceed to search the vehicle, discover the drugs, and make arrests. Thus, it is reasonable for an officer to believe that an alert will increase the risk that the occupants of the vehicle will attempt to flee or perhaps even attack the officer. In this case, Officer Struble was outnumbered at the scene, and he therefore called for backup and waited for the arrival of another officer before conducting the sniff. As a result, the sniff was not completed until seven or eight minutes after he delivered the warning. But Officer Struble could have proceeded with the dog sniff while he was waiting for the results of the records check on Pollman and before the arrival of the second officer. If he had chosen that riskier sequence of events, the dog sniff would have been completed before the point in time when, according to the Court, the authority to detain for the traffic stop ended. Thus, an action that would have been lawful had the officer made the *unreasonable* decision to risk his life became unlawful when the officer made the *reasonable* decision to wait a few minutes for backup. The rule is unlikely to have any appreciable effect on the length of future traffic stops. Most officers will learn the prescribed sequence of events even if they cannot fathom the reason for that requirement.

Point for Discussion

Length of Seizure

In *United States v. Sokolow*, 490 U.S. 1 (1989), believing that Sokolow was a drug courier, DEA agents approached him during a stopover in Los Angeles. Sokolow "appeared very nervous." Later, Sokolow arrived in Honolulu. He had not checked any luggage and proceeded directly to the street, and tried to hail a cab, where DEA agents approached him. One agent displayed his credentials, grabbed Sokolow by the arm, and moved him back onto the sidewalk. The agent asked Sokolow for his airline ticket and identification; Sokolow said that he had neither. He told the agents that his name was "Sokolow," but that he was traveling under his mother's maiden name, "Kray." Sokolow was escorted to the DEA office at the airport. There, his luggage was examined by a narcotics detector dog which alerted on Sokolow's brown shoulder bag. The agents arrested Sokolow and obtained a warrant to search the bag. They found no illicit drugs, but the bag did contain several suspicious documents indicating respondent's involvement in drug trafficking. The agents had the dog reexamine the remaining luggage, and this time the dog alerted on a medium-sized bag. Since it was too late for agents to obtain a second warrant, they allowed respondent to leave for the night, but kept his luggage. The next morning, the agents obtained a warrant and found 1,063 grams of cocaine inside the bag. The Court rejected the challenge: "Respondent points to the statement in *Royer*, that 'the investigative methods employed should be the least intrusive means reasonably available to verify or dispel the officer's suspicion in a short period of time.' That statement, however, was directed at the length of the investigative stop, not at whether the police had a less intrusive means to verify their suspicions before stopping Royer. The reasonableness of the officer's decision to stop a suspect does not turn on the availability of less intrusive investigatory techniques. Such a rule would unduly hamper the police's ability to make swift, on-the-spot decisions—here, respondent was about to get into a taxicab—and it would require courts to indulge in 'unrealistic second-guessing.' "

Hypo 1: *Length of Stop*

Suppose that the police stop a car for a broken tail light and an inoperable brake light. During the stop, they become suspicious that the driver may be involved in illegal drug activity based on several factors: the stop took place in an area with a high level of drug activity; the driver appeared quite nervous when stopped; and the driver gave evasive answers to the police questions. Once the police have dealt with the justifications for the initial stop, can the officer prolong the stop under these circumstances in order to bring in a drug sniffing dog? *See Commonwealth v. Cordero*, 74 N.E.3d 1282 (Mass. 2017).

Hypo 2: *Drug Couriers*

A state trooper, with 17 years experience, stops an east bound vehicle bearing Indiana license plates in Texas, for speeding on a highway that the officer knows as a "drug trafficking corridor" between Houston and Dallas, major drug distribution centers. The trooper approaches the passenger side of the vehicle and asks for identification and the vehicle's registration. The trooper notices that the driver appears to be extremely nervous—he is breathing heavily, his hands are shaking, and his carotid artery is visibly pulsing. The trooper asks the driver to accompany him to the patrol car where he states that he plans to issue a warning for speeding. He then asks her about her travel history. She replies that she and Pack (her boyfriend) had been visiting her aunt in Houston who was ill. The trooper radios dispatch and requests computer checks on Williamson's and Pack's licenses and criminal histories. The trooper then returns to the vehicle and asks Pack about the couple's travel history. Pack tells the trooper that he and Williamson were coming from Dallas, where they had visited friends, and that they had stayed with relatives in San Antonio. Pack said that he was not aware of any family Williamson might have in Texas or that were ill. Because of the circumstances, can the officer reasonably conclude that they are engaged in criminal drug activity and order a canine sniff? *See United States v. Pack*, 612 F.3d 341 (5th Cir. 2010); *see also People v. Devone*, 931 N.E.2d 70 (2010).

Hypo 3: *The Express Delivery Package*

Police believe that Jefferson might be involved in illegal narcotics operations, and ask postal officials to alert them if Jefferson receives a package. When a package arrives for him (the package was sent the day before and was guaranteed for two-day delivery), the police instruct postal officials to hold it until the next day so that it can be inspected. The next day, the police subject the package to a canine sniff and the dog alerts. The package is delivered to Jefferson at 5 p.m. that same day, and he is arrested. Did the police search the package? If not, was the "seizure" (since delivery of the package was delayed) impermissible? What if the delay placed delivery beyond the guaranteed delivery time? *See United States v. Jefferson*, 566 F.3d 928 (9th Cir. 2009).

Hypo 4: *The Bus & the Suspicious Baggage*

Narcotics detectives observe passengers exiting a bus at a depot, while the bus is being cleaned and refueled, and they also examine the cargo hold of the bus. An officer becomes suspicious of a bag in the hold that has a computer generated destination tag for Dayton, Ohio, but a handwritten note indicating that the bag is headed for Indianapolis, IN. The officer has never seen a bag with a handwritten note that overrode the computer generated tag. The bag is outfitted with a strong after-market padlock. The officer removes the bag from the bus and places it inside the bus terminal. When the passengers re-board the bus, three officers board as well, with an officer holding the bag and asking the owner to identify himself. When no one does, an officer asks each passenger individually whether he/she owns the bag. When Alvarez responds in the affirmative, he is asked to leave the bus and does. During the questioning that follows, Alvarez produces a claim ticket for the bag that corresponds to the name on the bag. The officer then handcuffs Alvarez in order to prevent him from fleeing, and takes him to a police office inside the station. In Alvarez's presence, the bag is subjected to a canine sniff and the dog alerts. The bag is taken to a police station where it is subjected to a scan that reveals the presence of cocaine. Were the police actions permissible under the Fourth Amendment? *See United States v. Alvarez-Manzo*, 570 F.3d 1070 (8th Cir. 2009).

Hypo 5: *The Briefcase & the Drug Tainted Money*

Because Fallon purchased a one-way train ticket with cash just 72 hours prior to departure, police conclude that he satisfies a drug courier profile. Police meet Fallon at the train and ask him to accompany them to an office in the station. He does. During the subsequent questioning, when police ask Fallon whether he is carrying drugs or money, he begins sweating. At some point, when Fallon admits that he is carrying a large quantity of money, police take the briefcase and open it without permission. Inside, they find more than $100,000. The officers then call in a drug sniffing dog who alerts to the case, and the police seize the briefcase and the money. Did the officers act properly? If you had been advising the police, how would you have instructed them to proceed? *See United States v. Marrocco*, 578 F.3d 627 (7th Cir. 2009).

Hiibel v. Sixth Judicial District Court

542 U.S. 177 (2004).

JUSTICE KENNEDY delivered the opinion of the Court.

The sheriff's department in Humboldt County, Nevada, received an afternoon telephone call reporting an assault by a man in a red and silver GMC truck and dispatched an officer to investigate. When the officer arrived at the scene, he found the truck parked on the side of the road. A man was standing by the truck, and a young woman was sitting inside. The officer observed skid marks in the gravel behind the vehicle, leading him to believe it had come to a sudden stop. The officer approached the man and explained that he was investigating a report of a fight. The man appeared to be intoxicated. The officer asked him if he had "any identification on him," which we understand as a request to produce a driver's license or some other form of written identification. The man refused and asked why the officer wanted to see identification. The officer responded that he was conducting an investigation and needed to see some identification. The man became agitated and insisted he had done nothing wrong. The officer explained that he wanted to find out who the man was and what he was doing. After continued refusals to comply with the request for identification, the man began to taunt the officer by placing his hands behind his back and telling the officer to arrest him and take him to jail. This routine kept up for several minutes: the officer asked for identification 11 times and was refused each time. After warning the man that he would be arrested if he continued to refuse to comply, the officer placed him under arrest.

The man, Larry Hiibel, was charged with "willfully resisting, delaying, or obstructing a public officer in discharging or attempting to discharge any legal duty of his office" in violation of Nev.Rev.Stat. (NRS) § 199.280 (2003). A Nevada statute defines the legal rights and duties of a police officer in the context of an investigative stop. Section 171.123 provides: "1. Any peace officer may detain any person whom the officer encounters under circumstances which reasonably indicate that the person has committed, is committing or is about to commit a crime. . . . 3. The officer may detain the person pursuant to this section only to ascertain his identity and the suspicious circumstances surrounding his presence abroad. Any person so detained shall identify himself, but may not be compelled to answer any other inquiry of any peace officer." Hiibel was convicted and fined $250. The Supreme Court of Nevada affirmed. We granted certiorari.

NRS § 171.123(3) is an enactment sometimes referred to as a "stop and identify" statute. Stop and identify statutes often combine elements of traditional vagrancy laws with provisions intended to regulate police behavior in the course of investigatory stops. The statutes vary, but all permit an officer to ask or require a suspect to disclose his identity. A few States model their statutes on the Uniform Arrest Act, a model code that permits an officer to stop a person reasonably suspected of committing a crime and "demand of him his name, address, business abroad and whither he is going." Warner, *The Uniform Arrest Act*, 28 VA. L.REV. 315, 344 (1942). Other statutes are based on the text of the Model Penal Code. The provision provides that a person who is loitering "under circumstances which justify suspicion that he may be engaged or about to engage in crime commits a violation if he refuses the request of a peace officer that he identify himself and give a reasonably credible account of the lawfulness of his conduct and purposes." In some States, a suspect's refusal to identify himself is a misdemeanor offense or civil violation; in others, it is a factor to be considered in whether the suspect has violated loitering laws. In other States, a suspect may decline to identify himself without penalty.

Stop and identify statutes have their roots in early English vagrancy laws that required suspected vagrants to face arrest unless they gave "a good Account of themselves," a power that itself reflected common-law rights of private persons to "arrest any suspicious night-walker, and detain him till he give a good account of himself." 2 W. HAWKINS, PLEAS OF THE CROWN, ch. 13, § 6, p. 130. (6th ed. 1787). In recent decades, the Court has found constitutional infirmity in traditional vagrancy laws. In *Papachristou v. Jacksonville*, 405 U.S. 156 (1972), the Court held that a traditional vagrancy law was void for vagueness. Its broad scope and imprecise terms denied proper notice to potential offenders and permitted police officers to exercise unfettered discretion in the enforcement of the law. The Court has recognized similar constitutional limitations on the scope and operation of stop and identify statutes. In *Brown v. Texas*, 443 U.S. 47 (1979), the Court invalidated a conviction for violating a Texas stop and identify statute on Fourth Amendment grounds. The Court ruled that the initial stop was not based on specific, objective facts establishing reasonable suspicion to believe the suspect was involved in criminal activity. Absent that factual basis for detaining the defendant, the Court held, the risk of "arbitrary and abusive police practices" was too great and the stop was impermissible. Later, the Court invalidated a modified stop and identify statute on vagueness grounds. In *Kolender v. Lawson*, 461 U.S. 352 (1983), a California law required a suspect to give an officer "credible and reliable" identification when asked to identify himself. The Court held that the statute was void because it provided no standard for determining what a suspect must do to comply with it, resulting in "virtually unrestrained power to arrest and charge persons with a violation."

Here there is no question that the initial stop was based on reasonable suspicion, satisfying the Fourth Amendment requirements noted in *Brown*. Further, petitioner has not alleged that the statute is unconstitutionally vague. The Nevada statute is narrower and more precise. In contrast to *Kolender*, the Nevada Supreme Court has interpreted NRS § 171.123(3) to require only that a suspect disclose his name. The statute does not require a suspect to give the officer a driver's license or any other document. Provided that the suspect either states his name or communicates it to the officer by other means—a choice, we assume, that the suspect may make—the statute is satisfied and no violation occurs.

Beginning with *Terry v. Ohio*, 392 U.S. 1 (1968), the Court has recognized that a law enforcement officer's reasonable suspicion that a person may be involved in criminal activity permits the officer to stop the person for a brief time and take additional steps to investigate further. To ensure that the resulting seizure is constitutionally reasonable, a *Terry* stop must be limited. The officer's action must be "justified at its inception, and reasonably related in scope to the circumstances which justified the interference in the first place." The seizure cannot continue for an excessive period of time or resemble a traditional arrest. Questions concerning a suspect's identity are a routine and accepted part of many *Terry* stops. Obtaining a suspect's name in the course of a *Terry* stop serves important government interests. Knowledge of identity may inform an officer that a suspect is wanted for another offense, or has a record of violence or mental disorder. On the other hand, knowing identity may help clear a suspect and allow the police to concentrate their efforts elsewhere. Identity may prove particularly important in cases such as this, where the police are investigating what appears to be a domestic assault. Officers called to investigate domestic disputes need to know whom they are dealing with in order to assess the situation, the threat to their own safety, and possible danger to the potential victim.

It has been an open question whether the suspect can be arrested and prosecuted for refusal to answer. The reasonableness of a seizure under the Fourth Amendment is determined "by balancing its intrusion on the individual's Fourth Amendment interests against its promotion of legitimate government interests." *Delaware v. Prouse*, 440 U.S. 648 (1979). The Nevada statute satisfies that standard. The request for identity has an immediate relation to the purpose, rationale, and practical demands of a *Terry* stop. The threat of criminal sanction helps ensure that the request for identity does not become a legal nullity. On the other hand, the Nevada statute does not alter the nature of the stop itself: it does not change its duration or its location.

Petitioner argues that the Nevada statute circumvents the probable cause requirement, in effect allowing an officer to arrest a person for being suspicious. A *Terry* stop must be justified at its inception and "reasonably related in scope to the circumstances which justified" the initial stop. It is clear in this case that the request for identification was "reasonably related in scope to the circumstances which justified" the stop. The officer's request was a commonsense inquiry, not an effort to obtain an arrest for failure to identify after a *Terry* stop yielded insufficient evidence. The stop, the request, and the State's requirement of a response did not contravene the guarantees of the Fourth Amendment.

Petitioner further contends that his conviction violates the Fifth Amendment's prohibition on compelled self-incrimination. As we stated in *Kastigar v. United States*,

406 U.S. 441 (1972), the Fifth Amendment privilege against compulsory self-incrimination "protects against any disclosures that the witness reasonably believes could be used in a criminal prosecution or could lead to other evidence that might be so used." Petitioner's refusal to disclose his name was not based on any articulated real and appreciable fear that his name would be used to incriminate him, or that it "would furnish a link in the chain of evidence needed to prosecute" him. Petitioner refused to identify himself only because he thought his name was none of the officer's business. The Fifth Amendment does not override the Nevada Legislature's judgment to the contrary absent a reasonable belief that the disclosure would tend to incriminate him. The narrow scope of the disclosure requirement is important. One's identity is, by definition, unique; yet it is a universal characteristic. Answering a request to disclose a name is likely to be so insignificant in the scheme of things as to be incriminating only in unusual circumstances. In every criminal case, it is known and must be known who has been arrested and who is being tried. Even witnesses who plan to invoke the Fifth Amendment privilege answer when their names are called to take the stand. Still, a case may arise where there is a substantial allegation that furnishing identity at the

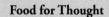
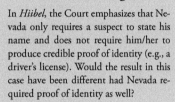

Food for Thought

In *Hiibel*, the Court emphasizes that Nevada only requires a suspect to state his name and does not require him/her to produce credible proof of identity (e.g., a driver's license). Would the result in this case have been different had Nevada required proof of identity as well?

time of a stop would have given the police a link in the chain of evidence needed to convict the individual of a separate offense. We need not resolve those questions here.

The judgment of the Nevada Supreme Court is *Affirmed*.

JUSTICE STEVENS, dissenting.

Given that citizens are not required to respond to police officers' questions during a *Terry* stop, it is no surprise that petitioner assumed that he had a right not to disclose his identity. The Court reasons that we should not assume that the disclosure of petitioner's name would be used to incriminate him or that it would furnish a link in a chain of evidence needed to prosecute him. But why else would an officer ask for it? And why else would the Nevada Legislature require its disclosure only when circumstances "reasonably indicate that the person has committed, is committing or is about to commit a crime"? If the Court is correct, then petitioner's refusal to cooperate did not impede the police investigation. The Nevada Legis-

Food for Thought

A dissenting Justice Breyer inquired whether a state, "in addition to requiring a stopped individual to answer 'What's your name?,' " can also require an answer to "What's your license number?" or "Where do you live?" How would you answer Justice Breyer's questions?

lature intended to provide its police officers with a useful law enforcement tool, and the very existence of the statute demonstrates the value of the information it demands.

Hypo 1: Hiibel*'s Limits*

In light of the Court's holding, consider the validity of the following laws mentioned in the majority opinion:

A) The Uniform Arrest Act's provisions which allow a police officer to stop a person reasonably suspected of committing a crime and "demand of him his name, address, business abroad and whither he is going."

B) The Model Penal Code's provisions which state that a person who is loitering "under circumstances which justify suspicion that he may be engaged or about to engage in crime commits a violation if he refuses the request of a peace officer that he identify himself and gives a reasonably credible account of the lawfulness of his conduct and purposes."

C) The rule in some States that a suspect's refusal to identify himself is a misdemeanor offense or civil violation.

D) The rule in some states that a suspect's refusal to identify himself is a factor to be considered in whether the suspect has violated loitering laws.

Hypo 2: *More on* Hiibel

Following *Hiibel*, when can the police demand identification? Consider the following scenarios: A) In an effort to be pro-active and "nip crime in the bud," a police officer decides to make routine stops of motorists to demand identification; B) At 3:00 am, a policeman sees a carload of teenagers driving in a residential neighborhood. The officer stops the teenagers to demand identification and information about their activities.

Hypo 3: *More on Requests for Identification*

Suppose that two police officers are on patrol in the middle of the afternoon, in an area that has been beset by a string of burglaries, when they see two men sitting on the front steps of a vacant building. The officers ask the men to justify their presence and to produce identification. Did the officers have sufficient cause to justify demanding that the men produce identification? *See Commonwealth v. Lyles*, 97 A.3d 298 (Penn. 2014).

Hypo 4: *The Men in the Alley*

Suppose that police are patrolling when they observe Brown and another man walking in opposite directions away from one another in an alley. The officers believe that the two had been together or were about to meet until the patrol car appeared. The officers stop one of the men, and ask him to identify himself and explain what he is doing. The other man disappears. The officer testifies that he stopped appellant because the situation "looked suspicious and we had never seen him in that area before." The area where appellant was stopped has a high incidence of drug traffic, but the officers did not suspect appellant of any specific misconduct, and did not have any reason to believe that he was armed. Appellant refused to identify himself and angrily asserted that the officers had no right to stop him. The man was then arrested under a state law which made it a crime for a person to refuse to give his name and address to an officer "who has lawfully stopped him and requested the information." Was the arrest for failure to produce identification legal and proper?

Hypo 5: *"Just Chilling"*

As Detective Ragland, a 17-year veteran, exits a restaurant and walks towards his unmarked vehicle, he notices a young male sitting in the driver's seat of an SUV. He also sees a second male in the passenger seat. The detective recognizes the second individual as Foster who he knows from a previous arrest for driving with a revoked license, as well as for a marijuana-related crime. The detective believes that Foster recognizes him as a police officer, and begins "shifting" his arms and "going haywire." However, the detective cannot see Foster's hands, but only his upper body and arms. As the detective walks past the SUV, he asks "What are ya'll doing?" Foster replies that they are "just chilling." The detective then leaves the parking lot in his car, goes across the street to a parking lot, and continues to observe the SUV. He does not see anyone enter or leave the vehicle. He then calls the police department and is informed that Foster is under investigation for a drug related offense. The detective calls for assistance and returns to the parked SUV with the other officer. The officers use their vehicles to block the SUV, exit their cars, and separately approach both sides of the SUV with their guns drawn. The officers ask Foster and the driver to show their hands, and the two comply. The detective then asks the driver for identification and the vehicle registration, and Foster opens the glove compartment to retrieve it. The moment the glove compartment opens, the detective sees a plastic bag containing a white powdery substance that he believes to be cocaine. Did the officers act properly in conducting this stop? *See United States v. Foster*, 634 F.3d 243 (4th Cir. 2011).

Hypo 6: *Warrant Checks on Pedestrians*

Shortly before midnight, a police officer on patrol sees three individuals exit an alleyway and begin walking down the middle of the street, side-by-side. One of the individuals is carrying a pit bull. The officer decides to question the individuals because they are walking in the middle of the street in violation of local law, and because there have been dog thefts in the area. The officer does not intend to cite the individuals, but he does intend to give them a verbal warning for walking in the street, to find out who they are, to find out why they are carrying the dog, and to determine whether the dog is stolen. The officer approaches the individuals, asks them to "hold up," and informs them that they are not permitted to walk in the middle of the street. He then talks to them about the dog. Satisfied with their explanations, he asks the individuals for their names. He immediately does a warrants check on each of them. Shortly thereafter, the dispatcher responds that there is an outstanding warrant for one of them (Burleson). The total duration of this initial encounter takes three to five minutes. After confirming Burleson's identity, the officer places him under arrest. At that point, Burleson admits that he has guns on him. Was the officer justified in extending the stop long enough to run a warrants check on the suspects? *See United States v. Burleson*, 657 F.3d 1040 (10th Cir. 2011).

Hypo 7: *The Encounter in the Park*

As police officers are riding bicycles through a park, they happen to notice a man and a woman sitting under a tree. Although the officers do not see the two engaged in any criminal activity, they regard it as "unusual" that a middle-aged couple would be in the park at that time of day (when it was usually frequented only by children and the elderly). The officers approach the man and the woman, ask to see identification, and then run a computer check on their names. Did the police act permissibly in requesting identification? *See State v. Ashbaugh*, 349 Or. 297, 244 P.3d 360 (2010).

Hypo 8: *Green Card*

A police officer spots a speeding pickup truck. As the truck passes, the driver brakes and both the driver and the passenger turn their heads away from the patrolman. When the officer follows the truck, the driver speeds up or slows down to lose him. The truck bears an out-of-state plate and the officer sees the truck "cross the center line several times." The officer decides to stop the vehicle because there are "indicators of someone impaired or suspicious activity." The officer asks the driver for his driver's license, the vehicle's registration, and proof of insurance. He also asks for identification from the front- and back-seat passengers. Two comply, but the third (Guijon) does not because he cannot speak English. When he is asked in Spanish, he produces a Lawful Permanent Resident Card ("Green Card") in the name of Daniel Gaitan. Guijon appears "very nervous" and "is shaking" as he does so. The patrolman then checks with headquarters for outstanding warrants and finds that there are none. The officer then decides to call the Bureau of Immigration and Customs Enforcement (ICE) "to verify the status of the permanent resident card." The entire process takes a number of minutes. Did the officer act properly? Should it matter whether a) the officer suspected Guijon's ID was false or altered, or belonged to someone else; b) suspected that, regardless of the validity of the ID, the defendant or one of the others might have been in the country unlawfully; c) checked with ICE as a matter of routine; or d) he simply had a hunch? Did the officer act properly? Was the stop of excessive length? *See United States v. Guijon-Ortiz*, 660 F.3d 757 (4th Cir. 2011). If, after checking with ICE, the officer still has concerns regarding Guijon's status, may he take Guijon to the ICE office which is approximately 15 minutes away? Does it matter that he gave the driver and the other passenger permission to leave, and gave them contact information for Guijon? Can ICE officers question Guijon regarding his immigration status? *See United States v. Guijon-Ortiz*, 660 F.3d 757 (4th Cir. 2011).

Maryland v. Buie

494 U.S. 325 (1990).

JUSTICE WHITE delivered the opinion of the Court.

Two men committed an armed robbery of a Godfather's Pizza restaurant in Prince George's County, Maryland. One of the robbers was wearing a red running suit. That same day, Prince George's County police obtained arrest warrants for respondent Jerome Edward Buie and his suspected accomplice, Lloyd Allen. Buie's house was placed under police surveillance. [Two days later], the police executed the arrest warrant for Buie. They first had a police secretary telephone Buie's house to verify that he was home. Six or seven officers proceeded to Buie's house. Once inside, the officers fanned out through the first and second floors. Corporal James Rozar announced that he would "freeze" the basement so that no one could come up and surprise the officers. With his revolver drawn, Rozar twice shouted into the basement, ordering anyone down there to come out. When a voice asked who was calling, Rozar announced three times: "this is the police, show me your hands." Eventually, a pair of hands appeared and Buie emerged from the basement. He was arrested, searched, and handcuffed. Thereafter, Detective Joseph Frolich entered the basement "in case there was someone else" there. He noticed a red running suit lying in plain view on a stack of clothing and seized it. The trial court denied Buie's motion to suppress the running suit, but the Court of Appeals of Maryland reversed. We granted certiorari.

Until the point of Buie's arrest the police had the right, based on the authority of the arrest warrant, to search anywhere in the house that Buie might have been found, including the basement. If Detective Frolich's entry into the basement was lawful, the seizure of the red running suit, which was in plain view and which the officer had probable cause to believe was evidence of a crime, was also lawful under the Fourth Amendment. The issue is what level of justification the Fourth Amendment required before Detective Frolich could legally enter the basement to see if someone else was there.

The ingredients to apply the balance struck in *Terry* and *Long* are present in this case. Possessing an arrest warrant and probable cause to believe Buie was in his home, the officers were entitled to enter and to search anywhere in the house in which Buie might be found. Once he was found, however, the search for him was over, and there was no longer that particular justification for entering any rooms that had not yet been searched.

That Buie had an expectation of privacy in those remaining areas of his house does not mean such rooms were immune from entry. In *Terry* and *Long* we were concerned with the immediate interest of the police officers in taking steps to assure themselves that the persons with whom they were dealing were not armed with, or able to gain immediate control of, a weapon that could unexpectedly and fatally be used against them. In the instant case, there is an analogous interest in taking steps to assure that the house in which a suspect is being, or has just been, arrested is not harboring other persons who are dangerous and who could unexpectedly launch an attack. The risk of danger in the context of an arrest in the home is as great as, if not greater than, it is in an on-the-street or roadside investigatory encounter. A *Terry* or *Long* frisk occurs before a police-citizen confrontation has escalated to the point of arrest. A protective sweep, in contrast, occurs as an adjunct to the serious step of taking a person into custody for the purpose of prosecuting him for a crime. Unlike an encounter on the street or along a highway, an in-home arrest puts the officer at the disadvantage of being on his adversary's "turf." An ambush in a confined setting of unknown configuration is more to be feared than it is in open, more familiar surroundings.

We recognized in *Terry* that "even a limited search of the outer clothing for weapons constitutes a severe, though brief, intrusion upon cherished personal security, and it must surely be an annoying, frightening, and perhaps humiliating experience." But we permitted the intrusion, which was no more than necessary to protect the officer from harm. Nor do we here suggest that entering rooms not examined prior to the arrest is a *de minimis* intrusion that may be disregarded. The arresting officers are permitted in such circumstances to take reasonable steps to ensure their safety after, and while making, the arrest. That interest is sufficient to outweigh the intrusion such procedures may entail. A warrant was not required. As an incident to the arrest the officers could, as a precautionary matter and without probable cause or reasonable suspicion, look in closets and other spaces immediately adjoining the place of arrest from which an attack could be immediately launched. There must be articulable facts which, taken together with the rational inferences from those facts, would warrant a reasonably prudent officer in believing that the area to be swept harbors an individual posing a danger to those on the arrest scene. A protective sweep, aimed at protecting the arresting officers, if justified by the circumstances, is nevertheless not a full search of the premises, but may extend only to a cursory inspection of those spaces where a person may be found. The sweep lasts no longer than is necessary to dispel the reasonable suspicion of danger and in any event no longer than it takes to complete the arrest and depart the premises.

The Fourth Amendment permits a properly limited protective sweep in conjunction with an in-home arrest when the searching officer possesses a reasonable belief based on specific and articulable facts that the area to be swept harbors an individual posing a danger to those on the arrest scene. We therefore vacate the judgment below and remand this case to the Court of Appeals for further proceedings not inconsistent with this opinion.

It is so ordered.

Justice Stevens, concurring.

The fact that respondent offered no resistance when he emerged from the basement is inconsistent with the hypothesis that the danger of an attack by a hidden confederate persisted after the arrest. Moreover, Officer Rozar testified that he was not worried about any possible danger when he arrested Buie. Officer Frolich supplied no explanation for why he might have thought another person was in the basement. He said only that he "had no idea who lived there." But Officer Frolich participated in the 3-day prearrest surveillance of Buie's home. No reasonable suspicion of danger justified the entry into the basement. If the officers were concerned about safety, one would expect them to do what Officer Rozar did before the arrest: guard the basement door to prevent surprise attacks. Officer Frolich might reasonably have "looked in" the already open basement door to ensure that no accomplice had followed Buie to the stairwell. But Officer Frolich did not merely "look in" the basement; he entered it. That strategy is a surprising choice for an officer, worried about safety, who need not risk entering the stairwell at all.

Justice Brennan, with whom Justice Marshall joins, dissenting.

Terry "permitted only brief investigative stops and extremely limited searches based on reasonable suspicion." This Court more recently has applied the rationale underlying *Terry* to a wide variety of more intrusive searches and seizures, prompting my continued criticism of the "emerging tendency on the part of the Court to convert the *Terry* decision" from a narrow exception into one that "swallows the general rule that searches are 'reasonable' only if based on probable cause." The majority offers no support for its assumption that the danger of ambush during planned home arrests approaches the danger of unavoidable "on-the-beat" confrontations in "the myriad daily situations in which policemen and citizens confront each other on the street." The Court's judgment that a protective sweep constitutes a "minimally intrusive" search akin to that involved in *Terry* markedly undervalues the nature and scope of the privacy interests involved. A protective sweep would bring within police purview virtually all personal possessions within the house

Take Note

In *Michigan v. Summers*, 452 U.S. 692 (1981), the occupant of a house was detained while a search warrant for the house was being executed. The Court held that the warrant made the occupant sufficiently suspicious to justify his temporary seizure: the "limited intrusion on the personal security" of the person detained was justified "by such substantial law enforcement interests" that the seizure could be made on articulable suspicion not amounting to probable cause. However, in *Bailey v. United States*, 568 U.S. 186 (2013), the Court held that the police did not have the authority to seize the occupant of a house, while executing a search warrant, when the occupant was some distance away from the premises to be searched and the only justification for the detention was to ensure the safety and efficacy of the search.

not hidden from view in a small enclosed space. Police officers searching for potential ambushers might enter every room including basements and attics; open up closets, lockers, chests, wardrobes, and cars; and peer under beds and behind furniture. The officers will view letters, documents, and personal effects that are on tables or desks or are visible inside open drawers; books, records, tapes, and pictures on shelves; and clothing, medicines, toiletries and other paraphernalia not carefully stored in dresser drawers or bathroom cupboards. While perhaps not a "full-blown" or "top-to-bottom" search, a protective sweep is much closer to it than to a "limited patdown for weapons" or a " 'frisk' of an automobile." The nature and scope of the intrusion sanctioned here are far greater than those upheld in *Terry* and *Long*. In light of the special sanctity of a private residence and the highly intrusive nature of a protective sweep, police officers must have probable cause to fear that their personal safety is threatened by a hidden confederate of an arrestee before they may sweep through the entire home. I would affirm the state court's decision to suppress the incriminating evidence. I respectfully dissent.

Points for Discussion

a. Securing the Premises

In *Illinois v. McArthur*, 531 U.S. 326 (2001), a woman asked police to accompany her to a trailer that she shared with her husband (Chuck) to help her retrieve her belongings. As the woman was leaving, she told police that her husband "had dope in there" and that he had "slid some dope underneath the couch." When the officer asked Chuck for permission to search the trailer, and he refused, another officer was sent to obtain a warrant, and told Chuck that he could not reenter the trailer unless accompanied by a police officer. Chuck reentered two or three times to get cigarettes and make phone calls, and each time an officer observed what Chuck did. A couple of hours later, when a warrant arrived, the police searched and found a marijuana pipe, a marijuana box, and a small amount of marijuana. The Court rejected the idea that Chuck was unlawfully seized when the officer refused to allow him to enter the trailer unaccompanied: "We cannot say that the warrantless seizure was *per se* unreasonable. It involves a claim of specially pressing or urgent law enforcement need, *i.e.*, 'exigent circumstances.' Moreover, the restraint was tailored to that need, limited in time and scope, and avoided significant intrusion into the home. Rather than employing a *per se* rule of unreasonableness, we balance the privacy-related and law enforcement-related concerns to determine if the intrusion was reasonable, and hence lawful, in light of the circumstances. The police had probable cause to believe that McArthur's trailer home contained evidence of a crime and contraband, namely, unlawful drugs. The police had good reason to fear that, unless restrained, McArthur would destroy the drugs before they could return with a warrant. The police made reasonable efforts to reconcile their law enforcement needs with the demands of personal privacy. They neither searched the trailer nor arrested McArthur before obtaining a warrant. Rather, they imposed a significantly less restrictive restraint, preventing McArthur only from entering the trailer unaccompanied. They left his home and his belongings intact—until a neutral Magistrate, finding probable cause, issued a warrant. The police imposed the restraint for a limited period of time, namely, two hours. This time period was no longer than reasonably necessary for the police, acting with diligence, to obtain the warrant." Justice Stevens dissented: "Illinois has decided that the possession of less than 2.5 grams of marijuana is a class C misdemeanor" and therefore is not "a law enforcement priority in the State of Illinois." Balancing the need versus the intrusion, he concluded that the majority got "the balance wrong" given McArthur's interest in the sanctity of his home.

b. Relying on "Wanted Fliers" to Establish "Reasonable Suspicion"

In *United States v. Hensley*, 469 U.S. 221 (1985), following an armed robbery, an informant told police that Hensley had driven the getaway car. Based on this information, the officer issued a "wanted flyer" which stated that Hensley was wanted for investigation of an aggravated robbery, described Hensley, stated the date and location of the alleged robbery, and asked other departments to pick up and hold Hensley in the event he was located. The flyer also warned other departments to use caution and to consider Hensley armed and dangerous. Based on the flyer, officers from another department stopped Hensley. When the officers spotted a revolver in plain view, they arrested Hensley. A search revealed other weapons. Based on the weapons, Hensley was convicted of being a convicted felon in possession of firearms. The Court upheld the stop, noting that admissibility turns on whether the officers who issued the flyer possessed probable cause to make the arrest. It does not turn on whether those relying on the flyer were themselves aware of the specific facts which led their colleagues to seek their assistance: "Reliance on a flyer or bulletin justifies a stop to check identification, to pose questions to the person, or to detain the person briefly while attempting to obtain further information. If the flyer has been issued in the absence of a reasonable suspicion, then a stop in the objective reliance upon it violates the Fourth Amendment. Of course, the officers making the stop may have a good-faith defense to any civil suit."

c. Can an Officer Order the Driver & Passengers to Exit a Lawfully-Stopped Vehicle?

In *Pennsylvania v. Mimms*, 434 U.S. 106 (1977), the Court held that a police officer may as a matter of course order the driver of a lawfully stopped car to exit the vehicle. In *Maryland v. Wilson*, 519 U.S. 408 (1997), the Court extended this rule to passengers. In *Wilson*, an officer attempted to stop a speeding vehicle, but the driver refused to stop. During the pursuit, the officer noticed that there were three people in the car and the two passengers turned to look at him several times, repeatedly ducking below sight level and then reappearing. As the officer approached the car on foot, the driver alighted and met him halfway. The driver was trembling and appeared extremely nervous, but nonetheless produced a valid driver's license. Hughes instructed him to return to the car and retrieve the rental documents, and he complied. During these events, Hughes noticed that the front-seat passenger (Wilson) was sweating and appeared extremely nervous. While the driver was looking for the rental papers, Hughes ordered Wilson out of the car. When Wilson exited, a quantity of crack cocaine fell to the ground. Wilson was then arrested and charged with possession of cocaine with intent to distribute. The Court held that the officer validly ordered Wilson to exit the vehicle Although there may have been no reason to conclude that the passenger has committed an offense, the Court found that the "same weighty interest in officer safety is present regardless of whether the occupant of the stopped car is a driver or passenger." The Court went on to note that in: "1994 alone, there were 5,762 officer assaults and 11 officers killed during traffic pursuits and stops. The fact that there is more than one occupant of the vehicle increases the possible sources of harm to the officer." "The possibility of a violent encounter stems not from the ordinary reaction of a motorist stopped for a speeding violation, but from the fact that evidence of a more serious crime might be uncovered during the stop. The motivation of a passenger to employ violence to prevent apprehension of such a crime is every bit as great as that of the driver." Justice Stevens dissented: "If a police officer has an articulable suspicion of possible danger, the officer may order passengers to exit the vehicle as a defensive tactic without running afoul of the Fourth Amendment." Justice Kennedy also dissented: "Traffic stops, even for minor violations, can take upwards of 30 minutes. When an officer commands passengers innocent of any violation to leave the vehicle and stand by the side of the road in full view of the public, the seizure is serious, not trivial. The command to exit ought not to be given unless there are objective circumstances making it reasonable for the officer to issue the order."

d. *Rettele* & the Naked Occupants

In *Los Angeles County v. Rettele,* 550 U.S. 609 (2007), police officers executed a search warrant at a house where they expected the occupants to be armed. Unaware that the actual suspects had moved out of the house three months earlier, the police found two individuals (a man and a woman) of a different race than the suspects in bed. The officers ordered the individuals to stand up even though they were naked, and made them stand there for a few minutes before they allowed them to dress. The individuals brought suit under 42 U.S.C. § 1983, claiming that their Fourth Amendment right to be free from unreasonable searches and seizures had been violated. They argued that a reasonable officer would have stopped the search upon discovering that respondents were of a different race than the suspects and would not have ordered respondents from their bed. The Court disagreed: "The deputies had no way of knowing whether the African-American suspects were elsewhere in the house. The presence of some Caucasians in the residence did not eliminate the possibility that the suspects lived there as well. The deputies, who were searching a house where they believed a suspect might be armed, possessed authority to secure the premises before deciding whether to continue with the search. In executing a search warrant officers may take reasonable action to secure the premises and to ensure their own safety and the efficacy of the search. The orders by the police, in the context of this lawful search, were permissible, and perhaps necessary, to protect the safety of the deputies. Blankets and bedding can conceal a weapon, and one of the suspects was known to own a firearm. The deputies needed a moment to secure the room and ensure that other persons were not close by or did not present a danger."

Hypo 1: *More on* Buie

Suppose that police arrest a man just inside the front door of his home. The arrest is pursuant to a warrant based on the man's violation of the terms of his supervised release. For their own safety, the police do a protective sweep of the house during which they find marijuana. Absent proof that someone else might be present, who presents a threat to the officers, are the police allowed to conduct a protective sweep? *See United States v. Bagley*, 877 F.3d 1151 (10th Cir. 2017); *United States v. Nelson*, 868 F.3d 885 (10th Cir. 2017). Suppose that the police go to a suspect's home to arrest him pursuant to a warrant. The warrant was issued because defendant failed to appear in court in response to charges of "disorderly conduct" (he played his stereo too loud late at night). The police are admitted to the house by the suspect's wife, and they call to him from the bottom of the stairs on the first floor, asking him to come downstairs. The suspect does come down, is handcuffed and taken to the kitchen. Before leaving, the police conduct a protective sweep of the upstairs. As you read *Buie*, is the protective sweep permissible? If not, why not? *See State v. McGrane*, 733 N.W.2d 671 (Iowa 2007). Suppose that the facts are the same except that the suspect is being arrested on drug charges, and the police have reason to believe that the suspect is dealing drugs out of his house. Does the nature of the charge alter the analysis? *See State v. McGrane*, 733 N.W.2d 671 (Iowa 2007).

Hypo 2: *Protective Sweeps*

Police were investigating Gorup on suspicion of dealing narcotics from his apartment. When they learn that Gorup is subject to an outstanding arrest warrant for a previous drug violation, detectives decide to conduct a "knock-and-talk investigation." The officers place Gorup (who is standing outside his apartment) under arrest and handcuff him. When the officers notice that there are other individuals inside, they decide to conduct a "protective sweep" of the apartment. It is unclear whether the other individuals can see either the police or Gorup. Is a protective sweep of the inside of the house permissible under these circumstances? Would it extend to a "small black zippered-type case" located on a table just inside the doorway? *See State v. Gorup*, 782 N.W.2d 16 (2010). Having probable cause to believe that Manuel was involved in a robbery and murder at a shop, police arrested him outside of his hotel room, forced him to the ground, and handcuffed him. Because the door to the room was open, the police immediately conducted a protective sweep of the room. One officer lifted the mattress and box spring from the foot of the bed to see if anyone was under it. When he did so, he heard a "clunking" sound and could see a gun in the box spring. Was it permissible for the officer to lift the mattress and box spring as part of a protective sweep? *See State v. Manuel*, 270 P.3d 828 (Ariz. 2011).

Hypo 3: *The Jacket*

Police detain a suspect while they search his home. Because the weather is chilly, and the police intend to take defendant outside, the police unilaterally decide to provide the suspect with a jacket and they choose the jacket from his closet. Before the police hand the jacket to the suspect, may they "frisk" the jacket to make sure that it does not contain a weapon or evidence? How would you respond to defendant's argument that, since the police have chosen to place the jacket within the area of defendant's "immediate control," they may not also search it? *See State v. Peterson*, 110 P.3d 699 (Utah 2005).

Hypo 4: *More on Knock & Talk*

Based on a tip from a confidential informant, police develop reason to believe that Basil is selling illegal drugs out of his house. In the course of the investigation, the police learn that "Basil" occupies the front bedroom in the basement apartment in which he resides. They also learn that he stays out late, sleeps late, usually departs from his apartment around noon, and has no known legal employment. The officers decide to go to Basil's home and conduct a "knock and talk." Three officers knock on the front door, and two more knock on the rear door after entering the fenced-in area of the yard. When a woman opens the back door, she mentions that there are other people in the apartment. At that point, officers Quinn and Salvetti pass through the apartment directly to the front bedroom. Quinn believes that this bedroom is occupied by "Basil."

Quinn has his gun drawn on the theory that Basil "could come out with a fire-arm or a gun or pose a danger." In the bedroom, underneath the bed, Quinn discovers a Hi-Point .380 caliber pistol with a defaced serial number. This pistol provides the basis of the firearm count with which Hassock is charged. Can the entry into the apartment be justified as a protective sweep? *See United States v. Hassock*, 631 F.3d 79 (2d Cir. 2011).

Hypo 5: *Helping the Co-Occupant*

After midnight, officers respond to a radio call that an individual has a gun at a residence. When they arrive, the officers see Vaz, who states that Simmons, his roommate, displayed a handgun during a dispute. Vaz requests that the offi-cers accompany him into the apartment so that he can retrieve his belongings. After entering, the officers conduct a protective sweep of the living room and kitchen, and then proceed down a hallway to the rear of the apartment where the bedrooms are located. As they do, the officers have their guns drawn and announce their presence. When they reach Simmons's bedroom, the officers find the bedroom door open, the room dimly lit, and Simmons lying in his bed. One officer sees a shiny object that he thinks might be the gun Vaz had described on a table next to the bed. When Simmons gets up and approaches the doorway, the officers instruct him to show his hands. Simmons complies, and is taken out into the hallway. Were the officers justified in removing Simmons from the bedroom? *See United States v. Simmons*, 661 F.3d 151 (2d Cir. 2011).

Hypo 6: *Searching Under the Mattress*

FBI agents execute an arrest warrant for a man that they believe to be "armed and dangerous." While two agents seize the subject of the warrant, other officers conduct a protective sweep of the remainder of the house. In one room, they find two teenage boys who they handcuff. Since the officers intend to place the boys on the bed, they look under the bed to make sure that there are no weapons there. In doing so, they find an illegal firearm. Did the officer's act consistently with the scope of a protective sweep in looking under the bed? *See United States v. Bennett*, 555 F.3d 962 (11th Cir. 2009).

Hypo 7: *Security Sweep of the Barricaded Home*

A man barricades himself in his house with a shotgun during a standoff with police. Eventually, the SWAT team is called in and zaps the man with a stun gun, thereby allowing the police to apprehend him. The man and his girlfriend claim that no one else is in the house. May the police nonetheless conduct a security sweep to make sure that there is no one else inside who poses a threat to them? *See Commonwealth v. Robertson*, 659 S.E.2d 321 (2008).

Hypo 8: *The Scope of a Protective Sweep*

A warrant authorizes the police to search the Aurora Tavern and the person of "Greg," a white male who works at the tavern, for possession of controlled substances. Police officers go to the tavern to execute the warrant, announce their purpose, and advise all present that they are going to conduct a "cursory search for weapons." The officers pat down each of the 13 customers. In patting down Greg, the officer feels what appears to be "a cigarette pack with objects in it." The officer retrieves the cigarette pack from Greg's pants pocket. Inside the pack he finds tinfoil packets containing a brown powdery substance which turns out to be heroin. Was the search of Greg constitutional? *See Ybarra v. Illinois*, 444 U.S. 85 (1979).

Hypo 9: *More on the Scope of a Protective Sweep*

Police officers have a warrant to arrest Johnson, but do not have a search warrant for his residence. An informant tells police that Johnson is staying in a particular house, is armed, and might have accomplices with him. The officers stake out the apartment. When Johnson's fiancée emerges, she tells the police that Johnson is inside alone. When Johnson steps outside, leaving the door ajar, the police arrest him. While handcuffing Johnson, the officer notices that Hamilton is observing from a distance, and Johnson tells Hamilton "they got me." Hamilton disappears. When other officers arrive, an officer conducts a "security check" of the house, including the bedroom, bathroom, and kitchen to verify that there are no armed individuals who might threaten the officers. In the bedroom, the officer discovers and seizes a gun sitting on a dresser and two bags of heroin lying in an open drawer. Did the police act properly in entering the apartment? *See United States v. Henry*, 48 F.3d 1282, 310 U.S.App.D.C. 431 (D.C.Cir.1995).

Delaware v. Prouse

440 U.S. 648 (1979).

MR. JUSTICE WHITE delivered the opinion of the Court.

A patrolman in a police cruiser stopped [respondent's automobile]. The patrolman smelled marihuana as he was walking toward the vehicle, and he seized marihuana in plain view on the car floor. At a hearing on respondent's motion to suppress, the patrolman testified that prior to stopping the vehicle he had observed neither traffic or equipment violations nor any suspicious activity, and that he made the stop only in order to check the driver's license and registration. The patrolman was not acting pursuant to any standards, guidelines, or procedures pertaining to document spot checks, promulgated by either his department or the State Attorney General. Characterizing the stop as "routine," the patrolman explained, "I saw the car in the area and wasn't answering any complaints, so I decided to pull them off." The trial court granted the motion to suppress.

The permissibility of a particular law enforcement practice is judged by balancing its intrusion on the individual's Fourth Amendment interests against its promotion of legitimate governmental interests. Implemented in this manner, the reasonableness standard usually requires, at a minimum, that the facts upon which an intrusion is based be capable of measurement against "an objective standard," whether this be probable cause or a less stringent test. The State of Delaware urges that these stops are reasonable under the Fourth Amendment because the State's interest in the practice as a means of promoting public safety upon its roads more than outweighs the intrusion entailed. We are aware of the danger to life and property posed by vehicular traffic and of the difficulties that even a cautious and an experienced driver may encounter. The States have a vital interest in ensuring that only those qualified to do so are permitted to operate motor vehicles, that these vehicles are fit for safe operation, and that licensing, registration, and vehicle inspection requirements are being observed. Automobile licenses are issued periodically to evidence that the drivers holding them are sufficiently familiar with the rules of the road and are physically qualified to operate a motor vehicle. The registration requirement and the related annual inspection requirement in Delaware are designed to keep dangerous automobiles off the road. Unquestionably, these provisions, properly administered, are essential elements in a highway safety program. Furthermore, we note that the State of Delaware requires a minimum amount of insurance coverage as a condition to automobile registration, implementing its legitimate interest in seeing to it that its citizens have protection when involved in a motor vehicle accident.

The question remains whether in the service of these important ends the discretionary spot check is a sufficiently productive mechanism to justify the intrusion upon Fourth Amendment interests which such stops entail. That question must be answered in the negative. Given the alternative mechanisms available, both those in use and those that might be adopted, we are unconvinced that the incremental contribution to highway safety of the random spot check justifies the practice under the Fourth Amendment. The foremost method of enforcing traffic and vehicle safety regulations is acting upon observed violations. Vehicle stops for traffic violations occur countless times each day; and on these occasions, licenses and registration papers are subject to inspection and drivers without them will be ascertained. Furthermore, drivers without licenses are presumably the less safe drivers whose propensities may well exhibit themselves. Finding an unlicensed driver among those who commit traffic violations is a much more likely event than finding an unlicensed driver by choosing randomly from the entire universe of drivers. The contribution to highway safety made by discretionary stops selected from among drivers generally will therefore be marginal at best. Furthermore, we find it difficult to believe that the unlicensed driver would not be deterred by the possibility of being involved in a traffic violation or having some other experience calling for proof of his entitlement to drive but that he would be deterred by the possibility that he would be one of those chosen for a spot check. In terms of actually discovering unlicensed drivers or deterring them from driving, the spot check does not appear sufficiently productive to qualify as a reasonable law enforcement practice under the Fourth Amendment.

Much the same can be said about the safety aspects of automobiles as distinguished from drivers. Many violations of minimum vehicle-safety requirements are observable, and something can be done about them by the observing officer, directly and immediately. In Delaware, as elsewhere, vehicles must carry and display current license plates, which themselves evidence that the vehicle is properly registered; and, under Delaware law, to qualify for annual registration a vehicle must pass the annual safety inspection and be properly insured. It does not appear, therefore, that a stop of a Delaware-registered vehicle is necessary in order to ascertain compliance with the State's registration requirements; and, because there is nothing to show that a significant percentage of automobiles from other States do not also require license plates indicating current registration, there is no basis for concluding that stopping even out-of-state cars for document checks substantially promotes the State's interest.

The marginal contribution to roadway safety possibly resulting from a system of spot checks cannot justify subjecting every occupant of every vehicle on the roads to a seizure—limited in magnitude compared to other intrusions but nonetheless constitutionally cognizable—at the unbridled discretion of law enforcement officials. Stopping apparently safe drivers is necessary only because the danger presented by some drivers is not observable at the time of the stop. When there is not probable cause to believe that a driver is violating any one of the multitude of applicable traffic and equipment regulations—or other articulable basis amounting to reasonable suspicion that the driver is unlicensed or his vehicle unregistered—we cannot conceive of any legitimate basis upon which a patrolman could decide that stopping a particular driver for a spot check would be more productive than stopping any other driver. This kind of standardless and unconstrained discretion is the evil the Court has discerned when in previous cases it has insisted that the discretion of the official in the field be circumscribed, at least to some extent. The "grave danger" of abuse of discretion does not disappear simply because the automobile is subject to state regulation resulting in numerous instances of police-citizen contact. There are certain "relatively unique circumstances" in which consent to regulatory restrictions is presumptively concurrent with participation in the regulated enterprise. Otherwise, regulatory inspections unaccompanied by any quantum of individualized, articulable suspicion must be undertaken pursuant to previously specified "neutral criteria."

An individual operating or traveling in an automobile does not lose all reasonable expectation of privacy simply because the automobile and its use are subject to government regulation. Automobile travel is a basic, pervasive, and often necessary mode of transportation to and from one's home, workplace, and leisure activities. Many people spend more hours each day traveling in cars than walking on the streets. Undoubtedly, many find a greater sense of security and privacy in traveling in an automobile than they do in exposing themselves by pedestrian or other modes of travel. Were the individual subject to unfettered governmental intrusion every time he entered an automobile, the security guaranteed by the Fourth Amendment would be seriously circumscribed.

Except in those situations in which there is at least articulable and reasonable suspicion that a motorist is unlicensed or that an automobile is not registered, or that either the vehicle or an occupant is otherwise subject to seizure for violation of law, stopping an automobile and detaining the driver in order to check his driver's license and the registration of the automobile are unreasonable under the Fourth Amendment.

MR. JUSTICE REHNQUIST, dissenting.

The State may require the licensing of those who drive on its highways and the registration of vehicles which are driven on those highways. If it may insist on these requirements, it obviously may take steps necessary to enforce compliance. The reasonableness of the enforcement measure chosen by the State is tested by weighing its intrusion on the motorists' Fourth Amendment interests against its promotion of the State's legitimate interests. The State's primary interest is in traffic safety, not in apprehending unlicensed motorists for the sake of apprehending unlicensed motorists. The whole point of enforcing motor vehicle safety regulations is to remove from the road the unlicensed driver before he demonstrates why he is unlicensed.

Points for Discussion

a.   Defining Reasonable Suspicion

In *United States v. Cortez*, 449 U.S. 411 (1981), border patrol agents stopped a van which they suspected contained illegal aliens. The Court held that the suspicion was "reasonable":

> When used by trained law enforcement officers, objective facts, meaningless to the untrained, can be combined with permissible deductions from such facts to form a legitimate basis for suspicion of a particular person and for action on that suspicion. The officers knew that the area was a crossing point for illegal aliens. They knew that it was common for persons to lead aliens through the desert from the border to Highway 86, where they could—by prearrangement—be picked up by a vehicle. Based upon clues they had discovered in the 2-month period prior to the events at issue, they believed that one such guide, whom they designated "Chevron," had a particular pattern of operations. By piecing together the information at their disposal, the officers tentatively concluded that there was a reasonable likelihood that "Chevron" would attempt to lead a group of aliens on [that] Sunday [night]. Someone with chevron-soled shoes had led several groups of aliens in the previous two months, yet it had been two weeks since the latest crossing. "Chevron," they deduced, was therefore due reasonably soon. "Chevron" tended to travel on clear weekend nights. Because it had rained on the Friday and Saturday nights of the weekend, Sunday was the only clear night of that weekend. The officers drew upon other objective facts known to them to deduce a time frame within which "Chevron" and the aliens were likely to arrive. They knew the time when sunset would occur; they knew about how long the trip would take. They were thus able to deduce that "Chevron" would likely arrive at the pickup point on Highway 86 in the time frame between 2 a.m. and 6 a.m. From objective facts, the officers also deduced the probable point on the highway—milepost 122—at which "Chevron" would likely rendezvous with a pickup vehicle. They deduced from the direction taken by the sets of "Chevron" footprints they had earlier discovered that the pickup vehicle would approach the aliens from, and return with them to, a point east of milepost 122. They therefore staked out a position east of milepost 122 and watched for vehicles that passed them going west and then, approximately one and a half hours later, [a van] passed them again, this time going east. From what they had observed about the previous groups guided by the person with "chevron" shoes, they deduced that "Chevron" would lead a group of 8 to 20 aliens. They therefore focused their attention on enclosed vehicles of that passenger capacity. In a 4-hour period the officers observed only one vehicle meeting that description. And it is not surprising that when they stopped the vehicle

on its return trip it contained "Chevron" and several illegal aliens. The limited purpose of the stop in this case was to question the occupants of the vehicle about their citizenship and immigration status and the reasons for the round trip in a short timespan in a virtually deserted area. No search of the camper or any of its occupants occurred until after respondent Cortez voluntarily opened the back door of the camper. The intrusion upon privacy associated with this stop was limited and reasonable.

b. Reasonable Suspicion & Revoked Licenses

In *Kansas v. Glover*, 140 S.Ct. 1183 (2020), an officer ran the license plate on a pickup truck and learned that the owner's driver's license had been suspended. Suspecting that the driver was the owner, the officer initiated a traffic stop, and ultimately arrested the driver-owner. The Kansas Supreme Court concluded that the officer did not have adequate cause to stop the truck because it involved an assumption that the owner was the driver of the truck and that he disregarded the suspension/revocation order. The Court disagreed: "We have previously recognized that States have a 'vital interest in ensuring that only those qualified to do so are permitted to operate motor vehicles and that licensing, registration, and vehicle inspection requirements are being observed.' *Delaware v. Prouse*, 440 U.S. 648, 658 (1979)." The officer "drew the commonsense inference that Glover was likely the driver of the vehicle, which provided more than reasonable suspicion to initiate the stop. Empirical studies demonstrate what common experience readily reveals: Drivers with revoked licenses frequently continue to drive and therefore to pose safety risks to other motorists and pedestrians."

Hypo 1: *The Evasive Camper*

A federal agent observes a pickup truck with a camper shell traveling in tandem with another vehicle for 20 miles in an area known to be frequented by drug traffickers. The agent testifies that campers are often used to transport large quantities of marihuana. The pickup truck in question appears to be heavily loaded, and the windows are covered with a quilted bed-sheet material. When the officer begins following the vehicles in a marked police car, both vehicles take evasive actions and start speeding. Is there sufficient cause to stop the camper? *See United States v. Sharpe*, 470 U.S. 675 (1985).

Hypo 2: *"Reasonable Suspicion"*

In *Alabama v. White*, 496 U.S. 325 (1990), police receive an anonymous call stating that Vanessa White will be leaving Lynwood Apartments at a particular time in a brown Plymouth station wagon with the right taillight lens broken, that she will be going to Dobey's Motel, and that she will be carrying an ounce of cocaine in a brown attache case. Officers go to the apartments, find a brown Plymouth station wagon with a broken right taillight, observe respondent leave the building (carrying nothing) and enter the station wagon. They follow the vehicle as it drives the most direct route to Dobey's Motel. When the vehicle is stopped just short of the motel, the officer tells respondent that she has been stopped because she is suspected of carrying cocaine. He asks if they may search the car and respondent consents. The officers find a locked brown brief case in the car, and, upon request, respondent provides the combination to the lock. The officers find cocaine in the brief case and place respondent under arrest. Did the police have reasonable suspicion for the stop?

Hypo 3: *DMV Computer Checks & Reasonable Suspicion*

A police officer, parked by the side of the road, runs the license plate numbers of passing motorists through a department of motor vehicles data base. When the search reveals that the license plate of a passing car has been suspended, the officer pulls the car over. During the stop, the officer runs the driver's license through the same data base and finds that it is suspended as well. Also, the officer realizes that the driver is intoxicated. Was it permissible for the officer to run the driver's license plate through the data base without any suspicion of criminal activity? *See People v. Bushey*, 75 N.E.3d 1165 (2017).

Food for Thought

Police receive a reliable tip that a drug courier would be driving on a particular highway in a black Toyota Camry on a particular day. The police stake the road out on the particular day and see a black Toyota Camry. However, they also see a RAV4 which appears to be traveling in tandem with the Camry. Do the police have sufficient cause to stop both the Camry and the RAV4? *See United States v. Belakhdhar*, 924 F.3d 925 (6th Cir. 2019).

Hypo 4: *The Lost Motorist*

A police officer concludes that the driver of an automobile is lost, and stops the driver to offer help. As the officer approaches the vehicle, he spots a bomb in plain view in the backseat. How might you argue that the officer acted properly? How might the driver respond? Are there instances when the police should stop someone to offer help (*i.e.*, a bridge is out and an officer wants to stop the motorist to inform him of this fact)?

Food for Thought

In some areas, the police have instituted "good driving" programs designed to reward "good drivers." Under these programs, officers pull drivers over (using their sirens and lights), and present the drivers with gift certificates and coupons for prizes. The purpose of these programs is to encourage better driving. Are "good driving" programs constitutional? Suppose, for example, that an officer pulls a driver over to award a certificate, notices contraband in the car, and arrests the driver. Can the state use the evidence against the driver? How might you argue that the evidence should be suppressed? How might the state respond? Is a "good driving" program more likely to be constitutional if the police provide drivers with bumper stickers designed to signal their participation in the "good driver" program, and only pull over cars that have such stickers on their bumpers?

Hypo 5: *Driving Slowly*

A police officer on routine patrol observes a driver traveling at 48 mph in a 65 mph zone. Based solely on the speed of the vehicle, does the officer have reasonable suspicion to stop the car? Must there be additional evidence, such as erratic driving or unusual behavior by the driver, to justify a stop? *See State v. Rincon*, 147 P.3d 233 (2006).

Hypo 6: *The Mistaken Stop*

A police officer stops a vehicle because it is registered to a woman with an outstanding warrant for her arrest. As he approaches the vehicle, he realizes that it is being driven by a man. Since the officer has already stopped the vehicle, he decides to ask the driver for his license and registration. Are the officer's actions permissible? *See People v. Cummings*, 6 N.E.3d 725 (Ill. 2014).

City of Indianapolis v. Edmond

531 U.S. 32 (2000).

JUSTICE O'CONNOR delivered the opinion of the Court.

In *Michigan Dept. of State Police v. Sitz*, 496 U.S. 444 (1990), and *United States v. Martinez-Fuerte*, 428 U.S. 543 (1976), we held that brief, suspicionless seizures at highway checkpoints for the purposes of combating drunk driving and intercepting illegal immigrants were constitutional. We now consider the constitutionality of a highway checkpoint program whose primary purpose is the discovery and interdiction of illegal narcotics.

In 1998, the city of Indianapolis began to operate vehicle checkpoints on Indianapolis roads in an effort to interdict unlawful drugs. The city conducted six such roadblocks between August and November that year, stopping 1,161 vehicles and arresting 104 motorists. Fifty-five arrests were for drug-related crimes, while 49 were for offenses unrelated to drugs. The overall "hit rate" of the program was approximately nine percent. At each checkpoint location, the police stop a predetermined number of vehicles. Approximately 30 officers are stationed at the checkpoint. Pursuant to written directives issued by the chief of police, at least one officer approaches the vehicle, advises the driver that he or she is being stopped briefly at a drug checkpoint, and asks the driver to produce a license and registration. The officer also looks for signs of impairment and conducts an open-view examination of the vehicle from the outside. A narcotics-detection dog walks around the outside of each stopped vehicle. Directives instruct the officers that they may conduct a search only by consent or based on the appropriate quantum of particularized suspicion. Officers must conduct each stop in the same manner until particularized suspicion develops, and the officers have no discretion to stop any vehicle out of sequence. The city agreed to operate the checkpoints in such a way as to ensure that the total duration of each stop, absent reasonable suspicion or probable cause, would be five minutes or less. Checkpoint locations are selected weeks in advance based on such considerations as area crime statistics and traffic flow. The checkpoints are generally operated during daylight hours and are identified with lighted signs reading, "NARCOTICS CHECKPOINT ___ MILE AHEAD, NARCOTICS K-9 IN USE, BE PREPARED TO STOP." Once a group of cars has been stopped, other traffic proceeds without interruption until all the stopped cars have been processed or diverted for further processing. The average stop for a vehicle not subject to further processing lasts two to three minutes or less.

Respondents James Edmond and Joell Palmer were each stopped at a narcotics checkpoint in September 1998. Respondents then filed suit on behalf of themselves and the class of all motorists who had been stopped or were subject to being stopped in the future at the checkpoints. The trial court denied the motion for a preliminary injunction. [The] United States Court of Appeals for the Seventh Circuit reversed. We granted certiorari and affirm.

The Fourth Amendment requires that searches and seizures be reasonable. A search or seizure is ordinarily unreasonable in the absence of individualized suspicion of wrongdoing. While such suspicion is not an "irreducible" component of reasonableness, we have recognized only limited circumstances in which the usual rule does not apply. For example, we have upheld certain regimes of suspicionless searches where the program was designed to serve "special needs, beyond the normal need for law enforcement." *See, e.g., Vernonia School Dist. 47J v. Acton*, 515 U.S. 646 (1995) (random drug testing of student-athletes); *Treasury Employees v. Von Raab*, 489 U.S. 656 (1989) (drug tests for United States Customs Service employees seeking transfer or promotion to certain positions); *Skinner v. Railway Labor Executives' Assn.*, 489 U.S. 602 (1989) (drug and alcohol tests for railway employees involved in train accidents or found to be in violation of particular safety regulations). We have also allowed searches for certain administrative purposes without particularized suspicion of misconduct, provided that those searches are appropriately limited. *See, e.g., New York v. Burger*, 482 U.S. 691 (1987) (warrantless administrative inspection of premises of "closely regulated" business); *Michigan v. Tyler*, 436 U.S. 499 (1978) (administrative inspection of fire-damaged premises to determine cause of blaze); *Camara v. Municipal Court*, 387 U.S. 523 (1967) (administrative inspection to ensure compliance with city housing code).

We have also upheld brief, suspicionless seizures of motorists at a fixed Border Patrol checkpoint designed to intercept illegal aliens, and at a sobriety checkpoint aimed at removing drunk drivers from the road. In addition, in *Delaware v. Prouse*, 440 U.S. 648 (1979), we suggested that a similar type of roadblock with the purpose of verifying drivers' licenses and vehicle registrations would be permissible. In none of these cases, however, did we indicate approval of a checkpoint program whose primary purpose was to detect evidence of ordinary criminal wrongdoing. In *Martinez-Fuerte*, we entertained Fourth Amendment challenges to stops at two permanent immigration checkpoints located on major United States highways less than 100 miles from the Mexican border. We noted the "formidable law enforcement problems" posed by the northbound tide of illegal entrants into the United States. We found that the balance tipped in favor of the Government's interests in policing the Nation's borders, and emphasized the difficulty of effectively containing illegal immigration at the border itself. We also stressed the impracticality of the particularized study of a given car to discern whether it was transporting illegal aliens, as well as the relatively modest degree of intrusion entailed by the stops. Although the stops did not occur at the border itself, the checkpoints were located near the border and served a border control function made necessary by the difficulty of guarding the border's entire length. In *Sitz*, we evaluated the constitutionality of a Michigan highway sobriety checkpoint program involving brief suspicionless stops of motorists so that police officers could detect signs of intoxication and remove impaired drivers from the road. Motorists who exhibited signs of intoxication were diverted for a license and registration check and, if warranted, further sobriety tests. This checkpoint program was clearly aimed at reducing the immediate hazard posed by the presence of drunk drivers on the highways, and there was an obvious connection between the imperative of highway safety and the law enforcement practice at issue. The gravity of the drunk driving problem and the magnitude of the State's interest in getting drunk drivers off the road weighed heavily in our determination that the program was constitutional.

In *Prouse*, we invalidated a discretionary, suspicionless stop for a spot check of a motorist's driver's license and vehicle registration. We acknowledged the States' "vital interest in ensuring that only those qualified to do so are permitted to operate motor vehicles, that these vehicles are fit for safe operation, and hence that licensing, registration, and vehicle inspection requirements are being observed." Accordingly, we suggested that "questioning of all oncoming traffic at roadblock-type stops" would be a lawful means of serving this interest in highway safety. We indicated in *Prouse* that we considered the purposes of such a hypothetical roadblock to be distinct from a general purpose of investigating crime. The State proffered the additional interests of "the apprehension of stolen motor vehicles and of drivers under the influence of alcohol or narcotics" in its effort to justify the discretionary spot check. We attributed the entirety of the latter interest to the State's interest in roadway safety. The interest in apprehending stolen vehicles may be partly subsumed by the interest in roadway safety. We observed that "the remaining governmental interest in controlling automobile thefts is not distinguishable from the general interest in crime control." Not only does the common thread of highway safety thus run through *Sitz* and *Prouse*, but *Prouse* itself reveals a difference in the Fourth Amendment significance of highway safety interests and the general interest in crime control. A vehicle stop at a highway checkpoint effectuates a seizure within the meaning of the Fourth Amendment. The fact that officers walk a narcotics-detection dog around the exterior of each car at the Indianapolis checkpoints does not transform the seizure into a search. *See United States v. Place*, 462 U.S. 696 (1983). An exterior sniff of an automobile does not require entry into the car and is not designed to disclose any information other than the presence or absence of narcotics. A sniff by a dog that simply walks around a car is "much less intrusive than a typical search."

The Indianapolis checkpoint program unquestionably has the primary purpose of interdicting illegal narcotics. The parties refer to the checkpoints as "drug checkpoints" and as "being operated in an effort to interdict unlawful drugs in Indianapolis." We have never approved a checkpoint program whose primary purpose was to detect evidence of ordinary criminal wrongdoing. Rather, our checkpoint cases have recognized only limited exceptions to the general rule that a seizure must be accompanied by some measure of individualized suspicion. We suggested in *Prouse* that we would not credit the "general interest in crime control" as justification for a regime of suspicionless stops. Consistent with this suggestion, each of the checkpoint programs that we have approved was designed primarily to serve purposes closely related to the problems of policing the border or the necessity of ensuring roadway safety. Because the primary purpose of the Indianapolis narcotics checkpoint program is to uncover evidence of ordinary criminal wrongdoing, the program contravenes the Fourth Amendment.

Petitioners propose several ways in which the narcotics-detection purpose of the instant checkpoint program may resemble the primary purposes of the checkpoints in *Sitz* and *Martinez-Fuerte*. The checkpoints in those cases had the same ultimate purpose of arresting those suspected of committing crimes. Securing the border and apprehending drunk drivers are, of course, law enforcement activities, and law enforcement officers employ arrests and criminal prosecutions in pursuit of these goals. If we were to rest at this high level of generality, there would be little check on the ability of the authorities to construct roadblocks for almost any conceivable law enforcement purpose. The Fourth Amendment would do little to prevent such intrusions from becoming a routine part of American life. Petitioners emphasize the severe and intractable nature of the drug problem as justification for the checkpoint program. There is no doubt that traffic in illegal narcotics creates social harms of the first magnitude. The law enforcement problems that the drug trade creates likewise remain daunting and complex, particularly in light of the myriad forms of spin-off crime that it spawns. The same can be said of various other illegal activities, if only to a lesser degree. But the gravity of the threat alone cannot be dispositive of questions concerning what means law enforcement officers may employ to pursue a given purpose. Rather, in determining whether individualized suspicion is required, we must consider the nature of the interests threatened and their connection to the particular law enforcement practices at issue. We are reluctant to recognize exceptions to the general rule of individualized suspicion where governmental authorities primarily pursue their general crime control ends.

Nor can the narcotics-interdiction purpose of the checkpoints be rationalized in terms of a highway safety concern similar to that present in *Sitz*. The detection and punishment of almost any criminal offense serves broadly the safety of the community, and our streets would no doubt be safer but for the scourge of illegal drugs. Only with respect to a smaller class of offenses, however, is society confronted with the type of immediate, vehicle-bound threat to life and limb that the sobriety checkpoint in *Sitz* was designed to eliminate.

Petitioners liken the anticontraband agenda of the Indianapolis checkpoints to the antismuggling purpose of the checkpoints in *Martinez-Fuerte*. Petitioners cite this Court's conclusion in *Martinez-Fuerte* that the flow of traffic was too heavy to permit "particularized study of a given car that would enable it to be identified as a possible carrier of illegal aliens," and claim that this logic has even more force here. The problem is that the same logic prevails any time a vehicle is employed to conceal contraband or other evidence of a crime. Further, the Indianapolis checkpoints are removed from the border context that was crucial in *Martinez-Fuerte*. We must look more closely at the nature of the public interests that such a regime is designed principally to serve.

The primary purpose of the Indianapolis checkpoints is to advance "the general interest in crime control." We decline to suspend the usual requirement of individualized suspicion where the police seek to employ a checkpoint primarily for the ordinary enterprise of investigating crimes. We cannot sanction stops justified only by the generalized and ever-present possibility that interrogation and inspection may reveal that a given motorist has committed some crime. There are circumstances that may justify a law enforcement checkpoint where the primary purpose would otherwise, but for some emergency, relate to ordinary crime control. For example, the Fourth Amendment would almost certainly permit an appropriately tailored roadblock set up to thwart an imminent terrorist attack or to catch a dangerous criminal who is likely to flee by way of a particular route. The exigencies created by these scenarios are far removed from the circumstances under which authorities might simply stop cars as a matter of course to see if there just happens to be a felon leaving the jurisdiction. While we do not limit the purposes that may justify a checkpoint program to any rigid set of categories, we decline to approve a program whose primary purpose is ultimately indistinguishable from the general interest in crime control.

Petitioners argue that the Indianapolis checkpoint program is justified by lawful secondary purposes of keeping impaired motorists off the road and verifying licenses and registrations. If this were the case, law enforcement authorities would be able to establish checkpoints for virtually any purpose so long as they also included a license or sobriety check. We examine the evidence to determine the primary purpose of the checkpoint program. A program driven by an impermissible purpose may be proscribed while a program impelled by licit purposes is permitted, even though the challenged conduct may be outwardly similar. Our holding today does nothing to alter the constitutional status of the sobriety and border checkpoints that we approved in *Sitz* and *Martinez-Fuerte*, or of the type of traffic checkpoint that we suggested would be lawful in *Prouse*. Our holding also does not affect the validity of border searches or searches at places like airports and government buildings, where the need for such measures to ensure public safety can be particularly acute. Our holding also does not impair the ability of police officers to act appropriately upon information that they properly learn during a checkpoint stop justified by a lawful primary purpose, even where such action may result in the arrest of a motorist for an offense unrelated to that purpose. We caution that the purpose inquiry is to be conducted at the programmatic level and is not an invitation to probe the minds of individual officers acting at the scene.

Because the primary purpose of the Indianapolis checkpoint program is indistinguishable from the general interest in crime control, the checkpoints violate the Fourth Amendment. The judgment of the Court of Appeals is accordingly affirmed.

It is so ordered.

CHIEF JUSTICE REHNQUIST, with whom JUSTICE THOMAS joins, and with whom JUSTICE SCALIA joins as to Part I, dissenting.

This case follows naturally from *Martinez-Fuerte* and *Sitz* and it is constitutionally irrelevant that petitioners hoped to interdict drugs. The seizure is objectively reasonable as it lasts, on average, two to three minutes and does not involve a search. The checkpoints are clearly marked and operated by uniformed officers who are directed to stop every vehicle in the same manner. We have already held that a "sniff test" by a trained narcotics dog is not a "search" within the meaning of the Fourth Amendment. There is nothing to indicate that the sniff lengthens the stop. Finally, the checkpoints' success rate—49 arrests for offenses unrelated to drugs—confirms the State's legitimate interests in preventing drunken driving and ensuring the proper licensing of drivers and registration of their vehicles. The "special needs" doctrine, which has been used to uphold certain suspicionless searches performed for reasons unrelated to law enforcement, is an exception to the general rule that a search must be based on individualized suspicion of wrongdoing. *See, e.g., Skinner v. Railway Labor Executives' Assn.*, 489 U.S. 602 (1989) (drug test search).

Point for Discussion

Discretion to Suspend Roadblock

In *Commonwealth v. Worthy*, 598 Pa. 470, 957 A.2d 720 (2008), the court held that police could exercise discretion to suspend a DUI roadblock long enough to alleviate a traffic jam, and then resume the roadblock. The court sustained the suspension even though state guidelines required that every car be stopped. The court found "substantial compliance" with the guidelines, even though police suspended the roadblock three times to alleviate heavy traffic.

> **FYI**
>
> In dicta, *Prouse* sanctioned roadside truck weigh-stations and inspection checkpoints. The Court recognized that some vehicles may be subjected to longer detention and more intrusive inspections than others.

Take Note

In *Illinois v. Lidster*, 540 U.S. 419 (2004), after a bicyclist was struck and killed by a motorist late one evening, the police decided to establish a checkpoint at about the same time of night at the same location in an effort to locate potential witnesses to the incident. The roadblock slowed traffic and created lines of up to 15 cars in each direction. Each vehicle was stopped for 15–20 seconds, was given a flier related to the fatal hit and run accident, and asked for assistance in solving the crime. Lidster, one of the motorists stopped, was found to be driving under the influence of alcohol. The Court rejected the idea that the roadblock was unconstitutional under *Edmond*: "The public concern was grave. Police were investigating a crime that had resulted in a human death. The stop's objective was to help find the perpetrator of a specific and known crime, not of unknown crimes of a general sort. The stop advanced this grave public concern to a significant degree. The police approximately tailored their checkpoint stops to fit important criminal investigatory needs. The stops took place about one week after the hit-and-run accident, on the same highway near the location of the accident, and at about the same time of night. Police used the stops to obtain information from drivers, some of whom might well have been in the vicinity of the crime at the time it occurred. Most importantly, the stops interfered only minimally with liberty of the sort the Fourth Amendment seeks to protect. Each stop required only a brief wait in line—a very few minutes at most. Contact with the police lasted only a few seconds. Police contact consisted simply of a request for information and the distribution of a flyer. Viewed subjectively, the contact provided little reason for anxiety or alarm. The police stopped all vehicles systematically. And there is no allegation here that the police acted in a discriminatory or otherwise unlawful manner while questioning motorists during stops."

Food for Thought

On New Year's Eve, the police establish a sobriety checkpoint on a divided interstate highway about a mile beyond an exit. Approximately one-half mile beyond the exit is a large sign that reads: "Sobriety checkpoint one mile ahead. Prepare to stop." On seeing the sign, some drivers make a u-turn over the median and head in the opposite direction. (State law permits u-turns on divided highways provided that the driver makes the turn in a "careful and prudent" manner) Do the police have reasonable suspicion to stop drivers who make u-turns? What arguments might be made on behalf of the police? How might the driver respond to those arguments? Would it matter that the signs were placed just before the entrance to a rest area, and that there is no actual roadblock ahead. Would the police have "reasonable suspicion" to stop any car that enters the rest area? Now, suppose that (in addition) the police had stationed a patrol car in the median of the interstate to monitor the reactions of drivers, and stop cars that seem to make a hurried exit into the rest area. *See State v. Hedgcock*, 277 Neb. 805, 765 N.W.2d 469 (2009).

Hypo 1: *Sobriety Checkpoints with Drug Sniffing Dogs*

Suppose that the police establish sobriety checkpoints rather than drug interdiction checkpoints, and the stated goal of the checkpoints is simply to catch drunk drivers. However, during the sobriety checks, officers walk drug sniffing dogs around the cars. Is the procedure permissible if it is "primarily" justified as a sobriety check and does not lengthen the stop?

Food for Thought

After *Martinez-Fuerte*, it is clear that ICE can establish "immigration checkpoints" inside the U.S. border in an effort to apprehend illegal immigrants. Suppose that ICE establishes one of these checkpoints, but it's primary objective is to apprehend those transporting illegal drugs. Under *Edmond*, would such checkpoints still be permissible? Would it matter whether ICE was seeking illegal narcotics that had been illegally transported across the U.S. border, or was simply trying to assist local police in apprehending drug transporters? *See United States v. Soto-Zuniga*, 837 F.3d 992 (9th Cir. 2016).

Hypo 2: *The "Terrorist" Plot*

Just weeks after the Madrid commuter rail bombings, the Massachusetts Bay Transit Authority (MBTA) received a tip suggesting that terrorists were plotting to attack a Boston rail station. Adjacent to the Sullivan MBTA subway station is an MBTA parking lot. One morning, an officer notices a white van with two occupants parked in the lot. The officer, who has been trained to identify terrorists, is concerned because it is unusual for vehicles to remain parked in the lot with occupants inside. From her experience, people use the lot to "park and ride," and they use a different lot to pick up or discharge passengers. Continuing to observe the vehicle, the officer realizes that there are more than two men in the van, and that they are writing notes. Her terrorism training makes her suspicious that the van's occupants could be planning where to plant explosives. If the men had been working for the MBTA, she would have expected them to have checked-in at the station and to have displayed a work permit. The officer decides to investigate. Walking past the van, she sees that it has a paper license plate over a regular license plate, which her training teaches her was suspicious. She also sees that the van has tinted windows, obscuring the view of the van's interior. She sees that there are more than five men sitting in the van, that no other vehicles in the lot have people sitting in them, that the men appear to be of Middle Eastern descent (with darker skin color). The officer then decides to approach the van, knock on the driver's side window, order everyone out, and ask them to identify themselves. The driver is of Mexican descent with a Texas driver's license, and the passengers have Brazilian passports with no indication of lawful entry into the United States. Did the officer act properly in approaching the van, demanding identification, and ordering the passengers out of the vehicle? *See United States v. Ramos*, 629 F.3d 60 (1st Cir. 2010).

Hypo 3: *The Anti-Poaching Checkpoint*

In order to combat poaching, park police are thinking about establishing vehicle checkpoints in order to question individuals about whether they intend to hunt or have hunted in the park (hunting is illegal). The checkpoint will be placed at park entrances and all vehicles will be stopped as they enter or leave the park. Rangers will post signs instructing drivers to prepare to stop, and the stops will be conducted by rangers in uniforms and reflective jackets. A ranger will approach the vehicle, identify himself as a ranger, state that he is conducting a hunting checkpoint, and ask the driver, "have you been hunting?" If the driver responds that he or she was not hunting, the ranger will not search the vehicle. Questioning will last 15 to 25 seconds, and drivers will sometimes have to wait in line for about one minute before being questioned. You work as an attorney for the park service and have been asked for an opinion regarding the constitutionality of the proposed roadblock. What advice would you give? *See United States v. Fraire*, 575 F.3d 929 (9th Cir. 2009).

Hypo 4: *Neighborhood Safety Zones*

Because a particular neighborhood suffers from an exceptionally high crime rate, including murders and gun-related crimes, police designate it as a "neighborhood safety zone." The police wish to establish vehicle checkpoints over a five-day period in order "to provide high police visibility, prevent and deter crime, safeguard officers and community members, and create safer neighborhoods." Under the program, the police will provide motorists with advance notice of the checkpoints, mark them with signs, barricades, lights, cones, and/or flares, and stop all vehicles entering the area, but will not stop pedestrians or vehicles leaving the area absent particularized suspicion. Officers will identify themselves and inquire whether the motorists have "legitimate reasons" for entering the area. Legitimate reasons include the fact that the motorist is 1) a resident; 2) is employed or on a commercial delivery; 3) is attending school or taking a child to school or day-care; 4) is related to a resident; 5) is elderly, disabled or seeking medical attention; or 6) is attempting to attend a verified organized civic, community, or religious event. If the motorist provides the officer with a legitimate reason, the officer will be authorized to request additional information sufficient to verify the motorist's stated reason for entry. Officers will deny entry to those motorists who do not have a legitimate reason for entry, who cannot substantiate their reason for entry, or who refuse to provide a legitimate reason. The police may not search a vehicle absent particularized suspicion. If you are counsel to the police department, how would you advise them regarding the constitutionality of the program? *See Mills v. District of Columbia*, 571 F.3d 1304 (D.C. Cir. 2009).

Food for Thought

How far can the "need" versus "intrusion" test be pushed? Suppose that, over the last five months, seven gruesome murders have been committed in Gainesville, Florida near the University of Florida campus. Even though the police have reason to believe that all of the murders were committed by a single person who lives in the area, they are not close to making an arrest and they believe that more murders will be committed in the near future. Desperate for information, the police establish roadblocks for the purpose of interviewing motorists. The police hope that one or more motorists will provide information that will lead to a break in the case. Given the "need" to find the murderer before another crime is committed, are the roadblocks constitutional? If the roadblocks prove unsuccessful, and another murder is committed, would the police be justified in making house-to-house searches in hopes of finding relevant evidence?

9. Border Searches

The government has always exercised broad authority to stop individuals seeking to enter the United States, to demand identification, and to search their persons and effects to make sure that contraband is not being smuggled. However, there are questions regarding the scope of governmental authority. Consider the following case.

United States v. Flores-Montano

<u>541 U.S. 149 (2004)</u>.

CHIEF JUSTICE REHNQUIST delivered the opinion of the Court.

Respondent, driving a 1987 Ford Taurus station wagon, attempted to enter the United States at the Otay Mesa Port of Entry in southern California. A customs inspector conducted an inspection of the station wagon, and requested respondent to leave the vehicle. The vehicle was then taken to a secondary inspection station where a second customs inspector inspected the gas tank by tapping it, and noted that the tank sounded solid. The inspector requested a mechanic under contract with Customs to come to the border station to remove the tank. Within 20 to 30 minutes, the mechanic arrived. He raised the car on a hydraulic lift, loosened the straps and unscrewed the bolts holding the gas tank to the undercarriage of the vehicle, and then disconnected some hoses and electrical connections. After the gas tank was removed, the inspector hammered off bondo (a putty-like hardening substance used to seal openings) from the top of the gas tank. The inspector opened an access plate and found 37 kilograms of marijuana bricks. The process took 15 to 25 minutes. A grand jury indicted respondent of unlawfully importing marijuana and possession of marijuana with intent to distribute. The District Court held that reasonable suspicion was required to justify the search and granted respondent's motion to suppress. The Court of Appeals affirmed. We granted certiorari and now reverse.

The reasons that might support a requirement of some level of suspicion in the case of highly intrusive searches of the person—dignity and privacy interests of the person being searched—simply do not carry over to vehicles. Complex balancing tests to determine what is a "routine" search of a vehicle, as opposed to a more "intrusive" search of a person, have no place in border searches of vehicles. The Government's interest in preventing the entry of unwanted persons and effects is at its zenith at the international border. Time and again, we have stated that "searches made at the border, pursuant to the longstanding right of the sovereign to protect itself by stopping and examining persons and property crossing into this country, are reasonable simply by virtue of the fact that they occur at the border." *United States v. Ramsey*, 431 U.S. 606 (1977). Congress, since the beginning of our Government, "has granted the Executive plenary authority to conduct routine searches and seizures at the border, without probable cause or a warrant, in order to regulate the collection of duties and to prevent the introduction of contraband into this country." *Montoya de Hernandez, supra*, at 537. The modern statute, 19 U.S.C. § 1581(a),[12] derived from a statute passed by the

---

[12]   Section 1581(a) provides: "Any officer of the customs may at any time go on board any vehicle at any place in the United States or, as he may be authorized, within a customs-enforcement area established under the Anti-Smuggling Act, or at any other authorized place, without as well as within his district, and examine and examine, inspect, and search the vessel or vehicle and every part thereof and any person, trunk, package, or cargo on board, and to this end may hail and stop such vessel or vehicle, and use all necessary force to compel compliance."

First Congress, and reflects the "impressive historical pedigree" of the Government's power and interest. It is axiomatic that the United States, as sovereign, has the inherent authority to protect, and a paramount interest in protecting, its territorial integrity.

Smugglers frequently attempt to penetrate our borders with contraband secreted in their automobiles' fuel tank. Over the past 5½ years, there have been 18,788 vehicle drug seizures at California ports of entry. Of those 18,788, gas tank drug seizures have accounted for 4,619 of the vehicle drug seizures, or approximately 25%. Instances of persons smuggled in and around gas tank compartments are discovered at San Ysidro and Otay Mesa at a rate averaging 1 approximately every 10 days.

Respondent urges that he has a privacy interest in his fuel tank, and that the suspicionless disassembly of his tank is an invasion of his privacy. The expectation of privacy is less at the border than it is in the interior. *Montoya de Hernandez, supra,* at 538. We have long recognized that automobiles seeking entry into this country may be searched. It is difficult to imagine how the search of a gas tank, which should be solely a repository for fuel, could be more of an invasion of privacy than the search of the automobile's passenger compartment.

Second, respondent argues that the Fourth Amendment "protects property as well as privacy," *Soldal v. Cook County,* 506 U.S. 56 (1992), and that the disassembly and reassembly of his gas tank is a significant deprivation of his property interest because it may damage the vehicle. He cannot, truly contend that the procedure of removal, disassembly, and reassembly of the fuel tank has resulted in serious damage to, or destruction of, the property. In fiscal year 2003, 348 gas tank searches conducted along the southern border were negative (*i.e.*, no contraband was found), the gas tanks were reassembled, and the vehicles continued their entry into the United States without incident. Respondent cites not a single accident involving the vehicle or motorist in the many thousands of gas tank disassemblies that have occurred at the border. A gas tank search involves a brief procedure that can be reversed without damaging the safety or operation of the vehicle. If damage to a vehicle were to occur, the motorist might be entitled to recovery. While the interference with a motorist's possessory interest is not insignificant when the Government removes, disassembles, and reassembles his gas tank, it nevertheless is justified by the Government's paramount interest in protecting the border.[3] We conclude that the Government's authority to conduct suspicionless inspections at the border includes the authority to remove, disassemble, and reassemble a vehicle's fuel tank. While some searches of property are so destructive as to require a different result, this was not one of them. The judgment of the United States Court of Appeals for the Ninth Circuit is therefore reversed, and the case is remanded for further proceedings consistent with this opinion.

---

[3]   Respondent also argued that he has a Fourth Amendment right not to be subject to delay at the international border and that the need for the use of specialized labor, as well as the hour actual delay here and the potential for even greater delay for reassembly are an invasion of that right. Delays of one to two hours at international borders are to be expected.

It is so ordered.

JUSTICE BREYER, concurring.

Customs keeps track of the border searches its agents conduct, including the reasons for the searches. This administrative process should help minimize concerns that gas tank searches might be undertaken in an abusive manner.

In *United States v. Martinez-Fuerte,* 428 U.S. 543 (1976), the Court upheld immigration roadblocks located within 100 miles of the United States border.

Food for Thought

In *United States v. Brignoni-Ponce*, 422 U.S. 873 (1975), the Court held that a roving patrol of law enforcement officers could stop motorists near an international border to briefly inquire about their residence status provided that the officers "reasonably suspect that vehicles contain aliens who are illegally in the country." But what constitutes "reasonable suspicion" that vehicles contain illegal aliens? Near the Mexican border, is there sufficient cause if an officer spots someone of Hispanic descent driving a vehicle? What more should be required?

Take Note

Under 19 U.S.C. § 1583 customs officials are required to hold a "reasonable suspicion" of criminal activity before opening and reading private mail being sent to foreign countries. However, under 19 U.S.C. § 5317(b), individuals who send more than $10,000 in currency or negotiable instruments, are required to submit a declaration form, and customs officials are allowed to conduct suspicionless searches. In *United States v. Seljan,* 547 F.3d 993 (9th Cir. 2008), the court upheld the actions of customs officials who read a private letter contained in a packet subject to a § 5317(b) form.

Food for Thought

Following the holding in *Flores-Montano*, suppose that customs officials believe that an entrant is trying to smuggle illegal drugs into the U.S.? What powers may they exercise? Rip out the seats? Tear luggage apart? Strip searches? Body cavity searches?

Hypo 1: *Advising the Border Patrol*

A mile inside the U.S.-Mexico border, in an area with sand dunes and valleys, border patrol agents spot an SUV coming from the direction of the Mexican border. The vehicle is moving unusually fast for the terrain, is not bearing the required orange safety flag and recreational permit, is traveling in a straight path uncharacteristic of recreational use, and the entire rear portion of the vehicle is covered by a black tarp (often used by drug smugglers to cover their vehicles). The officers want advice about whether they can stop the vehicle using a tire deflation device designed to flatten all four of the vehicle's tires and effectively render it inoperable. Under the circumstances, how would you advise them given that great effort (obtaining and mounting four new tires) to render the vehicle operable again? Is it relevant that drug smugglers generally refuse to yield to lights or sirens and frequently engage in desperate attempts to escape apprehension (*e.g.*, crossing freeway medians, driving into oncoming traffic, and leading officers on high-speed pursuits) that sometimes cause death to innocent bystanders? *See United States v. Guzman-Padilla*, 573 F.3d 865 (9th Cir. 2009).

Food for Thought

As a general rule, customs officials have the right to search individuals and any baggage or containers that they are carrying with them. Suppose that an individual arrives at the U.S. border carrying a laptop. Do customs officials have the right to examine the electronic contents of the laptop to make sure that the individual is not carrying illegal material (e.g., child pornography) into the country? Can they copy the contents of the laptop for later review? Alternatively, can they seize the laptop for a few days to a week so that it can be sent to a laboratory for more detailed examination? A new Department of Homeland Security regulation seems to give DHS officials broad authority to do all of these things. *See* U.S. Department of Homeland Security, Privacy Impact Assessment for the Border Searches of Electronic Devices (2009) 1, 6 (2009) (hereafter Homeland Security Assessment), http://www.dhs.gov/xlibrary/assets/privacy/privacy_pia_cbp_laptop.pdf. As of January, 2018, U.S. Customs and Border Patrol (CBP) has indicated that it interprets these rules as requiring a "reasonable suspicion" of criminal activity in order to conduct advanced searches or to copy the contents of smartphones or tablets. *See* Vanessa Romo & Joel Rose, *U.S. Customs and Border Protection Sets New Rules for Searching Electronic Devices, The Two-Way*, National Public Radio (Jan. 5, 2018). Is that enough of a change or should CBP be required to have at least probable cause, and perhaps a warrant, to search or copy the contents of these devices? Would the decision in *Riley* suggest that something more is required? *See United States v. Cotterman*, 709 F.3d 952 (9th Cir. 2013). Would you view the situation differently if customs detained the laptop for seven days, and mistakenly damaged it rendering the information unusable? *See Kam-Almaz v. United States*, 682 F.3d 1364 (Fed. Cir. 2012).

Hypo 2: *Searching for Text Messages*

Shommo is traveling to the United States from a foreign country, and is carrying an iPhone. Customs officials, who find the iPhone in his possession, want to review defendant's text messages and internet search history. You are the INS' counsel, and you receive a phone call inquiring whether it is permissible to do so. How would you advise the INS? Are such searches consistent with the justifications for allowing border searches? In deciding whether to examine a particular entrant's phone, could the INS take into account the entrant's ethnicity and country of origin? Would it matter that prior digital searches of computers and iPhones had uncovered digital pictures of high-level Al-Qaida officials and video clips of improvised explosive devices? *See* Joelle Tessler, *Lawmakers May Restrict Federal Agents' Searches of Laptops*, Courier-Journal, Dec. 14, 2008, at D-7, C 1–6. Does the *Riley* decision, *supra*, offer any guidance on this issue? *See United States v. Sanoonchi*, 48 F. Supp.3d 815 (D. Md. 2014). If cause should be required, suppose that ICE agents believe that a suspect may be shuttling illegal drugs between Columbia and the United States. Can ICE seize the suspect's laptop and gaming system and hold them for a week for electronic analysis? If the seizure is regarded as "non-routine," so that a "reasonable suspicion" of criminal activity should be required, would the following facts provide the required suspicion: the suspect made four trips to Colombia (a reputed drug capitol) in the prior five months; all of the trips were short (4–5 days); the suspect purchased the tickets with cash; the suspect did not know the last names of the people that he was visiting. *See United States v. Molina-Gomez*, 781 F.3d 13 (1st Cir. 2015).

Hypo 3: *More on Extended Border Searches*

In interviewing a suspected drug smuggler, Immigration and Customs Enforcement ("ICE") agents learn that he is involved in a large drug trafficking organization, as well as that he plans to meet a white Toyota Tacoma, which would serve as a "load vehicle," and a white PT Cruiser, which would serve as a "scout vehicle." He is supposed to meet the cars on the California side of the border at which point he will be led to a separate drop-off location The smuggler shows the agents a picture of the PT Cruiser on his cell phone, from which ICE agents can decipher a license plate number, 6CHU366. The following morning, Villasenor is observed driving a white PT Cruiser with the same license plate number to a nearby U.S. border checkpoint. A narcotics detection dog sniffs the car but fails to alert and the driver and car are allowed entry. Shortly thereafter, ICE agent Torregrosa is driving near the border crossing when he spots the PT

Cruiser, realizes that it is the vehicle that the smuggler referred to, and begins following it. Villasenor stops at a gas station, gets out while talking on his cell phone, but keeps looking at the border crossing. He then returns to his car and drives off without filling up. He then stops at another service station where he continues to talk on his phone and then drives off again. Torregrosa then stops the Cruiser. While a police officer (who assists the agent) writes Villasenor a ticket for failure to provide proof of insurance, Torregrosa calls in a drug sniffing dog. Forty-five minutes later, the dog arrives and alerts to the right rear panel on the car (the agents were unaware of the prior sniff). The agents look behind the panel and discover cocaine. Was the second dog sniff permissible? *See United States v. Villasenor*, 608 F.3d 467 (9th Cir. 2010).

10. Special Needs Searches

In a number of recent cases, the Court has established and developed a "special needs" exception to the warrant requirement. This exception, which especially applies in safety and administrative situations, allows the government to search or seize without probable cause and sometimes even without reasonable suspicion.

Take Note

A foundational decision is *Skinner v. Railway Labor Executives' Association*, 489 U.S. 602 (1989). In that case, the Court upheld Federal Railroad Administration (FRA) regulations mandating blood and urine tests of railroad employees involved in "major" train accidents, and authorizing railroads to administer breath and urine tests to employees who violate certain safety rules. The regulations were designed to combat the problem of drug and controlled substance abuse by railroad employees. The Court upheld the regulations, noting that the "governmental interest in ensuring the safety of the traveling public and of the employees themselves plainly justifies prohibiting covered employees from using alcohol or drugs on duty, or while subject to being called for duty." The Court emphasized that "Alcohol and other drugs are eliminated from the bloodstream at a constant rate, and blood and breath samples taken to measure whether these substances were in the bloodstream when a triggering event occurred must be obtained as soon as possible. The delay necessary to procure a warrant nevertheless may result in the destruction of valuable evidence." As a result, the Court concluded that the "Government interest in testing without a showing of individualized suspicion is compelling." Finally, the Court held that covered employees had a diminished expectation of privacy due to the nature of their jobs, and that "the privacy interests implicated by the search are minimal" because of the manner in which the tests were performed.

In *Bill v. Brewer*, 799 F.3d 1295 (9th Cir. 2015), *cert. denied*, 136 S.Ct. 1377 (2016), following a crime, police investigators sought DNA from police officers in order to exclude them as possible contributors of DNA to the crime scene. Before the request, the officers were told that they had been excluded as possible suspects, and that any DNA that they contributed would not be entered into the Combined DNA Index System (CODIS). The court upheld a lower court order requiring the officers to provide the DNA evidence through buccal swabs. Although the court concluded that a warrant could be invalidated if it unduly intruded on personal privacy, the court concluded that this order was not unduly intrusive.

Board of Education of Independent School District No. 92 of Pottawatomie County v. Earls

536 U.S. 822 (2002).

JUSTICE THOMAS delivered the opinion of the Court.

Tecumseh, Oklahoma, is a rural community about 40 miles southeast of Oklahoma City. In 1998, the School District adopted the Student Activities Drug Testing Policy, which requires all middle and high school students to consent to drug testing in order to participate in any extracurricular activity. In practice, the Policy has been applied only to competitive extracurricular activities sanctioned by the Oklahoma Secondary Schools Activities Association, such as the Academic Team, Future Farmers of America, Future Homemakers of America, band, choir, pom-pom, cheerleading, and athletics. Under the Policy, students are required to take a drug test before participating in an extracurricular activity, must submit to random drug testing while participating in that activity, and must agree to be tested at any time upon reasonable suspicion. The urinalysis tests are designed to detect only the use of illegal drugs, including amphetamines, marijuana, cocaine, opiates, and barbituates, not medical conditions or the presence of authorized prescription medications. Lindsay Earls was a member of the show choir, the marching band, the Academic Team, and the National Honor Society. Daniel James sought to participate in the Academic Team. Both challenged the Policy on Fourth Amendment grounds. The district court rejected respondents' claim and the court of appeals reversed. We granted certiorari.

Searches by public school officials, such as the collection of urine samples, implicate Fourth Amendment interests. *See Vernonia School Dist. 47J v. Acton*, 515 U. S. 646 (1995). We must therefore review the School District's Policy for "reasonableness," which is the touchstone of the constitutionality of a governmental search. Reasonableness usually requires a showing of probable cause. The probable-cause standard, however, "is peculiarly related to criminal investigations" and may be unsuited to determining the reasonableness of administrative searches where the "Government seeks to prevent the development of hazardous conditions." *Treasury Employees v. Von Raab*, 489 U. S. 656 (1989). A warrant and finding of probable cause are unnecessary in the public school context because such requirements "would unduly interfere with the maintenance of the swift and informal disciplinary procedures that are needed." *Vernonia, supra*, at 653.

Respondents argue that drug testing must be based at least on some level of individualized suspicion. We generally determine the reasonableness of a search by balancing the nature of the intrusion on the individual's privacy against the promotion of legitimate governmental interests. But we have long held that "the Fourth Amendment imposes no irreducible requirement of individualized suspicion." *United States v. Martinez-Fuerte*, 428 U. S. 543 (1976). "In certain limited circumstances, the Government's need to discover such latent or hidden conditions, or to prevent their development, is sufficiently compelling to justify the intrusion on privacy entailed by conducting such searches without any measure of individualized suspicion." *Von Raab, supra*, at 668. In the context of safety and administrative regulations, a search unsupported by probable cause may be reasonable "when 'special needs, beyond the normal need for law enforcement, make the warrant and probable-cause requirement impracticable.' " *Griffin v. Wisconsin*, 483 U. S. 868 (1987) (quoting T.L.O., supra, at 351 (Blackmun, J., concurring)).

This Court has previously held that "special needs" inhere in the public school context. While schoolchildren do not shed their constitutional rights when they enter the schoolhouse, "Fourth Amendment rights are different in public schools than elsewhere; the 'reasonableness' inquiry cannot disregard the schools' custodial and tutelary responsibility for children." In particular, a finding of individualized suspicion may not be necessary when a school conducts drug testing. In *Vernonia*, this Court held that the suspicionless drug testing of athletes was constitutional. The Court, however, did not simply authorize all school drug testing, but rather conducted a fact-specific balancing of the intrusion on the children's Fourth Amendment rights against the promotion of legitimate governmental interests. Applying *Vernonia*, we conclude that Tecumseh's Policy is also constitutional.

We first consider the nature of the privacy interest allegedly compromised by the drug testing. A student's privacy interest is limited in a public school environment where the State is responsible for maintaining discipline, health, and safety. Schoolchildren are routinely required to submit to physical examinations and vaccinations against disease. Securing order in the school environment sometimes requires that students be subjected to greater controls than those appropriate for adults. Respondents argue that because children participating in nonathletic extracurricular activities are not subject to regular physicals and communal undress, they have a stronger expectation of privacy than the athletes tested in *Vernonia*. This distinction was not essential to our decision in *Vernonia*, which depended primarily upon the school's custodial responsibility and authority. In any event, students who participate in competitive extracurricular activities voluntarily subject themselves to many of the same intrusions on their privacy as do athletes. Some of these clubs and activities require occasional off-campus travel and communal undress. All of them have their own rules and requirements for participating students that do not apply to the student body as a whole and a faculty sponsor monitors students for compliance with these rules. This regulation of extracurricular activities further diminishes the expectation of privacy among schoolchildren. We conclude that the students affected by this Policy have a limited expectation of privacy.

Next, we consider the character of the intrusion imposed by the Policy. Urination is "an excretory function traditionally shielded by great privacy." But the "degree of intrusion" on one's privacy caused by collecting a urine sample "depends upon the manner in which production of the urine sample is monitored." Under the Policy, a faculty monitor waits outside the closed restroom stall for the student to produce a sample and must "listen for the normal sounds of urination in order to guard against tampered specimens and to insure an accurate chain of custody." The monitor then pours the sample into two bottles that are sealed and placed into a mailing pouch along with a consent form signed by the student. This procedure is virtually identical to that reviewed in *Vernonia*, except that it additionally protects privacy by allowing male students to produce their samples behind a closed stall. Given that we considered the method of collection in *Vernonia* a "negligible" intrusion, the method here is even less problematic.

The Policy clearly requires that the test results be kept in confidential files separate from a student's other educational records and released to school personnel only on a "need to know" basis. Respondents contend that the intrusion on students' privacy is significant because the Policy fails to protect effectively against the disclosure of confidential information and, specifically, that the school "has been careless in protecting that information: for example, the Choir teacher looked at students' prescription drug lists and left them where other students could see them." But the choir teacher is someone with a "need to know," because during off-campus trips she needs to know what medications are taken by her students. In any event, there is no allegation that any other student did see such information. This one example of alleged carelessness hardly increases the character of the intrusion.

Moreover, the test results are not turned over to any law enforcement authority. Nor do the test results here lead to the imposition of discipline or have any academic consequences. The only consequence of a failed drug test is to limit the student's privilege of participating in extracurricular activities. Indeed, a student may test positive for drugs twice and still be allowed to participate in extracurricular activities. After the first positive test, the school contacts the student's parent or guardian for a meeting. The student may continue to participate in the activity if within five days of the meeting the student shows proof of receiving drug counseling and submits to a second drug test in two weeks. For the second positive test, the student is suspended from participation in all extracurricular activities for 14 days, must complete four hours of substance abuse counseling, and must submit to monthly drug tests. Only after a third positive test will the student be suspended from participating in any extracurricular activity for the remainder of the school year, or 88 school days, whichever is longer. Given the minimally intrusive nature of the sample collection and the limited uses to which the test results are put, we conclude that the invasion of students' privacy is not significant.

Finally, this Court must consider the nature and immediacy of the government's concerns and the efficacy of the Policy in meeting them. This Court has articulated the importance of the governmental concern in preventing drug use by schoolchildren. The drug abuse problem among our Nation's youth has hardly abated since *Vernonia* was decided in 1995. In fact, evidence suggests that it has only grown worse. As in *Vernonia*, "the necessity for the State to act is magnified by the fact that this evil is being visited not just upon individuals at large, but upon children for whom it has undertaken a special responsibility of care and direction." The health and safety risks identified in *Vernonia* apply with equal force to Tecumseh's children. Indeed, the nationwide drug epidemic makes the war against drugs a pressing concern in every school.

The School District has presented specific evidence of drug use at Tecumseh schools. Teachers testified that they had seen students who appeared to be under the influence of drugs and that they had heard students speaking openly about using drugs. A drug dog found marijuana cigarettes near the school parking lot. Police officers once found drugs or drug paraphernalia in a car driven by a Future Farmers of America member. And the school board president reported that people in the community were calling the board to discuss the "drug situation." We decline to second-guess the finding that "the School District was faced with a 'drug problem' when it adopted the Policy."

Respondents argue that there is no "real and immediate interest" to justify a policy of drug testing nonathletes. We have recognized that "a demonstrated problem of drug abuse is not in all cases necessary to the validity of a testing regime," but that some showing does "shore up an assertion of special need for a suspicionless general search program." The School District has provided sufficient evidence to shore up the need for its drug testing program. Furthermore, this Court has not required a particularized or pervasive drug problem before allowing the government to conduct suspicionless drug testing. In *Von Raab* the Court upheld the drug testing of customs officials on a purely preventive basis, without any documented history of drug use by such officials. In response to the lack of evidence relating to drug use, the Court noted that "drug abuse is one of the most serious problems confronting our society today," and that programs to prevent and detect drug use among customs officials could not be deemed unreasonable. Likewise, the need to prevent and deter the substantial harm of childhood drug use provides the necessary immediacy for a school testing policy. It would make little sense to require a school district to wait for a substantial portion of its students to begin using drugs before it was allowed to institute a drug testing program designed to deter drug use. Given the nationwide epidemic of drug use, and the evidence of increased drug use in Tecumseh schools, it was entirely reasonable for the School District to enact this particular drug testing policy.

Respondents argue that the testing of nonathletes does not implicate any safety concerns, and that safety is a "crucial factor" in applying the special needs framework. They contend that there must be "surpassing safety interests," or "extraordinary safety and national security hazards," in order to override the usual protections of the Fourth Amendment. Respondents are correct that safety factors into the special needs analysis, but the safety interest furthered by drug testing is undoubtedly substantial for all children, athletes and nonathletes alike. Drug use carries a variety of health risks for children, including death from overdose.

We reject the argument that drug testing must presumptively be based upon an individualized reasonable suspicion of wrongdoing because such a testing regime would be less intrusive. In this context, the Fourth Amendment does not require a finding of individualized suspicion, and we decline to impose such a requirement on schools attempting to prevent and detect drug use by students. Moreover, we question whether testing based on individualized suspicion would be less intrusive. Such a regime would place an additional burden on public school teachers who are already tasked with the difficult job of maintaining order and discipline and might unfairly target members of unpopular groups. The fear of lawsuits resulting from such targeted searches may chill enforcement of the program, rendering it ineffective in combating drug use. In any case, this Court has repeatedly stated that reasonableness under the Fourth Amendment does not require employing the least intrusive means, because "the logic of such elaborate less-restrictive-alternative arguments could raise insuperable barriers to the exercise of virtually all search-and-seizure powers." *Martinez-Fuerte*, 428 U. S., at 556–557, n. 12.

We find that testing students who participate in extracurricular activities is a reasonably effective means of addressing the School District's legitimate concerns in preventing, deterring, and detecting drug use. While in *Vernonia* there might have been a closer fit between the testing of athletes and the finding that the drug problem was "fueled by the 'role model' effect of athletes' drug use," such a finding was not essential to the holding. Drug testing of Tecumseh students who participate in extracurricular activities effectively serves the School District's interest in protecting the safety and health of its students.

Within the limits of the Fourth Amendment, local school boards must assess the desirability of drug testing schoolchildren. In upholding the constitutionality of the

Policy, we express no opinion as to its wisdom. We hold only that Tecumseh's Policy is a reasonable means of furthering the School District's important interest in preventing and deterring drug use among its schoolchildren. We reverse the judgment of the Court of Appeals.

It is so ordered.

JUSTICE BREYER, concurring.

The drug problem in our Nation's schools is serious in terms of size, the kinds of drugs being used, and the consequences of that use both for our children and the rest of us. The program at issue seeks to discourage demand for drugs by changing the school's environment in order to combat the single most important factor leading school children to take drugs, namely, peer pressure. It offers the adolescent a nonthreatening reason to decline his friend's drug-use invitations, namely, that he intends to play baseball, participate in debate, join the band, or engage in any one of half a dozen useful, interesting, and important activities. Not everyone would agree with this Court's characterization of the privacy-related significance of urine sampling as "negligible." But the testing program avoids subjecting the entire school to testing and it preserves an option for a conscientious objector. He can refuse testing while paying a price (nonparticipation) that is serious, but less severe than expulsion from the school. I cannot know whether the school's drug testing program will work. But the Constitution does not prohibit the effort.

JUSTICE GINSBURG, with whom JUSTICE STEVENS, JUSTICE O'CONNOR, and JUSTICE SOUTER join, dissenting.

The testing program upheld today is not reasonable. Petitioners' policy targets for testing a student population least likely to be at risk from illicit drugs and their damaging effects. *Vernonia* cannot be read to endorse invasive and suspicionless drug testing of all students upon any evidence of drug use, solely because drugs jeopardize the life and health of those who use them. Many children, like many adults, engage in dangerous activities on their own time; that the children are enrolled in school scarcely allows government to monitor all such activities. If a student has a reasonable subjective expectation of privacy in the personal items she brings to school, surely she has a similar expectation regarding the chemical composition of her urine.

While extracurricular activities are "voluntary" in the sense that they are not required for graduation, participation in such activities is a key component of school life, essential for students applying to college, and a significant contributor to the breadth and quality of the educational experience. Voluntary participation in athletics has a distinctly different dimension: Schools regulate student athletes discretely because competitive school sports by their nature require communal undress and, more important, expose students to physical risks that schools have a duty to mitigate.

Schools cannot offer a program of competitive athletics without intimately affecting the privacy of students. Interscholastic athletics require close safety and health regulation; a school's choir, band, and academic team do not. Student athletes' expectations of privacy are necessarily attenuated. On "occasional out-of-town trips," students like Lindsay Earls "must sleep together in communal settings and use communal bathrooms." But those situations are hardly equivalent to the routine communal undress associated with athletics.

In this case, respondents allege that the School District handled personal information collected under the policy carelessly, with little regard for its confidentiality.

Vernonia initiated its drug testing policy in response to "a large segment of the student body, particularly those involved in interscholastic athletics, in a state of rebellion." Tecumseh, by contrast, repeatedly reported to the Federal Government that drug use was not a major problem. *Vernonia* emphasized that "the particular drugs screened by Vernonia's Policy have been demonstrated to pose substantial physical risks to athletes." Despite nightmarish images of colliding tubas, the great majority of students are engaged in activities that are not safety sensitive to an unusual degree. There is a difference between imperfect tailoring and no tailoring. Nationwide, students who participate in extracurricular activities are significantly less likely to develop substance abuse problems than are their less-involved peers. Tecumseh's policy thus falls short doubly if deterrence is its aim: It invades the privacy of students who need deterrence least, and risks steering students at greatest risk for substance abuse away from extracurricular involvement that potentially may palliate drug problems. It is a sad irony that the School District seeks to justify its edict by trumpeting "the schools' custodial and tutelary responsibility for children." "That schools are educating the young for citizenship is reason for scrupulous protection of Constitutional freedoms

FYI

In *Griffin v. Wisconsin*, 483 U.S. 868 (1987), the Court upheld probationer searches conducted pursuant to a Wisconsin regulation permitting "any probation officer to search a probationer's home without a warrant as long as his supervisor approves and as long as there are 'reasonable grounds' to believe the presence of contraband." The Court held that a probation system presented a "special need" for the "exercise of supervision to assure that probation restrictions are in fact observed" and therefore the search was reasonable. Likewise, in *United States v. Knights*, 534 U.S. 112 (2001), when a judge imposed a similar restriction as a condition of probation, the Court upheld a search of the probationer's residence based on a reasonable suspicion that he was involved in criminal activity. The Court balanced the need for the search against the intrusion, and held that the search was justified. In assessing the intrusion, the Court held that probationers do not enjoy the same liberties as other citizens, "a court granting probation may impose reasonable conditions that deprive the offender of some freedoms enjoyed by law-abiding citizens," and that a probationer "is more likely than the ordinary citizen to violate the law." The Court held that the search could be justified based on a finding of reasonable suspicion that the probationer is involved in criminal activity.

of the individual, if we are not to strangle the free mind at its source and teach youth to discount important principles of our government as mere platitudes." *West Virginia Bd. of Ed. v. Barnette*, 319 U.S. 624, 637 (1943).

Food for Thought

Following the favorable decision in this case, suppose that the Tecumseh school district decides to adopt a drug testing program applicable to all students, not just those involved in extra-curricular activities. Based on the Court's decision, and the evidence before the Court, would such a program be constitutional? Would it matter whether the program involved only "random" drug testing (10 students per week chosen based on their names' position in the alphabet), or whether it involved an annual drug test of every student?

Hypo 1: *Direct Observation*

In an effort to ensure the integrity of the program referred to in the *Earls* case, could a school require that all urine samples be collected under the direct observation of school employees rather than in a closed stall?

Hypo 2: *Drug Interdiction Searches*

A public high school is thinking about adopting a drug interdiction policy designed to "balance each student's right to privacy" with "the need to maintain an appropriate learning environment." In particular, the policy would allow school administrators in conjunction with the police to screen student property using trained drug and weapons detection dogs. The policy permits dogs to sniff student lockers, desks, backpacks, and similar items. When the dogs are brought into a classroom, the students are asked to leave all items in the room, but to exit while the canine performs the sniff. The policy states that a student's possessions will only be searched if a drug dog has twice alerted on the same property. Suppose that the school has evidence suggesting that it frequently receives reports from students, parents, and teachers regarding the use of illegal and prescription drugs in school, and that schools officials handle drug related incidents on average three or more times per week, leading them to believe that "there is a drug problem" at the high school. Can the search be upheld under the special needs exception? *See Burlison v. Springfield Public Schools,* 708 F.3d 1034 (8th Cir. 2013).

Hypo 3: *Searching the Student's Car*

After receiving a report of a student "under the influence," the assistant principal of a school meets with the student who admits to taking a "green pill" given to him by another student. After sending the student for medical care, the assistant principal confronts the other student (Best) and questions him. Best denies giving the first student any pill although he admits giving another student a "nutritional supplement" and a search reveals that he has several white pills of unknown composition. The assistant principal then searches Best's car and finds drugs and drug paraphernalia. Was the assistant principal's search of the vehicle permissible under the Fourth Amendment? *See State v. Best*, 987 A.2d 605 (2010).

Hypo 4: *Advising the City*

The City of Mesa, Arizona, wishes to adopt a random drug testing program for firefighters in an effort to deter drug and alcohol use. In order to adopt a valid program, what findings must the City make in order to justify the program? How should the program be administered?

Hypo 5: *Terrorism & Football*

Florida's Tampa Sports Authority (TSA), concerned about the possibility of terrorists entering Raymond James Stadium, wants to conduct suspicionless pat-down searches of all individuals attending games at the Stadium. You are the attorney for the TSA. What must the TSA show in order to impose the pat-down search requirement? *See Johnston v. Tampa Sports Authority*, 442 F. Supp.2d 1257 (M.D. Fla. 2006).

Hypo 6: *Terrorism & Subways*

In response to subway attacks in other countries, the New York Police Department would like to implement a program of random, suspicionless, searches of items being carried by subway passengers. Suppose that you are the legal adviser to the NYPD. What must it show in order to create a valid "special

needs" program for such searches? For example, must it show that it is responding to a particular terrorist threat regarding its subway lines? Must it show that
the program will be effective in deterring potential terrorists? Must the NYPD
place warning signs at the entrances to subway stations warning riders that "by
choosing to ride on the subway, they agree to consent to random searches of
their persons and effects"? Must the program be random? *See MacWade v. Kelly*,
460 F.3d 260 (2d Cir. 2006).

Hypo 7: *Public School Teacher Drug Testing*

After two teachers are arrested for possession of illegal drugs, a school board
adopts a policy providing for random drug testing. The policy applies to all
school board employees (including Board Members) and provides for testing
under the following circumstances: a) a job application; b) reasonable suspicion
of drug or alcohol use; c) "routine" fitness-for-duty drug or alcohol testing; d)
"follow-up" drug or alcohol testing; e) "post-accident testing." The Policy provides that all supervisors and teachers must receive training on alcohol abuse
and the use of controlled substances, and for random drug testing of at least
10% percent of all employees annually. Employees are subject to a urine test
for alcohol, amphetamines, cannabinoids, cocaine, phencyclidine and opiates
or any other substance prohibited by statute. However, the testing also involves
searches for the presence of benzodiazepines, barbiturates, propoxyphene, and
methadone which include some commonly prescribed medications. When a
teacher reports for testing, only a nurse is in the testing room. After confirming
the teacher's identity, the nurse breaks open a package that contains a sample cup
and two vials. The teacher goes into the bathroom alone to produce the sample.
Upon completion, the nurse splits the sample into two vials, with the first to be
used for testing, and the second for confirmation, if necessary. The vials are then
sealed and the teacher signs a form stating that the samples are hers. The teacher
is then free to leave. Can the drug testing policy be justified on the basis that
teachers serve "*in an in loco parentis*" capacity and are charged with the responsibility for securing order and protecting students from harm while in their
custody." What about the argument that teachers should be unimpaired and
mentally and physically able to respond promptly to any emergency of which
they become aware? There have been situations in the schools which called for
quick and decisive actions by a teacher, including when a bleeding student fell
out of a chair, a student passed out in a classroom, a student who appeared to
be "high" and almost fell, and occasions when a student suffered a seizure in the
classroom. Is the policy valid? *See Smith County Education Association v. Smith
County Board of Education*, 781 F.Supp.2d 604 (M.D. Tenn. 2011).

Hypo 8: *Drug Testing & Librarians*

May a city require drug testing of all applicants for all city jobs? Jane Foeburn is denied a job as a librarian on the basis that she refused to take a drug test. If hired, Foeburn would have retrieved items from the book drop and returned them to the shelves. In challenging the denial, Foeburn claims that the city is unable to establish a "special need" for subjecting librarians to drug tests. The city disagrees. Who is correct? How might the city justify the testing? *See Lanier v. Woodburn*, 518 F.3d 1147 (9th Cir. 2008). Could a city drug test all welfare recipients as a prerequisite to eligibility? Would it matter that the city's goal is to make sure that the children of needy families are receiving adequate parental care? *See Marchwinski v. Howard*, 309 F.3d 330 (6th Cir. 2002).

Hypo 9: *Breathalyzers Following Police Killings*

The N.Y.C. police department is considering adopting a policy requiring that all police officers who kill or injure citizens with their guns submit to an immediate breathalyzer test to determine the amount of alcohol in their systems. Under the proposed policy, the initial test would be administered on site via a portable machine. If that test produces a positive result, the officer would be transported to a police facility for a second test with a non-portable machine. Suppose that you are the legal adviser to the police department and you are asked to advise it regarding the constitutionality of the policy. How might you respond? Now, suppose that you are hired by the police union to assist it in commenting on the proposed policy, what concerns or objections might you raise? *See Lynch v. New York City*, 589 F.3d 94 (2d Cir. 2009).

Food for Thought

In *Maryland v. King*, 569 U.S. 435 (2013), the Court suggested that DNA testing is changing rapidly, and might evolve to the point where DNA can be analyzed very quickly. Suppose that it is now possible to analyze DNA samples in a matter of seconds, and the Transportation Security Administration has decided that it would like to test the DNA of all airline passengers in order to more accurately determine the identity of those who are traveling. Can TSA mandate DNA screening, along with checks against governmental DNA data bases, for all airline passengers?

Ferguson v. City of Charleston

532 U.S. 67 (2001).

JUSTICE STEVENS delivered the opinion of the Court.

We must decide whether a state hospital's performance of a diagnostic test to obtain evidence of a patient's criminal conduct for law enforcement purposes is an unreasonable search if the patient has not consented to the procedure. More narrowly, the question is whether the interest in using the threat of criminal sanctions to deter pregnant women from using cocaine can justify a departure from the general rule that an official nonconsensual search is unconstitutional if not authorized by a valid warrant.

In 1988, staff members at the public hospital operated in the city of Charleston by the Medical University of South Carolina (MUSC) became concerned about an increase in the use of cocaine by patients who were receiving prenatal treatment. MUSC began to order drug screens performed on urine samples from maternity patients who were suspected of using cocaine. If a patient tested positive, she was referred to the county substance abuse commission for counseling and treatment. The incidence of cocaine use among the patients at MUSC did not appear to change. Four months later, Nurse Shirley Brown, case manager for the MUSC obstetrics department, heard that the police were arresting pregnant users of cocaine for child abuse.[6] Nurse Brown discussed the story with MUSC's general counsel who contacted Charleston's Solicitor to offer cooperation in prosecuting mothers whose children tested positive for drugs at birth. Solicitor Condon appointed a task force with representatives of MUSC, the police, the County Substance Abuse Commission and the Department of Social Services. Their deliberations led to MUSC's adoption of a document entitled "POLICY M-7," dealing with the subject of "Management of Drug Abuse During Pregnancy."

The first three pages of Policy M-7 set forth the procedure to be followed by the hospital staff to "identify/assist pregnant patients suspected of drug abuse." The first section, the "Identification of Drug Abusers," provided that a patient should be tested for cocaine through a urine drug screen if she met one or more of nine criteria.[7] It also stated that a chain of custody should be followed when obtaining and testing urine samples to make sure that the results could be used in subsequent criminal proceedings. The policy also provided for education and referral to a substance abuse clinic for patients who tested positive. It added the threat of law enforcement interven-

---

6   Under South Carolina law, a viable fetus has been regarded as a person and the ingestion of cocaine during the third trimester of pregnancy constitutes criminal child neglect.

7   Those criteria were as follows: 1. No prenatal care; 2. Late prenatal care after 24 weeks gestation; 3. Incomplete prenatal care; 4. Abruptio placentae; 5. Intrauterine fetal death; 6. Preterm labor "of no obvious cause"; 7. IUGR intrauterine growth retardation "of no obvious cause"; 8. Previously known drug or alcohol abuse; 9. Unexplained congenital anomalies.

tion which was regarded as essential to the program's success in getting women into treatment and keeping them there. The threat of law enforcement involvement was set forth in two protocols, the first dealing with the identification of drug use during pregnancy, and the second with identification of drug use after labor. Under the latter protocol, the police were to be notified without delay and the patient promptly arrested. Under the former, after the initial positive drug test, the police were to be notified (and the patient arrested) only if the patient tested positive for cocaine a second time or if she missed an appointment with a substance abuse counselor. In 1990, the policy was modified to give the patient who tested positive during labor, like the patient who tested positive during a prenatal care visit, an opportunity to avoid arrest by consenting to substance abuse treatment.

The policy contained forms for the patients to sign, as well as procedures for the police to follow when a patient was arrested. The policy prescribed the precise offenses with which a woman could be charged. If the pregnancy was 27 weeks or less, the patient was to be charged with simple possession. If it was 28 weeks or more, she was to be charged with possession and distribution to a person under the age of 18, the fetus. If she delivered "while testing positive for illegal drugs," she was also to be charged with unlawful neglect of a child. Under the policy, the police were instructed to interrogate the arrestee in order "to ascertain the identity of the subject who provided illegal drugs to the suspect." The policy made no mention of any change in the prenatal care of such patients, nor did it prescribe any special treatment for the newborns.

Petitioners are women who received obstetrical care at MUSC and who were arrested after testing positive for cocaine. Respondents include the city of Charleston, law enforcement officials, and representatives of MUSC. Petitioners' challenged the validity of the policy under various theories, including the claim that warrantless and nonconsensual drug tests conducted for criminal investigatory purposes were unconstitutional searches. Lower courts found for respondents. We granted certiorari.

Because the hospital seeks to justify its authority to conduct drug tests and to turn the results over to law enforcement agents without the knowledge or consent of the patients, this case differs from previous cases in which we have considered whether comparable drug tests "fit within the closely guarded category of constitutionally permissible suspicionless searches." In three cases, we sustained drug tests for railway employees involved in train accidents, *Skinner v. Railway Labor Executives' Assn.*, 489 U.S. 602 (1989), for United States Customs Service employees seeking promotion to certain sensitive positions, *Treasury Employees v. Von Raab*, 489 U.S. 656 (1989), and for high school students participating in interscholastic sports, *Vernonia School Dist. 47J v. Acton*, 515 U.S. 646 (1995). In the fourth case, we struck down such testing for candidates for designated state offices as unreasonable. *Chandler v. Miller*, 520 U.S. 305 (1997).

Those cases balanced the intrusion on the individual's interest in privacy against the "special needs" that supported the program. The invasion of privacy in this case is far more substantial. In the previous cases, there was no misunderstanding about the purpose of the test or the potential use of the test results, and there were protections against the dissemination of the results to third parties. The use of an adverse test result to disqualify one from eligibility for a particular benefit, such as a promotion or an opportunity to participate in an extracurricular activity, involves a less serious intrusion on privacy than the unauthorized dissemination of such results to third parties. The reasonable expectation of privacy enjoyed by the typical patient undergoing diagnostic tests in a hospital is that the results of those tests will not be shared with nonmedical personnel without her consent. In none of our prior cases was there any intrusion upon that kind of expectation.

The critical difference between those drug-testing cases and this one lies in the nature of the "special need" asserted as justification for the warrantless searches. In the earlier cases, the "special need" was one divorced from the State's general interest in law enforcement. In this case, the central and indispensable feature of the policy was the use of law enforcement to coerce the patients into substance abuse treatment. This fact distinguishes this case from circumstances in which physicians or psychologists, in the course of ordinary medical procedures aimed at helping the patient herself, come across information that under rules of law or ethics is subject to reporting requirements.

Respondents argue that their ultimate purpose—protecting the health of both mother and child—is a beneficent one. In this case, a review of the M-7 policy reveals that the purpose served by the MUSC searches "is indistinguishable from the general interest in crime control." "It is clear that an initial and continuing focus of the policy was on the arrest and prosecution of drug-abusing mothers." The document codifying the policy incorporates the police's operational guidelines. It devotes its attention to the chain of custody, the range of possible criminal charges, and the logistics of police notification and arrests. Nowhere does the document discuss medical treatment for either mother or infant, aside from treatment for the mother's addiction. Throughout the development and application of the policy, the Charleston prosecutors and police were extensively involved in the day-to-day administration of the policy. Police and prosecutors decided who would receive the reports of positive drug screens and what information would be included with those reports. Law enforcement officials helped determine the procedures to be followed when performing the screens. They had access to medical files on the women who tested positive, routinely attended the substance abuse team's meetings, and regularly received copies of team documents discussing the women's progress. Police took pains to coordinate the timing and circumstances of the arrests with MUSC staff.

While the ultimate goal of the program may well have been to get the women into substance abuse treatment and off of drugs, the immediate objective of the searches was to generate evidence for law enforcement purposes in order to reach that goal.[21] The threat of law enforcement may ultimately have been intended as a means to an end, but the direct and primary purpose of MUSC's policy was to ensure the use of those means. This distinction is critical. Because law enforcement involvement always serves some broader social purpose or objective, virtually any nonconsensual suspicionless search could be immunized under the special needs doctrine by defining the search solely in terms of its ultimate, rather than immediate, purpose. Such an approach is inconsistent with the Fourth Amendment. Given the primary purpose of the Charleston program, which was to use the threat of arrest and prosecution in order to force women into treatment, and given the extensive involvement of law enforcement officials at every stage of the policy, this case simply does not fit within the closely guarded category of "special needs."[23]

The fact that positive test results were turned over to the police does not merely provide a basis for distinguishing our prior cases applying the "special needs" balancing approach to the determination of drug use. It also provides an affirmative reason for enforcing the strictures of the Fourth Amendment. While state hospital employees, like other citizens, may have a duty to provide the police with evidence of criminal conduct that they inadvertently acquire in the course of routine treatment, when they undertake to obtain such evidence from their patients *for the specific purpose of incriminating those patients*, they have a special obligation to make sure that the patients are fully informed about their constitutional rights, as standards of knowing waiver require.

Respondents motive was benign rather than punitive. Such a motive, however, cannot justify a departure from Fourth Amendment protections, given the pervasive involvement of law enforcement with the development and application of the MUSC policy. While drug abuse is a serious problem, "the gravity of the threat alone cannot be dispositive of questions concerning what means law enforcement officers may employ to pursue a given purpose." The Fourth Amendment's general prohibition against nonconsensual, warrantless, and suspicionless searches necessarily applies to such a policy.

The judgment of the Court of Appeals is reversed, and the case is remanded for further proceedings consistent with this opinion.

---

[21] This case differs from *New York v. Burger,* 482 U.S. 691 (1987), because the discovery of evidence of other violations would have been incidental to the purposes of the administrative search. This policy was specifically designed to gather evidence of violations of penal laws. This case also differs from the roadblock seizure cases which did not involve "intrusive search of the body or the home" and distinguished checkpoints from cases dealing with "special needs."

[23] It is difficult to argue that the program here was designed simply to save lives. Amici claim a near consensus in the medical community that programs of the sort at issue, by discouraging women who use drugs from seeking prenatal care, harm, rather than advance, the cause of prenatal health.

It is so ordered.

JUSTICE KENNEDY, concurring in the judgment.

None of our special needs precedents has sanctioned the routine inclusion of law enforcement, both in the design of the policy and in using arrests, either threatened or real, to implement the system designed for the special needs objectives. The traditional warrant and probable cause requirements are waived on the explicit assumption that the evidence is not intended for law enforcement purposes. While the policy may well have served legitimate needs unrelated to law enforcement, it had a penal character with a far greater connection to law enforcement than other searches sustained under our special needs rationale. We recognize the legitimacy of the State's interest in fetal life and of the grave risk to the life and health of the fetus, and later the child, caused by cocaine ingestion. South Carolina can impose punishment upon an expectant mother who has so little regard for her own unborn that she risks causing lifelong damage and suffering.

An essential, distinguishing feature of the special needs cases is that the person searched has consented, though the usual voluntariness analysis is altered because adverse consequences, (e.g., dismissal from employment or disqualification from playing on a high school sports team), will follow from refusal. The consent, and the circumstances in which it was given, bear upon the reasonableness of the whole special needs program.

JUSTICE SCALIA, with whom THE CHIEF JUSTICE and JUSTICE THOMAS join as to Part II, dissenting.

The hospital's reporting of positive drug-test results to police is obviously not a search. At most it may be a "derivative use of the product of a past unlawful search," which "works no new Fourth Amendment wrong" and "presents a question, not of rights, but of remedies."

A search which has been consented to is not unreasonable. There is no contention that the urine samples were extracted forcibly. We have *never* held—or even suggested—that material which a person voluntarily entrusts to someone else cannot be given by that person to the police, and used for whatever evidence it may contain. There is no basis to "distinguish this case from circumstances in which physicians or psychologists, in the course of ordinary medical procedures

Food for Thought

Suppose that you are the legal adviser to MUSC. Following the decision in this case, you are asked for advice about how to establish a constitutionally permissible program for expectant mothers. How would you advise MUSC to proceed?

aimed at helping the patient herself, come across information that is subject to reporting requirements.

Hypo 1: *Suspicionless Drug Testing of Welfare Recipients*

Suppose that your state legislature is considering the possibility of requiring welfare recipients, as a condition of receiving government-provided monetary assistance, to submit to suspicionless drug testing. Under the proposed law, when an individual applies for public assistance, he is notified that he will be required to submit to and pay for drug testing as a condition of receiving benefits. If the applicant submits to the drug testing and tests negative, the cost of the test will be reimbursed to the applicant through a one-time increase in benefits. If the applicant tests positive for controlled substances, he is ineligible to receive benefits for one year, but can reapply in six months if he completes a substance abuse treatment program and passes another drug test, both at his own expense. Although an adult applicant who fails the drug test is ineligible for benefits, the applicant's dependent child may still receive benefits so long as the adult designates an appropriate payee to receive the child's benefits. However, the individual who wishes to serve as the payee must also submit to and pass mandatory drug testing to receive benefits for the child. In addition to the mandatory drug test, applicants are required to sign a release acknowledging their consent to be tested. How would you advise the legislature? Is the law valid? *See Lebron v. Secretary,* 710 F.3d 1202 (11th Cir. 2013).

Hypo 2: *The Fire Department Program*

A city fire department adopts a program of random suspicionless drug testing in an effort to control drug and alcohol use among firemen. The Program requires testing of firefighters in four situations: 1) if the Department has reasonable suspicion to believe an individual firefighter has abused drugs or alcohol; 2) after a firefighter is involved in an accident on the job; 3) following a firefighter's return to duty or as a follow-up to "a determination that a covered member is in need of assistance"; and 4) "on an unannounced and random basis spread reasonably throughout the calendar year." A computer selects the firefighters to be tested, and the Department notifies firefighters of their selection for random testing immediately before, during, or after work; the firefighters are tested within thirty minutes of their notification, with allowance for travel time to the laboratory for collection. Once at the laboratory, firefighters are permitted to use private bathroom stalls when providing urine samples, which are then inspected by a monitor for the proper color and temperature. A laboratory tests the sample for the presence of marijuana, cocaine, opiates, amphetamines, and phencyclidine. The laboratory initially tests the specimens by using an immuno-assay test and then confirms positive test results using the gas chromatography/mass spectrometry technique and report positive results to a Medical Review Officer (MRO), who would have a "detailed knowledge of possible alternate medical explanations." The MRO would review the results before giving the information to the Department's administrative official. Only positive tests would be reported to the Department. Before verifying a positive result, the MRO must contact the firefighter on a confidential basis. The Department would not release information in a firefighter's drug testing record outside the Department without the firefighter's consent. A firefighter whose test revealed a blood alcohol concentration in excess of that allowed under the Program or who tested positive for any of several specified drugs would be removed from all covered positions and would be evaluated by a substance abuse professional. The Department could discipline or terminate the employment of a firefighter who tested positive a second time or who refused to submit to a required test. The primary purpose of the random testing component would be "to deter prohibited alcohol and controlled substance use and to detect prohibited use for the purpose of removing identified users from the safety-sensitive work force." That purpose would advance the City's goal of establishing "a work environment that is totally free of the harmful effects of drugs and the misuse of alcohol." Is the program constitutional?

Hypo 3: *Additional Factors*

In the prior problem, which of the following facts might be determinative regarding the constitutionality of the program: A. The City asserts that it has a "special need" to test firefighters because they occupy safety-sensitive positions. The City alleges that random testing furthers this interest by deterring "prohibited alcohol and controlled substance use" and detecting "prohibited use for the purpose of removing identified users from the safety-sensitive work force." B. The fact that the record is devoid of any evidence of even a single instance of drug use among the firefighters to be tested but also of any evidence of accidents, fatalities, injuries, or property damage that can be attributed to drug or alcohol use by the City's firefighters. C. Can it be argued that it is reasonable to assume that anyone applying for a safety-sensitive position in a heavily regulated field of activity anticipates—and implicitly agrees to—a probing inquiry into the applicant's capacity to perform job-related duties.

Hypo 4: *The Conditional Release Program*

Norris is arrested for sexually abusing his stepdaughter, but is ultimately released under a conditional release program. Under that program persons awaiting trial may be freed if they agree to certain judicially-imposed conditions. To participate in the Program, Norris agreed that he would avoid contact with his stepdaughter and not use illegal drugs or consume alcoholic beverages. He also agreed that he would undergo random drug testing. Premier, a private corporation, conducts pretrial drug testing for the courts. Premier uses a "direct observation" method in obtaining urine samples for testing. Premier requires that a male lower his pants so that its employee may "directly observe the urine coming straight out of the body," and must "allow collector visibility of the participant's genitalia." Kentucky views the direct observation method as "essential." Is the testing regime valid? *See Norris v. Premier Integrity Solutions, Inc.*, 641 F.3d 695 (6th Cir. 2011).

11. Exigent Circumstances

The police can also dispense with a warrant when they are faced with "exigent circumstances." For example, there is a long line of cases which suggests that the police may make a warrantless entry into a home in order to prevent the imminent destruction of evidence. *See, e.g., Kentucky v. King*, 563 U.S. 452 (2011). Likewise, it has always been assumed that the police perform a "community caretaking" function which may give them the authority to make a warrantless entry into a private place in order to protect lives or property. For example, when a police officer hears shots followed by cries for help from a nearby apartment, the officer can enter the apartment to render emergency help and assistance. *See McDonald v. United States*, 335 U.S. 451 (1948). Likewise, "a warrant is not required to break down a door to enter a burning home to rescue occupants or extinguish a fire, or to bring emergency aid to an injured person." *See Wayne v. United States*, 318 F.2d 205 (D.C.Cir.1963). Under what other circumstances may police search without a warrant? Consider the following cases.

Take Note

In *Warden v. Hayden*, 387 U.S. 294 (1967), the Court held that the police may make a warrantless entry into a home when they are in "hot pursuit" of a fleeing armed robber: "The exigencies of the situation made a warrantless entry and search imperative. The police were informed that an armed robbery had taken place, and that the suspect had entered the house less than five minutes before they arrived. The Fourth Amendment does not require police officers to delay in the course of an investigation if to do so would gravely endanger their lives or the lives of others." The Court held that the police were also allowed to search the home for weapons: "The permissible scope of a search must, therefore, at the least, be as broad as may reasonably be necessary to prevent the dangers that the suspect at large in the house may resist or escape. The officer who found the clothes in the washing machine knew that the robber was armed and he did not know that some weapons had been found at the time he opened the machine. In these circumstances the inference that he was in fact also looking for weapons is fully justified."

Michigan v. Fisher

558 U.S. 45 (2009).

PER CURIAM.

Police officers responded to a complaint of a disturbance in Brownstown, Michigan. Officer Goolsby testified that, as he and his partner approached the area, a couple directed them to a residence where a man was "going crazy." Upon their arrival, the officers found a household in considerable chaos: a pickup truck in the driveway with its front smashed, damaged fence posts, and three broken house windows, the glass still on the ground outside. The officers also noticed blood on the hood of the pickup and on clothes inside of it, as well as on one of the doors to the house. Through a window, the officers could see respondent, Jeremy Fisher, inside the house, screaming and throwing things. The back door was locked, and a couch had been placed to block the front door. The officers knocked, but Fisher refused to answer. They saw that Fisher had a cut on his hand, and they asked him whether he needed medical attention. Fisher ignored these questions and demanded, with accompanying profanity, that the officers obtain a search warrant. Officer Goolsby then pushed the front door partway open and ventured into the house. Through the window of the open door he saw Fisher pointing a long gun at him. Officer Goolsby withdrew. Fisher was charged under Michigan law with assault with a dangerous weapon and possession of a firearm during the commission of a felony. The trial court granted Fisher's motion to suppress Goolsby's statement that Fisher pointed a rifle at him. The Michigan Court of Appeals affirmed and the Michigan Supreme Court denied leave to appeal. Because the decision of the Michigan Court of Appeals is contrary to our Fourth Amendment case law, particularly *Brigham City v. Stuart*, 547 U.S. 398 (2006), we grant the State's petition for certiorari and reverse.

"The ultimate touchstone of the Fourth Amendment," is "reasonableness." "Searches and seizures inside a home without a warrant are presumptively unreasonable," *Groh v. Ramirez*, 540 U.S. 551, 559 (2004), but that presumption can be overcome. For example, "the exigencies of the situation may make the needs of law enforcement so compelling that the warrantless search is objectively reasonable." *Mincey v. Arizona*, 437 U.S. 385, 393 (1978). *Brigham City v. Stuart*, 547 U.S. 398 (2006) identified one such exigency: "the need to assist persons who are seriously injured or threatened with such injury." Thus, law enforcement officers "may enter a home without a warrant to render emergency assistance to an injured occupant or to protect an occupant from imminent injury." This "emergency aid exception" does not depend on the officers' subjective intent or the seriousness of any crime they are investigating when the emergency arises. It requires only "an objectively reasonable basis for believing," that "a person within the house is in need of immediate aid," *Mincey, supra*, at 392. *Brigham City* illustrates the application of this standard. Police officers responded to a noise complaint in the early hours of the morning. "As they approached the house, they could hear an altercation occurring, some kind of fight." Following the tumult to the back of the house whence it came, the officers saw juveniles drinking beer in the backyard and a fight unfolding in the kitchen. They watched through the window as a juvenile broke free from the adults restraining him and punched another adult in the face, who recoiled to the sink, spitting blood. Under these circumstances, we found it "plainly reasonable" for the officers to enter the house and quell the violence, for they had "an objectively reasonable basis for believing both that the injured adult might need help and that the violence in the kitchen was just beginning."

A straightforward application of the emergency aid exception dictates that the officer's entry in this case was reasonable. As in *Brigham City*, the police officers were responding to a report of a disturbance. When they arrived they encountered a tumultuous situation in the house, and they also found signs of a recent injury, perhaps from a car accident, outside. As in *Brigham City*, the officers could see violent behavior inside. Although Officer Goolsby and his partner did not see punches thrown, they did see Fisher screaming and throwing things. It would be objectively reasonable to believe that Fisher's projectiles might have a human target (perhaps a spouse or a child), or that Fisher would hurt himself in the course of his rage. As in *Brigham City* the officer's entry was reasonable under the Fourth Amendment.

The Michigan Court of Appeals thought the situation "did not rise to a level of emergency justifying the warrantless intrusion into a residence." Although the court conceded that "there was evidence an injured person was on the premises," it found that "the mere drops of blood did not signal a likely serious, life-threatening injury." The court added that the cut Officer Goolsby observed on Fisher's hand "likely explained the trail of blood" and that Fisher "was very much on his feet and apparently able to see to his own needs." Officers do not need ironclad proof of "a likely serious, life-threatening" injury to invoke the emergency aid exception. The only injury police could confirm in *Brigham City* was the bloody lip they saw the juvenile inflict upon the adult. Fisher argues that the officers could not have been motivated by a perceived need to provide medical assistance, since they never summoned emergency medical personnel. This would have no bearing upon their need to assure that Fisher was not endangering someone else in the house. Moreover, even if the failure to summon medical personnel established that Goolsby did not subjectively believe, when he entered the house, that Fisher or someone else was seriously injured (which is doubtful), the test is not what Goolsby believed, but whether there was "an objectively reasonable basis for believing" that medical assistance was needed, or persons were in danger, *Brigham City, supra*, at 406.

It was error for the Michigan Court of Appeals to replace that objective inquiry into appearances with its hindsight determination that there was in fact no emergency. It does not meet the needs of law enforcement or the demands of public safety to require officers to walk away from a situation like the one they encountered here. Only when an apparent threat has become an actual harm can officers rule out innocuous explanations for ominous circumstances. "The role of a peace officer includes preventing violence and restoring order, not simply rendering first aid to casualties." *Brigham City, supra*, at 406. It sufficed to invoke the emergency aid exception that it was reasonable to believe that Fisher had hurt himself (albeit nonfatally) and needed treatment that in his rage he was unable to provide, or that Fisher was about to hurt, or had already hurt, someone else.

The petition for certiorari is granted. The judgment of the Michigan Court of Appeals is reversed, and the case is remanded for further proceedings not inconsistent with this opinion.

It is so ordered.

JUSTICE STEVENS, with whom JUSTICE SOTOMAYOR joins, dissenting.

A warrantless entry is justified by the "need to protect or preserve life or avoid serious injury." *Mincey v. Arizona, supra*, at 392. The State bears the burden of proof on that factual issue. Goolsby was not sure about certain facts—such as whether Fisher had a cut on his hand-but he did remember that Fisher repeatedly swore at the officers and told them to get a warrant, and that Fisher was screaming and throwing things. Goolsby also testified that he saw "mere drops" of blood outside Fisher's home. Goolsby did not testify that he had any reason to believe that anyone else was in the house. The factual question was whether Goolsby had "an objectively reasonable basis for believing that Fisher was seriously injured or imminently threatened with such injury." The trial judge found the police decision to leave the scene and not return for several hours-without resolving any potentially dangerous situation and without calling for medical assistance-inconsistent with a reasonable belief that Fisher was in need of immediate aid. The one judge who heard Goolsby's testimony was not persuaded that Goolsby had an objectively reasonable basis for believing that entering Fisher's home was necessary to avoid serious injury. We ought not usurp the role of the fact finder when faced with a close question of the reasonableness of an officer's actions, particularly in a case tried in a state court.

> **FYI**
>
> In *United States v. Santana*, 427 U.S. 38 (1976), after an undercover drug buy, the police went to "Mom" Santana's home to arrest her (Santana had provided drugs to the seller), and found her standing in the doorway with a brown paper bag in her hand. When the officers shouted "police," and displayed their identification, Santana retreated into her house. The officers followed through the open door and caught her in the vestibule. As she tried to pull away, the bag tilted and "two bundles of glazed paper packets with a white powder" fell to the floor. The Court upheld the entry into the house: " 'Hot pursuit' means some sort of a chase, but it need not be an extended hue and cry 'in and about the public streets.' The fact that the pursuit here ended almost as soon as it began did not render it any the less a 'hot pursuit' sufficient to justify the warrantless entry into Santana's house. Once Santana saw the police, there was a realistic expectation that any delay would result in destruction of evidence. Once she had been arrested the search, incident to that arrest, which produced the drugs and money was clearly justified."

Points for Discussion

a. More on the Emergency Exception

In *Ryburn v. Huff*, 565 U.S. 469 (2012), police responded to a call for distress from a high school where a student was rumored to have written a letter threatening to "shoot up" the school. Because of the threat, many parents had decided to keep their children at home. While interviewing students, the police learned that the student in question (Vincent) had been absent from school for two days and that he was frequently subjected to bullying. The officers had received training on targeted school violence and were aware that these characteristics are common among perpetrators of school shootings. As a result, the officers decided to interview the student at his home. When no one responded to a knock on the door, or to a phone call, the police called the mother's cell phone. The mother and Vincent then came out of the house, but refused a police request to discuss the matter inside the house. When asked about whether there were any guns in the house, the mother responded by "immediately turning around and running into the house." One of the officers, who was "scared because he didn't know what was in that house" and had "seen too many officers killed," entered the house behind her. Other officers, concerned for the first officer's safety, also entered the house. The officers ultimately concluded that the rumor was unfounded and left the house. The Court concluded that a reasonable police officer could have construed *Brigham City* as allowing an officer to enter a residence if the officer has a reasonable basis for concluding that there is an imminent threat of violence. The Court noted that the district court found that the police had an objectively reasonable basis for reaching such a conclusion.

Take Note

In *Kentucky v. King*, 563 U.S. 452 (2011), the Court rejected the position, adopted by some courts, that the exigent circumstances exception did not apply when the police "deliberately created the exigent circumstances with the bad faith intent to avoid the warrant requirement." The police made a warrantless entry into a home after they heard the occupants attempting to destroy evidence (drugs). The case was complicated by the fact that the police chose to knock on the door of the residence and announce their presence. When they did, the occupants engaged in hurried activities suggesting that they were trying to destroy evidence. As a result, the Court was presented with the question of whether the police could invoke the exigent circumstances exception when their conduct precipitated the evidence destruction. The Court upheld the entry and search: "Where, as here, the police did not create the exigency by engaging or threatening to engage in conduct that violates the Fourth Amendment, warrantless entry to prevent the destruction of evidence is reasonable and thus allowed." The Court refused to consider the subjective intentions of the police officers, choosing instead to focus on whether the police conduct was objectively justifiable. Even if the police have probable cause to obtain a warrant, they are not required to do so, but may proceed without a warrant so long as they do not violate the law. The Court held that the officers were entitled to knock on the door and announce their presence. If the occupants of the premises respond by attempting to destroy evidence, the police may make an immediate warrantless entry: "Occupants who choose not to stand on their constitutional rights but instead elect to attempt to destroy evidence have only themselves to blame for the warrantless exigent-circumstances search that may ensue."

Food for Thought

In *Evans v. Commonwealth*, 290 Va. 277, 776 S.E.2d 760 (2015), police officers are on patrol when they notice a marijuana smell emanating from an apartment. The officers stop, knock on the door, and explain their suspicions to a woman who opens the door. The woman denies that anyone is smoking marijuana and immediately slams the door. The officers then hear movement inside the apartment. Do exigent circumstances justify a warrantless entry into the apartment?

b. Homicide Scenes

In *Flippo v. West Virginia*, 528 U.S. 11 (1999), after Flippo's wife was found dead at a cabin in a state park, and Flippo was taken to a hospital (he claimed that he and his wife had been attacked), officers returned and searched the cabin where the two had been staying. In the cabin, they found photographs that were later used at Flippo's trial. The Court rejected the argument that the police had an automatic right to make a warrantless search of a "homicide crime scene."

c. Political Assassination

In *People v. Sirhan*, 7 Cal.3d 710, 102 Cal.Rptr. 385, 497 P.2d 1121 (1972), after Senator Robert Kennedy was murdered, the police took Sirhan Sirhan into custody, and searched his home where they found several items that were ultimately used against him (e.g., pages from his notebooks and an envelope). The court upheld the search: "The officers believed that there might be a conspiracy to assassinate political leaders in this country and that prompt action on their part was necessary. Their beliefs were entirely reasonable. The crime was one of enormous gravity. The victim was a major presidential candidate, and a crime of violence had already been committed against him. Although the officers did not have reasonable cause to believe that the house contained evidence of a conspiracy to assassinate prominent political leaders, the mere possibility that there might be such evidence in the house fully warranted the officers' actions. It is not difficult to envisage what would have been the effect on this nation if several more political assassinations had followed that of Senator Kennedy. Today when assassinations of persons of prominence have repeatedly been committed in this country, it is essential that law enforcement officers be allowed to take fast action in their endeavors to combat such crimes."

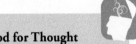

Food for Thought

Police receive a tip that there is "a dead body in apartment 618 of the Rhode Island Avenue Plaza." The police knock repeatedly and identify themselves as police officers. After ten minutes of knocking and identifying themselves, the police enter the apartment and find the body. Was it permissible for the police to enter without a warrant on the report of a "dead body?" How might the owner of the premises argue that the entry was improper? How might the state respond? What if the police had received a report of an "unconscious" rather than a "dead" body? *See Wayne v. United States*, 318 F.2d 205 (D.C.Cir.1963).

Take Note

When animals are kept in diseased or dangerous conditions, as well as when they are in immediate danger, governmental officials may seize those animals without a warrant. In addition, if the seized animals have communicable diseases, governmental officials may have the right to euthanize them. *See Recchia v. City of Los Angeles*, 889 F.3d 553 (9th Cir. 2018).

Hypo 1: *The "Foaming" Driver*

The police find Dunavan in a disabled car foaming at the mouth and unable to talk. The police remove Dunavan, send him to the hospital, and search the car for identification. The search reveals a Social Security card, $961 in cash, a motel key, a car rental agreement and two locked briefcases. Fearing for Dunavan's safety, and hopeful that they can find medical information, the police enter Dunavan's motel room and find two small keys which fit the briefcases. While there, the police are told that Dunavan is a diabetic and that he keeps insulin in one of the briefcases. Both briefcases are opened. The first is full of money, banded with Green Hills Branch Bank bands (that bank had been robbed earlier that day), marked with red dye and smelling of gas from a bank anti-robbery device. In the second brief case, the police find insulin and a syringe, along with a lot more money marked like the money in the first case. Based on the evidence found in the briefcases, the police charge Dunavan with the bank robbery. Dunavan moves to suppress. Can the police justify the search under the community caretaking exception? How might Dunavan argue that the exception does not apply? *See United States v. Dunavan*, 485 F.2d 201 (6th Cir.1973).

Food for Thought

Police receive an anonymous telephone call from a payphone, indicating that a man is beating a woman in a nearby house, and that the neighbors can hear loud screams. The police respond, but find that the house is quiet. They knock on both the front door and the back door, but no one answers. Having a "gut feeling" that someone in the house is in need of assistance, the police enter the house where they find a woman who has been severely beaten. The woman is rushed to the hospital where she dies. Did the police have sufficient cause to justify entering the house without a warrant? *See Commonwealth v. Davido*, 106 A.3d 611 (Penn. 2014).

Hypo 2: *The Light in the Vacant House*

Police respond to a call stating that the lights are on in a house which is believed to be vacant. The police enter the house, believing that a burglary might be in progress, in order to investigate. While conducting a protective sweep, the police discover marijuana plants growing in the basement. Can the entry and the search be justified under the community caretaking exception? *See United States v. McClain*, 430 F.3d 299 (6th Cir.2005).

Food for Thought

On a winter evening, a police officer observes a jeep with its headlights on parked in a "pull off" adjacent to the westbound lane of travel, but facing east. The car is eight feet from the roadway. It is a dark, cold night and there is snow on the ground, but the road markings are visible. The officer believes that it is "unusual" to see a car parked in such a manner. In addition, the officer recently covered a fatal motor vehicle accident in which a vehicle parked similarly to the defendant's was a contributing factor, and he believes that the manner in which the Jeep is parked violates state law. The officer stops "to check things out." He pulls behind the Jeep and activates his cruiser's blue lights and spotlight in order to alert occupants of the vehicle and other motorists to his presence. He does not know whether the vehicle is occupied, whether an accident has occurred, or whether any potential occupants need assistance. When he approaches the Jeep, he observes two men in the front seat and asks the passenger to lower his window. The officer then smells the odor of marijuana emanating from the vehicle, and charges the occupants with possession of drugs. Was the officer justified in his actions? *See State v. Boutin*, 161 N.H. 139, 13 A.3d 334 (2010).

Hypo 3: *Hot Pursuit?*

When a police officer sees an individual commit a traffic violation, he turns on his lights and siren intending to pull the driver over. The driver flees. Eventually, the driver arrives at a residence, quickly exits the vehicle, and enters the home. Under the hot pursuit doctrine, is the officer entitled to make a warrantless entry into the house? Should it matter that there is no indication that the fleeing individual is dangerous, or is about to destroy evidence? *See Trent v. Wade*, 776 F.3d 368 (5th Cir. 2015).

Hypo 4: *The Whimpering Dog*

The police receive a 911 call relating to gun shots being fired from a residence. Arriving at the residence, the police hear footsteps from within and whimpering. As it turns out, the whimpering is coming from a dog rather than from a person, but the officer thought that it was coming from a person. Can the officer enter the home to see if a person needs assistance? *See United States v. Evans*, 958 F.3d 1102 (11th Cir. 2020).

Hypo 5: *Arrested at Home*

Police receive a 911 call from a neighbor indicating that the owners of a nearby house are at work and that a white male wearing a black jacket and carrying a red backpack has scaled their fence and entered their backyard. Officers, responding to the call, enter the backyard of the home without a warrant (one scales the fence and another kicks open a padlocked gate). Before doing so, the officers see a red backpack lying against a porch in the backyard, and a white male wearing a black jacket in the yard. However, there are no signs of a forced entry into the house. When the officers order the man to the ground, the man responds that he lives at the house. As it turns out, he does, but the officers verify that fact only after they arrest the man and search his backpack, finding an unloaded handgun. By that point, the officers have also learned that the man is a felon. Did the police act properly in entering the backyard, in seizing the man, and in searching his backpack? *See United States v. Struckman*, 603 F.3d 731 (9th Cir. 2010).

Hypo 6: *The Static 911 Call*

When a 911 dispatcher receives a phone call from a residence that contains nothing but static, the dispatcher tries unsuccessfully to return the call, and then sends two police officers to the residence to investigate. The officers arrive twenty-five minutes after the 911 call at the house which is located in a rural area on a secluded lot. When they arrive, the gate is closed, but they walk through an opening next to the gate. They repeatedly knock on the front door and announce their presence, but they receive no response. The officers inspect the perimeter of the house and look into the windows, but see no signs of forced entry and cannot see nor hear anyone inside. The officers then walk up a second-floor balcony. There, they find a closed but unlocked sliding glass door. Through the glass, they can see some electronic boxes near the door and they notice that the house looks disheveled. The officers open the sliding glass door and announce their presence. They receive no response. The officers enter and conduct a sweep of the house "to ensure that no one was injured, unconscious, or deceased." During the search, they see drugs and drug paraphernalia in plain view. Did the officers act properly in entering the house? *See United States v. Martinez*, 643 F.3d 1292 (10th Cir. 2011).

Food for Thought

A woman, on returning to her apartment finds a bullet hole in a wall that she shares with her neighbor, and calls 911. The responding police knock on the neighbor's door, but nobody responds. May the police break into the adjoining apartment to make sure that everyone is ok? *See United States v. Timmann*, 741 F.3d 1170 (11th Cir. 2013).

Food for Thought

A woman is involved in an automobile collision which causes her car to roll over. Before the police arrive, the woman's husband arrives and drives her away. The police, worried that the woman may have been seriously injured because of the severity of the crash, decide to go to her home to make sure that she is ok. If nobody answers the door, may the police make a warrantless entry to check on the woman's well-being? *See State v. Saale*, 204 P.3d 1220 (Mont. 2009).

Hypo 7: *Flipping off the Police Officer*

John and Judy were driving to the home of Judy's son with John in the passenger seat. As they approach an intersection, John sees a police officer using a radar device to track the speed of vehicles. John expresses his displeasure by extending his middle finger over the car's roof. Judy is not speeding or committing any other traffic violation. The officer follows with lights flashing. The officer claims that he initiated the stop because he felt that John was trying to get his attention, that there might be a problem in the car, and that he just wanted to "assure the safety of the passengers." The officer also claims that he was concerned for the safety of the female driver because there might have been a "domestic dispute." Was the stop reasonable under the Fourth Amendment? *See Swartz v. Insogna*, 704 F.3d 105 (2d Cir. 2013).

Food for Thought

Vargas resided in a second-floor apartment. With his rent five days overdue, Vargas' landlord made several unsuccessful attempts to contact him by knocking on the door and leaving voice messages. Other tenants told the landlord that they had not seen Vargas for "several days" to "a week," that a bag of trash had been left on Vargas's front porch, and that Vargas's Jaguar convertible had not been moved. Ten days later, the landlord found Vargas's Jaguar still unmoved, covered in pollen, with its rear tires deflated, Vargas's mailbox was full, and the landlord's earlier letter had not been removed. The landlord again knocked on Vargas's door and called Vargas' phone without any response. At this point, the landlord called 911 and explained the situation. Police officers were dispatched to the scene for a "welfare check," and peered through a window but saw no one. With the landlord's help, the officers entered Vargas's apartment because they "had reasons to fear for his safety." Can the officers justify the entry under their "community caretaking" function? *See State v. Vargas*, 63 A.3d 175 (2013).

Hypo 8: *Offering Assistance*

Just after midnight, a police officer sees a vehicle pull off of the road and come to a stop on the shoulder of the road. In the area, there are only a few businesses, no houses, and only one traffic light. Believing that the driver needs assistance, the officer activates both his front-facing and rear-facing overhead red and blue lights to notify the driver that it is the police and not "some bad guy" who has pulled in behind him. The officer's sole reason for stopping is "to see if the driver has a problem or maybe is lost" and "to see if he needs assistance." The driver begins to drive away, but quickly stops. The officer stops the vehicle, notices a strong odor of alcohol coming from the vehicle, and notices that the driver's eyes are bloodshot and his speech slurred. Did the officer act properly in stopping the vehicle? *See Gonzales v. State*, 369 S.W.3d 851 (Tex. Crim. App. 2012).

Food for Thought

Suppose that anti-abortion protestors drive on city streets with trucks that depict large photos of aborted fetuses. Because of the potentially offensive nature of the material, the protestors cover the photos with tarps when going to and from protest sites. In addition, because of the potential for violence at protest sites, the protestors wear helmets and kevlar vests. A police officer on routine patrol happens to observe the trucks (covered by tarps) being driven by individuals with helmets and kevlar vests. Fearing a terrorist strike, the police officer decides to stop the trucks and search them. Did the officer act properly? *See Center for Bio-Ethical Reform, Inc. v. Springboro*, 477 F.3d 807 (6th Cir. 2007).

Take Note

In *Minnesota v. Olson,* 495 U.S. 91 (1990), following a robbery at a gasoline station, during which the station manager was fatally shot, the police apprehend the individual who actually killed the manager, but an accomplice escapes. Using information obtained from the get-away vehicle, police ascertain the name of the accomplice (Olson). The next day, the police receive a tip which states where Olson is staying and indicates that he is about to leave town. Police surround the residence, phone, and ask Olson to come out. The detective hears a male voice say, "tell them I left." At that point, the police enter the house, with guns drawn, to arrest Olson. At the police station, Olson made an inculpatory statement. The Court concluded that the police did not have exigent circumstances for entering the house without a warrant: "Although a grave crime was involved, respondent 'was known not to be the murderer but thought to be the driver of the getaway car,' and the police had already recovered the murder weapon." The police knew that the women with the suspect were under no threat of danger. Police squads surrounded the house. The time was 3 p.m., Sunday. It was evident the suspect was going nowhere. If he came out of the house he would have been promptly apprehended."

In *Vale v. Louisiana*, 399 U.S. 30 (1970), officers possessed a warrant for Vale's arrest and had information that he was residing at a particular place. After surveilling the house, the officers observed a car drive up and sound the horn. Vale, who was known to the officers, came out of the house and had a brief conversation with the driver. After looking up and down the street, he returned to the house and reappeared a few minutes later. He again looked up and down the street, went to the car, and leaned through the window. The officers were convinced that a narcotics sale was taking place. They immediately drove toward Vale. As he saw them, he turned and walked quickly toward the house. The officers called for Vale to stop as he reached the front steps of the house. Once the officers subdued Vale, they told him that they were going to search the house. After entering, the officers made a cursory inspection to ascertain if anyone else was present. At that point, Mrs. Vale and James Vale, mother and brother of defendant, returned home carrying groceries and were informed of the arrest and impending search. The search of a rear bedroom revealed a quantity of narcotics. The Court held that the search could not be justified under the "exigent circumstances" exception: "The officers were not responding to an emergency. They were not in hot pursuit of a fleeing felon. The goods ultimately seized were not in the process of destruction. Nor were they about to be removed from the jurisdiction. The officers were able to procure two warrants for Vale's arrest. They also had information that he was residing at the address where they found him. There is thus no reason to suppose that it was impracticable for them to obtain a search warrant. We decline to hold that an arrest on the street can provide its own 'exigent circumstance' so as to justify a warrantless search of the arrestee's house." Mr. Justice Black dissented: "Vale's arrest took place near the house, and anyone observing from inside would surely have been alerted to destroy the stocks of contraband which the police believed Vale had left there. The police were faced with the choice of risking the immediate destruction of evidence or entering the house and conducting a search. I cannot say that their decision to search was unreasonable."

Hypo 9: *The Screams*

Early afternoon, police officers hear screams coming from a nearby hotel. An officer determines that the screams are coming from room #7, and knocks on that door. When a male voice inquires as to who is knocking, the officers answer "the police." After several repetitions of this exchange a woman opens the door. The woman and another woman, the lessee of the room, state that they do not know of any cause for the screams, and one woman states that she might have had a nightmare. The officers then hear the flushing of a toilet in the bathroom, and see defendant emerge from the bathroom in his undershorts. An officer immediately enters the bathroom, observes pieces of currency floating in the commode, and retrieves them. The officer then pulls the chain of the water closet and recovers additional pieces of currency which have floated to the surface. Did the officer have sufficient cause to enter the bathroom and observe the commode? *See United States v. Barone*, 330 F.2d 543 (2d Cir.1964).

Food for Thought

Aware (based on a tip) that Hendrix is selling drugs from his house, two officers stake out the house while another officer telephones the residence. The telephoning officer asks for "Hendrix," receives an affirmative response, and warns him that the police are on their way to the house with a search warrant. The lights in the house go off, and there is a great deal of activity within the house for three or four minutes, then the lights come back on. Hendrix exits the residence, jumps in his Lincoln Continental, and drives away. An officer follows the Lincoln which travels a short distance and turns into a driveway on another street. Does the officer have adequate cause to stop Hendrix and search the vehicle? How would you argue the case for the State? How might Hendrix respond? Suppose that the officer does not stop the vehicle and search it, but rather simply follows it. He sees Hendrix stop and hurriedly exit. The officer goes to the car, peers in, and sees a set of scales commonly used for weighing cocaine, a lock box, a large suitcase, and a bottle of Inositol powder (used to dilute cocaine). The officer then enters the car, opens the suitcase and finds weapons inside. When he removes the scales and lock box from the back seat he observes a plastic bag with cocaine. A search warrant is subsequently obtained to open the lock box which contains a larger quantity of cocaine in plastic bags. Did the officer act properly? *See State v. Hendrix*, 782 S.W.2d 833 (Tenn.1989).

Hypo 10: *The Disturbance*

Just after midnight, police officers respond to a disturbance call at an apartment where there is yelling, screaming, and the sounds of objects being thrown. When they knock, a woman opens the door, appearing to be "extremely distraught and highly intoxicated," stumbling as she walks, and speaking in a slurred manner. However, she does not seem to have any injuries. The woman denies that there has been domestic violence, and states that she threw things because she discovered that her boyfriend was seeing other women. She states further that he is not there and she does not know where he has gone. The woman does state that there are babies in the apartment. During these events, the woman repeatedly asks the police to leave. Eventually, the woman is more emphatic: "Get out of my f * * * ing house!" The police refuse to leave because there is evidence of "a disturbance," even though there are no signs of injury, and the officers feel that they should investigate in order to ensure the safety of any babies in the apartment, and should run a warrant check on the woman. While they remain, the police observe a small, burned marijuana cigarette and arrest the woman. The officers search further and find two baggies containing traces of a white powdery substance. Did the officers act properly in refusing to leave the residence under these circumstances? *See Miller v. State*, 393 S.W.3d 255 (Tex. Crim. App. 2012).

Hypo 11: *Applying the "Community Caretaking" Exception*

A police officer is on patrol when he spots a dirt bike on the side of the road. He writes down the bike's vehicle identification number, enters the VIN in a computer, and drives away. When he learns that the bike is stolen, he returns to the scene, but the bike is gone. Later that day, he spots the same bike being ridden by an unknown male. Later, when he spots the bike in the back of a house, he walks around to the front yard and notices that the front door is open. He also sees candlelight through a boarded-up window on the first floor. The officer believes that the house is abandoned because it is in a state of severe disrepair, the backyard is full of trash, there are "boards on the door and the windows," the yard is covered in weeds and generally untended, there is nothing covering the windows on the second floor, and the two first floor windows on the front of the house are boarded up with plywood, and the front door is unlocked and ajar. The officer walks in the front door without knocking or announcing his presence. Inside the house, the officer finds Harrison with a gun, scales, pills, and cocaine base on the table next to him. Harrison lives at another address, but pays the owner for the use of the house and has the key in his possession. Did the officer act properly in entering the house? *See United States v. Harrison*, 689 F.3d 301 (3d Cir. 2012).

Hypo 12: *The 911 Call*

Early one morning, Infante called 911 to request that an ambulance be sent to his house. He explains that he sustained hand injuries when a propane tank exploded. Infante affirms that he is home alone. Asked whether anything is still burning or smoldering, he replies, "No, it just went bang big time." Infante states that he is out of danger and is securing his home because he is going out. The dispatcher advises him that help is on the way, and broadcasts a "fire call and rescue" regarding "a propane explosion" at the address where a "male, by himself, has a large cut, and hand injuries." Infante decides not to wait for an ambulance and drives himself to the hospital. Nevertheless, the fire department responds and sees Infante driving with his warning lights on. When they persuade Infante to stop for medical assistance, the paramedics observe that Infante has superficial "shrapnel" wounds and a hand wrapped in a bloody towel. A paramedic unwraps the towel and provides medical assistance. Afterwards, Infante leaves. Firemen nevertheless proceed to the site of the explosion. Finding no signs of an explosion on the outside, they call the 911 dispatcher who states that Infante indicated that the explosion occurred inside from a butane lighter. From the window, the officers see blood inside the house. The firemen decide to enter the house to search for the source of the explosion, and to "make sure there are no other hazards to the homeowner or the public." By this time, about one hour has elapsed since the original 911 call. Following the trail of blood down the cellar stairs, they observe marijuana plants and plant growing equipment, and continue to search for the source of the explosion. They eventually find three pipe-bombs. The officers immediately exit the house and call the police. Did the fireman act properly in entering the house under these circumstances? *See United States v. Infante*, 701 F.3d 386 (1st Cir. 2012).

Hypo 13: *Child Safety*

Lopez, an investigator with a state's Department of Family Services goes to investigate allegations of marijuana use at Turrubiate's home. Erin Guller, Turrubiate's girlfriend, and her six-month old child, also live there. When the investigator knocks, Turrubiate cracks the door open, and Lopez notices a strong odor of marijuana emanating from the home. Turrubiate claims that Guller and her child are not at home. Lopez immediately contacts his supervisor and the sheriff's department, and informs them that the home smells like marijuana. When Lopez returns with a police officer to investigate, and Turrubiate opens the door, Lopez again smells "a strong, fresh odor of marijuana" and determines that entry is required to "prevent the marijuana from being destroyed" while he obtains a warrant. As a result, Lopez and the officer forcibly enter the home, handcuff Turrubiate, and place him on the floor. They then search Turrubiate and the surrounding area for weapons, finding marijuana in Turrubiate's backpack. Were there sufficient exigent circumstances to justify a warrantless entry into the home? Is it relevant that Turrubiate did not destroy the marijuana after Lopez's initial visit? *See Turrubiate v. State*, 399 S.W.3d 147 (Tex. Crim. App. 2013).

Hypo 14: *Gunshots*

Late one evening, police respond to a 911 call regarding a series of gunshots. Over a dozen officers arrive, and they learn that a person has been shot in the leg. The officers remain in the neighborhood until about 4 a.m. Schmidt lives nearby in a house that shares a backyard with another duplex. The front and back of the duplexes are almost entirely enclosed by chain-link fences with "No Trespassing" signs, chain-link gates, and a wooden fence. About 1:00 a.m., an investigating officer approaches the duplex from the back alley. He notices bullet holes in a car parked on a concrete slab adjacent to the backyard and bullet holes in the duplex itself. He also notices a trail of about nine spent casings on the ground, including five casings right next to the duplex and one casing in the yard. The chain-link gate on the back alley side is open, and the officer, without a warrant, enters the backyard and pans the area with his flashlight. Does the officer have the right to enter the property in order to investigate? *See United States v. Schmidt*, 700 F.3d 934 (7th Cir. 2012).

Hypo 15: *More on Community Caretaking*

Suppose that the police are dispatched to a house based on a report of a need for medical care. When they arrive, they find a blood spattered door and a man who is covered in blood. They arrange an ambulance to take the man to the hospital. After the ambulance departs, the officers go to the back door of the house where they find more blood, and a blood trail that leads to a nearby house. The officers find blood on the door of that residence, and they hear loud noises coming from inside. The officers then call for backup. When the backup arrives, they enter the home to check on the residents. Seeing blood on the stairs, the officers continue upstairs where they find a door covered in blood. The officers demand entry and find a marijuana plant. Can the officers' actions be justified under the community caretaking doctrine? *See State v. Matalonis*, 2016 WI 7, 875 N.W.2d 567 (2016).

Food for Thought

During a bank robbery, a GPS device is inserted into a bag of stolen money. Tracking the GPS, the police receive information suggesting that the tracker is somewhere on a block where 92 vehicles are located. May the police block off the road, question the owners of all vehicles on the street, and use a tracking device to determine which vehicle has the GPS device? *See United States v. Paetsch*, 782 F,3d 1162 (10th Cir. 2015).

Food for Thought

Receiving a report from a landlord that he is unable to awaken defendant, who is unresponsive, the police enter the apartment to make sure that defendant is okay. After they enter, he wakes up and appears to be fine. Must the police leave or can they investigate further? What if they do not investigate further, but do see contraband lying in plain view? *See State v. Neighbors*, 328 P.3d 1081 (Kan. 2014).

Rochin v. California

342 U.S. 165 (1952).

MR. JUSTICE FRANKFURTER delivered the opinion of the Court.

Having "information that petitioner was selling narcotics," deputy sheriffs of the County of Los Angeles, went to the two-story dwelling house in which Rochin lived. Finding the outside door open, they entered and forced open the door to Rochin's room on the second floor. Inside they found petitioner sitting partly dressed on the side of the bed, upon which his wife was lying. On a "night stand" beside the bed the deputies spied two capsules. When asked "Whose stuff is this?" Rochin seized the capsules and put them in his mouth. A struggle ensued during which the officers attempted to extract the capsules. The force they applied proved unavailing against Rochin's resistance. He was handcuffed and taken to a hospital. At the direction of one of the officers a doctor forced an emetic solution through a tube into Rochin's stomach against his will. This "stomach pumping" produced vomiting. In the vomited matter were found two capsules which proved to contain morphine.

Regard for the requirements of the Due Process Clause "inescapably imposes upon this Court an exercise of judgment upon the whole course of the proceedings (resulting in a conviction) in order to ascertain whether they offend those canons of decency and fairness which express the notions of justice of English-speaking peoples even toward those charged with the most heinous offenses." These standards of justice are not authoritatively formulated anywhere. Due process of law is a summarized constitutional guarantee of respect for those personal immunities which, as Mr. Justice Cardozo twice wrote for the Court, are "so rooted in the traditions and conscience of our people as to be ranked as fundamental", or are "implicit in the concept of ordered liberty". *Palko v. State of Connecticut*, 302 U.S. 319.

The vague contours of the Due Process Clause do not leave judges at large. We may not draw on our merely personal and private notions and disregard the limits that bind judges in their judicial function. Even though the concept of due process of law is not final and fixed, these limits are derived from considerations that are fused in the whole nature of or judicial process. *See* Cardozo, The Nature of the Judicial Process; The Growth of the Law; The Paradoxes of Legal Science. These are considerations deeply rooted in reason and in the compelling traditions of the legal profession. The Due Process Clause places upon this Court the duty of exercising a judgment, within the narrow confines of judicial power in reviewing State convictions, upon interests of society pushing in opposite directions.

Due process of law thus conceived is not to be derided as resort to a revival of "natural law." To believe that this judicial exercise of judgment could be avoided by freezing "due process of law" at some fixed stage of time or thought is to suggest that the most important aspect of constitutional adjudication is a function for inanimate machines and not for judges, for whom the independence safeguarded by Article III of the Constitution was designed and who are presumably guided by established standards of judicial behavior.

Applying these general considerations, we are compelled to conclude that the proceedings by which this conviction was obtained do more than offend some fastidious squeamishness or private sentimentalism about combating crime too energetically. This is conduct that shocks the conscience. Illegally breaking into the privacy of the petitioner, the struggle to open his mouth and remove what was there, the forcible extraction of his stomach's contents—this course of proceeding by agents of government to obtain evidence is bound to offend even hardened sensibilities. They are methods too close to the rack and the screw to permit of constitutional differentiation.

On the facts of this case the conviction of the petitioner has been obtained by methods that offend the Due Process Clause. The judgment below must be reversed.

Reversed.

MR. JUSTICE BLACK, concurring.

If the Due Process Clause does vest this Court with such unlimited power to invalidate laws, I am still in doubt as to why we should consider only the notions of English-speaking peoples to determine what are immutable and fundamental principles of justice. One may well ask what avenues of investigation are open to discover "canons" of conduct so universally favored that this Court should write them into the Constitution? All we are told is that the discovery must be made by an "evaluation based on a disinterested inquiry pursued in the spirit of science, on a balanced order of facts."

MR. JUSTICE DOUGLAS, concurring.

The evidence obtained from this accused's stomach would be admissible in the majority of states where the question has been raised. Yet the Court now says that the rule which the majority of the states have fashioned violates the "decencies of civilized conduct." To that I cannot agree. It is a rule formulated by responsible courts with judges as sensitive as we are to the proper standards for law administration.

Mitchell v. Wisconsin

139 S.Ct. 2525 (2019).

JUSTICE ALITO announced the judgment of the Court and delivered an opinion, in which THE CHIEF JUSTICE, JUSTICE BREYER, and JUSTICE KAVANAUGH join.

We return to a topic that we have addressed twice in recent years: the circumstances under which a police officer may administer a warrantless blood alcohol concentration (BAC) test to a motorist who appears to have been driving under the influence of alcohol. We have previously addressed what officers may do in two broad categories of cases. First, an officer may conduct a BAC test if the facts of a particular case bring it within the exigent-circumstances exception to the Fourth Amendment's general requirement of a warrant. Second, if an officer has probable cause to arrest a motorist for drunk driving, the officer may conduct a breath test (but not a blood test) under the rule allowing warrantless searches of a person incident to arrest.

Today, we consider what police officers may do in cases in which the driver is unconscious and therefore cannot be given a breath test. In such cases, the exigent-circumstances rule almost always permits a blood test without a warrant. When a breath test is impossible, enforcement of the drunk-driving laws depends upon the administration of a blood test. And when a police officer encounters an unconscious driver, it is very likely that the driver would be taken to an emergency room and that his blood would be drawn for diagnostic purposes even if the police were not seeking BAC information. In addition, police officers most frequently come upon unconscious drivers when they report to the scene of an accident, and under those circumstances, the officers' many responsibilities—such as attending to other injured drivers or passengers and preventing further accidents—may be incompatible with the procedures that would be required to obtain a warrant. Thus, when a driver is unconscious, the general rule is that a warrant is not needed.

In *Birchfield v. North Dakota*, 136 S.Ct. 2160 (2016), we recounted the country's efforts over the years to address the terrible problem of drunk driving. Today, "all States have laws that prohibit motorists from driving with a BAC that exceeds a specified level." To help enforce BAC limits, every State has passed what are popularly called implied-consent laws. As "a condition of the privilege of" using the public roads, these laws require that drivers submit to BAC testing "when there is sufficient reason to believe they are violating the State's drunk-driving laws." Wisconsin's implied-consent law is much like those of the other 49 States and the District of Columbia. It deems drivers to have consented to breath or blood tests if an officer has reason to believe they have committed one of several drug- or alcohol-related offenses. *See* Wis. Stat. §§ 343.305(2), (3). Officers seeking to conduct a BAC test must read aloud a statement declaring their intent to administer the test and advising drivers of their options and the implications of their choice. If a driver's BAC level proves too high, his license will be suspended; but if he refuses testing, his license will be revoked and his refusal may be used against him in court. No test will be administered if a driver refuses—or "withdraws" his statutorily presumed consent. But "a person who is unconscious or otherwise not capable of withdrawing consent is presumed not to have" withdrawn it. More than half the States have provisions like this one regarding unconscious drivers.

The sequence of events that gave rise to this case began when Officer Alexander Jaeger of the Sheboygan Police Department received a report that petitioner Gerald Mitchell, appearing to be very drunk, had climbed into a van and driven off. Jaeger soon found Mitchell wandering near a lake. Stumbling and slurring his words, Mitchell could hardly stand without support. Jaeger judged a field sobriety test hopeless, if not dangerous, and gave Mitchell a preliminary breath test. It registered a BAC level of 0.24%, triple the legal limit for driving in Wisconsin. Jaeger arrested Mitchell for operating a vehicle while intoxicated and, as is standard practice, drove him to a police station for a more reliable breath test using better equipment. On the way, Mitchell's condition continued to deteriorate—so much so that by the time the squad car had reached the station, he was too lethargic even for a breath test. Jaeger therefore drove Mitchell to a nearby hospital for a blood test; Mitchell lost consciousness on the ride over and had to be wheeled in. Even so, Jaeger read aloud to a slumped Mitchell the standard statement giving drivers a chance to refuse BAC testing. Hearing no response, Jaeger asked hospital staff to draw a blood sample. Mitchell remained unconscious while the sample was taken, and analysis of his blood showed that his BAC, about 90 minutes after his arrest, was 0.222%.

Mitchell was charged with violating two related drunk-driving provisions. He moved to suppress the results of the blood test on the ground that it violated his Fourth Amendment right against "unreasonable searches" because it was conducted without a warrant. Wisconsin [claims] that its implied-consent law (together with Mitchell's free choice to drive on its highways) rendered the blood test a consensual one, thus curing any Fourth Amendment problem. The trial court denied Mitchell's motion to suppress, and a jury found him guilty. The Wisconsin Supreme Court affirmed Mitchell's convictions, and we granted certiorari to decide "whether a statute authorizing a blood draw from an unconscious motorist provides an exception to the Fourth Amendment warrant requirement."

"Our prior opinions have referred approvingly to the general concept of implied-consent laws that impose civil penalties and evidentiary consequences on motorists who refuse to comply." *Birchfield*, 136 S.Ct., at 2185. But our decisions have not rested on the idea that these laws create actual consent to all the searches they authorize. Instead, we have based our decisions on precedent regarding the specific constitutional claims while keeping in mind the wider regulatory scheme developed over the years to combat drunk driving. That scheme is centered on legally specified BAC limits for drivers—limits enforced by the BAC tests promoted by implied-consent laws. Over the last 50 years, we have approved many of the defining elements of this scheme. We have held that forcing drunk-driving suspects to undergo a blood test does not violate their constitutional right against self-incrimination. *See Schmerber v. California*, 384 U.S. 757 (1966). Nor does using their refusal against them in court. *See South Dakota v. Neville*, 459 U.S. 553 (1983). And punishing that refusal with automatic license revocation does not violate drivers' due process rights if they have been arrested upon probable cause; on the contrary, this kind of summary penalty is "unquestionably legitimate." *Neville, supra*, at 560.

These cases generally concerned the Fifth and Fourteenth Amendments, but motorists charged with drunk driving have also invoked the Fourth Amendment's ban on "unreasonable searches" since BAC tests are "searches." Though our precedent normally requires a warrant for a lawful search, there are well-defined exceptions to this rule. In *Birchfield*, we applied the "search-incident-to-arrest" exception to BAC testing of conscious drunk-driving suspects. We held that their drunk-driving arrests, taken alone, justify warrantless breath tests but not blood tests, since breath tests are less intrusive, just as informative, and (in the case of conscious suspects) readily available. We have also reviewed BAC tests under the "exigent circumstances" exception—which allows warrantless searches "to prevent the imminent destruction of evidence." *Missouri v. McNeely*, 569 U.S. 141, 149 (2013). In *McNeely*, we were asked if this exception covers BAC testing of drunk-driving suspects in light of the fact that blood-alcohol evidence is always dissipating due to "natural metabolic processes." We answered that the fleeting quality of BAC evidence alone is not enough. But in *Schmerber* it did justify a blood test of a drunk driver who had gotten into a car accident that gave police other pressing duties, for then the "further delay" caused by a warrant application really "would have threatened the destruction of evidence." *McNeely, supra*, at 152.

Like *Schmerber*, this case sits much higher than *McNeely* on the exigency spectrum. *McNeely* was about the minimum degree of urgency common to all drunk-driving cases. In *Schmerber*, a car accident heightened that urgency. Here Mitchell's medical condition did just the same. Mitchell's stupor and eventual unconsciousness deprived officials of a reasonable opportunity to administer a breath test. To be sure, Officer Jaeger managed to conduct "a preliminary breath test" using a portable machine when he first encountered Mitchell at the lake. But he had no reasonable opportunity to give Mitchell a breath test using "evidence-grade breath testing machinery." As a result, it was reasonable for Jaeger to seek a better breath test at the station; he acted with reasonable dispatch to procure one; and when Mitchell's condition got in the way, it was reasonable for Jaeger to pursue a blood test. As Justice SOTOMAYOR explained in her partial dissent in *Birchfield*: "There is a common misconception that breath tests are conducted roadside, immediately after a driver is arrested. While some preliminary testing is conducted roadside, reliability concerns with roadside tests confine their use in most circumstances to establishing probable cause for an arrest. The standard evidentiary breath test is conducted after a motorist is arrested and transported to a police station, governmental building, or mobile testing facility where officers can access reliable, evidence-grade breath testing machinery." Because the "standard evidentiary breath test is conducted after a motorist is arrested and transported to a police station" or another appropriate facility, the important question is what officers may do when a driver's unconsciousness (or stupor) eliminates any reasonable opportunity for that kind of breath test.

The Fourth Amendment guards the "right of the people to be secure in their persons against unreasonable searches" and provides that "no Warrants shall issue, but upon probable cause." A blood draw is a search of the person, so we must determine if its administration here without a warrant was reasonable. *See Birchfield*, 136 S.Ct., at 2174. Though we have held that a warrant is normally required, we have also "made it clear that there are exceptions to the warrant requirement." *Illinois v. McArthur*, 531 U.S. 326, 330 (2001). And under the exception for exigent circumstances, a warrantless search is allowed when "there is compelling need for official action and no time to secure a warrant." *McNeely, supra*, at 149. In *McNeely*, we considered how the exigent-circumstances exception applies to the broad category of cases in which a police officer has probable cause to believe that a motorist was driving under the influence of alcohol, and we do not revisit that question. Nor do we settle whether the exigent-circumstances exception covers the specific facts of this case. Instead, we address how the exception bears on the category of cases encompassed by the question on which we granted certiorari—those involving unconscious drivers. In those cases, the need for a blood test is compelling, and an officer's duty to attend to more pressing needs may leave no time to seek a warrant.

BAC tests are needed for enforcing laws that save lives. Highway safety is a vital public interest. We have called highway safety a "compelling interest," we have called it "paramount." Twice we have referred to the effects of irresponsible driving as "slaughter" comparable to the ravages of war. We have spoken of "carnage," and even "frightful carnage." The frequency of preventable collisions is "tragic" and "astounding." Behind this fervent language lie chilling figures, all captured in the fact that from 1982 to 2016, alcohol-related accidents took roughly 10,000 to 20,000 lives in this Nation every single year. In the best years, that would add up to more than one fatality per hour. When it comes to fighting these harms and promoting highway safety, specified BAC limits make a big difference. States resorted to these limits when earlier laws that included no "statistical definition of intoxication" proved ineffectual or hard to enforce. The maximum permissible BAC, initially set at 0.15%, was first lowered to 0.10% and then to 0.08%. Congress encouraged this process by conditioning the award of federal highway funds on the establishment of a BAC limit of 0.08%, and every State has adopted this limit. Many States, including Wisconsin, have passed laws imposing increased penalties for recidivists or for drivers with a BAC level that exceeds a higher threshold. As we noted in *Birchfield*, these tougher measures corresponded with a dramatic drop in highway deaths and injuries: From the mid-1970s to the mid-1980s, "the number of annual fatalities averaged 25,000; by 2014, the number had fallen to below 10,000."

Enforcing BAC limits requires a test that is accurate enough to stand up in court. And "extraction of blood samples for testing is a highly effective means of" measuring "the influence of alcohol." Enforcement of BAC limits also requires prompt testing because it is "a biological certainty" that "alcohol dissipates from the bloodstream at a rate of 0.01 percent to 0.025 percent per hour. Evidence is literally disappearing by the minute." *McNeely*, 569 U.S., at 169 (opinion of ROBERTS, C.J.). The ephemeral nature of BAC was "essential to our holding in *Schmerber*," which itself allowed a warrantless blood test for BAC. Even when we later held that the exigent-circumstances exception would not permit a warrantless blood draw in every drunk-driving case, we acknowledged that delays in BAC testing can "raise questions about accuracy." It is no wonder that implied-consent laws that incentivize prompt BAC testing have been with us for 65 years and now exist in all 50 States. *Birchfield*, 136 S.Ct., at 2169. These laws and the BAC tests they require are tightly linked to a regulatory scheme that serves the most pressing of interests. When a breath test is unavailable to promote those interests, "a blood draw becomes necessary." *McNeely*, 569 U.S., at 170 (opinion of ROBERTS, C.J.). Thus, in the case of unconscious drivers, who cannot blow into a breathalyzer, blood tests are essential for achieving the compelling interests described above. Indeed, not only is the link to pressing interests here tighter; the interests themselves are greater: Drivers who are drunk enough to pass out at the wheel or soon afterward pose a much greater risk. It would be perverse if the more wanton behavior were rewarded—if the more harrowing threat were harder to punish.

For these reasons, there clearly is a "compelling need" for a blood test of drunk-driving suspects whose condition deprives officials of a reasonable opportunity to conduct a breath test. The only question left, under our exigency doctrine, is whether this compelling need justifies a warrantless search because there is, furthermore, "no time to secure a warrant."

We held that there was no time to secure a warrant before a blood test of a drunk-driving suspect in *Schmerber* because the officer there could "reasonably have believed that he was confronted with an emergency, in which the delay necessary to obtain a warrant, under the circumstances, threatened the destruction of evidence." So even if the constant dissipation of BAC evidence alone does not create an exigency, *Schmerber* shows that it does so when combined with other pressing needs: "[1] the percentage of alcohol in the blood begins to diminish shortly after drinking stops, as the body functions to eliminate it from the system. Particularly in a case such as this, where [2] time had to be taken to bring the accused to a hospital and to investigate the scene of the accident, there was no time to seek out a magistrate and secure a warrant. Given these special facts, the attempt to secure evidence of blood-alcohol content in this case without a warrant was appropriate." Thus, exigency exists when (1) BAC evidence is dissipating and (2) some other factor creates pressing health, safety, or law enforcement needs that would take priority over a warrant application. Both conditions are met when a drunk-driving suspect is unconscious, so *Schmerber* controls: With such suspects, too, a warrantless blood draw is lawful.

In *Schmerber*, the extra factor giving rise to urgent needs that would only add to the delay caused by a warrant application was a car accident; here it is the driver's unconsciousness. Unconsciousness does not just create pressing needs; it is itself a medical emergency. It means that the suspect will have to be rushed to the hospital or similar facility not just for the blood test itself but for urgent medical care. Police can reasonably anticipate that such a driver might require monitoring, positioning, and support on the way to the hospital; that his blood may be drawn anyway, for diagnostic purposes, immediately on arrival; and that immediate medical treatment could delay (or otherwise distort the results of) a blood draw conducted later, upon receipt of a warrant, thus reducing its evidentiary value. All of that sets this case apart from the uncomplicated drunk-driving scenarios addressed in *McNeely*. Just as the ramifications of a car accident pushed *Schmerber* over the line into exigency, so does the condition of an unconscious driver bring his blood draw under the exception. In such a case, as in *Schmerber*, an officer could "reasonably have believed that he was confronted with an emergency."

Indeed, in many unconscious-driver cases, the exigency will be more acute. A driver so drunk as to lose consciousness is quite likely to crash, especially if he passes out before managing to park. And then the accident might give officers a slew of urgent tasks beyond that of securing (and working around) medical care for the suspect. Police may have to ensure that others who are injured receive prompt medical attention; they may have to provide first aid themselves until medical personnel arrive at the scene. In some cases, they may have to deal with fatalities. They may have to preserve evidence at the scene and block or redirect traffic to prevent further accidents. These pressing matters require responsible officers to put off applying for a warrant, and that would only exacerbate the delay—and imprecision—of any subsequent BAC test. In sum, all these rival priorities would put officers, who must often engage in a form of triage, to a dilemma. It would force them to choose between prioritizing a warrant application, to the detriment of critical health and safety needs, and delaying the warrant application, and thus the BAC test, to the detriment of its evidentiary value and all the compelling interests served by BAC limits. This is just the kind of scenario for which the exigency rule was born—just the kind of grim dilemma it lives to dissolve.

Mitchell objects that a warrantless search is unnecessary in cases involving unconscious drivers because warrants these days can be obtained faster and more easily. But even in our age of rapid communication, "warrants inevitably take some time for police officers or prosecutors to complete and for magistrate judges to review. Telephonic and electronic warrants may still require officers to follow time-consuming formalities designed to create an adequate record, such as preparing a duplicate warrant before calling the magistrate judge. And improvements in communications technology do not guarantee that a magistrate judge will be available when an officer needs a warrant after making a late-night arrest." *McNeely*, 569 U.S., at 155. With better technology, the time required has shrunk, but it has not disappeared. In the emergency scenarios created by unconscious drivers, forcing police to put off other tasks for even a relatively short period of time may have terrible collateral costs. That is just what it means for these situations to be emergencies.

When police have probable cause to believe a person has committed a drunk-driving offense and the driver's unconsciousness or stupor requires him to be taken to the hospital or similar facility before police have a reasonable opportunity to administer a standard evidentiary breath test, they may almost always order a warrantless blood test to measure the driver's BAC without offending the Fourth Amendment. We do not rule out the possibility that in an unusual case a defendant would be able to show that his blood would not have been drawn if police had not been seeking BAC information, and that police could not have reasonably judged that a warrant application would interfere with other pressing needs or duties. Because Mitchell did not have a chance to attempt to make that showing, a remand is necessary.

The judgment of the Supreme Court of Wisconsin is vacated, and the case is remanded for further proceedings.

It is so ordered.

Justice Thomas, concurring in the judgment.

"The imminent destruction of evidence" is a risk in every drunk-driving arrest and thus "implicates the exigent-circumstances doctrine." *McNeely*, 569 U.S., at 178. "Once police arrest a suspect for drunk driving, each passing minute eliminates probative evidence of the crime" as alcohol dissipates from the bloodstream. In many States, this "rapid destruction of evidence" is particularly problematic because the penalty for drunk driving depends in part on the driver's blood alcohol concentration. Because the provisions of Wisconsin law allow blood draws only when the driver is suspected of impaired driving, they fit easily within the exigency exception to the warrant requirement. The destruction of evidence alone is sufficient to justify a warrantless search. That the exigent-circumstances exception might ordinarily require "an evaluation of the particular facts of each case" does not foreclose us from recognizing that a certain, dispositive fact is always present in some categories of cases. Police officers may perform searches without a warrant when destruction of evidence is a risk. *United States v. Banks*, 540 U.S. 31, 38 (2003). The rule should be no different in drunk-driving cases.

Justice Sotomayor, with whom Justice Ginsburg and Justice Kagan join, dissenting.

The plurality's decision rests on the false premise that [it] is necessary to spare law enforcement from a choice between attending to emergency situations and securing evidence used to enforce state drunk-driving laws. The State of Wisconsin conceded that it had time to get a warrant to Mitchell's blood, and that should be the end of the matter. The warrant requirement is not a mere formality; it ensures that necessary judgment calls are made "by a neutral and detached magistrate," not "by the officer engaged in the often competitive enterprise of ferreting out crime." *Schmerber v. California*, 384 U.S. 757, 770 (1966). A warrant thus serves as a check against searches that violate the Fourth Amendment by ensuring that a police officer is not made the sole interpreter of the Constitution's protections.

Blood draws are "searches" under the Fourth Amendment. *Missouri v. McNeely*, 569 U.S. 141, 148 (2013). The blood draw also "places in the hands of law enforcement authorities a sample that can be preserved and from which it is possible to extract information beyond a simple BAC reading," *Birchfield v. North Dakota*, 136 S.Ct. 2160 (2016), such as whether a person is pregnant, is taking certain medications, or suffers from an illness. That "invasion of bodily integrity" disturbs "an individual's 'most personal and deep-rooted expectations of privacy.'" *McNeely*, 569 U.S., at 148. Unless there is too little time to do so, police officers must get a warrant before ordering a blood draw. Meanwhile, significant technological advances have allowed for "more expeditious processing of warrant applications." In the federal system, magistrate judges can issue warrants based on sworn testimony communicated over the phone or through "other reliable electronic means." In a sizable majority of States, police officers can apply for warrants "remotely through various means, including telephonic or radio communication, electronic communication such as e-mail, and video conferencing." *McNeely*, 569 U.S., at 154. And the use of "standard-form warrant applications" has streamlined the warrant process in many States as well, especially in this context. As a result, judges can often issue warrants in 5 to 15 minutes. Of course, securing a warrant will always take some time, and that time will vary case to case. As *McNeely* made clear, the exigency exception is appropriate only in those cases in which time is not on the officer's side.

In these cases, there is still a period of delay during which a police officer might take steps to secure a warrant. Of course, the police and other first responders must dutifully attend to any urgent medical needs of the driver and others at the scene. In many cases, the police will have enough time to address medical needs and still get a warrant before the putative evidence (i.e.,alcohol in the suspect's blood) dissipates. If police officers "are truly confronted with a 'now or never' situation," they will be able to rely on the exigent-circumstances exception to order the blood draw immediately. "Requiring a warrant whenever practicable helps ensure that when blood draws occur, they are indeed justified." *McNeely*, 569 U.S., at 174 (opinion of ROBERTS, C.J.).

JUSTICE GORSUCH, dissenting.

Application of the exigent doctrine in this area poses complex and difficult questions that neither the parties nor the courts below discussed. I would have dismissed this case and waited for a case presenting the exigent circumstances question.

Points for Discussion

a. Fingernail Scrapings

In *Cupp v. Murphy*, 412 U.S. 291 (1973), Murphy's wife died by strangulation at home with abrasions and lacerations on her throat, but no indication of a break-in. When Murphy, who did not live with his wife, agreed to come to the police station for questioning, the police noticed a dark spot on his finger. Suspecting that the spot might be dried blood, and aware that strangulation often leaves evidence under the assailant's fingernails, the police requested permission to take a sample of the spot. When Murphy refused, and was seen trying to remove the blood, the police took the sample without a warrant. The samples were found to include fabric from the victim's nightgown as well as traces of her skin and blood. The Court upheld the search: "Murphy was motivated to attempt to destroy what evidence he could without attracting further attention. Considering the existence of probable cause, the very limited intrusion undertaken incident to the station house detention, and the ready destructibility of the evidence, we cannot say that this search violated the Fourth and Fourteenth Amendments." Mr. Justice Marshall concurred: "If the Fourth Amendment permits a stop-and-frisk, it also permits fingernail scrapings in the circumstances of this case." Mr. Justice Douglas dissented in part: "Scraping a man's fingernails is an invasion of that privacy and it is tolerable, constitutionally speaking, only if there is a warrant for a search or seizure issued by a magistrate on a showing of 'probable cause' that the suspect had committed the crime. Murphy could have been detained while one was sought; and that detention would have preserved the perishable evidence the police sought."

b. Seizure for Breathalyzer Test

In *Welsh v. Wisconsin*, 466 U.S. 740 (1984), the police received reports indicating that Welsh had been driving under the influence. When Welsh's stepdaughter answered the door of his home, the police entered and proceeded upstairs to Welsh's bedroom where they found him lying naked in bed. The police arrested Welsh and took him to the police station where he refused to submit to a breathalyzer test. The Court concluded that the police acted improperly:

Before the government may invade the sanctity of the home, the burden is on the government to demonstrate exigent circumstances that overcome the presumption of unreasonableness that attaches to all warrantless home entries. When the government's interest is only to arrest for a minor offense, that presumption of unreasonableness is difficult to rebut, and the government usually should be allowed to make such arrests only with a warrant issued upon probable cause by a neutral and detached magistrate. The claim of hot pursuit is unconvincing because there was no immediate or continuous pursuit of the petitioner from the scene of a crime. Moreover, because the petitioner had already arrived home, and had abandoned his car at the

FYI

In *United States v. Smith*, 470 F.2d 377 (D.C.Cir.1972), defendant was charged with assault with intent to commit rape against a six year-old girl who was raped and left bleeding. The police asked defendant to undergo a benzidine test "to see if there was a show of blood." The mechanics of the test were outlined, and defendant was advised that if the test results were positive he would be charged with the offense; if negative, he would be released. Defendant replied that "he had no fear about the test because he knew it would be negative." The test was performed and there was a positive reaction. The court held that the test results were properly admitted: "The search was reasonable since it was necessary to conduct the test as promptly as possible because of the ease with which the evidence could be destroyed by a thorough washing. The simplicity of the test makes it unnecessary to have it conducted by a physician. It is a chemical test not a medical test and was properly administered by a trained police technician."

scene of the accident, there was little remaining threat to the public safety. The only potential emergency claimed by the State was the need to ascertain the petitioner's blood-alcohol level. The State of Wisconsin has chosen to classify the first offense for driving while intoxicated as a noncriminal, civil forfeiture offense for which no imprisonment is possible. Given this expression of the State's interest, a warrantless home arrest cannot be upheld simply because evidence of the petitioner's blood-alcohol level might have dissipated while the police obtained a warrant.

Justice White dissented: "A test under which the existence of exigent circumstances turns on the perceived gravity of the crime would significantly hamper law enforcement and burden courts with pointless litigation concerning the nature and gradation of various crimes. Nevertheless, this Court has long recognized the compelling state interest in highway safety."

Food for Thought

Suppose that police officers are watching a warehouse and observe a worker carrying bundles from the warehouse to a large bonfire and throwing them into the blaze. The officers have probable cause to believe that the bundles contain marijuana. Because there is only one person carrying the bundles, the officers believe it will take hours to completely destroy the drugs. During that time the officers likely could obtain a warrant. Must the officers sit idly by and watch the destruction of evidence while they wait for a warrant? Would it matter, as in a drunk driving case, that the ever-diminishing quantity of drugs may have an impact on the severity of the crime and the length of the sentence?

Hypo 1: *Surgical Bullet Removal*

During a robbery of a shop, the assailant is wounded. Twenty minutes later, police find defendant eight blocks from the robbery scene suffering from a gunshot wound to the chest. He tells police that he was shot when a man tried to rob him. When defendant arrives at the emergency room, the victim of the robbery sees defendant, and exclaims "that's the man that shot me." The police decide that defendant's story of himself being a robbery victim is untrue. Since the bullet in defendant's stomach constitutes evidence, the state seeks an order forcing him to undergo surgery to remove the bullet (lodged under his left collarbone). Defendant objects to the procedure which would take 45 minutes and involve a three to four percent chance of temporary nerve damage, a one percent chance of permanent nerve damage, and a one-tenth of one percent chance of death. The surgeon states that a general anesthetic would be desirable for medical reasons, and that the risks described above derive from the anesthetic. In light of *Rochin* and *Schmerber*, may a court order defendant to undergo the surgical procedure under a general anesthetic for removal of the bullet lodged in his chest? What arguments might you make on defendant's behalf? How might the state respond? *See Winston v. Lee*, 470 U.S. 753 (1985).

Food for Thought

Using modern technology, the police have the ability to remotely access computers. Thus, an FBI agent in Washington, D.C., has the capacity to remotely access an individual's home computer in Kansas City, Missouri. The FBI has increasingly used such remote access techniques, and did so in connection with a "darknet" site called Playpen. The techniques allow the FBI to remotely install software on computers which sends their IP addresses back to the FBI. The FBI claims that the use of these techniques have led to some 350 arrests for the possession of child pornography, and allowed it to rescue some 186 children from sexual abuse. Can the warrantless use of such remote techniques be justified under the exigent circumstances exception? Must there at least be probable cause to believe that the person being surveilled is involved with child pornography? *See United States v. Wagner*, 951 F.3d 1232 (10th Cir. 2020).

Hypo 2: *Searching the Pregnant Woman*

Defendant is arrested at home on a warrant charging her with selling cocaine. During the arrest, the officers see paraphernalia used in the heating and administering of heroin (*e.g.*, hypodermic needles, an eyedropper, water, copper wire, a "cooker" (a burned bottle cap with a wad of cotton) and white residue). Two policewomen take defendant (clad only in a nightgown and underpants) into the bathroom to search her, and tell her to strip, bend over, and spread her buttocks. It is difficult for defendant to bend over because she is seven months pregnant. The police women then look into her privates and find nothing. Because of cramped quarters and poor lighting in the bathroom, the officers decide that defendant should be searched a second time at the station. The detectives have information from a "reliable informer" that defendant is known to carry heroin in her vagina. At the station, defendant is again forced to disrobe and bend over, and a policewomen uses rubber gloves to spread her buttocks. Are such procedures permissible? *See United States v. McCauley*, 385 F.Supp. 193 (E.D.Wis.1974).

Hypo 3: *Abdominal Surgery*

When a hand-held metal detector suggests the presence of metal on a prison inmate, prison guards subject the inmate to a search and eventually to a strip search. When the search reveals nothing, the inmate is subjected to an x-ray that seems to reveal the presence of a foreign object in his stomach. Are prison officials allowed to subject the inmate to abdominal surgery to determine the nature of the object? Would the surgery be permissible if the inmate had undergone two bowel movements neither of which revealed a foreign object? *See Sanchez v. Pereira-Castillo*, 590 F.3d 31 (1st Cir. 2009).

Hypo 4: *Swabbing the Arrestee's Private Parts*

At 2:30 a.m., responding to a distress call, police find a highly distressed naked woman (D.L.) who claims to have been forced to engage in oral sex with a "fat white guy" in his twenties, with "short, dark hair wearing no shirt, black pants and smelling of alcohol." D.L.'s face is injured, bruised and bloody, she has bruises to her stomach and back, and she has scrape marks on her arms and legs. The officers go to the scene of the alleged crime (a garage), and "observe that two chairs have been knocked over outside the access door and that there is female clothing, including a bra, a shirt and a woman's shoe as well as condom wrappers strewn about on the ground as though a struggle had occurred." They also see a pair of jeans hanging off a "make-shift bed on the floor of the garage," and "blood on the floor adjacent to the bed." Based on the statements of D.L., along with the evidence in the garage, the officers determine that they "have probable cause to believe that a criminal-sexual-conduct crime has occurred and that the suspect is inside a nearby house possibly destroying evidence." They arrest the man, place him in the back of a squad car, and notice that he has numerous scratches on his chest, stomach, back, arms, as well as blood on his hands, his shirt is inside-out, and his pants and belt are undone. The officers then swab respondent's hands to take a sample of the blood because they fear that it will be washed or rubbed off. Can the swabbing be justified under the exigent circumstances doctrine? *See State v. Lussier*, 770 N.W.2d 581 (Minn. App. 2009).

Hypo 5: *Probing for Cocaine*

After receiving a tip that Gray is in possession of crack cocaine, police arrest him with on a warrant. Gray is taken to jail where a strip search is conducted, but Gray is "not fully cooperative." The police then do an extensive, two-hour search of Gray's vehicle, which also turns up nothing. Gray is then taken out of the general population and strip-searched a second time. As a part of his strip search, he is instructed to squat, pull his buttocks apart, and cough, in order to dislodge anything that may be concealed in the anus. Gray will only "slightly bend at the knees and give a faint cough." In addition, the police conduct a second search of the scene where they stopped Gray, and jail personnel conduct strip searches of all inmates who were in Gray's holding cell with him. None of these searches turns up any drugs or other contraband. At this point, the police present Gray with some options: he can undergo a third strip search; he can be placed in a cell with a waterless toilet; or he can consent to a rectal x-ray examination. Gray refuses to consent to any of these options. Based on all of these events and their education, training, and experience, police believe that the "only place" Gray could be concealing the crack cocaine is in his rectum. Suppose that you are the judge assigned to hear the request for a warrant. The affidavit states that police suspect Gray of concealing crack cocaine in his "anal cavity," and request the right to examine this cavity using "recognized medical procedures." Should you grant the request? *See United States v. Gray*, 669 F.3d 556 (5th Cir. 2012).

Hypo 6: *More on Probing for Cocaine*

In the prior problem, suppose that you have granted the request for a warrant, and the police decide to subject Gray to an x-ray. Gray is uncooperative with the x-ray technician, and the technician is unable to "get a good picture with the portable x-ray." The technician tries again with a stationary x-ray machine, but Gray will not lie still and will not stay "where he is told." Eventually, the x-ray technician obtains a usable picture, and notices something that he thinks could either be a gas pocket or a foreign object. The police then subject Gray to a digital exam. Have the police acted properly under the circumstances? If the digital exam is inconclusive, can the police undertake a proctoscopic examination of Gray's rectum? Essentially, what they want to do is to inset an illuminated tube up the anal canal and into the rectum, fill the rectum with air, causing the rectum walls to distend so that they can be examined. In order to administer the exam, medical personnel will subject Gray to two sedatives that will be administered intravenously. Doctors believe that the risks associated with the sedatives are low, and Gray's cardiovascular status will be monitored throughout the examination. The sedatives carry with them a risk of respiratory depression or arrest. Proctoscopy also has associated risks, including pain and potential anal bleeding or perforation, and are not usually conducted on uncooperative patients. Is the procedure permissible? Should police first resort to other procedures (e.g., watch and wait, or an enema) that would not require sedation? *See United States v. Gray*, 669 F.3d 556 (5th Cir. 2012).

Hypo 7: *Cutting the Baggie off*

After receiving a report indicating that Edwards brandished a firearm, police officers locate Edwards on a residential street and detain him. Since Edwards did not make any movements characteristic of someone who is armed, or who is engaged in a drug transaction, the officers are not "too worried." Once a search warrant is issued for Edwards' arrest, the officers request a police van to transport Edwards to the station. While they are waiting for the van, the officers subject Edwards to a pat-down search that reveals nothing. When the van arrives, the officers decide to search Edwards a second time before placing him in the van. While three male officers surround Edwards, one officer unfastens Edwards' belt, loosens it, and pulls Edwards' pants and underwear six or seven inches away from his body. The officers direct a flashlight beam inside both the front and the back of Edwards' underwear, and they notice a plastic sandwich baggie tied in a knot around Edwards' penis that appears to contain smaller blue ziplock baggies which contain "a white rocklike substance." Based on his training and experience, the officer concludes that the baggie and its contents are consistent with the packaging or distribution of a controlled substance. Did the officers act properly in examining Edwards so thoroughly? May the officers cut the baggie off of Edwards' penis with a knife? *See United States v. Edwards*, 666 F.3d 877 (4th Cir. 2011).

Food for Thought

Two people, who had been at defendant's home drinking tequila the evening before, got sick and were taken to the hospital. After the police learned that defendant had not gone to work that day, police went to defendant's home to check on his well-being. At the house, the police persuaded defendant to go to the hospital to "be checked out." After defendant left, the police entered the house and searched the tequila which was found to contain a date rape drug. Was it appropriate for the police to enter the house under these circumstances? *See Commonwealth v. Kaeppeler*, 42 N.E.3d 1090 (Mass. 2015).

Executive Summary

Warrant Requirement. The failure to obtain a search warrant is unreasonable under the Fourth Amendment unless the searching officers are acting pursuant to one or more of the recognized exceptions to the Warrant Requirement.

Affidavits. Search warrants are usually obtained from a neutral magistrate who must find probable cause to exist based on the information presented to the court in sworn (usually written) affidavits.

Defective Warrants. A search warrant is defective if it is not supported by probable cause set out in a supporting affidavit "on its face." A search warrant can also be challenged as defective by "going behind" the affidavit and establishing that the affiant included false information necessary to establish probable cause (or omitted information necessary to establish probable cause) recklessly or intentionally. Challenges to the supporting affidavits take place in pre-trial "*Franks*" hearings."

Particularity. Search warrants must particularly describe the place to be searched and the things to be seized. The description must be detailed enough to insure that the executing officers can reasonably ascertain and identify the place to be searched and the things to be seized. A search warrant lacking in particularity is unconstitutionally defective.

Search of Wrong Premises. The mistaken search of the wrong premises with a search warrant is not unconstitutional if the executing officers did not know or should not have known that the premises described in the warrant were described too broadly, and where the officers leave immediately when they learn that they are in the wrong place.

Knock & Announce Requirement. In the absence of exigent circumstances, officers executing a search warrant must a) announce their presence at the search premises; b) announce their purpose, i.e. that they have a warrant; and c) delay prior to entry for a sufficient time to permit the occupants to open the door. Typically, a delay of 15 to 20 seconds will suffice. "No-knock" entries are permitted, however, where the police have a specific reasonable suspicion that knocking and announcing would be dangerous, futile, or could lead to the destruction of evidence. In any event, the federal exclusionary rule does not apply to knock-and-announce violations.

Definition of the Term "Search." For many years, in defining the term "search" for purposes of the Fourth Amendment, the Court focused on whether a governmental had trespassed in, or intruded on, a constitutionally protected area. Constitutionally protected areas include a dwelling and the curtilage land around it. Protected areas include conversations inside a home, to information that a monitored tracking beeper that is tracked inside the home, to heat emanating from a home as captured in a thermal imaging device from outside the home, and to other information regarding the interior of a home that could not otherwise have been obtained without a physical intrusion.

"Reasonable Expectation of Privacy" Test. Beginning in the 1960s, the Court supplemented the "constitutionally protected area" approach with a "reasonable expectation of privacy" (REOP) test. In other words, when the government violates an individual's REOP, there is a search within the meaning of the Fourth Amendment. A REOP has been recognized in conversations one holds in a public telephone booth that the police record with a device from outside the booth, and in a bus passenger's luggage placed in overhead rack and squeezed to determine its contents. Otherwise, outside the home, the Court has somewhat narrowly construed the REOP test.

Constitutionally Protected Areas & Physical Trespass Intrusions. Both a home and the curtilage land around it are constitutionally protected areas, and therefore are protected against the physical intrusion of a government agent's entry and visual surveillance on the ground. Conversations in the home are protected from recording with a device that involves a physical intrusion. While a person's movement by car on public streets is generally not protected against monitoring by a GPS device, it is protected when the device is attached to the car by means of a physical intrusion.

Absence of a REOP. Over the years, the Court has construed the REOP test rather narrowly. Even in the protected area of the home, there is no Fourth Amendment protection from the recording of conversations by a government informant. Similarly, curtilage is protected only from physical entry on the ground, not from aerial surveillance from a helicopter or airplane flying in navigable air space. There is no REOP with regard to open fields, and therefore there is no protection against a government agent's entry and visual surveillance of open fields. There is no REOP protection from a search of garbage placed on a curb in front of a dwelling. Similarly, a narcotics-detection dog may sniff luggage in a public place or sniff the exterior of an automobile during a roadblock or traffic stop. Nor is there a valid privacy expectation for freedom from surveillance by means of a tracking beeper to monitor a person's movement by car on public streets.

Continuing Vitality of the Trespass Test. Based on the *Jones* case, the Court still uses the old physical trespass test in deciding whether the government has engaged in a search.

Recent Decisions on Privacy. In recent decisions, the Court seems somewhat more sympathetic to finding the existence of a search when the police use technologies to spy on citizens. For example, the government may not use thermal technology to determine the level of heat emanating from a home, cannot routinely go through an individual's cell phone incident to an arrest, and cannot access cell site historical data without a warrant.

The Role of Probable Cause. Probable cause is an integral part of the Fourth Amendment's prohibition against unreasonable searches and seizures. In order to obtain a warrant to search, among other things, a magistrate must find probable cause to believe that the fruits instrumentalities or evidence of crime can be found at the place to be searched. For an arrest warrant, there must be probable cause to believe that a crime has been committed and that the person to be arrested committed it. Some exceptions to the warrant requirement also require proof of probable cause.

The Meaning of Probable Cause. Applied literally, "probable cause" requires that a conclusion be "more probable than not." However, the courts have rarely applied the probable cause requirement literally. The Court has indicated that the probable cause determination is not "technical," but instead deals with "probabilities" and the "factual and practical considerations of everyday life on which reasonable and prudent men, not legal technicians, act." The question is whether there are sufficient "facts and circumstances" to lead a reasonable person to conclude that there is "reasonably trustworthy information" to support the conclusions reached.

The *Aguilar-Spinelli* Test. In *Spinelli v. United States*, 393 U.S. 410 (1969), the Court imposed a two-prong test for evaluating whether an informant's tip provided the police with probable cause. That test, called the *Aguilar-Spinelli* test because it was partly based on the holding in *Aguilar v. Texas*, 378 U.S. 108 (1964), provides that, in order for the police to rely on an informant's tip, that must find that the tip must set forth the "underlying circumstances" necessary to evaluate the factual accuracy of the tip, and must contain information suggesting that the informant is "credible" and "reliable."

The *Draper* Case. In *Draper v. United States*, 358 U.S. 307 (1959), the Court relaxed the "basis of information" prong of the *Aguilar-Spinelli* test. In that case, although the police had information regarding the informant's credibility (he had given correct information to the police in the past), he failed to state how he had obtained his information. However, the tip did contain a degree of detail, and the police were able to verify that detail, so the Court concluded that probable cause existed: "Independent police work case corroborated much more than one small detail." The Court concluded that the police verification suggested that, if the informant were correct about the various items of detail, then it was likely that he was correct about the ultimate conclusion (that the suspect would be carrying illegal drugs).

Gates' **Modification of the** *Aguilar-Spinelli* **Test.** In *Illinois v. Gates*, 462 U.S. 213 (1983), the Court modified the *Aguilar-Spinelli* test. That case involved a tip from an anonymous informant so that the police did not know anything about the informant's credibility. Likewise, the tip did not reveal how the informant came by the information so that neither prong of the test was satisfied. Although the Court suggested that an informant's "veracity," "reliability" and "basis of knowledge" are all "highly relevant in determining the value of his report," the Court concluded that they should be used simply to "illuminate the commonsense, practical question whether there is 'probable cause' to believe that contraband or evidence is located in a particular place." In other words, the Court did not regard the probable cause determination as "technical, but as sweeping in the factual and practical considerations of everyday life on which reasonable and prudent men, not legal technicians, act." In *Gates*, the Court concluded that probable cause existed even though neither prong of the *Aguilar-Spinelli* test was satisfied. Instead, the Court looked at the "totality of circumstances" and simply considered the *Aguilar-Spinelli* test as part of that analysis.

Probable Cause & Canine Drug-Sniffing. In *Florida v. Harris*, 568 U.S. 237 (2013), the Court concluded that the police could establish probable cause based on the "alert" of a drug-detection dog. In that case, although the dog had purportedly misfired during a couple of traffic stops, he had certified as reliable during his training, and the Court concluded that the training records were sufficient, in and of themselves, to prove the dog's reliability.

The Warrant Preference & Warrantless Searches. Despite the preference for a warrant, the Court has established numerous exceptions to the warrant requirement. The Court distinguishes between warrantless arrests and warrantless searches. Even though warrantless arrests (and seizures) are generally permissible, warrantless searches are disfavored and are "*per se* unreasonable subject only to a few specifically established and well-delineated exceptions." *Katz v. United States*, 389 U.S. 347, 357 (1967).

Plain View Exception. The "plain view" exception is an often-used exception to the warrant requirement. When the police are conducting a lawful search, and are in a place where they have the right to be, this exception allows them to observe and sometimes to seize items that they find in plain view. To be in plain view, the criminal nature of the item must be "immediately apparent." An item is not in "plain view" if the police must move it to determine its contraband status, but drugs hidden in an opaque balloon (of a type commonly used to carry drugs) are considered to be in "plain view."

Search Incident to Legal Arrest Exception. The search incident to legal arrest exception is one of the oldest and most well-established exceptions to the warrant requirement. It provides that, when the police make a legal arrest, they have the right to make a search incident to that arrest. The police can only search the area within the individual's "immediate control."

Requirements for a Valid Arrest. An arrest is the most serious form of seizure, and occurs when the police take a suspect into custody. The requirements for a valid arrest were articulated in *United States v. Watson*, 423 U.S. 411 (1976). In that case, the Court indicated that a peace officer is "permitted to arrest without a warrant for a misdemeanor or felony committed in his presence as well as for a felony not committed in his presence if there was reasonable ground for making the arrest." In *Atwater v. City of Lago Vista*, 532 U.S. 318 (2001), the Court held that police can make warrantless misdemeanor arrests "for all sorts of relatively minor offenses unaccompanied by violence." In evaluating the validity of an arrest, the courts should focus on the objective facts before the officer, and should not delve into the arresting officer's subjective intentions.

Arrests in Special Situations. In *Payton v. New York*, 445 U.S. 573 (1980), the Court held that, absent exigent circumstances, the police may not arrest an individual at home without a warrant. In *Steagald v. United States*, 451 U.S. 204 (1981), the Court held that a law enforcement officer may not search for the subject of an arrest warrant in the home of a third party without first obtaining a search warrant. *See also Minnesota v. Olson*, 495 U.S. 91 (1990).

Using Deadly Force to Effect an Arrest. In *Tennessee v. Garner*, 471 U.S. 1 (1985), the Court held that the Constitution prohibits the use of deadly force to make an arrest except when the arrestee "poses a threat of serious physical harm either to the officer or to others." In *Garner*, the suspect's youth, slightness, and lack of a weapon suggested that he did not pose a threat of physical danger to himself or others. In *Scott v. Harris*, 550 U.S. 372 (2007), the Court held that a police officer could attempt to stop a fleeing motorist (who refused to yield to pursuing police) by ramming the motorist's car from behind even though the ramming ultimately rendered the motorist a paraplegic. The Court rejected the notion that the officer had used deadly force in contravention of *Garner*.

Search Incident to Arrest of Automobiles. In *Arizona v. Gant*, 556 U.S. 332 (2009), the Court redefined the search incident to arrest exception as applied to someone who is arrested while driving in an automobile. In a prior case, *New York v. Belton*, 453 U.S. 454 (1981), the Court had held that when an officer lawfully arrests "the occupant of an automobile, he may, as a contemporaneous incident of that arrest, search the passenger compartment of the automobile" and any containers therein." *Gant* overruled *Belton* and held that the police may only search a car when the arrestee is unsecured and within reaching distance of the passenger compartment at the time of the search, or when it is "reasonable to believe evidence relevant to the crime of arrest might be found in the vehicle."

Cell Phone Searches Incident to Arrest. In *Riley v. California*, 134 U.S. 2473 (2014), because of the privacy implications, the Court held that the police do not have *carte blanche* to go through the contents of a cell phone incident to arrest. The Court concluded that "a warrant is generally required before such a search." "Even though the search incident to arrest exception does not apply to cell phones, other case-specific exceptions may still justify a warrantless search of a particular phone. Such exigencies could include the need to prevent the imminent destruction of evidence in individual cases, to pursue a fleeing suspect, and to assist persons who are seriously injured or who are threatened with imminent injury."

Booking Search Exception. Before jail or prison officials actually admit an individual to the inmate population, they will usually conduct a "booking search" for weapons or contraband that the individual may be carrying. In *Florence v. Board of Chosen Freeholders of the County of Burlington*, 566 U.S. 318 (2012), the Court concluded that jail or prison officials have the right to impose strip searches as part of these booking procedures. In *Maryland v. King*, 569 U.S. 435 (2013), the Court held that jail and prison officials could also require those incarcerated to submit to DNA analysis in order to verify their identities.

The Automobile Exception. The automobile exception is one of the oldest exceptions to the warrant requirement. It provides that, when the police have probable cause to believe that an automobile contains the fruits, instrumentalities or evidence of crime, they may search the vehicle without a warrant. The exception is justified by the mobility of vehicles (the circumstances giving rise to probable cause can arise unexpectedly, and vehicles can quickly disappear), as well as the fact that they are accompanied by a "diminished expectation of privacy." The scope of an automobile search allows the police to search anywhere in the vehicle that they have probable cause to believe that the fruits, instrumentalities or evidence of crime can be found. The exception includes the right to open closed containers if the police have probable cause to believe that contraband can be found in those containers.

Inventory Exception. There is also an "inventory" exception to the warrant requirement. The most common inventory search occurs when the police impound a vehicle. Inventory searches serve to protect an owner's property while it is in the custody of the police, to insure against claims of lost, stolen, or vandalized property, and to guard the police from danger. An inventory search can extend to the entire vehicle.

However, courts will sometimes focus on whether the jurisdiction has established policies or procedures regarding when vehicles can be impounded, and the scope of inventory searches.

Consent Searches. The consent exception is not really an "exception" to the warrant requirement. Any constitutional right can be waived, and citizens can waive their Fourth Amendment right to be free from governmental searches and seizures. The courts have struggled to determine what constitutes "consent." The question is whether the consent was voluntarily given or whether it was coerced. Issues of consent are determined by considering the totality of circumstances. Although an individual can consent even though an individual is unaware of the right to refuse consent, unawareness is a relevant consideration in the analysis.

Authority to Consent. Ordinarily, one would assume that only those who own or possess property would have the authority to consent to a search of that property. However, in *Illinois v. Rodriguez*, 497 U.S. 177 (1990), the Court held that a woman's consent to search an apartment was valid even though she did not live in the apartment (she used to live there and had a key without the owner's knowledge), if the police acted reasonably in relying on her purported consent: "The Constitution is no more violated when officers enter without a warrant because they reasonably (though erroneously) believe that the person who has consented to their entry is a resident of the premises, than it is violated when they enter without a warrant because they reasonably (though erroneously) believe they are in pursuit of a violent felon who is about to escape."

Objecting Co-Tenants. In *Georgia v. Randolph*, 547 U.S. 103 (2006), a wife granted the police consent to search their home in the presence of her objecting husband. The Court held that, even though both spouses would ordinarily be entitled to consent to a search since they have common authority over the premises, "shared social expectations" would not permit entry when one spouse was present and objecting" "A caller standing at the door of shared premises would have no confidence that one occupant's invitation was a sufficiently good reason to enter when a fellow tenant stood there saying, 'stay out.'" In the Court's subsequent decision in *Fernandez v. California*, 571 U.S. 292 (2014), the Court held that the other tenant had the authority to consent after the objecting tenant was removed from the premises (in that case, he was removed after arrest by the police).

The Administrative Inspection Exception. In *Camara v. Municipal Court*, 387 U.S. 523 (1967), the Court held that administrative inspections are subject to the Fourth Amendment's requirement of a warrant based on probable cause. However, the Court redefined the concept of "probable cause" by providing that the agency only need prove the existence of a reasonable administrative inspection plan, and show that it is time to search the particular premises under that plan, in order to establish probable cause to obtain a warrant. In a number of cases, the Court has held that certain "highly regulated industries" (e.g., firearms and liquor sellers) can be subjected to warrantless searches. Hotels do not qualify as "highly regulated industries."

Stop & Frisk Exception. In *Terry v. State of Ohio*, 392 U.S. 1 (1968), the Court articulated the "stop and frisk" exception to the warrant requirement. In doing so, the Court balanced the "governmental interest" or "need" against the level of intrusion on the individual, and held that when "a police officer observes unusual conduct which leads him reasonably to conclude in light of his experience that criminal activity may be afoot and that the persons with whom he is dealing may be armed and presently dangerous, where in the course of investigating this behavior he identifies himself as a policeman and makes reasonable inquiries, and where nothing in the initial stages of the encounter serves to dispel his reasonable fear for his own or others' safety, he is entitled for the protection of himself and others in the area to conduct a carefully limited search of the outer clothing of such persons in an attempt to discover weapons which might be used to assault him."

Strip Searches of High School Students. In *Safford Unified School District v. Redding*, 557 U.S. 364 (2009), although the Court held that school officials could search a high school student's backpack in an effort to find prescription strength Ibuprofen, but could not subject her to a strip search: "The meaning of such a search, and the degradation its subject may reasonably feel, place a search that intrusive in a category of its own demanding its own specific suspicions."

Other Investigative Stops. In addition to authorizing a "stop and frisk," in appropriate situations, *Terry* also authorizes the police to make "investigative stops" which are a form of seizure. The Court has recognized many different types of seizures ranging from an investigatory stop to an arrest. These seizures are subject to differing constitutional requirements. Most seizures are investigative in nature and can be relatively brief. Roadside stops usually fit this description. However, the police also "seize" individuals for fingerprinting, lineups or interrogation purposes. In *United States v. Mendenhall*, 446 U.S. 544 (1980), the Court held that the police may make investigative stops when they have a reasonable suspicion to believe that a suspect is involved in criminal activity. Balancing the need for the search against the level of intrusion, the Court justified these stops on the basis that they are generally of relatively brief duration and relatively less intrusive.

Defining an Investigative Stop. In *Mendenhall*, the Court held that an investigative stop occurs when a reasonable person in the suspect's position would not feel free to leave. However, if the suspect resists or flees, *California v. Hodari D.*, 499 U.S. 621 (1991), held that there is an investigative seizure "when the officer, by means of physical force or show of authority, has in some way restrained the liberty of a citizen."

Custodial Questioning. If the police wish to force an individual to go to the police station for questioning, or to participate in a lineup or to be fingerprinted, probable cause (rather than reasonable suspicion) is required.

Length of Investigative Stops. In *United States v. Place*, 462 U.S. 696 (1983), the Court held that the police exceeded the scope of a permissible investigative stop when they detained Place's luggage for 45 minutes (to allow a drug sniffing dog to be brought up) and then detained the luggage for 48 hours in order to obtain a warrant (after the dog alerted to it): "The length of the detention of Place's luggage precludes a conclusion that the seizure was reasonable in the absence of probable cause." The Court has made it clear that an investigative stop can be justified based on a reasonable suspicion because it "must be temporary and last no longer than is necessary to effectuate the purpose of the stop."

Demanding Identification. In *Hiibel v. Sixth Judicial District Court*, 542 U.S. 177 (2004), the Court held that the police may demand identification from individuals in certain situations: "It is clear in this case that the request for identification was 'reasonably related in scope to the circumstances which justified' the stop. The officer's request was a commonsense inquiry, not an effort to obtain an arrest for failure to identify after a *Terry* stop yielded insufficient evidence. The stop, the request, and the State's requirement of a response did not contravene the guarantees of the Fourth Amendment."

Protective Sweeps. In various situations, the Court has held that the police may conduct protective sweeps of homes to make sure that there are no threats to their safety. For example, when the police execute an arrest warrant, they may take steps to ensure "that the house in which a suspect is being, or has just been, arrested is not harboring other persons who are dangerous and who could unexpectedly launch an attack." The permitted sweep is "not a full search of the premises, but only a cursory inspection of those spaces where a person may be found. The sweep lasts no longer than is necessary to dispel the reasonable suspicion of danger and in any event no longer than it takes to complete the arrest and depart the premises." The Court has allowed the police to temporarily detain the occupant of a home while executing a warrant to search the home.

Police Stops of Automobiles. In *Delaware v. Prouse*, 440 U.S. 648 (1979), the Court held that the police may not stop motorists simply to check their driver's license and registration absent a reasonable suspicion that they are involved in criminal activity. The Court concluded that the primary method for enforcing traffic and vehicle safety regulations is by responding to observed violations of traffic laws. The Court was concerned about abuse of discretion if police officers were free to pull drivers over at will.

Roadblocks. In *Michigan Dept. of State Police v. Sitz*, 496 U.S. 444 (1990), and *United States v. Martinez-Fuerte*, 428 U.S. 543 (1976), the Court upheld brief, suspicionless seizures at highway checkpoints for the purposes of combating drunk driving and intercepting illegal immigrants. However, in *City of Indianapolis v. Edmond*, 531 U.S. 32 (2000), the Court invalidated a drug interdiction checkpoint, holding that it had "never approved a checkpoint program whose primary purpose was to detect evidence of ordinary criminal wrongdoing." In *Illinois v. Lidster*, 540 U.S. 419 (2004), the Court upheld a checkpoint designed to locate potential witnesses to a fatal accident involving a bicyclist: "The stops took place about one week after the hit-and-run accident, on the same highway near the location of the accident, and at about the same time of night. Police used the stops to obtain information from drivers, some of whom might well have been in the vicinity of the crime at the time it occurred."

The Border Exception. The government has always exercised broad authority to stop individuals seeking to enter the United States, to demand identification, and to search their persons and effects to make sure that contraband is not being smuggled. For example, in *United States v. Flores-Montano*, 541 U.S. 149 (2004), the Court held that border patrol agents could dismantle an automobile's gas tank to determine whether illegal drugs were being carried in the trunk.

Special Needs Searches. In a number of cases, the Court has developed a "special needs" exception to the warrant requirement. This exception, which especially applies in safety and administrative cases, allows the government to search or seize without probable cause and sometimes even without reasonable suspicion. For example, in *Skinner v. Railway Labor Executives' Association*, 489 U.S. 602 (1989), the Court upheld Federal Railroad Administration (FRA) regulations that required blood and urine tests of railroad employees involved in "major" train accidents, and authorizing railroads to administer breath and urine tests to employees who violate certain safety rules. In *Board of Education v. Earls*, 536 U.S. 822 (2002), the Court upheld mandatory drug testing for students involved in extracurricular activities. However, in *Ferguson v. City of Charleston*, 532 U.S. 67 (2001), the Court struck down a hospital's prenatal urine testing program that tested maternity patients for usage of illegal drugs and turned the results over to the police for prosecution. Although the patients agreed to the test, they were unaware that the results might be turned over to the police. The Court struck the program down: "The reasonable expectation of privacy enjoyed by the typical patient undergoing diagnostic tests in a hospital is that the results of those tests will not be shared with nonmedical personnel without her consent. In none of our prior cases was there any intrusion upon that kind of expectation."

Exigent Circumstances. The police can also dispense with a warrant when they are faced with "exigent circumstances." For example, there is a long line of cases which suggest that the police may make a warrantless entry into a home in order to prevent the imminent destruction of evidence. In addition, the police are regarded as having a "community caretaking" function, and are sometimes allowed to make warrantless entry into buildings when there is "an objectively reasonable basis for believing," that "a person within the house is in need of immediate aid."

Due Process Limitations. In *Rochin v. California*, 342 U.S. 165 (1952), the Court held that the police could not forcibly extract evidence from an individual's stomach (the police believed that Rochin had swallowed morphine to prevent the police from seizing it) by forcing emetic solution into his stomach. The Court concluded that the police conduct "shocks the conscience." In general, although the police do not need a warrant to force someone to take a breath test, designed to determine whether a driver is intoxicated, a warrant is generally now required for blood draws designed to test the level of alcohol in a driver's blood.

Major Themes

a. Warrants Uncommon—Although there is a constitutional warrant preference and a constitutional warrant requirement, in actuality, the overwhelming majority of searches and seizures occur—lawfully—without a warrant, pursuant to one of the recognized exceptions to the warrant requirement.

b. Coexisting Tests for Recognition of Protected Interests—Before 1967, the Court used the physical trespass test and provided Fourth Amendment protection only when a government surveillance method constituted a physical intrusion into a constitutionally protected area. In 1967, the Court endorsed a supplementary test in *Katz* to be used for determining whether Fourth Amendment protection should be recognized in scenarios that did not satisfy the physical trespass requirement. Under *Katz*, a person must exhibit an actual subjective expectation of privacy, and that expectation objectively must be recognized by society as reasonable. The Court continues to employ both tests today.

c. Complexity of *Katz* Test—In assessing whether an expectation of privacy is reasonable under *Katz*, the Court has considered a variety of factors. Some precedents find that no reasonable expectation exists when a defendant voluntarily conveys information to a third party or knowingly exposes the information to the public. Other precedents reach the same result when a government search technique discloses only limited information and requires no exposure of possessions. The dog sniff precedents focus the question whether the government surveillance method produces information that would previously have been unknowable without a physical intrusion, or whether relevant common law history supports a social consensus about privacy values.

d. The Probable Cause Requirement—The Fourth Amendment requires that all warrants be based (among other things) on probable cause, and some exceptions to the warrant requirement (e.g., the automobile exception) also require probable cause. "Probable cause" is not a technical term, but instead involves a commonsense determination regarding whether reasonable cause exists to believe that the fruits, instrumentalities or evidence of crime can be found at the place to be searched, or that the person to be arrested committed a crime.

e. **The Warrant Preference**—Although the courts impose a warrant "preference," meaning that warrantless searches are presumptively unconstitutional, the Fourth Amendment does not require a warrant as a precondition for a valid search. The Fourth Amendment requires only that searches be "reasonable."

f. **Exceptions to the Warrant Requirement**—Despite the warrant preference, there are multiple exceptions to the warrant requirement. Indeed, there are so many exceptions that they almost swallow the warrant preference.

For More Information

- JOHN BURKOFF, SEARCH WARRANT LAW DESKBOOK (semi-annual editions) (Thomson Reuters).

- THOMAS K. CLANCY, THE FOURTH AMENDMENT: ITS HISTORY AND INTERPRETATION (2d ed. 2013).

- Andrew Guthrie Ferguson, *The "Smart" Fourth Amendment*, 102 CORNELL L. REV. 547 (2017).

- Brandon Garrett & Seth Stoughton, *A Tactical Fourth Amendment*, 103 VA. L. REV. 211 (2017).

- Orin S. Kerr, *The Effect of Legislation on Fourth Amendment Protection*, 115 MICH. L. REV. 1117 (2017).

- Orin Kerr, *The Fourth Amendment and the Global Internet*, 67 STAN. L. REV. 285 (2015).

- WAYNE LaFAVE, SEARCH AND SEIZURE: A TREATISE ON THE FOURTH AMENDMENT (6th ed. 2017).

- Christopher Slobogin, *Policing as Administration*, 165 U. PA. L. REV. 91 (2016).

- RUSSELL L. WEAVER, JOHN M. BURKOFF, CATHERINE HANCOCK & STEVEN I. FRIEDLAND, PRINCIPLES OF CRIMINAL PROCEDURE Ch. 4 (7th ed. 2021).

Test Your Knowledge

To assess your understanding of the material in this chapter, click here to take a quiz.

CHAPTER 5

Entrapment

By the time the Supreme Court recognized the criminal law defense of entrapment in federal cases, the defense had been recognized by state courts for over 50 years and was supported by federal court precedents. However, in its earliest entrapment decision in *Sorrells v. United States, infra*, the Court was split regarding the definition and scope of the defense, and the same division marked the Court's opinion in *Sherman v. United States* (1958). That split remains evident today. The federal courts and a majority of state courts have adopted the *Sherman* majority's requirements for the entrapment defense, while a minority of state courts have chosen to follow the approach of the concurring justices in *Sherman*.

A. The Entrapment Defense

The so-called "subjective test" for the entrapment defense was established in *Sorrells v. United States* (1932) and reaffirmed in the following case. Consider the priorities expressed in the majority opinion and compare the views of the concurring justices. What reasons may explain why the subjective test is sufficiently controversial to provoke resistance among the state courts that adhere to the objective test instead?

1. Elements of Entrapment

Sherman v. United States

356 U.S. 369 (1958).

MR. CHIEF JUSTICE WARREN delivered the opinion of the Court.

[After Kalchinian was arrested for narcotics crimes, he agreed to act as a government informer and to identify others who could be persuaded to sell him drugs.] In late August 1951, he first met petitioner at a doctor's office where both were being treated to be cured of narcotics addiction. Several accidental meetings followed, either at the doctor's office or at the pharmacy where both filled their prescriptions. From mere greetings, conversation progressed to a discussion of mutual experiences and problems, including their attempts to overcome addiction to narcotics. Finally, Kalchinian asked petitioner if he knew of a good source of narcotics. He asked petitioner to supply him with a source because he was not responding to treatment and was suffering withdrawal symptoms. Petitioner tried to avoid the issue. Not until after repetitions of the request, predicated on Kalchinian's presumed suffering, did petitioner finally acquiesce. Several times thereafter he obtained a quantity of narcotics which he shared with Kalchinian. Each time petitioner told Kalchinian that the total cost of narcotics he obtained was twenty-five dollars and that Kalchinian owed him fifteen dollars. The informer thus bore the cost of his share of the narcotics plus the taxi and other expenses necessary to obtain the drug. After several such sales Kalchinian informed agents of the Bureau of Narcotics that he had another seller for them. On three occasions during November 1951 Government agents observed petitioner give narcotics to Kalchinian in return for money supplied by the Government. At the trial the factual issue was whether the informer had convinced an otherwise unwilling person to commit a criminal act or whether petitioner was already predisposed to commit the act and exhibited only the natural hesitancy of one acquainted with the narcotics trade. The issue of entrapment went to the jury, and a conviction resulted. Petitioner was sentenced to imprisonment for ten years. The Court of Appeals for the Second Circuit affirmed.

In *Sorrells v. United States*, 287 U.S. 435 (1932), this Court firmly recognized the defense of entrapment in the federal courts. The intervening years have in no way detracted from the principles underlying that decision. Criminal activity is such that stealth and strategy are necessary weapons in the arsenal of the police officer. However, "A different question is presented when the criminal design originates with the officials of the government, and they implant in the mind of an innocent person the disposition to commit the alleged offense and induce its commission in order that they may prosecute." The stealth and strategy become as objectionable police methods as the coerced confession and the unlawful search. Congress could not have intended that its statutes were to be enforced by tempting innocent persons into violations. However, the fact that government agents "merely afford opportunities or facilities for the commission of the offense does not" constitute entrapment. Entrapment occurs only when the criminal conduct was "the product of the creative activity" of law enforcement officials. To determine whether entrapment has been established, a line must be drawn between the trap for the unwary innocent and the trap for the unwary criminal.

We conclude from the evidence that entrapment was established as a matter of law. Petitioner was induced by Kalchinian. In Kalchinian's own words we are told of the accidental, yet recurring, meetings, the ensuing conversations concerning mutual experiences in regard to narcotics addiction, and then of Kalchinian's resort to sympathy. One request was not enough, for Kalchinian tells us that additional ones were necessary to overcome, first, petitioner's refusal, then his evasiveness, and then his hesitancy in order to achieve capitulation. Kalchinian not only procured a source of narcotics but apparently also induced petitioner to return to the habit. Finally, assured of a catch, Kalchinian informed the authorities so that they could close the net. Although he was not being paid, Kalchinian was an active government informer who had but recently been the instigator of at least two other prosecutions. Undoubtedly the impetus for such achievements was the fact that Kalchinian was himself under criminal charges for illegally selling narcotics and had not yet been sentenced. It makes no difference that the sales for which petitioner was convicted occurred after a series of sales. They were not independent acts subsequent to the inducement but part of a course of conduct which was the product of the inducement.

The Government sought to overcome the defense of entrapment by claiming that petitioner evinced a "ready complaisance" to accede to Kalchinian's request. Aside from a record of past convictions, the Government's case is unsupported. There is no evidence that petitioner himself was in the trade. When his apartment was searched after arrest, no

> **Take Note**
>
> Kalchinian ultimately received a suspended sentence in 1952, after the federal prosecutor informed the judge that Kalchinian had fulfilled his agreement to cooperate with the Government.

narcotics were found. There is no significant evidence that petitioner even made a profit on any sale to Kalchinian. The Government's characterization of petitioner's hesitancy to Kalchinian's request as the natural wariness of the criminal cannot fill the evidentiary void.

The Government sought to show that petitioner was ready and willing to sell narcotics should the opportunity present itself, based on petitioner's record of two past narcotics convictions. In 1942 petitioner was convicted of illegally selling narcotics; in 1946 he was convicted of illegally possessing them. However, a nine-year-old sales conviction and a five-year-old possession conviction are insufficient to prove petitioner had a readiness to sell narcotics at the time Kalchinian approached him, particularly when we must assume he was trying to overcome the narcotics habit at the time.

> **Food for Thought**
>
> One way to prove predisposition is to demonstrate a defendant's ready response to an inducement. What types of evidence may provide proof of such readiness that is synonymous with predisposition, as indicated in the *Sherman* opinion? Why did the Court conclude that the evidence was insufficient in *Sherman* to justify the jury's finding of predisposition, so that a finding of entrapment was required as a matter of law?

The case at bar illustrates an evil which the defense of entrapment is designed to overcome. The government informer entices someone attempting to avoid narcotics not only into carrying out an illegal sale but also into returning to the habit of use. Selecting the proper time, the informer then tells the government agent. The set-up is accepted by the agent without even a question as to the manner in which the informer encountered the seller. Thus the Government plays on the weaknesses of an innocent party and beguiles him into committing crimes which he otherwise would not have attempted. Law enforcement does not require methods such as this.

Food for Thought

The *Sherman* majority assumed that if the Government could have shown the defendant's predisposition, then the same successful scheme to set him up would not be "an evil" that required the remedy of acquittal based on the entrapment defense. What arguments could be used to justify this view? What arguments could be used to criticize it?

The judgment of the Court of Appeals is reversed and the case is remanded to the District Court with instructions to dismiss the indictment.

MR. JUSTICE FRANKFURTER, whom MR. JUSTICE DOUGLAS, MR. JUSTICE HARLAN, and MR. JUSTICE BRENNAN join, concurring in the result.

It is surely sheer fiction to suggest that "Congress could not have intended that its statutes were to be enforced by tempting innocent persons into violations." The courts refuse to convict an entrapped defendant, not because his conduct falls outside the proscription of the statute, but because, even if his guilt be admitted, the methods employed on behalf of the Government to bring about conviction cannot be countenanced. As Mr. Justice Holmes said in *Olmstead v. United States*, 277 U.S. 438, 470 (1925) (dissenting), in another connection, "For my part I think it a less evil that some criminals should escape than that the government should play an ignoble part." Public confidence in the fair and honorable administration of justice, upon which ultimately depends the rule of law, is the transcending value at stake.

The crucial question is whether the police conduct revealed in the particular case falls below standards for the proper use of governmental power. Of course in every case of this kind the intention that the particular crime be committed originates with the police, and without their inducement the crime would not have occurred. But it is perfectly clear that where the police in effect simply furnished the opportunity for the commission of the crime, that this is not enough to enable the defendant to escape conviction.

Make the Connection

Justice Holmes dissented in *Olmstead* from the Court's ruling that no Fourth Amendment "search" occurred when agents inserted wiretaps into telephone wires, given the lack of "actual physical invasion" into a "constitutionally protected area." He observed the federal agents in *Olmstead* violated a state criminal law, and that "the Government should not itself foster and pay for other crimes, when they are the means by which the evidence is to be obtained."

The intention referred to must be a predisposition to commit, whenever the opportunity should arise, crimes of the kind solicited, and in proof of such a predisposition evidence has often been admitted to show the defendant's reputation, criminal activities, and prior disposition. The danger of prejudice in such a situation, when the issue of entrapment must be submitted to the jury, is evident. The defendant must run the substantial risk that, in spite of instructions, the jury will allow a criminal record or bad reputation to weigh in its determination of guilt of the specific offense of which he stands charged. Furthermore, a test that looks to the character and predisposition of the defendant rather than the conduct of the police loses sight of the underlying reason for the defense of entrapment. No matter what the defendant's past record and present inclinations to criminality, certain police conduct to ensnare him into further crime is not to be tolerated by an advanced society. Permissible police activity does not vary according to the particular defendant concerned; surely if two suspects have been solicited at the same time in the same manner, one should not go to jail simply because he has been convicted before and is said to have a criminal disposition. Appeals to sympathy, friendship, the possibility of exorbitant gain, and so forth, can no more be tolerated when directed against a past offender than against an ordinary law-abiding citizen. Past crimes do not forever outlaw the criminal and open him to police practices, aimed at securing his repeated conviction, from which the ordinary citizen is protected. The whole ameliorative hopes of modern penology and prison administration strongly counsel against such a view.

This does not mean that the police may not act so as to detect those engaged in criminal conduct and ready and willing to commit further crimes should the occasion arise. It does mean that in holding out inducements they should act in such a manner as is likely to induce to the commission of crime only these persons and not others who would normally avoid crime and through self-struggle resist ordinary temptations. This test shifts attention from the record and predisposition of the particular defendant to the conduct of the police and the likelihood, objectively considered, that it would entrap only those ready and willing to commit crime. It is as objective a test as the subject matter permits and draws directly on the fundamental intuition that led in the first instance to the outlawing of "entrapment" as a prosecutorial instrument. The power of government is abused and directed to an end for which it was not constituted when employed to bring about the downfall of those who, left to themselves, might well have obeyed the law. Human nature is weak enough and

What's That?

Justice Frankfurter's reference to the "ameliorative hopes of modern penology" is an allusion to the consensus of criminal justice reformers in the *Sherman* era that rehabilitation was the primary purpose of punishment. This view found expression in the practice of sentencing defendants to "indeterminate" prison terms, with release made contingent upon a prisoner's successful rehabilitation as determined by corrections officials. *See* FRANCIS A. ALLEN, THE DECLINE OF THE REHABILITATIVE IDEAL (1981).

sufficiently beset by temptations without government adding to them and generating crime.

What police conduct is to be condemned, because likely to induce those not otherwise ready and willing to commit crime, must be picked out from case to case as new situations arise involving different crimes and new methods of detection. Particularly reprehensible in the present case was the use of repeated requests to overcome petitioner's hesitancy, coupled with appeals to sympathy based on mutual experiences with narcotics addiction. Evidence of the setting in which the inducement took place is of course highly relevant in judging its likely effect, and the court should also consider the nature of the crime involved, its secrecy and difficulty of detection, and the manner in which the particular criminal business is usually carried on. It is the province of the court and not the jury to protect the government from the prostitution of the criminal law. Only the court can do this with the degree of certainty that the wise administration of criminal justice demands.

Points for Discussion

a. What Is an Inducement?

Most courts recognize that an inducement requires more than "the fact that government agents initiated contact with the defendant and offered an ordinary opportunity to commit a crime." *United States v. Mayfield*, 771 F.3d 417, 431 (7th Cir. 2014) (en banc). In this context, the term "ordinary" means "something close to what unfolds when a sting operation mirrors the customary execution of the crime charged." For an inducement to exist, "Something more is required, either in terms of the character and degree of the government's persistence or persuasion, or the nature of the enticement or reward."

The "something more" that establishes an inducement has been described as "a special incentive" that "can consist of anything that materially alters the balance of risks and rewards bearing on a defendant's decision whether to commit the offense, so as to increase the likelihood that he will engage in the particular criminal conduct." *United States v. Poehlman*, 217 F.3d 692, 698 (9th Cir. 2000). Typically, an inducement involves "excessive pressure by the government or the government's taking advantage of an alternative, non-criminal type of motive." *Jacobson v. United States*,

503 U.S. 540, 550 (1992). For example, an inducement may take the form of a plea based on friendship or need, or it may offer positive incentives, such as "promises of reward," or negative incentives, such as "threats, coercive tactics, or harassment." Even "very subtle government pressure, if skillfully applied, can amount to inducement," such as the establishment of a "friendly relationship" as in *Sherman*, followed by a plea for empathy with a suffering friend. *Poehlman*, 217 F.3d at 698, 701–702.

Both the *Sherman* majority and concurrence required the existence of an inducement as the first step for establishing the entrapment defense. But the finding of an inducement leads to different consequences for a defendant with an entrapment claim, depending on which model of entrapment has been adopted. According to the *Sherman* majority's formula, the defendant's successful proffer of "some evidence" of inducement will open the door to a jury instruction that allows the jury to accept the defense and acquit the defendant. But the instruction also will tell the jury to convict if the prosecutor can prove beyond a reasonable doubt that the induced defendant was "predisposed" to commit the crime. By contrast, the second step required by the "objective test," as reflected in the *Sherman* concurrence, is for the trial judge to decide whether the defendant should be acquitted as a matter of law. The question for the judge to answer is whether the particular inducement would create a substantial risk that the crime would be committed by a hypothetical person who ordinarily would avoid crime.

b. Proving Predisposition

The Government may demonstrate a defendant's predisposition to commit a crime in one of several ways, including proving: 1) "an existing course of criminal conduct similar to the crime for which the defendant is charged"; 2) "an already formed design on the part of the accused to commit the crime for which he is charged"; or 3) the defendant's "willingness to commit the crime" as shown by his or her "ready response to the inducement." *United States v. Brunshtein*, 344 F.3d 91, 101 (2d Cir. 2003). Since *Sherman*, courts have looked to a wide variety of "factors" in assessing jury findings of predisposition. As enumerated in *United States v. Dion*, 762 F.2d 674 (8th Cir. 1985), *rev'd on other grounds*, 476 U.S. 734 (1986), those factors have included: 1) "the circumstances surrounding the illegal conduct"; 2) "the state of mind of a defendant before government agents make any suggestion that he shall commit a crime"; 3) "the defendant's reputation"; 4) "the conduct of the defendant during the negotiations with the undercover agent"; 5) "whether the defendant has refused to commit similar acts on other occasions"; 6) "the nature of the crime charged"; and 7) "the degree of coercion present in the instigation law officers have contributed to the transaction" relative to the "defendant's criminal background." Examples of additional "factors" include: 8) "whether the defendant engaged in the criminal activity for profit"; 9) "whether the defendant evidenced a reluctance to commit the offense that was overcome by government persuasion"; and 10) "the nature of the inducement or persuasion by the government." *United States v. Pillado*, 656 F.3d 754, 766 (7th Cir. 2011). Not until *Jacobson* (1992) did the Supreme Court clarify predisposition analysis by explicating the *Sorrells* admonition that government agents should not "implant in the mind" of the defendant "the disposition to commit the alleged offense" and then "induce its commission."

c. Persistent Split over Test

In advocating for the objective test, the concurring justices in *Sherman* echoed the position of the *Sorrells* dissenters, including Justice Brandeis, whose earlier advocacy of the objective test in *Casey v. United States*, 276 U.S. 413, 423 (1928) (dissenting opinion), prefigured the views of its defenders in *Sorrells* and *Sherman*: "The government may not provoke or create a crime and then punish the criminal, its creature. If such a one is guilty, it is because he yielded to the temptation presented by the officers. It does not follow that the court must suffer a detective-made criminal to be punished. To permit that would be tantamount to a ratification by the government of the officers' unauthorized and unjustifiable conduct."

Food for Thought

Suppose that Anne regularly sells cocaine to close friends but not to others because she is afraid of getting caught. When an undercover agent offers to buy drugs at the going rate from Anne, she rejects his offer. But when the agent offers Anne four times the normal price, she agrees to sell. If Anne is convicted and brings an appeal based on the entrapment defense, would she have a better chance of success in a jurisdiction using the *Sherman* majority's "subjective" test or the "objective" test advocated by the *Sherman* concurrence?

Four years after *Sherman*, the Model Penal Code endorsed the objective test for entrapment by requiring acquittal under the following circumstances: "A public law enforcement official or person acting in cooperation with such an official perpetrates an entrapment if for the purpose of obtaining evidence of the commission of an offense, he induces or encourages another person to engage in conduct constituting such offense by employing methods of persuasion or inducement that create a substantial risk that such an offense will be committed by persons other than those who are ready to commit it." Model Penal Code § 2.13. How does this provision resemble the objective test as expressed in Justice Frankfurter's concurring opinion in *Sherman*?

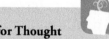

Food for Thought

The persistent debate over the competing tests has produced "substantial volatility" in state entrapment doctrines. Some state courts and legislatures have switched back and forth between the subjective and objective tests (or vice versa), and some states have adopted "an amalgamated approach." Joseph A. Colquitt, *Rethinking Entrapment*, 41 AM. CRIM. L. REV. 1389, 1402 (2004). What policy concerns may help to explain the continuing resistance to the subjective test?

Hypo 1: *Wartime Experiences*

In *Sorrells*, an undercover agent joined a group of defendant's friends during their visit to defendant's home, and repeatedly asked defendant to sell him some bootlegged whisky. Defendant brushed off these requests. When the agent learned that defendant was a veteran, the agent identified himself as a veteran, and conversed about their wartime experiences. When the agent made a third request for whisky, defendant left his house and returned with a half-gallon jug that he sold to the agent for five dollars. Defendant was convicted of crimes under the National Prohibition Act after the trial judge refused to give a jury instruction on entrapment. Was there sufficient evidence of inducement to apply the entrapment defense? If so, how might the government attempt to prove the defendant's predisposition at the new trial? *See Sorrells v. United States*, 287 U.S. 435 (1932).

Hypo 2: *Recruitment as Entrapment?*

After receiving a tip that some members of the San Antonio Police Department were willing to commit crimes in exchange for money, FBI agents created a reverse-sting operation using an undercover agent who posed as a drug dealer named Page. He offered to pay officers $2,500 in exchange for providing "security" during illegal drug transactions. Sally, a sergeant, heard about Page's operation and told Page that she wanted to participate. After Sally provided "security" for several transactions, Page asked whether she knew any other officers who might want to provide security. When Sally told Zeno, one of the new police cadets, about the lucrative opportunity available in Page's operation, Zeno told Sally, "I want in." Zeno received $2,500 from Page for providing security during one transaction, and Zeno was arrested along with the other officers involved in Page's sting. At Zeno's trial, defense counsel sought an entrapment instruction, arguing that: 1) Sally's acts in recruiting Zeno should be attributed to the Government; and 2) that there was sufficient evidence of Sally's inducement of Zeno because she was his superior officer and he was afraid of her. The trial judge denied the instruction. Should the appellate court affirm that ruling? *See United States v. Gutierrez*, 343 F.3d 415 (5th Cir. 2003).

Hypo 3: *Decoy Addict*

Undercover agents noticed Stan because he appeared to be a narcotics addict suffering from withdrawal. He was pale, twitching, shaking, and vomiting as the agents approached him. The agents decided to use Stan as a decoy. The agents gave Stan $50 and asked him to buy drugs for them, and he led them to a nearby intersection where he expected to find drug sellers. Finding no sellers, Stan called out to a passing stranger, Ricardo, saying, "I need a fix, I need your help, I'm really hurting. Please, just find me someone who can sell me something right away." Ricardo told Stan that he was sorry to see Stan in such terrible shape, and that he had heard some people say that drug sellers sometimes came to a nearby park. So Ricardo and Stan walked to the park, with the agents trailing them at a distance. At the park, Stan collapsed on a bench, while Ricardo took Stan's $50 and approached a woman who appeared to be selling drugs. Ricardo bought the drugs for Stan and when he gave them to Stan, Ricardo was arrested and charged with drug crimes. Ricardo's defense counsel asks for an entrapment instruction at trial. Was there sufficient evidence of inducement? *See Bradley v. Duncan*, 315 F.3d 1091 (9th Cir. 2002).

Hypo 4: *Sufficient Inducement?*

Bess is a police informant in Sheridan, Wyoming, who was paid for making drug buys of meth from targets identified by the police. One day Bess was invited to a party by one of the target sellers, Sal, who introduced Bess to George. Later at the party, George told Bess that if she could not obtain all the meth she wanted from Sal, George was willing to try to get it for her. Bess told the police about George and they directed Bess to make George one of her targets. George and Bess spent a lot of time in the local dog park together, waiting to meet with the meth dealers George happened to know, so that Bess can engage in her drug buys. Bess flirted with George by kissing him. After every successful buy, she promised to spend the night with George but never followed through. When George was charged with drug crimes, assume that Wyoming law endorsed the *Sherman* majority's subjective model for the entrapment defense. George's request for an entrapment instruction was denied based on "insufficient proof of inducement." The trial judge reasoned that Sal did not introduce Bess to George "at the behest of the State," that there was no "extraordinary effort by the State" to tempt George into providing meth to Bess, and that Bess "never offered to buy meth from George's sources at a premium price." George was convicted by the jury. Did the trial judge get it wrong? Should the appellate court reverse and remand for a new trial at which George should receive an entrapment instruction? *See Black v. State*, 464 P.3d 574 (Wyo. 2020).

2. Modern Developments

The *Jacobson* case was a milestone in entrapment because it shifted the emphasis of the predisposition concept from an examination of the defendant's response to an assessment of the question whether the defendant would have committed the crime without the government's involvement.

Jacobson v. United States

503 U.S. 540 (1992).

JUSTICE WHITE delivered the opinion of the Court, in which JUSTICE BLACKMUN, JUSTICE STEVENS, JUSTICE SOUTER and JUSTICE THOMAS, joined.

Because the Government overstepped the line between setting a trap for the "unwary innocent" and the "unwary criminal," *Sherman v. United States*, 356 U.S. 369, 372 (1958), and as a matter of law failed to establish that petitioner was independently predisposed to commit the crime for which he was arrested, we reverse the Court of Appeals' judgment affirming his conviction.

In February 1984, petitioner, a 56-year-old veteran-turned-farmer, who supported his elderly father in Nebraska, ordered two magazines and a brochure from a California adult bookstore. The magazines, entitled Bare Boys I and Bare Boys II, contained photographs of nude preteen and teenage boys. The contents of the magazines startled petitioner, who testified that he had expected to receive photographs of "young men 18 years or older." The young men depicted in the magazines were not engaged in sexual activity, and petitioner's receipt of the magazines was legal under both federal and Nebraska law. Within three months, the law with respect to child pornography changed; Congress passed the Act illegalizing the receipt through the mails of sexually explicit depictions of children. In the very month that the new provision became law, postal inspectors found petitioner's name on the mailing list of the California bookstore that had mailed him Bare Boys I and II. There followed over the next 2 ½ years repeated efforts by two Government agencies, through five fictitious organizations and a bogus pen pal, to explore petitioner's willingness to break the new law by ordering sexually explicit photographs of children through the mail.

The Government began its efforts in January 1985 when a postal inspector sent petitioner a letter supposedly from the American Hedonist Society, which in fact was a fictitious organization. The letter included a membership application and stated the Society's doctrine: that members had the "right to read what we desire, the right to discuss similar interests with those who share our philosophy, and finally that we have the right to seek pleasure without restrictions being placed on us by outdated puritan morality." Petitioner enrolled in the organization and returned a sexual attitude questionnaire that asked him to rank on a scale of one to four his enjoyment of various sexual materials, with one being "really enjoy," two being "enjoy," three being "somewhat enjoy," and four being "do not enjoy." Petitioner ranked the entry "preteen sex" as a two, but indicated that he was opposed to pedophilia.

Take Note

The *Jacobson* defendant was targeted by the Postal Service's Operation Looking Glass, a "reverse-sting" which resulted in 161 arrests and 147 convictions. Only the *Jacobson* prosecution led to a ruling that upheld the entrapment defense. By the time the Supreme Court decided his case in 1992, five years had passed since Jacobson's arrest in 1987 and he "had completed his sentence." Joseph A. Colquitt, *Rethinking Entrapment*, 41 AM. CRIM. L. REV. 1389, 1391, 1414 (2004). Jacobson received a three-year prison sentence that was suspended to 250 hours of community service and two years of probation.

For a time, the Government left petitioner alone. But then a new "prohibited mailing specialist" in the Postal Service found petitioner's name in a file, and in May 1986, petitioner received a solicitation from a second fictitious consumer research company, "Midlands Data Research," seeking a response from those who "believe in the joys of sex and the complete awareness of those lusty and youthful lads and lasses of the neophite [sic] age." The letter never explained whether "neophite" referred to minors or young adults. Petitioner responded: "Please feel free to send me more information, I am interested in teenage sexuality. Please keep my name confidential."

Petitioner then heard from yet another Government creation, "Heartland Institute for a New Tomorrow" (HINT), which proclaimed that it was "an organization founded to protect and promote sexual freedom and freedom of choice. We believe that arbitrarily imposed legislative sanctions restricting your sexual freedom should be rescinded through the legislative process." The letter also enclosed a second survey. Petitioner indicated that his interest in "preteen sex-homosexual" material was above average, but not high. In response to another question, petitioner wrote: "Not only sexual expression but freedom of the press is under attack. We must be ever vigilant to counter attack right wing fundamentalists who are determined to curtail our freedoms." HINT replied, portraying itself as a lobbying organization seeking to repeal "all statutes which regulate sexual activities, except those laws which deal with violent behavior, such as rape. HINT is also lobbying to eliminate any legal definition of 'the age of consent.'" HINT also provided computer matching of group members with similar survey responses; and, although petitioner was supplied with a list of potential "pen pals," he did not initiate any correspondence.

Nevertheless, the Government's "prohibited mailing specialist" began writing to petitioner, using the pseudonym "Carl Long." The letters employed a tactic known as "mirroring," which the inspector described as "reflecting whatever the interests are of the person we are writing to." Petitioner responded at first, indicating that his interest was primarily in "male-male items." Inspector "Long" wrote back: "My interests too are primarily male-male items. Are you satisfied with the type of VCR tapes available? Personally, I like the amateur stuff better if its [sic] well produced as it can get more kinky and also seems more real. I think the actors enjoy it more." Petitioner responded: "As far as my likes are concerned, I like good looking young guys (in their late teens and early 20s) doing their thing together." Petitioner's letters to "Long" made no reference to child pornography. After writing two letters, petitioner discontinued the correspondence.

By March 1987, 34 months had passed since the Government obtained petitioner's name from the mailing list of the California bookstore, and 26 months had passed since the Postal Service had commenced its mailings to petitioner. Although petitioner had responded to surveys and letters, the Government had no evidence that petitioner had ever intentionally possessed or been exposed to child pornography. At this point, the Postal Service wrote to petitioner as the "Far Eastern Trading Company Ltd." The letter began: "As many of you know, much hysterical nonsense has appeared in the American media concerning 'pornography' and what must be done to stop it from coming across your borders. This brief letter does not allow us to give much comment; however, why is your government spending millions of dollars to exercise international censorship while tons of drugs, which makes yours the world's most crime ridden country, are passed through easily." The letter went on to say: "We have devised a method of getting these to you without prying eyes of U.S. Customs seizing your mail. After consultations with American solicitors, we have been advised that once we have posted our material through your system, it cannot be opened for any inspection without authorization of a judge."

The letter invited petitioner to send for more information. It also asked petitioner to sign an affirmation that he was "not a law enforcement officer or agent of the U.S. Government acting in an undercover capacity for the purpose of entrapping Far Eastern Trading Company, its agents or customers." Petitioner responded. A catalog was sent, and petitioner ordered Boys Who Love Boys, a pornographic magazine depicting young boys engaged in various sexual activities. Petitioner was arrested after a controlled delivery of a photocopy of the magazine.

When petitioner was asked at trial why he placed such an order, he explained that the Government had succeeded in piquing his curiosity: "Well, the statement was made of all the trouble and the hysteria over pornography and I wanted to see what the material was. It didn't describe the—I didn't know for sure what kind of sexual action they were referring to in the Canadian letter."

In petitioner's home, the Government found the Bare Boys magazines and materials that the Government had sent to him in the course of its protracted investigation, but no other materials that would indicate that petitioner collected, or was actively interested in, child pornography. Petitioner was indicted for violating 18 U.S.C. § 2252(a)(2)(A). [This provision in the Child Protection Act of 1984 prohibits the conduct of "knowingly receiving any visual depiction" that has been mailed "if the producing of such visual depiction involves the use of a minor engaging in sexually explicit conduct and such visual depiction is of such conduct."] The trial court instructed the jury on the petitioner's entrapment defense, and petitioner was convicted.

There can be no dispute about the evils of child pornography or the difficulties that laws and law enforcement have encountered in eliminating it. Likewise, there can be no dispute that the Government may use undercover agents to enforce the law. "It is well settled that the fact that officers or employees of the Government merely afford opportunities or facilities for the commission of the offense does not defeat the prosecution. Artifice and stratagem may be employed to catch those engaged in criminal enterprises." *Sorrells v. United States*, 287 U.S. 435, 441 (1932).

In their zeal to enforce the law, however, Government agents may not originate a criminal design, implant in an innocent person's mind the disposition to commit a criminal act, and then induce commission of the crime so that the Government may prosecute. Where the Government has induced an individual to break the law and the defense of entrapment is at issue, as it was in this case, the prosecution must prove beyond reasonable doubt that the defendant was disposed to commit the criminal act prior to first being approached by Government agents.

Where the defendant is simply provided with the opportunity to commit a crime, the entrapment defense is of little use because the ready commission of the criminal act amply demonstrates the defendant's predisposition. Had the agents in this case simply offered petitioner the opportunity to order child pornography through the mails, and petitioner—who must be presumed to know the law—had promptly availed himself of this criminal opportunity, it is unlikely that his entrapment defense would have warranted a jury instruction.

But that is not what happened here. By the time petitioner finally placed his order, he had already been the target of 26 months of repeated mailings and communications from Government agents and fictitious organizations. Therefore, although he had become predisposed to break the law by May 1987, it is our view that the Government did not prove that this predisposition was independent and not the product of the attention that the Government had directed at petitioner since January 1985.

The prosecution's evidence of predisposition falls into two categories: evidence developed prior to the Postal Service's mail campaign, and that developed during the course of the investigation. The sole piece of pre-investigation evidence is petitioner's 1984 order and receipt of the Bare Boys magazines. But this is scant if any proof of petitioner's predisposition to commit an illegal act, the criminal character of which a defendant is presumed to know. It may indicate a predisposition to view sexually oriented photographs that are responsive to his sexual tastes; but evidence that merely indicates a generic inclination to act within a broad range, not all of which is criminal, is of little probative value in establishing predisposition.

Take Note

Justice White noted that "the proposition that the accused must be predisposed prior to contact with law enforcement officers is so firmly established that the Government conceded the point at oral argument." What the Government argued was that "the evidence it developed during the course of its investigation" was probative in demonstrating petitioner's predisposed "state of mind prior to the commencement of the Government's investigation."

Furthermore, petitioner was acting within the law at the time he received these magazines. Evidence of predisposition to do what once was lawful is not, by itself, sufficient to show predisposition to do what is now illegal, for there is a common understanding that most people obey the law even when they disapprove of it. Hence, the fact that petitioner legally ordered and received the Bare Boys magazines does little to further the Government's burden of proving that petitioner was predisposed to commit a criminal act. This is particularly true given petitioner's unchallenged testimony that he did not know until they arrived that the magazines would depict minors.

Petitioner's responses to the many communications prior to the ultimate criminal act were at most indicative of certain personal inclinations, including a predisposition to view photographs of preteen sex and a willingness to promote a given agenda by supporting lobbying organizations. Even so, petitioner's responses hardly support an inference that he would commit the crime of receiving child pornography through the mails. Furthermore, a person's inclinations and "fantasies are his own and beyond the reach of government." *Stanley v. Georgia*, 394 U.S. 552, 565 (1969).

On the other hand, the strong arguable inference is that, by waving the banner of individual rights and disparaging the legitimacy and constitutionality of efforts to restrict the availability of sexually explicit materials, the Government not only excited petitioner's interest in sexually explicit materials banned by law but also exerted substantial pressure on petitioner to obtain and read such material as part of a fight against censorship and the infringement of individual rights. For instance, HINT described itself as "an organization founded to protect and promote sexual freedom and freedom of choice" and stated that "the most appropriate means to accomplish its objectives is to promote honest dialogue among concerned individuals and to continue its lobbying efforts with State Legislators." Mailings from the equally fictitious American Hedonist Society, and the correspondence from the nonexistent Carl Long, endorsed these themes. Similarly, the mailing from the Far Eastern Trading Company in the spring of 1987 raised the spectre of censorship while suggesting that petitioner ought to be allowed to do what he had been solicited to do. The Postal Service solicitation described the concern about child pornography as "hysterical nonsense," decried "international censorship," and assured petitioner, based on consultation with "American solicitors," that an order that had been posted could not be opened for inspection without authorization of a judge.

Petitioner's ready response to these solicitations cannot be enough to establish beyond reasonable doubt that he was predisposed, prior to the Government acts intended to create predisposition, to commit the crime of receiving child pornography through the mails. The evidence that petitioner was ready and willing to commit the offense came only after the Government had devoted 2 ½ years to convincing him that he had or should have the right to engage in the very behavior proscribed by law. Rational jurors could not say beyond a reasonable doubt that petitioner possessed the requisite predisposition prior to the Government's investigation and that it existed independent of the Government's many and varied approaches to petitioner. As was explained in *Sherman*, where entrapment was found as a matter of law, "the Government may not play on the weaknesses of an innocent party and beguile him into committing crimes which he otherwise would not have attempted."

Food for Thought

At what point did the Government's repeated inducements create the petitioner's predisposition? What action can government agents take in a child pornography sting operation in order to avoid the creation of predisposition, thereby preserving their ability to show that a targeted person was "independently predisposed to commit the crime" at the time of the first government contact?

When the Government's quest for convictions leads to the apprehension of an otherwise law-abiding citizen who, if left to his own devices, likely would have never run afoul of the law, the courts should intervene. Because we conclude that this is such a case and that the prosecution failed, as a matter of law, to adduce evidence to support the jury verdict that petitioner was predisposed, independent of the Government's acts and beyond a reasonable doubt, to violate the law, we reverse the Court of Appeals' judgment affirming the conviction of Keith Jacobson.

JUSTICE O'CONNOR, with whom THE CHIEF JUSTICE and JUSTICE KENNEDY join, and with whom JUSTICE SCALIA joins except as to Part II, dissenting.

Government agents admittedly did not offer Mr. Jacobson the chance to buy child pornography right away. Instead, they first sent questionnaires in order to make sure that he was generally interested in the subject matter. Indeed, a "cold call" in such a business would not only risk rebuff and suspicion, but might also shock and offend the uninitiated, or expose minors to suggestive materials. Mr. Jacobson's responses to the questionnaires gave the investigators reason to think he would be interested in photographs depicting preteen sex.

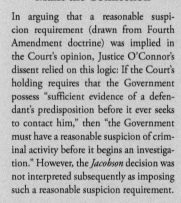

Make the Connection

In arguing that a reasonable suspicion requirement (drawn from Fourth Amendment doctrine) was implied in the Court's opinion, Justice O'Connor's dissent relied on this logic: If the Court's holding requires that the Government possess "sufficient evidence of a defendant's predisposition before it ever seeks to contact him," then "the Government must have a reasonable suspicion of criminal activity before it begins an investigation." However, the *Jacobson* decision was not interpreted subsequently as imposing such a reasonable suspicion requirement.

The Court, however, concludes that a reasonable jury could not have found Mr. Jacobson to be predisposed beyond a reasonable doubt on the basis of his responses to the Government's catalogs, even though it admits that, by that time he was predisposed to commit the crime. The Government, the Court holds, failed to provide evidence that Mr. Jacobson's obvious predisposition at the time of the crime "was independent and not the product of the attention that the Government had directed at petitioner." In so holding, the Court fails to acknowledge the reasonableness of the jury's inference from the evidence, and introduces a new requirement that Government sting operations have a reasonable suspicion of illegal activity before contacting a suspect.

The crux of the Court's concern is that the Government went too far and "abused" the " 'processes of detection and enforcement' " by luring an innocent person to violate the law. Consequently, the Court holds that the Government failed to prove beyond a reasonable doubt that Mr. Jacobson was predisposed to commit the crime. It was, however, the jury's task, as the conscience of the community, to decide whether Mr. Jacobson was a willing participant in the criminal activity here or an innocent dupe. Because I believe there was sufficient evidence to uphold the jury's verdict, I respectfully dissent.

Points for Discussion

a. *Jacobson's* Significance

Justice White noted in *Jacobson* that the 1980 Attorney General's Guidelines on FBI Undercover Operations limited the offering of an inducement to these two scenarios: 1) When "there is a reasonable indication, based on information developed through informants or other means, that the subject is engaging, has engaged, or is likely to engage in illegal activity of a similar type"; or 2) When "the opportunity for illegal activity has been structured so that there is reason for believing that persons drawn to the opportunity, or brought to it, are predisposed to engage in the contemplated illegal activity."

One year after *Jacobson*, an FBI bulletin provided the following advice to agents from an instructor at the FBI Academy: "

> First, while reasonable suspicion is not legally necessary to initiate an undercover investigation, officers should nonetheless be prepared to articulate a legitimate law enforcement purpose for beginning such an investigation. Second, they should, to the extent possible, avoid using persistent or coercive techniques, and instead, merely create an opportunity or provide the facilities for the target to commit the crime. Third, officers should document and be prepared to articulate the factors demonstrating a defendant was disposed to commit the criminal act prior to government contact." Paul Marcus, *Presenting, Back from the [Almost] Dead, the Entrapment Defense*, 47 Fla. L. Rev. 205, 237 (1995) (quoting Thomas V. Kukura, *Undercover Investigations and the Entrapment Defense*, FBI L. Enforcement Bull., April 1993, at 32).

Food for Thought

Professor Marcus argues that although *Jacobson* did not alter the elements of the entrapment defense, the decision was significant because the of the Court's emphasis on the need for appellate courts to engage in "more careful review of evidence concerning government activity and the defendant's state of mind." What are the benefits of "more careful" judicial scrutiny of cases in which the jury has rejected the entrapment defense? Does the FBI Bulletin from 1993 suggest that *Jacobson* encouraged more careful design of sting operations by government agents?

b. Interpretations of *Jacobson*

In *United States v. Gendron*, 18 F.3d 955 (1st Cir. 1994) (Breyer, J.), the court viewed the government's inability to prove the requisite type of predisposition in *Jacobson* as attributable to the government's use of inducements that were not "ordinary" but "special" in three respects: "First, the solicitations reflected a psychologically "graduated" set of responses to Jacobson's own noncriminal responses, beginning with innocent lures and progressing to frank offers. Second, the government's soliciting letters sometimes depicted their senders as 'free speech' lobbying organizations and fighters for the "right to read what we desire"; they asked Jacobson to 'fight against censorship and the infringement of individual rights.' Third, the government's effort to provide an "opportunity" to buy child pornography stretched out over two and a half years. Thus, the government's evidence did not show how Jacobson would have acted had he been faced with an ordinary 'opportunity' to commit the crime rather than a 'special' inducement."

A more complex interpretation of *Jacobson* appeared in *United States v. Hollingsworth*, 27 F.3d 1196, 1200 (7th Cir. 1994) (en banc): "We do not suggest that *Jacobson* adds a new element to the entrapment defense—'readiness' or 'ability' or 'dangerousness' on top of inducement and, most important, predisposition. (An inducement is significant chiefly as evidence bearing on predisposition; the greater the inducement, the weaker the inference that in yielding to it the defendant demonstrated that he was predisposed to commit the crime in question.) Rather, the Court clarified the meaning of predisposition. Predisposition is not a purely mental state, the state of being willing to swallow the government's bait. It has positional as well as dispositional force. The dictionary definitions of the word include 'tendency' as well as "inclination.' The defendant must be so situated by reason of previous training or experience or occupation or acquaintances that it is likely that if the government had not induced him to commit the crime some criminal would have done so; only then does a sting or other arranged crime take a dangerous person out of circulation. [I]f the defendant had the idea for the crime all worked out and lacked merely the present means to commit it, and if the government had not supplied them someone else very well might have, then that would be a case in which the government had merely furnished the opportunity to commit the crime to someone already predisposed to commit it."

Hollingsworth's "positional predisposition" approach has been viewed as an interpretation of *Jacobson*'s instruction "to ask what the defendant would have done without governmental involvement," by looking "not only to the defendant's mental state ('his disposition') but also to whether the defendant was able and likely, based

> **FYI**
>
> Notwithstanding *Hollingsworth*'s mixed reception in other circuits, the Seventh Circuit reaffirmed *Hollingsworth*'s interpretation of *Jacobson* by a vote of 8 to 2 in *United States v. Mayfield*, 771 F.3d 417, 436–437 (7th Cir. 2014) (en banc).

on experience, training, and contacts, to actually commit the crime (his 'position')." *United States v. Knox*, 112 F.3d 802, 807 (5th Cir. 1997).

Some courts have rejected the "positional predisposition" doctrine on the ground that it is not expressly supported in *Jacobson*'s reasoning. *See United States v. Cromitie*, 727 F.3d 194, 217 (2d Cir. 2013); *United States v. Thickstun*, 110 F.3d 1394, 1398

(9th Cir. 1997). These courts also cite the objections advanced by the *Hollingsworth* dissent:

> The *Hollingsworth* majority has changed the "ready" defendant from one who is inclined, feeling or exhibiting no reluctance, to one on the point of acting. Its holding will benefit not only the pathetic incompetents of the criminal world but also the very competent criminal who is sufficiently studied in his way of doing business so as to appear not too organized. The most problematic application of the new rule will come when a sting operation attracts a very willing but also not very well organized or inept first offender. A defendant's prior arrests and convictions, as well as his previous associations with drug traffickers, are strong indications of predisposition. Without that past record, however, would the neophyte's quick reply to an agent's invitation to "talk business" count as predisposition? Would his agreement to distribute drugs show a willingness, but not a readiness? There is, of course, no constitutional requirement that the Congress punish only activity that is *immediately dangerous*.

Hypo 1: *Special Teacher*

Mark's wife sought a divorce when she discovered that Mark liked crossdressing. He became lonely and depressed and started to visit "alternative lifestyle" discussion groups on the internet, looking for a female companion. Mark got a positive reaction from Shari, who told him that she thought cross-dressing was OK. When they exchanged emails, Mark described his status as a divorced father with two sons, and Shari shared her own biography as a mother of twin twelve-year-old daughters—her "sweethearts." Mark told Shari that he was "looking for a long-term relationship leading to marriage," and that he believed in strong family values and would treat Shari's children as his own. Shari told Mark that she was "looking for someone who understands us and does not let society's views stand in the way." When Shari told Mark that she was "looking for a special man teacher" for her sweethearts, Mark assured Shari that he would "teach her children proper morals and give support to them where it is needed." Ultimately, Shari asked Mark what he would teach her sweethearts "as a first lesson," if he were their "special man teacher." She advised him that, "If I disagree with something, I'll just say so. I do like to watch, though. I hope you don't think I'm too weird." Then Mark finally realized that Shari wanted him to play sex instructor, and he agreed to be a "special teacher" for her daughters. But he also kept saying that he wanted a relationship with her. After six months of exchanging emails, Shari invited Mark to her home. When he arrived, he discovered that Shari was an FBI agent whose assignment was to catch pedophiles on the internet. Mark was charged with the federal crime of attempted lewd acts with a minor. How will Mark's defense counsel argue that the necessary inducement evidence exists in this case? What arguments will defense counsel make to rebut the government's argument that Mark was predisposed? *See United States v. Poehlman*, 217 F.3d 692 (9th Cir. 2000).

Hypo 2: *Terrorist Designs*

Hussain is a Pakistani national who was paid to work undercover for the FBI in the Hudson River Valley with the goal of locating "disaffected Muslims who might be harboring terrorist designs on the United States." While attending a mosque in Newburgh, he portrayed himself as a wealthy businessman, and cultivated a friendship with Cromitie, an impoverished man who worshipped at the mosque and worked a night shift at Walmart. Cromitie's father was from Afghanistan. When Hussain asked Cromitie whether he would like to travel to Afghanistan, Cromitie said that he would, and added that he wanted to "do something to America," and to "die like a martyr and go to Paradise." The FBI instructed Hussain to tell Cromitie that he was a representative of a terrorist group in Pakistan (JeM). In response, Cromitie said that he wanted to join JeM. In September, Hussain mentioned to Cromitie that military planes flew from the nearby Newburgh Airport to take arms and ammunition to Afghanistan and Iraq. In response, Cromitie expressed his frustration with the United States, "taking down our Islamic countries" and disrespecting Muslims. Hussain asked Cromitie if he had ever thought of "doing something here in the U.S." and confided to Cromitie that he could obtain guns and rockets. In December, Hussain said, "Let's pick a target," and Cromitie said that he'd "like to get a synagogue." Later, Cromitie told Hussain that he was hard up for money, and Hussain said he could give Cromitie $250,000, that Hussain would train Cromitie how to use a rocket launcher, and that JeM would provide a missile. Hussain bought Cromitie a camera and drove him to the airport and to a synagogue to conduct surveillance. In May, Hussain drove Cromitie to a warehouse where three fake bombs and two fake missiles were stored. They put the bombs in Hussain's car and drove to a synagogue where the FBI arrested Cromitie. At his trial for terrorism crimes, the jury rejected Cromitie's entrapment defense.

See It

A documentary film entitled, "The Newburgh Sting" (2014), portrays the entrapment story in the *Cromitie* case described here and can be viewed at the HBO website.

What arguments will the prosecutor and defense counsel make on appeal regarding the defense of entrapment? *See United States v. Cromitie*, 727 F.3d 194 (2d Cir. 2013).

B. Due Process & "Outrageous Government Conduct"

In the post-*Sherman* era, some federal courts have recognized the need for a Due Process doctrine that could be used to reverse the conviction of a predisposed defendant who is apprehended by means of a police operation that rises to the level of "outrageous government conduct." However, the Supreme Court failed to endorse such a doctrine when the opportunity to do so arose in two cases in the 1970s. These precedents have had a chilling effect on the viability of a Due Process defense in some federal circuits today. The opinions in *United States v. Russell* (1973) and *Hampton v. United States* (1976) illustrate the Court's debates concerning the difficulties of identifying the characteristics of police operations that would justify the finding of a Due Process violation.

United States v. Russell

411 U.S. 423 (1973).

MR. JUSTICE REHNQUIST delivered the opinion of the Court.

[Russell was convicted of drug crimes by a jury that received an entrapment instruction but rejected his defense.] The Court of Appeals reversed the conviction for the reason that an undercover agent supplied an essential chemical for manufacturing the methamphetamine which formed the basis of Russell's conviction. The court concluded that as a matter of law, "a defense to a criminal charge may be founded upon an intolerable degree of governmental participation in the criminal enterprise." We reverse that judgment.

A federal agent offered to supply Russell and the Connolly brothers with the chemical phenyl-2-propanone (P2P), a necessary ingredient for making methamphetamine, in exchange for receiving half of the drug they produced. They accepted his offer and also agreed to show him their meth lab and to give him a meth sample. At their lab, the agent saw an empty bottle of P2P. Two days later, he brought a 100-gram bottle of P2P to the lab. One of the Connollys added it to a flask, while Russell cut up aluminum foil pieces and put them in the flask. A few foil pieces fell on the ground and the agent picked them up and added them. The next day, Russell delivered the promised batches of meth to the agent. One month later, the agent returned to the lab to find out whether the trio was still interested in their "business arrangement." One of the Connollys told the agent that he had obtained two bottles of P2P that he was still using. Soon thereafter, the agent executed a search warrant and found the two bottles at the lab.

On appeal, Russell conceded that the jury could have found him predisposed to commit the offenses, but argued that on the facts presented there was entrapment as a matter of law. The Court of Appeals agreed and expanded the traditional notion of entrapment to mandate dismissal based on a new defense that was held to rest on either of two alternative theories. One theory is based on district court decisions which have found entrapment, regardless of predisposition, whenever the government supplies contraband to the defendants. The second theory is based on a decision that reversed a conviction because a government investigator was so enmeshed in the criminal activity that the prosecution of the defendants was held to be repugnant to the American criminal justice system. *Greene v. United States*, 454 F.3d 783 (9th Cir. 1971). The court below held that these two rationales constitute the same defense, and "both theories are premised on fundamental concepts of due process and evince the reluctance of the judiciary to countenance 'overzealous law enforcement.'" 459 F.3d at 674 (quoting *Sherman v. United States*, 356 U.S. 369, 381 (1958) (Frankfurter, J., concurring)).

Defendant asks us to reconsider the theory of the entrapment defense and his contention is that the defense should rest on constitutional grounds. He argues that the level of the agent's involvement in the manufacture of the methamphetamine was so high that a criminal prosecution for the drug's manufacture violates the fundamental principles of due process. Defendant would have the Court adopt a rigid constitutional rule that would preclude any prosecution when the criminal conduct would not have been possible had not an undercover agent "supplied an indispensable means to the commission of the crime that could not have been obtained otherwise, through legal or illegal channels." Even if we were to surmount the difficulties attending the notion that due process of law can be embodied in fixed rules, the rule he proposes would not appear to be of significant benefit to him. On the record presented, he cannot fit within the terms of the very rule he proposes. Although P2P was difficult to obtain, it was by no means impossible. Defendants admitted making the drug both before and after those batches made with the P2P supplied by the agent. He testified that he saw an empty bottle labeled phenyl-2-propanone on his first visit to the laboratory, and when it was searched, two additional bottles labeled P2P were seized. Thus, the facts amply demonstrate that the P2P used in the illicit manufacture of methamphetamine not only *could* have been obtained without the intervention of the agent but was in fact obtained by these defendants.

While we may be presented with a situation in which the conduct of law enforcement agents is so outrageous that due process principles would absolutely bar the government from invoking judicial processes to obtain a conviction, the instant case is not of that breed. The agent's contribution of P2P to the criminal enterprise already in process was scarcely objectionable. The chemical is by itself a harmless substance and its possession is legal.

The illicit manufacture of drugs is not a sporadic, isolated criminal incident, but a continuing, though illegal, business enterprise. In order to obtain convictions for illegally manufacturing drugs, the gathering of evidence of past unlawful conduct frequently proves to be an all but impossible task. Thus in drug-related offenses law enforcement personnel have turned to one of the only practicable means of detection: the infiltration of drug rings and a limited participation in their unlawful present practices. Such infiltration is a recognized and permissible means of investigation; if that be so, then the supply of some item of value that the drug ring requires must, as a general rule, also be permissible. For an agent will not be taken into the confidence of the illegal entrepreneurs unless he has something of value to offer them. Law enforcement tactics such as this can hardly be said to violate "fundamental fairness" or [to be] "shocking to the universal sense of justice."

Food for Thought

In 1980, P2P was listed as a controlled substance. Would the *Russell* Court have reached a different result if P2P had been a controlled substance in 1973?

Defendant also urges, as an alternative, that we broaden the non-constitutional defense of entrapment in order to sustain the judgment of the Court of Appeals. He argues that the views of the minority in *Sorrells v. United States*, 287 U.S. 435 (1932), and *Sherman* should be adopted by law. We decline to overrule these cases. Since the defense is not of a constitutional dimension, Congress may address itself to the question and adopt any substantive definition of the defense that it may find desirable. The defense of entrapment was not intended to give the federal judiciary a "chancellor's foot" veto over law enforcement practices of which it did not approve. The decision of the Court of Appeals unnecessarily introduces an unmanageably subjective standard which is contrary to the holdings in

What's That?

A "chancellor's foot" veto stands for inequitable variability in court decisions. The term was coined by John Selden, a 17th-century barrister, who said, "One Chancellor has a long foot, another a short foot, a third an indifferent foot; 'tis the same thing in the Chancellor's conscience."

Sorrells and *Sherman*. The Court of Appeals was wrong when it sought to broaden the principle laid down in [those cases]. Its judgment is therefore reversed.

Mr. Justice Douglas, with whom Mr. Justice Brennan concurs, dissenting.

My view is that of Mr. Justice Frankfurter stated in *Sherman v. United States*, 356 U.S. 378 (1958) (concurring in result). The fact that the chemical ingredient supplied by the federal agent might have been obtained from other sources is quite irrelevant. Supplying the chemical ingredient used in the manufacture of this batch of "speed" made the United States an active participant in the unlawful activity. Federal agents play a debased role when they become the instigators of the crime, or partners in its commission, or the creative brain behind the illegal scheme. That is what the federal agent did here when he furnished the accused with one of the chemical ingredients needed to manufacture the unlawful drug.

Mr. Justice Stewart, with whom Mr. Justice Brennan and Mr. Justice Marshall join, dissenting.

The objective approach to entrapment advanced by the minority in *Sorrells* and *Sherman* is the only one truly consistent with the underlying rationale of the defense. This does not mean that the Government's use of undercover activity, strategy, or deception is necessarily unlawful. But when the agents' involvement in criminal activities goes beyond the mere offering of such an opportunity and when their conduct is of a kind that could induce or instigate the commission of a crime by one not ready and willing to commit it, then—regardless of the character or propensities of the particular person induced—I think entrapment has occurred. In that situation, the Government has engaged in the impermissible manufacturing of crime, and the federal courts should bar the prosecution in order to preserve the institutional integrity of the system of federal criminal justice. It is the Government's duty to prevent crime, not to promote it. Here, the Government's agent asked that the illegal drug be produced for him, solved his quarry's practical problems with the assurance that he could provide the one essential ingredient that was difficult to obtain, furnished that element as he had promised, and bought the finished product from the defendant—all so that the defendant could be prosecuted for producing and selling the very drug for which the agent had asked and for which he had provided the necessary component. Under the objective approach that I would follow, this defendant was entrapped, regardless of his predisposition or "innocence."

> **Food for Thought**
>
> Why did the *Russell* dissenters prefer to support the defendant's second argument that the objective test should be adopted for the entrapment defense in federal cases, instead of supporting the defendant's first argument based on Due Process?

Hampton v. United States

425 U.S. 484 (1976).

MR. JUSTICE REHNQUIST announced the judgment of the Court in an opinion in which THE CHIEF JUSTICE and MR. JUSTICE WHITE join.

When Hampton noticed needle marks in Hutton's arms, Hampton said that he needed money and knew where he could get some heroin to sell. Hampton did not realize that Hutton was a DEA informant. Hutton offered to find a buyer for the heroin so that Hampton could sell it. Then Hutton called another DEA agent to set up a meeting for the "buy." At the meeting, two DEA agents posed as narcotics dealers. Hampton brought a tinfoil packet of heroin and the agents paid him $145 after testing the heroin and pronouncing it "okay." Hampton offered to sell them more heroin, and the agents arranged for another "buy." When Hutton and Hampton arrived at the meeting, Hampton produced a tinfoil packet of heroin and asked for $500. Then he was arrested. At his trial, Hampton testified to an entirely different story. He admitted telling Hutton that he was short of cash, and claimed that Hutton's response was to propose that he could obtain a non-narcotic counterfeit drug from a pharmacist friend. The drug would produce the same reaction as heroin, so he and Hampton could make money by selling it to gullible acquaintances. At both meetings with the agents, Hampton believed that they were being duped into buying fake heroin. Hampton testified that it was Hutton who had supplied the drugs that Hampton sold to the agents, and that Hampton never realized that it was real heroin. At his trial, Hampton sought a non-standard jury instruction that provided: "The defendant asserts that he was the victim of entrapment. If you find that the narcotics were supplied to him by an informer in the employ of or acting on behalf of the government, then you must acquit the defendant because the law as a matter of policy forbids his conviction, and you need not consider the predisposition of the defendant to commit the defense charged." The trial judge denied the instruction and Hampton was convicted. The Court of Appeals affirmed the conviction, relying on *Russell*.

Defendant correctly recognizes that his case does not qualify as one involving "entrapment." He instead relies on the language in *United States v. Russell*, 411 U.S. 423, 431 (1974), that "we may some day be presented with a situation in which the conduct of law enforcement agents is so outrageous that due process principles would absolutely bar the government from invoking judicial processes to obtain a conviction." Defendant's case is different from *Russell*'s but the difference is one of degree not of kind. In *Russell* the ingredient supplied by the Government agent was a legal drug which the defendants demonstrably could have obtained from other sources besides the Government. Here the drug which the Government informant allegedly supplied to defendant both was illegal and constituted the *corpus delicti* for the sale of which he was convicted. The Government obviously played a more significant role in enabling him to sell contraband than it did in *Russell*. But in each case the Government agents were acting in concert with the defendant, and in each case either the jury found or the defendant conceded that he was predisposed to commit the crime for which he was convicted. The remedy of the criminal defendant with respect to the acts of Government agents, which, far from being resisted, are encouraged by him, lies solely in the defense of entrapment. Defendant's conceded predisposition rendered this defense unavailable to him.

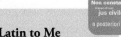

It's Latin to Me

The term *"corpus delicti"* means "body of crime," and it "stands for the principle that in order for a person to be convicted of a crime, it must be proved that the crime actually occurred."

To sustain defendant's contention here would run directly contrary to our statement in *Russell* that the defense of entrapment is not intended "to give the federal judiciary a 'chancellor's foot' veto over law enforcement practices of which it did not approve." The limitations of the Due Process Clause of the Fifth Amendment come into play only when the Government activity in question violates some protected right of the *defendant*. Here, the police, the Government informant, and the defendant acted in concert with one another. If the police engage in illegal activity in concert with a defendant beyond the scope of their duties, the remedy lies not in freeing the equally culpable defendant, but in prosecuting the police under the applicable provisions of state or federal law. But the police conduct here no more deprived defendant of any right secured to him by the United States Constitution than did the police conduct in *Russell* deprive Russell of any rights. *Affirmed*.

MR. JUSTICE POWELL, with whom MR. JUSTICE BLACKMUN joins, concurring in the judgment.

Defendant Hampton contends that the Government's supplying of contraband to one later prosecuted for trafficking in contraband constitutes a *per se* denial of due process. As I do not accept this proposition, I concur in the judgment of the Court. I am not able to join the plurality opinion, as it would unnecessarily reach and decide difficult questions not before us.

Hampton would distinguish *Russell* on the ground that here contraband itself was supplied by the Government, while the phenyl-2-propanone P2P supplied in *Russell* was not contraband. Given the characteristics of P2P, this is a distinction without a difference and *Russell* disposes of this case. But the plurality does not stop there. In discussing Hampton's Due Process contention, it enunciates a *per se* rule: "The remedy of the criminal defendant with respect to the acts of Government agents, which, far from being resisted, are encouraged by him, lies *solely* in the defense of entrapment." The plurality thus says that the concept of fundamental fairness inherent in the guarantee of due process would never prevent the conviction of a predisposed defendant, regardless of the outrageousness of police behavior in light of the surrounding circumstances. I do not understand *Russell* or earlier cases delineating the defense of entrapment to have gone so far, and there was no need for them to do so. Nor have we had occasion yet to confront Government over-involvement in areas outside the realm of contraband offenses. *Cf. United States v. Archer*, 486 F.2d 670 (2d Cir. 1973). I am unwilling to conclude that an analysis other than one limited to predisposition would never be appropriate under due process principles.

Take Note

In *United States v. Archer*, 486 F.2d 670, 676–77 (2d Cir. 1973), the court found it unnecessary to decide whether "outrageous government conduct" occurred because the conviction could be reversed on other grounds. The federal agents in *Archer* acquired evidence of a state prosecutor's acceptance of a bribe by "lying to New York police officers and committing perjury before New York judges and grand jurors." The court noted that the federal agents' operation displayed an "arrogant disregard for the sanctity of the state judicial and police processes," which was "substantially more offensive" than "common cases where government agents induce the sale of narcotics in order to make drug arrests."

MR. JUSTICE BRENNAN, with whom MR. JUSTICE STEWART and MR. JUSTICE MARSHALL concur, dissenting.

Defendant's claims in this case allege a course of police conduct that would plainly be held to constitute entrapment as a matter of law under the objective test, and I think that reversal of defendant's conviction also is compelled for those who follow the "subjective" approach to the defense of entrapment. I agree with Mr. Justice Powell that *Russell* does not foreclose imposition of a bar to conviction—based on due process principles—where the conduct of law enforcement authorities is sufficiently offensive, even though the individuals entitled to invoke such a defense might be "predisposed." In my view, the police activity in this case was beyond permissible limits.

Two facts sufficiently distinguish this case from *Russell*. First, the chemical supplied in that case was not contraband. In contrast, defendant claims that the very narcotic he is accused of selling was supplied by an agent of the government. Second, the defendant in *Russell* "was an active participant in an illegal drug manufacturing enterprise which began before the Government agent appeared on the scene and continued after the Government agent had left the scene." In contrast, the two sales for which defendant was convicted were allegedly instigated by Government agents and completed by the Government's purchase. The beginning and end of this crime thus coincided exactly with the Government's entry into and withdrawal from the criminal activity in this case, while the Government was not similarly involved in Russell's crime. Where the Government's agent deliberately sets up the accused by supplying him with contraband and then bringing him to another agent as a potential purchaser, the Government's role has passed the point of toleration. The Government is doing nothing less than buying contraband from itself through an intermediary and jailing the intermediary. There is little, if any, law enforcement interest promoted by such conduct; plainly it is not designed to discover ongoing drug traffic. That the accused is "predisposed" cannot possibly justify the action of government officials in purposefully creating the crime. No one would suggest that the police could round up and jail all "predisposed" individuals, yet that is precisely what set-ups like the instant one are intended to accomplish. Thus, this case is nothing less than an instance of "the Government seeking to punish for an alleged offense which is the product of the creative activity of its own officials." *Sorrells v. United States*, 287 U.S. 435, 451(1932).

Food for Thought

One problem for federal judges is how to articulate a Due Process concept of outrageous government conduct that does not simply mimic the standards of the objective test. As one judge noted, "the language used in both *Russell* and *Hampton* indicates that no such back-door reincarnation of the objective approach was intended." *United States v. Twigg*, 588 F.2d 373, 385 (3d Cir. 1978) (Adams, J., dissenting). What approaches to Due Process are expressed in the opinions in *Hampton*?

Points for Discussion

a. Need for Due Process Defense

The need for a Due Process defense for predisposed defendants was expressed in the Second Circuit's observation in *Archer* that it would be "unthinkable, for example, to permit government agents to instigate robberies and beatings merely to gather evidence to convict other members of a gang of hoodlums." Consider the similar policy judgment reflected in the Tenth Circuit's version of the "outrageous governmental conduct" defense that requires a defendant to bear the burden of proving either "(1) excessive government involvement in the creation of the crime, or (2) significant governmental coercion to induce the crime." *United States v. Pedraza*, 27 F.3d 1515, 1521 (10th Cir. 1994). Could defense counsel in *Russell* and *Hampton* argue that the facts of those cases met this Tenth Circuit standard? What counter-arguments would a prosecutor make regarding that question?

b. Rarely Successful Defense

The reasoning in *Russell* and *Hampton* persuaded the Sixth and Seventh Circuits to reject the establishment of a Due Process defense based on "outrageous government conduct." The First, Fourth, and Eleventh Circuits have recognized the potential existence of the defense, but have never reversed a conviction based on a defendant's Due Process claim. The Tenth Circuit has granted such relief only once. *See United States v. Dyke*, 718 F.3d 1281, 1285 (10th Cir. 2013). Even when courts have established criteria for the Due Process defense and encounter frequent claims, it is typical to see the "doctrine of outrageous police conduct" described as one that "must be sparingly applied and used only in the most egregious situations." *State v. Markwart*, 329 P.3d 108, 115 (Wash. App. 2014). Government operations that have been upheld as insufficiently outrageous include these examples: 1) agents purchasing "lewd table dances with public funds to gain evidence of violation of liquor rules"; 2) agents creating "a phony job recruiting center and soliciting the purchase of marijuana from a potential job applicant"; 3) agents selling "illegally imported bobcat hides and providing false forms intended to show that the hides were legal." *Id.* One repeatedly quoted perspective is that "the banner of outrageous misconduct is often raised but seldom saluted." *United States v. Santana*, 6 F.3d 1, 4 (1st Cir. 1993).

c. Articulation of Due Process Criteria

Some state courts that use the subjective test for entrapment have established criteria for the assessment of Due Process claims. One example appears in *State v. Lively*, 921 P.2d 1035 (Wash. 1996), which explains Due Process analysis as follows:

> In determining whether police conduct violates Due Process, this court has held that the conduct must be so shocking that it violates fundamental fairness. A Due Process claim based on outrageous conduct requires more than a mere demonstration of flagrant police conduct. Dismissal is reserved for only the most egregious circumstances. While some courts have limited the outrageous conduct defense to a "slim category of cases in which the police have been brutal, employing physical or psychological coercion against the defendant," other courts recognize the violation of Due Process standards in cases where the government conduct is so integrally involved in the offense that the government agents direct the crime from beginning to end, or where the crime is fabricated by the police to obtain a defendant's conviction, rather than to protect the public from criminal behavior.

> We agree with those courts which hold that in reviewing a defense of outrageous government conduct, the court should evaluate the conduct based on the "totality of the circumstances." There are several factors to consider when determining whether police conduct offends Due Process: whether the police conduct instigated a crime or merely infiltrated ongoing criminal activity; whether the defen-

Food for Thought

How could defense counsel in *Russell* and *Hampton* argue that the facts of those cases satisfied the Due Process criteria described in *Lively*? What counter-arguments would a prosecutor make regarding the facts of each case?

dant's reluctance to commit a crime was overcome by pleas of sympathy, promises of excessive profits, or persistent solicitation; whether the government controls the criminal activity or simply allows for the criminal activity to occur; whether the police motive was to prevent crime or protect the public; and whether the government conduct itself amounted to criminal activity or conduct "repugnant to a sense of justice."

Hypo 1: *Fencing Operation*

In an attempt to uncover information about illegal activity, the police set up an undercover operation and accept stolen property from people who steal the property or know that it is stolen. Then the police resell it to others who know the property is stolen. Because of the fencing operation, the police are able to crack a major theft ring. Eventually, the police shut down the operation and make a number of arrests for burglary, possession of stolen property, receiving stolen property, and other related crimes. Defendants claim that the government violated Due Process by establishing and operating the fencing operation. Did the government embroil itself to an intolerable degree in the criminal enterprise? *See State v. Brooks*, 633 P.2d 1345 (Wash. App. 1981).

Hypo 2: *Child Prostitution Sting*

Recognizing that child sexual abuse is a major problem, the police recruit young boys to work as prostitutes. The boys are encouraged to cooperate with the "johns" and to place themselves in revealing situations. At the appropriate point, the police break in and arrest the "John." Given the compelling nature of the child abuse problem, is this sting operation justifiable, or would it violate Due Process? *See State v. Jessup*, 641 P.2d 1185 (Wash. App. 1982).

Hypo 3: *Child Porn Site*

While investigating a child pornography website (Playpen), the FBI assumed control of the site and maintained it live for two weeks. During that time, defendant logged in to the website twelve times. Does the FBI's conduct "shock the conscience" so that it should be regarded as a violation of Due Process? *See United States v. Anzalone*, 923 F.3d 1 (1st Cir. 2019); *United States v. Vortman*, 801 Fed. Appx. 470 (9th Cir. 2020).

Hypo 4: *Plan to Marry*

As part of an undercover drug investigation, Koby Desai, an informant, arranged a cocaine purchase from Amy Lively by an undercover detective named David. A week later, Desai arranged for David to purchase more cocaine from Lively at Desai's apartment. Lively was arrested and charged with drug crimes. At her trial, Lively raised both the entrapment defense and the Due Process defense of "outrageous government conduct." She testified that she started drinking alcohol and using cocaine at age fourteen. She eventually entered a detoxification program, and began attending Alcoholics Anonymous/Narcotics Anonymous (AA/NA) meetings. Later, she had a relapse and entered a 28-day inpatient detoxification program. At this point, she had never sold or offered to sell drugs. She was not using drugs at the time of the offenses and had not used cocaine for several years. When Desai began working as a police informant, the police provided him with an apartment, including utilities, a car, and other living expenses. Desai began attending AA/NA meetings where he met Lively. Desai's attendance was approved by the drug squad. At trial, Lively testified that: 1) she had tried to kill herself after completing the program and was emotionally distraught; 2) Desai asked her out on a date and she started a sexual relationship with him because he was supportive and emotionally responsive; 3) she moved in with Desai and they made plans to marry; he promised to assist her in obtaining a divorce, and to fly her friends to California for the wedding; 4) Desai told Lively that he had a friend David (the undercover detective), who wanted to buy cocaine, and Desai asked her to obtain the drugs for David; 5) Desai's requests continued for two weeks before Lively finally agreed to obtain cocaine for David. Desai admitted lying repeatedly to Lively, but stated that he thought it was all right to lie to maintain his cover story. Assume that the Lively's entrapment defense will fail because of predisposition. What arguments can defense counsel make regarding the Due Process defense? *See State v. Lively*, 130 Wash.2d 1, 921 P.2d 1035 (1996) (en banc).

Hypo 5: *Phony Stash House*

The government sends a paid confidential informant (CI) to Phoenix with instructions to recruit people to help rob a non-existent cocaine stash house. CI went to bars in "a bad part of town" and looked for people who seemed to be "bad guys." CI had not been told to seek out people already engaged in criminal activity or even persons engaged in suspicious conduct. Rather, he trolled for targets in bars and eventually encountered Simpson who expressed a willingness to join in the robbery. CI introduced Simpson to his handler, Agent Z, who posed as a disgruntled former drug courier. Simpson asserted that he had criminal experience and introduced Z to Black. Agent Z fed the men details about the imaginary target (including the number of kilos of cocaine to be found in the imaginary stash house), and encouraged them to be sure to bring guns along. When the defendants met with Agent Z in preparation for the robbery, he led them to a warehouse where they were arrested. Is this an appropriate case for application of the Due Process defense? *See United States v. Black*, 750 F.3d 1053 (9th Cir. 2014) (Reinhardt, J.) (dissenting from denial of rehearing en banc).

See It

In 2014, USA Today launched an investigative series regarding the ATF sting operations in which targeted individuals were enticed by the prospect of large payments to steal drugs from a phony stash house supposedly operated by a Mexican drug ring. One of these operations led to the prosecution described in Hypo 5. Several indictments have been dismissed in similar prosecutions based on the Due Process defense of outrageous government conduct.

Executive Summary

Subjective Test for Entrapment. Assuming that a defendant produces some evidence of government inducement, the question is whether the government can show beyond a reasonable doubt that the defendant was predisposed to commit the crime.

Inducement. An inducement occurs when the government creates an opportunity plus a special incentive of some kind for the defendant to commit a crime.

Predisposition. The government must show that the defendant was predisposed to commit the crime before the inducement occurred, assuming that sufficient evidence of inducement exists. To prove disposition, the government may show that the defendant engaged in a similar existing course of conduct, or had an already formed design to commit the crime, or responded readily to the inducement.

Objective Test for Entrapment. A court using this test will rule in favor of a defendant, as a matter of law, when the type of inducement offered by the government was one that was likely to induce ordinary people, who would normally avoid crime, to yield to the inducement.

Due Process or Outrageous Government Conduct Defense. Courts that recognize the Due Process defense have pointed to a variety of factors that supply criteria for the inquiry whether government conduct is so shocking that it violates fundamental fairness. Such factors include the use of physical or psychological coercion, or the government direction of a crime from its initiation through to its conclusion. However, the federal and state courts that recognize the defense have rarely upheld the defense and reversed a conviction.

Major Themes

a. Split over Test for Entrapment Defense—The federal courts have followed the subjective test since the Court endorsed it in *Sherman*. However, a minority of states use the objective test because of the various weaknesses of the subjective test, including its toleration for government entrapment of predisposed defendants.

b. Split over Due Process Defense—The Court and some federal courts have declined to recognize this defense. However, other federal circuit courts have recognized the defense in order to allow predisposed defendants to argue that some inducements and government conduct are too outrageous to be tolerable as a matter of Due Process.

For More Information

- Joseph A. Colquitt, *Rethinking Entrapment*, 41 AM. CRIM. L. REV. 1389 (2004).

- WAYNE R. LAFAVE, CRIMINAL LAW § 9.8, at 529–550 (6th ed. 2017).

- PAUL MARCUS, *Presenting Back from the [Almost] Dead, The Entrapment Defense*, 47 FLA. L. REV. 205 (1995).

- RUSSELL L. WEAVER, JOHN M. BURKOFF, CATHERINE HANCOCK & STEVEN I. FRIEDLAND, PRINCIPLES OF CRIMINAL PROCEDURE Ch. 6 (7th ed. 2021).

- AMERICAN LAW INSTITUTE, MODEL PENAL CODE AND COMMENTARIES, Part I, § 2.13, Comments at 405–420 (1980).

Test Your Knowledge

To assess your understanding of the material in this chapter, click here to take a quiz.

CHAPTER 6

Police Interrogations & Confessions

A. Pre-*Miranda* Doctrines

Prior to the Court's landmark 1966 decision in *Miranda v. Arizona*, the Court used three doctrines to regulate police interrogations. Beginning in 1936, the Court began applying the Due Process Clause of the Fourteenth Amendment as a source of standards governing the admissibility of confessions in state courts; the same analysis came to be used for the Fifth Amendment Due Process standards in federal courts. The Court also developed the non-constitutional *McNabb-Mallory* doctrine to exclude some confessions under its supervisory powers to create evidence rules for federal courts. Finally, in 1964 the Court relied on Sixth Amendment right-to-counsel doctrine to limit post-indictment interrogations by undercover government agents.

Take Note

The doctrines established in the Court's Due Process and Sixth Amendment confession precedents remain good law today. However, the modern scope of each doctrine has been influenced in significant ways by *Miranda* doctrine, which delineates the rights of persons interrogated in police custody, and thereby serves to protect the exercise of the Fifth Amendment privilege against self-incrimination.

1. Pre-*Miranda* Due Process

Brown v. Mississippi

297 U.S. 278 (1936).

MR. CHIEF JUSTICE HUGHES delivered the opinion of the Court.

The violent acts used to procure the confessions of three African-American defendants were admitted at trial by the white sheriff and white men who helped him. After arrest, one defendant was "hanged by a rope to the limb of a tree" three times, "tied to a tree and whipped," and then released, "suffering intense pain and agony." A day or two later, the same man was arrested again, "severely whipped," and told that the whipping would continue "until he confessed" to murder, which he did. When the two other defendants were arrested and taken to jail, they were made to strip, "and they were laid over chairs and their backs were cut to pieces with a leather strap with buckles on it." They were told that the whipping would continue until they confessed. When they did confess, they "changed or adjusted their confession in all particulars of detail so as to conform to the demands of their torturers." The two-day trial began the day after arraignment when defendants received appointed counsel; defendants testified that their confessions were false, but they were convicted of murder and sentenced to death. They challenged their convictions on Due Process grounds.

The question is whether convictions, which rest solely upon confessions shown to have been extorted by brutality and violence, are consistent with the due process of law required by the Fourteenth Amendment. The state stresses that "exemption from compulsory self-incrimination in the courts of the states is not secured by any part of the Federal Constitution." But the question of the right of the state to withdraw the privilege against self-incrimination is not here involved. The compulsion to which the Fifth Amendment refers is that of the processes of justice by which the accused may be called as a witness and required to testify. Compulsion by torture to extort a confession is a different matter.

The state is free to regulate the procedure of its courts in accordance with its own conceptions of policy, unless in so doing it "offends some principle of justice so rooted in the traditions and conscience of our people as to be ranked as fundamental." The freedom of the state in establishing its policy is limited by the requirement of due process of law. Because a state may dispense with a jury trial, it does not follow that it may substitute trial by ordeal. The rack and torture chamber may not be substituted for the witness stand. The state may not permit an accused to be hurried to conviction under mob domination—where the whole proceeding is but a mask—without supplying corrective process. The state may not deny to the accused the aid of counsel. *Powell v. Alabama*, 287 U.S. 45 (1932). Nor may a state, through the action of its officers, contrive a conviction through the pretense of a trial which "deprives a defendant of liberty through a deliberate deception of court and jury by the presentation of testimony known to be perjured." *Mooney v. Holohan*, 294 U.S. 103, 112 (1935). The trial equally is a mere pretense where the state authorities have contrived a conviction resting solely upon confessions obtained by violence. The due process clause requires that government action "shall be consistent with the fundamental principles of liberty and justice which lie at the base of all our civil and political institutions." *Hebert v. Louisiana*, 272 U.S. 312 (1926). It would be difficult to conceive of methods more revolting to the sense of justice than those taken to procure the confessions of these defendants, and the use of the confessions thus obtained as the basis for conviction and sentence was a clear denial of due process.

Point for Discussion

Language of Voluntariness

Over time, the Court used Due Process doctrine to hold that only "voluntary" confessions are admissible, produced by the "free will" of the defendant. The Court rejected confessions that were extracted based on police "coercion," including inducements, threats, or deceptive stratagems. *See, e.g., Spano v. New York,* 360 U.S. 315 (1959) (involuntary confession obtained by tricks of lying police officer); *Lynumn v. Illinois,* 372 U.S. 528 (1963) (involuntary confession obtained by threat that defendant's children could be taken away).

Take Note

The purposes of the Due Process ban on involuntary confessions overlap with common law evidence doctrine that prohibits the admission of such evidence. The evidence doctrine was intended to insure the inadmissibility of "presumptively false evidence," whereas an additional purpose of the Due Process doctrine was to prevent unfairness "in the use of evidence whether true or false." *Lisenba v. California,* 314 U.S. 219, 236 (1941).

During the thirty years between *Brown* and *Miranda*, the Court relied on Due Process doctrine to invalidate confessions in more than twenty cases, while upholding confessions in less than half that number. Most of these decisions revealed sharp disagreements among the justices concerning the interpretation of the "voluntariness" concept. Over time, the Court expanded this concept to encompass various types of psychologically coercive interrogation strategies, and came to focus upon the customs of *incommunicado* police questioning as the ultimate source of the coercion problem. The concept of voluntariness continued to evolve in Due Process decisions even after *Miranda*.

Haynes v. Washington

373 U.S. 503 (1963).

MR. JUSTICE GOLDBERG delivered the opinion of the Court.

Haynes was arrested at night for robbing a gas station; he was taken to the police station and booked for "investigation" on the "small book," which meant that he was not allowed to make phone calls or to have visitors. During the interrogation that night, Haynes asked to call an attorney and to call his wife, but the police refused these requests, telling him that "he might make a call if he confessed." The next day, the police continued to reject his requests to call his wife during interrogation, while telling Haynes that after he "made a statement and cooperated with" the police, they "would see to it" that he could call his wife. During a third interrogation in the prosecutor's office, Haynes made further requests to call his wife, which were rejected again. He made incriminating statements during all three interrogations, and his second and third statements were transcribed. Haynes signed the second statement but refused to sign the third one, telling the prosecutor that "all the promises of all the officers I had talked to had not been fulfilled and so I would sign nothing under any conditions until I was allowed to call my wife to see about legal counsel." After he appeared at a preliminary hearing on the day after arrest, Haynes was returned to jail and held incommunicado while the police made repeated efforts to obtain his signature on the third statement. He was not allowed to call his wife until "some five or seven days after his arrest." The signed statement was admitted at his trial, and he was convicted of robbery; he argued that this statement was involuntary under Due Process standards.

Haynes was not taken before a magistrate and granted a preliminary hearing until he had acceded to demands that he give and sign the written statement. Nor is there any indication that prior to signing the written confession, or thereafter, Haynes was advised by authorities of his right to remain silent, warned that his answers might be used against him, or told of his rights respecting consultation with an attorney. Whether the confession was obtained by coercion or improper inducement can be determined only by an examination of all of the attendant circumstances. Haynes' undisputed testimony permits no doubt that [the confession] was obtained under a totality of circumstances evidencing an involuntary written admission of guilt. Haynes was alone in the hands of the police, with no one to advise or aid him, and he had "no reason not to believe that the police had ample power to carry out their threats," to continue, for a much longer period if need be, the incommunicado detention—as in fact was actually done. Confronted with the express threat of continued incommunicado detention and induced by the promise of communication with and access to family, Haynes understandably chose to make and sign the damning written statement.

We cannot blind ourselves to what experience unmistakably teaches: that even apart from the express threat, the basic techniques present here—the secret and incommunicado detention and interrogation—are devices adapted and used to extort confessions from suspects. The line between proper and permissible police conduct and techniques and methods offensive to due process is, at best, a difficult one to draw, particularly in cases such as this where it is necessary to make fine judgments as to the effect of psychologically coercive pressures and inducements on the mind and will of an accused. We are here impelled to the conclusion, from all of the facts presented, that the bounds of due process have been exceeded. History amply shows that confessions have often been extorted to save law enforcement officials the trouble and effort of obtaining valid and independent evidence; the coercive devices used here were designed to obtain admissions to complete a case in which there had already been obtained, by proper investigative efforts, competent evidence sufficient to sustain a conviction. The procedures here are no less constitutionally impermissible, and perhaps more unwarranted because so unnecessary.

Official overzealousness of the type which vitiates a conviction has only deleterious effects. Here it has put the State to the substantial additional expense of prosecuting the case through the appellate courts and will require even a greater expenditure in the event of retrial, as is likely. But it is the deprivation of the protected rights themselves which is fundamental and the most regrettable, not only because of the effect on the individual defendant, but because of the effect on our system of law and justice. Whether there is involved the brutal "third degree," or the more subtle, but no less offensive, methods here obtaining, official misconduct cannot but breed disrespect for law, as well as for those charged with its enforcement.

MR. JUSTICE CLARK, with whom MR. JUSTICE HARLAN, MR. JUSTICE STEWART and MR. JUSTICE WHITE, join, dissenting.

Haynes is neither youthful nor lacking in experience in law breaking. He is married and was a skilled sheet-metal worker temporarily unemployed. He had served time. He cannot be placed in the category of those types of people with whom our Due Process cases have ordinarily dealt, such as the mentally subnormal accused, the youthful offender, or the naive and impressionable defendant. There is no contention of physical abuse, no extended or repeated interrogation, no deprivation of sleep or food, no use of psychiatric techniques, and no threat of mob violence. In light of his age, intelligence and experience with the police, the comparative absence of any coercive circumstances, and the fact that he never evidenced a will to deny his guilt, his written confession was not involuntary.

The Court's Due Process precedents often relied on the defendant's special vulnerability to police coercion based on physical and mental attributes and life experiences. In *Spano v. New York*, 360 U.S. 315 (1959), the Court relied on a "totality of circumstances" analysis to invalidate a confession, including the defendant's attributes: "Spano was a foreign-born man of 25 with no past history of law violation. He had progressed only one-half years into high school and he had a history of emotional instability. He had suffered a cerebral concussion, and was found unacceptable for military service primarily because of psychiatric disorder. He had also failed the Army's intelligence test. He was subjected to questioning from early evening into the night by fifteen police officers, prosecutors, and others for virtually eight straight hours before he confessed. The questioners persisted in the face of his repeated refusals to answer on the advice of his attorney, and they ignored his reasonable requests to contact his attorney. The use of Bruno, a police cadet and 'childhood friend' of Spano's is another factor because Bruno's was the one face visible to Spano in which he could put some trust. The police officers instructed Bruno falsely to state that his job was in jeopardy unless Spano confessed, and that the loss of his job would be disastrous to his three children, his wife and his unborn child. Spano ultimately yielded to his false friend's entreaties. We conclude that Spano's will was overborne by official pressure, fatigue and sympathy falsely aroused after considering all the facts."

Points for Discussion

a. Inherent Coercion & Alternatives to Due Process

In *Stein v. New York*, <u>346 U.S. 156 (1953)</u>, the Court opined that some defendants might be especially resistant to police coercion, reasoning that, "What would be overpowering to the weak of will or mind might be utterly ineffective against an experienced criminal." However, *Stein* recognized that the defendant's attributes might be irrelevant in some cases, such as when "physical violence or threat of it invalidates confessions and is universally condemned by law," so "there is no need to weigh or measure its effects on the will of the individual victim." Another decision that focused on the inherently coercive nature of an interrogation strategy was *Ashcraft v. Tennessee*, <u>322 U.S. 143 (1944)</u>, where the Court determined that 36 hours of "third degree" interrogation inevitably would produce an involuntary confession.

Take Note

A number of justices were dissatisfied with the Due Process "totality" doctrine because it failed to provide clear, predictable, and uniform guidelines as to the boundaries of acceptable police conduct during interrogations. Moreover, the difficulties of defining "voluntariness" were magnified, as one justice observed, because "the trial on the issue of coercion is seldom helpful," as police "usually testify one way, the accused another," and the secrecy of interrogations gives defendants "little chance to prove coercion at trial." *Crooker v. California*, 357 U.S. 433 (1958) (Douglas, J., dissenting).

b. The Movement Towards *Per Se* Rules

The creation of *per se* rules for interrogations offered the promise of clearer guidelines for police and greater protections from coercion for interrogated people. One such rule was proposed by some justices in *Spano* who endorsed a *per se* Due Process right for an indicted defendant who asks for counsel during interrogation to be allowed to consult with counsel. *See Spano*, 360 U.S. at 324 (Douglas, J., concurring, joined by Justices Black and Brennan).

Hypo: *Interrogation of Juvenile*

Robert Gallegos, a 14-year-old boy, is arrested for assault, and when the victim dies from his injuries, Gallegos becomes a potential defendant in a homicide prosecution. During his detention in a juvenile facility, his mother attempts to visit him; but is told that she must wait at least three days until the next visiting day, a Monday, or wait six more days and visit on the next Thursday. By the time she visits Gallegos on a Thursday, he has signed a confession. He was detained incommunicado during this entire period. Before his confession, police tell Gallegos that he may ask to have his parents or an attorney present during the interrogation, but he does not make that request. Police also warn him that he does not have to make a statement and that he faces the possibility of a murder charge. His mother is informed by police that Gallegos has a right to counsel, but she did not obtain a lawyer for him. Gallegos later testifies that he was not threatened by the police and not questioned for long periods of time. Do the circumstances of his interrogation violate Due Process? *See Gallegos v. Colorado,* 370 U.S. 49 (1962).

2. The *McNabb-Mallory* Rule

During the post-*Brown* era, the Court supplemented the Due Process doctrine with the *McNabb-Mallory* rule that applied only in the federal courts. In *McNabb v. United States,* 318 U.S. 332 (1943), the Court created an exclusionary rule to enforce the command of 18 U.S.C. § 595, which requires that a federal officer who arrests any person must "take the defendant before the nearest judicial officer having jurisdiction for a hearing, commitment, or taking bail for trial." The *McNabb* rule allowed courts to exclude confessions obtained in a suspicious context, or when a federal officer delayed an arrestee's appearance in court so as to perform interrogation before counsel could be appointed. *McNabb* acknowledged that "Congress has not explicitly forbidden the use of evidence" procured in this way, but declared that the admission of such a confession "would stultify the policy" of that of § 595.

Take Note

The Court repeatedly rejected the argument that the *McNabb-Mallory* rule should be incorporated into Due Process doctrine and applied to the states, but some state courts chose to incorporate the rule into their own state law. *McNabb* and *Mallory* rested on the Supreme Court's supervisory authority over the federal courts.

In *Mallory v. United States,* 354 U.S. 449 (1957), the Court created an exclusionary rule to enforce the mandate of Rule 5(a) of the Federal Rules of Criminal Procedure, which requires arraignment of federal arrestees without "unnecessary delay." The *Mallory* Court reasoned that the purpose of this requirement was to insure that a person "may be advised of his rights" by a judicial officer "as quickly as possible" after arrest. Therefore, a court should invalidate a confession in a case such as *Mallory,* where the officers delayed arraignment for over four hours, used that time to procure a confession at police headquarters, and refrained from informing the arrestee "of his right to counsel," his right "to a preliminary examination before a magistrate," his right "to keep silent," and his right to know that "any statement made by him may be used against him." The *McNabb-Mallory* rule expressed the Court's concern that arrestees could be interrogated while remaining ignorant of their rights, as long as information about those rights was communicated only by judges at a hearing that came too late for arrestees to learn of those rights and exercise them.

FYI

In effect, the *McNabb-Mallory* doctrine was based on the assumption that the exclusion of some confessions would have a deterrent effect on police decisions to delay the access of arrestees to hearings and consultations with counsel.

In *Corley v. United States*, 556 U.S. 303 (2009), the Court held that Congress narrowed the *McNabb-Mallory* rule in Title II of the Omnibus Crime Control and Safe Streets Act of 1968, but did not eliminate it. That statute provides in § 3501(c) that a confession made by a federal defendant under arrest "shall not be inadmissible solely because of delay in bringing such person before a magistrate judge if such confession is made voluntarily within six hours of arrest." This six-hour period may be extended if further delay is "reasonable considering the means of transportation and the distance to be traveled to the nearest available magistrate." For confessions that occur more than six hours after arrest, the *McNabb-Mallory* doctrine applies for determinations whether there was "unnecessary" delay that requires exclusion of the confession from evidence.

3. Pre-*Miranda* Sixth Amendment Right to Counsel

After the Sixth Amendment right to counsel was incorporated into Due Process and applied to the states in 1963, two different approaches to regulating police interrogations appeared the next year. One approach is reflected in the following decision.

Massiah v. United States

377 U.S. 201 (1964).

MR. JUSTICE STEWART delivered the opinion of the Court.

Massiah was indicted for violating federal narcotics laws. He retained a lawyer, pleaded not guilty, and was released on bail. While he was free on bail a federal agent succeeded by surreptitious means in listening to incriminating conversations with a co-defendant who had agreed to hide a radio transmitter under his car seat to broadcast the conversations to the agent. These statements were introduced at Massiah's trial and he was convicted. He argued that his Sixth Amendment rights were violated by the agent's deliberate elicitation of his statements, after indictment and in the absence of his counsel.

Some justices opined in *Spano* that a confession is inadmissible when it is deliberately elicited by the police after the defendant has been indicted, and therefore is clearly entitled to a lawyer's help. A Constitution which guarantees a defendant the aid of counsel at a public trial could surely vouchsafe no less to an indicted defendant under interrogation by the police in a completely extrajudicial proceeding. Anything less might deny a defendant "effective representation by counsel at the only stage when legal aid and advice would help him." Since *Spano*, the New York courts have followed this rule: "Any secret interrogation of the defendant, from and after the finding of the indictment, without the protection afforded by the presence of counsel, contravenes the basic dictates of fairness in the conduct of criminal causes and the fundamental rights of person charged with crime." This view no more than reflects a constitutional principle established as long ago as *Powell v. Alabama*, 287 U.S. 45 (1932), where the Court noted that "during perhaps the most critical period of the proceedings from the time of their arraignment until the beginning of their trial, when consultation, thorough-going investigation and preparation are vitally important, the defendants are as much entitled to the aid of counsel during that period as at the trial itself."

We hold that Massiah was denied the basic protections of the Sixth Amendment when there was used against him at his trial evidence of his own incriminating words, which federal agents had deliberately elicited from him after he had been indicted and in the absence of his counsel. It is true that in *Spano* defendant was interrogated in a police station, while here the damaging testimony was elicited from the defendant without his knowledge while he was free on bail. But "if such a rule is to have any efficacy it must apply to indirect and surreptitious interrogations as well as those conducted in the jailhouse." We do not question that in this case it was entirely proper to continue an investigation of the suspected criminal activities of the defendant and his alleged confederates, even though the defendant had already been indicted. All that we hold is that the defendant's own incriminating statements could not constitutionally be used by the prosecution as evidence against him at his trial on the narcotics charge.

MR. JUSTICE WHITE, with whom MR. JUSTICE CLARK and MR. JUSTICE HARLAN join, dissenting.

I am unable to see how this case presents an unconstitutional interference with Massiah's right to counsel. Massiah was not prevented from consulting with counsel as often as he wished. No meetings with counsel were disturbed or spied upon. Preparation for trial was in no way obstructed. It is unsound to say that because Massiah had a right to counsel's aid before and during the trial, his out-of-court conversations and admissions must be excluded if obtained without counsel's consent or presence. The right to counsel has never meant as much before. Had there been no prior arrangements between Massiah's co-defendant and the police, his testimony would be readily admissible at Massiah's trial. But because the co-defendant had been cooperating with the police prior to his meeting with Massiah, his evidence is somehow transformed into inadmissible evidence despite the fact that the hazard to Massiah remains precisely the same—the defection of a confederate in crime.

Point for Discussion

The Sixth Amendment & Pre-Indictment Arrestees

Soon after *Massiah*, the Court extended the right to counsel to arrestees who were not yet indicted. In *Escobedo v. Illinois*, 378 U.S. 478 (1964), the Court held that the police violated the Sixth Amendment because the police investigation had "begun to focus on" the defendant in custody as "a particular suspect," the police had not "effectively warned" the defendant of "the right to remain silent," the defendant had "requested and been denied an opportunity to consult with his lawyer," and the police had elicited incriminating statements from him during questioning. Escobedo was repeatedly refused access to his lawyer even after the lawyer arrived at the police station, although they did come "into each other's view for a few moments." *Escobedo* reasoned that the right to counsel for indicted defendants was necessary both at trial and during the "completely extrajudicial proceeding" of police interrogation, and that it "should make no difference" that defendant had not yet been indicted. For the "right to use counsel at the formal trial" would be "a very hollow thing" if "for all practical purposes, the conviction is already assured" by pre-indictment interrogation of an arrestee. *Escobedo* acknowledged that the police need to use interrogations to investigate "an unsolved crime," but concluded that once the police "process shifts from investigatory to accusatory" so that the purpose of that process "is to elicit a confession," then the "adversary system begins to operate" for Sixth Amendment purposes.

Take Note

Escobedo's extension of the Sixth Amendment to the pre-indictment phase of an investigation was retracted in *Kirby v. Illinois*, 406 U.S. 682 (1972), which held that the right to counsel applies only to "critical stages" of a prosecution that occur after the commencement of "adversarial judicial proceedings." The event of arrest does not qualify as this type of proceeding. After *Kirby*, *Escobedo*'s Sixth Amendment rationale became untenable. The Court formally recognized this point in *Oregon v. Elstad*, 470 U.S. 298 (1985), and given the fact that *Miranda*'s Fifth Amendment rules had supplanted *Escobedo*'s holding, the *Elstad* Court decided to reinterpret *Escobedo* retrospectively as a Fifth Amendment decision.

The *Massiah* Court's prohibition on the elicitation of statements from indicted defendants was consistent with the alignment of the Sixth Amendment right to counsel with the commencement of adversarial judicial proceedings. Unlike *Escobedo*, *Massiah* was not made redundant by *Miranda*. *Massiah* rights apply to indicted persons who are not in custody, and to indicted persons who are questioned surreptitiously by government agents, whereas *Miranda* rights do not apply to persons in either category. The post-*Miranda* cases interpreting *Massiah* rights are presented later in this chapter.

B. The Fifth Amendment & *Miranda*

The Court's recognition of the shortcomings of Due Process doctrine led to the articulation of Fifth Amendment protections for interrogated persons in custody.

Miranda v. Arizona

384 U.S. 436 (1966).

MR. CHIEF JUSTICE WARREN delivered the opinion of the Court.

The question is whether the Fifth Amendment privilege "is fully applicable during a period of custodial interrogation." More specifically, we deal with the admissibility of statements obtained from an individual who is subjected to custodial police interrogation and the necessity for procedures which assure that the individual is accorded his privilege under the Fifth Amendment not to be compelled to incriminate himself or herself. The modern practice of in-custody interrogation is psychologically rather than physically oriented. Interrogation still takes place in privacy. Privacy results in secrecy and this in turn results in a gap in our knowledge as to what in fact goes on in the interrogation rooms. A valuable source of information about present police practices, however, may be found in various police manuals and texts which document procedures employed with success in the past. These texts are used by law enforcement agencies themselves as guides. The officers are told by the manuals that the "principal psychological factor contributing to a successful interrogation is privacy—being alone with the person under interrogation." The efficacy of this tactic has been explained as follows: "If at all practicable, the interrogation should take place in the investigator's office or at least in a room of his choice. In his own home he may be confident, indignant, or recalcitrant. He is more keenly aware of his rights and more reluctant to tell of his indiscretions of criminal behavior within the walls of his home. Moreover his family and other friends are nearby, their presence lending moral support. In his office, the investigator possesses all the advantages. The atmosphere suggests the invincibility of the forces of the law."

The manuals instruct the police to display an air of confidence in the suspect's guilt and from outward appearance to maintain only an interest in confirming certain details. The interrogator should direct his comments toward the reasons why the subject committed the act, rather than court failure by asking the subject whether he did it. The officers are instructed to minimize the moral seriousness of the offense, to cast blame on the victim or on society. These tactics are designed to put the subject in a psychological state where his story is but an elaboration of what the police purport to know already—that he is guilty. Explanations to the contrary are dismissed and discouraged. The texts thus stress that the major qualities an interrogator should possess are patience and perseverance: "The investigator will encounter many situations where the sheer weight of his personality will be the deciding factor. Where emotional appeals and tricks are employed to no avail, he must rely on an oppressive atmosphere of dogged persistence. He must interrogate steadily and without relent, leaving the subject no prospect of surcease. He must dominate his subject and overwhelm him with his inexorable will to obtain the truth. He should interrogate for a spell of several hours pausing only for the subject's necessities in acknowledgment of the need to avoid a charge of duress that can be technically substantiated. In a serious case, the interrogation may continue for days, with the required intervals for food and sleep, but with no respite from the atmosphere of domination. It is possible in this way to induce the subject to talk without resorting to duress or coercion."

The manuals suggest that the suspect be offered legal excuses for his actions in order to obtain an initial admission of guilt. Where there is a suspected revenge-killing, for example, the interrogator may say: "Joe, you probably didn't go out looking for this fellow with the purpose of shooting him. My guess is, however, that you expected something from him and that's why you carried a gun—for your own protection. You knew him for what he was, no good. Then when you met him he probably started using foul, abusive language and he gave some indication that he was about to pull a gun on you, and that's when you had to act to save your own life. That's about it, isn't it, Joe?" Having then obtained the admission of shooting, the interrogator is advised to refer to circumstantial evidence which negates the self-defense explanation. This should enable him to secure the entire story. One text notes that "Even if he fails to do so, the inconsistency between the subject's original denial of the shooting and his present admission of at least doing the shooting will serve to deprive him of a self-defense 'out' at the time of trial."

When the techniques described above prove unavailing, the texts recommend they be alternated with a show of some hostility. One ploy often used has been termed the "friendly-unfriendly" or the "Mutt and Jeff" act: "In this technique, two agents are employed. Mutt, the relentless investigator, who knows the subject is guilty and is not going to waste any time. He's sent a dozen men away for this crime and he's going to send the subject away for the full term. Jeff, on the other hand, is a kindhearted man. He disapproves of Mutt and his tactics and will arrange to get him off the case if the subject will cooperate. He can't hold Mutt off for very long. The subject would be wise to make a quick decision. The technique is applied by having both investigators present while Mutt acts out his role. Jeff may stand by quietly and demur at some of Mutt's tactics. When Jeff makes his plea for cooperation, Mutt is not present."

The interrogators sometimes are instructed to induce a confession out of trickery. In the identification situation, the interrogator may take a break in questioning to place the subject in a line-up. "The witness or complainant (previously coached, if necessary) studies the line-up and confidently points out the subject as the guilty party." Then the questioning resumes "as though there were now no doubt about the guilt of the subject." A variation on this technique is called the "reverse line-up": "The accused is placed in a line up, but this time he is identified by several fictitious witnesses or victims who associated him with different offenses. It is expected that the subject will become desperate and confess to the offense under investigation in order to escape from the false accusations."

The manuals also contain instructions for police on how to handle the individual who refuses to discuss the matter entirely, or who asks for an attorney or relatives. The examiner is to concede him the right to remain silent. "This usually has a very undermining effect. First of all, he is disappointed in his expectation of an unfavorable reaction on the part of the interrogator. Secondly, a concession of this right to remain silent impresses the subject with the apparent fairness of his interrogator." After this psychological conditioning, however, the officer is told to point out the incriminating significance of the suspect's refusal to talk: "Joe, you have a right to remain silent. That's your privilege and I'm the last person in the world who'll try to take it away from you. If that's the way you want to leave this, O.K. But let me ask you this. Suppose you were in my shoes and I were in yours and you called me in to ask me about this and I told you, 'I don't want to answer any of your questions.' You'd think I had something to hide, and you'd probably be right in thinking that. That's exactly what I'll have to think about you, and so will everybody else. So let's sit here and talk this whole thing over."

Few will persist in their initial refusal to talk, it is said, if this monologue is employed correctly. In the event that the subject wishes to speak to a relative or an attorney, the following advice is tendered: "The interrogator should respond by suggesting that the subject first tell the truth to the interrogator himself rather than get anyone else involved. If the request is for an attorney, the interrogator may suggest that the subject save himself or his family the expense of any such professional service, particularly if he is innocent of the offense. The interrogator may also add, 'Joe, I'm only looking for the truth, and if you're telling the truth, that's it. You can handle this by yourself.'"

From these representative samples of interrogation techniques, the setting pre-scribed by the manuals and observed in practice becomes clear. In essence: To be alone with the subject is essential to prevent distraction and to deprive him of any outside support. The aura of confidence in his guilt undermines his will to resist. To obtain a confession, the interrogator must "patiently maneuver himself or his quarry into a position from which the desired objective may be attained." When normal procedures fail to produce the needed result, the police may resort to deceptive stratagems such as giving false legal advice. It is important to keep the subject off balance, for example, by trading on his insecurity about himself or his surroundings. The police then persuade, trick, or cajole him out of exercising his constitutional rights. Even without employing brutality, the "third degree" or the specific stratagems described here, the very fact of custodial interrogation exacts a heavy toll on individual liberty and trades on the weakness of individuals.

In the four cases before us, we concern ourselves primarily with this interrogation atmosphere and the evils it can bring. In these cases, we might not find the defendants' statements to have been involuntary in traditional terms. However, in each, defendant was thrust into an unfamiliar atmosphere and run through menacing police inter-rogation procedures. To be sure, the records do not evince overt physical coercion or patent psychological ploys. The fact remains that in none of these cases did the officers undertake to afford appropriate safeguards at the outset of the interrogation to insure that the statements were truly the product of free choice.

It is obvious that such an interrogation environment is created for no purpose other than to subjugate the individual to the will of his examiner. This atmosphere carries its own badge of intimidation. To be sure, this is not physical intimidation, but it is equally destructive of human dignity. The current practice of incommunicado interrogation is at odds with one of our Nation's most cherished principles—that the individual may not be compelled to incriminate himself. Unless adequate protective devices are employed to dispel the compulsion inherent in custodial surroundings, no statement obtained from defendant can truly be the product of his free choice. From the foregoing, we can readily perceive an intimate connection between the privilege against self-incrimination and police custodial questioning.

The privilege against self-incrimination—the essential mainstay of our adversary system—is founded on a complex of values. All these policies point to one overriding thought: the constitutional foundation underlying the privilege is the respect a govern-ment—state or federal—must accord to the dignity and integrity of its citizens. To maintain a "fair state-individual balance," to require the government "to shoulder the entire load," to respect the inviolability of the human personality, our accusatory sys-tem of criminal justice demands that the government seeking to punish an individual produce the evidence against him by its own independent labors, rather than by the cruel, simple expedient of compelling it from his own mouth. In sum, the privilege is fulfilled only when the person is guaranteed the right "to remain silent unless he chooses to speak in the unfettered exercise of his own will." *Malloy v. Hogan*, 378 U.S. 1, 8 (1964). All the principles embodied in the privilege apply to informal compulsion exerted by law-enforcement officers during in-custody questioning. An individual swept from familiar surroundings into police custody, surrounded by antagonistic forces, and subjected to the techniques of persuasion described above cannot be otherwise than under compulsion to speak. As a practical matter, the compulsion to speak in the isolated setting of the police station may well be greater than in courts or other official investigations, where there are often impartial observers to guard against intimidation or trickery.

There can be no doubt that the Fifth Amendment privilege is available outside of criminal court proceedings and serves to protect persons in all settings in which their freedom of action is curtailed in any significant way from being compelled to incriminate themselves. We have concluded that without proper safeguards the process of in-custody interrogation of persons suspected or accused of crime contains inherently compelling pressures which work to undermine the individual's will to resist and to compel him to speak where he would not otherwise do so freely. In order to combat these pressures and to permit a full opportunity to exercise the privilege against self-incrimination, the accused must be adequately and effectively apprised of his rights and the exercise of those rights must be fully honored. It is impossible for us to foresee the potential alternatives for protecting the privilege which might be devised by Congress or the States in the exercise of their creative rule-making capacities. Our decision in no way creates a constitutional straitjacket which will handicap sound efforts at reform, nor is it intended to have this effect. We encourage Congress and the States to continue their laudable search for increasingly effective ways of protecting the rights of the individual while promoting efficient enforcement of our criminal laws. However, unless we are shown other procedures which are at least as effective in apprising accused persons of their right of silence and in assuring a continuous opportunity to exercise it, the following safeguards must be observed.

First, at the outset, if a person in custody is to be subjected to interrogation, he must first be informed in clear and unequivocal terms that he has the right to remain silent. For those unaware of the privilege, the warning is needed simply to make them aware of it—the threshold requirement for an intelligent decision as to its exercise. More important, such a warning is an absolute prerequisite in overcoming the inherent pressures of the interrogation atmosphere. The warning will show the individual that his interrogators are prepared to recognize his privilege should he choose to exercise it. The Fifth Amendment privilege is so fundamental to our system of constitutional rule and the expedient of giving an adequate warning as to the availability of the privilege so simple, we will not pause to inquire in individual cases whether the defendant was aware of his rights without a warning being given.

Second, the warning of the right to remain silent must be accompanied by the explanation that anything said can and will be used against the individual in court. This warning is needed in order to make him aware not only of the privilege, but also of the consequences of forgoing it. It is only through an awareness of these consequences that there can be any assurance of real understanding and intelligent exercise of the privilege. Moreover, this warning may serve to make the individual more acutely aware that he is faced with a phase of the adversary system—that he is not in the presence of persons acting solely in his interest.

Third, the right to have counsel present at the interrogation is indispensable to the protection of the Fifth Amendment privilege under the system we delineate today. A once-stated warning, delivered by those who will conduct the interrogation, cannot itself suffice to that end among those who most require knowledge of their rights. Even preliminary advice given to the accused by his own attorney can be swiftly overcome by the secret interrogation process. Thus, the need for counsel to protect the Fifth Amendment privilege comprehends not merely a right to consult with counsel prior to questioning, but also to have counsel present during any questioning if the defendant so desires. An individual need not make a pre-interrogation request for a lawyer. While such request affirmatively secures his right to have one, his failure to ask for a lawyer does not constitute a waiver. No effective waiver of the right to counsel during interrogation can be recognized unless specifically made after the warnings have been given. The accused who does not know his rights and therefore does not make a request may be the person who most needs counsel. Accordingly we hold that an individual held for interrogation must be clearly informed that he has the right to consult with a lawyer and to have the lawyer with him during interrogation under the system for protecting the privilege we delineate today. As with the warnings of the right to remain silent and that anything stated can be used in evidence against him, this warning is an absolute prerequisite to interrogation.

Fourth, if an individual indicates that he wishes the assistance of counsel before any interrogation occurs, the authorities cannot rationally ignore his request on the basis that the individual does not have or cannot afford a retained attorney. The privilege against self-incrimination secured by the Constitution applies to all individuals. The need for counsel to protect the privilege exists for the indigent as well as the affluent. The vast majority of confession cases involve those unable to retain counsel. Therefore, it is necessary to warn an interrogated person that if he is indigent a lawyer will be appointed to represent him. Without this additional warning, the admonition of the right to consult with counsel would often be understood as meaning only that he can consult with a lawyer if he has one or has the funds to obtain one. The warning of a right to counsel would be hollow if not couched in terms that would convey to the indigent the knowledge that he too has a right to have counsel present. As with the warnings of the right to remain silent and of the general right to counsel, only by effective and express explanation to the indigent of this right can there be assurance that he was truly in a position to exercise it.

Fifth, once warnings have been given, if the individual indicates in any manner, at any time prior to or during questioning, that he wishes to remain silent, the interrogation must cease. He has shown that he intends to exercise his Fifth Amendment privilege; any statement taken after the person invokes his privilege cannot be other than the product of compulsion, subtle or otherwise. Without the right to cut off questioning, the setting of in-custody interrogation operates on the individual to overcome free choice in producing a statement after the privilege has been once invoked. If the individual states that he wants an attorney, the interrogation must cease until an attorney is present. At that time, the individual must have an opportunity to confer with the attorney and to have him present during any subsequent questioning. If the individual cannot obtain an attorney and he indicates that he wants one before speaking to police, they must respect his decision to remain silent. This does not mean that each police station must have a "station house lawyer" present at all times to advise prisoners. It does mean that if police authorities conclude that they will not provide counsel during a reasonable period of time in which investigation in the field is carried out, they may refrain from doing so without violating the person's Fifth Amendment privilege so long as they do not question him during that time.

Sixth, if the interrogation continues without the presence of an attorney and a statement is taken, a heavy burden rests on the government to demonstrate that the defendant knowingly and intelligently waived his privilege against self-incrimination and his right to retained or appointed counsel. An express statement that the individual is willing to make a statement and does not want an attorney followed closely by a statement could constitute a waiver. But a valid waiver will not be presumed simply from the silence of the accused after warnings are given or simply from the fact that a confession was in fact eventually obtained. The fact of lengthy interrogation or incommunicado incarceration before a statement is made is strong evidence that the accused did not validly waive his rights because the fact that the individual eventually made a statement is consistent with the conclusion that the compelling influence of the interrogation finally forced him to do so. Moreover, any evidence that the accused was threatened, tricked, or cajoled into a waiver will, of course, show that the defendant did not voluntarily waive his privilege.

Finally, no distinction can be drawn between statements which are direct confessions and statements which amount to "admissions" of part or all of an offense. The privilege against self-incrimination does not distinguish degrees of incrimination. Similarly, no distinction may be drawn between inculpatory statements and statements alleged to be merely "exculpatory." If a statement were in fact truly exculpatory it would never be used by the prosecution. When an individual is in custody on probable cause, the police may seek out evidence in the field to be used at trial against him. Such investigation may include inquiry of persons not under restraint. General on-the-scene questioning as to facts surrounding a crime or other general questioning of citizens in the fact-finding process is not affected by our holding.

We hold that when an individual is taken into custody or otherwise deprived of his freedom by the authorities in any significant way and is subjected to questioning, the privilege against self-incrimination is jeopardized. Procedural safeguards must be employed to protect the privilege and in the absence of other fully effective measures, the following measures are required. He must be warned prior to any questioning that he has the right to remain silent, that anything he says can be used against him in a court of law, that he has the right to the presence of an attorney, and that if he cannot afford an attorney one will be appointed for him prior to any questioning if he so desires. Opportunity to exercise these rights must be afforded to him throughout the interrogation. After such warnings have been given, and such opportunity afforded him, the individual may knowingly and intelligently waive these rights and agree to answer questions or make a statement. But unless and until such warnings and waiver are demonstrated by the prosecution at trial, no evidence obtained as a result of interrogation can be used against him.

A recurrent argument made is that society's need for interrogation outweighs the privilege. But the Constitution has prescribed the rights of the individual when it provided in the Fifth Amendment that an individual cannot be compelled to be a witness against himself. That right cannot be abridged. Our decision does not in any way preclude police from carrying out their traditional investigatory functions. Although confessions may play an important role in some convictions, the cases before us present graphic examples of the overstatement of the "need" for confessions because even after police officers obtained "considerable" independent evidence against each defendant, they still conducted interrogations.

It is urged that an unfettered right to detention for interrogation should be allowed because it will often redound to the benefit of the person questioned. But the person who has committed no offense will be better able to clear himself after warnings with counsel present than without. Custodial interrogation, does not necessarily afford the innocent an opportunity to clear themselves. A serious consequence of the present practice is that many arrests "for investigation" subject large numbers of innocent persons to detention and interrogation. In one case here, police held four persons in jail for five days until one defendant confessed, although the police stated later that there was "no evidence to connect them with any crime."

Over the years the Federal Bureau of Investigation has compiled an exemplary record of effective law enforcement while advising any suspect or arrested person, at the outset of an interview, that he is not required to make a statement, that any statement may be used against him in court, that the individual may obtain the services of an attorney of his own choice and, more recently, that he has a right to free counsel if he is unable to pay. The practice of the FBI can readily be emulated by state and local enforcement agencies.

Judicial solutions to problems of constitutional dimension have evolved decade by decade. As courts have been presented with the need to enforce constitutional rights, they have found means of doing so. Where rights secured by the Constitution are involved, there can be no rule making or legislation which would abrogate them.

Mr. Justice Clark, dissenting.

I would continue to follow the Due Process rule. I would consider whether the police officer prior to custodial interrogation added the warning that the suspect might have counsel present at the interrogation and the warning that a court would appoint one at his request if he was too poor to employ counsel. In the absence of warnings, the burden would be on the State to prove that counsel was knowingly and intelligently waived or that in the totality of the circumstances, including the failure to give the necessary warnings, the confession was clearly voluntary.

Mr. Justice Harlan, whom Mr. Justice Stewart and Mr. Justice White join, dissenting.

The new rules are not designed to guard against police brutality or other unmistakably banned forms of coercion. Those who use third-degree tactics and deny them in court are equally able and destined to lie as skillfully about warnings and waivers. Rather, the thrust of the new rules is to negate all pressures, to reinforce the nervous or ignorant suspect, and ultimately to discourage any confession at all. What the Court largely ignores is that its rules impair, if they will not eventually serve wholly to frustrate, an instrument of law enforcement that has long and quite reasonably been thought worth the price paid for it. The Court's new code would markedly decrease the number of confessions. To warn the suspect that he may remain silent and remind him that his confession may be used in court are minor obstructions. To require also an express waiver by the suspect and an end to questioning whenever he demurs must heavily handicap questioning. To suggest or provide counsel for the suspect simply invites the end of the interrogation. How much harm this decision will inflict on law enforcement cannot be predicted with accuracy. We know that some crimes cannot be solved without confessions, that expert testimony attests to their importance in crime control, and that the Court is taking a real risk with society's welfare in imposing its new regime on the country. While passing over the costs and risks of its experiment, the Court portrays the evils of normal police questioning in exaggerated terms. Interrogation is no doubt often inconvenient and unpleasant for the suspect. However, it is no less so for a man to be arrested and jailed, to have his house searched, or to stand trial in court, yet all this may properly happen to the most innocent given probable cause, a warrant, or an indictment. Society has always paid a stiff price for law and order, and peaceful interrogation is not one of the dark moments of the law.

MR. JUSTICE WHITE, with whom MR. JUSTICE HARLAN and MR. JUSTICE STEWART join, dissenting.

Even if some confessions are coerced and present judicial procedures are believed to be inadequate to identify the confessions that are coerced and those that are not, it would still not be essential to impose the rule that the Court has fashioned. Transcripts or observers could be required, specific time limits, tailored to fit the cause, could be imposed, or other devices could be utilized to reduce the chances that otherwise indiscernible coercion will produce an inadmissible confession. By considering any answers to any interrogation to be compelled and by escalating the requirements to prove waiver, the Court, for all practical purposes, forbids interrogation except in the presence of counsel. Instead of confining itself to protection of the right against compelled self-incrimination the Court has created a limited Fifth Amendment right to counsel—or, as the Court expresses it, a "need for counsel to protect the Fifth Amendment privilege." There is every reason to believe that a good many criminal defendants who otherwise would have been convicted will now under this new version of the Fifth Amendment, either not be tried at all or will be acquitted if the State's evidence, minus the confession, is put to the test of litigation. Today's decision leaves open such questions as whether the accused was in custody, whether his statements were spontaneous or the product of interrogation, and whether the accused has effectively waived his rights, all of which are certain to prove productive of uncertainty during investigation and litigation.

Prior to *Miranda*, the Court sometimes referred to certain trial rights and procedures as "safeguards" that protect the right to a fair trial. For example, the Court described its judge-made exclusionary rule in *Brown* as one of the "procedural safeguards of due process" for the pre-trial stage of a criminal prosecution. *Chambers v. Florida*, 309 U.S. 227, 238 (1940). Later the Court identified the theory underlying Due Process doctrine as "a compound of two influences": the idea that the right to a fair trial with "procedural safeguards" should be viewed as an antidote to inquisitorial procedures like police interrogation; and the idea that the Fourteenth Amendment prohibition on coercion and the Fifth Amendment prohibition on compulsion are linked together. *Gallegos v. Colorado*, 370 U.S. 49, 55 (1962). *Miranda* continued to use the Due Process metaphor of "safeguards" in fashioning new methods for effectuating the Fifth Amendment privilege, and subsequent decisions reveal differing perspectives concerning the consequences of the labeling of *Miranda*'s requirements as "prophylactic safeguards." *Compare Withrow v. Williams*, 507 U.S. 680 (1993) *with United States v. Patane*, 542 U.S. 630 (2004) (plurality opinion).

Take Note

More than 30 years after *Miranda*, the Court addressed the constitutionality of 18 U.S.C. § 3501, which provided that confessions are admissible in federal courts if they are voluntarily given. In *Dickerson v. United States*, 530 U.S. 428 (2000), the Court held that § 3501 is unconstitutional. The Court noted that the *Miranda* opinion "is replete with statements indicating that the majority thought it was announcing a constitutional rule," and concluded that, "Congress may not legislatively supersede our decisions interpreting and applying the Constitution." However, *Dickerson* declined to hold that "the *Miranda* warnings are required by the Constitution, in the sense that nothing else will suffice to satisfy constitutional requirements." Instead, the Court held that, "the *Miranda* decision was based on the assumption that 'something more than the Due Process totality test was necessary' to prevent involuntary custodial confessions. Therefore, the totality test of § 3501 "cannot be sustained if *Miranda* is to remain the law." *Dickerson* found no justification for overruling *Miranda* because the decision "has become embedded in routine police practice to the point where the warnings have become part of our national culture" and because principles of *stare decisis* "weigh heavily against overruling it."

Points for Discussion

a.   *Miranda* Violations & Civil Damage Actions

In *Chavez v. Martinez*, 538 U.S. 760 (2003), Martinez alleged that he was coercively interrogated in violation of *Miranda*. Since he was never prosecuted, he could not seek suppression of his statements at trial; instead, he brought a civil suit under 42 U.S.C. § 1983 and claimed that the officer's actions violated his Fifth Amendment privilege, as well as his Due Process right to be free from coercive questioning. The Court concluded that Martinez could not establish a violation of his Fifth Amendment rights because the privilege only prevents a defendant from being "compelled in any criminal case to be a witness against himself." This right could not have been violated since "Martinez was never prosecuted for a crime."

b.   *Miranda* & *Habeas* Review

Food for Thought

Consider the fact that *Miranda* relied extensively on police interrogation manuals to support its decision. The curious thing about the decision is that the Court almost ignores the facts of the cases before it. If techniques like the "Mutt and Jeff" treatment were not used against *Miranda*, why did they receive so much attention in the Court's opinion?

In *Withrow v. Williams*, 507 U.S. 680 (1993), the Court held that even when a defendant has received a "full and fair chance to litigate" a *Miranda* claim in state court, the doctrine of *Stone v. Powell*, 428 U.S. 465 (1976), does not bar *habeas* review of that claim. However, *Miranda habeas* claims are subject to the requirements of the Antiterrorism and Effective Death Penalty Act of 1996 (AEDPA), so that a defendant must show that the state-court ruling on the *Miranda* claim "was contrary to, or involved an unreasonable application of, clearly established" federal law as determined by Court precedents under 28 U.S.C. § 2254(d)(1).

Food for Thought

Arguably, *Miranda* is a pro-prosecution ruling as well as a pro-defendant ruling. Prosecutors were critical of the decision which they regarded as "highly technical" and as sometimes mandating the exclusion of valuable evidence based on police violations of rules that may be difficult to interpret and easy to violate in good faith. On the other hand, it is not clear that the warning provides as much protection for suspects as the Court might have hoped. The warning is sometimes administered in a very perfunctory manner, and, in any event, does not eliminate the inherent coerciveness of the custodial interrogation situation. A suspect may still be isolated from the outside world in a police-dominated environment. Moreover, although suspects may receive the warning, they may not be familiar with the rules of evidence or the fact that seemingly innocent statements can be incriminating. Moreover, once a *Miranda* warning has been given, any resulting confession is much more likely to be regarded as voluntary and therefore admissible. So, are the *Miranda* warnings a panacea for the confessions problem?

Hypo: *Alternatives to Miranda*

Justice White's dissent proposed that specific alternatives, such as transcripts or observers, could serve as substitutes for the *Miranda* warnings. Subsequently, as technology has improved, and become considerably cheaper, it is possible to tape record all confessions. Would transcripts, observers or cameras be preferable to the *Miranda* warnings?

C. *Miranda*'s Application

In extending the privilege against self-incrimination to custodial interrogations, *Miranda* raised a host of questions regarding the scope and application of its requirements, and years of litigation have been required to define such terms as "custody," "interrogation," "adequate warnings," "voluntary, knowing and intelligent" waiver, "unambiguous invocations" of the rights to silence and counsel, and post-invocation "initiation" that nullifies an invocation.

1. Custody

The duty to give *Miranda* warnings arises only when the police interrogate a person who is in "custody." The concepts of "custody" and "interrogation" are distinct and must coexist during "custodial interrogation" in order to give rise to *Miranda* rights and duties. In *Thompson v. Keohane*, <u>516 U.S. 99 (1995)</u>, while the Court did not provide a precise definition of the term "custody," it did state that "the court must apply an objective test to resolve the ultimate inquiry: was there a formal arrest or restraint on freedom of movement of the degree associated with a formal arrest."

Stansbury v. California

<u>511 U.S. 318 (1994)</u>.

PER CURIAM.

The initial determination of custody depends on the objective circumstances of the interrogation, not on the subjective views harbored by either the interrogating officers or the person being questioned. In *Beckwith v. United States*, 425 U.S. 341 (1976), defendant, without being advised of his *Miranda* rights, made incriminating statements to Government agents during an interview in a private home. He later asked that *Miranda* "be extended to cover interrogation in non-custodial circumstances after a police investigation has focused on the suspect." We found his argument unpersuasive, explaining that it "was the compulsive aspect of custodial interrogation, and not the strength or content of the government's suspicions at the time the questioning was conducted, which led the Court to impose the *Miranda* requirements with regard to custodial questioning."

In *Berkemer v. McCarty*, 468 U.S. 420 (1984), we reaffirmed *Beckwith*. *Berkemer* concerned the roadside questioning of a motorist detained in a traffic stop. We decided that the motorist was not in custody for purposes of *Miranda* even though the traffic officer "apparently decided as soon as the motorist stepped out of his car that the motorist would be taken into custody and charged with a traffic offense." The reason was that the officer "never communicated his intention to" the motorist during the relevant questioning. Under *Miranda* "a policeman's unarticulated plan has no bearing on the question whether a suspect was 'in custody' at a particular time"; rather, "the only relevant inquiry is how a reasonable man in the suspect's shoes would have understood his situation."

It is well settled, then, that a police officer's subjective view that the individual under questioning is a suspect, if undisclosed, does not bear upon the question whether the individual is in custody for purposes of *Miranda*. The same principle obtains if an officer's undisclosed assessment is that the person being questioned is not a suspect.

In either instance, one cannot expect the person under interrogation to probe the officer's innermost thoughts. Save as they are communicated or otherwise manifested to the person being questioned, an officer's evolving but unarticulated suspicions do not affect the objective circumstances of an interrogation or interview, and thus cannot affect the *Miranda* custody inquiry. An officer's knowledge or beliefs may bear upon the custody issue if they are conveyed, by word or deed, to the individual being questioned. Those beliefs are relevant to the extent they would affect how a reasonable person in the position of the individual being questioned would gauge the breadth of his or her "freedom of action." Even a clear statement from an officer that the person under interrogation is a prime suspect is not, in itself, dispositive of the custody issue, for some suspects are free to come and go until the police decide to make an arrest. The weight and pertinence of any communications regarding the officer's degree of suspicion will depend upon the facts and circumstances of the particular case.

We think it appropriate for the California Supreme Court to consider this question of custody in the first instance. We therefore reverse its judgment and remand the case for further proceedings not inconsistent with this opinion.

Points for Discussion

a. Routine Traffic Stops

Stansbury relied on *Berkemer v. McCarty*, 468 U.S. 420 (1984), a case which held that "routine" traffic stops do not create custody for purposes of *Miranda:* "Two features of an ordinary traffic stop mitigate the danger that a person questioned will be induced 'to speak where he would not otherwise do so freely.' First, detention of a motorist pursuant to a traffic stop is presumptively temporary and brief. A motorist's expectations are that he will be obliged to spend a short period of time answering questions and waiting while the officer checks his license and registration, that he may then be given a citation, but that in the end he most likely will be allowed to continue on his way. In this respect, questioning incident to an ordinary traffic stop is quite different from station house interrogation, which frequently is prolonged, and in which the detainee often is aware that questioning will continue until he provides his interrogators the answers they seek. Second, circumstances associated with the typical traffic stop are not such that the motorist feels completely at the mercy of the police. To be sure, the aura of authority surrounding an armed, uniformed officer and the knowledge that the officer has some discretion in deciding whether to issue a citation, in combination, exert some pressure on the detainee to respond to questions. But the typical traffic stop is public, at least to some degree. This exposure to public view both reduces the ability of an unscrupulous policeman to use illegitimate means to elicit self-incriminating statements and diminishes the motorist's fear that, if he does not cooperate, he will be subjected to abuse. The fact that the detained motorist typically is confronted by only one or at most two officers further mutes his sense of vulnerability. In short, the atmosphere surrounding an ordinary traffic stop is substantially less 'police dominated' than that surrounding the kinds of interrogation at issue in *Miranda* itself, and in the subsequent cases in which we have applied *Miranda*."

Take Note

Stansbury refers to the perspective of the "reasonable person in the suspect's shoes" so that the defendant's personal characteristics may or may not be relevant to that "perspective." In *Yarborough v. Alvarado*, 541 U.S. 652 (2004), the Court explained that the "objective" aspect of the "reasonable person" standard is meant to further the clarity of the custody test, so that police officers do not have "to make guesses" about a person's subjective experiences before deciding how they may interrogate a person. The Court acknowledged that "the line between permissible objective facts and impermissible subjective experiences can be indistinct in some cases." However, the Court held that a person's "prior history with law enforcement" is irrelevant to the custody inquiry: "In most cases, police officers will not know a suspect's interrogation history. Even if they do, the relationship between a suspect's past experiences and the likelihood a reasonable person with that experience would feel free to leave often will be speculative. Suspects with prior law enforcement experience may understand police procedures and reasonably feel free to leave unless told otherwise. On the other hand, they may view past as prologue and expect another in a string of arrests. We do not ask police officers to consider these contingent psychological factors when deciding when suspects should be advised of their *Miranda* rights. The inquiry turns too much on the suspect's subjective state of mind and not enough on the "objective circumstances of the interrogation."

b. Voluntary Interview

Stansbury also relied on *Oregon v. Mathiason*, 429 U.S. 492 (1977), in which the Court held that a voluntary interview at the police station may not qualify as "custody" if the interview does not involve a "restraint on freedom of movement of the degree associated with a formal arrest." Several factors led the Court to conclude that the interview in that case was non-custodial: "Mathiason came voluntarily to the police station, where he was immediately informed that he was not under arrest. At the close of a half-hour interview Mathiason did in fact leave the police station without hindrance. A noncustodial situation is not converted to one simply because the questioning took place in a coercive environment. Any interview of one suspected of a crime by a police officer will have coercive aspects to it. But the requirement of *Miranda* warnings is not to be imposed simply because the questioning takes place in the station house, or because the questioned person is one whom the police suspect." Justice Marshall dissented, arguing that *Miranda* "requires us to distinguish situations that resemble the 'coercive aspects' of custodial interrogation from those that more nearly resemble 'general on-the-scene questioning or other general questioning of citizens in the fact-finding process.' " He emphasized that Mathiason was interrogated in "private" and "unfamiliar surroundings," while being subjected to "deceptive strategems" condemned in *Miranda*. Justice Stevens dissented, arguing that a parolee like

Mathiason "should always be warned" during a police interview because a "parolee is technically in legal custody continuously until his sentence has been served."

c.   Custody & Inmates

In *Mathis v. United States*, 391 U.S. 1 (1968), the Court held that a state prison inmate should have received *Miranda* warnings when he was interrogated by an IRS agent in an isolated prison location regarding potential violations of the tax code. The Court reasoned that even "routine" tax investigations can lead to criminal prosecutions, and that nothing in *Miranda* "calls for a curtailment of the warnings based on the reason why the person is in custody." However, in *Maryland v. Shatzer*, 559 U.S. 98 (2010), the Court held that the mere fact of imprisonment does not establish the existence of custody for *Miranda* purposes. During the time when inmates are neither interrogated nor "isolated with their accusers," but living instead in the "accustomed surroundings" of the "general prison population," the fact of incarceration alone "does not create the coercive pressures identified in *Miranda*." However, *Shatzer* held that *Miranda* warnings must be given to inmates in "interrogative custody." In *Howes v. Fields*, 565 U.S. 499 (2012), the Court held that courts must examine the totality of circumstances on a case-by-case basis in determining whether an inmate is in custody for *Miranda* purposes: "We have declined to accord talismanic power to the freedom-of-movement inquiry, and instead have asked whether the relevant environment presents the same inherently coercive pressures as the type of station house questioning at issue in *Miranda*." *Howes* concluded that an inmate was not in custody when he was interrogated in a conference room in which he was "not physically restrained or threatened," and was "told at the outset of the interrogation," and reminded later, "that he could leave and go back to his cell whenever he wanted." He was offered "food and water," and "the door to the conference room was sometimes left open." He never asked to go back to his cell. Justice Ginsburg's *Howes* dissent proposed that custody should be found to exist when an inmate is "subjected to 'incommunicado interrogation' " in a "police-dominated atmosphere," and placed "against his will" in an "inherently stressful situation," with his "freedom of action" "curtailed in any significant way." She noted that: "The deputies were armed, and they questioned the inmate in isolation for between five to seven hours into the early morning hours. He was not given his evening medications. Even though the inmate was told that he was free to return to his cell, he did not ask to do so because he believed, with good reason, that they would not have allowed him to leave. The officers had ignored his repeated statements that he did not want to speak to them."

d.   Juvenile Justice

In *J.D.B.* the Court held that a child's age is relevant to the determination of custody: "Neither officers nor courts can reasonably evaluate the effect of objective circumstances that are specific to children," such as the schoolhouse setting of an interrogation, "without accounting for the age of the child subjected to those circumstances." *J.D.B.* distinguished *Alvarado*: "Precisely because childhood yields objective conclusions—among others, that children are "most susceptible to influence" and 'outside pressures'—considering age in the custody analysis in no way involves a determination of how youth "subjectively affects the mindset" of any particular child." *J.D.B.* acknowledged that a child's age would not necessarily be "a determinative, or even a significant, factor in every case." But the Court rejected the State's argument that a child's age should never be relevant to the custody determination, because such a rule would "ignore the very real differences between children and adults" and would "deny children the full scope of the procedural safeguards that *Miranda* guarantees to adults."

Hypo 1: *Stansbury Facts*

Four police officers go to Stansbury's home near midnight, and ask him to accompany them to the police station for questioning as a possible witness in a homicide investigation. They offer him the choice of riding in the patrol car or driving himself to the station, and Stansbury chooses to accept the ride. In order to reach the interview room in the jail area, Stansbury must pass through a locked parking garage door and a locked jail entrance, both of which are locked from both the inside and the outside, and he is subjected to a pat-down search. Stansbury is not restrained in the interview room, and two police officers are present. Oliver, the interviewing officer, tells Stansbury that he is being questioned as a witness, and that he is not "under arrest." After 30 minutes of questioning, Oliver decides to give Stansbury the *Miranda* warnings when Stansbury mentions a potentially incriminating fact. Was Stansbury in custody before Oliver gave him the warnings? *Compare People v. Stansbury*, 889 P.2d 588 (Ca. 1995) and *People v. Elmarr*, 181 P.3d 1157 (Colo. 2008); *State v. Muntean*, 12 A.3d 518 (2010); *State v. Waring*, 701 S.E.2d 615 (2010); *United States v. Ambrose*, 668 F.3d 943 (7th Cir. 2012).

Food for Thought

A Fourth Amendment "seizure" occurs when an individual is subjected either to an investigative stop based on reasonable suspicion, or to a custodial arrest based on probable cause. Assume that a motorist dutifully stops at a police roadblock set up to catch drunk drivers. Is the motorist in custody for purposes of *Miranda*? If the motorist is not in custody, what circumstances might arise at the roadblock to justify a finding of custody so as to require *Miranda* warnings?

Hypo 2: *More on Traffic Stops*

Does a "custodial interrogation" occur if the officer conducts a traffic stop, asks the stopped driver to sit in the front seat of his police car, and the driver agrees to do so (while the officer sits in the driver's seat of the same car)? Suppose another police officer arrives, and stands outside of the passenger window of the stopped motorist's car? Does the situation change significantly if one of the officers tells the stopped driver that he is aware that she was recently arrested for possession of illegal drugs, and that he suspects her of being in possession of drugs? *See State v. Landis*, 794 N.W.2d 151 (2011); *see also People v. Thomas*, 247 P.3d 886 (2011).

Hypo 3: *Home Interviews*

What circumstances might transform a home interview into a custodial interrogation? Suppose that the questioning officer makes clear that the suspect is not under arrest, that the officer "just wants to talk," and that the suspect will not be arrested that day regardless of what he says. Is there "custody" if the officer suggests that the interview should take place in a quiet area, and the officer and the suspect move to a storage room (where they will not be heard by others) and close the door? *See United States v. Craighead*, 539 F.3d 1073 (9th Cir. 2008); *see also Mumford v. People*, 270 P.3d 953 (Colo. 2012). Would your view be different if seven police officers, all displaying guns, arrive to execute a search warrant at a woman's house, and order her to sit on the couch. Would it matter whether the police told the woman that she was not under arrest? *See State v. Mangual*, 85 A.3d 627 (Conn. 2014). Suppose that a nine year-old of limited intelligence is suspected of having murdered his infant brother. A police officer indicates a desire to talk to the boy. Sitting at the dining room table, at the family home, with the father present, the officer asks the boy "what happened?" in a conversational tone. Was the boy in custody? How does the boy's age enter into the analysis of custody and coercion issues? *See In re DLH, Jr.*, 32 N.E.3d 1075 (Ill. 2015).

Hypo 4: *Hospital Interview*

Jamison is taken to the emergency room where he tells a police officer, Maurice, that he was shot by a stranger who ran away. Maurice asks Jamison for the location of the shooting and arranges for a detective to come to the hospital to investigate. Maurice follows Jamison to a treatment room where Jamison is placed on a gurney while attending nurses cut away his clothing and treat the wounds on his leg. Maurice places bags on Jamison's hands, which is routine procedure to preserve evidence on the hands of shooting victims. After noticing that there are no bullet holes in Jamison's clothing, Officer Maurice asks him to recount what happened during the shooting, and Jamison admits that he shot himself with an illegal handgun. Was Jamison in custody and entitled to *Miranda* warnings? *See United States v. Jamison*, 509 F.3d 623 (4th Cir. 2007).

Food for Thought

The *J.B.D.* decision, discussed *supra*, discusses the idea that courts might be more inclined to find that a juvenile is in custody even though it might not find that an adult is in custody under similar circumstances. Let's think a bit about how the holding in *J.B.D.* might be applied. Suppose that a high school student, who is suspected of having given prescription pain killers to a fellow student, is sent to the principal's office. As he enters the officer, is the student now in "custody?" Would your view be different if the principal has called the police, waits until the police arrive, and then calls the student in for an interview? Does the age of the student matter? Would you be more likely to find "custody" when a middle school student is called to the principal's office than when a high school student is called? *See N.C. v. Commonwealth*, 396 S.W.2d 852 (Ky. 2013); *State v. Pearson*, 804 N.W.2d 260 (Iowa 2011).

Hypo 5: *More on Custody*

The police have a warrant to arrest McKenna for child molestation. Before making the arrest, they speak with him to see whether he has an alibi defense (*e.g.*, he was away at the time of the alleged molestation). The police drive to McKenna's restaurant, and ask whether he is willing to speak with them about a "private" matter. McKenna agrees to do so. For over an hour, while the police and McKenna are strolling outside of McKenna's restaurant, they discuss the allegations. At one point, McKenna indicates an intention to enter some woods. The interrogating officer tells McKenna that they need to stay in eyesight of an officer who is watching the interrogation from a nearby police car. Was McK enna in custody for purposes of *Miranda*? If so, when did the custody begin? *See State v. McKenna,* <u>103 A.3d 756 (N.H. 2014).</u>

Hypo 6: *Custody at the Border?*

An individual, who has been flagged for further scrutiny, arrives at the U.S. border. After some brief questioning, he is referred for "secondary questioning" which takes place in a small (10' x 10') room, lasts for two hours, and is focused on the belief that he is engaged in drug smuggling. Under these circumstances, is defendant in "custody" so that a *Miranda* warning is required? By contrast, is there "interrogation" when the suspect is asked only "routine" immigration questions at the border? *See United States v. Molina-Gomez,* <u>781 F.3d 13 (1st Cir. 2015).</u>

Hypo 7: *Custody During Street Encounters?*

Suppose that federal agents receive a tip from a gun dealer that an individual is purchasing guns for others (a federal crime). The officers follow the individual when he leaves the shop, and stop him for committing a traffic infraction. Knowing that the suspect has just purchased guns and ammunition, the officers approach the vehicle with their guns drawn. After a few minutes, they holster their guns, and tell him that he is not "under arrest." The officers speak to the suspect for a few minutes without administering a *Miranda* warning, and he makes incriminating statements. Was the suspect "in custody" for purposes of *Miranda*? *See United States v. Ortiz,* <u>781 F.3d 221 (5th Cir. 2015).</u>

Hypo 8: *Barricaded Suspect*

Police officers have probable cause to believe that Mack shot and wounded his wife and daughter, and have a warrant for his arrest. Mack barricades himself in a motel room with hostages and weapons. The agents surround Mack's room. When Mack does not respond to police requests to give himself up, communicated to him by bullhorn, the police bring in an FBI hostage negotiator who calls Mack on the telephone. For three hours, the FBI agent converses with Mack without giving him *Miranda* warnings. At Mack's trial, the prosecution seeks to introduce Mack's statements to the FBI agent. Was Mack in "custody" during the hostage negotiation and entitled to *Miranda* warnings? *See United States v. Mesa*, 638 F.2d 582 (3d Cir. 1980).

2. Interrogation

In order for *Miranda* to apply, not only must the suspect be in "custody," there must also be "interrogation." Just as the courts have struggled to define the term "custody," they have also struggled to define the term "interrogation."

Rhode Island v. Innis

446 U.S. 291 (1980).

MR. JUSTICE STEWART delivered the opinion of the Court.

A taxi driver was robbed shortly after midnight by a man with a sawed-off shotgun; the driver identified Innis as the robber from a photo array, and reported that he had dropped Innis off in the Mount Pleasant section of Providence. Five days earlier, another Providence taxi driver had been killed by a man with a shotgun. Around 4:30 a.m., Patrolman Lovell was cruising in a patrol car when he spotted Innis standing in the street. Lovell arrested Innis, who was unarmed, and advised him of his *Miranda* rights. Lovell and Innis waited in the patrol car and Lovell did not converse with Innis. A sergeant soon arrived and read Innis the *Miranda* warnings; minutes later Captain Leyden arrived with other officers and advised Innis again of his *Miranda* rights. Innis stated that he understood those rights and wanted to speak with a lawyer. Captain Leyden then directed that Innis should be placed in a "caged wagon," a four-door police car with a wire screen mesh between the front and rear seats, and be driven to the central police station. Three officers were assigned to accompany Innis to the police station. Captain Leyden then instructed the officers not to question Innis or intimidate or coerce him in any way.

While en route to the station, Patrolman Gleckman initiated a conversation with Patrolman McKenna concerning the missing shotgun. Gleckman testified: "I was stating that I frequent this area while on patrol and that because a school for handicapped children is located nearby, there's a lot of handicapped children running around in this area, and God forbid one of them might find a weapon with shells and they might hurt themselves." Patrolman McKenna testified: "I more or less concurred with Gleckman that it was a safety factor and that we should continue to search for the weapon." Patrolman Williams testified that he heard Gleckman say, "it would be too bad if the little—I believe he said a girl—would pick up the gun, maybe kill herself." Innis then interrupted the conversation, stating that the officers should turn the car around so he could show them where the gun was located. At the time, they had traveled no more than a mile, a trip encompassing only a few minutes. The police vehicle then returned to the scene of the arrest where a search for the shotgun was in progress. There, Captain Leyden again advised Innis of his *Miranda* rights and Innis replied that he understood those rights but that he "wanted to get the gun out of the way because of the kids in the area in the school." Innis then led the police to a nearby field, where he pointed out the shotgun under some rocks by the side of the road. The gun and his statements were introduced at his trial for kidnaping, robbery, and murder, and Innis was convicted. He argued that the gun and statements were inadmissible because of improper police interrogation after he invoked his right to counsel under *Miranda*.

The starting point for defining "interrogation" is *Miranda* where the Court observed that "by custodial interrogation, we mean questioning initiated by law enforcement officers after a person has been taken into custody or otherwise deprived of his freedom of action in any significant way." This passage might suggest that the *Miranda* rules were to apply only to those police interrogation practices that involve express questioning of a defendant while in custody. We do not, however, construe *Miranda* so narrowly. The concern of *Miranda* was that the "interrogation environment" created by the interplay of interrogation and custody would "subjugate the individual to the will of his examiner" and thereby undermine the privilege against compulsory self-incrimination. The police practices that evoked this concern included several that did not involve express questioning. For example, one of the practices was the use of line-ups in which a coached witness would pick the defendant as the perpetrator. This was designed to establish that the defendant was in fact guilty as a predicate for further interrogation. A variation on this theme was the so-called "reverse line-up" in which a defendant would be identified by coached witnesses as the perpetrator of a fictitious crime, with the object of inducing him to confess to the actual crime of which he was suspected in order to escape the false prosecution. *Miranda* also included in its survey of interrogation practices the use of psychological ploys, such as to "posit" "the guilt of the subject," to "minimize the moral seriousness of the offense," and "to cast blame on the victim or on society." It is clear that these techniques of persuasion, no less than express questioning, were thought, in a custodial setting, to amount to interrogation. This is not to say that all statements obtained by the police after a person has been taken into custody are to be considered the product of interrogation. As *Miranda* noted: "Volunteered statements of any kind are not barred by the Fifth Amendment." The special procedural safeguards outlined in *Miranda* are required not where a suspect is simply taken into custody, but rather where a suspect in custody is subjected to interrogation. 'Interrogation,' as conceptualized in *Miranda*, must reflect a measure of compulsion above and beyond that inherent in custody itself."

We conclude that the *Miranda* safeguards come into play whenever a person in custody is subjected to either express questioning or its functional equivalent. That is to say, the term "interrogation" refers also to any words or actions on the part of the police (other than those normally attendant to arrest and custody) that the police should know are reasonably likely to elicit an incriminating response from the suspect. The latter portion of this definition focuses primarily upon the perceptions of the suspect, rather than the intent of the police. This focus reflects the fact that the *Miranda* safeguards were designed to vest a suspect in custody with an added measure of protection against coercive police practices, without regard to objective proof of the underlying intent of the police.

Turning to the present case, we conclude that Innis was not "interrogated" within the meaning of *Miranda*. The conversation between Gleckman and McKenna included no express questioning of Innis. Rather, that conversation was, at least in form, nothing more than a dialogue between the two officers to which no response from Innis was invited. Moreover, it cannot be fairly concluded that Innis was subjected to the "functional equivalent" of questioning. It cannot be said that Gleckman and McKenna should have known that their conversation was reasonably likely to elicit an incriminating response from Innis. There is nothing in the record to suggest that the officers were aware that Innis was peculiarly susceptible to an appeal to his conscience concerning the safety of handicapped children. Nor is there anything to suggest that the police knew that he was unusually disoriented or upset at the time of his arrest.

The case thus boils down to whether, in the context of a brief conversation, the officers should have known that Innis would suddenly be moved to make a self-incriminating response. Given the fact that the entire conversation appears to have consisted of no more than a few off hand remarks, we cannot say that the officers should have known that it was reasonably likely that Innis would so respond. This is not a case where the police carried on a lengthy harangue in the presence of the suspect. Nor does the record support the contention by Innis that, under the circumstances, the officers' comments were particularly "evocative." It is our view that Innis was not subjected by the police to words or actions that the police should have known were reasonably likely to elicit an incriminating response from him.

MR. JUSTICE MARSHALL, with whom MR. JUSTICE BRENNAN joins, dissenting.

I agree with the Court's definition of "interrogation" within the meaning of *Miranda*. I am utterly at a loss to understand how this objective standard as applied to the facts before us can rationally lead to the conclusion that there was no interrogation. If the statements had been addressed to Innis, it would be impossible to draw such a conclusion. The simple message of the "talking back and forth" between Gleckman and McKenna was that they had to find the shotgun to avert a child's death. One can scarcely imagine a stronger appeal to the conscience of a suspect—any suspect—than the assertion that if the weapon is not found an innocent person will be hurt or killed. Not just any innocent person, but an innocent child—a little girl—a helpless, handicapped little girl on her way to school. The notion that such an appeal could not be expected to have any effect unless the suspect were known to have some special interest in handicapped children verges on the ludicrous. The appeal to a suspect to confess for the sake of others, to "display some evidence of decency and honor," is a classic interrogation technique. *See, e.g.*, F. INBAU & J. REID, CRIMINAL INTERROGATION AND CONFESSIONS 60–62 (2d ed. 1967). This is not a case where police officers speaking among themselves are accidentally overheard by a suspect. These officers were "talking back and forth" in close quarters with the handcuffed suspect, traveling past the very place where they believed the weapon was located. They knew respondent would hear their conversation, and they are chargeable with knowledge of and responsibility for the pressures to speak which they created.

Points for Discussion

a.   Public Safety Exception

In *New York v. Quarles*, 467 U.S. 649 (1984), the Court held that police officers may sometimes withhold the *Miranda* warnings until after they ask an arrestee questions that are "necessary to secure their own safety or the safety of the public." In *Quarles*, police received information from a rape victim, describing the clothing and height of her assailant, and reporting that the man had just entered a nearby supermarket carrying a gun. When the officers entered the store, a man matching the victim's description turned and ran. The officers pursued and caught the man, after losing sight of him briefly. When they stopped him at gunpoint and frisked him, the police discovered that the man was wearing an empty shoulder holster. One officer handcuffed the man in the presence of three other officers, and then asked the man about the location of the gun. When the man nodded in the direction of some empty cartons and said, "Over there," the police located the gun and then recited the *Miranda* warnings. *Quarles* held that the gun and the statement about its location were admissible at his trial for criminal possession of the weapon, under a "public safety" exception to *Miranda*: "The police, in the act of apprehending a suspect, were confronted with the immediate necessity of ascertaining the whereabouts of a gun which they had every reason to believe the suspect had just removed from his empty holster and discarded in the supermarket. So long as the gun was concealed somewhere in the supermarket, it posed more than one danger to the public safety: an accomplice might use it, a customer or employee might come upon it. If the police are required to recite the *Miranda* warnings before asking the whereabouts of the gun, suspects in Quarles' position might well be deterred from responding. Procedural safeguards which deter a suspect from responding were deemed acceptable in *Miranda* in order to protect the Fifth Amendment privilege; when the primary social cost of those added protections is the possibility of fewer convictions, the *Miranda* majority was willing to bear that cost. Here, had *Miranda* warnings deterred Quarles from responding to the question about the whereabouts of the gun, the police could not have insured that further danger to the public did not result from the concealment of the gun in a public area. The officer asked only the question necessary to locate the missing gun before advising Quarles of his rights. The exception which we recognize today, far from complicating the thought processes and the on-the-scene judgments of police officers, will simply free them to follow their legitimate instincts when confronting situations presenting a danger to the public safety."

The *Quarles* dissenters argued against the public safety exception, contending that the police had not shown a danger to public safety. They emphasized that *Miranda* was not based on a cost-benefit analysis, and that "society's need for interrogation" cannot "outweigh" the privilege against self-incrimination. In addition, the dissenters viewed the Court's claim that the "public was at risk" as "speculative": "Before the interrogation, Quarles had been 'reduced to a condition of physical powerlessness' and he was not believed to have an accomplice. When the questioning began, the arresting officers were sufficiently confident of their safety to put away their guns. Based on the interrogating officer's testimony that 'the situation was under control', the lower court found that 'nothing suggests that any of the officers was concerned for his own physical safety.' The conclusion that neither Quarles nor his missing gun posed a threat to the public's safety is amply supported by evidence that no customers or employees were wandering about the store, and Quarles' arrest took place during the middle of the night when the store was deserted except for clerks at the checkout counter. The police could easily have cordoned off the store and searched for the missing gun. Had they done so, they would have found the gun quickly because they were well aware that Quarles had discarded his weapon somewhere near the scene of the arrest."

b. Undercover Agent Exception

In *Illinois v. Perkins*, <u>496 U.S. 292 (1990)</u>, the Court held that when an undercover agent questions a suspect in custody, such questioning does not qualify as "interrogation" under *Miranda*, reasoning as follows: "Conversations between suspects and undercover agents do not implicate the concerns underlying *Miranda*. The essential ingredients of a 'police-dominated atmosphere' and compulsion are not present when an incarcerated person speaks freely to someone whom he believes to be a fellow inmate. Coercion is determined from the perspective of the suspect. It is the premise of *Miranda* that the danger of coercion results from the interaction of custody and official interrogation. Questioning by captors, who appear to control the suspect's fate, may create mutually reinforcing pressures that the Court has assumed will weaken the suspect's will, but where a suspect does not know that he is conversing with a government agent, these pressures do not exist. When the suspect has no reason to think that the listeners have official power over him, it should not be assumed that his words are motivated by the reaction he expects from his listeners. "When the agent carries neither badge nor gun and wears not 'police blue,' but the same prison gray" as the suspect, there is no 'interplay between police interrogation and police custody.' The use of undercover agents is a recognized law enforcement technique, often employed in the prison context to detect violence against correctional officials or inmates, as well as for the purposes of gathering evidence here."

FYI

The "routine booking question" exception derives from the *Miranda* Court's observation that police questions that are "normally attendant to arrest and custody" do not qualify as "interrogation." In *Pennsylvania v. Muniz*, 496 U.S. 582 (1990), the Court noted that "routine booking questions" typically are asked to secure "the biographical data necessary to complete booking or pretrial services," and held that an intoxicated driver could be asked booking questions about his or her "name, address, height, weight, eye color, date of birth, and current age." The government conceded that a sixth question for the driver was not a "routine booking question": "Do you know what the date was of your sixth birthday?" The Court concluded that this question violated the Fifth Amendment because it called for a "testimonial response": it called for defendant to "explicitly or implicitly relate a factual assertion or disclose information," and it subjected defendant to the "cruel trilemma" of "self-accusation, perjury, or contempt."

Food for Thought

In *Innis*, suppose that there had been a school for handicapped children in the vicinity of the defendant's arrest, and the police knew that Innis had a handicapped daughter who was six years old. After the officer made his remark about a handicapped girl killing herself, he states, "You know, I saw that happen once. It was just terrible. The little girl blew her own head right off." Would these facts alter the result in *Innis*?

Hypo 1: *Stolen Furs*

Defendant is arrested for the murder of a woman and the theft of her furs. After defendant invokes his right to remain silent, and is placed in a cell, the police place the stolen furs outside his cell. At that point, defendant makes several incriminating statements. Was defendant subjected to "interrogation" within the meaning of *Miranda*? *See People v. Ferro*, 472 N.E.2d 13 (N.Y. 1984).

Hypo 2: *Playing Audio Tapes*

Vallar is arrested at home for drug conspiracy, and taken to the police station, but is not given a *Miranda* warning. The police do not question Vallar, but they do make him listen to audio tapes of conversations between two of Vallar's friends implicating Vallar in the conspiracy. Vallar listens silently and says nothing. Then a detective gives Vallar a *Miranda* warning, and Vallar says, "OK, I will waive my rights," signs a waiver form, and makes incriminating statements during the subsequent interrogation. Did the playing of the audio tapes constitute interrogation under *Innis*? *See United States v. Vallar,* 635 F.3d 271 (7th Cir. 2011).

Hypo 3: *Creating an Evocative Situation*

A man is arrested for killing his son, is given a *Miranda* warning, and invokes his rights. When the man's wife is brought in for questioning, she asks to speak to her husband. The police grant the request, but keep a police officer in the room for security reasons. The man objects to his wife's presence, as well as to the presence of a tape recorder. Even though the man continuously asks his wife to remain silent, she makes several incriminating statements. Does placing the wife in the room with her husband, amount to interrogation? *See Arizona v. Mauro,* 481 U.S. 520 (1987).

Hypo 4: *The Blabbermouth*

A suspect in a stabbing incident is taken to the police station where the investigating detective tells the suspect that he has spoken with the arresting officer (the suspect made incriminating statements to the arresting officer). The suspect responds "I told it to him 14 times." The detective responds, "OK, do you want to tell it to me?" Did the officer's statement involve "interrogation" so that a *Miranda* warning was required? Should it matter that the detective knew that the suspect tended to be a "blabbermouth?" *See State v. Juranek,* 844 N.W.2d 791 (Neb. 2014).

Food for Thought

From reading the note about *Quarles*, do you have a clear understanding regarding when the public safety exception applies (and, equally importantly,) when it does not apply? Part of the difficulty is that most matters that involve the police implicate "public safety." Moreover, the facts of *Quarles* were not particularly compelling in terms of establishing the need to act in the public interest (the effort to locate a lost weapon). One can think of a variety of scenarios where the "public interest" might be more compelling (e.g., murder, robbery, rape), especially when the perpetrator is on the loose. As a result, if the exception is broadly applied, it has the potential to dramatically undercut the *Miranda* requirement. Can you think of criteria that courts could use to decide which situations are compelling enough to justify dispensing with the *Miranda* warning?

Hypo 5: *Meaning of* Quarles *& Its Application*

In which of the following situations would you apply the public safety exception:

A) Suppose that there are a series of murders in a community. Although the police are unable to locate the murderer, they have identified several suspects. Given the heinous nature of the crimes, if the police question each of the suspects without giving *Miranda* warnings, should a court rely on the *Quarles* public safety exception to find that the incriminating statements of one suspect are admissible?

B) A teenage boy has mysteriously disappeared. The police have probable cause to believe that Rubio has kidnapped the boy so they bring him to the stationhouse for questioning. Would the public safety exception justify the police in dispensing with a *Miranda* warning when they interrogate Rubio? *See United States v. Vega Rubio*, 2011 WL 220033 (D. Nev. 2011); *People v. Davis*, 208 P.2d 78 (Cal. 2009).

C) Suppose that the police discover an unexploded bomb near Times Square in N.Y.C. An investigation reveals that Shahzad may have planted the bomb. Shahzad is apprehended as he is trying to board a flight at JFK airport. If the police are fearful that Shahzad is part of a terrorist network that is planning to commit other crimes, may they interrogate him without giving him a *Miranda* warning? *See In re Terrorist Bombings of U.S. Embassies in East Africa*, 552 P.3d 93 (2d Cir. 2008); *United States v. Hasan*, 747 F. Supp.2d 642 (E.D. Va. 2010).

D) Responding to a 911 call about suspicious activity, the police find a man in a rural area with blood on his hunting coveralls. The man provides identification, and states that he is walking for his health and is wearing coveralls because of the cold. When the police ask the man about the blood, he invokes his right to remain silent. If the police fear that the blood relates to a homicide, may they question the man without providing him with a *Miranda* warning? *See People v. Doll,* 998 N.E.2d 384 (N.Y. 2013).

Hypo 6: *"Routine Booking Questions?"*

The police arrest Denise for stealing morphine tablets from a pharmacy. After Denise is given a *Miranda* warning, she states that she wants to remain silent. However, a police detective listens to the answers that Denise gives during the booking process. Some of the questions on a medical questionnaire inquire about drug use in order to help the facility decide whether the arrestee should be placed in jail or in a medical facility. Denise admits that she took one morphine tablet that day, and states that she has used morphine within the last 72 hours. Can these questions be regarded as "routine booking questions?" *See State v. Denney,* 218 P.3d 633 (Wash. App. 2009).

Hypo 7: *Border Crossing*

When Calzada's plane arrives at JFK airport from the Dominican Republic, a Customs & Border Patrol officer notices that her name is in a database of people that are subject to outstanding arrest warrants. She is escorted to a conference room for questioning to determine whether she should be admitted to the United States. In reviewing Calzada's documents, the officer notices that there is a passport application by someone of the exact same name with a photograph of a woman who looks nothing like Calzada. As she is questioned, Calzada admits that she is traveling under a false name, and is charged with identity theft and misuse of a passport. The prosecution admits that Calzada was not given a *Miranda* warning, but argues that there should be an exception for "routine border crossing" inquiries designed to determine whether a person may be admitted to the United States. How should the court rule? *See United States v. FNU LNU,* 653 F.3d 144 (2d Cir. 2011).

3. Adequate Warnings

When custodial interrogation takes place, the prosecution must prove that an adequate set of *Miranda* warnings were given before interrogation occurred. *Tague v. Louisiana*, 444 U.S. 469 (1980). To be adequate, warnings must "reasonably convey" the substance of the mandated warning. Warnings may be inadequate if they are incomplete or provide misleading information about a suspect's rights. Warnings can also be inadequate if they are "non-functional" in that the police fail to warn at the outset of an interrogation, and then deliver "midstream" warnings and continue the interrogation. If a court determines that the *Miranda* warnings were inadequate, then post-warning incriminating statements will be inadmissible. Thus, a claim that warnings were "inadequate" is distinct from a claim that an invalid waiver was obtained after adequate warnings were provided.

Florida v. Powell

559 U.S. 50 (2010).

JUSTICE GINSBURG delivered the opinion of the Court.

On August 10, 2004, law enforcement officers in Tampa, Florida, seeking to apprehend respondent Kevin Powell in connection with a robbery investigation, entered an apartment rented by Powell's girlfriend. After spotting Powell coming from a bedroom, the officers searched the room and discovered a loaded nine-millimeter handgun under the bed. The officers arrested Powell and transported him to headquarters. Once there, and before asking Powell any questions, the officers read Powell the standard Tampa Police Department Consent and Release Form 310 which states: "You have the right to remain silent. If you give up the right to remain silent, anything you say can be used against you in court. You have the right to talk to a lawyer before answering any of our questions. If you cannot afford to hire a lawyer, one will be appointed for you without cost and before any questioning. You have the right to use any of these rights at any time you want during this interview." Acknowledging that he had been informed of his rights, that he "understood them," and that he was "willing to talk" to the officers, Powell signed the form. He then admitted that he owned the handgun found in the apartment. Powell knew he was prohibited from possessing a gun because he had previously been convicted of a felony, but said he had nevertheless purchased and carried the firearm for his protection.

Powell was charged with possession of a weapon by a prohibited possessor. Contending that the *Miranda* warnings were deficient because they did not adequately convey his right to the presence of an attorney during questioning, he moved to suppress his inculpatory statements. The trial court denied the motion and convicted Powell. The Florida Supreme Court found that the advice Powell received was misleading because it suggested that Powell could "only consult with an attorney before questioning" and did not convey Powell's entitlement to counsel's presence throughout the interrogation. We granted certiorari and reverse.

To give force to the Constitution's protection against compelled self-incrimination, the Court established in *Miranda* "certain procedural safeguards that require police to advise criminal suspects of their rights under the Fifth and Fourteenth Amendments before commencing custodial interrogation." *Duckworth v. Eagan,* 492 U.S. 195, 201 (1989). Intent on "giving concrete constitutional guidelines for law enforcement agencies and courts to follow," *Miranda* prescribed the following four now-familiar warnings: "A suspect must be warned prior to any questioning that he has the right to remain silent, that anything he says can be used against him in a court of law, that he has the right to the presence of an attorney, and that if he cannot afford an attorney one will be appointed for him prior to any questioning if he so desires."

Miranda's third warning addresses our concern that "the circumstances surrounding in-custody interrogation can operate very quickly to overbear the will of one merely made aware of his privilege to remain silent by his interrogators." Responsive to that concern, as "an absolute prerequisite to interrogation," an individual held for questioning "must be clearly informed that he has the right to consult with a lawyer and to have the lawyer with him during interrogation." The question is whether the warnings Powell received satisfied this requirement.

The four warnings are invariable, but this Court has not dictated the words in which the essential information must be conveyed. *See California v. Prysock,* 453 U.S. 355 (1981) (per curiam). In determining whether police officers adequately conveyed the four warnings, reviewing courts are not required to examine the words "as if construing a will or defining the terms of an easement. The inquiry is simply whether the warnings reasonably 'convey to a suspect his rights as required by *Miranda*.'" *Duckworth,* 492 U.S. at 203 (quoting *Prysock,* 453 U.S. at 361).

Prysock and *Duckworth* inform our judgment. In *Prysock,* an officer informed the suspect of, *inter alia,* his right to a lawyer's presence during questioning and his right to counsel appointed at no cost. The Court of Appeals held the advice inadequate because it lacked an express statement that the appointment of an attorney would occur prior to the impending interrogation. We reversed. "Nothing in the warnings," we observed, "suggested a limitation on the right to the presence of appointed counsel different from the clearly conveyed rights to a lawyer in general, including the right to a lawyer before the suspect is questioned, while he is being questioned, and all during the questioning." In *Duckworth,* we upheld advice that communicated the right to have an attorney present during the interrogation and the right to an appointed attorney, but also informed the suspect that the lawyer would be appointed "if and when the suspect goes to court." The Court of Appeals "thought the 'if and when you go to court' language suggested that only those accused who can afford an attorney have the right to have one present before answering any questions." We thought otherwise. Under the relevant state law, "counsel is appointed at a defendant's initial appearance in court." The "if and when you go to court" advice "simply anticipated" a question the suspect might be expected to ask after receiving *Miranda* warnings, *i.e., "when* will he obtain counsel." We held that the warnings, "in their totality, satisfied *Miranda.*"

We reach the same conclusion in this case. The officers did not "entirely omit," any information *Miranda* required them to impart. They informed Powell that he had "the right to talk to a lawyer before answering any of their questions" and "the right to use any of his rights at any time he wanted during the interview." The first statement communicated that Powell could consult with a lawyer before answering any particular question, and the second statement confirmed that he could exercise that right while the interrogation was underway. In combination, the two warnings reasonably conveyed Powell's right to have an attorney present, not only at the outset of interrogation, but at all times. To reach the opposite conclusion, *i.e.,* that the attorney would not be present throughout the interrogation, the suspect would have to imagine an unlikely scenario: To consult counsel, he would be obliged to exit and reenter the interrogation room between each query. A reasonable suspect in a custodial setting who has just been read his rights would not come to the counterintuitive conclusion that he is obligated, or allowed, to hop in and out of the holding area to seek his attorney's advice. Instead, the suspect would likely assume that he must stay put in the interrogation room and that his lawyer would be there with him the entire time.

The Florida Supreme Court found the warning misleading because it believed the language suggested Powell could consult with an attorney only before the interrogation started. In context, the term "before" merely conveyed when Powell's right to an attorney became effective—namely, before he answered any questions at all. Nothing in the words used indicated that counsel's presence would be restricted after the questioning commenced. Instead, the warning communicated that the right to counsel carried forward to and through the interrogation: Powell could seek his attorney's advice before responding to "*any* of the officers' questions" and "*at any time during* the interview." Although the warnings were not the *clearest possible* formulation of *Miranda*'s right-to-counsel advisement, they were sufficiently comprehensive and comprehensible when given a commonsense reading.

Powell points out that law enforcement agencies, hoping to obtain uninformed waivers, will be tempted to end-run *Miranda* by amending their warnings to introduce ambiguity. But as the United States explained as *amicus curiae,* "law enforcement agencies have little reason to assume the litigation risk of experimenting with novel *Miranda* formulations," instead, it is "desirable police practice" and "in law enforcement's own interest" to state warnings with maximum clarity. For these reasons, "all federal law enforcement agencies explicitly advise suspects of the full contours of each

Miranda right, including the right to the presence of counsel during questioning." The standard warnings used by the Federal Bureau of Investigation are exemplary. They provide, in relevant part: "you have the right to talk to a lawyer for advice before we ask you any questions. you have the right to have a lawyer with you during questioning." This advice is admirably informative, but we decline to declare its precise formulation necessary to meet *Miranda*'s requirements. Different words were used in the advice Powell received, but they communicated the same essential message.

For the reasons stated, the judgment of the Supreme Court of Florida is reversed, and the case is remanded for further proceedings not inconsistent with this opinion.

It is so ordered.

JUSTICE STEVENS, with whom JUSTICE BREYER joins, dissenting.

In this case, the form regularly used by the Tampa police warned Powell only of the right to consult with a lawyer before questioning. The warning did not say anything about the right to have counsel present during interrogation. Although we have never required "rigidity in the *form* of the required warnings," *California v. Prysock*, 453 U.S. 355, 359 (1981) (per curiam), this is the first time the Court has approved a warning which, if given its natural reading, entirely omitted an essential element of a suspect's rights. When the relevant clause is given its most natural reading, it communicated that Powell could exercise the previously listed rights at any time. Yet the only previously listed right was the "right to talk to a lawyer *before* answer-ing any of the officers' questions." This warning did not reasonably convey the right to talk to a lawyer *after* answering some questions, much less implicitly inform Powell of his right to have a lawyer with him at all times during interrogation. Unlike the *Duckworth* warning, Powell's warning entirely failed to inform him of the separate and distinct right "to have counsel present during any questioning."

> **Food for Thought**
>
> Assume that a suspect receives a version of the warnings that is identical to those received by the *Powell* defendant, except that the so-called "catchall" warning ("You have the right to use any of these rights at any time you want during this interview") is *not* included in the language of the warnings. Would the Court still be inclined to find that the warnings are sufficient? *See United States v. Warren*, 642 F.3d 182 (3d Cir. 2011).

Hypo 1: *When a Suspect Knows the Warnings*

A police officer arrests defendant for a drug crime, and attempts to advise her regarding her *Miranda* rights. As the officer states, "You have the right to remain silent," the woman interrupts and tells the officer, "I know my rights, you don't have to tell me any more." The officer then asks the woman whether she is willing to waive her rights and identify her source of drugs, and the woman immediately says yes, and names Dan (a drug dealer) as her source. The prosecutor wants to introduce Jane's statement at her trial. Is this statement inadmissible because of inadequate *Miranda* warnings? *See United States v. Patane*, 542 U.S. 630 (2004).

Hypo 2: *The "Anything You Say" Warning*

Suppose that a police officer gives the following warning: "You have the right to remain silent, the right to the presence of an attorney if you so wish, you are not required to answer any questions and if you decide to answer questions you can stop and do so, and if you cannot afford an attorney one will be appointed before you answer any questions." How can Jane's counsel argue that these *Miranda* warnings are inadequate? *See United States v. Tillman*, 963 F.2d 137 (6th Cir. 1992). *Compare United States v. Rogers*, 659 F.3d 74 (1st Cir. 2011); *United States v. Moore*, 670 F.3d 222 (2d Cir. 2012).

Hypo 3: *Post-Waiver Break & Later Interrogation*

A police officer gives Larry a *Miranda* warning, and obtains a valid waiver. In response to questioning, Larry makes a statement denying any involvement in a homicide. Larry is returned to his cell. The next morning, the same officer drives Larry from the jail to his first appearance hearing. The officer says to Larry, "if you have anything to say, now is the time to do it, because once we get to the hearing it will be too late." Larry makes an incriminating statement. Is this statement admissible, or was the officer required to give him a new *Miranda* warning? *See United States v. Pruden*, 398 F.3d 241 (3d Cir. 2005).

Hypo 4: *"You Don't Need a Lawyer Present"*

Don is taken into custody and given a *Miranda* warning. When the officer asks Don whether he understands his rights, Don says, "Yes." Then the officer asks Don, "Do you want to make a statement now without a lawyer being present?" Don responds by asking her, "If I say yes, we're going to discuss the incident, right? Would I be setting myself up if we discuss the case without my lawyer?" The officer replies, "If we discuss any matters outside of the case, you don't need a lawyer present at all, period. When we discuss the case, when I ask you something specifically, or if you tell me something specifically, you have a right to have a lawyer present here. What you are doing here is giving up a right to have a lawyer present to tell me your side. You don't have to do that." Don responds, "All right. I know what you are saying." Then the officer says, "You understand that you do have rights. Do you want to make a statement at this time without a lawyer present?" Don says, "Yes," and makes incriminating statements. Did the officer violate *Miranda*? *See State v. Luckett,* 413 Md. 360, 993 A.2d 25 (2010).

Missouri v. Seibert

542 U.S. 600 (2004).

JUSTICE SOUTER announced the judgment of the Court and delivered an opinion, in which JUSTICE STEVENS, JUSTICE GINSBURG, and JUSTICE BREYER join.

A police officer made a "conscious decision" to withhold *Miranda* warnings from Seibert when interrogating her at the station, using an interrogation technique that he had been taught, to "question first, then give the warnings, and then repeat the question" until "I get the answer that the suspect has already provided once." Seibert made incriminating statements about her knowledge that her sons burned her mobile home with the expectation that an unrelated teenager living with the family would not be rescued from the fire. The initial interrogation lasted for 30 to 40 minutes, and then stopped for 20 minutes; then the same officer gave Seibert the *Miranda* warnings and she signed a waiver. During the interrogation that followed, the officer obtained incriminating statements that repeated the information in the pre-warnings statement. The pre-warning statement was suppressed at Seibert's trial, but the post-warning statement was admitted and Seibert was convicted of murder.

This case tests a police protocol for custodial interrogation that calls for giving no warnings of the rights to silence and counsel until interrogation has produced a confession. Then the interrogating officer follows it with *Miranda* warnings and leads the suspect to cover the same ground a second time. Because this midstream recitation of warnings following an interrogation and unwarned confession could not effectively comply with *Miranda's* constitutional requirement, we hold that a statement repeated after a warning in such circumstances is inadmissible.

The technique of interrogating in successive, unwarned and warned phases raises a new challenge to *Miranda*. One officer testified that the strategy of withholding *Miranda* warnings until after interrogating and drawing out a confession was promoted not only by his own department, but by a national police training organization and other departments in which he had worked. The Police Law Institute instructs that "officers may conduct a two-stage interrogation so that at any point during the pre-*Miranda* interrogation, usually after arrestees have confessed, officers may then read the *Miranda* warnings and ask for a waiver. If the arrestees waive their *Miranda* rights, officers will be able to repeat any subsequent incriminating statements later in court." Police Law Institute, Illinois Police Law Manual 83 (Jan. 2001–Dec. 2003).

The threshold issue when interrogators question first and warn later is whether the warnings effectively advise the suspect that he had a real choice about giving an admissible statement or that he could choose to stop talking if he had talked earlier? For unless the warnings could place a suspect who has just been interrogated in a position to make such informed choices, there is no practical justification for accepting the formal warnings as compliance with *Miranda*, or for treating the second stage of interrogation as distinct from the first, unwarned and inadmissible segment. By any objective measure, it is likely that if the interrogators employ the technique of withholding warnings until after interrogation succeeds in eliciting a confession, the warnings will be ineffective in preparing the suspect for successive interrogation, close in time and similar in content. Upon hearing warnings only in the aftermath of interrogation and just after making a confession, a suspect would hardly think he had a genuine right to remain silent, let alone persist in so believing once the police began to lead him over the same ground again. A more likely reaction on a suspect's part would be perplexity about the reason for discussing rights at that point. What is worse, telling a suspect that "anything you say can and will be used against you," without expressly excepting the statement just given, could lead to an entirely reasonable inference that what he has just said will be used, with subsequent silence being of no avail. Thus, when *Miranda* warnings are inserted in the midst of coordinated and continuing interrogation, they are likely to mislead and "deprive a defendant of knowledge essential to his ability to understand the nature of his rights and the consequences of abandoning them." By the same token, it would ordinarily be unrealistic to treat two spates of integrated and proximately conducted questioning as independent interrogations subject to independent evaluation simply because *Miranda* warnings formally punctuate them in the middle.

The State argues that a confession repeated at the end of an interrogation sequence envisioned in a question-first strategy is admissible on the authority of *Oregon v. Elstad,* 470 U.S. 298 (1985). In *Elstad,* the police went to the young suspect's house to take him into custody on a charge of burglary. Before the arrest, one officer spoke with the suspect's mother, while the other one joined the suspect in a "brief stop in the living room," where the officer said he "felt" the young man was involved in a burglary. The suspect acknowledged he had been at the scene. The Court assumed that the officer's initial failure to warn was an "oversight" that "may have been the result of confusion as to whether the brief exchange qualified as 'custodial interrogation'" At the outset of a later and systematic station house interrogation going well beyond the scope of the laconic prior admission, the suspect was given *Miranda* warnings and made a full confession. It is fair to read *Elstad* as treating the living room conversation as a good-faith *Miranda* mistake that was open to correction by careful warnings before systematic questioning. At the opposite extreme are the facts here, which by any objective measure reveal a police strategy adapted to undermine the *Miranda* warnings. The unwarned interrogation was conducted in the station house, and the questioning was systematic, exhaustive, and managed with psychological skill. The warned phase of questioning proceeded after a pause of only 15 to 20 minutes, in the same place as the unwarned segment. When the same officer who had conducted the first phase recited the *Miranda* warnings, he said nothing to counter the probable misimpression that the advice that anything Seibert said could be used against her also applied to the details of the inculpatory statement previously elicited. In particular, the police did not advise that her prior statement could not be used. Nothing was said or done to dispel the oddity of warning about legal rights to silence and counsel right after the police had led her through a systematic interrogation. The impression that the further questioning was a mere continuation of the earlier questions and responses was fostered by references back to the confession already given. It would have been reasonable to regard the two sessions as parts of a continuum, in which it would have been unnatural to refuse to repeat at the second stage what had been said before. These circumstances must be seen as challenging the comprehensibility and efficacy of the *Miranda* warnings to the point that a reasonable person in the suspect's shoes would not have understood them to convey a message that she retained a choice about continuing to talk. Because the question-first tactic effectively threatens to thwart *Miranda*'s purpose of reducing the risk that a coerced confession would be admitted, and because the facts here do not reasonably support a conclusion that the warnings given could have served their purpose, Seibert's post warning statements are inadmissible. The judgment of the Supreme Court of Missouri is *affirmed.*

JUSTICE O'CONNOR, with whom THE CHIEF JUSTICE, JUSTICE SCALIA and JUSTICE THOMAS join, dissenting.

We have previously rejected a theory that is indistinguishable from the one today's plurality adopts. In *Elstad,* we refused to recognize the "psychological impact of the suspect's conviction that he has let the cat out of the bag" because we refused to "endow those 'psychological effects' with 'constitutional implications.' To do so would "effectively immunize a suspect who responds to pre-warning questions from the consequences of his subsequent informed waiver," an immunity that "comes at a high cost to legitimate law enforcement activity." I would analyze the two-step interrogation procedure under the voluntary waiver standard of *Elstad* and leave this analysis for the Missouri courts to conduct on remand.

> Some lower courts follow the approach advocated by Justice Kennedy's concurring opinion in *Seibert* because he supplied the fifth vote for the result. His opinion reasoned as follows: "*Miranda*'s clarity is one of its strengths, and a multifactor test that applies to every two-stage interrogation may undermine that clarity. If the deliberate two-step strategy has been used, postwarning statements that are related to the substance of prewarning statements must be excluded unless curative measures are taken before the postwarning statement is made. Curative measures should ensure that a reasonable person in the suspect's situation would understand the import and effect of the *Miranda* warning and the *Miranda* waiver. For example, a substantial break in time and circumstances between the prewarning statement and the *Miranda* warning may suffice in most circumstances, as it allows the accused to distinguish between the two contexts and appreciate that the interrogation has taken a new turn. An additional warning that explains the likely inadmissibility of the prewarning custodial statement may be sufficient. No curative steps were taken in this case, however, and so the prewarning statements are inadmissible and the conviction cannot stand."

Point for Discussion

Seibert Dissenters & Involuntary Waiver

The *Seibert* dissenters rejected the *Seibert* plurality's interpretation of *Elstad* as a precedent that posed no barrier to creation of the inadequate warnings doctrine. This is because *Elstad* opined that, "A subsequent administration of mid-interrogation *Miranda* warnings to a suspect who has given a prior unwarned statement ordinarily should suffice to remove the conditions namely, the initial lack of warnings that made the earlier statement inadmissible." If the *Seibert* dissenters had prevailed, they would have relied on *Elstad* to reject the defendant's claim that the midstream warnings did not reasonably convey the *Miranda* rights. The dissenters would have required the defendant to show on remand that her waiver was not "voluntary" based on a showing of "actual coercion", defined under *Elstad* as "physical violence or other deliberate means calculated to break the suspect's will."

Food for Thought

Defendant is arrested for robbery and brought to the station in the morning. No *Miranda* warnings are given, and he makes no incriminating statements during questioning. Then defendant is given a polygraph exam without warnings, and the officers tell him that he "failed" the polygraph. In the afternoon, defendant is taken to court and a magistrate gives him the *Miranda* warning. Upon his return to the police station, the officers obtain a waiver from defendant, and then he makes his first incriminating statements. Under Kennedy's test, will the trial court find that the magistrate's warnings failed to reasonably convey the *Miranda* rights? How will the analysis change if the trial court uses the *Seibert* plurality's test? *See Martinez v. State*, 272 S.W.3d 615 (Tex. Crim. App. 2008).

Hypo 1: *"Question First" Approach & Good Faith*

In *Seibert* the police admitted that they were trained to use the "question-first" approach—to withhold the *Miranda* warnings deliberately until after an arrestee confesses. Assume that in a future case, the police testify that they did not intentionally use the "question-first" strategy, but that rather acted in good faith when they failed to give the initial warnings. What factors might a reviewing court consider in determining whether the police conduct resembles the "good faith mistake" of the police in *Elstad* or the intentional misconduct of the police in *Seibert*? *See Kelly v. State*, 997 N.E.2d 1045 (Ind. 2013).

Hypo 2: *Central Booking Interview Program*

A prosecutor directs that indigent defendants be subjected to preliminary custodial interrogation before arraignment. In the jurisdiction, arraignment occurs only after an arrestee's paperwork is completed by the police, the Criminal Justice Agency has interviewed the arrestee in order to make a recommendation concerning bail, the criminal complaint has been drafted, and the district attorney delivers the relevant paperwork to the court. Thereafter, the case is docketed, and the next available appearance is scheduled for the defendant. Under the prosecutor's direction, indigent defendants who are "administratively ready" for arraignment are diverted to an interrogation room where prosecutors read from a prepared script which informs defendant of "the charges" he or she will face when he "goes to court," and that "in a few minutes," you will be read your rights and "given an opportunity to explain what you did at that date, time, and place." Then the following is recited by a prosecutor: "If you have an alibi, give us as much information as you can, including the names of any people you were with. If your version of the events that day is different from what we have heard, this is your opportunity to tell us your story. If there is something you would like us to investigate concerning this incident, if you tell us, we will look into it. You do not have to talk to me. This will be the only opportunity you will have to talk to me before you go to court on these charges." Then the defendant is read the *Miranda* warnings. Defendants who have retained counsel are allowed to proceed directly to arraignment. Only indigent defendants who cannot retain an attorney are diverted to the interrogation room. However, diversion is based on subjective criteria. Does the program violate *Seibert? See People v. Perez,* 946 N.Y.S.2d 835 (N.Y. 2012).

4. Waiver

Even when the *Miranda* warnings are given, the prosecution must prove by a preponderance of the evidence that the suspect "voluntarily, knowingly and intelligently" waived the *Miranda* rights. In *Moran v. Burbine,* 475 U.S. 412 (1986), the Court summarized the waiver requirement as follows: "The inquiry has two distinct dimensions. First, the relinquishment of the right must have been voluntary in the sense that it was the product of a free and deliberate choice rather than intimidation, coercion, or deception. Second, the waiver must have been made knowingly and intelligently, with a full awareness of both the nature of the right being abandoned and the consequences of the decision to abandon it. Only if the 'totality of the circumstances surrounding the interrogation' reveal both an uncoerced choice and the requisite level of comprehension may a court properly conclude that the *Miranda* rights have been waived."

Berghuis v. Thompkins

560 U.S. 370 (2010).

JUSTICE KENNEDY delivered the opinion of the Court.

On January 10, 2000, a shooting occurred outside a mall in Southfield, Michigan. Among the victims was Samuel Morris, who died from multiple gunshot wounds. The other victim, Frederick France, recovered from his injuries and later testified. Thompkins, who was a suspect, fled. About one year later he was found in Ohio and arrested there. Two Southfield police officers traveled to Ohio to interrogate Thompkins, then awaiting transfer to Michigan. The interrogation began around 1:30 p.m. and lasted about three hours. The interrogation was conducted in a room that was 8 by 10 feet, and Thompkins sat in a chair that resembled a school desk. At the beginning of the interrogation, one of the officers, Detective Helgert, presented Thompkins with a form derived from the *Miranda* rule. It stated:

NOTIFICATION OF CONSTITUTIONAL RIGHTS AND STATEMENT

1. You have the right to remain silent.

2. Anything you say can and will be used against you in a court of law.

3. You have a right to talk to a lawyer before answering any questions and you have the right to have a lawyer present with you while you are answering any questions.

4. If you cannot afford to hire a lawyer, one will be appointed to represent you before any questioning, if you wish one.

5. You have the right to decide at any time before or during questioning to use your right to remain silent and your right to talk with a lawyer while you are being questioned.

Helgert asked Thompkins to read the fifth warning out loud. Thompkins complied. Helgert later said this was to ensure that Thompkins could read, and Helgert concluded that Thompkins understood English. Helgert then read the other four *Miranda* warnings out loud and asked Thompkins to sign the form to demonstrate that he understood his rights. Thompkins declined to sign the form. The record contains conflicting evidence about whether Thompkins then verbally confirmed that he understood the rights listed on the form.

At no point during the interrogation did Thompkins say that he wanted to remain silent, that he did not want to talk with the police, or that he wanted an attorney. Thompkins was "largely" silent during the interrogation, which lasted about three hours. He did give a few limited verbal responses such as "yeah," "no," or "I don't know." On occasion he communicated by nodding his head. Thompkins also said that he "didn't want a peppermint" that was offered to him by the police and that the chair he was "sitting in was hard." About 2 hours and 45 minutes into the interrogation, Helgert asked Thompkins, "Do you believe in God?" Thompkins made eye contact with Helgert and said "Yes," as his eyes "welled up with tears." Helgert asked, "Do you pray to God?" Thompkins said "Yes." Helgert asked, "Do you pray to God to forgive you for shooting that boy down?" Thompkins answered "Yes" and looked away. Thompkins refused to make a written confession, and the interrogation ended about 15 minutes later.

Thompkins was charged with first-degree murder, assault with intent to commit murder, and certain firearms offenses. He moved to suppress the statements made during the interrogation. He argued that he had not waived his right to remain silent, and that his inculpatory statements were inadmissible. The trial court denied the motion. The jury found Thompkins guilty on all counts and sentenced him to life in prison without parole. The state courts rejected his *Miranda* claim, as did the District Court. The Sixth Circuit reversed and we granted certiorari.

All concede that the warning given in this case was in full compliance with *Miranda*'s requirements. The dispute centers on the response—or nonresponse—from the suspect. Even absent the accused's invocation of the right to remain silent, the accused's statement during a custodial interrogation is inadmissible at trial unless the prosecution can establish that the accused "in fact knowingly and voluntarily waived *Miranda* rights" when making the statement. *North Carolina v. Butler*, 441 U.S. 369, 373 (1979). The waiver inquiry "has two distinct dimensions": waiver must be "voluntary in the sense that it was the product of a free and deliberate choice rather than intimidation, coercion, or deception," and "made with a full awareness of both the nature of the right being abandoned and the consequences of the decision to abandon it." *Moran v. Burbine*, 475 U.S. 412, 421 (1986).

Some language in *Miranda* could be read to indicate that waivers are difficult to establish absent an explicit written waiver or a formal, express oral statement. *Miranda* said "a valid waiver will not be presumed simply from the silence of the accused after warnings are given or simply from the fact that a confession was in fact eventually obtained." In addition, *Miranda* stated that "a heavy burden rests on the government to demonstrate that the defendant knowingly and intelligently waived his privilege against self-incrimination and his right to retained or appointed counsel." Decisions since *Miranda* demonstrate that waivers can be established even absent formal or express statements of waiver that would be expected in, say, a judicial hearing to determine if a guilty plea has been properly entered. The purpose of *Miranda* is to ensure that an accused is advised of and understands the right to remain silent and the right to counsel. Thus, "our cases have reduced the impact of *Miranda* on legitimate law enforcement while reaffirming the decision's core ruling that unwarned statements may not be used as evidence in the prosecution's case in chief." *Dickerson v. United States*, 530 U.S. 428, 443–444 (2000).

One of the first cases to decide the meaning and import of *Miranda* with respect to waiver was *Butler*, which interpreted the *Miranda* language concerning the "heavy burden" to show waiver in accord with usual principles of determining waiver, which can include waiver implied from all the circumstances. In a later case, the Court stated that this "heavy burden" is not more than the burden to establish waiver by a preponderance of the evidence. *Colorado v. Connelly*, 479 U.S. 157, 168 (1986). The prosecution does not need to show that a waiver of *Miranda* rights was express. An "implicit waiver" of the "right to remain silent" is sufficient to admit a suspect's statement into evidence. *Butler* made clear that a waiver of *Miranda* rights may be implied through "the defendant's silence, coupled with an understanding of his rights and a course of conduct indicating waiver." *Butler* therefore "retreated" from the "language and tenor of the *Miranda* opinion," which "suggested that the Court would require that a waiver be 'specifically made.' " *Connecticut v. Barrett*, 479 U.S. 523, 531–532 (1987) (Brennan, J., concurring in judgment).

If the State establishes that a *Miranda* warning was given and the accused made an uncoerced statement, this showing, standing alone, is insufficient to demonstrate "a valid waiver" of *Miranda* rights. The prosecution must make the additional showing that the accused understood these rights. Where the prosecution shows that a *Miranda* warning was given and that it was understood by the accused, an accused's uncoerced statement establishes an implied waiver of the right to remain silent.

Although *Miranda* imposes on the police a rule that is both formalistic and practical when it prevents them from interrogating suspects without first providing them with a *Miranda* warning, it does not impose a formalistic waiver procedure that a suspect must follow to relinquish those rights. As a general proposition, the law can presume that an individual who, with a full understanding of his or her rights, acts in a manner inconsistent with their exercise has made a deliberate choice to relinquish the protection those rights afford. As *Butler* recognized, *Miranda* rights can therefore be waived through means less formal than a typical waiver on the record in a court-room, given the practical constraints and necessities of interrogation and the fact that *Miranda*'s main protection lies in advising defendants of their rights.

The record shows that Thompkins waived his right to remain silent. First, there is no contention that Thompkins did not understand his rights; and it follows that he knew what he gave up when he spoke. Thompkins received a written copy of the *Miranda* warnings; Detective Helgert determined that Thompkins could read and understand English; and Thompkins was given time to read the warnings. Thompkins, furthermore, read aloud the fifth warning. He was thus aware that his right to remain silent would not dissipate after a certain amount of time and that police would have to honor his right to be silent and his right to counsel during the whole course of interrogation. Those rights, the warning made clear, could be asserted at any time. Second, Thompkins's answer to Detective Helgert's question about whether Thompkins prayed to God for forgiveness for shooting the victim is a "course of conduct indicating waiver" of the right to remain silent. If Thompkins wanted to remain silent, he could have said nothing in response to Helgert's questions, or he could have unambiguously invoked his *Miranda* rights and ended the interrogation. The fact that Thompkins made a statement about three hours after receiving a *Miranda* warning does not overcome the fact that he engaged in a course of conduct indicating waiver. Police are not required to rewarn suspects from time to time. Waiver is confirmed by the fact that Thompkins had given sporadic answers to questions throughout the interrogation. Third, there is no evidence that Thompkins's statement was coerced.

Thompkins does not claim that police threatened or injured him during the interrogation or that he was in any way fearful. The interrogation was conducted in a standard-sized room in the middle of the afternoon. The fact that Helgert's question referred to Thompkins's religious beliefs did not render Thompkins's statement involuntary. In these circumstances, Thompkins knowingly and voluntarily made a statement to police, so he waived his right to remain silent.

Thompkins argues that, even if his answer to Detective Helgert could constitute a waiver of his right to remain silent, the police were not allowed to question him until they obtained a waiver first. *Butler* held that courts can infer a waiver of *Miranda* rights "from the actions and words of the person interrogated." The *Miranda* rule and its requirements are met if a suspect receives adequate *Miranda* warnings, understands them, and has an opportunity to invoke the rights before giving any answers or admissions. Any waiver, express or implied, may be contradicted by an invocation at any time. If the right to counsel or the right to remain silent is invoked at any point during questioning, further interrogation must cease. Interrogation provides the suspect with additional information that can put his or her decision to waive, or not to invoke, into perspective. When the suspect knows that *Miranda* rights can be invoked at any time, he or she has the opportunity to reassess his or her immediate and long-term interests. Cooperation with the police may result in more favorable treatment for the suspect; the apprehension of accomplices; the prevention of continuing injury and fear; beginning steps towards relief or solace for the victims; and the beginning of the suspect's own return to the law and the social order it seeks to protect.

In order for an accused's statement to be admissible at trial, police must have given the accused a *Miranda* warning. If that condition is established, the court can proceed to consider whether there has been an express or implied waiver of *Miranda* rights. In making its ruling on the admissibility of a statement made during custodial questioning, the trial court considers whether there is evidence to support the conclusion that, from the whole course of questioning, an express or implied waiver has been established. Thus, after giving a *Miranda* warning, police may interrogate a suspect who has neither invoked nor waived his or her *Miranda* rights. It follows the police were not required to obtain a waiver of Thompkins's *Miranda* rights before commencing the interrogation.

The judgment of the Court of Appeals is reversed, and the case is remanded with instructions to deny the petition.

It is so ordered.

JUSTICE SOTOMAYOR, with whom JUSTICE STEVENS, JUSTICE GINSBURG, and JUSTICE BREYER join, dissenting.

The Court concludes that a criminal suspect waives his right to remain silent if, after sitting tacit and uncommunicative through nearly three hours of police interrogation, he utters a few one-word responses. This proposition marks a substantial retreat from the protection against compelled self-incrimination that *Miranda* has long provided during custodial interrogation. The State did not satisfy its "heavy burden" in proving waiver. *See, e.g., Tague v. Louisiana*, 444 U.S. 469, 470–471 (1980) (*per curiam*). A court may not presume waiver from a suspect's silence or from the mere fact that a confession was eventually obtained. *Butler* made clear that the prosecution bears a substantial burden in establishing an implied waiver. It is undisputed here that Thompkins never expressly waived his right to remain silent. His refusal to sign even an acknowledgment that he understood his *Miranda* rights evinces, if anything, an intent not to waive those rights. That Thompkins did not make the inculpatory statements at issue until after 2 hours and 45 minutes of interrogation serves as "strong evidence" against waiver. Thompkins' "actions and words" preceding the inculpatory statements do not evidence a "course of conduct indicating waiver." Although Thompkins "sporadically" participated in the interview, the opinion and the record are silent as to the subject matter or context of even a single question to which Thompkins purportedly responded, other than the exchange about God and the statements respecting the peppermint and the chair. It is objectively unreasonable under our clearly established precedents to conclude the prosecution met its "heavy burden" of proof on a record consisting of three one-word answers, following 2 hours and 45 minutes of silence punctuated by a few largely nonverbal responses to unidentified questions. When waiver is inferred during a custodial interrogation, there are sound reasons to require evidence beyond inculpatory statements themselves. *Miranda* and our cases are premised on the idea that custodial interrogation is inherently coercive. Requiring proof of a course of conduct beyond the inculpatory statements themselves is critical to ensuring that those statements are voluntary admissions and not the dubious product of an overborne will.

Food for Thought

Assume that you are the law clerk for a state supreme court justice who tells you that the court is considering whether to reject *Moran*. Your judge asks for your analysis of the possible alternative rules that could be adopted instead of the rules endorsed by the court. Describe the possible duties that might be imposed on police to inform an interrogated person that his attorney (either his previously retained attorney or one obtained for him by friends or family) is trying to contact him. Explain how the state court could resolve the problems that are likely to arise if such a duty is created, including the problems mentioned by the Moran majority. *Compare Commonwealth v. Mavredakis*, 725 N.E.2d 169 (2000); *People v. Bender*, 551 N.W.2d 71 (1996); *State v. Stoddard*, 537 A.2d 446 (1988).

Take Note

In *Colorado v. Spring*, 479 U.S. 564 (1987), the Court rejected defendant's argument that his written waiver was invalid because ATF agents did not tell him that they planned to question him not only about a federal firearms violation, but also about an unrelated homicide. After questioning defendant about the firearms crime, the agents asked him if he had a criminal record. He admitted that he had a juvenile record involving a shooting, and then the agents asked if he had ever shot anyone else. The defendant "mumbled" that "I shot another guy once," and then provided no further information. The Court found that defendant's waiver was voluntary because the non-disclosure of possible topics did not raise "any of the traditional indicia of coercion," and did not constitute the type of "police trickery and deception" that was condemned in *Miranda*. The Court concluded that defendant's waiver was knowing and intelligent because there was no allegation that he "failed to understand" the warning, or that he "misunderstood the consequences of speaking freely" to the police. The Court emphasized that defendant received a complete set of *Miranda* warnings before he signed the waiver, including the warning that "anything you say may be used against you." Noting that "there is no qualification of this broad and explicit warning," the Court held that defendant's "awareness of all the possible subjects of questioning in advance of interrogation" is not relevant to determining whether his waiver was voluntary, knowing, and intelligent.

Points for Discussion

a. Conditional Waivers with Limited Invocations

In *Connecticut v. Barrett*, 479 U.S. 523 (1987), defendant was arrested for sexual assault and given *Miranda* warnings. Defendant stated that "he would not give the police any written statements but that he had no problem talking about the incident." Then he made incriminating statements. Thirty minutes later, the police gave him warnings again and this time defendant said that he would not make a written statement unless his attorney was present, but had "no problem" talking about the crime, and he made a second oral statement. He also made a third oral statement that was tape-recorded after he received additional warnings, and after he stated again that he had no problem with talking but would not put anything in writing until his attorney arrived. The Court upheld the admissibility of all three statements: "Barrett's limited requests for counsel were accompanied by affirmative announcements of his willingness to speak to the authorities. Barrett made clear his intentions, and they were honored by police. To conclude that he invoked his right to counsel for all purposes requires a disregard of the ordinary

Food for Thought

How do you explain the fact that defendant was willing to make an oral statement, but completely unwilling to make an oral statement, without the presence of an attorney? Is it possible that defendant did not understand that oral admissions can be as damaging as written admissions? Is there another explanation for his aversion to written statements?

meaning of his statement. We reject the contention that Barrett's distinction between oral and written statements indicates an understanding of the consequences so incomplete that we should deem his limited invocation of the right to counsel effective for all purposes. The warnings made clear to Barrett that 'If you talk to any police officers, anything you say can and will be used against you in court.' We have never embraced the theory that a defendant's ignorance of the full consequences of his decisions vitiates their voluntariness."

b.   Efforts by Counsel to Contact a Custodial Defendant

In *Moran v. Burbine*, 475 U.S. 412 (1986) defendant was in custody when his sister retained a lawyer for him, and the lawyer telephoned the police in an effort to contact defendant prior to his interrogation. The lawyer was told that Burbine was not going to be interrogated because the police "were through with him for the night." However, police officers did interrogate Burbine an hour later without telling him about the lawyer's phone call. After receiving warnings, he waived his rights and made incriminating statements. The Court held that the waiver was valid because Burbine made a "voluntary decision to speak" with "full awareness and comprehension" of his rights: "Events occurring outside of the presence of the suspect and entirely unknown to him surely can have no bearing on the capacity to comprehend and knowingly relinquish a constitutional right. Although the 'deliberate or reckless' withholding of information is objectionable as a matter of ethics, such conduct is only relevant to the constitutional validity of a waiver if it deprives a defendant of knowledge essential to his ability to understand the nature of his rights and the consequences of abandoning them. We are not prepared to adopt a rule requiring that police inform a suspect of an attorney's efforts to reach him. While such a rule might add marginally to *Miranda*'s goal of dispelling the compulsion inherent in custodial interrogation, overriding practical considerations counsel against its adoption. The proposed rule would have the inevitable consequence of muddying *Miranda*'s otherwise relatively clear waters." Justice Stevens dissented, joined by two other justices, emphasizing that the police violated the ABA Standards for Criminal Justice, arguing that there should be "no constitutional distinction," between "a deceptive misstatement and the concealment by the police of the critical fact that an attorney retained by the accused or his family has offered assistance, either by telephone or in person."

c.   Mental Illness & Voluntary Waiver

In *Colorado v. Connelly*, 479 U.S. 157 (1986), the Court rejected defendant's argument that his waiver of *Miranda* rights was not "voluntary" because he was mentally ill at the time of the interrogation. When Connelly approached a police officer and spontaneously confessed to murder, the officer gave him *Miranda* warnings. In answering the officer's questions, Connelly stated that he understood his rights, denied that he had been drinking or taking drugs, and admitted that he had been a patient in several mental hospitals. The officer "perceived no indication whatsoever" that defendant was "suffering from any kind of mental illness" and so Connelly was interrogated after waiving his *Miranda* rights. The next day Connelly told his appointed counsel that "voices" had ordered him to make a confession, and expert testimony at trial showed that he was suffering from chronic schizophrenia. The Court held that there was no evidence of "police overreaching" or "official coercion" to nullify the "voluntariness" of Connelly's waiver, and it found that the interrogation did not violate Due Process "voluntariness" standards. The Due Process ruling in the case is presented in Part E, *infra*.

Hypo 1: *Applying Davis*

A homicide suspect is read a *Miranda* warning, and asked whether he wishes to waive his rights. The man responds "I don't want to talk right now," but states that he would be willing to "write it down." Has the man invoked his right to remain silent? *See State v. Piatnitsky*, 325 P.3d 167 (Wash. 2014). Suppose that instead the man states that "If you can bring me a lawyer that way I can tell you everything that I know and everything that I need to tell you and have someone to represent me." Has the man invoked his right to counsel? *See People v. Sauceda-Contreras*, 282 P.2d 379 (Cal. 2012).

Hypo 2: *Blurted-Out Confession*

Assume that Mike is in custody in an interrogation room with a police officer who states that he has been arrested for the crime of bank robbery. After the officer gives the *Miranda* warnings, Mike says, "I did it. I robbed the bank." If Mike makes this incriminating statement after receiving *Miranda* warnings, and then tells Kira, "I don't really understand my rights very well, and I'm not willing to sign a waiver form," has there been a waiver? May the officer ask whether Mike wishes to waive his rights without violating *Berghuis*? *Compare United States v. Plugh*, 576 F.3d 135 (2d Cir. 2009).

Food for Thought

Assume that defendant is arrested for bank robbery and is given *Miranda* warnings. When the officer asks whether he wishes to waive his rights, Mike says that he wants to know: 1) what the police will do if he says he wants to remain silent or that he wants to talk to a lawyer, 2) whether police are required to let him actually talk to a lawyer before interrogation if he says he wants to do that, and 3) whether the officer thinks it is a good idea for him to talk to a lawyer now. How should the officer be advised to respond to these questions in order to maximize the chance of obtaining a valid waiver from Mike?

Hypo 3: *Capacity for Knowing & Intelligent Waiver*

Garner's lawyer argues that his waiver was not "knowing and intelligent" because of his borderline IQ and the results of the "Grisso test" which show that he has a low capacity for understanding the concepts involved in a *Miranda* waiver. Should Garner's mental capacity bear on whether he has made a knowing and intelligent waiver? Or should the court hold that Garner must show that there was "some observable indication" to the interrogating police officer that he was incapable of understanding the *Miranda* warnings at the time of the waiver? *See Garner v. Mitchell*, 557 F.3d 257 (6th Cir. 2009).

Food for Thought

Assume that you are a prosecutor. You are asked by the police chief to create guidelines for obtaining waivers from people who are juveniles, who may be intoxicated, who may have language problems, or who may suffer from mental illness. What guidelines would you suggest in order to insure that valid waivers can be obtained from these persons?

Hypo 4: *Prior "Field Checks" & Waiver*

Hector, a 17 year-old high school dropout, has been approached repeatedly on the street by police officers conducting "field checks" that involve questioning and frisking without *Miranda* warnings. During these encounters, Hector always cooperated and answered all questions. One day, Officer Smith (who conducted a number of the field checks on Hector), placed Hector in cuffs, took him inside his home, recited the *Miranda* warnings, and told Hector, "Just show us where the drugs are." Hector tells Smith, "I can show you where the drugs are," and does so. The prosecution wants to use this statement at Hector's trial for drug posses sion. Did Hector waive his *Miranda* rights? *See United States v. Gonzalez,* 719 F. Supp. 2d 167 (D. Mass. 2010).

5. Invocations of *Miranda* Rights

The threshold issue in invocation litigation is whether the defendant effectively communicated an invocation to the interrogating officer after warnings. If so, then the officer must cut off questioning immediately without further waiver-seeking or interrogation.

If a person in custody receives *Miranda* warnings and "invokes" either the Fifth Amendment right to remain silent, or the "Fifth Amendment right to counsel," *Miranda* requires the police to cease questioning immediately. *Miranda* assumed that once a person is notified of her rights, she can be expected to notify the interrogating officer that she wishes to exercise these rights. In the absence of such notice, the officer may assume that she does not wish to exercise them and may seek and obtain a waiver.

Davis v. United States

512 U.S. 452 (1994).

JUSTICE O'CONNOR delivered the opinion of the Court.

Navy authorities suspected Davis of murder. After receiving *Miranda* warnings, Davis waived his right to remain silent and his right to counsel, both orally and in writing. After an hour and a half of questioning, Davis said, "Maybe I should talk to a lawyer." The interrogating officer testified that he responded by telling Davis "that if he wants a lawyer, then we will stop any questioning with him, that we weren't going to pursue the matter unless we have it clarified is he asking for a lawyer or is he just making a comment about a lawyer, and he said, 'No, I'm not asking for a lawyer,' and 'I don't want a lawyer.'" After a short break, the officers reminded Davis of his rights to silence and to counsel. The questioning continued for another hour until Davis stated, "I think I want a lawyer before I say anything else." Then the questioning ceased. Davis sought to suppress his statements on the theory that he invoked his right to counsel when he said, "Maybe I should talk to a lawyer"; therefore, the subsequent comments by the officer violated the *Miranda* duty to cut off questioning, and statements made by Davis after these comments were inadmissible. The trial court rejected this argument; Davis was convicted of murder and appealed on *Miranda* grounds.

If a suspect requests counsel at any time during an interview, he is not subject to further questioning, and this rule requires courts to "determine whether the accused actually invoked his right to counsel." *Smith v. Illinois*, 469 U.S. 91, 98 1984. To avoid difficulties of proof and to provide guidance to officers conducting interrogations, this is an objective inquiry. If a suspect makes a reference to an attorney that is ambiguous or equivocal in that a reasonable officer in light of the circumstances would have understood only that the suspect might be invoking the right to counsel, our precedents do not require the cessation of questioning. Rather, the suspect must unambiguously request counsel. "A statement either is an assertion of the right to counsel or it is not." *Smith*, 469 U.S. at 98. Although a suspect need not "speak with the discrimination of an Oxford don," he must articulate his desire to have counsel present sufficiently clearly that a reasonable police officer in the circumstances would understand the statement to be a request for an attorney. If the statement fails to meet the requisite level of clarity, the officers need not stop questioning the suspect. When officers reasonably do not know whether or not the suspect wants a lawyer, a cessation of questioning would needlessly prevent them from questioning when the suspect did not wish to have a lawyer present.

We recognize that requiring a clear assertion of the right to counsel might disadvantage some suspects—who because of fear, intimidation, lack of linguistic skills, or a variety of other reasons—will not articulate their right to counsel although they actually want to have a lawyer present. But if we were to require questioning to cease based on an ambiguous invocation, officers would be forced to make difficult judgment calls with the threat of suppression if they guess wrong. When a suspect makes an ambiguous or equivocal statement it will often be good police practice for the officers to clarify whether or not he actually wants an attorney, in order to help protect the rights of the suspect and to minimize the chance of a confession being suppressed. But we decline to adopt a rule requiring officers to ask clarifying questions.

The courts below found that the remark to the agents was not a request for counsel, and we see no reason to disturb that conclusion. The agents therefore were not required to stop questioning Davis, though it was entirely proper for them to clarify whether he wanted a lawyer. Because there is no ground for the suppression of his statements, the judgment of the Court of Military Appeals is

Affirmed.

JUSTICE SOUTER, with whom JUSTICES BLACKMUN, STEVENS and GINSBURG join, concurring in the judgment.

A rule barring government agents from further interrogation until they determine whether a suspect's ambiguous statement was meant as a request for counsel assures that a suspect's choice whether or not to deal with police through counsel will be "scrupulously honored" under *Miranda*. Moreover, this rule would relieve the officer for any responsibility for guessing "whether in fact the suspect wants a lawyer even though he hasn't said so" by assuring that the "judgment call" will be made by the party most competent to resolve the ambiguity, the individual suspect. I am not persuaded that even ambiguous statements require an end to all police questioning. The costs to society of losing confessions would be hard to bear where the suspect, if asked for his choice, would have chosen to continue. Here Davis's invocation was ambiguous and the officers properly confined their questions to verifying whether he meant to ask for a lawyer and so no *Miranda* violation occurred.

Points for Discussion

a.   Timing of Invocation

Neither *Miranda* nor *Davis* address the issue of whether *Miranda* rights can be invoked even before the *Miranda* warnings are communicated to a person. Some lower courts recognize the validity of pre-warning invocations of the right to counsel by those in custody and assume that the unambiguous invocation requirement should be effective. *See, e.g., Carr v. State*, 934 N.E.2d 1096 (Ind. 2010). However, other courts have relied on dicta from *McNeil v. Wisconsin*, 501 U.S. 171 (1991), as disallowing the "anticipatory invocation" of the *Miranda* right to counsel by anyone other than a person in custody. *See, e.g., State v. Hurst*, 258 P.3d 950 (Ct. App. 2011). *Compare State v. Davis*, 256 P.3d 1075 (2011) (En Banc).

b.   Incriminating Silence?

In *Harris v. New York*, 401 U.S. 222 (1971), the Court held that a defendant's statement, obtained in violation of *Miranda*, is admissible for purposes of impeaching the defendant's credibility at trial. The police violated *Miranda* by failing to give the defendant warnings, and so his incriminating statement about selling heroin was a "fruit" of the violation and therefore inadmissible in the prosecution's case in chief. The *Harris* defendant took the stand in order to testify that he sold baking powder rather than heroin, thus rebutting the testimony of a government witness that the substance sold was heroin. The prosecutor was allowed to cross-examine the defendant using the inadmissible statement to police, and the *Harris* Court validated this impeachment use of the otherwise inadmissible evidence. The Court reasoned that "the impeachment process undoubtedly provided valuable aid to the jury in assessing the defendant's credibility" and opined that "the shield provided by *Miranda*" should not be "perverted into a license to use perjury by way of defense, free from the risk of confrontation with prior inconsistent utterances." The *Harris* dissenters argued that the Court's rule would "seriously undermine" *Miranda*'s objective of "deterring" unconstitutional police practices. But the Court declared that "the benefits" of the impeachment process "should not be lost" merely "because of the speculative possibility that impermissible police conduct will be encouraged thereby." As in *Tucker*, the *Harris* Court expressed confidence that sufficient deterrence of *Miranda* violations would be provided by making *Miranda*-defective statements "unavailable to the prosecution in its case in chief."

In *Doyle v. Ohio*, 426 U.S. 610 (1976), the Court found a Due Process violation when a prosecutor used the fact of defendant's silence in response to *Miranda* warnings to impeach defendant's testimony at trial. The Court noted that "every post-arrest silence is insolubly ambiguous because of what the State is required to advise the person arrested," namely, the right to remain silent under *Miranda*. Therefore, an arrestee's "silence in the wake of the *Miranda* warnings may be nothing more than the arrestee's exercise of the *Miranda* rights." Although "the *Miranda* warnings contain no express assurance that silence will carry no penalty, the Court concluded that such an assurance "is implicit" and so it would violate the fairness concerns of Due Process "to allow the arrested person's silence to be used to impeach an explanation subsequently offered at trial."

The Court's later precedents consistently upheld the impeachment use of a person's silence in other contexts where such silence was not a response to the *Miranda* warnings. In *Jenkins v. Anderson*, 447 U.S. 231 (1980), the Court held that no violation occurred when the defendant's silence *before* arrest was used for impeachment purposes. This holding was justified on the grounds that "no governmental action" like *Miranda* warnings "induced the defendant to remain silent before arrest." The dissenters argued that pre-arrest silence is unlikely to be probative of the falsity of a defendant's trial testimony. Similarly, in *Fletcher v. Weir*, 455 U.S. 603 (1982), the Court found no *Doyle* violation when a defendant's silence *after* arrest occurred *before* warnings were given. *See also Brecht v. Abrahamson*, 507 U.S. 619 (1993). Even when a prosecutor commits a *Doyle* violation during cross-examination, the violation can be cured if the trial judge sustains a subsequent objection and instructs the jury to "ignore the prosecutor's question." *See Greer v. Miller*, 483 U.S. 756 (1987).

However, in *Salinas v. Texas*, 570 U.S. 178 (2013), the police sought to use defendant's conduct as evidence against him. In a non-custodial interview, during which defendant was not read the *Miranda* warnings before being asked whether his shotgun "would match the shells recovered at the scene of the murder," defendant declined to answer, "looked down at the floor, shuffled his feet, bit his bottom lip, clenched his hands in his lap, and began to tighten up." At trial, the prosecution sought to offer testimony regarding defendant's conduct: "We have before us no allegation that petitioner's failure to assert the privilege was involuntary, and it would have been a simple matter for him to say that he was not answering the officer's question on

Fifth Amendment grounds. Because he failed to do so, the prosecution's use of his noncustodial silence did not violate the Fifth Amendment. Our cases establish that a defendant normally does not invoke the privilege by remaining silent. We have also repeatedly held that the express invocation requirement applies even when an official has reason to suspect that the answer to his question would incriminate the witness."

Food for Thought

Worth was arrested, given *Miranda* warnings, and stated that he wanted his lawyer but could not recall the lawyer's name. The officer later asks Worth, "Have you come up with the name yet?" When he says "no," the officer asks, "What do you want to do?", and Worth says, "I guess I'll talk to you." The officer asks, "Even without an attorney?" Worth says, "OK," and then signs a waiver, making incriminating statements. Did Worth unambiguously invoke his right to counsel? *See Wedgeworth v. State*, 374 Ark. 373, 288 S.W.3d 234 (2008).

Hypo 1: *Clarifying Invocation*

Sid is arrested for burglary, taken to the police station, and given *Miranda* warnings. The officer then states, "Do you want to talk to me?" Sid replies, "I got nothin' to say." The officer states, "So that's a no?" Sid says nothing. The officer says, "I just need a yes or a no—so do you want to give your side of the story, yes or no?" Sid replies, "Okay, yes." The officer says, "Yes—meaning you want to answer questions?" Sid states, "Ah, perhaps. I'm not gonna say anything." The officer says, "Well, you can stop any time you want." Sid says, "Okay." Then the officer asks questions about the burglary and Sid makes incriminating statements. Did Sid invoke his rights and did the police respond appropriately? *See State v. Szpyrka*, 202 P.3d 5324 (App. 2008).

Hypo 2: *"I Am Doing My Right"*

An interrogation begins with casual conversation with police detectives, but the detectives eventually read *Miranda* warnings and state, "Do you understand the rights that I have explained to you? Yes or no?" Manzo states "I'm doing my right." A detective asks, "Okay, but do you understand them?" Manzo states, "I'm doing my right." Then the detective says, "OK—do you understand what he just read to you? I'm not asking you to tell me anything. I'm just asking do you understand what I told you?" Manzo replies, "Yes, I understand." A detective then says, "Okay. The point I made earlier is that I don't think you pulled the trigger, so I don't think you need to go down for life. Okay? You got your act together now, you got a job. You're staying clean, your girlfriend says you ain't doing dope. You're not hanging out down in the hood." Manzo then makes incriminating statements. Did Martin unambiguously invoke his right to remain silent? *See People v. Manzo*, <u>121 Cal.Rptr.3d 207 (2011)</u>.

Food for Thought

After Harden is informed of his rights, and while the officer is attempting to obtain a written acknowledgement, Harden says, "You said I could have a lawyer. I can't afford no lawyer," and the officer responds, "Well, you know, that's all stuff that could be worked out—my question to you, do you want to get this off your back; I can tell you've got a lot of pressure on you right now." If Harden makes incriminating statements, did he unambiguously invoke his right to counsel? *See Harden v. State*, <u>59 So.3d 594 (Miss. 2011)</u>.

Hypo 3: *Shaking Head*

After Clarke is arrested, and taken to the police station, he is given a *Miranda* warning. Clarke is then given a waiver form, told to read it, and the detective reviews verbally each of the rights described on the form. The detective then asks Clarke, "Do you want to discuss the charges? Clarke asks, "What happens if I don't speak to you?" The detective replies, "Nothing." Clarke says, "I just want to go home." The detective asks, "You just want to go home? So you don't want to speak?" At that point, Clarke shakes his head in a negative fashion. The detective then says, "OK." But the detective says, "When I said that 'nothing' would happen, that does not exclude us from charging you and detaining you here. You'll either be bailed, or you'll go to court in the morning to answer the charges. So it doesn't mean you'll get to walk out of here and go home now." If Clarke makes incriminating statements, can he argue that he unambiguously invoked his right to silence? *See Commonwealth v. Clarke*, <u>960 N.E.2d 306 (2012)</u>.

Hypo 4: *Can We Get Him Down Here Now?*

In *People v. Kutlak*, 364 P.3d 199 (Colo. 2016), defendant was in custody and had been given a *Miranda* warning. He then stated that he had a personal lawyer and asked "Can you get him down here now, or . . . . ?" The officer responded that it might be difficult to get the lawyer there now, and asked defen dant whether he wanted to continue with the interrogation, stating "It's entirely up to you." Defendant then stated that he would "take a dice roll" and continued with the interrogation. The court concluded that defendant did not clearly and unambiguously request counsel.

Hypo 5: *Request to Speak to Uncle*

Suppose that defendant is given a *Miranda* warning, and repeatedly asserts that he wishes to talk to his uncle before talking to the police. The police continue to ask him whether he wants to speak with them, and he repeats his request to speak to his uncle. Do his repeated requests to speak to his uncle constitute the equivalent of a request to remain silent? *See State v. Maltese*, 120 A.3d 197 (2015).

Food for Thought

Defendant is arrested for burglarizing a neighbor's apartment. At the time of the arrest, the police ask defendant whether he wants to speak with them. Defendant replies "No. You know everything anyway." At that point, the police give defendant a *Miranda* warning and inquire whether he wishes to speak with them. The defendant agrees to talk with the police and makes incriminating statements. Did the police fail to respect defendant's invocation of his right to remain silent? *See State v. Johansen*, 105 A.3d 433 (2014).

Hypo 6: *Anticipatory Invocation*

Suppose that defendant, who is the prime suspect in a murder that was committed in Philadelphia, is apprehended by juvenile authorities in Florida. A public defender in Philadelphia, at the request of defendant's father, sends him a form to sign which purports to invoke his *Miranda* rights, including both the right to remain silent and the right to counsel. Defendant signs the form and hands it to the authorities in Florida. Six days later, after defendant is extradited back to Philadelphia where he is given a *Miranda* warning, he waives his rights, and confesses to the murder. Was the anticipatory invocation of the *Miranda* warning valid against the subsequent waiver of rights? *See Commonwealth v. Bland*, 115 A.3d 854 (Pa. 2015).

Food for Thought

Suppose that a suspect is arrested and read a *Miranda* warning. At that point, the suspect says "I got a lawyer." A conversation ensues in which the arrestee tells the officer the name of the lawyer and the location of his office. The officer then says "do you want to use the lawyer or do you want to talk to me?" and the suspect responds "I could use him." At that point, the officer says "I don't know whether we can get him over here at this moment," and re-asks whether she wants to talk to the officer now. At that point, the suspect states "I'll talk with you." Did the officer act properly under *Miranda*? *See Downey v. State*, 144 So.3d 146 (Miss. 2014).

Hypo 7: *More on Invocation*

Before a juvenile is taken into custody by the police, his father admonishes him to request a lawyer before speaking. When the police bring the juvenile into an interrogation room, the following conversation occurs: "There wouldn't be any possible way that I could have a—a lawyer present while we do this?" Det. Woods: "Well, uh, what I'll do is, um—" Sessoms: "Yeah, that's what my dad asked me to ask you guys . . . uh, give me a lawyer." The officers then tell Sessoms that his accomplices have already told them what happened, and that the only way to tell his side of the story is to speak to the officers then and there without an attorney. Only after talking with him, softening him up, and warning him regarding the "risks" of speaking with counsel, did the detectives read Sessoms his *Miranda* rights. At that point, Sessoms agreed to talk and made incriminating statements. Was Sessoms' request for counsel unequivocal? *See Sessoms v. Grounds*, 768 F.3d 882 (9th Cir. 2014).

Food for Thought

After a suspect is given a *Miranda* warning, he tells police to call his girlfriend to obtain the contact information for his lawyer and "get him down here." Is the suspect's invocation sufficiently unambiguous? *See State v. Philpot*, 787 S.E.2d 181 (2016).

Hypo 8: *"I Ain't Signing Shit Without My Attorney"*

After a suspect was read a *Miranda* warning, he was asked to sign a form authorizing a search of his house. He responded: "I ain't signing shit without my attorney." Has the suspect made a "clear and unequivocal" invocation of his right to an attorney? Could a reasonable police officer conclude that he was willing to speak to the officers, but that he was unwilling to sign the consent to search form? *See State v. Holman,* 502 S.W.3d 621 (Mo., en banc, 2016).

6. Waiver-Seeking After Invocation

Once a suspect invokes either his *Miranda* rights or his right to remain silent, there may be a subsequent attempt to seek a waiver. The Court has recognized that an invocation does not necessarily provide permanent immunity from interrogation. Instead, the validity of a subsequent interrogation depends on whether a person reasserts the right to silence or the right to counsel. Later opportunities for officers to obtain waivers may arise after each type of invocation, but for different reasons.

Michigan v. Mosley

423 U.S. 96 (1975).

MR. JUSTICE STEWART delivered the opinion of the Court.

Mosley was arrested in the afternoon based on a tip that he had participated in two robberies at bars in Detroit. Detective Cowie brought Mosley to the Robbery Bureau on the fourth floor of the police headquarters, and gave him *Miranda* warnings. Mosley signed a "rights notification" form and then he said he did not want to answer any questions about the robberies. Cowie ceased the questioning, and took Mosley to a ninth-floor cell block. A few hours later, Detective Hill brought Mosley from the cell block to the fifth-floor office of the Homicide Bureau for questioning about the fatal shooting of Williams, who had been killed during an attempted holdup at a different bar. Hill read and explained the *Miranda* warnings to Mosley, and this time Mosley waived his rights. When Hill told Mosley that another man had implicated Mosley in the Williams homicide, Mosley made incriminating statements during the 15 minute interrogation that followed. These statements were admitted at Mosley's murder trial and he was convicted.

The issue is whether the conduct of the Detroit police that led to Mosley's incriminating statement violated *Miranda*. Resolution of the question turns almost entirely on the interpretation of a single passage in the *Miranda* opinion: "Once warnings have been given, the subsequent procedure is clear. If the individual indicates in any manner, at any time prior to or during questioning, that he wishes to remain silent, the interrogation must cease. At this point he has shown that he intends to exercise his Fifth Amendment privilege; any statement taken after the person invokes his privilege cannot be other than the product of compulsion, subtle or otherwise. Without the right to cut off questioning, the setting of in-custody interrogation operates on the individual to overcome free choice in producing a statement after the privilege has been once invoked."

This passage could be literally read to mean that a person who has invoked his "right to silence" can never again be subjected to custodial interrogation by any police officer at any time or place on any subject. Another possible construction of the passage would characterize "any statement taken after the person invokes his privilege" as inadmissible, even if it were volunteered by the person in custody. Or the passage could be interpreted to require only the immediate cessation of questioning, and to permit a resumption of interrogation after a momentary respite. It is evident that any of these possible literal interpretations would lead to absurd and unintended results. To permit the continuation of custodial interrogation after a momentary cessation would clearly frustrate the purposes of *Miranda* by allowing repeated rounds of questioning to undermine the will of the person being questioned. At the other extreme, a blanket prohibition against the taking of voluntary statements or a permanent immunity from further interrogation, regardless of the circumstances, would transform the *Miranda* safeguards into wholly irrational obstacles to legitimate police investigative activity, and deprive suspects of an opportunity to make informed and intelligent assessments of their interests. Moreover, *Miranda* prescribes different consequences for different kinds of invocations: an invocation of silence does not trigger the requirement of a lawyer's presence before interrogation can occur, but if "the individual states that he wants an attorney," then "the interrogation must cease until an attorney is present."

A reasonable and faithful interpretation of the *Miranda* opinion must rest on the intention of the Court to adopt "fully effective means to notify the person of his right of silence and to assure that the exercise of the right will be scrupulously honored." The critical safeguard is a person's "right to cut off questioning." Through the exercise of his option to terminate questioning he can control the time at which questioning occurs, the subjects discussed, and the duration of the interrogation. The requirement that law enforcement authorities must respect a person's exercise of that option counteracts the coercive pressures of the custodial setting.

A review of the circumstances leading to Mosley's confession reveals that his "right to cut off questioning" was scrupulously honored in this case. Before his initial interrogation, Mosley received warnings, orally acknowledged that he understood them, and signed a notification-of-rights form. When Mosley stated that he did not want to discuss the robberies, Detective Cowie immediately ceased the interrogation and did not try either to resume the questioning or in any way to persuade Mosley to reconsider his position. After an interval of more than two hours, Mosley was questioned by another police officer at another location about an unrelated holdup murder. He was given full and complete *Miranda* warnings at the outset of the second interrogation. The subsequent questioning did not undercut Mosley's previous decision not to answer Detective Cowie's inquiries. Detective Hill did not resume the interrogation about the robberies, but instead focused exclusively on the homicide, a crime different in nature and in time and place of occurrence from the robberies. The questioning of Mosley about an unrelated homicide was quite consistent with a reasonable interpretation of Mosley's earlier refusal to answer any questions about the robberies. For these reasons, we conclude that the admission in evidence of Mosley's incriminating statement did not violate *Miranda*.

MR. JUSTICE BRENNAN, with whom MR. JUSTICE MARSHALL joins, dissenting.

Miranda is not to be read to impose an absolute ban on resumption of questioning "at any time or place on any subject," or "to permit a resumption of interrogation after a momentary respite." *Miranda*'s terms, however, are not so uncompromising as to preclude the fashioning of guidelines to govern this case. Michigan law requires that the suspect be arraigned before a judicial officer "without unnecessary delay," certainly not a burdensome requirement. Alternatively, a requirement that resumption of questioning should await appointment and arrival of counsel for the suspect would be an acceptable and readily satisfied precondition to resumption. The Court expediently bypasses this alternative in its search for circumstances where renewed questioning would be permissible. Today's decision virtually empties *Miranda* of principle, for plainly the decision encourages police asked to cease interrogation to continue the suspect's detention until the police station's coercive atmosphere does its work and the suspect responds to resumed questioning.

Hypo 1: *Waiver Seeking About Same Crime*

Assume that Kevin is arrested for theft, receives *Miranda* warnings, and invokes his right to remain silent. Two hours later, the same officer comes to Kevin's cell, gives him the *Miranda* warnings again, and asks Kevin if he is willing to sign a waiver and talk about the theft. If Kevin now signs the waiver and makes incriminating statements, are they admissible? Would it matter if the officer waited only twenty minutes before coming back? *See Commonwealth v. Callendar*, 960 N.E.2d 910 (2012); *State v. Bauldwin*, 811 N.W.2d 267 (2012). Would it matter whether the same officer returned, or whether it was a different officer? *See United States v. Oquendo-Rivas*, 750 F.3d 12 (1st Cir. 2014). Suppose that the suspect reinitiates contact by asking "what happens next?," to which the officer replies that he intends to obtain a search warrant. Has the officer reinitiated the interrogation? *See State v. McKnight,* 319 P.3d 298 (Haw. 2013).

Hypo 2: *New Evidence*

Assume that when the officer in the prior hypo came to Kevin's cell two hours after Kevin's invocation of the right to remain silent, her justification for returning to seek a waiver was based on her discovery of new evidence about the same crime. She wanted to find out if Kevin was interested in hearing about the new evidence in order to reconsider his decision to remain silent. Would this change the arguments as to whether the officer violated *Miranda* when she returned and obtained the waiver from Kevin? Would it matter whether the officer mentioned the existence of new evidence at the time she gave Kevin the new *Miranda* warnings, before he signed the waiver? If Kevin were represented by an attorney, would an attorney want to know about new evidence? *See United States v. Guerra,* 237 F. Supp. 2d 795 (E.D. Mich. 2003).

Hypo 3: *No Additional Warnings*

When the officer in the prior hypo returned to seek a waiver from Kevin two hours after his invocation of the right to remain silent, she does not give Kevin the *Miranda* warnings again. Instead, she says, "Kevin, you remember me. Now that two hours have passed, I'm wondering whether you have changed your mind about remaining silent, and whether you are now willing to waive your rights and talk to me?" Assume that Kevin signs the waiver and makes incriminating statements. How does the officer's failure to provide the *Miranda* warnings again change the arguments as to whether she violated *Miranda*? *See State v. Hartley,* 511 A.2d 80 (1986).

Food for Thought

Assume that the officer in the prior hypo failed to obtain a signed waiver after two hours because Kevin invoked the right to silence a second time. Assume that every two hours during the next 12 hours, the officer returns like clockwork to Kevin's cell, gives him the *Miranda* warnings again, and seeks a waiver from Kevin concerning the theft crime. Each time, Kevin invokes the right to remain silent again, and the officer leaves. Then the officer returns one more time to Kevin's cell, gives him *Miranda* warnings and seeks a waiver. This time Kevin signs the waiver and makes incriminating statements. On these facts, did the officer violate *Miranda*? *See United States v. Barone,* 968 F.2d 1378 (1st Cir. 1992).

Hypo 4: *Invocation of Silence with Conditions*

Border patrol agents in San Diego arrest several occupants of a house for the crime of smuggling illegal immigrants into the country. An officer asks Jerry, one of the arrestees, whether he is willing to waive his rights and be questioned about his own citizenship and about other people in the house. Jerry says, "I'll make a statement about my citizenship, but I won't talk about other people." The agent says, "No, we want to talk about both your citizenship and that of the other people." Jerry responds, "I will only talk about my citizenship." Then the agent asks Jerry questions about his citizenship and about the people in the house and Jerry answers all the questions. Did the agent violate *Miranda* and *Mosley* by ignoring Jerry's attempt to invoke his right to silence on the subject of the people in the house? *See United States v. Soliz,* 129 F.3d 499 (9th Cir.1997).

Food for Thought

The *Mosley* Court observes "that when *Miranda* described the need to assure an arrestee that the exercise of the right to silence will be scrupulously honored," the "critical safeguard" that will achieve that assurance is an arrested person's "right to cut off questioning." However, the *Miranda* warnings do not inform an arrestee that such a *Miranda* "right" exists, or that the beneficial consequence of an invocation is that it gives rise to the police duty to cut off questioning. What additional information would be useful for arrestees to understand concerning the operation of their invocation rights and the implementation of *Mosley* power by police officers? Would it be desirable to add such requirements?

Edwards v. Arizona

451 U.S. 477 (1981).

JUSTICE WHITE delivered the opinion of the Court.

Edwards was arrested for theft and homicide crimes and was given *Miranda* warnings at the police station. Edwards said that he understood his rights and would submit to questioning. Then he was told that another suspect had implicated him, and he denied involvement in the crimes, gave a taped statement presenting an alibi defense, and said he wanted to "make a deal." One interrogating officer replied that he had no authority to do that, and gave Edwards the telephone number of the county prosecutor. Edwards made the call but hung up after a few moments and declared, "I want an attorney before making a deal." At that point, questioning ceased and Edwards was taken to jail. The next morning, two detectives asked to see Edwards, and the guard told Edwards that "he had" to talk to them, even though Edwards told the guard that he did not want to talk to anyone. The detectives told Edwards that they wanted to question him, and gave him *Miranda* warnings. Edwards said that he was willing to talk, but first he wanted to hear the taped statement of the alleged suspect who had implicated him. After listening to the statement for several minutes, Edwards agreed to make a statement as long as it was not recorded. When the detectives explained that they could testify in court about any unrecorded statement he made, Edwards replied, "I'll tell you anything you want to know, but I don't want it on tape." He made incriminating statements that were admitted at the trial that led to his conviction.

Although after initially being advised of his *Miranda* rights, the accused may himself validly waive his rights and respond to interrogation, the Court has strongly indicated that additional safeguards are necessary when the accused asks for counsel; we now hold that when an accused has invoked his right to have counsel present during custodial interrogation, a valid waiver of that right cannot be established by showing only that he responded to further police-initiated custodial interrogation even if he has been advised of his rights. An accused, having expressed his desire to deal with the police only through counsel, is not subject to further interrogation by the authorities until counsel has been made available to him, unless the accused himself initiates further communication, exchanges, or conversations with the police. *Miranda* itself indicated that the assertion of the right to counsel was a significant event and that once exercised by the accused, "the interrogation must cease until an attorney is present." Our later cases have maintained that view. In *Michigan v. Mosley,* 423 U.S. 96 (1975), the Court noted that *Miranda* had distinguished between the procedural safeguards triggered by a request to remain silent and a request for an attorney and required that interrogation cease until an attorney was present only if the individual stated that he wanted counsel.

Had Edwards initiated the meeting with the detectives, nothing would prohibit them from merely listening to his volunteered statements and using them against him at the trial. Absent interrogation, there would have been no infringement of the right that Edwards invoked. Here, the officers conducting the first interrogation ceased their questions when Edwards requested counsel as he had been advised he had the right to do. But without making counsel available to Edwards, the police returned to him the next day. This was not at his suggestion or request. Indeed, Edwards informed the detention officer that he did not want to talk to anyone. At the meeting, the detectives told Edwards that they wanted to talk to him and again advised him of his *Miranda* rights. Edwards stated that he would talk, but what prompted this action does not appear. He listened at his own request to part of the taped statement made by one of his alleged accomplices and then made an incriminating statement, which was used against him at his trial. We think it clear that Edwards was subjected to custodial interrogation within the meaning of *Innis*, and that this occurred at the instance of the authorities. His statement made without access to counsel, did not amount to a valid waiver and hence was inadmissible.

The concept of defendant's "initiation" that operates as a retraction of an invocation was defined in *Oregon v. Bradshaw*, 462 U.S. 1039 (1983), in which the defendant was arrested for furnishing liquor to a juvenile who died in a car accident. After defendant was given *Miranda* warnings, he denied involvement in the accident and invoked his right to counsel. The police officer cut off questioning. Soon thereafter, as "Bradshaw was being transferred to the county jail, some ten to fifteen miles away, Bradshaw inquired of a police officer, 'Well, what is going to happen to me now?' The officer answered by saying 'You do not have to talk to me. You have requested an attorney and I don't want you talking to me unless you so desire because anything you say—because—since you have requested an attorney, you know, it has to be at your own free will.' Bradshaw said he understood. There followed a discussion between Bradshaw and the officer concerning where Bradshaw was being taken and the offense with which he would be charged. The officer suggested that Bradshaw might help himself by taking a polygraph examination. Bradshaw agreed to do so, and he made incriminating statements during the examination the next day, after receiving warnings and waiving his rights during the polygraph procedure." The Court concluded that Bradshaw "initiated" the further conversation. While there are some types of inquiries (e.g., a request for a drink of water or a request to use a telephone) that are "so routine that they cannot be fairly said to represent a desire on the part of an accused to open up a more generalized discussion relating directly or indirectly to the investigation," the Court believed that "Bradshaw's question as to what was going to happen to him evinced a willingness and a desire for a generalized discussion about the investigation; it was not merely a necessary inquiry arising out of the incidents of the custodial relationship." In addition, the Court concluded that Bradshaw validly waived his rights. Justice Marshall, joined by three other justices, dissented, arguing that Bradshaw's question, which "came only minutes after invocation," was "a normal reaction to being taken from the police station and placed in a police car, obviously for transport to some destination." As a result, the dissent contended that it did not qualify as "initiation."

Points for Discussion

a. *Edwards* Invocation & Different Crimes

In *Arizona v. Roberson*, <u>486 U.S. 675 (1988)</u>, Roberson was arrested for burglary, given *Miranda* warnings, and invoked his right to counsel. Three days later, Roberson was still in custody when a different police officer, who was unaware of the earlier invocation, gave Roberson a new *Miranda* warning and sought to interrogate him about a different burglary. Roberson waived his rights and made incriminating statements about the other burglary. The Court interpreted *Edwards* as precluding the police from seeking a waiver regarding different crimes after invocation of the right to counsel: "Roberson's unwillingness to answer any questions without the advice of counsel indicated that he did not feel sufficiently comfortable with the pressures of custodial interrogation to answer questions without an attorney. This discomfort is precisely the state of mind that *Edwards* presumes to persist unless the suspect himself initiates further conversation about the investigation. *Edwards* laid down a rule designed to protect an accused from being badgered by police officers. After a person invokes the right to consult counsel, any further interrogation without counsel having been provided will surely exacerbate whatever compulsion to speak the suspect may be feeling. Police are free to inform the suspect of the facts of the second investigation as long as such communication does not constitute interrogation. We attach no significance to the fact that the officer who conducted the second interrogation did not know that respondent had made a request for counsel." Justice Kennedy, joined by Chief Justice Rehnquist, dissented, arguing that the Court's extension of *Edwards* to bar waiver-seeking for "separate and independent investigations" will deprive law enforcement of a useful investigative technique "routinely used to resolve major crimes." "When a person is arrested, his name and fingerprints are checked, and police frequently discover that this person "is wanted for questioning" for unrelated crimes. No *Edwards* protection is necessary from such questioning after invocation of counsel because 'the danger of badgering is minimal.' " The *Roberson* dissenters emphasized that *Mosley* supports the use of fresh *Miranda* warnings as sufficient protection before police engage in waiver-seeking and interrogation about a different crime; the warnings show a suspect that police respect his right to invoke, and to remind him that he may invoke his rights again.

b. Attempted Questioning After Consultation with Counsel

In *Minnick v. Mississippi*, <u>498 U.S. 146 (1990)</u>, defendant was arrested in San Diego for a murder committed in Mississippi. After he received *Miranda* warnings, he refused to sign a waiver and stated, "Come back Monday when I have a lawyer." The agents cut off questioning, and an appointed attorney met with defendant, warned him not to talk to anybody, and promised to get a court order to stop police interrogation. Three days later, a Mississippi sheriff came to question Minnick, and the jailer told Minnick that he must talk to the sheriff. After receiving *Miranda* warnings,

Minnick again refused to sign a waiver, but he started to talk to the sheriff "about how everybody was back in the county jail and what everybody was doing, and what the sheriff had heard from his Mama or his brother, Tracy, and several different other questions pertaining to such things as how the escape went down at the county jail." Minnick made further incriminating statements, which were admitted at his murder trial; he was convicted and received the death penalty. The Court rejected the argument that after a defendant invokes the right to counsel, and consults with counsel, the police no longer have a duty to cut off questioning, and may renew the attempt to seek a waiver: "When counsel is requested, interrogation must cease, and officials may not reinitiate interrogation without counsel present, whether or not the accused has consulted with his attorney. Minnick testified that though he resisted, he was required to submit to both the interviews. The compulsion to submit to interrogation followed his unequivocal request during the FBI interview that questioning cease until counsel was present. We decline to remove protection from police-initiated questioning based on isolated consultations with counsel who is absent when the interrogation resumes." Justice Scalia dissented, joined by Chief Justice Rehnquist, arguing that after consultation with counsel, a suspect would have a heightened awareness of his or her rights, especially of the right to remain silent, so that any police-initiated waiver and confession could no longer be presumed to be based on the suspect's ignorance of rights or on police coercion. Scalia concluded that the decision was unjustified because it "makes it impossible" for police to ask a prisoner who invokes and consults counsel whether "he has changed his mind" about waiving his rights.

Take Note

In *Maryland v. Shatzer*, 559 U.S. 98 (2010), the Court held that after a person in custody invokes the right to counsel, the *Edwards* prohibition on waiver-seeking will expire 14 days after the person's release from custody: "It may be envisioned that once a suspect invokes his *Miranda* right to counsel, the police will release the suspect briefly (to end the *Edwards* presumption) and then promptly bring him back into custody for reinterrogation. But once the suspect has been out of custody long enough (14 days) to eliminate its coercive effect, there will be nothing to gain by such gamesmanship." On the facts of *Shatzer*, the Court concluded that a break in custody occurred when the inmate defendant invoked his *Edwards* right during a custodial interrogation in prison concerning a prior crime in the outside world, and then was released back into the general inmate population. Therefore, his invocation expired 14 days after that event.

Hypo 1: *Refusal to Honor the Invocation*

Suppose that Ted is given *Miranda* warnings during interrogation and invokes his right to counsel under *Edwards* by saying, "I want a lawyer now." The interrogating officers ignore Ted's invocation and continues to interrogate.

Ted refuses to sign a waiver and repeatedly invokes his right to counsel during a three-hour interrogation during which he makes no incriminating statements. He is taken back to the jail. Five hours later he is brought back to the interrogation room for more questioning. Before he is given more warnings, Ted says, "What is going to happen to me now?" The police officer responds by saying, "We're going to resume our interrogation." At this point Ted makes incriminating statements. Did the police violate *Miranda*? *See Hill v. Brigano*, 199 F.3d 833 (6th Cir. 1999).

Hypo 2: *One Arrestee Speaking for Two*

Amy and her boyfriend Bo were arrested for burglary and placed in different interview rooms. Each received *Miranda* warnings and each invoked the right to counsel. They were taken to the courthouse for arraignment in the same police car. During the ride, Amy was silent, but Bo declared, "Take us to the station, let us talk together in private, and then we'll talk about the burglary." So the police returned to the station and Amy and Bo were allowed to speak privately. When the officers entered the room later, Amy was silent but Bo stated, "We're ready to talk, but we have to speak to you together." An officer recited the *Miranda* warnings again to Bo and Amy, asked them whether they understood their rights and were willing to waive them, and then gave Bo a waiver form, which Bo signed. Amy did not sign the form and remained silent. During the interrogation, Bo made incriminating statements. Amy made only one incriminating statement and was otherwise silent. Did the interrogation violate the *Miranda* rights of either Bo or Amy? *See United States v. Lafferty*, 503 F.3d 293 (3d Cir. 2007).

Hypo 3: *Initiation After* Edwards *Violation*

Although Dorsey was given *Miranda* warnings, and invoked his right to counsel, police detectives continued to interrogate him. When he tried to invoke his right to counsel several more times, the officers disparaged his request and continued. During thirteen hours of questioning, continuing through the night, Dorsey did not make any incriminating statements. He repeatedly told the officers that he needed sleep, and was taken to his cell at 8:00 a.m., but was informed that questioning would continue when he awoke. A few hours passed without interrogation after Dorsey woke up. At that point, Dorsey asked a guard if he could speak to one of the detectives, and then he told the detective that he was willing to talk. The interrogation continued without new *Miranda* warnings, and Dorsey made incriminating statements. Are the statements admissible? *See Dorsey v. United States*, 2 A.3d 222 (D.C. Ct. App. 2010); *Ex parte Williams*, 31 So.3d 670 (Ala. 2009).

Hypo 4: *"Tell the Story to Me"*

After Phil is arrested for robbery, detectives take him to an interrogation room, recite the *Miranda* warnings, and obtain a waiver of rights. For 45 minutes, one detective engages in general chat with Phil about his personal life, in order to put Phil at ease. The other detective returns and shouts that the robbery was a terrible crime and that Phil should confess. Phil responds, "I have changed my mind about talking and want to see an attorney immediately." At that point, the second detective leaves. The first detective then states, "Since you have invoked the right to counsel, I cannot speak to you. If you decide that you want to tell your story, you can do that. However, you must first affirm that you are willing to speak without counsel. I want to get your side of the story, but that is totally up to you." Did the detectives violate *Edwards*? *See Phillips v. State*, 425 Md. 210, 40 A.3d 25 (2012).

Hypo 5: *Arrestee in Jail*

Elliott is arrested for violating parole based on a tip that he had committed a robbery, and receives a *Miranda* warning. The arresting officer wants to interrogate Elliott, but Elliott invokes his right to counsel. The questioning ends and Elliott is placed in a cell. Three days later, he is in that cell when Cheryl, his parole officer, arrives at the jail to serve Elliott with parole-violation charges. Before meeting with Elliott, Cheryl talks to the arresting officer, and reviews the police report and the tip concerning the robbery. She then goes to Elliott's cell, serves him with the parole violation charges, and asks him to tell her about the robbery. Elliott makes incriminating statements. Are those statements admissible at his robbery trial? *See People v. Elliott*, 815 N.W.2d 575 (2012).

7. *Miranda* in International Contexts

When statements are elicited during overseas interrogations by foreign police in the absence of *Miranda* warnings, they must be suppressed "whenever United States law enforcement agents actively participate in questioning conducted by foreign authorities." Although the mere presence of U.S. agents at such an interrogation does not constitute the active or substantial participation, the "coordination and direction of an investigation or interrogation by U.S. agents does." *See United States v. Abu Ali*, 528 F.3d 210 (4th Cir. 2008). When *Miranda* applies to the interrogation of a foreign national overseas, U.S. agents must inform the person of his *Miranda* rights, including the right to consult with counsel, and they must stop questioning when that right is invoked. However, the following warning may be used to describe the arrestee's actual access to counsel: "Whether you can retain a lawyer, or have a lawyer appointed for you, and whether you can consult with a lawyer and have a lawyer present during questioning are matters that depend on local law, and we cannot advise you on such matters. If local authorities permit you to obtain counsel (retained or appointed) and to consult with a lawyer at this time, you may attempt to obtain and consult with an attorney before speaking with us. Similarly, if local authorities permit you to have a lawyer present during questioning by local authorities, your lawyer may attend any questioning by us." *See In re Terrorist Bombings of U.S. Embassies in East Africa*, 552 F.3d 93 (2d Cir. 2008).

D. Post-*Miranda* Sixth Amendment Law

For more than a decade after *Miranda*, the Court did not decide a confession case on Sixth Amendment grounds, and did not address questions relating to the relationship between the *Miranda* and *Massiah* rights to counsel. Although *Massiah* established Sixth Amendment protection for indicted defendants questioned by undercover agents, that decision did not explain how the protection would apply (if at all) during police questioning. In 1977 the Court provided that explanation, when it used *Massiah* to resolve a controversial case, and embarked upon the process of articulating the differences between *Massiah* and *Miranda* rights.

Brewer v. Williams

430 U.S. 387 (1977).

MR. JUSTICE STEWART delivered the opinion of the Court.

When an arrest warrant was issued for Williams in Des Moines for the crime of abduction, he was in Davenport. He sought the advice of a Des Moines attorney, who advised Williams to turn himself in to the Davenport police. Then Williams waited for the Des Moines police to pick him up. When Williams was arraigned in Davenport, he consulted with the local counsel. Williams received *Miranda* warnings from the police who arrested him, from the magistrate during arraignment, and from Detective Leaming when the Des Moines police arrived to pick up Williams. But he never received a waiver form, and Detective Leaming never sought an oral waiver or provided additional warnings during the 160-mile car trip to Des Moines. When Detective Leaming arrived in Davenport and heard about the police agreement that Williams would not be questioned during the trip, Leaming rejected the request of counsel to accompany Williams. The incriminating statements that Williams made during the trip were admitted at his murder trial. The Court found it unnecessary to reach the *Miranda* issues.

When the ride began, the detective and his prisoner embarked on a wide-ranging conversation covering a variety of topics, including the subject of religion. Leaming knew that Williams was a former mental patient and was deeply religious. Not long after reaching the interstate highway, Leaming delivered what has been referred to as the "Christian burial speech." Addressing Williams as "Reverend," the detective said: "I want to give you something to think about while we're traveling down the road. I want you to observe the weather conditions, it's raining, it's sleeting, it's freezing, driving is very treacherous, visibility is poor, it's going to be dark early this evening. They are predicting several inches of snow for tonight, and you are the only person that knows where this little girl's body is, that you yourself have only been there once, and if you get a snow on top of it you yourself may be unable to find it. Since we will be going right past the area on the way into Des Moines, I feel that we could stop and locate the body, that the parents of this little girl should be entitled to a Christian burial for the little girl who was snatched away from them on Christmas Eve and murdered. I feel we should stop and locate it on the way in rather than waiting until morning and trying to come back out after a snow storm and possibly not being able to find it at all." Leaming then stated: "I do not want you to answer me. I don't want to discuss it any further. Just think about it as we're riding down the road." After the car traveled another 100 miles, Williams made incriminating statements and told the officers how to find the body.

There can be no doubt that judicial proceedings had been initiated against Williams before the start of the automobile ride from Davenport to Des Moines. A warrant had been issued for his arrest, he had been arraigned on that warrant before a judge in a Davenport courtroom, and he had been committed by the court to confinement in jail. There can be no serious doubt that Leaming deliberately and designedly set out to elicit information from Williams just as surely as and perhaps more effectively than if he had formally interrogated him. The clear rule of *Massiah* is that once adversary proceedings have commenced against an individual, he has a right to legal representation when the government interrogates him.

The prosecutor argued that Williams waived his Sixth Amendment right to counsel. It was incumbent upon the State to prove "an intentional relinquishment or abandonment of a known right or privilege." *Johnson v. Zerbst*, 304 U.S. 458, 464 (1938). The record falls far short of sustaining the state's burden. Williams had been informed of and appeared to understand his right to counsel. But waiver requires not merely comprehension but relinquishment, and Williams' consistent reliance upon the advice of counsel in dealing with the authorities refutes any suggestion that he waived that right. Williams was advised not to make any statements before seeing his counsel in Des Moines, and was assured that the police had agreed not to question him. His statements while in the car "When I get to Des Moines and see my lawyer, I am going to tell you the whole story" were the clearest expressions by Williams himself that he desired the presence of an attorney before any interrogation took place. Even before making these statements, Williams had effectively asserted his right to counsel by having secured attorneys at both ends of the automobile trip, both of whom had made clear to the police that no interrogation was to occur during the journey. Williams knew of that agreement and, particularly in view of his consistent reliance on counsel, there is no basis for concluding that he disavowed it. Despite Williams' express and implicit assertions of his right to counsel, Leaming proceeded to elicit incriminating statements from Williams. Leaming did not preface this effort by telling Williams that he had a right to the presence of a lawyer, and made no effort at all to ascertain whether Williams wished to relinquish that right. The circumstances thus provide no reasonable basis for finding that Williams waived his right to the assistance of counsel.

MR. CHIEF JUSTICE BURGER, dissenting.

Williams made a valid waiver of his Fifth Amendment right to silence and his Sixth Amendment right to counsel when he led police to the body. The fundamental purpose of the Sixth Amendment is to safeguard the fairness of the trial and the integrity of the factfinding process. It appears suppression is mandated here for no other reason than the Court's general impression that it may have a beneficial effect on future police conduct.

MR. JUSTICE WHITE, with whom MR. JUSTICE BLACKMUN and MR. JUSTICE REHNQUIST join, dissenting.

Waiver is shown whenever the facts establish that an accused knew of a right and intended to relinquish it. Such waiver, even if not express, was plainly

FYI

When Williams was retried for murder, his statements about the location of the body were inadmissible, but the prosecutor relied on the "inevitable discovery" exception to the exclusionary rule to support the admission of location of the victim's body and condition. In *Nix v. Williams*, 467 U.S. 431 (1984), the Court upheld Williams' conviction, and ruled that the prosecutor made a sufficient showing that the police would have "inevitably" discovered the location of the body by following the police search procedures that were underway at the time, so the *Massiah* violation could be ignored.

shown here. The officers' conduct did not jeopardize the fairness of the defendant's trial or in any way risk the conviction of an innocent man, the risk against which the Sixth Amendment guarantee of assistance of counsel is designed to protect.

Take Note

The Court has identified a short list of events that qualify as "adversary judicial criminal proceedings," including a "formal charge, preliminary hearing, indictment, information, or arraignment." *Rothgery v. Gillespie County*, 554 U.S. 191, 198 (2008). Some of these events involve the defendant's appearance before a judicial officer, and other events involve only the participation of a prosecutor. If the Court decides to expand the *Rothgery* list in a future case, an event or procedure that involves neither element is unlikely to qualify as an "adversary judicial proceeding."

Points for Discussion

a. Contrasting "Deliberate Elicitation" with "Interrogation"

Following *Brewer*, the Court emphasized that the "deliberate elicitation" concept is central to the *Massiah* doctrine, and is distinct from *Miranda*'s "interrogation" concept. *Brewer* does not compare the two concepts, but *Brewer* was decided before *Innis* established the modern definition of "interrogation." However, *Brewer* explained deliberate elicitation by noting that the detective "purposely sought" to isolate the defendant "from his lawyers to obtain as much incriminating information as possible", and that the detective conceded "as much" at trial. In *Fellers v. United States*, 540 U.S. 519 (2004), the Court justified a finding of deliberate elicitation in simpler terms, noting that when the police arrived at the defendant's home, "they informed him that their purpose was to discuss his involvement in the distribution of methamphetamine and his association with certain charged co-conspirators." Therefore, the "ensuing discussion" violated defendant's right to counsel because it occurred "after he had been indicted, outside the presence of counsel, and in the absence of any waiver of his Sixth Amendment rights".

b. Comparing *Innis* & *Brewer*

Innis emphasized that the concepts of "interrogation" and "deliberate elicitation" are not interchangeable, but the Court used the *Brewer* facts to shape the definition of "interrogation" in *Innis*. For example, *Innis* states that "this is not a case in which the police carried on a lengthy harangue in the presence of a suspect," that the officers "were not aware that the defendant was peculiarly susceptible to an appeal to his conscience," that the officers' remarks in *Innis* were not "particularly evocative," and that their conversation "was nothing more than a dialogue between the two officers to which no response was invited." Surely not coincidentally, the scenario in *Brewer* presented the "perfect opposite" of *Innis* in these four respects. *Innis* implied that a finding of "interrogation" would have been justified in *Brewer* if the case had been decided on the basis of *Miranda* rather than *Massiah*.

Take Note

The *Massiah* right is more limited than the *Miranda* right because the Sixth Amendment right to counsel is "offense specific." Notably, *Brewer* held that after the defendant's Sixth Amendment right attached at his arraignment on an abduction charge, police violated that right by deliberately eliciting statements from him concerning an uncharged murder. However, in *Texas v. Cobb*, 532 U.S. 162 (2001), the Court interpreted *Massiah* as allowing police to question an indicted defendant about uncharged offenses that are "factually related" to the charged "offense," and imported the definition of "offense" from double jeopardy precedent into *Massiah* doctrine. *See Blockburger v. United States*, 284 U.S. 299, 304 (1932). Thus, under *Cobb*, police may question an indicted defendant about any uncharged offense that requires proof of a fact not required by the definition of the charged offense. The *Cobb* dissenters argued that police should be prohibited from deliberately eliciting information about uncharged offenses that are "closely related to" or "inextricably intertwined" with the charged offense. They predicted that the *Cobb* rule would operate to "remove a significant portion" of *Massiah*'s protection because prosecutors can so easily "spin out a series of offenses from a single criminal transaction."

Hypo: *"Deliberate Elicitation" & Comments Not Directed at Defendant*

Suppose that, instead of making the "Christian Burial Speech" to Williams, Detective Leaming and the other officer make a few off-hand remarks to each other. Leaming says, "They are predicting several inches of snow for tonight." The other officer replies, "Yes, and I sure hope that the people who are searching for the victim's body will find it so that she can receive a proper Christian burial." Suddenly, Williams blurts out the location of the body. Would the Court still be inclined to find that Leaming "deliberately elicited" incriminating statements from *Brewer*? If the case had been decided under *Miranda*, rather than under the Sixth Amendment, would the Court be inclined to find that Leaming's words were "reasonably likely to elicit an incriminating response?" Would it matter if Leaming had also stated the following to the other officer: "I am so afraid that the body of that little girl is out there somewhere in the snow where no one can find her on Christmas Eve, and that her grieving parents will never be able to give her a Christian burial."

Food for Thought

A statute requires a child protective services agency to inform the police when they have reasonable cause to believe that child sexual abuse has occurred, and also requires them to determine the scope of potential risks to the child. As part of this process, agency officials conduct interviews with alleged abusers, but are not allowed to ask suspected abusers whether they have been charged with a crime or whether they have counsel. In addition, they do not administer *Miranda* warnings. Should incriminating statements made to agency investigators be inadmissible at an abuser's trial? *See State v. Oliveira,* 961 A.2d 299 (R.I. 2008).

Kuhlmann v. Wilson

477 U.S. 436 (1986).

JUSTICE POWELL announced the judgment of the Court and delivered the opinion of the Court.

Kuhlmann was arraigned on charges of robbery and murder and placed in a cell with Lee, a prisoner who had agreed to act as a police informant. Lee agreed to listen to Kuhlmann's conversations and report his remarks to Detective Cullen, who wished to discover the identities of Kuhlmann's confederates. Cullen told Lee not to ask any questions, but simply to "keep his ears open." Kuhlmann first spoke to Lee about the crimes after he noticed that their cellblock window overlooked the taxi garage where the crimes had occurred. He said, "someone's messing with me," and told Lee the same story about the robbery that he gave the police at the time of his arrest. Lee advised Kuhlmann that his explanation "didn't sound too good," but Kuhlmann did not alter his story immediately. After a few days, Kuhlmann received a visit from his brother, who mentioned that members of his family were upset because they believed that Kuhlmann was guilty of murder. After the visit, Kuhlmann admitted to Lee that he and two other men had planned and carried out the robbery and murder. Lee reported Kuhlmann's statements to Detective Cullen, and gave Cullen the notes that he had written surreptitiously while sharing the cell with Kuhlmann. The trial court found that Cullen had instructed Lee "to ask no questions of Kuhlmann about the crime but merely to listen as to what Kuhlmann might say in his presence." The court determined that Lee obeyed these instructions, that he "at no time asked any questions with respect to the crime," and that he "only listened to Kuhlmann and made notes regarding what he had to say." The trial court also found that Kuhlmann's statements to Lee were "spontaneous" and "unsolicited."

The primary concern of the *Massiah* precedents is secret interrogation by investigatory techniques that are the equivalent of direct police interrogation. Since "the Sixth Amendment is not violated whenever—by luck or happenstance—the State obtains incriminating statements from the accused after the right to counsel has attached," a defendant does not make out a violation of that right simply by showing that an informant, either through prior arrangement or voluntarily, reported his incriminating statements to the police. *Maine v. Moulton,* 474 U.S. 159, 176 (1985). Rather, defendant must demonstrate that the police and their informant took some action, beyond merely listening, that was designed deliberately to elicit incriminating remarks. Cullen instructed Lee only to listen to Kuhlmann and Lee followed these instructions; "at no time did he ask any questions" of Kuhlmann concerning the pending charges and he "only listened" to Kuhlmann's statements. The only remark made by Lee was his comment that Kuhlmann's initial version of his participation in the crimes "didn't sound too good."

[The Court concluded that based on the state court's findings on the record there was no "deliberate elicitation" by Lee that violated the Sixth Amendment. The Court also noted that the record provided no information concerning the fact that Kuhlmann was placed in a cell overlooking the crime scene.]

JUSTICE BRENNAN, with whom JUSTICE MARSHALL joins, dissenting.

Under *Massiah* it is irrelevant whether the informant asks pointed questions about the crime or "merely engages in general conversation about it." Lee encouraged Kuhlmann to talk about his crime by conversing with him on the subject over the course of several days and by telling him that his exculpatory story would not convince anyone without more work. A disturbing visit from his brother, rather than a conversation with the informant, seems to have been the catalyst for Kuhlmann's confession. But the deliberate-elicitation standard requires consideration of the entire course of government behavior. Here the State intentionally created a situation in which it was foreseeable that Kuhlmann would make incriminating statements without the assistance of counsel—it assigned him to a cell overlooking the scene of the crime and designated a secret informant to be his cellmate. The informant, while avoiding direct questions, nonetheless developed a relationship of cellmate camaraderie with Kuhlmann and encouraged him to talk about his crime. Clearly the State's actions had a sufficient nexus with Kuhlmann's admission of guilt to constitute deliberate elicitation.

After *Massiah*, the Court was forced to define the term "government agent." The Court held that there must be an agency relationship between the informant and the government, and that such a relationship can be prompted by extensive "police involvement with the informant." Relevant factors can include promises of rewards, requests to obtain incriminating evidence, placement of the informant in a position to obtain such evidence, and initiation of a pre-existing plan to secure it. When a government agent has not "directed or steered" an informant toward the defendant, a court may decide that the informant did not achieve the status of "agent" and was merely "an entrepreneur who hoped to sell information to the government." *See State v. Swinton,* 268 Conn. 781, 847 A.2d 921 (2004). Some courts use a bright line test to define an "agent" which provides that an informant becomes a government agent "only when the informant has been instructed by the police to get information about the particular defendant." Other courts employ a case-by-case approach, requiring only "some evidence that an agreement, express or implied, between the individual and a government official existed at the time the elicitation took place." One court observed that, "To hold otherwise would allow the State to accomplish 'with a wink and a nod' what it cannot do overtly." *See Ayers v. Hudson,* 623 F.3d 301 (6th Cir. 2010).

Points for Discussion

a. When Informant Violates Instructions to "Listen and Don't Ask Questions"

The informant in *Massiah* deliberately elicited information from his co-defendant by "inducing Massiah to enter the informant's car and talk about the case." In later cases, government agents instructed informants "not to question" the target defendant and "not to initiate any conversations" about the charged crime. However, in *United States v. Henry,* 447 U.S. 264 (1980), when a disobedient informant violated these instructions by "stimulating" conversations with the defendant in order to elicit information, the Court found that he had engaged in "deliberate elicitation" attributable to the government. *Henry* left open the question whether it would violate *Massiah* for the government to place an informant "in close proximity" to defendant, as long as the informant "makes no effort to stimulate conversations about the crime charged." *Kuhlmann* provided a negative answer to that question.

b. Knowing Exploitation of the Opportunity to Confront the Accused Without Counsel

In *Maine v. Moulton,* 474 U.S. 159 (1985), the informant was a co-defendant who received a proposal from Moulton to meet "to plan their defense." The government supplied the informant with a wire that would transmit conversations to a listening agent. Although instructed "not to question" Moulton, the informant asked Moulton to remind him about the details of the crime, thereby "deliberately eliciting" Moulton's statements. The prosecutor argued that no *Massiah* violation occurred because Moulton proposed the meeting, not the informant. In rejecting that argument, the Court held that the informant's "wired" presence involved a "knowing exploitation by the State of an opportunity to confront the accused without counsel being present," which it equated with the "intentional creation of the opportunity to circumvent the right to counsel." No *Massiah* violation occurs where agents obtain a statement "by luck or happenstance," but the *Moulton* scenario did not fit that category.

c. Continuing Investigations After Indictment

The *Massiah* Court observed that it was "entirely proper to continue investigating the suspected criminal activities of the defendant," so that admissible evidence unrelated to the charged offense might be obtained and used in prosecutions for other crimes. In *Maine v. Moulton*, <u>474 U.S. 159 (1985)</u>, the Court rejected a prosecutor's proposal to restrict *Massiah* by allowing government agents to deliberately elicit statements about a charged offense whenever the government puts forward a "legitimate reason" to do so that goes beyond the simple need to investigate the charged crime. *Moulton* reasoned that it would be too difficult for courts to define the parameters of a "legitimate reason" and predicted that the proposed limitation would invite "abuse by law enforcement personnel in the form of fabricated investigations and would risk the evisceration" of *Massiah* rights.

Take Note

In *Kansas v. Ventris*, <u>556 U.S. 586 (2009)</u>, the Court held that an informant's inadmissible testimony about an indicted defendant's statements could be used to impeach defendant's inconsistent testimony at trial even though they were obtained in violation of *Massiah*. The Court held that *Massiah* is violated when impermissible deliberate elicitation occurs. *Ventris* concerned "the scope of the remedy for a violation that has already occurred." In the Court's view, the exclusion of *Massiah*-defective statements from the prosecutor's case in chief provides police with a "significant incentive" to comply with *Massiah*. *Ventris* concluded that the mere "speculative possibility" that police might violate *Massiah* in order to uncover impeachment evidence did not "trump the costs of allowing perjurious statements to go unchallenged." The *Ventris* dissenters argued that the "use of ill-gotten evidence during any phase of a criminal prosecution does damage to the adversarial process—the fairness of which the Sixth Amendment was designed to protect." They also emphasized that the admission of *Massiah*-defective evidence at trial was identified explicitly by the *Massiah* Court as a Sixth Amendment harm.

Food for Thought

Kuhlmann emphasized that the informant merely "listened" to the defendant and did not "ask questions" about the crime. Even though the informant did make one potentially evocative remark to the defendant, telling him that his story to the police "didn't sound too good," the Court did not view that comment as significant. Why not?

Hypo 1: *Developing the Evidence*

Suppose that you are a defense attorney who has been appointed to represent a defendant like Kuhlmann who has made incriminating statements to an informant prisoner in the defendant's cell block. What types of evidence might convince a court to exclude the defendant's statements based on a *Massiah* violation? Explain how you would go about obtaining such evidence.

Hypo 2: *Handing Letter to Officer*

When David was indicted, he requested and received counsel. However, Detective Flores, who was unaware of David's indictment and of counsel, had David brought to a large open area in the jail. When Detective Flores introduced himself as a police officer, David handed him a folded letter and said, "I've been waiting to talk to somebody." The letter contained incriminating statements which were admitted at David's trial. Did Officer Flores violate *Massiah* by "deliberately eliciting" information from David? *See State v. Maldonado*, 259 S.W.3d 184 (Tex. Crim. App. 2008).

Hypo 3: *Whereabouts of Witness*

Baker, who was charged with assaulting a man who threatened his girlfriend (Jen), was released on bail. Detective Ed thought that Baker might be trying to "hide" Jen from being interviewed by the prosecutor. When Ed went looking for Jen, Ed could not find her but he did find Baker. So he asked Baker, "Do you know the whereabouts of Jen?" Baker replied, "She is out for lunch with friends." Later Detective Ed discovered that Baker was lying and that Jen had taken a trip to Germany. At Baker's trial, Detective Ed testified about the lie, and the prosecutor urged the jury to infer that Baker's lie showed that he was attempting to conceal the location of a witness, which indicated his "consciousness of guilt." Did Detective Ed violate *Massiah* by "deliberately eliciting" information from Baker when asking the question about the whereabouts of Jen? *See Baker v. State*, 157 Md.App. 600, 853 A.2d 796 (2004).

Patterson v. Illinois

<u>487 U.S. 285 (1988)</u>.

JUSTICE WHITE delivered the opinion of the Court.

Patterson was arrested for battery and mob action and was suspected of murder. He was given *Miranda* warnings and he answered questions about the battery and mob action crimes, but denied knowing about the murder. The next day he was indicted for murder, taken from the lockup, and told that because he was now indicted, he was being transferred to another jail. When Patterson started to make incriminating statements, Officer Gresham interrupted him, gave him a *Miranda* form, and read the warnings aloud as Patterson read along with him. Patterson signed a waiver form and made incriminating statements to Gresham; during a later interview with a prosecutor, he received *Miranda* warnings again, waived his rights again, and made further incriminating statements.

Patterson's principal claim is that questioning him without counsel present violated the Sixth Amendment because he did not validly waive his right to have counsel present during the interviews. In the past, this Court has held that a waiver of the Sixth Amendment right to counsel is valid only when it reflects "an intentional relinquishment or abandonment of a known right or privilege." *Johnson v. Zerbst*, supra, at 464. In a case arising under the Fifth Amendment, we described this requirement as "a full awareness of both the nature of the right being abandoned and the consequences of the decision to abandon it." *Moran v. Burbine*, 475 U.S. 412, 421 (1986). Whichever of these formulations is used, the key inquiry in a case such as this one must be: Was the accused, who waived his Sixth Amendment rights during postindictment questioning, made sufficiently aware of his right to have counsel present during the questioning, and of the possible consequences of a decision to forgo the aid of counsel? In this case, by admonishing Patterson with the *Miranda* warnings, the state has met this burden and that petitioner's waiver of his right to counsel at the questioning was valid.

First, the *Miranda* warnings given Patterson made him aware of his right to have counsel present during the questioning. Second, the *Miranda* warnings also served to make Patterson aware of the consequences of a decision by him to waive his Sixth Amendment rights during postindictment questioning. He knew that any statement that he made could be used against him in subsequent criminal proceedings. This is the ultimate adverse consequence petitioner could have suffered by virtue of his choice to make uncounseled admissions to the authorities. This warning also sufficed to let him know what a lawyer could "do for him" during the postindictment questioning: namely, advise petitioner to refrain from making any such statements.

We reject the argument that a waiver of an accused's Sixth Amendment right to counsel should be "more difficult" to effectuate than waiver of a suspect's Fifth Amendment rights. We have never suggested that one right is "superior" or "greater" than the other. Instead, we have taken a more pragmatic approach to the waiver question—asking what purposes a lawyer can serve at the particular stage of the proceedings in question, and what assistance he could provide to an accused at that stage—to determine the scope of the Sixth Amendment right to counsel, and the type of warnings and procedures that should be required before a waiver of that right will be recognized.

Applying this approach, whatever warnings suffice for *Miranda*'s purposes will also be sufficient in the context of postindictment questioning. The State's decision to take an additional step and commence formal adversarial proceedings against the accused does not substantially increase the value of counsel to the accused at questioning, or expand the limited purpose that an attorney serves when the accused is questioned by authorities. Because the role of counsel at questioning is relatively simple and limited, we see no problem in having a waiver procedure at that stage which is likewise simple and limited. So long as the accused is made aware of the "dangers and disadvantages of self-representation" during post-indictment questioning by use of the *Miranda* warnings, his waiver of his Sixth Amendment right to counsel at such questioning is "knowing and intelligent."

JUSTICE BLACKMUN, dissenting.

After formal adversary proceedings against a defendant have been commenced, the Sixth Amendment mandates that the defendant not be "subject to further interrogation by the authorities until counsel has been made available to him, unless the accused initiates further communication, exchanges, or conversations with the police." The Sixth Amendment does not allow the prosecution to take undue advantage of any gap between the commencement of the adversary process and the time at which counsel is appointed for a defendant.

JUSTICE STEVENS, with whom JUSTICE BRENNAN and JUSTICE MARSHALL join, dissenting.

To say that the *Miranda* warnings lay a sufficient basis for accepting a waiver of the Sixth Amendment right to counsel because they make clear to an accused that a lawyer could advise him to refrain from making any incriminating statements is a gross understatement of the disadvantage of proceeding without a lawyer and an understatement of what a defendant must understand to give a knowing waiver. The *Miranda* warnings do not inform the accused that a lawyer might examine the indictment for legal sufficiency or that a lawyer is likely to be considerably more skillful at negotiating a plea bargain and that such negotiations may be most fruitful if initiated prior to any interrogation. The warnings do not even go so far as to explain to the accused the nature of the charges pending against him—advice that a court would insist upon before allowing a defendant to enter a guilty plea with or without the presence of an attorney. After indictment the adversary relationship between the state and the accused has solidified, so it inescapably follows that a prosecutor may not conduct private interviews with a charged defendant. Even the *Miranda* warnings themselves are a species of legal advice that is improper when given by the prosecutor or his or her agents, the police after indictment.

Point for Discussion

Request for Appointment of Counsel at Arraignment

In *Montejo v. Louisiana,* 556 U.S. 778 (2009), the Court overruled *Michigan v. Jackson,* 475 U.S. 625 (1986), which held that police officers were prohibited under the Sixth Amendment from initiating an interrogation once a defendant makes a post-adversarial proceeding assertion of his right to counsel. Defendant argued that the Court should extend the *Jackson* rule to a preliminary hearing at which defendant made no explicit request for counsel because under state law counsel was automatically appointed. Instead, the Court determined that *Montejo* illustrated why the *Jackson* rule was unworkable. According to *Montejo, Jackson* was based on an analogy to the *Edwards* prohibition on waiver-seeking after invocation of the Fifth Amendment *Miranda* right to counsel, which prohibition is "designed to prevent police from badgering a defendant into waiving his previously asserted *Miranda* rights." Logically, when a defendant has not requested counsel, he has no need to be protected against "badgering." The Court noted that *Jackson* "is only two decades old," and "eliminating it would not upset expectations." Finally, the Court concluded that *Jackson* did not recognize how "the marginal benefits" of its holding are "dwarfed" by "substantial costs" to the "truth-seeking process and the criminal justice system."

Justice Stevens' *Montejo* dissent, joined by three other justices, illustrates the values that underlie the *Jackson* rule. The dissenters emphasized that *Montejo* "flagrantly misrepresents *Jackson*'s underlying rationale," which it described as "to 'protect the unaided layman at critical confrontations with his adversary,' by giving him 'the right to rely on counsel as a "medium" between himself and the State.' *Jackson* concluded that arraigned defendants are entitled to 'at least as much protection' during interrogation as the Fifth Amendment affords unindicted suspects, and *Jackson* is firmly rooted in the unique protections afforded to the attorney-client relationship by the Sixth Amendment." The *Montejo* dissenters would have found that *Montejo* did not need an extension of the *Jackson* rule because the police officers violated his Sixth Amendment rights by seeking a waiver after counsel was automatically appointed at his preliminary hearing, and the police questioned him "without notice to, and outside the presence of, his lawyer" and "the Sixth Amendment is violated when the State obtains incriminating statements by knowingly circumventing the accused's right to have counsel present in a confrontation between the accused and a state agent." *Maine v. Moulton,* 474 U.S. 159, 176 (1985).

Food for Thought

In *Patterson*, the officer told defendant about his indictment. The Court reserved the question whether "an accused must be told that he has been indicted before a post-indictment Sixth Amendment waiver will be valid," noting that "the desirability of so informing the accused" is "a matter that can be reasonably debated." After *Patterson*, the consensus of lower courts is that the "failure to inform the defendant that he has been charged with the crime with respect to which he is making a statement does not vitiate an otherwise valid *Miranda* warning given at the interview where the statement was made." What arguments can be made on both sides of this issue? *See Johnson v. State,* 851 N.E.2d 372 (Ind.App. 2006).

Hypo: *Effect of Warnings*

Franco was indicted for murder but was not taken into custody. The next day, Franco retained a lawyer to represent himself, and she advised him not to talk to anyone without her. The lawyer also spoke to the prosecutor and Detective York to inform them of her representation. A few days later, Franco was arrested by Officer Howard who Franco told that he had hired a lawyer, and he placed a phone call to the lawyer. When the lawyer tried calling Franco's cell phone, she got no answer. Then she called the prosecutor, Detective York, and Officer Howard, but she got no answer and none of them returned her calls. In the interim, Officer Howard interrogated Franco after giving him *Miranda* warnings, obtained a waiver, and obtained incriminating statements. Should Franco's statements be regarded as admissible under *Patterson* because he received the *Miranda* warnings? *See State v. Franco,* 133 P.3d 164 (Kan. App. 2006).

Food for Thought

Patterson declared that "as a general matter" the *Miranda* warnings will "sufficiently apprise" a person of Sixth Amendment rights. But the Court also observed that there will be cases where a valid *Miranda* waiver "will not suffice for Sixth Amendment purposes" because "the Sixth Amendment's protection of the attorney-client relationship extends beyond *Miranda*'s protection of the right to counsel." What scenarios may fit this category of cases?

E. Post-*Miranda* Due Process Law

In the post-*Miranda* era, defendants continue to challenge their confessions as involving violations of Due Process. For those defendants who do not have viable *Miranda* or *Massiah* claims, a Due Process claim may be the only basis for arguing that their statements to police are inadmissible at trial. These defendants may lack *Miranda* arguments when they waive their rights, when they confess while not in "custody," when they are interrogated by secret agents, and when they face impeachment on the stand with *Miranda*-defective statements. Even defendants who qualify for *Massiah* rights may lose them through waivers provided to police interrogators. The Court's modern Due Process precedents continue to rely on a "totality" test, which now incorporates the factor of police compliance with *Miranda*. As in the pre-*Miranda* era, the Court remains divided about the meaning of coercion and about the appropriate interpretation of the "involuntariness" standard.

Mincey v. Arizona

437 U.S. 385 (1978).

MR. JUSTICE STEWART delivered the opinion of the Court.

Mincey was wounded during an exchange of fire with officers entering his house to arrest him for narcotics crimes; he was taken to the hospital and treated in intensive care. An officer died in the shootout, and that evening, Detective Hust came to interrogate Mincey about the shooting. Hust gave *Miranda* warnings to Mincey and told him that he was under arrest. Mincey could not talk because of the tube in his mouth, and so he wrote out his answers to Hust's questions. The interrogation lasted until almost midnight, and Hust repeatedly violated *Miranda* by ignoring Mincey's repeated invocations of the right to counsel. However, Mincey took the stand at his murder trial, and so his *Miranda*-defective statements could be used to impeach his testimony under *Harris*. Mincey's statements were admitted and he was convicted, despite his counsel's argument that his hospital statements were inadmissible for impeachment purposes because they were involuntary under Due Process standards.

If Mincey's statements were not the "product of a rational intellect and a free will," his conviction cannot stand. This Court is under a duty to make an independent evaluation of the record. Mincey had been seriously wounded and had arrived at the hospital "depressed almost to the point of coma," according to his physician. He complained to Detective Hust that the pain in his leg was "unbearable." He was evidently confused and unable to think clearly because some of his written answers were not entirely coherent. Finally, while Mincey was being questioned he was lying on his back on a hospital bed, encumbered by tubes, needles, and breathing apparatus. He was at "the complete mercy" of Detective Hust, unable to escape or resist the thrust of Hust's interrogations. In this debilitated and helpless condition, Mincey clearly expressed his wish not to be interrogated. As soon as Hust's questions turned to the details of the afternoon's events, Mincey wrote: "This is all I can say without a lawyer." Hust nonetheless continued to question him, and a nurse who was present suggested it would be best if Mincey answered. Hust ignored Mincey's second request for a lawyer and his third request made immediately thereafter. But despite Mincey's entreaties to be let alone, Hust ceased the interrogation only during intervals when Mincey lost consciousness or received medical treatment, and after each such interruption returned relentlessly to his task.

There were not present in this case some of the gross abuses that have led the Court in other cases to find confessions involuntary, such as beatings, or "truth serums." But "the blood of the accused is not the only hallmark of an unconstitutional inquisition." It is apparent from the record that Mincey's statements were involuntary. Mincey was weakened by pain and shock, isolated from family, friends, and legal counsel, and barely conscious, and his will was simply overborne. Due process of law requires that statements obtained as these were cannot be used in any way against a defendant at his trial.

Mr. Justice Rehnquist dissenting in part:

The Court ignores entirely some evidence of voluntariness. Mincey's nurse "testified that she had not given Mincey any medication and that he was alert and able to understand the officer's questions. She said that Mincey was in moderate pain but was very cooperative with everyone. The interrogating officer testified that Mincey did not appear to be under the influence of drugs and that his answers were generally responsive to the questions." While the interviews took place over a three-hour time span, they were not "very long; probably not more than an hour total for everything." Hust would leave the room whenever Mincey received medical treatment "or if it looked like he was getting a little bit exhausted." According to Hust, Mincey never "lost consciousness at any time." It was the testimony of both Detective Hust and Nurse Graham "that neither mental or physical force nor abuse was used on Mincey. Nor were any promises made." Mincey did not claim that he felt compelled by Detective Hust to answer the questions propounded. The trial court was entitled to conclude that notwithstanding Mincey's medical condition, his statements were admissible.

Colorado v. Connelly

479 U.S. 157 (1986).

CHIEF JUSTICE REHNQUIST delivered the opinion of the Court.

Connelly approached an officer in Denver and said without prompting that he had killed someone. The officer gave him *Miranda* warnings, and Connelly said he understood his rights and wanted to talk. In response to the officer's questions, Connelly denied that he had been taking drugs or drinking, but mentioned that he had been a patient in several mental hospitals. He told the officer he wanted to talk because his conscience had been bothering him. A detective gave *Miranda* warnings to Connelly again, and then asked him "what he had on his mind." Connelly told the officers that he killed a woman in November 1982 and he took the officers to the location of the killing. The officers did not perceive that Connelly was suffering from mental illness when he confessed. But after Connelly was held overnight, he became disoriented during an interview with the public defender the next morning and explained that "God's voice" told him to go to Denver and either confess to the murder or commit suicide. Experts at Connelly's preliminary hearing testified that he was suffering from chronic schizophrenia and was in a psychotic state at least as of the day before he confessed. Connelly argued that he did not confess voluntarily of his own "free will" but his confession was admitted at his trial and he was convicted of murder.

The Due Process cases since *Brown* have focused upon the crucial element of police overreaching. Absent police conduct causally related to the confession, there is simply no basis for concluding that any state actor has deprived a criminal defendant of due process of law. We do not agree that a defendant's mental condition, by itself and apart from its relation to official coercion, should ever dispose of the inquiry into constitutional "voluntariness." Connelly relies on *Blackburn v. Alabama,* 361 U.S. 199 (1960), and *Townsend v. Sain,* 372 U.S. 293 (1963), for the proposition that the "deficient mental condition of the defendants in those cases was sufficient to render their confessions involuntary." In *Blackburn,* the Court found that the petitioner was probably insane at the time of his confession and the police learned during the interrogation that he had a history of mental problems. The police exploited this weakness with coercive tactics and these tactics supported a finding that the confession was involuntary. Townsend presented a similar instance of police wrongdoing. In that case, a police physician had given Townsend a drug with truth-serum properties. These two cases demonstrate that while mental condition is surely relevant to an individual's susceptibility to police coercion, mere examination of the confessant's state of mind can never conclude the due process inquiry. The purpose of excluding evidence seized in violation of the Constitution is to substantially deter future violations of the Constitution. Only if we were to establish a brand new constitutional right—the right of a criminal defendant to confess to his crime only when totally rational and properly motivated—could respondent's present claim be sustained. We hold that coercive police activity is a necessary predicate to the finding that a confession is not "voluntary" within the meaning of the Due Process Clause of the Fourteenth Amendment. We also conclude that the taking of respondent's statements, and their admission into evidence, constitute no violation of that Clause.

JUSTICE BRENNAN, with whom JUSTICE MARSHALL joins, dissenting.

The Court's failure to recognize all forms of involuntariness or coercion as antithetical to due process reflects a refusal to acknowledge free will as a value of constitutional consequence. While police overreaching has been an element of every confession case, the Court has made clear that ensuring that a confession is a product of free will is an independent concern in our Due Process cases. No physical evidence links the defendant to the alleged crime. Police did not identify the alleged victim's body as the woman named by the defendant. Mr. Connelly identified the alleged scene of the crime, but it has not been verified that the unidentified body was found there or that a crime actually occurred there. There is not a shred of competent evidence in this record linking the defendant to the charged homicide. There is only Mr. Connelly's confession. Minimum standards of due process should require that the trial court find substantial indicia of reliability, on the basis of evidence extrinsic to the confession itself, before admitting the confession of a mentally ill person into evidence. To hold otherwise allows the State to imprison and possibly to execute a mentally ill defendant based solely upon an inherently unreliable confession. The officer and the detective were both aware of Connelly's five hospitalizations in mental institutions and this should be sufficient knowledge about Connelly's mental incapacity to render it "involuntary."

Arizona v. Fulminante

499 U.S. 279 (1991).

JUSTICE WHITE delivered the opinion of the Court.

Fulminante was serving a sentence for a firearms crime, and Sarivola was serving a short sentence for extortion, when they became friends and "came to spend several hours a day together" in a federal prison. Sarivola was a former police officer with organized crime experience in loansharking, and as a paid informant for the FBI he was "masquerading" in prison as an organized crime figure. When he asked Fulminante about a prison rumor that Fulminante had killed a child in Arizona, Fulminante repeatedly denied the allegation. When Sarivola passed this information to an FBI agent, he was instructed to "find out more." Sarivola learned more one evening as he and Fulminante walked together around the prison track. Sarivola said that he knew Fulminante was "starting to get some tough treatment and whatnot" from other inmates because of the rumor. Sarivola offered to protect Fulminante from his fellow inmates, but told him, "You have to tell me about it,' you know. I mean, 'For me to give you any help." Fulminante then made incriminating statements to Sarivola, which were admitted at Fulminante's murder trial; Fulminante was convicted, and argued on appeal that his statements were involuntary under Due Process standards.

In applying the totality of the circumstances test to determine that the confession to Sarivola was coerced, the state supreme court focused on a number of relevant facts. First, "because Fulminante was an alleged child murderer, he was in danger of physical harm at the hands of other inmates." Using his knowledge of these threats of receiving "rough treatment from the guys", Sarivola offered to protect Fulminante in exchange for a confession to the crime, and "in response to Sarivola's offer of protection, Fulminante confessed." The state court declared: "The confession was obtained as a direct result of extreme coercion and was tendered in the belief that the defendant's life was in jeopardy if he did not confess. This is a true coerced confession in every sense of the word." The Court noted that Fulminante dropped out of school in the fourth grade, that he is short in stature and slight of build, that he requested protective custody when he was in prison in his mid-twenties, and that he was once admitted to a psychiatric hospital in prison because he was unable to cope with the isolation. We normally give great deference to the factual findings of the state court and we agree that Fulminante's confession was coerced. A finding of coercion need not depend upon actual violence by a government agent; a credible threat is sufficient. "Coercion can be mental as well as physical, and the blood of the accused is not the only hallmark of an unconstitutional inquisition." *Blackburn v. Alabama,* 361 U.S. 199, 206 (1960). As in *Payne v. Arkansas,* 356 U.S. 560 (1958), where the Court found that a confession was coerced because the interrogating police officer had promised that if the accused confessed, the officer would protect the accused from an angry mob outside the jailhouse door, so too here, it was fear of physical violence, absent protection from his friend (and Government agent) Sarivola, which motivated Fulminante to confess. Given the credible threat of physical violence, we agree that Fulminante's will was overborne in such a way as to render his confession the product of coercion.

The dissenting opinion of CHIEF JUSTICE REHNQUIST, with whom JUSTICES O'CONNOR, KENNEDY, and SOUTER join:

Fulminante was no stranger to the criminal justice system: He had six prior felony convictions and had been imprisoned on three prior occasions. I am at a loss to see how the state supreme court found the confession involuntary. Since Fulminante was unaware that Sarivola was an FBI informant, there existed none of "the danger of coercion resulting from the interaction of custody and official interrogation." The conversations between Sarivola and Fulminante were not lengthy, and the defendant was free at all times to leave Sarivola's company. Sarivola at no time threatened him or demanded that he confess; he simply requested that he speak the truth about the matter. Fulminante was an experienced habitué of prisons, and presumably able to fend for himself. In concluding that Fulminante's confession was involuntary, the Court today a more expansive definition of that term than is warranted by any of our decided cases.

Practice Pointer

Before *Miranda*, some states allowed a jury to determine the "voluntariness" of a confession at trial, but the Court invalidated that procedure in *Jackson v. Denno*, 378 U.S. 368 (1964). The Court held that a pre-trial judicial hearing is required to determine voluntariness because a jury cannot be expected to produce a fair and reliable finding on this question during the trial on the issue of guilt. The prosecutor bears the burden of proving that a confession does not violate Due Process by a preponderance of the evidence. *See Lego v. Twomey*, 404 U.S. 477 (1972).

Point for Discussion

Harmless Error

Fulminante held that the admission of the defendant's confession made to an undercover agent was not harmless in that case; the Court also advised judges to "exercise extreme caution" before finding that the admission of a confession was harmless error, given "the risk that a given confession is unreliable, coupled with the profound impact that the confession has upon the jury."

Take Note

If a confession is admitted at trial, and is later held to be unconstitutional under Due Process standards, its admission may be found to be harmless error only if the prosecution shows that it was harmless beyond a reasonable doubt.

Food for Thought

Assume that you are a legal adviser to the local police department. The police chief wants to know whether, in light of the Court's Due Process decisions, police interrogators may continue to use the "Mutt and Jeff" technique described in the *Miranda* opinion. Consider the pro and con arguments that may be made.

Hypo 1: *"You're Going Home"*

Brown went voluntarily to the police station to be interviewed by detectives regarding an assault crime. Brown denied involvement, but asked the detectives, "But if I were involved, then what would the consequences be?" One detective replied: "I'm not going to sit here and tell you what a judge is going to do, and I can't tell you what the penalties are. I can't promise you anything or tell you anything. What I can tell you is that, no matter what you tell me or say to me, you're going home. If you tell me the assault happened, I'm not going to place you in handcuffs and arrest you. You're going home today." At this point, the other detective stated, "If you killed somebody, then you're not going home." When Brown looked startled, the detective said, "But no one has died. Just ignore me." During the next 40 minutes, both officers sought to persuade Brown to admit involvement. Finally, when Brown did make incriminating statements, one detective said, "Well, I hope you realize that I can't let you leave after what you just told us." Brown replied, "Yes, I know. And I'm in big trouble." Did the officers violate Brown's right to Due Process during the interrogation? *See Brown v. State*, 290 Ga. 865, 725 S.E.2d 320 (2012).

Food for Thought

To what extent should a suspect's vulnerabilities enter into the analysis? Suppose that an arrestee suffers from alcohol withdrawal and mental health problems. Would it be inappropriate for the questioning officer to focus on emotionally provocative topics and to ask leading questions? *See State v. Hoppe*, 661 N.W.2d 407 (Wis. 2003). What if the suspect has an IQ of 65. Suppose that the police ask leading questions that, while not technically coercive, require "yes" or "no" answers, all of which assume the defendant's guilt. Because of the suspect's limited intelligence, he does not challenge the fairness of the questions. *See United States v. Preston*, 2014 WL 18762669 (9th Cir.).

Hypo 2: *Lengthy Interrogations*

Now, let's think about how the courts might apply the due process test today. In which of the following situations would you conclude that police interrogation violated the due process clause?

A) A 17 year old (Doody) is brought in for questioning on a homicide charge, is read a *Miranda* warning, and agrees to speak to the police. It is 9:00 p.m. at night and the police question Doody until 10:00 a.m. the next morning. During this time, the police repeatedly tell Doody that he "must" answer their questions, and that the questioning will continue until "we get some answers." *See Doody v. Schriro,* 548 F.3d 847 (9th Cir. 2008); vacated sub. nom. *Doody v. Ryan,* 562 U.S. 956 (2010), remanded sub. nom. *Doody v. Ryan,* 649 F.3d 986 (9th Cir.2011); *see also Moore v. State,* 30 A.3d 945 (Md. App. 2011).

B) In the prior problem, suppose that the police did not tell Doody that he "must" respond, or that he would be forced to stay until "we get some answers," but they keep him at the police station for 55 hours. He is not continuously questioned, and has access to his father. At the end of the 55 hours, when he is not being questioned, he volunteers the fact that he committed the homicide. *See Carter v. Thompson,* 690 F.3d 837 (7th Cir. 2012).

Hypo 3: *Due Process & Threats*

Now, let's think about how the due process test might apply when the police make threats against a suspect. In all situations, assume that the suspect has waived his *Miranda* rights. Consider the following situations and decide whether there is a due process violation:

A) Police are interrogating a man regarding possible sexual molestation of his children. At one point, the police tell the man that they will seek a court order removing the children from the home unless he agrees to cooperate with them. At that point, the man makes incriminating statements. *See Stanton v. Commonwealth,* 349 S.W. 3d 914 (Ky. 2011).

B) Suppose that the police arrange a fake lineup (the "witness" is actually a police officer) at which the witness "identifies" the suspect as the perpetrator of the crime, and then the suspect makes incriminating statements. *See State v. Patton,* 826 A.2d 783 (N.J. Super. 2003); *Whittington v. State,* 809 A.2d 721 (Md. App. 2002).

C) Suppose that a baby was badly injured under suspicious circumstances and would probably die. The father is in custody and the mother is at the child's bedside. When the man refuses to talk to the police, the police state that they will arrest the wife and bring her in for questioning. At that point, the man makes incriminating statements. *See People v. Thomas*, 985 N.Y.S.2d 193, 8 N.E.3d 308 (N.Y. App. 2014).

D) Suppose that Bond, who is black, is being questioned regarding a possible homicide. He makes incriminating statements after the questioning officer urges Bond not to subject himself to the "racist whims" of a rural jury pool composed of "white people, Hispanic people, and others not from your hood." *See Bond v. State*, 9 N.E. 3d 134 (Ind. 2014).

E) A man is being investigated for sexual assault. During the interrogation, the man makes incriminating statements after he is told that he will likely be deported from the U.S. if he does not tell the truth. *See People v. Ramadon*, 314 P.3d 836 (Colo. 2013).

Hypo 4: *Due Process, Promises & Representations*

Which of the following statements would constitute due process violations (assume, again, that *Miranda* warnings were given and rights were waived) if the suspect makes incriminating statements:

A) Suppose that the police suggest that the district attorney might "go lighter" in terms of punishment recommendations if a suspect "comes clean." *See Harper v. State*, 722 So.2d 1267 (Miss.App. 1998); *State v. Polk*, 812 N.W.2d 670 (Iowa 2012).

B) Suppose that a man is being investigated for child sexual abuse. During the interrogation, the police tell the man that the victim's family doesn't want to "get him in trouble. They just want an apology." When the man does confess, and gives a letter of apology, the police seek to use both as evidence against him. *See Hill v. State*, 12 A.3d 1193 (Md. 2011).

C) An officer tells a suspect about some of the charges that will be brought against him, but refuses to detail all of them unless the suspect "comes clean." *See State v. Pyles*, 90 A.3d 1228 (N.H. 2014).

D) Before a suspect makes incriminating statements, the police conceal the fact that a warrant has been issued for his arrest, and assure him that he is not a "target" of their investigation. *See United States v. Boskic*, 545 F.3d 69 (1st Cir. 2008).

E) *Promises Regarding Girlfriend.* During an interrogation, a suspect is deeply concerned about the possible consequences to his girlfriend who was an accomplice to the crime so the police make a number of references to her during the interrogation. For example, they suggest that they don't need to dig deeper once they have nailed the culprit, and that these charges could be very disruptive to her life. Defendant makes incriminating statements thinking that he will gain a benefit for his girlfriend. However, the police make it clear that they are not empowered to make any deals regarding her, but the suspect seems convinced that his incriminating statements will help her get off. If the suspect makes incriminating statements, should they be regarded as coerced? *See United States v. Hufstetler*, 782 F.3d 19 (1st Cir. 2015).

F) *Promises of Leniency.* During an interrogation, a police officer tells a suspect that "if he tells the truth and is honest, we are not going to charge you with anything. You'll have your life, maybe you'll go into the Marines . . . and you'll chalk this up to a very scary time in your life." Perez then states that he has "some information," and he then confesses his involvement in a robbery during which Perez's accomplice killed the victim. Do the promises of leniency render the confession involuntary? What if the police promise a homeless woman leniency and also tell her that it will help her and her children find housing? *See People v. Perez*, 243 Cal.App.4th 863, 196 Cal.Rptr.3d 871 (2016); *Sharp v. Rohling*, 793 F.3d 1216 (10th Cir. 2015).

Executive Summary

The Due Process Test. In 1936, the Court recognized the Due Process Clause of the Fourteenth Amendment as a source for standards governing the admissibility of confessions in state courts; the same analysis came to be used for the Fifth Amendment Due Process standards applied in federal courts. The seminal case is *Brown v. Mississippi*, 297 U.S. 278 (1936), in which defendants were hung by their necks and beaten until they confessed. The Court found a due process violation: "It would be difficult to conceive of methods more revolting to the sense of justice than those taken to procure the confessions of these defendants, and the use of the confessions thus obtained as the basis for conviction and sentence was a clear denial of due process."

Due Process Standards. The vocabulary of due process came to be incorporated into Due Process law, as illustrated by the requirements that only "voluntary" confessions are admissible, that confessions must come from the "free will" of the defendant, rather than police "coercion" that includes inducements, threats, or deceptive stratagems.

From *Brown* to *Miranda*. During the thirty years between *Brown* and *Miranda*, the Court relied on Due Process doctrine to invalidate confessions in more than twenty cases, while upholding confessions in less than half that number. Most of those decisions revealed sharp disagreements among the justices concerning the interpretation of the "voluntariness" concept. Over time, the Court expanded this concept to encompass various types of psychologically coercive interrogation strategies, and came to focus upon the practice of *incommunicado* police questioning as the ultimate source of the coercion problem.

Defendant's Attributes. The Court's Due Process precedents often relied on the defendant's special vulnerability to police coercion, based on physical and mental attributes and life experiences.

Dissatisfaction with the Due Process Voluntariness Test. A number of justices were dissatisfied with the Due Process voluntariness test because it failed to provide clear, predictable, and uniform guidelines regarding the boundaries of acceptable police conduct during interrogations. Moreover, the difficulties of defining "voluntariness" were magnified, as one justice observed, because "the trial on the issue of coercion is seldom helpful," as police "usually testify one way, the accused another," and the secrecy of interrogations gives defendants "little chance to prove coercion at trial." *Crooker v. California*, 357 U.S. 433 (1958) (Douglas, J., dissenting).

The *McNabb-Mallory* Rule. During the post-*Brown* era, the Court supplemented the Due Process doctrine with the *McNabb-Mallory* rule that applied only in the federal courts. The Court repeatedly rejected the argument that this rule should be incorporated into Due Process doctrine and applied to the states, but some state courts chose to incorporate the rule into their own state law on their own. *McNabb* and *Mallory* rested on the Court's supervisory authority over the federal courts. In *McNabb v. United States*, 318 U.S. 332 (1943), the Court created an exclusionary rule to enforce the command of 18 U.S.C. § 595, which requires that a federal officer who arrests any person must "take the defendant before the nearest judicial officer having jurisdiction for a hearing, commitment, or taking bail for trial." *McNabb-Mallory* was partially overruled by congressional enactment.

The Sixth Amendment Right to Counsel. In *Massiah v. United States*, <u>377 U.S. 201 (1964)</u>, the Court applied the Sixth Amendment right to counsel to exclude a confession. The confession was extracted by surreptitious means from a defendant who had been indicted. After *Massiah*, the Court extended the right to counsel to arrestees who were not yet indicted. In *Escobedo v. Illinois*, <u>378 U.S. 478 (1964)</u>, the Court held that the police violated the Sixth Amendment because the police investigation had "begun to focus on" the defendant in custody as "a particular suspect," the police had not "effectively warned" the defendant of "the right to remain silent," the defendant had "requested and been denied an opportunity to consult with his lawyer," and the police had elicited incriminating statements from him during questioning. While *Massiah* remains good law today, *Escobedo* is no longer good law.

The Fifth Amendment & *Miranda*. In the Court's landmark decision in *Miranda v. Arizona*, <u>384 U.S. 436 (1966)</u>, the Court began applying the Fifth Amendment privilege to interrogations. Historically, the privilege had been applied at trial, but had not been applied to stationhouse interrogations. In *Miranda*, the Court expressed concern that police manuals suggested sophisticated tactics for evoking confessions from defendants, and provided the prophylactic remedy of requiring the police to give suspects the *Miranda* warning: "He must be warned prior to any questioning that he has the right to remain silent, that anything he says can be used against him in a court of law, that he has the right to the presence of an attorney, and that if he cannot afford an attorney one will be appointed for him prior to any questioning if he so desires." The right to counsel is a Fifth Amendment (rather than a Sixth Amendment) right to counsel. In other words, the right is imposed in order to protect the individual against compelled self-incrimination.

***Miranda* Applies to Custodial Interrogations.** *Miranda* does not apply to all interrogations, but only to "custodial interrogations." "Custody" is something more than a mere seizure (when a reasonable person would not feel free to leave) and is more akin to an arrest. "Interrogation" involves either explicit questioning or its functional equivalent (questioning that is reasonably likely to elicit an incriminating response.)

***Miranda* Procedures.** Once the warnings have been given, if the individual indicates, prior to or during questioning, that he wishes to remain silent, the interrogation must cease. If the individual states that he wants an attorney, the interrogation must cease until an attorney is present. If the individual cannot obtain an attorney and he indicates that he wants one before speaking to police, they must respect his decision to remain silent. If the interrogation continues without the presence of an attorney and a statement is taken, a heavy burden rests on the government to demonstrate that the defendant knowingly and intelligently waived his privilege against self-incrimination and his right to retained or appointed counsel.

Public Safety Exception. In *New York v. Quarles,* <u>467 U.S. 649 (1984)</u>, the Court held that police officers may sometimes withhold the *Miranda* warnings until after they ask an arrestee questions that are "necessary to secure their own safety or the safety of the public." The exception has remained relatively undefined and unapplied.

Routine Booking Question Exception. The *Miranda* Court observed that police questions that are "normally attendant to arrest and custody" do not qualify as "interrogation." In *Pennsylvania v. Muniz,* <u>496 U.S. 582 (1990)</u>, the Court noted that "routine booking questions" typically are asked to secure "the biographical data necessary to complete booking or pretrial services," and held that an intoxicated driver could be asked booking questions about his or her "name, address, height, weight, eye color, date of birth, and current age." The government conceded that a sixth question for the driver was not a "routine booking question": "Do you know what the date was of your sixth birthday?" The Court concluded that this question violated the Fifth Amendment because it called for a "testimonial response": it called for defendant to "explicitly or implicitly relate a factual assertion or disclose information," and make mental calculations that revealed his level of intoxication and it therefore subjected defendant to the "cruel trilemma" of "self-accusation, perjury, or contempt."

The Adequacy of *Miranda* Warnings. *Miranda* warnings must "reasonably convey" the substance of the mandated warning. Warnings may be inadequate if they are incomplete or provide misleading information about a suspect's rights. Warnings can also be inadequate if they are "non-functional" in that the police fail to warn at the outset of an interrogation, and then deliver "midstream" warnings and continue the interrogation. If a court concludes that the *Miranda* warnings were inadequate, then post-warning incriminating statements will be inadmissible. Thus, a claim that warnings were "inadequate" is distinct from a claim that an invalid waiver was obtained after adequate warnings were provided.

Waivers of *Miranda* Rights. The prosecution has the burden of proving that *Miranda* rights have been waived. The waiver inquiry "has two distinct dimensions": the waiver must be "voluntary in the sense that it was the product of a free and deliberate choice rather than intimidation, coercion, or deception," and must be "made with a full awareness of both the nature of the right being abandoned and the consequences of the decision to abandon it." A waiver will not be presumed from silence. However, waivers do not have to be formal or explicit. Even if a suspect neither invokes nor waives his rights, and is largely silent, he can implicitly waive his rights through limited responses such as nodding his head. However, the prosecution must still establish that the suspect understood his rights. The prosecution need not inform the suspect of the topics about which he/she will be questioned.

Police Conduct Following Invocation of Rights. If a suspect invokes either the right to remain silent, or the right to counsel, all questioning must cease. However, if a suspect makes a reference to an attorney that is ambiguous or equivocal, so that a reasonable officer in light of the circumstances would have understood only that the suspect might be invoking the right to counsel, the police need not terminate questioning. The suspect must unambiguously request counsel.

Waiver-Seeking After Invocation. The court has held that, once an individual invokes his right to remain silent, that invocation does not preclude all future questioning. In one case, after the police respected the suspect's invocation of rights, another police officer came to the suspect's cell a few hours later and gave a new warning. The Court held that the subsequent waiver was valid. However, when an individual invokes the right to counsel, the police may not seek a further waiver unless the suspect initiates the conversation. However, in *Maryland v. Shatzer*, 559 U.S. 98 (2010), the Court held that after a person in custody invokes the right to counsel, the prohibition on waiver-seeking will expire 14 days after the person's release from custody.

Post-*Miranda* Sixth Amendment Law. For more than a decade after *Miranda*, the Court did not decide a confession case on Sixth Amendment grounds, and did not address questions relating to the relationship between the *Miranda* and *Massiah* rights to counsel. However, in *Brewer v. Williams*, 430 U.S. 387 (1977), the Court made it clear that the Sixth Amendment right to counsel continues to apply to interrogations, but only after adversarial proceedings have commenced. In *Brewer*, the Court concluded that the police had "deliberately elicited" a confession from a suspect.

Attachment of the Sixth Amendment Right to Counsel. The Court has identified a short list of events that qualify as "adversary judicial criminal proceedings," including a "formal charge, preliminary hearing, indictment, information, or arraignment." *Rothgery v. Gillespie County,* 554 U.S. 191, 198 (2008). Some of these events involve the defendant's appearance before a judicial officer, and other events involve only the participation of a prosecutor.

Sixth Amendment Right to Counsel Is "Offense Specific." In *Texas v. Cobb,* 532 U.S. 162 (2001), the Court interpreted *Massiah* as allowing police to question an indicted defendant about uncharged offenses that are "factually related" to the charged "offense," and imported the definition of "offense" from double jeopardy precedent into *Massiah* doctrine. Thus, under *Cobb*, police may question an indicted defendant about any uncharged offense that requires proof of a fact not required by the definition of the charged offense.

Post-*Miranda* Due Process Law. In the post-*Miranda* era, defendants continue to challenge their confessions based on police violations of Due Process; for those defendants who do not have viable *Miranda* or *Massiah* claims, a Due Process claim may be the only basis for arguing that their statements to police are inadmissible at trial. These defendants lack *Miranda* arguments if they confess while not in "custody," when they are interrogated by secret agents, and when they face impeachment on the stand with *Miranda*-defective statements. Even defendants who qualify for *Massiah* rights may lose them through waivers provided to police interrogators. The Court's modern Due Process precedents continue to rely on a "totality" test, which now incorporates the factor of police compliance with *Miranda*. As in the pre-*Miranda* era, the Court remains divided about the meaning of coercion and about the appropriate interpretation of the "voluntariness" standard.

Major Themes

a. The Search for a Panacea—For nearly a century, the courts have struggled with how to ensure that confessions are voluntary rather than coerced. In attempting to deal with these problems, courts have used various approaches for protecting suspects, including the Due Process voluntariness test, the *McNabb-Mallory* rule, the Sixth Amendment right to counsel, and the Fifth Amendment privilege against self-incrimination.

b. Modern Approaches—While none of the Court's approaches have been entirely satisfactory, the courts continue to regularly use all of the approaches except for the *McNabb-Mallory* test. Thus, courts will sometimes reject confessions under Due Process, under the Sixth Amendment right to counsel, and under the Fifth Amendment privilege against self-incrimination.

c. Differing Approaches—The various approaches have differing requirements. For example, for due process analysis, the focus is on whether a confession was "voluntary" or "coerced." Due process concerns can arise at any point in the criminal process. By contrast, the Fifth Amendment privilege against self-incrimination (as reflected in *Miranda*) focuses on whether a suspect who is being subjected to "custodial interrogation" has been given a *Miranda* warning, and whether the suspect validly waived his rights. The Sixth Amendment right to counsel only applies once adversarial proceedings have commenced, and focuses on whether defendant was provided with, or waived, counsel.

For More Information

- Ric Simmons & Renee McDonald Hutchins, Learning Criminal Procedure (2d ed. 2019).

- Wayne R. LaFave, Jerold H. Israel, Nancy J. King & Orin S. Kerr, Criminal Procedure (6th ed. 2017).

- Russell L. Weaver, John M. Burkoff, Catherine Hancock & Steven I. Friedland, Principles of Criminal Procedure Ch. 5 (7th ed. 2021).

Test Your Knowledge

To assess your understanding of the material in this chapter, click here to take a quiz.

CHAPTER 7

Identification Procedures

A. The Nature & Constitutional Implications of Identification Processes

Eyewitness identification may be a particularly potent form of evidence in a criminal proceeding. Inherent in such evidentiary methods, however, are significant reliability risks. Accurate identification depends upon perception and recall that are free of distortion. A multiplicity of factors, individually or collectively, may operate under a given set of circumstances to impair either process. The ability to perceive may be skewed by physical realities such as distance, observation time, light and the field or content of activity. Stereotypes and cultural assumptions also may interfere with perceptual acuity. Even accurate perception may be undermined by suggestive questioning, faded memory and mental tendencies to convert assumption or expectation into reality.

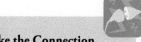

Make the Connection

Like searches, seizures and custodial interrogation, identification procedures constitute a basic methodology for building a criminal case. Compulsory generation of an identifying characteristic, such as a writing exemplar, voice sample or fingerprint, could be understood as a seizure or self-incrimination. However, case law establishes that unlike searches and seizures, identification processes are not governed by the Fourth Amendment. Nor do they implicate the Fifth Amendment guarantee against self-incrimination.

1. The Problem: The Unreliability of Eyewitness Identification

Many believe "that the human brain operates more or less as a mechanical recording device" so that individuals record their memories as if "on a memory tape." Frederic D. Woocher, *Note, Did Your Eyes Deceive You? Expert Psychological Testimony on the Unreliability of Eyewitness Identification*, 29 STAN. L. REV. 969, 971–89 (1977). Under this view, when a person wishes to recall a memory, he/she "simply selects the appropriate memory tape and plays it back, producing a faithful recounting of the original perception." *Id.* In fact, memory does not function in that way at all. When people perceive events, they frequently pay attention to only a limited number of environmental stimuli. Even as to those stimuli that they actually observe, "or pay attention to," "the representation of an event stored in memory undergoes constant change; some details are added or altered unconsciously to conform the original memory representation to new information about the event, while others simply are forgotten." *Id.* Likewise, there can be distortion when a memory is retrieved.

Part of the problem stems from the fact that individuals can only perceive a limited number of stimuli at any one time, and therefore they develop "unconscious strategies to aid in the selectivity of perceptual processes and ultimately to concentrate attention on the most necessary and useful details." *Id.* However, these "perceptual shortcuts and strategies," while generally useful and effective in daily life, can "lead to inaccurate perceptions when the eye must make the fine distinctions necessary to observe and recognize faces accurately." *Id.* In most cases, individuals are not aware of these shortcuts or the fact that they create perceptual inaccuracies. The net effect is that even trained observers can encounter difficulties recounting the physical characteristics of individuals that they encounter. Lay witnesses have even more difficulty, and frequently cannot be precise in their recollections of faces. Witnesses can also be imprecise in their estimates of how much time passed has during a sudden event, such as a crime. When individuals are involved in "sudden action-packed events such as crimes, people almost always overestimate the length of time involved because the flurry of activity leads them to conclude that a significant amount of time has passed." *Id.* Time simply elapses more slowly "when the observer is caught in an anxiety-producing situation." *Id.*

Eyewitness perceptual inaccuracies can be caused by a variety of factors. For one thing, crimes are often "brief, fast-moving events; the victim and witnesses consequently will have difficulty getting a sufficiently good 'look' to allow them to process enough visual features of the event and the offender to make a reliable subsequent recognition." *Id.* Such perceptual difficulties are likely to arise when a "crime occurs suddenly, and the witness is thus unprepared to focus perceptual attention on the important features of the event." *Id.* A second factor that creates perceptual inaccuracies is anxiety. Although "victim's will sometimes assert that 'I was so frightened that his face is etched in my memory forever,' "the evidence shows "that perceptual abilities actually decrease significantly when the observer is in a fearful or anxiety-provoking situation." *Id.* Indeed, extreme anxiety can cause a witness to shut off "in order to block out and avoid recognition of stimuli that might produce anxiety." *Id.* Perceptual inaccuracies are also caused by stereotypes: "a victim may unwittingly distort her perception of an assailant to include physical features that the victim associates with the personality traits typified by the criminal's behavior." *Id.* Further, individuals have greater difficulty identifying people who are of a different race than their own.

Even if an individual clearly viewed a crime perpetrator's characteristics, his later descriptions may be inaccurate. Eyewitnesses are usually asked to give verbal descriptions of perpetrators of crimes, but verbal descriptions are often imprecise and potentially inaccurate. While police investigators may seek detailed, precise and complete descriptions of the perpetrator, eyewitnesses rarely remember with that level of specificity. Moreover, memories tend to deteriorate over time. In addition, "because of a psychological need to reduce uncertainty and eliminate inconsistencies, witnesses have a tendency not only to fill any gaps in memory by adding extraneous details but also to change mental representations unconsciously so that they 'all make sense.' " *Id*. In other words, memory is an "active" rather than a "static" process so that an individual's perception of events can change over time, and can be affected by many different factors, including media reports, mug shots, or even the observation of a defendant in a lineup.

Eyewitness identifications can also be influenced by social psychological factors. When viewing a lineup, a witness is likely to assume that the police believe that the perpetrator is in the lineup, and may feel pressure to pick the individual who most closely resembles the perpetrator—even if the eyewitness is not certain sure that the identification is accurate. Plus, if the eyewitness is the victim, he may have hostility towards the perpetrator; something which makes him susceptible to police suggestion which can exist by virtue of the way that the police have arranged the lineup (e.g., is the suspected perpetrator physically similar to, or different than, the other participants, or does the suspected perpetrator have one distinctive physical characteristic that the other suspects do not possess?), as well as by the police officer's voice intonation or other gestures. *Id*. Suggestiveness can also be created when the police arrange a photo display in advance of an actual lineup. If suggestiveness encourages the eyewitness to pick an individual out of the lineup, it is quite likely that the eyewitness will pick the same individual out of an actual lineup, and identify that person at trial.

Point for Discussion

Characteristics of Voice

Referencing *Katz v. United States*, the Court has held that no reasonable expectation of privacy exists in publicly exposed traits. As a result, in *United States v. Dionisio*, 410 U.S. 1, 14 (1973), the Court rejected defendant's argument that disclosure of his voice implicated Fourth Amendment interests, observing that: "the physical characteristics of a person's voice, its tone and manner, as opposed to the content of a specific conversation, are constantly exposed to the public. Like a man's facial characteristics, or handwriting, his voice is repeatedly produced for others to hear. No person can have a reasonable expectation that others will not know the sound of his voice any more than he can reasonably expect that his face will be a mystery to the world."

Take Note

Although acknowledging that identification procedures elicit incriminating information, the Court has also held that they do not implicate the Fifth Amendment. In rejecting a privilege against self-incrimination claim in the context of identification procedures, the Court characterized such evidence as nontestimonial. For example, in *Gilbert v. California*, 388 U.S. 263, 266 (1967), it held that: "the taking of handwriting exemplars did not violate petitioner's Fifth Amendment privilege against self-incrimination. The privilege reaches only compulsion of 'an accused's communications, whatever form they might take, and the compulsion of responses which are also communications.' One's voice and handwriting are, of course, means of communication. It by no means follows, however, that every compulsion of an accused to use his voice or write (compels) a communication within the cover of the privilege. A mere handwriting exemplar, in contrast to the content of what is written, like the voice or body itself, is an identifying physical characteristic outside its protection."

Despite the general irrelevance of the Fourth and Fifth Amendments to identifications (although Fourth Amendment interests may be implicated when a person is seized for purposes of obtaining identification, *Hayes v. Florida*, 470 U.S. 811 (1985)), identification procedures are not without significant constitutional protection. Like other criminal investigative methods, identification processes may implicate due process. Case law also has established that the right to counsel may attach to identification proceedings. Contrasted with the pervasive applicability of the due process clause, however, Sixth Amendment protection is limited to identification procedures employed "at or after the time that adversarial judicial proceedings have been initiated." *Kirby v. Illinois*, 406 U.S. 682, 688 (1972) (plurality opinion).

Hypo: *Display of Platinum Teeth*

Suppose that defendant has teeth made of platinum. Because the victim of an assault claims that his assailant had special teeth, the judge orders defendant to reveal his teeth to the witness and the jury. Defendant objects that the display of his teeth would constitute self-incrimination. He also claims that he will be unduly prejudiced because the platinum teeth make him look "particularly fierce," and therefore will encourage the jury to convict him of the crime. Can defendant be required to exhibit his teeth? *See State v. Gonzalez*, 359 Wisc.2d 1, 856 N.W.2d 850 (2014).

B. The Sixth Amendment

The right to counsel in an identification context is dependent upon whether the proceeding occurs at a stage of the process that is critical enough that counsel's presence "is necessary to preserve the defendant's basic right to a fair trial." *United States v. Wade,* 388 U.S. 218, 227 (1967). Seminal case law reflects the Court's sense that post-indictment line-ups not only satisfy the "critical stage" requirement but also present profound risks to a fair trial.

United States v. Wade

388 U.S. 218 (1967).

MR. JUSTICE BRENNAN delivered the opinion of the Court.

The federally insured bank in Eustace, Texas, was robbed. A man with a small strip of tape on each side of his face entered the bank, pointed a pistol at the female cashier and the vice president, the only persons in the bank at the time, and forced them to fill a pillowcase with money. The man then drove away with an accomplice who had been waiting in a stolen car. An indictment was returned against respondent, Wade, and two others for conspiring to rob the bank, and against Wade and the accomplice for the robbery itself. Wade was arrested and counsel was appointed to represent him. Fifteen days later an FBI agent, without notice to Wade's lawyer, arranged to have the two bank employees observe a lineup made up of Wade and five or six other prisoners conducted in a courtroom of the local county courthouse. Each person in the line wore strips of tape as allegedly worn by the robber and upon direction each said something like "put the money in the bag," the words allegedly uttered by the robber. Both bank employees identified Wade as the bank robber. At trial the two employees, when asked on direct examination if the robber was in the courtroom, pointed to Wade. The prior lineup identification was then elicited from both employees on cross-examination. Wade was convicted.

Neither the lineup itself nor anything shown by this record that Wade was required to do in the lineup violated his privilege against self-incrimination. The privilege "protects an accused only from being compelled to testify against himself, or otherwise provide the State with evidence of a testimonial or communicative nature."

The fact that the lineup involved no violation of Wade's privilege against self-incrimination does not, however, dispose of his contention that the courtroom identifications should have been excluded because the lineup was conducted without notice to and in the absence of his counsel. It is urged that the assistance of counsel at the lineup was indispensable to protect Wade's most basic right as a criminal defendant—

his right to a fair trial at which the witnesses against him might be meaningfully cross-examined.

The Government characterizes the lineup as a mere preparatory step in the gathering of the prosecution's evidence, not different—for Sixth Amendment purposes—from various other preparatory steps, such as systematized or scientific analyzing of the accused's fingerprints, blood sample, clothing, hair, and the like. We think there are differences which preclude such stages being characterized as critical stages at which the accused has the right to the presence of his counsel. Knowledge of the techniques of science and technology is sufficiently available, and the variables in techniques few enough, that the accused has the opportunity for a meaningful confrontation of the Government's case at trial through the ordinary processes of cross-examination of the Government's expert witnesses and the presentation of the evidence of his own experts. The denial of a right to have his counsel present at such analyses does not therefore violate the Sixth Amendment; they are not critical stages since there is minimal risk that his counsel's absence at such stages might derogate from his right to a fair trial.

But the confrontation compelled by the State between the accused and the victim or witnesses to a crime to elicit identification evidence is peculiarly riddled with innumerable dangers and variable factors which might seriously, even crucially, derogate from a fair trial. The vagaries of eyewitness identification are well-known; the annals of criminal law are rife with instances of mistaken identification. Mr. Justice Frankfurter once said: "What is the worth of identification testimony even when uncontradicted? The identification of strangers is proverbially untrustworthy. The hazards of such testimony are established by a formidable number of instances in the records of English and American trials. These instances are recent—not due to the brutalities of ancient criminal procedure." A major factor contributing to the high incidence of miscarriage of justice from mistaken identification has been the degree of suggestion inherent in the manner in which the prosecution presents the suspect to witnesses for pretrial identification. Suggestion can be created intentionally or unintentionally in many subtle ways. The dangers for the suspect are particularly grave when the witness' opportunity for observation was insubstantial, and thus his susceptibility to suggestion the greatest. Moreover, "it is a matter of common experience that, once a witness has picked out the accused at the line-up, he is not likely to go back on his word later on, so that in practice the issue of identity may (in the absence of other relevant evidence) for all practical purposes be determined there and then, before the trial."

The pretrial confrontation for purpose of identification may take the form of a lineup, also known as an "identification parade" or "showup," as in the present case, or presentation of the suspect alone to the witness. Risks of suggestion attend either form of confrontation and increase the dangers inhering in eyewitness identification. But as with secret interrogations, there is serious difficulty in depicting what transpires at lineups and other forms of identification confrontations. "Privacy results in secrecy and this in turn results in a gap in our knowledge as to what in fact goes on." The defense can seldom reconstruct the manner and mode of lineup identification for judge or jury at trial. Those participating in a lineup with the accused may often be police officers; in any event, the participants' names are rarely recorded or divulged at trial. The impediments to an objective observation are increased when the victim is the witness. Lineups are prevalent in rape and robbery prosecutions and present a particular hazard that a victim's understandable outrage may excite vengeful or spiteful motives. In any event, neither witnesses nor lineup participants are apt to be alert for conditions prejudicial to the suspect. If they were, it would likely be of scant benefit to the suspect since neither witnesses nor lineup participants are likely to be schooled in the detection of suggestive influences. Improper influences may go undetected by a suspect, guilty or not, who experiences the emotional tension which we might expect in one being confronted with potential accusers. Even when he does observe abuse, if he has a criminal record he may be reluctant to take the stand and open the admission of prior convictions. Moreover any protestations by the suspect of the fairness of the lineup made at trial are likely to be in vain; the jury's choice is between the accused's unsupported version and that of the police officers. In short, the accused's inability effectively to reconstruct at trial any unfairness that occurred at the lineup may deprive him of his only opportunity meaningfully to attack the credibility of the witness' courtroom identification.

The potential for improper influence is illustrated by the circumstances surrounding the prior identifications in the three cases we decide today. In the present case, the testimony of the identifying witnesses elicited on cross-examination revealed that those witnesses were taken to the courthouse to await assembly of the lineup. The courtroom faced a hallway observable to the witnesses through an open door. The cashier testified that she saw Wade "standing in the hall" within sight of an FBI agent. Five or six other prisoners later appeared in the hall. The vice president testified that he saw a person in the hall in the custody of the agent who "resembled the person that we identified as the one that had entered the bank."

The vice of suggestion created by the identification in *Stovall v. Denno*, 388 U.S. 293, 302 (1967), was the presentation to the witness of the suspect alone handcuffed to police officers. It is hard to imagine a situation more clearly conveying the suggestion to the witness that the one presented is believed guilty by the police. The few cases that have surfaced reveal the existence of a process attended with hazards of serious unfairness to the criminal accused and strongly suggest the plight of the numerous defendants who are unable to ferret out suggestive influences in the secrecy of the confrontation. We do not assume that these risks are the result of police procedures intentionally designed to prejudice an accused. Rather they derive from the dangers inherent in eyewitness identification and the suggestibility inherent in the context of the pretrial identification. Williams & Hammelmann, in one of the most comprehensive studies of such forms of identification, said, "The fact that the police have little or no doubt that the man put up for identification has committed the offense, and that their chief pre-occupation is with the problem of getting sufficient proof, because he has not 'come clean,' involves a danger that this persuasion may communicate itself even in a doubtful case to the witness in some way." Williams & Hammelmann, *Identification Parades, Part I,* (1963) CRIM.L.REV. 479, 483

Insofar as the accused's conviction may rest on a courtroom identification in fact the fruit of a suspect pretrial identification which the accused is helpless to subject to effective scrutiny at trial, the accused is deprived of that right of cross-examination which is an essential safeguard to his right to confront the witnesses against him. Even though cross-examination is a precious safeguard to a fair trial, it cannot be viewed as an absolute assurance of accuracy and reliability. In the present context, where so many variables and pitfalls exist, the first line of defense must be the prevention of unfairness and the lessening of the hazards of eyewitness identification at the lineup itself. The trial which might determine the accused's fate may well not be that in the courtroom but at the pretrial confrontation, with the State aligned against the accused, the witness the sole jury, and the accused unprotected against the overreaching, intentional or unintentional, and with little or no effective appeal from the judgment there rendered by the witness—"that's the man."

Since it appears that there is grave potential for prejudice, intentional or not, in the pretrial lineup, which may not be capable of reconstruction at trial, and since presence of counsel itself can often avert prejudice and assure a meaningful confrontation at trial, there can be little doubt that for Wade the postindictment lineup was a critical stage of the prosecution at which he was "as much entitled to such of counsel as at the trial itself." Thus both Wade and his counsel should have been notified of the impending lineup, and counsel's presence should have been a requisite to conduct of the lineup, absent an "intelligent waiver." No substantial countervailing policy considerations have been advanced against the requirement of the presence of counsel. Concern is expressed that the requirement will forestall prompt identifications and result in obstruction. As for the first, in the two cases in which the right to counsel is today held to apply, counsel had already been appointed and no argument is made that notice to counsel would have prejudicially delayed the confrontations. Moreover, we leave open the question whether the presence of substitute counsel might suffice where notification and presence of the suspect's own counsel would result in prejudicial delay. To refuse to recognize the right to counsel for fear that counsel will obstruct the course of justice is contrary to the basic assumptions upon which this Court has operated in Sixth Amendment cases. We rejected similar logic in *Miranda* concerning presence of counsel during custodial interrogation. In our view counsel can hardly impede legitimate law enforcement; on the contrary, law enforcement may be assisted by preventing the infiltration of taint in the prosecution's identification evidence. That result cannot help the guilty avoid conviction but can only help assure that the right man has been brought to justice.

Legislative or other regulations, such as those of local police departments, which eliminate the risks of abuse and unintentional suggestion at lineup proceedings and the impediments to meaningful confrontation at trial may also remove the basis for regarding the stage as "critical." But neither Congress nor the federal authorities have seen fit to provide a solution. What we hold today "in no way creates a constitutional straitjacket which will handicap sound efforts at reform, nor is it intended to have this effect."

We come now to the question whether the denial of Wade's motion to strike the courtroom identification by the bank witnesses at trial because of the absence of his counsel at the lineup required the grant of a new trial at which such evidence is to be excluded. We do not think this disposition can be justified without first giving the Government the opportunity to establish by clear and convincing evidence that the in-court identifications were based upon observations of the suspect other than the lineup identification. Where the admissibility of evidence of the lineup identification itself is not involved, a *per se* rule of exclusion of courtroom identification would be unjustified. A rule limited solely to the exclusion of testimony concerning identification at the lineup itself, without regard to admissibility of the courtroom identification, would render the right to counsel an empty one. The lineup is most often used to crystallize the witnesses' identification of the defendant for future reference. We have already noted that the lineup identification will have that effect. The State may then rest upon the witnesses' unequivocal courtroom identifications, and not mention the pretrial identification as part of the State's case at trial. Counsel is then in the predicament in which Wade's counsel found himself—realizing that possible unfairness at the lineup may be the sole means of attack upon the unequivocal courtroom identification, and having to probe in the dark in an attempt to discover and reveal unfairness, while bolstering the government witness' courtroom identification by bringing out and dwelling upon his prior identification. Since counsel's presence at the lineup would equip him to attack not only the lineup identification but the courtroom identification as well, limiting the impact of violation of the right to counsel to exclusion of evidence only of identification at the lineup itself disregards a critical element of that right.

The proper test to be applied in these situations is "Whether, granting establishment of the primary illegality, the evidence to which instant objection is made has been come at by exploitation of that illegality or instead by means sufficiently distinguishable to be purged of the primary taint." Application of this requires consideration of various factors; for example, the prior opportunity to observe the alleged criminal act, the existence of any discrepancy between any pre-lineup description and the defendant's actual description, any identification prior to lineup of another person, the identification by picture of the defendant prior to the lineup, failure to identify the defendant on a prior occasion, and the lapse of time between the alleged act and the lineup identification. It is also relevant to consider facts which, despite the absence of counsel, are disclosed concerning the conduct of the lineup.

On the record before us we cannot make the determination whether the in-court identifications had an independent origin. We therefore vacate the conviction pending a hearing to determine whether the in-court identifications had an independent source, or whether, in any event, the introduction of the evidence was harmless error, and for the District Court to reinstate the conviction or order a new trial, as may be proper.

Mr. Justice Black, dissenting in part and concurring in part.

The Government forced Wade to stand in a lineup, wear strips on his face, and speak certain words, in order to make it possible for government witnesses to identify him as a criminal. Being forced by the Government to help convict himself and to supply evidence against himself by talking outside the courtroom is equally violative of his constitutional right not to be compelled to be a witness against himself. The assistance of counsel at the lineup is also necessary to protect the defendant's in-custody assertion of his privilege against self-incrimination, for counsel may advise the defendant not to participate in the lineup or to participate only under certain conditions.

Mr. Justice White, whom Mr. Justice Harlan and Mr. Justice Stewart join, dissenting in part and concurring in part.

The premise for the Court's rule is not the general unreliability of eyewitness identifications nor the difficulties inherent in observation, recall, and recognition. The Court assumes a narrower evil—improper police suggestion which contributes to erroneous identifications. I do not share this pervasive distrust of official investigations.

It may be asked, what possible state interest militates against requiring the presence of defense counsel at lineups? After all, he *may* do some good, he *may* upgrade the quality of identification evidence in state courts and he can scarcely do any harm. Absent some reliably established constitutional violation, the processes by which the States enforce their criminal laws are their own prerogative. I would not require counsel's presence at pretrial identification procedures. Some counsel may advise their clients to refuse to make any movements or to speak any words in a lineup or even to appear in one. The impact on truthful factfinding is obvious. Others will not only observe what occurs and develop possibility for later cross-examination but will hover over witnesses and begin their cross-examination then, menacing truthful factfinding as thoroughly as the Court fears the police now do. There is an implicit invitation to counsel to suggest rules for the lineup and to manage and produce it as best he can. I doubt that the Court's new rule, absent some clearly defined limits on counsel's role, will measurably contribute to more reliable pretrial identifications. The State is entitled to investigate and develop its case outside the presence of defense counsel. This includes the right to have private conversations with identification witnesses.

MR. JUSTICE FORTAS with whom THE CHIEF JUSTICE and MR. JUSTICE DOUGLAS join, concurring in part and dissenting in part.

The accused may not be compelled in a lineup to speak the words uttered by the person who committed the crime. It is the kind of volitional act—the kind of forced cooperation by the accused—which is within the historical perimeter of the privilege against compelled self-incrimination. I agree that the accused must be advised of and given the right to counsel before a lineup.

Take Note

Crucial to *Wade*'s outcome was the Court's recognition that lineups could be managed or manipulated in various ways. The logical extension of that understanding is that identification methods which are a function of scientific review, such as fingerprinting, blood sampling, and hair, fiber or DNA analysis, do not trigger the right to counsel. Given the standardization of analysis characterizing such testing, *Wade* stressed "that the accused has the opportunity for a meaningful confrontation of the Government's case at trial through the ordinary processes of cross-examination of the Government's expert witnesses and the presentation of the evidence of his own experts." Such analysis and distinction illuminates an overarching concern with the right to counsel not independently but as a means of facilitating a fair trial when other protections would be inadequate. Elaborating on this theme, the Court in *Gilbert v. California*, 388 U.S. 263, 266 (1967), concluded that "The taking of handwriting exemplars was not a 'critical' stage of the criminal proceedings entitling petitioner to the assistance of counsel. Putting aside the fact that the exemplars were taken before the indictment and appointment of counsel, there is minimal risk that the absence of counsel might derogate from his right to a fair trial. If an unrepresentative exemplar is taken, this can be brought out and corrected through the adversary process at trial since the accused can make an unlimited number of additional exemplars for analysis and comparison by government and defense handwriting experts. Thus, "the accused has the opportunity for a meaningful confrontation of the State's case at trial through the ordinary processes of cross-examination of the State's expert handwriting witnesses and the presentation of the evidence of his own handwriting experts."

Point for Discussion

Pre-Charge Showup

In *Kirby v. Illinois*, 406 U.S. 682 (1972), the Court was asked to extend the exclusionary rule to identification testimony (a showup) that took place before the defendant had been indicted or otherwise formally charged with any criminal offense. The Court refused: "A person's Sixth and Fourteenth Amendment right to counsel attaches only at or after the time that adversary judicial proceedings have been initiated against him. The initiation of judicial criminal proceedings is far from a mere formalism. It is the starting point of our whole system of adversary criminal justice. It is only then that the government has committed itself to prosecute, and only then that the adverse positions of government and defendant have solidified. It is then that a defendant finds himself faced with the prosecutorial forces of organized society, and immersed in the intricacies of substantive and procedural criminal law." Mr. Justice Brennan dissented: "Counsel is required at confrontations because "the dangers inherent in eyewitness identification and the suggestibility inherent in the context of the pretrial identification," mean that protection must be afforded to the "most basic right of a criminal defendant—his right to a fair trial at which the witnesses against him might be meaningfully cross-examined." Hence, "the initiation of adversary judicial criminal proceedings," is completely irrelevant. There inhere in a confrontation for identification conducted after arrest the identical hazards to a fair trial that inhere in such a confrontation conducted 'after the onset of formal prosecutional proceedings.' "

Food for Thought

You have been hired to represent a suspect who is going to be placed in a lineup. After *Wade,* you know that you have to be concerned about the possibility of "suggestiveness" during the lineup. How is suggestiveness created? In other words, when you go to the lineup, what sorts of problems should you be looking for?

Food for Thought

You attend the actual lineup and find that it is unduly suggestive. What is your role? Do you object?

Food for Thought

In *Rothgery v. Gillespie County,* 554 U.S. 191 (2008), the Court reaffirmed the idea "that the right to counsel guaranteed by the Sixth Amendment applies when adversary proceedings commence." The Court held that the adversary process can commence with "the initiation of adversary judicial criminal proceedings-whether by way of formal charge, preliminary hearing, indictment, information, or arraignment," as well as by "the first appearance before a judicial officer at which a defendant is told of the formal accusation against him and restrictions are imposed on his liberty." The Court relied on *Brewer v. Williams,* 430 U.S. 387, 398 (1977), and *Michigan v. Jackson,* 475 U.S. 625, 629 (1986). The Court went on to hold that the right attaches whether or not a public prosecutor is aware of the initial proceeding.

Hypo 1: *The Need for Counsel*

Is counsel really necessary in a lineup situation? Why isn't it possible for the suspect to "observe" and "report" to his/her attorney regarding circumstances at the lineup? Based on such observations, would it be possible for the attorney to cross-examine witnesses at trial?

Hypo 2: *The Basis for a Challenge*

If the lineup is suggestive, but you are present, you won't be able to challenge the result of the identification on Sixth Amendment right to counsel grounds. So, on what basis do you challenge it?

Hypo 3: *Pre-Adversarial Proceedings Lineups*

Suppose that a lineup occurs before the suspect has been indicted or formally charged, and the suspect is forced to appear without the benefit of counsel. The suspect is identified by the witness, and the suspect is ultimately indicted. You have been appointed to represent him. After *Wade*, you know that you cannot object to the pre-trial identification (or, for that matter, to an in-court identification by the same witness) on Sixth Amendment right to counsel grounds. On what basis might you object if you believe that the process was tainted?

United States v. Ash

413 U.S. 300 (1973).

MR. JUSTICE BLACKMUN delivered the opinion of the Court.

On the morning of August 26, 1965, a man with a stocking mask entered a bank in Washington, D.C., and began waving a pistol. He ordered an employee to hang up the telephone and instructed all others present not to move. Seconds later a second man, also wearing a stocking mask, entered the bank, scooped up money from tellers' drawers into a bag, and left. The gunman followed, and both men escaped through an alley. The robbery lasted three or four minutes. A Government informer, Clarence McFarland, told authorities that he had discussed the robbery with Charles J. Ash, Jr., the respondent. Acting on this information, an FBI agent, in February 1966, showed five black-and-white mug shots of Negro males of generally the same age, height, and weight, one of which was of Ash, to four witnesses. All four made uncertain identifications of Ash's picture. At this time Ash was not in custody and had not been charged. On April 1, 1966, an indictment was returned charging Ash and a codefendant, John L. Bailey, in five counts related to this bank robbery. In preparing for trial, the prosecutor decided to use a photographic display to determine whether the witnesses he planned to call would be able to make in-court identifications. Shortly before the trial, an FBI agent and the prosecutor showed five color photographs to the four witnesses who previously had tentatively identified the black-and-white photograph of Ash. Three of the witnesses selected the picture of Ash, but one was unable to make any selection. None of the witnesses selected the picture of Bailey which was in the group. This post-indictment identification provides the basis for respondent Ash's claim that he was denied the right to counsel at a "critical stage" of the prosecution.

The Government argued in *Wade* that if counsel was required at a lineup, the same forceful considerations would mandate counsel at other preparatory steps in the "gathering of the prosecution's evidence," such as, for particular example, the taking of fingerprints or blood samples. The Court concluded that there were differences. Rather than distinguishing these situations from the lineup in terms of the need for counsel to assure an equal confrontation at the time, the Court recognized that there were times when the subsequent trial would cure a one-sided confrontation between prosecuting authorities and the uncounseled defendant. In other words, such stages were not "critical." Referring to fingerprints, hair, clothing, and other blood samples, the Court explained: "Knowledge of the techniques of science and technology is sufficiently available, and the variables in techniques few enough, that the accused has the opportunity for a meaningful confrontation of the Government's case at trial through the ordinary processes of cross-examination of the Government's expert witnesses and the presentation of the evidence of his own experts."

The structure of *Wade*, viewed in light of the careful limitation of the Court's language to "confrontations," makes it clear that lack of scientific precision and inability to reconstruct an event are not the tests for requiring counsel in the first instance. These are, instead, the tests to determine whether confrontation with counsel at trial can serve as a substitute for counsel at the pretrial confrontation. If accurate reconstruction is possible, the risks inherent in any confrontation still remain, but the opportunity to cure defects at trial causes the confrontation to cease to be "critical."

A substantial departure from the historical test would be necessary if the Sixth Amendment were interpreted to give Ash a right to counsel at the photographic identification in this case. Since the accused himself is not present at the time of the photographic display, and asserts no right to be present, no possibility arises that the accused might be misled by his lack of familiarity with the law or overpowered by his professional adversary. Similarly, the counsel guarantee would not be used to produce equality in a trial-like adversary confrontation. Rather, the guarantee was used by the Court of Appeals to produce confrontation at an event that previously was not analogous to an adversary trial. Even if we were willing to view the counsel guarantee in broad terms as a generalized protection of the adversary process, we would be unwilling to go so far as to extend the right to a portion of the prosecutor's trial-preparation interviews with witnesses. Although photography is relatively new, the interviewing of witnesses before trial is a procedure that predates the Sixth Amendment. The counterbalance in the American adversary system for these interviews arises from the equal ability of defense counsel to seek and interview witnesses himself. That adversary mechanism remains as effective for a photographic display as for other parts of pretrial interviews. No greater limitations are placed on defense counsel in constructing displays, seeking witnesses, and conducting photographic identifications than those applicable to the prosecution. Selection of the picture of a person other than the accused, or the inability of a witness to make any selection, will be useful to the defense in precisely the same manner that the selection of a picture of the defendant would be useful to the prosecution. In this very case, for example, the initial tender of the photographic display was by Bailey's counsel, who sought to demonstrate that the witness had failed to make a photographic identification. Although we do not suggest that equality of access to photographs removes all potential for abuse, it does remove any inequality in the adversary process itself and thereby fully satisfies the historical spirit of the Sixth Amendment's counsel guarantee.

The argument has been advanced that requiring counsel might compel the police to observe more scientific procedures or might encourage them to utilize corporeal rather than photographic displays. This Court has recognized that improved procedures can minimize the dangers of suggestion. Pretrial photographic identifications, however, are hardly unique in offering possibilities for the actions of the prosecutor unfairly to prejudice the accused. Evidence favorable to the accused may be withheld; testimony of witnesses may be manipulated; the results of laboratory tests may be contrived. In many ways the prosecutor, by accident or by design, may improperly subvert the trial. The primary safeguard against abuses of this kind is the ethical responsibility of the prosecutor, who, as so often has been said, may "strike hard blows" but not "foul ones." If that safeguard fails, review remains available under due process standards.

We are not persuaded that the risks inherent in the use of photographic displays are so pernicious that an extraordinary system of safeguards is required. We hold that the Sixth Amendment does not grant the right to counsel at photographic displays conducted by the Government for the purpose of allowing a witness to attempt an identification of the offender.

MR. JUSTICE STEWART, concurring in the judgment.

A photographic identification is quite different from a lineup, for there are substantially fewer possibilities of impermissible suggestion when photographs are used, and those unfair influences can be readily reconstructed at trial. It is true that defendant's photograph may be markedly different from the others displayed, but this unfairness can be demonstrated at trial from a comparison of the photographs or from the witness' description of the display. The photographs could be arranged in a suggestive manner, or that by comment or gesture the prosecuting authorities might single out the defendant's picture. But these are the kinds of overt influence that a witness can easily recount and that would serve to impeach the identification testimony. In short, there are few possibilities for unfair suggestiveness—and those rather blatant and easily reconstructed. Accordingly, an accused would not be foreclosed from effective cross-examination of an identification witness simply because his counsel was not present at the photographic display. For this reason, a photographic display cannot fairly be considered a "critical stage" of the prosecution.

Mr. Justice Brennan, with whom Mr. Justice Douglas and Mr. Justice Marshall join, dissenting.

The "dangers of mistaken identification set forth in *Wade* are applicable to photographic as well as corporeal identifications." To the extent that misidentification may be attributable to a witness' faulty memory or perception, or inadequate opportunity for detailed observation during the crime, the risks are obviously as great at a photographic display as at a lineup. "Because of the inherent limitations of photography, which presents its subject in two dimensions rather than the three dimensions of reality, a photographic identification, even when properly obtained, is clearly inferior to a properly obtained corporeal identification." In this sense at least, the dangers of misidentification are even greater at a photographic display than at a lineup.

As in the lineup situation, the possibilities for impermissible suggestion in the context of a photographic display are manifold. Such suggestion, intentional or unintentional, may derive from three possible sources. First, the photographs themselves might tend to suggest which of the pictures is that of the suspect. Differences in age, pose, or other physical characteristics of the persons represented, and variations in the mounting, background, lighting, or markings of the photographs all might have the effect of singling out the accused. Second, impermissible suggestion may inhere in the manner in which the photographs are displayed to the witness. Third, gestures or comments of the prosecutor at the time of the display may lead an otherwise uncertain witness to select the "correct" photograph. "Regardless of how the initial misidentification comes about, the witness is apt to retain in his memory the image of the photograph rather than of the person actually seen."

As with lineups, the defense can "seldom reconstruct" at trial the mode and manner of photographic identification. Preservation of the photographs affords little protection to the unrepresented accused. Although retention of the photographs may mitigate the dangers of misidentification due to the suggestiveness of the photographs themselves, it cannot in any sense reveal to defense counsel the more subtle, and therefore more dangerous, suggestiveness that might derive from the manner in which the photographs were displayed or any accompanying comments or gestures. The accused cannot rely upon the witnesses themselves to expose these latter sources of suggestion, for the witnesses are not "apt to be alert for conditions prejudicial to the suspect. The witnesses are hardly "likely to be schooled in the detection of suggestive influences." Finally, the accused is not even present at the photographic identification, thereby reducing the likelihood that irregularities in the procedures will ever come to light. The difficulties of reconstructing at trial an uncounseled photographic display are at least equal to, and possibly greater than, those involved in reconstructing an uncounseled lineup.

This Court's decisions suggest that a "stage" of the prosecution must be deemed "critical" for the purposes of the Sixth Amendment if it is one at which the presence of counsel is necessary "to protect the fairness of the trial itself." *Wade* envisioned counsel's function at the lineup to be primarily that of a trained observer, able to detect the existence of any suggestive influences and capable of understanding the legal implications of the events that transpire. Having witnessed the proceedings, counsel would then be in a position effectively to reconstruct at trial any unfairness that occurred at the lineup, thereby preserving the accused's fundamental right to a fair trial on the issue of identification. There simply is no meaningful difference, in terms of the need for attendance of counsel, between corporeal and photographic identifications. Applying established and well-reasoned Sixth Amendment principles, a pretrial photographic display, like a pretrial lineup, is a "critical stage" of the prosecution at which the accused is constitutionally entitled to the presence of counsel.

Point for Discussion

Wade's Vitality

Post-*Ash* law establishes the continuing vitality of *Wade* in post-charging circumstances. In *Moore v. Illinois,* 434 U.S. 220, 224 (1977), the Court reiterated the basic premise that counsel must be present for a showup or one-on-one confrontation. The *Wade-Ash-Moore* line of decisions indicates that the right of counsel extends only to post-charging procedures requiring the presence and identification of the defendant. Prior to charging, counsel is not required even at a line-up or show-up. The distinction between pre-charging and post-charging circumstances is rooted in Sixth Amendment text that references "criminal prosecutions." In reviewing arguments for extending the *Wade* rule to pre-charging circumstances, the Court in *Kirby v. Illinois* reiterated the significance of actual judicial criminal proceedings rather than police investigations.

Hypo: *More on Photographic Displays*

In conducting a photographic identification, should it matter whether the photographs are presented simultaneously or in succession? Suppose that a witness is simultaneously shown photos of eleven different individuals, and is told to look at the photographs and to make an identification "if she can." She does, pointing out defendant as the culprit. Does due process require that the photographs be shown sequentially? Does it matter whether the police comment, positively or negatively, as the witness makes comments on the suspects? *See Commonwealth v. Thomas*, 476 Mass. 451, 68 N.E.3d 1161 (Mass. 2017).

C. Due Process Considerations

Even though the Sixth Amendment may not govern an identification proceeding, because of its timing or circumstance, constitutional review is not necessarily precluded. As a guarantor of procedural fairness, due process claims may be asserted in any investigative or adjudicative context. Due process review imposes upon claimants a significant task of demonstrating that identification methods were "unnecessarily suggestive and conducive to mistaken identification." *Stovall v. Denno*, 388 U.S. 293, 302 (1967). Unlike *Gilbert* and *Wade*, which referenced the Sixth Amendment's relevance to defendants identified in person, *Stovall v. Denno* involved a pre-indictment one-on-one identification. The *Stovall* decision represents the seminal articulation of due process principles governing identification procedures.

In *Stovall v. Denno*, 388 U.S. 293 (1967), Dr. Paul Behrendt was stabbed to death in the kitchen of his home. During the murder, Behrendt's wife was stabbed 11 times. She was hospitalized for major surgery to save her life. The police, without affording petitioner time to retain counsel, arranged with her surgeon to bring petitioner to her hospital room about noon, the day after the surgery. Petitioner was handcuffed to one of five police officers who, with two district attorneys, brought him to the hospital room. Petitioner was the only African-American in the room. Mrs. Behrendt identified him from her hospital bed after being asked by an officer whether he "was the man" and after petitioner repeated at the direction of an officer a "few words for voice identification." None of the witnesses could recall the words that were used. Mrs. Behrendt and the officers testified at the trial to her identification of petitioner in the hospital room, and she also made an in-court identification of petitioner in the courtroom. Petitioner claimed that the in-hospital identification was unconstitutionally obtained, but the Court disagreed: "A claimed violation of due process of law in the conduct of a confrontation depends on the totality of the circumstances surrounding it, and the record in the present case reveals that the showing of Stovall to Mrs. Behrendt in an immediate hospital confrontation was imperative." The Court quoted from the lower court opinion: "Here was the only person in the world who could possibly exonerate Stovall. Her words, and only her words, 'He is not the man' could have resulted in freedom for Stovall. The hospital was not far distant from the courthouse and jail. No one knew how long Mrs. Behrendt might live. Faced with the responsibility of identifying the attacker, with the need for immediate action and with the knowledge that Mrs. Behrendt could not visit the jail, the police followed the only feasible procedure and took Stovall to the hospital room. Under these circumstances, the usual police station line-up was out of the question." *See also Simmons v. United States,* 390 U.S. 377, 384 (1968) (although the identification process included repetitive use of the suspect's picture, the Court found that there was a need for swift police action to determine whether police "were on the right track" and that the risk of misidentification was insignificant). A year later, in *Foster v. California,* the Court determined that an identification procedure was so suggestive, and reliability so undermined, that due process was denied.

Foster v. California

394 U.S. 440 (1969).

Mr. Justice Fortas delivered the opinion of the Court.

Petitioner was charged with the armed robbery of a Western Union office. The day after the robbery one of the robbers, Clay, surrendered to the police and implicated Foster and Grice. Except for the robbers themselves, the only witness to the crime was Joseph David, the late-night manager of the Western Union office. After Foster had been arrested, David was called to the police station to view a lineup. There were three men in the lineup. One was petitioner. He is a tall man—close to six feet in height. The other two men were short—five feet, five or six inches. Petitioner wore a leather jacket which David said was similar to the one he had seen underneath the coveralls worn by the robber. After seeing this lineup, David could not positively identify petitioner as the robber. He "thought" he was the man, but he was not sure. David then asked to speak to petitioner, and petitioner was brought into an office and sat across from David at a table. Except for prosecuting officials there was no one else in the room. Even after this one-to-one confrontation David still was uncertain whether petitioner was one of the robbers: "truthfully—I was not sure," he testified at trial. A week or 10 days later, the police arranged for David to view a second lineup. There were five men in that lineup. Petitioner was the only person in the second lineup who had appeared in the first lineup. This time David was "convinced" petitioner was the man. At trial, David testified to his identification of petitioner in the lineups. He also repeated his identification of petitioner in the courtroom. The only other evidence against petitioner which concerned the particular robbery with which he was charged was the testimony of the alleged accomplice Clay.

This case presents a compelling example of unfair lineup procedures. In the first lineup, petitioner stood out from the other two men by his height and by the fact that he was wearing a leather jacket similar to that worn by the robber. When this did not lead to positive identification, the police permitted a one-to-one confrontation between petitioner and the witness. This Court pointed out in *Stovall* that "the practice of showing suspects singly to persons for the purpose of identification, and not as part of a lineup, has been widely condemned." Even after this the witness' identification of petitioner was tentative. So some days later another lineup was arranged. Petitioner was the only person in this lineup who had also participated in the first lineup. This finally produced a definite identification. The suggestive elements in this identification procedure made it all but inevitable that David would identify petitioner whether or not he was in fact "the man." In effect, the police repeatedly said to the witness, "*This* is the man." This procedure so undermined the reliability of the eyewitness identification as to violate due process.

Point for Discussion

Irreparable Misidentification

Determining whether an identification procedure is "impermissible," even if suggestive, requires attention to concerns that compete with and may supersede optimum integrity and regularity. The *Simmons* Court referenced reliability and terminal prejudice factors as a potential offset to suggestive procedures. In *Neil v. Biggers*, the Court stressed that "irreparable misidentification" was "the primary evil to be avoided."

Neil v. Biggers

409 U.S. 188 (1972).

MR. JUSTICE POWELL delivered the opinion of the Court.

Respondent was convicted of rape and was sentenced to 20 years' imprisonment. The State's evidence consisted in part of testimony concerning a station-house identification of respondent by the victim. The District Court held that the claims were not barred and, after a hearing, held in an unreported opinion that the station-house identification procedure was so suggestive as to violate due process. The Court of Appeals affirmed. We granted certiorari to decide whether the identification procedure violated due process.

The victim testified at trial that on the evening of January 22, 1965, a youth with a butcher knife grabbed her in the doorway to her kitchen:

"A. He grabbed me from behind, and grappled—twisted me on the floor. Threw me down on the floor.

"Q. And there was no light in that kitchen?

"A. Not in the kitchen.

"Q. So you couldn't have seen him then?

"A. Yet, I could see him, when I looked up in his face.

"Q. In the dark?

"A. He was right in the doorway—it was enough light from the bedroom shining through. Yes, I could see who he was.

"Q. You could see? No light? And you could see him and know him then?

"A. Yes."

When the victim screamed, her 12-year-old daughter came out of her bedroom and also began to scream. The assailant directed the victim to "tell her [the daughter] to shut up, or I'll kill you both." She did, and was then walked at knifepoint about two blocks along a railroad track, taken into a woods, and raped. She testified that "the moon was shining brightly, full moon." After the rape, the assailant ran off, and she returned home, the whole incident having taken between 15 minutes and half an hour.

She then gave the police what the trial court characterized as "only a very general description," describing him as "being fat and flabby with smooth skin, bushy hair and a youthful voice." Additionally, she testified at the *habeas corpus* hearing that she had described her assailant as being between 16 and 18 years old and between five feet ten inches and six feet tall, as weighing between 180 and 200 pounds, and as having a dark brown complexion. This testimony was substantially corroborated by that of a police officer who was testifying from his notes. On several occasions over the course of the next seven months, she viewed suspects in her home or at the police station, some in lineups and others in showups, and was shown between 30 and 40 photographs. She told the police that a man pictured in one of the photographs had features similar to those of her assailant, but identified none of the suspects. On August 17, the police called her to the station to view respondent, who was being detained on another charge. In an effort to construct a suitable lineup, the police checked the city jail and the city juvenile home. Finding no one at either place fitting respondent's unusual physical description, they conducted a showup instead. The showup consisted of two detectives walking respondent past the victim. At the victim's request, the police directed respondent to say "shut up or I'll kill you." The testimony was not altogether clear as to whether the victim first identified him and then asked that he repeat the words or made her identification after he had spoken. In any event, the victim testified that she had "no doubt" about her identification.

We turn to the central question, whether under the "totality of the circumstances" the identification was reliable even though the confrontation procedure was suggestive. The factors to be considered in evaluating the likelihood of misidentification include the opportunity of the witness to view the criminal at the time of the crime, the witness' degree of attention, the accuracy of the witness' prior description of the criminal, the level of certainty demonstrated by the witness at the confrontation, and the length of time between the crime and the confrontation. Applying these factors, we disagree with the District Court's conclusion.

The District Court focused unduly on the relative reliability of a lineup as opposed to a showup, the issue on which expert testimony was taken at the evidentiary hearing. We find that the District Court's conclusions on the critical facts are unsupported by the record and clearly erroneous. The victim spent a considerable period of time with her assailant, up to half an hour. She was with him under adequate artificial light in her house and under a full moon outdoors, and at least twice, once in the house and later in the woods, faced him directly and intimately. She was no casual observer, but rather the victim of one of the most personally humiliating of all crimes. Her description to the police, which included the assailant's approximate age, height, weight, complexion, skin texture, build, and voice, might not have satisfied Proust but was more than ordinarily thorough. She had "no doubt" that respondent was the person who raped her. In the nature of the crime, there are rarely witnesses to a rape other than the victim, who often has a limited opportunity of observation. The victim here, a practical nurse by profession, had an unusual opportunity to observe and identify her assailant. She testified at the *habeas corpus* hearing that there was something about his face "I don't think I could ever forget."

Take Note

Biggers stressed that, even if an identification procedure is unnecessarily suggestive, the due process inquiry does not end. *Stovall* intimated that suggestiveness itself might be sufficient to make an identification inadmissible. *Stovall v. Denno*, 388 U.S. 293, 302 (1967). *Biggers* previewed a redirection of case law, emphasizing that suggestiveness is merely a factor, and that due process inquiry will be driven primarily by considerations of reliability.

There was, to be sure, a lapse of seven months between the rape and the confrontation. This would be a seriously negative factor in most cases. Here, however, the testimony is undisputed that the victim made no previous identification at any of the showups, lineups, or photographic showings. Her record for reliability was thus a good one, as she had previously resisted whatever suggestiveness inheres in a showup. Weighing all the factors, we find no substantial likelihood of misidentification. The evidence was properly allowed to go to the jury.

Manson v. Brathwaite

432 U.S. 98 (1977).

MR. JUSTICE BLACKMUN delivered the opinion of the Court.

Jimmy Glover, a trooper of the Connecticut State Police, in 1970 was assigned to the Narcotics Division in an undercover capacity. On May 5 of that year, about 7:45 p.m., and while there was still daylight, Glover and Henry Brown, an informant, went to an apartment building at 201 Westland, in Hartford, for the purpose of purchasing narcotics from "Dickie Boy" Cicero, a known narcotics dealer. Cicero lived on the third floor of that apartment building. Glover and Brown entered the building, observed by back-up Officers D'Onofrio and Gaffey, and proceeded to the third floor. Glover knocked at the door of one of the two apartments served by the stairway. The area was illuminated by natural light from a window in the third floor hallway. The door was opened 12 to 18 inches in response to the knock. Glover observed a man standing at the door and, behind him, a woman. Brown identified himself. Glover then asked for "two things" of narcotics. The man at the door held out his hand, and Glover gave him two $10 bills. The door closed. Soon the man returned and handed Glover two glassine bags. While the door was open, Glover stood within two feet of the person from whom he made the purchase and observed his face. Five to seven minutes elapsed from the time the door first opened until it closed the second time. Glover and Brown then left the building about eight minutes after their arrival. Glover drove to headquarters where he described the seller to D'Onofrio and Gaffey. Glover at that time did not know the identity of the seller. He described him as being "a colored man, approximately five feet eleven inches tall, dark complexion, black hair, short Afro style, high cheekbones, and of heavy build. He was wearing at the time blue pants and a plaid shirt." D'Onofrio, suspecting from this description that respondent might be the seller, obtained a photograph of respondent from the Records Division of the Hartford Police Department. He left it at Glover's office. D'Onofrio was not acquainted with respondent personally but did know him by sight and had seen him "several times" prior to May 5. Glover, when alone, viewed the photograph for the first time upon his return to headquarters on May 7; he identified the person shown as the one from whom he had purchased the narcotics.

Respondent was charged, in a two-count information, with possession and sale of heroin. At trial, the photograph from which Glover had identified respondent was received in evidence without objection on the part of the defense. Glover testified that, although he had not seen respondent in the eight months that had elapsed since the sale, "there was no doubt whatsoever" in his mind that the person shown on the photograph was respondent. Glover also made a positive in-court identification without objection. No explanation was offered by the prosecution for the failure to utilize a photographic array or to conduct a lineup. The jury found respondent guilty on both counts and was affirmed by the Connecticut Supreme Court. Thereafter, respondent filed a petition for *habeas corpus*, which the court of appeals granted. The court felt that evidence as to the photograph should have been excluded, regardless of reliability, because the examination of the single photograph was unnecessary and suggestive. In the court's view, the evidence was unreliable in any event.

Petitioner acknowledges that "the procedure was suggestive because only one photograph was used and unnecessary" because there was no emergency or exigent circumstance. The respondent proposes a *per se* rule of exclusion that he claims is dictated by the demands of the Fourteenth Amendment's guarantee of due process. Since the decision in *Biggers*, the Courts of Appeals appear to have developed at least two approaches to such evidence. The first, or *per se* approach focuses on the procedures employed and requires exclusion of the out-of-court identification evidence, without regard to reliability, whenever it has been obtained through unnecessarily suggestive confrontation procedures. The justifications advanced are the elimination of evidence of uncertain reliability, deterrence of the police and prosecutors, and "assurance against the awful risks of misidentification." The second, or more lenient, approach is one that continues to rely on the totality of the circumstances. It permits the admission of the confrontation evidence if, despite the suggestive aspect, the out-of-court identification possesses certain features of reliability. Its adherents feel that the *per se* approach is not mandated by the Due Process Clause of the Fourteenth Amendment. This second approach is ad hoc and serves to limit the societal costs imposed by a sanction that excludes relevant evidence from consideration and evaluation by the trier of fact.

There are, of course, several interests to be considered and taken into account. The driving force behind our prior holdings was concern with the problems of eyewitness identification. Usually the witness must testify about an encounter with a total stranger under circumstances of emergency or emotional stress. The witness' recollection of the stranger can be distorted easily by the circumstances or by later actions of the police. Thus, *Wade* and its companion cases reflect the concern that the jury not hear eyewitness testimony unless that evidence has aspects of reliability. Both approaches are responsive to this concern. The *per se* rule, however, goes too far since its application automatically and peremptorily, and without consideration of alleviating factors, keeps evidence from the jury that is reliable and relevant. The second factor is deterrence. Although the *per se* approach has the more significant deterrent effect, the totality approach also has an influence on police behavior. The police will guard against unnecessarily suggestive procedures under the totality rule, as well as the *per se* one, for fear that their actions will lead to the exclusion of identifications as unreliable. The third factor is the effect on the administration of justice. Here the *per se* approach suffers serious drawbacks. Since it denies the trier reliable evidence, it may result, on occasion, in the guilty going free. Also, because of its rigidity, the *per se* approach may make error by the trial judge more likely than the totality approach. And in those cases in which the admission of identification evidence is error under the *per se* approach but not under the totality approach—cases in which the identification is reliable despite an unnecessarily suggestive identification procedure-reversal is a Draconian sanction. Certainly, inflexible rules of exclusion that may frustrate rather than promote justice have not been viewed recently by this Court with unlimited enthusiasm.

It is true that *Biggers* referred to the pre-*Stovall* character of the confrontation in that case. But that observation was only one factor in the judgmental process. It does not translate into a holding that post-*Stovall* confrontation evidence automatically is to be excluded. We conclude that reliability is the linchpin in determining the admissibility of identification testimony for both pre-and post-*Stovall* confrontations. The factors to be considered are set out in *Biggers*. These include the opportunity of the witness to view the criminal at the time of the crime, the witness' degree of attention, the accuracy of his prior description of the criminal, the level of certainty demonstrated at the confrontation, and the time between the crime and the confrontation. Against these factors is to be weighed the corrupting effect of the suggestive identification itself. We turn, then, to the facts of this case and apply the analysis:

1. *The opportunity to view.* Glover testified that for two to three minutes he stood at the apartment door, within two feet of the respondent. The door opened twice, and each time the man stood at the door. The moments passed, the conversation took place, and payment was made. Glover looked directly at his vendor. It was near sunset, but the sun had not yet set, so it was not dark or even dusk or twilight. Natural light from outside entered the hallway through a window. There was natural light, as well, from inside the apartment.

2. *The degree of attention.* Glover was not a casual or passing observer, as is often the case with eyewitness identification. Glover was a trained police officer on duty—and specialized and dangerous duty—when he called at the third floor of 201 Westland. Glover was a Negro and unlikely to perceive only general features of "hundreds of Hartford black males." It is true that Glover's duty was that of ferreting out narcotics offenders and that he would be expected in his work to produce results. But it is also true that, as a specially trained, assigned, and experienced officer, he could be expected to pay scrupulous attention to detail, for he knew that he would have to

find and arrest his vendor. In addition, he knew that his claimed observations would be subject later to close scrutiny and examination at trial.

3.   *The accuracy of the description.* Glover's description was given to D'Onofrio within minutes after the transaction. It included the vendor's race, height, build, the color and style of his hair, and the high cheekbone facial feature. It also included clothing the vendor wore. No claim has been made that respondent did not possess the physical characteristics so described. D'Onofrio reacted positively at once. Two days later, when Glover was alone, he viewed the photograph D'Onofrio and identified its subject as the narcotics seller.

4.   *The witness' level of certainty.* There is no dispute that the photograph in question was that of respondent. Glover testified: "There is no question whatsoever." This positive assurance was repeated.

5.   *The time between the crime and the confrontation.* Glover's description of his vendor was given to D'Onofrio within minutes of the crime. The photographic identification took place only two days later. We do not have here the passage of weeks or months between the crime and the viewing.

These indicators of Glover's ability to make an accurate identification are hardly outweighed by the corrupting effect of the challenged identification. Although identifications arising from single-photograph displays may be viewed with suspicion, we find little pressure on the witness to acquiesce in the suggestion that such a display entails. D'Onofrio left the photograph at Glover's office and was not present when Glover first viewed it two days after the event. There thus was little urgency and Glover could view the photograph at his leisure. Since Glover examined the photograph alone, there was no coercive pressure to make an identification arising from the presence of another. The identification was made in circumstances allowing care and reflection.

Although it plays no part in our analysis, this assurance as to the reliability of the identification is hardly undermined by the facts that respondent was arrested in the very apartment where the sale had taken place, and that he acknowledged his frequent visits to that apartment.

Surely, we cannot say that under the circumstances of this case there is "a very substantial likelihood of irreparable misidentification." Such evidence is for the jury. We are content to rely upon the good sense and judgment of American juries, for evidence with some element of untrustworthiness is customary grist for the jury mill. Juries are not so susceptible that they cannot measure intelligently the weight of identification testimony that has some questionable feature.

Of course, it would have been better had D'Onofrio presented Glover with a photographic array including "so far as practicable a reasonable number of persons similar to any person then suspected whose likeness is included in the array." The use of that procedure would have enhanced the force of the identification and would have avoided the risk that the evidence would be excluded as unreliable. But we are not disposed to view D'Onofrio's failure as one of constitutional dimension to be enforced by a rigorous and unbending exclusionary rule. The defect, if there be one, goes to weight and not to substance.

The criteria laid down in *Biggers* are to be applied in determining the admissibility of evidence offered by the prosecution concerning a post-*Stovall* identification, and those criteria are satisfactorily met and complied with here.

The judgment of the Court of Appeals is *reversed.*

MR. JUSTICE STEVENS, concurring.

The Court's decision to fashion new rules to minimize the danger of convicting the innocent on the basis of unreliable eyewitness testimony can be performed "more effectively by the legislative process than by a somewhat clumsy judicial fiat." The Federal Constitution does not foreclose experimentation by the States in the development of such rules.

MR. JUSTICE MARSHALL, with whom MR. JUSTICE BRENNAN joins, dissenting.

The Court wrongly evaluates the *Biggers* factors. First, the Court acknowledges that one of the factors, deterrence of police use of unnecessarily suggestive identification procedures, favors the *per se* rule. Indeed, such a rule would make it unquestionably clear to the police they must never use a suggestive procedure when a fairer alternative is available. Conduct would quickly conform to the rule. Second, the Court gives passing consideration to the dangers of eyewitness identification recognized in the *Wade* trilogy. The dangers of mistaken identification are too great to permit unnecessarily suggestive identifications. Finally, the Court errs in its assessment of the relative impact of the two approaches on the administration of justice. The Court relies most heavily on this factor, finding that "reversal is a Draconian sanction" in cases where the identification is reliable despite an unnecessarily suggestive procedure used to obtain it. In so doing, the Court disregards two significant distinctions between the *per se* rule advocated in this case and the exclusionary remedies for certain other constitutional violations. First, the *per se* rule is not "inflexible." Where evidence is suppressed as the fruit of an unlawful search, it may well be lost to the prosecution. Identification evidence, however, can by its very nature be readily and effectively reproduced. The in-court identification, permitted under *Wade* and *Simmons* if it has a source independent of an uncounseled or suggestive procedure, is one example. Similarly, when a prosecuting attorney learns that there has been a suggestive confrontation, he can easily arrange another lineup conducted under scrupulously fair conditions. Second, other exclusionary rules have been criticized for preventing jury consideration of relevant and usually reliable evidence in order to serve an interest unrelated to guilt or innocence, such as discouraging illegal searches or denial of counsel. Suggestively obtained eyewitness testimony is excluded because of its unreliability and concomitant irrelevance. Its exclusion both protects the integrity of the truth-seeking function of the trial and discourages police use of needlessly inaccurate and ineffective investigatory methods.

Indeed, impermissibly suggestive identifications are not merely worthless law enforcement tools. They pose a grave threat to society at large in a more direct way than most governmental disobedience of the law. For if the police and the public erroneously conclude, on the basis of an unnecessarily suggestive confrontation, that the right man has been caught and convicted, the real outlaw must still remain at large. Law enforcement has failed and has left society unprotected from the depredations of an active criminal. The Court's totality test will allow unreliable and misleading evidence to be put before juries. Equally important, it will allow dangerous criminals to remain on the streets while citizens assume that police action has given them protection.

Despite my strong disagreement with the Court over the proper standards to be applied, I am pleased that its application of the totality test does recognize the continuing vitality of *Stovall*. In assessing the reliability of the identification, the Court mandates weighing "the corrupting effect of the suggestive identification" against the "indicators of a witness' ability to make an accurate identification." The Court holds that a due process identification inquiry must take account of the suggestiveness of a confrontation and the likelihood that it led to misidentification, as recognized in *Stovall* and *Wade*. Thus, even if a witness did have an otherwise adequate opportunity to view a criminal, the later use of a highly suggestive identification procedure can render his testimony inadmissible. Assuming applicability of the totality test enunciated by the Court, the facts of the present case require that result.

I consider first the opportunity that Officer Glover had to view the suspect. Careful review of the record shows that he could see the heroin seller only for the time it took to speak three sentences of four or five short words, to hand over some money, and later after the door reopened, to receive the drugs in return. The entire face-to-face transaction could have taken as little as 15 or 20 seconds. During this time, Glover's attention was not focused exclusively on the seller's face. He observed that the door was opened 12 to 18 inches, that there was a window behind the door, and that there was a woman behind the man. Glover was, also concentrating on the details of the transaction. The observation thus may have been as brief as 5 or 10 seconds.

Glover was a police officer trained in and attentive to the need for making accurate identifications. Nevertheless, both common sense and scholarly study indicate that while a trained observer such as a police officer "is somewhat less likely to make an erroneous identification than the average untrained observer, the mere fact that he has been trained is no guarantee that he is correct in a specific case. Moreover, "identifications made by policemen in highly competitive activities, such as undercover narcotic agents, should be scrutinized with special care."

Another factor—the witness' degree of certainty in making the identification—is worthless as an indicator that he is correct. Even if Glover had been unsure initially about his identification of respondent's picture, by the time he was called at trial to present a key piece of evidence for the State that paid his salary, it is impossible to imagine his responding negatively to such questions as "is there any doubt in your mind whatsoever" that the identification was correct. The Court finds that because the identification procedure took place two days after the crime, its reliability is enhanced. While such temporal proximity makes the identification more reliable than one occurring months later, the greatest memory loss occurs within hours after an event. Thus, the reliability of an identification is increased only if it was made within several hours of the crime. If the time gap is any greater, reliability necessarily decreases.

Finally, the Court makes much of the fact that Glover gave a description of the seller to D'Onofrio shortly after the incident. Despite the Court's assertion that because "Glover himself was a Negro and unlikely to perceive only general features of 'hundreds of Hartford black males,' as the Court of Appeals stated," the description given by Glover was actually no more than a general summary of the seller's appearance. We may discount entirely the seller's clothing, for that was of no significance. Indeed, to the extent that Glover noticed clothes, his attention was diverted from the seller's face. Glover merely described vaguely the seller's height, skin color, hairstyle, and build. He did say that the seller had "high cheekbones," but there is no other mention of facial features, nor even an estimate of age. Conspicuously absent is any indication that the seller was a native of the West Indies, certainly something which a member of the black community could immediately recognize from both appearance and accent.

The evidence of Glover's ability to make an accurate identification is far weaker than the Court finds. The procedure used to identify respondent was both extraordinarily suggestive and strongly conducive to error. In dismissing "the corrupting effect of the suggestive identification" procedure, the Court virtually grants the police license to convict the innocent. By displaying a single photograph of respondent to the witness Glover under the circumstances in this record almost everything that could have been done wrong was done wrong.

In the first place, there was no need to use a photograph at all. Because photos are static, two-dimensional, and often outdated, they are "clearly inferior in reliability" to corporeal procedures. Worse still was the display to Glover of only a single picture, rather than a photo array. Such single-suspect procedures have "been widely condemned." They give no assurance that the witness can identify the criminal from among a number of persons of similar appearance, surely the strongest evidence that there was no misidentification. The use of a single picture (or the display of a single live suspect) is a grave error because it dramatically suggests to the witness that the person shown must be the culprit. Why else would the police choose the person? It is deeply ingrained in human nature to agree with the expressed opinions of others—particularly others who should be more knowledgeable—when making a difficult decision. In this case, the pressure was not limited to that inherent in the display of a single photograph. Glover knew that D'Onofrio, an experienced Hartford narcotics detective, familiar with local drug operations, believed respondent to be the seller. There was at work both loyalty to another police officer and deference to a better-informed colleague. Finally, there was Glover's knowledge that without an identification and arrest, government funds used to buy heroin had been wasted.

There is no doubt that even in D'Onofrio's absence, a clear and powerful message was telegraphed to Glover as he looked at respondent's photograph. He was emphatically told that "*this* is the man," and he responded by identifying respondent then and at trial "whether or not he was in fact 'the man.' " There was "a very substantial likelihood of misidentification." The suggestive display of respondent's photograph to Glover likely erased any independent memory that Glover had retained of the seller from his barely adequate opportunity to observe the criminal.

Take Note

Review of identification procedures has been characterized by less demanding criteria than those governing confessions. Even if found reliable, an involuntary confession is inadmissible. *Jackson v. Denno*, 378 U.S. 368, 376 (1964). Relevant case law, when involuntary confessions were concerned, reflects not only an inclination to exclude such evidence but an insistence upon excusing the jury when arguments on admissibility are heard. Although the impact of an inadmissible identification may be as profound as that of a confession, the admissibility question may be resolved with the jury present. *Watkins v. Sowders*, 449 U.S. 341, 349 (1981). Beyond finding reliability an offset to suggestiveness, the Court also may reference an independent source of identification or harmless error as a factor that supports admissibility.

Food for Thought

Recall the earlier problem in which a lineup occurs before the suspect has been indicted or formally charged, and the suspect is forced to appear without the benefit of counsel. When the suspect is identified by the witness, and the suspect is ultimately indicted, you are appointed to represent him. You object that neither identification should be permitted. Now you need to develop proof to support your objection. What type of proof would be convincing and probative? How would you develop it?

Hypo 1: *Bail Hearing Identification*

Shortly after noon, the victim awakened from a nap to find a man holding a knife in the doorway to her bedroom. The man entered the bedroom, threw her face down on the bed, and choked her until she was quiet. After covering his face with a bandana, the intruder partially undressed the victim, forced her to commit oral sodomy, raped her, and left. When police arrived, the victim gave a description of her assailant. Although she did not know who he was and had seen his face for only 10 to 15 seconds during the attack, she thought he was the same man who had made offensive remarks to her in a neighborhood bar the night before. In the week that followed, police showed the victim two groups of photographs. From the first group of 200 she picked about 30 men who resembled her assailant in height, weight, and build. From the second group of 10, she picked two or three. One of these was petitioner. Police arrested petitioner at his apartment and held him overnight pending a preliminary hearing. The next morning, a policeman accompanied the victim to court for the hearing. The policeman told her she was going to view a suspect and should identify him if she could. He also asked her to sign a complaint that named petitioner as her assailant. At the hearing, petitioner's name was called and he was led before the bench. The judge told petitioner that he was charged with rape and deviate sexual behavior. The judge then called the victim, who had been in the courtroom waiting for the case to be called, to come before the bench. The State's Attorney stated that police had found evidence linking petitioner with the offenses. He asked the victim whether she saw her assailant in the courtroom, and she pointed at petitioner. At trial, the victim testified that she had identified petitioner as her assailant at the preliminary hearing. She also testified that petitioner was the man who had raped her. Was petitioner's right to counsel, or his right to due process, violated by the pretrial identification? Should the witness be allowed to make an in-court identification of petitioner or to testify regarding the pre-trial identification? What arguments might be made on the defendant's behalf? How might the state respond to those arguments? *See Moore v. Illinois,* 434 U.S. 220 (1977).

Food for Thought

As we have seen, even though a defendant cannot object to a photographic identification on Sixth Amendment right to counsel grounds, he might be able to raise a due process objection. If you are appointed to represent a defendant confronted by this situation, what types of evidence might help you establish a due process violation? How might you develop the evidence?

Hypo 2: *More on Show Ups*

Police observe a night club because rival gangs congregate there, and problems sometimes develop. Several men run out of the club, and then a BMW pulls up with a driver and passenger who are covered in blood. The police seal off the club and order all male patrons to submit to a "show up" with the former BMW occupants. The process takes forty minutes. Palacios is identified as one of the perpetrators. Although the results of the show up are admitted at Palacios trial, the surviving BMW occupant (the other died on the night of the incident) was unable to identify Palacios as one of the perpetrators. Nevertheless, Palacios is convicted. In subjecting the males to the show up, were they "seized" within the meaning of the Fourth Amendment? If so, was the seizure permissible? Was the show up permissible and admissible at trial? *See Palacios v. Burge,* 589 F.3d 556 (2d Cir. 2009).

Hypo 3: *More on Identification Admissibility*

During the night, two men (Clark and Henderson) forcefully enter an apartment to collect money owed to Clark. While Harper (the victim) and Clark go to a different room to discuss things, the other man (Henderson) points a gun at Womble and tells him, "Don't move, you're not involved in this." Womble testifies that he "got a look at" the stranger, but not "a real-good look." Womble did overhear Clark and Harper arguing in the other room. Harper said, "do what you got to do," after which Womble heard a gunshot. Womble then walks into the room, sees Clark holding a handgun, offers to get Clark the $160, and urges him not to shoot Harper again. As Clark leaves, he warns Womble, "Don't rat me out, I know where you live." Harper dies from the gunshot wound. When approached by the police, Womble initially lies regarding being able to identify the perpetrator. He later admits that he lied because he "didn't want to get involved" for fear that they will retaliate against his elderly father. Womble leads the investigators to Clark, who eventually gives a statement about his involvement and identifies the person who accompanied him as Henderson. The officers then ask Womble to view a photographic array that involves seven "filler" photos and a photo of Henderson. The eight photos all depict headshots of white men between the ages of twenty-eight and thirty-five, with short hair, goatees, and similar facial features. Womble quickly eliminates five of the photos. He then reviews the remaining three, discounts one more, and says that he "isn't 100 percent sure of the final two pictures." Officers believe that Womble is holding back because of fear. Ruiz said Womble was "nervous, upset about his father." In an effort to calm Womble, McNair "tells him to focus, calm down, relax and that any type of protection that he needs, any threats against him would be put to rest by the Police Department." Ruiz adds, "just do what you have to do, and we'll be out of here." In response, Womble says that he "can make an identification." The exchange lasts less than one minute. Then Officer McNair reshuffles the eight photos and again displays them to Womble sequentially. This time, when Womble sees defendant's photo, he slams his hand on the table and exclaims, "that's the guy." From start to finish, the entire process takes fifteen minutes. Womble does not recant his identification, but testifies that he felt that Detective McNair was "nudging" him to choose defendant's photo, and "that there was pressure" to make a choice. Should the results of the photo identification be admitted at trial? Why or why not? *See State v. Henderson,* 208 N.J. 208, 27 A.3d 872 (N.J. 2011).

Food for Thought

A police officer responds to a burglary alarm, reportedly involving two black men and one white man. When he arrives at the house, the officer sees that the door has been forced open and that there are no lights on. He also sees that there is a staircase to the second floor that faces away from the front door towards the rear sliding-glass door. The base of the staircase is fifteen feet away and the sliding glass door is another three feet away. After hearing movement upstairs, the officer yells "police," and then he hears two individuals run down the stairs and bolt out the sliding glass door. Each man glances at the officer, but only for a brief "second." One is a "heavyset white male of medium complexion, and the other is a black male, not as heavy, with cornrows in his hair, light skin color, wearing a black jacket." Suppose that other police officers (who came to provide backup) apprehend several men a few minutes later, and the initial police officer identifies them based on the initial encounter. If you represent the defendant, how would you challenge the officer's identification of the man? *See Byrd v. State,* 25 A.3d 761 (Del. 2011).

Hypo 4: *More on the* Byrd *Problem*

Now, let's add a few facts to the prior problem. While the events are in progress, a third officer arrives on the scene, notices a black male (who turns out to be Denzel Butler) and an older woman (Butler's mother) standing in front of the house adjacent to the crime scene property, and decides to talk to Butler and his mother. Butler tells the officer that, earlier in the day, he saw three men in the street. He spoke briefly to one of the men with whom he had attended high school. Would your conclusion in the prior problem be different if the officer's testimony was supported by Butler's testimony and identification? *See Byrd v. State,* 25 A.3d 761 (Del. 2011).

Hypo 5: *In-Court Identifications*

Do in-court identifications present special difficulties for defendants when the witness has not previously made an out-of-court identification? After all, defendant is likely to be sitting at the defense table, and therefore there is a suggestion of guilt because the state is prosecuting defendant. Of course, the advantage of an in-court identification is that there is no prior suggestive out-of-court identification. Should courts be particularly wary of first-time in-court identifications? *See Commonwealth v. Crayton,* 21 N.E.3d 157 (Mass. Sup. Jud. Ct., Middlesex, 2015). What steps, if any, could a trial court take to overcome the suggestiveness inherent in an in-court identification?

Hypo 6: *More on In-Court Identifications*

Would it matter if there had been a prior inconclusive out-of-court identification? Suppose that a man is the only eyewitness to a murder, but he had only a fleeting opportunity to view the perpetrator. He is shown a non-suggestive photographic display and fails to make an identification. He does suggest that defendant might be the perpetrator, and asks to see a side view of him (at the scene of the crime, the eyewitness had only a side view of the murderer). However, none is available. At trial, under oath, the eyewitness is asked whether he sees the perpetrator in the courtroom. The eyewitness immediately identifies defendant who is sitting with defense counsel. The defense objects that the identification is unduly suggestive under the circumstances, especially given the fact that defendant is sitting at the defense table, and obviously has been singled out for prosecution, and given the prior failure to make an identification. Should the in-court identification be admissible? Should any additional proof be required of the prosecution? *See Commonwealth v. Collins*, 21 N.E.3d 528 (Mass. 2014).

Hypo 7: *Witness Identifications & Videos*

Suppose that the culprit of a crime is captured on video committing the crime, but the video is a bit fuzzy. A police detective circulates a picture of the culprit to other police officers, and one is able to identify the culprit as defendant. At trial, should the fellow officer be able to testify regarding the identity of the culprit? Or should the judge leave it to the jury to view the video itself, compare the image on the video to defendant, and make its own determination regarding whether defendant is the culprit? *See People v. Thompson*, 49 N.E.3d 393 (2016).

Hypo 8: *The Man in the Mask*

A man wearing a ski mask exposes himself to a young girl. Before the police ask the girl to identify the man in a showup, they tell her that they caught the man, and they dress him in a jacket similar to that worn by the culprit. She admits on cross-examination that she did not see the culprit's face at the scene of the crime, but claims that she can identify the jacket on the suspect as the one worn by the culprit. At the show-up, she is unable to identify the suspect's face but does identify the suspect based on the jacket. Is the girl's identification admissible? *See State v. Jones*, 224 N.J. 70, 128 A.3d 1096 (2016).

Perry v. New Hampshire

565 U.S. 338 (2012).

Justice Ginsburg delivered the opinion of the Court.

Around 3 a.m. on August 15, 2008, Joffre Ullon called the Nashua, New Hampshire, Police Department and reported that an African-American male was trying to break into cars parked in the lot of Ullon's apartment building. Officer Nicole Clay responded to the call. Upon arriving at the parking lot, Clay heard what "sounded like a metal bat hitting the ground." She then saw petitioner Perry standing between two cars. Perry walked toward Clay, holding two car-stereo amplifiers in his hands. A metal bat lay on the ground behind him. Clay asked Perry where the amplifiers came from. "I found them on the ground," Perry responded. Meanwhile, Ullon's wife, Nubia Blandon, woke her neighbor, Alex Clavijo, and told him she had just seen someone break into his car. Clavijo immediately went downstairs to the parking lot to inspect the car. He first observed that one of the rear windows had been shattered. On further inspection, he discovered that the speakers and amplifiers from his car stereo were missing, as were his bat and wrench. Clavijo then approached Clay and told her about Blandon's alert and his own subsequent observations. By this time, another officer had arrived at the scene. Clay asked Perry to stay in the parking lot with that officer, while she and Clavijo went to talk to Blandon. Clay and Clavijo then entered the apartment building and took the stairs to the fourth floor, where Blandon's and Clavijo's apartments were located. They met Blandon in the hallway just outside the open door to her apartment. Asked to describe what she had seen, Blandon stated that, around 2:30 a.m., she saw from her kitchen window a tall, African-American man roaming the parking lot and looking into cars. Eventually, the man circled Clavijo's car, opened the trunk, and removed a large box.[2] Clay asked Blandon for a more specific description of the man. Blandon pointed to her kitchen window and said the person she saw breaking into Clavijo's car was standing in the parking lot, next to the police officer. Perry's arrest followed this identification. About a month later, the police showed Blandon a photographic array that included a picture of Perry and asked her to point out the man who had broken into Clavijo's car. Blandon was unable to identify Perry.

Perry was charged in New Hampshire state court with one count of theft by unauthorized taking and one count of criminal mischief. He moved to suppress Blandon's identification on the ground that admitting it at trial would violate due process. Blandon witnessed what amounted to a one-person showup in the parking lot, Perry asserted, which all but guaranteed that she would identify him as the culprit. The New Hampshire Superior Court denied the motion. We granted certiorari to resolve a division of opinion on the question whether the Due Process Clause requires a trial judge to conduct a preliminary assessment of the reliability of an eyewitness identification made under suggestive circumstances not arranged by the police.

The Constitution protects a defendant against a conviction based on evidence of questionable reliability, not by prohibiting introduction of the evidence, but by affording the defendant means to persuade the jury that the evidence should be discounted as unworthy of credit. Constitutional safeguards available to defendants to counter the State's evidence include the Sixth Amendment rights to counsel, *Gideon v. Wainwright,* 372 U.S. 335 (1963); compulsory process, *Taylor v. Illinois,* 484 U.S. 400 (1988); and

---

[2]   The box, which Clay found on the ground near where she first encountered Perry, contained car-stereo speakers.

confrontation plus cross-examination of witnesses, *Delaware v. Fensterer,* 474 U.S. 15 (1985) (*per curiam*). Apart from these guarantees, state and federal statutes and rules ordinarily govern the admissibility of evidence, and juries are assigned the task of determining the reliability of the evidence presented at trial. Only when evidence "is so extremely unfair that its admission violates fundamental conceptions of justice," have we imposed a constraint tied to the Due Process Clause. *See, e.g., Napue v. Illinois,* 360 U.S. 264, 269 (1959).

Contending that the Due Process Clause is implicated here, Perry relies on a series of decisions involving police-arranged identification procedures. In *Stovall v. Denno,* 388 U.S. 293 (1967), a witness identified the defendant as her assailant after police officers brought the defendant to the witness' hospital room. Although the police-arranged showup was undeniably suggestive, the Court held that no due process violation occurred. Crucial to the Court's decision was the procedure's necessity: The witness was the only person who could identify or exonerate the defendant; the witness could not leave her hospital room; and it was uncertain whether she would live to identify the defendant in more neutral circumstances. A year later, in *Simmons v. United States,* 390 U.S. 377 (1968), the Court held that when a witness identifies the defendant in a police-organized photo lineup, the identification should be suppressed only where "the photographic identification procedure was so unnecessarily suggestive as to give rise to a very substantial likelihood of irreparable misidentification." The Court rejected the defendant's due process challenge to admission of the identification. In contrast, the Court held in *Foster v. California,* 394 U.S. 440 (1969), that due process required the exclusion of an eyewitness identification obtained through police-arranged procedures that "made it all but inevitable that the witness would identify the defendant."

Synthesizing previous decisions, we set forth in *Neil v. Biggers,* 409 U.S. 188 (1972), and reiterated in *Manson v. Brathwaite,* 432 U.S. 98 (1977), the approach appropriately used to determine whether the Due Process Clause requires suppression of an eyewitness identification tainted by police arrangement. The Court emphasized, first, that due process concerns arise only when law enforcement officers use an identification procedure that is both suggestive and unnecessary. Even when the police use such a procedure, suppression of the resulting identification is not the inevitable consequence. A rule requiring automatic exclusion, the Court reasoned, would "go too far," for it would "keep evidence from the jury that is reliable and relevant," and "may result, on occasion, in the guilty going free." The Court held that the Due Process Clause requires courts to assess, on a case-by-case basis, whether improper police conduct created a "substantial likelihood of misidentification." "Reliability [of the eyewitness identification] is the linchpin" of that evaluation, the Court stated in Brathwaite. Where the "indicators of a witness' ability to make an accurate identification" are "outweighed by the corrupting effect" of law enforcement suggestion, the identification should be suppressed. Otherwise, the evidence (if admissible in all other respects) should be submitted to the jury.[5]

Applying this "totality of the circumstances" approach, the Court held in *Biggers* that law enforcement's use of an unnecessarily suggestive showup did not require suppression of the victim's identification of her assailant. Notwithstanding the improper procedure, the victim's identification was reliable: She saw her assailant for a considerable period of time under adequate light, provided police with a detailed description of her attacker long before the showup, and had "no doubt" that the defendant was the person she had seen. Similarly, the Court concluded in *Brathwaite* that police use of an unnecessarily suggestive photo array did not require exclusion of the resulting identification. The witness, an undercover police officer, viewed the defendant in good light for several minutes, provided a thorough description of the suspect, and was certain of his identification. Hence, the "indicators of the witness' ability to make an accurate identification were hardly outweighed by the corrupting effect of the challenged identification."

Perry concedes that, in contrast to every case in the *Stovall* line, law enforcement officials did not arrange the suggestive circumstances surrounding Blandon's identification. The rationale underlying our decisions, Perry asserts, supports a rule requiring trial judges to prescreen eyewitness evidence for reliability any time an identification is made under suggestive circumstances. We disagree. Perry's argument depends, in large part, on the Court's statement in *Brathwaite* that "reliability is the linchpin in determining the admissibility of identification testimony." If reliability is the linchpin of admissibility under the Due Process Clause, Perry maintains, it should make no difference whether law enforcement was responsible for creating the suggestive circumstances that marred the identification.

Perry has removed our statement in *Brathwaite* from its mooring. *Brathwaite*'s reference to reliability appears in a portion of the opinion concerning the appropriate remedy *when the police use an unnecessarily suggestive identification procedure*. The Court adopted a judicial screen for reliability as a course preferable to a *per se* rule requiring exclusion of identification evidence whenever law enforcement officers employ an improper procedure. The due process check for reliability comes into play only after the defendant establishes improper police conduct. The very purpose of the check is to avoid depriving the jury of identification evidence that is reliable, *notwithstanding* improper police conduct. A primary aim of excluding identification evidence obtained under unnecessarily suggestive circumstances is to deter law enforcement use of improper lineups, showups, and photo arrays in the first place. Alerted to the pros-

---

[5]   Among "factors to be considered" in evaluating a witness' "ability to make an accurate identification," the Court listed: "the opportunity of the witness to view the criminal at the time of the crime, the witness' degree of attention, the accuracy of his prior description of the criminal, the level of certainty demonstrated at the confrontation, and the time between the crime and the confrontation." *Manson v. Brathwaite*, 432 U.S. 98 (1977).

pect that identification evidence improperly obtained may be excluded, police officers will "guard against unnecessarily suggestive procedures." This deterrence rationale is inapposite in cases, like Perry's, in which the police engaged in no improper conduct. The defendants in *Coleman* contended that a witness' in-court identifications violated due process, because a pretrial stationhouse lineup was "so unduly prejudicial and conducive to irreparable misidentification as fatally to taint the later identifications." The Court rejected this argument. No due process violation occurred, the plurality explained, because nothing "the police said or did prompted the witness' virtually spontaneous identification of the defendants." True, Coleman was the only person in the lineup wearing a hat, the plurality noted, but "nothing in the record showed that he was required to do so."

Perry and the dissent place significant weight on *United States v. Wade*, 388 U.S. 218 (1967), describing it as a decision not anchored to improper police conduct. In fact, the risk of police rigging was the very danger to which the Court responded in *Wade* when it recognized a defendant's right to counsel at postindictment, police-organized identification procedures. Perry's argument would open the door to judicial preview, under the banner of due process, of most, if not all, eyewitness identifications. External suggestion is hardly the only factor that casts doubt on the trustworthiness of an eyewitness' testimony. Many other factors bear on "the likelihood of misidentification"—for example, the passage of time between exposure to and identification of the defendant, whether the witness was under stress when he first encountered the suspect, how much time the witness had to observe the suspect, how far the witness was from the suspect, whether the suspect carried a weapon, and the race of the suspect and the witness. There is no reason why an identification made by an eyewitness with poor vision, for example, or one who harbors a grudge against the defendant, should be regarded as inherently more reliable, less of a "threat to the fairness of trial," than the identification Blandon made in this case. To embrace Perry's view would thus entail a vast enlargement of the reach of due process as a constraint on the admission of evidence.

Perry maintains that the Court can limit the due process check he proposes to identifications made under "suggestive circumstances." Even if we could rationally distinguish suggestiveness from other factors bearing on the reliability of eyewitness evidence, Perry's limitation would still involve trial courts, routinely, in preliminary examinations. Most eyewitness identifications involve some element of suggestion. Indeed, all in-court identifications do. Out-of-court identifications volunteered by witnesses are also likely to involve suggestive circumstances. For example, suppose a witness identifies the defendant to police officers after seeing a photograph of the defendant in the press captioned "theft suspect," or hearing a radio report implicating the defendant in the crime. Or suppose the witness knew that the defendant ran with the wrong crowd and saw him on the day and in the vicinity of the crime. Any of these circumstances might have "suggested" to the witness that the defendant was the person the witness observed committing the crime.

Perry maintains that eyewitness identifications are a uniquely unreliable form of evidence. We do not doubt either the importance or the fallibility of eyewitness identifications. Indeed, in recognizing that defendants have a constitutional right to counsel at postindictment police lineups, we observed that "the annals of criminal law are rife with instances of mistaken identification." *Wade*, 388 U.S. at 228. We have concluded in other contexts that the potential unreliability of a type of evidence does not alone render its introduction at the defendant's trial fundamentally unfair. *See, e.g., Ventris*, 556 U.S. at 594. The fallibility of eyewitness evidence does not, without the taint of improper state conduct, warrant a due process rule requiring a trial court to screen such evidence for reliability before allowing the jury to assess its creditworthiness.

Our unwillingness to enlarge the domain of due process rests, in large part, on our recognition that the jury, not the judge, traditionally determines the reliability of evidence. We also take account of other safeguards built into our adversary system that caution juries against placing undue weight on eyewitness testimony of questionable reliability. These protections include the defendant's Sixth Amendment right to confront the eyewitness. Another is the defendant's right to the effective assistance of an attorney, who can expose the flaws in the eyewitness' testimony during cross-examination and focus the jury's attention on the fallibility of such testimony during opening and closing arguments. Eyewitness-specific jury instructions, which many federal and state courts have adopted, likewise warn the jury to take care in appraising identification evidence. State and federal rules of evidence, moreover, permit trial judges to exclude relevant evidence if its probative value is substantially outweighed by its prejudicial impact or potential for misleading the jury. *See, e.g.,* Fed. Rule Evid. 403. In appropriate cases, some States also permit defendants to present expert testimony on the hazards of eyewitness identification evidence.

Many of the safeguards just noted were at work at Perry's trial. During her opening statement, Perry's court-appointed attorney cautioned the jury about the vulnerability of Blandon's identification. While cross-examining Blandon and Officer Clay, Perry's attorney constantly brought up the weaknesses of Blandon's identification. Perry's counsel reminded the jury of these frailties during her summation. After closing arguments, the trial court read the jury a lengthy instruction on identification testimony and the factors the jury should consider when evaluating it. The court also instructed the jury that the defendant's guilt must be proved beyond a reasonable doubt, and specifically cautioned that "one of the things the State must prove beyond a reasonable doubt is the identification of the defendant as the person who committed the offense."

Given the safeguards generally applicable in criminal trials, protections availed of by the defense in Perry's case, we hold that the introduction of Blandon's eyewitness testimony, without a preliminary judicial assessment of its reliability, did not render Perry's trial fundamentally unfair. Finding no convincing reason to alter our precedent, we hold that the Due Process Clause does not require a preliminary judicial inquiry into the reliability of an eyewitness identification when the identification was not procured under unnecessarily suggestive circumstances arranged by law enforcement. Accordingly, the judgment of the New Hampshire Supreme Court is *Affirmed.*

JUSTICE THOMAS, concurring.

The *Stovall* line of cases is premised on a "substantive due process" right to "fundamental fairness." Those cases are wrongly decided because the Fourteenth Amendment's Due Process Clause is not a "secret repository of substantive guarantees against 'unfairness.' " *BMW of North America, Inc. v. Gore,* 517 U.S. 559 (1996) (Scalia, J., dissenting). I would limit the suggestive eyewitness identification cases to the precise circumstances that they involved.

JUSTICE SOTOMAYOR, dissenting.

Eyewitness identifications' unique confluence of features—unreliability, susceptibility to suggestion, powerful impact on the jury, and resistance to the ordinary tests of the adversarial process—can undermine the fairness of a trial. The admission at trial of out-of-court eyewitness identifications derived from impermissibly suggestive circumstances that pose a very substantial likelihood of misidentification violates due process. The Court today announces that that rule does not even "come into play" unless the suggestive circumstances are improperly "police-arranged." Our due process concern, arises not from the act of suggestion, but rather from the corrosive effects of suggestion on the reliability of the resulting identification. The Court's holding ignores our precedents' acute sensitivity to the hazards of intentional and unintentional suggestion alike and unmoors our rule from the very interest it protects, inviting arbitrary results. And it recasts the driving force of our decisions as an interest in police deterrence, rather than reliability.

The "driving force" behind *Wade, Gilbert,* and *Stovall* was "the Court's concern with the problems of eyewitness identification"—specifically, "the concern that the jury not hear eyewitness testimony unless that evidence has aspects of reliability." *Manson v. Brathwaite,* 432 U.S. 98, 111 (1977). We have singled out a "major factor contributing" to that proverbial unreliability: "the suggestibility inherent in the context of the pretrial identification." Our precedents make no distinction between intentional and unintentional suggestion. To the contrary, they explicitly state that "suggestion can be created intentionally or unintentionally in many subtle ways."

Moore v. Illinois, 434 U.S. 220 (1977). Even police acting with the best of intentions can inadvertently signal "that's the man." *Wade,* 388 U.S. at 236.

In *Wade,* we noted that the "potential for improper influence [in pretrial confrontations] is illustrated by the circumstances." Our precedents focus not on the act of suggestion, but on suggestion's "corrupting effect" on reliability. *Brathwaite,* 432 U.S. at 114. Eyewitness evidence derived from suggestive circumstances is uniquely resistant to the ordinary tests of the adversary process. An eyewitness who has made an identification often becomes convinced of its accuracy. *"Regardless of how the initial misidentification comes about,* the witness thereafter is apt to retain in his memory the image of the photograph rather than of the person actually seen, reducing the trustworthiness of subsequent courtroom identification." *Simmons v. United States,* 390 U.S. 377, 383 (1968). Suggestion bolsters that confidence.

At trial, an eyewitness' artificially inflated confidence in an identification's accuracy complicates the jury's task of assessing witness credibility and reliability. It also impairs the defendant's ability to attack the eyewitness' credibility. That in turn jeopardizes the defendant's basic right to subject his accuser to meaningful cross-examination. *See Wade,* 388 U.S. at 235. The end result of suggestion, whether intentional or unintentional, is to fortify testimony bearing directly on guilt that juries find extremely convincing and are hesitant to discredit.

Consistent with our focus on reliability, we have declined to adopt a *per se* rule excluding all suggestive identifications. "reliability is the linchpin" in deciding admissibility. *Brathwaite,* 432 U.S. at 114. To protect that evidentiary interest, we have applied a two-step inquiry: First, defendant has the burden of showing that the eyewitness identification was derived through "impermissibly suggestive" means. *Simmons,* 390 U.S. at 384. Second, if defendant meets that burden, courts consider whether the identification was reliable under the totality of the circumstances. That step entails considering the witness' opportunity to view the perpetrator, degree of attention, accuracy of description, level of certainty, and the time between the crime and pretrial confrontation, then weighing such factors against the "corrupting effect of the suggestive identification." *Brathwaite,* 432 U.S. at 108, 114.

The majority today categorically exempts all eyewitness identifications derived from suggestive circumstances that were not police-manipulated—however suggestive, and however unreliable—from our due process check. Police intent is now paramount. The arrangement-focused inquiry will sow needless confusion. The vast majority of eyewitness identifications that the State uses in criminal prosecutions are obtained in lineup, showup, and photograph displays arranged by the police. Our precedents reflect that practical reality. Our due process concerns were not predicated on the source of suggestiveness. Rather, "it is the likelihood of misidentification which violates a defendant's right to due process," *Biggers,* 409 U.S. at 198. Whether the police have created the suggestive circumstances intentionally or inadvertently, the resulting identification raises the same due process concerns. The majority's approach lies in tension with our precedents. Whereas our precedents were sensitive to intentional and unintentional suggestiveness alike, today's decision narrows our concern to intentionally orchestrated suggestive confrontations. The majority insists that our precedents "aim to deter police from rigging identification procedures," so our rule should be limited to applications that advance that "primary aim" and "key premise." The majority emphasizes that we should rely on the jury to determine the reliability of evidence. But jurors find eyewitness evidence unusually powerful and their ability to assess credibility is hindered by a witness' false confidence in the accuracy of his or her identification. That disability in no way depends on the intent behind the suggestive circumstances. The majority also suggests that applying our rule beyond police-arranged suggestive circumstances would entail a heavy practical burden, requiring courts to engage in "preliminary judicial inquiry" into "most, if not all, eyewitness identifications." But that is inaccurate. The burden of showing "impermissibly suggestive" circumstances is the defendant's, so the objection falls to the defendant to raise. Today's decision nonetheless precludes even the possibility that an unintended confrontation will meet that bar, mandating summary dismissal of every such claim at the threshold.

The empirical evidence demonstrates that eyewitness misidentification is "the single greatest cause of wrongful convictions in this country." A staggering 76% of the first 250 convictions overturned due to DNA evidence since 1989 involved eyewitness misidentification. Study after study demonstrates that eyewitness recollections are highly susceptible to distortion by post-event information or social cues; that jurors routinely overestimate the accuracy of eyewitness identifications; that jurors place the greatest weight on eyewitness confidence in assessing identifications even though confidence is a poor gauge of accuracy; and that suggestiveness can stem from sources beyond police-orchestrated procedures. The majority today nevertheless adopts an artificially narrow conception of the dangers of suggestive identifications.

Hypo 1: *The Ex-Girlfriend & the Pregnant Wife*

JC received a late evening call from his ex-girlfriend, Cecilia Chen. JC stated that he was happily married and expecting a child. Defendant told him that she had recently broken up with her boyfriend, and wondered "how things might have turned out" had they remained together. Chen cried. Several days later, Helen (JC's wife), who was 5 months pregnant, received a phone call asking for JC. The caller explained that she was calling about a mortgage with Bank of America (the Kims had no such mortgage). The caller ID listed "Foley's Liquor Store"—located nearby. Helen went back to sleep but was awakened by the sound of knocking. When she responded, she saw a young woman she did not know. The woman explained that her car had broken down and asked to use a phone. Helen offered the woman a cell phone, but the woman said she needed to use the bathroom. Helen let the woman enter the house and noticed a computer cord sticking out of her left sleeve. Helen then called JC to tell him about the strange phone call and the woman. While they were speaking, the woman returned from the bathroom, grabbed Helen, and stabbed her with a kitchen knife in the shoulder. JC called 911. Helen fought back. The woman also tried to use the computer cord to choke Helen. Eventually, Helen disarmed her attacker. As Helen was about to strike her, the woman said, "Don't do anything to hurt your baby." Helen froze and the woman ran off.

When the police responded, Helen described her assailant as an Asian or Filipino woman, about 5'4", wearing a black jacket, gray hood, dark pants, brown boots, and black gloves. Helen added that her attacker was about twenty to twenty-five years old, weighed between 110 and 120 pounds, and wore black frame glasses and a gray scarf. The police were unable to locate the attacker, but recovered a pair of black-rimmed glasses, a steak knife, and a computer cord. The neighbor provided a similar description to the police within two hours of the attack. In a signed statement, the neighbor stated, "I didn't see her face except for a second when she turned." Helen, who was unable to sleep after the incident, drew a picture of her assailant. When JC saw the picture, he stated that "it looked a little familiar." JC then accessed Chen's personal website and showed Helen five to ten pictures of Chen on the computer. When she saw one particular picture, Helen "just jumped" and was "ninety percent positive" that Chen was her attacker. Helen said she was not completely certain because Chen was smiling and not wearing glasses in the picture, unlike her assailant. In response, Helen's sister, who was also present, drew eyeglasses onto printed copies of two of the pictures. Helen testified that she looked at the photos about five more times during the first month after the attack. The Kims brought copies of the photos to the police station later in the day. Helen also worked with a police sketch artist who drew a composite sketch. She later testified that the sketch did not completely resemble her attacker. Twenty-two months after the attack, the police presented a photo array to Helen and the neighbor for the first time. Detective Clancy used the photo array out of a "concern" that the website pictures might have prejudiced Helen. Both selected defendant's picture. At trial, defense counsel argued that Helen's identification was based on seeing photos that her husband showed her rather than on her memory of the attack. The prosecution argued that "the procedure followed by the police was not impermissibly suggestive." Should the identifications be admitted? Do defendant's arguments go only to the weight of the identifications rather than their admissibility. Does the identification satisfy the *Biggers* criteria? *See State v. Chen,* 27 A.3d 930 (N.J. 2011).

> ## Hypo 2: *More on Private Suggestive Identifications*
>
> Suppose that a man (the victim) runs into an old acquaintance in a bar. The man recognizes the acquaintance from having played youth football with him. A couple of hours later, the man is attacked by someone that he recognizes as the acquaintance. The man goes on the internet, finds a My Space picture of the acquaintance, and gives it to the police. The police construct a photo display of possible suspects which includes the picture that the victim found on the internet, and asks the victim whether he can identify his assailant. The man picks the acquaintance out of the display. Should the identification be excluded on due process grounds? *See State v. Johnson*, 312 Conn. 687, 94 A.3d 1173 (2014).

Executive Summary

Concerns Regarding Eyewitness Identification Techniques. Although eyewitness identifications constitute a particularly potent form of evidence in criminal proceedings, they involve significant reliability risks. A reliable identification depends upon both accurate perception and recall, matters that can be distorted by many factors, including distance, observation time, light, the field or content of activity, stereotypes, cultural assumptions, suggestive questioning, faded memory and mental tendencies that tend to convert assumption or expectation into reality.

The Fourth Amendment & Personal Traits. *United States v. Dionisio*, 410 U.S. 1, 14 (1973), observed that an individual's personal traits receive no special protection under the Fourth Amendment: "the physical characteristics of a person's voice, its tone and manner, as opposed to the content of a specific conversation, are constantly exposed to the public. Like a man's facial characteristics, or handwriting, his voice is repeatedly produced for others to hear. No person can have a reasonable expectation that others will not know the sound of his voice any more than he can reasonably expect that his face will be a mystery to the world."

The Fifth Amendment & Identification Procedures. Personal traits are also not protected against disclosure by the privilege against self-incrimination because they are regarded as nontestimonial. In *Gilbert v. California*, 388 U.S. 263, 266–67 (1967), the Court stated that "the taking of handwriting exemplars did not violate petitioner's Fifth Amendment privilege against self-incrimination. The privilege reaches only compulsion of 'an accused's communications, whatever form they might take, and the compulsion of responses which are also communications and not 'compulsion which makes a suspect or accused the source of real or physical evidence.' One's voice and handwriting are, of course, means of communication. It by no means follows that every compulsion of an accused to use his voice or write (compels) a communication within the privilege. A mere handwriting exemplar, in contrast to the content, like the voice or body itself, is an identifying physical characteristic outside its protection."

Right to Counsel & Identification Procedures. Case law has established that the right to counsel may attach to identification proceedings. Contrasted with the pervasive applicability of the due process clause, however, Sixth Amendment protection is limited to identification procedures employed "at or after the time that adversarial judicial proceedings have been initiated." *Kirby v. Illinois,* 406 U.S. 682, 688 (1972) (plurality opinion).

Identifications & "Critical Stage" Analysis. The right to counsel in an identification context is dependent upon whether the identification occurs at a stage of the process that is critical enough that counsel's presence "is necessary to preserve the defendant's basic right to a fair trial." *United States v. Wade,* 388 U.S. 218, 227 (1967). Seminal case law reflects the Court's sense that post-indictment line-ups not only satisfy the "critical stage" requirement but also present profound risks to a fair trial.

Possibility for Irreparable Mistaken Identification. In *United States v. Wade,* the Court held that the Sixth Amendment right to counsel applies to post-adversarial proceedings because of the possibility of irreparable mistaken identification, and counsel's presence is needed to give counsel the opportunity to meaningfully cross-examine witnesses. The Court concluded that there is "grave potential for prejudice, intentional or not, in the pretrial lineup, which may not be capable of reconstruction at trial, and since presence of counsel itself can often avert prejudice and assure a meaningful confrontation at trial, the postindictment lineup was a critical stage of the prosecution" at which a defendant is entitled to counsel.

Right to Counsel Inapplicable to Pre-Adversarial Identification Proceedings. In *Kirby v. Illinois,* 406 U.S. 682 (1972), the Court declined to extend the exclusionary rule to identification testimony (a showup) that took place *before* the defendant had been indicted or otherwise formally charged with any criminal offense. The Court held: "The initiation of judicial criminal proceedings is far from a mere formalism. It is the starting point of our whole system of adversary criminal justice. For it is only then that the government has committed itself to prosecute, and only then that the adverse positions of government and defendant have solidified. It is then that a defendant finds himself faced with the prosecutorial forces of organized society, and immersed in the intricacies of substantive and procedural criminal law."

Defining the Commencement of Adversarial Proceedings. In *Rothgery v. Gillespie County,* 554 U.S. 191 (2008), the Court reaffirmed the idea "that the right to counsel guaranteed by the Sixth Amendment applies when adversary proceedings commence." The Court held that the adversary process can commence with "the initiation of adversary judicial criminal proceedings-whether by way of formal charge, preliminary hearing, indictment, information, or arraignment," as well as by "the first appearance before a judicial officer at which a defendant is told of the formal accusation against him and restrictions are imposed on his liberty."

The Right to Counsel & Photographic Displays. The Court has refused to extend the right to counsel to pre-trial identification procedures involving photographic displays. The Court concluded that it was "not persuaded that the risks inherent in the use of photographic displays are so pernicious that an extraordinary system of safeguards is required."

Due Process & Pre-Adversarial Process Identifications. As a guarantor of procedural fairness, due process claims may be asserted in any investigative or adjudicative context. The standards of review requires a demonstration that the identification methods used were "unnecessarily suggestive and conducive to mistaken identification." *Stovall v. Denno*, 388 U.S. 293, 302 (1967). In *Foster v. California*, 394 U.S. 440 (1969), the Court suppressed an identification that was deemed to be so suggestive that it "so undermined the reliability of the eyewitness identification as to violate due process."

The Focus on Reliability. In *Neil v. Biggers,* 409 U.S. 188 (1972), the Court concluded that the possibility of "irreparable mistaken identification" is the "primary evil sought to be avoided." The focus is on whether, even if an identification is suggestive, is it reliable? That issue is to be determined by considering a variety of factors, including the "opportunity of the witness to view the criminal at the time of the crime, the witness' degree of attention, the accuracy of the witness' prior description of the criminal, the level of certainty demonstrated by the witness at the confrontation, and the length of time between the crime and the confrontation."

Suggestiveness in the Absence of State Action. In *Perry v. New Hampshire,* 565 U.S. 228 (2012), the Court held that courts need not pre-screen cases for reliability when the suggestive circumstances of a pre-trial identification were not arranged by law enforcement officers, but rather by private individuals independently of state action. Rather, the Court concluded that the identification's reliability could be tested "through the rights and opportunities generally designed for that purpose, notably, the presence of counsel at postindictment lineups, vigorous cross-examination, protective rules of evidence, and jury instructions on both the fallibility of eyewitness identification and the requirement that guilt be proved beyond a reasonable doubt."

Major Themes

a. Concerns Regarding Eyewitness Identification Techniques—Although eyewitness identifications may be a particularly potent form of evidence in criminal proceedings, such evidence presents significant reliability risks. Even though an accurate identification depends upon accurate perception and recall, many factors can distort both perception and recall.

b. The Right to Counsel and Identification Procedures—The right to counsel attaches to some identification proceedings that are employed "at or after the time that adversarial judicial proceedings have been initiated." There is "grave potential for prejudice, intentional or not, in the pretrial lineup, which may not be capable of reconstruction at trial, and since presence of counsel itself can often avert prejudice and assure a meaningful confrontation at trial, the postindictment lineup was a critical stage of the prosecution" at which a defendant is entitled to counsel.

c. Right to Counsel Inapplicable to Pre-Adversarial Identification Proceedings—Courts have refused to extend the exclusionary rule to identifications (e.g., a showup or lineup) that take place *before* the defendant has been indicted or otherwise formally charged with a criminal offense. The courts have also refused to extend the right to counsel to pre-trial identification procedures involving photographic displays.

d. Due Process and Pre-Adversarial Process Identifications—As a guarantor of procedural fairness, due process claims may be asserted in any investigative or adjudicative context. The focus is on whether the identification methods used were "unnecessarily suggestive and conducive to mistaken identification." However, even if an identification is suggestive, the ultimate question is whether it is "reliable." That issue is to be determined by considering a variety of factors, including the "opportunity of the witness to view the criminal at the time of the crime, the witness' degree of attention, the accuracy of the witness' prior description of the criminal, the level of certainty demonstrated by the witness at the confrontation, and the length of time between the crime and the confrontation."

e. Suggestiveness in the Absence of State Action—Courts need not pre-screen cases for reliability when the suggestive circumstances of a pre-trial identification were not arranged by law enforcement officers, but by private individuals independently of state action. Rather, the Court concluded that the identification's reliability could be tested "through the rights and opportunities generally designed for that purpose, notably, the presence of counsel at postindictment lineups, vigorous cross-examination, protective rules of evidence, and jury instructions on both the fallibility of eyewitness identification and the requirement that guilt be proved beyond a reasonable doubt."

f. Eyewitness Identifications—Such identifications involve a significant risk of irreparable mistaken identification.

g. Identifications After Commencement of Adversarial Proceedings—After the commencement of adversarial proceedings, criminal defendants have the right to the assistance of counsel.

h. Suggestive Circumstances—Even when an identification is made under suggestive circumstances, it will not be excluded from evidence if the identification is deemed to be "reliable."

i. Variety of Factors—In determining whether an identification is reliable, courts consider a variety of factors, including the: "opportunity of the witness to view the criminal at the time of the crime, the witness' degree of attention, the accuracy of the witness' prior description of the criminal, the level of certainty demonstrated by the witness at the confrontation, and the length of time between the crime and the confrontation."

For More Information

- Wayne R. LaFave, Jerold H. Israel, Nancy J. King & Orin S. Kerr, Criminal Procedure (6th ed. 2017).

- Russell L. Weaver, John M. Burkoff, Catherine Hancock & Stephen I. Friedland, Principles of Criminal Procedure (7th ed. 2021).

Test Your Knowledge

To assess your understanding of the material in this chapter, click here to take a quiz.

CHAPTER 8

The Exclusionary Rule

The exclusionary evidence rule precludes the state from using evidence seized in violation of a defendant's constitutional rights to convict the defendant of a crime.

A. The Exclusionary Rule's Application to Federal & State Proceedings

Although the United States Supreme Court's 1914 decision in *Weeks v. United States*, 232 U.S. 383 (1914), held that the exclusionary rule applies in federal court proceedings, that decision failed to extend the rule to state court proceedings.

> **Make the Connection**
>
> Although the exclusionary rule is frequently applied when the police conduct an illegal search or seizure in violation of the Fourth Amendment, it is also applied to violations of other constitutional rights (*e.g.*, evidence obtained from unconstitutional lineups and interrogations).

Wolf v. Colorado

338 U.S. 25 (1949).

MR. JUSTICE FRANKFURTER delivered the opinion of the Court.

The security of one's privacy against arbitrary intrusion by the police—which is at the core of the Fourth Amendment—is basic to a free society. It is therefore implicit in "the concept of ordered liberty" and enforceable against the States through the Due Process Clause. The knock at the door, whether by day or by night, as a prelude to a search, without authority of law but solely on the authority of the police, did not need the commentary of recent history to be condemned as inconsistent with the conception of human rights enshrined in the history and the basic constitutional documents of English-speaking peoples.

Accordingly, we have no hesitation in saying that were a State affirmatively to sanction such police incursion into privacy it would run counter to the guaranty of the

Fourteenth Amendment. But the ways of enforcing such a basic right raise questions of a different order. How such arbitrary conduct should be checked, what remedies against it should be afforded, the means by which the right should be made effective, are all questions that are not to be so dogmatically answered as to preclude the varying solutions which spring from an allowable range of judgment on issues not susceptible of quantitative solution.

In *Weeks v. United States*, 232 U.S. 383 (1914), this Court held that in a federal prosecution the Fourth Amendment barred the use of evidence secured through an illegal search and seizure. This ruling was not derived from the explicit requirements of the Fourth Amendment. The decision was a matter of judicial implication. Since then it has been frequently applied and we stoutly adhere to it. But the question is whether the basic right to protection against arbitrary intrusion by the police demands the exclusion of logically relevant evidence obtained by an unreasonable search and seizure because, in a federal prosecution for a federal crime, it would be excluded. One would suppose this to be an issue to which men with complete devotion to the protection of the right of privacy might give different answers. When most of the English-speaking world does not regard as vital to such protection the exclusion of evidence thus obtained, we must hesitate to treat this remedy as an essential ingredient of the right. The contrariety of views of the States is particularly impressive. Before the *Weeks* decision 27 States had passed on the admissibility of evidence obtained by unlawful search and seizure. 26 States opposed the *Weeks* doctrine. 1 State anticipated the *Weeks* doctrine. Since the *Weeks* decision 47 States have passed on the *Weeks* doctrine. 20 passed on it for the first time. 6 followed the *Weeks* doctrine. 14 rejected the *Weeks* doctrine. 26 States reviewed prior decisions contrary to the *Weeks* doctrine. Of these, 10 States have followed *Weeks*, overruling or distinguishing their prior decisions. 16 States adhered to their prior decisions against *Weeks*. 1 State adhered to its prior formulation of the *Weeks* doctrine. As of today 30 States reject the *Weeks* doctrine, 17 States are in agreement with it. Of 10 jurisdictions within the United Kingdom and the British Commonwealth of Nations which have passed on the question, none has held evidence obtained by illegal search and seizure inadmissible.

The jurisdictions which have rejected the *Weeks* doctrine have not left the right to privacy without other means of protection.[1] Indeed, the exclusion of evidence is a remedy which directly serves only to protect those upon whose person or premises something incriminating has been found. We cannot, therefore, regard it as a depar-

---

[1]   The common law provides actions for damages against the searching officer; against one who procures the issuance of a warrant maliciously and without probable cause; against a magistrate who has acted without jurisdiction in issuing a warrant; and against persons assisting in the execution of an illegal search. One may also without liability use force to resist an unlawful search. Statutory sanctions provide for the punishment of one maliciously procuring a search warrant or willfully exceeding his authority in exercising it. Some statutes more broadly penalize unlawful searches. Virginia also makes punishable one who issues a general search warrant or a warrant unsupported by affidavit. A few States have provided statutory civil remedies. And in one State, misuse of a search warrant may be an abuse of process punishable as contempt of court.

ture from basic standards to remand such persons, together with those who emerge scatheless from a search, to the remedies of private action and such protection as the internal discipline of the police, under the eyes of an alert public opinion, may afford. Granting that in practice the exclusion of evidence may be an effective way of deterring unreasonable searches, it is not for this Court to condemn as falling below the minimal standards assured by the Due Process Clause a State's reliance upon other methods which, if consistently enforced, would be equally effective. We cannot brush aside the experience of States which deem the incidence of such conduct by the police too slight to call for a deterrent remedy not by way of disciplinary measures but by overriding the relevant rules of evidence. There are, moreover, reasons for excluding evidence unreasonably obtained by the federal police which are less compelling in the case of police under State or local authority. The public opinion of a community can far more effectively be exerted against oppressive conduct on the part of police directly responsible to the community itself than can local opinion, sporadically aroused, be brought to bear upon remote authority pervasively exerted throughout the country.

We hold, therefore, that in a prosecution in a State court for a State crime the Fourteenth Amendment does not forbid the admission of evidence obtained by an unreasonable search and seizure.

Affirmed.

MR. JUSTICE BLACK, concurring.

The federal exclusionary rule is not a command of the Fourth Amendment but is a judicially created rule of evidence which Congress might negate.

MR. JUSTICE RUTLEDGE, dissenting.

I reject the conclusion that the mandate embodied in the Fourth Amendment, although binding on the states, does not carry with it the one sanction—exclusion of evidence taken in violation of the Amendment's terms—failure to observe which means that "the protection of the 4th Amendment might as well be stricken from the Constitution." *Weeks v. United States*, 232 U.S. 383. The Amendment without the sanction is a dead letter. Twenty-nine years ago this Court, speaking through Justice Holmes, refused to permit the Government to subpoena documentary evidence which it had stolen, copied and then returned, for the reason that such a procedure "reduces the Fourth Amendment to a form of words." *Silverthorne Lumber Co. v. United States*, 251 U.S. 385, 392. But the version of the Fourth Amendment today held applicable to the states hardly rises to the dignity of a form of words; at best it is a pale and frayed carbon copy of the original, bearing little resemblance to the Amendment the fulfillment of whose command I had heretofore thought to be "an indispensable need for a democratic society." The view that the Fourth Amendment itself forbids the introduction of evidence illegally obtained in federal prosecutions is one of long standing and firmly established. It is too late in my judgment to question it now.

MR. JUSTICE MURPHY, with whom MR. JUSTICE RUTLEDGE joins, dissenting.

There is but one alternative to the rule of exclusion. That is no sanction at all. This has been perfectly clear since 1914, when a unanimous Court decided *Weeks*. "If letters and private documents can be seized and held and used in evidence against a citizen accused of an offense," we said, "the protection of the 4th Amendment, declaring his right to be secure against such searches and seizures, is of no value, and might as well be stricken from the Constitution." "It would reduce the Fourth Amendment to a form of words." Holmes, J., for the Court, in *Silverthorne Lumber Co. v. United States*, 251 U.S. 385. Today the Court wipes those statements from the books with this bland citation of "other remedies." Little need be said concerning the possibilities of criminal prosecution. Self-scrutiny is a lofty ideal, but its exaltation reaches new heights if we expect a District Attorney to prosecute himself or his associates for well-meaning violations of the search and seizure clause during a raid the District Attorney or his associates have ordered. A trespass action for damages is a venerable means of securing reparation for unauthorized invasion of the home. But what an illusory remedy this is, if by "remedy" we mean a positive deterrent to police and prosecutors tempted to violate the Fourth Amendment. The measure of damages is simply the extent of the injury to physical property. If the officer searches with care, he can avoid all but nominal damages. Are punitive damages possible? Perhaps. But a few states permit none, whatever the circumstances. In those that do, the plaintiff must show malice, and surely it is not unreasonable to assume that one in honest pursuit of crime bears no malice toward the search victim. If that burden is carried, recovery may be defeated by the rule that there must be physical damages before punitive damages may be awarded. In addition, some states limit punitive damages to the actual expenses of litigation. Others demand some arbitrary ratio between actual and punitive damages. Even assuming the ill will of the officer, his reasonable grounds for belief that the home he searched harbored evidence of crime is admissible in mitigation of punitive damages. The bad reputation of the plaintiff is likewise admissible. If the evidence seized was actually used at a trial, that fact has been held a complete justification of the search, and a defense against the trespass action. And even if the plaintiff hurdles all these obstacles, and gains a substantial verdict, the individual officer's finances may well make the judgment useless—for the municipality, of course, is not liable without its consent. Is it surprising that there is so little in the books concerning trespass actions for violation of the search and seizure clause?

One remedy exists to deter violations of the search and seizure clause. That is the rule which excludes illegally obtained evidence. Only by exclusion can we impress upon the zealous prosecutor that violation of the Constitution will do him no good. Only when that point is driven home can the prosecutor be expected to emphasize the importance of observing constitutional demands in his instructions to the police. If proof of the efficacy of the federal rule were needed, there is testimony in abundance in the recruit training programs and in-service courses provided the police in states which follow the federal rule. This is an area in which judicial action has positive effect upon the breach of law; and without judicial action, there are simply no effective sanctions. Today's decision will do inestimable harm to the cause of fair police methods in our cities and states. Even more important, it must have tragic effect upon public respect for our judiciary. The Court now allows what is indeed shabby business: lawlessness by officers of the law. Since the evidence admitted was secured in violation of the Fourth Amendment, the judgment should be reversed.

Points for Discussion

a.   Section 1983 Actions

Are there other, more effective, remedies for Fourth Amendment violations? For example, would the § 1983 remedy provide an effective deterrent for police misconduct? That statute provides as follows: "Every person who, under color of any statute, ordinance, regulation, custom or usage, of any State or Territory, subjects, or causes to be subjected, any citizen of the United States or other person within the jurisdiction thereof to the deprivation of any rights, privileges, or immunities secured by the Constitution and laws, shall be liable to the party injured in an action at law, suit in equity, or other proper proceeding for redress." It is difficult to recover under § 1983 when the governing law is uncertain. *Monroe v. Pape*, 365 U.S. 167 (1961), construed § 1983 as applicable to suits against individual governmental officials. However, in *Pierson v. Ray*, 386 U.S. 547 (1967), the Court held that police officers are protected by qualified immunity "if they act in good faith and with probable cause in making an arrest under a statute that they believe to be valid." In *Gomez v. Toledo*, 446 U.S. 635 (1980), the Court held that defendant has the burden of proving qualified immunity in a 1983 action.

b.   *Bivens* Actions

Since § 1983 actions are generally unavailable when the offending official is a federal agent or employee, suits against such officials are often based directly on the Constitution itself. These so-called "*Bivens*" actions, named for the holding in *Bivens v. Six Unknown Named Agents*, 403 U.S. 388 (1971), are claims based directly on the Fourth Amendment itself: "It is well settled that where legal rights have been invaded, and a federal statute provides for general right to sue for such invasion, federal courts may use any available remedy to make good the wrong done." In *Carlson v. Green*, 446 U.S. 14 (1980), the Court held that the availability of relief under the Federal Tort Claims Act did not bar a *Bivens* action. Finally, in *Anderson v. Creighton*, 483 U.S. 635 (1987), the Court imposed a good faith defense in *Bivens* actions which provided that "a federal law enforcement officer may not be held personally liable for money damages if a reasonable officer could have believed that the search comported with the Fourth Amendment."

FYI

In *Ziglar v. Abbasi*, 137 S.Ct. 1843 (2017), the Court limited *Bivens'* scope. Following the 9/11 terrorist attacks, the U.S. Government took hundreds of illegal aliens into custody, and allegedly subjected them to harsh prison conditions (*e.g.,* lights were left on in detainees' cells 24 hours a day, the cells were tiny, detainees were not given basic hygiene procedures, were allowed virtually no exercise or recreation, and were subjected to physical abuse). When plaintiffs sued, not only under *Bivens* but under a federal statute, the Court noted that it had become cautious about extending *Bivens'* actions because of separation of powers concerns. Indeed, the Court emphasized that it has refused to expand *Bivens* over the last thirty years. The Court deferred to Congress, noting that, in "most instances, the Legislature is in the better position to decide whether the public interest would be served by imposing a new substantive legal liability," and suggested that the courts should hesitate to act "in the absence of affirmative action by Congress." The Court was moved by the potential impact of *Bivens* actions on all aspects of government, including the impact of such suits on Government employees who are sued personally, as well as the projected costs and consequences to the Government itself when the tort and monetary liability mechanisms of the legal system are used to bring about the proper formulation and implementation of public policies." As a result, the Court did not view *Bivens* actions as "a proper vehicle for altering an entity's policy," or for holding officers responsible for the acts of their subordinates. In addition, the Court was worried that "the discovery and litigation process would either border upon or directly implicate the discussion and deliberations that led to the formation of the policy in question," and they have shown deference to what the Executive Branch has determined is "essential to national security." The Court held that the detainees had other means for challenging the conditions of their confinement. Likewise, in *Hernandez v. Mesa*, 885 F.3d 811 (5th Cir. 2018), the Court refused to extend *Bivens* to a suit by the parents of a 15 year-old boy who was killed by border patrol agents who shot across the border into Mexico. Even though no federal statute authorized such a trans-national cause of action, the Court refused to extend *Bivens* to this situation, concluding that to do so "would interfere with the political branches' oversight of national security and foreign affairs."

c. The Possibility of Injunctive Relief

The injunctive remedy might seem particularly appropriate when the police have engaged in a pattern of misconduct. However, in *Rizzo v. Goode*, 423 U.S. 362 (1976), the Court imposed significant barriers to injunctive relief against police officials. That case involved a claim that the police had

Food for Thought

Given the limitations, do *Bivens* actions against federal officials, coupled with § 1983 actions against state officials, provide an effective remedy?

engaged in an "assertedly pervasive pattern of illegal and unconstitutional mistreatment" against "minority citizens in particular and against all Philadelphia residents in general." Plaintiffs presented 250 witnesses who described some 40-odd incidents. The trial court ordered petitioners to draft "a comprehensive program for dealing adequately with civilian complaints" for its approval. The Supreme Court concluded that injunctive relief was inappropriate:

> We doubt whether an Art. III case or controversy exists. In *O'Shea v. Littleton*, 414 U.S. 488 (1974), plaintiffs alleged that a county magistrate and judge, had embarked on a continuing, intentional practice of racially discriminatory bond setting, sentencing, and assessing of jury fees. No specific instances involving the individual respondents were set forth in the prayer for injunctive relief. Even though some of the named respondents had in fact "suffered from the alleged unconstitutional practices," the Court concluded that "past exposure to illegal conduct does not in itself show a present case or controversy regarding injunctive relief, however, if unaccompanied by any continuing, present adverse effects." The Court further recognized that while "past wrongs are evidence bearing on whether there is a real and immediate threat of repeated injury," the attempt to anticipate under what circumstances the respondents there would be made to appear in the future before petitioners "takes us into the area of speculation and conjecture." These observations apply here with even more force, for the individual respondents' claim to "real and immediate" injury rests not upon what the named petitioners might do to them in the future such as set a bond on the basis of race but upon what one of a small, unnamed minority of policemen might do to them in the future because of that unknown policeman's perception of departmental disciplinary procedures. This hypothesis is even more attenuated than those allegations of future injury found insufficient in *O'Shea* to warrant invocation of federal jurisdiction. Thus, insofar as the individual respondents were concerned, we think they lacked the requisite "personal stake in the outcome"; *i.e.,* the order overhauling police disciplinary procedures. Considerations of federalism are additional factors weighing against the granting of relief. The District Court's injunctive order here, significantly revising the internal procedures of the Philadelphia police department, was indisputably a sharp limitation on the department's "latitude in the 'dispatch of its own internal affairs.' " Principles of federalism also have applicability where injunctive relief is sought, not against the judicial branch of the state government, but against those in charge of an executive branch of an agency of state or local governments such as petitioners here.

Hypo 1: *The Serial Murderer*

Serial murders are committed in the New Orleans area. The police search for the murderer, trying to find him before he kills again. Weeks pass, more murders occur, and still the murderer has not been found. The police suspect Yoplait of the crimes, but do not have probable cause to arrest him. In a desperate attempt to solve the crime and prevent further murders, the police illegally search Yoplait's apartment (the police lack both a search warrant and probable cause), and find conclusive evidence of Yoplait's involvement in the murders (Yoplait liked to keep gory pictures of the people he killed). Suppose that, under *Wolf*, the exclusionary rule does not apply in state court proceedings. Does Yoplait have adequate alternative remedies available to him? Consider the following possibilities:

A) Suppose that Yoplait brings a civil suit against <u>the police officers</u> claiming that the police officers trespassed, as well as that they converted his property. If Yoplait prevails, is a jury likely to give him a large damage award?

B) Of course, it is possible for the jury to award punitive damages. Is the jury likely to award punitive damages against the police in a case like this?

C) Public opinion can provide a powerful deterrent to police misconduct. Is the public likely to rise up in outrage over the illegal search?

D) Is the prosecutor likely to criminally prosecute the police for this illegal search (or, for that matter, is the police disciplinary board likely to bring disciplinary charges)?

Hypo 2: *More on the Serial Murderer*

In thinking about the prior hypo, would you answer the questions differently if the evidence showed a pervasive pattern of police misconduct? Suppose that there is evidence that New Orleans police routinely violate citizens' civil rights by illegally stopping motorists, "roughing them up," and illegally searching cars. Suppose that a motorist brings a civil suit against the police officers claiming intentional violations of his rights (e.g., assault, battery, kidnapping). Consider the following avenues for relief: a) damages in a tort action; b) punitive damages; c) public opinion; d) criminal prosecution of the offending police. Are any of these remedies likely to provide an effective deterrent to police misconduct?

Hypo 3: *The Innocent Suspect*

Now, let's consider one more scenario. Suppose that the police intentionally search someone's home without a warrant or probable cause. Would it matter that the subject of the search was innocent, and that the police were completely mistaken about the subject's involvement in criminal activity? For example, suppose that the police illegally search a medical doctor's home believing that he is involved in illicit drug trafficking. The police are in error about this fact because, while listening to a wiretap, they *thought* they heard a reference to the doctor. Are the following remedies likely to be effective for this violation: a) Civil suit for damages? b) Punitive damages? c) Public opinion? d) Criminal prosecution? e) Disciplinary sanctions?

Mapp v. Ohio

367 U.S. 643 (1961).

MR. JUSTICE CLARK delivered the opinion of the Court.

Appellant was convicted of possession of lewd and lascivious books, pictures, and photographs in violation of Ohio law. The Supreme Court of Ohio upheld the conviction though "based upon evidence seized during an unlawful search of defendant's home." The State says that even if the search were made without authority, or otherwise unreasonably, it is not prevented from using the unconstitutionally seized evidence at trial, citing *Wolf v. People of State of Colorado.*, 338 U.S. 25 (1949). Prior to *Wolf*, almost two-thirds of the States were opposed to the use of the exclusionary rule, now, despite *Wolf*, more than half, by their own legislative or judicial decision, have wholly or partly adopted or adhered to the *Weeks* rule. Significantly, among those now following the rule is California, which, according to its highest court, was "compelled to reach that conclusion because other remedies have completely failed to secure compliance with the constitutional provisions." *People v. Cahan*, 1955, 282 P.2d 905. *Wolf* concluded that "other means of protection" have been afforded "the right to privacy." The experience of California that such other remedies have been worthless and futile is buttressed by the experience of other States. The obvious futility

772 CRIMINAL PROCEDURE: INVESTIGATIVE A Contemporary Approach

of relegating the Fourth Amendment to the protection of other remedies has been recognized by this Court since *Wolf*. Likewise, time has set its face against what *Wolf* called the "weighty testimony" of *People v. Defore*, 1926, 150 N.E. 585. There Justice (then Judge) Cardozo, rejecting adoption of the *Weeks* exclusionary rule in New York, said that "the Federal rule as it stands is either too strict or too lax." The force of that reasoning has been largely vitiated by later decisions of this Court. It plainly appears that the factual considerations supporting the failure of the *Wolf* Court to include the *Weeks* exclusionary rule when it recognized the enforceability of the right to privacy against the States in 1949, while not basically relevant to the constitutional consideration, could not, in any analysis, now be deemed controlling.

Today we again examine *Wolf*'s constitutional documentation of the right to privacy free from unreasonable state intrusion, and close the only courtroom door remaining open to evidence secured by official lawlessness in flagrant abuse of that basic right, reserved to all persons as a specific guarantee against that very same unlawful conduct. We hold that all evidence obtained by searches and seizures in violation of the Constitution is, by that same authority, inadmissible in a state court. Since the Fourth Amendment's right of privacy has been declared enforceable against the States through the Due Process Clause of the Fourteenth, it is enforceable by the same sanction of exclusion as is used against the Federal Government. Were it otherwise, the assurance against unreasonable federal searches and seizures would be "a form of words", valueless and undeserving of mention in a perpetual charter of inestimable human liberties and the freedom from state invasions of privacy would be so ephemeral and so neatly severed from its conceptual nexus with the freedom from all brutish means of coercing evidence as not to merit this Court's high regard as a freedom "implicit in the concept of ordered liberty." At the time that the Court held in *Wolf* that the Amendment was applicable to the States through the Due Process Clause, cases had steadfastly held that as to federal officers the Fourth Amendment included the exclusion of the evidence seized in violation of its provisions. In extending the substantive protections of due process to all constitutionally unreasonable searches—state or federal—it was logically and constitutionally necessary that the exclusion doctrine—an essential part of the right to privacy—be also insisted upon as an essential ingredient of the right newly recognized by the *Wolf* case. The admission of the new constitutional right could not consistently tolerate denial of its most important constitutional privilege, namely, the exclusion of the evidence which an accused had been forced to give by reason of the unlawful seizure. To hold otherwise is to grant the right but in reality to withhold its privilege and enjoyment. Only last year the Court itself recognized that the purpose of the exclusionary rule "is to deter—to compel respect for the constitutional guaranty in the only effectively available way—by removing the incentive to disregard it." *Elkins v. United States*, 364 U.S. 206, 217 (1960).

We are aware of no restraint, similar to that rejected today, conditioning the enforcement of any other basic constitutional right. The right to privacy, no less

CHAPTER 8 *The Exclusionary Rule*

important than any other right carefully and particularly reserved to the people, would stand in marked contrast to all other rights declared as "basic to a free society." This Court has not hesitated to enforce as strictly against the States the rights of free speech and of a free press, the rights to notice and to a fair, public trial, including the right not to be convicted by use of a coerced confession, however logically relevant it be, and without regard to its reliability. Nothing could be more certain than that when a coerced confession is involved, "the relevant rules of evidence" are overridden without regard to "the incidence of such conduct by the police." Why should not the same rule apply to what is tantamount to coerced testimony by way of unconstitutional seizure of goods, papers, effect, documents, etc.? As to the Federal Government, the Fourth and Fifth Amendments and, as to the States, the freedom from unconscionable invasions of privacy and the freedom from convictions based upon coerced confessions do enjoy an "intimate relation" in their perpetuation of "principles of humanity and civil liberty secured only after years of struggle." *Bram v. United States,* 1897, 168 U.S. 532. They express "supplementing phases of the same constitutional purpose—to maintain inviolate large areas of personal privacy." *Feldman v. United States,* 1944, 322 U.S. 487. The philosophy of each Amendment and of each freedom is complementary to, although not dependent upon, that of the other in its sphere of influence—the very least that together they assure in either sphere is that no man is to be convicted on unconstitutional evidence.

Our holding that the exclusionary rule is an essential part of both the Fourth and Fourteenth Amendments is not only the logical dictate of prior cases, it also makes very good sense. There is no war between the Constitution and common sense. Presently, a federal prosecutor may make no use of evidence illegally seized, but a State's attorney across the street may, although he supposedly is operating under the enforceable prohibitions of the same Amendment. Thus the State, by admitting evidence unlawfully seized, serves to encourage disobedience to the Federal Constitution which it is bound to uphold. In non-exclusionary States, federal officers, being human, were invited to and did step across the street to the State's attorney with their unconstitutionally seized evidence. Prosecution on the basis of that evidence was then had in a state court in utter disregard of the enforceable Fourth Amendment. If the fruits of an unconstitutional search had been inadmissible in both state and federal courts, this inducement to evasion would have been sooner eliminated. Federal-state cooperation in the solution of crime under constitutional standards will be promoted, if only by recognition of their now mutual obligation to respect the same fundamental criteria in their approaches. Denying shortcuts to only one of two cooperating law enforcement agencies tends naturally to breed legitimate suspicion of "working arrangements" whose results are equally tainted.

There are those who say, as did Justice (then Judge) Cardozo, that under our constitutional exclusionary doctrine "the criminal is to go free because the constable has blundered." *People v. Defore,* 150 N.E. at page 587. In some cases this will undoubtedly be the result. But, as was said in *Elkins,* "there is another consideration—the imperative of judicial integrity." The criminal goes free, if he must, but it is the law that sets him free. Nothing can destroy a government more quickly than its failure to observe its own laws, or worse, its disregard of the charter of its own existence. As Mr. Justice Brandeis, dissenting, said in *Olmstead v. United States*, 1928, 277 U.S. 438: "Our government is the potent, the omnipresent teacher. For good or for ill, it teaches the whole people by its example. If the government becomes a lawbreaker, it breeds contempt for law; it invites every man to become a law unto himself; it invites anarchy." Nor can it lightly be assumed that, as a practical matter, adoption of the exclusionary rule fetters law enforcement. In *Elkins v. United States*, 364 U.S. at page 218, the Court noted that "The federal courts have operated under the exclusionary rule of *Weeks* for almost half a century; yet it has not been suggested either that the Federal Bureau of Investigation has thereby been rendered ineffective, or that the administration of criminal justice in the federal courts has thereby been disrupted. Moreover, the experience of the states is impressive. The movement towards the rule of exclusion has been halting but seemingly inexorable."

The ignoble shortcut to conviction left open to the State tends to destroy the entire system of constitutional restraints on which the liberties of the people rest. Having recognized that the right to privacy embodied in the Fourth Amendment is enforceable against the States, and that the right to be secure against rude invasions of privacy by state officers is constitutional in origin, we can no longer permit that right to remain an empty promise. Because it is enforceable in the same manner and to like effect as other basic rights secured by the Due Process Clause, we can no longer permit it to be revocable at the whim of any police officer who chooses to suspend its enjoyment. Our decision, founded on reason and truth, gives to the individual no more than that which the Constitution guarantees him, to the police officer no less than that to which honest law enforcement is entitled, and, to the courts, that judicial integrity so necessary in the true administration of justice.

The judgment of the Supreme Court of Ohio is reversed and the cause remanded for further proceedings not inconsistent with this opinion.

Reversed and remanded.

Mr. Justice Black, concurring.

The Fourth Amendment, standing alone, would not be enough to bar the introduction into evidence against an accused of papers and effects seized from him in violation of its commands. For the Fourth Amendment does not itself contain any provision expressly precluding the use of such evidence, and I am extremely doubtful that such a provision could properly be inferred from nothing more than the basic command against unreasonable searches and seizures. When the Fourth Amendment's ban against unreasonable searches and seizures is considered together with the Fifth

Amendment's ban against compelled self-incrimination, a constitutional basis emerges which not only justifies but actually requires the exclusionary rule. In *Boyd v. United States*, the Court declared itself "unable to perceive that the seizure of a man's private books and papers to be used in evidence against him is substantially different from compelling him to be a witness against himself."

Mr. Justice Douglas, concurring.

The facts of this case show—as would few other cases—the casual arrogance of those who have the untrammeled power to invade one's home and to seize one's person.

Mr. Justice Harlan, whom Mr. Justice Frankfurter and Mr. Justice Whittaker join, dissenting.

I would not impose upon the States this federal exclusionary remedy. It is said that "the factual grounds upon which *Wolf* was based" have since changed, in that more States now follow the *Weeks* exclusionary rule. While that is true, one-half of the States still adhere to the common-law non-exclusionary rule. The preservation of a proper balance between state and federal responsibility in the administration of criminal justice demands patience on the part of those who might like to see things move faster. Problems of criminal law enforcement vary widely from State to State. One State may conclude that the need for embracing the *Weeks* rule is pressing because other remedies are unavailable or inadequate to secure compliance with the substantive Constitutional principle involved. Another, though equally solicitous of Constitutional rights, may choose to pursue one purpose at a time, allowing all evidence relevant to guilt to be brought into a criminal trial, and dealing with Constitutional infractions by other means. This Court should continue to forbear from fettering the States with an adamant rule in criminal law enforcement.

In *Weeks*, in implementing the Fourth Amendment, we occupied the position of a tribunal having the ultimate responsibility for developing the standards and procedures of judicial administration within the judicial system over which it presides. Here we review state procedures whose measure is to be taken not against the specific substantive commands of the Fourth Amendment but under the flexible contours of the Due Process Clause. I do not believe that the Fourteenth Amendment empowers this Court to mold state remedies effectuating the right to freedom from "arbitrary intrusion by the police."

In requiring exclusion of an involuntary statement of an accused, we are concerned not with an appropriate remedy for what the police have done, but with something which is regarded as going to the heart of our concepts of fairness in judicial procedure. "Ours is the accusatorial as opposed to the inquisitorial system."

Watts v. State of Indiana, 338 U.S. 49. The trial defense to which an accused is entitled should not be rendered an empty formality by reason of statements wrung from him, for then "a prisoner has been made the deluded instrument of his own conviction." 2 HAWKINS, PLEAS OF THE CROWN (8th ed., 1824), c. 46, § 34. The coerced confession analogy works strongly against what the Court does today. This Court can increase respect for the Constitution only if it rigidly respects the limitations which the Constitution places upon it, and respects as well the principles inherent in its own processes. In the present case we exceed both, and our voice becomes only a voice of power, not of reason.

Point for Discussion

The Exclusionary Rule in Forfeiture Proceedings

In *One 1958 Plymouth Sedan v. Commonwealth of Pennsylvania*, 380 U.S. 693 (1965), the Court applied the exclusionary rule to a forfeiture proceeding because of the "quasi-criminal" nature of that proceeding. That case involved the forfeiture of an automobile found to be carrying liquor without Pennsylvania tax seals.

Food for Thought

Consider then Chief Justice Burger's dissent in *Bivens v. Six Unknown Named Agents*, 403 U.S. 388 (1971):

Rejection of evidence does nothing to punish the wrong-doing official, while it may, and likely will, release the wrong-doing defendant. It deprives society of its remedy against one lawbreaker because he has been pursued by another. It protects one against whom incriminating evidence is discovered, but does nothing to protect innocent persons who are the victims of illegal but fruitless searches. Instead of continuing to enforce the suppression doctrine inflexibly, rigidly, and mechanically, we should discontinue what the experience of over half a century has shown neither deters errant officers nor affords a remedy to the totally innocent victims of official misconduct. I do not propose that we abandon the suppression doctrine until some meaningful alternative can be developed. The public interest would be poorly served if law enforcement officials were suddenly to gain the impression that all constitutional restraints on police had somehow been removed—that an open season on "criminals" had been declared. The problems of both error and deliberate misconduct by law enforcement officials call for a workable remedy. Private damage actions against individual police officers concededly have not adequately met this requirement.

An entirely different remedy is necessary but it is beyond judicial power. Congress should develop an administrative or quasi-judicial remedy against the government itself to afford compensation and restitution for persons whose Fourth Amendment rights have been violated. The venerable doctrine of respondeat superior in our tort law provides an entirely appropriate conceptual basis for this remedy. Such a statutory scheme would have the added advantage of providing some remedy to the completely innocent persons who are sometimes the victims of illegal police conduct—something that the suppression doctrine, of course, can never accomplish. A simple structure would suffice. Congress could enact a statute along the following lines: a) a waiver of sovereign immunity as to the illegal acts of law enforcement officials committed in the performance of assigned duties; b) the creation of a cause of action for damages sustained by any person aggrieved by conduct of governmental agents in violation of the Fourth Amendment or statutes regulating official conduct; c) the creation of a tribunal, quasi judicial in nature or perhaps patterned after the United States Court of Claims to adjudicate all claims under the statute; d) a provision that this statutory remedy is in lieu of the exclusion of evidence; and (e) a provision directing that no evidence, otherwise admissible, shall be excluded from any criminal proceeding because of violation of the Fourth Amendment. I doubt that lawyers serving on such a tribunal would be swayed either by undue sympathy for officers or by the prejudice against "criminals" that has sometimes moved lay jurors to deny claims. In addition to awarding damages, the record of the police conduct would become a relevant part of an officer's personnel file so that the need for additional training or disciplinary action could be identified or his future usefulness as a public official evaluated. Finally, appellate judicial review could be made available on much the same basis that it is now provided as to district courts and regulatory agencies. This would leave to the courts the ultimate responsibility for determining and articulating standards. Once the constitutional validity of such a statute is established, it can reasonably be assumed that the States would develop their own remedial systems on the federal model. Steps along these lines would move our system toward more responsible law enforcement on the one hand and away from the irrational and drastic results of the suppression doctrine on the other.

Does Chief Justice Burger's proposal make sense? Is it a better alternative?

B. Modern Decisions Construing the Scope of the Exclusionary Rule

Because of the perceived "costs" associated with the exclusionary rule (*i.e.*, the loss of evidence, the reversal of convictions, and the difficulty of convicting without suppressed evidence), some police and law enforcement officials have pressed for limitations on the exclusionary rule. One suggested limitation involves the so-called "good faith" exception to the exclusionary rule.

United States v. Leon

468 U.S. 897 (1984).

JUSTICE WHITE delivered the opinion of the Court.

The Fourth Amendment contains no provision expressly precluding the use of evidence obtained in violation of its commands, and an examination of its origin and purposes makes clear that the use of fruits of a past unlawful search or seizure "works no new Fourth Amendment wrong." *United States v. Calandra,* 414 U.S. 338 (1974). The wrong condemned by the Amendment is "fully accomplished" by the unlawful search or seizure itself, and the exclusionary rule is neither intended nor able to "cure the invasion of the defendant's rights which he has already suffered." *Stone v. Powell,* 428 U.S. 465, 540 (1976) (White, J., dissenting). The rule thus operates as "a judicially created remedy designed to safeguard Fourth Amendment rights generally through its deterrent effect, rather than a personal constitutional right of the party aggrieved." *United States v. Calandra,* 414 U.S. at 348. Whether the exclusionary sanction is appropriately imposed in a particular case is "an issue separate from the question whether the Fourth Amendment rights of the party seeking to invoke the rule were violated by police conduct." Only the former question is currently before us, and it must be resolved by weighing the costs and benefits of preventing the use in the prosecution's case in chief of inherently trustworthy tangible evidence obtained in reliance on a search warrant issued by a detached and neutral magistrate that ultimately is found to be defective. The substantial social costs exacted by the exclusionary rule have long been a source of concern. "Unbending application of the exclusionary sanction to enforce ideals of governmental rectitude would impede unacceptably the truth-finding functions of judge and jury." *United States v. Payner,* 447 U.S. 727 (1980). An objectionable collateral consequence is that some guilty defendants may go free or receive reduced sentences as a result of favorable plea bargains.[6] Particularly when law enforcement officers have acted in objective good faith or their transgressions have been minor, the magnitude of the benefit conferred on guilty defendants offends basic concepts of the criminal justice system. Indiscriminate application of the exclusionary rule may well "generate disrespect for the law and administration of justice." "As with any remedial device, application of the rule has been restricted to those areas where its remedial objectives are thought most efficaciously served." *United States v. Calandra,* 414 U.S., at 348. Close attention to those remedial objectives has characterized our recent decisions concerning the scope of the Fourth Amendment exclusionary rule. The Court has not seriously questioned, "in the absence of a more efficacious sanction, the continued application of the rule to suppress evidence from the prosecution's case where a Fourth Amendment violation has been substantial and deliberate." *Franks v. Delaware,* 438 U.S. 154 (1978). Nevertheless, the balancing approach "forcefully suggests that the exclusionary rule be modified to permit the introduction of evidence obtained in the reasonable good-faith belief that a search or seizure was in accord with the Fourth Amendment." *Illinois v. Gates,* 462 U.S. 213, 255 (1983) (White, J.,

---

[6]   One study suggests that the rule results in the nonprosecution or nonconviction of between 0.6% and 2.35% of individuals arrested for felonies. The estimates are higher for crimes which depends heavily on physical evidence. Thus, the loss of felony drug charges is probably in the range of 2.8% to 7.1%. Many researchers have concluded that the impact of the exclusionary rule is insubstantial, but the small percentages mask a large absolute number of felons who are released. "Any rule of evidence that denies the jury access to clearly probative and reliable evidence must bear a heavy burden of justification, and must be carefully limited to the circumstances in which it will pay its way by deterring official unlawlessness." *Illinois v. Gates,* 462 U.S. 213, 257 (1983) (White, J., concurring). Because the rule can have no substantial deterrent effect in the situations under consideration in this case, it cannot pay its way in those situations.

concurring). In *Stone v. Powell*, the Court emphasized the costs of the exclusionary rule, expressed its view that limiting the circumstances under which Fourth Amendment claims could be raised in federal *habeas corpus* proceedings would not reduce the rule's deterrent effect, and held that a state prisoner who has been afforded a full and fair opportunity to litigate a Fourth Amendment claim may not obtain federal *habeas* relief on the ground that unlawfully obtained evidence had been introduced at his trial. Proposed extensions of the exclusionary rule to proceedings other than the criminal trial itself have been evaluated and rejected under the same analytic approach. In *Calandra*, we declined to allow grand jury witnesses to refuse to answer questions based on evidence obtained from an unlawful search or seizure since "any incremental deterrent effect which might be achieved by extending the rule to grand jury proceedings is uncertain at best." Similarly, in *United States v. Janis*, 428 U.S. 433 (1976), we permitted the use in federal civil proceedings of evidence illegally seized by state officials since the likelihood of deterring police misconduct through such an extension of the exclusionary rule was insufficient to outweigh its substantial social costs. In so doing, we declared that, "if the exclusionary rule does not result in appreciable deterrence, then, clearly, its use in the instant situation is unwarranted." It does not follow from the emphasis on the exclusionary rule's deterrent value that "anything which deters illegal searches is thereby commanded by the Fourth Amendment." In determining whether persons aggrieved solely by the introduction of damaging evidence unlawfully obtained from their co-conspirators or co-defendants could seek suppression, for example, we found that the additional benefits of such an extension of the exclusionary rule would not outweigh its costs. Standing to invoke the rule has thus been limited to cases in which the prosecution seeks to use the fruits of an illegal search or seizure against the victim of police misconduct. Even defendants with standing to challenge the introduction in their criminal trials of unlawfully obtained evidence cannot prevent every conceivable use of such evidence. Evidence obtained in violation of the Fourth Amendment and inadmissible in the prosecution's case in chief may be used to impeach a defendant's direct testimony. A similar assessment of the "incremental furthering" of the ends of the exclusionary rule led us to conclude in *United States v. Havens*, 446 U.S. 620 (1980), that evidence may be used to impeach statements made by a defendant in response to "proper cross-examination reasonably suggested by the defendant's direct examination." When considering the use of evidence obtained in violation of the Fourth Amendment in the prosecution's case in chief, we have declined to adopt a *per se* or "but for" rule that would render inadmissible any evidence that came to light through a chain of causation that began with an illegal arrest. We also have held that a witness' testimony may be admitted even when his identity was discovered in an unconstitutional search. The perception underlying these decisions—that the connection between police misconduct and evidence of crime may be sufficiently attenuated to permit the use of that evidence at trial—is a product of considerations relating to the exclusionary rule and the constitutional principles it is designed to protect.[7] In view of this purpose, an assessment of the flagrancy of the police misconduct constitutes an important step in the calculus.

We have not recognized any form of good-faith exception to the Fourth Amendment exclusionary rule. But the balancing approach that has evolved during the years of experience with the rule provides strong support for the modification currently urged upon us. Because a search warrant "provides the detached scrutiny of a neutral magistrate, which is a more reliable safeguard against improper searches than the hurried judgment of a law enforcement officer 'engaged in the often competitive enterprise of ferreting out crime,' " we have expressed a strong preference for warrants and declared that "in a doubtful or marginal case a search under a warrant may be sustainable where without one it would fall." *United States v. Ventresca*, 380 U.S. 102 (1965). Reasonable minds may differ on the question whether a particular affidavit establishes probable cause, and the preference for warrants is most appropriately effectuated by according "great deference" to a magistrate's determination. Deference to the magistrate, however, is not boundless. The deference accorded to a magistrate's finding of probable cause does not preclude inquiry into the knowing or reckless falsity of the affidavit on which that determination was based. The courts must also insist that the magistrate purport to "perform his 'neutral and detached' function and not serve merely as a rubber stamp for the police." A magistrate failing to "manifest that neutrality and detachment demanded of a judicial officer when presented with a warrant application" and who acts instead as "an adjunct law enforcement officer" cannot provide valid authorization for an otherwise unconstitutional search. Reviewing courts will not defer to a warrant based on an affidavit that does not "provide the magistrate with a substantial basis for determining the existence of probable cause." Even if the warrant application was supported by more than a "bare bones" affidavit, a reviewing court may properly conclude that, notwithstanding the deference that magistrates deserve, the warrant was invalid because the magistrate's probable-cause determination reflected an improper analysis of the totality of the circumstances, or because the form of the warrant was improper in some respect.

Only in the first of these three situations has the Court set forth a rationale for suppressing evidence obtained pursuant to a search warrant; in the other areas, it has simply excluded such evidence without considering whether Fourth Amendment interests will be advanced. To the extent that proponents of exclusion rely on its behavioral effects on judges and magistrates in these areas, their reliance is misplaced. First, the exclusionary rule is designed to deter police misconduct rather than to punish the errors of judges and magistrates. Second, there exists no evidence suggesting that judges and magistrates are inclined to ignore or subvert the Fourth Amendment or that lawlessness among these actors requires application of the extreme sanction of

---

[7]   Where there is a close causal connection between the illegal seizure and the confession, not only is exclusion of the evidence more likely to deter similar police misconduct, but the evidence is more likely to compromise the integrity of the courts." *Dunaway v. New York* 442 U.S. 200, 217 (1979).

exclusion. Third, we discern no basis for believing that exclusion of evidence seized pursuant to a warrant will have a significant deterrent effect on the issuing judge or magistrate. Many of the factors that indicate that the exclusionary rule cannot provide an effective "special" or "general" deterrent for individual offending law enforcement officers apply as well to judges or magistrates. To the extent that the rule is thought to operate as a "systemic" deterrent, it can have no such effect on individuals empowered to issue search warrants. Judges and magistrates are not adjuncts to the law enforcement team; as neutral judicial officers, they have no stake in the outcome of particular criminal prosecutions. The threat of exclusion cannot significantly deter them. Imposition of the exclusionary sanction is not necessary meaningfully to inform judicial officers of their errors, and we cannot conclude that admitting evidence obtained pursuant to a warrant while at the same time declaring that the warrant was somehow defective will in any way reduce judicial officers' professional incentives to comply with the Fourth Amendment, encourage them to repeat their mistakes, or lead to the granting of all colorable warrant requests.[18]

If exclusion of evidence obtained pursuant to a subsequently invalidated warrant is to have any deterrent effect, it must alter the behavior of individual law enforcement officers or the policies of their departments. One could argue that applying the exclusionary rule in cases where the police failed to demonstrate probable cause in the warrant application deters future inadequate presentations or "magistrate shopping" and thus promotes the ends of the Fourth Amendment. Suppressing evidence obtained pursuant to a technically defective warrant supported by probable cause also might encourage officers to scrutinize more closely the form of the warrant and to point out suspected judicial errors. We find such arguments speculative and conclude that suppression of evidence obtained pursuant to a warrant should be ordered only in those unusual cases in which exclusion will further the purposes of the exclusionary rule. We have frequently questioned whether the exclusionary rule can have any deterrent effect when the offending officers acted in the objectively reasonable belief that their conduct did not violate the Fourth Amendment. Even assuming that the rule effectively deters some police misconduct and provides incentives for the law enforcement profession to conduct itself in accord with the Fourth Amendment, it cannot be expected to deter objectively reasonable law enforcement activity. This is particularly true when an officer acting with objective good faith has obtained a search warrant from a judge or magistrate and acted within its scope. In most such cases, there is no police illegality and thus nothing to deter. It is the magistrate's responsibility to determine whether the officer's allegations establish probable cause and, if so, to issue a warrant comporting with the requirements of the Fourth Amendment. In the ordinary case, an officer cannot be expected to question the magistrate's probable-cause determination or his judgment that the form of the warrant is technically sufficient. Penalizing the officer for the magistrate's error, rather than his own,

---

[18] If a magistrate serves merely as a "rubber stamp" for the police or is unable to exercise mature judgment, closer supervision or removal provides a more effective remedy than the exclusionary rule.

cannot logically contribute to the deterrence of Fourth Amendment violations.[22] The marginal or nonexistent benefits produced by suppressing evidence obtained in objectively reasonable reliance on a subsequently invalidated search warrant cannot justify the substantial costs of exclusion. "Searches pursuant to a warrant will rarely require any deep inquiry into reasonableness" for "a warrant issued by a magistrate normally suffices to establish" that a law enforcement officer has "acted in good faith in conducting the search." *United States v. Ross,* 456 U.S. 798 (1982). Nevertheless, the officer's reliance on the magistrate's probable-cause determination and on the technical sufficiency of the warrant he issues must be objectively reasonable,[23] and it is clear that in some circumstances the officer[24] will have no reasonable grounds for believing that the warrant was properly issued. Suppression therefore remains an appropriate remedy if the magistrate or judge in issuing a warrant was misled by information in an affidavit that the affiant knew was false or would have known was false except for his reckless disregard of the truth. The exception will also not apply where the issuing magistrate wholly abandoned his judicial role in the manner condemned in *Lo-Ji Sales, Inc. v. New York,* 442 U.S. 319 (1979); in such circumstances, no reasonably well trained officer should rely on the warrant. Nor would an officer manifest objective good faith in relying on a warrant based on an affidavit "so lacking in indicia of probable cause as to render official belief in its existence entirely unreasonable." Finally, depending on the circumstances, a warrant may be so facially deficient—*i.e.*, in failing to particularize the place to be searched or the things to be seized—that the executing officers cannot reasonably presume it to be valid.

In limiting the suppression remedy, we leave untouched the probable-cause standard and the various requirements for a valid warrant. The good-faith exception, turning as it does on objective reasonableness, should not be difficult to apply in practice. When officers have acted pursuant to a warrant, the prosecution should ordinarily be able to establish objective good faith without a substantial expenditure of judicial time. Nor are we persuaded that application of a good-faith exception to searches conducted pursuant to warrants will preclude review of the constitutionality of the search or seizure, deny needed guidance from the courts, or freeze Fourth Amendment

---

[22] When a Fourth Amendment violation has occurred because the police have reasonably relied on a warrant issued by a detached and neutral magistrate but ultimately found to be defective, "the integrity of the courts is not implicated." *Illinois v. Gates,* 462 U.S., at 259, n.14 (White, J., concurring.)

[23] We eschew inquiries into the subjective beliefs of law enforcement officers who seize evidence pursuant to a subsequently invalidated warrant. Our good-faith inquiry is confined to the objectively ascertainable question whether a reasonably well trained officer would have known that the search was illegal despite the magistrate's authorization. In making this determination, all of the circumstances—including whether the warrant application had previously been rejected by a different magistrate—may be considered.

[24] We consider the objective reasonableness, not only of the officers who executed a warrant, but also of the officers who obtained it or who provided information material to the probable-cause determination. Nothing suggests that an officer could obtain a warrant on the basis of a "bare bones" affidavit and then rely on colleagues who are ignorant of the circumstances under which the warrant was obtained to conduct the search.

law in its present state.[25] There is no need for courts to adopt the inflexible practice of always deciding whether the officers' conduct manifested objective good faith before turning to the question whether the Fourth Amendment has been violated. If resolution of a particular Fourth Amendment question is necessary to guide future action by law enforcement officers and magistrates, nothing will prevent reviewing courts from deciding that question before turning to the good-faith issue. Indeed, it frequently will be difficult to determine whether the officers acted reasonably without resolving the Fourth Amendment issue. Reviewing courts could decide in particular cases that magistrates under their supervision need to be informed of their errors and so evaluate the officers' good faith only after finding a violation. In other circumstances, those courts could reject suppression motions posing no important Fourth Amendment questions by turning immediately to a consideration of the officers' good faith.

When the principles we have enunciated today are applied to this case, the judgment cannot stand. Leon has contended that no reasonably well trained police officer could have believed that there existed probable cause to search his house. Officer Rombach's application for a warrant clearly was supported by much more than a "bare bones" affidavit. The affidavit related the results of an extensive investigation and provided evidence sufficient to create disagreement among thoughtful and competent judges as to the existence of probable cause. Under these circumstances, the officers' reliance on the magistrate's determination of probable cause was objectively reasonable, and application of the extreme sanction of exclusion is inappropriate.

Accordingly, the judgment of the Court of Appeals is *Reversed*.

JUSTICE BRENNAN, with whom JUSTICE MARSHALL joins, dissenting.

I have witnessed the Court's gradual but determined strangulation of the exclusionary rule. It appears that the Court's victory over the Fourth Amendment is complete. Today the Court sanctions the use in the prosecution's case in chief of illegally obtained evidence against the individual whose rights have been violated. The language of deterrence and of cost/benefit analysis creates an illusion of technical precision and ineluctability. When the Court's analysis is examined, it is clear that we have not been treated to an honest assessment of the merits of the exclusionary rule, but have instead been drawn into a curious world where the "costs" of excluding illegally obtained evidence loom to exaggerated heights and where the "benefits" of such exclusion are made to disappear with a mere wave of the hand.

The Court treats the exclusionary rule as merely a "judicially created remedy designed to safeguard Fourth Amendment rights through its deterrent effect, rather than a personal constitutional right." The Fourth Amendment, like other provisions

---

[25] Although the exception might discourage presentation of insubstantial suppression motions, the magnitude of the benefit conferred on defendants by a successful motion makes it unlikely that litigation of colorable claims will be substantially diminished.

of the Bill of Rights, restrains the power of the government. The judiciary is responsible, no less than the executive, for ensuring that constitutional rights are respected. Because seizures are executed principally to secure evidence, and because such evidence generally has utility in our legal system only in the context of a trial, the admission of illegally obtained evidence implicates the same constitutional concerns as the initial seizure of that evidence. By admitting unlawfully seized evidence, the judiciary becomes a part of what is a single governmental action prohibited by the terms of the Amendment. The right to be free from the initial invasion of privacy and the right of exclusion are coordinate components of the central embracing right to be free from unreasonable searches and seizures. From *Weeks to Olmstead*, the Court plainly understood that the exclusion of illegally obtained evidence was compelled not by judicially fashioned remedial purposes, but rather by a direct constitutional command.

The deterrence theory is misguided and unworkable. The Court has frequently bewailed the "cost" of excluding reliable evidence. The Amendment directly contemplates that some reliable and incriminating evidence will be lost; therefore, it is not the exclusionary rule, but the Amendment itself that has imposed this cost. The entire enterprise of attempting to assess the benefits and costs of the exclusionary rule in various contexts is a virtually impossible task for the judiciary to perform honestly or accurately. To the extent empirical data are available regarding the general costs and benefits of the exclusionary rule, such data have shown that the costs are not as substantial as critics have asserted, and that while the exclusionary rule may well have certain deterrent effects, it is extremely difficult to determine with any degree of precision whether the incidence of unlawful conduct by police is now lower than it was prior to *Mapp*. The Court has sought to turn this uncertainty to its advantage by casting the burden of proof upon proponents of the rule. In this case, the affidavit filed by the police officers failed to provide a basis on which a neutral and detached magistrate could conclude that there was probable cause to issue the warrant. The application for a warrant was based on information supplied by a confidential informant of unproven reliability that was over five months old. Although the police conducted an independent investigation, the additional information failed to corroborate the details of the tip and was "as consistent with innocence as with guilt." The warrant, therefore, should never have issued. Stripped of the authority of the warrant, the conduct of these officers was plainly unconstitutional—it amounted to nothing less than a naked invasion of the privacy of respondents' homes without the requisite justification demanded by the Fourth Amendment. It was necessary that the evidence be suppressed.

The Court's opinion suggests that this order imposed a grave and presumably unjustifiable cost on society. Such a suggestion is a gross exaggeration. Since the bulk of the evidence seized was plainly admissible, the Government would still be able to present a strong case following the suppression order. The Court suggests that society has been asked to pay a high price—in terms either of setting guilty persons free or of impeding the proper functioning of trials—as a result of excluding relevant physical evidence in cases where the police, in conducting searches and seizing evidence, have made only an "objectively reasonable" mistake concerning the constitutionality of their actions. But what evidence is there to support such a claim? Recent studies have demonstrated that the "costs" of the exclusionary rule—calculated in terms of dropped prosecutions and lost convictions—are quite low. Federal and state prosecutors very rarely drop cases because of search and seizure problems. A 1979 study reported that only 0.4% of all cases declined for prosecution by federal prosecutors were declined primarily because of illegal search problems. The study shows that only 0.2% of all felony arrests are declined for prosecution because of potential exclusionary rule problems.[11] Of course, these data describe only the costs attributable to the exclusion of evidence in all cases; the costs due to the exclusion of evidence in the narrower category of cases where police have made objectively reasonable mistakes must necessarily be even smaller. The Court mistakenly weighs the aggregated costs of exclusion in all cases, irrespective of the circumstances that led to exclusion, against the potential benefits associated with only those cases in which evidence is excluded because police reasonably but mistakenly believe that their conduct does not violate the Fourth Amendment. When such faulty scales are used, it is little wonder that the balance tips in favor of restricting the application of the rule.

The key to the Court's holding is the belief that the prospective deterrent effect of the exclusionary rule operates only in those situations in which police officers, when deciding whether to go forward with some particular search, have reason to know that their planned conduct will violate the requirements of the Fourth Amendment. The Court's argument captures only one comparatively minor element of the deterrent purposes of the exclusionary rule. To be sure, the rule operates to deter future misconduct by individual officers who have had evidence suppressed in their own cases. What the Court overlooks is that the deterrence rationale is not designed to be a form of "punishment" of individual police officers for their failures to obey the restraints imposed by the Fourth Amendment. Instead, "exclusionary rule encourages those who formulate law enforcement policies, and the officers who implement them, to incorporate Fourth Amendment ideals into their value system." *Stone v. Powell*, 428 U.S., at 492. It is only through such an institution wide mechanism that information concerning Fourth Amendment standards can be effectively communicated to rank-and-file officers.

Application of the rule to even those situations in which individual police officers have acted on the basis of a reasonable but mistaken belief that their conduct was authorized can still be expected to have a considerable long-term deterrent effect. If evidence is consistently excluded in these circumstances, police departments will

---

[11]   A recent National Institute of Justice NIJ study showed that 4.8% of all cases that were declined for prosecution by California prosecutors were rejected because of illegally seized evidence—only 0.8% of all arrests. The number of prosecutions that are dismissed or result in acquittals in cases where evidence has been excluded—the data show that the Court's assessment of the rule's costs has been exaggerated.

surely instruct their officers to devote greater care and attention to providing sufficient information to establish probable cause when applying for a warrant, and to review with some attention the form of the warrant that they have been issued, rather than automatically assuming that whatever document the magistrate has signed will necessarily comport with Fourth Amendment requirements. After today's decisions, that institutional incentive will be lost. The Court's "reasonable mistake" exception to the exclusionary rule will tend to put a premium on police ignorance of the law. Armed with the assurance that evidence will always be admissible whenever an officer has "reasonably" relied upon a warrant, police departments will be encouraged to train officers that if a warrant has simply been signed, it is reasonable, without more, to rely on it. Moreover, the good-faith exception will encourage police to provide only the bare minimum of information in future warrant applications. The police will know that if they can secure a warrant, so long as the circumstances of its issuance are not "entirely unreasonable," all police conduct pursuant to that warrant will be protected from judicial review. The long-run effect will be to undermine the integrity of the warrant process.

Given the relaxed standard for assessing probable cause established *Illinois v. Gates*, 462 U.S. 213 (1983), the Court's newly fashioned good-faith exception, when applied in the warrant context, will rarely, if ever, offer any greater flexibility for police than the *Gates* standard already supplies. When the public demands that those in government increase their efforts to combat crime, it is all too easy for those government officials to seek expedient solutions. The relaxation of Fourth Amendment standards seems a tempting, costless means of meeting the public's demand for better law enforcement. In the long run we as a society pay a heavy price for such expediency. Once lost, rights are difficult to recover.

JUSTICE STEVENS, concurring in the judgment in No. 82–963, and dissenting in No. 82–1771.

The exclusionary rule is designed to prevent violations of the Fourth Amendment. Today's decisions do grave damage to that deterrent function. Under the majority's new rule, even when the police know their warrant application is probably insufficient, they retain an incentive to submit it to a magistrate, on the chance that he may take the bait. The exclusionary rule cannot deter when the authorities have no reason to know that their conduct is unconstitutional. But when probable cause is lacking, a reasonable person would not believe there is a fair likelihood that a search will produce evidence of a crime. Under such circumstances well-trained professionals must know that they are violating the Constitution. The Court's approach encourages the police to seek a warrant, even if they know the existence of probable cause is doubtful, can only lead to an increased number of constitutional violations. The Court's decision tarnishes the role of the judiciary in enforcing the Constitution. Courts simply cannot escape their responsibility for redressing constitutional violations if they admit evidence obtained through unreasonable searches and seizures, since the entire point of police conduct that violates the Fourth Amendment is to obtain evidence for use at trial. It is true that the exclusionary rule exerts a high price—the loss of probative evidence of guilt. But that price is one courts have been required to pay to serve important social goals. That price is also one the Fourth Amendment requires us to pay, assuming as we must that the Framers intended that its strictures "shall not be violated." We could facilitate the process of administering justice by ignoring the entire Bill of Rights—but it is the very purpose of a Bill of Rights to identify values that may not be sacrificed to expediency. In a just society those who govern, as well as those who are governed, must obey the law.

Food for Thought

About one-third of the states have rejected the good faith exception to the exclusionary rule under their own state constitutions. Illustrative is the holding of the New Jersey Supreme Court in *State v. Novembrino*, 519 A.2d 820 (N.J. 1987): "The exclusionary rule's function is not merely to deter police misconduct. The rule also serves as the indispensable mechanism for vindicating the constitutional right to be free from unreasonable searches. Because the good-faith exception would undermine the constitutionally-guaranteed standard of probable cause, and in the process disrupt the highly effective procedures employed by our criminal justice system to accommodate that constitutional guarantee without impairing law enforcement, we decline to recognize a good-faith exception to the exclusionary rule. We see no need to experiment with the fundamental rights protected by the fourth-amendment counterpart of our State Constitution." Consider also *State v. Marsala*, 579 A.2d 58 (Conn. 1990): "A good faith exception to the exclusionary rule would have several negative effects. First, the good faith exception would encourage police to expend less effort in establishing the necessary probable cause and more effort in locating a judge who might be less exacting when ruling on whether an affidavit has established probable cause. Second, the "exception implicitly tells magistrates that they need not take care in reviewing warrant applications, since their mistakes will have virtually no consequence." Finally, it is unlikely "that overburdened courts will take the time to write advisory opinions on search and seizure law when they can easily admit the evidence under the good faith exception." The exclusionary rule is not designed to "punish" anyone. It is designed to deter future police misconduct and ensure institutional compliance with the warrant requirements of our state constitution. The relevant inquiry is whether the sanction of the exclusionary rule is appropriate where the officer believed that he was doing everything correctly, but in fact had not supplied the issuing authority with information sufficient to meet the constitutional requirement of probable cause. If evidence is consistently excluded, police departments will surely instruct their officers to devote greater care to providing sufficient information to establish probable cause when applying for a warrant, and to review the form of the warrant that they have been issued, rather than automatically assuming that whatever document the magistrate has signed will comport with Fourth Amendment requirements." Do you agree with these state court decisions?

In *Malley v. Briggs*, 475 U.S. 335 (1986), a police officer unconstitutionally arrested plaintiffs by presenting a judge with a complaint and a supporting affidavit which failed to establish probable cause. Plaintiffs sued the officers for damages. The Court held that the officers were protected by qualified immunity, but only if they acted "reasonably": "The question is whether a reasonably well-trained officer in petitioner's position would have known that his affidavit failed to establish probable cause and that he should not have applied for the warrant. If such was the case, the officer's application for a warrant was not objectively reasonable, because it created the unnecessary danger of an unlawful arrest." Does the possibility of a civil suit sufficiently deter police misconduct?

In *Groh v. Ramirez*, 540 U.S. 551 (2004), the Court concluded that Bureau of Alcohol, Tobacco and Firearm (ATF) agents did not act reasonably when they executed a search warrant. The warrant failed to provide an adequate description of the place to be searched, and the Court held that the officers who executed the warrant were not entitled to qualified immunity. The Court concluded that the warrant was so "facially deficient" that the officers could not presume it to be valid. Despite *Groh*'s holding, courts are often deferential to judgments made by the police, especially when they have relied on a warrant issued by a magistrate, and courts are therefore reluctant to impose damage awards. *See Messerschmidt v. Millender*, 565 U.S. 535 (2012).

Points for Discussion

a. Good Faith & "Technical Errors"

Massachusetts v. Sheppard, 468 U.S. 981 (1984) was a "companion case" to *Leon*. In *Sheppard*, the Court extended *Leon* to a case involving a warrant invalidated because of a technical error on the part of the issuing judge: "Suppressing evidence because the judge failed to make all the necessary clerical corrections despite his assurances that such changes would be made will not serve the deterrent function that the exclusionary rule was designed to achieve."

b. Good Faith Reliance on an Invalid Statute

In *Illinois v. Krull*, 480 U.S. 340 (1987), the Court extended the good faith exception to instances when the police acted in objectively reasonable reliance upon a statute authorizing warrantless administrative searches, but where the statute was ultimately found to violate the Fourth Amendment: "The application of the exclusionary rule to suppress evidence obtained by an officer acting in objectively reasonable reliance on a statute would have as little deterrent effect on the officer's actions as would the exclusion of evidence when an officer acts in objectively reasonable reliance on a warrant. Unless a statute is clearly unconstitutional, an officer cannot be expected to question the judgment of the legislature that passed the law. If the statute is subsequently declared unconstitutional, excluding evidence obtained pursuant to it prior to such a judicial declaration will not deter future Fourth Amendment violations by an officer who has simply fulfilled his responsibility to enforce the statute as written." Justice O'Connor dissented: "Statutes authorizing unreasonable searches were the core concern of the Framers of the Fourth Amendment. Both the history of the Fourth Amendment and this Court's later interpretations of it, support application of the exclusionary rule to this situation."

c. Reliance on Prior Precedent

In *Davis v. United States*, <u>564 U.S. 229 (2011)</u>, the police conducted a search in reliance on prior Court precedent. However, that precedent (*New York v. Belton*), which allowed police to routinely search the interior of a vehicle as part of a search incident to legal arrest, was overruled by a later decision (*State v. Gant*). The Court again focused on the deterrence rationale, and held that the costs of excluding the evidence outweighed the potential benefits: "The question is whether to apply the exclusionary rule when the police conduct a search in objectively reasonable reliance on binding judicial precedent. The officers who conducted the search did not violate Davis's Fourth Amendment rights deliberately, recklessly, or with gross negligence. Nor does this case involve any 'recurring or systemic negligence' on the part of law enforcement. The police acted in strict compliance with binding precedent, and their behavior was not wrongful. Unless the exclusionary rule is to become a strict-liability regime, it can have no application. We have 'never applied' the exclusionary rule to suppress evidence obtained as a result of nonculpable, innocent police conduct. All that exclusion would deter is conscientious police work. When binding appellate precedent specifically *authorizes* a particular police practice, well-trained officers should use that tool to fulfill their crime-detection and public-safety responsibilities." Likewise, following the Court's decision in *Carpenter v. United States*, 138 S.Ct. 2206 (2018), which held that police must have a warrant in order to access historical cell site records, the question arose whether pre-*Carpenter* access of those records should be admissible under the good faith exception to the warrant requirement. In *United States v. Zodhiates*, 901 F.3d 137 (2d Cir. 2018), and *United States v. Rojas-Reyes*, 2018 WL 3439082 (S.D. Ind. 2018), lower courts applied that exception.

d. Bookkeeping Errors

In *Herring v. United States*, <u>555 U.S. 135 (2009)</u>, a police officer made an arrest, based on an outstanding arrest warrant, but the warrant was invalid due to a negligent bookkeeping error by another police employee. The arrest led to information that Herring was in possession of illegal drugs, and a firearm (which was prohibited since he was a

> **Food for Thought**
>
> Reread *Mapp v. Ohio*. Does your reading suggest that the exclusionary rule is premised solely on principles of deterrence, or does it suggest that the rule is based on other considerations as well (e.g., the "imperative" of judicial integrity, or the Fourth Amendment itself—in other words, that the rule is "constitutionally required")?

convicted felon). Focusing on the deterrence rationale for exclusion, and the cost-benefit test, the Court held that the evidence need not be excluded, emphasizing that exclusion has generally only been applied to flagrant misconduct: "To trigger the exclusionary rule, police conduct must be sufficiently deliberate that exclusion can meaningfully deter it, and sufficiently culpable that such deterrence is worth the price paid by the justice system." The Court concluded that the bookkeeping error did not rise to that level, and was not "so objectively culpable as to require exclusion." Exclusion might have been justified if the police had been "reckless in maintaining a warrant system, or knowingly made false entries to lay the groundwork for future false arrests." Justice Ginsburg, joined by three other justices, dissented, arguing that exclusion is needed to discourage police error and to protect innocent individuals against improper arrest: "Negligent recordkeeping errors by law enforcement threaten individual liberty, are susceptible to deterrence by the exclusionary rule, and cannot be remedied effectively through other means."

Food for Thought

Would *Leon*'s logic suggest that the good faith exception should apply when an officer makes a warrantless search in "good faith" (not in reliance on an invalid statute or prior judicial precedent)? For example, the officer believes that he has probable cause to search a vehicle, and therefore can invoke the automobile exception to the warrant requirement, but he is wrong in concluding that probable cause exists. Does *Leon*'s rationale extend to warrantless searches of this type?

Hypo 1: *Application of the Good Faith Exception*

Suppose that the police receive information implicating Powell in the theft of a police vehicle, and apply for a search warrant authorizing them to obtain a sample of the suspect's hair as well as a buccal swab. However, the warrant application does not state that the police have hair samples or other evidence from the car against which samples from the suspect can be compared. Moreover, although the affidavit indicates that the police have probable cause to believe that defendant has committed a crime, the warrant does not specifically indicate which crime. There is a potential implication of a car theft because the warrant application refers to informants who implicated Powell in that theft. Should the good faith exception apply if a reviewing court determines that the warrant application was not supported by probable cause? *See State v. Powell*, 325 P.3d 1162 (Kan. 2014).

Hypo 2: *More on Application of the Good Faith Exception*

Suppose that the police obtain a search warrant for a suspect's computer in order to search for child pornography. They do so based on his computer address and proof that his computer accessed child pornography some nine months earlier. Later, a court concludes that the evidence of prior access was "stale," and therefore probable cause did not exist for issuance of the warrant. The court emphasizes that there is a difference between someone who accidentally accesses a child porn site, and does not click on any images, and someone who seeks out that site and downloads images, concluding that the intentional downloader might hoard the images that he downloaded, but that one who accidentally accessed the site would not. Despite the absence of probable cause, should the search be upheld under the good faith exception? *See United States v. Raymonda*, 780 F.3d 105 (2d Cir. 2015).

Hypo 3: *Good Faith & the "Dark Web"*

Police investigators are searching the "dark web" looking for evidence of child pornography. The difficulty is that the web can be accessed from all over the U.S., indeed from all over the world. Suppose that a federal district judge in Virginia issues a warrant for a search in Colorado. If the judge does not have the jurisdiction to issue a Colorado warrant, but federal investigators rely on the warrant in "good faith," should evidence produced by the search be admissible under the good faith exception? *See United States v. Ortiz-Cervantes*, 868 F.3d 695 (8th Cir. 2017); *United States v. Workman*, 863 F.3d 1313 (10th Cir. 2017).

Hudson v. Michigan

547 U.S. 586 (2006).

JUSTICE SCALIA delivered the opinion of the Court, except as to Part IV.

When the police arrived to execute a warrant, they announced their presence, but waited only a short time—perhaps "three to five seconds"—before turning the knob of the unlocked front door and entering Hudson's home. Hudson moved to suppress all the inculpatory evidence drugs and a loaded gun, arguing that the premature entry violated his Fourth Amendment rights. The evidence was admitted and Hudson's appeal was rejected. We granted certiorari.

The common-law principle that law enforcement officers must announce their presence and provide residents an opportunity to open the door is an ancient one. *See Wilson v. Arkansas*, 514 U.S. 927 (1995). Since 1917, this traditional protection has been part of federal statutory law and is currently codified at 18 U.S.C. § 3109. *Wilson* concluded that it was also a command of the Fourth Amendment. It is not necessary to knock and announce when "circumstances present a threat of physical violence," or if there is "reason to believe that evidence would likely be destroyed if advance notice were given," or if knocking and announcing would be "futile," *Richards v. Wisconsin*, 520 U.S. 385 (1997). We require only that police "have a reasonable suspicion under the particular circumstances" that one of these grounds for failing to knock and announce exists, and we have acknowledged that "this showing is not high."

When the knock-and-announce rule does apply, it is not easy to determine precisely what officers must do. How many seconds' wait are too few? Our "reasonable wait time" standard, *see United States v. Banks*, 540 U.S. 31 (2003), is necessarily vague. *Banks* (a drug case, like this one) held that the proper measure was not how long it would take the resident to reach the door, but how long it would take to dispose of the suspected drugs—but that such a time (15 to 20 seconds in that case) would necessarily be extended when, for instance, the suspected contraband was not easily concealed. If our *ex post* evaluation is subject to such calculations, it is unsurprising that, *ex ante,* police officers about to encounter someone who may try to harm them will be uncertain how long to wait.

Michigan has conceded that the entry was a knock-and-announce violation. The issue here is remedy. Suppression of evidence has always been our last resort, not our first impulse. The exclusionary rule generates "substantial social costs," *United States v. Leon*, 468 U.S. 897 (1984), which sometimes include setting the guilty free and the dangerous at large. We have therefore been "cautious against expanding" it, and "have repeatedly emphasized that the rule's 'costly toll' upon truth-seeking and law enforcement objectives presents a high obstacle for those urging its application," *Pennsylvania Bd. of Probation and Parole v. Scott*, 524 U.S. 357 (1998). We have rejected "indiscriminate application" of the rule, and have held it to be applicable only "where its remedial objectives are thought most efficaciously served,"—that is, "where its deterrence benefits outweigh its 'substantial social costs,' " *Scott, supra*, at 363 (quoting *Leon, supra*, at 907).

We did not always speak so guardedly. Dicta in *Mapp* suggested wide scope for the exclusionary rule. But we have long since rejected that approach. In *Leon*, we explained that "whether the exclusionary sanction is appropriately imposed in a particular case, is 'an issue separate from the question whether the Fourth Amendment rights of the party seeking to invoke the rule were violated by police conduct.' " Exclusion may not be premised on the mere fact that a constitutional violation was a "but-for" cause of obtaining evidence. But-for causality is only a necessary, not a sufficient, condition for suppression. In this case, the constitutional violation of an illegal *manner* of entry was *not* a but-for cause. Whether that preliminary misstep had occurred *or not,* the police would have executed the warrant they had obtained, and would have discovered the gun and drugs inside the house. The more apt question in such a case is 'whether, granting establishment of the primary illegality, the evidence to which instant objection is made has been come at by exploitation of that illegality or instead by means sufficiently distinguishable to be purged of the primary taint.' " *Wong Sun v. United States*, 371 U.S. 471 (1963) (*quoting* J. MAGUIRE, EVIDENCE OF GUILT 221 (1959)).

Attenuation can occur when the causal connection is remote. Attenuation also occurs when, even given a direct causal connection, the interest protected by the constitutional guarantee that has been violated would not be served by suppression of the evidence obtained. In *New York v. Harris*, 495 U.S. 14 (1990), where an illegal warrantless arrest was made in Harris' house, we held that "suppressing Harris' statement taken outside the house would not serve the purpose of the rule that made Harris' in-house arrest illegal. The warrant requirement for an arrest in the home is imposed to protect the home, and anything incriminating the police gathered from arresting Harris in his home, rather than elsewhere, has been excluded, as it should have been; the purpose of the rule has thereby been vindicated."

Cases excluding the fruits of unlawful warrantless searches say nothing about the appropriateness of exclusion to vindicate the interests protected by the knock-and-announce requirement. Until a valid warrant has issued, citizens are entitled to shield "their persons, houses, papers, and effects," U.S. Const., Amdt. 4, from the government's scrutiny. Exclusion of the evidence obtained by a warrantless search vindicates that entitlement. The interests protected by the knock-and-announce requirement are quite different—and do not include the shielding of potential evidence from the government's eyes. One of those interests is the protection of human life and limb, because an unannounced entry may provoke violence in supposed self-defense by the surprised resident. Another interest is the protection of property. The knock and announce rule gives individuals "the opportunity to comply with the law and to avoid the destruction of property occasioned by a forcible entry." *Richards*, 520 U.S., at 393. Thirdly, the knock-and-announce rule protects those elements of privacy and dignity that can be destroyed by a sudden entrance. "The brief interlude between announcement and entry with a warrant may be the opportunity that an individual has to pull on clothes or get out of bed." It assures the opportunity to collect oneself before answering the door. What the knock-and-announce rule has never protected, however, is one's interest in preventing the government from seeing or taking evidence described in a warrant. Since the interests that *were* violated in this case have nothing to do with the seizure of the evidence, the exclusionary rule is inapplicable.

Quite apart from the requirement of unattenuated causation, the exclusionary rule has never been applied except "where its deterrence benefits outweigh its 'substantial social costs,' " *Scott*, 524 U.S., at 363. The costs here are considerable. In addition to the grave adverse consequence that exclusion of relevant incriminating evidence always entails (viz., the risk of releasing dangerous criminals into society), imposing that massive remedy for a knock-and-announce violation would generate a constant flood of alleged failures to observe the rule, and claims that any asserted *Richards* justification for a no-knock entry had inadequate support. The cost of entering this lottery would be small, but the jackpot enormous: suppression of all evidence, amounting in many cases to a get-out-of-jail-free card. Courts would experience the reality that "the exclusionary rule frequently requires extensive litigation to determine whether particular evidence must be excluded." *Scott, supra*, at 366. Unlike the warrant or *Miranda* requirements, compliance with which is readily determined, what constituted a "reasonable wait time" in a particular case (or how many seconds the police in fact waited), or whether there was "reasonable suspicion" of the sort that would invoke the *Richards* exceptions, is difficult to determine and even more difficult for an appellate court to review.

Another consequence of the incongruent remedy Hudson proposes would be police officers' refraining from timely entry after knocking and announcing. The amount of time they must wait is necessarily uncertain. If the consequences of running afoul of the rule were so massive, officers would be inclined to wait longer than the law requires—producing preventable violence against officers in some cases, and the destruction of evidence in others. We deemed these consequences severe enough to produce our unanimous agreement that a mere "reasonable suspicion" that knocking and announcing "under the particular circumstances, would be dangerous or futile, or that it would inhibit the effective investigation of the crime," will cause the requirement to yield. *Richards, supra*, at 394.

Next to these "substantial social costs" we must consider the deterrence benefits, existence of which is a necessary condition for exclusion. *United States v. Calandra*, 414 U.S. 338 (1974). The value of deterrence depends upon the strength of the incentive to commit the forbidden act. Viewed from this perspective, deterrence of knock-and-announce violations is not worth a lot. Violation of the warrant requirement sometimes produces incriminating evidence that could not otherwise be obtained. But ignoring knock-and-announce can realistically be expected to achieve absolutely nothing except the prevention of destruction of evidence and the avoidance of life-threatening resistance by occupants of the premises—dangers which, if there is even "reasonable suspicion" of their existence, *suspend the knock-and-announce requirement anyway*. Massive deterrence is hardly required.

It seems to us not true that without suppression there will be no deterrence of knock-and-announce violations at all. Even if this assertion were accurate, it would not necessarily justify suppression. Assuming that civil suit is not an effective deterrent, one can think of many forms of police misconduct that are similarly "undeterred." When a confessed suspect in the killing of a police officer, arrested (along with incriminating evidence) in a lawful warranted search, is subjected to physical abuse at the station house, would it seriously be suggested that the evidence must be excluded, since that is the only "effective deterrent"? What, other than civil suit, is the "effective deterrent" of police violation of an already-confessed suspect's Sixth Amendment rights by denying him prompt access to counsel? Many would regard these violated rights as more significant than the right not to be intruded upon in one's nightclothes—and yet nothing but "ineffective" civil suit is available as a deterrent. And the police incentive for those violations is arguably greater than the incentive for disregarding the knock-and-announce rule.

Hudson complains that "it would be very hard to find a lawyer to take a case such as this," but Congress has authorized attorney's fees for civil-rights plaintiffs. Even if we thought that only large damages would deter police misconduct (and that police somehow are deterred by "damages" but indifferent to the prospect of large § 1988 attorney's fees), we do not know how many claims have been settled, or indeed how many violations have occurred that produced anything more than nominal injury. Lower courts are allowing colorable knock-and-announce suits to go forward. As far as we know, civil liability is an effective deterrent here. Another development that deters civil-rights violations is the increasing professionalism of police forces, including a new emphasis on internal police discipline. There have been "wide-ranging reforms in the education, training, and supervision of police officers." S. WALKER, TAMING THE SYSTEM: THE CONTROL OF DISCRETION IN CRIMINAL JUSTICE 1950–1990, p. 51 (1993). Failure to teach and enforce constitutional requirements exposes municipalities to financial liability. It is not credible to assert that internal discipline, which can limit successful careers, will not have a deterrent effect. There is also evidence that the increasing use of various forms of citizen review can enhance police accountability.

In sum, the social costs of applying the exclusionary rule to knock-and-announce violations are considerable; the incentive to such violations is minimal to begin with, and the extant deterrences against them are substantial—incomparably greater than the factors deterring warrantless entries when *Mapp* was decided. Resort to the massive remedy of suppressing evidence of guilt is unjustified.

For the foregoing reasons we affirm the judgment of the Michigan Court of Appeals.

It is so ordered.

JUSTICE KENNEDY, concurring in part and concurring in the judgment.

The continued operation of the exclusionary rule is not in doubt. Today's decision determines only that in the specific context of the knock-and-announce requirement, a violation is not sufficiently related to the later discovery of evidence to justify suppression.

JUSTICE BREYER, with whom JUSTICE STEVENS, JUSTICE SOUTER, and JUSTICE GINSBURG join, dissenting.

In *Wilson,* we traced the lineage of the knock-and-announce rule back to the 13th century and concluded that "there was 'little doubt that the Framers of the Fourth Amendment thought that the method of an officer's entry into a dwelling was among the factors to be considered in assessing the reasonableness of a search or seizure." An unreasonable search or seizure is, constitutionally speaking, an illegal search or seizure. The driving legal purpose underlying the exclusionary rule, namely, the deterrence of unlawful government behavior, argues strongly for suppression. Failure to apply the exclusionary rule would make the Fourth Amendment's promise a hollow one, reducing it to "a form of words," "of no value" to those whom it seeks to protect. What reason is there to believe that alternative remedies (such as private damages actions under 42 U.S.C. § 1983), which the Court found inadequate in *Mapp,* can adequately deter unconstitutional police behavior? The need for deterrence—the critical factor driving this Court's Fourth Amendment cases—argues with at least comparable strength for evidentiary exclusion.

The Court has declined to apply the exclusionary rule only: (1) where there is a specific reason to believe that application of the rule would "not result in appreciable deterrence," or (2) where admissibility in proceedings other than criminal trials was at issue. Neither of these two exceptions applies here. The first does not apply because there is no reason to think that, in the case of knock-and-announce violations by the police, "the exclusion of evidence at trial would not sufficiently deter future errors," or "further the ends of the exclusionary rule in any appreciable way." It is difficult for me to see how the presence of a warrant that does not authorize the entry in question has anything to do with the "inevitable discovery" exception or otherwise diminishes the need to enforce the knock-and-announce requirement through suppression. The knock-and-announce rule protects the occupants' privacy by assuring them that government agents will not enter their home without complying with those requirements (among others) that diminish the offensive nature of any such intrusion. The knock-and-announce requirement is no less a part of the "centuries-old principle" of special protection for the privacy of the home than the warrant requirement. The Court is therefore wrong to reduce the essence of its protection to "the right not to be intruded upon in one's nightclothes." Failure to comply with the knock-and-announce rule renders the related search unlawful. And where a search is unlawful, the law insists upon suppression of the evidence consequently discovered, even if that evidence or its possession has little or nothing to do with the reasons underlying the unconstitutionality of a search. Ordinarily a court will simply look to see if the unconstitutional search produced the evidence.

Food for Thought

In *State v. Cable*, 51 So.3d 434 (Fla. 2010), applying its state constitution, the Florida Supreme Court held that a violation of Florida's knock-and-announce statute vitiated the ensuing arrest and required suppression of evidence obtained in connection with it. The court concluded that, "even if probable cause exists for the arrest of a person, our statute is violated by an unannounced intrusion in the form of a breaking and entering any building, including a private home, except (1) where the person within already knows of the officer's authority and purpose; (2) where the officers are justified in the belief that the persons within are in imminent peril of bodily harm; (3) if the officer's peril would have been increased had he demanded entrance and stated the purpose, or (4) where those within made aware of the presence of someone outside are then engaged in activities which justify the officers in the belief that an escape or destruction of evidence is being attempted." The court reasoned as follows: "A citizen's obligation to respond to a request to allow a law enforcement officer into his or her home depends on the purpose of the law enforcement officer's request. While a citizen has every right to refuse entry to an officer who may be merely seeking information or conducting an investigation, the citizen has no right to refuse entry by an officer whose purpose in seeking entry is to execute an arrest warrant or search warrant. Before law enforcement officials may properly enter a private building to effect an arrest and 'use all necessary and reasonable force to enter any building or property,' § 901.19(1), Fla. Stat., they are required to announce their purpose." Is the Florida approach preferable?

Hypo 1: *The Delayed Search*

Pursuant to a warrant authorizing them to search for stolen and forged checks, the police search defendant's home. During the search, they find two locked safes capable of holding checks. Police seize the safes and transport them to the police station. A state court finds that it would have been permissible for the police to search the safes at the time of the original search, but that it was impermissible to seize them and search them later. Under *Hudson*, does the violation of defendant's possessory rights require exclusion of evidence found in the safes (methamphetamine)? What arguments might you make on the defense's behalf? *See State v. Powell*, 306 S.W.3d 761 (Tex. Crim. App. 2010).

Hypo 2: *More on Deterrence*

After some suspicious transactions, police investigate two fraudulent bank accounts opened in the name of "Ousmane Diallo" using a passport from Guinea. However, they are unable to locate Diallo. When a man named Fode Fofana arrives at a U.S. airport under conditions that flag him for additional screening, he is individually questioned and searched. During the search, a TSA agent finds envelopes containing large amounts of cash, as well as two envelopes with "something hard and unbendable," but unidentifiable. The TSA agent opens the envelopes and finds three passports bearing Fofana's picture, but with different names. One passport contains the name "Ousmane Diallo." Because of the passport, later determined to be illegal, police link Fofana to the fraudulent bank accounts. Fofana moves to suppress the seized passports as the fruit of an illegal search, as well as to suppress information regarding his identity, on the basis that TSA did not have the authority to open the envelopes. If the passports are excluded, must the court also exclude evidence regarding the link between Fofana and Diallo? Is sufficient deterrence obtained by the fact that the passports are excluded? *See United States v. Fofana*, <u>666 F.3d 985 (6th Cir. 2012)</u>.

Hypo 3: *The Exclusionary Rule & State Law*

While investigating a cocaine ring, a state warrant authorizes the police to eavesdrop on digital pager communications. Consistently with Title III of the Omnibus Crime Control and Safe Streets Act of 1968, as amended by Title I of the Electronic Communications Privacy Act of 1986, the warrant specifically requires the police to capture, keep and store the communications on a police department computer "in a manner that will protect the records from editing and alteration." The warrant also authorizes the monitoring of communications via a duplicate or "clone" paging device, which would display the same information as that shown on the device being monitored. When the police chose to monitor the clone pager, and fail to comply with a local law requiring that the information be stored on a police department computer, defendant moved to suppress the evidence. Assuming that the warrant was supported by probable cause, and was otherwise in order, should noncompliance with the ECPA's recording requirement trigger application of the exclusionary rule? *See United States v. Amanuel*, <u>615 F.3d 117 (2d Cir. 2010)</u>.

Hypo 4: *Arrest by an Officer in Excess of Jurisdiction*

On Christmas Eve, a city officer observes an automobile traveling in excess of the speed limit on a road near the city limits. The officer mistakenly believes that the road is within the city limits. The officer begins pursuit with the intention of giving the driver a warning. However, the driver does not respond to the officer's blue lights, increases his speed, and runs a stop sign. When the officer finally catches up to the driver, he realizes that the driver has been driving under the influence of alcohol. If the officer does not have the authority to exercise police powers outside of the city limits, should the evidence of intoxication be suppressed? Should it matter that the officer acted in good faith? *See Delker v. State*, 50 So.3d 300 (Miss. 2010).

Hypo 5: Jones *& the Good Faith Exception*

As you may recall, in *United States v. Jones*, 565 U.S. 400 (2012), the Court held that the police violated the Fourth Amendment when they attached a GPS tracking device to a vehicle in order to track the vehicle's movements. The Court's prior decisions, particularly *United States v. Knotts*, 460 U.S. 276 (1983), had held that the police could track GPS devices without violating the Fourth Amendment. However, the facts were somewhat different in *Knotts*, because rather than attaching a GPS device to Knotts' car, the police inserted the GPS device in a bottle of chloroform before Knotts purchased it. Lower court decisions had construed *Knotts* as applying to situations when the police attach a GPS device to a suspect's vehicle. Should evidence obtained through direct attachment be admitted under the good faith exception? *See Kelly v. State*, 82 A.3d 205 (Md. 2013); *United States v. Aguiar*, 737 F.3d 251 (2d Cir. 2013); *United States v. Smith*, 741 F.3d 1211 (11th Cir. 2013).

Hypo 6: *Good Faith &* Jardines

In *Florida v. Jardines*, 569 U.S. 1 (2013), the Court invalidated a canine sniff at an individual's residence as a violation of the Fourth Amendment. If lower court decisions had held that a dog sniff under similar circumstances was permissible, does the good faith exception apply? *See State v. Scull*, 843 N.W.2d 859 (Wis. App. 2014); *see also State v. Scull*, 862 N.W.2d 562 (Wis. 2015); *United States v. Davis*, 760 F.3d 901 (8th Cir. 2014); *United States v. Gutierrez*, 760 F.3d 750 (7th Cir. 2014).

C. The Rule's Application in Other Contexts

Should the exclusionary rule apply in other contexts (*e.g.*, civil proceedings)? Consider the following case.

United States v. Janis

428 U.S. 433 (1976).

MR. JUSTICE BLACKMUN delivered the opinion of the Court.

Los Angeles police obtained a warrant directing a search for bookmaking paraphernalia at two specified apartments in the city and on the respective persons of Morris Levine and respondent Max Janis. The warrant was issued by a judge of the Municipal Court of the Los Angeles Judicial District. It was based upon the affidavit of Officer Leonard Weissman. After the search, both the respondent and Levine were arrested and the police seized from respondent property consisting of $4,940 in cash and certain wagering records. Officer Weissman telephoned an agent of the United States Internal Revenue Service and informed the agent that Janis had been arrested for bookmaking activity. With the assistance of Weissman, who was familiar with bookmakers' codes, the revenue agent analyzed the wagering records and determined the gross volume of respondent's gambling activity for the five days immediately preceding the seizure. Weissman informed the agent that respondent had been engaged in bookmaking during the 77-day period from September 14 through November 30, 1968, the day of the arrest. Respondent had not filed any federal wagering tax return pertaining to bookmaking activities for that 77-day period. Based exclusively upon its examination of the evidence so obtained by the Los Angeles police, the Internal Revenue Service made an assessment jointly against respondent and Levine for wagering taxes, under § 4401 of the Internal Revenue Code of 1954, in the amount of $89,026.09, plus interest. The assessment having been made, the Internal Revenue Service exercised its statutory authority, under 26 U.S.C. § 6331, to levy upon the $4,940 in cash in partial satisfaction of the assessment against respondent. Charges were filed in due course against respondent and Levine in Los Angeles Municipal Court for violation of the local gambling laws. The judge concluded that the evidence had been illegally obtained, and granted a motion to quash the warrant. In June 1969 respondent filed a claim for refund of the $4,940. The claim was not honored, and respondent filed suit. The Government counterclaimed for the substantial unpaid balance of the assessment. In pretrial proceedings, it was agreed that the "sole basis of the computation of the civil tax assessment was the items obtained pursuant to the search warrant and the information furnished to (the revenue agent) by Officer Weissman with respect to the duration of alleged wagering activities." Respondent then moved to suppress the evidence seized, and all copies thereof in the possession of the Service, and to quash the assessment. The District Court granted the motion to suppress. Because of the obvious importance of the question, we granted certiorari.

In the complex and turbulent history of the rule, the Court never has applied it to exclude evidence from a civil proceeding, federal or state. In the present case we are asked to create judicially a deterrent sanction by holding that evidence obtained by a state criminal law enforcement officer in good-faith reliance on a warrant that later proved to be defective shall be inadmissible in a federal civil tax proceeding. Clearly, the enforcement of valid laws would be hampered by so extending the exclusionary rule, and concededly relevant and reliable evidence would be rendered unavailable. In evaluating the need for a deterrent sanction, one must first identify those who are to be deterred. In this case it is the state officer who is the primary object of the sanction. Two factors suggest that a sanction in addition to those that presently exist is unnecessary. First, the local law enforcement official is already "punished" by the exclusion of the evidence in the state criminal trial. That, necessarily, is of substantial concern to him. Second, the evidence is also excludable in the federal criminal trial so that the entire criminal enforcement process, which is the concern and duty of these officers, is frustrated.

Jurists and scholars have recognized that the exclusionary rule imposes a substantial cost on the societal interest in law enforcement by its proscription of what concededly is relevant evidence. And alternatives that would be less costly to societal interests have been the subject of extensive discussion and exploration. If the exclusionary rule is the "strong medicine" that its proponents claim it to be, then its use in the situations in which it is now applied (resulting in frustration of the Los Angeles police officers' good-faith duties as enforcers of the criminal laws) must be assumed to be a substantial and efficient deterrent. Assuming this efficacy, the additional marginal deterrence provided by forbidding a different sovereign from using the evidence in a civil proceeding surely does not outweigh the cost to society of extending the rule to that situation. If, on the other hand, the exclusionary rule does not result in appreciable deterrence, then, clearly, its use in the instant situation is unwarranted.

We conclude that exclusion from federal civil proceedings of evidence unlawfully seized by a state criminal enforcement officer has not been shown to have a sufficient likelihood of deterring the conduct of the state police so that it outweighs the societal costs imposed by the exclusion. This Court, therefore, is not justified in so extending the exclusionary rule. Imposition of the exclusionary rule in this case is unlikely to provide significant, much less substantial, additional deterrence. It falls outside the offending officer's zone of primary interest. The extension of the exclusionary rule would be an unjustifiably drastic action by the courts in the pursuit of what is an undesired and undesirable supervisory role over police officers. In the situation before us, we do not find sufficient justification for the drastic measure of an exclusionary rule. There comes a point at which courts, consistent with their duty to administer the law, cannot continue to create barriers to law enforcement in the pursuit of a supervisory role that is properly the duty of the Executive and Legislative Branches. We therefore hold that the judicially created exclusionary rule should not be extended to forbid the use in the civil proceeding of one sovereign of evidence seized by a criminal law enforcement agent of another sovereign.

The judgment of the Court of Appeals is reversed, and the case is remanded for further proceedings consistent with this opinion.

It is so ordered.

MR. JUSTICE BRENNAN, with whom MR. JUSTICE MARSHALL concurs, dissenting.

The exclusionary rule is a necessary and inherent constitutional ingredient of the protections of the Fourth Amendment.

MR. JUSTICE STEWART, dissenting.

Federal officials responsible for the enforcement of the wagering tax provisions regularly cooperate with federal and local officials responsible for enforcing criminal laws restricting or forbidding wagering. Similarly, federal and local law enforcement personnel regularly provide federal tax officials with information, obtained in criminal investigations, indicating liability under the wagering tax. The pattern is one of mutual cooperation and coordination, with the federal wagering tax provisions buttressing state and federal criminal sanctions. If state police officials can effectively crack down on gambling law violators by the simple expedient of violating their constitutional rights and turning the illegally seized evidence over to Internal Revenue Service agents on the proverbial "silver platter," then the deterrent purpose of the exclusionary rule is wholly frustrated. "If, on the other hand, it is understood that the fruit of an unlawful search by state agents will be inadmissible in a federal trial, there can be no inducement to subterfuge and evasion with respect to federal-state cooperation in criminal investigation." *Elkins v. United States*, 364 U.S. 206, 222 (1960).

Points for Discussion

a.   The Exclusionary Rule & Immigration Proceedings

Janis was followed by the Court's decision in *Immigration and Naturalization Service v. Lopez-Mendoza*, 468 U.S. 1032 (1984), in which the Court refused to apply the exclusionary rule in a deportation proceeding even though the officials who conducted an unlawful arrest were the same officials who brought a subsequent deportation proceeding (in other words, there was no "intrasovereign" violation). The Court justified its decision as follows:

Several factors significantly reduce the deterrent value of the exclusionary rule in a civil deportation proceeding. First, deportation will still be possible when evidence not derived directly from the arrest is sufficient to support deportation. Since the person and identity of the respondent are not themselves suppressible, the INS must prove only alienage, and that will sometimes be possible using evidence gathered independently of, or sufficiently attenuated from, the original arrest. There is no provision which forbids drawing an adverse inference from the fact of standing mute. The second factor is a practical one. In the course of a year the average INS agent arrests almost 500 illegal aliens. Over 97.5% apparently agree to voluntary deportation without a formal hearing. When an occasional challenge is brought, the arresting officer is most unlikely to shape his conduct in anticipation of the exclusion of evidence at a formal deportation hearing. Third, and perhaps most important, the INS has its own comprehensive scheme for deterring Fourth Amendment violations by its officers. Evidence seized through intentionally unlawful conduct is excluded by Department of Justice policy from the proceeding for which it was obtained. The INS also has in place a procedure for investigating and punishing immigration officers who commit Fourth Amendment violations. The INS's attention to Fourth Amendment interests reduces the likely deterrent value of the exclusionary rule. Deterrence must be measured at the margin. Finally, the deterrent value of the exclusionary rule in deportation proceedings is undermined by the availability of alternative remedies for institutional practices by the INS that might violate Fourth Amendment rights.

On the other side of the scale, the social costs of applying the exclusionary rule in deportation proceedings are unusual and significant. Applying the exclusionary rule in proceedings that are intended not to punish past transgressions but to prevent their continuance or renewal would require the courts to close their eyes to ongoing violations of the law. This Court has never before accepted costs of this character in applying the exclusionary rule. Sandoval is a person whose unregistered presence in this country, without more, constitutes a crime. His release within our borders would immediately subject him to criminal penalties. His release would clearly frustrate the express public policy against an alien's unregistered presence in this country. Even the objective of deterring Fourth Amendment violations should not require such a result. The constable's blunder may allow the criminal to go free, but we have never suggested that it allows the criminal to continue in the commission of an ongoing crime. Other factors also weigh against applying the exclusionary rule in deportation proceedings. The INS currently operates a deliberately simple deportation hearing system, streamlined to permit the quick resolution of very large numbers of deportation actions, and it is against this backdrop that the costs of the exclusionary rule must be assessed. Finally, the INS advances the credible argument that applying the exclusionary rule to deportation proceedings might well result in the suppression of large amounts of information that had been obtained entirely lawfully. INS arrests occur in crowded and confused circumstances. In these circumstances we are persuaded that the *Janis* balance between costs and benefits comes out against applying the exclusionary rule in civil deportation hearings held by the INS.

Justice Brennan, dissenting, argued that "the Government has an obligation to obey the Fourth Amendment; that obligation is not lifted simply because the evidence was to be used in civil deportation proceedings." Justice White, also dissenting, contended that: "Because INS agents are law enforcement officials whose mission is analogous to that of police officers and because civil deportation proceedings are to INS agents what criminal trials are to police officers, the costs and benefits of applying the exclusionary rule in civil deportation proceedings do not differ from the costs and benefits of applying the rule in ordinary criminal proceedings." Justice Marshall also dissented: "There is no other way than exclusion to achieve 'the twin goals of enabling the judiciary to avoid the taint of partnership in official lawlessness and of assuring the people—all potential victims of unlawful government conduct—that the government would not profit from its lawless behavior.' "

b.   More on the Exclusionary Rule & Deportation Proceedings

In *Lopez-Rodriguez v. Mukasey*, 536 F.3d 1012 (9th Cir. 2008), the court applied the exclusionary rule in a deportation proceeding on the basis that the Fourth Amendment violation was "egregious." In that case, officers entered the suspects' home without a warrant, consent or exigent circumstances.

c.   The Exclusionary Rule in Grand Jury Proceedings

In *United States v. Calandra*, 414 U.S. 338 (1974), the Court refused to apply the exclusionary rule to a witness summoned to appear and testify before a grand jury who refused to answer questions on the ground that they were based on evidence obtained from an unlawful search and seizure. The Court justified its decision as follows: "This extension of the exclusionary rule would seriously impede the grand jury. Because the grand jury does not finally adjudicate guilt or innocence, it has traditionally been allowed to pursue its investigative and accusatorial functions unimpeded by the evidentiary and procedural restrictions applicable to a criminal trial. Any incremental deterrent effect which might be achieved by extending the rule to grand jury proceedings is uncertain at best. Such an extension would deter only police investigation consciously directed toward the discovery of evidence solely for use in a grand jury investigation. The incentive to disregard the requirement of the Fourth Amendment solely to obtain an indictment from a grand jury is substantially negated by the inadmissibility of the illegally seized evidence in a subsequent criminal prosecution of the search victim. A prosecutor would be unlikely to request an indictment where a conviction could not be obtained." Justice Brennan dissented: "The exclusionary rule is 'an essential part of both the Fourth and Fourteenth Amendments,' that 'gives to the individual no more than that which the Constitution guarantees him, to the police officer no less than that to which honest law enforcement is entitled, and, to the courts, that judicial integrity so necessary in the true administration of justice.' "

Food for Thought

In *Sanchez-Llamas v. Oregon*, 548 U.S. 331 (2006), the Court refused to apply the exclusionary rule to a violation of Article 36 of the Vienna Convention on Consular Relations. Article 36 provides that, when a national of one country is detained by authorities in another, the authorities must notify the consular officers of the detainee's home country if the detainee so requests, and must inform the detainee of his right to request consular assistance. Sanchez-Llamas was detained for shooting a police officer, and given a *Miranda* warning, but was not informed of his right to consular assistance. He sought to suppress his statements because of non-compliance with Article 36. After noting that Article 36 does not provide for the remedy of suppression, the Court held that U.S. law does not require suppression: "It is beyond dispute that we do not hold a supervisory power over the courts of the several States. Where a treaty does not provide a particular remedy, either expressly or implicitly, it is not for the federal courts to impose one on the States through lawmaking of their own. Even if Sanchez-Llamas is correct that Article 36 implicitly requires a judicial remedy, the Convention equally states that Article 36 rights 'shall be exercised in conformity with the laws and regulations of the receiving State.' Under our domestic law, the exclusionary rule is not a remedy we apply lightly. The violation of the right to consular notification, in contrast, is at best remotely connected to the gathering of evidence." Justice Breyer, joined by Justices Stevens and Souter, dissented: "*Sometimes* suppression could prove the only effective remedy. And, if that is so, then the Convention, which insists upon effective remedies, would require suppression in an appropriate case."

Hypo 1: *More on the Exclusionary Rule's Application to Civil Proceedings*

Does *Janis* suggest that the exclusionary rule should never be applied in administrative proceedings? Suppose that the *Janis* search had been conducted by IRS investigators rather than by the police. Would the Court's "cost-benefit" analysis require exclusion of the evidence when the IRS sought to use it? Suppose that IRS investigators enter Grace Harlow's home in hopes of finding evidence of illegal gambling. The investigators are acting without a warrant even though one is required. When Harlow confronts the investigators, they beat and restrain her. Ultimately, the investigators uncover evidence of illegal gambling and seek to use that evidence against Harlow in a civil tax proceeding. If you are hired to represent Harlow, how can you distinguish *Janis* and argue that the exclusion ary rule should be applied to Harlow's case? How might the IRS respond to those arguments? In light of *Lopez-Mendoza*, is the Court likely to apply the exclusionary rule in administrative proceedings? When will the "benefits" of the exclusionary rule outweigh the "costs" in a manner that justifies application of the exclusionary rule in an administrative proceeding?

Hypo 2: *The Exclusionary Rule & Cooperative Investigations*

The police and the IRS often work together on criminal investigations. Suppose that Janis can prove that the police and the IRS were working together in investigating him? Under such circumstances, should the Court apply the exclusionary rule? Would it matter whether the IRS was actually involved and helped plan the illegal search?

Hypo 3: *Evaluating Calandra*

Do you agree with *Calandra*'s conclusion that a prosecutor would have no incentive to seek an indictment based on evidence that could not be admitted at trial? Suppose that the prosecutor believes that defendant is part of a conspiracy to commit bank robberies, and uses the illegal evidence to indict one of the conspirators. What advantage might the prosecutor gain from the simple fact of the indictment?

D. The Scope of the Exclusionary Rules

The exclusionary rule is subject to various rules and doctrines that expand or contract the scope of the rule.

1. Standing

Standing concepts limit the exclusionary rule's application. In the Fifth Amendment area, the Court treats the privilege against self-incrimination as "personal" and has held that it can only be asserted by the person whose rights have been violated. This limitation is seemingly implicit in the Fifth Amendment itself which states that "no person shall be compelled in any criminal case to be a witness against himself." U.S. Const., Amend. V. As the Court stated in *Hale v. Henkel*, 201 U.S. 43 (1906): "The right of a person under the 5th Amendment to refuse to incriminate himself is purely a personal privilege of the witness. It was never intended to permit him to plead the fact that some third person might be incriminated by his testimony, even though he were the agent of such person. A privilege so extensive might be used to put a stop to the examination of every witness who was called upon to testify before the grand jury with regard to the doings or business of his principal, whether such principal were an individual or a corporation."

Even though the Fourth Amendment is not phrased in such personal terms, the Court has also applied the standing requirement to Fourth Amendment violations. In *Alderman v. United States*, 394 U.S. 165 (1969), the Court stated: "Fourth Amendment rights are personal rights which, like some other constitutional rights, may not be vicariously asserted. If the police make an unwarranted search of a house and seize tangible property belonging to third parties, the homeowner may object to its use against him, not because he had any interest in the seized items as 'effects' protected by the Fourth Amendment, but because they were the fruits of an unauthorized search of his house, which is itself expressly protected by the Fourth Amendment."

At one point, the standing requirement was modified by an "automatic standing" rule articulated in *Jones v. United States*, 362 U.S. 257 (1960). Jones, who was prosecuted for the possession of narcotics, moved to suppress evidence obtained via a search warrant on the basis that the warrant had been issued without probable cause. The judge denied the motion for lack of standing, and the Court reversed: "Since narcotics charges may be established through proof solely of possession of narcotics, a defendant seeking to comply with the conventional standing requirement has been forced to allege facts the proof of which would tend, if indeed not be sufficient, to convict him. He has been faced, not only with the chance that the allegations made on the motion to suppress may be used against him at the trial, but also with the encouragement that he perjure himself if he seeks to establish 'standing' while maintaining a defense to the charge of possession. The possession on the basis of which petitioner is to be and was convicted suffices to give him standing under any fair and rational conception of the requirements of Rule 41(e)."

Rakas v. Illinois

439 U.S. 128 (1978).

MR. JUSTICE REHNQUIST delivered the opinion of the Court.

A police officer on routine patrol received a radio call notifying him of a robbery of a clothing store and describing the getaway car. Shortly thereafter, the officer spotted an automobile which he thought might be the getaway car. After following the car, he and several other officers stopped the vehicle. The occupants of the automobile, petitioners and two female companions, were ordered out of the car and two officers searched the interior of the vehicle. They discovered a box of rifle shells in the glove compartment, which had been locked, and a sawed-off rifle under the front passenger seat. After discovering the rifle and the shells, the officers placed petitioners under arrest. Petitioners moved to suppress the rifle and shells on the ground that the search violated the Fourth and Fourteenth Amendments. They conceded that they did not own the automobile and were simply passengers; the owner of the car had been the driver. Nor did they assert that they owned the rifle or the shells seized. The prosecutor challenged petitioners' standing to object to the lawfulness of the search of the car. The trial court held that petitioners lacked standing and denied the motion to suppress the evidence. Petitioners were convicted and the conviction was affirmed.

Petitioners urge us to relax or broaden the rule of standing enunciated in *Jones v. United States*, 362 U.S. 257 (1960), so that any criminal defendant at whom a search was "directed" would have standing to contest the legality of that search and object to the admission of evidence obtained as a result of the search. Alternatively, petitioners argue that they have standing to object to the search under *Jones* because they were "legitimately on the premises" at the time of the search. *Jones* focuses on whether the person seeking to challenge the legality of a search was himself the "victim" of the search or seizure. Adoption of the so-called "target" theory advanced by petitioners would in effect permit a defendant to assert that a violation of the Fourth Amendment rights of a third party entitled him to have evidence suppressed at his trial. We decline to extend the rule of standing. As we stated in *Alderman v. United States*, 394 U.S. 165, 174 (1969), "Fourth Amendment rights are personal rights which, like some other constitutional rights, may not be vicariously asserted." A person who is aggrieved by an illegal search and seizure only through the introduction of damaging evidence secured by a search of a third person's premises or property has not had any of his Fourth Amendment rights infringed. Since the exclusionary rule is an attempt to effectuate the guarantees of the Fourth Amendment, it is proper to permit only defendants whose Fourth Amendment rights have been violated to benefit from the rule's protections. There is no reason to think that a party whose rights have been infringed will not, if evidence is used against him, have ample motivation to move to suppress it. Even if such a person is not a defendant in the action, he may be able to recover damages for the violation of his Fourth Amendment rights, or seek redress under state law for invasion of privacy or trespass.

In support of their target theory, petitioners rely on the following quotation from *Jones*: "In order to qualify as a 'person aggrieved by an unlawful search and seizure' one must have been a victim of a search or seizure, one against whom the search was directed, as distinguished from one who claims prejudice only through the use of evidence gathered as a consequence of a search or seizure directed at someone else." This statement suggests that the language was meant merely as a parenthetical equivalent of the previous phrase "a victim of a search or seizure." To the extent that the language might be read more broadly, it is dictum which was impliedly repudiated in *Alderman* and which we now expressly reject. In *Alderman*, Mr. Justice Fortas argued that the Court should "include within the category of those who may object to the introduction of illegal evidence 'one against whom the search was directed.' " The Court rejected this theory holding that persons who were not parties to unlawfully overheard conversations or who did not own the premises on which such conversations took place did not have standing to contest the legality of the surveillance, regardless of whether or not they were the "targets" of the surveillance. Mr. Justice Harlan identified administrative problems posed by the target theory: "The target rule would entail very substantial administrative difficulties. In the majority of cases, the police plant a bug with the expectation that it may well produce leads to a large number of crimes. A lengthy hearing would then be necessary in order to determine whether the police knew of an accused's criminal activity at the time the bug was planted and whether the police decision to plant a bug was motivated by an effort to obtain information against the accused or some other individual. I do not believe that this administrative burden is justified in any substantial degree by the hypothesized marginal increase in Fourth Amendment protection." We cannot but give weight to practical difficulties such as those foreseen by Mr. Justice Harlan in the quoted language.

Conferring standing to raise vicarious Fourth Amendment claims would necessarily mean a more widespread invocation of the exclusionary rule during criminal trials. *Alderman* counseled against such an extension of the exclusionary rule: "We are not convinced that the additional benefits of extending the exclusionary rule to other defendants would justify further encroachment upon the public interest in prosecuting those accused of crime and having them acquitted or convicted on the basis of all the evidence which exposes the truth." Each time the exclusionary rule is applied it exacts a substantial social cost for the vindication of Fourth Amendment rights. Relevant and reliable evidence is kept from the trier of fact and the search for truth at trial is deflected. Since our cases generally have held that one whose Fourth Amendment rights are violated may successfully suppress evidence obtained in the course of an illegal search and seizure, misgivings as to the benefit of enlarging the class of persons who may invoke that rule are properly considered when deciding whether to expand standing to assert Fourth Amendment violations. We can think of no decided cases that would have come out differently had we concluded, as we do now, that the type of standing requirement discussed in *Jones* and reaffirmed today is more properly subsumed under substantive Fourth Amendment doctrine. The better analysis forthrightly focuses on the extent of a particular defendant's rights under the Fourth Amendment, rather than on any theoretically separate, but invariably intertwined concept of standing.

The issue of standing involves two inquiries: first, whether the proponent of a particular legal right has alleged "injury in fact," and, second, whether the proponent is asserting his own legal rights and interests rather than basing his claim for relief upon the rights of third parties. The question is whether the challenged search or seizure violated the Fourth Amendment rights of a criminal defendant who seeks to exclude the evidence obtained. That inquiry requires a determination of whether the disputed search and seizure has infringed an interest of the defendant which the Fourth Amendment was designed to protect. We are under no illusion that by dispensing with the rubric of standing used in *Jones* we have rendered any simpler the determination of whether the proponent of a motion to suppress is entitled to contest the legality of a search and seizure. But we think the decision of this issue will rest on sounder logical footing.

Petitioners, who were passengers occupying a car which they neither owned nor leased, seek to analogize their position to that of the defendant in *Jones*. In *Jones*, petitioner was present at the search of an apartment which was owned by a friend. The friend had given Jones permission to use the apartment and a key to it, with which Jones had admitted himself on the day of the search. He had a suit and shirt at the apartment and had slept there "maybe a night," but his home was elsewhere. At the time of the search, Jones was the only occupant of the apartment because the lessee was away for several days. Under these circumstances, this Court stated that while one wrongfully on the premises could not move to suppress evidence obtained as a result of searching them, "anyone legitimately on premises where a search occurs may challenge its legality." Petitioners argue that their occupancy of the automobile was comparable to that of Jones in the apartment and that they therefore have standing to contest the legality of the search—or as we rephrased the inquiry, that they, like Jones, had their Fourth Amendment rights violated by the search.

We do not question the conclusion in *Jones*. Nonetheless, we believe that the phrase "legitimately on premises" coined in *Jones* creates too broad a gauge for measurement of Fourth Amendment rights. Applied literally, this statement would permit a casual visitor who has never seen, or been permitted to visit, the basement of another's house to object to a search of the basement if the visitor happened to be in the kitchen at the time of the search. Likewise, a casual visitor who walks into a house one minute before a search commences and leaves one minute after the search ends would be able to contest the legality of the search. The first visitor would have absolutely no interest or legitimate expectation of privacy in the basement, the second would have none in the house, and it advances no purpose served by the Fourth Amendment to permit either of them to object to the lawfulness of the search. We think that *Jones* stands for the unremarkable proposition that a person can have a legally sufficient interest in a place other than his own home so that the Fourth Amendment protects him from unreasonable governmental intrusion into that place. In defining the scope of that interest, arcane distinctions developed in property and tort law between guests, licensees, invitees, and the like, ought not to control. But the *Jones* statement that a person need only be "legitimately on premises" in order to challenge the validity of the search of a dwelling place cannot be taken in its full sweep beyond the facts of that case.

Katz held that capacity to claim the protection of the Fourth Amendment depends not upon a property right in the invaded place but upon whether the person who claims the protection of the Amendment has a legitimate expectation of privacy in the invaded place. Jones had a legitimate expectation of privacy in the premises he was using and therefore could claim the protection of the Fourth Amendment with respect to a governmental invasion of those premises, even though his "interest" in those premises might not have been a recognized property interest at common law.[12] In abandoning "legitimately on premises" for the doctrine that we announce today, we are rejecting blind adherence to a phrase which at most has superficial clarity and which conceals underneath that thin veneer all of the problems of line drawing which must be faced in any conscientious effort to apply the Fourth Amendment. We would not wish to be understood as saying that legitimate presence on the premises is irrelevant to one's expectation of privacy, but it cannot be deemed controlling.

Judged by this analysis, petitioners' claims must fail. They asserted neither a property nor a possessory interest in the automobile, nor an interest in the property seized. The fact that they were "legitimately on the premises" in the sense that they were in the car with the permission of its owner is not determinative of whether they had a legitimate expectation of privacy in the particular areas of the automobile searched. It is unnecessary to decide whether the same expectations of privacy are warranted in a car as in a dwelling place in analogous circumstances. Petitioners' claim is one which would fail even in an analogous situation in a dwelling place, since they made no showing that they had any legitimate expectation of privacy in the glove compartment or area under the seat of the car in which they were merely passengers. Like the trunk of an automobile, these are areas in which a passenger qua passenger would not normally have a legitimate expectation of privacy. *Jones* and *Katz* involved significantly different factual circumstances. Jones not only had permission to use the apartment of his friend, but also had a key to the apartment with which he admitted himself on the day of the search and kept possessions in the apartment. Except with respect to his friend, Jones had complete dominion and control over the apartment and could

---

[12] A "legitimate" expectation of privacy means more than a subjective expectation of not being discovered. A burglar plying his trade in a cabin may have a subjective expectation of privacy, but it is not one which the law recognizes as "legitimate." Legitimate expectations must have a source outside of the Fourth Amendment, either by reference to concepts of real or personal property law or to understandings that are recognized and permitted by society. Expectations of privacy need not be based on a common-law interest in real or personal property, or on the invasion of such an interest. But the Court has not altogether abandoned use of property concepts in determining the presence or absence of the privacy interests protected by that Amendment. In *Alderman*, the Court held that an individual's property interest in his own home was so great as to allow him to object to electronic surveillance of conversations emanating from his home, even though he himself was not a party to the conversations. On the other hand, even a property interest in premises may not be sufficient to establish a legitimate expectation of privacy with respect to particular items located on the premises or activity conducted thereon.

exclude others from it. Likewise in *Katz*, the defendant occupied the telephone booth, shut the door behind him to exclude all others and paid the toll, which "entitled him to assume that the words he uttered into the mouthpiece would not be broadcast to the world." Katz and Jones could legitimately expect privacy in the areas which were the subject of the search and seizure each sought to contest. No such showing was made by petitioners with respect to those portions of the automobile which were searched.[17]

The Illinois courts were correct in concluding that it was unnecessary to decide whether the search of the car might have violated the rights secured to someone else by the Fourth and Fourteenth Amendments to the United States Constitution. Since it did not violate any rights of these petitioners, their judgment of conviction is

Affirmed.

MR. JUSTICE POWELL, with whom THE CHIEF JUSTICE joins, concurring.

None of the passengers had control of the vehicle or the keys. It is unrealistic to suggest that these passengers had any reasonable expectation that the car in which they had been riding would not be searched after they were lawfully stopped and made to get out. The minimal privacy that existed is not comparable to that of an individual in his place of abode.

MR. JUSTICE WHITE, with whom MR. JUSTICE BRENNAN, MR. JUSTICE MARSHALL, and MR. JUSTICE STEVENS join, dissenting.

When a person is legitimately present in a private place, his right to privacy is protected from unreasonable governmental interference even if he does not own the premises. An expectation of privacy does not hinge on ownership. Surely a person riding in an automobile next to his friend the owner, or a child or wife with the father or spouse, must have some protection. If a nonowner may consent to a search merely because he is a joint user or occupant of a "premises," then that same nonowner must have a protected privacy interest.

The Court asserts that it is not limiting the bar against unreasonable searches to the protection of property rights, but in reality it is doing exactly that.[18] Petitioners

---

[17] Our dissenting Brethren criticize our "holding" that unless one has a common-law property interest in the premises searched, one cannot object to the search. To the contrary, we have taken pains to reaffirm the statements in *Jones* and *Katz* that "arcane distinctions developed in property law ought not to control."

[18] The Court's reliance on property law concepts is shown by its suggestion that visitors could "contest the lawfulness of the seizure of evidence or the search if their own property were seized during the search." What difference should that property interest make to constitutional protection against unreasonable searches, which is concerned with privacy? A passenger in a car expects to enjoy the privacy of the vehicle whether or not he happens to carry some item along for the ride. Even a person living in a barren room without possessions is entitled to expect that the police will not intrude without cause.

were in a private place with the permission of the owner. If that is not sufficient, what would be? It is hard to imagine anything short of a property interest that would satisfy the majority. Insofar as the Court's rationale is concerned, no passenger in an automobile, without an ownership or possessory interest and regardless of his relationship to the owner, may claim Fourth Amendment protection against illegal stops and searches of the automobile in which he is rightfully present. The Court approves the result in *Jones*, but it fails to give any explanation why the facts in *Jones* differ, in a fashion material to the Fourth Amendment, from the facts here.[15] More importantly, how is the Court able to avoid answering the question why presence in a private place with the owner's permission is insufficient?

As a control on governmental power, the Fourth Amendment assures that some expectations of privacy are justified and will be protected from official intrusion. If protected zones of privacy can only be purchased or obtained by possession of property, then much of our daily lives will be unshielded from unreasonable governmental prying, and the reach of the Fourth Amendment will have been narrowed to protect chiefly those with possessory interests in real or personal property. *Katz* firmly established that the Fourth Amendment was intended as more than simply a trespass law applicable to the government. Katz had no possessory interest in the public telephone booth; Katz was simply legitimately present. And the decision in *Katz* was based not on property rights, but on the theory that it was essential to securing "conditions favorable to the pursuit of happiness" that the expectation of privacy in question be recognized. One could say that perhaps the Constitution provides some degree less protection for the personal freedom from unreasonable governmental intrusion when one does not have a possessory interest in the invaded private place. But that would only change the extent of the protection; it would not free police to do the unreasonable.

The Court's holding is contrary to the everyday expectations of privacy that we all share. If the owner of the car had not only invited petitioners to join her but had said to them, "I give you a temporary possessory interest in my vehicle so that you will share the right to privacy that I own," then the majority would reverse. But people seldom say such things, though they may mean their invitation to encompass them if only they had thought of the problem. If the nonowner were the spouse or child of the owner, would the Court recognize a sufficient interest? If so, would distant relatives somehow have more of an expectation of privacy than close friends? What if the nonowner were driving with the owner's permission? *Katz* expressly recognized protection for such passengers. Why should Fourth Amendment rights be present when one pays a cabdriver for a ride but be absent when one is given a ride by a friend?

---

[15] Jones had permission to use the apartment, had slept in it one night, had a key, had left a suit and a shirt there, and was the only occupant at the time of the search. Petitioners here had permission to be in the car and were occupying it at the time of the search. Thus the only distinguishing fact is that Jones could exclude others from the apartment by using his friend's key. But petitioners and their friend the owner had excluded others by entering the automobile and shutting the doors.

This decision invites police to engage in patently unreasonable searches every time an automobile contains more than one occupant. Should something be found, only the owner of the vehicle, or of the item, will have standing to seek suppression, and the evidence will presumably be usable against the other occupants. The danger of such bad faith is especially high in cases where the officers are only after the passengers.

Take Note

The concept of "automatic standing," first articulated in *Jones*, did not survive long after the *Rakas* decision. The Court laid the groundwork for the rule's demise in *Simmons v. United States*, 390 U.S. 377 (1968), a case in which petitioner was arrested for armed robbery based on an illegal search of a house. Petitioner testified that he thought he was the owner of the seized items. Using a self-incrimination analysis, the Court held that petitioner's testimony could not be used against him: "when a defendant testifies in support of a motion to suppress evidence on Fourth Amendment grounds, his testimony may not be admitted against him at trial on the issue of guilt unless he makes no objection." *But see United States v. Kahan*, 415 U.S. 239 (1974) (Court refused to apply *Simmons* to a prosecution for perjury: "*Simmons* barred the use of pretrial testimony at trial to prove its incriminating content. Here, by contrast, the incriminating component of respondent's pretrial statements derives not from their content, but from respondent's knowledge of their falsity."). The Court followed with its decision in *United States v. Salvucci*, 448 U.S. 83 (1980): "Defendants charged with crimes of possession may only claim the benefits of the exclusionary rule if their own Fourth Amendment rights have been violated. The automatic standing rule of *Jones* is therefore overruled. The 'dilemma' identified in *Jones*, that a defendant charged with a possessory offense might only be able to establish his standing to challenge a search and seizure by giving self-incriminating testimony admissible as evidence of his guilt, was eliminated by our decision in *Simmons. Simmons* grants a form of 'use immunity' to those defendants charged with nonpossessory crimes. We decline to use possession of a seized good as a substitute for a factual finding that the owner of the good had a legitimate expectation of privacy in the area searched." Justice Marshall dissented: "*Simmons* does not provide complete protection against the 'self-incrimination dilemma.' The use of the testimony for impeachment purposes would subject a defendant to precisely the same dilemma, unless he was prepared to relinquish his constitutional right to testify in his own defense, and would thereby create a strong deterrent to asserting Fourth Amendment claims. One of the purposes of *Jones* and *Simmons* was to remove such obstacles. Moreover, the opportunity for cross-examination at the suppression hearing may enable the prosecutor to elicit incriminating information beyond that offered on direct examination to establish the requisite Fourth Amendment interest. Even if such information could not be introduced at the subsequent trial, it might be helpful to the prosecution in developing its case or deciding its trial strategy. The furnishing of such a tactical advantage to the prosecution should not be the price of asserting a Fourth Amendment claim." The automatic standing rule is still applied by some state courts under their state constitutions. *See Commonwealth v. Enimpah*, 106 A.3d 695 (Penn. 2014).

In *Byrd v. United States*, 138 S.Ct. 1518 (2018), defendant was stopped while he was driving a rental car that he was not authorized to drive because the rental agreement required that he be listed as an additional driver. The stop ultimately led to a search which uncovered heroin. The Court rejected the argument that a driver who is not listed on a rental agreement lacks an expectation of privacy in the automobile based on the rental company's lack of authorization. The Court emphasized that car-rental agreements contain numerous restrictions (*e.g.*, prohibitions against driving on unpaved roads), and the Court was unwilling to hold that a violation of any of these provisions eliminates a driver's REOP. The Court did not resolve the question of whether Byrd had no REOP because he obtained the car under false pretenses (using a confederate to rent the vehicle because he could not have rented it due to his criminal record), thereby committing fraud on the rental company. That issue was not raised in the lower courts.

Food for Thought

Does *Rakas* use any standard other than property principles to define the expectation of privacy test? If so, what are those principles? Does *Rakas* apply the "expectation of privacy" test in the same manner as *Katz*? If not, how do you explain the difference in application?

Hypo 1: *Denying Ownership*

The police wish to search a vehicle that is on a car transport carrier. They inquire of a man, standing near the vehicle, whether they may conduct the search. The man denies that he owns the vehicle. After the police conduct the search, and find contraband, and eventually link the man to the vehicle, he wants to challenge the search as a violation of the Fourth Amendment. Can the man establish standing to challenge the search after he originally denied ownership of the vehicle? *See United States v. Castellanos*, 716 F.3d 828 (4th Cir. 2013). Likewise, does a passenger in an automobile have standing to challenge a search of his luggage that was left in the trunk of another person's automobile? Does it matter whether the luggage has tags identifying the owner? Does it matter whether, at the time of the search, the owner claimed ownership of the bag, and demanded that the police not search the bag? *See United States v. Iraheta*, 764 F.3d 455 (5th Cir. 2014).

Food for Thought

Consider Justice Fortas' opinion, concurring and dissenting, in *Alderman*: "In recognition of the principle that lawlessness on the part of the Government must be stoutly condemned, this Court has ruled that the Government may not profit from its fruits. For reasons which are related more to convenience and judicial prudence than to constitutional principles, courts of all states except California and of the federal system have allowed in evidence material obtained by police agents in direct and acknowledged violation of the Fourth Amendment. They have allowed this evidence except where a defendant who moves for suppression of the material can show that his personal right of privacy was violated by the unlawful search or seizure. If the exclusionary rule follows from the Fourth Amendment itself, there is no basis for confining its invocation to persons whose right of privacy has been violated by an illegal search. The Fourth Amendment is couched in terms of a guarantee that the Government will not engage in unreasonable searches and seizures. It is a general prohibition, a fundamental part of the constitutional compact, the observance of which is essential to the welfare of all persons. Accordingly, the necessary implication is that any defendant against whom illegally acquired evidence is offered, whether or not it was obtained in violation of his right to privacy, may have the evidence excluded. The Fourth Amendment is an assurance to all that the Government will exercise its formidable powers to arrest and to investigate only subject to the rule of law." Do you agree with Justice Fortas?

Hypo 2: *Rakas & Familial Relations*

In *Rakas*, Justice White asks whether the Court would have reached the opposite result (in other words, it would have found that "standing" existed), had the passengers been related to the driver. Suppose that you have been hired to represent the driver's teenage son. Following a search of the car, the police find illegal drugs (rather than a shotgun) under the seat. Would the son have standing to challenge the search if he had been a passenger in his father's car? In light of the *Rakas* decision, how would you argue the case on his behalf?

Hypo 3: *More on Passenger Standing*

In *Rakas*, the police also found shotgun shells in the glove compartment. Would a passenger have standing to challenge the search if the glove compartment was locked, and the passenger had possession of the key? Would it matter whether the owner/driver also had a key? Would your decision be affected by the fact that the passenger (who was not the owner of the car) was driving the car, and the owner was in the passenger seat? *See United States v. Almeida*, 748 F.3d 41 (1st Cir. 2014).

Hypo 4: *Challenging the Stop*

Would the result in *Rakas* have been different if, instead of challenging the search, the passengers had claimed that the police illegally stopped the car in which they were riding? How might Rakas have argued that he has standing to challenge the illegal stop? Would his standing to challenge the stop also give him standing to challenge the subsequent search?

Hypo 5: *Jones & Passenger Standing*

Now, recall the holding in *United States v. Jones* (discussed in chapter 4) which held that the police commit a trespass when they attach a GPS device to a vehicle in order to track it. Under *Jones*, we know that the owner of the vehicle has standing to challenge the attachment of the GPS system. What about a passenger in the vehicle? *See United States v. Davis*, 750 F.3d 1186 (10th Cir. 2014). Would a driver, who did not own the vehicle, but simply borrowed it, have standing to challenge the GPS? *See United States v. Gibson*, 708 F.3d 1256 (11th Cir. 2013).

Hypo 6: *Standing to Challenge Corporate Office Searches*

IRS agents obtain warrants authorizing a search of a corporation's headquarters and principal business offices for evidence of health care fraud and tax evasion. The search leads to an indictment, alleging a conspiracy with physicians, cardiac diagnostic providers, and others to bill for work that they did not actually perform. Subsequently, the corporation and its officers challenge the warrant on the basis that it fails the particularity requirement. Does the corporation have standing to challenge the warrant? Do corporate officers or part owners of the corporation also have standing to challenge the warrant? *See United States v. SDI Future Health, Inc.*, 553 F.3d 1246 (9th Cir. 2009).

Hypo 7: *Standing in an Internet Age*

The police believe that defendant is transmitting child pornography via the internet. In an effort to catch defendant, the police obtain a warrant to search Google's computer records regarding defendant's internet search requests. When the Google search uncovers information that incriminates defendant, defendant moves to suppress on the basis that the Google search was a "fishing expedition" that was not justified based on probable cause. Does defendant have standing to challenge the Google search?

Hypo 8: *Fraudulent Access to Property*

Rigmaiden uses a fake identity to rent an apartment, as well as to purchase a computer and aircard that he uses to perpetrate tax fraud. When the police track the aircard, the IP address for the computer, and search the apartment, Rigmaiden claims that the police violated his REOP. Can Rigmaiden have a REOP in property obtained through a fake identity? *See United States v. Rigmaiden*, 2013 WL 1932800 (Ariz.).

Hypo 9: *More on Standing*

Suppose that a woman consents to a body cavity search that reveals the existence of illegal drugs. A reviewing court concludes that the consent was coerced for a variety of reasons: the police held the woman under difficult conditions for several hours; the police implied that they had obtained a warrant for the search when they had not; and the woman appeared groggy when she gave the consent. After the appellate court concludes that the evidence cannot be used against the woman, the prosecution tries to use it to prosecute her husband. Can the evidence be introduced against the husband? More to the point, can he object to the coercive tactics used against his wife, and use those tactics to obtain exclusion of the evidence against himself? Would it matter that the police conduct is regarded as so "egregious" as to violate due process? *See United States v. Anderson*, 772 F.3d 969 (2d Cir. 2014).

Minnesota v. Olson

495 U.S. 91 (1990).

JUSTICE WHITE delivered the opinion of the Court.

A lone gunman robbed an Amoco gasoline station in Minneapolis, Minnesota, and fatally shot the station manager. A police officer heard the dispatcher report and suspected Joseph Ecker. The officer and his partner drove immediately to Ecker's home, arriving at about the same time that an Oldsmobile arrived. The driver of the Oldsmobile took evasive action, and the car spun out of control and came to a stop. Two men fled the car on foot. Ecker, who was later identified as the gunman, was captured shortly thereafter inside his home. The second man escaped. Inside the abandoned Oldsmobile, police found a sack of money and the murder weapon. They also found a title certificate with the name Rob Olson crossed out as a secured party, a letter addressed to a Roger R. Olson of 3151 Johnson Street, and a videotape rental receipt made out to Rob Olson and dated two days earlier. The police verified that a Robert Olson lived at 3151 Johnson Street. The next morning, a woman identifying herself as Dianna Murphy called the police and said that a man by the name of Rob drove the car in which the gas station killer left the scene and that Rob was planning to leave town by bus. About noon, the same woman called again, gave her address and phone number, and said that a man named Rob had told a Maria and two other women, Louanne and Julie, that he was the driver in the Amoco robbery. The caller stated that Louanne was Julie's mother and that the two women lived at 2406 Fillmore Northeast. Police officers were sent to 2406 Fillmore to check out Louanne and Julie. When police arrived they determined that the dwelling was a duplex and that Louanne Bergstrom and her daughter Julie lived in the upper unit but were not home. Police spoke to Louanne's mother, Helen Niederhoffer, who lived in the lower unit. She confirmed that a Rob Olson had been staying upstairs but was not then in the unit. She promised to call the police when Olson returned. At 2 p.m., a "probable cause arrest bulletin," was issued for Olson's arrest. The police were instructed to stay away from the duplex. At approximately 2:45 p.m., Niederhoffer called police and said Olson had returned. The detective-in-charge instructed police officers to go to the house and surround it. He then telephoned Julie from headquarters and told her Rob should come out of the house. The detective heard a male voice say, "tell them I left." Julie stated that Rob had left, whereupon at 3 p.m. the detective ordered the police to enter the house. Without seeking permission and with weapons drawn, the police entered the upper unit and found respondent hiding in a closet. Less than an hour after his arrest, respondent made an inculpatory statement at police headquarters.

The trial court denied respondent's motion to suppress his statement which was admitted into evidence and Olson was convicted of first-degree murder, three counts of armed robbery, and three counts of second-degree assault. The Minnesota Supreme Court reversed, holding that respondent had a sufficient interest in the Bergstrom home to challenge the legality of his warrantless arrest there, that the arrest was illegal because there were no exigent circumstances to justify a warrantless entry, and that respondent's statement was tainted by that illegality and should have been suppressed. We granted the State's petition for certiorari and now affirm.

It was held in *Payton v. New York*, 445 U.S. 573 (1980), that a suspect should not be arrested in his house without an arrest warrant, even though there is probable cause to arrest him. The purpose of the decision was not to protect the person of the suspect but to protect his home from entry in the absence of a magistrate's finding of probable cause. The State argues that Olson's relationship to the premises does not satisfy the 12 factors which in its view determine whether a dwelling is a "home." We need go no further than to conclude that Olson's status as an overnight guest is alone enough to show that he had an expectation of privacy in the home that society is prepared to recognize as reasonable.

The facts of this case are similar to those in *Jones v. United States*, 362 U.S. 257 (1960). In *Jones*, the defendant was arrested in a friend's apartment during the execution of a search warrant and sought to challenge the warrant as not supported by probable cause. "Jones testified that the apartment belonged to a friend, Evans, who had given him the use of it, and a key, with which Jones had admitted himself on the day of the arrest. Jones testified that he had a suit and shirt at the apartment, that his home was elsewhere, that he paid nothing for the use of the apartment, that Evans had let him use it 'as a friend,' that he had slept there 'maybe a night,' and that at the time of the search Evans had been away in Philadelphia for about five days."[6] The Court ruled that Jones could challenge the search of the apartment because he was "legitimately on the premises." Although the "legitimately on the premises" standard was rejected in *Rakas* as too broad, *Rakas* explicitly reaffirmed the factual holding in *Jones*. *Rakas* thus recognized that, as an overnight guest, Jones was much more than just legitimately on the premises. We do not understand *Rakas* to hold that an overnight guest can never have a legitimate expectation of privacy except when his host is away and he has a key. To hold that an overnight guest has a legitimate expectation of privacy in his host's home merely recognizes the everyday expectations of privacy that we all share. Staying overnight in another's home is a longstanding social custom that serves functions recognized as valuable by society. Society recognizes that a houseguest has a legitimate expectation of privacy in his host's home. From the overnight guest's perspective, he seeks shelter in another's home precisely because it provides him with privacy, a place where he and his possessions will not be disturbed by anyone but his host and those his host allows inside. We are at our most vulnerable when we are asleep because we cannot monitor our own safety or the security of our belongings. Although we may spend all day in public places, when we cannot sleep in our own home we

---

[6] Olson, who had been staying at Ecker's home for several days before the robbery, spent the night of the robbery on the floor of the Bergstroms' home, with their permission. He had a change of clothes with him at the duplex.

seek out another private place to sleep, whether it be a hotel room, or the home of a friend. Society expects at least as much privacy in these places as in a telephone booth—"a temporarily private place whose momentary occupants' expectations of freedom from intrusion are recognized as reasonable," *Katz*, 389 U.S., at 361 (Harlan, J., concurring).

That the guest has a host who has ultimate control of the house is not inconsistent with the guest having a legitimate expectation of privacy. The houseguest is there with the permission of his host, who is willing to share his house and his privacy with his guest. It is unlikely that the guest will be confined to a restricted area of the house; and when the host is away or asleep, the guest will have a measure of control over the premises. The host may admit or exclude from the house as he prefers, but it is unlikely that he will admit someone who wants to see or meet with the guest over the objection of the guest. On the other hand, few houseguests will invite others to visit them while they are guests without consulting their hosts; but the latter, who have the authority to exclude despite the wishes of the guest, will often be accommodating. The point is that hosts will more likely than not respect the privacy interests of their guests, who are entitled to a legitimate expectation of privacy despite the fact that they have no legal interest in the premises and do not have the legal authority to determine who may or may not enter the household. If the untrammeled power to admit and exclude were essential to Fourth Amendment protection, an adult daughter temporarily living in the home of her parents would have no legitimate expectation of privacy because her right to admit or exclude would be subject to her parents' veto. Because respondent's expectation of privacy in the Bergstrom home was rooted in "understandings that are recognized and permitted by society," it was legitimate, and respondent can claim the protection of the Fourth Amendment. We therefore affirm the judgment of the Minnesota Supreme Court.

It is so ordered.

Take Note

In *Minnesota v. Carter*, 525 U.S. 83 (1998), a police officer peered through a gap in a closed window blind into a ground floor apartment, and observed respondent bagging cocaine. The Court held that respondent lacked standing to challenge the officer's action because he was a temporary out-of-state visitor to the apartment: "If we regard the overnight guest in *Olson* as typifying those who may claim the protection of the Fourth Amendment in the home of another, and one merely 'legitimately on the premises' as typifying those who may not do so, the present case is obviously somewhere in between. The purely commercial nature of the transaction engaged in here, the relatively short period of time on the premises, and the lack of any previous connection between respondents and the householder, all lead us to conclude that respondents' situation is closer to that of one simply permitted on the premises. Any search which may have occurred did not violate their Fourth Amendment rights."

Points for Discussion

a. Controlled Substances in Another's Purse

In *Rawlings v. Kentucky*, 448 U.S. 98 (1980), petitioner was convicted of trafficking and possession of controlled substances based on evidence seized during the search of a purse. Petitioner, who was staying at a friend's home, carried drugs in a green bank bag. He asked a woman friend whether she would carry it for him and she said "yes." Shortly after she agreed to do so, the police arrived. In response to a police request, Cox poured the contents of her purse onto a coffee table, and told petitioner "to take what was his." Petitioner immediately claimed ownership of the controlled substances. The trial court admitted the drugs against him, holding that petitioner lacked standing to challenge the search: "At the time petitioner dumped thousands of dollars worth of illegal drugs into Cox's purse, he had known her for only a few days and had never sought or received access to her purse. Nor did petitioner have any right to exclude other persons from access. Even assuming that petitioner's version of the bailment is correct and that Cox did consent to the transfer of possession, the precipitous nature of the transaction hardly supports a reasonable inference that petitioner took normal precautions to maintain his privacy. The record contains a frank admission that he had no subjective expectation that Cox's purse would remain free from governmental intrusion. While petitioner's ownership of the drugs is undoubtedly one fact to be considered, *Rakas* emphatically rejected the notion that 'arcane' concepts of property law ought to control the ability to claim the protections of the Fourth Amendment. Petitioner had no legitimate expectation of privacy in Cox's purse." Justice Marshall dissented: "When the government seizes a person's property, it interferes with his constitutionally protected right to be secure in his effects. That interference gives him the right to challenge the reasonableness of the government's conduct, including the seizure. If the defendant's property was seized as the result of an unreasonable search, the seizure cannot be other than unreasonable. *Jones* and *Katz* expanded our view of the protections afforded by the Fourth Amendment by recognizing that privacy interests are protected even if they do not arise from property rights. But that recognition was never intended to exclude interests that had historically been sheltered by the Fourth Amendment."

b. Search of a Union Office

In *Mancusi v. DeForte*, 392 U.S. 364 (1968), DeForte was convicted of conspiracy, coercion and extortion based on evidence seized from a union office where DeForte and several other union officials worked. The search was conducted without a warrant and over DeForte's objections. The Court held that DeForte had standing to object to the search even though the papers belonged to the union: "One has standing to object to a search of his office, as well as of his home. If DeForte had occupied a 'private' office in the union headquarters, and union records had been seized from a desk or a filing cabinet in that office, he would have had standing. In such a 'private' office, DeForte would have been entitled to expect that he would not be disturbed except by personal or business invitees, and that records would not be taken except with his permission or that of his union superiors. The situation was not fundamentally changed because DeForte shared an office with other union officers. DeForte still could reasonably have expected that only those persons and their personal or business guests would enter the office, and that records would not be touched except with their permission or that of union higher-ups. It is irrelevant that the Union or some of its officials might validly have consented to a search of the area where the records were kept, regardless of DeForte's wishes, for it is not claimed that any such consent was given." Justice Black dissented: "A corporate or union official suffers no personal injury when the business office he occupies as an agent of the corporation or union is invaded and when records he has prepared and safeguarded as an agent are seized. The organization has every right to challenge such intrusions if the seizure is illegal, the records can be suppressed in a prosecution against the organization, and if no prosecution is initiated, the organization can obtain return of all the documents by bringing a civil action. Such intrusions, however, involve absolutely no invasion of the 'personal privacy' or security of the agent or employee as an individual, and he has no right to seek suppression of records that the corporation or union itself has made no effort to regain."

Hypo 1: *The Protective Order*

Suppose that, rather than simply being an overnight guest, Olson had previously been in an intimate relationship with the woman who owned the house. However, after Olson became violent, she obtained a protective order prohibiting him from coming within 500 feet of her. The police receive a report, indicating that the woman has allowed Olson (the bank robber) into the house. Does Olson still have a REOP inside the house? *See United States v. Cortez-Dutreiville*, 743 F.3d 881 (3d Cir. 2014).

Hypo 2: *Motel Rooms*

Police receive a tip regarding "suspicious activity" at a nearby motel and they respond. One officer stands behind a motel room (outside a frosted bathroom window) while the other two officers approach the front door. When the officers knock on the door, the third officer sees the bathroom light go on and a figure bending over. The third officer bursts through the window, believing that evidence is being flushed down the toilet. When the officers at the door hear the commotion, they burst through the door and observe two brothers in the room with counterfeit money, women, drugs, and guns. At trial, one woman testified that one brother paid for the rooms and told the other brother to "rent them for the group's use." Did the other brothers have a reasonable expectation of privacy in the motel room? *See United States v. Domenech*, 623 F.3d 325 (6th Cir. 2010).

Hypo 3: *Standing & GPS Tracking Systems*

Drug Enforcement Agency agents are alerted to a drug trafficking operation in Iowa. Using magnetic strips, they place a GPS tracking device on the bumper of a Ford truck while it is parked in a Walmart parking lot in Des Moines. The tracking device allows police to follow the truck back and forth to Denver. Investigators access the device to change the battery seven times during the course of the investigation, each time while the vehicle is parked in a public place. The device can relay the location of the vehicle only while the vehicle is outdoors, and Iowa investigators work with Denver police to monitor the truck while it is in Denver. In addition, they install stationary "pole cameras" in two locations in Des Moines. During the investigation, investigators see Acosta riding in Ford used in the drug ring, and he is seen at a house on Broadway that appears to be the transfer point for drugs. However, Acosta neither owns nor drives the Ford, but is only an occasional passenger therein. Does Acosta have standing to contest the installation and use of the GPS device? *See United States v. Marquez*, 605 F.3d 604 (8th Cir. 2010).

Hypo 4: *Cell Phone Monitoring*

Investigating a drug ring, the police wire an undercover agent so that they can overhear cell phone conversations between criminals. Does a participant in the conversations (who did not know about the confederate or the consent) have standing to challenge the police monitoring of the conversations? What about one of the criminals who participated in the endeavor, but not in the conversations? *See United States v. Marquez*, 605 F.3d 604 (8th Cir. 2010).

Hypo 5: *Standing & the Unclaimed Duffle Bag*

Drug enforcement authorities receive a tip that defendant, who is traveling by bus, is carrying illegal drugs. When the bus stops at a rest area, an officer informs the passengers that he is conducting an investigation, and needs to check their baggage claim tickets. When the passengers claim their luggage, one large duffel bag remains unclaimed. The officer asks defendant if the bag belongs to him, and defendant replies, "No." After a drug-detection dog alerts to the unclaimed duffel bag. Police search the bag and find heroin, as well as identification cards with defendant's name. Given that defendant denied that the duffle bag belonged to him, does he have standing to challenge the search? *See State v. Carvajal*, 202 N.J. 214, 996 A.2d 1029 (2010).

Hypo 6: *Standing & the Evicted Tenant*

A landlord obtains an eviction order requiring defendant to vacate the premises within three days, and authorizing the constable to put the landlord in possession. Unable to find defendant at home, officers attach a copy of the order to defendant's door on two occasions over the next week. At that point, the constable decides to forcibly remove defendant and his possessions. Before he does, he runs an identity check and learns that defendant has two felony convictions. When the police arrive, defendant is present, the police secure him, and conduct a security sweep of the home. In plain view, they find marijuana. Given the eviction order, did defendant have standing to challenge the search of the house? *See United States v. Curlin*, 638 F.3d 562 (7th Cir. 2011).

Hypo 7: *Standing & the Use of an Alias*

Alejandro pays for two hotel rooms and directs Rogelio to rent them for their use. Both are in one of the rooms when the police arrive. Does the fact that Alejandro used an agent to rent the rooms deprive him of standing to challenge a search of the rooms? Does the fact that Rogelio registered for the rooms under an alias deprive him of standing to challenge the search? Would you reach the same result if a celebrity's agent registers him for a room under an alias in order to avoid paparazzi? *See United States v. Domenech*, 623 F.3d 325 (6th Cir. 2010).

Hypo 8: *The Escaping Thief*

An undercover store detective, who believes that defendant is engaged in shoplifting, approaches him. A scuffle ensues. When the detective grabs the back of defendant's jacket, defendant slips out of the jacket and runs away. In the jacket, the detective finds stolen merchandise and a cell phone (which the police used to identify defendant). Does defendant have standing to challenge the search of his jacket and his cell phone given that he voluntarily left them behind? *See State v. Dailey*, 2010 WL 3836204 (Ohio App. 3 Dist. 2010).

Hypo 9: *Dogs in the Aunt's Backyard*

Betts keeps dogs in his aunt's backyard. He used to live at the home, and she allows him to keep the dogs there and to enter daily in order to water and feed his dogs. The backyard was fenced on three sides with wire fencing, and on the fourth side with a wood privacy fence. The dogs are kept approximately 70 yards from the road in the center of the back yard. Some of the dogs are chained to their dog-houses, and others are in pens. Does Betts have standing to challenge a warrantless entry into the backyard to inspect and seize the dogs? *See State v. Betts*, 397 S.W. 3d 198 (Tex. Crim. App. 2013).

United States v. Payner

447 U.S. 727 (1980).

MR. JUSTICE POWELL delivered the opinion of the Court.

Respondent Payner was indicted on a charge of falsifying his 1972 federal income tax return in violation of 18 U.S.C. § 1001. The indictment alleged that respondent denied maintaining a foreign bank account at a time when he knew that he had such an account in the Bahama Islands. The Government's case rested on a loan guarantee agreement dated April 28, 1972, in which respondent pledged the funds in his account as security for a $100,000 loan.

The events are not in dispute. The Internal Revenue Service launched an investigation into the financial activities of American citizens in the Bahamas. The project, known as "Operation Trade Winds," was headquartered in Jacksonville, Fla. Suspicion focused on the Castle Bank in 1972, when investigators learned that a suspected narcotics trafficker had an account there. Special Agent Richard Jaffe of the Jacksonville office asked Norman Casper, a private investigator and occasional informant, to learn what he could about the Castle Bank and its depositors. Casper cultivated his friendship with Castle Bank vice president Michael Wolstencroft. Casper introduced Wolstencroft to Sybol Kennedy, a private investigator and former employee. When Casper discovered that the banker intended to spend a few days in Miami in January 1973, he devised a scheme to gain access to the bank records he knew Wolstencroft would be carrying in his briefcase. Agent Jaffe approved the basic outline of the plan. Wolstencroft arrived in Miami on January 15 and went directly to Kennedy's apartment. At about 7:30 p.m., the two left for dinner at a Key Biscayne restaurant. Shortly thereafter, Casper entered the apartment using a key supplied by Kennedy. He removed the briefcase and delivered it to Jaffe. While the agent supervised the copying of approximately 400 documents taken from the briefcase, a "lookout" observed Kennedy and Wolstencroft at dinner. The observer notified Casper when the pair left the restaurant, and the briefcase was replaced. The documents photographed that evening included papers evidencing a close working relationship between the Castle Bank and the Bank of Perrine, Fla. Subpoenas issued to the Bank of Perrine ultimately uncovered the loan guarantee agreement at issue in this case.

The District Court found that the United States, acting through Jaffe, "knowingly and willfully participated in the unlawful seizure of Michael Wolstencroft's briefcase." According to that court, "the Government affirmatively counsels its agents that the Fourth Amendment standing limitation permits them to purposefully conduct an unconstitutional search and seizure of one individual in order to obtain evidence against third parties." The documents seized from Wolstencroft provided the leads that ultimately led to the discovery of the critical loan guarantee agreement. Although the search did not impinge upon the respondent's Fourth Amendment rights, the District Court believed that the Due Process Clause of the Fifth Amendment and the inherent supervisory power of the federal courts required it to exclude evidence tainted by the Government's "knowing and purposeful bad faith hostility to any person's fundamental constitutional rights." The Court of Appeals for the Sixth Circuit affirmed. We granted certiorari and reverse.

Respondent lacks standing under the Fourth Amendment to suppress the documents illegally seized from Wolstencroft. The [lower courts] believed, however, that a federal court should use its supervisory power to suppress evidence tainted by gross illegalities that did not infringe the defendant's constitutional rights. We understand the commendable desire to deter deliberate intrusions into the privacy of persons who are unlikely to become defendants in a criminal prosecution. No court should condone the unconstitutional and possibly criminal behavior of those who planned and executed this "briefcase caper." But our cases do not command the exclusion of evidence in every case of illegality. The illegality must be weighed against the considerable harm that would flow from indiscriminate application of an exclusionary rule.

The exclusionary rule "has been restricted to those areas where its remedial objectives are most efficaciously served." The Court has acknowledged that the suppression of probative but tainted evidence exacts a costly toll upon the ability of courts to ascertain the truth in a criminal case. Our cases have consistently recognized that unbending application of the exclusionary sanction to enforce ideals of governmental rectitude would impede unacceptably the truth-finding functions of judge and jury. After all, it is the defendant, and not the constable, who stands trial. The same societal interests are at risk when a criminal defendant invokes the supervisory power to suppress evidence seized in violation of a third party's constitutional rights. The supervisory power is applied with some caution even when the defendant asserts a violation of his own rights. In *United States v. Caceres*, 440 U.S. 741 (1979), we refused to exclude all evidence tainted by violations of an executive department's rules. And in *Elkins v. United States*, 364 U.S. 206 (1960), the Court called for a restrained application of the supervisory power. "Any apparent limitation upon the process of discovering truth in a federal trial ought to be imposed only upon the basis of considerations which outweigh the general need for untrammeled disclosure of competent and relevant evidence in a court of justice."

We conclude that the supervisory power does not authorize a federal court to suppress otherwise admissible evidence on the ground that it was seized unlawfully from a third party not before the court. Our Fourth Amendment decisions have established beyond any doubt that the interest in deterring illegal searches does not justify the exclusion of tainted evidence at the instance of a party who was not the victim of the challenged practices. The values assigned to the competing interests do not change because a court has elected to analyze the question under the supervisory power instead of the Fourth Amendment. In either case, the need to deter the underlying conduct and the detrimental impact of excluding the evidence remain precisely the same.

The District Court erred, therefore, when it concluded that "society's interest in deterring bad faith conduct by exclusion outweighs society's interest in furnishing the trier of fact with all relevant evidence." Were we to accept this use of the supervisory power, we would confer on the judiciary discretionary power to disregard the considered limitations of the law it is charged with enforcing. We hold that the supervisory power does not extend so far.

The judgment of the Court of Appeals is

Reversed.

MR. JUSTICE MARSHALL, with whom MR. JUSTICE BRENNAN and MR. JUSTICE BLACKMUN join, dissenting.

This Court has on several occasions exercised its supervisory powers over the federal judicial system in order to suppress evidence that the Government obtained through misconduct. The rationale for such suppression is twofold: to deter illegal conduct by Government officials, and to protect the integrity of the federal courts. The Court has stressed the need to use supervisory powers to prevent the federal courts from becoming accomplices to such misconduct. The need to use the Court's supervisory powers to suppress evidence obtained through governmental misconduct was perhaps best expressed by Mr. Justice Brandeis in his famous dissenting opinion in *Olmstead v. United States*, 277 U.S. 438 (1928): "Decency, security and liberty alike demand that government officials shall be subjected to the same rules of conduct that are commands to the citizen. In a government of laws, existence of the government will be imperiled if it fails to observe the law scrupulously. If the Government becomes a lawbreaker, it breeds contempt for law; it invites every man to become a law unto himself; it invites anarchy. To declare that in the administration of the criminal law the end justifies the means—to declare that the Government may commit crimes in order to secure the conviction of a private criminal—would bring terrible retribution. Against that pernicious doctrine this Court should resolutely set its face." If the federal court permits the introduction of evidence, the intended product of deliberately illegal Government action, to be used to obtain a conviction, it places its imprimatur upon such lawlessness and thereby taints its own integrity. The present case falls within that category. The District Court found a deliberate decision by Government agents to violate the constitutional rights of Wolstencroft for the explicit purpose of obtaining evidence against persons such as Payner. The actions of the Government agents— stealing the briefcase, opening it, and photographing all the documents inside—were patently in violation of the Fourth Amendment rights of Wolstencroft and plainly in violation of the criminal law. The Government knew exactly what information it wanted. Similarly, the Government knew that it wanted to prosecute persons such as Payner, and it made a conscious decision to forgo any opportunity to prosecute Wolstencroft in order to obtain illegally the evidence against Payner and others. Since the supervisory powers are exercised to protect the integrity of the court, rather than to vindicate the constitutional rights of the defendant, it is hard to see why the Court today bases its analysis entirely on Fourth Amendment standing rules. The federal judiciary should not be made accomplices to the crimes of Casper, Jaffe, and others.

2. "Fruit of the Poisonous Tree" Doctrine

When the exclusionary rule is applied, it prohibits the prosecution from using evidence directly obtained from a constitutional violation. Thus, if the police coerce a suspect into confessing, the exclusionary rule prohibits the use of that confession. The "derivative evidence rule," also known as the "Fruit of the Poisonous Tree" doctrine, prohibits the police from using evidence "derived" (or indirectly obtained) from the direct evidence.

Brown v. Illinois

422 U.S. 590 (1975).

MR. JUSTICE BLACKMUN delivered the opinion of the Court.

Petitioner Richard Brown was arrested for murder while attempting to enter his Chicago apartment. The arrest was illegal because the police lacked probable cause. The police took petitioner to the police station. During the 20-minute drive Nolan again asked Brown, who was sitting with him in the back of the car, whether his name was Richard Brown and whether he owned a 1966 Oldsmobile. Brown evaded these questions or answered them falsely. Upon arrival at the station house Brown was placed in a central interrogation room. The room was bare except for a table and four chairs. He was left alone, without handcuffs, for some minutes while the officers obtained the file on the homicide. They returned with the file, sat down, one across from Brown and the other to his left, and spread the file on the table in front of him. The officers warned Brown of his rights under *Miranda*. They then informed him that they knew of an incident that had occurred in a poolroom when Brown, angry at having been cheated at dice, fired a shot from a revolver into the ceiling. Brown answered: "Oh, you know about that." Lenz informed him that a bullet had been obtained from the ceiling of the poolroom and had been taken to the crime laboratory to be compared with bullets taken from the victim's body. Brown responded: "Oh, you know that, too." At this point—it was about 8:45 p.m.—Lenz asked Brown whether he wanted to talk about the homicide. Petitioner answered that he did. For the next 20 to 25 minutes Brown answered questions put to him by Nolan, as Lenz typed. This questioning produced a two-page statement in which Brown acknowledged that he and a man named Jimmy Claggett visited Corpus on the evening of May 5; that the three for some time sat drinking and smoking marihuana; that Claggett ordered him at gunpoint to bind Corpus' hands and feet with cord from the headphone of a stereo set; and that Claggett, using a .38-caliber revolver sold to him by Brown, shot Corpus three times through a pillow. The statement was signed by Brown. Later that night, after the police apprehended Claggett, Brown was again placed in the interrogation room. He was given coffee and was left alone, for the most part, until 2 a.m. when Assistant State's Attorney Crilly arrived. Crilly, too, informed Brown of his *Miranda* rights. After a half hour's conversation, a court reporter appeared. Once again the *Miranda* warnings were given. Crilly told him that he "was sure he would be charged with murder." Brown gave a second

> **FYI**
>
> If an illegal stop leads to a confession, the derivative evidence rule might prohibit the prosecution from using the confession as evidence. As the Court stated in *Nardone v. United States*, 308 U.S. 338 (1939), "the essence of a provision forbidding the acquisition of evidence in a certain way is that not merely evidence so acquired shall not be used before the Court but that it shall not be used at all."

statement, providing a factual account of the murder substantially in accord with his first statement, but containing factual inaccuracies with respect to his personal background. When the statement was completed, at about 3 a.m., Brown refused to sign it. An hour later he made a phone call to his mother. At 9:30 that morning, about 14 hours after his arrest, he was taken before a magistrate. At trial, the State introduced evidence of both statements, and the jury found petitioner guilty of murder. The conviction was affirmed on appeal.

In *Wong Sun v. United States*, 371 U.S. 471 (1963), the Court pronounced the principles to be applied when the issue is whether statements and other evidence obtained after an illegal arrest or search should be excluded. In that case, federal agents elicited an oral statement from defendant Toy after forcing entry at 6 a.m. into his laundry, at the back of which he had his living quarters. The agents followed Toy to the bedroom and placed him under arrest. There was no probable cause. Toy's statement, which bore upon his participation in the sale of narcotics, led the agents to question another person, Johnny Yee, who actually possessed narcotics. Yee stated that heroin had been brought to him earlier by Toy and another Chinese known to him only as "Sea Dog." Under questioning, Toy said that "Sea Dog" was Wong Sun. Toy led agents to a multifamily dwelling where, he said, Wong Sun lived. Gaining admittance to the building through a bell and buzzer, the agents climbed the stairs and entered the apartment. One went into the back room and brought Wong Sun out in handcuffs. After arraignment, Wong Sun was released on his own recognizance. Several days later, he returned voluntarily to give an unsigned confession. This Court ruled that Toy's declarations and the contraband taken from Yee were the fruits of the agents' illegal action and should not have been admitted as evidence against Toy. The statement did not result from "an intervening independent act of a free will," and was not "sufficiently an act of free will to purge the primary taint of the unlawful invasion." With respect to Wong Sun's confession, however, the Court held that in the light of his lawful arraignment and release on his own recognizance, and of his return voluntarily several days later to make the statement, the connection between his unlawful arrest and the statement "had become so attenuated as to dissipate the taint." The Court said: "We need not hold that all evidence is 'fruit of the poisonous tree' simply because it would not have come to light but for the illegal actions of the police. Rather, the more apt question is 'whether, granting establishment of the primary illegality, the evidence to which instant objection is made has been come at by exploitation of that illegality or instead by means sufficiently distinguishable to be purged of the primary taint.' MAGUIRE, EVIDENCE OF GUILT, 221 (1959)."

The exclusionary rule thus was applied in *Wong Sun* primarily to protect Fourth Amendment rights. Protection of the Fifth Amendment right against self-incrimination was not the Court's paramount concern there. To the extent that the question whether Toy's statement was voluntary was considered, it was only to judge whether it "was sufficiently an act of free will to purge the primary taint of the unlawful invasion." The Court in *Wong Sun*, as is customary, emphasized that application of the exclusionary rule on Toy's behalf protected Fourth Amendment guarantees in two respects: "in terms of deterring lawless conduct by federal officers," and by "closing the doors of the federal courts to any use of evidence unconstitutionally obtained."

The Illinois courts refrained from resolving the question whether Brown's statements were obtained by exploitation of the illegality of his arrest. They assumed that the *Miranda* warnings, by themselves, assured that the statements (verbal acts, as contrasted with physical evidence) were of sufficient free will as to purge the primary taint of the unlawful arrest. This Court has described the *Miranda* warnings as a "prophylactic rule," and as a "procedural safeguard," employed to protect Fifth Amendment rights against "the compulsion inherent in custodial surroundings." The function of the warnings relates to the Fifth Amendment's guarantee against coerced self-incrimination, and the exclusion of a statement made in the absence of the warnings, serves to deter the taking of an incriminating statement without first informing the individual of his Fifth Amendment rights.

Although, almost 90 years ago, the Court observed that the Fifth Amendment is in "intimate relation" with the Fourth, the *Miranda* warnings thus far have not been regarded as a means either of remedying or deterring violations of Fourth Amendment rights. Frequently, rights under the two Amendments may appear to coalesce since "the 'unreasonable searches and seizures' condemned in the Fourth Amendment are almost always made for the purpose of compelling a man to give evidence against himself, which in criminal cases is condemned in the Fifth Amendment." The exclusionary rule, however, when utilized to effectuate the Fourth Amendment, serves interests and policies that are distinct from those it serves under the Fifth. It is directed at all unlawful searches and seizures, and not merely those that happen to produce incriminating material or testimony as fruits. In short, exclusion of a confession made without *Miranda* warnings might be regarded as necessary to effectuate the Fifth Amendment, but it would not be sufficient fully to protect the Fourth. *Miranda* warnings, and the exclusion of a confession made without them, do not alone sufficiently deter a Fourth Amendment violation.

Thus, even if the statements in this case were found to be voluntary under the Fifth Amendment, the Fourth Amendment issue remains. In order for the causal chain, between the illegal arrest and the statements made subsequent thereto, to be broken, *Wong Sun* requires not merely that the statement meet the Fifth Amendment standard of voluntariness but that it be "sufficiently an act of free will to purge the primary taint." *Wong Sun* thus mandates consideration of a statement's admissibility in light of the distinct policies and interests of the Fourth Amendment. If *Miranda* warnings were held to attenuate the taint of an unconstitutional arrest, regardless of how wanton and purposeful the Fourth Amendment violation, the effect of the exclusionary rule would be substantially diluted. Arrests made without warrant or without probable cause, for questioning or "investigation," would be encouraged by the knowledge that evidence derived therefrom could be made admissible at trial by the simple expedient of giving *Miranda* warnings. Any incentive to avoid Fourth Amendment violations would be eviscerated by making the warnings, in effect, a "cure-all," and the constitutional guarantee against unlawful searches and seizures could be reduced to "a form of words."

It is possible, of course, that persons arrested illegally may decide to confess, as an act of free will unaffected by the initial illegality. But the *Miranda* warnings, alone and *per se*, cannot always make the act sufficiently a product of free will to break, for Fourth Amendment purposes, the causal connection between the illegality and the confession. They cannot assure that the Fourth Amendment violation has not been unduly exploited. The question whether a confession is the product of a free will under *Wong Sun* must be answered on the facts of each case. No single fact is dispositive. The workings of the human mind are too complex, and the possibilities of misconduct too diverse, to permit protection of the Fourth Amendment to turn on such a talismanic test. The *Miranda* warnings are an important factor in determining whether the confession is obtained by exploitation of an illegal arrest. But they are not the only factor to be considered. The temporal proximity of the arrest and the confession, the presence of intervening circumstances, and, particularly, the purpose and flagrancy of the official misconduct are all relevant. The voluntariness of the statement is a threshold requirement. And the burden of showing admissibility rests on the prosecution.

The State failed to sustain the burden of showing that the evidence in question was admissible under *Wong Sun*. Brown's first statement was separated from his illegal arrest by less than two hours, and there was no intervening event of significance whatsoever. His situation is remarkably like that of James Wah Toy in *Wong Sun*. And the second statement was clearly the result and the fruit of the first.[12] The illegality here, moreover, had a quality of purposefulness. The impropriety of the arrest was obvious; awareness of that fact was virtually conceded by the two detectives when they repeatedly acknowledged that the purpose of their action was "for investigation" or for "questioning." The detectives embarked upon this expedition for evidence in the hope that something might turn up. The manner in which Brown's arrest was affected gives the appearance of having been calculated to cause surprise, fright, and confusion.

We decide only that the Illinois courts were in error in assuming that the *Miranda* warnings, by themselves, under *Wong Sun* always purge the taint of an illegal arrest. The judgment of the Supreme Court of Illinois is reversed and the case is remanded for further proceedings not inconsistent with this opinion.

---

[12]   The fact that Brown had made one statement, believed by him to be admissible, and his cooperation with the arresting and interrogating officers in the search for Claggett, with his anticipation of leniency, bolstered the pressures for him to give the second, or at least vitiated any incentive on his part to avoid self-incrimination.

It is so ordered.

MR. JUSTICE POWELL, with whom MR. JUSTICE REHNQUIST joins, concurring in part.

The point at which the taint can be said to have dissipated should be related, in the absence of other controlling circumstances, to the nature of that taint. That police have not succeeded in coercing the accused's confession through willful or negligent misuse of the power of arrest does not remove the fact that they may have tried. The impermissibility of the attempt, and the extent to which such attempts can be deterred by the use of the exclusionary rule, are of primary relevance in determining whether exclusion is an appropriate remedy. The basic purpose of the rule is to remove possible motivations for illegal arrests. Given this purpose the notion of voluntariness has practical value in deciding whether the rule should apply to statements removed from the immediate circumstances of the illegal arrest. If an illegal arrest merely provides the occasion of initial contact between the police and the accused, and because of time or other intervening factors the accused's eventual statement is the product of his own reflection and free will, application of the exclusionary rule can serve little purpose: the police normally will not make an illegal arrest in the hope of eventually obtaining such a truly volunteered statement. In a similar manner, the role of the *Miranda* warnings in the *Wong Sun* inquiry is indirect. To the extent that they dissipate the psychological pressures of custodial interrogation, *Miranda* warnings serve to assure that the accused's decision to make a statement has been relatively unaffected by the preceding illegal arrest. Correspondingly, to the extent that the police perceive *Miranda* warnings to have this equalizing potential, their motivation to abuse the power of arrest is diminished. Bearing these considerations in mind, and recognizing that the deterrent value of the Fourth Amendment exclusionary rule is limited to certain kinds of police conduct, the following general categories can be identified.

Those most readily identifiable are on the extremes: the flagrantly abusive violation of Fourth Amendment rights, on the one hand, and "technical" Fourth Amendment violations, on the other. In my view, these extremes call for significantly different judicial responses. I would require the clearest indication of attenuation in cases in which official conduct was flagrantly abusive of Fourth Amendment rights. In such cases, I would consider the equalizing potential of *Miranda* warnings rarely sufficient to dissipate the taint. In such cases the deterrent value of the exclusionary rule is most likely to be effective, and the corresponding mandate to preserve judicial integrity, most clearly demands that the fruits of official misconduct be denied. I thus would require some demonstrably effective break in the chain of events leading from the illegal arrest to the statement, such as actual consultation with counsel or the accused's presentation before a magistrate for a determination of probable cause, before the taint can be deemed removed. At the opposite end of the spectrum lie "technical" violations of Fourth Amendment rights where, for example, officers in good faith arrest an individual in reliance on a warrant later invalidated or pursuant to a statute that subsequently is declared unconstitutional. I would not require more than proof that effective *Miranda* warnings were given and that the ensuing statement was voluntary in the Fifth Amendment sense. Absent aggravating circumstances, I would consider a statement given at the station house after one has been advised of *Miranda* rights to be sufficiently removed from the immediate circumstances of the illegal arrest to justify its admission at trial.

Points for Discussion

a. Illustrating the FOPT Doctrine

After *Brown*, the Court has decided several similar cases. In *Dunaway v. New York*, <u>442 U.S. 200 (1979)</u>, the Court held that the police violated petitioner's rights when they seized him and took him to the stationhouse for custodial questioning absent probable cause. Because of the illegal seizure, the Court refused to admit petitioner's incriminating statements at the stationhouse: "The situation in this case is virtually a replica of the situation in *Brown*. Petitioner was seized without probable cause in the hope that something might turn up, and confessed without any intervening event of significance." Chief Justice Rehnquist dissented: "The connection between petitioner's allegedly, unlawful detention and the incriminating statements and sketches is sufficiently attenuated to permit their use at trial. Where police have acted in good faith and not in a flagrant manner, I would require no more than that proper *Miranda* warnings be given and that the statement be voluntary within the meaning of the Fifth Amendment." *See also Taylor v. Alabama*, <u>457 U.S. 687 (1982)</u> (Court suppressed confession when "petitioner was arrested without probable cause in the hope that something would turn up, and he confessed shortly thereafter without any meaningful intervening event" even though he was given three *Miranda* warnings).

In *Rawlings v. Kentucky*, <u>448 U.S. 98 (1980)</u>, petitioner was convicted of trafficking in, and possession of, various controlled substances. The conviction was based, in part, on statements made by petitioner at the scene of the arrest. Even though the Court concluded that petitioner was illegally detained at the time he made the statements, the Court held that the connection between the seizure and the statements was sufficiently attenuated: "Petitioner received *Miranda* warnings only moments before he made his incriminating statements. Petitioner and his companions were detained for a period of approximately 45 minutes. The three people sat quietly in the living room, or at least initially, moved freely about the first floor of the house. Petitioner's admissions were apparently spontaneous reactions to the discovery of his drugs in Cox's purse, and this factor weighs heavily in favor of a finding that petitioner acted 'of free will unaffected by the initial illegality.' The conduct of the police does not rise to the level of conscious or flagrant misconduct. Petitioner has not argued that his admission to ownership of the drugs was anything other than voluntary." Justice Marshall dissented: "Petitioner's admissions, far from being 'spontaneous,' were made in response to Vanessa Cox's demand that petitioner 'take what was his.' Her statement was the direct product of the illegal search of her purse. That search was made possible only because the police refused to let anyone in the house depart unless they 'consented' to a body search; that detention was illegal."

Take Note

In *United States v. Patane*, <u>542 U.S. 630 (2004)</u>, a plurality of the Court held that police failure to give the *Miranda* warnings did not require suppression of the physical fruits of a defendant's unwarned statements. After officers arrested Patane, but before they gave him complete *Miranda* warnings, they asked him about the location of a gun. He told them the location and they seized it. A plurality held that the statement was inadmissible, but that the gun was admissibile: "Introduction of the nontestimonial fruit of a voluntary statement, such as Patane's gun, does not implicate the Self-Incrimination Clause. The admission of such fruit presents no risk that a defendant's coerced statements will be used against him at a criminal trial and 'the exclusion of unwarned statements is a complete and sufficient remedy' for any perceived *Miranda* violation. There is simply no need to extend the prophylactic rule of *Miranda* to require the exclusion of physical evidence. Although the Court requires the exclusion of the physical fruit of actually coerced statements, it must be remembered that statements taken without sufficient *Miranda* warnings are presumed to have been coerced only for certain purposes and then only when necessary to protect the privilege against self-incrimination. We decline to extend that presumption further." Justices Kennedy, joined by Justice O'Connor, concurred, opining that "the important probative value of reliable physical evidence" made it "doubtful that exclusion of the gun can be justified by a deterrence rationale." The *Patane* dissenters argued that the admissible status of physical evidence "fruits" of *Miranda* violations would serve as an "invitation to law enforcement officers to flout *Miranda* when there may be physical evidence to be gained."

b. A Witness as a "Fruit" of an Illegal Search

In *United States v. Ceccolini*, <u>435 U.S. 268 (1978)</u>, while the police were investigating illegal gambling, Biro, a police officer entered respondent's place of business (a flower shop), went behind the customer counter and spent his break talking with his friend, an employee of the shop. During the conversation, he spotted an envelope with money lying on the cash register. Biro picked up the envelope, examined its contents, and discovered that it contained not only money but betting slips. He placed the envelope back on the register and, without telling his friend what he had seen, asked her who owned it. She replied that the envelope belonged to respondent, and that he had instructed her to give it to someone. Later, when respondent testified before a grand jury that he had never taken bets, Hennessey gave contrary testimony. The Court held that the friend's testimony was not subject to exclusion: "The testimony given by the witness was an act of her own free will in no way coerced or even induced by official authority as a result of Biro's discovery of the policy slips. Nor were the slips themselves used in questioning. Substantial periods of time elapsed between the time of the illegal search and the initial contact with the witness, and between the latter and the testimony at trial. While the knowledge to which Hennessey testified at trial can be logically traced back to Biro's discovery of the policy slips both the identity of Hennessey and her relationship with the respondent were well known to those investigating the case. There is not the slightest evidence to suggest that Biro entered the shop or picked up the envelope with the intent of finding tangible evidence bearing on an illicit gambling operation, much less any suggestion that he entered the shop and searched with the intent of finding a willing and knowledgeable witness to testify against respondent."

Likewise, in *Michigan v. Tucker*, 417 U.S. 433 (1974), a plurality held that a witness's testimony could be used by the prosecution, notwithstanding the fact that the identity of the witness was obtained from defendant's statement in violation of *Miranda*. The Court reasoned that where the police committed the *Miranda* violation in good faith, "the deterrent effect" of reducing future *Miranda* violations would not be "significantly augmented" by excluding the testimony of "a third party who was subject to no custodial pressures." Defendant did not receive complete *Miranda* warnings, and therefore the statement he made after waiver, identifying the name of an alibi witness, was inadmissible at his trial. Although the witness's name and testimony were "fruits" of the *Miranda* violation, they were deemed admissible.

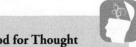

Food for Thought

What might the police have done differently in *Brown* that might have altered the result?

Utah v. Strieff

136 S.Ct. 2056 (2016).

JUSTICE THOMAS delivered the opinion of the Court.

In December 2006, someone called the South Salt Lake City police's drug-tip line to report "narcotics activity" at a particular residence. Narcotics detective Fackrell investigated the tip. Over the course of a week, Fackrell conducted intermittent surveillance of the home. He observed visitors who left a few minutes after arriving at the house. These visits were sufficiently frequent to raise his suspicion that the occupants were dealing drugs. One of those visitors was respondent Edward Strieff. Fackrell observed Strieff exit the house and walk toward a nearby convenience store. In the store's parking lot, Officer Fackrell detained Strieff, identified himself, and asked Strieff what he was doing at the residence. As part of the stop, Officer Fackrell requested Strieff's identification, and Strieff produced his Utah identification card. Officer Fackrell relayed Strieff's information to a police dispatcher, who reported that Strieff had an outstanding arrest warrant for a traffic violation. Officer Fackrell then arrested Strieff pursuant to that warrant. When Officer Fackrell searched Strieff incident to the arrest, he discovered a baggie of methamphetamine and drug paraphernalia. The State charged Strieff with unlawful possession of methamphetamine and drug paraphernalia. Strieff moved to suppress the evidence, arguing that the evidence was inadmissible because it was derived from an unlawful investigatory stop. The prosecutor conceded that Officer Fackrell lacked reasonable suspicion for the stop but argued that the evidence should not be suppressed because a valid arrest warrant attenuated the connection between the unlawful stop and discovery of the contraband. The trial court admitted the evidence. The Utah Court of Appeals affirmed. The Utah Supreme Court reversed. We granted certiorari and reverse.

Because officers who violated the Fourth Amendment were traditionally considered trespassers, individuals subject to unconstitutional searches or seizures historically enforced their rights through tort suits or self-help. In the 20th century, the exclusionary rule—the rule that often requires trial courts to exclude unlawfully seized evidence in a criminal trial—became the principal judicial remedy to deter Fourth Amendment violations. *See, e.g., Mapp v. Ohio,* 367 U. S. 643 (1961). The exclusionary rule encompasses both the "primary evidence obtained as a direct result of an illegal search or seizure" and "evidence later discovered and found to be derivative of an illegality," the so-called "fruit of the poisonous tree." *Segura v. United States,* 468 U. S. 796 (1984). But the significant costs of this rule have led us to deem it "applicable only where its deterrence benefits outweigh its substantial social costs." *Hudson v. Michigan,* 547 U. S. 586 (2006). "Suppression of evidence has always been our last resort, not our first impulse." *Ibid.*

We have recognized several exceptions to the rule. Three of these exceptions involve the causal relationship between the unconstitutional act and the discovery of evidence. First, the independent source doctrine allows trial courts to admit evidence obtained in an unlawful search if officers independently acquired it from a separate, independent source. *See Murray v. United States,* 487 U. S. 533 (1988). Second, the inevitable discovery doctrine allows for the admission of evidence that would have been discovered even without the unconstitutional source. *See Nix v. Williams,* 467 U. S. 431 (1984). Third is the attenuation doctrine: Evidence is admissible when the connection between unconstitutional police conduct and the evidence is remote or has been interrupted by some intervening circumstance, so that "the interest protected by the constitutional guarantee that has been violated would not be served by suppression of the evidence obtained." *Hudson, supra,* at 593.

Turning to the attenuation doctrine, we address whether this doctrine applies at all to a case where the intervening circumstance that the State relies on is the discovery of a valid, pre-existing, and untainted arrest warrant. The Utah Supreme Court declined to apply the attenuation doctrine because it read our precedents as applying the doctrine only "to circumstances involving an independent act of a defendant's 'free will' in confessing to a crime or consenting to a search." We disagree. The attenuation doctrine evaluates the causal link between the government's unlawful act and the discovery of evidence, which often has nothing to do with a defendant's actions. The logic of our prior attenuation cases is not limited to independent acts by the defendant.

It remains to address whether the discovery of a valid arrest warrant was a sufficient intervening event to break the causal chain between the unlawful stop and the discovery of drug-related evidence on Strieff's person. The three factors articulated in *Brown v. Illinois,* 422 U. S. 590 (1975), guide our analysis. First, we look to the "temporal proximity" between the unconstitutional conduct and the discovery of evidence to determine how closely the discovery of evidence followed the unconstitutional search. Second, we consider "the presence of intervening circumstances." Third, and "particularly" significant, we examine "the purpose and flagrancy of the official misconduct." In evaluating these factors, we assume that Officer Fackrell lacked reasonable suspicion to initially stop Strieff. Because we conclude that the warrant breaks the causal chain, we have no need to decide whether the warrant's existence alone would make the initial stop constitutional even if Officer Fackrell was unaware of its existence. The first factor, temporal proximity between the initially unlawful stop and the search, favors suppressing the evidence. Our precedents have declined to find that this factor favors attenuation unless "substantial time" elapses between an unlawful act and when the evidence is obtained. Here, Officer Fackrell discovered contraband on Strieff's person only minutes after the illegal stop. Such a short time interval counsels in favor of suppression. The second factor, the presence of intervening circumstances, strongly favors the State. In *Segura,* 468 U. S. 796, the Court addressed similar facts to those here and found sufficient intervening circumstances to allow the admission of evidence. There, agents had probable cause to believe that apartment occupants were dealing cocaine. They sought a warrant. In the meantime, they entered the apartment, arrested an occupant, and discovered evidence of drug activity during a limited search for security reasons. The next evening, the Magistrate Judge issued the search warrant. This Court deemed the evidence admissible notwithstanding the illegal search because the information supporting the warrant was "wholly unconnected with the arguably illegal entry and was known to the agents well before the initial entry." *Segura,* of course, applied the independent source doctrine because the unlawful entry "did not contribute in any way to discovery of the evidence seized under the warrant." But *Segura* suggested that the existence of a valid warrant favors finding that the connection between unlawful conduct and the discovery of evidence is "sufficiently attenuated to dissipate the taint." In this case, the warrant was valid, it predated Officer Fackrell's investigation, and it was entirely unconnected with the stop. Once Officer Fackrell discovered the warrant, he had an obligation to arrest Strieff. "A warrant is a judicial mandate to an officer to conduct a search or make an arrest, and the officer has a sworn duty to carry out its provisions." *United*

States v. Leon, 468 U. S. 897, 920 (1984). Officer Fackrell's arrest of Strieff thus was a ministerial act that was independently compelled by the pre-existing warrant. Once Officer Fackrell was authorized to arrest Strieff, it was undisputedly lawful to search Strieff as an incident of his arrest to protect Officer Fackrell's safety. *See Arizona v. Gant,* 556 U. S. 332 (2009).

Finally, the third factor, "the purpose and flagrancy of the official misconduct" also strongly favors the State. The exclusionary rule exists to deter police misconduct. *Davis v. United States,* 564 U. S. 229 (2011). The third factor reflects that rationale by favoring exclusion only when the police misconduct is most in need of deterrence—that is, when it is purposeful or flagrant. Officer Fackrell was at most negligent. In stopping Strieff, Officer Fackrell made two good-faith mistakes. First, he had not observed what time Strieff entered the suspected drug house, so he did not know how long Strieff had been there. Fackrell thus lacked a sufficient basis to conclude that Strieff was a short-term visitor who may have been consummating a drug transaction. Second, because he lacked confirmation that Strieff was a short-term visitor, Fackrell should have asked Strieff whether he would speak with him, instead of demanding that Strieff do so. Officer Fackrell's stated purpose was to "find out what was going on in the house." Nothing prevented him from approaching Strieff simply to ask. But these errors in judgment hardly rise to a purposeful or flagrant violation of Strieff's Fourth Amendment rights. While Officer Fackrell's decision to initiate the stop was mistaken, his conduct thereafter was lawful. The officer's decision to run the warrant check was a "negligibly burdensome precaution" for officer safety. *Rodriguez v. United States,* 575 U. S. ___ (2015) (slip op., at 7). Officer Fackrell's search was a lawful search incident to arrest. Moreover, there is no indication that this unlawful stop was part of any systemic or recurrent police misconduct. The stop was an isolated instance of negligence that occurred in connection with a bona fide investigation of a suspected drug house. Officer Fackrell saw Strieff leave a suspected drug house. His suspicion about the house was based on an anonymous tip and his personal observations.

Applying these factors, we hold that the evidence discovered on Strieff's person was admissible because the unlawful stop was sufficiently attenuated by the pre-existing arrest warrant. Although the illegal stop was close in time to Strieff's arrest, that consideration is outweighed by two factors supporting the State. The outstanding arrest warrant for Strieff's arrest is a critical intervening circumstance that is wholly independent of the illegal stop. The discovery of that warrant broke the causal chain between the unconstitutional stop and the discovery of evidence by compelling Officer Fackrell to arrest Strieff. It is especially significant that there is no evidence that Officer Fackrell's illegal stop reflected flagrantly unlawful police misconduct.

Strieff argues that the attenuation doctrine should not apply because the officer's stop was purposeful and flagrant. But Officer Fackrell sought information from Strieff to find out what was happening inside a house whose occupants were legitimately suspected of dealing drugs. This was not a suspicionless fishing expedition "in the hope that something would turn up." For the violation to be flagrant, more severe police misconduct is required than the mere absence of proper cause for the seizure. Second, Strieff argues that, because of the prevalence of outstanding arrest warrants in many jurisdictions, police will engage in dragnet searches if the exclusionary rule is not applied. We think that this outcome is unlikely. Such wanton conduct would expose police to civil liability. *See* 42 U. S. C. § 1983; *Monell v. New York City Dept. of Social Servs.,* 436 U. S. 658 (1978). In any event, the *Brown* factors take account of the purpose and flagrancy of police misconduct. Were evidence of a dragnet search presented here, the application of the Brown factors could be different. But there is no evidence that the concerns that Strieff raises with the criminal justice system are present in South Salt Lake City, Utah.

We hold that the evidence Officer Fackrell seized as part of his search incident to arrest is admissible because his discovery of the arrest warrant attenuated the connection between the unlawful stop and the evidence seized from Strieff incident to arrest. The judgment of the Utah Supreme Court, accordingly, is reversed.

It is so ordered.

JUSTICE SOTOMAYOR, with whom JUSTICE GINSBURG joins as to Parts I, II, and III, dissenting.

This case allows the police to stop you on the street, demand your identification, and check it for outstanding traffic warrants—even if you are doing nothing wrong. If the officer discovers a warrant for a fine you forgot to pay, courts will now excuse his illegal stop and will admit into evidence anything he happens to find by searching you after arresting you on the warrant. I dissent.

II

When "lawless police conduct" uncovers evidence of lawless civilian conduct, this Court has long required later criminal trials to exclude the illegally obtained evidence. *Mapp v. Ohio*, 367 U. S. 643 (1961). The "exclusionary rule" removes an incentive for officers to search without proper justification. It also keeps courts from being "made party to lawless invasions of the constitutional rights of citizens by permitting unhindered governmental use of the fruits of such invasions." *Id.,* at 13. But when courts admit illegally obtained evidence as well, they reward "manifest neglect if not an open defiance of the prohibitions of the Constitution." *Weeks,* 232 U. S., at 394.

The officer found the drugs only after learning of Strieff's traffic violation; and he learned of Strieff's traffic violation only because he unlawfully stopped Strieff to check his driver's license. These factors confirm that the officer discovered Strieff's drugs by exploiting his own illegal conduct. The officer did not ask Strieff to volunteer his name only to find out, days later, that Strieff had a warrant against him. The officer illegally stopped Strieff and immediately ran a warrant check. The officer's sole reason for stopping Strieff was investigative—he wanted to discover whether drug activity was going on in the house Strieff had just exited. The warrant check was not an "intervening circumstance" separating the stop from the search for drugs. It was part and parcel of the officer's illegal "expedition for evidence in the hope that something might turn up." *Brown,* 422 U. S., at 605. Because the officer found Strieff's drugs by exploiting his own constitutional violation, the drugs should be excluded.

III

The officer stopped Strieff without suspecting him of committing any crime. By his own account, the officer did not fear Strieff. Moreover, the safety rationale is conspicuously absent. A warrant check on a highway "ensures that vehicles on the road are operated safely and responsibly." We allow such checks during legal traffic stops because the legitimacy of a person's driver's license has a "close connection to roadway safety." The officer's sole purpose was to fish for evidence. The majority casts his unconstitutional actions as "negligent" and therefore incapable of being deterred by the exclusionary rule. Even officers prone to negligence can learn from courts that exclude illegally obtained evidence. Indeed, they are perhaps the most in need of education, whether by the judge's opinion, the prosecutor's future guidance, or an updated manual on criminal procedure. If the officers are in doubt about what the law requires, exclusion gives them an "incentive to err on the side of constitutional behavior." *United States v. Johnson,* 457 U. S. 537, 561 (1982). Most striking about the Court's opinion is its insistence that the event here was "isolated," with "no indication that this unlawful stop was part of any systemic or recurrent police misconduct." Outstanding warrants are surprisingly common. The States and Federal Government maintain databases with over 7.8 million outstanding warrants, the vast majority for minor offenses. Most officers act in "good faith" and do not set out to break the law. That does not mean these stops are "isolated instances of negligence." The New York City Police Department long trained officers to "stop and question first, develop reasonable suspicion later."

IV

Although many Americans have been stopped for speeding or jaywalking, few may realize how degrading a stop can be when the officer is looking for more. This Court has allowed an officer to stop you for whatever reason he wants—so long as he can point to a pretextual justification after the fact. *Whren v. United States,* 517 U. S. 806 (1996). The officer does not even need to know which law you might have broken so long as he can later point to any possible infraction—even one that is minor, unrelated, or ambiguous. This case involves a *suspicionless* stop, one in which the officer initiated this chain of events without justification. This case tells everyone, white and black, guilty and innocent, that an officer can verify your legal status at any time.

JUSTICE KAGAN, with whom JUSTICE GINSBURG joins, dissenting.

This case requires the Court to determine whether excluding the fruits of Officer Douglas Fackrell's unjustified stop would significantly deter police from committing similar constitutional violations in the future. That inquiry turns on application of the "attenuation doctrine." First, the closer the "temporal proximity" between the unlawful act and the discovery of evidence, the greater the deterrent value of suppression. Second, the more "purposeful" or "flagrant" the police illegality, the clearer the necessity, and better the chance, of preventing similar misbehavior. And third, the presence (or absence) of "intervening circumstances" makes a difference: The stronger the causal chain between the misconduct and the evidence, the more exclusion will curb future constitutional violations. Each of those considerations points toward suppression: Nothing in Fackrell's discovery of an outstanding warrant so attenuated the connection between his wrongful behavior and his detection of drugs as to diminish the exclusionary rule's deterrent benefits.

The temporal proximity factor "favors suppressing the evidence." After all, Fackrell's discovery of drugs came just minutes after the unconstitutional stop. The majority chalks up Fackrell's Fourth Amendment violation to a couple of innocent "mistakes." It is not disputed that Fackrell stopped Strieff without reasonable suspicion. The illegality here had a quality of purposefulness. The impropriety of the stop was obvious. Fackrell embarked upon this expedition for evidence in the hope that something might turn up." Finally, consider whether any intervening circumstance "broke the causal chain" between the stop and the evidence. Fackrell's discovery of an arrest warrant—the only event the majority thinks intervened—was an eminently foreseeable consequence of stopping Strieff. The department's standard detention procedures—stop, ask for identification, run a check—are partly designed to find outstanding warrants. Find them they will, given the staggering number of such warrants on the books.

The majority's misapplication of *Brown*'s three-part inquiry creates unfortunate incentives for the police—indeed, practically invites them to do what Fackrell did here. So long as the target is one of the many millions of people in this country with an outstanding arrest warrant, anything the officer finds in a search is fair game for use in a criminal prosecution. From here on, he sees potential advantage in stopping individuals without reasonable suspicion—exactly the temptation the exclusionary rule is supposed to remove. The majority places Fourth Amendment protections at risk.

Hypo 1: *Identification as the "Fruit" of an Unlawful Arrest*

A woman was accosted and robbed at gunpoint by a man in the women's restroom at the Washington Monument. Six days later, two other women were assaulted and robbed in the same restroom. All three women gave the same description of the robber: a young male, 15–18 years old, approximately five feet, eight inches tall, slender in build, with a very dark complexion and smooth skin. When an officer spied respondent (who matched the description) in the vicinity of the restrooms, the officer took him into custody and transported him to the station where he was photographed and released. The detention was arguably illegal because, although the officer had a "reasonable suspicion," he lacked probable cause. Afterwards, police showed the victim of the first robbery an array of photographs. Although she had failed to identify the robber after previously viewing more than 100 pictures, she immediately identified respondent as her assailant. Afterwards, respondent was taken into custody and forced to participate in a lineup where he was positively identified by two victims. At respondent's trial, should the court suppress the photographic identifications and the lineup identification because of the illegal seizure? How would you argue the case for defendant? How might the prosecution respond? *See United States v. Crews*, <u>445 U.S. 463 (1980)</u>.

Hypo 2: *More on Identifications as "Fruits"*

In the prior hypo, instead of offering the photographic and lineup identifications in court, suppose that the prosecution seeks to have the witnesses identify respondent in court on the basis of their independent recollections. Should the witnesses be allowed to do so despite the illegal seizure? How would you argue the case for the defendant? How might the prosecution respond? How should the court rule? *See United States v. Crews*, <u>445 U.S. 463 (1980)</u>.

Hypo 3: *Confession as the "Fruit" of a Payton Violation?*

The police had probable cause to arrest Harris, but they arrested him at his home without an arrest warrant in contravention of *Payton v. New York*. Harris was *Mirandized* and admitted to committing a murder. Harris was then taken to the stationhouse where he was given a second *Miranda* warning and made a written incriminating statement. After reading Harris his rights a third time, the police videotaped his confession. Should the confession be suppressed as the "fruit" of an illegal arrest? *See New York v. Harris*, 495 U.S. 14 (1990).

Hypo 4: *Illegal Search Followed by Consent*

Police conduct a warrantless and illegal entry into defendant's garage, and use a drug sniffing dog that confirms the existence of marijuana. The police then leave the premises. When defendant's wife returns home, they ask her for permission to search the house, and she consents. Aware that the dog has alerted to the garage, police go there first and find a large quantity of marijuana. Should the prior illegal search render the subsequent consent invalid? How would you argue the case for the defendant? *State v. Guillen*, 223 P.3d 658 (Az. 2010).

Nix v. Williams

467 U.S. 431 (1984).

CHIEF JUSTICE BURGER delivered the opinion of the Court.

In *Brewer v. Williams*, the Court reversed Williams' murder conviction because it was based on a confession obtained in violation of his Sixth Amendment right to counsel. The Court found that the confession was deliberately elicited by the "Christian burial speech" that a police officer gave to respondent on route from Davenport to Des Moines. At Williams' second trial, the prosecution did not offer Williams' statements into evidence, nor did it seek to show that Williams had directed the police to the child's body. However, evidence of the condition of her body as it was found, articles and photographs of her clothing, and the results of post mortem medical and chemical tests on the body were admitted. The trial court concluded that the State had proved by a preponderance of the evidence that, if the search had not been suspended and Williams had not led the police to the victim, her body would have been discovered "within a short time" in essentially the same condition as it was actually found.

The trial court also ruled that if the police had not located the body, "the search would clearly have been taken up again where it left off, given the extreme circumstances of this case and the body would have been found in short order." In finding that the body would have been discovered in essentially the same condition as it was actually found, the court noted that freezing temperatures had prevailed and tissue deterioration would have been suspended. The challenged evidence was admitted and the jury again found Williams guilty of first-degree murder; he was sentenced to life in prison. After respondent's conviction was affirmed, he sought a writ of *habeas corpus* challenging his conviction. The court denied the writ. The Eighth Circuit Court of Appeals reversed finding that, whether or not the body would have been discovered, suppression was required because the police acted in bad faith. We granted certiorari and we reverse.

The "vast majority" of courts, both state and federal, recognize an inevitable discovery exception to the exclusionary rule. We are now urged to adopt and apply the so-called ultimate or inevitable discovery exception to the exclusionary rule.

Williams contends that evidence of the body's location and condition is "fruit of the poisonous tree," *i.e.*, the "fruit" or product of Detective Leaming's plea to help the child's parents give her "a Christian burial," which this Court had already held equated to interrogation. The doctrine requiring courts to suppress evidence as the tainted "fruit" of unlawful governmental conduct had its genesis in *Silverthorne Lumber Co. v. United States*, 251 U.S. 385 (1920); there, the Court held that the exclusionary rule applies not only to the illegally obtained evidence itself, but also to other incriminating evidence derived from the primary evidence. The holding was carefully limited, for the Court emphasized that such information does not automatically become "sacred and inaccessible." "If knowledge of such facts is gained from an independent source, they may be proved like any others."

The core rationale consistently advanced by this Court for extending the exclusionary rule to evidence that is the fruit of unlawful police conduct has been that this admittedly drastic and socially costly course is needed to deter police from violations of constitutional and statutory protections. This Court has accepted the argument that the way to ensure such protections is to exclude evidence seized as a result of such violations notwithstanding the high social cost of letting persons obviously guilty go unpunished for their crimes. On this rationale, the prosecution is not to be put in a better position than it would have been in if no illegality had transpired. By contrast, the derivative evidence analysis ensures that the prosecution is not put in a worse position simply because of some earlier police error or misconduct. The independent source doctrine allows admission of evidence that has been discovered by means wholly independent of any constitutional violation. That doctrine, although closely related to the inevitable discovery doctrine, does not apply here; Williams' statements to Leaming indeed led police to the child's body. The independent source doctrine teaches us that the interest of society in deterring unlawful police conduct and the public interest in having juries receive all probative evidence of a crime are properly balanced by putting the police in the same, not a worse, position than they would have been in if no police error or misconduct had occurred. When the challenged evidence has an independent source, exclusion of such evidence would put the police in a worse position than they would have been in absent any error or violation. Thus, while the independent source exception would not justify admission of evidence in this case, its rationale is wholly consistent with and justifies our adoption of the ultimate or inevitable discovery exception to the exclusionary rule.

Cases implementing the exclusionary rule "begin with the premise that the challenged evidence is the product of illegal governmental activity." *United States v. Crews*, 445 U.S. 463 (1980). This does not end the inquiry. If the prosecution can establish by a preponderance of the evidence that the information ultimately or inevitably would have been discovered by lawful means—here the volunteers' search—then the deterrence rationale has so little basis that the evidence should be received.[5] Anything less would reject logic, experience, and common sense.

The requirement that the prosecution must prove the absence of bad faith would place courts in the position of withholding from juries relevant and undoubted truth that would have been available to police absent any unlawful police activity. That view would put the police in a worse position than they would have been in if no unlawful conduct had transpired. Of equal importance, it wholly fails to take into account the enormous societal cost of excluding truth in the search for truth in the administration of justice. Nothing in this Court's prior holdings supports any such formalistic, pointless, and punitive approach. The Court of Appeals concluded that if an absence-of-bad-faith requirement were not imposed, "the temptation to risk deliberate violations of the Sixth Amendment would be too great, and the deterrent effect of the Exclusionary Rule reduced too far." We reject that view. A police officer who is faced with the opportunity to obtain evidence illegally will rarely, if ever, be in a position to calculate whether the evidence sought would inevitably be discovered. On the other hand, when an officer is aware that the evidence will inevitably be discovered, there will be little to gain from taking any dubious "shortcuts" to obtain the evidence. Significant disincentives to obtaining evidence illegally—including the possibility of departmental discipline and civil liability—also lessen the likelihood that the ultimate or inevitable discovery exception will promote police misconduct.

---

[5]   Williams argues that the preponderance-of-the-evidence standard is inconsistent with *United States v. Wade*, 388 U.S. 218 (1967). In requiring clear and convincing evidence of an independent source for an in-court identification, the Court gave weight to the effect an uncounseled pretrial identification has in "crystallizing the witnesses' identification of the defendant for future reference." The Court noted as well that possible unfairness at the lineup "may be the sole means of attack upon the unequivocal courtroom identification," and recognized the difficulty of determining whether an in-court identification was based on independent recollection unaided by the lineup identification. By contrast, inevitable discovery involves no speculative elements but focuses on demonstrated historical facts capable of ready verification or impeachment and does not require a departure from the usual burden of proof at suppression hearings.

In these circumstances, the societal costs of the exclusionary rule far outweigh any possible benefits to deterrence that a good-faith requirement might produce.

Williams contends that because he did not waive his right to the assistance of counsel, the Court may not balance competing values in deciding whether the challenged evidence was properly admitted. He argues that the Sixth Amendment exclusionary rule is designed to protect the right to a fair trial and the integrity of the factfinding process. Williams contends that, when those interests are at stake, the societal costs of excluding evidence obtained from responses presumed involuntary are irrelevant in determining whether such evidence should be excluded. We disagree. Exclusion of physical evidence that would inevitably have been discovered adds nothing to either the integrity or fairness of a criminal trial. Here, Detective Leaming's conduct did nothing to impugn the reliability of the evidence in question—the body of the child and its condition as it was found, articles of clothing found on the body, and the autopsy. Suppression, in these circumstances, would do nothing whatever to promote the integrity of the trial process, but would inflict a wholly unacceptable burden on the administration of criminal justice. Nor would suppression ensure fairness on the theory that it tends to safeguard the adversary system of justice. If the government can prove that the evidence would have been obtained inevitably and, therefore, would have been admitted regardless of any overreaching by the police, there is no rational basis to keep that evidence from the jury in order to ensure the fairness of the trial proceedings. The State has gained no advantage at trial and the defendant has suffered no prejudice. Indeed, suppression of the evidence would operate to undermine the adversary system by putting the State in a worse position than it would have occupied without any police misconduct.

More than a half century ago, Judge, later Justice, Cardozo made his seminal observation that under the exclusionary rule "the criminal is to go free because the constable has blundered." Prophetically, he went on to consider "how far-reaching in its effect upon society" the exclusionary rule would be when "the pettiest peace officer would have it in his power through overzeal or indiscretion to confer immunity upon an offender for crimes the most flagitious." Someday, Cardozo speculated, some court might press the exclusionary rule to the outer limits of its logic—or beyond—and suppress evidence relating to the "body of a murdered" victim because of the means by which it was found. When, as here, the evidence in question would inevitably have been discovered without reference to the police error or misconduct, there is no nexus sufficient to provide a taint and the evidence is admissible.

Three courts independently reviewing the evidence have found that the body of the child inevitably would have been found by the searchers. The prosecution offered the testimony of Agent Ruxlow of the Iowa Bureau of Criminal Investigation. Ruxlow had organized and directed some 200 volunteers who were searching for the child's body. The searchers were instructed "to check all the roads, the ditches, any culverts. If they came upon any abandoned farm buildings, they were instructed to go onto the property and search those abandoned farm buildings or any other places where a small child could be secreted." Ruxlow testified that he marked off highway maps of Poweshiek and Jasper Counties in grid fashion, divided the volunteers into teams of four to six persons, and assigned each team to search specific grid areas. Ruxlow also testified that, if the search had not been suspended because of Williams' promised cooperation, it would have continued into Polk County, using the same grid system. Although he had previously marked off into grids only the highway maps of Poweshiek and Jasper Counties, Ruxlow had obtained a map of Polk County, which he said he would have marked off in the same manner had it been necessary for the search to continue. The search commenced at approximately 10 a.m. and moved westward through Poweshiek County into Jasper County. At approximately 3 p.m., after Williams volunteered to cooperate with the police, Detective Leaming, who was in the police car with Williams, sent word to Ruxlow and the other Special Agent directing the search and the search was suspended at that time. The search was not resumed once it was learned that Williams had led the police to the body, which was found two and one-half miles from where the search had stopped in what would have been the easternmost grid to be searched in Polk County. There was testimony that it would have taken an additional three to five hours to discover the body if the search had continued; the body was found near a culvert, one of the kinds of places the teams had been specifically directed to search. It is clear that the search parties were approaching the actual location of the body, and we are satisfied that the volunteer search teams would have resumed the search had Williams not earlier led the police to the body and the body inevitably would have been found. The evidence asserted by Williams as newly discovered, *i.e.*, certain photographs of the body and deposition testimony of Agent Ruxlow made in connection with the federal *habeas* proceeding, does not demonstrate that the material facts were inadequately developed in the suppression hearing in state court or that Williams was denied a full, fair, and adequate opportunity to present all relevant facts at the suppression hearing.

The judgment of the Court of Appeals is reversed, and the case is remanded for further proceedings consistent with this opinion.

It is so ordered.

JUSTICE STEVENS, concurring in the judgment.

Admission of the victim's body, if it would have been discovered anyway, means that the trial was not the product of an inquisitorial process; that process was untainted by illegality. The good or bad faith of Detective Leaming is therefore simply irrelevant. If the trial process was not tainted as a result of his conduct, this defendant received the type of trial that the Sixth Amendment envisions. The prosecution cannot escape responsibility for a constitutional violation through speculation. The need to adduce proof sufficient to discharge its burden, and the difficulty in predicting whether such proof will be available or sufficient, means that the inevitable discovery rule does not permit state officials to avoid the uncertainty they would have faced but for the constitutional violation. The majority refers to the "societal cost" of excluding probative evidence. The more relevant cost is that imposed on society by police officers who decide to take procedural shortcuts instead of complying with the law. What is the consequence of the shortcut that Detective Leaming took when he decided to question Williams in this case and not to wait an hour or so until he arrived in Des Moines? The answer is years and years of unnecessary but costly litigation. Thanks to Detective Leaming, the State of Iowa has expended vast sums of money and countless hours of professional labor in his defense. That expenditure surely provides an adequate deterrent to similar violations; the responsibility for that expenditure lies not with the Constitution, but rather with the constable. I concur.

JUSTICE BRENNAN, with whom JUSTICE MARSHALL joins, dissenting.

The "inevitable discovery" exception to the exclusionary rule is consistent with the requirements of the Constitution. I would require clear and convincing evidence before concluding that the government had met its burden of proof on this issue. Increasing the burden of proof serves to impress the fact finder with the importance of the decision and thereby reduces the risk that illegally obtained evidence will be admitted. I would remand this case for application of this heightened burden of proof by the lower courts.

Point for Discussion

Independent Source

In *Segura v. United States*, 468 U.S. 796 (1984), the police had probable cause to search Segura's apartment. However, because it was evening, they decided to secure the apartment until a warrant could be obtained the next day. After entering, the police made a limited check to make sure that no one was present who might pose a threat to their safety or destroy evidence. During this search, the police found evidence of drug trafficking in plain view, but did not disturb it. Because of administrative delays, the warrant was not obtained until 5 p.m. the next day, and the apartment was not searched until 6 p.m. (19 hours after the initial entry). The search turned up the items discovered the night before, as well as cocaine, 18 rounds of ammunition, more than $50,000 cash, and records of narcotics transactions. Defendants were convicted of conspiring to distribute cocaine, and of distributing and possessing with intent to distribute cocaine based in part on the evidence seized. The Court concluded that the initial seizure of the apartment was "reasonable," and that there was an "independent source" for the evidence: "Whether the initial entry was illegal or not is irrelevant to the admissibility of the challenged evidence because there was an independent source for the warrant. None of the information on which the warrant was secured was derived from or related in any way to the initial entry into petitioners' apartment; the information came from sources wholly unconnected with the entry and was known to the agents well before the initial entry. It is therefore beyond dispute that the information possessed by the agents before they entered the apartment constituted an independent source for the discovery and seizure of the evidence now challenged. The valid warrant search was a 'means sufficiently distinguishable' to purge the evidence of any 'taint' arising from the entry." The Court rejected the argument that suppression was appropriate because the evidence might have been destroyed had the officers not secured the apartment: "the essence of the dissent is that there is some 'constitutional right' to destroy evidence. This concept defies both logic and common sense." Justice Stevens, joined by three other justices, dissented, arguing that "the agents' access to the fruits of the authorized search was a product of illegal conduct. If Segura had not returned home that night, or the next day, it is probable that the occupants of the apartment would have become concerned and might have destroyed the records of their illegal transactions, or removed some of the evidence. If so, that evidence would not have been accessible to the agents when the warrant finally was executed. If the evidence would not have been available to the agents at the time they executed the warrant had they not illegally entered and impounded petitioners' apartment, then it cannot be said that the agents' access to the evidence was 'independent' of the prior illegality. If we are to give more than lipservice to protection of the core constitutional interests that were violated in this case, some effort must be made to isolate and then remove the advantages the Government derived from its illegal conduct."

In *State v. Winterstein*, 167 Wash.2d 620, 220 P.3d 1226 (2009), the State of Washington's Supreme Court held that the inevitable discovery doctrine is incompatible with Washington's Constitution: "Based on the intent of the framers of the Washington Constitution, we have held that the choice of their language 'mandates that the right of privacy shall not be diminished by the judicial gloss of a selectively applied exclusionary remedy.' Because the intent was to protect personal rights rather than curb government actions, 'whenever the right is unreasonably violated, the remedy must follow.' The constitutionally mandated exclusionary rule provides a remedy for individuals whose rights have been violated and protects the integrity of the judicial system by not tainting the proceedings with illegally obtained evidence. Because of textual differences, state action may be valid under the Fourth Amendment but violate article I, section 7." Is the Washington approach preferable?

Food for Thought

In *Nix*, the Court emphasized the fact that the weather was sub-freezing and that the victim's body was preserved by the cold against deterioration. Had the search taken place in mid-summer, should the Court have reached a different result? Would that fact have made the discovery less "inevitable?"

Hypo 1: *Proving Inevitable Discovery*

In a murder case like *Nix*, the prosecution is able to prove inevitability by pointing to the fact that a search was already underway, and demonstrating that this search was likely to have uncovered the body. But suppose that the search had not begun at the time of the so-called Christian Burial Speech. Would it still have been possible for the prosecution to show inevitability? If so, how?

Hypo 2: *Inevitable Discovery & the Kidnapped Girl*

A teenage girl disappears, and police believe that she has been kidnapped. Johnson becomes a suspect when the police search the girl's cell phone, and find sexually explicit messages from him. If the police decide to make an illegal warrantless search of Johnson's home, can they argue that any evidence that they found would have been "inevitably discovered" because of the cell phone messages? Would you apply the exception if Johnson made calls to the girl's cell phone just prior to her disappearance? What if GPS tracking data shows that Johnson's phone had traveled from New Mexico (where he lived) to California (where the girl lived), and back, just prior to the disappearance? What if a police investigator goes to Johnson's home, peers through the window, and sees Johnson engaged in sex with an unidentified teenage girl? *See United States v. Christy*, 810 F. Supp. 2d 1219 (D. Mexico 2014).

Food for Thought

Suppose that a police officer randomly pulls a motorist over and illegally searches his car (without a warrant, probable cause, or any other basis for the search). The trial court suppresses the evidence as the fruit of an illegal search. Would it be possible for the prosecution to prove inevitable discovery? If so, how?

Hypo 3: *The Inventory Exception & Inevitable Discovery*

When Ruckes is stopped for speeding, police learn that his license has been suspended and place him under arrest. The officer searches the vehicle and finds that it contains cocaine and a firearm (prohibited because he is a convicted felon). Although the search is invalid under *Arizona v. Gant*, the state claims that the evidence should be admitted under the inevitable discovery doctrine. The state claims that Ruckes would not have been allowed to drive the car away given the license suspension, could not have driven the car anyway because he was arrested, and there was no one else available to assume control of the car. Hence, the police would have impounded the vehicle and subjected it to an inventory search that would have turned up the cocaine and the firearm. Should the inevitable discovery doctrine apply under such circumstances? *See United States v. Ruckes*, 586 F.3d 713 (9th Cir. 2009). Would it matter whether local procedures specifically permit impoundment of a vehicle whenever an individual is found to be driving without a valid license? *See United States v. Cartwright*, 630 F.3d 610 (2010).

Hypo 4: *Inevitable Discovery & Subpoenas*

The government, trying to prove health care fraud, obtains a doctor's medical records pursuant to a search of his offices. When the doctor moves to suppress the records, the government claims that discovery of the records was "inevitable" because the government could have subpoenaed the records. How does the government go about proving that the discovery was "inevitable"? Would it matter whether the government had served subpoenas on this particular doctor in the past or on other doctors? Would it matter whether the government had actually contemplated obtaining this particular information by subpoena? *See United States v. Lazar*, 604 F.3d 230 (6th Cir. 2010).

Hypo 5: *An Independent Source?*

Working with the police, Sutton (an informer) makes telephone calls and sends texts to Moody (a suspected dealer) requesting methamphetamine, and she arranges to meet him to complete the transaction. Law enforcement officials stop Moody on his way to meet with Sutton. During the stop, the police examine Moody's cell phone records and note that he has made a number of phone calls to a person identified in the cell phone records only as "G." Moody is convicted of distribution of illegal narcotics. Following Moody's release from prison, he resumes selling methamphetamine. One of the people to whom he regularly sells is Donald Blair who resells it to others. Eventually, Blair, who is cooperating with the police, seeks to make a controlled purchase of methamphetamine from Moody. Law enforcement place audio/video recording devices in Blair's house, and Blair himself is outfitted with a recording device. While Moody is at Blair's apartment and under the surveillance of officers, Moody receives a call from a man later identified as Moody's methamphetamine source ("G"). Moody indicates during the phone conversation that he will leave Blair's apartment to meet his methamphetamine source to obtain additional supplies. Surveillance officers follow Moody to a nearby truck stop where they observe a blue vehicle pull up beside Moody's truck. A Hispanic male (later identified as Gonzalo Gutierrez or "G") leaves the blue vehicle and enters Moody's truck. He remains in Moody's truck for approximately two minutes and then returns to his vehicle and drives away. Officers follow both Moody and Gutierrez, and eventually stop Gutierrez for speeding. Gutierrez is arrested and his vehicle is impounded. During an inventory search of the vehicle, officers find $6,290 in cash and a cell phone. Some of the currency seized from Gutierrez's vehicle matches the currency Blair gave to Moody earlier that day. Suppose that the police officers' initial search and seizure of Moody's cell phone (in which they learned about "G") was illegal. Did the police develop an independent source for the information so that there is nothing prohibiting the admission of that evidence against either Moody or Gutierrez? *See United States v. Moody*, 664 F.3d 164 (7th Cir. 2011).

Hypo 6: *Proving Inevitable Discovery*

Suppose that the police have probable cause to obtain a search warrant for a home. They suspect that there is a marijuana growing operation inside the house because a bail bondsman informed police that he saw it. Instead of obtaining a warrant, the police go immediately to the house where they seek consent to search. Although the consent is given, a reviewing court later finds that the consent is invalid. Is the evidence obtained as a result of the search admissible anyway under the inevitable discovery exception? Should it matter whether police have taken any steps towards obtaining a warrant? *See Rodriguez v. State*, 187 So.3d 841 (Fl. 2015).

Executive Summary

The Exclusionary Rule's Function. The exclusionary evidence rule precludes the state from using evidence seized in violation of a defendant's constitutional rights to convict the defendant of a crime. Although the rule is frequently applied to violations of Fourth Amendment rights, it can be invoked to exclude evidence obtained in violation of other constitutional rights as well. The exclusionary rule has been applied in federal cases since the Court's 1914 decision in *Weeks v. United States,* 232 U.S. 383 (1914). However, the Court did not mandate its application in state proceedings until 1961 in *Mapp v. Ohio,* 367 U.S. 643 (1961).

The Good Faith Exception to the Exclusionary Rule. Because of the perceived "costs" of the exclusionary rule, in *United States v. Leon,* 468 U.S. 897 (1984), the Court created the "good faith" exception to the exclusionary rule. In doing so, the Court emphasized that the exclusionary rule is not constitutionally mandated, but instead is a judicially created remedy that is designed to safeguard Fourth Amendment rights by deterring police misconduct. Emphasizing the "substantial social costs" that the rule imposes, including the fact some guilty defendants may go free or receive reduced sentences as a result of favorable plea bargains, the Court concluded that the costs are too high "when law enforcement officers have acted in objective good faith [reliance on a search warrant] or their transgressions have been minor."

The *Leon* Balancing Test. In *Leon,* the Court established a balancing test to use in evaluating the propriety of applying the exclusionary rule in a given case. The Court balances the costs of exclusion (principally, the notion that an innocent individual might go free) against the benefits (deterrence of police misconduct). In *Leon,* because the police relied in good faith on a warrant issued by a neutral and detached magistrate, the Court concluded that the costs of exclusion outweighed the benefits because one cannot hope to deter police who are acting in good faith reliance on a magistrate's finding of probable cause.

Situations When the Good Faith Exception Is Inapplicable. The Court has found that good faith does not exist when the magistrate or judge who issued a warrant was misled by information in an affidavit that the affiant knew was false or would have known was false except for his reckless disregard of the truth, when the issuing magistrate wholly abandoned his judicial role, when the warrant is based on an affidavit "so lacking in indicia of probable cause as to render official belief in its existence entirely unreasonable," or "when the warrant is so facially deficient—*i.e.,* in failing to particularize the place to be searched or the things to be seized—that the executing officers cannot reasonably presume it to be valid." In these circumstances, the executing officers may be subject to civil liability.

Proceedings When the Exclusionary Rule Does Not Apply. The Court has refused to apply the exclusionary rule in a variety of contexts: in grand jury proceedings when witnesses are asked about evidence obtained from an unlawful search or seizure; in federal civil proceedings; when a warrant is invalid because of a "technical error" by the issuing judge; when the police made a warrantless search in good faith reliance on a local law authorizing warrantless searches; when the police relied in good faith on precedent that was later overruled; when a police officer made an arrest based on an outstanding arrest warrant, but the warrant was invalid due to a negligent bookkeeping error; and when police officers, executing a search warrant, violated the "knock and announce" requirement. Although *Leon*'s logic suggest that the good faith exception should apply when an officer makes a warrantless search in "good faith," the Court has extended the good faith exception to some warrantless searches (*e.g.*, good faith reliance on an invalid statute authorizing warrantless searches). However, as a general rule, the exception does not apply to warrantless searches.

Standing, the Exclusionary Rule, & the Fifth Amendment. Standing concepts limit the exclusionary rule's application. In the Fifth Amendment area, the Court treats the privilege against self-incrimination as "personal" and has held that it can only be asserted by the person whose rights have been violated. Even though the Fourth Amendment is not phrased in such personal terms, the Court has also applied the standing requirement to Fourth Amendment violations. At one point, the standing requirement was modified by an "automatic standing" rule. Automatic Standing no longer exists.

Standing in the Fourth Amendment Context. In the Fourth Amendment context, an individual can establish standing by showing that he owns or possesses the place that was searched, or that the police violated his "reasonable expectation of privacy" (REOP). Although an overnight guest may have a REOP in the place where he is staying, those who visit a house for only a short period of time may not. An individual who puts contraband in a friend's purse may not have a REOP in the purse.

Fruit of the Poisonous Tree Doctrine. When the exclusionary rule is applied, it prohibits the prosecution from using evidence directly obtained from a constitutional violation. Thus, if the police coerce a suspect into confessing, the exclusionary rule prohibits the use of that confession. The "derivative evidence rule," also known as the "Fruit of the Poisonous Tree" doctrine, prohibits the police from using evidence "derived" from the direct evidence. In some instances, it is possible to "purge the taint" of illegal conduct so that it will not be treated as "fruit of the poisonous tree. The administration of *Miranda* warnings can be a factor in purging the taint, but it is only a factor. Courts will examine a variety of factors in determining whether the taint of a confession has been purged, including "the temporal proximity of the arrest and the confession, the presence of intervening circumstances, and, particularly, the purpose and flagrancy of the official misconduct are all relevant. The voluntariness of the statement is a threshold requirement. And the burden of showing admissibility rests on the prosecution." The Court has held that police failure to give the *Miranda* warnings does not require suppression of the physical fruits of a defendant's unwarned statements, and they have held that a witness located through an illegal search need not be suppressed. In addition, courts have refused to apply the exclusionary rule when the "fruits" would have inevitably been discovered, as well as when the police have an "independent source" for the evidence.

Major Themes

a. The Exclusionary Rule's Function—The exclusionary evidence rule precludes the state from using evidence seized in violation of a defendant's constitutional rights to convict the defendant of a crime. In general, the exclusionary rule is applied when the benefits of applying it (deterrence of police misconduct) outweigh the costs. As a result, the Court has refused to apply the rule in some situations in which the police act in good faith, as well as in various other situations.

b. Limitations and Expansions of the Exclusionary Rule—The courts have applied a variety of principles that limit application of the exclusionary rule, including the requirement of standing and the concept of harmless error. They have also applied the "fruit of the poisonous tree" doctrine that tends to expand the scope of the exclusionary rule.

For More Information

- Wayne R. LaFave, Jerold H. Israel, Nancy J. King & Orin S. Kerr, Criminal Procedure (6th ed. 2017).

- Russell L. Weaver, John M. Burkoff, Catherine Hancock & Steven I. Friedland, Principles of Criminal Procedure Ch. 8 (7th ed. 2021).

Test Your Knowledge

To assess your understanding of the material in this chapter, click here to take a quiz.

Index

References are to pages.

Page numbers 859–1468, set out below,
are found in Weaver, Burkoff, and Hancock's
Criminal Procedure, A Contemporary Approach (3rd ed. 2021).